We do not know where we are or where we are going if we do not know where we have been, and these two sprawling volumes do just that: they take us on a fascinating tour of our field's past and present. Given the scope of Brown's research, even long-time adepts will learn much.

—**DALE C. ALLISON JR.,** Richard J. Dearborn Professor of
New Testament, Princeton Theological Seminary

As professor at Fuller Theological Seminary for thirty-two years, Colin Brown (1932–2019) was a well-known exponent of Christology with a strong emphasis on historical and theological method. Aside from books covering such topics as Karl Barth, miracles, and philosophical theology, some of his best work concerned the reception of Jesus in modern scholarship. Anticipated by *Jesus in European Protestant Thought* (1985), his achievement culminates in this posthumous two-volume treatment of research on the historical Jesus (here painstakingly edited by Craig A. Evans). Brown here reconstitutes his topic away from the classic and still-dominant scholarly template for these quests, both by stressing the importance of Jesus research well before Schweitzer and by extending his purview to chronicle the exciting and far-reaching debates of the later twentieth century.

—**MARKUS BOCKMUEHL,** Dean Ireland's Professor of the
Exegesis of Holy Scripture, University of Oxford

With characteristic lucidity, learning, and touches of humor, Colin Brown here examines what it means to think critically about Jesus. Against the claim that the quest of the historical Jesus is a purely modern pursuit, he demonstrates that theology from the beginning of Christianity has pressed to understand Jesus in his own terms. Brown is a master at putting differing views into conversation with one another, sometimes across time, in his sweeping, socially sensitive account of what investigators have proposed and how scholarship might tool up to face present and future challenges. Evangelical theology in particular is the richer for this precise, creative, well-written account, which sets out its own arguments alongside those it discusses, and breathes the quiet confidence that faith is often best served by rigorous inquiry.

—**BRUCE CHILTON,** Bernard Iddings Bell Professor of
Philosophy and Religion, Bard College

Not since the grand survey of Albert Schweitzer at the beginning of the twentieth century have we seen—especially in English—such a vast review of academic (and at times popular) literature on the historical Jesus. The differences from Schweitzer's opus are many. Besides the obviously wider and more international scope of the survey, as well as the inclusion of often neglected scholars (notably from England), Dr. Brown is at pains to offer not just a synopsis but also a fair and balanced evaluation of each scholar's work. Naturally, there will always be room for disagreement, especially when the reader reaches Dr. Brown's presentation of his own position at the end of the second volume. But such honest expression of his own views (voiced at times throughout the two volumes) is what makes this massive work more than a list of names and dates. In that sense, it is a true history, echoing the original meaning of the term in Herodotus. A final word of thanks must go to Dr. Craig Evans, who undertook the selfless task of putting the manuscript into final shape after the unfortunate death of Dr. Brown.

—**JOHN P. MEIER,** Warren Professor of Theology Emeritus, University of Notre Dame

Colin Brown (d. 2019) dedicated the better part of his career to mastering the primary and secondary literature on the quests of the historical Jesus. In *A History of the Quests for the Historical Jesus*, Brown (with Craig A. Evans) offers a comprehensive, reliable, and insightful guide to the variety of original quests (beginning with the New Testament), the New Quest, the Third Quest, the Jewish Jesus, and ongoing phases of the movement, highlighting how the social circumstances of the individual participants influenced the discussion.

—**CLARE K. ROTHSCHILD,** professor of Scripture studies at Lewis University, professor extraordinary in the Department of Ancient Studies at Stellenbosch University

In this comprehensive two-volume study, the late Colin Brown brings together the rich fruits of his lifelong studies on Jesus in Christian theology. In contrast to what is usual in Western tradition, the author does not begin his "quest of the historical Jesus" with Reimarus and Schweitzer, but with the time of Jesus itself. Another remarkable characteristic is that the interpretation of Jesus is deeply embedded in the intellectual, political, and religious situation of the respective period and region. In this way, Colin Brown develops a broad framework for the study of Jesus in Christian theology. For future Jesus research, this thorough study is an indispensable tool.

—**JENS SCHRÖTER,** professor of New Testament exegesis and theology and ancient Christian apocrypha, Humboldt University

Brown and Evans break the boundaries of the "three-quest scenario" to move in multiple fresh directions. The result is a one-stop resource for historical Jesus research that uncovers historical, exegetical, and theological treasures.

—**ELIZABETH E. SHIVELY,** senior lecturer in New Testament, St. Mary's College, University of St. Andrews, Scotland

The result of years of labour and reflection, this is a fresh, lucid, and insightful history of life of Jesus research that will be a vital addition to any library where the subject is taught. Moving away from standard models, Brown creates a nuanced schematic history and also points to a new path ahead. Important too are his own erudite contributions to key topics.

—**JOAN E. TAYLOR,** professor of Christian origins and Second Temple Judaism, King's College London

A History of the Quests for the Historical Jesus is a remarkable achievement that makes for a significant contribution to the field of historical Jesus research. Colin Brown provides an in-depth, detailed, and learned analysis of the study of the historical Jesus, taking the changing cultural context into regard as he skillfully guides the readers through the centuries. This is an important book that fills a definite gap in scholarship.

—**CECILIA WASSÉN,** senior lecturer of New Testament exegesis, Uppsala University, Sweden

A HISTORY OF THE QUESTS FOR THE HISTORICAL JESUS

FROM THE BEGINNINGS OF CHRISTIANITY
TO THE END OF WORLD WAR II

VOLUME 1

COLIN BROWN
WITH CRAIG A. EVANS

ZONDERVAN ACADEMIC

A History of the Quests for the Historical Jesus, Volume 1
Copyright © 2022 by The Colin Brown and Olive Margaret Brown Trust

Requests for information should be addressed to:
Zondervan, *3900 Sparks Dr. SE, Grand Rapids, Michigan 49546*

Zondervan titles may be purchased in bulk for educational, business, fundraising, or sales promotional use. For information, please email SpecialMarkets@Zondervan.com.

Library of Congress Cataloging-in-Publication Data

Names: Brown, Colin, 1932- author. | Evans, Craig A., editor.
Title: A history of the quests for the historical Jesus / Colin Brown, edited by Craig A. Evans.
Description: Grand Rapids : Zondervan, 2022. | Includes bibliographical references and index.
  | Contents: volume 1. From the beginnings of Christianity to the end of World War II
  -- volume 2. From the post-war era through contemporary debates.
Identifiers: LCCN 2022012653 (print) | LCCN 2022012654 (ebook) | ISBN 9780310125488
  (hardcover ; v. 1) | ISBN 9780310125617 (hardcover ; v. 2) | ISBN 9780310125495 (ebook ;
  v. 1) | ISBN 9780310125624 (ebook ; v. 2)
Subjects: LCSH: Jesus Christ--Biography--History and criticism. | Jesus Christ--Historicity. |
  Jesus Christ--History of doctrines.
Classification: LCC BT303.2 .B765 2022 (print) | LCC BT303.2 (ebook) | DDC
  232.9/08--dc23/eng/20220513
LC record available at https://lccn.loc.gov/2022012653
LC ebook record available at https://lccn.loc.gov/2022012654

All Scripture quotations, unless otherwise indicated, are taken from the New Revised Standard Version Bible. Copyright © 1989, Division of Christian Education of the National Council of the Churches of Christ in the United States of America. Used by permission. All rights reserved.

Scripture quotations marked KJV are taken from the King James Version. Public domain.

Scripture quotations marked RSV are taken from the Revised Standard Version of the Bible. Copyright © 1952 [2nd edition 1971] by the Division of Christian Education of the National Council of the Churches of Christ in the United States of America. Used by permission. All rights reserved.

Scripture quotations marked NIV are taken from The Holy Bible, New International Version®, NIV® Copyright ©1973, 1978, 1984, 2011 by Biblica, Inc.® Used by permission of Zondervan. All rights reserved worldwide. www.Zondervan.com. The "NIV" and "New International Version" are trademarks registered in the United States Patent and Trademark Office by Biblica, Inc.®

Any internet addresses (websites, blogs, etc.) and telephone numbers in this book are offered as a resource. They are not intended in any way to be or imply an endorsement by Zondervan, nor does Zondervan vouch for the content of these sites and numbers for the life of this book.

All rights reserved. No part of this publication may be reproduced, stored in a retrieval system, or transmitted in any form or by any means—electronic, mechanical, photocopy, recording, or any other—except for brief quotations in printed reviews, without the prior permission of the publisher.

Cover design: Studio Gearbox
Cover photos: ANL, Georgio G, Everett Collection–Shutterstock; GeorgiosArt–Getty Images; Zondervan;
  Harvard University; Public Domain
Interior Design: Kait Lamphere

Printed in the United States of America

---

22 23 24 25 26 27 28 29 30 31 32 /LSC/ 15 14 13 12 11 10 9 8 7 6 5 4 3 2 1

CONTENTS

Editor's Preface ix
Introduction xi

Part 1: Quests before Schweitzer

1. The First Quest 3
2. Evolution of Orthodoxy 63
3. Post-Reformation Alternatives 121
4. Deism and the Historical Jesus 183

Part 2: The European Scene

5. Schweitzer and the Old Quest 239
6. From Old Quest to New 303
7. The No Quest in Europe to World War II 361
8. The No Quest in Europe after World War II 411

Abbreviations 469
Bibliography 471
Index of Subjects 625
Index of Names 647
Index of Ancient Writings 658

EDITOR'S PREFACE

REGRETTABLY, Professor Colin Brown did not have the opportunity to write a preface for his lengthy and learned work that appears in these two volumes. Not long after he finished a first draft of *A History of the Quests for the Historical Jesus* he became ill, and a few months later in 2019, he passed away at the age of eighty-seven. It has fallen to me to edit and finish his work.

Brown was born in Bradford, England, in 1932. He was ordained in the Church of England in 1958 and became vice principal of Tyndale Hall Theological College, which later became Trinity College, Bristol. Brown earned his BA at Liverpool University, an MA from Nottingham University, and a PhD from the University of Bristol. In 1978 he joined the faculty of Fuller Theological Seminary in Pasadena, California, where he remained until his retirement in 2010.

I taught summer school at Fuller for twenty-five consecutive years, and it was thanks to these regular visits that I became acquainted with Colin Brown. He and I often took lunch together and then sat in his office discussing various aspects of Jesus research. It was in this collegial setting that I learned about his book—which he thought he could finish in about five years, but at the time of his death he had been at it for two decades!

As I sifted through two large boxes of drafts and notes, I came to appreciate the extent of Colin's labors. He had read thousands of books, chapters, and journal articles in English, French, and German. As I worked through his 1,500-page manuscript, I was struck by the depth of his learning. Colin had mastered the relevant primary and secondary literature and, at the same time, had gained a great deal of insight into

A History of the Quests for the Historical Jesus

the lives of the major scholars themselves. It became clear that the social settings of the thinkers who influenced the discussion had a profound influence on them as well.

In my opinion Colin's most significant contribution in the present work was his decision to abandon the framework of Albert Schweitzer's survey of Jesus research, which began with the posthumous publications of a lengthy manuscript penned by Hermann Samuel Reimarus. Colin rightly recognized that there were several important precursors whose contributions to Jesus research had been overlooked or underestimated. Colin also wisely steered his discussion away from the three-quest schema that has been in vogue for more than a century. The result is a stimulating and insightful analysis of this rich and complicated field of study. Colin's expertise in epistemology and his critical assessment of supernaturalism equipped him to undertake this onerous task at a level that few in the field can equal.

Failure to publish what will be regarded as Colin Brown's *magnum opus* would have been an egregious sin of omission. But we have managed to publish his work thanks to the generosity and diligence of Nancy Rothwell, trustee of the Colin Brown estate, and the good people at Zondervan, who early on recognized the value of Colin's book and agreed to publish it in good time and in its full form. For this I am very grateful to Katya Covrett and Dr. Stan Gundry, as well as to Matt Estel for copyediting, to Vanessa Carroll, Becky Danley, and Lynn Wilson for assistance in proofing, and to Sandra Judd for indexing. It is my hope that readers at all levels of expertise will benefit from this learned work.

C. A. Evans
Houston Baptist University

INTRODUCTION

FOR MORE than a century, historical-Jesus studies were shaped by one man and one book. The man was Albert Schweitzer (1875–1965), brilliant philosopher and theologian, internationally renowned organist and musicologist, medical missionary in the jungles of West Africa, and Nobel Laureate. Schweitzer's book was published in Gothic script in 1906, with a title that threatened to consign it to university library shelves of unread books—*Von Reimarus zu Wrede. Eine Geschichte der Leben-Jesu-Forschung*—"From Reimarus to Wrede: A History of Life-of-Jesus Research."[1]

The title suggested a pedantic catalogue of biographies written between dates set by writers known only to scholars. The Gothic script remained for decades to come. However, in the second enlarged edition the subtitle of the 1st edition supplied the title for the entire book. The new title gave the impression that the book was indeed the definitive *History of Life-of-Jesus Research*. The names of Reimarus and Wrede dropped out of sight,[2] but at the expense of concealing their significance in Schweitzer's narrative.

At first the academic community gave Schweitzer's book a mixed reception. The turnaround came with the English translation under the title *The Quest of the Historical Jesus: A Critical Study of Its Progress from Reimarus to Wrede* (1910). In the preface Cambridge professor F. C.

---

1. Albert Schweitzer, *Von Reimarus zu Wrede: Eine Geschichte des Leben-Jesu-Forschung* (Tübingen: Mohr Siebeck, 1906).

2. My 1951 copy of the sixth photomechanical reprint of the second edition (1913) is entitled simply *Geschichte der Leben-Jesu-Forschung* (Tübingen: Mohr Siebeck, 1951). The Gothic script remains.

A History of the Quests for the Historical Jesus

Burkitt assured readers of the book's significance. It set before them "as no other book has ever done, the history of the struggle which the best-equipped intellects of the modern world have gone through in endeavoring to realize for themselves the historical personality of our Lord."[3] Over the years Schweitzer's book achieved near canonical status as the definitive account of what its English title promised to deliver. Even those who questioned Schweitzer's portrait of Jesus could not deny the verve of his narrative or his mastery of material.

Canonical status was reasserted in the English-speaking world by publication of *The Quest of the Historical Jesus*, first complete edition (2000).[4] The work was in fact a revision of William Montgomery's original translation, with supplementary chapters from the second German edition of 1913. Schweitzer wrote them in response to developments between 1906 and 1912. The foreword by Dennis Nineham, the notes by the editor, and the appreciation of Schweitzer by Marcus J. Borg offered no serious critical assessment of Schweitzer's contribution or account of developments after 1912. For all intents and purposes, Schweitzer had given the definitive account of the quest of the historical Jesus.[5]

Today it is customary to speak of three quests: the original quest chronicled by Schweitzer, the New Quest initiated in Germany in the 1950s by members of the Bultmann school, and the subsequent Third Quest popularized by Marcus Borg, N. T. Wright, and others. However, there is reason to think that the notion of three quests owes more to the entrepreneurial spirit of British publishers than to scholars actually engaged in Jesus studies.

It began with the title given to the English translation of Schweitzer's book, published in London by A. & C. Black, which introduced the word *Quest*. Their word choice intimated a narrative akin to *Raiders of the Lost Ark* or at least suggested that the Jesus of history was quite different from the Christ of Christian tradition and the Jesus of liberal Protestantism. This goal was, in fact, what Schweitzer had in mind. The feeling of excitement generated by the quest was heightened by Montgomery's

---

3. Albert Schweitzer, *The Quest of the Historical Jesus: A Critical Study of Its Progress from Reimarus to Wrede*, trans. W. Montgomery (London: Black, 1910), xvii.

4. Albert Schweitzer, *The Quest of the Historical Jesus*, 1st complete ed., ed. John Bowden (London: SCM, 2000; Minneapolis: Fortress, 2001).

5. A more incisive and comprehensive appraisal of Schweitzer and his influence was given by James M. Robinson in his introduction to a paperback reprint of the first English edition of the *Quest* (New York: Macmillan, 1968), xi–xxxiii.

Introduction

translation. However, the editor of the "first complete edition" found it "bombastic." It needed correction to bring it into line with "Schweitzer's clear, matter-of-fact and often witty prose."[6]

History repeated itself half a century later in connection with a paper presented to the Oxford Congress on the Four Gospels (1957) by a brilliant young American scholar, James M. Robinson. The paper was entitled, "The Kerygma and the Quest of the Historical Jesus."

Discussions with the editor of the SCM Press in London about turning the paper into a book led to the proposal of getting rid of jargon and entitling the book *A New Quest of the Historical Jesus*. The editor's suggestion was finally agreed upon. Later, Robinson described it as "an afterthought."[7]

Robinson's intention was not to start a New Quest but to carry forward ideas set out by Rudolf Bultmann in *Jesus and the Word* (1926). His aim was not to create a "post-Bultmann" Jesus but to understand the historical Jesus *through* existential response to the kerygma. Robinson, however, became both the historian of the New Quest and its leading advocate in the New World.

Given this history, it was almost inevitable that the term *Third Quest* should be coined to describe approaches that were different from the other two quests. It gained currency through N. T. Wright. Wright used it in his capacity as editor of a handbook of New Testament scholarship published by the Oxford University Press and later in his own writings.[8] Unlike its predecessors, the Third Quest stressed the Jewishness of Jesus. However, it is not clear whether it was intended to cover all writers who shared this emphasis,[9] or whether membership of the Third Quest was limited to those who subscribed to a particular methodology.

Bultmann defined authenticity with regard to recognizing genuine traditions about Jesus in terms of the criterion of *double dissimilarity*— dissimilar to both Judaism and Christianity, thus characterizing the

---

6. Schweitzer, *Quest*, 1st complete ed., xi.

7. James M. Robinson, *A New Quest of the Historical Jesus, and Other Essays* (Philadelphia: Fortress, 1983), 5. This edition adds a few previously published essays to Robinson's *A New Quest of the Historical Jesus*, SBT 25 (London: SCM, 1959).

8. Stephen Neill and Tom Wright, *The Interpretation of the New Testament, 1861–1986*, 2nd ed. (Oxford: Oxford University Press, 1988), 367–403, esp. 397–403; N. T. Wright, *Jesus and the Victory of God*, Christian Origins and the Question of God 2 (Minneapolis: Fortress, 1996), 83–124.

9. Wright named some twenty scholars, including the present author (*Jesus and the Victory of God*, 84).

xiii

A History of the Quests for the Historical Jesus

authentic teaching of Jesus by its "distinctive eschatological temper."[10] In response, Wright proposed a criterion of *double similarity and double dissimilarity* for identifying authentic passages relating to Jesus. "It is thus decisively *similar* to both the Jewish context and in the early Christian world, and at the same time importantly *dissimilar.* . . . [W]hen something can be seen to be credible (though perhaps deeply subversive) within first-century Judaism, *and* credible as the implied starting point (though not the exact replica) of something in later Christianity, there is a strong possibility of our being in touch with the genuine history of Jesus."[11]

This is not the place to pursue this debate further. Right now, it is more important to note that the term *Third Quest* implies only *two* previous quests. It suggests that Schweitzer was right to begin with Reimarus and that Reimarus had no predecessors. However, it is a reminder of Schweitzer's omissions. He focused on writers in Germany and France. He ignored Martin Kähler's critique. He also ignored Jewish scholarship and perceptions of Jesus outside the domain of New Testament studies.[12]

The three-quest scenario ignores many developments outside its purview. It is not for nothing that the facetious term *No Quest* was coined to denote the vast areas outside the three-quest scenario. It is in this facetious sense that *No Quest* is used in the present book to discuss contributions outside the confines of the three quests. Schweitzer's *Quest of the Historical Jesus* was not the impartial historical investigation that it is often imagined to be. As we shall see in due course, it was a monument of self-vindication.

My work has its origins in the Hensley Henson Lectures in the University of Oxford, which I was honored to give in 1993. Their title was "The Question of Miracle and the Quest of the Historical Jesus." Behind the topic was my doctoral work in the University of Bristol. It was

---

10. Rudolf Bultmann, *The History of the Synoptic Tradition*, trans. John Marsh (Oxford: Blackwell, 1963), 205.

11. Wright, *Jesus and the Victory of God*, 132.

12. Vincent A. McCarthy, *Quest for a Philosophical Jesus: Christianity and Philosophy in Rousseau, Kant, Hegel and Schelling* (Macon, GA: Mercer University Press, 1986); Paul K. Moser, ed., *Jesus and Philosophy: New Essays* (Cambridge: Cambridge University Press, 2009). On Jesus in popular culture and fiction, see, e.g., R. Laurence Moore, *Touchdown Jesus: The Mixing of Sacred and Secular in American History* (Louisville: Westminster John Knox, 1973); Richard Wightman Fox, *Jesus in America: Personal Savior, Cultural Hero, National Obsession* (San Francisco: HarperSanFrancisco, 2004); Margaret E. Ramey, *The Quest for the Fictional Jesus: Gospel Rewrites, Gospel (Re)interpretation, and Christological Portraits Within Jesus Novels* (Eugene, OR: Pickwick, 2013).

Introduction

eventually published in the United States, where I have lived since 1978. The book bears the title *Jesus in European Protestant Thought, 1778–1860*.[13] Also behind the topic of my lectures was my investigation into the changing role of miracles in the history of theology and philosophy, *Miracles and the Critical Mind*.[14]

Every guest speaker in a distinguished lecture series is faced by the choice of whether to publish the lectures more or less as delivered or to develop them into a more substantial book. With the encouragement of colleagues, I decided upon the latter course. While I have tried not to lose sight of my original aim of investigating changing attitudes toward miracles in the quest, I have chosen to explore it in contexts wider than a short lecture series permitted.

Along the way I have abandoned Albert Schweitzer as a guide to the course of the quest of the historical Jesus. I have also abandoned the three-quest scenario because of its shortsighted limitations. Although it may seem like reinventing the wheel, we have no option but to start again with our eyes open to the pitfalls of the past. We need a willingness to listen to what others have to say and to try to understand where they are coming from. The quest of the historical Jesus involves hermeneutics as well as exegesis—a merging of horizons, beliefs, and philosophies.

To help readers navigate through the labyrinth of conflicting ideas, I offer below what I call a "road map," which sets out the argument chapter by chapter. In addition, each chapter has its own list of topics. I make no claims to completeness. What I offer is the results of a personal pilgrimage, which has experienced many changes of heart and mind over the years.

I end this introduction on a personal note. Some readers may wonder why the author of this book, who has spent much of his career teaching systematic theology, should presume to trespass on an area commonly regarded as the preserve of New Testament scholars. I offer two explanations.

The first has to do with the nature of the quest of the historical Jesus. From the outset it has been a multidisciplinary enterprise, involving more than biblical studies. In the modern era it has become ever more complex.

---

13. Colin Brown, *Jesus in European Protestant Thought, 1778–1860*, Studies in Historical Theology 1 (Durham: Labyrinth, 1985; repr., Pasadena: Fuller Theological Seminary Press, 2008).

14. Colin Brown, *Miracles and the Critical Mind* (Grand Rapids: Eerdmans, 1984; repr., Pasadena, CA: Fuller Theological Seminary Press, 2006).

Biblical study cannot be divorced from philosophy, hermeneutics, historical theology, archaeology, sociology, the study of antiquity and its literature and languages. This list is not intended to be exhaustive. It merely gives some idea of the range of disciplines that are relevant to the quest. No one can achieve mastery in all these fields. But one can be attentive to the expertise of others.

The second explanation has to do with my understanding of systematic theology. In my opinion it has nothing to do with teaching systems like Calvinism or Arminianism or an infallible method. It has more to do with exploration than with indoctrination. For much of my career, teaching systematic theology has involved asking three questions over and over again: What do we believe? Why do we believe the things that we believe? How do we put it together?

In seeking answers I am guided by my study of Scripture, the ecumenical confessions of faith, and a host of scholars past and present. In my last decade of classroom teaching, I added a fourth question: How are our beliefs influenced by culture?

In short, my approach is like what medieval scholars termed *Quaestiones Disputatae* or what Karl Rahner called *Theological Investigations*.[15] The historical Jesus is important to every question we ask and try to answer.

A Road Map

Quests of the Historical Jesus contains twenty-one chapters on specialized subjects. Each chapter begins with a brief introduction and table of contents. The aim of this road map is to give an overview of the book. It takes the form of a guide to help to readers navigate their way through the labyrinth of its contents by explaining the underlying strategy and tactics. The strategy identifies four major areas of investigation. The tactics explain the issues discussed in the chapters in the four areas.

The first area of investigation, "Quests before Schweitzer," consists of chapters 1–4. They explore the background necessary for appraising

---

15. I am also indebted to Rahner regarding the Trinity: one God who subsists in three distinct manners of subsisting. See Karl Rahner, *The Trinity*, trans. Joseph Donceel, introduction by Catherine Mowry LaCugna (New York: Crossroad, 2010), 113.

Introduction

Schweitzer's *Quest*. On a deeper level they serve to understand the separation of Christianity and Judaism as well as the emerging "orthodoxies" of both faiths. From the sixteenth century on, Europe underwent significant religious and intellectual climate changes, culminating in deism. These changes precipitated the *modern* quest of the historical Jesus.

The second area of investigation (chaps. 5–8), "The European Scene," explores quests of the historical Jesus in Europe. It begins with a reappraisal of Schweitzer and his narrative of the quest from Reimarus to himself. It then examines the rise of the history of religions school, form criticism, and dialectical theology. The dominant figure was Rudolf Bultmann. However, Bultmann's combination of radical criticism with dialectical theology bordered on docetism. Under the leadership of Ernst Käsemann, Bultmann's former students embarked on the short-lived New Quest of the Historical Jesus.

The term *No Quest* is used facetiously to denote ongoing quests that flew under Bultmann's radar screen. It includes major contributions to understanding the world of Jesus—the languages, history, and culture of Second Temple Judaism—and early reclamations of Jesus. On the darker side was the rise of National Socialism and its impact on Jesus studies. In the postwar period Joachim Jeremias and Oscar Cullmann were the most prominent advocates of recognizing the importance of the historical investigation of Jesus.

The third area of investigation (chaps. 9–15), "Britain and North America," focuses on developments in the English-speaking world. It retraces our steps in order to assess the impact of European scholarship. We begin with Britain and a discussion of the role of Anglican Church politics in historical Jesus studies. We then turn to the universities of Oxford and Cambridge and the part they played in introducing Schweitzer and his *Quest* to English readers. In the early part of the twentieth century William Sanday at Oxford and F. C. Burkett at Cambridge were the towering figures. As the century wore on, their place was taken by B. H. Streeter, C. H. Dodd, and T. W. Manson. Among the key figures after the Second World War were John Macquarrie, Austin Farrer, David Daube, W. D. Davies, and J. D. M. Derrett.

The twentieth century witnessed the growing importance on the world stage of American scholarship. Up until then, American schools were primarily colleges preparing men for the professions. It was the custom for scholars to go to Europe to round off their education.

xvii

A History of the Quests for the Historical Jesus

The twentieth century saw major American universities emerge as research institutions. In view of this transformation, Jesus studies are examined at four leading schools: Princeton Theological Seminary and the divinity schools at Yale, Chicago, and Harvard. The focus then shifts to the rise and fall of the New Quest in America. It takes the form of four case studies of leading participants during and after the episode: James M. Robinson, Schubert M. Ogden, Reginald H. Fuller, and Norman Perrin. The segment concludes with discussion of the endeavors of Paul Tillich and Hans Frei to detach Christology from its dependence on the vagaries of historical criticism, as well as Leander H. Keck's response.

The fourth area of investigation (chaps. 16–21), "Ongoing Issues," reviews the contemporary state of scholarship. The word *ongoing* is used in two ways. In chapter 16 it refers to an issue that spans a period of time. The role of Apollonius of Tyana as a rival to Jesus has been debated for centuries. In chapter 17 *ongoing* refers to the influence of Friedrich Nietzsche. Nietzsche's nihilism attracted Albert Schweitzer and continues to influence contemporary philosophy. The remaining chapters are devoted to current issues: methods, criteria, sources (chap. 18), Jesus the Jew (chap. 19), and a two-part reassessment of the historical Jesus today (chaps. 20–21).

I. Quests before Schweitzer

CHAPTER 1: THE FIRST QUEST. A case is made for thinking that the quest of the historical Jesus did not begin in Europe in the eighteenth-century Age of Enlightenment. It began in Jesus' lifetime when a delegation of scribes was sent from Jerusalem to Galilee to investigate Jesus. Oddly enough, the purpose of their mission could be described in words taken from the title of Reimarus's final *Fragment*. Their goal was to investigate the *aims of Jesus and his disciples*. The answers were different, but the questions were the same.

The scribes' verdict was that Jesus was casting out demons by Beelzebul, the prince of demons; Satan had got into him, and he was leading multitudes astray. Jesus fit the profile laid out in Deuteronomy 13:1–5. Such a prophet was guilty of a capital offence. According to the mandates of the Torah, prophets and dreamers of dreams who performed signs and wonders in order to lead astray should be put to death. Evil should be purged from the people of Israel.

Introduction

Mark's gospel gives a succinct narrative of events. Jesus had come from Galilee for the express purpose of being baptized by John the Baptist in the Jordan. As Jesus was coming out of the water, he experienced the Spirit of God swooping down upon him like a dove. A voice from heaven declared that Jesus was the Son of God.

After John's arrest Jesus returned to Capernaum on the north end of the Sea of Galilee, not to his family home in Nazareth. Capernaum was the initial center of his operations. Jesus began by calling the nucleus of a band of disciples. Eventually their number rose to twelve. In the meantime, Jesus established his reputation as a teacher, healer, and exorcist.

Some people thought him mad. His family tried to restrain him. Following the scribes' verdict, the family tried again. Jesus' mother, brothers, and sisters made the long journey from Nazareth in the hill country to Capernaum to reason with him. Jesus refused to meet them and opted for his family of followers who did the will of God. From now on relations with his biological family were dysfunctional. It was evident that Jesus must get out of Capernaum. Jesus and the Twelve escaped in a boat under the protection of darkness. The remainder of Jesus' life was spent on the move. It was not a matter of choice. Henceforth, Jesus lived the life of a fugitive with nowhere to lay his head.

Mark's gospel was written to vindicate Jesus. Mark stressed the anointing of Jesus by the Spirit at his baptism. It made him the Anointed One, the Christ, the Son of God. This anointing was the source of Jesus' authority. It was seen as a fulfillment of prophecy about the One on whom the Spirit of the Lord would come. His mission was to baptize Israel with the Spirit of God.

In form and genre, Mark's gospel represents the state of the art in Jewish Hellenistic literature. Mark's composition as a *tragic epic* can be traced back to Aristotle's *Poetics*. It has a five-act structure with a prologue and an epilogue.[16] The prologue sets out the dynamics of the action that followed. The epilogue transforms the tragedy of Jesus' death and burial into a triumphant ending: news of his resurrection.

In Aristotle, the rules for narrating fiction and history were the same. Fiction described the kind of events that could happen; history dealt with events that had happened.[17] Tragedies were performed by actors;

---

16. Aristotle recommended three acts, but by the time of Horace five acts were in vogue.

17. Dennis R. MacDonald identified affinities between the Gospels and Homeric epics: *The*

xix

A History of the Quests for the Historical Jesus

epics were narrated by a single person. The reason why performances of Mark today are so successful stems from the fact that it was written to be narrated.

The gospels of Matthew and Luke were built on Mark's framework. John was different. His gospel was also a vindication of Jesus. But as we shall see, John took a different course.

CHAPTER 2: EVOLUTION OF ORTHODOXY. Chapter 2 examines the "parting of the ways" that separated Christianity from Judaism and the formation of orthodoxy in both faiths. The separation had begun already in the time of the New Testament. Their respective orthodoxies were developed in isolation from each other. It is one of the great tragedies of history that in their formative years communication ceased and hostility prevailed. Jewish teachers, especially in the Babylonian Talmud, vented their frustration in coded caricatures of Jesus.

In the Christian creeds and the decrees of the ecumenical councils, Jesus became a virtual gentile. The conciliar decrees defined orthodoxy in terms of metaphysical theology that mediated between warring theological factions. They were more concerned with conceptual formulations of Jesus' divinity and humanity than with his life and teaching. They omitted to say that Jesus was Jewish.

No mention was made of the role of God's Spirit—apart from in Jesus' conception—or the controversies with Jewish authorities that occupy so much of the canonical Gospels. In the Nicene Creed only a punctuation mark separates "became incarnate from the Virgin Mary, and was man" from "For our sake he was crucified under Pontius Pilate." The ancient creeds and the definitions of Nicea and Chalcedon remained authoritative statements of orthodoxy in both the Catholic Church and the Protestant Reformation.

CHAPTER 3: POST-REFORMATION ALTERNATIVES. Chapter 3 examines discontent within Protestantism, beginning with *voices of dissent*—the protests of Servetus regarding the doctrine of the Trinity and the Arminian conflict within Calvinism. The chapter then traces the rise of *anti-Trinitarianism* as it took shape in Socinianism and Unitarianism.

Homeric Epics and the Gospel of Mark (New Haven, CT: Yale University Press, 2000); *Mythologizing Jesus: From Jewish Teacher to Epic Hero* (Lanham, MD: Rowman & Littlefield, 2015); *The Gospels and Homer, Intimations of Greek Epic in Mark and Luke-Acts*, vol. 1, *The New Testament and Greek Literature* (Lanham, MD: Rowman & Littlefield, 2015). My own proposals stress Hellenistic influence over the *form* of Mark but give greater weight to the Jewish context with regard to *content*.

Introduction

In England the greatest scientist of the age, Sir Isaac Newton, wrote more (unpublished) manuscripts on theology than he did on science. He was fiercely critical of Nicea and its defender Athanasius. Newton's friends William Whiston and Samuel Clarke were charged with reviving Arianism, the heresy condemned at the Council of Nicea.

The final part of the chapter is devoted to the rise of skepticism in view of its critical role in later thought. Modern European skepticism may be traced to *Pyrrhonism*, the revival of interest in the ancient Greek skeptic Pyrrho through the writings of Sextus Empiricus. Pyrrhonism influenced the rationalism of René Descartes and the skepticism of David Hume.

Hume is often described as an *empiricist* in philosophy. The term betrays an unrecognized connection with Sextus Empiricus. Hume saw himself as a moderate Pyrrhonist. Systematic doubt was ultimately self-destructive, but a modicum of doubt was useful. In Hume's day, miracles had come to be viewed as legitimation of Christianity as a *belief system*. Hume, like Thomas Hobbes and Benedictus de Spinoza before him, questioned whether evidence for them was adequate to bear this burden.

CHAPTER 4: DEISM AND THE HISTORICAL JESUS. The previous chapter dealt with what might be called "intellectual climate change." Chapter 4 begins with a review of British deism. It is followed by discussion of deism in America and Germany.

British deism was amorphous. Leading figures include Lord Herbert of Cherbury, Charles Blount, John Toland, Anthony Collins, Thomas Woolston, and Matthew Tindal. All but Tindal were private scholars. Their unity, if it existed at all, could be defined by what they opposed: institutional Christianity. Blount introduced English readers to Apollonius of Tyana, a rival to Jesus. An anonymous work outlined the rational pantheism of Spinoza. Toland criticized *mysteries* in religion and propagated his own brand of Spinozism.

Anthony Collins, a friend of John Locke and member of the English gentry, published two anonymous treatises after Locke's death that undermined predictive prophecy. Appeal to prophecy, particularly in Matthew, was regarded a one of the twin pillars of Christian apologetics: prophecy and miracles. Collins's exact scholarship showed that passages credited with foretelling Jesus and his times actually were fulfilled in their own times. Collins planned a critical treatment of miracles but was preempted by Thomas Woolston.

xxi

Woolston was a former Cambridge scholar who was deprived of his fellowship on grounds of mental instability. He gained notoriety for a series of pamphlets—the social media of the age—that he marketed himself. Woolston called them *Discourses on the Miracles of Our Saviour.* They were progressively more hostile and defamatory. If the gospel miracle stories bore any truth, it was as *allegories.* Whether this claim is credible—or whether it was a case of *theological lying*—is disputed. Woolston was tried and convicted for blasphemy. The case became a *cause célèbre.*

Unitarianism and deism spread to America. The most famous representative was Thomas Jefferson, framer of the Declaration of Independence and third president of the United States. Under the influence of the English Unitarian Joseph Priestley, Jefferson was won over from deism to Unitarianism. An outcome was the unpublished *Jefferson Bible.* It was actually a scissors-and-paste version of the four canonical Gospels. Jefferson compiled it by snipping verses from printed versions of the Bible and pasting them in a book. He cut out all references to the supernatural. Jefferson was convinced that one day Unitarianism would become the religion of America.

Knowledge of British deism was widespread in German intellectual circles. Modern scholarship has shown that Reimarus possessed a comprehensive collection of deists in his personal library. Schweitzer was reliant on the extracts of Reimarus's work posthumously edited by Lessing. The full text of Reimarus's *Apology or Defense of the Rational Worshippers of God* was first published in 1972 and reveals extensive knowledge of the deists whom Reimarus ranked among the "rational worshippers of God."

Immanuel Kant is remembered as the philosopher of Protestantism. It might be more accurate to see him as the philosopher of deism. He described God as a postulate of practical reason but insisted that knowledge of God could not be inferred from it. He rejected revelation and did not refer to Jesus by name. Kant insisted that morality was based on unconditional moral laws. Although he castigated the Fragmentist, he also denounced priestcraft. He preferred to speak of "the personified idea of the Good principle." The great teacher of natural religion who figured in *Religion within the Boundaries of Mere Reason* was more a project of thought embodying ideal morality than a historical figure. Kant was closer to being a deist than the Christian theist he claimed to be.

xxii

Introduction

II. The European Scene

CHAPTER 5: SCHWEITZER AND THE OLD QUEST. Chapter 5 examines the origin and contents of Albert Schweitzer's *The Quest of the Historical Jesus: A Critical Study of Its Progress from Reimarus to Wrede* (1906; ET 1910).

Before Schweitzer embarked on his career in theology, he obtained a doctorate in philosophy from the University of Strassburg. The subject of his 1899 dissertation was Kant's philosophy of religion from *Critique of Pure Reason* to *Religion within the Boundaries of Mere Reason*. Regardless of whatever else he got from Kant, it seems that from then on Schweitzer was set on a course for constructing theology within the boundaries of mere reason. Before he became an admirer of Nietzsche, Schweitzer was a devotee of Kant. This enthusiasm is understandable if we remove, as Schweitzer did in his dissertation, the postulate of God from Kant's later critical philosophy.

The starting point of Schweitzer's *Quest* was Lessing's extracts from an unpublished text by Heinrich Samuel Reimarus. Lessing published them as *Fragments of an Unnamed Author*, using the subterfuge that he had discovered them in his capacity as librarian to the Duke of Brunswick at Wolfenbüttel. The extracts are frequently referred to as the *Wolfenbüttel Fragments*.

What is not often realized is the fact that the *Quest* was written as a monumental vindication of an earlier work. In 1901 Schweitzer published a two-volume dissertation on the Lord's Supper for his qualification to teach theology at Strassburg. Volume 1 (first published in English translation in 1982) was devoted to proving that Jesus did not intend the Last Supper to be replicated down the ages. Volume 2 outlined events leading up to the Last Supper and was published in English translation in 1914 with the title *The Mystery of the Kingdom of God: The Secret of Jesus' Messiahship and Passion*.

Schweitzer had begun to form his ideas about eschatology and the kingdom of God as early as 1894. Johannes Weiss had persuaded him that Jesus understood the kingdom of God *eschatologically*, as the advent of a new world order. Jesus came to believe that his death as a martyr would inaugurate it. However, on the same day that Schweitzer's book was published, William Wrede published a book on the same subject that overshadowed Schweitzer. Wrede contended that the messianic secret was characteristic of Mark's gospel but could not be traced back to Jesus himself.

Wrede's book set Schweitzer on a course of self-vindication. He would

xxiii

show that readers ultimately would be confronted by the choice between Wrede's *thoroughgoing skepticism* and his own *thoroughgoing eschatology*. In point of fact, it was a choice between different forms of skepticism. As a modern thinker, Schweitzer was no less skeptical about eschatology than Wrede. However, for Schweitzer eschatology was the key to understanding the actions of Jesus.

Along the way leading up to this ultimate choice were three critical turning points. Each marked a phase from which there was no turning back. The first presented the choice between a "purely historical" Jesus and the supernatural Jesus of tradition. The leading proponent of the "purely historical" Jesus was D. F. Strauss. Strauss's career led him from graduate studies at Tübingen under F. C. Baur, to enthusiasm for Hegel in Berlin, and to disenchantment with Schleiermacher. The outcome was Strauss's *The Life of Jesus Critically Examined* (1835–36). The gospel miracles were the product of myth making based on alleged fulfillment of Old Testament narratives about what the Messiah would do. Strauss's book earned him a place in the history of scholarship at the expense of sacrificing his academic career. In later life Strauss wrote a second life of Jesus, which dropped his earlier Hegelianism in favor of Kantianism.

The second turning point was the elimination of John's gospel from historical study. Schweitzer credited it to F. C. Baur and the Tübingen school and to his own mentor, H. J. Holtzmann. The third turning point was the triumph of Johannes Weiss's eschatological Jesus over the noneschatological Jesus of liberal Protestantism. The final confrontation pitted Schweitzer's thoroughgoing eschatology against the thoroughgoing skepticism of Wrede.

Many readers today remember Schweitzer from the paragraph that concluded the first edition of his *Quest*. "He comes to us as One unknown, without a name, as of old, by the lake-side, He came to those men who knew Him not. He speaks to us the same word: 'Follow thou me!' and sets us the task which He has to fulfil for our time. He commands. And to those who obey Him, whether they be wise or simple, He will reveal Himself in the toils, the conflicts, the sufferings which they shall pass through in His fellowship, and, as an ineffable mystery, they shall learn in their own experience Who He is."[18]

There is something ironical about citing an incident described in

---

18. Schweitzer, *Quest* (1968 repr.), 403.

Introduction

John 21:9–19, a gospel that Schweitzer dismissed as unhistorical, having already announced the exclusion of the supernatural from serious history. Taken out of context, the passage reads like a rehabilitation of orthodoxy. Taken in context, it pictures what was left among the rubble that remained from Schweitzer's demolition of traditional belief and critical scholarship. B. H. Streeter was nearer the truth than he perhaps realized when he described Schweitzer's portrait of Jesus as "a little like the Superman of Nietzsche dressed in Galilean robes."[19] Schweitzer had long been an admirer of Nietzsche and his vision of the *Übermensch*. Schweitzer himself saw his results as the triumph of mysticism as the alternative to orthodoxy and critical positivism.

CHAPTER 6: FROM OLD QUEST TO NEW. Chapter 6 traces the trajectory of Jesus research from Wilhelm Bousset and the history of religions school in the early years of the twentieth century to the last great representative of that school, Rudolf Bultmann. Together with Schweitzer, Bousset and Bultmann set the agenda for much of the scholarship of the twentieth century. Bultmann declared his conviction that the central theme of Bousset's *Kyrios Christos* (1913) was also that of New Testament theology—the *history* of belief in Christ.[20]

According to Bousset, pre-Pauline Palestinian theology viewed Jesus as a cult figure. He was given the title *Kyrios* ("Lord"), which was derived from the mystery cults. Paul introduced a mysticism that turned Jesus into a supraterrestrial power. Paul did not proclaim the faith *of* Jesus, but faith *in* Jesus. In Paul's writings Jesus became the Last Adam and the sender of the Spirit. The estrangement of "the Johannine circle" from the primitive figure of Jesus of Nazareth was nothing short of docetism.

Bultmann was heir to Bousset in a double sense. On Bousset's death in 1920, Bultmann succeeded to his chair at Giessen. Bousset's convictions and agenda regarding the stratification of early Christianity provided the basis for Bultmann's own account. Bultmann was a pioneer of form criticism. However, the English term does not do full justice to what the German *Formgeschichte* (literally, "form history") implies.

---

19. B. H. Streeter, "The Historic Christ," in *Foundations: A Statement of Christian Belief in Terms of Modern Thought by Seven Oxford Men*, ed. B. H. Streeter (London: Macmillan, 1912), 77.

20. Wilhelm Bousset, *Kyrios Christos: Geschichte des Christusglaubens von den Anfängen des Christentums bis Irenaeus* (Göttingen: Vandenhoeck & Ruprecht, 1913; 5th ed., 1965); ET: *Kyrios Christos: A History of the Belief in Christ from the Beginnings of Christianity to Irenaeus*, introduction by Rudolf Bultmann, trans. John E. Steely (Nashville: Abingdon, 1970), 8–9.

A History of the Quests for the Historical Jesus

To Bultmann, what was important was not merely the classification of different forms embedded in the writings of the New Testament. It was also their *history* (*Geschichte*), which he analyzed at great length in successive editions of *The History of the Synoptic Tradition* (1921). The Gospels were not biographies depicting historical events in the life, death, and resurrection of the Son of God. They were collections of stories compiled to satisfy the curiosity of believing communities about the one who gave rise to the kerygma. "Mark was the creator of this sort of Gospel; the Christ myth gives his book, the book of secret epiphanies, not indeed a biographical unity, but a unity based upon the myth of the kerygma."[21] Matthew and Luke followed suit.

In one important respect, Bultmann parted company from Bousset. Bousset belonged to the world of cultural Protestantism. Early in his career Bultmann embraced the dialectical theology of Karl Barth. Instead of rejecting liberal theology like Barth did, Bultmann came to believe that dialectical theology made historical critical study more fruitful.

This combination of belief in the transcendent act of God with radical criticism, together with the history-of-religions understanding of the thought world of the New Testament, resulted in the demythologizing program that characterized Bultmann's later writings. The message of Jesus was the *presupposition* of New Testament theology rather than part of that theology. "Christian faith did not exist until there was a Christian *kerygma;* i.e., a *kerygma* proclaiming Jesus Christ—specifically Jesus Christ the Crucified and Risen One—to be God's eschatological act of salvation."[22]

The New Quest was launched by Bultmann's former students in the 1950s. They felt that Bultmann's radical emphasis was vulnerable to charges of docetism. Jesus was reduced to a shadowy figure whose historical reality was discounted if the exalted Lord of the kerygma was severed from the humiliated Lord in history. Ernst Käsemann, Ernst Fuchs, Günther Bornkamm, and Hans Conzelmann were among those who voiced concerns. However, in an address to the Heidelberg Academy of Sciences (1959), Bultmann brought about the end of the New Quest, rebuking his former students by name. It was not their critical skills that

---

21. Bultmann, *The History of the Synoptic Tradition*, 371.

22. Bultmann, *Theologie des Neuen Testaments* (Tübingen: Mohr Siebeck, 1948); ET: *Theology of the New Testament*, trans. Kendrick Grobel, 2 vols. (New York: Scribner's, 1951–55; London: SCM, 1952–55), 1:3.

Introduction

were at fault. It was their *theological* failure to grasp that the kerygma had changed the "once" of the historical Jesus into the "once for all" of the church's proclamation. The proclaimer had become the proclaimed.

CHAPTER 7: THE NO QUEST IN EUROPE TO WORLD WAR II. Chapter 7 examines developments outside the purview of Schweitzer and the history of religions school. It has three sections: "Early Reclamations of Jesus"; "The Recovery of Jesus' World"; and "Later Reclamations of Jesus." The term *reclamation* draws attention to the fact that Protestant, Catholic, Jewish, and Nazi scholars zealously reclaimed Jesus in their narratives of their heritage.

The early reclamations of Jesus began with a lecture series delivered *extempore* at the University of Berlin in the Winter Semester of 1899–1900. The lectures were delivered by the eminent church historian Adolf Harnack. His theme was the "essence of Christianity," a hot topic of the day. The English translation was given the title *What Is Christianity?* (1901). Sales far outstripped those of Schweitzer's work on the messianic secret. By the time of the fourteenth printing in 1927, Harnack's work had shipped 71,000 copies.

For Harnack, Jesus was first and foremost a teacher. His message could be summed up under three headings: the kingdom of God and its coming, God the Father and the infinite value of the human soul, and the higher righteousness and the commandment to love. Echoing the language of Nietzsche but inverting its meaning, Harnack insisted that the teaching of Jesus amounted to a "transvaluation of all values."

Harnack's view of the essence of Christianity found widespread approval among liberal protestants. A different view was taken by the leading Old Testament scholar, Julius Wellhausen, who in his later career turned to New Testament studies: "Jesus was not a Christian but a Jew. . . . His teaching, according to Mark, is almost entirely a polemic directed against the scribes and Pharisees. . . . He undermined the uniform binding authority of the Law. He took the Decalogue out of its context and reduced its scope to love of God and one's neighbor. . . . He demanded purity of heart and of actions, which were directed not to God but to human beings."[23]

Harnack's lectures drew a swift reply from Alfred Loisy, leader of

---

23. Julius Wellhausen, *Einleitung in die drei ersten Evangelien* (Berlin: Reimer, 1905; 2nd ed., 1911), 102.

xxvii

the French modernist movement in the Roman Catholic Church. Loisy's remark that "Jesus announced the kingdom of God, and what came was the church"[24] is widely taken to mean that the church was an anticlimax. In context, it meant the opposite. Building on John Henry Newman's idea of the development of doctrine, Loisy argued that the church was the outworking in history of Jesus' preaching about the kingdom. Harnack had made the mistake of thinking that an adult person's identity was understood by examining the person in infancy.

Irish Catholic modernist George Tyrrell famously summed up Loisy's case in the remark: "The Christ that Harnack sees, looking back through nineteen centuries of Catholic darkness, is only the reflection of a Liberal Protestant face, seen at the bottom of a deep well."[25]

Reform rabbi Leo Baeck complained that Harnack was ignorant of Jewish sources, especially rabbinic haggadic tradition. Jesus had a thoroughly Jewish outlook. The day had come for gentiles to absorb Israel's teaching.

Joseph Klausner was born in Lithuania to Jewish parents. He earned a doctorate from the University of Heidelberg and spent his early career in Odessa on the Black Sea. A Zionist, he emigrated to Palestine, eventually teaching Hebrew language and literature at the Hebrew University of Jerusalem. Klausner's *Jesus of Nazareth* (1921; ET 1925) demonstrates exceptional thoroughness in research and a deep appreciation of his subject. Klausner dismissed Harnack's Jesus as a product of "the liberal anti-Jewish Germany of the early twentieth century."[26] Wellhausen fared scarcely better. Klausner argued that Jesus, as a Jew, had one idea: to implant the nation with the idea of the coming Messiah and to prepare them for it. Jesus' ethical ideals surpassed those of Hillel. But apart from that, he gave nothing to the nation and to Jewish national life.

The second section of chapter 7 is devoted to the recovery of Jesus' world. The importance of the subject was recognized by Emil Schürer. His *History of the Jewish People in the Time of Jesus Christ* (1877) was originally intended as a textbook. Its various editions culminated in the

---

24. Alfred Loisy, *L'Évangile et L'Église* (Paris: Nourry, 1902; 5th ed., 1929), 153 (author's translation).

25. George Tyrrell, *Christianity at the Cross-Roads* (New York: Longmans, Green, 1909; repr., London: Allen & Unwin, 1963), 49.

26. Joseph Klausner, *Jesus of Nazareth: His Life, Times, and Teaching*, trans. Herbert Danby (London: Allen & Unwin, 1925), 96.

Introduction

extensively revised form of the multivolume reference work *The History of the Jewish People in the Age of Jesus Christ* (1973–87), edited by Geza Vermes and others. The work is like an immense background without a portrait—since Jesus himself makes only fleeting appearances.

The *Kommentar zum Neuen Testament aus Talmud und Midrasch* (1922–61), or "Hand-Commentary to the New Testament drawn from Talmud and Midrash," is commonly called "Strack-Billerbeck." The names are those of the project's founder, Hermann L. Strack, and its primary researcher, Paul Billerbeck. Later volumes were edited by Joachim Jeremias. The work was conceived as a means of initiating readers into the world of Judaism by noting parallels with the Talmud and Midrashic exegesis. However, it assumed that rabbinic Judaism represented normative Judaism and predated the important Dead Sea Scrolls. Additionally, nonexperts had a difficult time judging the relevance of alleged parallels in the absence of expert guidance.

The languages spoken by Jesus were explored by a number of scholars. In *The Words of Jesus* (1898; 2nd ed., 1930; ET 1902) Gustaf Dalman sought to ascertain the meaning of Jesus' words, as they would have been heard by Aramaic-speaking hearers. Dalman's *Jesus-Jeshua* (1922; ET 1929) argued the case that Jesus knew three languages: Aramaic, his mother tongue; Greek, the language of commerce and government; and Hebrew, the language of Scripture and theological discourse. Dalman went on to show how his interpretation affected our understanding of Jesus' words in the synagogue, the Sermon on the Mount, his final Passover meal, and his words from the cross. In an appendix, Dalman made a comparison between Jewish proverbs and maxims and those of Jesus.

Adolf Deissmann drew attention to the Greco-Roman world in *Light from the Ancient East* (1908; 4th ed., 1923; ET 1927). Deissmann maintained that the language of the New Testament was not a form of Semitic Greek barely understandable in the Hellenistic world but was the everyday Greek known as Koine Greek. A planned dictionary of New Testament Greek failed to come to fruition. It fell to Walter Bauer to produce the standard work used by scholars the world over *A Greek-English Lexicon of the New Testament and Other Early Christian Literature* (1928; 3rd English ed., 2000).

Gerhard Kittel, a leading authority on Judaism, gave his name to the reference work known in English as the *Theological Dictionary of the New*

A History of the Quests for the Historical Jesus

Testament, 10 vols. (1964–76). Actually Kittel edited only the first four volumes; the remaining six were edited by Gerhard Friedrich. The project went back to Adolf Deissmann's desire to place the vocabulary of the New Testament into living linguistic connection with its contemporary world. However, the task of identifying the distinctive features of New Testament language proved in retrospect more complex than contributors to the *Dictionary* thought. The grouping of words by a common stem led to interpretations based on etymology that did not do justice to usage.

The links between Kittel and National Socialism cast a dark shadow on the *Dictionary*'s achievements. Kittel joined the National Socialist Party in 1933. The same year he gave a public lecture on "the Jewish Question," which recommended separating Jewish Christians from gentile churches. Karl Barth, Martin Buber, Ernst Lohmeyer, and Adolf Schlatter (to whom the *Theological Dictionary* was dedicated) were among those who disowned Kittel's views. After World War II, Kittel was not allowed to return to his professorial chair or resume editorship of the *Dictionary*.

The third section of chapter 7 examines three later reclamations of Jesus. The first is the work of Adolf Schlatter, the Tübingen professor who taught many of the major theologians of the twentieth century. Among them were Karl Barth, Ernst Käsemann, Ernst Fuchs, and Gerhard Kittel. Schlatter's biblical commentaries shunned critical introductions and interaction with other scholars. On the other hand, they were crammed with citations in Greek and Hebrew from Josephus, the Mishnah, the Talmuds, and other primary sources. They show the Jesus of the Gospels deeply rooted in the world of Judaism and the importance of Jewish literature for understanding him. The historical Jesus was the Christ of faith, who was to be found by entering into the world of the text. To reach Jesus we must listen to the Evangelists.

By contrast, Rudolf Otto's approach was through the phenomenology of religion. His seminal work on *The Holy* (1917) identified the concept as the *numinous* mystery that produces awe and fear while it also attracts and exalts. Otto's last major work *The Kingdom of God and the Son of Man* (1934; ET 1938) built on this idea. Jesus was a Galilean charismatic itinerant preacher and healer.

As a Galilean, Jesus did not belong to official Judaism. At first, Jesus thought that he was the representative of the Son of Man. Later he saw himself as the Son of Man. The Last Supper was a prophetic sign showing his willingness to assume his messianic obligation to suffer.

Introduction

The working of the Spirit of God through Jesus' healing and exorcisms were manifestations of the dawning kingdom of God.

Walter Grundmann did more than anyone to bolster the pro-Nazi German Christians. He had earned his doctorate under Kittel and later assisted him in work on his *Theological Dictionary*. He became a professor at the University of Jena and director of research at the nearby Institute for Investigation into Jewish Influence on German Church Life and Its Eradication. In 1940 he published *Jesus der Galiläer und das Judentum* ("Jesus the Galilean and Judaism") with a view to giving a scholarly answer to the burning question of the day. This book is well remembered by New Testament scholars for asserting that Jesus "was no Jew."

Grundmann explored two avenues. The first was Jesus' message and clash with Judaism. Jesus was a "charismatic" who possessed an inner vision. Inevitably, it brought him into conflict with official Judaism. Jesus repudiated charges of impurity, being in league with the devil, and leading people astray. It was Jesus' adversaries who killed prophets and opposed the will of God. For a Jew to declare himself Son of God was blasphemous, but it was not so for the Romans. The Jews adopted the cynical ploy of representing Jesus as a dangerous political messiah. The act of handing Jesus over to the Romans for execution revealed the chasm between Jesus and Judaism.

The other avenue that Grundmann explored was Jesus' ethnic background. Grundmann claimed that for most of its history Galilee had been separate politically and ethnically from Judea. He inferred that Jesus was not a Jew but descended from one of the ethnic streams existing in Galilee. The Gospel genealogies and narratives linking Jesus' birth to Bethlehem in Judea were untenable fabrications, devised to foster acceptance of Jesus' Davidic descent and messiahship. Jesus was a servant, not a messianic ruler.

After World War II, Grundmann protested that his former actions were designed to save the church from Nazi oppression. He became a leading theologian in the communist German Democratic Republic. Among his many postwar writings was his massive account of *The History of Jesus Christ* (1956; 3rd ed., 1961). It dropped Grundmann's former attempts to make Jesus an Aryan. Otherwise, it fits the description coined by the nineteenth-century French writer Alphonse Karr: *Plus ça change, plus c'est la même chose*, or "The more it changes, the more it is the same thing."

A History of the Quests for the Historical Jesus

CHAPTER 8: THE NO QUEST IN EUROPE AFTER WORLD WAR II. One way of exploring this theme would be to examine articles in leading theological journals. In the case of the *Theologische Rundschau*, research was facilitated by the compilation of reports by Werner Georg Kümmel over a period of forty years.[27] Chapter 8, however, is more limited in scope. It focuses on three scholars who attracted international attention: Ethelbert Stauffer, Joachim Jeremias, and Oscar Cullmann.

Ethelbert Stauffer, professor of New Testament at Erlangen, wrote a series of books designed to locate Jesus in the worlds of Rome and Judaism for the benefit of general readers. They include *Christ and the Caesars* (1955), *Jerusalem und Rom* (1957), and *Jesus and His Story*, which was published in different translations in England (1960) and the United States (1959). Though popular in style, his works have endnotes rich with primary sources. Stauffer promised to stick to facts and omit interpretations, including his own. However, one interpretation must be considered: Jesus' interpretation of himself. It was impossible to fit John into the Synoptics' chronology, but it was possible to fit the Synoptics into John's.

Stauffer traced the Sanhedrin's decision to destroy Jesus to the raising of Lazarus (John 11:38–50). He used Mark for events leading to Jesus' conviction for blasphemy. On the question of Jesus' identity, Stauffer argued that Jesus did not refer to himself as the Messiah. He used Son of Man more frequently than any other title, often as a direct counter to Messiah. Jesus' most important self-designation was "I am he." It led to Jesus' condemnation. "I am" was the divine self-designation found in the Hebrew Scriptures. On the lips of Jesus, it was the "historical epiphany of God."

To some reviewers, Stauffer represented a step back into the precritical era. He paid no attention to genre, and his use of John seemed out of date. His claim to stick to facts, independent of interpretation, appeared naïve and positivistic. But to say this is not to deny that Stauffer's work contained important insights. Among them is his pioneering work in seeking to uncover the roots of hostility that Jesus aroused. These roots raised their own far-reaching hermeneutical questions.

In 1956 Joachim Jeremias delivered a seminal paper on "The Present

---

27. Werner Georg Kümmel, *Vierzig Jahre Jesusforschung (1950–1990)*, ed. Helmut Merklein, 2nd ed., BBB 91 (Weinheim: Beltz Athenäum, 1994).

Introduction

State of the Debate about the Problem of the Historical Jesus." He saw gains in the Bultmann school's attention to the kerygma. But he also saw grave dangers in surrendering the affirmation "the Word became flesh" and in ignoring the "salvation history [*Heilsgeschichte*]" of God's activity in Jesus of Nazareth. The church was in danger of docetism when Christ became an idea. It was dangerous to put the proclamation of Paul in the place of the good tidings of Jesus. On one level, Jeremias was sending a warning to the church and to its theologians. On another level, he was describing the agenda for his life's work, which took place primarily from the University of Göttingen.

Jeremias had already begun addressing this agenda in *The Eucharistic Words of Jesus* (1935, subsequently enlarged). The Last Supper was a Passover meal with a fourfold structure. In the gospel narratives of the meal, Jeremias detected Jesus' *ipsissima vox*—that is, his distinctive manner of speaking. There were three elements: the phrase "Truly I say to you"; the use of the *theological passive* for God's activity through Jesus; and a predilection for similitudes, comparisons, and parabolic expressions. Jeremias interpreted the injunction "Do this in my remembrance" as a plea that God would remember Jesus' death as a Maranatha cry.

Jeremias's study of *The Parables of Jesus* went through numerous editions, culminating in the sixth German edition (1962; ET 1963). Following in the footsteps of Adolf Jülicher, Jeremias rejected allegorical interpretation. Parables were not the prime means of spreading the gospel; this was done through other ways, such as communal meals, the offer of forgiveness, and the call to follow Jesus, which embodied God's outreach through Jesus to sinners. The parables were *defenses* of these actions and what they signified. Characteristic themes were as follows: now is the day of salvation, God's mercy for sinners, the great assurance, the imminence of catastrophe, it may be too late, the challenge of the hour, realized discipleship, the Via Dolorosa and the exaltation of the Son of Man, the consummation, and Jesus' acts as parabolic actions. The parables challenged hearers to come to a decision about Jesus' person and mission. The secret of the kingdom of God (Mark 4:11) was *eschatology* that was *in process of realization*.

The Prayers of Jesus (1967) brought together studies of key themes. Jeremias interpreted the word *Abba* as a unique expression of Jesus' personal intimacy with his heavenly Father. He suggested that the word derived from the childhood expression *Daddy*. *Abba* denoted the total

xxxiii

A History of the Quests for the Historical Jesus

surrender of the Son to the Father. The Lord's Prayer is preserved in two forms in the Gospels. Matthew's longer form (6:9–13) reflects liturgical tradition in Jewish Christian communities. Luke's shorter form (11:2–4) suggests gentile Christian tradition. Jeremias interpreted both forms eschatologically. The petition regarding "bread" asked God for sustenance in the end time. The petition regarding "temptation" referred not to everyday temptations but to deliverance from the time of trial in the end time.

Oscar Cullmann was one of the most versatile New Testament scholars of his day. Among his range of studies was an early investigation of the dating of the *Gospel of Thomas*. Another was on the date of Christmas, which could not be December 25. The early church did not celebrate Christmas in the same way they celebrated Easter. The only hint of the time of year given in the New Testament comes in Luke's account of the shepherds. December was too cold for shepherds to keep watch over their flocks outdoors at night. The adoption of December 25 was in line with the emperor Constantine's policy of uniting the worship of Christ with that of the sun, whose chief festival coincided with the winter solstice. The decision was comparable with Constantine's edict of 321 CE, which made the day of the sun (which coincided with the Lord's Day) the authorized day of rest throughout the empire.

Cullmann's *Peter: Disciple, Apostle, Martyr* was a contribution to the quest of the historical Peter, yet it indirectly involved the historical Jesus.[28] The case for connecting Jesus with the church (*ekklēsia*, Matt 16:18) was rejected by the Bultmann school. It was not just because the passage contains one of only three instances of *ekklēsia* in the Gospels, which are all in Matthew. The idea of the church seemed incompatible with the imminent coming of the kingdom of God. Cullmann pointed out that *ekklēsia* was common in the Old Testament to denote the people of God. Confession of Jesus as Messiah implied the existence of a messianic people.

The idea of *Heilsgeschichte* gained prominence in the nineteenth century through J. C. K. Hofmann. For Cullmann, God's saving actions in Christ were the dominant theme of theology. In contrast with Greek cyclical views of time and the more recent views of Schweitzer, Bultmann,

---

28. Oscar Cullmann, *Peter: Disciple, Apostle, Martyr; A Historical and Theological Study*, trans. Floyd V. Filson, 2nd ed. (London: SCM, 1962).

Introduction

and Barth, Cullmann set out a linear view of time in *Christ and Time* (1946; rev. ET 1964). He returned to the subject in his last major work, *Salvation and History* (1965; ET 1967). Echoing the language of World War II, Cullmann compared *Heilsgeschichte* with D-Day (the Allied invasion of Europe) and VE-Day (Victory in Europe Day). Christ had won the decisive battle (D-Day). The final victory (VE-Day) would be Christ's *parousia*.

Jeremias and Cullmann were the theological superstars of the postwar scene. When on tour, they packed university auditoriums. Chapter 8 would not be complete without noting the less-than-enthusiastic comments of the generation that followed. Nevertheless, Jeremias and Cullmann merit a second hearing.

III. Britain and North America

CHAPTER 9: ANGLICAN CHURCH POLITICS AND THE HISTORICAL JESUS. The Church of England, also known as the Anglican Church, occupies a unique position in English history. Since the Reformation in the sixteenth century it has been the legally established national church in England. Over the years, other denominations acquired legal recognition. However, church-state relations in national life have been monopolized by the Anglican Church. The two ancient English universities of Oxford and Cambridge were uniquely tied to the Anglican Church until well into the reign of Queen Victoria. All this meant that theological dissent within the Anglican Church had legal implications. The ensuing discussion focuses on two critical issues: programmatic essays calling for the church to adapt to the times and revisionist clergy who stirred up controversy.

The section on "Essays Calling for Change" discusses four Anglican symposia, each of which mapped out controversial theological programs. *Essays and Reviews* (1860) was a mild, rambling attempt by Oxford broadchurch scholars to introduce readers to the world of modern scholarship. It backfired with disastrous results.

Lux Mundi ("Light of the World," 1889) was the work of clergy with links to Oxford. Its central thesis argued that whatever adjustments may be required by modern scholarship, the incarnation must remain the church's central belief. In addressing the theme of "The Holy Spirit and

Inspiration," the editor, Charles Gore, introduced to Anglican readers the idea of kenosis. Jesus' differences with modern scholars over historical details of the Old Testament might be understood in light of the divine self-emptying of certain divine attributes—omnipotence, omniscience, and omnipresence—during the period when God became man. To opponents, Gore's proposal was tantamount to surrendering the incarnation altogether.

Foundations (1912), edited by B. H. Streeter, was closer in spirit to *Essays and Reviews* than it was to *Lux Mundi*. Although its authors were born in the age of Queen Victoria, their review of the foundations of Christianity was directed at the post-Victorian age. *Essays Catholic and Critical* (1926), edited by E. G. Selwyn, was a synthesis in the tradition of *Lux Mundi* for readers living in the post–World War I era.

The section on "Revisionist Clergy" focuses on individuals who sparked controversies over Christology and the historical Jesus. A common factor was the figure of Charles Gore—not the *avant garde* liberal Catholic of 1889 but the diocesan bishop and guardian of creedal orthodoxy.

CHAPTER 10: JESUS AT OXFORD AND CAMBRIDGE. The chapter has three main sections. Section 1 reviews early precritical Lives of Jesus under the heading "Victorian Perspectives."

Section 2 examines "Jesus at Oxford." William Sanday pioneered Jesus scholarship in England. He introduced F. C. Burkitt at Cambridge to the work of Wrede and Schweitzer. In so doing, he flamed Burkitt's enthusiasm for Schweitzer and eschatology. Sanday's own early enthusiasm for Schweitzer waned, but his determination to reconcile faith and scientific criticism endured.

Sanday's *Christologies Ancient and Modern* (1910) was intended as a prelude to a *magnum opus* on the life of Christ, which he did not live to write. In his attempt to restate Christology for the modern age, Sanday drew on William James's work on the unconscious mind as a model for understanding divine immanence and reconceptualizing the divinity of Christ. Sanday returned to the topic in *Personality in Christ and in Ourselves* (1911). The two books were republished in a single volume *Christology and Personality* (1911).

Sanday was one of the first British scholars to chair a regular research seminar, which launched in 1894. One tangible outcome was *Studies in the Synoptic Problem* (1911). Members of the seminar, such as Sir John Hawkins, W. C. Allen, and B. H. Streeter, went on to make their own distinguished contributions to scholarship.

Introduction

Section 3 of chapter 10 discusses the work at Cambridge of F. C. Burkitt and J. M. Creed. Burkitt was responsible for introducing Schweitzer to the English-speaking world through the translation of Schweitzer's *Quest of the Historical Jesus* by his former student William Montgomery. However, Burkitt distanced himself from Schweitzer's "consistent eschatology." Eschatology was important for putting the world in perspective but not for constructing a timetable of events. Later in life, Burkitt showed himself aware of Bultmann and form criticism. But he repudiated the form-critical account of Jesus traditions created by communities, as figments of the imagination.

J. M. Creed's commentary on *Luke* (1930) drew on form criticism and filled a gap in British scholarship. His Hulsean Lectures on *The Divinity of Christ* (1938), which saw Christ as "one with the creative word of God," found a way of expressing the divinity and humanity of Christ without becoming entangled in the thickets of ancient controversies.

CHAPTER 11: THE NEXT GENERATION. Chapter 11 discusses scholarship in the generation that followed that of Sanday, Streeter, Burkitt, and Creed. Although Oxford and Cambridge remained important, younger universities also played a significant part, as did some of the theological colleges dedicated to training ordinands for ministry.

Section 1, "The Shadows of Schweitzer and Bultmann," discusses the influences of Schweitzer and Bultmann in shaping the agendas of C. H. Dodd, T. W. Manson, and Vincent Taylor. Each felt compelled to present alternatives.

Dodd was educated at Oxford but spent his teaching career at Manchester and Cambridge. In *The Parables of the Kingdom* (1935; rev. 1961) Dodd proposed "realized eschatology" in opposition to Schweitzer's "thoroughgoing eschatology." In response to Bultmann's view of the Synoptic Gospels as late collections of stories about Jesus, Dodd suggested that analysis of the apostolic preaching in Acts showed distinctive patterns that fitted the framework of Mark. In *History and the Gospel* (1938), Dodd used form criticism to identify a consistent picture of Jesus in different genres and contexts—a unique historical personality characterized by his welcoming attitude to the outcasts of society. In retirement he returned to Oxford, where his studies began and published two major works about John: *The Interpretation of the Fourth Gospel* (1953) and *Historical Tradition in the Fourth Gospel* (1963).

T. W. Manson was educated at Glasgow and Cambridge. He followed

Dodd at Manchester, where he spent the remainder of his academic career. In a groundbreaking book on *The Teaching of Jesus* (1931), Manson argued that Jesus' view of the Son of Man was derived principally from Daniel 7:13. The Son of Man depicted the righteous, faithful remnant of Israel in their trials and ultimate vindication. "Son of Man" was a vocational title that Jesus originally applied to himself *and* to his followers in their common vocation to renew Israel as the righteous remnant.

The passion predictions applied to Jesus *and* the disciples. However, after reaching Jerusalem and Jesus' action in the temple, Judas changed his mind and betrayed Jesus to the authorities. The other disciples fell away. Jesus was left standing *alone* as the Son of Man. In other writings Manson was highly critical of claims made on behalf of form criticism.

Vincent Taylor spent most of his career at Headingly College, Leeds, in the North of England, training ordinands for the Methodist ministry. At the same time he made numerous contributions to scholarship. *The Formation of the Gospel Tradition* (1933) introduced form criticism to British readers. It remains one of the outstanding treatments of the subject. Whereas German form criticism was largely negative, Taylor suggested positive uses. In midcareer Taylor brought to nonspecialists accounts of scholarship on the person and work of Christ. His commentary on the Greek text of *Mark* (1952) has been described as "a no-stone-left-unturned interpretation of the Second Gospel."[29]

Section 2 addresses "New Questions and Old." It begins by noting two scholars who became prominent toward the end of this generation of scholarship. Both stood apart from the mainstream.

John Macquarrie taught in his early career at the University of Glasgow, where he had been an undergraduate student. He introduced British readers to demythologized existentialism in *An Existentialist Theology* (1955) and *The Scope of Demythologizing* (1960). He also translated Heidegger and wrote the survey *Twentieth-Century Religious Thought* (1963). Macquarrie's *Principles of Christian Theology* (1963) outlined existentialist approaches to systematic theology.

While at Union Seminary in New York (1962–70), Macquarrie joined the Anglican Church. He returned to Britain as Regius Professor of Divinity at Oxford (1970–86). In what many regard as his most enduring work, *Jesus Christ in Modern Thought* (1990), Macquarrie signaled

---

29. Robert Brawley, "Vincent Taylor," in *DMBI*, 962.

Introduction

rapprochement with orthodoxy. He moved further along this road in *Christology Revisited* (1998). It framed Christology in terms of "the absolute paradox," the apparent contradiction that Christ was both human and divine.

Austin Farrer spent most of his adult life at Oxford. His writings were characterized by fascination with symbolism and disdain for Q. Farrer's commentaries on Matthew and Mark and Bampton Lectures on *The Glass of Vision* (1948) were built around the idea that images were "the stuff of inspiration," the medium of divine and human encounter. Farrer's celebrated essay "On Dispensing with Q" (1953) was the starting point of the subsequent movement, headed by his student Michael Goulder, that contended that Q was a redundant hypothesis.

"New Questions and Old" concludes by drawing attention to the distinctive contributions of three scholars: David Daube, W. D. Davies, and J. D. M. Derrett. Davies pioneered modern insights into the relationship of Christianity and Judaism. Daube and Derrett were eminent legal scholars, who drew on their expertise in the field of law to illuminate biblical interpretation.

The closing section of the chapter presents retrospective reflections on the period under discussion.

CHAPTER 12: PRINCETON AND YALE. The next four chapters are devoted to developments in North America. Up to the beginning of the twentieth century, American theology was shaped largely by imported European ideas. The centers of higher learning were originally colleges preparing men for the professions. The importation from Germany of the PhD degree in the latter part of the nineteenth century helped to turn colleges into research institutions. Chapters 12 and 13 explore this transformation in four major centers: Princeton Theological Seminary and the divinity schools of Yale, Chicago, and Harvard.

In the nineteenth century, Princeton Theological Seminary was the bastion of Presbyterian Calvinism in the face of deism, Unitarianism, and liberalism. The last great protagonist of that tradition was Benjamin B. Warfield. Like many predecessors and successors, Warfield went to Europe to round off his education. He differed from them in applying his compendious knowledge of European scholarship to his indefatigable war on liberal ideas from Europe. To Warfield, the key that unlocked the New Testament was the patristic idea of the two natures of Christ: divinity and humanity. It also provided the test of orthodoxy and veracity.

Benjamin W. Bacon was Warfield's junior contemporary by roughly a decade. A Yale graduate, Bacon taught at Yale for most of his professional life. Whereas for Warfield the key to the New Testament was the doctrine of the two natures of Christ, for Bacon that key was higher criticism. Bacon applied German Pentateuchal criticism to the New Testament. His most famous contribution was his account of Matthew's portrait of Jesus as a new Moses, and Matthew's gospel as a new Pentateuch (*Studies in Matthew*, 1930). What is not always remembered is that, for Bacon, these were retrograde steps. They turned Jesus into a teacher of the law. Matthew's *neolegalism* obscured Jesus' affinity with the protests of the prophets of the post-Deuteronomic age against "book-religion." Like the prophets, Jesus was driven by the vision of the living God of goodness and truth.

CHAPTER 13: CHICAGO AND HARVARD. The University of Chicago was a relative newcomer among America's premier universities, and Harvard is its oldest.

The University of Chicago was founded in 1891 as a Baptist institution, supported by the munificence of John D. Rockefeller. Its first president was William Rainey Harper, a Yale PhD who had taught Hebrew at the Chicago Baptist Union Seminary. Harper insisted that the university should have a divinity school, and he should be named professor of Old Testament. Underlying all this was the aspiration that the fledgling university would become the Yale of the West. There was another aspiration: the missionary zeal shared by Harper and his faculty for spreading the gospel of modern scholarship.

Over the years, the university became separated from its Baptist roots, due at least in part to the alarm of Baptist ministers in Chicago over disturbing liberal tendencies of some of the divinity school's faculty. Meanwhile, zeal to bring scholarship to the public at large intensified. Whereas original members of the Chicago faculty shared a literary and linguistic orientation, social factors became increasingly important in the generation dominated by Shailer Mathews and Shirley Jackson Case.

Harvard College was founded by Puritan settlers in 1636. In the early nineteenth century it swung from Congregationalism to Unitarianism. Under the presidency of Charles William Eliot, the focus of the divinity school changed from what were considered sectarian interests to the scientific study of religion. Meanwhile, Andover Theological Seminary was founded nearby as a more orthodox alternative institution for the

Introduction

training of ministers. At its foundation Andover was better endowed than Harvard, and its curriculum was possibly more rigorous. But by 1908 Andover's future looked uncertain, and its theological differences with Harvard were no longer acute. The result was that Andover relocated, and the two schools became affiliated. In 1922 a full merger was proposed. However, it was thwarted by legal action. The entire Andover faculty resigned. Andover was forced into closure until it merged with a Baptist college to form the Andover Newton Theological School (1965).

One of the former Andover faculty members was the Harvard-educated Quaker, Henry Joel Cadbury. Later as a Harvard professor, Cadbury was acknowledged as a worldwide authority on Luke-Acts and its Greco-Roman environment. Cadbury is also remembered for his contrarian books on historical-Jesus scholarship. The most famous was *The Peril of Modernizing Jesus* (1937), which argued that the more Jesus was depicted in modern terms, the further he was removed from his own culture. In reading the Gospels we need to recognize our prejudices and presuppositions and learn the "mentality" of the Jesus movement. Cadbury was wary of ascribing a program or plan to Jesus. His moral teaching usually addressed *ad hoc* situations. Messiahship was not something he aspired to; God put it upon him. Whatever success or failure befell him, Jesus accepted as God's will for him.

Jesus: What Manner of Man? (1947) sought to be "more positive." It focused on Jesus' habits of thought and argument. Cadbury endorsed the view of the British Jewish scholar Claude Montefiore that Jesus taught "an excess or virtue." Cadbury called it "a demand for a surplus." Did Jesus live up to it? Mark 10:45 indicates that he did.

In *The Eclipse of the Historical Jesus* (1964) Cadbury berated the Bultmann school. Bultmann's preoccupation with the kerygma of the cross and resurrection meant that the Jesus of theology began where the Jesus of history left off. Bultmann made the apostle Paul the effective founder of Christianity. The flight from history was accelerated by Barth's theology of the word and Tillich's philosophy of being.

CHAPTER 14: JESUS IN AMERICA: THE NEW QUEST. Chapter 14 examines the contributions of four scholars during and after the New Quest: James M. Robinson, Schubert M. Ogden, Reginald H. Fuller, and Norman Perrin. Robinson, Fuller, and Perrin were enthusiastic supporters, though each in his own way. Ogden was critical.

On the demise of the New Quest, the four went their separate ways.

A History of the Quests for the Historical Jesus

Ogden stayed on course, developing what he called "a priori Christology." Perrin's theological pilgrimage led him into literary criticism and hermeneutics. He died while his work was still in progress. Fuller and Robinson returned to their theological roots. In his later years, Fuller described himself as a "pre-Tractarian high churchman." He became the elder theological statesman of the Episcopal Church in America.

In his first career Robinson pioneered the New Quest. After Bultmann's fateful Heidelberg lecture, he embarked on a second and even third career. All three had bearing on the historical Jesus. The second career was devoted to the editorship of the *Nag Hammadi Library*, the Coptic texts discovered in Upper Egypt after the Second World War. Robinson's third career centered on Q. Robinson was a key figure in the International Q Project, which led to *The Critical Edition of Q* (2000). On the basis of his Q studies, Robinson attempted to reconstruct the Q community and the historical Jesus according to Q.

CHAPTER 15: CHRISTOLOGY WITHOUT THE HISTORICAL JESUS? The two leading advocates of Christology without the historical Jesus were both German expatriates living in America. Both found America a place of refuge from Nazi tyranny. Both sought to rescue Christology from the vicissitudes of historical criticism.

Paul Tillich was a student of Martin Kähler. In America he taught at several major schools. His teaching was a twentieth-century restatement of the nineteenth-century Idealism of F. W. J. von Schelling. Tillich's theology of Being analyzed Being in terms of human estrangement from the Ground of Being. Jesus was the symbolic "bearer of the New Being" in which estrangement was overcome. For Tillich, symbols were the means by which human beings participate in the *reality of Being*. The truth of biblical narratives was not literal or historical. They expressed truth in much the same way as Expressionist painting expressed truth, as expressions of the essence of Being.

Hans Frei was brought to the United States by his parents. Eventually he became an Episcopal priest and was attracted to the theology of Karl Barth through H. Richard Niebuhr at Yale. Frei's work on *The Eclipse of Biblical Narrative* (1974) was a forerunner of what came to be called "Yale theology" or "postliberalism." He urged return to seeking meaning *in* the text rather than trying to find what lay *behind* it. In *The Identity of Jesus Christ* (1975) Frei argued that Christ's identity is grasped through believing the *fact* that Jesus has been raised from the dead. God's presence in

xlii

Jesus Christ becomes "identical with his effective act of self-presentation" through the narrative of the New Testament.

The final part of chapter 15 examines Leander E. Keck's analysis of the state of historical-Jesus studies beginning with *A Future for the Historical Jesus* (1971). In the 1970s Keck edited a series on "The Lives of Jesus," which made available classic texts from Reimarus to Shailer Mathews. A "central aim" of the series was "to encourage a fresh discovery of and a lively debate with this tradition so that our own work may be richer and more precise."[30]

Keck became dean and professor of biblical theology at Yale Divinity School. A feature of his career was the dialogue with Keck and prominent contemporaries. The chapter concludes with reflections on Keck's *Who Is Jesus? History in Perfect Tense* (2001).

IV. Ongoing Issues

CHAPTER 16: APOLLONIUS AND THE "DIVINE MAN." The figure of Apollonius of Tyana as a rival to Jesus of Nazareth has sparked controversy from the third century to modern times. Some twentieth-century scholars identified Jesus and Apollonius as examples of the generic "divine man." The editor and translator of the current Loeb Classical Library edition of Philostratus's *Life*, Christopher P. Jones, viewed it as largely "fiction." "Philostratus built up a picture of an ascetic holy man that was to resonate with pagans like Hierocles, and (more important for the survival of the work) with devout ecclesiastics like Photius."[31]

With regard to similarities with New Testament narratives, not only stories about Jesus but also narratives about Peter and Paul invite comparison. The similarities seem to be confined to what may be found in Luke and in Acts. They prompt the question whether Luke-Acts was a *source* that Philostratus drew upon as a model.

CHAPTER 17: NIETZSCHE AND JESUS. Friedrich Nietzsche played no personal part in the quests for the historical Jesus. He died in 1900 some six years before the publication of the original German edition of Schweitzer's *Quest*. Various sources affirm that Schweitzer admired

---

30. See Keck's foreword to the series that is printed in each volume.
31. Philostratus, *Life* (LCL), 1:12.

A History of the Quests for the Historical Jesus

Nietzsche. Both Nietzsche and Schweitzer were engaged in deconstruction and reconstruction.

Nietzsche arrived at his concept of the *Übermensch* through a lengthy progress toward nihilism that celebrated "the death of God." Since God was dead, objective values had died with him. The *Übermensch* created, lived, and died by his self-imposed values. Chapter 5 suggested that the *Übermensch* provided Schweitzer with a model for reconstructing Jesus in the wake of his deconstruction of orthodoxy and liberalism.

Nietzsche himself did not identify Jesus with the *Übermensch*. Perhaps it would have been too much of a concession to Christianity. He admired Jesus but despised Christianity for advocating compassion for the weak. It represented the opposite of his view of the *Übermensch*. In one of his last writings, *The Anti-Christ: A Curse on Christianity* (1888), Nietzsche pictured Jesus in terms of what physiologists of his day called the *holy idiot*, a combination of the sublime, sickness, and childlikeness.

CHAPTER 18: METHODS, CRITERIA, SOURCES. This chapter is the first of four chapters devoted to topics that are at the center of ongoing debate. Section 1 examines three leading advocates of distinctive criteria and methodology: John Dominic Crossan, E. P. Sanders, and John P. Meier.

John Dominic Crossan's *The Historical Jesus: The Life of a Mediterranean Peasant* (1991) was the most ambitious attempt to identify Jesus in light of the history of the Roman Empire, systematic study of canonical and noncanonical texts, and social theory. The first part of the book was devoted to a review of method. Before discussing the historical Jesus, Crossan analyzed in detail the historical, social, and economic context of the Roman Empire. The *Pax Romana* exacted a terrible toll on conquered societies. Their rulers were reduced to the status of clients of Rome. The land of Israel was no exception. This analysis provided the context for determining the role of Jesus in Jewish society. Crossan found it by seeking the bedrock of historical truth.

Crossan interpreted sources by compiling an elaborate inventory of texts identified by chronological stratification and multiple attestation. Of the 522 identified items, only 180 were attested by more than one source. The rest were discounted. Canonical texts were frequently dated later than apocryphal sources. An example was the *Secret Gospel of Mark*, which Crossan ranked prior to the canonical gospel of Mark, but is regarded widely as a forgery today. On the basis of the grid constituted by the *Pax Romana* and the inventory of texts, Crossan identified Jesus

Introduction

as a Mediterranean peasant bent on subverting the status quo, through communal meals and free healing. He assumed the role of a wandering Jewish Cynic.

Like Crossan, E. P. Sanders sought to uncover the bedrock of historical truth about Jesus. However, his criteria and method were entirely different. *Jesus and Judaism* (1985) began with an assessment of what Sanders took to be the eight most secure facts about Jesus according to modern scholarship. He then searched for explanation. Jesus' action in the temple was the dominant paradigm for understanding Jesus. Sanders insisted that it was neither a cleansing nor a judgment. It was a prophetic sign, part of Jesus' restoration program, signifying that the end of an era was at hand. The temple would be destroyed, so that a new and perfect temple might arise and with it a renewed Israel.

John P. Meier, a priest of the Roman Catholic Church, was the author of the most ambitious study of the historical Jesus undertaken by any scholar of any faith. His five-volume project is titled *A Marginal Jew: Rethinking the Historical Jesus* (1991–2016). Jesus was marginal in several ways. His death on a cross was one that Romans reserved for criminals. To Jews it was a sign of God's curse. Jesus came from humble origins. He lacked the formal training of the scribal literate. He rarely was mentioned in secular literature.

Meier distinguished between "the real Jesus" (who is beyond historical recovery), "the theological Jesus" (the Christ of Christian theology), and "the historical Jesus" (who inevitably is a modern construct). Meier identified five *useful* criteria: embarrassment, discontinuity, multiple attestation, coherence, and rejection.

The different conclusions of Crossan, Sanders, and Meier lead to revisiting the role of criteria (section 2). Like most writers discussed in this book, Crossan, Sanders, and Meier were more interested in the *historical value* of sources than in their *genre and format*. I contend that the two questions cannot be separated.

For now, I wish to draw attention to the obvious. In the case of Crossan, Sanders, and Meier—as throughout this book—there is a correlation between criteria and conclusions. Criteria shape conclusions. Facts are not like fish swimming about in the ocean that can be caught with the right tackle. Facts are products of observation, beliefs, and judgment. They involve data beliefs, data background beliefs, and control beliefs.

As Meier observed, the historical Jesus is a construct. But so too is

xlv

A History of the Quests for the Historical Jesus

the theological Jesus. Both constructs are based on narratives. If, for purposes of illustration and simplification, we can talk separately about the historical and theological, both involve three basic forms of constructs. Primary constructs are the constructs embedded in the primary sources (however we may define them). Secondary constructs are constructs made by interpreters (scholars, teachers, pastors, etc.). Tertiary constructs are constructs made by hearers and readers. Through the interplay of these constructs we apprehend and understand what generates them.

With regard to criteria, even the criteria of double dissimilarity and double similarity does not guarantee authenticity. It is more an approximation or definition of parameters of plausibility. In the book *The Quest for the Plausible Jesus* (2002), Gerd Theissen and Dagmar Winter draw attention to the importance of plausibility. They propose the criterion of historical plausibility as a correction to the criterion of dissimilarity. Historical plausibility has two subcriteria: the plausibility of effects and the plausibility of context.

The next sections of chapter 18 focus on sources outside the Synoptic Gospels: John (section 3), Paul (section 4), and sources other than Scripture (section 5). Rather than attempt to summarize in this roadmap these vast fields of research, I wish to draw attention to critical turning points.

With regard to John, three turning points may be noted. The first is Raymond E. Brown's comment on John 1:14. "Too often we read John 1:14, 'The Word became flesh,' in the light of the Matthean and Lucan infancy narratives and assume that the moment of becoming flesh should automatically be interpreted as the conception/birth of Jesus. There is reason to believe that the evangelist himself regarded the whole human life of Jesus from its beginning as the career of the Word-become-flesh."[32]

The second observation also refers to John 1:14. It is the comment of Craig A. Evans regarding the statement "the word [λόγος, *logos*] became flesh and dwelt [ἐσκήνωσεν, *eskēnōsen*; literally, "tabernacled"] among us." The term *dwelt* alludes to the tabernacle in the Old Testament. It was the locus of God's presence among his people. Evans commented: "Jesus is presented as the fleshly dwelling of the *logos*, that which has existed with God from eternity and that which enlightens the world."[33]

---

32. Raymond E. Brown, *The Community of the Beloved Disciple* (New York: Paulist, 1979), 152–53.

33. Craig A. Evans, *Word and Glory: On the Exegetical and Theological Background of John's Prologue*, JSNTSup 89 (Sheffield: JSOT Press, 1993), 185–86.

Introduction

The third observation draws attention to the case made by Allison A. Trites, A. E. Harvey, Andrew T. Lincoln, and others. John's gospel takes the form of legal case after the manner of prophetic lawsuits in the Old Testament. If so, there are wide-ranging implications for the interpretation of John and John's relationship to the Synoptic Gospels.

With regard to Paul and Jesus, attention is drawn to D. M. Baillie's interpretation of 2 Corinthians 5:19: "God was in Christ reconciling the world to himself." Like John, Paul had the tabernacle in mind as the locus of God's presence. Formerly, it was through the tabernacle that God lived, walked, and was among his people (2 Cor 6:16; cf. Lev 26:12). For Paul, Christ now superseded the tabernacle and its successor, the temple. He was known through the experience of grace. However, there was more to Baillie than what he let on in *God Was in Christ*.

With regard to outside sources (section 5), Josephus's so-called *Testimonium Flavianum* is the most explicit reference by an outside authority. It even appears to take a favorable view. However, many scholars think that the text has been doctored. The section contains a review of the pros and cons of this debate. It also advises readers to examine it in context, especially in light of the narrative followed (Josephus, *Ant.* 18.65–80).

The discussion of outside sources then moves on to the relevance to the Jesus of the Dead Sea Scrolls and the Nag Hammadi codices.

The concluding section draws attention to "Other Voices" in the debate about methods, criteria, and sources.

CHAPTER 19: THE JEWISH JESUS. This chapter takes the opportunity to review scholars who have not received close attention in the discussion so far. Each has figured prominently on the larger stage of international scholarship. They represent the spectrum of scholarly opinion, Jewish and non-Jewish.

Jewish viewpoints are represented by Paula Fredriksen, Amy-Jill Levine, Walter Homolka, and Daniel Boyarin. Christian viewpoints are represented by Bruce Chilton, N. T. Wright, Stanley E. Porter, and Tom Holmén. Maurice Casey was a self-described agnostic. The views discussed are illuminating but are far from representing a consensus.

CHAPTER 20: JESUS: TWO THOUSAND YEARS LATER, PART 1. Chapter 20 is the first of two concluding chapters that try to assess contemporary answers to the age-old questions about the identity and intentions of Jesus.

xlvii

A History of the Quests for the Historical Jesus

Section 1 deals with Jesus' name and titles. The Latin name *Jesus* contextualized him for Latin-speaking Western Christendom. It did so at the expense of concealing Semitic forms of his name, *Yeshuah* or *Yeshu*, that were used during his lifetime. His name pointed to Yahweh as Israel's savior. In the Old Testament LXX and Jewish Hellenist literature, the name was translated as *Joshua*, who led Israel's bloody conquest of the Promised Land. There are grounds for seeing Jesus not as a new Moses but as a new Joshua engaged in a peaceful conquest of sanctification and renewal.

Son of Man was a concept derived from Daniel 7:13, where it denoted the righteous remnant that was ultimately vindicated and exalted by God. There are grounds for thinking that in the Gospels Son of Man is a vocational title representing Jesus *and* his followers. However, his followers fell away at the crucial moment, and Jesus alone fulfilled the vocation to the end.

Son of God was a messianic title connected with the Spirit's *anointing* of Jesus as the Christ—the Anointed One—and the voice from heaven. "You are my Son, the Beloved; with you I am well pleased." In the Synoptic Gospels the "messianic secret" also involved a "Melchizedek secret," which is explained in chapter 21 (4.1).

Section 2 is devoted to a question that has come to the forefront of contemporary debate—the role of memory, testimony, and the historicity of the Gospel narratives. The discussion focuses on two areas of lively debate: Scandinavian/Nordic scholarship, and viewpoints in Britain and North America. On one side are those who draw attention to the fallibility of memory, particularly group memory. On the other side are those who contend that the entire fabric of civilized society rests on trust of testimony, which is subject to confirmation or disconfirmation. In the final analysis, the testimony of eyewitnesses is crucial.

Section 3 highlights a facet of Jesus' teaching that is sometimes overlooked. Jesus' teaching was not only oral. He also used prophetic signs in his teaching capacity. In doing so, Jesus continued a long line of Jewish biblical tradition.

Section 4 draws attention to the growing body of literature on Galilee, its terrain, politics, and relationship with Judea. Under the Hasmonean dynasty it had come under the domination of the Jerusalem temple hierarchy. Galilee had been invaded by Roman armies and had become part of Herod's kingdom. On Herod's death, his kingdom

Introduction

was divided, and his son Antipas was made ruler of Galilee. Antipas embarked on an ambitious building program, which included new capital cities—first Sepphoris and later Tiberias. There is no record of Jesus setting foot in either city. Antipas was responsible for the death of John the Baptist. Jesus called him a jackal and refused to be deterred from going to Jerusalem by his plotting.

Section 5 notes the importance of sociology to the study of Jesus. Sociology identifies the invisible rules and conventions that affect conduct: power, honor and shame, family and households, patrons and clients, laws and their implementation. The section draws from major surveys and studies of particular issues.

Section 6 approaches the politics of Jesus from two angles: the Zealots and Rome. The question of the Zealots tends to divide American and European scholars. In Josephus's account of the war with Rome, the Zealot faction enters the discussion only after the outbreak of war. From this fact, American scholars have inferred that the Zealots were not a factor in the time of Jesus. On the other hand, European scholars argue that the Zealots date from before the birth of Jesus.[34] They point to the long history of continuous political unrest and violence in the belief that the land belonged to Yahweh, not foreign invaders. Josephus had his own reasons for not naming them. He wanted to put the blame for the war with Rome on extremists who seized power in the course of the war. In his eyes, Israel's defeat was a divine judgment for opposing Rome.

The role of Rome has prompted a resurgence of investigation. The Gospels throw more light on the subject than has been imagined in years gone by. The world in which Jesus lived and died was in political and economic turmoil. What Jesus taught and did had far-reaching political implications. The kingdom of God called for love, nonviolence, and reconciliation. Jesus did not align himself with any party or faction.

CHAPTER 21: JESUS: TWO THOUSAND YEARS LATER, PART 2. Section 1 on holiness and purity draws attention to these fundamental components of Jewish religion and life. Jesus flouted convention by his physical contacts with the unclean and by the company he kept. Instead of being made unclean, Jesus practiced a "contagious holiness," which made the unclean *clean*. His actions involved conflicting paradigms.

---

34. See especially Martin Hengel, *The Zealots: Investigations into the Jewish Freedom Movement in the Period from Herod I until 70 A.D.*, trans. David Smith (Edinburgh: T&T Clark, 1989).

A History of the Quests for the Historical Jesus

The paradigms of Jesus' adversaries were grounded on the Torah, the law of Moses. Jesus taught that his actions fulfilled the Law and the Prophets.

Section 2 draws attention to the vast literature devoted to healing and exorcism. Jesus' actions expressed his concern for making people whole in the wider context of the restoration of Israel. There were no professional doctors who practiced medicine in the land of Israel in Jesus' day. Medicine was associated with magic in the surrounding areas. Jesus' success in exorcism, coupled with the following that he was attracting, made it easy to draw negative conclusions, such as the Beelzebul charge. In modern times, Morton Smith revived the charge of magic.

Section 3 examines the apocalyptic and the eschatological. It concludes with discussion of the "Apocalyptic Discourse" in Mark 13:3–37 (par.). The discourse poses the question whether it is about events in the immediate future, the end of the world, or both. There is strong evidence for the former. The "abomination of desolation set up where it ought not to be" nearly came about through the plan of Gaius Caligula to set up a statue of himself in the Jerusalem Temple. It was averted only by the emperor's own assassination (41 CE).

Cosmic language was used in Old Testament prophecy to denote the divine dimension of this-worldly calamities. Allusion to Christ's coming poses the question: "In which direction?" In Daniel 7:13 it referred to the coming of the Son of Man *to* the Ancient of Days. In this light, the disciples were asking about the earthly sign of the heavenly exaltation of the Son of Man (Matt 24:3). However, in view of the cosmic significance of the temple, their question could indeed be about the sign of "the end of the age."

Section 4 is devoted to the circumstances surrounding Jesus' death. In view of allusions in the narratives to Psalm 118, Jesus' plan to go to Jerusalem was a reenactment of the psalm. It involved ritual admission to the temple of a king who had been rejected. However, instead of being welcomed by the priests inside, Jesus' entry through "the gates of righteousness" proved to be entry to "the gates of Hades," the realm of the dead.

An immense body of literature is devoted to the trial of Jesus. However, study of the gospel narratives raises the question whether Jesus was given a formal trial. Following his nighttime arrest, Jesus was taken to the house of the high priest for pretrial interrogation. Because

Introduction

of disagreement among witnesses regarding allegations about planned destruction of the temple, the case against Jesus collapsed. It was to have been presented to a formal meeting of the Sanhedrin during daylight hours.

At this point, the high priest asked a question, which used the same words as the narratives of Peter's confession. It revived the charge, made by the deputation of scribes sent to investigate Jesus back in Galilee. Instead of asking about Beelzebul, the high priest asked point-blank: "Are you the Messiah [ὁ χριστός, *ho christos*], the Son of the Blessed One?" Jesus replied, "I am; and 'you will see [ὄψεσθε, *opsesthe*, plural] the Son of Man seated at the right hand of the Power,' and 'coming with the clouds of heaven'" (Mark 14:62; cf. Ps 110:1; Dan 7:13).

Jesus not only replied, "I am" (meaning "yes"), he gave a *prophecy* of the *sign* of exaltation of the Son of Man, which the hearers themselves would live to see. God would come in judgment, with the Son of Man seated at his right hand. God's presence was a place to which only the high priest could aspire. The members of the Sanhedrin agreed with the high priest's verdict of blasphemy. Jesus was judged culpable on account of a claim that merited capital punishment.

The formal meeting of the Sanhedrin the next morning made the decision to hand Jesus over to Pontius Pilate. Pilate had come to Jerusalem from his residence in Caesarea to keep his eye on events during the Passover. Blasphemy was a capital offence in the Torah but not in Roman law. Jesus was condemned and executed as the insurgent "King of the Jews." Legal formality to the proceedings came when Pilate delivered his verdict from his judge's bench (John 19:13–16).

The final sections of chapter 21 discuss the questions of the veneration of Jesus (section 5) and genre and history (section 6). The New Testament narratives were careful to stress that the Father was the unique object of worship and veneration. Jesus was the anointed Son who made him known. With regard to genre, I contend that it is of prime importance in pursuit of the historical Jesus. My survey concludes with reflections on recent interpretations of kenosis in light of Philippians 2:6–11 and its context in Greek literature and language.

PART 1

QUESTS BEFORE SCHWEITZER

CHAPTER 1

THE FIRST QUEST

IT IS CUSTOMARY to think that the quest of the historical Jesus began in the eighteenth century with the rise of historical consciousness in the Age of Enlightenment. In this chapter I propose a case for thinking that the First Quest began already in the lifetime of Jesus. Curiously enough, this first-century quest addressed essentially the same question as did H. S. Reimarus, whom Albert Schweitzer credited with inaugurating the quest: What were the intentions of Jesus and his disciples? However, the quest during Jesus' lifetime and the quest of the eighteenth century had entirely different worldviews and produced radically different answers. My argument will serve as a backdrop for reviewing the evolution of what we might call "proto-orthodoxy" and—in view of their comparative neglect of healing and exorcism[1]—more recent quests of the historical Jesus.

> 1. The Initial Conflict: Mark's Narrative
>   1.1. Mark's Spirit Christology
>   1.2. Jesus and Satan/Beelzebul
>   1.3. Capernaum: Calling and Healing
>   1.4. Jesus' Critics

---

1. A notable exception is Morton Smith, *Jesus the Magician* (New York: Harper & Row, 1978). On the question of miracles as magic, see David E. Aune, "Magic in Early Christianity," in *Apocalypticism, Prophecy, and Magic in Early Christianity: Collected Essays*, WUNT 199 (Grand Rapids: Baker Academic, 2008), 369–420; Colin Brown, "Synoptic Miracle Stories: A Jewish Religious and Social Setting," *Foundations and Facets Forum* 2, no. 4 (1986): 55–76; Eric Eve, *The Jewish Context of Jesus' Miracles*, JSNTSS 231 (London: Sheffield Academic Press, 2002). An earlier version of Aune's article was published as "Magic in Early Christianity," *ANRW*, 2.23.2 (1980): 1507–57.

1.5. Jesus the Father's Agent
1.6. The Beelzebul Charge
1.7. The Hermeneutical Divide
1.8. The Stubborn and Rebellious Son
1.9. End of Ministry in Capernaum
2. Narratives and History
2.1. Criteria and Authenticity
2.2. Reception History
3. Gospel Narratives: An Overview
3.1. Mark
3.2. Matthew and Luke
3.3. John

1. The Initial Conflict: Mark's Narrative

The First Quest was initiated early in Jesus' public activity. It is easy to miss it since only Mark identified it as such with his observation about the Beelzebul charge made by the scribes who came down from Jerusalem (3:22). Matthew and Luke both related the Beelzebul charge together with Jesus' rejoinder about sin against the Holy Spirit. However, Matthew and Luke omitted the Jerusalem scribes, giving different details (Matt 12:22–32; Luke 11:14–23; 12:10). Mark traced the Beelzebul charge to this delegation of scribes who were experts in Torah scholarship.[2] Scribes bore responsibility to interpret, teach, and participate in judicial matters. Evidently, disturbing reports about the activities of Jesus had reached Jerusalem. So the scribes were sent on a fact-finding mission. Their presence in Galilee may be regarded as the inauguration of the First Quest. Mark observed tersely: "And the scribes who came down from Jerusalem [οἱ γραμματεῖς οἱ ἀπὸ Ἱεροσολύμων καταβάντες] said, 'He has Beelzebul, and by the ruler of the demons he casts out demons'"

---

2. Emil Schürer, *The History of the Jewish People in the Age of Jesus Christ (175 B.C.–A.D. 135)*, ed. Geza Vermes et al. (Edinburgh: T&T Clark, 1979), 2:322–36. Although the word *Torah* is commonly translated as "law," it also means "instruction," "teaching," and "guidance." Strictly speaking, Torah refers to the five books of Moses, the Pentateuch (i.e., Genesis, Exodus, Leviticus, Numbers, Deuteronomy). In broader senses it was extended to the whole of the Hebrew Scriptures and the revelation ultimately derived from Moses. Recent discussion includes Michael Tait and Peter Oakes, eds., *Torah in the New Testament: Papers Delivered at the Manchester-Lausanne Seminar of June 2008*, LNTS 401 (London: T&T Clark, 2009).

The First Quest

(Mark 3:22; cf. Matt 12:24; Luke 11:15).[3] In connection with the later dispute over purity, Mark mentioned that the Pharisees were joined by "some of the scribes who had come from Jerusalem" (7:1). Mark's gospel is a carefully crafted narrative of events leading up to the charges in chapter 3 and the events that followed. There is more to it than meets the modern reader's eye.

Mark's gospel is not a biography in the modern sense. It offers no psychological analysis, no information about Jesus' early years, and next to nothing about his family background. Instead, Mark begins by giving prominence to three incidents that had far-reaching consequences: Jesus' baptism in the Jordan by John the Baptist (for which he came specially from Nazareth of Galilee); the descent of the Spirit following the baptism; and the words of the heavenly voice, "You are my Son, the Beloved, with you I am well pleased" (Mark 1:11; cf. Matt 3:17; Luke 3:22). Each of these incidents merits attention in light of the unfolding events.

1.1. Mark's Spirit Christology.[4] If we read John's baptism as an alternative to the purification rites of the Torah or as a forerunner to Christian baptism, we may miss the point. John is not criticizing the Torah rites, and in any case, the waters of the Jordan were regarded as ritually impure.

3. For further discussion of the importance of scribes *from Jerusalem* in the investigation of Jesus in the context of reports of his being "a miracle worker," see Roland Deines, "Religious Practices and Religious Movements in Galilee: 100 BCE–200 CE," in *Galilee in the Late Second Temple and Mishnaic Periods*, vol. 1, *Life, Culture, and Society*, ed. David A. Fiensy and James Riley Strange (Minneapolis: Fortress, 2014), 78–111, here 89–93.

4. Various forms of Spirit Christology have been put forward in recent years. G. W. H. Lampe (*God as Spirit*, Bampton Lectures 1976 [Oxford: Clarendon, 1977]) argued that the Spirit was not a separate person in the Trinity but a bridge-word indicating the immanence of God.

Roger Haight urged Catholics to think of Spirit Christology as a viable option today (*Jesus, Symbol of God* [Maryknoll, New York: Orbis, 1999]). In this regard, see also Piet Schoonenberg, *Der Geist, das Wort und der Sohn. Eine Geist-Christologie* (Regensberg: Friedrich Pustet, 1992); Birgit Blankenberg, *Gottes Geist in der Theologie Piet Schoonenbergs* (Mainz: Matthias-Grünewald, 2000).

Among works that attempted to combine Spirit Christology with traditional creedal theology are Gerald F. Hawthorne, *The Presence and the Power* (Dallas: Word, 1991); and Ralph Del Colle, *Christ and Spirit: Spirit-Christology in Trinitarian Perspective* (Oxford: Oxford University Press, 1994).

The most comprehensive account of Spirit Christology is the work of James D. G. Dunn, *Jesus and the Spirit: A Study of the Religious and Charismatic Experience of Jesus and the First Christians as Reflected in the New Testament* (London: SCM, 1975); Dunn, *Christology in the Making: A New Testament Inquiry into the Origins of the Doctrine of the Incarnation*, 2nd ed. (Grand Rapids: Eerdmans, 1989); Dunn, *The Christ and the Spirit: Collected Essays*, vol. 1, *Christology*, and vol. 2, *Pneumatology* (Grand Rapids: Eerdmans, 1998). Dunn (*Jesus and the Spirit*, 92, Dunn's italics) contends for a Christology from below: "If we can indeed properly speak of the 'divinity' of the *historical* Jesus, we can only do it in terms of his experience of God: *his 'divinity' means his relationship with the Father as son and the Spirit of God within him.*"

Quests before Schweitzer

The Jordan was, and still is, important as the eastern boundary of the land of Israel. In biblical history the southern reaches of the Jordan served as the entry point of the promised land and its conquest under Joshua. In this light, John's activity may be seen as a symbolic reenactment of Joshua's crossing of the Jordan (Josh 3–4). His preaching summoned the inhabitants of Judea and Jerusalem to reenter the promised land as a penitent, reconsecrated Israel in preparation for the coming reign of God. In receiving John's baptism, Jesus identified himself with John's renewal movement.[5]

As Jesus was coming out of the water he saw the heavens being torn apart and the Spirit swooping down on him like a dove (Mark 1:10).[6] Jesus' reception of the Spirit was described in apostolic preaching as the event that made him the Christ, the Anointed One (ὁ χριστός). "That message spread throughout Judea, beginning in Galilee after the baptism that John announced: how God anointed [ἔχρισεν] Jesus of Nazareth with the Holy Spirit and with power; how he went about doing good and healing all who were oppressed by the devil, for God was with him" (Acts 10:37–38). The occasion for this proclamation, attributed to Peter, was the reception into the church of gentile believers. A similar account was Peter's words at Pentecost, calling Israel to repent. "Jesus of Nazareth, a man attested to you by God with deeds of power, wonders, and signs that God did through him among you, as you yourselves know" (Acts 2:22). In both cases *God was acting through* Jesus of Nazareth.[7]

These examples from Acts, together with the Spirit Christology that emerges in Mark, may exemplify what Gerd Theissen called "cross-section evidence": "recurring items of content, or formal motifs and structures in different streams of tradition." Alternatively they may exemplify genre-constancy: "features and motifs that have maintained themselves in different genres."[8]

---

5. Colin Brown, "What Was John the Baptist Doing?" *BBR* 7 (1997): 37–50. Jesus' appointment of "twelve" is consistent with the theme of Israel's renewal.

6. Leander E. Keck, "The Spirit and the Dove," *NTS* 17 (1970): 41–67; S. Gero, "The Spirit as a Dove at the Baptism of Jesus," *NovT* 18 (1977): 17–35; Joel Marcus, *Mark 1–8*, AB 27A (New York: Doubleday, 2000), 158–67.

7. In similar vein, Luke's narrative of disciples on the Emmaus road records their description of Jesus as "a prophet mighty in deed and word [ἀνὴρ προφήτης δυνατὸς ἐν ἔργῳ καὶ λόγῳ ἐναντίον τοῦ θεοῦ καὶ παντὸς τοῦ λαοῦ] before God and all the people" (Luke 24:19). The Mishnah used similar terminology in a list of great men, whose like would not be seen again. Haninah ben Dosa was described as a "man of deed," i.e., wonder worker (*m. Sotah* 9:15).

8. Gerd Theissen and Dagmar Winter, *The Quest for the Plausible Jesus: The Question of Criteria*, trans. M. Eugene Boring (Louisville: Westminster John Knox, 2002), 178.

The First Quest

Jesus heard a voice from heaven saying: "You are my Son, the Beloved; with you I am well pleased" (Mark 1:11). The "voice" is commonly identified by scholars as an instance of direct divine communication, which rabbis termed a *Bath Qol* or *Bat Kol* (lit. "daughter of a voice").[9] To identify the appellation *my Son* with the second person of the Trinity, as defined by later ecumenical councils, is anachronistic. In Jewish writings the term *Son of God* was used in a variety of senses. In each case it referred to heavenly or human beings who were not divine personally but who stood in a special relation to God.[10] The subtext of the oracle in Mark 1:11 (cf. Matt 3:17; Luke 3:22; John 3:34) stressed the *kingly* appointment of Jesus (Ps 2:7; 2 Sam 7:14) with echoes of the chosen servant on whom God had put his Spirit (Isa 42:1).[11]

This line of interpretation is pursued in Sam Janse's comprehensive study of the reception of Psalm 2 in the early church. Janse argues that Mark structured his gospel on the depiction of kingship in Psalm 2. "The principal figure of Psalm 2, who is threatened and attacked by his enemies, is by virtue of the divine word God's king and God's Son. Mark essentially says: this principal figure is Jesus Christ."[12] The motif of Jesus as the kingly "Son of God" appears at the beginning, middle, and end of Mark's gospel in the accounts of the baptism (1:11), transfiguration

---

9. Another instance is Mark 9:7 in the transfiguration scene. John 1:33–34 gives a variant account in which God said to John: "'He on whom you see the Spirit descend and remain is the one who baptizes with the Holy Spirit.' And I myself have seen and have testified that this is the Son of God." See also John 12:28–30, where God speaks from heaven and the people think it is either thunder or the voice of an angel.

10. Christopher M. Tuckett notes "sons of God" as heavenly beings (Gen 6:2; Deut 32:8; Pss 24:1; 89:7; Dan 3:25), the nation of Israel (Exod 4:22; Deut 32:5–6; Jer 31:9, 20; Hos 11:1), righteous Israelites (Sir 4:10; Wis 2:17–18; 2:13; 5:5; *Jub.* 1:24–25), and kingly connotations (2 Sam 7:14; Pss 2:7; 89:26–27). See Tuckett, *Christology and the New Testament: Jesus and His Earliest Followers* (Louisville: Westminster John Knox, 2001), 23. Anthony E. Harvey (*Jesus and the Constraints of History*, Bampton Lectures, 1980 [London: Duckworth; Philadelphia: Westminster, 1982], 154–73) urged that *Son of God* must be understood within the constraints of monotheism.

The Sermon on the Mount implies that peacemakers and righteous disciples shall be called sons of God (Matt 5:9, 16). The address to God as "Our Father" (Matt 6:9) or "Father" (Luke 11:2) in the Lord's Prayer encourages disciples to engage in a filial relation with God.

11. Joel Marcus, *The Way of the Lord: Christological Exegesis of the Old Testament in the Gospel of Mark* (Louisville: Westminster John Knox, 1992), 48–79.

12. Sam Janse, *"You Are My Son": The Reception History of Psalm 2 in Early Judaism and the Early Church*, Contributions to Biblical Exegesis and Theology (Leuven: Peeters, 2009), 158. On the biblical background, see Adela Yarbro Collins and John J. Collins, *King and Messiah as Son of God: Divine, Human, and Angelic Messianic Figures in Biblical and Related Literature* (Grand Rapids: Eerdmans, 2008). For the Roman-world perspective, see Michael Peppard, *The Son of God in the Roman World: Divine Sonship in Its Social and Political Context* (Oxford: Oxford University Press, 2011).

Quests before Schweitzer

(9:7), and triumphant death (15:39). This basic theme was taken over by Matthew and Luke.

Mark's account of Jesus' baptism was preceded by a catena of three biblical prophecies (Mark 1:2–3; cf. Exod 23:20; Mal 3:1; Isa 40:3), stressing preparation for the coming reign of God. Their link with the name Isaiah suggests that Mark's gospel was the fulfillment of the prophecy of Isaiah.[13] Mark adds the prophecy of John the Baptist with its echoes of God pouring out his Spirit on all flesh (Joel 2:28). "I have baptized you with water, but he will baptize you with the Holy Spirit [ἐν πνεύματι ἁγίῳ]" (Mark 1:8).[14]

Christian tradition has interpreted this prophecy as an allusion to reception of the Spirit in baptism and conversion. The charismatic tradition takes it to refer to Pentecost and gifts of the Spirit following conversion. In both cases it would mean that the prophecy had only a postmortem fulfillment, so far as the earthly Jesus was concerned. It would have no relevance to Jesus' activity as narrated by Mark. John's prophecy is frequently conflated with Acts 1:5 and 11:16. The conflation ignores the fact that the prophecies in Acts were addressed to *disciples* about what will happen to them at Pentecost. John's prophecy was addressed to *Jews* who had come to him for baptism.

These observations are bound up with my thesis that the central

---

13. See Joel Marcus (n11 above). Marcus cogently argues that the opening words of Mark are a conflation of three passages (Exod 23:20; Mal 3:1; Isa 40:3). Together they represent Mark's gospel as "The Gospel according to Isaiah" (Marcus, *The Way of the Lord*, 10–47). See also Rikki E. Watts, *Isaiah's New Exodus and Mark*, WUNT 88 (Tübingen: Mohr Siebeck, 1997).

Although Mark contains only two references to the name Isaiah (1:2; 7:6), Isaiah's critique of the state of Israel was applied by Jesus to teachers of his day. "Isaiah prophesied rightly about you hypocrites, as it is written, 'This people honors me with their lips, but their hearts are far from me; in vain do they worship me, teaching human precepts as doctrines'"(7:6–7; cf. Isa 29:13). After Jesus' action in the Temple, Jesus adapted Isaiah's parable of the vineyard in a way that depicted himself as the son that the tenants put to death (12:1–6; cf. Isa 5:1–7). It led to the decision to arrest and have him executed (12:12).

14. James D. G. Dunn has made a strong case for considering the Q version of John's prophecy to be the original form ("Spirit-and-Fire Baptism," in *The Christ and the Spirit*, 2:93–117). It was essentially a prophecy regarding the inauguration of the new age (112). The note of judgment was transformed by what Jesus' death meant for him (cf. Luke 12:49–50). However, if Mark knew of the words "and with fire," he deliberately omitted them. His account stressed purification and the role that it played in Jesus' activity. Mark's narrative also recognized the possibility of "unquenchable fire," for disciples whose actions gave offence (9:43–48). In referring to his own "baptism" (10:39), Jesus' words appear to allude to the rite of baptism and at the same time his death, which his adversaries would see as a purification (Colin Brown, "The Jesus of Mark's Gospel," in *Jesus Then and Now: Images of Jesus in History and Christology*, ed. Marvin Meyer and Charles Hughes [Harrisburg, PA: Trinity Press International, 2001], 38; see n14 below).

theme of Mark's gospel is the consequences of the coming of the Spirit upon Jesus that made him the Christ, the Anointed One. The sundry actions of Jesus narrated by Mark show ways in which Jesus fulfilled John's prophecy in his lifetime and in his death. They embody different aspects of the purification and sanctification of Israel, beginning with Jesus' encounter with the man "with an unclean spirit [ἐν πνεύματι ἀκαθάρτῳ]" (1:23), which may be described as the first act of baptism with "the Holy Spirit [ἐν πνεύματι ἁγίῳ]" (1:8). This event was followed by other acts of purification and sanctification: the cleansing of the leper (1:40–42) and the remission of the paralytic's sin (2:5–11). Other facets of fulfillment come to light as Mark's story proceeds.[15]

Mark's narrative is not monolithic in the sense of presenting only one viewpoint. Mark presents various perspectives in addition to his own—those of the scribes and the Pharisees, Herod Antipas, and common people. Early identifications of Jesus were largely negative and, from Mark's perspective, inadequate. It is against this background that Peter confessed Jesus as the Anointed One (8:27–29).[16] To understand Mark's narrative, it is important to adopt reading strategies to help identify different viewpoints. Here I shall concentrate on conflicting viewpoints that are relevant for understanding the First Quest.

1.2. Jesus and Satan/Beelzebul. Mark depicts Jesus as the resolute adversary of Satan,[17] and a righteous upholder of the Torah. The forty

---

15. Brown, "The Jesus of Mark's Gospel," 26–53. My current research explores Mark in detail in a book I hope to write provisionally entitled *Hearing Mark for the First Time*. The project is an attempt to envisage how Mark's first hearers heard his narrative. I have attempted to envisage how this project might work out for the Synoptic Gospels in Colin Brown, "With the Grain and against the Grain: A Strategy for Reading the Synoptic Gospels," *HSHJ*, ed. Stanley E. Porter and Tom Holmén (Leiden: Brill, 2011), 1:619–49. For a sketch of how this approach might apply to the Fourth Gospel, see chap. 18. [Editor's note: Professor Brown was unable to finish *Hearing Mark for the First Time*.]

16. The idea that there was in Judaism a generally accepted profile of the Messiah belongs to the precritical era of Christian belief. Modern scholarship indicates a variety of conceptions entertained among competing forms of Judaism. See Jacob Neusner, William Scott Green, Ernest Frerichs, eds., *Judaisms and Their Messiahs at the Turn of the Christian Era* (Cambridge: Cambridge University Press, 1987); James H. Charlesworth, ed., *The Messiah: Developments in Earliest Judaism and Christianity*, First Princeton Symposium on Judaism and Christian Origins (Minneapolis: Fortress, 1992); John J. Collins, *The Scepter and the Star: Messianism in Light of the Dead Sea Scrolls*, 2nd ed. (Grand Rapids: Eerdmans, 2010). Anthony E. Harvey urged that we must work with the "provisional hypothesis" that *Christ* was not "the application to Jesus of a title which had wide currency, but of the identification made by Christians of Jesus 'who was called Christ' with the coming one who was occasionally described as 'anointed'" (*Jesus and the Constraints of History*, 82).

17. Richard H. Bell, "Demon, Devil, Satan," in *DJG* (2nd ed.), 193–202. The name Satan is used in the Old Testament in the sense of "accuser." In the Synoptic Gospels it is used interchangeably with Beelzebul, meaning "Baal the prince" or "Baal of the high house." "Baal"

days of testing by Satan in the wilderness[18] were the consequence of the Spirit's driving (1:12–13). It was not a test of whether Jesus was the second person of the Trinity as defined by later creeds; it was a test of his sonship as defined by the voice from heaven. The combat with Satan was a portent of things to come in the form of apocalyptic dualism.[19] Jesus, empowered by the Spirit of God, was locked in constant mortal combat with the forces of evil, corruption, and death.

Mark stressed the continuity of Jesus' mission with that of John the Baptist. "Now after John was arrested, Jesus came to Galilee, proclaiming the good news of God [κηρύσσων τὸ εὐαγγέλιον τοῦ θεοῦ], and saying, 'The time is fulfilled, and the kingdom of God has come near; repent, and believe in the good news [ἐν τῷ εὐαγγελίῳ]'" (1:14–15; cf. 1:4).

1.3. Capernaum: Calling and Healing. Broadly speaking, the narratives culminating in the Beelzebul charge consist of episodes, which are characterized by two alternating themes. For purposes of identification, the first theme may be termed the *call to discipleship and following Jesus.* The second theme may be termed *exorcism and healing.*[20] The first theme features Jesus seeking people and summoning them to follow him. The second theme focuses on people seeking Jesus. In Mark's narrative of healings the only person named, Bartimaeus (10:46), was also the last person to be "made well." The healing occurred as Jesus entered the final stage of his fateful journey to Jerusalem. It was a unique case of the two themes coinciding. On regaining his sight, Bartimaeus followed Jesus "on the way" (10:52). The choice of healings described in Mark seems to have been governed by the symbolism of the human body and the number of the tribes of Israel plus one representative of the gentile world.[21]

---

signifies "lord." Devil derives from the Greek διάβολος, "slanderer," and is often used as an alias for Satan. In the Synoptic Gospels the kingdom of God stands over against the kingdom of Satan. See Craig A. Evans, "Exorcisms and the Kingdom: Inaugurating the Kingdom of God and Defeating the Kingdom of Satan," in *Key Events in the Life of the Historical Jesus: A Collaborative Exploration of Context and Coherence*, ed. Darrell L. Bock and Robert L. Webb, WUNT 247 (Tübingen: Mohr Siebeck, 2009), 151–79.

18. Susan R. Garrett, *The Temptations of Jesus in Mark's Gospel* (Grand Rapids: Eerdmans, 1998).

19. Recent studies of dualism include Armin Lange, Eric M. Meyers, Bennie H. Reynolds III, and Randall Styers, eds., *Light against Darkness: Dualism in Ancient Mediterranean Religion and the Contemporary World*, JAJS 2 (Göttingen: Vandenhoeck & Ruprecht, 2011).

20. Mark generally distinguishes between exorcism and healing, although exorcism was a form of healing. See Bell, "Demon, Devil, Satan," 196–98, for differences of emphasis in the Gospels, and differences between Jesus' exorcisms and those of other exorcists.

21. Austin Farrer, *St. Matthew and St. Mark* (London: Black, 1954), 23. Farrer noted that

The First Quest

The first episode in Jesus' public activity is devoted to the *call to discipleship and following Jesus* theme: the call of the first four disciples, Simon, his brother Andrew, James the son of Zebedee, and his brother John (1:16–20). All four were fishermen. Simon and Andrew were given the promise: "Follow me and I will make you fish for people" (1:17). All four immediately left their work and followed Jesus.[22] Simon, later named Peter (3:16),[23] James, and John would play major roles in subsequent events.

The next episode changes abruptly to the theme of *exorcism and healing* with events in the synagogue at Capernaum on the Sabbath (1:21–28). The event caused Jesus' fame to spread through Galilee. It is not immediately clear why Jesus returned to Galilee or why he chose Capernaum[24] as his base of operations (1:21; 2:1; 3:1). Perhaps it was because he came from Galilee (1:9), and Capernaum was a convenient location. The city was situated in territory governed by Herod Antipas, who had sanctioned John's execution. However, it was relatively distant from Perea, where, according to Josephus, John's execution took place.[25]

Mark described the healing of twelve Israelites plus one gentile, corresponding to the twelve tribes of Israel plus a representative of the gentile world. The number also corresponds to the number of the disciples plus the tax collector Levi. Levi's occupation disqualified him from being a true Israelite. The healings form a kind of composite of the human body afflicted by typical ailments of the day: the unclean spirit (1:25), Simon's mother-in-law's fever (1:31), leprosy (1:41), paralysis (2:11), the withered hand (3:5), Legion (5:8), a dead girl (5:23), the unclean woman (5:29), the possessed Syrophoenician girl (7:29), the deaf mute (7:34), the blind Bethsaidan (8:25), the epileptic boy (9:25), and blind Bartimaeus (10:46).

22. Cf. Martin Hengel, *The Charismatic Leader and His Followers*, trans. James Greig (New York: Crossroad, 1981).

23. Martin Hengel, *Saint Peter: The Underestimated Apostle*, trans. Thomas H. Trapp (Grand Rapids: Eerdmans, 2010), 36–48; Marcus Bockmuehl, *The Remembered Peter in Ancient Reception and Modern Debate*, WUNT 262 (Tübingen: Mohr Siebeck, 2010); Bockmuehl, *Simon Peter in Scripture and Memory: The New Testament Apostle in the Early Church* (Grand Rapids: Baker Academic, 2012), 20–27, 153–63.

24. Virgilio C. Corbo, "Capernaum," *ABD*, 1:866–69; John J. Rousseau and Rami Arav, *Jesus and His World: An Archaeological and Cultural Dictionary* (Minneapolis: Fortress, 1995), 39–47; Gerd Theissen and Annette Merz, *The Historical Jesus: A Comprehensive Guide*, trans. John Bowden (London: SCM; Minneapolis: Fortress, 1996), 162–78; Stephano De Luca, "Capernaum," and Yardenna Alexandre, "Galilee," in *The Oxford Encyclopedia of the Bible and Archaeology*, ed. Daniel M. Master (Oxford: Oxford University Press, 2013), 1:168–80, 1:423–34, respectively.

25. Mark recorded John's execution in a kind of flashback but did not indicate the location (6:14–20). Josephus identified it as Machaerus (*Ant.* 18.117–19); cf. Morten Hørning Jensen, *Herod Antipas in Galilee: The Literary and Archaeological Sources on the Reign of Herod Antipas and Its Socio-Economic Impact on Galilee*, 2nd ed., WUNT II/215 (Tübingen: Mohr Siebeck, 2006). On the death of Herod the Great, his son Herod Antipas was made tetrarch of Galilee (4 BCE–39 CE). When the Romans deposed Archelaus in 6 CE, Antipas was given Perea, the separate territory east of the Jordan extending south to the northern part of the Dead Sea. The palatial stronghold of Machaerus was located in the south of Perea.

Quests before Schweitzer

Jesus (at least in later life) seems to have avoided the capital cities of Herod Antipas: first Sepphoris[26] and then Tiberias.[27]

Capernaum was located on the northern shore of the Sea of Galilee some two miles west of the Jordan. It stood on the *Via Maris* ("Way of the Sea"), which linked Damascus to Ptolemais and Caesarea Maritima, and was conveniently situated for escape (if need be) to the adjoining territory of Herod Philip, tetrarch of the territories north and east of the Jordan. Capernaum was also a convenient base from which to reach the homeland of the lost northern tribes of Israel.[28] In light of subsequent events, all these factors seem relevant.

From the outset, Jesus' public activity was characterized by observance of the Torah and, for want of better terminology, extraordinary behavior.[29] Jesus made a point of waiting for the Sabbath to begin teach-

---

26. Sepphoris was strategically located in the mountains of lower Galilee some eighteen miles from the Mediterranean and about the same distance from Tiberias on the Sea of Galilee. It is thought to have been the northern outpost of Herod the Great. On his death a revolt against the Romans was put down by Varus (4 BCE; cf. Josephus, *J.W.* 2.68; *Ant.* 17.289). Antipas made Sepphoris his capital and made it militarily impregnable (Josephus, *Ant.* 18.27). Nazareth was located some four miles down the mountain from Sepphoris. It is thought that Joseph and Jesus may have found employment there as carpenters and builders (Gk. τέκτων), but Sepphoris is not mentioned in the New Testament. See further Rebecca Martin Nagy, Carol L. Meyers, Eric M. Meyers, and Zeev Weiss, eds., *Sepphoris in Galilee: Crosscurrents of Culture* (Winona Lake, IN: Eisenbrauns, 1996); Carol Meyers and Eric M. Meyers, "Sepphoris," in *The Oxford Encyclopedia of the Bible and Archaeology*, 2:336–48.

27. Tiberias (named in honor of the emperor Tiberius [14–37 CE]) was founded around 20 CE by Herod Antipas to replace Sepphoris as his main residence. It was situated between the steep hills to the west and the lake shoreline. Josephus identified the area as "the best region of Galilee on Lake Gennesaritis" (*Ant.* 18.36)—also called the Sea of Galilee and Lake Tiberias. Josephus noted that the new settlers were "a promiscuous rabble," including forced labor. During construction, tombs were discovered, which rendered the settlers unclean for seven days (*Ant.* 18.37; cf. Num 19:11–22). Even today, the area is avoided by religiously observant Jews. Jesus may have avoided it because of its uncleanness and the presence of Herod Antipas. The only references to Tiberias in the New Testament are John 6:21, 23; 21:1. See further James F. Strange, "Tiberias," *ABD* 6:547–49; John J. Rousseau and Rami Arav, "Tiberias," in *Jesus and His World: An Archaeological and Cultural Dictionary* (Minneapolis: Fortress, 1995), 316–18; Shulamit Miller, "Tiberias," in *The Oxford Encyclopedia of the Bible and Archaeology* 2:429–37.

28. Brant Pitre, *Jesus, the Tribulation, and the End of Exile: Restoration Eschatology and the Origin of the Atonement*, WUNT 204 (Tübingen: Mohr Siebeck, 2005).

29. Among recent studies that examine Jesus' continuity with Judaism and divergence is Tom Holmén, ed., *Jesus in Continuum*, WUNT 289 (Tübingen: Mohr Siebeck, 2012). Articles include Darrell L. Bock, "What Did Jesus Do That Got Him into Trouble? Jesus in the Continuum of Early Judaism–Early Christianity," 171–210; and Christopher Tuckett, "Jesus and the Sabbath," 411–42.

Bock notes among early "minor irritants": association with tax collectors and sinners; forgiveness of sins; Sabbath incidents; authority and exorcisms; purity. These are "solidified" by later "major incidents": temple cleansing and declaration before leadership of future vindication.

The First Quest

ing in the synagogue[30] at Capernaum. However, he taught as "one having authority, and not as the scribes" (1:22). Jesus' teaching was interrupted by a man with an unclean spirit. The episode (1:23–26) represented a clash between two spirits: a demonic spirit that had taken possession of the man and the Spirit of God that had anointed Jesus. The encounter prompted the response "What is this? A new teaching—with authority [διδαχὴ καινὴ κατ᾽ ἐξουσίαν]! He commands even the unclean spirits, and they obey him" (1:27). The remark about subjection of the spirits resurfaced in the charges, "He has Beelzebul, and by the ruler of the demons he casts out demons" (3:22).

Typically, the unclean spirit's description of Jesus as "the Holy One of God" (1:24) is taken as an acknowledgment of Jesus' true identity. However, Jesus made a point of rejecting the testimony of spirits (1:34; 3:11–12). If he had accepted their testimony, it would have given weight to the charge that Beelzebul had given him mastery over the spirits. Graham H. Twelftree contends that, in the context of ancient exorcism, naming may be seen as an attempt to gain power. Here it was a form of self-defense in an attempt to gain power over Jesus.[31] By commanding the spirit to be silent and depart, Jesus demonstrated the superiority of the Spirit of God that anointed him.

The episode may be read on two levels. Paul W. Hollenbach's social historical approach sees such instances of possession as the outcome of

---

Like others in the same volume Bock does not treat as "major"—or indeed at all—questions of the first commandment and apostasy latent in the Beelzebul charge or disregard for the fifth commandment in connection with family ties.

Tuckett concludes that almost all the contexts involving Jesus and the Sabbath concern healing and miracles. "Jesus' actions are to be seen as bestowing and/or 'saving' 'life'—and hence his actions override even Sabbath law" (441).

30. Recent accounts of synagogues in the time of Jesus include Lee I. Levine, "Synagogue," in *The Oxford Handbook of Jewish Daily Life in Roman Palestine*, ed. Catherine Hezser (Oxford: Oxford University Press, 2010), 521–44; Lester L. Grabbe, "Synagogue and Sanhedrin in the First Century," in *HSHJ*, 2:1724–45; Anders Runesson, "Synagogue," in *DJG*, 903–11.

31. Graham H. Twelftree, *Jesus the Exorcist: A Contribution to the Study of the Historical Jesus*, WUNT 54 (Tübingen: Mohr Siebeck, 1993), 53–71; cf. Hans Dieter Betz, ed., *The Greek Magical Papyri in Translation, Including the Demotic Spells* (Chicago: University of Chicago Press, 1986; 2nd ed., 1992).

Clinton Wahlen also identified this episode as an exorcism in virtue of the power of the Holy Spirit (*Jesus and the Impurity of Spirits in the Synoptic Gospels*, WUNT 185 [Tübingen: Mohr Siebeck, 2004], 81–92, 170–75). However, Wahlen's main interest lay in comparison of the Synoptic accounts. He drew a sharp distinction in Mark (as contrasted with Matthew and Luke) between exorcism of a demon and healing of the sick (88).

colonial oppression.[32] Hollenbach examined cases of abnormal behavior in dire situations and noted comparable behavior in New Testament descriptions. Peter G. Bolt argues that Mark's hearers would have understood demons as the spirits of the departed, and Jesus' action as the initial skirmish with the powers of death.[33] Bolt examined the use of δαίμων (which he translated as "daimon" in preference to the more common "demon") and its cognates in a wide range of Greco-Roman texts and other sources. People "in the ancient world would simply assume the connection between *daimons* and the spirits of the dead."[34] Hearers of Mark's narrative would make the same connection when Mark used as an alternative πνεῦμα ἀκάθαρτον, "unclean spirit."[35]

In the case of the episode in the synagogue at Capernaum, Bolt admitted that it contained no direct reference to spirits of the dead. However, there was the underlying assumption about the common identity of unclean spirits and *daimons*. Moreover, there were links with the world of magic: naming, binding (φιμώθητι),[36] and violence and noise on exit. The most important point was the spirit's question (v. 24): "Have you come to destroy us?" Bolt concludes, "The *daimon's* question raises the possibility that Jesus had come to destroy these beings. If so, he would thus also end their manipulation by magicians and the resulting evil effects, thus breaking the fear of such influences and effects by which large segments of the populace were held. The question raises the exciting possibility that Jesus was about to unlock the stranglehold of the dead on the living."[37]

The next episode describes the return from the synagogue to Simon's house and the healing of his mother-in-law's fever (1:29–31). At first sight the incident appears to have relatively minor importance as one of the less

---

32. Paul W. Hollenbach, "Jesus, Demoniacs, and Public Authorities: A Socio-Historical Study," *JAAR* 49 (1981): 567–88; Hollenbach, "Recent Historical Jesus Studies and the Social Sciences," in *SBL 1983 Seminar Papers* (Chico, CA: Scholars, 1983), 61–78; Hollenbach, "Help for Interpreting Jesus' Exorcisms," in *SBL 1993 Seminar Papers* (Atlanta: Scholars, 1993), 119–28.

33. Peter G. Bolt, "Jesus, the Daimons and the Dead," in *The Unseen World: Christian Reflections on Angels, Demons and the Heavenly Realm*, ed. Anthony N. S. Lane (Grand Rapids: Baker, 1996), 75–102. Cf. Peter G. Bolt, *Jesus' Defeat of Death: Persuading Mark's Early Readers*, SNTSMS 125 (Cambridge: Cambridge University Press, 2003); *The Cross from a Distance: Atonement in Mark's Gospel* (Downers Grove, IL: InterVarsity Press, 2004).

34. Bolt, "Jesus, the Daimons and the Dead," 75.

35. Bolt, "Jesus, the Daimons and the Dead," 77n3.

36. The verb φιμόω (*phimoō*) means "muzzle," or "silence." It was used in exorcism and is found in the narrative of the stilling of the storm (4:39). *BDAG*, 1060.

37. Bolt, "Jesus, the Daimons and the Dead," 97.

The First Quest

spectacular healings attributed to Jesus. It turns out to have major consequences. It brings together the two themes of *exorcism and healing* and the *call to discipleship and following Jesus*. In Mark's narrative Jesus "took her by the hand and lifted her up. Then the fever left her, and she began to serve them." Simon's house seems to have become the base of Jesus' activity in Galilee so long as it lasted (1:33; 2:1; 3:19, 31). Simon's mother's serving extended to becoming the matriarch of his new family. This role was indicated when Jesus' biological mother and brothers came to the house to remonstrate with him after the Beelzebul charge (3:31). The crowd around Jesus inside the house informed Jesus that they were outside. He declined to see them asking, "Who are my mother and brothers?" Looking around him, he said, "Here are my mother and my brothers! Whoever does the will of God is my brother and sister and mother" (3:33–35).

The next four episodes are all devoted to the theme of *healing and exorcism*. The first two give general accounts; the second two give more detailed descriptions. The first of the general accounts describes what happened when the Sabbath was over (1:32–34). By waiting until sundown to bring the sick and the possessed to the house for healing and exorcism, the entire city of Capernaum showed their fidelity to the Torah. Jesus cured various diseases. He cast out many demons, forbidding them to speak "because they knew him" (1:34). The following morning, very early Jesus went out alone to pray.[38] When Simon and his companions found him, Jesus explained that his mission was to "proclaim the message" in the neighboring towns, "for that is what I came out to do" (1:38). This led to the second general account: Jesus' mission throughout Galilee "proclaiming the message in their synagogues and casting out demons" (1:39).

The story of Jesus healing of the leper (1:40–45) was the first of the two more detailed descriptions of a healing. The event proved to be a major turning point, marking the start of Jesus' alienation from the authorities in Jerusalem. Mark gives no indication of time or place, but presumably it was not a built-up area because lepers had to be segregated from communities for fear of contagion.

To see the story in perspective, we need to see it in context of Jewish history and religion. The term *leprosy* covers a variety of diseases.[39]

---

38. Mark stresses the role of solitary prayer at crucial turning points in Jesus' life (1:35; 6:46; 14:35, 39).

39. The biblical laws for treatment of conditions commonly called leprosy are given in Lev 13–14; see David P. Wright and Richard M. Jones, "Leprosy," in *ABD*, 4:277–82; R. I. Zwi

15

Even in the Second Temple period, professional doctors practiced medicine in the Diaspora but not in the land of Israel itself. On the one hand, the history of medicine in the surrounding nations was associated with magic. On the other hand, the Torah declared that Yahweh alone was Israel's healer (Exod 15:26; Deut 32:39). Sickness and healing were signs of God's punishment and favor. Sickness was seen widely as evidence of demonic powers. Where recovery occurred through prophets, as in the cases of Elijah (1 Kgs 17:17–24) and Elisha (2 Kgs 5:1–15), the prophet was God's agent in healing. Trained physicians first appeared in the Jewish Diaspora. They were commended in the Wisdom of Ben Sira "for their gift of healing comes from the Most High" (Sir 38:2). Where the "physician" (ἰατρός) is mentioned (e.g., Mark 2:17; 5:26), the connotation is that of a healer rather than a medical doctor in the modern sense of the term.[40]

In the purity system of the Torah, priests functioned as public health inspectors, which is why Jesus' commanded the leper to say nothing to anyone and to show himself to the priest "and offer for your cleansing what Moses commanded, as a testimony to them" (1:44; cf. Lev 14:2–32). To fulfil this injunction the man would have had to go all the way to the temple in Jerusalem.

By obeying Jesus' injunction, the man would have confronted the authorities with the question of how he had been healed. Jesus had not only responded to the man's plea, "If you choose, you can make me clean" (1:40), but also *touched* him and said, "I do choose. Be made clean!" (1:41). According to the Torah, this act would have made Jesus himself unclean. Jesus' touch went beyond Elisha's treatment of Naaman, where no physical contact was made (2 Kings 5). The incident illustrates Mark's portrait of Jesus as one who communicates holiness and purity.

Klaus Berger traced the root of the ensuing conflict with the Pharisees to different conceptions of purity.[41] The Pharisees had a "defensive"

Werblowsky and Geoffrey Wigoder, "Leprosy," *ODJR*, 414. A more exhaustive review in the context of the Torah purity system is given by Jacob Milgrom, *Leviticus 1–16*, AB 3 (New York: Doubleday, 1991), 768–889.

40. Howard Clark Kee, *Miracle in the Early Christian World: A Study in Sociohistorical Method* (New Haven and London: Yale University Press, 1983); Kee, *Medicine, Miracle and Magic in New Testament Times*, SNTSMS 55 (Cambridge: Cambridge University Press, 1986); Kee, "Medicine and Healing," *ABD* 4:659–64.

41. Klaus Berger, "Jesus als Pharisäer und frühe Christen als Pharisäer," *NovT* 30 (1988): 231–62; cf. Jerome H. Neyrey, "The Idea of Purity in Mark's Gospel," *Semeia* 35 (1986): 91–128.

attitude, which avoided contact with whatever defiled, and followed prescribed rituals when contact was unavoidable. Jesus' disregard of "defensive" purity violated Pharisaic practice. His practice of "offensive" holiness conveyed purity to the unclean in virtue of his anointing by the Spirit.[42] Crispin H. T. Fletcher-Louis saw the "contagious holiness" as an aspect of "a programmatic statement of Jesus' claim to a high-priestly identity as 'the holy one of God.'"[43]

These differences were enough to alienate orthodox Jews. Nevertheless, Howard Clark Kee noted a fundamental continuity with Jewish tradition. Kee observed, "The role of Jesus as healer was by no means an accommodation of an itinerant prophet-preacher to Hellenistic culture, but was in direct continuity with the Old Testament of what God was doing in the New Age, for the salvation of his people and for the healing of the nations. Jesus is pictured in the gospel tradition as pre-eminently the agent of Yahweh the Healer."[44] However, the leper's disregard of Jesus' instructions about showing himself to the priests ensured that "Jesus could no longer go into a town openly, but stayed out in the country; and people came to him from every quarter" (1:45). From that point on, Jesus' relations with the Jerusalem hierarchy went irrevocably downhill.

The healing of the paralytic (2:1–12) introduces another aspect of purification: forgiveness of sin. It also raises the question of authority, which is an issue that surfaces at crucial junctures in Mark's narrative (1:22, 27; 2:10; 3:15; 6:7; 11:28, 29, 33). Jesus' pronouncement, "Son, your sins are forgiven" (2:5), prompted the question in the minds of the scribes present in the synagogue: "Why does this man speak thus? It is blasphemy! Who can forgive sins but God alone?" (2:7 RSV).

1.4. Jesus' Critics. Before we examine the blasphemy charge, it is important to note that from now on in Mark's narrative complaints against Jesus seems to alternate between those leveled by scribes and those leveled by Pharisees.[45] Lester L. Grabbe observes that the term *scribe* (γραμματεύς) was widely used in Greek literature for those gifted

---

42. Berger, "Jesus als Pharisäer," 247.
43. Crispin H. T. Fletcher-Louis, "Jesus as the High Priestly Messiah," *JSHJ* 4 (2006): 155–75; and *JSHJ* 5 (2007): 57–79.
44. Kee, *Medicine, Miracle, and Magic in New Testament Times*, 125.
45. For comprehensive overview of the situation see the articles in William Horbury, W. D. Davies, and John Sturdy, eds., *The Cambridge History of Judaism*, vol. 3, *The Early Roman Period* (Cambridge: Cambridge University Press, 1999).

with the skill of writing who occupied a variety of positions involving drafting documents and administration. In the Jewish world they were employed mainly in provincial administration and the Jerusalem temple.[46] Their role as students of the Torah was eulogized by Ben Sira (Sir 38:24–39:11).

Mark indicates different classes of scribes. The scribes in Mark 2:6 appear to be locally based administrators and interpreters of the Torah. This would account for their presence in the synagogue at Capernaum on the Sabbath and might also account for the congregation's astonishment at the difference between Jesus and the scribes (1:22; 2:12). The "scribes of the Pharisees" (2:16) may indicate scribes drawn from the Pharisaic community. The scribes "who came down from Jerusalem" (3:22; cf. 7:1) suggests they were high level Torah experts sent to investigate Jesus regarding disturbing reports from Galilee.

Gregory Thellman sees the Pharisees as the main opposition group to Jesus in Galilee.[47] Their primary concern was with praxis and purity. Jacob Neusner's contention, that the Pharisees sought to maintain purity on the same level as that required in the temple cult, makes sense in the Galilean context.[48] Participation in temple rites on a regular basis would be impossible in regions as remote as Galilee. But purity ritual practices could be followed anywhere. Pharisees are mentioned again in Mark 12:13 in connection with the lawfulness of paying tribute to

---

46. Lester L. Grabbe, "Scribes," in *EHJ*, 554–55; M. J. Cook, *Mark's Treatment of the Jewish Leaders*, NovTSup 51 (Leiden: Brill, 1978); Daniel R. Schwartz, *Studies in the Jewish Background of Christianity*, WUNT 60 (Tübingen: Mohr Siebeck, 1992); Lester L. Grabbe, *Priests, Prophets, Diviners, Sages: A Socio-Historical Study of Religious Specialists in Ancient Israel* (Valley Forge, PA: Trinity Press International, 1995); Christine Schams, *Jewish Scribes in the Second Temple Period*, JSOTSup 291 (Sheffield: Sheffield Academic Press, 1998); John P. Meier, *A Marginal Jew: Rethinking the Historical Jesus*, vol. 3, *Companions and Competitors* (New York: Doubleday, 2001), 289–647; Marcus, "The Scribes and the Pharisees," in *Mark 1–8*, 519–24.

47. Thellman, "Scribes," in *DJG*, 840–45, here 842.

48. Jacob Neusner, *The Rabbinic Traditions about the Pharisees before 70* (Leiden: Brill, 1971); Neusner, *From Politics to Piety: The Emergence of Pharisaic Judaism* (Englewood Cliffs, NJ: Prentice-Hall, 1973); Neusner and Bruce D. Chilton, eds., *In Quest of the Historical Pharisees* (Waco TX: Baylor University Press, 2007). The latter includes articles in the long-running debate with E. P. Sanders. Discussions of that debate include James D. G. Dunn, *Jesus, Paul and the Law: Studies in Mark and Galatians* (London: SPCK, 1990), 61–88.

Major studies include Steve Mason, *Flavius Josephus on the Pharisees: A Composition-Critical Study* (Leiden: Brill, 1991); E. P. Sanders, *Judaism, Practice and Belief: 63 BCE–66 CE* (Philadelphia: Trinity Press International, 1992); Anthony Saldarini, *Pharisees, Scribes, and Sadducees in Palestinian Society* (Grand Rapids: Eerdmans, 2001). For a brief discussion and bibliography see Lynn H. Cohick, "Pharisees," in *DJG* (2nd ed.), 673–79.

The First Quest

Caesar. However, they do not appear to have taken part in the arrest and conviction of Jesus.

Scribes, on the other hand, figure consistently in questions of authority and accusations that could lead to capital punishment. Thellman observes, "The Jerusalem priest-scribe (elder) is always referred to in either the context of Jesus' death (Mark 8:31; 10:33; 11:18, 27; 14:1, 53; 15:1, 31) or where they challenge his authority (Mark 11:15–19, 27–33). Jesus' authority and scriptural interpretation are central issues where scribes are mentioned alone."[49]

The question of blasphemy figured from the early days of Jesus' activity to the charge on which Jesus was convicted at his interrogation before the Sanhedrin (14:64).[50] For now we shall focus on the scribes' reaction to Jesus' words to the paralytic who was brought to Jesus in the crowded house at Capernaum (2:1–12). Jesus' responded, "Son, your sins are forgiven" (2:5). The unspoken reaction of the scribes was to ask, "Why does this fellow speak in this way? It is blasphemy! Who can forgive sins but God alone?" (2:7). Jesus justified his action by saying that he spoke in this way "so that you may know that the Son of Man has authority on earth to forgive sins" (2:10). Without exploring the question of Jesus and the Son of Man,[51] we may note that Jesus claimed to have a delegated authority as justification for his action.[52]

Abuse of the divine name was punishable by death (Lev 24:10–11, 14–16, 23; *m. Sanh.* 7:5). But Jesus did not invoke the divine name. He pronounced forgiveness, employing the theological passive, "Your sins are forgiven."[53] Jesus acted as God's agent in declaring the paralytic forgiven and healed, just as he had cast out the unclean spirit and declared the leper clean. It is in the implicit claim to be God's *agent* (Hebrew, *shaliach*,

---

49. Thellman, "Scribes," in *DJG*, 842.

50. See below, chap. 19, §8 on "The Death of Jesus" for discussion of the interrogation of Jesus and the blasphemy charge.

51. See below, chap. 18, §2 on "Jesus, Son of Man, Son of God, Christ."

52. Darrell L. Bock links Jesus' reply with his eventual exaltation and vindication fulfilling the prophecies of Ps 110:1 and Dan 7:13–14 as the Son of the Blessed and Son of Man. See Bock, "Jesus as Blasphemer," in *Who Do My Opponents Say That I Am? An Investigation into the Accusations against Jesus*, ed. Scot McKnight and Joseph B. Modica, LNTS 327 (London: T&T Clark, 2008), 76–94.

53. Maximilian Zerwick, *Biblical Greek, Illustrated by Examples*, Scripta Pontificii Instituti Biblici 114 (Rome: Pontifical Biblical Institute, 1963), §236, 76, cf. §2, 1–2. In rabbinic literature this passive construction is rare. Joachim Jeremias saw use of the theological passive as characteristic of the *ipsissima vox* of Jesus. See Jeremias, *The Prayers of Jesus*, trans. John Bowden, SBT Second Series 6 (London: SCM, 1967), 115.

Quests before Schweitzer

i.e., someone who is sent)—especially if the rabbinic axiom that a man's agent is as himself (*m. Berakhot* 5:5) applies here—that the alleged blasphemy lies. It was unthinkable for the scribes to entertain the notion that someone outside the temple system should have such a role.

1.5. Jesus the Father's Agent. As Mark's narrative unfolds, the notion of Jesus as God's agent and the twelve disciples as Jesus' agents— and thus ultimately as *God's agents*—becomes increasingly important, even more so if linked with T. W. Manson's contention that Jesus saw the Son of Man in Daniel 7:13 as a vocational summons. In Daniel's vision, the Son of Man signified the righteous remnant of Israel. In Jesus' vision, Jesus together with his disciples was called to serve as that remnant. However, one by one the disciples fell away, leaving Jesus *alone* as the Son of Man.[54]

The next three episodes return to issues related to the theme of the *Call to Discipleship and Following Jesus*. The first relates the call of Levi son of Alphaeus, and the reaction of "the scribes of the Pharisees" (2:13– 17). The later member of the twelve disciples, James son of Alphaeus (3:18), may have been Levi's brother. In the first century most people with the name Levi were Levites, who as hereditary descendants of the biblical Levi performed service in the temple. Since the scribes were also probably Levites, the objection that Jesus ate with tax collectors and sinners may have been something of a family quarrel.[55]

Levi may have been the black sheep of the family, who disgraced his relatives by becoming a tax collector (τελώνης). The position might more accurately be translated as "toll collector" since it involved collection of dues on transported goods.[56] Such posts were farmed out to the highest bidder, who was free to charge as much as he wished. Their dishonesty was proverbial. According to the Mishnah, the entry of a tax collector into a house made the house unclean (*m. Tohor.* 7:6). Jesus encountered Levi sitting in his tax booth. Levi immediately answered Jesus' call to follow him.

In a pattern similar to the call of Simon, Jesus ate a meal in his house (2:15; cf. 1:29–31). However, many guests attended Levi's dinner,

---

54. See below, chap. 11, §1.2; chap. 18, §2.

55. Marcus, *Mark 1–8*, 225.

56. John R. Donahue, "Tax Collector," in *ABD*, 6:337–38; Fritz Herrenbrück, *Jesus und die Zöllner. Historische und neutestamentlich-exegetische Untersuchungen*, WUNT 41 (Tübingen: Mohr Siebeck, 1990).

The First Quest

including "many tax collectors and sinners" as well as Jesus, his disciples, and many followers.[57] The question of the scribes of the Pharisees— "Why does he eat with tax collectors and sinners?" (2:16)—carries the insinuation that the cost of the meal was met by ill-gotten gain. Jesus' reply—that those well have no need of a healer, but only those who are sick. The reply may be read that Pharisaic practice sufficed for the righteous. However, in context there was biting irony: "I have come to call not the righteous but sinners" (2:17).

This pronouncement has an implicit triadic structure, which was noted by W. D. Davies, Dale C. Allison Jr., and Glen H. Stassen in connection with the teaching of the Sermon on the Mount.[58] It is arguable that this triadic structure characterizes the Jesus of the canonical evangelists, but for now comments must be limited to Mark and the *First Quest*. The triads consist of (1) the vicious circle of destructive behavior, (2) traditional Torah-based piety, and (3) the "transforming initiative" of Jesus' radical teaching and praxis, which fulfills the Law and the Prophets. The first two options fail to break the cycle of destructive behavior. The third alone achieves this objective. In the case of those attending Levi's banquet, only Jesus' "transforming initiative" could break the destructive cycle that gripped their lives.

Levi's banquet and the parables in Mark 4:1–33 also support Joachim Jeremias's view that Jesus' proclamation of the good news to sinners took the form of his offer of forgiveness and call to follow him. The parables were not addressed to sinners but to critics as "a defence of the Good News."[59] Jeremias saw the feasts that Jesus attended as "prophetic signs" of the new age.[60]

---

57. Even if "the scribes of the Pharisees" were not among the invited guests, as outsiders they could hardly have failed to notice what was going on. Use of the verb κατάκειμαι, recline (2:15), suggests a well-to-do standard of dining.

58. W. D. Davies and Dale C. Allison Jr., *Matthew*, ICC (Edinburgh: T&T Clark, 1988), 1:86–87; Glen H. Stassen, "The Fourteen Triads of the Sermon on the Mount (Matthew 5:21–7:12)," *JBL* 122, no. 2 (2003): 267–308. In a personal conversation with Glen H. Stassen, my late colleague assured me that his mentor, W. D. Davies, believed that the triadic structure had wider application, as Stassen himself also believed. It is exemplified in the episodes that immediately follow. Other examples include Jesus' teaching on purity (7:1–23), lifestyle and service (10:1–45), and in the Temple court (12:13–44).

59. Joachim Jeremias, *The Parables of Jesus*, trans. S. H. Hooke, rev. ed. (London: SCM, 1963), 145.

60. Jeremias, *The Parables of Jesus*, 227. See below, chap. 8, §2; chap. 18, §6. See also Craig L. Blomberg, "The Authenticity and Significance of Jesus' Table Fellowship with Sinners," in Bock and Webb, *Key Events in the Life of the Historical Jesus*, 215–50.

Quests before Schweitzer

Levi's banquet and the following two episodes form a kind of triptych, giving glimpses into the lifestyle of Jesus and his disciples. They share the common theme of food and eating—ranging from abundance to poverty, with fasting in the middle. In all three scenes Pharisees raised objections.

Jesus' attitude to fasting (2:18–22) was problematic to both the disciples of John and the Pharisees.[61] Why did the disciples of Jesus not fast, whereas John's did? The only fast in the Torah was connected with the Day of Atonement (Lev 16:29–31; 23:26–32). Nevertheless, abstention from food was a recognized expression of mourning and repentance (Jonah 3:7–8).[62] Jesus did not oppose fasting, but he questioned its appropriateness at the present time. Fasting was not appropriate at weddings (Isa 62:5). The image of Jesus as a bridegroom (cf. Matt 25:1–12) evoked the prophetic metaphor of marriage—often strained—between Yahweh and Israel (Hos 2; Ezek 16; Jer 2:2; Isa 54:5).[63] Jesus proceeded to give what may be the first passion prediction. The day would come when the bridegroom would be taken away, and then the disciples would fast (2:20). The miniature parable of the bridegroom was followed by two further miniature parables: the new patch sewn on an old cloak (2:21) and new wine in old wine skins (2:22). All three parabolic images indicated that traditional piety was inadequate and incompatible with Jesus' radical alternative. They also supported Jeremias's contention that parables were defences of Jesus' actions.

The third episode involving food and eating is the narrative of the disciples plucking grain on the Sabbath (2:23–28). There are at least two ways of envisaging the scene. The first way is to picture the disciples going for a Sabbath stroll among the fields. They decided to have a snack. Unfortunately, hostile Pharisees were patrolling the fields on the lookout for Sabbath breakers. E. P. Sanders questioned the authenticity of this scenario on two grounds. First, Pharisees did not spend their Sabbaths in Galilean grainfields in the hope of catching transgressors. Second was his now widely questioned claim that Pharisees preferred to live in or near Jerusalem and were unlikely to visit Galilee.[64] This latter claim is weakened by the well-known case in which Pharisees took part in

---

61. Rainer Riesner, "The Question of the Baptist's Disciples on Fasting," *HSHJ*, 4:3305–3347.
62. R. I. Zwi Werblowsky and Geoffrey Wigoder, "Fasts," in *ODJR*, 251.
63. Marcus, *Mark 1–8*, 237.
64. E. P. Sanders, *Jesus and Judaism* (Philadelphia: Fortress, 1985), 265.

The First Quest

a delegation to Galilee to investigate Josephus's orthodoxy.[65] Maurice Casey argued that the passage could be translated back into Aramaic as a presumed source, and that it may be seen as an instance of legitimate halakhic discussion of what one may be permitted to do on the Sabbath.[66]

The second way of envisaging the scene makes several stipulations. The first is that the disciples, who had left their livelihoods to follow Jesus, qualified for the social security of the day that allowed the needy to glean from the edges of fields (Lev 19:9). This was known as *Pe'ah* and was the subject of a tractate in the Mishnah. What the disciples gathered was not eaten on the spot but taken back to Capernaum for a meal.

The second stipulation is to acknowledge that the issue at stake was not gleaning *per se* but gleaning on the Sabbath. In order to determine what was permitted on the Sabbath (Exod 20:8–11; Deut 5:12–15), rabbinic scholars, who were the successors of the Pharisees, noted thirty-nine cases of work. The underlying guiding principle of their determinations was that work benefiting human beings was proper on the six working days of the week. However, such work was not allowed on the Sabbath, which belonged to God.[67]

The third stipulation concerns Jesus' reply to the Pharisees. Jesus justified the disciples' action by comparing it with what David did when he and his companions were hungry and in need of food. "[David] entered the house of God . . . and ate the bread of the Presence, which is not lawful for any but the priests to eat, and he gave some to his companions" (2:26; cf. 1 Sam 21:1–6; Lev 24:8–9).[68] Both interpretations of the episode recognize that the Pharisees' complaint was ostensibly about the disciples. But they recognize also that Jesus himself was the real target, especially in light of the rabbinic dictum that a man's agent was as himself.

Jesus' invocation of David and the bread of Presence seems overblown and not strictly apt if what the disciples were doing was no more than helping themselves to a snack. However, in light of the alternative way of envisaging the scene, questions of parallels emerge but are not answered

---

65. Josephus, *Life*, 197–98.

66. Maurice Casey, *Aramaic Sources of Mark's Gospel*, SNTSMS 102 (Cambridge: Cambridge University Press, 1998), 138–73.

67. *M. Shabb.* 7:2; cf. D. A. Carson, ed., *From Sabbath to Lord's Day: A Biblical, Historical, and Theological Investigation* (Grand Rapids: Zondervan, 1982).

68. The reference to Abiathar (Mark 2:26) is problematic and is omitted from some manuscripts.

Quests before Schweitzer

directly. David was on the run from Saul. He and his hungry followers ate the bread of the Presence as a last resort. Was the disciples' plucking grain a similar situation of last resort? Was Jesus comparing his situation with that of Saul's enmity for David? Was Jesus already thinking of his mission in terms of being, in some sense, the Son of David?[69]

From the standpoint of form criticism, the episode took the form of a "controversy dialogue" (German, "Streitgespräch") with question, counterquestion, appeal to Scriptural authority, and concluding pronouncement.[70] The dialogue concludes: "The Sabbath was made for man, not man for the Sabbath. So the Son of Man is Lord even of the Sabbath" (2:27–28 NIV). The appeal to the origin of the Sabbath rest in creation indicates a reversal of rabbinic interpretation. Since God rested from his labors in creation on the seventh day and hallowed it, God intended the Sabbath for human rest and renewal (cf. Gen 2:2–3). If the "man" of Mark 2:27 refers to the first man (Heb. *adam*, "man"), then the Son of Adam is lord even of the Sabbath. If the Son of Man refers to the righteous remnant, Jesus and his disciples, the pronouncement gives them authority over the Pharisees on the how the Sabbath should be kept.

At this point a pattern begins to emerge regarding authority. The opponents of Jesus based their criticism on the Torah. Jesus defended his disciples' action by appealing to the Torah (God resting on the seventh day) and the Prophets (David and the bread of Presence).[71]

The next episode—the man with a withered hand on the Sabbath in the synagogue at Capernaum (3:1–6)—returns to the theme of *exorcism and healing*. It proved to be a test case for Jesus with regard to his stance in the previous episode. The latter centered on gathering food; the present episode centered on healing. Both involved activity on the Sabbath. Onlookers watched to see what Jesus would do. Whereas the

---

69. Cf. Mark 10:47–48; 11:10; 2:35–37. See also Donald A. Hagner, "Jesus and Synoptic Sabbath Controversies," in Bock and Webb, *Key Events in the Life of the Historical Jesus*, 251–92.

70. The term gained currency through Rudolf Bultmann, *The History of the Synoptic Tradition*, trans. John Marsh (Oxford: Blackwell, 1963), 39–54. Bultmann located their origin in early Christian conflicts with Judaism, which were historicized in the form in stories about the historical Jesus. Others, like Jeremias, traced these differences to conflicts involving the historical Jesus.

Controversy dialogues figure at critical points in Mark's subsequent narrative. They include discussions of purity (7:1–13); marriage and divorce (10:2–9); and Jesus' authority regarding his action in the Temple (11:27–12:11).

71. In the Hebrew canon the books of Samuel were counted among the Former Prophets. See David Noel Freedman, *The Unity of the Hebrew Bible* (Ann Arbor: University of Michigan Press, 1993).

The First Quest

question of gathering food on the Sabbath was raised by the Pharisees, Jesus now asked, "Is it lawful to do good or to do harm on the sabbath, to save life or to kill?" (3:4). Healing implied work, which was disallowed. It could be argued that even chronic sufferers could wait a day longer until the Sabbath was over. In disputed cases, penalties for infringing even strict rules were applied leniently.[72] However, if the infringement of the Sabbath implied incitement to apostasy, it was a different matter.

Jesus' question was met with silence. Angered and grieved by their hardness of heart, Jesus commanded the man to stretch out his hand, and it was restored (3:5). Perhaps the language evoked memories of the strong hand and outstretched arm in a holy war,[73] suggesting incitement to arms. At any rate, the incident prompted an unholy alliance between the Pharisees and the Herodians,[74] between the holiness party and the supporters of Herod Antipas, the ruler of Galilee, to conspire to destroy Jesus. The Pharisees were concerned about repeated breaches of the Sabbath. The Herodians appear to have viewed Jesus as a political threat.[75] The collusion of the Pharisees and the Herodians involved a double irony: doing harm on the Sabbath when one should do good (3:4) and plotting to destroy someone who had just restored another person (3:6).

In later episodes Jesus continued to observe the Sabbath, as when he came to his hometown of Nazareth and taught in the synagogue (6:1–2). But the Sabbath question seems to recede in importance for the Pharisees behind other aspects of purity (7:1–23) and opportunities for entrapment: signs, divorce and remarriage, taxes to Caesar.[76] The different groups

---

72. E. P. Sanders, *Jewish Law from Jesus to the Mishnah: Five Studies* (London: SCM; Philadelphia: Trinity Press International, 1990), 6–23. See also Nina L. Collins, *Jesus, the Sabbath and the Jewish Debate: Healing on the Sabbath in the 1st and 2nd Centuries CE*, LNTS 474 (London: T&T Clark, 2014).

73. Deut 4:34; 5:15; 7:19; 11:2; 26:6; 1 Kgs 8:42; 2 Chr 6:32; Ps 136:12; Jer 21:5; 32:21; Ezek 20:33–34.

74. The term *Herodians* appears only in Mark 3:6 and 12:13. It may have been coined by the Romans in the Latin formation *Herodiani*. See Theissen and Merz, *The Historical Jesus*, 233–34.

75. Herod Antipas seems to have viewed Jesus as a reincarnation of John the Baptist (Mark 6:16). According to Josephus, Herod feared that the crowds that John attracted would lead to upheaval. He ordered John's execution as a preemptive strike (*Ant.* 18.118–19).

76. The Pharisees' request for a sign (8:11–12) is usually taken at face value as an invitation to help them make up their minds about following Jesus. But if he had performed a sign, it could have been construed as material evidence before impeccable witnesses—namely, themselves—that Jesus was the kind of prophet described in Deut 13:1–5, who led astray by signs and wonders.

The Pharisees' question about divorce and remarriage (10:2–9) was asked in the region of Perea by the Jordan, where John the Baptist had been arrested and executed for denouncing the conduct of Herod Antipas for divorcing his wife and marrying Herodias. If Jesus agreed with John,

Quests before Schweitzer

opposing Jesus seem to have focused on different issues. Their common ground was that the issues were capital offences.[77] The two episodes following the scene in the synagogue deal respectively with the themes of *exorcism and healing* and *the call to discipleship and following Jesus*. Together they have the effect of exponentially exacerbating the situation.

The first of these episodes describes what proved to be the end of Jesus' activity in Capernaum (3:7–12). Mark's description indicates that Jesus was now a national figure. He moved to the sea followed by "a great multitude" drawn from places that he would eventually pass through: Tyre, Sidon, Perea, Judea, and Jerusalem. To avoid the crush, Jesus instructed the disciples to have a boat ready (3:9). The sick were healed through touching him (3:10). Unclean spirits who shouted, "You are the Son of God," were commanded not to make him known (3:11–12).

In the next episode, Jesus called and commissioned the twelve apostles (3:13–19). The site is simply called "the mountain," a symbolic place where heaven and earth meet, recalling Moses and the elders (Exod 24:9–11). The appointment of the Twelve is widely associated with the twelve tribes of Israel (cf. Luke 22:28–30). In this episode Mark distinguishes the Twelve, whom Jesus named apostles, from the wider group of followers and disciples. Elsewhere they were also called disciples.[78]

Mark alone mentions their *threefold* role (3:14–15). First, and perhaps most important for Mark's subsequent narrative, is that they "should be

---

he risked the same fate as John. If he gave an answer that sided with Antipas, he would in effect renounce John's baptism of Jesus and John's prophecy about the one that would come after him.

The Pharisees and Herodians again sought to entrap Jesus by putting to him the question of paying taxes to Caesar (12:13–17). Jesus' answer, "Give to the emperor the things that are the emperor's, and to God the things that are God's," effectively made them answer their own question. See further Brown, "The Jesus of Mark's Gospel," 26–53, esp. 36–39.

77. The Pharisees were concerned with the *praxis of purity*—keeping the Sabbath, purity laws affecting health, food, marriage, payment of taxes to Caesar (see previous note). With regard to the two latter issues, they could make common cause with the Herodians. The scribes—as theologians—and the Sanhedrin at large were concerned with blasphemy and apostasy (2:7; 14:61–64).

78. The reference to "apostles" may be an interpolation from Luke 6:13. However, external evidence is thought to warrant its inclusion in the text. See Bruce M. Metzger, *A Textual Commentary on the Greek New Testament*, 2nd ed. (New York: United Bible Societies, 1994), 75. In Greek the noun ἀπόστολος and verb ἀποστέλλω convey the notion of sending. The more generic term *disciple* (μαθητής) carries overtones of being a learner and pupil in contrast with a teacher.

For surveys, see Terence Paige, "Apostleship, Evangelism, Witness," in *EHJ*, 22–25; Eckhard J. Schnabel, "Apostle," in *DJG*, 34–45; Veronica Koperski, "Disciples, Discipleship," in *EHJ*, 160–63; Michael J. Wilkins, "Disciple and Discipleship," in *DJG*, 202–12. For more extensive discussion, see Meier, *A Marginal Jew*; C. Clifton Black, *The Disciples according to Mark: Markan Redaction in Current Debate*, JSNTSup 27 (Sheffield: Sheffield Academic Press, 1989).

The First Quest

with him" (KJV). This is in accord with T. W. Manson's view of the long-term vision of Jesus: that the disciples together with Jesus were to form the righteous remnant, the kingdom of the saints, the ideal contained in the term *Son of Man*.[79] In fulfillment of this vision, Jesus appointed the Twelve to send them out "to proclaim the message, and to have authority to cast out demons."

All three Synoptic Gospels list the names of the Twelve. Within the scope of the present account, it is impossible to discuss them all. Attention may be drawn to the following. The first in all three lists is Simon—the first to be called by Jesus (1:16)—who was given the name Peter (Mark 3:16; cf. Matt 4:18; Luke 6:14).[80] The lists represent wide diversity, including the last two to be named, Simon the (former?) Zealot[81] and Judas Iscariot, whom the Gospels identify as the one who betrayed Jesus.[82]

The brief bridging episode (Mark 3:20–21) that leads to the Beelzebul charge can be read in at least two ways, depending on how one reads two Greek terms. The choice between the two readings affects significantly the way one views the subsequent events. The first way is that followed by Joel Marcus,[83] and it is supported by (among others) the

---

79. T. W. Manson, *The Teaching of Jesus: Studies in Its Form and Content* (Cambridge: Cambridge University Press, 1931), 227. For further discussion, see chap. 11, §1.2 below.

80. Perhaps the Greek Πέτρος (*Petros*, "Rock") or Aramaic Κηφᾶς (*Kēphas*, "Rock") was originally a nickname given by Jesus that replaced "Simon" as the followers of Jesus became a community. It suggests a foundational role.

81. Mark identifies him as "Simon the Cananaean" (3:18; cf. Matt 10:4). Luke has "Simon, who was called the Zealot" (Luke 6:15; cf. Acts 1:13), which is a translation of the Aramaic "Cananaean." On this, see Martin Hengel, *The Zealots: Investigations into the Jewish Freedom Movement from Herod I to 70 A.D.*, trans. David Smith (Edinburgh: T&T Clark, 1989), 69–70, 338, 392.

The ideal figure of the Zealot movement was Phinehas, who led a war against Midian in the time of Moses and speared an Israelite man and a Midianite woman who were having sex (Num 25). Hengel traced the Zealot movement to a movement that Josephus called the fourth "philosophy" of Judaism. (The other three "philosophies" were all mainstream movements: the Pharisees, the Sadducees, and the Essenes) The "fourth philosophy" was founded by Judas the Galilean who rebelled against Roman taxation in 6 BCE. Josephus held the "philosophy" as ultimately responsible for the war with Rome (66–70 CE) but avoided naming it (*Ant.* 18.23–25).

82. The name Judas reflects the Greek form Ἰούδας corresponding to the English name Judah, the fourth son of Jacob and the eponymous ancestor of the tribe of Judah. It was commonly used as an honorable name with rich associations. Judas Maccabeus was a Hasmonean hero. Judas was the name of one of Jesus' brothers (6:3). However, Judas Iscariot seems to fit the profile of the trusted bosom friend who ate the bread but lifted up his heel against the psalmist (Ps 41:9). See further William Klassen, "Judas Iscariot," in *ABD*, 3:1091–96; Marvin Meyer, "Jesus, Judas Iscariot, and the *Gospel of Judas*," in Holmén, *Jesus in Continuum*, 113–32.

83. Marcus, *Mark 1–8*, 269–87.

Quests before Schweitzer

NRSV translation. It takes εἰς οἶκον to mean "home" and οἱ παρ αὐτοῦ to mean "his family." It carries the implication that "home" meant Nazareth because that is where Jesus grew up and where his family lived (cf. 6:1). Marcus accepts this implication and suggests that Mark 3:20–35 has a chiastic structure, centered on the parable of the strong man, framed by charges of "demonic agency," beginning and ending with "Jesus' relatives."[84] He observes that "Mark is the harshest of all the Gospels in its depiction of Jesus' relation to all his family."

Without wishing to quarrel about that observation, I read the episode differently. To begin with, it seems strange that, having appointed the twelve apostles, Jesus would abandon his project and walk some thirty miles to Nazareth in the hill country.[85] In Mark's narrative, Nazareth and family had hitherto played no part. Jesus' ministry in Nazareth lay in the future, and he was amazed at the unbelief that he encountered (6:1–6a). The words εἰς οἶκον (lit. "to/at a house") were more likely to refer to the house in Capernaum where Jesus was currently living and οἱ παρ αὐτοῦ (lit. "those by him") to "those around him."[86] It is not unlikely that it was the same house, which had likewise drawn crowds when they learned that Jesus was "at home" (ἐν οἴκῳ, 2:1).

In view of these considerations it seems more likely that Mark 3:20–21 refers to those around Jesus who tried to restrain him because people in Capernaum were saying that Jesus had gone "out of his mind" (ἐξέστη).[87] On this reading, the episode was directly related to the appointment of the Twelve, which for some may have been the last straw. The citizens of Capernaum would have known Simon, Andrew, James and John, who had left their trade to follow Jesus. Others among the Twelve may have been known for dubious reputations. Where would it all lead?

1.6. The Beelzebul Charge. The Beelzebul charge was not a snap judgment or an expression of pent-up frustration on the part of jealous rivals. It was the deliverance of deliberate investigation, arising from age-old hermeneutical procedure for dealing with apostasy. In the final analysis it was rooted in the monotheism of the Ten Commandments (Exod 20:2–17; Deut 5:6–21). More specifically the charge reflected

---

84. Marcus, *Mark 1–8*, 278–79.

85. Ken Dark, "Nazareth," in *The Oxford Encyclopedia of the Bible and Archaeology*, 2:164–68.

86. Yarbro Collins, *Mark: A Commentary*, ed. Harold W. Attridge, Hermeneia (Minneapolis: Fortress, 2007), 226–27; BDAG, 698–99, 756–57.

87. BDAG, 350.

The First Quest

Torah instructions regarding the prophet who led astray by means of signs and wonders.

> If a prophet arises among you, or a dreamer of dreams, and gives you a sign or a wonder, and the sign or wonder which he tells you comes to pass, and if he says, "Let us go after other gods," which you have not known, "and let us serve them," you shall not listen to the words of that prophet or to that dreamer of dreams; for the LORD your God is testing you, to know whether you love the LORD your God with all your heart and with all your soul. You shall walk after the LORD your God and fear him, and keep his commandments and obey his voice, and you shall serve him and cleave to him. But that prophet or that dreamer of dreams shall be put to death, because he has taught rebellion against the LORD your God, who brought you out of the land of Egypt and redeemed you out of the house of bondage, to make you leave the way in which the LORD your God commanded you to walk. So you shall purge the evil from the midst of you. (Deut 13:1–5 RSV)

Capital punishment was not limited to the guilty prophet. The inhabitants and livestock of towns that fell into apostasy were to be put to the sword, their habitations destroyed and never rebuilt (Deut 13:12–18). These traditions were preserved in the Dead Sea Scrolls (11QTemple 55:2–19), the Mishnah (*Sanh.* 7:4; 10:4), and the warnings of Mark 13:22. A contemporary comment on Deuteronomy 13 was given by Philo (c. 20 BCE–45 CE), the Hellenistic Jewish philosopher of Alexandria (*The Special Laws*, 1.315–316; cf. 4.50–52 on the "false prophet," ψευδοπροφήτης; *Life of Moses*, 1.277). Philo justified the severity of Deuteronomic laws by attributing them to the care that God had for his children, as "sons of God" (υἱοὶ τοῦ θεοῦ).[88]

Miraculous healings and exorcisms alone were not the issue. It was their role in connection with teaching that led followers astray. In the case of Jesus, it was the combination of exorcism with novel teaching and practice. Jesus attracted large crowds and deliberately formed of a band of followers, described in the two alternating themes used above in describing the First Quest. The Jerusalem scribes focused on *two* issues:

---

88. Philo, *The Special Laws*, 1.318 (LCL, *Philo* 7, trans. F. H. Coulson, 284).

Quests before Schweitzer

"he has Beelzebul [Βεελζεβοὺλ ἔχει]," and "by the ruler of demons he casts out demons [ἐν τῷ ἄρχοντι τῶν δαιμονίων ἐκβάλλει τὰ δαιμόνια]" (3:22; cf. Matt 12:24; 9:34; Luke 11:15). The alien deity that had taken hold of Jesus and empowered him was Beelzebul, alias Satan. Jesus had given himself to Beelzebul, and in return the ruler of the demons had given him power over the demons.[89]

Jesus' rejoinder took the form of *two* brief parables, directed at the *two* charges, followed by a pronouncement. The parables were riddles. Both pointed to the self-contradictory nature of the charges. The first pictured a kingdom or house that if divided could not stand (3:24–26). The second compared the situation to plundering the property of a strong man, who must first be bound before his house can be plundered (3:27). They suggest a double reference. On the one hand, there is the allusion to Satan as the *prince of demons* and the *strong man*. But there was also a cryptic allusion to earthly kingdoms—the fraught relationship between Roman emperors and their client rulers of the house of Herod. The conversion of Levi the tax collector, the agent of Antipas and ultimately the Romans, could be seen as an instance of fractured earthly rule and also of plundering the strong man's goods.

The two riddles were followed by Jesus' pronouncement about unforgivable sin: "Truly I tell you, people will be forgiven for their sins and whatever blasphemies they utter; but whoever blasphemes against the Holy Spirit can never have forgiveness, but is guilty of an eternal sin" (3:28–29). Over the centuries countless people have wondered whether, wittingly or unwittingly, they had committed the unforgivable sin. However, Mark inserted a comment showing how he understood the pronouncement: "For they had said, 'He has an unclean spirit'" (3:30). In other words, Mark wanted it to be understood that the words and actions of Jesus followed from the empowering of the Holy Spirit described in Mark's prologue (1:8, 10). The accusers, who attributed to Satan the manifest work of God's Spirit, were guilty of an eternal sin.[90]

---

89. On Beelzeboul (Βεελζεβούλ) and this passage, see BDAG, 173; Yarbro Collins, *Mark*, 228–34; Dwight D. Sheets, "Jesus as Demon-Possessed," in *Who Do My Opponents Say That I Am?*, 27–49; Michael Labahn, "'The 'Darker Side of Power'—Beelzebul: Manipulated or Manipulator? Reflections on the History of a Conflict in the Traces Left in the Memory of Its Narrators," *HSHJ*, 4: 2911–45. Mediums and wizards were likewise judged (Lev 19:27; 20:27; CD 12:2–3; *m. Sanh.* 7:7).

90. Remarkably, the term *Holy Spirit* is rare in the Hebrew Scriptures but common in the New Testament. There are only three instances in the Masoretic text of the Old Testament, which

The First Quest

1.7. The Hermeneutical Divide. What may not be immediately apparent to modern readers is the fact that the conflicts surrounding Jesus turned on fundamentally different belief systems with conflicting understandings of hermeneutics. Anthony C. Thiselton defines hermeneutics as follows: "Hermeneutics explores how we read, understand, and handle texts, especially those written in another time or in a context of life different from our own. Biblical hermeneutics investigate more specifically how we read, understand, apply, and respond to biblical texts."[91] Thiselton's definition is helpful in understanding the differences between scribes, the Jewish community that they represented, and Mark and the early Christian community to which he belonged.

They approached questions of authority and perception in radically different ways. The Torah, in the sense of the Pentateuch, was uniquely important for orthodox Jews. The revised edition of Schürer's *History of the Jewish People in the Age of Jesus Christ* gives the following assessment: "Despite the collocation of the Prophets and the Writings with the Torah, at no time were they placed on the same footing as the Torah: the Torah has always occupied the higher place. In it is set down, in writing and in full, the original revelation given to Israel. The Prophets and the Writings merely hand down the message still further."[92]

This outlook stands in stark contrast with that of Mark, who from the outset made it clear that the gospel of Jesus fulfilled the message of the prophets—especially Isaiah—as well as the message of John the

---

occur in Ps 51:11 and Isa 63:10–11. The psalmist's plea not to be cast from God's presence and that God will not take away from him his "holy Spirit" may be understood as a plea that God will not take away the Spirit that sustains life. See John R. Levison, *The Spirit in First Century Judaism*, AGJU 29 (Leiden: Brill, 1997), 68. Levison takes the references in Isaiah to refer to "the corporate experience of Israel and cannot, therefore, be understood as the spirit that individual humans possess from birth until death" (65). The term *holy Spirit* became more widely used to describe God's presence among Jews, both Palestinian and Diaspora, in the Greco-Roman era (105). Widespread use in Christian communities may be in part a protest that the Spirit that had anointed Jesus, and which they themselves experienced, was *holy*, not Satanic or evil.

In subsequent research Levison found significant evidence substantiating the role of purification by the Spirit notably in the Dead Sea Scrolls and even the expression Holy Spirit (CD 7:4; 5:11–13; 1QHa 20:11–12; Levison, "Spirit, Holy," *The Eerdmans Dictionary of Early Judaism*, ed. John J. Collins and Daniel C. Harlow [Grand Rapids: Eerdmans, 2010], 1252–54). It amply documents Levison's contention that his article offers evidence to dispel the misconception that Judaism was "spiritually arid." However, it does not contradict the above suggestion about the wholesale Christian adoption of the term *Holy Spirit* in the face of the claims of Jesus' opponents that the spirit that motivated Jesus was anything but holy.

91. Anthony C. Thiselton, *Hermeneutics: An Introduction* (Grand Rapids: Eerdmans, 2009), 1.

92. Schürer, *The History of the Jewish People in the Age of Jesus Christ*, 2:319.

Quests before Schweitzer

Baptist. Moreover, Jesus was to be understood in light of his anointing by the Holy Spirit and the voice from heaven. Jesus himself did not seek to abolish the Torah, but he interpreted it in light of the kingdom of God. Markus Tiwald comments: "Jesus does not abolish the Torah by referring to the basileia, but rather the approaching basileia reveals the true meaning of the Torah as established by God at the beginning of time and as it will be restored at the end of times."[93]

To orthodox Jews, sources of revelation outside the Torah were relatively unimportant. *The Oxford Dictionary of the Jewish Religion* makes the comment: "The *bat qol*, like other forms of heavenly pronouncement, was not necessarily accepted in halakhic matters, since the rabbis held that the Torah 'is not in heaven' (*Dt.* 30.12) and that legal decisions had to be arrived at by the established hermeneutic and discursive methods (*B. M.* 59b)."[94] The vision associated with the voice from heaven could be construed as akin to the private revelation connected with the false prophet and dreamer of dreams (Deut 13:1–5). On the subject of dreams, Joseph Dan comments: "With the exception of Joseph and Daniel (both of whom interpreted dreams in foreign courts), dream interpretation by Jews is absent from the Bible. *Numbers* 12.6–7 considers prophetic experiences to be dreamlike visions, with the notable exception of the face-to-face encounter between God and Moses. Jeremiah, however, contrasts the 'word of God' given to true prophets with the dream revelations claimed by false prophets (*Jer.* 23)."[95] Jeremiah himself was no stranger to hostility, pain, and rejection. Ultimately, the test was resolved by fidelity to God and outcomes of the prophet's teaching, which is also the theme of the parables in Mark 4. The conflict that emerged in the First Quest was essentially a clash over *authority* and *hermeneutics*, much like the remainder of Mark's narrative.

The issue crystallized by the Beelzebul charge has both grammatical and hermeneutical dimensions. The grammatical dimension turns on the use of the preposition ἐν ("in," "with," or "by") followed by an indication of power or agency. The preposition is used of unclean spirit: ἐν πνεύματι

---

93. Markus Tiwald, "Jewish-Christian Trajectories in Torah and Temple Theology," in Holmén, *Jesus in Continuum*, 402.

94. Daniel Sperber, "Bat Qol," *ODJR*, 104.

95. Joseph Dan, "Dreams," *ODJR*, 207–8, esp. 207. Philo wrote a lengthy treatise in defense of dreams as a vehicle of divine revelation—dreams in the Pentateuch (*On Dreams, That They Are God-Sent*, LCL 275).

The First Quest

ἀκαθάρτῳ, "with an unclean spirit" (1:23; 5:2). The same grammatical construction is used to describe the scribes' charge: ἐν τῷ ἄρχοντι τῶν δαιμονίων ἐκβάλλει τὰ δαιμόνια, "by the ruler of the demons he casts out demons" (3:22). But the same grammatical construction is also used to describe the agency of the Holy Spirit. John the Baptist prophesied: "He will baptize you with the Holy Spirit [βαπτίσει ὑμᾶς ἐν πνεύματι ἁγίῳ]" (1:8; cf. 3:30; Matt 12:28; Luke 11:18–19). The Greek grammatical construction regarding agency is the same for unclean spirits, Beelzebul, and the Holy Spirit. However, the divide between the scribes' representation and Mark's was determined by the hermeneutical dimension of background beliefs regarding authority and who empowered Jesus to cast out unclean spirits.[96]

The findings of the Jerusalem scribes represented a summary judgment that was to be reported to the high council, the Sanhedrin.[97] Although the delegation lacked the authority to implement its judgment on the spot, it laid the foundation for the Sanhedrin's later condemnation of Jesus by identifying Jesus as a false prophet who leads astray through signs. The scribes' verdict provided the sanction that the Herodians needed to destroy Jesus in their own territory: Galilee (cf. 3:6).

The hermeneutical divide raises the question of Jesus as a teacher. In *Jesus and Judaism*, E. P. Sanders bracketed the question. His criterion of a good hypothesis was that "it should situate Jesus believably in Judaism and yet explain why the movement initiated by him eventually broke with Judaism."[98] With this in mind, he conducted a personal survey of

---

96. The same considerations apply to accounts in Matt 12:24, 27; and Luke 11:15, 18–19.

97. The term συνέδριον (*synedrion*) was used both for local councils and for the high council in Jerusalem presided over by the ruling high priests and composed of former high priests, elders, and scribes (BDAG, 967). This high council was responsible for religious, legal, and governmental affairs. Its origin may be traced to the era of Ezra and Nehemiah. In New Testament times its powers were limited by the appointment by Augustus of a procurator for Judea as a province of the Roman Empire (6 CE). The procurator was entrusted with "full powers, including capital punishment" (Josephus, *J.W.* 2.117; cf. John 18:31). See also Schürer, *The History of the Jewish People in the Age of Jesus Christ*, 2:199–226; Graham H. Twelftree, "Sanhedrin," in *EHJ*, 544–45; Twelftree, "Sanhedrin," in *DJG*, 836–40.

98. Sanders, *Jesus and Judaism*, 18. Sanders traced this stipulation back to the Jewish scholar Joseph Klausner. In so doing, Sanders unwittingly raised the question of whether the inauguration of the so-called Third Quest of the historical Jesus should be rightly credited to Klausner in the 1920s! See Klausner's epoch-making book *Jesus of Nazareth: His Life, Times, and Teaching*, trans. Herbert Danby (London: Allen & Unwin, 1925), 10. Klausner differed from Sanders in making Jesus' *moral teaching*, with apparently scant concern for the nation of Israel, the reason why Jews could not accept Jesus. See below, chap. 7, §1.3.

scholarship in order to compile a list of eight "almost indisputable facts." These would serve as bedrock for subsequent explanation.[99] Sanders began his book with the "controversy about the temple" (which was actually number five on his list). Discussing Jesus as a teacher did not make the cut because focusing on Jesus as a teacher was futile and misleading. For one thing, there was no consensus about what he taught or what kind of a teacher he was. For another, the enterprise of recovering the teaching of Jesus made the unspoken assumption that Jesus was first and foremost a teacher. Moreover, Sanders did not see a connection between Jesus as a teacher and the crucifixion.[100]

Rainer Riesner was more confident about Jesus' role as a teacher, both as a self-designation (Mark 14:14; and Matt 10: 24–25; Luke 6:40) and in situating his teaching within Jewish faith and practice.[101] Bruce D. Chilton made a landmark study of Jesus in relation to the Aramaic translation, the Targum of Isaiah.[102] From a different angle, Ben Witherington III made important contributions to the study of Jesus' wisdom teaching and prophetic role.[103]

David A. deSilva explored the question of what Jesus and his half-brothers were taught as boys. The answer was to be found through comparing teaching in the New Testament with apocryphal and pseudepigraphal literature.[104] Concentration on this literature precluded from consideration what Jesus might have been taught about the book of Daniel directly. Daniel was written in Hebrew and Aramaic (Dan 2:4b–7:28) and long lingered on the boundary of the Hebrew canon.[105]

---

99. Sanders, *Jesus and Judaism*, 10–11.

100. Sanders, *Jesus and Judaism*, 4.

101. Rainer Riesner, *Jesus als Lehrer*, 3rd ed., WUNT II/7 (Tübingen: Mohr Siebeck, 1988); Riesner, "Teacher, Teaching Forms and Styles," in *EHJ*, 624–30; Riesner, "From Messianic Teacher to the Gospels of Jesus Christ," *HSHJ*, 1:405–46; "Teacher," in *DJG*, 934–39.

102. Bruce D. Chilton, *A Galilean Rabbi and His Bible: Jesus' Use of the Interpreted Scripture of His Time* (Wilmington, DE: Glazier, 1984).

103. Ben Witherington III, *Jesus the Sage: The Pilgrimage of Wisdom* (Minneapolis: Fortress, 1994); Witherington, *Jesus the Seer: The Progress of Prophecy* (Minneapolis: Fortress, 1999).

104. David A. deSilva, *The Jewish Teachers of Jesus, James, and Jude: What Earliest Christianity Learned from the Apocrypha and Pseudepigrapha* (Oxford: Oxford University Press, 2012).

105. John J. Collins, *Daniel: With an Introduction to Apocalyptic Literature* (Grand Rapids: Eerdmans, 1984); John J. Collins with Adela Yarbro Collins, *Daniel: A Commentary on the Book of Daniel*, ed. Frank Moore Cross, Hermeneia (Minneapolis: Fortress, 1993); John J. Collins, Peter W. Flint, Cameron VanEpps, eds., *The Book of Daniel: Composition and Reception*, 2 vols., VTSup 83 (Leiden: Brill, 2001); Lorenzo DiTommaso, "Daniel, Book of," in *The Eerdmans Dictionary of Early Judaism*, ed. John J. Collins and Daniel C. Harlow (Grand Rapids: Eerdmans, 2010), 513–16.

DeSilva contended that the author of the Parables of Enoch took Daniel 7:13–14 "as his starting point for developing the 'Son of Man' as an eschatological agent."[106] However, he conceded that it was difficult to demonstrate the "direct dependence" of Jesus on 1 Enoch. Jesus seemed to know about the traditions associated with 1 Enoch but did not necessarily draw on them directly.[107] Indeed, it is difficult to avoid the conclusion that, in Mark at least, the Son of Man image looks more like that of Daniel 7:13–14 than that of 1 Enoch with all its embellishments.[108]

Chris Keith reopened the question of the conflict between Jesus and the scribal elite.[109] From the standpoint of the scribes, Jesus was a theologically illiterate former manual worker who presumed the status of having scribal-literate authority. Keith's proposal did not depend on catalysts such as healing, exorcism, or messianic claims, though it did not preclude them. The Pharisees appear to fade out in its final phase of Jesus' arrest and execution, and the Romans played no significant part in the early conflict. They were uninterested in Jewish theological questions but were very concerned with unrest in Jerusalem during Passover. Chris Keith's concern is with the final escalation. "When the scribal-literate authorities engaged Jesus in debates over Scripture and authority in order to expose him as a pretender to the position scribal-literate teacher, there was an interesting and ironic contrast between the intended effects of those engagements and their actual effects. By admitting Jesus to public dialogue, they enabled some audiences to come to a conclusion that was precisely the opposite from the one they intended when, at least on occasion, Jesus was the winner of the debate. . . . The scribal elite attempted to put out a fire with gasoline."[110] I concur with Chris Keith's assessment, but with one stipulation. The fuse that ignited the final conflagration was a very long one, reaching back to Jesus' time in Capernaum.

---

106. DeSilva, *The Jewish Teachers of Jesus, James, and Jude*, 133.

107. DeSilva, *The Jewish Teachers of Jesus, James, and Jude*, 139.

108. DeSilva compared Dan 7:9–10 with 1 Enoch 46:1; 47:3 and noted the close association of the Enthroned One with the Son of Man (1 Enoch 46:1, 3; 48:2). Finally, Enoch himself was translated from earth in a chariot and saw the earliest human ancestors (70:1–4). He was named Son of Man before angelic hosts, which were described in detail (71:8–14).

109. Chris Keith, *Jesus' Literacy: Scribal Culture and the Teacher from Galilee*, LNTS 413 (New York: T&T Clark, 2011); Keith, *Jesus against the Scribal Elite: The Origins of the Conflict* (Grand Rapids: Baker Academic, 2014).

110. Keith, *Jesus against the Scribal Elite*, 157.

Quests before Schweitzer

1.8. The Stubborn and Rebellious Son. The next episode (3:31–35) illustrates a further breach of Torah tradition. It involves Jesus' mother, brothers, and the complete breakdown of his family relations. Although it may not be immediately apparent,[111] the episode turns on the fifth commandment and consequences of disobedience. Jesus' mother and brothers (in the absence of a father) came to the crowded house and called for him. Jesus refused to meet them, disowning them with the reply: "'Who are my mother and my brothers?' And looking at those who sat around him, he said, 'Here are my mother and my brothers! Whoever does the will of God is my brother and sister and mother'" (3:33–35).[112]

The background to this episode is given in the case law procedure for breaking the fifth commandment set out in Deuteronomy 21:18–21 (RSV, emphasis added):

---

111. The issue seems to be sidestepped by the comment of *The Jewish Annotated New Testament*. "New religious movements often create 'fictive families' of social networks outside of traditional families, with members called 'brothers and sisters,' 'saints,' and so on" (*The Jewish Annotated New Testament: New Revised Standard Bible Translation*, ed. Amy-Jill Levine and Marc Zvi Brettler [Oxford: Oxford University Press, 2011], 67).

On the other hand, Jacob Milgrom maintained that the Decalogue would fail if it were not rooted in ritual observance, central to family life (*Leviticus 1–16*, 736). David Noel Freedman saw rebellion as the central theme of Deuteronomy. He attached particular importance to violation of the fifth commandment in the fifth book of the Torah with regard to the formation of the Hebrew canon (*The Unity of the Hebrew Bible*, 24–25). The contrast between the wise son and the foolish son was a major theme of wisdom literature.

Procedure for dealing with the stubborn and rebellious was discussed in various contemporary sources, including Josephus, *Ant.* 4.263–264; *Against Apion* 2.206; and Philo, *On Drunkenness* 14; *Special Laws* 2.232. References in the Talmud indicate division of opinion over whether the provisions of Deuteronomy 21 were actually implemented, or whether they were intended merely as a warning. However, it should be noted that the conditional promise of long life attached to the fifth commandment was not intended as a reward for good behavior. It was a warning of legal penalties for disobedience.

Some authorities hold that implementation of the procedure required the presence of both the father and mother. Others argue that the mother was introduced into the procedure in biblical law in order to limit the power of the *pater familias*. See further, Daniel Sinclair, "Ben Sorer U-Moreh," in *ODJR*, 114; Joseph B. Modica, "Jesus as Glutton and Drunkard: The 'Excesses of Jesus,'" in *Who Do My Opponents Say That I Am?*, 50–75.

112. The only reference in Mark to Mary (Miriam) by name is Mark 6:3, which described Jesus' return to the synagogue at his "hometown," Nazareth. None of Jesus' family actually appeared. People asked: "'Is not this the carpenter, the son of Mary and brother of James and Joses and Judas and Simon, and are not his sisters here with us?' And they took offense at him." Mark contains no references to Joseph. Jesus' break with his family was complete, although Jesus maintained respect for the Fifth Commandment (7:10–12; 10:7; 19; cf. Exod 20:12; Deut 5:16). He also recognized that discipleship could involve breakdown of family relationships (10:29).

The First Quest

If a man has *a stubborn and rebellious son*, who will not obey the voice of his father or the voice of his mother, and, though they chastise him, will not give heed to them, then his father and his mother shall take hold of him and bring him out to the elders of his city at the gate of the place where he lives, and they shall say to the elders of his city, "This our son is *stubborn and rebellious*, he will not obey our voice; he is *a glutton and a drunkard.*" Then all the men of the city shall stone him to death with stones; so you shall purge the evil from your midst; and all Israel shall hear, and fear.

The phrases put in italics are particularly relevant. Jesus' reputation as a stubborn and rebellious son is made more explicit by Matthew and Luke. In Mark's narrative, if Jesus did not qualify as a stubborn and rebellious son before his mother and brothers called on him, he himself did so by renouncing his blood ties and adopting a new family.

1.9. End of Ministry in Capernaum. The episodes described in Mark 3:20–35 represent mounting degrees of alienation. The three views connected with different groups—neighbors in Capernaum (he is out of his mind), the scribes (he is possessed by Beelzebul), and his family (the gravity of being a stubborn and rebellious son)—amounted to the number of witnesses needed in a law case (Deut 19:15; 17:6; Num 35:30; cf. Matt 18:16; 2 Cor 13:1; 1 Tim 5:19; Heb 10:28). However, like the witnesses at the hearing before the Sanhedrin, the views did not add up to agreement (14:59). Nevertheless, they marked the beginning of the end of Jesus' activity in Capernaum. The end took place on the lakeshore with such a large crowd that Jesus boarded a boat and taught the multitude on the shore (4:1).

Mark presents a selection of parables that Jesus taught (4:33). To the crowd he spoke only in parables designed to challenge "those outside" (4:11). Their meaning was explained only to insiders in private: the disciples (4:34). To them was given "the secret [τὸ μυστήριον] of the kingdom of God" (4:11).

In subsequent chapters of this book, we shall examine various interpretations of Jesus' parables. For now I want to concentrate on the role that Mark's selection plays in his narrative so far. Mark indicates that he chose the following parables out of many: the sower (4:3–9), the lamp (4:21–25), the seed (4:26–29), and the mustard seed (4:30–32). Jesus spoke only in parables to the crowd but explained the parable of the sower to the disciples (4:10–20). The parable of the lamp, which follows the private explanation of the parable of the sower, focuses on the disciples' future role and conduct amid adversity.

The parables addressed to the crowd were parables about seed and growth. Although it is not immediately clear, they amounted to a farewell address. Although the hearers were not to know it, Jesus' time in Capernaum was at an end. From now on, Jesus' ministry was itinerant, made necessary by mounting rejection alongside the accusations that we just reviewed.

Jesus' justification for teaching only in parables was grounded in a paraphrase of the divine instructions given to Isaiah. These instructions followed Isaiah's consecration as God's prophet to Israel. Isaiah was to preach God's word, whether or not people heeded it, even to the point where the land was laid waste and only a stump was left. That stump would be the "holy seed" for the future (Isa 6:13). Mark's paraphrase of Isaiah's mandate to preach reads: "in order that 'they may indeed look, but not perceive, and may indeed listen, but not understand; so that they may not turn again and be forgiven'" (Mark 4:12; cf. Isa 6:9–10).

The word of God was to be preached regardless of human obduracy. Hearers had opportunity to hear and listen: "Let anyone with ears to hear listen!" (4:9). However, the parable of the sower, which Rikki E. Watts suggests could more accurately be called *the parable of the soils*,[113] indicates causes of opposition and indifference. Seed that fell on the path was snatched away by Satan before it had chance to take root (4:15). Seed that fell on rocky ground indicated shallow reception (4:16). Since it lacked roots, it withered in the face of trouble or persecution (4:17). Seed that fell among thorns was choked by worldly cares (4:18–19). But seed that fell on good soil, those who heard and received the word, bore fruit thirty, sixty, and a hundredfold (4:20). The instructions given to the disciples (4:21–25) were a reality check regarding what they might expect. Jesus exhorted them to be like a light in a dark place.

Albert Schweitzer regarded the messianic secret, Jesus' inner conviction that he was the Christ, as the central motive of Jesus. William Wrede argued that the secret could be traced no further than Mark's gospel, not to Jesus himself. The debate over the *messianic secret* was one

---

113. Watts, *Isaiah's New Exodus and Mark*, 205.

The First Quest

of the major debates of the twentieth century.[114] However, it should be noted that the term μυστήριον (*mysterion*, "secret," "mystery") occurs in the Gospels only in Mark 4:11 and the parallels (Matt 13:11; Luke 8:10), where it has the sense of "private counsel of God."[115] In none of these passages does it refer to *messiahship* and the part it played in Jesus' motivation. The *mystery* was about the private wisdom of God with regard to human obstinacy, indifference, and response to his word. It was about opposition, indifference, and encouragement. In that sense, the parable of the sower might be regarded as a forerunner of the passion predictions, warning the disciples of opposition and disappointments that they would face in following Jesus and the prophecy of Isaiah.[116]

The final parables of growth (4:26–31) express confidence in the ultimate outcome. They represent Jesus' last public utterance in Capernaum. In Mark the narrative of the stilling of the storm (4:35–41) is a sequel to the mounting rejection Jesus had experienced. Neighbors thought him mad. Scribes from Jerusalem accused him of being possessed by Beelzebul. Relations with family came to a disastrous end.

Like Elijah before him (1 Kings 19),[117] Jesus was obliged to flee for his life. In structuralist analysis the episode is classified as a generic "rescue miracle."[118] In Mark the sea crossing represents a tactical retreat under cover of darkness. "On that day, when evening had come, he said to them, 'Let us cross over to the other side.' And leaving the crowd behind, they took him with them in the boat, just as he was. Other boats were with him" (4:35–36). These details are absent from the narratives in Matthew 8:23–27 and Luke 8:22–25. The allusion to "other boats" raises the question of whether they contained friends and supporters, the merely curious, or enemies keeping track of him.

---

114. Christopher Tuckett, ed., *The Messianic Secret*, Issues in Religion and Theology 1 (London: SCPK; Philadelphia: Fortress, 1983), contains a selection of important contributions.

115. BDAG, 622.

116. It would be a mistake to conclude that Mark's gospel was uniquely Isaianic. All three Synoptic Gospels give versions of Isa 6:9, though Matt 13:13 is abbreviated, and Luke 8:10 is even more so. All three Synoptic Gospels cite the prophecy of Isaiah (40:3) in connection with the appearance of John (Mark 1:2; cf. Matt 3:1; Luke 3:4).

117. Barnabas Lindars, "Elijah, Elisha and the Gospel Miracles," in *Miracles: Cambridge Studies in Their Philosophy and History*, ed. C. F. D. Moule (London: Mowbray, 1965), 63–79.

118. Gerd Theissen, *The Miracle Stories of the Early Christian Tradition*, trans. Francis McDonagh, ed. John Riches (Philadelphia: Fortress, 1983), 99–103; Meier, *A Marginal Jew*, 2:924–33.

Quests before Schweitzer

The description of Jesus being asleep in the stern recalls the prophet Jonah asleep on a ship in a similar predicament (4:38; cf. Jonah 1:5). Jesus, like Jonah, was a prophet under judgment. In the book of Jonah the ship and its crew were saved and the storm calmed by the sinful Jonah being thrown overboard. If the disciples' boat had sunk, and its occupants drowned, it would have been seen as a judgment. Catastrophe was averted by Jesus' treating the storm as a demonic attack, described in terms employed in exorcism.[119] In "great awe" the disciples asked, "Who then is this, that even the wind and the sea obey him?" (4:41). In the Old Testament stilling of the sea is something that only God could do: "You rule the raging of the sea; when its waves rise, you still them" (Ps 89:9). In the meantime, the storm foreshadowed things to come.

2. Narratives and History

In talking about the First Quest, I make no pretensions to being privy to the Jerusalem scribes' deliberations or to the extent of their knowledge about Jesus. What I have done is to draw attention to their place in Mark's narrative and in so doing offer an analytic construct of the first four chapters of Mark's narrative. I have two reasons for doing this. The first is to give readers an understanding of what the quests of the historical Jesus are about by sketching an account of the beginnings of the quest. All too often people talk about the quests without examining the primary evidence. The second reason for offering my construct is to draw attention to the fact that all reading and hearing involves interpretation and construal.

This second reason applies to ordinary actions like making a grocery list. When we get to the store we have to interpret the words and how they apply to items on the shelves so that we may make purchases. The Bible is not a kind of telescope that enables us to see directly what happened in the past. It is itself an endless source of constructs in words, which invite us to form our own understanding of what the words relate to.

---

119. The verb ἐπιτιμάω (*epitimaō*, "rebuke," the wind, 4:39) is used in connection with exorcism (1:25; 9:25; BDAG, 384). φιμόω (*phimoō*, "be silent," lit. "be muzzled," 4:39) is also used in exorcism (1:25; BDAG, 1060).

The First Quest

2.1. Criteria and Authenticity. In the course of the quests scholars have tried to identify criteria for authenticating the words and actions of Jesus. John P. Meier reminds readers of the distinction between "the real Jesus" and the "historical Jesus."[120] "We cannot know the 'real' Jesus through historical research, whether we mean his total reality or just a reasonably complete biographical portrait. We can, however, know the 'historical Jesus.'"[121] "The historical Jesus is not the real Jesus, but only a fragmentary hypothetical reconstruction of him by modern means of research."[122] The "theological Jesus" is the Christ of Christian theology. As a Catholic critical historian, Meier feels able to hand over to the theologians the investigation of the latter "according to their own proper methods and criteria." The "historical Jesus" must be investigated historically, using five "primary criteria": embarrassment, discontinuity with Judaism(s) and the early church, multiple attestation, coherence, and reasons for Jesus' rejection and execution.[123]

Meier's multivolume *A Marginal Jew* is an incomparable resource and, for me, a constant companion. However, I find his method both too pessimistic and too optimistic. In a word, it is too attached to positivism. A significant body of scholars has already moved away from "authenticity," as Chris Keith and Anthony Le Donne have shown recently.[124] On the one hand, the five "primary criteria" do not deliver agreed, unassailable, judgment-free, authentic data. They are more like declarations of intent, boundary markers of what is feasible. On the other hand, criteria like "embarrassment" and "rejection and execution" seem only marginally relevant. Meier admitted that the latter did not function like the others. Whereas the previous four help to determine whether a saying or deed was "authentic," the fifth directed attention to Jesus' violent end. Meier observed, "A Jesus whose words and deeds would not alienate people, especially powerful people, is not the historical Jesus."[125] However, this criterion is not a litmus test of whether the preceding four criteria have got it right. Embarrassment is a theme that runs through all

---

120. Meier, *A Marginal Jew*, 1:21–31.
121. Meier, *A Marginal Jew*, 1:24.
122. Meier, *A Marginal Jew*, 1:31.
123. Meier, *A Marginal Jew*, 1:167–95.
124. Chris Keith and Anthony Le Donne, eds., *Jesus, Criteria, and the Demise of Authenticity* (New York: T&T Clark, 2012).
125. Meier, *A Marginal Jew*, 1:177.

four canonical Gospels and, in my view, a major reason why they were written in the first place.

From a philosophical standpoint, the quest for objective, authentic facts is questionable. Alasdair McIntyre maintained a sustained polemic against the separation of facts from judgment and traditions:

> There are not two distinguishable items, a judgment on the one hand, and that portrayed in the judgment on the other, between which a relationship of correspondence can hold or fail to hold. The commonest candidate, in modern versions of what is all too often taken to be *the* correspondence theory of truth, for that which corresponds to a judgment in this way is a fact. But facts, like telescopes and wigs for gentlemen, were a seventeenth-century invention. . . . It is of course and always was harmless, philosophically and otherwise, to use the word "fact" of what a judgment states. What is and was not harmless, but highly misleading, was to conceive of a realm of facts independent of judgment or of any other form of linguistic expression, so that judgments or statements or sentences could be paired off with facts, truth or falsity being the alleged relationship between such paired items.[126]

Nicholas Wolterstorff rejected foundationalism in the sense of seeking indubitable foundations as the basis of certitude. No one has ever succeeded in showing the relation of the theories that we are warranted in accepting or rejecting to such a set of facts. There is no general logic of the sciences that would provide a general rule for a warranted theory of acceptance or rejection. As an alternative, Wolterstorff proposed that in weighing theories we need to distinguish between data beliefs, data-background beliefs, and control beliefs. Yet none of those beliefs provides the foundation. Rather, they function together. What functions as data-background belief or control belief on one occasion may be examined as data belief on another.[127] Other writers use the term *paradigm* for what

---

126. Alasdair McIntyre, *Whose Justice? Which Rationality?* (Notre Dame, IN: University of Notre Dame Press, 1998), 357–58. See also Trevor Hart, *Faith Thinking: The Dynamics of Christian Theology* (Downers Grove, IL: InterVarsity Press, 1996); Michael Polanyi, *Personal Knowledge: Towards a Post-Critical Philosophy*, Gifford Lectures, Aberdeen, 1951–1952 (London: Routledge, 1958); Polanyi, *The Tacit Dimension*, Terry Lectures, Yale, 1962 (London: Routledge, 1967).

127. Nicholas Wolterstorff, *Reason within the Bounds of Religion* (Grand Rapids: Eerdmans, 1976; 2nd ed., 1984), 69–70.

The First Quest

Wolterstorff describes as a *control belief*.[128] Advantages and disadvantages come with both terms.[129] On Wolterstorff's view, it may be argued that theories, beliefs, and world-views are not tested by appeal to single or several observable facts. Rather, they die "the death of a thousand qualifications."[130] Many explanations are accepted or rejected not because of observed facts, but because of differences over *control beliefs* or *paradigms*. Cases in point are controversies already noted in discussion of Mark's narrative. They recur in subsequent quests.

2.2. Reception History. A paradigm-shift in interpretation began with the publication of Hans-Georg Gadamer's *Wahrheit und Methode* (1960), or *Truth and Method*.[131] Gadamer's central question was with "understanding" (German, *Verstehen*). The operation was more like

---

128. Thomas S. Kuhn, *The Structure of Scientific Revolutions* (Chicago: University of Chicago Press, [1962]; 2nd ed., 1970); Ian G. Barbour, *Myths, Models, and Paradigms: The Nature of Scientific and Religious Language* (London: SCM; New York: Harper & Row, 1974); Earl R. MacCormac, *Metaphor and Myth in Science and Religion* (Durham, NC: Duke University Press, 1976).

129. The advantage of using the word *belief* is its reminder that there are components of trust and faith in science as well as religion. They occur not only in paradigms, which entail trusting the validity of the work of countless researchers in their formation. The same applies to the use of data and background information, supporting the data and its selection. Wolterstorff's account of the structure of argument applies to other fields, such as medicine, history, economics, and law. However, use of the word *belief* may suggest that Wolterstorff was talking only about religious belief and religious claims, where it is also applicable.

The advantage of the word *paradigm* is that it is relatively neutral. Its main disadvantage is that it conceals the components of faith and trust involved in scholarship. It is also used to denote commonly accepted practices within disciplines, and shared convictions at large. Earl R. MacCormac comments on the latter: "Revolutionary science occurs when a paradigm-shift takes place. Abandoning one paradigm is always accompanied by the acceptance of another paradigm. Newtonian mechanics were not abandoned until relativity theory was accepted. Before a paradigm-shift occurs, there is a crisis among believers in the old paradigm" (*Metaphor and Myth in Science and Religion*, 22). The same phenomenon appears to occur in religions.

130. Antony Flew, "Theology and Falsification," in *New Essays in Philosophical Theology*, ed. Antony Flew and Alasdair MacIntyre (London: SCM, 1955), 97.

131. In 1949 Hans-Georg Gadamer (1900–2002) became professor of philosophy at Heidelberg, where he achieved international acclaim. His early work was devoted to Plato, Aristotle, and Greek philosophy. He published *Wahrheit und Methode* at the age of sixty. *Truth and Method*, trans. Joel Weinsheimer and Donald G. Marshall (Tübingen: Mohr Siebeck, 1965) is based on the second German edition; it has been revised and reprinted and is now in paperback (London, New York: Bloomsbury Academic, 2013). Collected articles are reprinted in *Philosophical Hermeneutics*, trans. and ed. David E. Linge (Berkeley: University of California Press, 1977).

The vast literature includes Joel C. Weinsheimer, *Gadamer's Hermeneutics: A Reading of Truth and Method* (New Haven, CT: Yale University Press, 1985); Robert J. Dostal, ed., *The Cambridge Companion to Gadamer* (Cambridge: Cambridge University Press, 2002). For Gadamer's significance for theology, see Anthony C. Thiselton, *The Two Horizons: New Testament Hermeneutics and Philosophical Description with Special Reference to Heidegger, Gadamer, Bultmann, and Wittgenstein* (Grand Rapids: Eerdmans, 1980), 293–326; Thiselton, *New Horizons in Hermeneutics: The Theory and Practice of Transforming Biblical Reading* (Grand Rapids: Zondervan, 1992); Thiselton, *The*

43

Quests before Schweitzer

"coming to an understanding with someone" (German, *Verständigung*) and "agreement" (German, *Einverständnis*).[132] Gadamer rejected the idea that philosophical hermeneutics should be assimilated to the methods of the natural sciences. He rejected Schleiermacher's view that primary concern should be with discovery of the author's original intent. Nor did he share the Enlightenment's passion for removing preconception or prejudice (German, *Vorurteil*) so that the truth could be laid bare. Preconceptions and prejudice have a part to play in developing our understanding.

Two aspects of Gadamer's *Truth and Method* are particularly relevant to the present discussion. The first is *Wirkungsgeschichte*, "the reality of history in that it is the history of realization. What is real works—that is, in realizing itself it works itself out."[133] In *Truth and Method* it is called "history of effect." Gadamer himself did not regard it as something new. Nor was it a new branch of research but a new demand on "historical consciousness." This demand occurs

> every time a work of art or an aspect of the tradition is led out of the twilight region between tradition and history so that it can be seen openly in terms of its own meaning. . . . If we are trying to understand a historical phenomenon from the historical distance that is characteristic of our hermeneutical situation, we are always already affected by history. It determines in advance what will appear as an object of investigation, and we more or less forget half of what is really there—in fact, we miss the whole truth of the phenomenon—when we take its immediate appearance as the whole truth.[134]

The other relevant aspect of Gadamer's hermeneutics follows from the first. He described it as the "fusion of horizons" (German, *Horizontverschmeltzung*), that is, the horizons of the past and those of the present. Gadamer explained:

Hermeneutics of Doctrine (Grand Rapids: Eerdmans, 2007); Thiselton, *Hermeneutics* (Grand Rapids: Eerdmans, 2009), 206–27, etc.

132. Weinsheimer and Marshall, introduction to *Truth and Method*, xv.

133. Weinsheimer, *Gadamer's Hermeneutics*, 181.

134. Gadamer, *Truth and Method*, 311.

The First Quest

In fact the horizon of the present is continually in the process of being formed because we are continually having to test all our prejudices. An important part of this testing occurs in encountering the past and in understanding the tradition to be formed from which we come. Hence the horizon of the present cannot be formed without the past. There is no more an isolated horizon of the present in itself than there are historical horizons which have to be acquired. *Rather, understanding is always the fusion of these horizons supposedly existing by themselves.* We are familiar with this kind of fusion chiefly from earlier times and their naivete about themselves and their heritage. In a tradition this process of fusion is always going on, for there old and new are always combining into something of living value, without either being explicitly foregrounded from the other.[135]

Anthony C. Thiselton thinks that *Wirkungsgeschichte* is best understood as "history of influences," meaning "both the influence of readers on texts and the influence of text on readers . . . a two-way process and method of shaping traditions."[136] With this we are brought to "reception theory" and its leading exponent, Hans Robert Jauss.[137] This is not the place to attempt a summary of Jauss or reduplicate other discussions.[138] I shall limit my comments to two issues: Jauss's modification of Gadamer and recognition that Gadamer's method may be applied to biblical interpretation.

Jauss acknowledged fundamental agreement between his own

---

135. Gadamer, *Truth and Method*, 317. Gadamer's italics.

136. Thiselton, *Hermeneutics*, 316.

137. Hans Robert Jauss (1921–76) served as an officer on the Russian front in the Second World War. After postwar imprisonment he studied philosophy, philology, history, and literature. Among his teachers were Martin Heidegger and Hans-Georg Gadamer. He obtained doctorates at the University of Heidelberg. Jauss was appointed to a professorial chair at the newly founded University of Constance, where he was a member of what became known as the Constance school. Jauss's inaugural lecture on "Literary History as a Challenge to Literary Theory" is regarded as programmatic for reception theory. It is reprinted in Jauss, *Toward an Aesthetic of Reception*, trans. Timothy Bahti, introduction by Paul de Man, Theory and History of Literature 2 (Minneapolis: University of Minnesota Press, 1982). See also Jauss, *Aesthetic Experience and Literary Hermeneutics*, trans. Michael Shaw, introduction by Wlad Godzich, Theory and History of Literature 3 (Minneapolis: University of Minnesota Press, 1982).

138. Discussions include Osmond Rush, *The Reception of Doctrine: An Appropriation of Hans Robert Jauss' Reception Aesthetics and Literary Hermeneutics*, TGST 19 (Rome: Pontifical Gregorian University, 1997); Thiselton, *The Hermeneutics of Doctrine*, 98–104; Thiselton, *Hermeneutics*, 316–20; Robert Evans, *Reception History, Tradition and Biblical Interpretation: Gadamer and Jauss in Current Practice*, Scriptural Traces: Critical Perspectives on the Reception and Influence of the Bible 4, LNTS 510 (New York: T&T Clark, 2014).

endeavor to envisage literary history on the basis of reception and Gadamer's principle of historical influence. However, Jauss believed that Gadamer's preoccupation with the classical world needed modification.[139] Progressive understanding "must consider the history of literature in a threefold manner: diachronically in the interrelationships of the reception of literary works . . . synchronically in the frame of reference of the same moment, as well as in the sequence of such frames . . . and finally in the relationship of immanent literary development to the general process of history."[140]

Jauss recognized that his theory of reception with regard to European literature was also applicable to biblical interpretation. He welcomed the encyclical of Pope Pius XII *Divino afflante spiritu* (1943) with its recognition of the place of modern theories of literary genres in biblical exegesis.[141] Jauss saw the form critical work of Gunkel and Bultmann as examples of biblical exegesis that fitted his own overall framework.[142]

Anthony C. Thiselton notes several instances of the application of reception theory to New Testament interpretation. They include the work of Ulrich Luz on Matthew,[143] Ulrich Wilckens on Romans,[144] Judith Kovacs and Christopher Rowland on the book of Revelation,[145] and his own work on 1 Corinthians.[146] I venture to suggest that Mark's gospel could be added to the list of works appropriate for study in light of reception history.

In recent years attention has been drawn to oral performance as the

---

139. Jauss, *Towards an Aesthetic of Reception*, 30.

140. Jauss, *Towards an Aesthetic of Reception*, 32.

141. Jauss, *Towards an Aesthetic of Reception*, 100.

142. Jauss, *Towards an Aesthetic of Reception*, 101.

143. Ulrich Luz, *Matthew 1–7: A Commentary*, trans. James E. Crouch (Minneapolis: Augsburg; Edinburgh: T&T Clark, 1989); Luz, *Matthew 8–20*, trans. James E. Crouch and Wilhelm C. Linss (Minneapolis: Augsburg; London, SCM, 2001); Luz, *Matthew 21–28*, trans. James E. Crouch and Wilhelm C. Linss (Minneapolis: Fortress; London, SCM, 2005).

144. Ulrich Wilckens, *Der Brief an die Römer*, 3 vols., EKKNT (Neukirchen: Neukirchener, 1978–82).

145. Judith Kovacs and Christopher Rowland, *Revelation* (Oxford: Blackwell, 2004). See also Christopher Rowland and Crispin H. T. Fletcher-Louis, eds., *Understanding, Studying, and Reading: New Testament Essays in Honour of John Ashton*, JSNTSup 153 (Sheffield: Sheffield Academic Press, 1998); Michael Lieb, Emma Mason, Jonathan Roberts, and Christopher Rowland, eds., *The Oxford Handbook of the Reception History of the Bible* (Oxford: Oxford University Press, 2011); Zoë Bennett and David B. Gowler, eds., *Radical Christian Voices and Practice: Essays in Honour of Christopher Rowland* (Oxford: Oxford University Press, 2012).

146. Anthony C. Thiselton, *The First Epistle to the Corinthians: A Commentary of the Greek Text*, NIGTC (Grand Rapids: Eerdmans, 2000).

The First Quest

original form of Mark.[147] It has spawned a new branch of study: biblical performance criticism.[148] Attention is focused on questions like the role of the narrator, settings, plot, characters, and audience.[149] In general, the standpoint is *contemporary* literary criticism.

Without wishing to detract from this line of investigation, my personal interest in Mark's genre was sparked by a comment by Martin Hengel. It recommended that Mark should be read as oral performance in the tradition of Aristotle's *Poetics*.

> In terms of extent, construction and inner drama the Second Gospel remains a work which can be illuminated in an amazing way by the rules which Aristotle established in connection with the successful form of literary mimesis. . . . The Second Gospel probably developed out of living teaching and was composed for solemn reading in worship. The short cola, often with a rhythmic shape, point to oral recitation in the assembled community. The Gospel was written for the audience to listen to, and therefore is anything but an artificial literary composition written at a desk, stuck together from obscure written sources, countless notes and flysheets.[150]

My article on "The Jesus of Mark's Gospel" was my first shot at following up on Hengel and the scholars mentioned in his endnotes.[151]

---

147. David Rhoads, Joanna Dewey, Donald Michie, *Mark as Story: An Introduction to the Narrative of a Gospel*, 3rd ed. (Minneapolis: Fortress, 2012); cf. Robert M. Fowler, "Reader Response Criticism: Figuring Mark's Reader," in *Mark and Method: New Approaches to Biblical Studies*, ed. Janice Capel Anderson and Stephen D. Moore, 2nd ed. (Minneapolis: Fortress, 2008), 54–93.

148. The series on Biblical Performance Criticism published by Cascade Books, Eugene, Oregon, includes: Antoinette Clark Wire, *The Case for Mark Composed in Performance* (2011); Joanna Dewey, *The Oral Ethos of the Early Church: Speaking, Writing, and the Gospel of Mark* (2013); Richard A. Horsley, *Text and Tradition in Performance and Writing* (2013).

149. Matthew Ryan Hauge and Christopher W. Skinner, *Character Studies in the Gospel of Mark*, LNTS 483 (London: T&T Clark, 2014). Edwin K. Broadhead uses narrative analysis in *Teaching with Authority: Miracles and Christology in the Gospel of Mark*, JSNTSup 74 (Sheffield: Sheffield Academic Press, 1994).

150. Martin Hengel, *Studies in the Gospel of Mark*, trans. John Bowden (Philadelphia: Fortress, 1985), 36, 52; cf. Hengel, "Literary, Theological, and Historical Problems in the Gospel of Mark," *The Gospel and the Gospels*, ed. Peter Stuhlmacher, trans. John Bowden and John Vriend (Grand Rapids: Eerdmans, 1991), 209–51.

151. Brown, "The Jesus of Mark's Gospel," 26–53. Whereas Hengel followed Aristotle's three-act format, I think that Mark adopted the five-act format known to Horace. Aristotle's *Poetics* held that tragedy and epic followed the same basic rules, except that tragedy was acted, the epic was narrated. Fiction dealt with the kind of events that could happen; history dealt with

In it I proposed reading Mark as a tragic epic in five acts separated by blocks of commentary. Mark began with a prologue, which introduced the main characters and set up the dynamics of the action that followed. Mark's epilogue, with its story of the women and the empty tomb, turned what would have been a tragedy into a triumph. Since writing the article I have further tested the hypothesis, episode by episode, in a private seminar. What I have sketched above, under the heading of "The First Quest," is a summary of the prologue (1:1–15), act 1 (1:16–3:35), the first block of commentary (4:1–33), and the opening scene of act 2 (4:35–41).

3. Gospel Narratives: An Overview

The above account of Mark focuses on two main issues: the investigation undertaken by the scribes from Jerusalem (3:22) and Mark's account of what preceded and followed it. The two accounts are not to be confused since Mark was hardly privy to the scribes' deliberations, and we know only their verdict. Mark's gospel embodied the First Quest. What he gave was *his* reception of their verdict and events surrounding it. My account outlines *my* reception of Mark.

I have treated Mark's narrative as what Nicholas Wolterstorff called *data beliefs*. To help me interpret Mark, I have identified sundry *data-background beliefs* and have drawn on the best scholarship available to me—Jewish and Christian—in assessing their scope and relevance. I have not yet described my control beliefs, but they may become apparent in due course. For now, I wish to state that they too are open to change where data and background warrant it. This applies to ultimate control beliefs, such as what Christians believe about the Trinity and incarnation. The two are interrelated and are not exempt from scrutiny.[152]

In what follows, I wish to draw attention to similarities and differences in the canonical Gospels, first by sketching Mark in outline, then

---

events that did happen. The common aim was to produce a *catharsis* or purifying response from the audience. Aristotle identified three recurring elements: discovery or recognition, reversal, and suffering. They are found abundantly in Mark. Among those who have pursued this line of investigation are Gilbert Bilezikian, Friedrich Gustav Lang, Benoît Standaert, Mary Ann Beavis, and Morna D. Hooker (See Brown, "The Jesus of Mark's Gospel," 47n30).

152. Colin Brown, "Trinity and Incarnation: In Search of Contemporary Orthodoxy," *Ex Auditu* 7 (1991): 83–100.

The First Quest

by looking at Matthew and Luke together, and finally drawing attention to the different perspective of John.

3.1. Mark. First, I will set out my view of Mark more fully, and then I shall offer brief comments on issues in those parts of his narrative that I have not yet examined. With regard to *content*, I regard Mark as thoroughly Jewish. With regard to *genre*, I situate Mark in the context of the Hellenistic culture that permeated Second Temple Judaism.[153]

Among precedents for treating sacred history in dramatic form is the *Exagoge* of Ezekiel the Tragedian, which tells the story of the exodus from Egypt.[154] Dennis R. MacDonald has investigated the possible influence of Homeric epics on Mark.[155] My proposal is that, remembering that Christians were a persecuted minority sect at the time, Mark set out to write a vindication of Jesus using the best genre available to him, the tragic epic.

Aristotle described tragedy and epic in terms of μίμησις, which scholars transliterate as *mimēsis* or translate as "representation."[156] The actions depicted should arouse pity and fear in order to accomplish a catharsis of the emotions. Whereas the poet describes the kind of event that can happen, the historian describes events that have happened. Pity and fear have their greatest effect when incidents occur in consequence of each other.

---

153. Martin Hengel, *Judaism and Hellenism: Studies in Their Encounter in Palestine during the Early Hellenistic Period*, trans. John Bowden, 2 vols. (London: SCM, 1974); Hengel in collaboration with Christoph Markschies, *The 'Hellenization' of Judaea in the First Century after Christ* (repr., Eugene, OR: Wipf & Stock, 2003); John J. Collins and Gregory E. Sterling, eds., *Hellenism in the Land of Israel*, Christianity and Judaism in Antiquity 13 (Notre Dame, IN: University of Notre Dame Press, 2001); Erich S. Gruen, *Heritage and Hellenism: The Reinvention of Jewish Tradition* (Berkeley: University of California Press, 1998; repr., 2002).

154. Fragments of this work from the second century BCE depicting the exodus are reproduced in *The Old Testament Pseudepigrapha*, ed. James H. Charlesworth (Garden City, NY: Doubleday, 1985), 2:803–19; cf. Robert Doran, "The High Cost of a Good Education," in Collins and Sterling, *Hellenism in the Land of Israel*, 94–115; Gruen, *Heritage and Hellenism*, 129–35.

155. Dennis R. MacDonald, *The Homeric Epics and the Gospel of Mark* (New Haven, CT: Yale University Press, 2000); MacDonald, *Two Shipwrecked Gospels: The Logoi of Jesus and Papias's Exposition of Logia about the Lord* (Atlanta: SBL Press, 2012).

156. The following account is based on Aristotle's *Poetics*, translated by Stephen Halliwell, LCL 199 (Cambridge, MA: Harvard University Press, 1995); cf. Halliwell, *The Aesthetics of Mimesis: Ancient Texts and Modern Problems* (Princeton, NJ: Princeton University Press, 2002). Discussions of *mimesis* include Gunter Gebauer and Christoph Wulf, *Mimesis: Culture—Art—Society*, trans. Don Reneau (Berkeley: University of California Press, 1995); Gary Potolsky, *Mimesis* (New York: Routledge, 2006); Scott R. Garrels, ed., *Mimesis and Science: Empirical Research on Imitation and the Mimetic Theory of Culture and Religion* (East Lansing, MI: University of Michigan Press, 2011). See also Joel L. Watts, *Mimetic Criticism and the Gospel of Mark* (Eugene, OR: Wipf & Stock, 2013).

Quests before Schweitzer

There are three key elements: recognition, reversal, and suffering. They achieve their best effect, when they are related. Aristotle maintained that there should be a single action that unfolded in three phases separated by the performance of the chorus. By the time of Horace and Seneca, the chorus had become obsolete, and the five-act format was recognized, with some tragedies even being narrated rather than acted.

Mark adopted the five-act format with a prologue and an epilogue. The prologue (1:1–13) tersely narrates the critical elements that precipitate the action that follows.[157] The epilogue (15:40–16:8) transforms what would have been a tragic end into the message of resurrection hope. The five acts are separated by blocks of teaching commenting on the previous action, whether monologues by Jesus or dialogues involving Jesus' response to the questions or observations of others. As such, the blocks of teaching replaced the role once occupied by the chorus. The expression καὶ εὐθύς, "and suddenly" (replaced in modern times by sundry translations so as to avoid monotony) occurs some 110 times, serving as a marker between episodes. The five acts follow a definite pattern. I have given them titles in order to identify them.

Act 1 describes "The Beginnings of Conflict" (1:14–3:35). It begins with Jesus coming to Capernaum and calling his first disciples. It ends with Jesus disowning his biological family. The parables that follow (4:1–33) serve as commentary on reaction to Jesus and his message and as a bridge to what was to come.

Act 2 carries the title "The Conflict Spreads" (4:35–6:56). In some ways the second act repeats act 1 on a larger scale and mainly outside Galilee. Whereas the initial conflict of act 1 involved a man with an unclean spirit, the initial conflict in act 2 involves the encounter with Legion, using the same Greek vocabulary. The theme of purification is continued with episodes involving the woman with the flow of blood and Jairus's deceased daughter. In what now would be called a *flashback*, we hear of the fate of John the Baptist.[158] Consecutive episodes give hints of Jesus' role and identity.

The narrative of John's fate is followed by retreat to "a deserted

---

157. Cf. Morna D. Hooker, "The Beginning of the Gospel," in *The Future of Christology: Essays in Honor of Leander W. Keck*, ed. Abraham J. Malherbe and Wayne A. Meeks (Minneapolis: Fortress, 1993), 18–28.

158. By narrating John's fate as a *flashback*, Mark was able to preserve his five-act structure, which would have been otherwise difficult.

The First Quest

place." Nevertheless, crowds followed Jesus, who "had compassion for them because they were like sheep without a shepherd" (6:34). The words recall a similar incident in biblical history. Moses used the same expression when he was facing death and anxious about having a successor. He worried Israel would be "like sheep without a shepherd" (Num 27:17). The Lord directed him to Joshua the son of Nun, "a man in whom is the spirit" (Num 27:18). The names of Joshua and Jesus are *the same* in Greek and Hebrew. In short, Jesus was called to be not a new Moses, who saw the promised land from afar, but a new Joshua. The incident of Jesus' walking on the Sea of Galilee (recalling Joshua's crossing of the Jordan) marked the beginning of a new, nonviolent conquest.[159]

The dispute between "the Pharisees and some of the scribes" about purity (Mark 7:1–23) serves as a block of teaching separating acts 2 and 3 and highlights fundamental differences between them. Jesus followed Isaiah in stressing the heart as the source of impurity. Mark interpreted it as a declaration that all foods were clean (7:19).

Act 3 marks "The Climax" (7:24–9:34). It began inauspiciously with Jesus in hiding "in the region of Tyre." His whereabouts was discovered by a gentile Syrophoenician woman, who importuned him regarding her demon-possessed daughter.[160] It proved to be a turning point with regard to the gentiles. The episode contains intertextual echoes of Elijah and healing (1 Kgs 17:8–24) and Jonah's reluctance to go to the Nineveh. The climax of the entire narrative—as discovery followed by reversal—is Peter's declaration that Jesus is the Christ, the one anointed by God (8:29), which is followed by Jesus' rebuke of Peter for suggesting that Jesus' suffering and death would deflect from his mission (8:33).

In Aristotle's terminology the episode entails discovery, reversal, and suffering. Peter's confession marked the inauguration of Jesus' fateful pilgrimage to Jerusalem. Jesus responded by beginning to teach the disciples that the Son of Man must undergo great suffering and be rejected by the elders, chief priests, and scribes and be killed and rise again (8:31–32). The transfiguration (9:2–8), which took place on the way, ratified Jesus' identity as God's Son, a status higher than that of Moses or Elijah.

The teaching at the conclusion of act 3 (9:35–10:45) focuses on the

---

159. Brown, "The Jesus of Mark's Gospel," 36; cf. J. D. M. Derrett, "Why and How Jesus Walked on the Sea," in *Studies in the New Testament* (Leiden: Brill, 1986), 92–110.

160. Pablo Alonso, *The Woman Who Changed Jesus: Crossing Boundaries in Mk 7.24–30*, BTS 11 (Leuven: Peeters, 2011).

Quests before Schweitzer

way of the Son of Man and would-be disciples. The allusion to baptism and drinking the same cup as Jesus (10:38–39) suggests a double reference: the impending events in Jerusalem, and the context of baptism and eucharist in the oral delivery of Mark's narrative.

Act 4 (10:46–12:44) is "The Dénouement," that is, the unraveling of events when Jesus reached Jerusalem and entered the temple. The underlying motif was the ritual of Psalm 118, in which the postulant sought admission to the temple, and the priests inside opened "the gates of righteousness" with the greeting "Blessed is the one who comes in the name of the Lord."[161] However, when Jesus reached the temple, there was no greeting (11:11). The temple gates turned out to be the gates of death.

Only on the following day did Jesus perform the action that is generally called "the cleansing of the temple."[162] When asked about his authority to act as he did, Jesus replied, "Did the baptism of John come from heaven, or was it of human origin?" (11:30). The counterquestion seems at first irrelevant and evasive. In fact, it led directly to the answer to the question. If the temple authorities were prepared to admit that John was a prophet sent by God, Jesus' next question would be, "Why then did you not believe him?" (11:31). However, the burden of John's preaching was "I have baptized you with water; but he will baptize you with the Holy Spirit" (1:8). Sensing where Jesus' line of questioning was leading, the delegation refused to give an answer. In turn, Jesus declined to answer their question. He began to speak in parables, culminating with the citation from Psalm 118:22–23 about the stone that the builders rejected being made the cornerstone (12:10–11). The incident led to the decision to arrest Jesus, but not immediately (12:12).

The three questions put to Jesus in the temple during his final days of his public activity were designed to entrap him. They run parallel to the testing that preceded his public activity (12:13–34; cf. 1:12–13). The questions were asked by representatives of the three main groups opposed to

---

161. Colin Brown, "The Gates of Hell and the Church," in *Church, Word, and Spirit: Historical and Theological Essays in Honor of Geoffrey W. Bromiley*, ed. James E. Bradley and Richard A. Muller (Grand Rapids: Eerdmans, 1987), 15–43; Brown, "The Gates of Hell: An Alternative Approach," in *SBL Seminar Papers 1987*, ed. Kent Harold Richards (Atlanta: Scholars, 1987), 357–67.

162. Craig A. Evans, "From 'House of Prayer' to 'Cave of Robbers': Jesus' Prophetic Criticism of the Temple Establishment," in *The Quest for Context and Meaning: Studies in Biblical Intertextuality in Honor of James A. Sanders*, ed. Craig A. Evans and Shemaryahu Talmon, BibIntS 28 (Leiden: Brill, 1997), 417–42.

The First Quest

Jesus. In the case of the first two questions, Jesus exposed the inconsistency of the questioners. The third resulted in the solitary scribe endorsing Jesus.

The first question was posed by Pharisees and Herodians, acting as proxy for the temple establishment (12:13; cf. 11:27). Did the Torah permit paying tribute to Caesar? (12:14–17). The fact that the questioners themselves produced a coin bearing Caesar's image showed the insincerity of the question. Jesus' answer, "Give to the emperor the things that are the emperor's, and to God the things that are God's," threw the question back to the questioners. After that, the Pharisees and Herodians fade from Mark's narrative.

The second question was posed by *Sadducees*, whose strict Torah-based theology endorsed Levirate marriage. The Torah instructed a man to marry his deceased brother's wife and raise children for him (12:18–27; cf. Deut 25:5–10). The Sadducees' denial of life after death put them in conflict with the Pharisees. They put forward what they thought was a *reductio ad absurdum* involving multiple brothers who married the same woman. Whose wife would she be in the resurrection? Jesus reminded them of what they had overlooked.

The third question was put by a solitary *scribe* who asked what was the greatest commandment of the Torah (12:28–34). The question itself implied that not all parts of the Torah were equally authoritative. It was also a test of Jesus' orthodoxy. Jesus' answer put the matter beyond doubt with his unequivocal affirmation of the Shema: "Hear, O Israel: the Lord our God, the Lord is one; you shall love the Lord your God with all your heart, and with all your soul, and with all your mind, and with all your strength" (12:29–30; cf. Deut 6:4–5; *m. Ber.* 9:5). Jesus then added a second commandment, which was also based on the Torah: "You shall love your neighbor as yourself" (12:31; cf. Lev 19:18).[163] The scribe's endorsement—"This is much more important than all whole burnt offerings and sacrifices"—placed him firmly in the prophetic tradition (12:33; cf. 1 Sam 15:22; Hos 6:6; Mic 6:6–8). Jesus replied, "You are not far from the kingdom of God" (12:34).

Jesus ended with a question of his own. How could the scribes say that the Messiah [ὁ χριστός] was the son of David when David himself

---

163. On the universality of the Golden Rule, see Jacob Neusner and Bruce Chilton, eds., *The Golden Rule: Analytical Perspectives* (Lanham MD: University Press of America, 2009).

Quests before Schweitzer

declared by the Holy Spirit [ἐν τῷ πνεύματι τῷ ἁγίῳ]:[164] "The Lord said to my Lord, 'Sit at my right hand, until I put your enemies under your feet'" (12:36; cf. Ps 110:1)?[165] The question went unanswered. However, it resurfaced during the interrogation of Jesus by the Sanhedrin.

Jesus went on to warn the crowd against the scribes. The final act of his public ministry was his comment on the widow who put two copper coins into the temple treasury. Whereas others had put in more money, the widow had put in all that she had (ὅλον τὸν βίον αὐτῆς, lit. "her whole life"). She was an abiding example of fulfilling the two great commandments. The teaching section at the end of act 4 deals with judgment (13:1–37).[166]

Act 5 narrates "The Catastrophe" (14:1–15:39). It begins with the decision to arrest Jesus and ends with his death. Along the way it describes the anointing at Bethany in the house of Simon the leper, the Passover meal, Jesus' arrest in Gethsemane, and the interrogation before the Sanhedrin. The latter seems to have been a preliminary nighttime hearing, prior to a formal trial. However, it was cut short by Jesus' testimony, which was deemed blasphemous, making a formal trial unnecessary.

A feature of the interrogation is the high priest's question, which is verbally identical in Greek with Peter's confession: Σὺ εἶ ὁ Χριστός. (8:29; cf. 14:61).[167] The difference between the two is that Peter's words implied recognition and commitment, whereas the high priest's expressed incredulity and rejection. The coincidence may be due to Mark's dramatic skill. The Synoptic Gospels' accounts of the high priest's words differ in detail, which may be explained by differences of audience. I am not suggesting that the accounts were fabricated. Rather, what the different accounts convey—to use terminology that Joachim Jeremias used for the words of Jesus—is the *ipsissima vox* of the high priest rather than his *ipsissima verba*.

After failing to attempt to get consistent witness against Jesus, regarding what he had said about the temple, the high priest asked Jesus, "Are you the Messiah, the Son of the Blessed One?" Jesus said, "I am; and 'you will see the Son of Man seated at the right hand of the Power,' and 'coming with the clouds of heaven'" (14:61–62; citing Ps 110:1; Dan 7:13).

---

164. The exact phrase occurs in the prophecy of John the Baptist (1:8; cf. 1:23; 3:30; 5:2; 11:28–33).

165. Martin Hengel, "'Sit at My Right Hand!' The Enthronement of Christ at the Right Hand of God and Psalm 110:1," in *Studies in Early Christology* (Edinburgh: T&T Clark, 1995), 119–225.

166. Brown, "The Jesus of Mark's Gospel," 39–40.

167. Colin Brown, "The Hermeneutics of Confession and Accusation," *CTJ* 30 (1995): 460–71.

The First Quest

The combination of allusions brought together two themes that defined Jesus' activity. The significance of Psalm 110 was a matter of public record since Jesus himself had recently raised it in the temple precincts. Jesus' sonship had been declared by the voice from heaven after his baptism and reaffirmed in the transfiguration. Jesus' vocation regarding the Son of Man was defined by Daniel 7:13. Together they represented a hermeneutic that threatened the Torah-based hermeneutic of the temple hierarchy.

Jesus' reply took the form of a prophecy accompanied by a sign, which fit the profile described in Deuteronomy 13:1–6 of the prophet who led astray by sign and wonders.[168] Moreover, it was given before impeccable witnesses—the assembled Sanhedrin. In a symbolic act on hearing *blasphemy* the high priest tore his clothes (*m. Sanh.* 7:5). He asked, "'Why do we still need witnesses? You have heard his blasphemy! What is your decision?' All of them condemned him as deserving of death" (14:63–64).[169] It brought to full circle the charge that scribes had entertained from the beginning (2:7).

In the events that followed, Jesus was mocked as a false prophet and "King of the Jews."[170] Mark depicted the procession to Golgotha as a Roman triumphal march in which conquered victims were led through the streets on their way to execution.[171] The episodes concerning the rending of the temple veil and the centurion were not signs that the Holy Place was open to all, and that the centurion was converted to Jesus. The veil was not the inner veil through which only the high priest passed on the Day of Atonement. It was the outer veil that separated the Holy Place from the profane world. Its rending was a portent of doom, which signaled that the divine presence had departed.[172] The centurion's cry, "Truly this

---

168. Among scholars who see Deuteronomy 13 as crucial to understanding Jesus' condemnation are Otto Betz and August Strobel: Betz, "Probleme des Prozesses Jesu," *ANRW*, 2.25.1 (1982): 565–647; Strobel, *Die Stunde der Wahrheit. Untersuchung zum Strafverfahren gegen Jesu*, WUNT 21 (Tübingen: Mohr Siebeck, 1980).

169. Darrell L. Bock, *Blasphemy and Exaltation in Judaism and the Final Examination of Jesus: A Philological Study of the Key Jewish Themes Impacting Mark 14:61–64*, WUNT 106 (Tübingen: Mohr Siebeck, 1998; Bock, "Blasphemy and the Jewish Examination of Jesus," in *Key Events in the Life of the Historical Jesus*, ed. Bock and Robert L. Webb, 589–667.

170. Brown, "The Jesus of Mark's Gospel," in Meyer and Hughes, *Jesus Then and Now*, 41; cf. Craig A. Evans, *Mark 8:27–16:20*, WBC 34B (Nashville: Nelson, 2001), lxxx–xciii, 486–512.

171. Thomas Schmidt, "Mark 15:16–32: The Crucifixion Narrative and the Roman Triumphal Procession," *NTS* 41 (1995): 1–18.

172. Raymond E. Brown, *The Death of the Messiah: From Gethsemane to the Grave; A Commentary on the Passion Narratives in the Four Gospels* (New York: Doubleday, 1994), 2:1099–1102.

man was God's Son" (15:39), was a cry of defeat.[173] It was a counterpart to 1:1, bringing Mark's narrative of the life of Jesus to its close.

If Mark's gospel had ended at 15:39, it would have remained a tragic epic. However, the epilogue (15:40–16:8) transformed tragedy into triumph. Like the prologue, the epilogue is set in locations not normally habited by Jews. The text itself is notoriously contested. The various alternative endings are testimony to the discomfort that many have felt with the best-attested text. This is not the place to repeat my arguments for believing that Mark's gospel ended with the women who visited the tomb, not daring to tell even the disciples "for they were afraid [ἐφοβοῦντο γάρ]" (16:8).[174] However, three observations are in order. First, to recognize women as the first witnesses of the empty tomb in a culture that rejected the witness of women altogether was in keeping with Paul's hermeneutic regarding authority—but not Mark's.[175] Second, fear was a major motif in Aristotle's concept of tragedy and also in biblical religion, where fear was an appropriate response to divine acts (Deut 5:29; 13:4; 31:12–13; Ps 2:11; Prov 1:7; cf. Mark 4:41; 5:33). Third, the young man—an angel—in the tomb and the women who entered were evidently not defiled, despite the tradition that corpses and graves caused defilement (Lev 21:1–2, 11–12; Num 6:6; 19:14–22; Matt 23:27; Luke 11:44). Jesus had performed the ultimate purification.

My review of Mark calls in question the common view that Jesus' public activity had three phases: a lengthy itinerant ministry in Galilee, a shorter ministry in Jerusalem, linked by a brief travel narrative. The initial ministry was based in Capernaum. On its abrupt termination he returned to Galilee only for a brief visit, marked by indifferent reception in Nazareth (6:1–6). Jesus spent most of his time—between leaving Capernaum and going to Jerusalem—in areas outside Galilee. My reading of Mark also calls in question the widely held view that Jesus' itinerant activity was largely a matter of choice and social conditions.[176]

---

173. John Pobee, "The Cry of the Centurion—A Cry of Defeat," in *The Trial of Jesus: Cambridge Studies in Honour of C. F. D. Moule*, ed. Ernst Bammel, SBT Second Series, 13 (London: SCM, 1970), 91–102.

174. Brown, "The Jesus of Mark's Gospel," in Meyer and Hughes, *Jesus Then and Now*, 42, 52, nn106–12.

175. Paul omitted women from his list of witnesses to the resurrection of Jesus (1 Cor 15:3–9), which was in keeping with his policy of being a Jew to Jews, and "under the law" to those "under the law" (1 Cor 9:19–20).

176. Gerd Theissen, *Sociology and Early Palestinian Christianity*, trans. John Bowden

The First Quest

Even the instructions about what the Twelve are *not to take* on their mission (6:6–13; cf. Matt 10:5–14; Luke 9:1–6) may not indicate ascetic itinerancy, but sacred urgency. The Mishnah records similar requirements for entering the Temple Mount.[177] After the Beelzebul charge Jesus was a fugitive for the remainder of his activity.[178]

3.2. Matthew and Luke. By and large, Matthew and Luke follow Mark's narrative outline. However, they differ from Mark and from each other at crucial points. Matthew and Luke both have conception and birth narratives. Some scholars are inclined to think that Matthew tells Joseph's story whereas Luke tells Mary's. Both have genealogies, but Matthew traces Jesus' paternal history back to Abraham, and Luke goes back to Adam. The genealogies also differ over details—not least Matthew's inclusion of women. Matthew and Luke give different versions of the Lord's Prayer. Matthew gives the Sermon on the Mount in some detail. Luke's Sermon on the Plain is much shorter, but it gives pronouncements of woe paired with the Beatitudes. Luke has a lengthy travel narrative and a sequence of parables not given in the other canonical Gospels. They differ in their accounts of the passion and resurrection. Luke indicates that his gospel is the first of two books, the second being the Acts of the Apostles. These differences receive comment in later chapters.

Matthew followed Mark's sequence in placing the Beelzebul charge after the healing of the man with the withered hand and the conspiracy of the Pharisees about how to destroy Jesus. However, Matthew prefaced it with a citation from Isaiah 42:1–4 (Matt 12:18–21). The passage was seen as fulfillment of the prophecy about the chosen servant on whom God would put his Spirit. The ensuing dialogue about the Spirit and speaking against the Spirit contains the pronouncement: "But if it is by the Spirit of God that I cast out demons, then the kingdom of God has come to you" (12:28).

The accusatory language in Matthew has been studied from a

(Philadelphia: Fortress, 1978); Theissen, "Jesus as Itinerant Teacher: Reflections from Social History on Jesus' Roles," in *Jesus Research: The First Princeton-Prague Symposium on Jesus*, ed. James H. Charlesworth and Petr Pokorný (Grand Rapids: Eerdmans, 2009), 98–122.

177. "One should not enter the Temple mount with his walking stick, his overshoes, his money bag, or with dust on his feet" (*m. Ber.* 9:5, Neusner's translation).

178. D. Neale, "Was Jesus a *Mesith*? Public Response to Jesus and His Ministry," *TynBul* 44 (1993): 89–101; J. Duncan M. Derrett, "Jesus as a Seducer (ΠΛΑΝΟΣ = MAT'EH)," *Bijdragen* 55 (1994): 43–55.

sociological viewpoint by Bruce J. Malina and Jerome H. Neyrey with very interesting results.[179] They used two models: the cultural cosmology of witchcraft societies, and witches and witchcraft accusations. Not only was Jesus perceived as a male witch (9:34; 12:24), so were his disciples (10:25) and John the Baptist (11:18). But the accusers were tarred with the same brush (10:38; 12:43–45; 13:38–39; 23:15).

Luke also connected Jesus' exorcisms with Spirit Christology and the presence of the kingdom. "But if it is by the finger of God that I cast out the demons, then the kingdom of God has come to you" (Luke 11:20).[180] However, Luke introduced his Spirit Christology in a scene in the synagogue at Nazareth, which he placed close to the beginning of Jesus' public activity (Luke 4:16–30). The account is unique to Luke. In it Jesus was given the Isaiah scroll, from which he read: "The Spirit of the Lord is upon me, because he has anointed me to bring good news to the poor. He has sent me to proclaim release to the captives and recovery of sight to the blind, to let the oppressed go free, to proclaim the year of the Lord's favor" (4:18–19; Isa 61:1–2; cf. 58:6).

Jesus announced, "Today this scripture has been fulfilled in your hearing" (4:21). At first all spoke well of him, amazed at the words spoken by "Joseph's son." Things turned sour, when he demurred at repeating the works that he had performed in Capernaum. When Jesus drew attention to the works performed by Elijah and Elisha among the gentiles, the crowd took it upon themselves to initiate his death by stoning. D. Neale suggested that the measure was the first step in carrying out the procedures prescribed in Deuteronomy 13, perhaps in self-exoneration. For Luke, the event turned Jesus into a fugitive with nowhere to lay his head (Luke 9:58).[181] The Beelzebul charge came later (11:15, 18–19).

Investigation into sickness, healing, miracles, and the pervasive role of magic in the Greco-Roman and Jewish worlds has proceeded unabated.[182]

---

179. Bruce J. Malina and Jerome H. Neyrey, *Calling Jesus Names: The Social Value of Labels in Matthew*, Foundations and Facets (Sonoma, CA: Polebridge, 1988).

180. On the terminology, see Edward J. Woods, *The 'Finger of God' and Pneumatology in Luke-Acts*, JSNTSup 205 (Sheffield: Sheffield Academic Press, 2001).

181. See n169.

182. On healing see Klaus Seybold and Ulrich B. Mueller, *Sickness and Healing*, trans. Douglas W. Stott (Nashville: Abingdon, 1981); John Wilkinson, *The Bible and Healing* (Edinburgh: Handsel; Grand Rapids: Eerdmans, 1991); Stevan L. Davies, *Jesus the Healer: Possession, Trance, and the Origin of Christianity* (New York: Continuum, 1995); John Christopher Thomas, *The Devil, Disease and Deliverance: Origins of Illness in New Testament Thought* (London: Sheffield Academic Press, 1998); Graham H. Twelftree, *Jesus the Miracle Worker: A Historical and Theological Study*

The First Quest

Earlier I drew attention to the fact that in Mark the wording of Peter's confession and the high priest's question was identical in Greek. Matthew followed the same pattern but elaborated on it, suggesting perhaps that the high priest was conducting an exorcism. Peter confessed, "You are the Messiah, the Son of the living God" (16:16). The high priest made the demand: "I put you under oath before the living God [ἐξορκίζω σε κατὰ τοῦ θεοῦ τοῦ ζῶντος], tell us if you are the Messiah, the Son of God" (26:63). The high priest was putting Jesus—who so far had remained silent—under a solemn oath to speak. However, the verb ἐξορκίζω (*exorkizō*) was used in exorcisms in the sense of coercing a demonic spirit through superior power.[183] In that case, the high priest was using the divine name to coerce the spirit that possessed him. As in Mark, Jesus' reply was judged blasphemous. Even after his death, Jesus and his followers were suspected of being impostors with supernatural pretensions (Matt 27:63–64).

Both Matthew and Luke mention Jesus' reputation for being a glutton and a drunkard (Matt 11:19; Luke 7:34). The phrase denoted more than eating and drinking habits. It was in fact a *formulaic code* used in the process of dealing with a defiant son who violated the fifth commandment. In Mark the question of Jesus as a stubborn and rebellious son comes to light at the end of act 1 (Mark 3:31–35). It plays a larger part in Luke, who also records the episode (8:19–21), as does Matthew (12:46–50).

The parable of the prodigal son (Luke 15:11–32) is based on the notion of *the stubborn and rebellious son*. The parable is replete with terminology and allusions drawn from Deut 21:18–21. It is a riddle in

---

(Downers Grove, IL: InterVarsity Press, 1999); Craig S. Keener, *Miracles: The Credibility of the New Testament Accounts*, 2 vols. (Grand Rapids: Baker Academic, 2012); Amanda Witmer, *Jesus, the Galilean Exorcist: His Social and Political Context*, LNTS 459 (London: T&T Clark, 2012).

On the demonic and magic in the ancient world, see Robert Detweiler and William G. Doty, eds., *The Daemonic Imagination: Biblical Text and Secular Story*, AARSR 60 (Atlanta: Scholars, 1990); Matthew Dickie, *Magic and Magicians in the Greco-Roman World* (New York: Routledge, 2001); Wendy Cotter, *Miracles in the Greco-Roman World: A Sourcebook* (New York: Routledge, 1999); Naomi Janowitz, *Magic in the Roman World* (New York: Routledge, 2001); Armin Lange, Hermann Lichtenberger, and K. F. Diethard Römheld, eds., *Die Dämonen/Demons: The Demonology of Israelite-Jewish and Early Christian Literature in Context of Their Environment* (Tübingen: Mohr Siebeck, 2003); Daniel Ogden, *Magic, Witchcraft and Ghosts in the Greek and Roman Worlds: A Sourcebook*, 2nd ed. (Oxford: Oxford University Press, 2009); Gideon Bohak, *Ancient Jewish Magic: A History* (Cambridge: Cambridge University Press, 2008; repr. 2011).

An important resource is *The Greek Magical Papyri in Translation, Including the Demotic Spells*, edited by Hans Dieter Betz. It translates and expands the Greek texts in Karl Preisendanz, *Papyri Graecae Magicae*, 2 vols., 2nd ed. (Stuttgart: Teubner, 1973–74).

183. Brown, "The Hermeneutics of Confession and Accusation," 469–70; cf. *LSJ*, 598.

Quests before Schweitzer

defense of Jesus' acceptance of sinners, inviting the question: Which of the two sons in the parable is really the stubborn and rebellious son?[184] The parable of the two sons sent to work in the father's vineyard poses the same question (Matt 21:28–32). The parable justifies the position that Jesus takes in Matthew's account of the interchange between Jesus and the authorities regarding Jesus' action in the temple (Matt 21:12–13; Mark 11:15–18; Luke 19:45–46).

The unjust steward (Luke 16:1–8) represents the other side of the coin.[185] It belongs to the same cycle as the parables in Luke 15 and follows directly after the parable of the prodigal son. Whereas the latter is universally loved as one of Jesus' most heartwarming parables, the unjust steward is a headache. The character of the unjust steward seems like a junk-bond artist who defrauds his master and gets praised for doing so. Such a reading detaches it from the preceding cycle of parables and from their overarching context as Jesus' reply to the Pharisees and scribes. They complained about Jesus welcoming and eating with tax collectors and sinners (15:1–2). My interpretation is based partly on the work of J. D. M. Derrett, who calculated that the steward remitted usurious interest on loans owed by the debtors. I suggest that the steward is Jesus himself, who as the Father's agent released sinners from burdens, not least those imposed by the scribes and Pharisees. Like the steward in the parable, Jesus found welcome from outsiders when he was rejected. The parables in Luke 15 focus on God's love of the lost. The unjust steward focuses on the agent mediating that love and how he was received.

3.3. John. John's gospel paints a different picture from that of the Synoptic Gospels. John has a prologue (1:1–18) and an epilogue (21:1–24), but they are very different from Mark's. The prologue is about the Word becoming flesh. The epilogue is about the risen Christ encountering his disciples. The Synoptic Gospels focus on Jesus' fateful action in the temple as the climax, which led to his death. John positioned the cleansing of the temple early his narrative (2:13–25). The Synoptic Gospels narrate only the final journey to Jerusalem. In John there are numerous

---

184. Colin Brown, "The Parable of the Rebellious Son(s)," *SJT* 51 (1998): 391–405. See also Howard Clark Kee, "Jesus: A Glutton and Drunkard," in *Authenticating the Words of Jesus*, ed. Bruce D. Chilton and Craig A. Evans, NTTS 28/1 (Leiden: Brill, 1999), 311–32.

185. Colin Brown, "The Unjust Steward: A New Twist?" in *Worship, Theology and Ministry in the Early Church: Essays in Honor of Ralph P. Martin*, ed., Michael J. Wilkins and Terence Paige, JSNTSup 87 (Sheffield: Sheffield Academic Press, 1992), 121–45.

The First Quest

confrontations in or outside the temple (5:14; 7:14, 28; 8:2, 20, 59; 9:1–41; 10:22–23; 11:56; 18:20).

Some scholars have suggested that while it is virtually impossible to fit John into synoptic chronology, the Synoptic Gospels could be fit into John's. Even so, there are major differences in style and content. John replaces the short, enigmatic parables of the synoptic Jesus with a series of discourses on a range of topics. They include the bread of life (6:35–65); the living water (7:37–39); the light of the world (8:12–20); Jesus' word (8:21–59); Jesus the good shepherd and door of the sheep (10:1–30); the way to the Father (14:1–30); the vine (15:1–11). Sometimes Jesus was interrupted by questions or objections, which gave him opportunity to explain further. Throughout there was confrontation with adversaries.

The synoptic account of the Last Supper as a Passover meal is replaced by Jesus' washing the disciples' feet (13:1–11). Instead of the Gethsemane scene, John gives the lengthy prayer, frequently called Jesus' High Priestly Prayer (17:1–26). John records an encounter with Annas, who then sends Jesus to Caiaphas (18:19–24). In turn, Caiaphas sends him to Pilate (18:28). Pilate caves in to pressure after the taunt that he is no friend of Caesar if he sets free one who claims to be a king (19:12).

There are no exorcisms in John, but Jesus himself was accused of being a Samaritan and having a demon (8:48–49). The charge was linked with works and construed as leading astray (7:12) and blasphemy (10:33, 36). John describes the works of Jesus as *signs*. Seven are described in detail: the wedding feast at Cana (2:1–11); the nobleman's son (4:46–54); the lame man by the pool (5:1–18); the feeding of the five thousand (6:1–15); Jesus walking on the sea (6:16–21); the man born blind (9:1–41); the raising of Lazarus (11:1–44). The last named sign prompted the high priest to say, "This man is performing many signs. If we let him go on like this, everyone will believe in him, and the Romans will come and destroy both our holy place and our nation" (11:47–48).

The Jesus of John's gospel attributes his words and works to the Father: "The words that I say to you I do not speak on my own; but the Father who dwells in me does his works" (14:10; cf. 10:37–38). From early times to the present, controversy has raged over John's portrait of Jesus. It shows no signs of abating.

One important thing that all four New Testament Gospels have in common is the public inscription that announced the reason for Jesus' execution: "Jesus, king of the Jews" (Matt 27:37; Mark 15:26; Luke

Quests before Schweitzer

23:38; John 19:19).[186] Ironically, so far as we know, these were the first words written about the Jesus of history, and these words corroborate a significant element in how the disciples of Jesus and the public, if not Jesus himself, viewed the founder of Christianity.

---

186. There are, of course, variations in the wording, but the gist is not controversial.

CHAPTER 2

EVOLUTION OF ORTHODOXY

THIS SECOND CHAPTER sets the scene for the quests that followed. It addresses the following topics:

1. Vermes versus Newman
2. The Formation of Orthodoxies
    2.1. The Parting of the Ways
    2.2. Judaism and Jesus
    2.3. Early Church Fathers and Jesus
    2.4. The Arian Controversy
    2.5. Councils and Confessions
3. The Sixteenth-Century Reformation
    3.1. Luther and Jesus
    3.2. Calvin and Jesus
4. Vermes Revisited

1. Vermes versus Newman

The word *Evolution* in the title of this chapter may be understood in two conflicting senses. The first carries with it a sense of unfolding, akin to John Henry Newman's notion of development in *An Essay on the Development of Christian Doctrine* (1845). Newman's *Essay* was published more than a decade before Charles Darwin's theory of biological evolution in *The Origin of Species* (1859). In both books the idea of adaptation to environment played a key role. Newman wrote his book in the final stages of his personal evolution from Anglican evangelicalism to Roman Catholicism, as he wrestled with the problem of the gross differences between the contemporary Catholic Church and primitive Christianity.

Newman's solution was to think of Catholic development like the growth of a plant from a seed, or an adult person from a baby. Doctrinal development was rooted in the idea of the *Word become flesh* (John 1:14), as its implications were worked out in different environments and cultures down through the ages. In order to distinguish between authentic developments and corruptions, Newman suggested that the former were recognizable by seven marks: preservation of idea, continuity of principles, power of assimilation, early anticipation, logical sequence, preservative additions, and chronic continuance.[1]

The second sense of doctrinal evolution is that of Geza Vermes, whose personal odyssey was even more dramatic than Newman's.[2] In *Christian Beginnings: From Nazareth to Nicaea* (2012) Vermes described changing perceptions of Jesus as an evolution from charismatic Galilean prophet to deification. "The way of thinking of the Church Fathers was very different from that of Jesus. The principal task the prophet from Nazareth set in front of his Galilean followers was the pursuit of the kingdom of God in the immediate here and now. By the early fourth century the practical, charismatic Judaism preached by Jesus was transformed into an intellectual religion defined and regulated by dogma." Vermes intended his book as a guide "along the evolutionary path from the Jesus of history toward the Christ deified at the Council of Nicaea."[3]

---

1. Among reprints of Newman's *An Essay on the Development of Christian Doctrine* (1845) is the edition of J. S. Cameron (Harmondsworth: Penguin, 1974). For background see Adrian Nichols, *From Newman to Congar: The Idea of Doctrinal Development from the Victorians to the Second Vatican Council* (Edinburgh: T&T Clark, 1990); Frank M. Turner, *John Henry Newman: The Challenge to Evangelical Religion* (New Haven, CT: Yale University Press, 2002). A contemporary Catholic counterpart to Newman is Gerald O'Collins, *Christology: A Biblical, Historical, and Systematic Study of Jesus*, 2nd ed. (Oxford: Oxford University Press, 2009).

2. Geza Vermes (1924–2013) was born in Hungary of Jewish parents. In a vain hope to escape Nazi persecution they converted to Catholicism. Vermes himself became a Catholic priest, obtaining a doctorate from the University of Louvain. He became internationally known as translator of the Dead Sea Scrolls. He came to England, where he obtained a lectureship at the University of Newcastle. Vermes moved to Oxford, where he became professor of Jewish Studies, and eventually joined the Liberal Jewish Synagogue of London. Vermes published his life story under the title *Providential Accidents: An Autobiography* (London: SCM, 1998). Details of other writings will be given in due course.

3. Geza Vermes, *Christian Beginnings: From Nazareth to Nicaea* (London: Penguin, 2012; New Haven, CT: Yale University Press, 2013), xvi.

The purpose of this chapter is not to adjudicate between Newman and Vermes—at least not for now—but to identify factors that shaped ways in which Jesus was perceived.

2. The Formation of Orthodoxies

The use of the word *Orthodoxies* in the plural is deliberate, since it applies to Judaism as well as to Christianity. Christological orthodoxy—both Jewish and Christian—was formed in the first five centuries. The following is a quick tour of highlights—or lowlights—depending on one's point of view.

2.1. The Parting of the Ways. The term *parting of the ways* is now part of contemporary theological vocabulary. It refers to the separation of Christianity from Judaism that took place approximately in the period between 70 and 135 CE.[4] The first date marked the fall of Jerusalem and destruction of the temple in the disastrous war with Rome. The second date marked the defeat and death of Shimon Bar Kochba in the battle, which ended the final uprising against the Romans. His reported capture of Jerusalem and restoration of sacrifice under the high priest El'azar raised hopes that he was the Messiah.[5] Bar Kochba's defeat and death consolidated Roman rule and was perhaps even more catastrophic than the first war with Rome. Jerusalem was turned into a Roman colony, renamed *Colonia Aelia Capitolina*. Jerusalem became in effect a pagan city.[6] Jews were forbidden to enter on pain of death.

The New Testament itself may be seen as a record of the parting of the ways, though scholars differ on interpreting the role of particular books. Dale C. Allison Jr. made an impressive case for seeing Jesus as a New Moses. He concluded that Matthew was written to *prevent* the

---

4. *Jews and Christians: The Parting of the Ways A.D. 70 to 135*, The Second Durham-Tübingen Research Symposium on Earliest Christianity and Judaism (Durham, September 1989), ed. James D. G. Dunn (Tübingen: Mohr Siebeck, 1992). Dunn had earlier set out his own views from a Christian perspective in *The Parting of the Ways Between Christianity and Judaism and Their Significance for the Character of Christianity* (London: SCM; Philadelphia: Trinity Press International, 1991). For a Jewish perspective, see Shaye J. D. Cohen, *From the Maccabees to the Mishnah*, 3rd ed. (Louisville: Westminster John Knox, 2014).

5. Bar Kochba was a sobriquet, meaning "Son of the Star," alluding to Num 24:17, which was taken as prophecy of his role as Messiah.

6. Peter Schäfer, *The History of the Jews in the Greco Roman World* (New York: Routledge, 2003), 145–61.

Quests before Schweitzer

parting of the ways. The evangelist wrote "with an almost Jeremian sense of foreboding, a man who solemnly undertook to write a powerful and persuasive book which would endorse the pre-Christian past and prohibit the disassociation of Christianity from Judaism, a book which would demonstrate that the Messiah himself followed in the footsteps of the lawgiver, and that therefore to abandon Moses is to abandon Jesus."[7] Yet Allison undermined his own argument almost at the outset by admitting that the biblical Joshua was remarkably like Moses. "Surely it would be a dull or uninformed reader who does not recognize that the life of Joshua is to a significant degree a replay of the life of Moses. Joshua completed the work left undone by his predecessor, with the result that the conquest of Canaan fulfilled the promise of the exodus from Egypt. We may say that the conqueror of the land is 'almost a second Moses.'"[8]

Joshua's similarity with Moses was not lost on Jesus ben Sirach, to whom is attributed authorship of the book known as *Ecclesiasticus*, or the *Wisdom of Jesus Son of Sirach*. Ben Sirach observed: "Joshua [LXX: Ἰησοῦς, Jesus] son of Nun was mighty in war, and was the successor of Moses in the prophetic office. He became, as his name implies ["The Lord is salvation"], a great savior of God's elect, to take vengeance on the enemies that rose against them, so that he might give Israel its inheritance" (Sir 46:1). The passage suggests that Sirach viewed *Joshua the son of Nun*, as *the prophet like Moses*, whom God would raise up, and in whose mouth God would put his word (Deut 18:15, 18). In short, Allison's argument works even better for a Joshua typology. After all, Jesus and Joshua bore the same name. Moses saw the promised land only at a distance. It was under Joshua that the conquest actually took place. However, Joshua's interpretation of the law of Moses led to unimaginable bloodshed. Jesus of Nazareth led a different conquest of the land with his peaceful interpretation of the law of Moses.

Allison argued that Matthew's gospel was written to stave off the parting of the ways. Graham N. Stanton argued that Matthew' Gospel was written for a situation in which the ways had already parted. "Matthew wrote his gospel as a 'foundation document' for a cluster of Christian communities, probably in Syria in the mid 80s. The evangelist

---

7. Dale C. Allison Jr., *The New Moses: A Matthean Typology* (Minneapolis: Fortress, 1993), 290.

8. Allison, *The New Moses*, 26; citing E. M. Good, "Joshua, Son of Nun," *IDB* 2:996. Allison meticulously documents the argument (23–28).

Evolution of Orthodoxy

and the original recipients of his gospel saw themselves as 'a new people', minority Christians over against both Judaism and the Gentile world at large."[9] Matthew "repeatedly re-enforces Christian convictions concerning the significance of Jesus which shaped the community of the 'new people.' *God himself* has disclosed to the 'new people' that Jesus is the son of God (3.17; 11.25–71; 16.17; 17.5). Jesus was sent on *God's initiative* (1.20; 10.40; 21.37). Through Jesus, *God is present with his people* (1.23; 8.23–7; 14.22–33; 18.20; 28.30); these verses have deep roots in Old Testament references to the presence of God with his people: an old theme is transposed into a new key."[10]

The parting of the ways enabled both Christianity and Judaism to survive as separate entities, but their separation brought loss to both as they lost touch with the first-century situation. In chapter 1, I argued that the separation began in Jesus' lifetime. It was not simply his identity and activity that were the cause. Surrounding that issue were fundamental *hermeneutical factors* that reached further back in time.

2.2. Judaism and Jesus. Before going further, it may be helpful to identify texts that played a part in the emergence of Judaism.[11] It is now widely recognized that no single Judaism ever existed. The Mishnah (oral instruction) is the foundational text for Talmudic law and tradition. The text dates from c. 200 CE. Yehudah ha-Nasi' (Rabbi Judah the Prince), who lived in Palestine, is credited with being the final editor of the Mishnah. The sages mentioned in the Mishnah, Tosefta, and early commentaries are known as Tannaim (scholars who studied, taught,

---

9. Graham N. Stanton, *A Gospel for a New People: Studies in Matthew* (Edinburgh: T&T Clark, 1992); cf. Stanton, "Matthew's Christology and the Parting of the Ways," in *Jews and Christians*, 99–116; Daniel M. Gurtner, Joel Willitts, and Richard A. Burridge, eds., *Jesus, Matthew's Gospel and Early Christianity: Studies in Memory of Graham N. Stanton*, LNTS 43 (London: T&T Clark, 2011).

10. Stanton, *A Gospel for a New People*, 378–79.

11. For overviews, see Jacob Neusner, *Introduction to Rabbinic Literature* (New York: Doubleday, 1994); John J. Collins and Daniel C. Harlow, eds., *The Eerdmans Dictionary of Early Judaism* (Grand Rapids: Eerdmans, 2010). Bruce D. Chilton and Jacob Neusner have edited an anthology of texts representing classical Christianity and Rabbinic Judaism focusing on seven critical issues: *Classical Christianity and Rabbinic Judaism: Comparing Theologies* (Grand Rapids: Baker Academic, 2004).

An inventory of texts was commissioned by the British Academy: *Handbook of Jewish Literature from Late Antiquity, 135–700 CE*, ed. Eyal Ben-Eliyahu, Yehudah Cohn, and Fergus Millar (Oxford: Oxford University Press for the British Academy, 2012). See also Alexander Samely, in collaboration with Philip Alexander, Rocco Bernasconi, and Robert Hayward, *Profiling Jewish Literature in Antiquity: An Inventory, from Second Temple Texts to the Talmuds* (Oxford: Oxford University Press, 2013).

67

Quests before Schweitzer

and maintained tradition). The classical period of the Tannaim began after Hillel (first century BCE) and Shammai (c. 50 BCE–30 CE) and ended after R. Yehudah ha-Nasi' in the early third century CE.

The Mishnah consists of sixty-three tractates arranged by topics in six divisions, taking the form of interpretations of the Torah and frequently naming past sages. This written collection maintained the continuity of Jewish life by discussion of the institutions of the sacred cult after the temple had been destroyed and sacrifice could be no longer practiced. Central to the discussion was the maintenance of Israel's holiness—how to prevent disruption and deal with it when it occurred. The two principal English editions are *The Mishnah*, translated by Herbert Danby (Oxford: Oxford University Press, 1933); and *The Mishnah: A New Translation*, translated by Jacob Neusner (New Haven, CT: Yale University Press, 1988). Whereas Danby's text is set in continuous paragraphs, Neusner's is arranged in alphabetized paragraphs, designed to distinguish the often anonymous opinions of contributors to the discussion.

The Tosefta (supplement, collection), also dating from the third century CE, is arranged in the same six divisions, containing tractates. It is a compilation of oral law, supplementing the Mishnah. In addition, there were commentaries on the Torah: Mekhilta (Exodus), Sifra (Leviticus), Sifré to Numbers, and Sifré to Deuteronomy. The term *Midrash* (investigation, examination) refers to the explanation of texts, to the discovery of meaning other than literal, and to works that incorporated them.

Talmud (teaching) is the name given to two great compilations of teaching, based on the Mishnah, and distinguished respectively as the Talmud Yerushalmi (Palestinian Talmud, or Talmud of the Land of Israel) and the Talmud Bavli (Babylonian Talmud). The two collections are associated with the two main centers of Jewish learning forming a "dual Torah." Together they constitute the foundation documents of the Jewish ideal of social order and how it may be realized.[12]

The Palestinian Talmud was redacted sometime around 400 CE. Originally it consisted of *gemara* (learning), commentary on the Mishnah without its text. Initially scholars traveled between the two centers for consultation. Whereas the Palestinian Talmud stopped abruptly, the

---

12. Hermann L. Strack and Günter Stemberger, *An Introduction to the Talmud and Midrash*, trans. Markus Bockmuehl (Edinburgh: T&T Clark, 1991; Minneapolis: Fortress, 1992); Charlotte Elisheva Fonrobert and Martin S. Jaffee, eds., *The Cambridge Companion to the Talmud and Rabbinic Literature* (Cambridge: Cambridge University Press, 2007).

scholars in Babylonia continued for another century and a half. The term *Yerushalmi* is a medieval misnomer, since it was produced outside Jerusalem. The Palestinian Talmud is generally considered less authoritative than the more discursive Babylonian Talmud. On the surface the two Talmuds look alike, but the Bavli shows greater depth in its discourse.[13]

The Babylonian Talmud was produced by Amoraim (interpreters), rabbis living in Babylonia (c. 200–700 CE) who succeeded the Tannaim. Their teaching was expressed in a variety of genres and addressed a wider range of topics. However, it covered only thirty-seven of the Mishnah's sixty-three tractates.[14] The Bavli contains Halakah (*the walk*), which comprises legal material showing how Israel should *walk* in the way of the Lord, and Haggadah (*narrative*), which are stories, aphorisms, and homilies that amplify Halakah. Current scholarship sees them as related.

Before discussing Jesus in the Talmud, it is important to note recent views of the prehistory of Judaism. While welcoming Neusner's contribution to recognition of the variety of Judaisms, Gabriele Boccaccini and others urge that greater attention should be paid to the roots of Rabbinic Judaism. Boccaccini traced them to ancient Enochian Judaism, which competed with priestly Zadokite Judaism.[15] Enochian Judaism was linked with the biblical Enoch, who was reputed to have lived three hundred and sixty-five years (Gen 5:21–23). Genesis 5:24—"Enoch walked with God; then he was no more, because God took him"—was the source of endless speculation.[16] After the Babylonian exile and the end of the Davidic monarchy leadership was claimed by the Zadokites, who traced

---

13. The only complete translation is that by Jacob Neusner assisted by other scholars, *Talmud of the Land of Israel: A Preliminary Translation and Explanation*, 3 vols. (Chicago: University of Chicago Press, 1984–93).

14. Two translations exist in English. The older one is that edited by Isadore Epstein, *The Babylonian Talmud*, 36 vols. (London: Soncino, 1935–52). A new version, using form analysis, was edited by Jacob Neusner, 75 vols. (Atlanta: Scholars, 1984–95).

15. Gabriele Boccaccini, *The Roots of Rabbinic Judaism: An Intellectual History from Ezekiel to Daniel* (Grand Rapids: Eerdmans, 2002); Boccaccini, *Beyond the Essene Hypothesis: The Parting of the Ways between Qumran and Enochic Judaism* (Grand Rapids: Eermans, 1998); Gabriele Boccaccini, ed., *Enoch and the Messiah Son of Man: Revisiting the Messiah Son of Man* (Grand Rapids: Eerdmans, 2007).

16. 1 Enoch is the oldest of three pseudepigrapha devoted to Enoch. It is dated between the second century BCE and the first century, but the oldest complete versions are much later Ethiopic texts. However, there are many earlier fragments, including discoveries at Qumran. 1 Enoch is recognized as a composite document. The section of Similitudes or Parables (chaps. 37–71) deal with the coming judgment, the Son of Man (who is finally revealed as Enoch), and numerous other secrets. See the translation and introduction by Ephraim Isaac (*OTP* 1:5–89).

their descent from Zadok, the supporter of David and Solomon. The Zadokite dynasty of high priests dominated pre-Maccabean Judaism.

The Maccabean revolt marked an important step in the evolution of a protorabbinic tradition. Daniel signaled the emergence of a "third way" between Enochic and Zadokite Judaism. The book was far removed from the Dream Visions of Enoch "in which the angelic world is seen out of control" and no reference is made to the Mosaic covenant. "Enoch reveals that Israel is caught by demonic forces and without divine protection, and Michael is relegated to the passive position of onlooker—all until the time established by God for definitive intervention."[17] Daniel shared the apocalyptic worldview of the Enochic tradition but rejected many of its speculations, while drawing them into the Zadokite tradition. Daniel "opposed the Enochite doctrine of the superhuman origin of evil and strenuously defended the tenets of Zadokite Judaism: the covenant (based on the Mosaic Torah) and the legitimacy of the Second Temple."[18] The suffering of the righteous became the norm of their existence. Only "with great caution" may one "label Daniel as the first protorabbinic text. The boundaries of the apocalyptic group that produced Daniel were not yet so well defined. The text itself was open to diametrically opposite interpretations."[19] Yet eventually Daniel was received into the rabbinic canon of Scripture.

David Noel Freedman made a strong case for believing that the book of Daniel was not part of the original Jewish canon of Scripture and only accepted later when various new factors were taken into consideration.[20] It would seem that canonical acceptance came in stages and was not general until the end of the first century CE.[21]

Any appeal to Daniel made by Jesus may have been seen by adversaries as yet another example of claiming authority outside the Torah. On the other hand, Jesus' appeal to Daniel may well have been a factor

---

17. Boccaccini, *The Roots of Rabbinic Judaism*, 185.
18. Boccaccini, *The Roots of Rabbinic Judaism*, 206.
19. Boccaccini, *The Roots of Rabbinic Judaism*, 207.
20. David Noel Freedman contended that Daniel dealt with an era outside the original canon. "With Daniel, we enter into the world of apocalyptic visions, coded messages, revelations through dreams, and angelic interpreters. The message of the book is to be faithful, even to death, in the face of pagan persecution" (*The Unity of the Hebrew Bible*, 96). Only later was the concept of the canon extended in light of events in the Maccabean and later times.
21. Klaus Koch, "Stages in the Canonization of the Book of Daniel," *The Book of Daniel: Composition and Reception*, ed. John J. Collins and Peter W. Flint, 2:421–46; Boccaccini, *The Roots of Rabbinic Judaism*, 206.

Evolution of Orthodoxy

in the acceptance of Daniel into the Christian canon. Synoptic accounts of Jesus' use of the term Son of Man show him as radical. The Son of Man figure that was the guardian of Israel was neither Enoch nor an archangel. *Son of Man* was a vocational title for the righteous remnant envisaged by Jesus. It meant being faithful to Israel's God unto death as a prerequisite of vindication—like earlier models of righteousness in Daniel. The Synoptic Gospels depict not only the *radical role* to which Jesus believed himself called. That role also involved *a radical hermeneutic.*

In the past, Christian scholarship largely discounted allusions to Jesus in the Talmud as garbled and unreliable. In addition to being relatively late, they occur only in the Babylonian Talmud. Peter Schäfer proposed that the stories about Jesus and his family were "deliberate and highly sophisticated counternarratives to the stories about Jesus' life and death in the Gospels—narratives that presuppose a detailed knowledge of the New Testament, and in particular of the Gospel of John."[22] Schäfer, professor of Jewish studies at Princeton University, argued that the Bavli allusions to Jesus become more coherent when examined thematically. They were not random memories of ordinary Jews. They were written by rabbis who sought to produce a counternarrative "meant to shake the foundations of the Christian message."[23] Such an enterprise was possible only in Babylonia. At the time when the Palestinian Talmud was completed, Jerusalem had become a gentile city under Roman rule, after which Constantine became increasingly predisposed to Christianity. By contrast Babylonia was remote from the centers of the Byzantine Empire and enjoyed relative freedom of expression.

With regard to Jesus' personal background, Schäfer identified the enigmatic names of Ben Stada and Ben Padera/Pantera as allusions to Jesus' illegitimacy.[24] The charge contradicted patristic interpretations of the gospel narratives of Jesus' conception and birth. Comment on this issue will be postponed to the next section, where the allusions may be compared with the teaching of the church fathers. In the meantime,

---

22. Peter Schäfer, *Jesus in the Talmud* (Princeton, NJ: Princeton University Press, 2007), 8. Schäfer suggested that rabbinic knowledge of John's gospel may have been obtained via Tatian's second-century harmony gospels, the *Diatessaron*, or the fifth-century Syriac translation of the Gospels, the *Peshitta* (8, 122–23).

23. Schäfer, *Jesus in the Talmud*, 10.

24. Schäfer, *Jesus in the Talmud*, 15–24. The two principal passages were *b. Shab.* 104b; *b. Sanh.* 67a; cf. Celsus' claim that Jesus' father was a Roman soldier named Pantera (*apud* Origen, *Contra Celsum* 1.32). The Hebrew *ben* means "son of."

it may be noted that one born from an illegitimate union, a *mamzer*, was excluded from the assembly of the Lord to the tenth generation (Deut 23:2–6).[25] Suspicions in the New Testament that Jesus may have been the offspring of an illegitimate union may be traced to Matthew 1:19 and John 8:41–42.

The Bavli went on to describe Jesus as a son or disciple who turned out badly. The descriptions involved repeated sexual innuendoes.[26] Jesus was a frivolous disciple,[27] a heretical teacher of the Torah,[28] and a magician.[29] With regard to the execution of Jesus, Schäfer discussed at length the *baraita* (pericope external to the Mishnah) *b. Sanh.* 43a,[30] which describes how Yeshu was hanged on the eve of the Passover. For forty days before the execution a herald went forth, crying that he was about to be stoned, because he had enticed Israel to apostasy. Anyone who had anything to say in his favor should come forward and plead on his behalf. But since no one came forward, he was hanged. In biblical law (Deut 21:22–23) hanging was not a means of execution but a public display of the victim's corpse after stoning. The display was intended to instill fear, but it was not to last beyond sundown lest the land be defiled.

Schäfer saw the detail about the herald as a *contradiction* of the passion prediction in the Gospels. The mode of execution was according to Jewish law rather than Roman law. The story was intentionally a counternarrative to the Gospels. The day of execution coincided with that of ben Stada. Schäfer saw the narrative details as confirmation not of the historicity of the Gospel accounts but of rabbinic knowledge of the gospel accounts. It was a "creative" rereading of them and proudly proclaimed Jewish responsibility for execution of a blasphemer and idolater—not the Messiah and Son of God.

Another *baraita* narrates the fate of five disciples who were put to death as followers of Jesus.[31] The judges tell the last of the five that his

---

25. Daniel Sinclair, "Adultery," and "Mamzer," in *ODJR*, 20–21, 439–40, respectively; Scot McKnight, "Jesus as *MAMZER* ('Illegitimate Son')," in *Who Do My Opponents Say That I Am?*, ed. Scot McKnight and Joseph B. Modica, 133–63. Hints that Jesus may have been the offspring of an illegitimate union may be traced to Matt 1:19 and John 8:41–42.

26. Schäfer, *Jesus in the Talmud*, 25–33; cf. *b. Sanh.* 103a.

27. Schäfer, *Jesus in the Talmud*, 34–40.

28. Schäfer, *Jesus in the Talmud*, 41–51.

29. Schäfer, *Jesus in the Talmud*, 52–62.

30. Schäfer, *Jesus in the Talmud*, 63–74.

31. Schäfer, *Jesus in the Talmud*, 75–81.

death honors God more than a thanksgiving sacrifice. In a final Bavli narrative, Jesus is pictured in hell.[32] Schäfer construed it as a literary counterpart to the gospel resurrection narratives and to the Eucharist together with the bread-of-life discourse in John 6. Jesus shared eternal torment along with the archenemies of Israel, including Titus, the conqueror of Jerusalem. Jesus was condemned to sit forever in boiling excrement. Schäfer surmised that the punishment may be linked to Jesus' teaching on purity.[33] The *baraita* carried the implication that the Christian church, far from being the new Israel, was made up of fools misled by a cunning deceiver.

In a subsequent study, Schäfer explored how Judaism and Christianity may have shaped each other.[34] Certain figures—David, Metatron, the Messiah, angels, and Adam—were assigned a place in Judaism similar to that played by Jesus in Christianity. Schäfer also coedited a symposium on research on the medieval anti-Christian "Life Story of Jesus"— *Toledot Yeshu.*[35]

2.3. Early Church Fathers and Jesus. In Peter Schäfer's construal, the Babylonian Talmud reveals implacable resentment on the part of those who composed its allusions to Jesus. The parallel development in Christian writings reveals a trajectory that began with dialogue and ended with Jesus as a virtual gentile. This section will examine the first phase of that trajectory. The second and third phases—the Arian controversy and the ensuing councils and confessions—will be discussed in the sections that follow.[36]

---

32. Schäfer, *Jesus in the Talmud*, 82–94.

33. Schäfer, *Jesus in the Talmud*, 91; cf. Matt 15:17–20; Mark 7:18–23.

34. Peter Schäfer, *The Jewish Jesus: How Judaism and Christianity Shaped Each Other* (Princeton: Princeton University Press, 2012).

35. Peter Schäfer, Michael Meerson, Yaacov Deutsch, eds., *Toledot Yeshu ("The Life Story of Jesus") Revisited, A Princeton Conference*, TSAJ 143 (Tübingen: Mohr Siebeck, 2011). Schäfer and Meerson have produced a critical edition of the *Toledot Yeshu* manuscript and an English translation: *Toledot Yeshu: The Life Story of Jesus*, vol. 1, *Introduction and Translation*, TSAJ 159 (Tübingen: Mohr Siebeck, 2014); *Toledot Yeshu: The Life Story of Jesus*, vol. 2, *Critical Edition*, TSAJ 159 (Tübingen: Mohr Siebeck, 2014).

36. Recent discussions of the evolution of Christology include: Anna Marmodoro and Jonathan Hill, eds., *The Metaphysics of the Incarnation* (Oxford: Oxford University Press, 2011); Matthew W. Bates, *The Birth of the Trinity: Jesus, God, and Spirit in the New Testament and Early Christian Interpretations of the Old Testament* (Oxford: Oxford University Press, 2015); Niels Henrik Gregersen, ed., *Incarnation: On the Scope and Depth of Christology* (Minneapolis: Fortress, 2015); Francesca Aran Murphy and Troy A. Stefano, eds., *The Oxford Handbook of Christology* (Oxford: Oxford University Press, 2015).

Justin Martyr (d. c. 165) is considered the most important apologist of the second century.[37] Justin was born into a pagan family. He became a teacher of Platonic philosophy before converting to Christianity, which he described as the "only reliable and profitable philosophy" (*Dialogue* 8). Three of his writings have survived: two *Apologies against the Gentiles* and the *Dialogue with Trypho*. Graham N. Stanton saw continuity between the New Testament charges against Jesus and Justin's defense of Jesus. Three issues were closely connected: magic, false prophecy, and the work of the devil.

An example of Justin's response shows how he linked miracles with the fulfillment of Old Testament prophecy and the glorification of God. Jesus' actions were like those of Elijah. They "glorified the Maker of all things as God and Father, and proclaimed the Christ sent from Him, as His Son, a thing which the false prophets who are filled with seducing and unclean spirits never do, but dare to work miracles of a sort to amaze men, and give glory to the spirits of error and demons" (*Dialogue* 7.3; cf. 108).[38]

A central teaching of the Apologist was the concept of Logos. It appealed to the Jewish tradition's belief in creation and revelation by the divine word. It also appealed to Stoic philosophy with its belief in Logos—the reason that permeated reality. Justin dedicated his *First Apology* to the Stoic emperor Antoninus Pius. He argued that the Logos that enlightened Socrates in rejecting demons was revealed *personally* in the man called Jesus Christ. In obedience to Christ his followers also rejected demons (*First Apology* 5). His followers also say "that the Word, who is the First-Begotten of God, was born without sexual union, Jesus Christ our teacher, and that He was crucified and died and rose again and ascended into heaven" (*First Apology* 21).[39]

---

37. Berthold Altaner, *Patrology*, trans. Hilda C. Graef (Freiburg: Herder; London: Nelson, 1958), 120. The term Apologist refers to Greek and Latin authors who wrote reasoned defenses of the Christian faith in response to pagan and Jewish objections. Discussions include Robert M. Grant, *Greek Apologists of the Second Century* (Philadelphia: Westminster, 1988); Grant, *Jesus after the Gospels: The Christ of the Second Century* (Louisville: Westminster John Knox, 1990). Modern editions of Justin include *St. Justin Martyr: The First and Second Apologies*, Ancient Christian Writers 56, trans. Leslie William Barnard (New York: Paulist, 1997); *Selections from Justin Martyr's Dialogue with Trypho*, ed. R. P. C. Hanson (London: Lutterworth, 1963); Justin Martyr, *Dialogue with Trypho*, trans. Thomas B. Falls, rev. by Thomas P. Halton, ed. Michael Slusser (Washington, DC: Catholic University Press of America, 2003).

38. Graham N. Stanton, "Jesus of Nazareth: A Magician and a False Prophet Who Deceived God's People?," in *Jesus and the Gospel* (Cambridge: Cambridge University Press, 2004), 227–47, here 237–38.

39. *St. Justin Martyr*, ed. Barnard, 37. Justin went on to argue that Christian beliefs were comparable with similar beliefs in the Greco-Roman world.

Evolution of Orthodoxy

In *Dialogue with Trypho* Justin drew comparisons between the act of speaking and divine begetting:

> When we utter any word, we originate this word [λόγον γεννῶμεν] but do not produce it by means of division, as if the reason [word] in us were thereby reduced. But the process is like what we see when fire is kindled from another. . . . The account of wisdom will supply me with a testimony here, wisdom which is this same God begotten [γεννηθείς] by the Father of the universe, who exists also as Word and Wisdom and Power and Glory of its begetter [γεννήσαντος].[40]

In a comparison of Justin with Irenaeus regarding tradition and the Gospels, Graham N. Stanton noted that Irenaeus wrote *Against the Heresies* barely a generation after Justin's death. Justin appears to have known four gospels, though he never named any of the evangelists. Irenaeus knew Justin's writings, and the two may have even met in Rome. However, there were major differences, not least Irenaeus's insistence on the fourfold written gospel.[41]

In a recent major study, John Behr stressed the importance of seeing Irenaeus in context.[42] Knowledge of his life is sketchy. Irenaeus was a disciple of Polycarp, who was believed to have had ties to the apostles. Irenaeus was a priest in Lyons and succeeded the martyred bishop Photinus. Irenaeus composed his abiding legacy over a period of time—the five books of *The Refutation and Overthrowal of Knowledge Falsely So-Called*, better known as *Against the Heresies*.[43]

Before going further, two points need clearing up. The first is that Irenaeus did not set out to write a heresiology. Nor did he use the label *gnostic* as a technical description. His aim was to expose the errors of those who had dissociated from mainstream catholic Christianity. The second point is that the word *refutation* should be seen in the context of a Hellenistic philosophical demonstration.[44] In the tradition of Aristotle

---

40. *Dialogue with Trypho*, trans. R. P. C. Hanson, §61, 39; Greek text Migne, PG 6:615.

41. Graham N. Stanton, "Jesus Traditions and the Gospels in Justin Martyr and Irenaeus," in *Jesus and the Gospel*, 92–109.

42. John Behr, *Irenaeus of Lyons: Identifying Christianity*, Christian Theology in Context (Oxford: Oxford University Press, 2013).

43. Behr, *Irenaeus of Lyons*, 13. Behr considers the longer title more applicable to the first two books.

44. Behr, *Irenaeus of Lyons*, 11.

Quests before Schweitzer

and Epicurus, Irenaeus believed that "first principles" could not be demonstrated by historical investigation or empirical evidence. Rather, a hypothesis was needed to function as a criterion or canon of truth. *Against the Heresies* should be read as Irenaeus's endeavor to articulate this canon of truth.

Against the Heresies presents a global view of sin and salvation from a selective biblical perspective. It exhibited the divine symmetry disclosed by precritical reading of Scripture. "In the first Adam we offended God by not performing his command; in the Second Adam we have been reconciled, becoming 'obedient unto death'" (*Heresies* 5.16.3; cf. Phil 2:8). "As through a tree we were made debtors to God, so through a tree we receive the cancellation of our debt" (5.17.3). "Eve by her disobedience brought death upon herself and on all the human race: Mary, by her obedience brought salvation" (3.22.4). At the heart of this symmetry was Irenaeus's vision of recapitulation. "Man is in all respects the handiwork of God; thus he consummates man in himself: he was invisible and became visible; incomprehensible and made comprehensible; impassible and made passible; the Word, and made man; consummating all things in himself" (3.16.6). The Word and the Spirit were the two hands of God. "Through the Word and the Spirit God made, ordered and governs all things, and gives them being" (1.22.1).[45]

Irenaeus is widely recognized as the founder of a way of thinking that survives to the present day. He may be rightly called the church's first systematic theologian. Not only did he construct a comprehensive belief system, but he also practiced a way of thinking theologically. This approach may be described as *theological interpretation*. Another description uses the German term *Sachexegese* (which may be paraphrased as *subject matter exegesis*). It has been described as "the effort to interpret the words of the Bible in light of the Bible's own central concern, i.e. God. The term is approximately equivalent to theological exegesis or theological interpretation."[46]

---

45. For these and many other comparable citations see Henry Bettenson, *The Early Christian Fathers: A Selection from the Writings of the Fathers from St. Clement of Rome to St. Athanasius* (London: Oxford University Press, 1956), 89–140; and the discussion in J. N. D. Kelly, *Early Christian Doctrines* (New York: Harper & Row, 1960; rev. 1978), passim. A recent reappraisal of Irenaeus's teaching on the Spirit is Anthony Briggman, *Irenaeus of Lyons and the Theology of the Holy Spirit*, Oxford Early Christian Studies (Oxford: Oxford University Press, 2012).

46. Richard N. Soulen and R. Kendall Soulen, *Handbook of Biblical Criticism*, 4th ed. (Louisville: Westminster John Knox, 2011), 186.

Evolution of Orthodoxy

Superficially, theological interpretation appears to enjoy a vantage point superior to that of the scholar who investigates narratives of alleged historical events. The vulnerability of theological interpretation becomes evident when we compare its truth claims with narratives of the same events from ground level. For example, consider the theological interpretations of the significance of Jesus' death compared with narratives of events leading up to it. We have different sets of explanations running on separate tracks.[47] It is not immediately obvious which narratives are more plausible and which are the product of vivid imagination, or how they relate to each other.

The Achilles' heel of theological interpretation is disclosed by the fact that no theologian enjoys the privileged position of sharing God's unique perspective. Perspectives are conditioned by cultural, temporal, theological horizons, and related ways of thinking. A classic example is the discussion of God's reasons for becoming a man by Anselm of Canterbury (c. 1033–1109). Anselm's *Cur deus homo* pushed *theological interpretation* to its limits by promising a rationale of incarnation and atonement, even if nothing were known of Christ (see the preface). Anselm dismissed the tradition of Irenaeus as beautiful but like pictures painted on water or on air (*Cur deus homo*, 1.3–4). However, Anselm's account was itself found wanting for precisely the same culturally conditioned reasons that Anselm claimed as its strength. Other attempts to claim privileged position for theological interpretation are exemplified by Luther, Barth, and Moltmann.[48]

Over time, as Christian theology moved further from the Jewish world of the first century, certain trends became increasingly apparent.

---

47. A vigorous challenge to Christology "from above" in the name of Christology "from below" was made by Wolfhart Pannenberg in *Jesus—God and Man*, trans. Lewis L. Wilkins and Duane A. Priebe (London: SCM, 1968), 33–49. He argued that the primary task of Christology was to show how it is grounded rather than assuming it. Pannenberg's critique included the practice of approaching Christology from soteriology. He attempted to ground atonement in the circumstances leading to the condemnation of Jesus for blasphemy.

48. Luther's theological interpretation, based of his view of the "theology of the cross" and the centrality of justification by faith, will be discussed below (§3). Barth's early theology was dominated by dialectical theology and the notion of God as "Wholly Other." Barth's later theology replaced dialectical theology by the postulate that God had made a covenant with humanity on the basis of the union of divine and human nature in the incarnation. See Colin Brown, *Karl Barth and the Christian Message* (London: Tyndale, 1967). Moltmann's theology was based on his conceptions of hope, "the crucified God," and the social Trinity. See Jürgen Moltmann, *Experiences in Theology: Ways and Forms of Christian Theology*, trans. Margaret Kohl (Minneapolis: Fortress, 2000). On Moltmann's theological exegesis, see especially pp. xxi–xxii.

Quests before Schweitzer

Son of God became the equivalent of *God the Son*, or simply *the Son*. The word *Father*, which previously served as a metaphor for Godhead, came to mean *Father of the Son*.[49] Interest in the activity of Jesus was replaced by focus on his birth and death. Jesus' life and teaching found no place in the formulations of the church councils and the creeds. Reading them today, one would scarcely guess that Jesus was Jewish.

These issues began to appear in the church fathers, as already discussed. They became more prominent with the rise of Monarchianism. The term goes back to at least Novatian's treatise on the Trinity (c. 250 CE) and mistakenly identifies Adoptionism and Modalism as two forms of the attempt to salvage the dogma that God is a one.[50] Adoptionism represented the view held by intellectual rationalists, that Jesus was an ordinary man who received divine powers at his baptism and was deified through his resurrection. It was also known as Dynamic Monarchianism in view of the δύναμις ("power") that came upon Jesus at baptism. Modalism was more widely espoused. An early proponent was Noetus, who believed that since there was only one God, the Father also suffered through Christ's suffering. This view came to be called Patripassianism in view of the suffering of the Father (Latin, *pater*) that it entailed. Sabellius was reputed to have used the analogy of the sun. The sun was a single entity, which radiates both warmth and light. The Son and the Spirit were different modes of the one God.

Tertullian (c. 150–c. 225) was an African church father and leading Latin apologist. He came from a pagan family, was brought up in Carthage, and received an education in rhetoric. Tertullian converted to

---

49. Kelly, *Early Christian Doctrines*, 83–108, 112, and passim. The patristic procedure of reading *personal preexistence* language and *theodramatic utterances* back into the Old Testament and the New Testament is exemplified by Matthew W. Bates, *The Birth of the Trinity: Jesus, God and Spirit in New Testament and Early Christian Interpretations of the Old Testament* (Oxford: Oxford University Press, 2015). At the same time, Bates criticizes as "somewhat weak" Simon J. Gathercole's argument for Jesus' preexistence from the Synoptic "I have come sayings." See Gathercole, *The Preexistent Son: Recovering the Christologies of Matthew, Mark, and Luke* (Grand Rapids: Eerdmans, 2006); cf. *The Birth of the Trinity*, 51. He also admits that his own "prosopological exegesis" (i.e., interpretation entailing dialogue between divine persons) by itself does not entail more than "ideal preexistence" (50).

Bates concludes, "I am seeking to signal that prosopological exegesis, among other factors, was essential to how Jesus Christ was from our earliest Christian sources understood to be divine—namely, as the Son who converses with the person of the Father through the Spirit in a time-transcending fashion (with the Spirit also occasionally speaking directly as a person)" (204).

50. Kelly, *Early Christian Doctrines*, 115–23. The two movements were both concerned with God's oneness, or *monarchia*.

Christianity as an adult and may have been a priest. Tertullian's *Against Praxeas* was the most notable early treatise on the Trinity—and in that context also on the incarnation.[51] Praxeas was a nickname meaning "Busybody," given to an unknown opponent. At Rome he "managed two pieces of the devil's business: . . . he put to flight the Paraclete and crucified the Father" (*Against Praxeas* 1). By this, Tertullian meant that Praxeas had persuaded the bishop of Rome to condemn Montanist prophecy (which Tertullian himself had espoused) and to embrace Patripassianism.

Tertullian expressed in Latin the Logos Christology of the Greek fathers, using the Latin *sermo* for Logos. In view of Proverbs 8:22, 25 and Genesis 1:3, he concluded that the Word came forth from God at the beginning of creation (*Against Praxeas* 6). The Son was "a second" (*secundum*), a "Person" (*persona*) beside the Father, participating in the divine substance (*substantia*). "Whatever therefore the substance of the Word was, that I call a Person [*quaecuneque ergo substant sermonis fuit, illam dico personam*], and for it I claim the name of Son: and while I acknowledge him as the Son I maintain that he is another [*secundum*] beside the Father" (*Against Praxeas* 7). The Spirit was "a third," like an irrigation canal leading from the river. The Son was not cut off from his source, just as "the shoot is not shut off from the root nor the river from the spring nor the beam from the sun, any more than the Word is shut off from God" (*Against Praxeas* 8).

Tertullian resolutely rejected Patripassianism. The Son suffered and died in his humanity, and in his suffering and death he was separated from the Father.

> "But in what way did the Son suffer, if the Father also did not suffer with him?" The difference begins from the Son, and not from the Father. For also if a river is defiled by some muddying, although the one substance comes down from the spring and there is no interruption at the spring, yet the malady of the river will not attach to the spring; and though the water which suffers [injury] belongs to the spring, so long as it suffers not in the spring but in the river it is not the spring that suffers, but the river which [has come] from the spring. (*Against Praxeas* 29)

---

51. Latin text and English translation with commentary by Ernest Evans, *Tertullian's Treatise Against Praxeas* (London: SPCK, 1948).

Quests before Schweitzer

Likewise the Spirit did not suffer. Jesus' cry of dereliction (Matt 27:46; Mark 15:34) indicated that Jesus suffered only in his manhood. "Yet the Father did not forsake the Son, since the Son placed his own spirit in the Father's hands . . . for while the spirit remains in the flesh the flesh cannot die at all" (*Against Praxeas* 30).

Much of the Trinitarian vocabulary of the Western church was taken over from Tertullian,[52] including the term *Trinity*, which he introduced early in the treatise against Praxeas. The term signified that Father, Son, and Spirit share "unity of substance" while guarding "the mystery of that economy which disposes the unity into trinity [*in trinitatem*], setting forth Father and Son and Spirit as three, three however not in quality but in sequence, not in substance but in aspect, not in power but in [its] manifestation, yet of one substance and one quality and one power, seeing it is but one God from whom those sequences and aspects and manifestations are reckoned out in the name of the Father and the Son and the Holy Spirit" (*Against Praxeas* 2).

Origen (c. 185–254) is considered by many experts to be the greatest scholar of Christian antiquity. He was also one of the most controversial. In early life he was closely associated with the church in Alexandria; in later life he traveled widely. In philosophy he was a Middle Platonist. In personal life he was an ascetic. Much of his work was devoted to biblical interpretation. The result was an amalgam of biblical interpretation expressed in terms of Middle Platonism, devoted to making Christian faith and life intelligible to the world that he lived in.[53] Origen was known as "Adamantios," man of steel or diamond. He died following torture in the persecution under the emperor Decius. On account of his speculative teaching on apocatastasis— the ultimate reconciliation and restoration of all God's creatures, including the devil—he was condemned posthumously as a heretic.

Within this sketch of trends in patristic Christology it is impossible to review Origen's entire legacy.[54] Focus must be limited to Christology—in particular the Son's relationship with the Father and his double origin. Much of Origen's vast output has been lost. The first of two works,

---

52. Evans, *Against Praxeas*, 38–58. J. N. D. Kelly cautions against reading modern notions of personality into the term *persona*. Originally the term meant the mask of an actor. Tertullian used *persona* to connote "the concrete presentation of an individual" (*Early Christian Doctrines*, 115).

53. R. P. C. Hanson, *Allegory and Event: A Study of the Sources and Significance of Origen's Interpretation of Scripture* (London: SCM, 1959).

54. Among the best surveys is Henri Crouzel, *Origen: The Life and Thought of the First Great Theologian*, trans. A. S. Worrall (Edinburgh: T&T Clark; San Francisco: Harper & Row, 1989).

Evolution of Orthodoxy

especially relevant to the present discussion, survives in Latin translation and Greek fragments. It is usually referred to by its Latin title *De Principiis* (Greek, *Peri Archon*), or *On the First Principles* (220–240 CE). It was the first manual of dogmatics, treating the triune God, angels and their fall, man as a fallen spirit imprisoned in the body, redemption, moral theology, and Scripture.

The other work, *Contra Celsum* (*Against Celsus*), also known by its Latin title, was written sometime after Origen reached the age of sixty, perhaps on the occasion of the celebration of Rome's millennium (247–48 CE). Origen wrote it at the prompting of his friend Ambrose, who urged him to refute *The True Word* by the deceased pagan philosopher Celsus. The massive refutation took the form of a sentence-by-sentence critique, so that it is possible to reconstruct Celsus's argument from Origen's text. The standard English edition is the translation by Henry Chadwick.[55] Celsus's work has been reconstructed by R. Joseph Hoffmann under the title *On the True Doctrine*. Hoffmann described Celsus as "the first of the New Testament demythologizers," the forerunner of "D. F. Strauss, Arthur Drews, and Rudolf Bultmann."[56] We shall look first at Origen and Celsus and then offer comments.

Origen's teaching followed in the footsteps of his immediate predecessors—only it was more sharply defined and drew upon Middle Platonism. Strictly speaking, the Father alone was God (cf. John 17:3). The Son was "a second God," who as the Logos of the Father derived his being from the Father (*Contra Celsum* 5.39). Creation followed from the Father's perfection, which required that he should have objects on which to lavish his goodness and power.

Origen's rationale for the incarnation was integrated into a Platonic metaphysic of the universe with its view of the preexistence of souls. As a Platonist, Origen believed that souls were eternal and immortal. Whereas all other souls underwent a premundane fall and became sinful human beings, one preexisting soul—that of Jesus—did not. "We say that the Logos dwelt in the soul of Jesus and was united with it in a closer union

---

55. Origen, *Contra Celsum*, trans. with introduction and notes by Henry Chadwick (Cambridge: Cambridge University Press, 1953; repr. 2003).

56. Celsus, *On the True Doctrine: A Discourse against the Christians*, trans. R. Joseph Hoffmann (Oxford: Oxford University Press, 1987), 37. In the introduction, Hoffmann reviewed earlier anti-Christian polemic (5–24), pagan opposition to Christianity (24–29), and Celsus's identity and argument (29–44).

Quests before Schweitzer

than that of any other soul, because he alone has been able perfectly to receive the highest participation in him who is the Logos and the very Wisdom, and the very Righteousness himself" (*Contra Celsum* 5.39).

On the subject of Jesus' birth and identity, Origen addressed at length Celsus's charge that Jesus was illegitimate. Citing an anonymous Jew, Celsus claimed that Jesus' mother had been "turned out by the carpenter who was betrothed to her, as she had been convicted of adultery and had a child by a certain soldier named Panthera" (*Contra Celsum* 1.32). The name *Panthera* figures in the Talmud and was a common name among Roman soldiers. From the standpoint of Jesus' detractors, it was important to brand him as a *mamzer*—that is, the offspring of an illicit union of a Jewish parent with a non-Jew. Such parentage would place him outside mainstream Judaism.[57] However, this handicap would be nullified with "Joseph, son of David" (Matt 1:20; cf. 1:15–16) as Mary's husband.

Origen dismissed Celsus's story as a fabricated myth concocted "to get rid of the miraculous conception by the Holy Spirit." The fact that an alternative narrative in Matthew 1:18–25 was preserved by Christian tradition, argued for its authenticity. Otherwise, it would have been suppressed. Origen claimed that virginal conception was entirely consistent with the Platonic view of the preexistence of souls. Moreover, his argument served to explain the sinlessness of Jesus. "Why then should there not be a certain soul that takes a body which is entirely miraculous, which has something in common with men in order to be able to live with them, but which has something out of the ordinary, in order that the soul may remain uncontaminated by sin?" (*Contra Celsum* 1.33).

This point led to discussion of the prophecy of Isaiah 7:10–14 (cf. Matt 1:23), which foretold that "the offspring of a virgin who according to the promised sign should give birth to a child whose name was significant of his work, showing that God would be with men" (*Contra Celsum* 1.34). Celsus apparently did not know of the prophecy or willfully suppressed it. Origen went on to stress that the Greek παρθένος (*parthenos*) meant a literal virgin[58] and that the prophecy should be understood as the prediction of a miracle.

---

57. Chadwick notes discussions of references to "Jesus ben Panthera" in the Talmud and Panthera in other literature (*Contra Celsum*, 31n3). On *mamzer* see Daniel Sinclair, *ODJR*, 441–42.

58. BDAG, 776, observes that in classical Greek *parthenos* denoted a person, generally a young woman of marriageable age, with or without focus on virginity. In early Christian literature it indicated someone who had never engaged in sexual intercourse, a virgin, or chaste person.

Evolution of Orthodoxy

Origen located the prophecy of the sign in the time of King Ahaz (Isa 7:10–17) in the eighth century BCE, but he saw its fulfillment centuries later in the birth of Jesus. God promised a sign to Ahaz that a virgin would conceive and bear a son with the name Immanuel ("God with us"). Before the child was weaned, the dreaded Syro-Ephraimite invasion came to pass. Origen asked rhetorically, "What sort of a sign would it be if a young woman not a virgin bore a son? And which would be more appropriate as the mother of Emmanuel, that is 'God with us', a woman who had intercourse with a man and conceived by female passion, or a woman who was still chaste and pure and a virgin?" (*Contra Celsum* 1.35).[59]

Other fabrications of Celsus included the claim that Jesus "was brought up in secret and hired himself out as a workman in Egypt, and after having tried his hand at certain magical powers he returned from there, and on account of those powers gave himself the title of God" (*Contra Celsum* 1.38). Again Origen answered rhetorically, "I do not know why a magician should have taken the trouble to teach a doctrine which persuades every man do every action before God who judges each man for all his works, and to instil this conviction in his disciples whom he intended to use as the ministers of his teaching."

Celsus mocked the notion of divine paternity. "And because [Mary] was beautiful did God have sexual intercourse with her although by nature He cannot love a corruptible body?" (*Contra Celsum* 1.39). The question looks like an allusion to "the sons of God" and "the daughters of men" who "were fair" (Gen 6:2). Origen dismissed Celsus's rhetoric with contempt.

Henry Chadwick contended that Celsus was not a second-century Voltaire.[60] Celsus's book on *The True Word* indicated that he believed that there was a *true doctrine* held from ancient times. This tradition was maintained in Judaism, albeit in a corrupt form. Christianity was a recent and even more corrupt manifestation. Celsus's Jew served as a spokesman against Christianity, which was a secret, illegal society that ought not be tolerated. He ridiculed the narrative of the Spirit descending on Jesus like a dove. It was simply a bird swooping down. In an imaginary address to

---

59. Chadwick noted similar arguments in Justin, *Dialogue* 84; Tertullian, *Adversus Judaeos* 9; and *Adversus Marcionem* 3.13 (34n4).

60. Chadwick, *Contra Celsum*, xvi–xxii.

Quests before Schweitzer

Jesus he asked, "What trustworthy witness saw this apparition, or who heard a voice from heaven adopting you as son of God? There was not proof except for your word and the evidence which you may produce of one of the men who were punished with you" (*Contra Celsum* 1.41).

Celsus's Jew applied to Jesus his own warning: "There will come among you others also who employ similar miracles, wicked men and sorcerers. . . . Is it not a miserable argument to infer from the same works that he is a god while they are sorcerers? . . . Why should we conclude from these works that the others were more wicked than this fellow, taking the witness of Jesus himself?" (*Contra Celsum* 1.53; cf. Matt 24:24; Mark 13:22; Deut 13:1–5). In similar vein, the Jew went on to raise "the question whether anyone who really died ever rose again with the same body" (*Contra Celsum* 1.57), a question that would be asked repeatedly in the quests of the historical Jesus.

This is not the place to attempt to resolve the question of the virgin birth.[61] However, some observations are in order, especially as they relate to the "parting of the ways." When viewed in the perspective of the separation of Christianity and Judaism, Matthew's birth and infancy narratives look rather different. Continuity with Judaism is stressed, while claiming that the birth of Jesus marked a new beginning. Rather than presenting random proof texts, Matthew's first two chapters present a coherent narrative.

---

61. A cross section of works that treat the subject at length includes the following: Hans von Campenhausen, *The Virgin Birth in the Theology of the Ancient Church*, trans. Frank Clarke, Studies in Historical Theology 2 (London: SCM; Naperville, IL: Allenson, 1964); Heiko A. Oberman, *The Virgin Mary in Evangelical Perspective*, with introduction by Thomas F. O'Meara, Facet Books Historical Series 20 (Philadelphia: Fortress, 1971); Raymond E. Brown, Karl P. Donfred, Joseph A. Fitzmyer, John Reumann, eds., *Mary in the New Testament* (Philadelphia: Fortress, 1968); Raymond E. Brown, *The Virginal Conception and Bodily Resurrection of Jesus* (London: Geoffrey Chapman, 1973); Jane Schaberg, *The Illegitimacy of Jesus: A Feminist Theological Interpretation of the Infancy Narratives* (New York: Crossroad, 1990); Richard A. Horsley, *The Liberation of Christmas: The Infancy Narratives in Social Context* (New York: Crossroad, 1989); Geoffrey Parrinder, *Son of Joseph: The Parentage of Jesus* (Edinburgh: T&T Clark, 1992); Elisabeth Schüssler Fiorenza, *Jesus—Miriam's Child, Sophia's Prophet: Critical Issues in Feminist Christology* (New York: Continuum, 1994); Raymond E. Brown, *The Birth of the Messiah: A Commentary on the Infancy Narratives in the Gospels of Matthew and Luke* (New York: Doubleday, [1977] 1993); Gerd Lüdemann, *Virgin Birth? The Real Story of Mary and Her Son Jesus*, trans. John Bowden (Harrisburg, PA: Trinity Press International, 1998); George J. Brooke, ed., *The Birth of Jesus: Biblical and Theological Reflections* (Edinburgh: T&T Clark, 2000); Joseph Ratzinger, Pope Benedict XVI, *Jesus of Nazareth: The Infancy Narratives*, trans. Philip J. Whitmore (New York: Image, 2012); Andrew T. Lincoln, *Born of a Virgin? Reconceiving Jesus in the Bible, Tradition, and Theology* (Grand Rapids: Eerdmans, 2013); Steve Moyise, *Was the Birth of Jesus according to Scripture?* (Eugene, OR: Cascade, 2013).

Evolution of Orthodoxy

Matthew's gospel begins with a genealogy (1:1–16). It is divided into three divisions, each consisting of fourteen generations (1:17). The first division spans what might be called the golden age from Abraham to David. The second represents the age of decline from Solomon to the deportation to Babylon. The third spans the unfinished restoration of Israel from the deportation to the birth of the Messiah (τοῦ Χριστοῦ, *tou Christou*). The names are predominantly male. Their paternal role is denoted in each case by the verb ἐγέννησεν (*egennēsen*, "begat," "was the father of"; e.g., "Abraham was the father of [ἐγέννησεν] Isaac"; 1:2).

The list of names in the second division of generations devoted to Israel's decline includes Ahaz (1:9), to whom the sign of Isaiah 7:14 was given. In the first division devoted to the rise of Israel, four women are mentioned—Tamar (1:3), Rahab (1:5), Ruth (1:5), and the unnamed "wife of Uriah" (1:6). In each case they are preceded by the preposition ἐκ (*ek*) or ἐξ (*ex*), "by" (NRSV). The genealogy concludes with a carefully worded reference to Mary. "Jacob the father of [ἐγέννησεν] Joseph the husband [τὸν ἄνδρα] of Mary, of whom Jesus was born, who is called the Messiah [ἐξ ἧς ἐγεννήθη Ἰησοῦς ὁ λεγόμενος Χριστός]" (1:16). In short, Joseph was not the *biological* father of Jesus, the Messiah.

The account of Mary's conception shared the same grammatical pattern as that of the four women in the genealogy who preceded her. Some were non-Israelites. All had past histories of trauma and sexual degradation.[62] The narratives (with the exceptions on those concerning Boaz and Joseph) bring nothing but shame to the memory of the male participants.

---

62. The story of Tamar (Matt 1:3) is told in Gen 38. She was married to Er, the first son of Judah who was put to death for his wickedness. Following the tradition of levirate marriage (Deut 25:5–10), which laid down the duty of a brother to raise children for his deceased brother, Judah gave Tamar to Onan. However, Onan spilled his semen, and Onan was put to death. At this point Judah told Tamar to remain a widow until his youngest son would be old enough to fulfil the levirate law. When the third son failed to keep the promise, Tamar disguised herself and had twins by Judah, who thought he was having sex with a temple prostitute. The elder twin, Perez, was the ancestor of David (Ruth 4:18–22; Matt 1:3).

The story of Rahab (Matt 1:5), the "harlot" of Jericho, is told in Joshua 2 and 6. She harbored two spies sent by Joshua, and was instrumental in the capture of Jericho, and thus of the subsequent conquest of the promised land. Matthew's genealogy identifies Rahab as the mother of Boaz (Matt 1:5), the husband of Ruth. Rahab is celebrated among the biblical examples of faith (Heb 11:31).

The book of Ruth identifies Ruth (Matt 1:5) as a Moabitess who, on the death of her first husband, chose to remain with her mother-in-law, Naomi, and accompany her to Bethlehem. She gleaned barley in the field of Boaz, who turned out to be a kinsman. Prompted by Naomi, she adorned herself and visited Boaz at night and offered herself to him. The reference to uncovering his "feet" (Ruth 3:4) is widely understood as uncovering his genitals. However, mindful of the levirate law (Ruth 4:1–12), Boaz refused to take her since another kinsman had prior right. However,

Quests before Schweitzer

The stories present a sharp reminder of the checkered course of Israel's history. The genealogy sets Mary firmly in this tradition, and in so doing places it at the beginning of Matthew's gospel. It thus provides a frame of reference for the remainder of Matthew's narrative.

The grammatical pattern is repeated in the brief account of Jesus' birth. "Now the birth [ἡ γένεσις] of Jesus the Messiah took place in this way. When his mother Mary had been engaged to Joseph, but before they lived together, she was found to be with child from the Holy Spirit [ἐκ πνεύματος ἁγίου]" (1:18). The foregoing discussion of Greek vocabulary and grammar may seem obscure. However, it has far-reaching theological significance, as John P. Meier pointed out. "The idea of virginal conception, whatever its origins, is not rooted in pagan ideas of impregnation by a god. Rather the theological affirmation made by the evangelists—whatever its historical basis—is that the Holy Spirit, who in early Christian tradition was associated with the power that raised Jesus from the dead (cf. Rom 1:3–4; 8:11), is likewise the eschatological power that brought about Jesus' virginal conception. Both signs are seen by the NT authors as signs of the end time."[63]

Meier pointed out that the same applies to Luke 1:26–38. Both narratives stress the role of the Spirit. The Greek word for "spirit," πνεῦμα (*pneuma*), is a neuter noun. However, the Hebrew רוּחַ (*ruach*) is predominantly feminine. The role of the Spirit in the conception of Jesus in Matthew 1:18 and 1:20 (the words of the angel to Joseph) conforms to the pattern noted above with regard to the women in Matthew's genealogy. In other words, the Holy Spirit played a *female* part in the conception narratives.[64] Similar interpretations were proposed by Jürgen

---

the kinsman formally declined, and the marriage of Boaz and Ruth was consummated. Their son Obed was the father of Jesse, the father of David (Ruth 4:17, 22; Matt 1:5–6).

The fourth woman is identified by the genealogy as "the wife of Uriah" (Matt 1:6). In 2 Sam 11:3, she is identified as Bathsheba, the wife of Uriah the Hittite. King David saw her bathing from a rooftop, seduced her, and made her pregnant. David then sent Uriah to certain death in battle. As a consequence David was rebuked by the prophet Nathan, and the child died soon after birth. Later Bathsheba bore David a son, Solomon (2 Sam 12:24).

A recent discussion of the women in Matthew's genealogy is given by Lincoln, *Born of a Virgin?*, 78–83.

63. John P. Meier, *A Marginal Jew: Rethinking the Historical Jesus*, vol. 1, *The Roots of the Problem and the Person* (New York: Doubleday, 1991), 221. See also Brown, *The Birth of the Messiah*, 160–61, 517–31.

64. In Luke, the angel's words to Mary have nothing to do with impregnation. The promise that "the power of the Most High will overshadow [ἐπισκιάσει] you" refers to providential protection (Luke 1:35). Elsewhere ἐπισκιάζω refers to the divine presence, such as a cloud overshadowing

Evolution of Orthodoxy

Moltmann and the nineteenth-century Catholic scholar Matthias J. Scheeben. Moltmann observed that Mary "should not be thought of as the human woman who becomes pregnant by the Holy Spirit, imagined in male terms.... The Holy Spirit would rather be the great virginal, life-engendering mother of all the living, and as such the divine archetype of Mary, the mother of Jesus Christ."[65]

The NRSV version of the angel's instruction to Joseph reads: "She will bear a son, and you are to name him Jesus, for he will save his people from their sins" (1:21). As it stands, this (and similar translations) present a confusing jumble of Latin and English. The name *Jesus* bears no relation to the promise of saving from sin. *Jesus* is a Latin name and was probably not used by Joseph or anyone else during Jesus' lifetime—except possibly by the Roman authorities and the soldiers who crucified him. The Latin name *Jesus* was used by Tertullian and other Latin authors. It gained currency in the Western church and ultimately replaced other forms as the standard name. On the plus side, the process might be seen as contextualizing the universal significance of *Jesus*. On the minus side, the contextualization was achieved at the cost of turning him into a virtual gentile. It severed ties of the New Testament name Ἰησοῦς (*Iesous*) with the Joshua of biblical history, who in Greek versions of the Old Testament bore the identical name.

In Hebrew the name of Joshua (יְהוֹשֻׁעַ [*Yehoshua*], abbreviated to יֵשׁוּעַ [*Yeshua*]) was connected with the verb ישׁע (*yashah*, "deliver," "save"). It came to mean, "Yahweh saves," or "May Yahweh save."[66] Joshua was the name of Moses's successor, who through the aid of Yahweh saved Israel from enemies as the nation settled in the promised land. Joshua became a popular Jewish name. However, it fell eventually into disuse on account of its connection with Christianity. The angel's explanation to Joseph gave the name a somewhat different meaning. *Yeshua* would not engage in military conquest but would "save his people from their sins" (1:21).

Matthew saw a connection with Isaiah 7:14: "All this took place to fulfill what had been spoken by the Lord through the prophet:

---

the disciples at the transfiguration (Matt 17:5; Mark 9:7; Luke 9:34; cf. BDAG, 378–79). It has this meaning in Hebrew Scripture (cf. Pss 17:8; 36:7; 57:1; 63:7; 91:1).

65. Jürgen Moltmannn, *The Way of Jesus Christ: Christology in Messianic Dimensions*, trans. Margaret Kohl (San Francisco: HarperSanFrancisco, 1990), 83–84; cf. Matthias Joseph Scheeben, *The Mysteries of Christianity*, trans. Cyril Vollert (St. Louis: Herder, 1864; repr. 1947), 124–89.

66. Meier, *A Marginal Jew*, 1:205–8.

'Look, the virgin shall conceive and bear a son, and they shall name him Emmanuel,' which means, 'God with us'" (1:23). As we have seen, Origen took Isaiah 7:14 as a prediction that foretold the virgin birth of Jesus. He dismissed the alternative that the prophecy predicted the conception of a child as a sign that God was with his people. Before the child was weaned, the invasion feared by Ahaz would be gone (Isa 7:16–17). Origen asked dismissively, "What sort of a sign would it be if a young woman not a virgin bore a son?" (*Contra Celsum* 1.35). It invites the retort, "What kind of a sign was it that did not address the time of Ahaz but took hundreds of years to come about?" In the prophecy, the name *Immanuel* was given to the child born in the time of Ahaz as a sign that Yahweh was with his people. The name *Yeshua* was given to Mary's child as a sign of the role that God had for him in saving his people from their sins (1:21).

Future generations of theologians and apologists would seize on miracles and fulfilled prophecy as proofs of the truth of Christianity as a belief system. Christian beliefs were true because only God could perform such feats, which vouched for the truth of the system. Skeptics were quick to point out fallacies. They pointed out that the kind of fulfilled prophecy cited in Matthew's birth narrative were not predictions regarding the distant future but allusions to earlier events. Origen's interpretation of Matthew 1:23 and Isaiah 7:14 was an instance of the fallacy. But it is questionable whether the same judgment should be applied to Matthew.

Fulfillment formulae in Matthew form a pattern that is best understood in light of the "parting of the ways." They establish roots in the history of Israel and Hebrew Scripture while claiming that Israel's past points to Jesus as the Messiah. Matthew identified landmarks in biblical history that were comparable with his narrative of Jesus' birth and early years. The former were well known, but the latter were seemingly insignificant since they centered on Joseph, Mary, and Mary's son. Nevertheless, in God's providential wisdom, those latter events were even more significant. In that sense, the latter events *fulfilled* the former events. In the terminology of contemporary hermeneutics, the earlier events provided subtexts for intertextual understanding of Matthew's narrative.

The point of the virgin's conception of a son was not the virginity of the mother but the child who would be named *Immanuel*—which means "God with us." The child was the sign that the dreaded danger of invasion would pass before he was weaned (Isa 7:14–17; cf. Matt 1:23).[67]

Raymond E. Brown noted that the fulfillment theme ran throughout Matthew's opening chapters—both where fulfillment formula was explicitly cited and also in allusions.[68] Allusions appear in Matthew's opening words regarding "the genealogy of Jesus the Messiah, the son of David, the son of Abraham" (1:1). The "son of Abraham" motif becomes apparent in the genealogy that begins with Abraham. The magi (2:1–2) represent fulfillment of the promise to Abraham that by his offspring "all the nations of the earth gain blessing for themselves" (Gen 22:18). The "son of David" motif was made explicit in the genealogy through the naming of David as the father of Solomon (1:6). It was further developed by the reply of the chief priests and scribes to Herod's question regarding the birthplace of the Messiah. Their answer was drawn from Micah 5:1 and 2 Samuel 5:2. The former text identified the location as Bethlehem, the birthplace of David (1 Sam 17:12). The latter drew attention to the king as ruler and shepherd.[69]

Dreams played an important part in Matthew's narrative. Joseph's dreams recall the part that they played in the life of his namesake Joseph, who also experienced forced sojourn in Egypt (Gen 37–50). The magi were warned in a dream of Herod's evil intent. As a result they returned to their own country by another road (2:12). In the first of Joseph's dreams an angel of the Lord told him not to fear taking Mary as his wife (1:20). In a second dream an angel told him to take the child and his mother to Egypt (2:13). Matthew interpreted their return as fulfillment of the pronouncement, "Out of Egypt I have called my son" (Matt 2:15; cf. Hos 11:1; Exod 4:22). Hosea's words were clearly not intended as a prediction about the return of the holy family. The citation draws attention to how the story of Jesus mirrored that of the nation.

The story of Herod's massacre of infant males mirrored the grief occasioned by the exile. The matriarch Rachel is depicted as weeping

---

67. Brown, *The Birth of the Messiah*, 148. As a Catholic biblical scholar, Brown asserted the importance of distinguishing between exegesis and church dogmatics. He discussed virginal conception in an appendix (517–33).

68. Brown, *The Birth of the Messiah*, 184.

69. For discussion of the star seen by the magi as an astronomical phenomenon see Mark Kidger, *The Star of Bethlehem: An Astronomer's View* (Princeton, NJ: Princeton University Press, 1999). An astrological interpretation is argued by Michael R. Molnar, *The Star of Bethlehem: The Legacy of the Magi* (New Brunswick, NJ: Rutgers University Press, 1999).

for her children (Matt 2:18; Jer 31:15). The Holy Family returned after Herod's death, settling in Nazareth out of reach from Herod's son Archelaus. The family's move to Nazareth is described as fulfillment of what had been spoken by the prophets, "He will be called a Nazorean" (2:23).[70]

Earlier reference was made to Origen's view of the double origin of the Son. So far the discussion has focused on his view of the virgin birth in time. However, the preexistence of the Son as a "second God" raised the question of the Son's origin. Previous church fathers were aware of the problem.[71] It gave rise to the question of eternal generation. Origen used the expression "beget eternally"[72] to denote an act of the immutable God outside time.

Maurice Wiles argued persuasively that the idea of eternal generation was bound up with the way that the early fathers interpreted the begetting of wisdom in the LXX translation of Proverbs 8:25 ("before the hills he begat me") and Psalm 110 (109):3 ("before the morning star I begat thee").[73] However, impetus for applying the thought of begetting was bound up with the way the fathers had come to understand *Son of God* as *God the Son* and hence *Father* as *Father of the Son*. There were, in effect, two acts of begetting: one in time when Jesus was (in the language of the creeds) "conceived by the Holy Spirit" and another in eternity when (in the language of Origen) the unbegotten Father begat the Son by an eternal act.

2.4. The Arian Controversy. Arianism dates from the dispute of the Alexandrian presbyter Arius (d. 336) with his bishop, Alexander, over the divinity of Christ. In the eyes of Arius, Alexander was a Sabellian who regarded the Father, the Son, and Spirit as mere manifestations of the

---

70. The prophecy combines several motifs. See Brown, *The Birth of the Messiah*, 209–13, 218–19. They include the location in Nazareth and allusion to the shoot (*nezer*) that that would spring from the stump of Jesse (Isa 11).

71. Justin Martyr spoke of utterance of words as analogous to begetting (see n39).

72. *Homily on Jeremiah* 9.4 (Migne, PG 13.357); *De Principiis* 1.2.4; cf. Kelly, *Early Christian Doctrines*, 128–32.

73. Maurice Wiles, "Eternal Generation," in *Working Papers in Doctrine* (London: SCM, 1976), 18–27. See also in the same volume "Some Reflections on the Origins of the Doctrine of the Trinity" (1–17), where Wiles cautions against making arbitrary statements about the inner life of God.

Irenaeus declined to speculate on the process by which the word was begotten or put forth in view of the warning in Isa 53:8 LXX: "Who shall explain his generation?" The Word coexists with the Father from eternity (*Heresies* 2.30.9; 4.20.3; cf. Kelly, *Early Christian Doctrines*, 105).

one godhead. Arius himself believed that Jesus was a human being and therefore a creature who could not share the full divinity of the Father.

Twentieth-century scholarship embarked on what could be called a quest of the historical Arius, his followers, and of his archenemy the successor to Alexander, Athanasius (c. 296–373).[74] Rowan Williams, former Lady Margaret Professor of Divinity at Oxford and later archbishop of Canterbury, rejected the charge that Arius was driven philosophically. Rather, Arius was a man of faith who sought to "develop a biblically based *and* rationally consistent catechesis." He was an "academic" like his Alexandrian predecessors, Clement and Origen, caught up in conflict with "catholic" institutionalism.[75]

Bishop R. P. C. Hanson (1916–1988), who held chairs at Nottingham, Durham, and Manchester, saw the underlying problem of the Arian controversy as that of "how to reconcile two factors which were part of the very fabric of Christianity: monotheism, and the worship of Christ as divine."[76] The term *Arian* was notoriously difficult to define, and those who came after Arius did not regard him as the founder of a school.[77] Hanson endorsed the theological achievements of Athanasius but could not excuse his "mendacity" and "gangsterism."[78] Hanson's work highlights the problem with the orthodox dogma of the impassibility of God—that God is immune from suffering. Athanasius had argued that Jesus had to be fully God and fully man in order to save humanity.[79] The Arians countered that Jesus suffered and died and thus could not be God like the immutable, impassible Father.[80] To say with the orthodox that Jesus suffered only in his humanity but not in his divinity[81] sounds strained and implausible.

Maurice Wiles (1923–2005), Regius Professor of Divinity at Oxford,

---

74. Robert C. Gregg and Dennis E. Groh, *Early Arianism: A View of Salvation* (Philadelphia: Fortress, 1981); Michael R. Barnes and Daniel H. Williams, eds., *Arianism after Arius: Essays on the Development of the Fourth Century Trinitarian Conflicts* (Edinburgh: T&T Clark, 1993).

75. Rowan Williams, *Arius: Heresy and Tradition* (Grand Rapids: Eerdmans, [1987] 2002), 111, 87.

76. R. P. C. Hanson, *The Search for the Christian Doctrine of God: The Arian Controversy, 318–381* (Edinburgh: T&T Clark, 1988), xx. See also Rowan Williams, "Article Review: R. P. C. Hanson's *The Search for the Christian Doctrine of God*," *SJT* 45 (1992): 101–11.

77. Hanson, *The Search for the Christian Doctrine of God*, 127.

78. Hanson, *The Search for the Christian Doctrine of God*, 244, 254.

79. Athanasius, *On the Incarnation of the Word*, §§7–9.

80. Hanson, *The Search for the Christian Doctrine of God*, 109–10, 562–72.

81. This was the view of Athanasius. It is found as early as Ignatius, *Ephesians* 7 and received classic expression in Tertullian, *Against Praxeas*.

saw the issues raised by Arianism as perennial.[82] Like Williams and Hanson, he noted the Scriptures to which Arius appealed: the High Priestly Prayer of Jesus with its reference to the Father as "the only true God" (John 17:3); the description of "the blessed and only Sovereign, the King of kings, the Lord of lords. It is he alone who has immortality" (1 Tim 6:15–16); the doxological ascription to "the only wise" God (Rom 16:27); Jesus' reminder to the rich young ruler that "no one is good but God alone" (Mark 10:18).[83] It was not clear that the allusion to word and Spirit in creation (Ps 33:6) implied the existence of separate divine entities. Wisdom, personified as God's agent in creation, appeared as God's first created work (Prov 8:22). Christ, like Moses before him, was "faithful" over God's house (Heb 3:6). For Paul, "There is one God, the Father, from whom are all things and for whom we exist, and one Lord, Jesus Christ, through whom are all things and through whom we exist" (1 Cor 8:6). Two key passages imply that the titles Lord and God were conferred on Jesus as a result of his faithfulness (Phil 2:5–11; Heb 1:8–9).[84] Arius appealed to ecclesiastical tradition, showing that it did not uniformly support his opponents, and to philosophical tradition, which stressed the unchanging transcendence of the Father.[85]

The dispute initiated by Arius spread rapidly, despite his condemnation by a synod at Alexandria (c. 320). Popular unrest threatened to disrupt the peace recently secured by Constantine between East and West in the Roman Empire. Constantine summoned the church's first general council. The Council of Nicea (325 CE) produced a formula and condemned Arius but proved to be merely the first painful step in the endeavor to establish peace and orthodoxy.

2.5. Councils and Confessions. The Council of Nicea began by rejecting an Arian creed. Eusebius of Caesarea, who stood in the tradition of Origen and was an early supporter of Arius, introduced the baptismal creed of his own church. But the creed that was ultimately accepted is thought to be based on the baptismal creed of the church of Jerusalem—supplemented by the insertion (supported by Constantine) of the phrase

---

82. Maurice Wiles, *Archetypal Heresy: Arianism through the Centuries* (Oxford: Oxford University Press, 1996); cf. John Macquarrie, "The Theological Legacy of Maurice Wiles," *ATR* 88 (2006): 597–616.
83. Wiles, *Archetypal Heresy*, 10.
84. Wiles, *Archetypal Heresy*, 15.
85. Wiles, *Archetypal Heresy*, 17–26.

Evolution of Orthodoxy

"*homoousion* [ὁμοούσιον, 'consubstantial,' or 'of one substance'] with the Father." The phrase occurs in a section affirming belief in the Father, "all powerful, maker of all things, both seen and unseen. And in one Lord Jesus Christ, the Son of God, the only-begotten from the Father, that is from the substance of the Father [ἐκ τῆς οὐσίας τοῦ πατρός], God from God, light from light, true God from true God, begotten not made, consubstantial with Father [ὁμοούσιον τῷ πατρί], through whom all things came to be."[86]

In addition to condemning Arius and his followers, the council anathematized those who held Arian slogans such as "there was once when he was not" and "before he was begotten he was not." However, the Arians were not finished, and traditionalists were lukewarm about the innovations. Fierce controversy raged for much of the fourth century. During that period, the leading advocate of Nicene theology was Athanasius (c. 296–373), who attended Alexander at the council and succeeded him as bishop of Alexandria in 328. By refusing to compromise, Athanasius incurred the wrath of powerful Arians and was not above resorting to violence himself. He was exiled several times before his party eventually triumphed at the Council of Constantinople (381).

Among the numerous writings of Athanasius is what many regard as the classic treatment of Christology, *On the Incarnation*.[87] The leading authority on fourth-century Christology, Frances M. Young, saw Athanasius's argument as the solution to the divine dilemma caused by the tension between God's love and human sin and disobedience. "The answer was the incarnation. The Logos took a human body capable of dying: when the Logos died the death owed by all humanity, the debt to God's honour was paid and death itself was overcome. The corrupt nature of humanity was re-created when the body of the Logos was raised and clothed in incorruptibility. The indwelling Logos restored the lost image of god to humanity, and God was reconciled to himself."[88] In common with many others, Thomas G. Weinandy credited Nicea

---

86. *Decrees of the Ecumenical Councils*, ed. Norman P. Tanner (London: Sheed & Ward; Washington, DC: Georgetown University Press, 1990), 1:5.
87. Athanasius, *Contra Gentes and De Incarnatione*, ed. and trans. Robert W. Thomson (Oxford: Clarendon, 1971). *On the Incarnation* was widely held to be an early composition on account of its lack of references to Arius and Nicea. Modern opinion is inclined to favor a later date, as it may be the working of Irenaeus in response to Eusebius's *Theophania*.
88. Frances M. Young, with Andrew Teal, *From Nicaea to Chalcedon: A Guide to the Literature and Its Background* (Grand Rapids: Baker Academic, 1983; 2nd ed., 2010), 55.

with having "established the foundational dogmatic truths concerning the Son's existence as God and as man."[89]

Re-creation was central to Athanasius's understanding of salvation. The Word "became man that we might become divine [ἐνηνθρώπησεν, ἵνα ἡμεῖς θεοποιηθῶμεν]; and he revealed himself through a body that we might receive an idea of the invisible Father; and he endured insults from men that we might inherit incorruption" (*On the Incarnation* 54.3).[90] The appeal of Arius was basically cosmological. Athanasius ultimately triumphed through his argument that salvation depended on the Son sharing the essential nature of the Godhead perfectly.[91]

The creed that is widely known as the Nicene Creed, and as such is widely used in liturgy today, was the form attributed to the Council of Constantinople (381 CE) as "the faith of the 150 fathers" by the Council of Chalcedon (451 CE).[92] This creed is longer than the text of Nicea and, among other changes, dropped the phrase "from the substance of the Father" as an explanation of *homoousios* as well as the anathemas. It added sections on the Holy Spirit and belief in the church, baptism, and the resurrection of the dead. It may have originated as the baptismal creed of the Church of Constantinople.

In the meantime, the focus of Christology began to change from whether Jesus was God to how his divine person related to his humanity. As throughout the patristic period, in the background was the premise that God was immutable and impassible. Two schools of thought dominated the debates between Nicea and Chalcedon—the schools of Alexandria and Antioch. The rival schools have been distinguished as Word-Flesh Christology versus Word-Man Christology.[93] The terminology signified the difference between the Word assuming human nature and the Word assuming the identity of a particular man. However, because the two schools used overlapping terminology, Frances Young

---

89. Thomas G. Weinandy, "Trinitarian Christology: The Eternal Son," in *The Oxford Handbook of the Trinity*, ed. Gilles Emery, and Matthew Levering (Oxford: Oxford University Press, 2011), 387–99, here 389.

90. Athanasius, *Contra Gentes and De Incarnatione*, 268–69. A similar thought in the New Testament is that of becoming "participants in the divine nature [θείας κοινωνοὶ φύσεως]" (2 Pet 1:4).

91. Young, *From Nicaea to Chalcedon*, 53, 71.

92. *Decrees of the Ecumenical Councils*, 1:1–24.

93. R. V. Sellers, *Two Ancient Christologies: A Study of the Christological Thought of the Schools of Alexandria and Antioch in the Early History of Christian Doctrine* (London: SPCK, 1940); R. V. Sellers, *The Council of Chalcedon: A Historical and Doctrinal Survey* (London: SPCK, 1953).

(along with other scholars) proposed rewording the question, "Who was the subject of the incarnate experiences of Jesus Christ?" Young's answer was as follows: "For the Alexandrians the subject remained the Word, who though transcendent accommodated himself to the conditions of human nature. For the Antiochenes, the corollary of Nicea could not possibly be regarded as the immediate subject of the incarnate experiences without blasphemous denigration of his essential divinity; naturally this produced a dualistic Christology in which the unity of the Christ as the Word was hard to maintain."[94] Both schools faced difficulties, and both produced advocates accused of heresy.

Two leading figures associated with the school of Alexandria were judged heretical—Apollinaris and Eutyches. Apollinaris (c. 310–c. 390), Bishop of Laodicea and friend of Athanasius, fiercely opposed Arianism and Adoptionism. Most of his extensive writings are lost. From what can be recovered, his regular description of the incarnation was "one nature" (μία φύσις)—"one incarnate nature of the divine Word."[95] The Word was embodied in the God-man, apparently replacing the human soul. Jesus was different from other men, insofar as he was "born in human likeness. And being found in human form" (Phil 2:7). Apollinarianism was condemned by the Cappadocian Father, Gregory of Nazianzus, in the famous comment: "What has not been assumed cannot be restored; for it is what is united with God that is saved" (*Epistle* 101).[96]

Eutyches (c. 378–454) was archimandrite of a large monastery at Constantinople and enjoyed considerable influence at the imperial court. He is remembered as the founder of a virtually docetic form of Monophysitism (belief that Christ had only one nature). Pope Leo formulated the Western answer to Eutyches in his famous *Tome*. A change of emperor sealed Eutyches's fate. He was deposed and exiled by the Council of Chalcedon (451). When pressed, Eutyches admitted that Christ was "of two natures," but "after the union I confess one nature." There may have been some ambiguity about the word φύσις, whether it meant "nature" or "concrete existence," as it did for other Alexandrians. However, Eutyches's denial that Jesus' manhood was consubstantial with human manhood was judged incompatible with orthodoxy.

---

94. Young, *From Nicaea to Chalcedon*, 242.
95. Altaner, *Patrology*, 363; Kelly, *Early Christian Doctrines*, 293.
96. Kelly, *Early Christian Doctrines*, 297.

The bitter conflict between the schools of Antioch and Alexandria dated from earlier decades. It came to a head with the running conflict between Nestorius (c. 351–c. 451) and Cyril (d. 444), patriarch of Alexandria. Nestorius embraced Antiochene theology during monastic studies at Antioch. He was appointed patriarch of Constantinople at the instigation of Emperor Theodosius II. Nestorius set about ridding the city of heretics and schismatics. Conflict flared up over application of the term *theotokos* (Θεοτόκος, one who gave birth to God) to the Virgin Mary. For the Alexandrians *theotokos* was not only a term used in devotion but also a test of orthodoxy insofar as it safeguarded against Adoptionism. Cyril saw denial of *theotokos* as tantamount to saying that Mary bore *two* sons artificially linked together.[97] *Theotokos* meant that the birth of Jesus was the occasion when the Logos was fused with humanity hypostatically for the sake of salvation.[98]

Nestorius preferred to speak of a voluntary *conjunction* of divine and human nature. Because change and suffering were appropriate to humanity but not divinity, Nestorius argued that it was better to use words like *anthropotokos* (man bearing) and *christotokos* (Christ bearing). In the hope of vindication, Nestorius asked Theodosius II to convene a council. However, the Third Ecumenical Council held at Ephesus (431) resulted in further condemnation of Nestorius and affirmation of Cyril.[99] The so-called Union Symbol (433) was a conciliatory synthesis of both positions, which reconciled the two parties for a time. But Nestorius was steadily losing ground. In 436 he was banished to Upper Egypt, where he eventually died.

The Fourth Ecumenical Council (451) was held in the city of Chalcedon in Asia Minor opposite Byzantium. It was convened by the Emperor Marcian to deal with the Eutychian heresy. The council canonized Cyril's two letters condemning Nestorianism and Leo's *Tome* condemning Eutychianism. The Chalcedonian formula consisted of a patchwork of statements drawn from tradition, and the rival schools of Alexandria and Antioch. Whereas Nicea had defined the consubstantiality of the Son with the Father, Chalcedon insisted on the Son's consubstantiality with humanity.

---

97. Kelly, *Early Christian Doctrines*, 313–14.
98. Young, *From Nicaea to Chalcedon*, 278.
99. *Decrees of the Ecumenical Councils*, 1:37–74.

[The Son was] truly God and truly man, of a rational soul and body, consubstantial with the Father as regards his divinity, and the same consubstantial with us as regards his humanity [ὁμοούσιον τῷ πατρὶ κατὰ τὴν θεότητα καὶ ὁμοούσιον ἡμῖν τὸν αὐτὸν κατὰ ἀνθρωπότητα], like us in all things except for sin; begotten before the ages from the Father as regards his divinity, and in the last days the same for us and the same for us for our salvation from Mary, the virgin God-bearer [Μαρίας τῆς παρθένου τῆς θεοτόκου], as regards his humanity; one and the same Christ, Son, Lord, only-begotten, acknowledged in two natures which undergo no confusion, no change, no division, no separation; at no point was the difference between the two natures taken away through the union, but rather the property of both natures is preserved and comes together in a single person and a single subsistent being [εἰς ἓν πρόσωπον καὶ μίαν ὑπόστασιν συντρεχούσης]. He is not parted or divided into two persons, but is one and the same only-begotten Son, God, Word, Lord Jesus Christ, just as the prophets taught from the beginning.[100]

The omission of Cyril's "hypostatic union" was a victory for the Antiochenes. But the confession also contained elements that preserved Alexandrian terminology stressing the essential unity of the divine and human. They include reference to Mary, the virgin *theotokos*, and the phrases "a single person and a single subsistent being," "not parted or divided into two persons, but is one and the same only-begotten Son, God, Word, Lord Jesus Christ."

Chalcedon did not put an end to the christological debate, which dragged on for several centuries. However, for present purposes regarding the evolution of orthodoxy, we have gone far enough. Chalcedon with its double *homoousios* regarding deity and humanity set the boundaries of Western orthodoxy, and agenda for future debate. From the Western dogmatic standpoint, it represented the climax of patristic achievement. In retrospect certain limitations are obvious. Chalcedon did not resolve the debate but set guidelines separating orthodoxy from heresy. It said nothing about the life and death of Jesus. The Holy Spirit played no part. Jesus had a universal significance. Apparently it had nothing to do

---

100. *Decrees of the Ecumenical Councils*, 1:86.

with being Jewish—apart perhaps from claims right at the end about the witness of the prophets.

At the risk of being overly detailed, the above account makes no claims to be comprehensive.[101] Its purpose was to identify and document points on the trajectory of the evolution of orthodoxy.

Among the many comments that could be cited, those of Morna D. Hooker are among the most insightful. In a contribution to the Festschrift for Maurice Wiles, she examined the distance between the New Testament and Chalcedon. She conceded that, given the philosophical climate, Chalcedon was probably "an inevitable development." Nevertheless, it was not "a proper development from what is said about Christ in the New Testament."[102] She summed up her argument by making three observations.

First, Chalcedon was intended to be a bastion against heresy. It was necessary to define which heretical views were excluded. On the other hand, in the days when the New Testament was being written, Judaism was the orthodoxy, and Christianity the heresy. Chalcedon and the New Testament belong to totally different historical contexts. Second, the New Testament writers were concerned about the activity of God. "What had been for our New Testament writers helpful images used to describe their experience of God have [in the formula of Chalcedon] become doctrines which themselves need to be defined and analysed." Third, the New Testament writers belong to a Jewish context, not a Greek philosophical one. The debate at Chalcedon would have made no sense at all to those

---

101. Recent discussion includes the massive collection of studies commemorating the anniversary of Chalcedon. Aloys Grillmeier and Heinrich Bacht, eds., *Das Konzil von Chalkedon: Geschichte und Gegenwart*, 3 vols. (Würzburg: Echter-Verlag, 1951). Grillmeier expanded his original contribution in *Christ in Christian Tradition*, vol. 1, *From the Apostolic Age to Chalcedon (451)*, trans. John Bowden (London: Mowbrays, [1965]; 2nd ed., 1975); vol. 2, *From Chalcedon to Justinian (451) to Gregory the Great (590–604)*, part 1, trans. Pauline Allen and John Cawte (Atlanta: John Knox, 1987). Other works include E. J. Fortman, *The Triune God: A Historical Study of the Doctrine of the Trinity* (Philadelphia: Westminster, 1972); Cristopher Stead, *Divine Substance* (Oxford: Clarendon, 1977); Stephen T. Davis, Daniel Kendall and Gerald O'Collins, eds., *The Trinity: An Interdisciplinary Symposium on the Trinity* (Oxford: Oxford University Press, 1999); Stephen T. Davis, Daniel Kendall, and Gerald O'Collins, eds., *The Incarnation: An Interdisciplinary Symposium on the Incarnation of the Son of God* (Oxford: Oxford University Press, 2002); John Hick, *The Metaphor of God Incarnate: Christology in a Pluralistic Age* (London: SCM; Louisville: Westminster John Knox, [1993], 2005).

102. Morna D. Hooker, "Chalcedon and the New Testament," in *The Making and Remaking of Christian Doctrine: Essays in Honour of Maurice Wiles*, ed. Sarah Coakley and David Pailin (Oxford: Clarendon, 1993), 73–93.

accustomed to thinking in Jewish terms. Moreover, the issues were quite different. The New Testament writers were not concerned with divine and human nature and being. "Their concern was to show that it was the same God who had been at work in the past who was now at work in Christ, and that his new work in Christ was the fulfilment of everything that had gone before: hence the importance of showing his superiority to Moses."[103] Professor Hooker's observations indicate the gulf between contemporary biblical scholars and philosophical theologians.

Two further observations may be added. The first is that incarnation and Trinity were not two separate doctrines. They belonged to a cluster of mutually defining terms and ideas. *Trinitas* is found as early as Tertullian in the context of his discussion of Patripassianism in *Against Praxeas*. Jesus suffered crucifixion in his manhood, but the deity of Father and Son remained beyond suffering. *Incarnatio* occurred in the Latin title of Athanasius's *On the Incarnation*. In conciliar pronouncements it appeared in the Latin text of the Council of Ephesus (431). The only begotten Son (*Filium unigenitum*) became incarnate (*incarnatum*) and was made man (*hominem factum*).[104] Both *incarnation* and *Trinity* go back to notions of God in which the Father was the Father of the Son. However, the review of the "First Quest" in the preceding chapter and the convoluted history of patristic Christology pose the question of whether early church theology has proprietary rights to determine the meaning of *incarnation* and *Trinity* today.

The second observation has to do with the use of creeds and definitions. The definition of Chalcedon set boundaries of heresy for the warring schools of Antioch and Alexandria. By contrast, the Nicene Creed was linked with liturgical practice both in its prehistory and subsequent use in baptism and eucharist.[105] In modern times the *Lambeth Quadrilateral* included the Apostles' Creed and the Nicene Creed among its proposals for ecumenical unity. The Apostles' Creed was recommended as the condition for baptism,[106] and the Nicene Creed as

---

103. Hooker, "Chalcedon and the New Testament," 86–88. See also the Festschrift for Professor Hooker: John Barclay and John Sweet, eds., *Early Christian Thought in Its Jewish Context* (Cambridge: Cambridge University Press, 1996).

104. *Decrees of the Ecumenical Councils*, 1:41.

105. On creeds in baptism and catechesis see J. N. D. Kelly, *Early Christian Creeds* (London: Longmans, Green, 1950), 30–61. On the use of the Niceno-Constantinopolitan Creed in baptism and eucharist see pp. 344–57.

106. In much of Christian tradition the Apostles' Creed was believed to date from the New Testament apostles. However, the title Apostles' Creed (or *symbolum apostolorum*) dates from

summary of Christian faith.[107] However, both creeds are problematic regarding Christology.

Jürgen Moltmann pointed out that in the Nicene and Apostles' Creeds "there is either nothing at all, or really no more than a comma between 'and was made man, he suffered' or 'born and suffered.'" Moltmann did not propose to change the creeds, but he suggested that we should add at least in thought something along the following lines:

> Baptized by John the Baptist,
> Filled with the Holy Spirit:
> To preach the kingdom to the poor,
> To heal the sick,
> To receive those who have been cast out,
> To revive Israel for the salvation of the nations,
> And to have mercy on all people.[108]

3. The Sixteenth-Century Reformation

The previous discussion makes no pretense at being a comprehensive account of early Christology. Rather, it sought to identify impulses and influential personalities in the evolution of orthodoxy. The present section seeks to follow this trajectory through the two most influential figures in the Protestant Reformation of the sixteenth century.

3.1. Luther and Jesus. The beginning of the Reformation is commonly dated from Luther's Ninety-Five Theses of 1517.[109] Martin Luther

---

390 CE, and nothing comparable with its contents can be traced to the New Testament. However, creedal fragments and a 'rule of faith' are another matter (Kelly, *Early Christian Creeds*, 1–29).

107. The *Lambeth Quadrilateral* was a proposal for church unification adopted by the conference of bishops of the Anglican Communion at the archbishop of Canterbury's London residence at Lambeth in 1888. Versions of the proposal were adopted at successive Lambeth Conferences. The four basic principles were (1) Scripture as the rule and ultimate standard of faith; (2) acceptance of the Apostles' Creed and Nicene Creed, as defined above; (3) acceptance of the two dominical sacraments, and (4) acceptance of the "historic episcopate."

108. Moltmann, *The Way of Jesus Christ*, 150.

109. For background, see H. J. Hillerbrand, *The Reformation in Its Own Words* (New York: Harper & Row; London: SCM, 1964); David Bagchi and David C. Steinmetz, eds., *The Cambridge Companion to Reformation Theology* (Cambridge: Cambridge University Press, 2004).

On Luther, see John Dillenberger, ed., *Martin Luther: Selections from His Writings* (New York: Doubleday, 1961); I. D. K. Siggins, *Martin Luther's Doctrine of Christ* (New Haven, CT: Yale University Press, 1970); David C. Steinmetz, *Luther in Context* (Grand Rapids: Baker, 1995;

(1483–1546) was a member of the order of Augustinian Hermits. He was ordained priest in 1507. The following year he became a professor at the newly founded University of Wittenberg. In 1515 he was made vicar of his order, responsible for eleven monasteries. During this early period Luther became increasingly aware of the significance of Augustine's teaching on sin and grace. Human beings were unable to respond to God without divine grace. They could be justified only through faith by the righteousness of Christ being imputed to them.

The Ninety-Five Theses were a protest against the sale of indulgences—time in purgatory could be remitted by donations to the church. The theses were intended for scholarly debate. Luther's concern is summed up in the first one: "When our Lord and Master Jesus Christ said 'Repent' he wanted the entire life of believers to be one of penitence."[110] The theses became a signal for national unrest, enflamed by Luther's writings calling for reform. A series of interviews and debates led to Luther's conviction of forty-one errors and excommunication by the papal bull *Exsurge Domine* (1520).[111] The following year he was summoned to appear before Emperor Charles V at an assembly of princes and electors of the Holy Roman Empire: the Diet of Worms. On his refusal to recant, Luther was placed under the imperial ban.[112]

Fearing for Luther's safety, the elector of Saxony arranged for him to be abducted and taken in hiding to the Wartburg castle. Here Luther spent eight months incognito, working on his German translation of the New Testament, based on Erasmus's Greek text.[113] Political attempts to curb the spread of Lutheranism were made at the Diets of Speyer (1526 and 1529). In response to efforts to end toleration of reform in Catholic

---

2nd ed. 2002); Robert Kolb, Irene Dingel, L'Ubomír Batka, eds., *The Oxford Handbook of Martin Luther's Theology* (Oxford: Oxford University Press, 2014). The standard edition of Luther's works is the *D. Martin Luthers Werke* (Weimar: Böhlau, 1883–1993). In references it is referred to as WA (Weimarer Ausgabe). The standard English translation is *Luther's Works*, ed., Helmut T. Lehmann and Jarolav Pelikan, 54 vols. (St. Louis: Muhlenberg; Philadelphia: Concordia, 1955–76).

110. Hillerbrand, *The Reformation in Its Own Words*, 51.
111. Hillerbrand, *The Reformation in Its Own Words*, 80–84.
112. Hillerbrand, *The Reformation in Its Own Words*, 85–100.
113. Hillerbrand, *The Reformation in Its Own Words*, 379–89. However, Luther and Erasmus were soon locked in controversy over free will. Erasmus accused Luther of extremism by underestimating cooperation with God in salvation in *De Libero Arbitrio* (1524). Luther replied with *De Servo Arbitrio* (1525). Freedom was a consequence of salvation—not a precondition. Otherwise, man's will was in bondage. Erasmus's *Hyperapistes* (1526) was a rejoinder. See *Luther and Erasmus: Free Will and Salvation*, trans. and ed. E. Gordon Rupp, LCC 17 (London: SCM; Philadelphia: Westminster, 1969).

regions, five princes and fourteen cities lodged a formal "protest" in 1529. From then on, supporters of reform were known as "Protestants."

In 1530 Charles V made an attempt to secure religious and political unity by convening a diet at Augsburg. Lutherans were invited to submit a statement of their beliefs and concerns. In response, the *Confession of Augsburg* was drafted by Luther's colleague Philip Melanchthon (1497–1560). It was conciliatory in tone, stressing affinity with the early church. The first part contained twenty-one articles of faith. The second part reviewed current abuses. The emperor handed over the *Confession* to conservative Catholic theologians, who formally rejected it. The Lutherans responded with an *Apology for the Augsburg Confession* (1530–31). The *Confession of Augsburg* became the first authoritative Lutheran statement of faith.[114]

Luther's Christology revised patristic tradition, but it fits neither contemporary conservatism nor liberalism. If anything, it is more like a precritical version of Bultmann's stress on the kerygma of the cross and resurrection.[115] In concluding his *Preface to the New Testament* (1522, revised 1546), Luther assured readers that they were now in position to judge the best books.

> John's Gospel and St. Paul's epistles, especially that to the Romans, are the true kernel and marrow of all the books.... For in them you do not find many works and miracles of Christ described, but you do find described in masterly fashion how faith in Christ overcomes sin, death and hell, and gives life, righteousness and salvation. This is the real nature of the gospel.... If I had to do without one or the other—the works or the preaching of Christ—I would rather do without the works than without his preaching. For the works do not help me, but his words give life as he himself says [John 6:63].... John's Gospel is the one, fine, true and chief gospel, and is far, far to be preferred over the other three and placed high above them.[116]

---

114. Jaroslav Pelikan and Valerie Hotchkiss, eds., *Creeds and Confessions of Faith in the Christian Tradition*, 3 vols. (New Haven, CT: Yale University Press, 2003), 2:49–118. Luther did not attend the Diet of Augsburg, since technically he was an outlaw.

115. See below, chap. 6.

116. *Luther's Works*, 35, 361–62.

Luther described his theology as a *theologia crucis* (theology of the cross) in contrast with a *theologia gloriae* (theology of glory). The terms figured in theses prepared for the Heidelberg Disputation (1518):

> 18. It is certain that man must utterly despair of his own ability before he is prepared to receive the grace of Christ. 19. That person does not deserve to be called a theologian who looks upon the invisible things of God as though they were clearly perceptible in those things which have actually happened [Rom 1:20]. 20. He deserves to be called a theologian, however, who comprehends the visible and manifest things of God seen through suffering and the cross. 21. A theology of glory calls evil good and good evil. A theology of the cross calls the thing what it actually is.[117]

The *cross* was a symbol making a soteriological claim. It was a statement of how God works against sin, first through his "alien work" of condemnation and then through his "proper work" of redemption and justification.[118]

Melanchthon echoed Luther's thoughts in the book that became the first textbook of Lutheran theology *Loci Communes* (1521). It was based on lectures on Romans dealing with the most common theological topics. In a dedicatory letter Melanchthon explained his departure from the approaches of John of Damascus and Peter Lombard. "We do better to adore the mysteries of Deity than to investigate them." Such mysteries included the unity and Trinity of God and the manner of the incarnation.

---

117. Hillerbrand, *The Reformation in Its Own Words*, 55–56; cf. Vítor Westhelle, "Luther's Theologia Crucis," in *The Oxford Handbook of Martin Luther's Theology*, 156–67.

118. Scott Hendrix, "Luther," in *The Cambridge Companion to Reformation Theology*, 39–56, here 45. Luther's terminology was based on his precritical exegesis of Isa 28:21, in which God's "alien work" of condemnation was the precondition of God's "proper work" of redemption.

On the medieval background of Luther's exegetical method see Wilhelm Pauck's introduction to *Luther: Lectures on Romans*, Library of Christian Classics 15 (London: SCM; Philadelphia: Westminster, 1961), xiii–lxvi. In his *Lectures on Galatians* (1535) Luther commented on the fourfold method of exegesis set out in the *Quadriga*. "The letter lets you know what happened, and allegory what you must believe; the moral sense what you must do, and anagoge what you may hope for." Luther had come to think of it as artificial, robbing people of true instruction. He became highly critical of Origen's stress on allegory. However, Luther's imaginative interpretation of the Old Testament suggests that he never fully rid himself of allegory.

On Luther and Melanchthon see also Henning Graf Reventlow, *History of Biblical Interpretation*, vol. 3, *Renaissance, Reformation, Humanism*, trans. James O. Duke, SBL Resources for Biblical Study 62 (Atlanta: Society of Biblical Literature, 2010), 65–87, 87–94.

"But as for the one who is ignorant of other fundamentals, namely, 'The Power of Sin,' 'The Law,' and "Grace,' I do not see how I can call him a Christian. For from these things Christ is known, since to know Christ means to know his benefits, and not as *they* teach, to reflect upon his natures and the modes of his incarnation."[119]

The Confession of Augsburg (1530) affirmed Lutheran continuity with Catholic Christology. In part 1 dealing with "Chief Articles of Faith," the confession stressed that continuity, while also asserting soteriology as the proper approach to Christology. The first article was devoted to the identity of God. It began by affirming solidarity with Nicea, regarding "the unity of the divine essence and of the three persons." In common with church fathers, Lutherans believed that *person* did not mean "a part or quality in another, but that which properly subsists" (art. 1). Before proceeding to the Son, the confession inserted discussion of original sin, which was traced to Adam. "Our churches condemn the Pelagians and others who deny that the vice of origin is sin and who obscure the glory of Christ's merit and benefits by contending that man can be justified before God by his own strength and reason" (art. 2). In response, article 3 on the "Son of God" reaffirmed the Apostles' Creed, stressing the inseparable union of Christ's divine and human natures and his death as "a sacrifice not only for original sin but also for all other sins and to propitiate God's wrath."[120]

Luther's *theologia crucis* did not imply commitment to historical investigation of the circumstances of Jesus' execution. Rather, the cross was the symbol of the cosmic drama of divine righteousness that was played out in earthly events. Vítor Westhelle observed, "Jesus on the cross was not the Anselmian settling of accounts. He was God as a gift in a sacrificial act of revelation that at the same time discloses the human condition and God's hidden identification with it."[121]

---

119. Wilhelm Pauck, ed., *Melanchthon and Bucer*, LCC 19 (London: SCM; Philadelphia: Westminster, 1969), 21–22.

120. Pelikan and Hotchkiss, eds., *Creeds and Confessions of Faith in the Christian Tradition*, 2:58–62; *Die Bekenntnisschriften der evangelisch-lutherischen Kirche, herausgegeben im Gedenkjahr der Augsburgischen Konfession 1530*, 3rd ed. (Göttingen: Vandenhoeck & Ruprecht, 1956), 52–55. There were no major differences between the Reformers and the Catholic Church over the conciliar definitions of the Trinity. See Scott R. Swain, "The Trinity in the Reformers," in *The Oxford Handbook of the Trinity*, ed. Gilles Emery and Matthew Levering (Oxford: Oxford University Press, 2011), 227–33.

121. Vítor Westhelle, "Luther's *Theologia Crucis*," in *The Oxford Handbook of Martin Luther's Theology*, 162.

The question of the humanity and divinity of Christ was answered by Lutheranism in distinctive ways, which separated it from Catholicism and also from other forms of Protestantism. It came to the fore in two areas. The first was the Lord's Supper.[122] Luther attacked transubstantiation in his treatise on how the church was kept in bondage through the seven sacraments, *The Babylonian Captivity of the Church* (1520). The Lord's Supper was a testament or will, promising the forgiveness of sins to heirs who received it by faith. At the Marburg Colloquy (1529) Luther and Melanchthon met with Swiss Reformer Ulrich Zwingli, accompanied by Johannes Oecolampadius, and Martin Bucer with a view to achieving Protestant unity. Hopes were shattered by Luther's insistence on the real presence of Christ promised by Jesus himself at the Last Supper. It was a sacramental union beyond explanation.

The second area concerned how to understand the humanity and divinity of Christ in his state of humiliation on earth. Ironically, attempts made by Lutheran theologians to explain how the divine and human attributes were related threatened to reverse the distinction between *theologia crucis* and *theologia gloriae*. The controversy shook the Lutheran Church to its foundations. There was wide agreement on the coinherence or mutual indwelling (περιχώρησις, *perichōrēsis*; Latin, *circumincessio*) of the persons of the Trinity and of Christ's divine and human natures.[123] The latter was implicit in Luther's understanding of the real presence of Christ—in his humanity and divinity—in the Lord's Supper. Tension arose over how to understand these natures during Jesus' earthly life and state of humiliation (*status humiliationis*). The humiliation consisted not confined to the sufferings of Christ. It was also inherent in the renunciation, nonuse, and concealment of divine attributes that belonged to his humanity as a result of the incarnation.

Underlying the debate was the interpretation of Philippians 2:5–11 and the meaning of "emptied himself" in that that passage. *Kenosis* (κένωσις; Latin, *exinanitio*; "emptying") provoked intense controversy in the nineteenth century and is still a live issue.[124] Whereas Calvinists saw the Word as the preexistent subject of *kenosis*, Lutherans saw the

---

122. Gordon A. Jensen, "Luther and the Lord's Supper," in *The Oxford Handbook of Martin Luther's Theology*, 322–32.

123. On terminology, see Richard A. Muller, *Dictionary of Latin and Greek Theological Terms, Drawn Principally from Protestant Scholastic Theology*, 2nd ed. (Grand Rapids: Baker Academic, 2017).

124. See below, chaps. 10 and 21.

incarnate person of the Word as the subject. Lutherans agreed that the incarnation involved κρύψις (*krypsis*, hiding or hiddenness) of the divinity of Christ. They fought bitterly about its implications. The more moderate faculty at Giessen University argued that the *krypsis* involved concealment and limited use of the attributes. The faculty at Tübingen argued that the incarnate Christ maintained full possession and use of the attributes, even though they were partially hidden.

The *Formula of Concord* (1577) attempted to bring resolution through a comprehensive statement of Lutheran teaching, reaffirming the Confession of Augsburg and rebuking Calvinism.[125] Its articles contained statements of controversies, affirmations, and negations. Article 8 discussed at great length "The Pure Teaching of the Christian Church Concerning the Person of Christ." Its reaffirmation of the hypostatic *union* rejected the Calvinist view:

> As when two boards are glued together and neither gives anything to or takes anything from the other. On the contrary, here is the highest communion which God truly has with man. Out of this personal union and the resultant exalted and ineffable sharing there flows everything human that is said or believed about God and everything divine that is said and believed about Christ the man. The ancient fathers have illustrated this union and sharing of the natures by the analogy of an incandescent iron and the union of body and soul in man.[126]

3.2. Calvin and Jesus. John Calvin (1509–64)[127] was born in France and studied in Paris, where he acquired knowledge of classics

---

125. Pelikan and Hotchkiss, eds., *Creeds and Confessions of Faith in the Christian Tradition*, 2:166–203; cf. Irene Dingel, "Luther's Legacy in Late Reformation and Protestant Orthodoxy," in *The Oxford Handbook of Martin Luther's Theology*, 525–39.

126. Art. 8, Affirmative 5 (Pelikan and Hotchkiss, eds., *Creeds and Confessions of Faith in the Christian Tradition*, 2:191; cf. *Bekenntnisschriften*, 806).

127. For contemporary sources relating to Calvin, see Hillerbrand, *The Reformation in Its Own Words*, 170–213. Citations from Calvin's *Institutes* are taken from *Calvin: Institutes of the Christian Religion*, 2 vols., ed. John T. McNeill, trans. Ford Lewis Battles, Library of Christian Classics, vols. 21–22 (London: SCM; Philadelphia: Westminster, 1961). Calvin's commentaries were based on lectures and fill volumes 23–55 of the *Corpus Reformatorum*. They cover both Old Testament and New Testament. A selection of extracts was edited by Joseph Haroutunian assisted by Louise Pettibone Smith, *Calvin: Commentaries*, Library of Christian Classics 23 (London: SCM; Philadelphia: Westminster, 1969). Selected treatises were translated by J. K. S. Reid, *Calvin:*

and humanism. His first book discussed Seneca's *On Clemency* (1532). Calvin's Protestant sympathies caused him to flee from Paris to escape persecution. Eventually he made his way to Basel, where he published in Latin an exposition of the Apostles' Creed,[128] which he called *The Institute of the Christian Religion* (1536). The Latin *institutio* meant basic *instruction*. Calvin prefaced his book by a lengthy letter addressed to the French King Francis vindicating reform and urging toleration. Over the years, the *Institutes* were enlarged considerably. What began as a catechetical manual changed in the 1539 edition to a book more like Melanchthon's *Loci Communes*, a review of the main topics of theology. The final Latin edition (1559) consisted of four books on the knowledge of God and how it should be fostered in church and society.

In 1536 Calvin was persuaded to assist in establishing the reformation in Geneva. After two years he was forced to leave over differences with the city council, which insisted on adopting Zwinglian practices. In 1541 he was invited to return. From that point on, Calvin devoted himself to establishing a theocratic regime. The regime's status was tarnished by the burning of Servetus as a heretic (1553). It was not until 1559 that Calvin's status was changed from resident alien to citizen. By then his position had become unchallenged. In addition to the *Institutes*, Calvin wrote numerous biblical commentaries based on public lectures, treatises, and letters.

Whereas the world of Luther was that of the late Middle Ages, the world of Calvin was that of Scripture colored by Renaissance learning. Calvin's knowledge of classical philosophy may not have been systematic, but it was not as hostile as Luther's. He referred to philosophic insights when he thought that they would illuminate his discussion.[129] A case in point was Calvin's view of the *twofold knowledge of God*, which formed the basis of his *Institutes*. Knowledge of God rested partly on nature and partly on revelation. Human beings were endowed with a "sense of divinity" or "sense of [the] deity," which was "the seed of religion" (*Institutes* 1.3.1; 1.4.1).

Theological Treatises, Library of Christian Classics 22 (London: SCM; Philadelphia: Westminster, 1964). On Calvin's biblical interpretation, see Reventlow, *History of Biblical Interpretation*, 115–37.

128. "I call it the Apostles' Creed without concerning myself in the least as to its authorship. . . . I have no doubt that at the very beginning of the church, in the apostolic age, it was received as a public confession by the consent of all—wherever it originated" (*Institutes*, 1.13.18).

129. Charles Partee, *Calvin and Classical Philosophy* (Leiden: Brill, 1977), 146.

This truth was recognized by "the eminent pagan" who observed that no nation so barbarous as to be without "a deep-seated conviction that there is a God."[130] It was complemented by the facts that the universe was founded as "a spectacle of God's glory," and evidence of divine providence in human affairs (1.5.5–7). On the other hand, sin dimmed discernment. "Unless aided by spectacles we discern nothing distinctly . . . unless Scripture guides us in seeking God, we are immediately confused" (1.14.1).

Revelation, in the form of Scripture, was the *second source* of knowledge of God. It clarified natural knowledge and gave knowledge beyond what could be known by natural means. It revealed (among other things) the eternal deity of the Son (1.13.7), his deity in the Old Testament (1.13.9), the demonstration of his deity by his miracles (1.13.13), and the deity of the Spirit (1.13.14). In short, Scripture revealed the divine Trinity, "one essence of God, which contains three persons" (1.13.1–29).

Calvin contended that God was "the Author" of Scripture. "Thus, the highest proof of Scripture derives in general from the fact that God in person speaks in it" (1.7.4). It is "self-authenticated; hence, it is not right to subject it to proof and reasoning. And the certainty it deserves with us, it attains by the testimony of the Spirit. For even if it wins reverence for itself by its own majesty, it seriously affects us only when it is sealed on our hearts through the Spirit. Therefore, illumined by his power, we believe neither by our own nor by anyone else's judgment that Scripture is from God. . . . It has flowed to us from the very mouth of God by the ministry of men" (1.7.5). Calvin went on to discuss "firm proofs" of "the credibility of Scripture" (1.8). They included its superiority to human wisdom, the sincerity of its narrative, its miraculous accompaniment, and continuous use down the ages. At best, these "proofs" supported credibility. They did not amount to demonstration that Scripture was the Word of God. This could be proved only by the internal testimony of the Spirit: God speaking his Word through Scripture.[131]

In the previous chapter we discussed the role of data beliefs, data background beliefs, and control beliefs in making truth claims. For Calvin, data beliefs and control beliefs were furnished by Scripture. Data background beliefs were also derived Scripture. But they were affected

---

130. The reference in *Institutes* 1.3.1 is to Cicero, *On the Nature of the Gods*, 1.16.43.
131. The apostles' witness was guided by Christ's Spirit "in a certain measure dictating the words" (4.8.8). They were "sure and genuine scribes of the Holy Spirit" (4.8.9).

by his understanding of civil government and sixteenth-century views of the physical world.

Calvin's commentaries on Scripture were delivered as lectures before being committed to print. Paul was treated before the Gospels. John appeared first (1553),[132] followed by *A Harmony of the Gospels, Matthew, Mark and Luke* (1555).[133] In compiling a harmony, Calvin was following ancient tradition. He justified doing so in the hope of providing "a welcome and useful short-cut to the three narratives in a continuous line." It also enabled readers to see points of likeness and difference.[134] The harmony followed Matthew's outline, while not losing sight of the perspective provided by Calvin and Scripture as a whole.

In a wider sense Calvin's theology as a whole was an endeavor to show the harmony of God's work and in creation, providence, and salvation. The sovereignty of God implied that "he does whatever he pleases" (Ps 115:3; *Institutes* 1.16.3). Everything proceeds from his "set plan . . . nothing takes place by chance" (1.16.4). "Not one drop of rain falls without God's sure command" (1.16.5). Passages of Scripture that speak of God repenting (e.g., Gen 6:6; 1 Sam 15:1; Jer 18:8) were explained as figures of speech, events that merely seemed to imply changes of mind (1.17.12–13). The existence of evil was not merely permitted by God (1.18.1). God used the deeds of the godless, but God himself was not to be blamed (1.18.4).

Calvin placed his discussion of predestination in the context of grace. It is succinctly summarized in the title of book 3, chapter 21: "Eternal Election, by Which God Has Predestined Some to Salvation, Others to Destruction." Later he summarized, "As Scripture, then, clearly shows, we say that God once established by his eternal and unchangeable plan those whom he long before determined once for all to receive unto salvation, and those whom, on the other hand, he would devote to destruction" (3.21.8). It was entirely "without regard to human worth; but by his just and irreprehensible and incomprehensible judgment he has barred the door of life to those whom he has given over to damnation."

---

132. Calvin, *The Gospel according to St. John*, 2 vols., trans. T. H. L. Parker (Grand Rapids: Eerdmans, 1961).

133. Calvin, *A Harmony of the Gospels, Matthew, Mark and Luke*, 3 vols., trans. A. W. Morrison and T. H. L. Parker (Grand Rapids: Eerdmans, 1972).

134. *Harmony* 1:xiii-xiv. The earliest known harmony was the *Diatessaron* of Tatian. Calvin's was preceded by Andreas Osiander's *Gospel Harmony* (1537). See further Reventlow, *History of Biblical Interpretation*, 3:132–33.

Between the discussions of providence in book 1 and predestination in book 3, Calvin placed his discussion of "The Knowledge of God the Redeemer in Christ, First Disclosed to the Fathers under the Law, and then to Us in the Gospel" (book 2). The harmony of God's plan began with the fall and revolt of Adam. Calvin's discussion embraced law and grace in the Old and New Testaments, showing that God had to become man in order to fulfil the office of mediator (2.12.1–7).

On the question of the two natures of Christ, Calvin dissociated himself from Lutheranism and adhered strictly to the formula of Chalcedon. The expression that "the Word was made flesh" (John 1:14) was not to be understood "in the sense that the Word was turned into flesh or confusedly mingled with flesh. Rather, that because he chose for himself the virgin's womb as a temple in which to dwell, he who was the Son of God became Son of man—not by confusion of substance, but by unity of person. . . . For we affirm his divinity so joined and united with his humanity that each retains its distinctive nature unimpaired, and yet these two natures constitute one Christ" (2.14.1).[135] In earlier editions of the *Institutes*, Calvin followed tradition in depicting Christ as king and high priest. In the final Latin edition of 1559 he added the prophetic office (1.15.2). The concept may have been derived from Bucer in 1536,[136] though it was introduced earlier by Andreas Osiander at the Diet of Augsburg (1530).[137] For Calvin the three offices indicated the

---

135. Calvin explained that when two substances were joined, each retained its distinctive nature. Similarly, soul did not become body nor body soul (for literature see *Institutes* 2:482n1). The Lutheran *Formula of Concord* (art. 8) noted the same examples but drew different conclusions (see above, n126).

With regard to the *persons* of the Trinity, Calvin appears to have followed the Augustinian tradition of Aquinas's relational understanding. Aquinas defined divine personhood in terms of "realities subsisting in the divine nature [*res subsistentes in divina natura*]" (author's translation of *Summa Theologiae* 1a, 30, 1 from *Summa Theologiae* 6, ed. and trans. Ceslaus Veleck [New York: Blackfriars, 1965], 64–65; cf. Denys Turner, *Thomas Aquinas: A Portrait* [New Haven, CT: Yale University Press, 2013], 126–31). To Calvin, *person* meant "a 'subsistence' in God's essence, which, while related to the others is distinguished by an incommunicable quality [*Personam igitur voco subsistentiam in Dei essentia, quae ad alios relata, proprietate incommunicabili distinguitur*]" (*Institutes* 1.13.6, trans. Battles; Latin, *Opera Selecta*, ed. P. Barth and W. Niesel [Munich: Kaiser, 1957], 3:116).

A modern version is the contention of Karl Rahner: "The one God subsists in three distinct manners of subsisting. . . . The Father, the Son, and Spirit are the one God each in a different manner of subsisting and in this sense we may count 'three' in God" (*The Trinity*, trans. Joseph Donceel [New York: Crossroad, [1970], 2010], 113–14).

136. *Institutes* 1:495n7.

137. The following citation from Osiander is taken from Wolfhart Pannenberg, *Jesus—God and Man*, trans. Lewis L. Wilkins and Duane A. Priebe (London: SCM, 1968), 213. "Since Christ

divine *purpose* conferred on Christ and the benefits they extended to believers through his work in communicating the knowledge of God and bestowing redemption.

The divinity of Christ was "demonstrated by his miracles" (1.13.13). Prophets and apostles performed miracles by their God-given gifts. Christ's miracles "showed forth his own power." The *Prefatory Address to King Francis*, to whom the first edition of the *Institutes* was dedicated, gave a preview of conflicts that were to come. Catholic opponents had complained about the novelty of Reformed teaching. They insisted that God had not forsaken his ancient church. As proof they drew attention to continuing miracles in the Catholic Church. Calvin replied that they were like the ancient Donatists, who overwhelmed the simplicity of the multitudes with "the battering ram" of miraculous claims. Calvin saw himself as a second Augustine who met their claims with Christ's warning that false prophets would come with signs and wonders that would deceive (if possible) the elect (Matt 24:24). Similarly Paul warned against sins and lying wonders of the Antichrist (2 Thess 2:9). But the true church was not lacking in miracles—those of Christ in Scripture. Catholic claims were "sheer delusions of Satan," performed to lead astray (Deut 13:2–6). It does not seem to have occurred to Calvin that Deuteronomy 13:2–6 may have been the basis of charges against Jesus in his lifetime.[138] Calvin's skirmish over the evidential role of miracles was merely the opening round of controversy that would rage long after his death.

Controversy with Lutherans centered on a different issue. Lutheranism was characterized by the view that the incarnation showed that the finite was capable of the infinite (*finitum capax infiniti*). Christ's humanity participated in the divine attributes. Calvinism rejected this proposal,

---

thus is called an Anointed One and only the prophets, kings, and high priests were anointed, one notes well that all three of these offices rightly belong to him: the prophetic office, since he alone is our teacher and master, Matt. 23:8ff.; the office of the king, since he reigns forever after the order of Melchizedek, Ps. 110:4. Thus it is his office that he is our wisdom, righteousness, sanctification, and redemption, as Paul testifies in I Cor., ch. 1."

Pannenberg was doubtful about the derivation of the prophetic office from Jesus' anointing, and about whether Jesus acted like a prophet in the Old Testament sense. Subsequently he acknowledged the "typological significance" of the threefold offices in theological tradition (*Systematic Theology*, trans. Geoffrey W. Bromiley [Grand Rapids: Eerdmans, 1994], 2:446–47).

Josephus recorded that John Hyrcanus enjoyed "three of the greatest privileges": rule of the nation, the office of high priest, and the gift of prophecy (*Ant.* 13.300). The observation suggests that this combination of gifts was deemed remarkable in Second Temple Judaism.

138. The question is not raised in the *Prefatory Address* (*Institutes*, 17–18) or discussion of the Beelzebul charge in *Harmony*, 1:33–53.

maintaining that the finite was not capable of the infinite (*finitum non est capax infiniti*). The debate extended to the cosmic functions of the Word during the incarnation. The Lutheran Johann Brenz insisted that Jesus exercised these functions as God and man, albeit in a hidden way (*krypsis*). Calvinists believed that the Word exercised them independently of Jesus' humanity. Calvin argued that it was "absurd" to imagine that the Word of God was

> confined within the narrow prison of an earthly body. This is mere impudence! For even if the Word in his immeasurable essence united with the nature of one person, we do not imagine that he was contained therein. Here is something marvelous: the Son of God descended from heaven in such a way that, without leaving heaven, he willed to be borne in the virgin's womb, to go about on earth, and to hang upon the cross; yet he continuously filled the world even as he had done from the beginning! (2.13.4)

The issue came to be called the *extra Calvinisticum*, the Calvinistic extra, a term of disrespect coined by Lutherans.[139] *The Formula of Concord* adopted a mitigated form of *krypsis* to explain the Lutheran understanding of the role of the two natures of Christ.[140] The Reformed Church set out its alternative in *The Heidelberg Catechism*.[141] To readers not familiar

---

139. Muller, *Dictionary of Greek and Latin Theological Terms*, 111.

140. Article 8 explained that this limited form of *krypsis* depended on Christ's will. "[16] 11. According to the personal union he always possessed this majesty. But in the state of humiliation he dispensed with it and could therefore truly increase in age, wisdom, and favor with God and men [Luke 2:52], for he did not always disclose this majesty, but only when it pleased him. Finally, after his resurrection he laid aside completely the form of a slave [Phil. 2:7] (not the human nature) and was established in the full use, revelation, and manifestation of his divine majesty" (Pelikan and Hotchkiss, eds., *Creeds and Confessions of Faith in the Christian Tradition*, 2:192; cf. the Antitheses [36–38] 17–19, 2:194).

141. The Reformed Church rejected the view that incarnation implied that Jesus' human nature was a kind of receptacle or container, which set limits on the divine presence and activity. It found expression in the Heidelberg Catechism (1563). Question 48 posed the question, "But are not the two natures in Christ separated from each other . . . if the humanity is not wherever the divinity is?" The answer was, "Not at all; for if the divinity is incomprehensible and everywhere present, it must follow that the divinity is indeed beyond the bounds of the humanity which it has assumed, and is nonetheless ever in that humanity as well, and remains personally united to it" (Pelikan and Hotchkiss, eds., *Creeds and Confessions of Faith in the Christian Tradition*, 2:438; cf. Calvin, *Institutes* 2.13.4).

See further E. David Willis, *Calvin's Catholic Christology: The Function of the So-Called Extra Calvinisticum in Calvin's Theology*, Studies in Medieval and Reformed Thought 2 (Leiden: Brill, 1966); Geoffrey W. Bromiley, "The Reformers and the Humanity of Christ," in *Perspectives on*

with the controversy, the whole debate may seem obscure and remote. But to those committed to orthodox doctrines of the personal divinity of Jesus, the issue was crucial. It turns on the question of how to think of divine attributes of the second person of the Trinity—omnipotence, omniscience, and omnipresence—together with his cosmic functions during the period of the incarnation. The question resurfaced in the nineteenth century with the proposal that kenosis—emptying or non-use of divine attributes—helped to envisage Jesus as a historical person. Conservatives objected that kenosis undermined Jesus' divinity. In the twentieth century conservatives appealed to kenosis and krypsis as ways of preserving orthodoxy. We shall examine the debates in later chapters.

4. Vermes Revisited

At the beginning of this chapter we noted Geza Vermes's critique of orthodoxy in *Christian Beginnings: From Nazareth to Nicaea*. Christian orthodoxy transformed Jesus from a charismatic Galilean prophet into a figure of intellectual religion, defined and regulated by dogma. Vermes covered the ground discussed above in §2 on "The Formation of Orthodoxies." I leave readers to make their own comparisons. In closing this chapter, I offer some observations on Vermes's construct of the historical Jesus.

The research foundations for Vermes's view of Jesus were laid in two scholarly investigations. The first was an article on the meaning of the term Son of Man in Aramaic.[142] Vermes laid out a convincing argument

---

Christology: Essays in Honor of Paul K. Jewett, ed. Marguerite Shuster and Richard Muller (Grand Rapids: Zondervan, 1991), 79–104, especially 99–100.

The *extra Calvinisticum* appears to have been anticipated by Cyril of Alexandria in a passage from his Third Letter to Nestorius (430 CE), which led to the Council of Ephesus the following year. "We declare that the flesh was not changed into the nature of the Godhead and that neither was the inexpressible nature of God the Word converted into the nature of flesh. He is, indeed, utterly unchangeable and immutable, ever remaining, as the Bible says, the same; even when a baby whose swaddling clothes at the bosom of the Virgin who bore him, he still filled the whole creation as God and was co-regent with his sire—for deity is measureless, sizeless and admits of no bounds.... No, he was actually united with flesh, without being changed into it, and brought about the sort of residence in it which a man's soul can be said to have in relation to its body" (Cyril of Alexandria, *Select Letters*, ed. and trans. Lionel R. Wickham, Oxford Early Christian Texts [Oxford: Clarendon, 1983], 17–19).

142. Geza Vermes, "The Use of *bar nas/bar nasa* in Jewish Aramaic," in an appendix to Matthew Black, *An Aramaic Approach to the Gospels and Acts* (Oxford: Oxford University Press, 1946; 3rd ed., 1967), 310–28.

that *bar-nas* (son of man) in Aramaic literature was an alternative way for saying "I." The second contained detailed research into rabbinic literature concerning the first-century figure of Hanina ben Dosa.[143] Vermes saw him as a Galilean charismatic miracle worker who shared common characteristics with Jesus of Nazareth. These two pieces of research provided the foundations for much of what may be described as a Jewish one-man quest of the historical Jesus.

Jesus the Jew: A Historian's Reading of the Gospels (1973; 2nd ed., 1981) was prompted by two contradictory pictures that Vermes found in the New Testament. On the one hand, the Synoptic Gospels portrayed a Jewish holy man of the first century who was a preacher, healer, and exorcist. This Jesus delivered moral exhortations concerning the impending arrival of the kingdom of God. On the other hand, John and Paul depicted Jesus as an otherworldly savior.

The Jesus of history was "neither the Christ of the Church, nor the apostate bogey-man of Jewish popular tradition." He fitted Vermes's profile of the holy man (*Hasid*) and "man of deed" (miracle worker). This profile was shaped by Honi the rainmaker (d. 65 BCE), who was reputed to have drawn a circle that he refused to leave until God gave rain (*m. Ta'an.* 3:8). Even more important was Jesus' younger contemporary, the Galilean charismatic Hanina ben Dosa.[144]

The Hanina tradition of charismatic Judaism was modeled on the northern miracle-working prophets Elijah and Elisha. Hanina ben Dosa was a man of prayer, renowned for successfully interceding for the sick, even at a distance, and helping the needy.

The earliest strand is found in the Mishnah, where Hanina is reputed to have said that fluency in reciting the Tefillah intercession for the sick was a sign that God would answer his prayer favorably. Otherwise the afflicted would die (*m. Ber.* 5:5). Hanina was described as a "man of deed," the last of the line of miracle workers in Judaism (*m. Sotah* 9:15; cf. Luke 24:19). Moral maxims attributed to him displayed warmhearted piety (*'Abot* 3:9–10). Talmudic tradition embellished his memory, elevated him to the status of rabbi, and avoided reporting any clash with rabbinic Judaism. Scholarship after Vermes regularly designated Jesus and Hanina

---

143. "Hanina ben Dosa," *Journal of Jewish Studies* 23 (1972): 28–50; 24 (1974): 51–64; reprinted in Vermes, *Post-Biblical Jewish Studies*, SJLA 8 (Leiden: Brill, 1978), 214.

144. Vermes, *Jesus the Jew: A Historian's Reading of the Gospels* (London: Collins, 1973; 2nd ed., Philadelphia: Fortress, 1981), 58–82.

Evolution of Orthodoxy

ben Dosa as examples of the same type of Galilean *Hasidim*, who because of their familiarity with God were designated sons of God.[145]

Vermes challenged previous interpretations of the title *Son of Man*. It was not a title of rank that Jesus used to designate himself. It was nowhere attested as a title in Aramaic writings of the relevant period. Rather, it was an Aramaic circumlocution, which a speaker might use to avoid either a taboo subject or to avoid sounding boastful.[146]

Vermes found it "noteworthy" that Josephus's reference to Jesus as a "wise man" (σοφὸς ἀνήρ) and "performer of marvelous deeds" (παραδόξων ἔργων ποιητής) "fitted so well into the historical context" that he had constructed.[147] The citations come from a passage known as the *Testimonium Flavianum*, which is generally regarded as a piece of Christianized editing, making it seem that Josephus confessed Jesus as the Messiah. Vermes dismissed the Christian rewriting, leaving a substratum of genuine text.

Scholars are divided over whether Josephus took a positive view of Jesus (along the lines of Vermes) or whether the passage was an ironic dismissal.[148] On the latter reading, Jesus ranked among the sophists, wonder workers, and troublemakers whose activities led to the war with Rome.[149] The *Testimonium* may serve as external evidence of Jesus' existence as well as the circumstances of his death. Josephus added that "Pilate on hearing him accused by men of the highest standing amongst us, had him condemned to be crucified" (*Ant.* 18.64). The importance that Josephus attached to Jesus was minimal compared with the story he proceeded to relate with considerable relish of the seduction in the temple of Isis in Rome of the lady Paulina by Decius Mundus, who posed as a god (*Ant.* 18.65–80).

Jesus the Jew was followed by *Jesus and the World of Judaism* (1983; republished as *Jesus in His Jewish Context*, 2003) and *The Religion of Jesus the Jew* (1993). Together the books form a trilogy representing not a scholarly consensus or comprehensive engagement with other scholars but "one man's reading of the Synoptic Gospels." These sources "to some extent at least, recount history" in reporting "the life and message of Jesus," and

---

145. *Jesus the Jew*, 206–10.
146. *Jesus the Jew*, 160–91.
147. *Jesus the Jew*, 79; cf. Josephus, *Ant.* 18.3.
148. Robert E. Van Voorst, *Jesus outside the New Testament: An Introduction to the Ancient Evidence* (Grand Rapids: Eerdmans, 2000), 81–104.
149. Rebecca Gray, *Prophetic Figures in Late Second Temple Jewish Palestine: The Evidence from Josephus* (Oxford: Oxford University Press, 1993).

were "unaffected by accretions deriving from the creative imagination of nascent Christianity." However, the resurrection and parousia were attributable to the doctrinal and apologetic needs of the early church.[150]

Jesus in His Jewish Context took the occasion to rebut criticisms of his earlier interpretations of the Son of Man and of Josephus, adducing examples from Josephus where the same vocabulary was used in a nonderogatory way, reiterating his view that "Josephus deliberately chose his words reflecting a not unsympathetic neutral stand." At the same time, Vermes disowned the Talmudic portrait of Jesus the magician (*b. Sanhedrin* 43b).[151]

The Religion of Jesus the Jew began by examining Jesus in relation to the Judaism of his age: his faithful interpretation of the law; his charismatic authority; and his use of proverbs and parables. Vermes then turned to the idea of God as King and Father in light of Jesus' eschatological enthusiasm and finally to Jesus "the religious man." Jesus' religion was "authentically Jewish" but displayed "specific features partly attributable to the eschatological-apocalyptic spirit which permeated the age in which he lived, and partly, on the subjective level, to his own turn of mind."[152] Believing that the kingdom of God was imminent and that very little time remained, Jesus urged Israelites to "seek first the kingdom" and amend their lives in unconditional repentance and faithfulness to the Torah. Jesus died for having done the wrong thing (causing a commotion), at the wrong place (in the temple), at the wrong time (just before the Passover). His death was a tragedy. His faithfulness held firm until the terrible moment when Jesus realized that God had abandoned him (Mark 15:34). Despite this overwhelming blow, his followers were soon convinced that Jesus had been raised, not least by their success as healers, preachers, and exorcists in his name. Fortified by the genius of Paul of Tarsus, they awaited Jesus' return in glory.[153] As the door was closed on Vermes's trilogy on the historical Jewish Jesus, another door opened on a new series of books by Vermes on Jesus' posthumous fortunes in what became known as Christianity.[154]

---

150. Geza Vermes, *Jesus in His Jewish Context* (London: SCM; Minneapolis: Fortress, 2003), 14–26.
151. Vermes, *Jesus in His Jewish Context*, 80–98.
152. Geza Vermes, *The Religion of Jesus the Jew* (London: SCM, 1993), 184.
153. Vermes, *The Religion of Jesus the Jew*, 207.
154. Later books include Geza Vermes, *The Changing Faces of Jesus* (London: Lane; Penguin, 2000); Vermes, *The Passion* (London: Lane; Penguin, 2005); Vermes, *The Nativity: History*

Vermes provoked considerable interest among scholars and the wider world in understanding Jesus in his Jewish context. However, Vermes's peers in the research of early Judaism have raised questions about bracketing Jesus with Hanina ben Dosa as members of a common type of Galilean wonder-working charismatic holy man. David Flusser (1917–2000), the eminent Jewish scholar who taught early Christianity and Judaism at the Hebrew University in Jerusalem, highly valued the comparison of Jesus with Hanina ben Dosa and Honi. As members of God's household, it was natural that all three should be regarded as "sons" and that they should address God as "Father." However, "If Jesus was like a son to God, this denoted more than the mere sonship of the miracle-workers. For him, sonship was also the consequence of his election through the heavenly voice at his baptism."[155] The "jubilation" that Jesus experienced (Matt 11:25–27) was comparable with Essene hymn writing.

Séan Freyne (1935–2013), professor of theology and director of Mediterranean and Near Eastern studies at Trinity College, Dublin, expressed doubt about the role that Vermes assigned to Hanina ben Dosa.[156] He cited Jacob Neusner and his school as representatives of a more exacting methodology. Freyne questioned the conflation of Hanina as a "man of deed" (miracle worker) with the *hasid* (holy man)—categories that were kept separate in the description of Hanina in connection with other great figures (*m. Sotah* 9:15). Hellenistic Judaism downplayed the role of miracles, which in Hanina's case were linked with answers to prayer rather than to personal miraculous endowment. His reputation as a teacher rests on scant evidence. The stories told in the Babylonian

---

and Legend (New York: Doubleday, 2006); Vermes, *The Resurrection: History and Myth* (New York: Doubleday, 2008); Vermes, *The Real Jesus: Then and Now* (Minneapolis: Fortress, 2010); Vermes, *Jesus in the Jewish World* (London: SCM, 2010); Vermes, *The True Herod* (London: T&T Clark, 2014).

155. David Flusser, *Jesus* (Jerusalem: Magness; Hebrew University, Jerusalem, 1968; revised in collaboration with R. Steven Notley, 1997), 119.

156. Séan Freyne, "The Charismatic," in *Ideal Figures in Ancient Judaism: Profiles and Paradigms*, ed. John J. Collins and George W. E. Nickelsburg, Septuagint and Cognate Studies Series 12 (Chico, CA: Scholars, 1980), 223–58. In his posthumously published *The Jesus Movement and Its Expansion: Meaning and Mission* (Grand Rapids: Eerdmans, 2014) Freyne noted Vermes's interpretation of *bar 'enash* (son of man) (147n25). He also noted the "counter-position" of Adela Yarbro Collins, "The Influence of Daniel in the New Testament," in John J. Collins, *Daniel: A Commentary on the Book of Daniel*, Hermeneia (Minneapolis: Fortress, 1993), 90–112. See also *The Jesus Movement*, 168–76, where Freyne discussed the role of the disciples together with Jesus in the Gospel interpretations of Dan 7:13.

and Palestinian Talmuds are not found in the Mishnah. Nor could Honi be classified under the same category. There is no significant evidence that Hanina led a group of wandering charismatic healers or gathered a community with eschatological expectations.

It remains to be said that there is no record of Hanina ben Dosa leading others astray from the Torah. In that respect, he was utterly different from Jesus of Nazareth, who from the early days of his public activity was accused of being possessed by Beelzebub.

Looking back on the evolution of orthodoxy, two twentieth-century comments deserve attention. The first is a remark made by Albert Schweitzer in the opening chapter of *The Quest of the Historical Jesus*. It gives his assessment of the impact of the Council of Chalcedon and why he thought that the quest of the historical Jesus was so long in coming.

> When at Chalcedon the West overcame the East, its doctrine of the two natures dissolved the unity of the personality of Jesus, and thereby cut off the possibility of a return to the historical Jesus. The contradiction was elevated into a law. But the manhood was so far admitted as to preserve in appearance, the rights of history. Thus by a deception the formula kept the life prisoner and prevented the leading spirits of the Reformation from grasping the idea of a return to the historical Jesus.[157]

The second comment was made some forty years later by the Scottish theologian D. M. Baillie in *God Was in Christ* (1948). The book surveyed the contemporary scene, examining a vast array of scholars, including Baillie's mentors and personal friends—among them Barth, Brunner, and Bultmann.

> It has always, indeed, been of the essence of Christian orthodoxy to make Jesus wholly human as well as wholly divine, and in the stories of the controversies which issued in the first four General Councils it is impressive to see the Church contending as resolutely for His full humanity as His full divinity. But the Church was building better than it knew, and its ecumenical decisions were wiser than its

---

157. Albert Schweitzer, *The Quest of the Historical Jesus*, 1st complete ed., ed. John Bowden (London: SCM, 2000; Minneapolis: Fortress, 2001), 5.

individual theologians in this matter. Or should we rather say that it did not fully realize the implications of declaring that in respect of his human nature Christ is consubstantial with ourselves?[158]

Schweitzer and Baillie represented diametrically opposed viewpoints. The chapters that follow are devoted to conflicts that arose from the commitments described by Schweitzer and Baillie.

---

158. D. M. Baillie, *God Was in Christ: An Essay on Incarnation and Atonement* (London: Faber and Faber; New York: Scribner's, 1948), 11.

CHAPTER 3

POST-REFORMATION ALTERNATIVES

THE SIXTEENTH CENTURY saw the emergence of two main streams of the Protestant Reformation. The Magisterial Reformation comprised the legally recognized churches that enjoyed the backing of governments—in Europe the Lutheran, Reformed, and Calvinist Churches. In England their counterpart was the Church of England, also known as the Anglican Church.[1] These churches were the progenitors of many of the denominations that today are called "mainline." Scripture was the supreme authority, but alongside reform they also stressed continuity with the church of the first four centuries. Generally, they embraced the christological formulations of the ecumenical councils. As the Anglican Articles of 1571 put it, the three Creeds—the Nicene, the Athanasian, and "that which is commonly called the Apostles' Creed"—"ought thoroughly to be received and believed; for they can be proved by the most certain warrants of Holy Scripture" (article 8; cf. articles 20–21 on the authority of the church and general councils).[2]

The more heterogeneous Radical Reformation embraced diverse

---

1. H. J. Hillerbrand, *The Reformation in Its Own Words* (New York: Harper & Row; London: SCM, 1964), 298–371; David Bagchi and David C. Steinmetz, eds., *The Cambridge Companion to the Reformation* (Cambridge: Cambridge University Press, 2004), 150–93.
2. Jaroslav Pelikan and Valerie Hotchkiss, eds., *Creeds and Confessions of Faith in the Christian Tradition*, vol. 2, *Creeds and Confessions of the Reformation Era* (New Haven, CT: Yale University Press, 2003), 525–40, here 530–31.

forms of belief and polity.[3] It included varieties of Anabaptists, who sought to restore the life and beliefs of the New Testament church, including believers' baptism. It also included millenarian movements and those who contended that the Magisterial Reformation did not go far enough, especially where the Trinity and Jesus were concerned. In the background was the revival of ancient skepticism known as Pyrrhonism, which actually predated the Reformation.

Christological criticism took two main forms: criticism of orthodox interpretation of Scripture, and skepticism about miracles and prophecy and their foundational role in belief systems. What follows is a selective, personal overview. It comes with two caveats. First, the order in which topics are reviewed is partly chronological, but also partly thematic. Some of the issues date from the lifetime of Calvin. Second, this chapter should be read in conjunction with the review of deism in the next chapter. The issues discussed in these two chapters were entwined.

1. Voices of Dissent
    1.1. Servetus and the Trinity
    1.2. The Arminian Controversy
2. Anti-Trinitarianism
    2.1. Socinianism
    2.2. The Spread of Unitarianism
3. Revival of the Arian Controversy
    3.1. Newton
    3.2. Whiston
    3.3. Clarke
4. The Rise of Skepticism
    4.1. Descartes and Pyrrhonism
    4.2. Pascal and Pyrrhonism
5. Skepticism, Belief, and Society
    5.1. Hobbes
    5.2. Spinoza
    5.3. Locke
    5.4. Hume

---

3. George H. Williams, *The Radical Reformation* (Philadelphia: Westminster; London: Weidenfeld and Nicolson, 1962; 3rd ed. Kirksville, MO: Sixteenth Century Journal, 1992); Hillerbrand, *The Reformation in Its Own Words*, 214–97.

1. Voices of Dissent

This section is devoted to two issues. Both were concerned with what might be called Protestant metanarratives—the identity and role of Jesus and God's saving activity in the world. The first issue is the claim of Michael Servetus that orthodox Christianity misunderstood and misrepresented the language of Scripture with regard to the Trinity and Jesus. The second issue centers on the Calvinist understanding of divine activity and God's eternal purposes for humankind. Neither of these issues involved investigation of the *historical* Jesus. Rather, they were concerned with *theological* interpretations of his role. They are included here as part of the history of interpretation.

1.1. Servetus and the Trinity. The case of the polymath Michael Servetus (c. 1511–1553) was the most notorious but by no means unique instance of questioning the Trinity and the divinity of Jesus.[4] A native of Spain, Servetus became convinced that the doctrine of the Trinity needed restating if the church were to make any headway with Moors and Jews. In 1531 Servetus launched the first of his salvos, *Concerning the Errors of the Trinity*.

Servetus's opening argument reveals a mind acutely aware of critical issues embedded in formulations regarding the Trinity, but at the same time it was precritical in its affirmations about Jesus as the Son of God. Servetus's outlook—like that of the Socinians and the latter-day Arians—seems to owe more to his respect for the authority of Scripture than to incipient rationalism. Servetus's comments suggest a revival of Modalism insofar as the man Jesus, the Son, was the mode of the Father's self-revelation.

> Any discussion of the Trinity should start with the man. That Jesus, surnamed Christ, was not a hypostasis but a human being is taught both by the early fathers and in the Scriptures, taken in their literal sense, and is indicated by the miracles that he wrought. He, and not the Word, is also the miraculously born Son of God in fleshly form, as the Scriptures teach—not a hypostasis, but an actual Son.

---

4. Others included Martin Cellarius (1499–1564), Bernardino Ochino (1487–1564), and Juan de Valdés (c. 1490–1541); cf. Earl Morse Wilbur, *A History of Unitarianism: Socinianism and Its Antecedents* (Cambridge, MA: Harvard University Press 1945).

He is God sharing God's divinity in full, and the theory of a communicatio idiomatum is a confusing sophistical quibble. This does not imply two gods, but only a double use of the term God, as is clear from the Hebrew use of the term. Christ, being one with God the Father, equal in power, came down from heaven and assumed flesh as a man. In short, all the Scriptures speak of Christ as a man.

The doctrine of the Holy Spirit as a third separate being lands us in practical tritheism no better than atheism, even though the unity of God be insisted upon. Careful interpretation of the usual proof-texts shows that they teach not a union of three beings in one, but a harmony between them. The Holy Spirit as a third person of the Godhead is unknown in Scripture. It is not a separate being, but an activity of God himself. The doctrine of the Trinity can neither be established by logic nor proved from Scripture, and is in fact inconceivable. . . .

Jesus taught that he himself was the Son of God. Numerous heresies have sprung from this philosophy, and fruitless questions have arisen out of it. Worst of all, the doctrine of the Trinity incurs the ridicule of the Mohammedans and the Jews. It arose out of Greek philosophy rather than the belief that Jesus is the Son of God; and he will be with the Church only if it keeps his teaching.[5]

What followed was a minute examination of biblical texts, interspersed with occasional patristic references. Servetus ended with an appeal to the Fourth Gospel. He reiterated his premise:

God is in all ways incomprehensible, unimaginable; nor can we form any conception of God unless he adapts himself to us under some form which we are capable of perceiving; and this the Master shows to us in John v. 37. . . . The divine being came to be flesh, and we have seen him, and he has given us a mind to know him, and

---

5. M. Servetus, *Concerning the Errors of the Trinity*, cited from *The Two Treatises of Servetus on the Trinity: On the Errors of the Trinity Seven Books, A.D. MCXXXI; Dialogues on the Trinity Two Books; On the Righteousness of Christ's Kingdom Four Chapters*, trans. Earl Morse Wilbur, HTS 16 (Cambridge, MA: Harvard University Press; London: Oxford University Press, 1932; repr., Eugene, OR: Wipf & Stock, 2013), 3 (italics used in the text). For further background, see Williams, *The Radical Reformation*; Hillerbrand, *The Reformation in Its Own Words* (New York: Harper & Row; London: SCM, 1964), 214–97; see also extracts from Servetus and texts relating to his execution on pp. 273–97.

the Father through him, to whom be glory and dominion forever, Amen, Amen, ever world without end. Selah.[6]

The following year Servetus repeated his attack in the form of the much briefer but no less tenacious *Dialogues on the Trinity*. For nearly a decade Servetus, the controversialist, retired from the public eye. He reemerged as a respected physician in the French city of Lyons with the name of Michael de Villeneuve. The name was adapted from *Villanovanus*, which he had earlier used in Paris, where he had studied medicine. In the meantime, having obtained copies of Calvin's writings, Servetus embarked on a lengthy exchange of letters with the Geneva Reformer.[7]

Convinced that he could win over Calvin to his way of thinking, Servetus sent drafts of his own *Christianismi Restitutio*, "Restoration of Christianity," which he conceived as a correction of Calvin's *Institutio Christianae Religionis*. Weary of the correspondence and reluctant to devote an entire book to answering Servetus, Calvin sent him a copy of his *Institutes*. Convinced of his destiny to fight under the Archangel Michael for the restoration of the church from Antichrist, Servetus published his *Christianismi Restitutio* (1553).[8] He arranged for its sale in several towns in France, Italy, and Germany, as well as Geneva. Calvin possessed a copy, perhaps a gift from the author.

In Vienne, Servetus's identity was discovered accidentally, and the Catholic Inquisition in Lyons took prompt action. But before proceedings were completed, Servetus escaped. He was convicted *in absentia*, and the inquisition had to satisfy itself by burning his effigy. En route to Italy, Servetus was apprehended in Geneva. He was tried on a number of charges, including blasphemy and attempting to destroy the foundations of Christianity.[9] The court felt that it could not pass a lesser sentence than that of the Catholic Inquisition.[10] Calvin's role was that of an expert witness. He urged a less agonizing form of execution than burning.

---

6. Servetus, *Concerning the Errors of the Trinity*, 184.

7. Servetus, *Thirty Letters to Calvin, Preacher to the Genevans; and Sixty Signs of the Kingdom of the Antichrist Which Is Now at Hand*, trans. Christopher A. Hoffman and Marian Hiller (Lewiston, NY; Queenston, ON: Mellen, 2010).

8. Servetus, *The Restoration of Christianity*, trans. Christopher A. Hoffman and Marian Hiller (Lewiston, NY; Queenston, ON: Mellen, 2007).

9. Hillerbrand, *The Reformation Its Own Words*, 285–87.

10. William G. Naphy, "Calvin's Geneva," *The Cambridge Companion to John Calvin*, ed. Donald K. McKim (Cambridge: Cambridge University Press, 2004), 25–37, here 32–33.

Guillaume Farel, who accompanied Servetus to the stake, recorded that to the last Servetus refused to confess that Jesus was the eternal Son of God.[11]

1.2. The Arminian Controversy. It is a convenient—but misleading— generalization to describe all forms of European Protestantism, outside Lutheranism, as Calvinism.[12] Two other misconceptions are that Calvin was the inventor of Calvinism[13] and that Arminianism came into being as the alternative to Calvinism.

Jacobus Arminius (1560–1609)[14] was the Latinized name of the Dutch pastor and theologian Jacobus Harmenszoon, who was orphaned at an early age. Arminius became a student at the newly founded Reformed University of Leiden, which was not indifferent to Lutheran, Zwinglian, and Anabaptist views. He later studied at Geneva under Calvin's interpreter Theodore Beza with interludes at Basel and Padua. At the time Padua was the foremost Italian university, but little is known of his stay there. In 1587 he received a call to a pastorate in Amsterdam

---

11. Hillerbrand, *The Reformation in Its Own Words*, 290.

12. John T. McNeill, *The History and Character of Calvinism* (Oxford: Oxford University Press, 1954); Darryl G. Hart, *Calvinism: A History* (New Haven, CT: Yale University Press, 2013). The term *Calvinism* seems to have had a derogatory origin. It was used by Calvin's Protestant opponents at Bern in 1548, with reference to both Calvin and Farel. See Heiko Oberman, "Calvin and Farel," in *John Calvin and the Reformation of the Refugees* (Geneva: Droz, 2009), 195–222; W. Stephen Gunter, *Arminius and His Declaration of Sentiments: An Annotated Translation with Introduction and Theological Commentary* (Waco, TX: Baylor University Press, 2012), 30.

13. See especially Richard A. Muller, *Christ and the Decree: Christianity and Predestination in Reformed Theology from Calvin to Perkins*, Studies in Historical Theology 1 (Durham, NC: Labyrinth, 1986); Muller, *The Unaccommodated Calvin: Studies in the Foundation of a Theological Tradition* (Oxford: Oxford University Press, 2000); Muller, *After Calvin: Studies in the Development of a Theological Tradition* (Oxford: Oxford University Press, 2003); Muller, *Post-Reformation Reformed Dogmatics: The Rise and Development of Reformed Orthodoxy, ca. 1520 to ca. 1725*, 4 vols. (Grand Rapids: Baker Academic, 2003); *Calvin and the Reformed Tradition: On the Work of Christ and the Order of Salvation* (Grand Rapids: Baker Academic, 2012).

Muller observed, "As often noted, Calvin stands in relation to the Reformed tradition as one second-generation codifier among others, arguably the most prominent of the group if not always the primary voice.... Calvin did not originate this tradition; he was not the sole voice in its early codification; and he did not serve as the norm for its development" (*Calvin and the Reformed Tradition*, 68).

14. Carl Bangs, *Arminius: A Study in the Dutch Reformation* (1985; repr., Eugene, OR: Wipf & Stock, 1998). Bangs wrote an introduction to the edited reprint of the London edition of his writings, *The Works of Arminius*, trans. James and Williams Nichols, 3 vols. (1825–75; Grand Rapids: Baker, 1999). Recent studies include Richard A. Muller, *God, Creation, and Providence in the Thought of Jacob Arminius: Sources and Directions of Scholastic Protestantism in the Era of Early Orthodoxy* (Grand Rapids: Baker, 1991); as well as Gunter, *Arminius and His Declaration of Sentiments*; and Keith D. Stanglin and Thomas H. McCall, *Jacob Arminius: Theologian of Grace* (Oxford: Oxford University Press, 2012).

and was ordained the following year. During this period his study of Romans led him to reexamine the strict doctrine of predestination in light of Paul's teaching on justification by faith and grace. Opponents charged him with Pelagianism and teachings inconsistent with those of Calvin and Beza.

In 1603 Arminius's call to teach at Leiden brought him into bitter conflict with another Leiden professor, Franciscus Gomarus (1563–1641), over Gomarus's supralapsarianism—the view that God predestined all human beings to salvation or damnation even before the fall. Tensions soon became public, though they did not prevent the election in 1605 of Arminius as *Rector Magnificus* of Leiden University. However, the appointment made him a more conspicuous target for his enemies. Fears of heresy led to Synods of North and South Holland to require ministers to expound the Heidelberg Catechism every Sunday afternoon. Mounting tension led to both Arminius and Gomarus making oral presentations to the High Court of the States of Holland at The Hague. Subsequently, they were asked to make written submissions. Arminius requested that he might appear again and also put his argument in writing. His request was granted, and on October 30, 1608, Arminius delivered in Dutch his oral statement, accompanied by his written submission.

The written version was subsequently published in Latin as *Declaratio Sententiae de Predestinatione*. The English translation of the title, *Declaration of Sentiments*, is perhaps misleading. Today the word *sentiments* (which was lacking in the original submission) suggests an emotional outpouring. However, among the meanings of the Latin *sententia* are "opinion" and "judgment." In Arminius's title *sententiae* is the genitive singular case. *Sententia* (the nominative singular) later appeared in the Latin title of the Canons of Dort: *Sententia, de Divina Predestinatione, et Annexis ei Capitibus*.[15] What Arminius presented to the States General was his considered *opinion*—a concise, factual review of the controversy, his understanding of predestination, and of the issues at stake. The *Declaratio Sententiae de Predestinatione* amounted to a written deposition presented to the States General, accompanying his oral presentation, on the subject of predestination.

---

15. Philip Schaff, ed., *Creeds of Christendom* (Grand Rapids: Eerdmans, 1877; repr., Grand Rapids: Baker, 1977), 3:551. *Sententia* was also used in the Socinian controversy to denote a judgment or point of view.

Arminius began by reviewing recent history of the controversy and his own involvement. He then turned to the central issue of predestination, "the election of some to salvation and the reprobation of others to damnation."[16] Although some members of the Dutch churches and the University of Leiden taught this doctrine, there was no consistent uniform opinion. The doctrine had never been affirmed by a general council and was not in the Belgic Confession[17] and Heidelberg Catechism,[18] which offered no support.[19] Arminius proceeded to examine the malign

---

16. Gunter, *Arminius and His Declaration of Sentiments*, 103.

17. The Belgic Confession (1561) and the Heidelberg Catechism (1563) constituted the articles of faith of the Reformed Church in the Netherlands. They were composed against the background of the Council of Trent (1545–63), which was in its final stages of formulating the Catholic response to the Protestant Reformation.

The term *Belgic* alludes to the Low Countries (Belgium and Holland), which formed part of the monarchy inherited by Philip II (1502–67), the king of Spain, in 1556. The principal author of the Belgic Confession was Guido de Brès, who composed the original version in French. A copy was presented to King Philip in the hope of securing toleration. The text stressed continuity with the early church as well as the distinctive emphases of the Reformed Church. Its thirty-seven articles outlined Reformed theology regarding Scripture, sin, election, incarnation, justification, church, sacraments, civil government, and the last judgment.

Spanish Hapsburg rule continued until the unification of the northern provinces recognized by the treaty known as the Union of Utrecht (1579). In 1581 the United Provinces declared their independence. The Twelve Years Truce (1609) effectively marked the end of Spanish claims.

For Latin text, see *Bekenntnisschriften und Kirchenordnungen der nach Gottes Wort reformierten Kirche*, ed. Wilhelm Niesel, 3rd ed. (Zollikon-Zürich: Evangelischer, 1938), 119–36. For English translation, see Pelikan and Hotchkiss, eds., *Creeds and Confessions of Faith in the Christian Tradition*, 2:405–26.

18. The Heidelberg Catechism (1563) was commissioned by Frederick III, elector of the Palatinate. Frederick was a Lutheran with Reformed leanings who wanted to assert biblical teaching in what was a strongly Lutheran enclave within the primarily Catholic Holy Roman Empire. Heidelberg, situated near the confluence of the Neckar and the Rhine, was the capital of the Palatinate and site of the oldest German university (founded 1386). The principal author of the Catechism was Caspar Olevianus, though its introduction credited the entire university faculty with authorship.

The Catechism consisted of 129 questions, divided into three main parts: (1) "Man's Misery," (2) "Man's Redemption," and (3) "Thankfulness." The questions were arranged in fifty-two sections called "Lord's Days," so that they could be taught consecutively on fifty-two Sundays of the year. The Heidelberg Catechism is regarded as the most pastoral and enduring of the Protestant confessions.

The practice of catechetical preaching began in the early days of the Reformation in Luther's Wittenberg and Calvin's Geneva, and the Reformed Church in the Netherlands adopted the practice in the late sixteenth century. A synod in The Hague (1586) recommended that pastors explain Christian doctrine as set out in the Heidelberg Catechism on Sundays in the afternoon sermon.

German text in *Bekenntnisschriften*, 149–81. English translation in Pelikan and Hotchkiss, eds., *Creeds and Confessions of Faith in the Christian Tradition*, 2:427–57. The 450th anniversary of the Catechism was celebrated in the comprehensive survey *Power of Faith—450 Years of the Heidelberg Catechism*, ed. Karla Apperloo-Boersma and Herman J. Selderhuis (Göttingen: Vandenhoeck & Ruprecht, 2013).

19. Gunter, *Arminius and His Declaration of Sentiments*, 112. Arminius examined articles 14 and 16 of the Belgic Confession and questions 20 and 54 of the Heidelberg Catechism, which were the passages most likely to discuss predestination.

Post-Reformation Alternatives

character of double predestination.[20] Double predestination was repugnant to the nature of God and in conflict with both human nature and creation. It was injurious to the glory of God, dishonorable to Christ, and a misrepresentation of the gospel.

Arminius then turned to his own understanding of predestination. It was based on four divine decrees.

I. The first specific and absolute decree regarding the salvation of sinful humanity: God decreed to appoint his Son, Jesus Christ, as Mediator, Redeemer, Savior, Priest and King in order that he might destroy sin by his own death, so that by his obedience he might obtain the salvation of the lost through disobedience, and by his power communicate this salvation.

II. In the second precise and absolute decree, God decided graciously to accept those who repent and believe in Christ, and for Christ's sake and through him to effect the final salvation of penitents and believers who persevere to the end in their faith. Simultaneously God decreed to leave in sin and under divine wrath all impenitent persons and unbelievers, damning them as alienated from Christ.

III. The third divine decree: God decided to administer in a sufficient and efficacious manner the means necessary for repentance and faith—this being accomplished according to divine wisdom, by which God knows what is proper and becoming both to his mercy and severity. And all this proceeds according to divine justice, by which God is prepared to adopt whatever his wisdom may prescribe and carry out.

IV. From these decrees the fourth proceeds, by which God decreed to save and to damn certain particular persons. This decree has its foundation in divine foreknowledge, through which God has known from all eternity those individuals who through the established means of his prevenient grace would persevere in faith. Likewise, in divine foreknowledge, God knew those who would not believe and persevere.[21]

---

20. Gunter, *Arminius and His Declaration of Sentiments*, 113–35.
21. Gunter, *Arminius and His Declaration of Sentiments*, 135.

Arminius went on to list twenty propositions arising from his view of predestination, and to enlarge upon the subjects of divine providence, free will, grace, perseverance, the divinity of the Son, and justification. His discussion seems designed to preempt charges of heresy. Arminius concluded with a call for a national synod to review the situation. If the synod judged that the Belgic Confession required amendment, the Dutch churches had the authority to do so. But since the Heidelberg Catechism belonged to the wider church, Arminius suggested that—if his interpretation of the divine decrees was judged inconsistent with it—submission to it should not be mandatory.[22]

The States General accepted Arminius's case and judged that he was within the parameters of Reformed theology. However, Arminius died from tuberculosis the following year. His close friend Johannes Uitenbogaert compiled a list of five Arminian articles drawn from the *Declaration of Sentiments* under the title *Articuli Arminiani sive Remonstrata* (1610).[23] In English they are known as *The Remonstrance*. It was signed by more than forty supporters. The Remonstrants, as they were called, petitioned for a synod to revise the Belgic Confession and the Heidelberg Catechism.

The text of *The Remonstrance* was brief. Article 1 declared that God's eternal purpose was to save the fallen humankind through Christ, by the grace of the Holy Spirit though faith (John 3:16). Article 2 declared that Christ died for all, but it required the response of faith to be effective (John 3:16; 1 John 2:2). Article 3 insisted that human beings do not have saving grace in themselves; they need to be born again in Christ, through the Spirit, and be renewed in order to understand, think, and will what is good. Without Christ they can do nothing (John 15:5). Article 4 maintained that human beings need prevenient grace before conversion and continued grace throughout their lives, but grace was "not irresistible" (Acts 7). Article 5 explained that grace was sufficient to prevent Satan or anyone from plucking the believer out of Christ's hand (John 10:28). Nevertheless, it was possible to forsake the faith and turn back to the world.

The appointment of an Arminian to succeed Arminius led to the resignation of Gomarus, who continued to wage an implacable war against

---

22. Gunter, *Arminius and His Declaration of Sentiments*, 155–57.
23. Pelikan and Hotchkiss, eds., *Creeds and Confessions of Faith in the Christian Tradition*, 2:547–50.

Post-Reformation Alternatives

the Remonstrants, culminating at the Synod of Dort (Dordrecht) (1618–19) with their crushing defeat. The outcome was a foregone conclusion. Although delegates from abroad were invited, Dutch Arminian delegates were admitted only after the synod had begun and then treated as defendants.

The Canons of Dort were set out under "Five Heads of Doctrine" in the form of positive and negative articles.[24] Its outline followed the topics listed in *The Remonstrance*, rejecting each point one by one. The first head dealt at great length with divine predestination, which entailed unconditional election based on God's eternal decree. There were no human grounds—not even faith—to merit election. It also entailed the damnation of the wicked. However, this did not make God responsible for their sin. The second head, dealing with the death of Christ and human redemption, taught substitutionary satisfaction. Because redemption is effectual, atonement is limited. Christ died only for the elect. The third and fourth heads were linked together, teaching total depravity, the extension of sin to all human acts and affections, and irresistible grace. God was the sole author of salvation, producing both the will to believe and the act of believing. The fifth head taught the doctrine of the perseverance of the saints: those who were truly converted would persevere because of the faithfulness of God.

The synod confirmed the authority of the Belgic Confession and Heidelberg Catechism. Some two hundred Arminian clergy were deprived. Henceforth, the Canons of Dort were ranked as the third confessional document of the Dutch Reformed Church. The States General sentenced the scholar and statesman Hugo Grotius (1583–1645) to life imprisonment. However, his wife arranged his escape in a consignment of books, and he settled in Paris in 1621. J. van Oldenbarnevelt, who had served thirty-three years as attorney general, was beheaded on a political false charge of treason.

In England the anti-Calvinistic movement, led by Archbishop Laud (1573–1645), was branded as "Arminian" by opponents. It is doubtful whether there was much direct influence from the work of Arminius

---

24. Pelikan and Hotchkiss, eds., *Creeds and Confessions of Faith in the Christian Tradition*, 2:569–600. The mnemonic TULIP—Total depravity, Unconditional election, Limited atonement, Irresistible grace, and Preservation of the saints—may be helpful for memorizing "The Five Points of Calvinism." However, it does not do justice to the Canons of Dort insofar as it distorts their structure and argument.

himself. The Westminster Confession of Faith (1647) followed the same path as Dort by placing discussion of predestination as the context for discussing creation and Christ the mediator.[25] It remained in force in Britain during the Commonwealth period.[26] It was adopted by the Church of Scotland (1690), and by the general synod of the Presbyterian Church in colonial America (1729). It is the official confession of the Church of Scotland, the Presbyterian Church (USA), and other Presbyterian churches. In revised form it was adopted by English Congregationalists in the Savoy Declaration (1658) and by London Baptists (1677).

The eighteenth-century evangelical revival in both Britain and America was divided over Arminianism. John Wesley (1703–91) embraced Arminian teaching, whereas George Whitefield (1714–70) followed Calvinism. The Methodist tradition in general was Arminian.

Some traditions still regard the division that came to a head at Dort as the defining issue today.[27] Others (like myself) see the issue as rival metanarratives, or grand narratives, locked in mortal combat over which

---

25. Following chapters on Scripture and the Trinity, chapter 3 was devoted to God's eternal decree. It began: "1. God the great Creator of all things doth uphold, direct, dispose, and govern all creatures, actions, and things, from the greatest to the least, by his most wise and holy providence, according to his infallible foreknowledge, and the free and immutable counsel of his own will, to the praise and glory of his wisdom, power, justice, and mercy. 2. Although in relation to the foreknowledge and decree of God, all things come to pass immutably and infallibly, yet, by the same provision, he ordereth them to fall out, according to the nature of second causes, either necessarily, freely or contingently."

Chapter 5 dealt with providence. It frankly admitted that it could not solve the problem raised by divine determinism. "4. The almighty power, unsearchable wisdom, and infinite goodness of God so far manifest themselves in his providence, that it extendeth even to the first fall, and all other sins of angels and men—and not by a bare permission, but such as he hath joined with it a most wise and powerful bounding, and ordering and governing of them, in manifold dispensation to his own holy ends, yet so, as the sinfulness thereof proceedeth only from the creature, and not from God, who being most holy and righteous, neither is, nor can be, the author and approver of sin" (Pelikan and Hotchkiss, eds., *Creeds and Confessions of Faith in the Christian Tradition*, 2:[601–49], 610, 612–13).

26. The Westminster Confession was the work of the Puritan divines who met at the Westminster Assembly for the purpose of revising the Thirty-Nine Articles of the Church of England. It was adopted in the brief period of the Commonwealth during the Protectorate of Oliver Cromwell (1653–58), when Presbyterianism replaced the Anglican Church. The Westminster Confession remained in force in England until the Restoration of the monarchy (1660).

27. See, for example, the discussions in Clark Pinnock, Richard Rice, John Sanders, William Hasker, and David Basinger, *The Openness of God: A Biblical Challenge to the Traditional Understanding of God* (Downers Grove, IL: InterVarsity Press, 1994); Donald K. McKim, *The Westminster Handbook to Reformed Theology* (Louisville: Westminster John Knox, 2001); Roger E. Olson, *Arminian Theology: Myths and Realities* (Downers Grove, IL: InterVarsity Press, 2006); F. Leroy Forlines, *Classical Arminianism: A Theology of Salvation* (Nashville: House, 2011); Roger E. Olson, *Against Calvinism* (Grand Rapids: Zondervan, 2011).

paradigms should govern biblical interpretation. In terms of the epistemology used in previous chapters to analyze the structure of knowledge, the distinction may be made between data beliefs, data background beliefs, and control beliefs. The primary conflict over Arminianism centered on predestination and divine decrees. Scripture was ransacked in search of data beliefs. The opposing parties appealed to the Belgic Confession and the Heidelberg Catechism as data background belief. The ultimate conflict turned on control beliefs. These seem to have functioned on two levels, which may be described as public and private.

In the *Declaratio* that Arminius submitted to the States General, he operated on the public level by framing the issue of divine decrees in terms of God's decrees to appoint his Son as Mediator and Savior from sin and graciously accept penitent believers. God provided the efficacious means necessary for repentance and faith. The salvation or condemnation of particular persons was founded on divine foreknowledge of who would respond and who would not to his prevenient grace. Arminius's presentation was cogently expressed in language that educated, biblically literate laymen could grasp.

However, on the more private level, Arminius interacted with an intense ongoing academic debate within both Catholic and Protestant scholasticism. Evidence of this involvement is preserved in accounts of his classroom activity and encounters with his academic peers. Richard A. Muller reopened investigation of this side of Arminius in his monograph on *God, Creation, and Providence in the Thought of Jacob Arminius* (1991). An issue that did not appear in the *Declaratio Sententiae* was Arminius's deep knowledge of prior Catholic discussions of providence and free will. Muller noted his "superb theological library," containing the writings of Aquinas and major Catholic interpreters as well as the Reformed tradition.[28] By itself the catalogue of books was not an accurate guide to Arminius's thought. However, identification of themes and arguments in Arminius's writings facilitated comparison with sources for discerning the structure of his thought. Central was the vision of God as Creator and Re-Creator.[29]

---

28. Muller, *God, Creation, and Providence*, 44–47; cf. the catalogue of Arminius's library compiled in 1610. The collection contained Luis de Molina's *Concordia liberi arbitrii cum gratia donis, divina praescientia, povidentia, praedestione et reprobatione* (1588) among the large number of Catholic writings.
29. Muller, *God, Creation, and Providence*, 71.

Muller concluded that Arminius modified Thomist intellectualism in the direction of Luis de Molina's idea of *scientia media*, or "middle knowledge." It allowed him to think of God's decrees regarding particular creatures and events as not directly willed by God. Providence was subordinate to God's eternal decree regarding creation. God eternally decided either to do or to permit everything that occurs in time. This internal decree preceded and grounded the external act, providence.[30] "Of the three major systematic models arising out of Protestantism, the Reformed, the Lutheran, and the Arminian, only one, the Arminian, proved genuinely open to the new rationalism, particularly in its more empirical and inductive forms."[31]

It remains to be said that much of current biblical scholarship does not support the double predestination teaching of Dort.[32] In the important passage, Romans 8:28–39, the central thought is not God's predestination of some to salvation and others to perdition. The verb προορίζω (*proorizō*), meaning "decide beforehand," "predetermine,"[33] refers to God's purpose that the called be conformed to the image of his Son, the first-born among many brethren. As such, the called—Jew and gentile—will be justified and ultimately glorified. God's faithfulness is manifested through his love in Christ, which remains constant, regardless of what terrible things may befall them. This interpretation does not preclude divine initiative and action in the lives of individuals and events (cf. Rom 9:1–33). But it does not imply the divine determination of *all* events. So far as the Arminian controversy as a whole was concerned, the Jesus of the Synoptic Gospels and his world seem to have disappeared from view.

2. Anti-Trinitarianism

Anti-Trinitarianism predates Socinianism, which gave impetus to its spread and formulation in what came to be called Unitarianism. The complex relationship between anti-Trinitarianism/Unitarianism and

---

30. Muller, *God, Creation, and Providence*, 250, cf. 280–82.
31. Muller, *God, Creation, and Providence*, 285.
32. See, for example, James D. G. Dunn, *Romans*, 2 vols., WBC 38A, 38B (Dallas: Word, 1988), 1:464–513; Robert Jewett, *Romans: A Commentary*, Hermeneia (Minneapolis: Fortress, 2007), 504–620.
33. BDAG, 873.

Post-Reformation Alternatives

Socinianism may perhaps be best understood by approaching it through a sketch of the careers of Laelius and Faustus Socinus.

2.1. Socinianism. The term *Socinianism* derives from the Latinized name of two Italian religious teachers who were uncle and nephew, though they spelled their surnames differently. The uncle, Lelio Francesco Maria Sozini (1525–62), alias Laelius Socinus, was a lawyer and in his day was the more prominent of the two. Fausto Paolo Sozzini (1539–1604), alias Faustus Socinus, pursued a more checkered career but despite his early neglected education exerted more influence.

Realizing that his interests lay more in theology than law, Laelius Socinus was drawn to Venice, which was then the center of Protestantism in Italy. He went on to visit other centers of the Reformation. In the course of his travels Laelius Socinus came to Geneva, where he incurred the suspicions of Calvin about his orthodoxy. To allay these doubts Heinrich Bullinger urged him to write a confession of faith (1555).[34] He did so, but without the word *credo*, "I believe." The resulting statement of belief was largely negative. "I do not assert that the Father is the same as the Son and the Holy Spirit. I do not suppose that there to be three Jehovahs, our coessential gods; I do not divide the person of Christ into two Christs, nor accept any confusion of his natures." He abhorred and abominated "the dogmas of Servetus [who had perished at the stake not long previously] and the whole Arian theology." He concluded by expressing his hope in the resurrection and meeting the return of Christ in the air. Laelius Socinus spent the remainder of his days in Zurich.

Faustus Socinus was, like his uncle, born in Siena.[35] He moved to Lyons, where he wrote a critique of the divinity of Christ.[36] On returning to Italy (1563), he served as a courtier before moving to Basel (1578). Here a chance meeting with the Huguenot pastor Jacques Couvet led to a protracted debate in which Couvet and Socinus tried to convert each other. The outcome was Socinus's *magnum opus* entitled *De Jesu Christo*

---

34. Pelikan and Hotchkiss, eds., *Creeds and Confessions of Faith in the Christian Tradition*, 2:704–8.

35. An early account by Joshua Toulmin, *Memoirs of the Life, Character, Sentiments and Writings, of Faustus Socinus* (1777) has been published in facsimile by Ecco Print Editions, n.d.

36. A modern facsimile reprint of his critique of Erasmus, *De Unigeniti filii Dei Existentia in Erasmum Iohannnis, et Faustum Socinum Disputatio*, 2nd ed. (Racovia, 1626) has been published by Kessinger, n.d.

Servatore (On Jesus Christ the Savior).[37] Although completed in 1578, it was not published until 1594, well after his arrival in Poland.

Faustus Socinus interpreted the significance of Jesus from the vantage point of Roman private law. Christ saved humankind through his teaching and example, not as the penal substitute for sins. Virtue and religion were matters of choice. Human nature was not changed by the sin of Adam. When Adam sinned, he lost access to the tree of life (Gen 2:9; 3:22–24). Human beings have no innate, natural knowledge of God. Christ came to persuade men and women to live moral lives. His life was an embodiment of his teaching. Those who committed themselves to following his example were assured that God would forgive their sins and give them eternal life. However, God retained the right to punish sinners if he so wished. In this respect, God's authority was like that of mortal rulers.

On completion of *De Jesu Christo Servatore*, Socinus moved to Transylvania in the hope that his liberal views would be welcomed and serve as a moderating force. Anti-Trinitarianism was already established in Transylvania and Poland before his arrival in either country. Much of Transylvania (modern Romania) had been won over to Lutheranism in the 1530s. The Hungarian parts were more favorable to Swiss Calvinism, especially with regard to the eucharist. King John Sigismund maintained a policy of religious liberty, while personally favoring Unitarianism. Socinus's teaching was moderate compared with that of Bishop Francis Dávid who was overthrown and died in prison in 1579. Shortly afterward the Transylvanian Confession of Faith was adopted. It emphasized Jesus as Son of God and Messiah without mentioning the Trinity.[38] The same year, Socinus moved to Poland, where he spent the remainder of his days.

---

37. A partial translation was made by Alan W. Gomez, "Faustus' Socinus' *De Jesu Christo Servatore*, Part III, Historical Introduction, Translation, and Notes" (PhD diss., Fuller Theological Seminary, 1990); see also John Charles Godbey. "A Study of Faustus Socinus's De Jesu Christo Servatore" (PhD diss., University of Chicago, 1968). See further Williams, *The Radical Reformation*, 746–63; Sarah Mortimer, *Reason and Religion in the English Revolution: The Challenge of Socinianism*, Cambridge Studies in Early Modern British History (Cambridge: Cambridge University Press, 2010), 13–33.

The Arminian Hugo Grotius replied with his *Defensio Fidei Catholicae de Satisfactione Christi adversus Faustum Socinum Senensem* (1617). Drawing on his legal background, Grotius depicted God as the moral governor of the universe. Jesus' death reveals the seriousness of sin. On the debate see Robert S. Franks, *The Work of Christ: A Historical Study of Christian Doctrine* ([1918]; London: Nelson, 1962), 362–409; L. W. Grensted, *A Short History of the Doctrine of Atonement* (Manchester: Manchester University Press; London: Longmans, Green, 1920), 281–306.

38. Pelikan and Hotchkiss, eds., *Creeds and Confessions of Faith in the Christian Tradition*, 2:745–48.

Post-Reformation Alternatives

In Poland Socinus met with a mixed reception. In some cities his presence was felt as a moderating influence. Other cities were unreceptive. Unitarianism was already established by *The Catechesis and Confession of Faith of the Polish Brethren* (1579), which has been identified as the first formulation of Unitarian faith and practice.[39] It predates the influence of both Laelius and Faustus Socinus. It shared the outlook of other European Anabaptist groups but was distinguished by its anti-Nicene stance. Jesus was "a most perfect prophet," "a most holy priest," and "a most invincible king." He should be believed "most high after God." The Holy Spirit was "the power of God, whose fullness God gave to his only-begotten Son, our Lord, in order that we may take, as adopted sons, from his fullness."

Socinus was refused communion with Polish Unitarian churches and participation in the direction of their affairs. Nevertheless, he was enabled to publish freely. *De Jesu Christo Servatore* finally appeared in 1594. He was able to promote his views on the unity of God and the humanity of Jesus Christ. Following his death, Socinian teaching was given formulation in the *Racovian Catechism*, published in Polish at Raków 1605.[40] Raków was an early center of Socinian teaching. The catechism drew on the existing confession, together with drafts by Socinus himself.

The *Racovian Catechism* was hardly a catechism in the customary sense. It was more like a treatise in question and answer form on the person of Christ. It had preliminary sections on the authority of Scripture, salvation, and the knowledge of God, followed by what amounted to a postscript on the church. The central theme was that reason and Scripture taught that there was only one God.[41] Following the tradition of Servetus, the catechism taught that Jesus was a man but not an ordinary man in light of his conception by the Holy Spirit and virgin birth. "For being conceived by the Holy Spirit, and born of a virgin, without the intervention of any human being, he had properly no father besides God."[42] In the tradition of Calvin, sections 5, 6, and 7 were devoted to the offices of Christ as Prophet, Priest, and King.

---

39. Pelikan and Hotchkiss, eds., *Creeds and Confessions of Faith in the Christian Tradition*, 2:711–44.

40. The edition used in the following discussion is *The Racovian Catechism, with Notes and Illustrations, Translated from the Latin, to Which Is Prefixed a Sketch of the History of Unitarianism in Poland and the Adjacent Countries*, trans. Thomas Rees (London: Longman, 1818; facsimile repr., Kessinger Legacy, n.d.).

41. *The Racovian Catechism*, section 3, chap. 1, 26–48.

42. *The Racovian Catechism*, section 4, chap.1, 52–53.

Quests before Schweitzer

Nine chapters were devoted to the prophetic office, but only one each to the other two. The catechism systemically reviewed the proof texts of its opponents. Typically, the answer is given that it cannot be proved from those texts that "Christ possesses a divine nature: indeed the contrary is rather to be inferred; for since he is the WORD of the one God, it is evident that he is not that one God."[43]

The prophetic office consisted "in perfectly manifesting to us, confirming, and establishing, the hidden Will of God."[44] In the chapters that followed, the catechism enlarged on the theme of how Jesus compressed the law of Moses into two commandments but added others like the Lord's Prayer and the Sermon on the Mount.[45] The prophetic office included discussion of believers' baptism, the Lord's Supper, the promise of eternal life, the promise of the Holy Spirit, the death of Christ, faith, free will, and justification. The catechism ended with much briefer sections on the priestly and kingly offices of Christ and on the church.

In conclusion, it may be observed that the threefold offices of Christ, as prophet, priest, and king, which are widely regarded as a characteristic of Calvinism, were also a characteristic of early Unitarianism. However, the offices were interpreted in completely different ways. For Unitarians, their appeal consisted in the characteristic *human* aspects of Jesus' activity.

2.2. The Spread of Unitarianism. Anti-Trinitarianism and Socinianism played a significant part in religious and civil life in the seventeenth century.[46] The *Racovian Catechism* was published in German (1608) and Latin (1609). A copy of the Latin version, which was dedicated to King James I of England, was ceremonially burned. A similar fate was accorded to the English translation by John Biddle, which was condemned by Oliver Cromwell and the British Parliament in 1652.

John Biddle (1615–62) was the leading pioneer of English Anti-Trinitarianism.[47] A graduate and tutor of Magdalen Hall, Oxford, he became a schoolmaster at the Crypt School in Gloucester, where

---

43. *The Racovian Catechism*, section 4, chap. 1, 139–40.
44. *The Racovian Catechism*, section 5, 169.
45. *The Racovian Catechism*, section 5, chap. 1, 173–238.
46. H. John McLachlan, *Socinianism in Seventeenth-Century England* (Oxford: Oxford University Press, 1951); Sarah Mortimer, *Reason and Religion in the English Revolution: The Challenge of Socininianism* (see above, n37); Paul C. H. Lim, *Mystery Unveiled: The Crisis of the Trinity in Early Modern England*, Oxford Studies in Historical Theology (Oxford: Oxford University Press, 2012).
47. Lim, *Mystery Unveiled*, 38–68.

he began a tireless search of Scripture for evidence of the Trinity. He concluded that it was an illogical and nonbiblical interpolation. His *Twelve Questions or Arguments from Scripture, wherein . . . the Deity of the Holy Spirit is clearly and fully refuted* (1647) was burned by the hangman. Other writings provoked public outcry. They included *A Confession of Faith Touching the Holy Trinity* (1648; repr., 1691). Biddle was imprisoned several times and exiled to the Scilly Isles by Oliver Cromwell. On his return, he was arrested and died in prison. A particular irony of the situation lay in the fact that Biddle claimed biblical authority for his views. It was a belief that he had in common with the Westminster Confession of Faith (1647), which gave absolute priority to Scripture. "The authority of the Holy Scripture, for which it ought to be believed and obeyed, dependeth not on the testimony of any man, or church, but wholly upon God (who is truth itself) the author thereof; and therefore ought to be received because it is the word of God."[48]

In England Unitarianism centered initially on the conventicle founded in London by John Biddle. Theophilus Lindsey (1723–1808) seceded from the Church of England and began conducting Unitarian worship in Essex Street, London (1774). Meanwhile, Lindsey's friend and Presbyterian minister turned Unitarian Joseph Priestley (1733–1804) sharply criticized the ideas of the preexistence and divinity of Christ and the satisfaction theory of atonement. Today Priestley is remembered as a scientist and discoverer of oxygen. He was also a prolific Unitarian author. Among his writings were *An Appeal to the Serious and Candid Professors of Christianity* (1770), *Institutes of Natural and Revealed Religion* (3 vols., 1772–74), *A Harmony of the Evangelists, in Greek* (1777), *A Harmony of the Evangelists, in English* (1780), *An History of the Corruptions of Christianity* (2 vols., 1782), and *An History of Early Opinions concerning Jesus Christ* (1786).[49]

---

48. Pelikan and Hotchkiss, eds., *Creeds and Confessions of Faith in the Christian Tradition*, 2:[601–49], 606. The Westminster Confession was the last major confession of the Reformation period. It was the work of the Westminster Assembly, which met in the Jerusalem Chamber of Westminster Abbey for the purpose of reforming the articles and polity of the Church of England so as to conform with Puritan Reformed theology. For background, see John Morrill, "The Puritan Revolution," in *The Cambridge Companion to Puritanism*, ed. John Coffey and Paul C. H. Lim (Cambridge: Cambridge University Press, 2008), 67–88.

49. See further Robert E. Schofield, *The Enlightenment of Joseph Priestley: A Study of His Life and Work from 1733 to 1773* (University Park, PA: Pennsylvania State University Press, 1997); Lester Kieft and Bennett R. Willeford Jr., eds., *Joseph Priestley, Scientist, Theologian, and Metaphysician: A Symposium Celebrating the Two Hundredth Anniversary of the Discovery of Oxygen by Joseph Priestley in 1774* (Lewisburg, PA: Bucknell University Press, 1980).

When rioting broke out in Birmingham in 1780 against Priestley's support of the French Revolution, the mob broke into his house and destroyed his belongings. Priestley went to America (1794), where he was welcomed by Thomas Jefferson. He spent the last ten years of his life in Pennsylvania and was instrumental in turning Jefferson toward Unitarianism.[50]

3. Revival of the Arian Controversy

Socinianism was characterized by repudiation and secession. English Arians of the seventeenth and eighteenth centuries—or perhaps more accurately, scholars suspected of Arianism—questioned the formularies of orthodoxy while striving to remain within the fold of the Anglican Church.[51] Modern reassessment of Arianism parallels that undertaken by seventeenth- and eighteenth-century Anglican divines.

3.1. Newton. It may seem strange to count among their number the greatest scientist of the age, the Lucasian Professor of Mathematics at Cambridge and later Master of the Mint, Sir Isaac Newton (1642–1727). All three leading English "Arians"—Newton, William Whiston, and Samuel Clarke—were scientists and biblical scholars. They were also closely connected. Newton was deeply religious and an almost obsessive student of the Bible. His *Philosophiae Naturalis Principia Mathematica* (1687) contained an argument for what today would be called "intelligent design"—the existence of a transcendent, omnipotent, and perfect Supreme Being, based on the order of the universe.

The only theological work that Newton wrote for publication was *The Chronology of the Ancient Kingdoms Amended* (1728). His *Observations upon the Prophecies of Daniel, and the Apocalypse of St. John* (1733) were published posthumously by his nephew. Extracts from Newton's theological manuscripts, estimated at one million words (housed chiefly in Cambridge, Jerusalem, and Wellesley, Massachusetts), have been published in modern times. Treatises on revelation and the day of judgment illustrate his method of interpretation and his vision of the millennium.[52] Newton urged

---

50. See below, chap. 4, §2.2.
51. On Arianism, see above, chap. 2, §3.
52. Extracts from Newton's theological writings were published by Herbert McLachlan under the title *Theological Manuscripts* (Liverpool: Liverpool University Press, 1950). For more

literal interpretation, keeping close to the uniform sense of words and paying attention to language and context. He believed that the restitution of all things is found in all the prophets and that after the day of judgment the earth would continue eternally to be inhabited by mortals.

Newton was a conforming member of the Church of England, though unlike most faculty at Oxford and Cambridge at the time, he was not ordained. It was vital to him as a Christian academic that he should not be in holy orders. Newton received a special dispensation from King Charles II that he should not be obliged to receive them. Privately he questioned the orthodox formulations of the Trinity and their history. Newton's unpublished papers include "Queries regarding the Word 'Homoousios',"[53] and "Paradoxical Questions concerning the Morals and Actions of Athanasius and His Followers." According to Newton, the adoption of ὁμοούσιος, *homoousios*, at Nicea was misguided. The bishops had allowed the unbaptized emperor Constantine to impose it against the wishes of the majority. Many bishops would have preferred to, and in fact did, add *homoiousios*—of like (but not identical) substance—to their subscription. Newton argued, "When therefore the Father or Son are called God, we are to understand it not metaphysically but in a moral monarchical sense."[54] The real damage was done by later interpretation, especially by Athanasius, in promoting belief in the equality of the substances of the Father and the Son.[55]

Maurice Wiles concluded that Newton was more anti-Athanasian than pro-Arian.[56] Newton saw himself as a faithful follower of primitive

---

recent discussion see Frank E. Manuel, *The Religion of Sir Isaac Newton*, The Freemantle Lectures 1973 (Oxford: Clarendon, 1974); Richard S. Westfall, *Never at Rest: A Biography of Isaac Newton* (Cambridge: Cambridge University Press, 1980); Wiles, *Archetypal Heresy*, 77–93; James E. Force and Richard Popkin, eds., *The Books of Nature and Scripture: Recent Essays on Natural Philosophy, Theology, and Biblical Criticism in the Netherlands of Spinoza's Time and the British Isles of Newton's Time*, International Archives of the History of Ideas 139 (Dordrecht, Netherlands: Kluwer Academic, 1994); Richard S. Westfall, *ODNB* (2004), 40:705–24; I. Bernard Cohen and George E. Smith, eds., *The Cambridge Companion to Newton* (Cambridge: Cambridge University Press, 2002); Rob Iliffe, *Priest of Nature: The Religious Worlds of Isaac Newton* (Oxford: Oxford University Press, 2017).

On biblical interpretation, see especially Manuel, *The Religion of Sir Isaac Newton*, 107–36; Maurizio Mamiani, "Newton on Prophecy and the Apocalypse," and Scott Mandelbrote, "Newton and Eighteenth-Century Christianity," in *The Cambridge Companion to Newton*, 387–408, and 409–30.

53. Keynes MS 11; McLachlan, *Theological Manuscripts*, 44–47; Wiles, *Archetypal Heresy*, 89.
54. Martin Bodmer MS, On the Church (C-H 33); Wiles, *Archetypal Heresy*, 89.
55. Keynes MS 11; Maclachlan, *Theological Manuscripts*, 45; Wiles, *Archetypal Heresy*, 90.
56. Wiles, *Archetypal Heresy*, 92. Thomas C. Pfizenmaier ("Was Isaac Newton an Arian?" *Journal of the History of Ideas* 58 [1997]: 57–80) rejects the charge of Arianism.

Christianity as taught by Scripture and practiced in the second and third centuries. However, his colleague William Whiston, after discussing his doubts with Newton, felt "much more inclined to what has been of late called Arianism."[57]

3.2. Whiston. The Rev. William Whiston (1667–1752)[58] was a Cambridge graduate in mathematics, at one time vicar of Lowestoft, and later assistant to Newton. Whiston was also Newton's handpicked successor to the Lucasian Chair of Mathematics in 1703 when Newton became Master of the Mint. Whiston's *New Theory of the Earth* (1696)[59] combined science and biblical exegesis. Like Newton, Whiston was a student of biblical chronology and prophecy.[60] Like Newton, he insisted on literal interpretation of prophecy. And like Newton, his study of the early church led him to "suspect that the Athanasian doctrine of the Trinity was not the doctrine of those early ages."[61]

By nature less circumspect than Newton, Whiston wrote to archbishops Tennison of Canterbury and Sharp of York in 1708 in the hope of bringing the Church of England to a more accommodating position. His endeavors backfired, and Whiston's reputation as an Arian led to his removal from the professorship (1710) and sustained attacks in convocation. Whiston moved to London, where he taught and wrote privately on numerous aspects of science.

Whiston rejected what he called "gross Arianism," which the Council of Nicea rightly condemned.[62] He instead embraced the teaching of the anti-Athanasians, who might more accurately be described as Eusebians.[63]

---

57. William Whiston, *Historical Memoirs of the Life and Writings of Dr. Samuel Clarke* (London: Gyles and Roberts, 1730), 13; cited by Wiles, *Archetypal Heresy*, 93.

58. James E. Force, *William Whiston: Honest Newtonian* (Cambridge: Cambridge University Press, 1985); Wiles, *Archetypal Heresy*, 93–110. Primary sources are William Whiston, *An Account of the Convocation's Proceedings with Relation to Mr. Whiston* (London: Baldwin, 1711); and William Whiston, *Memoirs of the Life and Writings of Mr. William Whiston* (London: self-published, 1749); Stephen D. Snobelen, *ODNB* (2004), 58:502–6.

59. Whiston, *A New Theory of the Earth from Its Original, to the Consummation of All Things* (London: Robert, 1696).

60. Whiston, *A Short View of the Chronology of the Old Testament and of the Harmony of the Four Evangelists* (Cambridge: Cambridge University Press, 1702). Whiston was the Boyle Lecturer in 1707.

61. Whiston, *Historical Memoirs of the Life and Writings of Dr. Samuel Clarke*, 12; Wiles, *Archetypal Heresy*, 94.

62. Whiston, "The Council of Nicea Vindicated," in *Three Essays* (London: self-published, 1713), 4; Wiles, *Archetypal Heresy*, 98.

63. Wiles, *Archetypal Heresy*, 98; cf. J. Lienhart, "The 'Arian' Controversy: Some Categories Reconsidered," *Theological Studies* 48 (1987): 419. Eusebius (c. 260–340), Bishop of Caesarea

In 1713 Whiston published a *Liturgy of the Church of England Reduced Nearer to the Primitive Standard Proposed for Public Consideration*. It drew on the *Apostolic Constitutions*, which Whiston erratically believed were communicated by Christ after his resurrection.[64] Whiston lingered in the Church of England some thirty-seven years after his removal from Cambridge. In 1747 he joined the Baptists. Today Whiston is remembered less for his "Arianism" than for his translation of the works of Josephus (1737) that remains in print.[65]

3.3. Clarke. Samuel Clarke (1675–1729) became a Newtonian at Cambridge. He translated Newton's *Opticks* into Latin in order to make Newton's ideas more accessible on the continent of Europe.[66] Clarke established his reputation through two sets of Boyle Lectures (1704–5), which defended rational theology against the criticisms of Hobbes, Spinoza, and the deists.[67] In 1709 he was appointed rector of St. James's, Piccadilly, in the heart of London, where his preaching attracted wide attention.[68] Among his admirers was Dr. Samuel Johnson.

Clarke's reputation for Arianism was based on his *Scripture Doctrine of the Trinity* (1712).[69] It provoked ferocious controversy leading the Lower House of Convocation to seek Clarke's condemnation. The Upper House of Bishops decided not to require retraction on condition that Clarke

---

and author of the *Ecclesiastical History*, was an opponent of Athanasius and accepted the Nicene formula with reluctance. Whiston listed seventeen "Suspicions Concerning Athanasius." See Whiston, *Primitive Christianity Revived*, vol. 1, *An Historical Preface* (London: self-published, 1711), cxvi–cxxvii. They were followed by *Athanasius Convicted of Forgery. In a Letter to Mr. Thirlby* (London: self-published, 1712).

64. Wiles, *Archetypal Heresy*, 104, 106.

65. Whiston, *The Genuine Works of Flavius Josephus, Complete and Unabridged*, new updated ed. (Peabody, MA: Hendrickson, 1987; 16th printing, 2001).

66. Isaac Newton, *Isaaci Newtoni Optices Libri tres, Accedunt ejusdem Lectiones Opticae, et Opuscula Omnia ad Lucem et Colores Pertinentia* (Patavii: Typis Seminarii apud Joannem Manfré, 1773); cf. Alan E. Shapiro, "Newton's Optics and Atomism," in *The Cambridge Companion to Newton*, 227–55. For Clarke's life and thought see John Gascoigne, *ODNB* (2004), 11:912–16.

67. The lectures were originally sixteen sermons published in two volumes (1705–6). Later they were given the title *A Discourse Concerning the Being and Attributes of God, the Obligations of Natural Religion, and the Truth and Certainty of the Christian Revelation* (London: Botham, 1716). They were reprinted in *The Works of Samuel Clarke, D.D.* (London: Knapton, 1738; facsimile repr., New York: Garland, 1978), 2:513–733. They are followed by letters in answer to critics.

68. Sermons fill the first two of the four volumes of Clarke's works.

69. Clarke, *Works*, 4:i–xiv, 1–447. The text is followed by Clarke's replies to *Waterland's Queries* (449–534), his account of the proceedings in Convocation (535–58), and further replies (559–74). See further Wiles, *Archetypal Heresy*, 110–34; Thomas C. Pfizenmaier, *The Trinitarian Theology of Dr. Samuel Clarke (1675–1729): Context, Sources, and Controversy*, Studies in the History of Christian Thought 75 (Leiden: Brill, 1997).

would cease to write on the subject.[70] The latter phase of his life was marked by correspondence with Leibniz defending Newton's teaching and discussing the nature of free will.[71]

The *Scripture Doctrine of the Trinity* was divided into three parts. Part 1 consisted of an inventory of "all the *Texts* in the New Testament . . . relating to the Doctrine of the Trinity," grouped in four chapters dealing respectively with God the Father, the Son of God, the Spirit of God, and passages referring to all three. For cross-referencing purposes they were numbered 1–1251, though some texts inevitably appeared more than once. Frequently, they were accompanied by annotations from the fathers and recent authors (occasionally distancing Clarke from the Socinians[72]).

Part 2 set out fifty-five propositions intended to formulate and elucidate the doctrine embedded in the texts listed in part 1. Clarke regularly cross-referenced his interpretation by noting other supporting texts. He quoted extensively from the fathers, setting out the English translation and the Greek or Latin in parallel columns, and was not afraid to join issue with authorities ancient and modern, sometimes at length.

Part 3 identified 186 passages from the Book of Common Prayer arranged thematically like part 1, which supported the unique deity of the Father and the subordination of the Son and the Spirit. By contrast, the doxology and the controversial so-called Creed of St. Athanasius "*may seem in some respect to* differ *from the foregoing* Doctrine."[73]

The thrust of Clarke's argument is caught in the following propositions from part 2. "*The* Father Alone *is* Self-existent, Underived, Unoriginated, Independent. He Alone *is* of None, *either by* Creation, Generation, Procession, *or* Any Other Way whatsoever" (§5). "*The* Son is not Self-existent; *but derives his* Being *and All his* Attributes *from the* Father, *as from the* Supreme Cause" (§12). "*The Scripture, speaking of* the Spirit of God, *never*

---

70. Norman Sykes, *William Wake, Archbishop of Canterbury 1657–1737* (Cambridge: Cambridge University Press, 1957), 2:154–60.

71. Clarke, *Works*, 4:575–710; H. G. Alexander, ed., *The Leibniz-Clarke Correspondence: Together with Extracts from Newton's Principia and Opticks* (New York: Philosophical Library, 1956); Domenico Bertoloni Meli, "Newton and the Leibiz-Clarke Correspondence," in *The Cambridge Companion to Newton*, 455–64. Raków was an early center of Socinian teaching.

72. See, for instance, §830, Clarke, *Works*, 4:85 ("If ye loved me, ye would rejoice, because I said, I go unto the Father: for my Father is *Greater* than I"). The Socinian interpretation—that the Father is greater than the human nature of Christ—is "flat and insipid." "The plain Meaning of the Words, is, that *God the Father* is *greater* than *the Son* absolutely: That *He that begat*, must need (for that reason, and upon that Account,) be *greater* than *he that is begotten* of Him."

73. Clarke, *Works*, 4:205.

mentions any Limitations of Time, *when he derived his Being from the Father; but supposes him to have existed with the Father from the Beginning*" (§21).

Clarke repudiated the characteristic Arian slogans "that the Son was made" (§14) and "that there was a time when the Son was not" (§16). "*The* reason *why the* Son *in the New Testament is sometimes stiled* God, *is not upon account of his* metaphysical Substance, *how Divine soever; but of his* relative Attributes *and Divine* Authority *(communicated to him from the Father over* Us)" (§25). "*The* Son, *before his Incarnation, was* with God, *was* in the Form of God, *and* had Glory with the Father" (§47). "*This* Honour *the Scripture directs to be paid to Christ; not upon account of his* metaphysical Essence *or* Substance, *and* abstract Attributes; *but of his* Actions *and* Attributes relative *to* Us; *his* Condescension *in becoming* Man, *who was the* Son of God; Redeeming, *and* Interceding for, *us; his* Authority, Power, Dominion, *and* Sitting upon the Throne of God his Father, *as our* Law-giver, *our* King, *our* Judge, *and our* God" (§51). "*The* Honour *paid in this manner to the* Son, *must (as before) always be understood as redounding ultimately to the* Glory *of* God the Father" (§52).

Clarke's great contribution was to identify the issues and to lay out with great precision the pertinent data from Scripture, the fathers, modern authors, and the Anglican liturgy. To adversaries like Daniel Waterland, Master of Magdalene College, Cambridge, Clarke had relapsed into Arianism.[74] A more measured judgment is that of Thomas C. Pfizenmaier: "Clarke's thought represents a re-emergence of the views of Origen, Eusebius of Caesarea, and in a sense, of the Eastern tradition in general. Clarke was not an Arian, nor an Athanasian, but a Eusebian."[75] Clarke's method represented what Pfizenmaier characterizes as "the emerging historical consciousness which was growing in its challenge to dogmatic theology."[76] That method was exemplified by Petavius in patristics[77] and

---

74. Wiles, *Archetypal Heresy*, 116–17; cf. Waterland, *Vindication of Christ's Divinity, Being a Defence of Some Queries Relating to Dr. Clarke's Scheme of the Trinity* (1719) and three further volumes (discussion in Pfizenmaier, *The Trinitarian Theology of Dr. Samuel Clarke*, 197–216). John Edwards described Whiston and Clarke as revivers of the heretical opinions of "the Racovian gentlemen." Whiston took a negative view, accusing Clarke of equivocation and lack of frankness (Wiles, *Archetypal Heresy*, 114–15).
75. Pfizenmaier, *The Trinitarian Theology of Dr. Samuel Clarke*, 140.
76. Pfizenmaier, *The Trinitarian Theology of Dr. Samuel Clarke*, 198.
77. Dionysius Petavius (1583–1652) made fundamental contributions to the study of ancient chronology and to the study of doctrine in *De Theologicis Dogmatibus* (4 vols. 1644–1650). He acknowledged imperfections in patristic theology when judged by later standards and called into question the standard view of monolithic adherence that the Ante-Nicene fathers shared the

Quests before Schweitzer

Richard Simon in biblical studies.[78] At the same time, it might be said to be an application of the scientific method of the day to historical theology in its rigorous assembling and classification of evidence, and its attempt to demonstrate propositions by adducing evidence. In his historical critical handling of the church fathers, Clarke represented the way of the future. In handling the New Testament, Clarke (like Newton and Whiston) remained in the precritical age, taking the text at its apparent face value and drawing logical deductions. But the precritical reading of the Bible had already begun to be challenged elsewhere.

4. The Rise of Skepticism

The debates discussed so far exhibited varying degrees of skepticism. We turn now to a systematic form of skepticism that shook the foundations of religion, science, and philosophy. In France it was called *la crise pyrrhonienne*—the Pyrrhonian crisis. Much of the credit for recognizing the significance of Pyrrhonism belongs to Richard H. Popkin. Popkin observed: "With the rediscovery in fifteenth and sixteenth centuries of writings of the Greek Pyrrhonist Sextus Empiricus, the arguments and views of the Greek skeptics became part of the philosophical core of the religious struggles then taking place. The problem of finding a criterion of truth, first in theological disputes, was then later raised with

---

convictions of the Post-Nicene fathers. In this, he was followed by Clarke, though Clarke rarely named him. References to Petavius would not have strengthened his argument in the eyes of his enemies (*The Trinitarian Theology of Dr. Samuel Clarke*, 156). However, Clarke did join issue with Bishop George Bull's celebrated *Defensio Fidei Nicaenae* (1685), which was largely a critique of Petavius.

78. Richard Simon (1638–1712) pioneered the historical critical study of the Bible. His *Histoire critique du Vieux Testament* (1678) was suppressed, and few copies of the original survived. However, imperfect French editions were produced in Holland between 1680 and 1685. An English translation made by "a Person of Quality" with the title *A Critical History of the Old Testament* was published in London in 1682. Simon reviewed the problem of the text of the Old Testament and the question of Mosaic authorship. Simon's works include *Critical Enquiries into the Various Editions of the Bible* (ET: 1684), *Histoire critique du Nouveau Testament* (Rotterdam, 1689) and *Nouvelles observations sur le texte et les versions du Nouveau Testament* (Paris, 1695). His work on the New Testament was introduced into German scholarship by J.S. Semler (*Kritische Schriften über das Neue Testament*, 3 vols. 1776–80). See further Colin Brown, "Enlightenment Period," in *Dictionary of Biblical Criticism and Interpretation*, ed. Stanley E. Porter (New York: Routledge, 2007), 91–101; Henning Graf Reventlow, *History of Biblical Interpretation*, vol. 4: *From the Enlightenment to the Twentieth Century*, Resources for Biblical Study 63 (Atlanta: Society of Biblical Literature, 2010).

regard to natural knowledge, leading to *la crise pyrrhonienne* of the early sixteenth century."[79]

The new skepticism, known as Pyrrhonism, was engendered by Sextus Empiricus's account of the Greek skeptic Pyrrho (d. c. 270 BCE) in his book *Outlines of Pyrrhonism*.[80] Pyrrhonists took from Sextus Empiricus (c. 200 CE) skepticism about the reliability of the senses and the ability of reason to discover ultimate truth. An early outpost was the Jesuit Collège de la Flèche in Anjou, where René Descartes and his lifelong friend Marin Mersenne received their early education.

4.1. Descartes and Pyrrhonism. The period in which René Descartes (1596–1650) lived was marked by religious wars in Europe, the convulsions of the Synod of Dort in Holland, and the English Civil War. In his younger days Descartes embarked on a military career during which he found leisure to pursue science. Scientific observation led to dissatisfaction with medieval philosophy and to the determination to make his philosophy more akin to scientific method. Descartes's move to Holland (1628–49) gave him greater freedom to think. However, he withheld publication of his treatise on *The World*, following the condemnation of Galileo in 1633. He was persuaded to move to Sweden by Queen Christina in 1649, but the harsh winters cut short his life.

Descartes's most important philosophical works published in his lifetime were his *Discourse on Method* (1637) and his *Meditations on First*

---

79. Richard H. Popkin, *The History of Scepticism from Savonarola to Bayle* (Oxford: Oxford University Press, 2003), 1. Studies of skepticism include Michael Hunter and David Wootton, eds., *Atheism from the Reformation to the Enlightenment* (Oxford: Clarendon, 1992; repr., 2003).

80. Richard H. Popkin notes that it was Savonarola (1452–98) who introduced Sextus Empiricus into the modern discussion. At the time when he was in charge of the convent of San Marco, there were five manuscript copies of the writings of Sextus Empiricus in the library, including one that belonged to the Florentine humanist Pico della Mirandola (*The History of Scepticism from Savonarola to Bayle*, 6). On the reception of Sextus Empiricus in the sixteenth century, see Popkin, *The History of Scepticism from Savonarola to Bayle*, 17–79. The thinker who most absorbed his influence was Michel de Montaigne (1533–92).

Editions include *Sextus Empiricus*, trans. R. G. Bury, LCL, 4 vols. (London: Heinemann; Cambridge, MA: Harvard University Press, 1933–49); and Sextus Empiricus, *Outlines of Scepticism*, ed. and trans. Julia Annas and Jonathan Barnes, 2nd ed. (Cambridge: Cambridge University Press, 2000); cf. also Julia Annas and Jonathan Barnes, *The Modes of Scepticism: Ancient Texts and Modern Interpretations* (Cambridge: Cambridge University Press, 1985).

The terms *empiricism* and *empiricist* initially had negative connotations that appear to be linked with the name Sextus Empiricus. As designations for that style of philosophy that stresses observation and inference, the terms gained currency from the time of Kant, who regarded Aristotle as "the chief of the *empiricists*" and Locke as his latter-day successor (*Critique of Pure Reason*, 2nd ed. [1787], "The Transcendental Doctrine of Method," chap. 4).

Philosophy (1641).[81] The former was written in French and only later translated into Latin. The latter was composed in Latin and consisted of six sets of reflections on selected topics, together with objections by learned colleagues, and Descartes's response to them. It was formally presented to the Sorbonne as *Meditations on First Philosophy in Which Are Demonstrated the Existence of God and the Distinction between the Human Soul and the Body.*

The conventional view of Descartes as the inventor of modern philosophy based on systematic doubt and the perception of the individual self requires qualification. The so-called "Cartesian doubt," which sought to doubt everything, was not in fact the invention of Descartes. Moreover, the commonly used title *Discourse on Method* gives the impression that Descartes was propounding the correct method in *all* disciplines. In fact, Descartes's goal was more focused. Descartes was describing a method in *the physical sciences*, which would not be vulnerable to the doubts of the Pyrrhonists. This is made clear by the Cambridge edition of Descartes's *Philosophical Writings*, which translates the title as *Discourse on the Method of Rightly Conducting One's Reason and Seeking the Truth in the Sciences, and in Addition the Optics, the Meteorology and the Geometry, Which Are Essays in This Method* (1637).[82] Most (if not all) of the appended essays were actually written first. Descartes sought to describe practice rather than theory. The work was intended to address the Pyrrhonist challenge to science. In religion, Descartes maintained traditional Catholic faith.

Descartes challenged the Pyrrhonists by playing their own game of systematic doubt. "I resolved to pretend that all the things that had ever entered my mind were no more true than the illusions of my dreams. But immediately I noticed that while I was trying thus to think everything

---

81. These works are included in *The Philosophical Writings of Descartes*, 2 vols. trans. John Cottingham, Robert Stoothoff, and Dugald Murdoch (Cambridge: Cambridge University Press, 1984–85). A third volume contains *The Correspondence*, trans. John Cottingham, Robert Stoothoff, Dugald Murdoch, and Anthony Kenny (Cambridge: Cambridge University Press, 1991).

Studies include: John Cottingham, ed., *The Cambridge Companion to Descartes* (Cambridge: Cambridge University Press, 1992); John Cottingham, ed., *Descartes*, Oxford Readings in Philosophy (Oxford: Oxford University Press, 1998); Geneviève Rodis-Lewis, *Descartes: His Life and Thought*, trans. Jane Marie Todd (Ithaca, London: Cornell University Press, 1998); Desmond M. Clarke, *Descartes: A Biography* (Cambridge: Cambridge University Press, 2006); David Cunning, ed., *The Cambridge Companion to Descartes' Meditations* (Cambridge: Cambridge University Press, 2014).

82. *The Philosophical Writings of Descartes*, 1:111. In a letter to Mersenne of March, 1636, Descartes proposed an even more elaborate title (*The Philosophical Writings of Descartes*, 3:50–52).

was false, it was necessary that I, who was thinking this, was something. And observing that this truth '*I am thinking, therefore I exist*' [French, *je pense donc je suis*; Latin, *cogito ergo sum*] was so firm and sure that all the most extravagant suppositions of the sceptics were incapable of shaking it, I decided that I could accept it without scruple as the first principle of the philosophy I was seeking."[83] It was not reached by means of a syllogism in logic. Some facts were impossible to doubt. They include the fact that one is doubting; hence "I am thinking, therefore I exist."[84] The fact was tacitly presupposed by the skeptics themselves in their expressions of doubt.[85]

As friends pointed out, *cogito ergo sum* was a formula that Augustine had used centuries earlier in response to the skeptics of his day. In a letter to Andreas Colvius, Descartes acknowledged the omission, which he claimed to have verified by checking the writings of Augustine in the University of Leiden's library. However, whereas Augustine used the expression in connection with his view of human beings as the image of God, Descartes used it to maintain that "this *I* which is thinking is *an immaterial substance* with no bodily element."[86] In so doing, Descartes opened the door to endless discussion about what may be predicated on the basis of *cogito ergo sum*.[87]

In building his case against skepticism Descartes needed to find further support for indubitable beliefs. No demonstration known to him gave assurance of the existence of their object. He found it in the idea of a perfect being, which "included existence in the same way as—or even more evidently than—the idea of a triangle includes the equality of its three angles to two right angles, or the idea of a sphere includes the equidistance on the surface from the centre. Thus, I concluded it is at least as certain as any geometrical proof that God, who is this perfect being, is or

---

83. *Discourse on the Method*, part 4 (*The Philosophical Writings of Descartes*, 1:127).
84. *The Philosophical Writings of Descartes*, 1:127.
85. Popkin, *The History of Scepticism from Savonarola to Bayle*, 151.
86. Letter date 14 November 1640 (*Philosophical Writings of Descartes*, 3:159). See Augustine, *On the Trinity* 10.10; 15.12.21; *City of God* 11.26; *On Free Will* 2.3.7; *On True Religion* 73; *Against the Academicians* 3.11.25–26; *On the Blessed Life* 2.2.7. Further discussion in Gerard O'Daly, "The Response to Skepticism and the Mechanism of Cognition," and Gareth B. Matthews, "Knowledge and Illumination," in *The Cambridge Companion to Augustine*, ed. Eleonore Stump and Norman Kretzmann (Cambridge: Cambridge University Press, 2001), 159–70, 171–85. Desmond M. Clarke (*Descartes: A Biography*, 210) suggests that Descartes's oversight regarding Augustine may have been an example of Descartes "dissembling again and exaggerating the novelty of his argument."
87. Peter Marki, "The Cogito and Its Importance," in *The Cambridge Companion to Descartes*, 140–73.

exists."[88] Descartes countered the scholastic maxim that there was nothing in intellect that had not been previously in the senses with the triumphant claim that "it is certain that the ideas of God and the soul have never been in the senses." God was the ultimate guarantor of valid sense perception.

However, cracks in Descartes's foundationalist edifice began to appear in the *Meditations*. The *First Meditation* was devoted to the question: What can be called into doubt? It concluded with Descartes's admission that he had not yet achieved his goal of identifying indubitable truth. "I shall stubbornly and firmly persist in this meditation; and, even if it is not in my power to know any truth, I shall at least do what is in my power, that is, guard against assenting to any falsehood, so that the deceiver, however cunning and powerful he may be, will be able to impose on me in the slightest degree. But this is an arduous undertaking, and a kind of laziness brings me back to normal life."[89]

Descartes's methodology placed epistemology before ontology. It involved a hypothetical absolute foundation, accepting the Pyrrhonist agenda of subjecting every proposition to maximum doubt. Charles Larmore reached the following verdict: "Reason, [Descartes] believed, requires that we dispose of every possible error, since only so can reason determine by its own lights the basic structure of the world. That is the basis of the rule, announced at the outset of the First Meditation, that only indubitable beliefs will do. The trouble is that no beliefs, or none of substantive import, can satisfy this standard. In other words, there can be no absolute beginnings."[90]

Similar conclusions were drawn by contemporary readers of the *First Meditation*. Descartes was denounced as a dangerous Pyrrhonist.[91] Since succeeding *Meditations* depended on the *First*, the problem was compounded. In the words of Richard H. Popkin, Descartes turned out to be a *sceptique malgré lui*—a skeptic in spite of himself. "Pyrrhonism was to remain a specter haunting European philosophy while philosophers struggled to find a way to overcome complete theoretical doubt, or to discover how to accept it without destroying all human certitude."[92]

---

88. *The Philosophical Writings of Descartes*, 1:129.
89. *The Philosophical Writings of Descartes*, 2:15.
90. Charles Larmore, "The First Meditation: Skeptical Doubt and Certainty," in *The Cambridge Companion to Descartes' Meditations*, 48–67, here 65–66.
91. Popkin, *The History of Scepticism from Savonarola to Bayle*, 158–73.
92. Popkin, *The History of Scepticism from Savonarola to Bayle*, 173.

Descartes's circle included Marin Mersenne (1588–1648) and his friend Pierre Gassendi (1592–1655). Both were clerics, and both were mitigated Pyrrhonists. Mersenne[93] shrank from rigorous skepticism in practice. He conceded that we could not prove anything certain in physics. However, Mersenne's *La Vérité des Sciences contre les Sceptiques ou Phyrrhoniens* (1625) argued that even if the skeptics could not be refuted, we could have knowledge that was requisite for our purposes in life.

Pierre Gassendi was professor of philosophy at Aix and moved to Paris in 1645.[94] In his earlier work he maintained that knowledge of the real nature of things was impossible, but he later adopted a more moderate skepticism. We could know something about appearances, which could be tested by seeking to verify propositions. His view of the universe was a form of Epicurean atomism.

4.2. Pascal and Pyrrhonism. Pascal and Descartes were contemporaries in more than the chronological sense. Both were born in France. Both made contributions to science. Both were Catholic laymen, and both were opposed to Pyrrhonism. However, their paths diverged widely. They appear to have met only once (September 23–24, 1647), when their discussion centered on the theory of the vacuum and experiments on atmospheric pressure.[95] Their views on religion, philosophy, and how to handle Pyrrhonism could not have been more different.

Blaise Pascal (1623–61)[96] was the son of Étienne Pascal, who later became commissioner of taxes for Upper Normandy. His mother died when he was a child. Pascal was educated at home, along with his two sisters. Throughout his life he had a sickly constitution. From an early age he was gifted in mathematics. Among Pascal's achievements was the invention of a digital calculator to help his father in his profession. In 1646 Pascal came into contact with the Jansenists—named after Cornelius Jansen, whose *Augustinus* (1640) set out a doctrine of grace that opponents denounced as divine determinism. Jansenism was condemned by the Jesuits of the Sorbonne (at the time the theology faculty) and later by Pope Innocent X (1563). However, Pascal was increasingly

---

93. Popkin, *The History of Scepticism from Savonarola to Bayle*, 112–20.
94. Popkin, *The History of Scepticism from Savonarola to Bayle*, 120–27.
95. Henry Philips, "Pascal's Reading and Inheritance of Montaigne and Descartes," in *The Cambridge Companion to Pascal*, ed. Nicholas Hammond (Cambridge: Cambridge University Press, 2003), 20–39, here 30–31.
96. Ben Rogers, "Pascal's Life and Times," in *The Cambridge Companion to Pascal*, 4–19.

drawn to the Jansenist theology of grace and spirituality, which centered on the convent of Port-Royal outside Paris. His younger sister Jacqueline was professed there as a nun.

The great turning point in Pascal's life occurred on November 23, 1654, with his experience of a "night of fire." His account—which gives the precise date—was stitched into the lining of his jacket as a "Memorial." The nearest that Pascal came to writing a book was a series of anonymous ironical letters. In them Pascal adopted the persona of an outsider explaining to a friend in the provinces the conflict between the Jesuits and the Jansenists. They were entitled *Lettres provenciales* (1656–57).[97] During this period, perhaps beginning with the "Memorial," Pascal began jotting down thoughts for a projected apologetic, which he did not live to write. Today these notes are known as Pascal's *Pensées*.[98] Pascal lived long enough to institute the first horse-drawn omnibus service in Paris. The *Pensées* were posthumously published with a preface by his nephew Etienne Périer: *Pensées de M. Pascal sur la religion et sur quelques autres sujets, qui ont esté trouvés après sa mort parmy ses papiers*, or "Thoughts of Monsieur Pascal on Religion and Some Other Subjects Which Have Been Found after His Death among His Papers."[99]

The "Memorial" records a life-changing experience. It involved a fundamental change of outlook and orientation that took place between about 10:30 in the evening and half past midnight. The following is an extract:

---

97. Richard Parish, "Pascal's *Lettres Provenciales*: From Flippancy to Fundamentals," in *The Cambridge Companion to Pascal*, 182–200.

98. Nicholas Hammond, "Pascal's *Pensées* and the Art of Persuasion," in *The Cambridge Companion to Pascal*, 235–52. The *Pensées* are available in various editions, which depend on how French editors have arranged the order of Pascal's notes.

99. Pascal left bundles of notes, some of which carried titles, but others were just thoughts jotted down. In the 1960s Louis Lafuma produced a French edition based on a copy made for Pascal's surviving sister. It is known as Copy A. Another version (Copy B) was that of Philippe Sellier (1976), which corresponded to the order in which Pascal left his notes—some with titles, and others that could not be ordered. The translation of A. J. Krailsheimer (Harmondsworth: Penguin, 1966; rev. ed., 1995) largely incorporates Copy A. *Pensées and Other Writings*, trans. Honor Levi, introduction and notes by Anthony Levi, World's Classics (Oxford: Oxford University Press, 1995) has much of Copy B, plus other material. It provides better background material. Whereas other translations and discussions try to help readers by glossing *Pyrrhonist* as "sceptic," the Levi edition serves them better by retaining Pascal's terminology regarding the Pyrrhonists. The more recent edition of Roger Ariew (Indianapolis: Hackett, 2004) follows Copy B and gives references to the numbering of both Sellier and Lafuma. Citations and page references that follow are to the Levi edition.

> Fire.
> God of Abraham, God of Isaac, God of Jacob.
> not of philosophers and scholars.
> Certainty, joy, certainty, emotion, sight, joy
> God of Jesus Christ.
> *Deum meum et Deum vestrum*
> [My God and your God, John 20:17].
>
> Your God will be my God. Ruth [1:16]. . . .
> This is life eternal, that they might know you,
> the only true God, and him whom you sent,
> [John 17:3]
>
> Jesus Christ
> Jesus Christ
> I have cut myself off from him. I have fled from him,
> denied him, crucified him
> Let me never be cut off from him.
> He can only be kept by the ways taught in the Gospel.
> Sweet and total renunciation.
> Total submission to Jesus Christ and my director.
> Everlasting joy for one's day of tribulation on earth. . . .[100]

Although the Pensées contain no systematic discussions of Descartes and Pyrhhonism, Pascal left no doubt what he thought of them. The following comment is typical: "Descartes useless and uncertain."[101] The Pyrrhonists fared no better:

> We know the truth not only by means of reason but also by means of the heart. It is through the heart that we know the first principles, and reason which has no part in this knowledge vainly tries to contest them. The Pyrrhonists who have only reason as the object of their attack are working ineffectually. We know that we are not dreaming, however powerless we are to prove it by reason.

---

100. *Pensées*, ed. Anthony Levi, 178.
101. *Pensées*, ed. Anthony Levi, §444, 105.

This powerlessness proves only the weakness of our reason, not the uncertainty of our entire knowledge as they claim.[102]

The conflict between rationalism and Pyrrhonism, together with role of gambling in the society in which Pascal lived, provided the context for the famous passage known as "Pascal's Wager."[103] Pascal envisaged an imaginary conversation in which he compared the situation posed by Pyrrhonism to life's great gamble. His argument took various forms. At the core was the fact that in life one could not evade making choices, not least between faith and skepticism. At the lowest material level it could be compared to making a bet. The chances of winning and losing were equal. If one bet on God and won, you won twice—in this life *and* in the world to come. If you lost, you lost nothing.

5. Skepticism, Belief, and Society

It lies outside the scope of this discussion to pursue questions regarding the making of modernity.[104] However, it is worthwhile to examine four major views regarding the impact of skepticism on belief and society. Their relation to the quest of the historical Jesus is indirect but important insofar as they impinge on his identity and the legitimation of Christianity as a belief system.

5.1. Hobbes. Much of Thomas Hobbes's life (1588–1679)[105] was overshadowed by war and bloodshed. He was born in the year of the

---

102. *Pensées*, ed. Anthony Levi, §142, 35; cf. §110, 28. The passage follows a brief critique of Pyrrhonism (§141, 35). A lengthier critique is given in §164, 41–43. Pascal's religious epistemology is summed up in the remark: "The heart has its reasons which reason itself does not know" (§680, 158). Anthony Levi comments: "Merely rational belief, unsupported by the infusion by God of religious feeling in the soul, is without avail in the supernatural order of grace, justification, and salvation. Pascal is also remembering that any theory of faith must accept the religious authenticity of simple uneducated belief" (231).

103. *Pensées*, ed. Anthony Levi, §680, 152–58; cf. A. W. F. Edwards, "Pascal's Work on Probability," and Jon Elster, "Pascal and Decision Theory," in *The Cambridge Companion to Pascal*, 40–52 and 53–74, respectively.

104. See Jonathan I. Israel, *Radical Enlightenment: Philosophy and the Making of Modernity 1650–1750* (Oxford: Oxford University Press, 2001); Roy Porter, *The Creation of the Modern World: The Untold Story of the British Enlightenment* (New York: Norton, 2000).

105. Tom Sorell, ed., *The Cambridge Companion to Hobbes* (Cambridge: Cambridge University Press, 1996); A. P. Martinich, *Hobbes: A Biography* (Cambridge: Cambridge University Press, 1999); Popkin, *The History of Skepticism from Savonarola to Bayle*, 189–207.

Post-Reformation Alternatives

Spanish Armada, which was planned as part of Catholic Europe's conquest of England and feared as an apocalyptic sign of the end time. In later life Hobbes remarked of his premature birth that fear was his twin.[106]

Hobbes lived through the transition of the Elizabethan Age to that of the Stuarts, the English Civil War, the beheading of King Charles I (1649), and the commonwealth of Oliver Cromwell. On the eve of the Civil War, Hobbes fled to France, where he served for a time as tutor to the prince of Wales (1646–48). He lived to see the restoration of the Stuarts in the person of King Charles II and the return of the Church of England with the Book of Common Prayer (1662) as the legally authorized prayer book. On the continent of Europe, the Thirty Years' War (1618–1648) pitted Catholics against Protestants, and nation against nation. Hobbes's political writings sought a way of coping with religious tyranny.

Hobbes spent some years in Paris (1629–31, 1634, 1637, and 1640–51), where he did much of his thinking and writing. As a supporter of the monarchy in the conflict with parliament, he chose exile in France to evade arrest. When he arrived in Paris in 1640, he stayed with a member of the Mersenne-Gassendi circle, Jacques du Bose. Du Bose was a friend of Samuel Sorbière, who was working on a French translation of Sextus Empiricus. Hobbes thus became acquainted with the avant-garde intellectual skeptics in Paris. He also had contact with the Arminian Hugo Grotius, who had found refuge in Paris from the orthodox Dutch Calvinists. Hobbes got to know Descartes and was bewildered how such an intelligent man could be so wrong about philosophy.[107] On his return to England Hobbes submitted to parliament.

Hobbes's political treatise *Leviathan, or the Matter, Form and Power of a Commonwealth, Ecclesiastical and Civil* (1651; Latin edition, 1668),[108]

---

106. Martinich, *Hobbes*, 2.
107. Martinich, *Hobbes*, 164. On publishing his *Mediatationes de Prima Philosophiae* (Paris: Soly, 1641), Descartes circulated the work among friends inviting comments and criticisms. The Third Set of Objections was "by a celebrated English philosopher" (*The Philosophical Writings of Descartes*, 2:121–37). Hobbes raised sixteen objections, which had a Pyrrhonist character. Descartes curtly dismissed them though they were not without philosophical merit. Hobbes's second objection, "I am a thinking thing" concluded: "The knowledge of the proposition 'I exist' thus depends on the knowledge of the proposition 'I am thinking'; and knowledge of the latter proposition depends on our ability to separate thought from the matter that is thinking. So it seems that the correct inference is that the thinking thing is material rather than immaterial" (123).
108. Thomas Hobbes, *Leviathan*, ed. Noel Malcolm, 3 vols. (Oxford: Clarendon, 2012) contains critical editions of both the English and Latin texts. It is published as part of a projected series of Hobbes's collected writings. See also Patricia Springborg, ed., *The Cambridge Companion to Hobbes's Leviathan* (Cambridge: Cambridge University Press, 2007).

was published two years after the execution of Charles I. Its title derived from the awesome sea monster of the Hebrew Scriptures (Job 3:8; 41:1; Pss 74:14; 104:26; Isa 27:1), which Hobbes used as a metaphor for the state and its powers. In the course of his argument, Hobbes laid out a theory of natural law as the basis of society and a view of representative government, which replaced the divine right of kings.

Hobbes sent a copy of *Leviathan* to Prince Charles, who forbade him to come into his presence. However, after the Restoration of the Monarchy, King Charles II awarded Hobbes a pension of £100 a year. In 1666 *Leviathan* was censured by Parliament, and a bill was brought to the House of Commons aimed at punishing atheism. It was dropped perhaps through the intervention of the king, but Hobbes was forbidden to publish anything again in England. His later works were published in Holland.

Hobbes subjected to harsh scrutiny the role of miracles as divine sanction in religion and politics. His discussion in chapter 37 of *Leviathan* heralded the genre of "theological lying."[109] It was a genre, which on the surface presented a viewpoint or argument as the author's own conviction, but it signaled to the discerning reader that the author thought otherwise. Formally Hobbes defined miracles in a way to which a believer could not take exception: "*A* MIRACLE *is a work of God, (besides His operation by way of nature, ordained in the Creation,) done, for the making manifest to his elect the mission of an extraordinary Minister for their salvation.*"[110] But he went on to warn that "ignorance and aptitude to error" over "natural causes" led people to suppose supernatural origins for natural events. Invoking the warnings of Deuteronomy 13 and 18 against false prophets, Hobbes urged that miraculous claims be tested by all possible means. The sovereign state under God—as "God's Lieutenant"—had the right to demand conformity in public. However, in private a man was free "to beleeve or not to beleeve in his heart those acts that have been given out for Miracles."[111]

---

109. David Berman, "Deism, Immortality, and the Art of Theological Lying," in *Deism, Masonry, and the Enlightenment: Essays Honoring Alfred Owen Aldridge*, ed. J. A. Leo Lemay (Newark, DE: University of Delaware Press; London: Associated University Presses, 1987), 61–78; cf. David Berman, *A History of Atheism in Britain: From Hobbes to Russell* (New York: Croom Helm, 1988), 48–69; Jeffrey R. Collins, "Thomas Hobbes: 'Father of Atheists,'" in *Atheism and Deism Revalued: Heterodox Religious Identities in Britain, 1650–1800*, ed. Wayne Hudson, Diego Lucci, and Jeffrey R. Wigglesworth (Farnham: Ashgate, 2014), 25–43.

110. Hobbes, *Leviathan*, ed. Malcolm, 3:688.

111. Hobbes, *Leviathan*, ed. Malcolm, 3:696; cf. Hobbes, *The Elements of Law, Natural and Public* (1640); Martinich, *Hobbes*, 235–53. See also Richard Tuck, "The 'Christian Atheism' of Thomas Hobbes," in *Atheism from the Reformation to the Enlightenment*," ed. Michael Hunter and

Post-Reformation Alternatives

Richard H. Popkin concluded:

> The skeptical element here in both moral and religious cases lies in Hobbes' conviction that there is no rational means for deciding between either competing moral or competing religious claims. Hence Hobbes has denied that there is any rational criterion of knowledge in these areas. Since it is necessary for social reasons that moral and religious decisions be made, the sovereign makes the decision (arbitrarily from the viewpoint of rational evidence for the decision), and the decision is to be accepted by the populace as if it were true.[112]

5.2. Spinoza. Baruch Spinoza (1632–77) (or Benedictus de Spinoza, to use the Latinized form of the name he assumed) was a secular Jewish thinker, whose home was in Calvinist Holland. As a maker of modernity, his life enjoys unrivalled interest among contemporary scholars.[113] Spinoza was born in Amsterdam of Jewish parents who were refugees from Portugal. Some years before his birth, the Netherlands had proclaimed religious freedom of thought. It opened the doors of refuge to those who fled persecution or who could not get their books published

---

David Wootton, 111–30. Tuck concluded that Hobbes was confronted by a dilemma raised by the political situation in England. He could not follow the course of radical independence. The alternative was the state taking over the church and controlling it through parliament. Ultimately, it would cause an avalanche in which Christianity itself would be buried.

112. Popkin, *The History of Skepticism from Savonarola to Bayle*, 201.

113. *Tractatus Theologico-Politicus*, ed. Carl Gebhard (Heidelberg: Winter, 1925); trans. Samuel Shirley, with introduction by Brad S. Gregory (Leiden: Brill, 1989). Vol. 1 of *The Collected Works of Spinoza*, trans. and ed. Edwin Curley (Princeton: Princeton University Press, 1985) contains Spinoza's posthumously published *Ethica* (1677). A recent translation of Spinoza's *Tractatus Theologico-Politicus* is *Theological-Political Treatise*, Cambridge Texts in the History of Philosophy, ed. Jonathan Israel, trans. Michael Silverthorne and Jonathan Israel (Cambridge: Cambridge University Press, 2007). See also Curley, *The Collected Works of Spinoza*, 2:65–354.

Recent studies include Don Garrett, ed., *The Cambridge Companion to Spinoza* (Cambridge: Cambridge University Press, 1996); Olli Koistinen, ed. *The Cambridge Companion to Spinoza's Ethics* (Cambridge: Cambridge University Press, 2009); Yitzhak Y. Melamed and Michael A. Rosenthal, eds., *Spinoza's Theological-Critical Treatise: A Critical Guide* (Cambridge: Cambridge University Press, 2010); Steven Nadler, *A Book Forged in Hell: Spinoza's Treatise and the Birth of the Secular Age* (Princeton, NJ: Princeton University Press, 2011); Susan James, *Spinoza on Philosophy, Religion, and Politics: The Theologico-Political Treatise* (Oxford: Oxford University Press, 2012); Daniel B. Schwartz, *The First Modern Jew: Spinoza and the History of an Image* (Princeton: Princeton University Press, 2012). On Spinoza's influence on the German Enlightenment see Winfried Schröder, *Spinoza in der deutschen Frühaufklärung* (Würzburg: Königshausen und Neumann, 1987).

in the countries of their birth. However, this did not prevent the young Spinoza from being expelled from the synagogue in 1656 for his heterodox views of the Bible. He moved away from Amsterdam, and for some years lived near Leiden. He then moved to Voorburg and then to The Hague, where he lodged in modest circumstances. His principal income came from grinding and polishing lenses for microscopes and telescopes. This occupation was a factor in his premature death. Additional financial support came from friends. He refused a chair of philosophy at Heidelberg, fearing that it might curtail his unorthodox views.

Spinoza published only two books in his lifetime. The first was a geometrical demonstration of Descartes's philosophy (1663) initially conceived to assist a student whom he was informally tutoring.[114] The second was his *Tractatus Theologico-Politicus* (1669), which was published anonymously with a fictitious title page. In the meantime, Spinoza was working on the definitive statement of his philosophy, *Ethica*.[115] The work was posthumously published by friends along with other writings as *Opera Posthuma* (1677) of an author identified as B.D.S.

Two decades after Hobbes's *Leviathan*, Spinoza's *Tractatus Theologico-Politicus* (*Theological-Political Treatise*, 1669) pushed skepticism about revealed religious knowledge to its limits. At the same time, as Richard H. Popkin remarks, Spinoza "was completely antisceptical with regard to 'rational knowledge,' that is metaphysics and mathematics."[116]

The fictitious title page[117] contained both misinformation and information. The misinformation was about the book's provenance. It gave the date of publication as 1670, instead of 1669. It announced that the book was published in Hamburg—not Amsterdam, the actual place of publication. The publisher's name, Heinrich Kuhnraht, was probably

---

114. Spinoza, *Parts I and II of Descartes's Principles of Philosophy Demonstrated in the Geometric Manner* (1663).

115. *Ethics, Demonstrated in Geometrical Order and Divided into Five Parts*. The work was presented as a series of deductive theorems in the manner of Euclidian geometry. A critical edition of *Ethics* in translation was made by Edwin Curley in *The Collected Works of Spinoza*, vol. 1 (Princeton, NJ: Princeton University Press, 1985). Extracts were published in *A Spinoza Reader*, which included an introduction by Stuart Hampshire (Princeton, NJ: Princeton University Press, 1994). It was republished as Benedict de Spinoza, *Ethics* (New York: Penguin, 1996).

116. Popkin, *The History of Skepticism from Savonarola to Bayle*, 239; cf. Alan Donagan, "Spinoza's Theology" and Richard H. Popkin, "Spinoza and Bible Scholarship," in *The Cambridge Companion to Spinoza*, 343–82 and 383–407, respectively.

117. *Theological-Political Treatise*, ed. Jonathan Israel, 1.

Post-Reformation Alternatives

an arcane joke.[118] With regard to information, the treatise's subtitle set out what the book was about: *Several Discourses Which Demonstrate That Freedom to Philosophize May Not Only Be Allowed Without Danger to Piety and the Stability of the Republic but Cannot Be Refused Without Destroying the Peace of the Republic and Piety Itself.* For good measure, the title page demonstrated the treatise's religious ecumenicity by quoting a verse from the New Testament: "By this we know that we remain in God, and God remains in us, because he has given us his spirit" (1 John 4:13).

Chapter 6 of the treatise was devoted to showing the inadmissibility of miracles on rational grounds. There could be no contravention of the laws of nature, for the laws of nature were the laws of God. This proposition should be understood within the context of Spinoza's pantheism, which posited one single substance—*deus sive natura*, God or nature[119]—which many contemporaries saw as a form of atheism. God is not the transcendent Creator of nature; *God is Nature*. Miracles either did not happen or were susceptible to natural explanation.

Spinoza began his discussion with the observation: "Just as men habitually call that knowledge which surpasses human understanding 'divinity', so they likewise classify any phenomenon whose cause is unknown by common people 'divine' or a work of God."[120] He proceeded to argue that, even if we could draw conclusions from miracles, we could not infer the existence of God, or anything substantive.

---

118. The name was that of the mystical writer Heinrich Kuhnraht (1560–1605). The name may also contain a pun together with a hint on what the work was about. In German *kühn* means "bold," "daring," and *Rat* means "counsel." Heinrich is a common German name. In other words, the book contains bold counsel for all who are prepared to give it a fair hearing. *Rat* was also the name of the council of the free imperial city of Hamburg.

119. In his discussion on God in part 1 of his *Ethics* (*The Collected Works of Spinoza*, 1:408–446) Spinoza set out his pantheistic view of God and the world. "P15: Whatever is, is in God, and nothing can be or be conceived without God." "P18: God is the immanent, not the transitive cause of all things." "P. 29: In nature there is nothing contingent, but all things have been determined from the necessity of the divine nature to exist and produce an effect in a certain way." He explained his view by means of his distinction between *Natura naturans* and *Natura naturata.*

"[By] *Natura naturans* we must understand what is in itself and conceived through itself, *or* such attributes of substance as express an eternal and infinite essence. . . . God, insofar as he is considered as a free cause. But by *Natura naturata* I understand whatever follows from the necessity of God's nature, *or* from any of God's attributes, that is, all the modes of God's attributes insofar as they are considered as things which are in God, and can near be nor conceived without God."

120. *Theological-Political Treatise*, ed. Jonathan Israel, 81.

We therefore conclude that we cannot come to know God and his existence and providence from miracles, the former being much better inferred from the fixed and unalterable order of nature. In reaching this conclusion I am speaking of a miracle simply as a phenomenon which surpasses, or is thought to surpass, human understanding. For in so far as it is conceived to destroy or interrupt the order of nature or conflict with its laws, to that extent (as we have just shown) not only would it give us no knowledge of God, it would actually take away the knowledge we naturally have and make us doubt about God and all things.[121]

Spinoza explicitly ruled out "any difference between a phenomenon which is contrary to nature and a phenomenon which is above nature.... For since a miracle does not occur outside of nature but within nature itself, even if it is said to be above nature, it must still necessarily interrupt the order of nature which otherwise we conceive to be fixed and unalterable by God's decrees."[122] In addition, he appealed to "Scripture's authority" in support of his view.

Even though Scripture nowhere explicitly tells us this, it may readily be inferred from the command of Moses in Deuteronomy 13 to condemn a false prophet to death even if he performs miracles. He says: (even though) "the sign or wonder that he foretold to you shall come to pass, etc., do not" (nevertheless) "listen to the words of that prophet, etc., for the Lord your God is testing you", etc. It plainly follows from this that miracles can be performed by false prophets, and that unless men are duly strengthened by a true knowledge and love of God, they may just as easily embrace false gods as a consequence of miracles as the true God; for he adds: "since Jehovah

---

121. *Theological-Political Treatise*, ed. Jonathan Israel, 86.
122. *Theological-Political Treatise*, ed. Jonathan Israel, 86–87. Spinoza proceeded to review the way that narratives of biblical miracles, including the healing on the blind man in John 9, indicated that they required "something other than what is called the absolute command of God" (*Treatise*, 90).

Spinoza concluded "without reservation that all things that are truly reported to have happened in Scripture necessarily happened according to the laws of nature as all things do. If anything is found which can be demonstrated conclusively to contradict the laws of nature or which could not possibly follow from them, we must accept in every case that it was interpolated into the Bible by blasphemous person. For whatever is contrary to nature, is contrary to reason, and what is contrary to reason, is absurd, and accordingly to be rejected" (*Treatise*, 91).

your God is testing you so as to know whether you love him with all you heart and with all your soul".[123]

In bringing Deuteronomy 13 into the discussion, Calvin, Hobbes, and Spinoza proved themselves more biblically literate than many later participants in the debate. However, none of them seems to have discerned the implications of this passage and its relevance to the quest of the historical Jesus. In my judgment, Deuteronomy 13 was implicit in the Beelzebul charge, which was at the center of what I called the First Quest in chapter 1. The point was not simply a question of miraculous power. It was also a matter of using inexplicable healing powers to attract a following in the service of what was presumed to be an alien deity.

Hugo Grotius had earlier drawn attention to the possible application to Jesus of Deuteronomy 13 in *De Veritate Christianae Religionis* ("On the Truth of the Christian Religion," 1627). However, he promptly dismissed its relevance on the grounds that Jesus' actions were directed toward the glory of God, and his teaching expressly forbade worship of false gods.[124]

In the ensuing discussion Spinoza pursued another course. In chapter 7 Spinoza turned to the interpretation of Scripture. Here he depicted Jesus not as subverter of the law but as its "teacher." He was concerned above all to save Israel from ruin by calling them back to the moral teaching of the law. In this sense, Jesus was the successor to Jeremiah, whose prophetic teaching had likewise failed to avert calamity.

> Had Jesus given these commands [the moral teaching of the Sermon on the Mount] as legislator, he would have destroyed the Law of Moses by this edict. But he openly commends the Law (see Matthew 5:17); consequently we must examine who it was exactly that said these things, to whom and at what time. Certainly, it was Christ who uttered them, but he was not laying down ordinances as legislator. Rather he was offering doctrine as a teacher, because (as we have shown above) it was less external actions that he sought to

---

123. *Theological-Political Treatise*, ed. Jonathan Israel, 87; cf. Deut 13:2–4. Spinoza noted that "miracles may also be performed by imposters" was "proved" by Deut 13 and Matt 24:24 (*Treatise*, 96).

124. Hugo Grotius, *The Truth of the Christian Religion, with Jean Le Clerc's Notes and Additions*, trans. John Clarke (1742), ed. with introduction by Maria Rosa Antognazza (Indianapolis: Liberty Fund, 2012), 192–93. For further discussion see below, chap. 4.

correct than peoples' minds. He pronounced these words to people who were oppressed and living in a corrupt state where justice was completely neglected, and he saw the ruin of that state was imminent.

This very doctrine that Christ taught at a time when the city's desolation was imminent, we see that Jeremiah had also expounded at the time of the first destruction of the city (see Lamentations 3). . . . Hence, the prophets offered this teaching only at a time of oppression, and it is nowhere promulgated as a law.[125]

Instead of achieving its goal of toleration and free speech, the *Theological-Political Treatise* met with condemnation from both the Jewish and Christian communities. The States of Holland and the States General formally banned the treatise, together with Lodewijk Meijer's *Philosophia S. Scripturae Interpres* ("Philosophy, Interpreter of Sacred Scripture," 1666) and Hobbes's *Leviathan*.[126]

In 1676, the year before his death, Spinoza was visited by Leibniz. The German philosopher publicly disowned him but privately was preoccupied by his ideas.[127] Following Spinoza's death, the States of Holland and the States General issued a more comprehensive ban (1678), condemning all his teachings and threatening authors, publishers, and printers with heavy fines and long terms of imprisonment for violations. Underlying the ban was not only Spinoza's critical understanding of Scripture but also his hermeneutic that gave priority to philosophy in the hermeneutics of Scripture.

A century later, the Christian philosopher F. H. Jacobi initiated in Germany what was called the *Pantheismusstreit*, pantheism controversy.[128] Jacobi claimed that Gotthold Ephraïm Lessing toward the end of his life had admitted to him that he was a Spinozist. Moses Mendelssohn, Lessing's long-standing friend and leader of the Jewish Enlightenment,

---

125. *Theological-Political Treatise*, ed. Jonathan Israel, 103.

126. Meijer was a friend and advocate of Spinoza. See Nadler, *A Book Forged in Hell*, 120–26, 129–31, 134–35. Spinoza and Meijer had the same publisher, Jan Rieuwertsz, who also published Descartes; cf. *A Book Forged in Hell*, 216–39.

127. Matthew Stewart gives a vivid reconstruction of the encounter in *The Courtier and the Heretic: Leibniz, Spinoza, and the Fate of God in the Modern World* (New York: Norton, 2006).

128. Kurt Weinberg, "Patheismusstreit," in *The Encyclopedia of Philosophy*, ed. Paul Edwards (New York: Macmillan, 1967), 6:35–37; Micah Gottlieb, *Faith and Freedom: Moses Mendelssohn's Theological-Political Thought* (Oxford: Oxford University Press, 2011).

was outraged. The controversy eventually involved Kant and Goethe. In view of Lessing's role in the quest of the historical Jesus, the admission to Jacobi—if true—sheds light on events that began to unfold in the 1770s. We shall discuss the question further in chapter 5.

5.3. Locke. John Locke (1632–1704) was born in the same year as Spinoza. He was the son of a west-country landowner and lawyer. At Christ Church, Oxford, Locke was awarded a studentship, which was tenable for life—being the equivalent of a fellowship at other colleges. At the time Puritanism was at its zenith. Locke held a variety of positions including censor of moral philosophy and lecturer in Greek. At Oxford he became increasingly interested in science and medicine and received his medical degree in 1665. In 1666 he was granted a dispensation from taking Holy Orders on the grounds that ordination would distract him from his scientific studies. The following year Locke joined the household of Lord Ashley, future earl of Shaftesbury. Locke performed surgery on Ashley, and Ashley credited him for saving his life. In 1668 Locke was elected a fellow of the Royal Society of London for Improving Natural Knowledge.

In 1671 Locke wrote the first drafts of his epoch-making contribution to philosophy *An Essay Concerning Human Understanding*.[129] The book was eventually published in 1689, though the title page bore the date 1690. Because of health problems, Locke lived in France for some time (1675–79), mainly in Paris and Montpellier. Here he read Descartes, got to know disciples of Gassendi, and became acquainted with Pyrrhonism.[130]

Toward the end of the Stuart monarchy Locke found it prudent to live in Holland (1683–89) because of his links with Shaftesbury and others who were implicated in a failed attempt to overthrow James II because of his Catholic leanings.[131] In Holland he entered the most productive intel-

---

129. An abridged version of *An Essay Concerning Human Understanding* was edited by A. S. Pringle-Pattison [1924], rev. by Peter H. Nidditch (Oxford: Clarendon, 1974). Quotations below are cited from Pringle-Pattison's edition. A version based on the posthumous 5th edition of 1706 was edited by Roger Woolhouse (London: Penguin, 1997, 2004). See also Vere Chappell, ed., *The Cambridge Companion to Locke* (Cambridge: Cambridge University Press, 1994); G. A. J. Rogers, ed., *Locke's Philosophy: Context and Content* (Oxford: Oxford University Press, 1994); Alan P. F. Sell, *John Locke and the Eighteenth-Century Divines* (Cardiff: University of Wales Press, 1997); Lex Newman, ed., *The Cambridge Companion to Locke's "Essay Concerning Human Understanding"* (Cambridge: Cambridge University Press, 2007).

130. Popkin, *The History of Scepticism from Savonarola to Bayle*, 257–61; J. R. Milton, "Locke's Life and Times," in *The Cambridge Companion to Locke*, 5–25, here 12–13.

131. Milton, "Locke's Life and Times," 14–17.

lectual phase of his career. He completed his *Essay Concerning Human Understanding* and his *First Letter on Toleration*. He made contact with other political exiles from England and elsewhere, including Pierre Bayle, as well as Dutch intellectuals. Locke did not return to England until after the Glorious Revolution of 1688, which brought William of Orange (William III) to the throne. In his later years Locke served in a variety of government posts including on the council for trade and plantations.

Locke never married. For health reasons he moved out of London. From 1691 to his death in 1704 he lived in Essex in the home of Sir Francis and Lady Masham. Lady Masham was the daughter of the Cambridge Platonist Ralph Cudworth. In his final days she read the Psalms to him.

In retirement Locke wrote three theological works. One was published in his lifetime: *The Reasonableness of Christianity, As Delivered in the Scriptures* (1695; 2nd ed., 1696).[132] The other two were published posthumously: *A Discourse of Miracles* (1706); and *A Paraphrase and Notes on the Epistles of St. Paul* (6 vols., 1705–7).

J. R. Milton commented on *Paraphrase*:

> The anti-Trinitarianism, which critics had rightly claimed to detect in his earlier writings, is again present, though understandably implicit rather than explicit form. Despite his wide reading in Socinian literature, he seems not to have been a pure Socinian, but rather to have adopted a position closer to Arianism. More generally, the *Paraphrase* reveals the deeply religious character of Locke's mind. It shows, much more clearly than *The Reasonableness of Christianity*, that the Christian vocabulary of Locke's earlier works cannot be interpreted as a pious façade or (less implausibly) a mere residue in a mind already secular but either reluctant or unable to acknowledge itself as such.[133]

In philosophy Locke adopted the mitigated skepticism of the Royal Society regarding what could and could not be known scientifically. The Royal Society received its charter from King Charles II in 1662.

---

132. Discussion below is based on the abridged edition, edited by Ian T. Ramsey, *The Reasonableness of Christianity with A Discourse of Miracles and Part of A Third Letter Concerning Toleration* (London: Black, 1958).

133. Milton, "Locke's Life and Times," 123–24.

Post-Reformation Alternatives

Early members included clergy, bishops, and laymen who were interested in science. Among their number was Joseph Glanvill of Bath Abbey and a chaplain to the king. Glanvill advocated what R. M. Burns called "the principle of context."[134]

> 'Tis not the doing wonderful things that is the only evidence that the holy Jesus was from God, and his doctrine true; but the conjunction of other circumstances, the holiness of his life, the reasonableness of his religion, and the excellency of his designs, added credit to his works, and strengthened the great conclusion, that he would be no other than the Son of God, and Saviour of the World.[135]

A similar view was advocated by Sir Robert Boyle (1627–91), the founder of chemistry and son of the Earl of Cork. Sir Robert, who was a founding member of the Royal Society, was an ardent Bible student. In his will was left the sum of £50 a year for the annual Boyle Lectures against "infidels." Boyle composed numerous treatises defending the harmony of scientific method and faith.

> If a supernatural effect be wrought to authorize a doctrine yet plainly contradicts these truths [the general principles of religion], I cannot judge such a miracle to be divine. . . . But if the revelation backed by a miracle proposes nothing that contradicts any of these truths . . . and much more if it proposes a religion that illustrates and confirms them; then I think myself obliged to admit both the miracle, and the religion it attests.[136]

The point of this digression on Glanvill and Boyle is to indicate that the views on miracles presented by Locke were in the tradition of situating miracles in the kind of context stipulated by proponents.

Locke's *Essay Concerning Human Understanding* was skeptical of the possibility of innate knowledge, as Descartes had claimed.

---

134. R. M. Burns, *The Great Debate on Miracles: From Joseph Glanvill to David Hume* (Lewisburg, PA: Bucknell University Press; London: Associated University Presses, 1981), 50.

135. Joseph Glanvill, *Saducismus Triumphatus* (London: Lowndes, 1689; repr., Gainesville, FL: Scholar's Facsimiles and Reprints, 1966), 101; cited from Burns, *The Great Debate on Miracles*, 50.

136. Boyle Manuscripts, Royal Society, 7 folios, 120–22; cited from Burns, *The Great Debate on Miracles*, 55.

Locke's repudiation of innate knowledge as derived from experience is summed up in the following statement about ideas.

> Let us then suppose the mind to be, as we say, white paper, void of all characters, without any ideas; how comes it to be furnished? Whence comes it by that vast store, which the busy and boundless fancy of man has painted on it with an almost endless variety? Whence has it all the materials of reason and knowledge? To this I answer, in one word, from EXPERIENCE; in that all our knowledge is founded, and from that it ultimately derives itself. Our imagination wither employed either external sensible objects, or about the internal operations of our minds, perceived and reflected upon by ourselves, is that which supplies our understandings of all the materials of thinking. These two are the fountains of knowledge, from whence all the ideas we have, or can naturally have, do spring. (*Essay* 2.1.2)

In book 4 Locke drew the following conclusions about knowledge in general: "Since the mind, in all its thoughts and reasonings, hath no other immediate object but its own ideas, which it alone does or can contemplate, it is evident that our knowledge is only conversant about them" (*Essay* 4.1.1). "Knowledge is the perception of the agreement or disagreement of two ideas" (*Essay* 4.1.2; cf. 4.3).

This may suggest that Locke was committed to a representative theory of perception, which limited knowledge to knowledge of ideas. However, the above quotations were accompanied by discussion of three kinds of knowledge: intuitive, demonstrative, and sensitive. Intuitive knowledge provided the greatest certainty and was basic to demonstration and knowledge acquired through the senses.

> Thus the mind perceives that white is not black, that a circle is not a triangle, that three are more than two, and equal to one and two. Such kind of truths the mind perceives at the first sight of the ideas together, by bare intuition, without the intervention of any other idea; and this kind of knowledge is the clearest and most certain that human frailty is capable of. . . . It is on this intuition that depends all the certainty and evidence of our knowledge, which certainty everyone finds so great, that he cannot imagine, and

therefore cannot require, a greater. . . . Certainty depends so wholly on this intuition, that in the next degree of knowledge, which I call demonstrative, this intuition is necessary in all the connexions of the intermediate ideas, without which we cannot attain knowledge and certainty. (*Essay*, 4.2.1)[137]

Probability was by its character relative. Locke defined *probability* as "the appearance of agreement upon fallible proofs" (*Essay*, 4.15.1). In this regard one must weigh the pros and cons relative to experience. The claim of ability to walk on water is feasible in cold climates but less so in the tropics, where ice is not part of common experience. Locke's story about the king of Siam, which was probably in circulation in Holland during Locke's exile, is a relevant example. The Dutch ambassador told the king that in his country in cold weather water became so hard that an elephant could walk on it. "To which the king replied, 'Hitherto I have believed the strange things that you have told me, because I look upon you as a sober fair man; but now I am sure you lie'" (*Essay*, 4.15.5). Locke went on to observe: "*Analogy* in these matters is the only help we have, and it is from that alone we draw all our grounds of probability" (*Essay*, 4.16.12).

Toward the end of his *Essay*, Locke embarked upon a discussion of how revelation might fit into this scheme of human understanding. He did so by means of drawing the following distinctions:

> (1) *According to reason* are such propositions whose truth we can discover by examining and tracing those ideas we have from sensation and reflection, and by natural deduction find to be true or probable. (2) *Above reason* are such propositions whose truth or probability we cannot by reason derive from those principles. (3) *Contrary to reason* are such propositions as are inconsistent with or irreconcilable to our clear and distinct ideas. Thus the existence of God is according to reason; the existence of more than one God is contrary to reason; the resurrection of the dead above reason. (*Essay* 4.17.23)

The credibility of the propositions that are above reason must be established by facts that are according to reason and empirically grounded.

---

137. For discussion, see Vere Chappell, "Locke's Theory of Ideas," in *The Cambridge Companion to Locke*, 26–55; Popkin, *The History of Scepticism from Savonarola to Bayle*, 258–61.

Reason is natural revelation, whereby the eternal Father of light and Fountain of all knowledge communicates to humankind the portion of truth that he has laid within the reach of their natural faculties. Revelation is natural reason enlarged by a new set of discoveries communicated by God immediately that reason vouches for the truth of by the testimony and proofs it gives that they come from God. (*Essay* 4.19.4)

Miracles, especially those that fulfilled prophecy,[138] were foundational in establishing truth claims involving propositions that were above reason. In *A Discourse of Miracles* Locke insisted that any definition of a miracle must contain a double reference: to the divine and to the observer. He defined a miracle as "a sensible operation, which, being above the comprehension of the spectator, and in his opinion contrary to the established course of nature, is taken by him to be divine."[139]

Miracles were not to be valued for their own sake or for their revelatory content. Rather, they functioned as credentials for validating the divine character of revelation. "To know that any revelation is from God, it is necessary to know that the messenger that delivers it is sent from God himself. Let us see then whether miracles, in my sense, be not such credentials, and will not infallibly direct us right in the search of divine revelation."[140] Locke postulated further qualifications: miracles must honor God; they must fulfil prophecy; they cannot be expected to attest to trivialities or serve as a substitute for rational inquiry; natural explanations cannot be ruled out in given cases.

Locke did not use miracles to establish belief in God.[141] His view of

---

138. *The Reasonableness of Christianity*, §§55–61. "For Locke, the miracles of Jesus are only significant because they were prophesied" (James E. Force, "Hume and Johnson on Prophecy and Miracles in Historical Context," in *Philosophy, Religion and Science in the Seventeenth and Eighteenth Centuries*, ed. John W. Yolton (Rochester, NY: University of Rochester Press, 1994), 127–39, here 129. Sir Isaac Newton also believed in fulfilled prophecy as a guarantee of the reasonableness of Christianity; cf. Newton, *Observations upon the Prophecies of Daniel and the Apocalypse of St. John* (London: Darby and Brown, 1733); cf. Frank E. Manuel, *The Religion of Isaac Newton*, Freemantle Lecture 1973 (Oxford: Clarendon, 1974).

139. Locke, *The Reasonableness of Christianity*, 79. The argument developed the views of reason, faith, and revelation set out in *An Essay Concerning Human Understanding*, 4.16, 4.18. Locke declared: "To convince men of this, he did his miracles; and their assent to, or not assenting to this, made them to be, or not to be of his Church; believers, or not believers," 33; cf. Colin Brown, *Miracles and the Critical Mind* (Grand Rapids: Eerdmans, 1984; repr., Pasadena, CA: Fuller Theological Seminary Press, 2006), 42–46.

140. Locke, *The Reasonableness of Christianity*, 80.

141. Human beings were capable of "*knowing certainly that there is a God*" on other grounds (*Essay* 4.10.1–19).

miracles is in line with what we have noted about his view of revelation. It did not contradict what was already known and accepted by reason. Rather, it enlarged the understanding and enabled one to perceive new truth. Miracles, therefore, function within the wider context of what is already known and believed about God. Their character confirms that the one who performs them does not deviate from the known character of God. The God who is attested by the miracle is the same as the one who is known on other grounds.

Miracles were not simply wonders that defied explanation but attestations from God confirming the revelation associated with the miracle. This is the thrust of Nicodemus's remark to Jesus: "Rabbi, we know that you are a teacher come from God; for no one can do these signs that you do apart from the presence of God" (John 3:2).[142] Or as Locke put it,

> If we will direct our thoughts by what has been, we must conclude that miracles, as the credentials of a messenger delivering a divine religion, have no place but upon a supposition of one only true God....
>
> For example, Jesus of Nazareth professes himself sent from God: He with a word calms a tempest at sea. This one looks on as a miracle, and consequently cannot but receive his doctrine. Another thinks this might be the effect of chance, or skill in the weather and no miracle, and so stands out; but afterwards seeing him walk on the sea, owns that for a miracle and believes; which yet upon another has not that force, who suspects it may possibly be done by the assistance of a spirit. But yet the same person, seeing afterwards Our Saviour cure an inveterate palsy by a word, admits that for a miracle, and becomes a convert. Another, overlooking it in this instance, afterwards finds a miracle in his giving sight to one born blind, or in raising the dead, or his raising himself from the dead, and so receives his doctrine as a revelation coming from God. By all which it is plain, that where the miracle is admitted, the doctrine cannot be rejected; it comes with the assurance of a divine attestation to him that allows the miracle, and he cannot question its truth.[143]

---

142. Locke, *The Reasonableness of Christianity*, 82.
143. Locke, *The Reasonableness of Christianity*, 81–82.

Similar arguments may be found in writers who differed from Locke in other respects: the Newtonian, Samuel Clarke,[144] and the latitudinarian Edward Stillingfleet,[145] who had denounced Locke's *Essay Concerning Human Understanding* as detrimental to the Trinitarian faith. The ambivalence about Locke lives on. The main body of scholars are inclined—with reservations—to take his writings at face value. However, among those who urge that Locke should be read with caution is Michael P. Zuckert, professor of political science at the University of Notre Dame.[146] His central concern was political theory. He built on the work of Leo Strauss who contended that Locke was a Hobbesian, but argued that Locke moved beyond Hobbes.[147] Zuckert even spoke—with deference to Pascal—of a "Lockean Wager" regarding Locke's arguments. Locke signaled in various ways uncertainty about his arguments for the existence of God.[148] Zuckert urged the need of circumspection with regard to "Lockean hermeneutics."[149] However, Zuckert stopped short of Matthew Stewart's suggestion that at bottom Locke shared Spinoza's view of God.[150]

Richard H. Popkin described Locke's view of knowledge as "a sort of semi-scepticism that could be read as a justification for empirical science."[151] Alan P. Sell concluded that Locke "was not a deist or Socinian, still less an atheist. He was a Christian." What that meant was expressed by Locke's dying words: "in perfect charity with all men and in sincere communion with the whole church of Christ, by whatever names Christ's followers call themselves."[152]

---

144. The miracles of Jesus afforded a "compleat *Demonstration* of our Saviour's being a Teacher sent from God"; Samuel Clarke, *A Discourse Concerning the Unchangeable Obligations of Natural Religion and the Truth and Certainty of the Christian Revelation*, Boyle Lectures for 1705 (Clarke, *Works*, 2:701).

145. Edward Stillingfleet, "Now what convictions there can be to any sober mind concerning *Divine authority* in any person without such a *power of miracles* going along with him, when he is to deliver some new doctrine to the world to be believed, I confess I do not understand"; Edward Stillingfleet, *Origines Sacrae* (London: Mortlock, 1663), 143.

146. Michael P. Zuckert, *The Natural Rights Republic: Studies in the Foundation of the American Political Tradition* (Notre Dame, IN: University of Notre Dame Press, 1996); Zuckert, *Launching Liberalism: On Lockean Political Philosophy* (Lawrence: University Press of Kansas, 2002).

147. Leo Strauss, *Natural Right and History* (Chicago: University of Chicago Press, 1954).

148. Zuckert, *Launching Liberalism*, 8; cf. Zuckert's discussion of Locke and the Old Testament and Christianity (129–66).

149. Zuckert, *Launching Liberalism*, 25–106.

150. Matthew Stewart, *Nature's God: The Heretical Origins of the American Republic* (New York: Norton, 2014), 146–49.

151. Popkin, *The History of Scepticism from Savonarola to Bayle*, 260.

152. Sell, *John Locke*, 273, 277.

Finally, I would like to add my own opinion, which concurs with much of this discussion. I read Locke's *Essay* and theological writings as akin to what in the nineteenth century Kierkegaard called thought-projects—hypothetical, provisional attempts to identify the paradoxes of reality.[153] Kierkegaard recognized that his own thought-projects would be judged unsatisfactory. Locke's discussion of miracles in terms of credentials of a messenger from God is at best provisional. Any single miracle on its own may not serve as a sufficient credential. Locke remained reticent about the content of the message. But given the qualifications that Locke made, miracle stories serve as pointers to divine transcendence.

5.4. Hume. David Hume (1711–1776)[154] is remembered today as perhaps the most acute of the British philosophers in the empiricist tradition. However, there are grounds for tracing the influence of Epicurus but concluding that Hume thought of himself as a mitigated Pyrrhonist.[155]

Hume entered the University of Edinburgh at the age of twelve and left two or three years later without taking a degree. He tried his hand

---

153. Søren Kierkegaard, *Philosophical Fragments, Johannes Climacus*, ed. and trans. Howard C. Hong and Edna H. Hong (Princeton, NJ: Princeton University Press, 1985); cf. Colin Brown, *Jesus in European Protestant Thought, 1778–1860*, Studies in Historical Theology 1 (Durham: Labyrinth, 1985; repr., Pasadena: Fuller Seminary Press, 2008), 140–59.

154. Ernest Campbell Mossner, *The Life of David Hume*, 2nd ed. (Oxford: Clarendon, 1980). A comprehensive overview of Hume's thought is David Fate Norton and Jacqueline Taylor, eds. *The Cambridge Companion to Hume*, 2nd ed. (Cambridge: Cambridge University Press, 2009). An appendix contains Hume's two autobiographical sketches: "A Kind of History of My Life" (1734), and "My Own Life" (1776) (515–29). For additional background see Alexander Broadie, ed., *The Cambridge Companion to the Scottish Enlightenment* (Cambridge: Cambridge University Press, 2003).

155. On the influence of Sextus Epicurus see Hume's *Enquiry Concerning Human Understanding*, in *Enquiries Concerning Human Understanding and Concerning the Principles of Morals*, ed. L. A. Selby-Bigge, rev. by P. H. Nidditch, 3rd ed. (Oxford: Clarendon, 1975), 11, §§102–15. On Hume's *mitigated* Pyrrhonism, see *Enquiry* 12, §§129–30; cf. David Hume, *An Enquiry Concerning Human Understanding: A Critical Edition*, trans. and ed. Tom L. Beauchamp, Clarendon Edition of the Works of David Hume (Oxford: Clarendon, [2000] 2007), xxxiv–xxxv, 116–23, 192–200; Donald L.M. Baxter, "Hume's Theory of Space and Time in Its Skeptical Context," in *The Cambridge Companion to Hume*, 105–46, esp. 112–21; Robert J. Fogelin, "Hume's Skepticism," in *The Cambridge Companion to Hume*, 209–37.

Hume rejected Pyrrhonism or *"excessive* skepticism" as self-destructive," but "a more *mitigated* skepticism, or ACDEMICAL philosophy . . . may be more durable and useful," when it corrects the excessive variety "by common sense and reflection" (*Critical Edition*, 120). Hume concluded his *Enquiry* with a reflection that was both a rhetorical flourish and a concise expression of his mind: "When we run of libraries, persuaded by the principles, what havoc must we make? If we take in our hand any volume; of divinity or school metaphysics, for instance; let us ask, *Does it contain any abstract reasoning regarding quantity and number?* No. *Does it contain any reasoning concerning matter of fact and existence?* No. Commit it then to the flames: For it can contain nothing but sophistry and illusion" (123).

at law and business but soon gave up. The account of what followed is recorded in Hume's words, entitled *My Own Life*,[156] which he composed in April 1776 knowing that he was terminally ill with cancer and had not long to live.

Following his lack of success in business Hume went to France. He resided mainly in La Flèche, Anjou, where Descartes had received his early education, and where Hume enjoyed the library and hospitality of the Jesuit fathers. At La Flèche he wrote much of *A Treatise of Human Nature*. Its publication in London (1738) "fell *dead-born from the press*; without reaching such distinction as even to excite a Murmur among the Zealots."[157] Following his failure to win a chair in the University of Edinburgh, Hume accepted an invitation to tutor the mentally unstable Marquis of Annandale. After that he became secretary to General St. Clair, who led an abortive expedition to Brittany. Hume later accompanied the general in embassies in Vienna and Turin.

Hume resolved to make a second attempt to publish his ideas.[158] He reworked book 1 of the treatise and restored the discussion of miracles that he had intended to include. The new book was entitled *Philosophical Essays Concerning Human Understanding* (1748). The 1758 edition bore the title *Enquiry Concerning Human Understanding*. It paralleled Hume's *Enquiry Concerning the Principles of Morals* (1751), which was based on book 3 of his prior treatise.

Once again Hume's efforts resulted in disappointment. "On my return from Italy, I had the Mortification to find all England in a Ferment on account of Dr. Middleton's Free Enquiry; while my Performance was entirely overlooked and neglected."[159] The "Performance" was his *Enquiry*, which met the same public indifference that greeted his other philosophical writings. The work that eclipsed Hume's was Conyers Middleton's *A Free Inquiry into the Miraculous Powers, Which Are Supposed to Have Subsisted in the Christian Church from the Earliest Ages through Several Successive Centuries. By Which It Is Shewn, That We Have No Sufficient Reason to Believe, upon the Authority of the Primitive Fathers,*

---

156. Mossner, *The Life of David Hume*, 591; cf. *The Cambridge Companion to Hume*, 526.
157. Hume, *My Own Life* (1776).
158. The *Enquiry* may, like Hume's *Letter from a Gentleman*, be an answer to critics, rebuilding his reputation, following Hume's failure to obtain a chair at Edinburgh University (Beauchamp, ed., *Critical Edition*, xvii–xix).
159. Mossner, *The Life of David Hume*, 612; *The Cambridge Companion to Hume*, 525.

That Any Such Powers Were Continued to the Church, after the Days of the Apostles (1749).[160]

Having failed to gain an academic position at Glasgow University, Hume became librarian to the faculty of advocates in Edinburgh (1752). Here he found the leisure and materials to write the most successful work published in his lifetime—his multivolume *History of England* (1752–57). During Hume's later years he published only one work, which addressed religion—a slim volume that offered little comfort to the orthodox and their adversaries *The Natural History of Religion* (1757).[161] There is evidence of a draft as early as 1751, but the subject matter of Hume's *Dialogues Concerning Natural Religion* contributed to their posthumous publication (1779).[162]

Hume lived in Paris (1763–66), where he was a popular figure in literary circles. He even entertained hopes of retiring to France. However, war intervened. On returning to England he was accompanied by Rousseau. It was a relationship that went sour. Back in London, Hume served as undersecretary in the Northern Department, a position which gave him responsibility for preferments in the Scottish Episcopal Church. He returned to Edinburgh in 1769.

Hume's contribution to the quest of the historical Jesus was indirect but substantial, albeit in a negative way. He did not discuss Jesus directly, but like the work of Conyers Middleton, which for a time outshone Hume's, it raised troubling questions about the Christian faith. Middleton's *Free Inquiry* and Hume's *Enquiry* appeared toward the end

---

160. Conyers Middleton, *A Free Inquiry into the Miraculous Powers* (1749) facsimile reprint (New York: Garland, 1976); cf. Brown, *Miracles and the Critical Mind*, 64–72. Conyers Middleton (1683–1750) was briefly a fellow of Trinity College, Cambridge, and for a time university librarian. He was noted for his writing style, which was overshadowed by his reputation as a latitudinarian and controversialist.

161. Hume's *The Natural History of Religion* was published in *Four Dissertations* (1757). A modern text was edited by H. E. Root (London: Black, 1956). The work gave Hume's view of anthropology, beginning with polytheism as the "primary religion." Religion had a bad influence on humankind. The whole was "an enigma, an inexplicable mystery," with the various species of religion opposing each other. Hume preferred to make his "escape into the calm, though obscure, regions of philosophy" (70).

162. A modern edition of the *Dialogues* was edited by Norman Kemp Smith (1935). Reprints include *Dialogues Concerning Natural Religion* (Indianapolis: Bobbs-Merrill, n.d.). They were modeled on Cicero, *On the Nature of the Gods*. Hume took the opportunity to discuss the ontological and cosmological arguments for the existence of God (cf. Brown, *Christianity and Western Thought: A History of Philosophers, Ideas and Movements* [Downers Grove, IL: InterVarsity Press, 1990], 1:251–55). Hume gave the concluding advice: "to be a philosophical sceptic is, in a man of letters, the first and most essential step towards being a sound believing Christian" (part 13, 228).

of the deist controversy and were to some extent retreading ground covered by writers that will be discussed in the next chapter. The reason for discussing them at the end of a chapter on post-Reformation alternatives lies in the fact that they represent the culmination of those alternatives.

Middleton's work was an extended critique of patristic miracle stories. Its methodology prompted John Wesley to suspect that the criteria could be applied equally to the New Testament and that Middleton was striving "to overthrow the whole Christian system."[163] In response Wesley composed a monograph-length letter to the author by way of refutation.[164] Neither Middleton nor Hume discussed the historical Jesus, but their questioning of miracles implicitly raised the question of the historicity of the gospel narratives and the identity of Jesus. History has reversed the situation described by Hume. Today Middleton's work is read by historians, whereas Hume's essay "Of Miracles,"[165] which appears as section 10 of his *Enquiry*, occupies center stage in any discussion of the subject.

Hume's argument[166] questioned the viability of basing religious belief on miracles and proposed criteria for assessing testimony to miracles,

---

163. Journal, January 28, 1749. See *The Works of John Wesley* 20, *Journals and Diaries* 3, ed. W. Reginald Ward and Richard P. Heitzenrater (Nashville: Abingdon, 1991), 262.

164. Letter to Middleton dated January 4, 1749. See *The Letters of the Rev. John Wesley, A.M.*, ed. John Telford (London: Epworth, 1931), 2:312–88.

165. Hume originally entitled his work *Philosophical Essays Concerning Human Understanding*. References are to Hume's *Enquiries Concerning Human Understanding and Concerning the Principles of Morals*, based on the posthumous 1777 ed., ed. L. A. Selby-Bigge, 3rd ed. rev. by P. H. Nidditch (Oxford: Clarendon, 1975); and also to the *Critical Edition* (see n155).

166. For more detailed discussion, see A. Flew, *Hume's Philosophy of Belief: A Study of His First Enquiry* (New York: Humanities, 1961), 166–213; Richard Swinburne, *The Concept of Miracle* (London: Macmillan; St. Martin's, 1970); Burns, *The Great Debate on Miracles*; J. C. A. Gaskin, *Hume's Philosophy of Religion* (Atlantic Highlands, NJ: Humanities, [1978]; 2nd ed., 1988), 135–65; J. L. Mackie, *The Miracle of Theism: Arguments for and against the Existence of God* (Oxford: Clarendon, 1982), 13–29; Brown, *Miracles and the Critical Mind*, 79–100; Robert J. Fogelin, *Hume's Skepticism in the Treatise of Human Nature* (New York: Routledge, 1985); David Basinger and Randall Basinger, *Philosophy and Miracle: The Contemporary Debate*, Problems in Contemporary Philosophy 2 (Lewiston: Mellon, 1986); Richard Swinburne, ed., *Miracles* (New York: Macmillan; London: Collier Macmillan, 1989); Robert A. H. Larmer, *Water into Wine? An Investigation of the Concept of Miracle* (Montreal: McGill-Queen's University Press, 1988); T. C. Williams, *The Idea of the Miraculous: The Challenge to Science and Religion* (New York: St. Martin's, 1990); Keith E. Yandell, *Hume's "Inexplicable Mystery": His Views on Religion* (Philadelphia: Temple University Press, 1992); J. Houston, *Reported Miracles: A Critique of Hume* (Cambridge: Cambridge University Press, 1994); Robert Bruce Mullin, *Miracles and the Modern Religious Imagination* (New Haven, CT: Yale University Press, 1996); R. Douglas Geivett and Gary R. Habermas, eds., *In Defence of Miracles: A Comprehensive Case for God's Action in History* (Downers Grove, IL: InterVarsity Press, 1997); Robert J. Fogelin, *A Defense of Hume on Miracles* (Princeton, NJ: Princeton University Press, 2003); J. C. A. Gaskin, "Hume on Religion," in *The Cambridge Companion to Hume*, 480–513.

which struck at the heart of traditional apologetics. The argument turned on the empirical character of the laws of nature in which belief is to be proportioned to evidence.[167] It led to a definition, which at the same time constituted a refutation: "A miracle is a violation of the laws of nature; and as a firm and unalterable experience has established these laws, the proof against a miracle, from the very nature of the fact, is as entire as any argument from experience can possibly be imagined."[168]

This definition was further qualified by a second definition that Hume gave in a footnote: "A miracle may accurately be defined, *a transgression of a law of nature by a particular volition of the Deity, or by the interposition of some invisible agent.*"[169] Some interpreters have seen in this second definition precisely the conditions that would warrant belief in a transgression of the laws of nature. But Hume thought that the problems attached to testimony to the miraculous were such that either the "miracle" would turn out to have a natural explanation or testimony to it would never be strong enough to warrant credence in the face of near-uniform experience.

Hume went on to exploit the weak and inconclusive character of testimony to the miraculous: the questionable character of the witnesses to alleged events performed in locations where detection of fraud was impossible,[170] human propensity to gossip and enlarge upon the

---

167. *Enquiry* §87. "The Indian prince, who refused to believe the first relations concerning the effects of frost, reasoned justly. . . . [reports about ice] bore so little analogy to those events, of which he had a constant and uniform experience. Though they were not contrary to his experience, they were not conformable to it" (§89).
  Discussion of this analogy was one of the most widely discussed issues in the *Enquiry*. Hume's allusion to the Indian prince may be indebted to Butler's *Analogy* rather than Locke's king of Siam (*Essay* 4.15.5). Hume inserted it in the second edition (1750). See Beauchamp, *Critical Edition*, 172–73.

168. *Enquiry* §90. Augustine and Aquinas both denied that miracles were violations of the laws of nature (Beauchamp, *Critical Edition*, 173). On their definition, genuine miracles were not violations of the created order of nature.
  It should be borne in mind that the Latin *miraclum* suggests a wonder, marvel, or amazing event. Augustine discussed the issue in a number of places. He held that there was no impropriety in saying that God did something that was contrary to nature if we meant that it was *contrary to what we know of nature* (*Against Faustus* 26.3; cf. *The Literal Meaning of Genesis* 6:13–14, 18; 9:17–18; *City of God* 21.8). Aquinas followed in the Augustinian tradition. He defined a miracle as "an event that occurs outside the natural run of things [Latin, *aliquid fit praeter ordinem naturae*]" (*Summa Theologiae* 1.110.4; Blackfriars Edition); cf. *Summa contra Gentiles* 3.2.99–102.

169. *Enquiry* §90 (Hume's emphasis). The second definition appears designed to address ancient and modern testimonies to the miraculous making explicit theistic claims, which Hume discussed in part 2, §92–98. See the literature noted by Beauchamp, *Critical Edition*, xxxi, 177–83.

170. *Enquiry* §92.

truth,[171] the fact that miracles "chiefly abound among ignorant barbarous nations" and that civilized people give credence to them on the credit of "ignorant and barbarous ancestors,"[172] and that truth claims based on miracles of rival religions cancelled each other out.[173]

Although the gospel narratives were not mentioned directly, Hume had set a trap for the unwary apologist who might appeal to the miracles described in them. Hume identified a number of examples that might conceivably falsify his argument but also served to discredit comparable stories in the Bible: Tacitus's report of "one of the best attested miracles in all profane history," that is, Vespasian in the temple of Serapis in Alexandria healing a blind man by his spittle and a lame man by the touch of his foot;[174] recent reports from Paris of the miracles at the tomb of François de Pâris;[175] and the hypothetical raising from the dead of Queen Elizabeth I after three months of certified internment.[176] "And what," asked Hume with a flourish that echoed the epistle to the Hebrews, "have we to oppose to such a cloud of witnesses, but the absolute impossibility or miraculous nature of the events, which they relate? And this surely, in the eyes of all reasonable people, will alone be regarded as sufficient refutation."[177] He concluded that what he had said

---

171. *Enquiry* §93.

172. *Enquiry* §94. Hume noted that from time to time miracle workers were exposed through chance accident, as in the case of Alexander of Abonoteichus, who was exposed by Lucian of Samosata. "But, though much to be wished, it does not always happen, that every Alexander meets with a Lucian, ready to expose and detect his impostures" (*Enquiry* §94; cf. Lucian, *Alexander the False Prophet*, in *Lucian*, trans. A. M. Harmon, LCL 4 [1925]: 174–253). Alexander achieved fame in remote Paphlagonia between 150 and 170, purporting to deliver oracles through the snake symbol of Asclepius, which turned out to be a contraption constructed by Alexander; cf. Steven J. Scherrer, "Signs and Wonders in the Imperial Cult: A New Look at a Roman Religious Institution in the Light of Rev 13:13–15," *JBL* 103 (1984): 599–610.

173. *Enquiry* §95.

174. *Enquiry* §96; cf. Tacitus, *Histories* 4.81; cf. *Tacitus*, trans. C. H. Moore, LCL 2 (London: Heinemann, 1931), 159–161; Suetonius, *Lives: The Deified Vespasian* 7; cf. *Suetonius*, trans. J. C. Rolfe, LCL 2 (London: Heinemann, 1914), 299.

175. *Enquiry* §96. The stories centered on the recently deceased Jansenist, François de Pâris (1690–1727), whose tomb rapidly became a miraculous shrine, which was closed by royal authority amidst religious and political ferment. The affair was widely known in the eighteenth century. Middleton refused to credit the events, though he allowed that they were better attested than miracles in the early church (*Free Inquiry*, 223–26). John Wesley also refused to credit them, but saw no analogy between them and the miracles in the early church and the Gospels (*Letters* 2:374). On the circumstances see Robert B. Kreiser, *Miracles, Convulsions, and Ecclesiastical Politics in Early Eighteenth-Century Paris* (Princeton, NJ: Princeton University Press, 1978).

176. *Enquiry* §99.

177. *Enquiry* §96; cf. Heb 12:1.

about miracles applied equally to prophecy, which was only another form of miracle pressed into service as "an argument for a divine mission or an authority from heaven."

> So that, upon the whole, we may conclude, that the *Christian Religion* not only was at first attended with miracles, but even at this day cannot be believed by any reasonable person without one. Mere reason is insufficient to convince us of its veracity: And whoever is moved by *Faith* to assent to it, is conscious of a continued miracle in his own person, which subverts all the principles of his understanding, and gives him a determination to believe what is most contrary to custom and experience.[178]

The argument poses many questions. Was it consistent for one who elsewhere had defined causal connections as something that "we *feel* in the mind"[179] to invoke the closed causal system of natural law to deny the possibility of exceptions? Was Hume a defender or an opponent of Newtonian science? Was Hume's argument an exercise in applying proto-Bayesian probability theory?[180] Has not Hume's emphasis on miracles as *violations* overlooked the possibility of divine immanent activity in the ordering of unusual events? Can history rule out the miraculous? Can science identify it? Can we ever know that an event has been caused by God? Such questions are the stuff of which philosophy of religion examinations are made. As significant as these questions are, my present purpose does not permit me to offer answers.[181]

---

178. *Enquiry* §101.

179. *Enquiry* §59; cf. §60; cf. Hume, *A Treatise of Human Nature*, ed. L. A. Selby-Bigge (Oxford: Clarendon, [1888] 1967), 1.3.14.

180. Cf. David Owen, "Hume versus Price on Miracles and Prior Probabilities," in Swinburne, ed., *Miracles*, 115–32. The theorem of Thomas Bayes (1702–61) was published posthumously in 1763, but it may have been known to Hume. It stated that the probability of a hypothesis relative to evidence and antecedent knowledge is equal to the probability of the hypothesis relative to antecedent knowledge multiplied by the probability of evidence relative to the hypothesis and antecedent knowledge and divided by the probability of the evidence relative to antecedent knowledge. Thus evidence improbable antecedently, but likely to obtain if the hypothesis raises the probability of a hypothesis most likely to be true. However, the problem with the theorem lies in assigning exact values to evidence and antecedent probabilities. David Wootton has made a strong case for locating Hume's argument as a response to French thought ("Hume's 'Of Miracles': Probability and Irreligion," *Studies in the Philosophy of the Scottish Enlightenment*, ed. M. A. Stewart [Oxford: Oxford University Press, 1990], 191–229).

181. For works offering answers, see n168.

The insertion of a discussion of miracles in a volume of *Enquiries Concerning Human Understanding* seemed "quite superfluous" to Hume's Victorian editor, L. A. Selby-Bigge.[182] But this verdict overlooks two factors: Hume's own pronouncements and the role that miracles had come to play in belief systems. At the outset Hume announced his satisfaction at having found "a decisive argument" that must "*silence* the most arrogant bigotry and superstition, and free us from their impertinent solicitations."[183] The argument was essentially negative and defensive.[184] Hume had not demonstrated the impossibility of miracles, especially if one grants their possibility within the context of a theistic belief system.[185] It was the foundational role of miracles in establishing such a system that was the primary object of attack.

> Every miracle, therefore, pretended to have been wrought in any of these religions (and all of them abound in miracles), as its direct scope is to establish the particular system to which it is attributed; so has it the same force, though more indirectly, to overthrow every other system. In destroying a rival system, it likewise destroys the credit of those miracles, on which that system was established; so that all the prodigies of different religions are to be regarded as contrary facts, and the evidences of these prodigies, whether weak or strong, as opposite to each other.[186]

David Owen commented: "Hume argued that the evidence of testimony in favor of miracles could never be good enough to provide a

---

182. *Enquiries*, viii, cf. xix.
183. *Enquiry* §86.
184. Flew, *Hume's Philosophy of Belief*, 176.
185. Cf. William Paley, *View of the Evidences of Christianity* (Cambridge: Hall & Son, [1794]; 4th ed., 1864), 2. Richard Swinburne offered a simplified version of Bayes' theorem regarding probability. He noted the importance of inclining factors and the relevance of "Weltanschauung:" "If any of these arguments have any weight, we would need only slender historical evidence of certain miracles to believe in their occurrence, just as we need only slender historical evidence of certain miracles to have reasonable grounds for belief in the occurrence of events whose occurrence is rendered probable by natural laws" (*The Concept of Miracle*, 68).
186. *Enquiry* §94. Whether Hume's contention that all religions have miracles and are used to establish belief systems is true is another matter. Swinburne pointed out that the major religions do not in fact make appeal to miracles in this way (*The Concept of Miracle*, 17–18, 60–61). Nor did they function in the ancient world to establish mutually exclusive belief systems. See Howard Clark Kee, *Miracle in the Early Christian World: A Study in Sociohistorical Method* (New Haven, CT: Yale University Press, 1983).

Post-Reformation Alternatives

rational basis for the foundation of a religion. . . . [It was designed] as an argument against a certain way of trying to rationally ground belief in Christianity."[187] Similar conclusions are shared by others.[188] They are supported by Hume's correspondence,[189] including the exchange with George Campbell in which Hume described how he first propounded his argument some years earlier in the Jesuit College at La Flèche.[190] The letters corroborate the view that Hume thought of his argument as a defense against both Protestant and Catholic apologetics in relation to the place that miracles had come to occupy in apologetics in the

---

187. In Swinburne, ed., *Miracles*, 132.

188. Terence Penelhum (*Hume* [London: Macmillan, 1975], 178) thought that the argument showed that, "Even if it is rational for a believer to expect some miracles to have occurred, it is not rational to *become* a believer on the basis of reports of them." The implausibility of a story may neutralize but not wholly demolish testimony. Similarly J. L. Mackie noted that it was one thing for theists to postulate the feasibility of miracles. It was something entirely different if the context of the debate is about the truth of theism itself. The intrinsic probability is that the event was not miraculous or that it did not occur and that the testimony is faulty in some way. "This entails that it is pretty well impossible that reported miracles should provide a worthwhile argument for theism addressed to those who are initially inclined to atheism or even to agnosticism" (*The Miracle of Theism*, 27). Likewise J. C. A. Gaskin (*Hume's Philosophy of Religion*, 165) described the argument as a systematic attack on "the reasonableness of belief in revealed religion."

189. See Hume's comments on the text prior to publication of George Campbell's *Dissertation on Miracles* (1762) in his undated letter to the Rev. Hugh Blair in the autumn of 1761 (*The Letters of David Hume*, ed. J. Y. T. Greig, [Oxford: Clarendon, 1932; repr., New York: Garland, 1983], §188, 1:348–51). Hume described Campbell as "certainly a very ingenious man, tho a little too zealous for a philosopher" (351). The letter repeats in summary Hume's earlier position, reiterating Hume's view of the connection between miracles and beliefs: "I never read of a miracle in my life, that was not meant to establish some new point of doctrine. . . . If a miracle proves a doctrine to be revealed from God, and consequently true, a miracle can never be wrought for a contrary doctrine. The facts are therefore as incompatible as the doctrines" (350–51). On Campbell, see Jeffrey M. Suderman, *Orthodoxy and Enlightenment: George Campbell in the Eighteenth Century*, McGill-Queen's Studies in the History of Ideas 32 (Montreal: McGill-Queen's University Press, 2001).

190. In a letter to Campbell following publication of the latter's "performance" in response to his argument, Hume cordially acknowledged Campbell's acumen and personal spirit but felt obliged to stick to his rule of not responding to critics. He did, however, inform Campbell that he might be amused to learn of the origin of his argument. In discussion with a learned Jesuit in the cloisters of the College of La Flèche during the time in which Hume was writing *A Treatise of Human Nature* (1735–37), the Jesuit told of a miracle that had been performed there. Hume outlined his objections whereupon the Jesuit observed "that it was impossible for that argument to have any solidity, because it operated equally against the Gospel as the Catholic miracles;— which observation I thought proper to admit as a sufficient answer" (letter to Campbell, June 7, 1762, *Letters* §194, 1:260–361). See *Enquiry* §96 for Hume's skepticism concerning miracles in the Catholic Church.

Hume deemed it prudent not to publish the argument in the *Treatise* but finally threw caution to the wind and published it in 1748. See Hume's letter to Henry Home, December 2, 1737 (*New Letters of David Hume*, ed. Raymond Klibansky and Ernest C. Mossner [Oxford: Clarendon, 1954; repr., New York: Garland, 1983], §1, 1–3); Letter to Henry Home, February 9, 1748 (*The Letters of David Hume*, §62, 1: 111).

establishment of divinely sanctioned truth claims. It was, like Hume's other arguments, a form of mitigated Pyrrhonism. Hume thought that consistent Pyrrhonism stultified all thought and action. In its place he advocated "a more *mitigated* scepticism or *academical* philosophy," using "a small tincture of Pyrrhonism."[191] The benefits of a "*mitigated scepticism* which may be of advantage to mankind, and which may be the natural result of the Pyrrhonian doubts and scruples, is the limitation of our enquiries to such subjects as are best adapted to the narrow capacity of human understanding."[192] Hume's philosophy in general and his discussion of miracles in particular exemplify this "*mitigated* scepticism," the natural result of "Pyrrhonian doubts and scruples."

Readers who have read only Hume's essay and his remarks about Middleton in "My Own Life" might be pardoned if they concluded that Hume felt piqued at finding that Middleton had beaten him to the winning post by publishing a novel critique of miracles. In point of fact, both Middleton and Hume were plowing over old ground. All of Hume's points had been made in the deist controversy.[193] Middleton's objections to patristic miracle stories were in principle the same as Hume's to miracle stories in general.[194] Hume's unique contribution was his elegant, concise formulation of the argument.

---

191. *Enquiry* §129. The "*academical* philosophy" refers to the skepticism of the Greek Middle Academy in the second century BCE.

192. *Enquiry* §130.

193. Burns, *The Great Debate on Miracles*, 141; cf. 70–141.

194. In response to six theses set out by John Chapman's *Eusebius* (Cambridge, 1739), Middleton proposed the following counter theses: "1. That they were all of such a nature, and performed in such a manner, as would inject a suspicion of fraud and delusion. 2. That the cures and beneficial effects of them, were either false, or imaginary, or accidental. 3. That they tend to confirm the idlest of all errors and superstitions. 4. That the integrity of the witnesses is either highly questionable, or their credulity at least so gross, as to render them unworthy of any credit. 5. That they were not onely vain and unnecessary, but generally speaking, so trifling also, as to excite nothing but contempt. And lastly, that the belief and defence of them, are the onely means in the world, that can possibly support, or that does in fact give any sort of countenance, to the modern impostures in the Romish Church" (Middleton, *A Free Inquiry*, 175–176). Similarities of language suggest that not only Middleton, but Hume may have been responding to Chapman (cf. Brown, *Miracles and the Critical Mind*, 64–72).

As with Hume, the principal objection was bound up with probability. "Ordinary facts, related by a credible person, furnish no cause of doubting from the nature of the thing: but if they be strange and extraordinary, doubts naturally arise, and in proportion as they approach towards the marvellous, those doubts still increase and grow stronger: for mere honesty will not warrant them; we require other qualities in the historian; a degree of knowledge, experience, and discernment, sufficient to judge of the whole nature and circumstances of the case: and if any of these be wanting, we necessarily suspend our belief" (Middleton, *A Free Inquiry*, 217).

Hume's methodology prompted Antony Flew to endorse C. S. Peirce's observation that "the whole of modern 'higher criticism' of ancient history in general, and of Biblical history in particular, is based on the same logic that is used by Hume."[195] This verdict claims too much. The only results that Hume achieved or allowed were negative. Hume showed no interest in recovering the historical Jesus. On the other hand, his argument highlighted the importance of analogy in making historical judgments, the interplay between science and history in determining what is feasible, and the fact that Christian origins cannot be isolated from the cultural and religious world of their day. These issues are still with us today. Hume's legacy with regard to miracles was not to prove their impossibility but to question their credibility and make succeeding generations nervous about appealing to them in order to establish a belief system. Hume's arguments had a chilling effect on investigators of the historical Jesus, who became increasingly hesitant about stressing the miraculous.

---

195. Flew, *Hume's Philosophy of Belief,* 179, citing C. S. Peirce, *Values in a Universe of Chance,* ed. P. P. Wiener (New York: Doubleday Anchor, 1958), 292–93. See Brown, *Miracles and the Critical Mind,* 72–77, for Edward Gibbon's attitude to the miraculous, and 103–36 for growing skepticism in Europe.

CHAPTER 4

DEISM AND THE HISTORICAL JESUS

ALBERT SCHWEITZER dated the quest of the historical Jesus from Hermann Samuel Reimarus (1694–1768), whom Schweitzer claimed had "no predecessors."[1] This chapter completes the task begun in the first two chapters of identifying predecessors and the intellectual and cultural climates in which they lived. I begin with a word of caution. The title of this chapter does not imply that the authors discussed here were generic deists. It may be more appropriate to speak of deisms, rather than deism.[2] Some authors may not even qualify as deists when measured by conventional views of deism. Two common threads run through the chapter. The first is that whatever else they believed or did not believe, the writers repudiated the orthodox doctrine of the Trinity and the pre-existent sonship of Jesus. The second is the pervasive influence of British writing. We shall consider the following:

1. British Deism
    1.1. Deism as Alternative to Orthodoxy and Pyrrhonism
    1.2. The Assault on Prophecy and Miracles
    1.3. Deism in Decline

---

1. *The Quest of the Historical Jesus*, 26 (details given below in chap. 5).
2. Cf. Wayne Hudson, "Introduction: Atheism and Deism Revived," and "Atheism and Deism Demythologized," in *Atheism and Deism Revalued: Heterodox Religious Identities in Britain, 1650–1800*, ed. Wayne Hudson, Diego Lucci, and Jeffrey R. Wigglesworth (Farnham: Ashgate, 2014), 1–12, 13–23.

2. Deism in America
   2.1. Early American Deists
   2.2. Jefferson's Lives of Jesus
3. Deism in Germany
   3.1. German Reception of English Deism
   3.2. Reimarus and the English Deists
   3.3. Kant's Deism
4. Retrospect

1. British Deism

1.1. Deism as Alternative to Orthodoxy and Pyrrhonism. In his celebrated *Dictionary of the English Language* (1755), Dr. Samuel Johnson defined *deist* as "a man who follows no particular religion but only acknowledges the existence of God, without any other article of faith." The word seems to have been used by Calvin's disciple Pierre Viret to describe an unidentified group who professed "belief in God as creator of heaven and earth but reject Jesus Christ and his doctrines."[3] In Viret's

---

3. Pierre Viret, *Instruction Chrestienne*, 2, Geneva, 1564 ("Epistre"). Etymologically the term derives from the Latin *deus* (God). It may be compared with *theism*, which derives from the Greek θεός, *theos* (God). Whereas theism denotes belief in a God who is both transcendent and immanent, deism precludes immanent divine activity in the world.

The classic contemporary survey is that of John Leland (1691–1766), *A View of the Principal Deistical Writers That Have Appeared in England in the Last and Present Century; with Observations upon Them, and Some Account of the Answers That Have Been Published against Them. in Several Letters to a Friend*, 2 vols. (London: Dod, 1744; 3rd ed., 1757); *A Supplement to the First and Second Volume of the View of the Deistical Writers. Containing Additions and Illustrations Relating to Those Volumes. in Several Letters to a Friend. to Which Is Added, Reflections on the Late Lord Bolingbroke's Letters on the Study and Use of History, as It Relates to the Holy Scriptures . . . with a Large Index to the Three Volumes*, 3rd ed. (London: Dod, 1756).

More recent studies include Leslie Stephen, *History of English Thought in the Eighteenth Century*, 2 vols. ([1876]; repr. of 3rd ed., 1902, New York: Harcourt Brace; London: Rupert-Hart Davis, 1962); Norman L. Torrey, *Voltaire and the English Deists* (New Haven, CT: Yale University Press, 1930; repr., Archon, 1967); John Redwood, *Reason, Ridicule and Religion: The Age of Enlightenment in England, 1660–1750* (London: Thames and Hudson, 1976), 134–55; Henning Graf Reventlow, *The Authority of the Bible and the Rise of the Modern World*, trans. John Bowden (London: SCM, 1984; Philadelphia: Fortress, 1985), 289–410; William Baird, *History of New Testament Research*, vol. 1, *From Deism to Tübingen* (Minneapolis: Fortress, 1992), 31–57; Richard H. Popkin, "The Deist Challenge," in *From Persecution to Toleration*, ed. Ole Peter Grell, Jonathan I. Israel, and Nicholas Tyacke (Oxford: Oxford University Press, 1991), 195–215; J. A. I. Champion, *The Pillars of Priestcraft Shaken: The Church of England and Its Enemies, 1660–1730*, Cambridge Studies in Early Modern History (Cambridge: Cambridge University Press, [1992] repr., 2014); Michael Hunter and David Wootton, eds., *Atheism from the Reformation to the*

sense, the deists were opposed to atheism, but by Dr. Johnson's day *deist* had become used internationally as a euphemism for *atheist*.[4]

Deism is commonly dated from the publication in Paris in 1624 of Edward Herbert's *De Veritate, Prout distinguitur a Revelatione, a Verisimili, a Possibli, et a Falso*.[5] More recently, Herbert (c. 1582–1648) has been called a naturalist and protodeist.[6] Herbert was a soldier, courtier, duelist, and diplomat. He attended Oxford University without completing a degree.

In 1619 Herbert was appointed King James I's ambassador to France with instructions to renew the oath of alliance between the kings of England and France and to maintain peaceful relations. In Paris he gained access to intellectual society. He was abruptly recalled in 1624 and rewarded with the Irish barony of Castle Island and the English barony of Cherbury (1629).

Before leaving Paris, Herbert completed *De Veritate* and with the approval of Grotius published it privately. The first edition was dedicated to "the whole human race," but the second edition (1633) and the final edition (1645) were dedicated to "every reader of sound and unprejudiced judgement." The work sought to develop a rational religion in response to Pyrrhonian skepticism and Protestant and Catholic orthodoxy. It argued

---

Enlightenment (Oxford: Clarendon, [1992]; repr., 2003); James A. Herrick, *The Radical Rhetoric of the English Deists: The Discourse of Skepticisim, 1680–1750* (Columbia: University of South Carolina Press, 1997); Jonathan I. Israel, *Radical Enlightenment: Philosophy and the Making of Modernity, 1650–1750* (Oxford: Oxford University Press, 2001); Richard H. Popkin, *The History of Scepticism from Savonarola to Bayle* (Oxford: Oxford University Press, 2003); Henning Graf Reventlow, *History of Biblical Interpretation*, vol. 4, *From the Enlightenment to the Twentieth Century*, trans. Leo G. Perdue, SBL Resources for Biblical Study 63 (Atlanta: Society of Biblical Literature, 2010); Hudson, Lucci, and Wigglesworth, eds., *Atheism and Deism Revalued*.

The following discussion is indebted to my earlier studies, *Miracles and the Critical Mind* (Grand Rapids: Eerdmans, 1984; repr., Pasadena, CA: Fuller Seminary Press, 2006), 47–77; and *Jesus in European Protestant Thought, 1778–1860*, Studies in Historical Theology 1 (Durham, NC: Labyrinth, 1985; repr., Pasadena, CA: Fuller Seminary Press, 2008), 36–50.

4. In the first of the Boyle Lectures Richard Bentley preached on "The Folly of Atheism, And (what is now called) DEISM; Even with Respect to the *Present Life*" (1692). He claimed to have "detected the mere *Deists* of our Age to be no better than disguised *Atheists*" (*The Works of Richard Bentley*, ed. Alexander Dyce [1838; repr., New York: AMS, 1966], 3:25).

5. An English translation was made by Merrick H. Carré from the 1645 edition, *On Truth, as It Is Distinguished from Revelation, the Probable, the Possible, and the False*, University of Bristol Studies 6 (Bristol: Arrowsmith, 1937). Herbert was the British ambassador in Paris at the time. Thomas Halyburton called Herbert "the father of English deism." His *Natural Religion Insufficient, and Revealed Necessary to Man's Happiness in His Present State* (1714) contains detailed accounts of Herbert and Blount (*The Works of Thomas Halyburton* [Glasgow: Blackie & Son, 1837], 253–501). See also David A. Pailin, *ODNB*, 26:663–69.

6. Israel, *Radical Enlightenment*, 629, 791.

that all religions were based on five innate principles or common notions independent of special revelation: the existence of God, that God should be worshiped, that virtue joined with piety is the chief element of worship, that repentance is a duty that expiates evil, and that there would be rewards and punishments in the afterlife.

The work was damned with faint praise by Gassendi and openly criticized by Descartes and Locke. In the measured words of Gassendi, "The truth in my view is well hidden from the Eyes of men and Monsieur Herbert seems to me to have gone a little too fast and to have a high opinion of his view when he recently condemned the arguments of the Sceptics."[7] The enlarged edition of *De Veritate* (1645) included an attack on revealed religion. Some copies included *De causis errorum: una cum tractatu de religione laici, et appendice ad sacerdotes; necnon quibusdam poematibus*, which also appeared separately.[8]

Charles Blount (1654–93) was educated at home on account of his father's opposition to the debauchery of undergraduate university life.[9] Blount married in 1672. The ceremony took place in Westminster Abbey. He had three sons and a daughter. About the time of his marriage, Blount inherited land in Islington, London, and was given the family estate of Blount's Hall in Staffordshire, where he lived the life of a country gentleman and man of letters. He also participated in fashionable London life. Blount's writings were either anonymous or published under a pseudonym.

Blount's first publication was a defense (1673) of John Dryden's play *The Conquest of Granada*. Dryden rewarded him with a complimentary

---

7. Letter of Gassendi to Diodati, August 29, 1634, in Mersenne, *Correspondance* 4 (1955): 337, quoted by Popkin, *The History of Scepticism from Savonarola to Bayle*, 123; cf. Gassendi, *Ad Librum D. Edoarti Herberti, De Veritate, Epistola*.

8. "Concerning the Causes of Errors, with a Treatise Concerning Religion for the Laity, and an Appendix to Priests; with Certain Poems" (cf. David A. Pailin, *ODNB*, 26:666). *De religione gentilium errorumque apud eos causis* ("Concerning the Religion and Errors of the Gentiles with Their Causes") was published in Amsterdam (1663), with an English version (1705).

9. An incomplete collection of his writings was edited by Charles Gilden, *The Miscellaneous Works of Charles Blount, Esq . . . To which is Prefixed the Life of the Author, and an Account and Vindication of his Death* (London, 1695). On Blount see J. A. Redwood, "Charles Blount (1654–93), Deism and English Free Thought," *Journal of the History of Ideas* 35 (1974): 490–98; Dario Pfanner, *ODNB*, 6:294–95.

Although most scholars regard Blount and Toland as Deists, David Berman contended that careful study of their language indicates that they were atheists ("Disclaimers as Offence Mechanisms in Charles Blount and John Toland," in Hunter and Wootton, *Atheism from the Reformation to the Enlightenment*, 255–72). Both rejected theism as nonsense. "Only the determined material God of pantheism exists, and he (or it) is really no God" (272).

reference in *The Life of Lucian*, which was prefixed to *The Works of Lucian* (1711) and was partly translated by Blount. In an address on *A Just Vindication of Learning* (1679) under the pseudonym Philopatris, Blount urged Parliament not to renew the Licensing Order, which legalized censorship. The act was eventually allowed to expire (1694)[10] but only after Blount's suicide. His suicide took place after the death of Blount's wife in 1693 and the denial of Blount's petition to marry her sister (which at the time was illegal).

Blount's deistic writings date from his essay *Anima Mundi* (1679), which bore the false imprint of Amsterdam. Drawing on the work of Montaigne and other skeptics, Blount put forward an argument for the immortality of the soul, which was deliberately ambiguous and unconvincing. Ostensibly, it was a case for the immortality of the soul, but the argument was so absurd as to qualify it as an example of "theological lying."

Shortly after Hobbes's death Blount edited anonymously extracts from *Leviathan* under the title of *The Last Sayings, or Dying Legacy of Mr. Thomas Hobbes* (1680). The influence of Hobbes and Lord Herbert appears in Blount's next two works, also published in 1680. *Great Is Diana of the Ephesians, or the Original of Idolatry, Together with the Politick Institution of the Gentiles Sacrifices* was published anonymously with the imprint "Cosmopoli" (London). Under the guise of an attack on pagan sacrifice, it was thinly veiled critique of priestcraft and institutional Christianity.

The figure of Apollonius of Tyana began to appear in apologetics from the time of Hugo Grotius.[11] His significance lay in his reputation

---

10. The Licensing Order (1643) dated from the time of Charles I. It required prepublication licensing, registration of materials, including names of author, printer, and publisher. It permitted search, seizure, and destruction of offensive literature, and the arrest and imprisonment of offenders. The Stationers Company was given a monopoly of the printing trade. John Milton's *Areopagitica* (1644) was written in protest. The Licensing Order was permitted to lapse (1694) due to pressure for a more open society. It came about through the Glorious Revolution of 1688, under which the Stuart monarchy was replaced by the reign of William and Mary.

11. Grotius's *De Veritate Religionis Christianae* (1627) was written partly as a response to Lord Herbert's *De Veritate* (which the author had given to Grotius) and partly as a handbook for Dutch voyagers to help them confute the challenges of non-Christian religions (*The Truth of the Christian Religion*, trans. John Clarke [1743], repr. with Jean Le Clerc's notes and additions, ed. Maria Rosa Antognazza [Indianapolis: Liberty Fund, 2012]). Grotius maintained that the works of Apollonius "were such as did not require a Power truly Divine, that is, Omnipotent" (176). He attributed the healing miracles of Vespasian to God's choice of him "to be the Executioner of his Judgments on the *Jews*" (178; cf. Tacitus, *Histories* 4). Grotius was also aware of Deut 13 and its possible application to Jesus but dismissed its relevance on the grounds that Jesus expressly forbade worship of false gods (99–102, 190–93).

as a holy teacher and miracle worker of the first century whose activities appeared to diminish the uniqueness of Jesus. This implication was not lost on readers of Blount's translation of *The Two First Books of Philostratus concerning the Life of Apollonius Tyaneus, Written Originally in Greek with Philological Notes on Each Chapter* (1680).[12] The first two books covered Apollonius's early travels. However, public outcry prevented further publication. From this point on, the figure of Apollonius as a rival to Jesus has hovered in the background of critical discussion.[13]

The Life of Apollonius was followed in 1683 by a tract attributed to Blount, *Miracles No Violations of the Laws of Nature*. It drew heavily on Spinoza's critique in *Tractatus Theologico-Politicus* and contained unacknowledged quotations from Thomas Burnet and Hobbes.[14]

John Toland (1670–1722) was born in Ireland, reputedly the illegitimate son of a Catholic priest. At the age of sixteen he rejected Catholicism, and for a time his guardians hoped that he would become a Presbyterian minister. In 1690 he graduated with an MA from Edinburgh University. He went on the Universities of Leiden and Utrecht, where he learned the exegetical methods of Spinoza, Bayle, and Richard Simon. Toland's eloquence, together with gifts as a linguist and social climber, brought him in contact with such notables as Leibniz, the Dutch Remonstrant theologians Philip van Limborch and Jean Le Clerc, the Electress Sophia, and her daughter Sophie Charlotte, the queen of Prussia. Following travels in Europe (1707–10), Toland returned to England, where he continued to publish. In common with many investors, he lost his money in the South Sea Bubble of 1720. His health rapidly deteriorated, and he died in poverty two years later.

A landmark work in the history of deism was John Toland's *Christianity Not Mysterious, Showing That There Is Nothing in the Gospel Contrary to Reason, nor above It; and That No Christian Doctrine Can Properly Be Call'd a Mystery* (1695; with the imprint 1696).[15] It is thought

---

12. The notes were taken partly from an anonymous "Dialogue between a tutor and his pupil" (Dario Pfanner, *ODNB*, 6:294). The "tutor" is thought to be Lord Herbert.

13. Apollonius figured in the polemics of Thomas Woolston. For further discussion of Apollonius, see chap. 16.

14. A facsimile reprint of the anonymous work has been published by EEBO Editions. On grounds of style and content J. A. Redwood (*Journal of the History of Ideas* 35 [1974]: 494) thought that the popular ascription of the work to Blount was justified.

15. Toland, *Christianity Not Mysterious* (facsimile repr., New York: Garland, 1978). See also E. C. Mossner, *EP* 8:141–43; Robert E. Sullivan, *John Toland and the Deist Controversy: A Study in*

to be the first major controversial work to be published after the lapse of the Licensing Order. Toland was merely twenty-five years of age. His book purported to popularize Locke's defense of belief in revealed truth, which was credibly attested and not contrary to reason. In fact, it was a polemic against "mysteries."[16] Toland countered Locke by arguing that unintelligible belief could not be the object of faith, because assent could not be given to anything that was not understood. Toland's work proved to be a decisive step toward the position adopted by Reimarus in launching the quest of the historical Jesus in Germany, and it was indeed used by Reimarus. With regard to miracles, Toland claimed: "Now whatever is contrary to *Reason* can be no *Miracle*, for it has been sufficiently prov'd already that Contradiction is only another word for Impossible or Nothing. The *miraculous* Action therefore must be something in itself intelligible and possible, tho the manner of doing it extraordinary."[17]

Toland talked darkly about the intrusion of pagan ideas and *priestcraft*, which, when duly stripped away, left Jesus as a preacher of "the purest Morals."[18] He pronounced Jesus to be the end of the law and its fulfillment (Rom 10:4; Matt 5:17).

> So having stripp'd the Truth of all those external Types and Ceremonies which made it difficult before, he rendred it easy and obvious to the meanest Capacities. His Disciples and Followers kept to this Simplicity for some considerable time, tho very early divers Abuses began to get a footing amongst them. The converted *Jews*, who continu'd mighty fond of their *Levitical* Rites and Feasts, would willingly retain them and be Christians too. Thus what at the Beginning was but only tolerated in weaker Brethren, became

---

Adaptation (Cambridge, MA: Harvard University Press, 1982); Stephen H. Daniel, *John Toland: His Methods, Manners, and Mind* (Montreal: McGill Queen's University Press, 1984); J. A. I. Champion, *Republican Learning: John Toland and the Crisis of Christian Culture* (Manchester: Manchester University Press, 2003); Stephen H. Daniel, *ODNB*, 54:894–98.

16. J. A. I. Champion maintained that "the conflict was not only about the competing epistemological hierarchy of revelation and reason but about who or what institution held the authoritative interpretation of truth" (*The Pillars of Priestcraft Shaken*, 10).

17. Toland, *Christianity Not Mysterious*, 150. In this regard Toland was following Pierre Bayle. Elsewhere, he claimed that not a third of the miracles reported in the Pentateuch were real (Daniel, *John Toland*, 125). Ian Leask claimed that a primary impulse was the argument against miracles in Spinoza's *Tractatus* ("The Undivulged Event in Toland's *Christianity Not Mysterious*," in *Atheism and Deism Revalued*, ed. Wayne Hudson et al., 63–80).

18. Toland, *Christianity Not Mysterious*, 158.

afterwards a part of *Christianity* it self, under the Pretence of *Apostolick* Prescription or Tradition.[19]

Toland's *Life of Milton* (1698) cast doubt on the authenticity of the New Testament. Its sequel, *Aymntor: Or, A Defence of Milton's Life* (1698), contained a discussion of the canon in light of patristic evidence under the heading "A Catalogue of Books attributed in the Primitive Times to Jesus Christ, his Apostles and other eminent Persons: With several important Remarks and Observations relating to the Canon of Scripture." Toland's *Letters to Serena* (1704),[20] that is, Queen Sophie Charlotte, contained attacks on Spinoza's account of motion and Newton's invocation of divine agency, but his *Socinianism Truly Stated* (1705) not only gave currency to the word *pantheist* but was essentially an argument for pantheism.[21]

Of Toland's numerous convoluted writings, the one that appears to promise discussion of the historical Jesus was *Nazarenus* (1718). In fact, such discussion is very difficult to find behind Toland's account of the "original plan." The book's title page indicates three parts. The first took the form of a very long letter entitled *Nazarenus: Or, Jewish, Gentile, and Mahometan Christianity. Containing the History of the Antient Gospel, and the Modern Gospel of the Mohametans, Attributed to the Same Apostle: This Last Gospel Being Now First Made Known among Christians*. Accompanying this letter was *The Original Plan of Christianity Occasionally Explain'd in the History of the Nazarens, Whereby Diverse Controversies about This Divine (but Highly Perverted) Institution May Be Happily Terminated*. The work also included a further letter on an Irish manuscript about Celtic Christianity. The entire work bore Toland's name. The first and second editions were both dated 1718.[22]

Toland claimed that be had discovered the text of a Mohammedan

---

19. Toland, *Christianity Not Mysterious*, 158–59.
20. Facsimile repr., New York: Garland, 1976.
21. The term *pantheist* was appropriated from Joseph Raphson, who referred to *panthei* and *pantheismus* in his *De spatio reali, sue, Ente infinito* (1697) (Daniel, *ODNB*, 54:897).
22. Justin Champion, *John Toland: Nazarenus*, British Deism and Free Thought 1 (Oxford: Voltaire Foundation, 1999). F. Stanley Jones, ed., *The Rediscovery of Jewish Christianity: From Toland to Baur*, History of Biblical Studies 5 (Atlanta: Society of Biblical Literature, 2012), contains critical essays, Toland's preface, and letter 1, based on the 2nd 1718 edition (167–242). The essayists contend that the concept of early Jewish Christianity dates from Toland, not F. C. Baur and the Tübingen School. This critical impulse began in Britain before making its way to Germany. References below are to the text edited by F. Stanley Jones.

gospel, previously unknown to Christians in 1709, while in Amsterdam.[23] What Toland called "the original plan of Christianity" arose from the fact that the earliest church consisted of converted Jews and gentiles, "The Jews, tho associating with the converted Gentiles, and acknowledging them for brethren, were still to observe their own Law thro-out all generations; and that the Gentiles who became so farr Jews . . . as to acknowledge ONE GOD, were not however to observe the Jewish Law: but that both of them were to be ever after united in one body or fellowship."[24] Toland claimed, "For the most part I am only a historian, resolv'd to make no Reflections but what my facts will naturally suggest, which facts are generally collected from the *Bible* and the *Fathers*."[25]

The first Christians were not called "Jesseans" after Jesus, nor even "Christians" after Christ, until they were so called at Antioch (Acts 11:26). Their original name was "Nazarenes" or "Ebionites" in view of Jesus' concern for the poor (Matt 11:5; cf. James 2:5).[26] Toland concluded that Jews needed to add to their observance of the law the "inward Regeneration and the Faith of the *Gospel*."[27] The "Original Plan of Christianity" did not involve abrogation of the law of Moses. "Jewish Christians were ever bound to observe the law of Moses, and the gentile Christians who liv'd among them, only the Noachic precepts of abstinence from blood and things offer'd to Idols: for the Moral Law was both then and before, and ever will be, of indispensable obligation to all men."[28]

---

23. *The Rediscovery of Jewish Christianity*, 170; cf. Pierre Lurbe, "John Toland's *Nazarenus* and the Original Plan of Christianity," *The Rediscovery of Jewish Christianity*, 45–66. Toland's reconstruction "eerily echoes" the concerns of his own eighteenth-century countrymen (64). Making Jesus as "a mere man" divinely conceived by Mary looked distinctly Unitarian (63). Lurbe concluded: "Whether Toland was a deist, pantheist, or a 'concealed atheist' is a moot point; that his scholarship was at times faulty is beyond doubt, and his conclusions cannot be taken for granted" (64). His main contribution was to bring apocryphal literature to the fore.

24. *The Rediscovery of Jewish Christianity*, 171.

25. *The Rediscovery of Jewish Christianity*, 190.

26. *The Rediscovery of Jewish Christianity*, 204. Toland cited patristic tradition linking the Ebionites with the Hebrew word *ebion*, "poor."

27. *The Rediscovery of Jewish Christianity*, 228.

28. *The Rediscovery of Jewish Christianity*, 229; cf. Acts 15:19–20. The laws given to Noah, prior to the Law given to Moses, were regarded in Jewish tradition as binding on all (Marc Shapiro, "Noahic Laws," *ODJR*, 504–5). Toland cited the support of Cicero, who "divinely" wrote about "true law" (*The Rediscovery of Jewish Christianity*, 229–30).

On the appropriation of Cicero by Toland and Anthony Collins see Giovanni Tarantino, "Collins's Cicero, Freethinker," in *Atheism and Deism Revalued*, ed. Wayne Hudson et al., 81–99. Collins' library was well stocked with Greek and Latin classics. Tarantino sees Collins in the tradition of Cicero—one who believed in the existence of the gods in public, but not in private.

Nazarenus is not an easy read. Perhaps it repays to read it backward from the end, as well as forward, in order to discern the forest from the trees. Even so, the reader has to contend with what David Berman—the world authority on the subject—called "theological lying."[29] Toland's title is ambiguous. *Nazarenus* is a Latin singular noun that could refer to Jesus himself or to a member of the community that Toland identified as Ebionites or Nazarenes.

The Greek Ναζωραῖος (*Nazōraios*) linked Jesus with Nazareth in the Galilean hill country where he grew up (Matt 2:23; cf. Luke 2:39–40; 18:37). Pontius Pilate used the word in his interrogation of Jesus (John 18:5–7), and it was the *titulus* affixed to the cross (John 19:19). It served in Acts as a designation of Jesus (Acts 2:22; 3:6; 4:10; 6:14; 22:8). Since *Jesus* was a common name, Ναζωραῖος served to identify him specifically by linking him with the village from which he came. Paul was accused of being a ringleader of the sect of the Nazarenes (Acts 24:5). In his hearing before Agrippa, Paul protested his former Jewish orthodoxy, which included doing many things "against the name of Jesus of Nazareth [Ἰησοῦ τοῦ Ναζωραίου]" (Acts 26:9).

As we saw in chapter 1, Jesus' public activity was initially linked with Capernaum, not Nazareth. People thought him mad (Mark 3:21), and Jesus broke with his family in Nazareth (Mark 3:31–35). When he briefly returned to Nazareth, Jesus met with indifference and unbelief (Mark 6:1–6). According to Luke, Jesus' reception in Nazareth rapidly turned from acceptance to hostility. It resulted in an attempt on his life by throwing him over a cliff (Luke 4:28–30). In view of the hilly terrain around Nazareth, such an episode was feasible, whereas it would not have been at Capernaum on the shore of the Sea of Galilee. Following the Beelzebul charge (Mark 3:22), Jesus left Galilee.

As will be seen in later chapters, twentieth-century scholars were reluctant to claim that Jesus had an "original plan" for Jews and gentiles. Henry Joel Cadbury saw such talk as symptomatic of the *perils of*

---

29. David Berman, "Disclaimers as Offence Mechanisms in Charles Blount and Johan Toland," in Hunter and Wootton, *Atheism from the Reformation to the Enlightenment*, 255–72. With regard to Blount's and Toland's protestations of orthodoxy, Berman contended: "*Either* Blount and Toland were orthodox rather boring Christians, *or* they were theological liars" (257). Berman compared Toland's treatment of "mysteries" in *Christianity Not Mysterious*, with belief in X "without any idea of X." It was like saying "we can believe in *blictri*, nonsense. In short, the God of theism is *blictri* for Toland; only the determined material god of pantheism exists, and he (or it) is really no God" (272).

modernizing Jesus. Joachim Jeremias was acutely aware of tensions created by the gentile mission. Jewish eschatology envisaged the gentiles coming to Jerusalem. The reality of the post-Pentecostal situation resulted in recognition by the Jerusalem church of the importance of reaching out to gentiles where they lived. The situation described in Acts 15 dealt with whether the law of Moses should be imposed on gentile converts. The council decided that it should not—the Noahic laws sufficed (Acts 15:19-20).

Matt Jackson-McCabe saw Toland's concept of Jewish Christianity as Toland's own invention. "[It] represents little more than a humanistic retelling of Trinitarian Christianity's myth of Christian origins. What had formerly been told as the story of a transcendent god manifesting itself historically in the form of a particular Jewish man has in Toland's hands become the story of a transcendent spirituality manifesting itself historically in Judaism itself, and indeed in humanity more generally."[30]

Toland's *Tetradymus* (1718) was a collection of four essays, the first of which denied the miraculous character of the Exodus cloud and pillar of fire. The fourth and final essay defended *Nazarenus*. Toland's *Pantheisticon. Sive Formula Celebrandae Sodalitatis Socratae* (1720) has been viewed variously as a literary hoax, an exposition of pantheism, disguised atheism, and a modernized version of Freemasonry.[31] In the 1960s Alan Richardson observed that ever since Toland's day *free-thinking* has been a synonym for *atheism*.[32]

1.2. The Assault on Prophecy and Miracles. While Toland was making his pilgrimage from Roman Catholicism to pantheism, Anthony Collins was preparing a frontal assault on one of the main buttresses of orthodox apologetics—the claim that Jesus fulfilled the prophecies of the Hebrew Bible.

Anthony Collins (1676–1729)[33] belonged to the landed gentry and was a justice of the peace. He was born in the county of Middlesex, northwest of London. He was educated at Eton College, Windsor,

---

30. Matt Jackson-McCabe, "The Invention of Jewish Christianity in John Toland's *Nazarenus*," in *The Rediscovery of Jewish Christianity*, 67–90, here 89.
31. Ernest Campbell Mossner, "Anthony Collins," in *EP*, 8:143.
32. Richardson, *History Sacred and Profane*, Bampton Lectures for 1962 (London: SCM, 1964), 273.
33. Mossner, "Anthony Collins," 144–46; James O'Higgins, *Anthony Collins: The Man and His Works*, International Archives of the History of Ideas 35 (The Hague: Martinus Nijhoff, 1970); J. Dybikowski, "Anthony Collins," in *ODNB*, 12:692–94.

and King's College, Cambridge, though he did not acquire a degree. He studied law at the Middle Temple, but he did not relish legal study and was never called to the bar.[34] In 1698 Collins married the daughter of the banker Sir Francis Child. She died prematurely in 1703, leaving behind four children. Collins received land from his father in the county of Essex northeast of London. Here he met John Locke, whom he visited on at least five occasions in the last eighteen months of Locke's life.[35] Locke was delighted with Collins's comprehensive knowledge of his *Essay*. When Locke died in 1704, he left Collins some of his books and made him cotrustee for a legacy of £3,000 for the son of Sir Francis and Lady Masham. Only after Locke's death did Collins drastically move away from Locke's position.

Collins's acquaintance with Toland seems to have begun before Locke's death, though it never amounted to close friendship.[36] Toland dedicated to Collins some of his writings, and Collins's vast library contained forty-eight of them.[37] Despite some resemblances, James O'Higgins concluded that "there was nothing in Collins remotely resembling Toland's pantheism, hinted at in the latter's early works and fully developed in *Pantheisticon*."[38] Whereas Toland's pantheism was tantamount to atheism, Collins never abandoned belief in God. Collins was also acquainted with Matthew Tindal and possessed twenty-seven of his writings, including four copies of *Christianity as Old as the Creation*.[39]

In 1707 Collins published the first of several works advocating free speech in the realm of religion and attacking institutions that repressed it. They reached their climax in 1712 with *A Discourse of Free-Thinking, Occasion'd by The Rise and Growth of a Sect call'd Free-Thinkers*.[40] For a

---

34. O'Higgins, *Anthony Collins*, 2–3.
35. O'Higgins, *Anthony Collins*, 4–8. An expression of Locke's esteem for Collins is conveyed in a letter dated October 29, 1703: "Beleive [sic] it my good Friend to Love truth for truths sake is the principal part of humane perfection in this world and the seed plot of all other virtues, and if I mistake not you have as much of it as ever I met in any body" (Letter to Collins, October 29, 1703; *The Correspondence of John Locke*, ed. E. S. De Beer [Oxford: Clarendon, 1989], 8:97). Collins's polemical works were published after Locke's death.
36. O'Higgins, *Anthony Collins*, 13–15.
37. O'Higgins, *Anthony Collins*, 37.
38. O'Higgins, *Anthony Collins*, 14.
39. O'Higgins, *Anthony Collins*, 37.
40. The date given on the title page of Anthony Collins, *A Discourse of Free Thinking* was 1713. Facsimile reprint together with Richard Bentley's *Remarks* and Collins's *Philosophical Inquiry* (New York: Garland, 1978).

time it was thought that the author was Toland. Collins urged: "The Subject of which Men are deny'd the right to think by the Enemys of *Free-Thinking*, are of all others those of which Men have not only a *Right to think*, but of which they are oblig'd in duty to think; *viz.* such as *of the Nature and Attributes of the Eternal Being* or God, *of the Truth and Authority of Books esteem'd Sacred*, and *of the Sense and Meaning of those Books*; or in one word, *of religious Questions*."[41] This work was followed by what many regard as the best and most successful of Collins's philosophical writings, *A Philosophical Inquiry Concerning Human Liberty* (1717).[42] In contrast with deists, who urged free will, Collins laid out a case for determinism.

Between 1717 and 1724 Collins fell silent. In this period he moved to Essex, where he lived the life of a country gentleman and rose to become a justice and county treasurer. In 1717 Collins acquired an estate at Great Baddow, where he moved his books to form one of the most extensive private libraries in England.[43] Collins was a lifelong collector of books, some of which were purchased on trips to Holland and other excursions. The library included classics and a substantial number of subversive works, which formed the basis of Collins's attacks on orthodoxy.

Collins sought to meet the self-imposed obligation of his 1712 *Discourse* in *A Discourse of the Grounds and Reasons of the Christian Religion* (1724).[44] It provoked so many replies that a sequel was required. Collins titled it *The Scheme of Literal Prophecy Consider'd; in a View of the Controversy, Occasion'd by a Late Book, Intitled, a Discourse of the Grounds and Reasons of the Christian Religion* (1726).

A Discourse of the Grounds and Reasons of the Christian Religion was divided into two parts. The first examined the nature of Hebrew prophecy in light of the use made of it in the New Testament. It struck at the heart of Locke's public position, which appealed to the miracles as the fulfillment of Old Testament prophecy.

---

41. Collins, *A Discourse of Free Thinking*, 32.

42. O'Higgins, *Anthony Collins*, 96–110.

43. O'Higgins, *Anthony Collins*, 23–39; Giovanni Tarrantino, "Collins's Cicero, Freethinker," in *Atheism and Deism Revalued*, ed. Wayne Hudson et al., 81–99. The extent of the collection is known with some precision through two catalogues—one compiled by Collins himself and the other compiled after his death for auction purposes.

44. Facsimile repr., New York: Garland, 1976. A facsimile reprint of the 1741 edition has been published by Eighteenth Century Collections Online Print Editions together with a reprint of the 1727 edition of *The Scheme of Literal Prophecy Consider'd*.

> If the proofs for christianity from the Old Testament be not valid; if the arguments founded on those books be not conclusive; and the *prophesies* cited from then be not fulfill'ed; then has christianity no just foundation: for the foundation on which Jesus and his apostles built it is then invalid and false. Nor can *miracles*, said to be wrought by Jesus and his apostles, in behalf of christianity, avail anything in the case: for *miracles* can never render a foundation valid, which is itself invalid; can never make a false inference true; can never make a *prophesy* fulfill'd, which is not fulfill'd; and can never make out a MESSIAS, or Jesus for the MESSIAS, if both are not mark'd out in the Old Testament.[45]

Indeed, in light of warnings about false prophets who perform signs contrary to the Law, "We have directions from the Old Testament itself [Deut 13:1–2] not to regard such miracles."[46]

The second part of the 1724 *Discourse* was a ferocious attack on William Whiston's *Essay towards Restoring the Text of the Old Testament, and for Vindicating the Citations Thence Made in the New Testament* (1722). Whiston dismissed Surenhusius's explanation that New Testament exegesis was influenced by Jewish nonliteral methods. Instead, he proposed that the New Testament writers had quoted the Old Testament literally. However, the text of the Old Testament had been corrupted by rabbis to make it seem as if the apostles had not argued literally. Collins subjected Whiston's argument to remorseless ridicule. He paid tribute to Whiston's character and learning but regretted that "his judgment does not seem to be equal to his sagacity, learning, zeal, and integrity."[47]

Crucial to Collins's overall position was what he saw as the patent misapplication to Jesus of prophetic texts in Matthew. Foundational in this regard was Matthew 1:22–23 (citing Isa 7:14): "Now all this was done, that it might be fulfilled which was spoken of the Lord by the prophet, saying, Behold, a virgin shall be with child, and shall bring forth a son, and they shall call his name Emmanuel, which being interpreted is, God with us" (KJV).[48] In the context of Isaiah, the sign offered

---

45. Collins, *A Discourse of the Grounds and Reasons of the Christian Religion*, 31–32.
46. Collins, *A Discourse of the Grounds and Reasons of the Christian Religion*, 32.
47. Collins, *A Discourse of the Grounds and Reasons of the Christian Religion*, 278; cf. O'Higgins, *Anthony Collins*, 170–71.
48. Collins, *A Discourse of the Grounds and Reasons of the Christian Religion*, 40–46, 60–70;

to Ahaz was that of a child to be born of a young woman. The danger posed by the two invading kings would pass before the child learned to refuse evil and choose the good. This prophecy was not fulfilled by Jesus in the literal sense. To Collins it seemed lame to say that it was fulfilled "in a secondary, or typical, or mystical, or allegorical sense; that is, the said prophesy, which was then literally fulfill'd by the birth of the prophet's son, was again fulfill'd by the birth of Jesus, as being an event of the same kind, and intended to be signify'd, either by the prophet, or by God, who directed the prophet's speech."[49]

Matthew 2:15 (citing Hos 11:1) refers to the return from Egypt of the holy family: "And was there until the death of Herod: that it might be fulfilled which was spoken of the Lord by the prophet, saying, Out of Egypt have I called my son" (KJV).[50] In context Hosea's prophecy referred to Israel's exodus from Egypt. It could be made to apply to Jesus only "mystically or allegorically." Matthew 2:23 states: "He came and dwelt in a city called Nazareth: that it might be fulfilled which was spoken by the prophets, He shall be called a Nazarene" (KJV). Collins observed that this "citation does not *expressly* occur in any place in the Old Testament, and therefore the Old Testament cannot be literally fulfill'd therein."[51]

Matthew 11:14 (citing Mal 4:5) identified John the Baptist with Elijah: "And if ye will receive it, this is Elias, which was for to come." However, Malachi 4:5 clearly makes a prophecy about Elijah: "Behold, I will send you Elijah the prophet before the coming of the great and dreadful day of the Lord" To Collins this is one of "so many undoubted instances" that show "the Old and New Testament to have no manner of connection . . . but to be in an *irreconcilable state*."[52] In commenting on Jesus' use of parables, Matthew 13:34–35 alludes to Isaiah 6:9: "All these things spake Jesus unto the multitude in parables; and without a parable spake he not unto them: That it might be fulfilled which was spoken

---

The Scheme of Literal Prophecy, 306–309. The texts cited in this discussion are taken from the KJV, reflecting Collins's usage, but it should be noted that Collins did not always cite the text in full.

49. Collins, *A Discourse of the Grounds and Reasons of the Christian Religion*, 44.

50. Collins, *A Discourse of the Grounds and Reasons of the Christian Religion*, 46–47; *The Scheme of Literal Prophecy*, 313–16.

51. Collins, *A Discourse of the Grounds and Reasons of the Christian Religion*, 47; *The Scheme of Literal Prophecy*, 316–18.

52. Collins, *A Discourse of the Grounds and Reasons of the Christian Religion*, 48; cf. *The Scheme of Literal Prophecy*, 318–19.

by the prophet, saying, I will open my mouth in parables; I will utter things which have been kept secret from the foundation of the world." To Collins, it was a patent mistake to apply the prophecy to Jesus' hearers, since it was "manifest, that, according to the literal sense, it relates to the obstinate *Jews*, who liv'd in the time of Isaiah."[53]

Collins appealed to the authority of Hugo Grotius's *Annotationes in Novum Testamentum* in support of the claim that "most, if not all, the prophecies quoted from the Old Testament in the New Testament" were not grounded in literal interpretation.[54] Grotius had broken with dogmatic exegesis in favor of philological criticism. But the key to understanding the New Testament's method of interpretation was supplied by the Dutch Hebraist Surenhusius, whose attention had been drawn to Talmudic exegesis by a friendly rabbi.[55] Following Surenhusius, Collins observed that "the Jewish doctors are used to detach passages from their connection, and put a sense upon them, which has no relation to what goes before or follows after."[56] The construction that Collins put on this method of exegesis was another example of what David Berman called "the art of theological lying."[57] It was the art practiced by Blount, Toland, Collins, and Tindal of making fideistic professions, while signaling, either by some code or by patent weakness of the argument, that the

---

53. Collins, *A Discourse of the Grounds and Reasons of the Christian Religion*, 48; cf. *The Scheme of Literal Prophesy*, 319–21.

54. Collins, *A Discourse of the Grounds and Reasons of the Christian Religion*, 49; cf. *Hugonis Grotii Annotationes in Novum Testamentum* (3 parts, 1641–50), ed. E. de Windheim (1755–57).

55. Collins, *A Discourse of the Grounds and Reasons of the Christian Religion*, 60.

56. Collins, *A Discourse of the Grounds and Reasons of the Christian Religion*, 71. Collins cited Surenhusius, *Tractatus in quo secudum Veterum Theologorum Hebraeorum formulas allegandi, & modus interpretandi, conciliantur loca ex V. in Nov. Test. Allegata* (Amsterdam, 1713), thesis 9.

Surenhusius alias Guilielmus Surenhusius (1666–1729) was professor of oriental languages at the Amsterdam Athenaeum. His edition of the Mishnah (1698–1703) printed the six divisions with the Hebrew text with Latin translation in parallel columns with the commentaries of Bartenora and Maimonides again with the Hebrew and Latin in parallel columns. Surenhusius, who was a supporter of the Jewish community, considered the Mishnah to be superior to the *Codex juris civilis*, since Jewish law promoted personal virtue, and not general law and order.

Collins's knowledge of Surenhusius was derived from Michael de la Roche, *Memoirs of Literature*, which were published serially and collected in *Memoirs of Literature. Containing a Large Account of Many Valuable Books, Letters and Dissertations upon Several Subjects, Miscellaneous Observations, etc.* (London: Kaplock, 1722); cf. *A Discourse of the Grounds and Reasons of the Christian Religion*, 54.

57. David Berman, "Deism, Immortality, and the Art of Theological Lying," in *Deism, Masonry, and the Enlightenment: Essays Honoring Alfred Owen Aldridge*, ed. J. A. Leo Lemay (Newark, DE: University of Delaware Press; London: Associated University Presses, 1987), 61–78.

statement was to be taken as irony or nonsense. "If therefore christianity is grounded on *allegory*, converted gentiles must be convinc'd by allegory, and become *allegorists* or *mystical Jews*, no less than converted Jews. For the religion itself, to which they were converted, was *allegory*, or christianity as taught *allegorically* in the Old Testament."[58] In plain English, orthodox Christianity was irrational fantasy. At bottom, Collins was what later would be called a positivist who saw truth as literal correspondence with facts and who—despite the fact that he is widely regarded as a deist—might more accurately be described as an atheist.[59] However, Collins was an Anglican who saw no inconsistency in not believing in the supernatural.[60]

At the end of *The Scheme of Literal Prophecy*, Collins promised to do for miracles what he had just done for prophecy and thus complete the assault on the remaining pillar of apologetics.[61] He was preempted by Thomas Woolston (1670–1731), who had already jumped into the fray with a book attacking Collins on prophecy. It was to be followed by a series of pamphlets on miracles, which again presented Woolston's unique perspective.

Thomas Woolston (1670–1731)[62] belonged to a totally different world

---

58. Collins, *A Discourse of the Grounds and Reasons of the Christian Religion*, 92. Although Collins referred to Origen, Eusebius, Jerome, other church fathers, and more recent commentators, he lumped together typical, mystical, and allegorical exegesis. Such exegesis was *ipso facto* erroneous, because it was not "obvious and literal." "Almost all christian *commentators* on the Bible, and *advocates* for the christian religion, both antient and modern, have judg'd [the proofs taken from the Old Testament] to be apply'd in a secondary, or typical, or mystical, or allegorical sense, that is, in a sense different from the obvious and literal sense, which they bear in the Old Testament" (Collins, *A Discourse of the Grounds and Reasons of the Christian Religion*, 40).

59. David Berman summed up Collins's thought as "Atheology" (David Berman, *A History of Atheism in Britain: From Hobbes to Russell* [New York: Croom Helm, 1988], 70–92).

60. O'Higgins, *Anthony Collins*, 199.

61. "I shall begin with a *Discourse upon the Miracles recorded in the old and new Testament*; which is almost transcrib'd" (*The Scheme of Literal Prophecy*, 419). N. L. Torrey believed that Collins withheld the now lost manuscript on the appearance of Woolston's *Discourses* (*Voltaire and the English Deists*, 59). Collins left his extensive library to his second wife, Elizabeth Collins, who had it auctioned, and his manuscripts to Collins's longstanding friend Pierre Des Maizeaux. The latter's reviews of Collins's works had attracted the attention of readers in Europe. Disappointed that Collins had left him only £50 in his will, Des Maizeaux sold the manuscripts to Elizabeth Collins, who suppressed them (Dybikowski, "Anthony Collins," in *ODNB*, 12:694).

62. A *Life* of Woolston is given in the first volume of Woolston's *Works*, 5 vols. (London, 1733). See also the contemporary review by Thomas Stackhouse, *A Fair State of the Controversy between Mr. Woolston and His Adversaries* (London, 1730). More recent accounts include: Ernest Campbell Mossner, "Thomas Woolston," *EP* 8:347–48; Torrey, *Voltaire and the English Deists*, 59–103; William H. Trapnell, *Thomas Woolston: Madman and Deist?* (Bristol: Thoemes, 1994); and Trapnell, "Thomas Woolston," in *ODNB*, 60:284–86.

than that of Collins. He was, if anything, closer to Toland, who was born a year after Woolston but predeceased him by nearly a decade. Woolston was born in Northampton, a county town some seventy miles northwest of London. He studied theology at Sidney Sussex College, Cambridge, where his MA was followed by a BD and a fellowship. Perhaps the Cambridge BD curriculum's emphasis on oral debate encouraged Woolston's proclivity for controversy. He claimed to have derived his ideas about typology and allegorical interpretation from Origen in his early thirties while working on his BD. Details, however, are sketchy.[63]

Woolston's first book, *The Old Apology for the Truth of the Christian Religion against the Jews and the Gentiles Revived* (1705), attacked a shallow tradition-literalist interpretation of Scripture. It was followed by a series of pamphlets challenging the clergy to refute him. Questions were raised about his mental stability, and in 1720 he was deprived of his fellowship. From 1721 Woolston lived mostly in London, supported by an allowance from his brother of £30 a year.

Woolston retaliated by publishing a presentation that he had made as part of his BD qualification, *The Exact Fitness of the Time in Which Christ Was Manifested in the Flesh, Demonstrated by Reason, Against the Objections of the Old Gentiles and Modern Unbelievers* (1722). He dedicated it mockingly to the master of Sidney Sussex College, a practice he employed on other occasions to pillory opponents. As in other publications, Woolston made a point of targeting authorities.

The Moderator between an Infidel and an Apostate (1725) drew on Woolston's study of allegory and the church fathers. It was a portent of things to come. The infidel was Anthony Collins, and the apostate was Edward Chandler, bishop of Lichfield, who replied to Collins in *A Defence of Christianity from the Prophecies of the Old Testament* (1725).[64] Woolston conceded Collins's contention that the only way of proving

---

63. Trapnell, *Thomas Woolston*, 33. Trapnell conceded that we do not have any precise information, apart from Woolston's own admission that he was about thirty when he began to think in the "allegorical Way." This would place him in the sixth year of preparation for his BD. Trapnell noted Whiston's observation that Woolston derived his allegorical interpretation from Origen. See William Whiston, *Memoirs of the Life and Writings of Mr. William Whiston* (London: self-published, 1749), 1:198.

Trapnell concluded that Woolston himself took the step of seeing truth in Scripture only through figurative interpretation. "Conflating figure with spirit, another bold assumption, he rejected *the letter* and embraced *the spirit*. Neither clear, nor coherent, nor thorough, the scheme betrays the mediocrity of the scholar and the theologian who conceived it."

64. Trapnell, *Thomas Woolston*, 92–100. *The Moderator* was followed by two supplements.

Jesus' messiahship to the Jews was through his completion of prophecy. He accused Chandler of playing a double game of literal and allegorical interpretation. As moderator, Woolston proposed his own view of reading the New Testament as thoroughly allegorical as a compromise solution. If Augustine were still alive, he would have ridiculed literal interpretation of miracles in favor of the mystical interpretation. Only the allegorical interpretation of Jesus' miracles and resurrection was defensible.

Woolston's six *Discourses on the Miracles of Our Saviour in View of the Present Controversy between Infidels and Apostates* (1727–29)[65] were eventually published as a single book. Originally, they appeared as separate pamphlets. Pamphlets were the social media of the age, especially for impoverished controversialists who published them out of their own pockets. Purchasers of Woolston's *Discourses* were advised by the title page that they were "Printed for the Author, and Sold by him next door to the *Star*, in *Aldermanbury*, and by the Booksellers of *London*, and *Westminster*." They were priced at one shilling each.

Woolston's six individual discourses were each dedicated ironically to a bishop of the Anglican Church who had previously wronged him. The *First Discourse* was dedicated to Edmund Gibson, bishop of London, who was reminded of his part in the prosecution of Woolston in writing *The Moderator*.[66] Taking up the argument of *The Moderator*, Woolston claimed that the gospels offered "no Sanctuary" for those who would base their apologetic appeal on miracles. Miracle stories offered no support for Jesus' "Authority and Messiahship." Some of the stories, "as recorded by the Evangelists, were never wrought, but are only related as prophetical and parabolical Narratives of what will be mysteriously and more wonderfully done by him."[67]

Woolston examined fifteen miracles stories (some more than once) culminating in the resurrection. In general, they were pronounced absurd,

---

65. Thomas Woolston, *Six Discourses on the Miracles of Our Saviour and Defences of His Discourses, 1727–1730* (New York: Garland, 1979). This facsimile edition is based on the 5th edition. Each discourse follows its original pagination. The volume also contains the two-part facsimile of Woolston's *Defence*. Both are dedicated to the bishops of St. David's and London and other adversaries. The second is addressed to Sir Robert Raymond, lord chief justice of the Court of King's Bench, who presided over Woolston's conviction.

The most comprehensive account of the deistic debate on miracles in its historical context is R. M. Burns, *The Great Debate on Miracles: From Joseph Glanvill to David Hume* (Lewisburg, PA: Bucknell University Press; London: Associated University Presses, 1981), 70–95.

66. Woolston, *First Discourse* (1727), iii–viii.

67. Woolston, *First Discourse*, 3.

incredible, and immoral. With an eye to the Protestant tradition from Calvin to Locke that true miracles had a morally elevating, God-honoring character, Woolston tartly commented on the miracle at Cana:

> If *Apollonius Tyanaeus*, and not *Jesus*, had been the Author of this Miracle, we should often have reproached his Memory with it. It is said of *Apollonius Tyanaeus*, that a Table was all on a sudden, at his Command, miraculously spread with Variety of nice Dishes for the Entertainment of himself and his Guests; which Miracle, our *Divines* can tell, makes not at all to his Credit, in as much as it was done for the Service and Pleasure of luxurious Appetites.[68]

The star of Bethlehem was "a *Will-a-Whisp*."[69] In some instances Woolston put forward psychosomatic and natural explanations. The woman in Luke 13, bound by Satan for eighteen years, was pronounced by Woolston to be "freed from the whimsical Imagination of being *Satan-ridden*."[70] "Reasonably then speaking, there was not much in the Disease and Cure of this Woman."[71]

The account of the lame man by the Pool of Bethesda (John 5) "absolutely destroys the Fame and Credit of *Jesus* for a Worker of Miracles" because of his omission to heal the rest of the afflicted.[72] The significance of the story lay in its anti-Jewish allegorical interpretation. The five porches by the pool indicated, as the church fathers taught, "the five Books of *Moses*, which are as so many Doors of Entrance into the House of Wisdom, or of the Grace of *Christ*."[73]

The clay made of dust and spittle in John 9:6 "would sooner put a

---

68. Woolston, *First Discourse*, 51.
69. Woolston, *First Discourse*, 56.
70. Woolston, *Second Discourse* (1727), 27. The second *Discourse* was dedicated to Edward Chandler, bishop of Lichfield, with whom Woolston crossed swords in *The Moderator*.
71. Woolston, *Second Discourse*, 31.
72. Woolston, *Third Discourse* (1728), 49. The third *Discourse* was dedicated to Richard Smalbroke, bishop of St. David's, who had denounced Woolston in a sermon preached to the Societies for the Reformation of Manners (1727). He also published *A Vindication of the Miracles of Our Blessed Saviour in Which Mr. Woolston's Discourses on Them Are Particularly Examined* (1729, 1730).
73. Woolston, *Third Discourse*, 58, alluding to Theophilus of Antioch and Augustine. It had long been thought that no such pool existed in Jerusalem. However, a pool matching John's description was discovered in the late nineteenth century, adjacent to the medieval church of St. Anne. Shrines dedicated to Asclepius, the god of healing, indicate the pool's association with healing in ancient times. See James H. Charlesworth, "Reinterpreting John: How the Dead Sea

Man's Eyes out than restore a blind one to his Sight."[74] Again following patristic exegesis, learned from his study of Origen, Woolston pronounced the true meaning of the story to be allegorical.

> And the Cure of Mankind of the Blindness of his Understanding, by the *Spirit's* being temper'd with the *Letter* of the Scriptures, which is the most mystical *Eye-Salve*, will not only be a most stupendous Miracle, but a Proof of *Jesus's Messiahship* beyond all contradiction, in as much as by such opening of the Eyes of our Understandings, which have been hitherto dark, we shall see, how he is the Accomplishment of the Law and the Prophets.[75]

While such allegorical interpretation was attractive to the church fathers, it was clearly unacceptable to the rational divines of the eighteenth century as a means of establishing the Christian faith. To Woolston, it merely demonstrated the preposterous character of that faith. If the miracle stories were "literally true, as our *Divines* do believe," they are "enough to turn our Stomachs against such a Prophet; and enough to make us take him for a *Conjuror*, a *Sorcerer*, and a *Wizard*, rather than the Messiah and Prophet of the most High God."[76]

The *Fifth Discourse* was a prelude to the final discourse, which was devoted to the resurrection of Jesus. The *Fifth Discourse* was dedicated to

---

Scrolls Have Revolutionized Our Understanding of the Gospel of John," *Bible Review* 9, no. 1 (1993): 19–25, 54.

Recent discussions include Craig S. Keener, *The Gospel of John: A Commentary* (Peabody, MA: Hendrickson, 2003), 1:636–39; and Urban C. von Wahlde, "Archaeology and John's Gospel," *Jesus and Archaeology*, ed. James H. Charlesworth (Grand Rapids: Eerdmans, 2006), 523–86, here 559–66. Von Wahlde observed: "The Johannine account speaks of (1) its location near the Sheep Gate; (2) the name of the pool as Bethesda; (3) the fact that it has five porticos; (4) the fact of intermittent turbulence in the water. All these details are corroborated through literary and archeological evidence of the site" (566). Robin Thompson, "Healing at the Pool of Bethesda: A Challenge to Asclepius?" *BBR* 27 (2017): 65–84. Thompson reviews the archaeological evidence relating to the pool of Bethesda (or Bethzatha) and concludes that it is doubtful that the pool was associated with Asclepius prior to 70 CE.

74. Woolston, *Fourth Discourse* (1728), 11. The *Discourse* was dedicated to Francis Hare, a Cambridge scholar and renowned preacher. He was Bishop of St. Asaph, and later of Chichester. Woolston's dedication mocked Hare's book *The Difficulties and Discouragements Which Attend the Study of the Scriptures.*

75. Woolston, *Fourth Discourse*, 22. Woolston gave numerous patristic references, noting the comments of Origen, Theophilus, and others. However, unlike Woolston, the patristic writers treated the story as literal, having allegorical significance.

76. Woolston, *First Discourse*, 15.

Quests before Schweitzer

Thomas Sherlock, who was a leading apologist for orthodoxy and would later emerge as the most famous of Woolston's critics. The discourse was devoted to the three gospel narratives of Jesus raising the dead: Jairus's daughter (Matt 9:18–26; Mark 5:21–43; Luke 8:40–56), the widow of Nain's son (Luke 7:11–17), and Lazarus (John 11:1–44). Toward the end of his discussion Woolston made the general observation: "That none of these three rais'd Persons had been long enough dead to amputate all Doubt of *Jesus's* miraculous Power in their Resurrection."[77] With regard to Lazarus, Woolston observed, "It is in the Opinion of the Fathers a Type of the general and mystical resurrection of Mankind in the Perfection of Time. But this is a most copious Subject; and unless I could here thoroughly handle it, I had much better say nothing."[78]

In closing the fifth discourse, Woolston laid out his personal credo in six articles. In each of the six Woolston made it clear that authority and ministry depended on the church fathers. The following are the first two.

> *Imprimis*, I believe on the Authority of the Fathers, that the Ministry of the Letter of the *Old* and *New* Testament is downright *Antichristianism*.
>
> *Item*, I believe upon the Authority of the Fathers, that the Miracles of *Jesus*, as recorded by the Evangelists, *literally* understood, are the *lying Wonders* of Antichrist.[79]

In the final discourse, Woolston introduced a rabbi who promised to convert to Christianity if the resurrection of Jesus could be proved. But the accounts were soon pronounced to be a ridiculous "romance," putting the rabbi in mind of "Robinson Cruso's filling his Pockets with Biskets, when he had neither Coat, Wastecoat, nor Breeches on."[80] In short, the resurrection of Jesus was "the most manifest, the most bare-faced, and the most self-evident Imposture that ever was put upon the World."[81]

Although the Licensing Order had been allowed to lapse, making it possible for free thinkers like Toland to express their views openly,

---

77. Woolston, *Fifth Discourse* (1728), 26.
78. Woolston, *Fifth Discourse*, 64–65.
79. Woolston, *Fifth Discourse*, 68.
80. Woolston, *Sixth Discourse* (1728), 31. The *Discourse* was dedicated to John Potter, former Regius Professor, bishop of Oxford (1715), and archbishop of Canterbury (1737). Daniel Defoe's widely popular *The Life and Strange Surprising Adventures of Robinson Crusoe* was published in 1719.
81. Woolston, *Sixth Discourse*, 27.

Deism and the Historical Jesus

blasphemy laws remained in force. They were subsumed in common law under subversive libel regarding undermining the authority of church and state. Moves to prosecute Woolston were considered already in response to *The Moderator*, which had outlined Woolston's argument. Further moves were set in motion by the *Discourses*. Warrant for Woolston's arrest followed the appearance of the *Fourth Discourse*. The *Sixth Discourse* appeared two weeks before the jury of the King's Bench Court found Woolston guilty of blasphemy.[82] Woolston was remanded to the King's Bench Prison in Southwark. He waited five months before receiving sentence, which kept being postponed in the hope that Woolston would cease to publish. Woolston refused. His *Discourses* were selling well and provided a source of income.

Sentence was finally passed by the Lord Chief Justice. Woolston received a year's imprisonment and a fine of £25 for each of the first four *Discourses*. Woolston refused to pay. He purchased the right to live at home instead of the overcrowded prison. When he died, Woolston was still technically a prisoner, despite the efforts of Samuel Clarke and others to procure his release.

Woolston defended himself in a two-part *Defence* (1729–30), and a five-volume edition of his *Works*, prefaced by his *Life*, which was published in 1733. In the meantime the first of some sixty replies appeared.[83] The most influential, both in Britain and in Europe through translation, came from the pen of the bishop named in the mock-dedication of Woolston's *Fifth Discourse*.

Thomas Sherlock (1678–1761) was educated at Eton College and Cambridge University, where he was elected a fellow of St. Catharine's College in 1698 and awarded the degree of Doctor of Divinity in 1714. He became master of the temple, dean of St. Paul's, master of St. Catherine's, and vice-chancellor of Cambridge University. He was successively bishop of Bangor (1728), Salisbury (1734), and London (1748 until his death). He declined the sees of York (1743) and Canterbury (1747) on grounds of ill health.[84] In addition, Sherlock was the C. S. Lewis of his day.

Taking his cue from Woolston's trial, Sherlock's *Tryal of the Witnesses*

---

82. For details of the case and conviction, see Trapnell, *Thomas Woolston*, 57–79.
83. William Lane Craig, *The Historical Argument for the Resurrection of Jesus during the Deist Controversy*, Texts and Studies in Religion 23 (Lewiston: Mellon, 1985), 255.
84. Edward Carpenter, *Thomas Sherlock, 1678–1761: Bishop of Bangor 1728; of Salisbury 1734; of London 1748* (London: SPCK, 1936); Colin Haydon, *ODNB*, 50:322–24.

of the Resurrection (1729) reversed the roles.[85] The scene was an amicable discussion among gentlemen of the Inns of Court, who decide to reopen the case, putting the apostles on trial instead of Woolston, appointing counsels for defense and prosecution, together with a judge. Questions like those of fraud and deceit, which were later to be treated by Hume, and evidence that was "insufficient to support the Credit of so extraordinary an Event" constituted key issues in the judge's summary.[86]

With regard to the former, the judge noted that the apostles might be sincerely mistaken, but Woolston's case required them to be demonstrable cheats. With regard to the latter issue, Sherlock drew upon an analogy discussed by Locke before him and Butler, Hume, and sundry others after him: the role of analogy, based on present limited knowledge and experience, in determining what may or may not be possible. The point was raised by the defense counsel's question of whether it was legitimate for a man who had lived only in the tropics to deny the possibility of water becoming solid. The counsel carried the day with the rhetorical question: "And what has the Gentleman said upon this Occasion against the Resurrection, more than any Man who never saw Ice might say against an Hundred honest Witnesses, who assert that Water turns to Ice in cold Climates?"[87]

Thomas Woolston was an enigma in his lifetime and remains so in posterity. He is widely identified as a deist but does not conform to any of the typical deistic profiles. If any consistent pattern can be found in his

---

85. Facsimile reprint of the 11th edition of Thomas Sherlock, *The Tryal of the Witnesses* (1743) and *The Use and Intent of Prophecy* (1728) (New York: Garland, 1978).

86. Sherlock, *The Tryal of the Witnesses*, 87–88.

87. Sherlock, *The Tryal of the Witnesses*, 60. Locke introduced the analogy in *An Essay Concerning Human Understanding* 4, 15, 5 (336) in the form of a discussion between the king of Siam and the Dutch ambassador, who tells the king that in his country it is possible under certain circumstances for a man, or even an elephant, to walk on water. Whereupon the king replies that hitherto he has always believed the ambassador when he told of strange things, but now he knows that he is lying. Evidently Locke learned the story in Holland.

Joseph Butler endorsed the argument in his *Analogy* (1736), introduction §3. It reappears in Hume's *Enquiry* §89, where Hume declares (contrary to Locke) that the "Indian Prince . . . reasoned justly." The case of the Indian prince further appeared in Sir Walter Scott's *The Talisman* (1825), chap. 2, and in J. S. Mill, *A System of Logic*, 8th ed. (London: Longmans, 1925), 411. J. C. A. Gaskin thinks that Hume's use of the argument indicates that he was seeking to answer Sherlock, rather than Locke, who did not use it to substantiate reports of miracles, or Butler, who mentioned it in the course of general remarks on probability (*Hume's Philosophy of Religion*, 150–52, 239n25). However, it would seem that Hume was familiar with other versions of the argument. In Sherlock it concerns "a Man who lives in a warm Climate." Butler used the term *prince*, alluding to Locke's "King of Siam."

public pronouncements, it lies in two claims. The first is his adherence to mysticism and the allegorical interpretation of Scripture. The second, which springs from the first, is his scathing denunciation of everyone who did not adopt this standpoint as an infidel and follower of the Antichrist. Yet the mysticism and allegorical interpretation—though vehemently recommended as the alternative to literalism—received nothing like the attention that Woolston devoted to his critique of literalism.

Woolston protested that his beliefs were based on "the Authority of the Fathers," yet the church fathers themselves did not view allegorical interpretation and literal interpretation as mutually exclusive. The two were complementary. Moreover, it was the fathers who created the orthodoxy of the creeds and councils. In short, Woolston's stance and the persona that he presented to the world raise the question of whether Woolston's oeuvre was a massive instance of "theological lying." At least to his own satisfaction, he had demolished the edifice of supernaturalism. In its place he offered unconvincing protestations of mystical piety and allegory. It was a world in which—to all intents and purposes—*God was dead.*

1.3. Deism in Decline. Matthew Tindal's *Christianity as Old as the Creation: Or, the Gospel, a Republication of the Religion of Nature* (1730)[88] is commonly described as "the Bible of deism." In fact, it is a rambling tirade, published while Woolston was still alive, toward the end of Tindal's career.

Matthew Tindal (1655–1733) was elected a fellow of All Souls, Oxford, in 1688, a position from which it was virtually impossible to dislodge anyone. Jonathan I. Israel describes Tindal as "not much of a thinker and practically devoid of originality."[89] His significance "lies not in his intellectual contribution but his effectiveness in transmitting the ideas of others," especially Spinoza's. Tindal's title was ironically taken from one of Bishop Sherlock's sermons, cited on his title page: "The Religion of the Gospel, is the true original Religion of Reason and Nature.—And its Precepts declarative of that original Religion, which was as old as the Creation."[90]

---

88. Matthew Tindal, *Christianity as Old as the Creation* (1730; facsimile repr., New York: Garland, 1978).

89. Israel, *Radical Enlightenment*, 620; cf. B. W. Young, "Matthew Tindal," in *ODNB*, 54:814–17.

90. Tindal, *Christianity as Old as the Creation*. Tindal believed that God's goal in creation

Tindal inverted Sherlock's intended meaning. He refrained from the kind of all-out attack on miracles that characterized Woolston's writings. He was content to insert barbed comments. He anticipated Hume's argument that nothing could be proved from miracles, because all parties appealed to them claiming their own to be "divine" and those of their opponents to be "diabolical."[91] In response to Clarke, Tindal retorted, "If the Doctrines themselves, from their internal Excellency, do not give us certain proof of the will of God, no traditional Miracles can do it; because one Probability added to another will not amount to Certainty."[92]

Tindal's book is littered with comments on the morals of Old Testament heroes, the barbarity of sacrifice,[93] the absurdity of Adam and Eve,[94] and relentless criticism of clerical practices. His position is summed up in the remark that "the Law of Nature either is, or is not, a perfect law; if the first, 'tis not capable of Addition; if the last, does it not argue Want of Wisdom in the Legislator [?]."[95] Tindal called himself a Christian deist.

> The Difference between those, who wou'd engross the Name of Christians to themselves, and these *Christian Deists*, as I may justly call them; is, that the former dare not examine into the Truth of Scripture Doctrines, lest they shou'd seem to question the Veracity of the Scriptures; whereas the Latter, who believe not the Doctrines, because contain'd in Scripture; but Scripture on Account of the Doctrines; are under no such Apprehension: For having critically examin'd those Doctrines that Reason, which God has giv'n them to distinguish Religion from Superstition; they are sure not to run into any Errors of Moment; notwithstanding the confess'd Obscurity of the Scriptures; and those many Mistakes that have crept into the Text, whether by Accident, or Design.[96]

---

was human happiness (cf. Jeffrey R. Wigglesworth, "God Can Require Nothing of Us, but What Makes for Our Happiness: Matthew Tindal on Toleration," in *Atheism and Deism Revalued*, ed. Wayne Hudson, et al., 139–55). Tindal's argument was a secularized version of Locke's appeal for religious toleration.

91. Tindal, *Christianity as Old as the Creation*, 159.
92. Tindal, *Christianity as Old as the Creation*, 374.
93. Tindal, *Christianity as Old as the Creation*, 85–104, 126.
94. Tindal, *Christianity as Old as the Creation*, 385–89.
95. Tindal, *Christianity as Old as the Creation*, 135, cf. 373.
96. Tindal, *Christianity as Old as the Creation*, 371. Tindal's observation about the truth of Scripture anticipated that of Lessing: "The religion is not true because the evangelists and apostles

Tindal's Christian deism did not need Jesus.[97]

Thomas Chubb (1679–1747), like Matthew Tindal, professed to be a Christian deist who regularly attended his parish church.[98] Whereas Tindal was an Oxford scholar, Chubb was self-taught. But this did not prevent him from mastering the rationalist thought of the day and responding to the likes of Samuel Clarke in *The Comparative Excellence and Obligation of Moral and Positive Duties* (1730) and *A Discourse concerning Reason with Regard to Religion and Divine Revelation* (1731).[99] Chubb's argument for free will provoked a reply from no less a figure than Jonathan Edwards in the New World.[100] Chubb's *The True Gospel of Jesus Christ Asserted* (1732) and *The True Gospel of Jesus Christ Vindicated* (1739) identified Christianity with the principles of natural religion. His *Discourse on Miracles, Considered as Evidence to Prove the Divine Original of a Revelation* (1741; corrected ed., 1742) shows signs of influence by Toland and Woolston.

The Welsh Christian deist Thomas Morgan (d. 1743) became a medical doctor following his dismissal from the ministry soon after 1720 on account of his extreme views.[101] Combining Lord Herbert's common notions with the biblical criticism of Toland and Chubb (whom he later criticized[102]), Morgan sought to exploit ambiguities in Scripture.

---

taught it; but they taught it because it is true" (Henry Chadwick, ed., *Lessing's Theological Writings* [London: Black, 1956], 18).

97. The title page of *Christianity as Old as the Creation* identifies the work as "Volume I." A second volume, which may have discussed Jesus, was begun but not published in Tindal's lifetime. Only thirty-two pages were printed. When Tindal died, a forged letter deprived his nephew of Tindal's property. The story that the manuscript fell into the hands of Edmund Gibson, bishop of London, who burned it (Stephen, *English Thought in the Eighteenth Century*, 1:114; Torrey, *Voltaire and the English Deists*, 105) is now thought to be spurious.

98. Chubb's *Posthumous Works*, 2 vols. (1748) contain the author's farewell to his readers (1745), which indicated that he regarded the mission of Jesus as divine, but could not accept his personal divinity. His friend William Whiston called him "one of the most foolish and injudicious of our modern Unbelievers" (*Memoirs* [1749], 276; cf. Clive Probyn, *ODNB*, 11:566–68).

99. Facsimile reprint of both works in one volume (New York: Garland, 1978).

100. Edwards devoted nineteen pages to Chubb in his *magnum opus* on *The Freedom of the Will* (1754).

101. Peter Harrison, "Thomas Morgan," in *ODNB* 39 (2004): 148–49.

102. Morgan attacked Chubb's optimistic assessment of human nature in *A Letter to Mr. T. Chubb Occasioned by His Vindication of Human Nature* (1727), and criticized him again in *A Defence of Natural and Revealed Religion* (1728). On Chubb and Morgan see Jeffrey R. Wigglesworth, "'God always acts suitable to his character as a wise and good being': Thomas Chub and Thomas Morgan on Miracles and Providence," in *Atheism and Deism Revalued*, ed. Wayne Hudson et al., 157–72. The book drew on Woolston's earlier study of the use of allegory by Origen and other church fathers.

History was a matter of probabilities. The idea of infallibility was fostered by priests for selfish purposes. Religion was a purely internal affair. Morgan's writings include *A Collection of Tracts, Relating to the Right of Private Judgement, the Sufficiency of Scripture, and the Terms of Church-Communion; Upon Christian Principles: Occasion'd by the Late Trinitarian Controversy* (1726), a *Letter to Eusebius* (1739) and *The Moral Philosopher, in a Dialogue between Philalethes, a Christian Deist, and Theophanes, a Christian Jew* (2 vols., 1737–39).

Viscount Bolingbroke (1678–1751), the Tory statesman and libertine, added little that was new. He left writings to be published posthumously.[103] Dr. Johnson regarded him as a "blunderbuss against religion and morality," and David Hume pronounced his works to be unoriginal and feeble.[104] Perhaps the thinker that took him most seriously was Thomas Jefferson.

Peter Annet (1693–1769) was the last of the old-line of British deists. His writings have been described as "a bridge between the early critical deists, such as Woolston and Collins, and the more political deists of the later eighteenth century, such as Paine."[105] They include *The Resurrection of Jesus Considered* (1744) and sequels that took up the theme of Woolston's trial and Sherlock's reply.[106] Annet argued that Jesus only appeared to die. Annet's assault on miracles, including those in the Old Testament, in *The Free Enquirer* (1761) brought a charge of blasphemous libel, to which he pleaded guilty. He was imprisoned for a month, pilloried twice, made to do hard labor for a year, fined, and put under bond of security for life. This was deemed a "mitigated" sentence by the court in view of his poverty and old age. Annet was the last person to suffer physical punishment for heterodox opinions.[107]

---

103. Henry St. John, *The Philosophical Works of the Late Right Honorable Henry St. John, Lord Viscount Bolingbroke*, 5 vols. (London, 1754–77; facsimile repr., New York: Garland, 1977); cf. Walter M. Merrill, *From Statesman to Philosopher: A Study in Bolingbroke's Deism* (New York: Philosophical Library, 1949).

104. E. C. Mossner, *EP* 1:332. H. T. Dickinson observes that "Bolingbroke's reputation was never substantial and, after the publication of his essays, it has never recovered" (*ODNB* 48:[614–28], 627).

105. James A. Herrick, "Peter Annet," in *ODNB*, 2:239–40, here 240.

106. Subsequent writings include *The Resurrection Reconsidered* (1744?), *The Resurrection Stripped of All Defence* (1745?), and *The Resurrection of Jesus Demonstrated to Have No Proof* (1745?). Other anti-religious works include *The Conception of Jesus Considered as the Foundation of the Christian Religion* (1744), and *Supernaturals Examined* (1747).

107. James A. Herrick, "Blasphemy in the Eighteenth Century: Contours of a Rhetorical

The most enduring reply to deism came from the pen of Joseph Butler (1692–1752), written at a time when Butler was a country clergyman living at Stanhope in Weardale in the diocese and county of Durham. Its title indicated Butler's apologetic strategy for refuting deism: *The Analogy of Religion, Natural and Revealed to the Constitution and Course of Nature* (1736).[108]

Butler had originally intended to become a Presbyterian minister, preparing at the dissenting academy of Samuel Jones first in Gloucester and then in Tewkesbury. There he received a more rigorous education than the one he later got at Oriel College, Oxford. Jones introduced Butler to Locke's *Essay Concerning Human Understanding* and Clarke's Boyle Lectures of 1704–5, *A Demonstration of the Being and Attributes of God*. The latter marked the beginning of a relationship, much of it carried out through correspondence, which shaped Butler's thinking. Butler decided to seek ordination in the Church of England, which enabled him to enter Oriel College. He graduated in 1718 and was ordained deacon and priest the same year. In 1719 Butler was appointed preacher at the Rolls Chapel, London, from which came the *Fifteen Sermons Preached at the Rolls Chapel*. They are regarded as among the most significant ethical discourses of the age.[109] Butler received the degree of DCL in 1733. He went on to become bishop of Bristol (1738–50) and bishop of Durham (1750–52).

In *The Analogy of Religion* Butler raised the debate above personal polemics, although the work was in part a reply to Tindal's *Christianity as Old as the Creation* (1730). Tindal's title was taken from one of Bishop Sherlock's sermons and was mockingly used to argue that there was nothing in Christianity that could not be found in the religion of nature. Butler sought to rectify the argument, replying that:

Crime," in *Atheism and Deism Revalued*, ed. Wayne Hudson et al., 101–18. Herrick notes the case of Jacob Ilive (1730–63), a printer and pamphleteer who also suffered physical punishment for blasphemy (112–15). Herrick describes his crime as "an exotic theology to that codified in the Christian creeds, a refurbished narrative belonging to the first centuries of the Christian era" (115).

108. Repr. in *The Works of Joseph Butler, D.C.L.*, ed. W. E. Gladstone, 2 vols. (Oxford: Clarendon; New York: Macmillan, 1896); cf. Brown, *Miracles and the Critical Mind*, 58–63; Christopher Cunliffe, "Joseph Butler," in *ODNB*, 9:173–80.

109. Butler, *Works*, 2:31–274. Among Butler's targets was the psychological egoism of Hobbes.

> Though natural religion is the foundation and principal part of Christianity, it is not in any sense the whole of it. . . . Christianity is a republication of natural religion. It instructs mankind in the moral system of the world: that it is the work of an infinitely perfect Being, and under his government; that virtue is his law; and that he will finally judge mankind in righteousness and render to all according to their works, in a future state. . . . Revelation is further, an authoritative publication of natural religion, and so affords the evidence and truth of it. Indeed the miracles and prophecies recorded in Scripture, were intended to prove a particular dispensation of Providence, the redemption of the world by the Messiah: but this does not hinder, but that they also prove God's general providence over the world, as our moral Governor and Judge.[110]

At the outset Butler had acknowledged that "probable evidence, in its very nature, affords but an imperfect kind of information; and is to be considered as relative to beings of limited capacities." With God, knowledge was otherwise. "But to us, probability is the very guide of life."[111] In response to the claim that miracles were improbable, Butler asked, "If there be the presumption of millions to one, against the most common facts; what can a small presumption, additional to this, amount to, though it be peculiar?"[112] In the end, miracles must not be compared with "common natural events . . . but to the extraordinary phenomena of nature. And then the comparison will be between the presumption against miracles, and the presumption against such uncommon appearances, suppose, as comets, and against there being any such powers in nature as magnetism and electricity, so contrary to the properties of other bodies not endued with these powers."[113]

Joseph Butler made no direct contribution to the quest of the historical Jesus. He appears to have had little or no understanding of, or interest in, the world of Second Temple Judaism. His view of miracles as external evidential support for truth claims belongs not to critical history but to the apologetic tradition that extended from the Reformation era to his own day and beyond. Butler's main contributions were to draw attention

---

110. Butler, *Works*, 1:188–89.
111. Butler, *Works*, 1:5.
112. Butler, *Works*, 1:218.
113. Butler, *Works*, 1:219.

to the role of probability in perception and argument and to challenge the assumption of the deists that reason was inevitably on their side.

2. Deism in America

2.1. Early American Deists. In America deism exerted a profound influence on the minds of Benjamin Franklin, George Washington, Thomas Jefferson, and other founding fathers of the United States.[114] Deism found expression in Ethan Allen's *Reason the Only Oracle of Man, Or a Compenduous* [sic] *System of Natural Religion* (1784), which blasted institutional Christianity and ridiculed the Bible.[115] Ten years later Thomas Paine sought to rescue deism from French atheism and at the same time to present Christianity as a species of atheism in *The Age of Reason: Being an Investigation of True and Fabulous Theology* (2 vols., 1794–96).[116]

On a popular level an attempt was made by the blind, former Presbyterian and Universalist preacher Elihu Palmer (1764–1806)[117] to spread deism among the lower classes. Palmer settled in New York City as a freelance speaker, where he founded a deistic society to which he preached on Sunday evenings. The society was known successively as the Philosophical Society, the Theistical Society, and the Society of Columbian Illuminati. He promoted his ideas through two weeklies: *Temple of Reason* (1803–5) and *Prospect: View of the Moral World* (1803–6). To him, Moses, Mohammed, and Jesus were all impostors.

2.2. Jefferson's Lives of Jesus. Two works that specifically dealt with the historical Jesus were unpublished pieces compiled by Thomas Jefferson (1743–1826), the framer of the Declaration of Independence

---

114. Gustav Adolf Koch, *Religion of the American Enlightenment* ([1933]; repr., New York: Crowell, 1969); Herbert M. Morais, *Deism in Eighteenth Century America* (New York: Columbia University Press, 1934; repr., New York: Russell & Russell, 1960); Herbert F. May, *The Enlightenment in America* (Oxford: Oxford University Press, 1976); Matthew Stewart, *Nature's God: The Heretical Origins of the American Republic* (New York: Norton, 2014); Steven K. Green, *Inventing a Christian America: The Myth of the Religious Founding* (Oxford: Oxford University Press, 2015).

115. Ethan Allen, *Reason the Only Oracle of Man* ([1784]; repr., New York: Kraus, 1970).

116. On Paine's use of the Bible, see Edward H. Davidson and William J. Scheick, *Paine, Scripture and Authority: The Age of Reason as Religious and Political Idea* (Bethlehem, PA: Lehigh University Press; London: Associated University Presses, 1994).

117. T. P. Thigpen, *Dictionary of Christianity in America*, ed. Daniel G. Reid et al. (Downers Grove, IL: InterVarsity Press, 1990), 860.

and third president of the United States (1801–9).[118] Jefferson had acquired firsthand knowledge of European culture during his travels as assistant to and later successor of Benjamin Franklin as minister to France (1784–89).

In the 1760s Jefferson experienced a religious crisis, which led him to reject the Trinitarian orthodoxy of Anglicanism and to embrace natural religion.[119] His thoughts on religion were copied in a commonplace book, his so-called "Literary Bible," consisting of extracts from ancient and modern writers and philosophers. The almost sixty pages extracted from Bolingbroke form the longest single entry and are the only writings to deal specifically with Christianity. They constitute a deistic credo, which declared it inconceivable that a just God "sent his only begotten son, who had not offended him, to be sacrificed by men, who had offended him, that he might expiate their sins, and satisfy his own anger."[120] The miracles that Jesus supposedly worked—"equivocal at best"—were accepted only by superstitious followers and their successors.

Jefferson was deeply influenced by Joseph Priestley's *History of the Corruptions of Christianity* (1782), which convinced him that one could be a Christian without believing in the Trinity and the divinity of Christ.[121] Jefferson and Priestley (1733–1804) became friends following the latter's move to the United States in 1794 after his home, books, writings, and laboratory were destroyed in the Birmingham riots. Jefferson was so impressed by Priestley's pamphlet on *Jesus and Socrates Compared* (1803) that he resolved to adopt the comparative method as a means to promote his own views. The result was his "Syllabus of an Estimate of the Merit

---

118. Thomas Jefferson, *The Life and Morals of Jesus of Nazareth. Extracted Textually from the Gospels in Greek, Latin, French, and English*, published in facsimile with an introduction by Cyrus Adler (Washington, DC: Government Printing Office, 1904). This edition is now superseded by *Jefferson's Extracts from the Gospels: "The Philosophy of Jesus" and "The Life and Morals of Jesus"*, ed. Dickinson W. Adams and Ruth W. Lester, introduction by Eugene R. Sheridan, *The Papers of Thomas Jefferson*, second series (Princeton, NJ: Princeton University Press, 1983).

See also the facsimile Smithsonian ed. of *The Jefferson Bible: The Life and Morals of Jesus of Nazareth Extracted Textually from the Gospels in Greek, Latin, French and English*, with essays by Harry R. Rubenstein, Barbara Clark Smith, and Janice Stagnitto Ellis (Washington, DC: Smithsonian, 2011).

119. *Jefferson's Extracts from the Gospels*, 5.

120. *Jefferson's Extracts from the Gospels*, 6; citing Gilbert Chinard, ed., *The Literary Bible of Thomas Jefferson* (Baltimore: Johns Hopkins Press, 1928), 56–57.

121. *Jefferson's Extracts from the Gospels*, 15. The *Corruptions* had originally been published in Birmingham. Jefferson possessed a copy of the 1793 edition of the two-volume work, which had been printed in London. He is thought to have read it sometime in the 1790s.

of the Doctrines of Jesus, Compared with Those of Others" (1803)[122] and "The Philosophy of Jesus" (1804).

The "Syllabus" was intended to review the teaching of Jesus in comparison with "the moral principles inculcated by the most esteemed of the sect of antt. [sic] philosophy, or of individuals; particularly Pythagoras, Socrates, Epicurus, Cicero, Epictetus, Seneca, Antoninus."[123] Turning to Jesus, Jefferson observed that "his parentage was obscure, his condition poor, his education null, his natural endowments great, his life correct and innocent; he was meek, benevolent, patient, firm, disinterested, and of the sublimest eloquence."[124] Nevertheless, "the doctrines which he delivered were defective as a whole" on account of the facts that Jesus himself wrote nothing, his teaching was committed to "the most unlettered and ignorant of men," and that "he fell an early victim to the jealousy and combination of the altar and throne" before he could develop "a compleat system of morals."[125]

---

122. The "Syllabus" was appended to a letter dated April 21, 1803, to the Philadelphia physician and social reformer Dr. Benjamin Rush (*Jefferson's Extracts from the Gospels*, 331–36). Rush and Jefferson had been members of the Continental Congress and had worked together to advance the causes of American independence and union. But whereas Jefferson regarded republicanism as essentially secular, the theologically universalist Rush saw it as part of a divine plan to establish the kingdom of God on earth. He urged Jefferson to adopt a more positive view of Christianity and the divinity of Christ.

In the letter of April 21, 1803, Jefferson wrote: "To the corruptions of Christianity, I am indeed opposed; but not to the genuine precepts of Jesus himself. I am a Christian, in the only sense in which he wished anyone to be; sincerely attached to his doctrines, in preference to all others; ascribing to himself every human excellence, and believing he never claimed any other."

Jefferson went on to remark that Priestley's *Jesus and Socrates Compared* had prompted him to arrange his own "Syllabus" "as I wished to see executed, by someone of more leisure and information for the task than myself. This I now send you, as the only discharge of my promise I can probably ever execute."

In a letter to Priestley, dated April 9, 1803 (*Jefferson's Extracts from the Gospels*, 327–29), Jefferson referred to his promise to Rush to write him a letter giving his view of "the Christian system." He went on to give Priestley a condensed version of the "Syllabus" he later sent to Rush. Aware of the "incorrectness" of the Jews' ideas of the deity, Jesus "endeavored to bring them to the principle of pure deism, and juster notions of the attributes of god [sic], to reform their moral doctrines to the standard of reason, justice, and philanthropy, and inculcate the belief of a future state." Despite the imperfect preservation of his teaching, the fragments that remain "shew a master workman, that his system of morality was the most benevolent and sublime that has ever been taught; and eminently more perfect than those of any of the antient philosophers." The letter was published twice in Jefferson's lifetime, first by an English Unitarian in the belief that it would lend prestige to rational religion, and then by an American Calvinist who wanted to discredit Unitarians.

123. *Jefferson's Extracts from the Gospels*, 332.
124. *Jefferson's Extracts from the Gospels*, 332–33.
125. *Jefferson's Extracts from the Gospels*, 333.

Quests before Schweitzer

> The question of his being a member of the god-head, or in direct communication with it,
> claimed for him by some of his followers, and denied by others,
> is foreign to the present view, which is merely an estimate of the intrinsic merit of his doctrines.
> 1. He corrected the Deism of the Jews, confirming them in their belief of one only god,
>   and giving them juster notions of his attributes and government.
> 2. His moral doctrines relating to kindred and friends were more pure and perfect, that those of the most correct of the philosophers, and greatly more so than those of the Jews.
>   And they went far beyond both in inculcating universal philanthropy.[126]

Jefferson urged Priestley to develop the comparison further, but Priestley died in February 1804. That same month Jefferson began his own "digest" of the moral teachings of Jesus. Using Priestley's *Harmony of the Evangelists in English* and *Harmony of the Evangelists in Greek*, which were given him by Priestley himself, a pair of identical English editions and a Greek-Latin edition, Jefferson constructed his own harmony based on Priestley's.[127] "The Philosophy of Jesus" was completed between February 4 and March 10, 1804.[128] Jefferson made a list of what he considered to be moral teachings of Jesus, and over a period of several evenings clipped out passages and pasted them in double columns on forty-six octavo sheets. He seems to have abandoned his intention of producing a Greek text and comparison with other philosophers on account of pressure of the presidency.

---

126. *Jefferson's Extracts from the Gospels*, 333–34.
127. A harmony is a presentation of the four Gospels in a single narrative designed to harmonize discrepancies in the form of a continuous narrative. The earliest known harmony is Tatian's *Diatessaron* (second century). The genre flourished after the Reformation but disappeared with the advent of higher criticism. In a letter to Priestley (January 29, 1804) Jefferson expressed thanks for Priestley's *Harmony* and told him of his intention to produce his own. "With a view to do this for my own satisfaction, I had sent to Philadelphia to get two testaments Greek of the same edition, and two English with a design to cut out morsels of morality, and paste them on the leaves of a book, in a manner you describe in forming your Harmony" (*Jefferson's Extracts from the Gospels*, 340).
128. *Jefferson's Extracts from the Gospels*, 27.

Deism and the Historical Jesus

Although the text of the work is now lost,[129] the title page has survived. It reads: "The Philosophy of Jesus of Nazareth extracted from the account of his life and doctrines as given by Mathew [sic], Mark, Luke, & John. being [sic] an abridgement of the New Testament for the use of the Indians unembarrassed by matters of fact or faith beyond the level of their comprehensions."[130] The allusion to "Indians" was ironic. It referred to Jefferson's Federalist opponents and their allies, whose political and religious obscurantism was seen by the president as a danger to the republic.[131] Jefferson was motivated not only by a desire to rebut assaults on his character but also to set out a moralistic, demystified version of Christianity upon which all persons of good will could agree.[132] However, he appears to have used the work almost exclusively for private study.

The more ambitious "Life and Morals of Jesus of Nazareth" includes texts narrating the career of Jesus in addition to his moral teaching. It was a private search for religious truth, conceived shortly before Jefferson began his second term in 1804 and completed by 1820.[133] It is characterized by a Unitarian focus on the ethics of Jesus. Jesus did not constitute a complete system, since he died before reaching full intellectual maturity.[134]

Jefferson entitled his work "The Life and Morals of Jesus of Nazareth Extracted Textually from the Gospels in Greek, Latin, French & English."[135] Like "The Philosophy of Jesus," it was literally a scissors and paste production. Jefferson had no compunction about cutting verses in half in order to eliminate the supernatural. He included the birth narratives but cut out references to the virginal conception and the Holy Spirit.[136] He likewise excised mention of the Spirit in the account of

---

129. A modern reconstruction has been made on the basis of an extant list of texts and copies of the KJV New Testaments from which Jefferson clipped verses (account of the reconstruction and facsimile in *Jefferson's Extracts from the Gospels*, 45–53, 55–105).
130. *Jefferson's Extracts from the Gospels*, 55.
131. *Jefferson's Extracts from the Gospels*, 28.
132. *Jefferson's Extracts from the Gospels*, 13–15.
133. *Jefferson's Extracts from the Gospels*, 30, 38. Photocopy of the text, 127–297.
134. *Jefferson's Extracts from the Gospels*, 40.
135. In selecting and arranging his material, Jefferson was influenced by the Unitarian Joseph Priestley's *Socrates and Jesus Compared* (Philadelphia, 1803). *Jefferson's Extracts from the Gospels*, 20–23.
136. Jefferson denounced the Trinity in numerous letters (*Jefferson's Extracts from the Gospels*, 40). Among them is a lengthy letter to William Short (August 4, 1820) in which he describes Jesus as a religious reformer. "Moses had either not believed in a future state of existence, or had not thought it essential to be explicitly taught to his people. Jesus inculcated that doctrine with emphasis and precision. Moses had bound the Jews to many idle ceremonies, mummeries and

Jesus' baptism. The temptation story was omitted, as were narratives of miracles and exorcisms. The Sermon on the Mount was reproduced extensively. Jefferson included parables that emphasized social responsibility, denunciations of the Pharisees, and the prophecy of the destruction of Jerusalem. The Last Supper was edited so as to include the Johannine account of the footwashing and the announcement of betrayal but omit the synoptic sayings about the bread and wine.

Jesus was condemned by the Sanhedrin for blasphemously claiming to be the Son of God. The narrative concluded with the burial of Jesus and the sealing of the tomb. Essentially Jefferson's work was a harmony of the evangelists or, to be more precise, a harmony of Matthew and Luke, largely following Matthew's narrative outline, with occasional insertions from Mark and John. Theologically, it had moved away from the negative deism of Jefferson's early years to embody the Unitarianism that Jefferson believed would become "the general religion of the United States."[137]

3. Deism in Germany

3.1. German Reception of English Deism. The purpose of this section is to draw attention to the fact that British deism was well known on the continent of Europe long before the publication in 1778 of Reimarus's study, which Schweitzer deemed to mark the beginning of the quest of the historical Jesus. If the discussion has the character of an annotated bibliography, it will have achieved its purpose of substantiating this contention. Voltaire acquired a firsthand knowledge of the deist controversies during his time in England (1726–29). His personal library

---

observances of no effect towards producing the social utilities which constitute the essence of virtue. Jesus exposed their futility and insignificance. . . . The office of reformer of the superstitions of a nation is ever dangerous. Jesus had to walk on the perilous confines of reason and religion. . . . That Jesus did not mean to impose himself on mankind as the son of god [sic] physically speaking I have been convinced by the writings of men more learned than myself in that lore. But that he might conscientiously believed himself inspired from above, is very possible" (*Jefferson's Extracts from the Gospels*, 396–97).

137. In a letter to James Smith (December 8, 1822) Jefferson expressed his opinion that "the unity of the supreme being [was not] ousted from the Christian creed by the force of reason, but by the sword of civil government wielded at the will of the fanatic Athanasius. . . . I confidently expect that the present generation will see Unitarianism become the general religion of the United States" (*Jefferson's Extracts from the Gospels*, 409).

included many deist works, which he drew upon in his own writings.[138] In 1701 John Toland was made secretary to the embassy to Hanover. He was introduced to the court in Berlin and became recognized on the European continent for his heterodox ideas.[139]

During the half-century prior to publication of Reimarus's first *Fragment* in 1774, deism was discussed in Germany. J. L. Mosheim gave an early account of Toland in his *Vindicia Antiquae Christianorum Disciplinae contra Tolandi Nazarenum* (1720). Woolston was discussed by Heinrich Christian Lemker in *Historische Nachrichten von Th. Woolstons Schicksal, Schriften und Streitigkeiten* (1740)[140] and by Carl Christian Woog in *De Vita et Scriptis Thomae Woolstoni* (1743). Christian Kortholt wrote *De Matthaeo Tindalio dissertatio* (1734), and Christian Gottloeb Jöcher lectured on Tindal at Leipzig. Toland, Tindal, Collins, Woolston, and Lord Herbert, together with Spinoza, Locke, Newton, and Clarke, were among the notables deemed worthy of inclusion in the original four volumes of Jöcher's *Allgemeines Gelehrten-Lexicon* (1750).[141] Many of the writings of the deists and their opponents were translated into French and German.[142] In 1741 Johann Lorenz Schmidt published his translation of Tindal's *Christianity as Old as the Creation*.[143] Schmidt was suggested mischievously by Lessing as the putative author of the *Fragments* in order to distract suspicion from Reimarus.[144]

---

138. See Torrey, *Voltaire and the English Deists*. Torrey devoted entire chapters to Voltaire and Collins, Woolston, Tindal, Middleton, and Annet. He considered Chubb and Bolingbroke as "minor influences."

139. Daniel, *John Toland*, 10.

140. William H. Trapnell considered Lemker's work to be the most thorough but marred by dogmatic literalism (*Thomas Woolston*, 183–84).

141. Repr., Hildesheim: Olms, 1960.

142. Gotthard Victor Lechler, *Geschichte des englischen Deismus* (Suttgart, Tübingen, 1841; repr. with foreword by Günter Gawlick, Hildesheim: Olms, 1965). For details of English books translated into German together with reviews, see Mary Bell Price and Lawrence Marsden Price, *The Publication of English Humaniora in Germany in the Eighteenth Century*, University of California Publications in Modern Philology 44 (Berkeley: University of California Press, 1955). This work complements their earlier *English Literature in Germany* (Berkeley: University of California Press, 1934). On theology in the German Enlightenment, see Karl Aner, *Die Theologie des Lessingzeit* ([1929]; repr., Hildesheim: Olms, 1964; Wolfgang Philipp, *Das Werden der Aufklärung in theologiegeschichtlicher Sicht*, FSTR 3 (Göttingen: Vandenhoeck & Ruprecht, 1957). Further literature in *TRE*, 8:404–6; *RGG*[4] 2:619, 622.

143. *Beweis, dass das Christenthum so ald wie die Welt sey, nebst Herrn Jacob Fosters Widerlegung desselben* (Frankfurt, 1741).

144. Lessing, *Sämtliche Schriften*, ed. Karl Lachmann and Franz Muncker, 36 vols. (Leipzig: Göschen, 1838–1924), 12:255; cf. Brown, *Jesus in European Protestant Thought*, 279n7. Schmidt was the author of the *Wertheimer Bibel*, which was a free translation with rationalistic notes. Only

Several works offered surveys of the field of debate. G. W. Alberti published *Briefe betreffend den allerneusten Zustand der Religion und der Wissenschaften in Gross-Britanien* (1752–54). John Leland's *View of the Principal Deistical Writings* (1754–56) appeared in translation by Heinrich Gottlob Schmid (1755–56).[145] Leland's work was reviewed by G. E. Lessing in *Briefe die neueste Literatur betreffend*.[146] In 1755 Urban Gottlob Thorschmid published his *Critische Lebensgeschichte Anton Collins*. It was followed by Thorschmid's *Versuch einer vollständigen Engelländischen Freydenker-Bibliothek, in welcher aller Schriften der berühmtesten Freydenker nebst dem Schutzschriften für die christliche Religion . . . aufgestellt werden* (4 vols., 1765–67). In 1759 J. A. Trinius published a *Freydenker-Lexikon, oder Einleitung in die Geschichte der neueren Feygeister, ihrer Schriften, und deren Widerlegungen*. Other contemporary sources of information were the *Allgemine Deutsche Bibliothek*, the *Göttingsche gelehrte Anzeigen* and S. J. Baumgarten's *Nachrichten von einer Hallischen Bibliothek* (8 vols., 1748–51) and *Nachrichten von merkwürdigen Büchern* (12 vols., 1752–58).

In a study commemorating Reimarus, Günter Gawlick argued that deism was the principal feature of the religious philosophy of the Enlightenment.[147] Moshe Pelle commented: "In Germany, birthplace of the Hebrew *Haskalah*—Enlightenment—deism received its inspiration from English deism and less from its French counterpart."[148] Pelle went on to say that "Reimarus was the deist *par excellence* of the German *Aufklärung*. He was the first to relinquish the Leibnizian belief in har-

---

the Pentateuch actually appeared. Like the English Deists, he rejected appeal to prophecy and miracles. He also translated Spinoza's *Ethics*. Schmidt died at Wolfenbüttel, where Lessing purported to have discovered the *Fragments*.

145. *Abriss der vornehmsten deistischen Schriften, die in dem vorigen und gegenwärtigen Jahrhunderte in Engeland bekandt geworden sind; nebst Anmerkungen über dieselben un Nachrichten von den gegen sie hearausgekommenen Antworten. In verschieden Briefen an einen guten Freund* (Hannover: Schmid, 1755–56).

146. *Sämtliche Schriften*, 5:443–45, §134.

147. "Der Deismus als Grundzug der Religionsphilosophie der Aufklärung," in *Hermann Samuel Reimarus (1694–1768). Ein "bekannter Unbekannte" der Aufklärung in Hamburg*, Vorträge der Tagung der Joachim Jungius-Gesellschaft der Wissenschaften, Hamburg am 12. und 13. Oktober 1972 (Göttingen: Vandenhoeck & Ruprecht, 1973), 15–43.

148. Moshe Pelle, "The Impact of Deism on the Hebrew Literature of the Enlightenment in Germany," *Eighteenth-Century Studies* 6 (1972–73): 35–59, here 42; cf. Christoph Voigt, *Der englische Deismus in Deutschland. Eine Studie zur Rezeption englisch-deutscher Literatur in den Zeitschriften und Kompendien des 18. Jahrhunderts*, BHT 121 (Tübingen: Mohr Siebeck, 2003); F. Stanley Jones, "From Toland to Baur: Tracks of the History of Research into Jewish Christianity," in *The Rediscovery of Christianity from Toland to Baur*, 123–36.

mony between divine revelation and reason, and to side with Bayle."[149] On the other hand, he exonerated Moses Mendelssohn—the "father" of the Jewish Enlightenment, grandfather of the composer, and friend of both Reimarus and Lessing—of charges of being a deist. "Though he was influenced by the deistic movement . . . , and although he shared some of its views, he was hardly part of it. . . . Mendelssohn Judaized—if one may use the term—a few deistic principles and rejected many others."[150]

3.2. Reimarus and the English Deists. In light of the above, the ground was well prepared for the controversy surrounding the anonymous *Fragments of an Unnamed Author* that Lessing extracted from Reimarus's unpublished "Apology or Defense of the Rational Worshippers of God." It will be discussed in the next chapter in connection with Albert Schweitzer's account of *The Quest of the Historical Jesus*. The "Rational Worshippers of God" were the deists.

At this point it may be helpful to give a sketch of Reimarus and the history of his private manuscript entitled *Apologie oder Schutzschrift für die vernünftigen Verehrer Gottes*. The manuscript was first published in its entirety in 1972.[151] What Schweitzer based his history on were extracts posthumously published by G. E. Lessing as *Fragmente eines Ungenannten* ("Fragments of an Unnamed [Writer]," or "Fragments of an Anonymous [Writer]").[152]

Hermann Samuel Reimarus (1694–1768) was born in Hamburg, where he spent most of his life. His family belonged to the cultural elite of the city. In 1708 he entered the Johanneum, where his father was among his teachers. In 1710 he transferred to Akademische Gymnasium, which was located in the same building. Among his teachers were the classics

---

149. *Eighteenth-Century Studies* 6 (1972–73): 44.

150. *Eighteenth-Century Studies* 6 (1972–73): 46–47. In support Pelle cites numerous references, including his own book in Hebrew, in lengthy footnotes. On Mendelssohn and his relationship with Reimarus and Lessing, see Alexander Altmann, *Moses Mendelssohn: A Biographical Study* (Tuscaloosa, AL: University of Alabama Press; London: Routledge & Kegan Paul, 1973).

151. Hermann Samuel Reimarus, *Apologie oder Schutzschrift für die vernünftigen Verehrer Gottes*, Im Auftrag der Joachim Jungius-Gesellschaft der Wissenschaften in Hamburg herausgegeben von Gerhard Alexander, 2 vols. (Frankfurt: Suhrkamp, 1972).

152. Current reappraisals of Reimarus include *Hermann Samuel Reimarus (1694–1768). Ein "bekannter Unbekannter" der Aufklärung in Hamburg*; and the major comprehensive study by Dietrich Klein, *Hermann Samuel Reimarus (1694–1768)*, Beiträge zur historischen Theologie 145 (Tübingen: Mohr Siebeck, 2009). In addition to examining in detail the historical development of Reimarus's thought, Klein analysed his *Apology* in the context of biblical criticism, and the philosophical theology of *The Principal Truths of Natural Religion*.

scholar Johann Albert Fabricius and the Hebraist Johann Christoph Wolf. Advanced courses in his final years were regarded as university equivalents. In 1714 Reimarus moved to Jena, where he studied theology, philosophy, and oriental languages. During a period at Leipzig, Reimarus was introduced to British empirical philosophy. He completed his studies at Wittenberg, where he received a university teaching qualification. He received his habilitation for a study of Machiavellianism before Machiavelli.

Reimarus made a study trip to Holland and England in 1720–21. Little is known of his activities there, but it seems that he got to know deism first hand.[153] On his return Reimarus was appointed rector of a high school in Wismar. He returned to Hamburg in 1728 on his appointment of professor of oriental languages at his alma mater. Eventually he became the institution's rector. Shortly after his appointment Reimarus married the daughter of Fabricius. Of their seven children, only three survived him. The respected physician Johann Albert Hinrich Reimarus and his sister Elise played significant parts in the course of subsequent events through their relationship with Gotthold Ephraïm Lessing.

The Reimarus household was a center of intellectual life in Hamburg. Here the respected professor embarked on a double life. The public *persona* was that of a scholar, editor, and author of learned academic treatises. In the early 1730s he completed and published the Job commentary of the late Johann Adolf Hofmann. He followed it by completing Fabricius's commentary on Roman history by Dio Cassius. Reimarus then turned to works in philosophy and natural science that led to his admission to the St. Petersburg Academy of Sciences. *Die vornehmsten Wahrheiten der natürlichen Religion* ("The Principal Truths of Natural Religion," 1754) and *Vernunftlehre* ("Rationality," 1756) were followed by *Allgemeine Betrachtungen über die Triebe der Tiere* ("General Observations on the Behavior of Animals," 2 vols., 1760).

Parallel to his public activity was Reimarus's biblical research that he kept secret—even from his wife. He ventured on publishing occasional ancillary pieces anonymously and even toyed with publishing the text

---

153. We know of the visit through the memorial address by J. G. Büsch "Memoriae Immortali H. S. Reimari," cited in the autobiography of Reimarus's son, Dr. J. A. H. Reimarus, *De Vita Sua Commentarius* (Hamburg, 1815), 9. The visit is confirmed by others including Henning Graf Reventlow, "Das Arsenal der Bibelkritik des Reimarus: Die Auslegung der Bibel, insbesondere des Alten Testaments, bei den englischen Deisten," in *Hermann Samuel Reimarus (1694–1768)*, 45.

of the manuscript. However, fear of political repercussions prevailed.[154] Drafts of Reimarus's *Apology* as it evolved were seen by only a privileged circle.

Reimarus made a lengthy study of the English deists. His personal library included most of their works, which in the words of Henning Graf Reventlow formed Reimarus's "arsenal of biblical criticism."[155] The unpublished manuscript from which the *Fragments* were extracted contains references to Toland, Shaftesbury, Collins, Woolston, Tindal, Chubb, Morgan, and Middleton.[156] Only Annet appears to have escaped his notice. Among the "rational worshippers of God" whom Reimarus defended was Gabriel da Costa, but his thought seems more indebted to the English deists than to European writers.

There were, however, major differences between the British deists and Reimarus. British deism was largely negative and at times egregiously speculative. At best Jesus was a shadowy preacher of a rational religion that had marked resemblances to liberal Protestantism. Judaism figured only rarely in the picture. Reimarus's defense of deism involved meticulous critique of Moses and the Old Testament exodus narratives. The *Apology* distinguished sharply between the intentions of Jesus and those of his disciples. Those of Jesus began by being lofty—the moral reform of Judaism—but were ultimately misguided in the belief that his martyr's death would establish the kingdom of God on earth. The intentions of Jesus' disciples were self-serving. They invented the resurrection narratives and compounded their fraud by propagating the message that Jesus would return. In short, Reimarus was deeply indebted to the British deists in his deconstruction of Protestant orthodox supernaturalism. His construction of an alternative historical narrative about the intentions of Jesus and his disciples was his own creation.

---

154. Dietrich Klein, *Hermann Samuel Reimarus*, 60–67.
155. Reventlow, "Das Arsenal der Bibelkritik des Reimarus," in *Ein "bekannter Unbekannte" der Aufklärung in Hamburg*, 44–65; Dietrich Klein, *Hermann Samuel Reimarus*, 133–48.
Reventlow (60) noted the observation in M. Loeser's dissertation on *Die Kritik des Hermann Samuel Reimarus am Alten Testament* (PhD diss., Berlin, Ev.-theol. F., 1941), 29, that the catalog in the Hamburger Staats- und Universitätsbibliothek of Reimarus's library indicated that Reimarus possessed most of the deists' writings.
156. In an earlier study A. C. Lundsteen suggested that in many places the impression cannot be avoided that Reimarus's work was "a plagiarism of English Deistic authors to the point of verbal reproduction" (*Hermann Samuel Reimarus und die Anfänge der Leben-Jesu-Forschung* [Copenhagen: Olsen, 1939], 138). However, it should be remembered that the *Apology* was not a published work but a draft in progress.

Quests before Schweitzer

3.3. Kant's Deism. It may seem anachronistic to include here reflections on Immanuel Kant (1724–1804), the leading philosopher of the age who spent his entire life in Königsberg, the capital city of East Prussia.[157] The inclusion is justified on two counts. First, Kant's religious philosophy represents the ultimate, most sophisticated development of deism. Second, (as we shall see in the next chapter) Albert Schweitzer wrote his first doctoral dissertation on Kant's philosophy of religion. It included discussion of Kant's *Religion within the Boundaries of Mere Reason*. Schweitzer followed Kant insofar as Schweitzer's account of Jesus fell strictly within the *boundaries of mere reason*.

In 1793 Kant wrote to his friend Carl Friedrich Stäudlin, professor of theology at Göttingen, about his goals in philosophy.

> The plan I prescribed for myself a long time ago calls for an examination of the field of pure philosophy with a view to solving three problems: (1) What can I know? (metaphysics). (2) What ought I to do? (moral philosophy). (3) What may I hope? (philosophy of religion). A fourth question ought to follow, finally: What is man? (anthropology, a subject on which I have lectured for over twenty years). With the enclosed work [*Die Religion innerhalb der Grenzen der blossen Vernunft*], I have tried to complete the third part of my plan. In this book I have proceeded conscientiously and with genuine respect for the Christian religion but also with a fitting candor, concealing nothing but rather presenting openly the way in which I believe that a possible union of Christianity with the purest practical reason is possible.... The complete education of a biblical theologian should unite into one system the products of his own powers and whatever contrary lessons he can learn from philosophy. (My book is that sort of combination.) By assessing his

---

157. See further Brown, *Jesus in European Protestant Thought*, 58–67; Brown, *Christianity and Western Thought: A History of Philosophers, Ideas and Movements* (Downers Grove, IL: InterVarsity Press, 1990), 1:309–29; Michel Despland, *Kant on History and Religion, with a Translation of Kant's "On the Failure of All Attempted Philosophical Theodicies"* (Montreal: McGill-Queen's University Press, 1973); Philip J. Rossi and Michael Wreen, eds., *Kant's Philosophy of Religion Reconsidered*, The Indiana Series in the Philosophy of Religion (Bloomington: Indiana University Press, 1991); Chris L. Firestone and Stephen R. Palmquist, eds., *Kant and the New Philosophy of Religion*, Indiana Series in the Philosophy of Religion (Bloomington: Indiana University Press, 2006); Paul Geyer, ed., *The Cambridge Companion to Kant and Modern Philosophy* (Cambridge: Cambridge University Press, 2006); Paul Geyer, ed., *The Cambridge Companion to Kant's Critique of Pure Reason* (Cambridge: Cambridge University Press, 2010).

doctrines from the point of view of rational grounds, he shall be armed against any future attack.[158]

The title of Kant's book has been variously translated. The new standard edition is entitled *Religion within the Boundaries of Mere Reason*.[159] It suggests that the religion Kant commended was to be reconfigured within the parameters of "mere reason." The opening words of the preface to the first edition threw down the challenge:

> So far as morality is based on the conception of the human being as one who is free but who also, just because of that, binds himself through his reason to unconditional laws, it is in need neither of the idea of another being above him in order that he recognize his duty, nor, that he observe it of an incentive other than the law itself.... Hence on its own behalf morality in no way needs religion (whether objectively, as regards willing or subjectively, as regards capability) but is self-sufficient by virtue of pure practical reason.[160]

However, morality "inevitably leads to religion, and through religion extends itself to the idea of a mighty moral lawgiver outside the human being, in whose will the ultimate ends (of the creation of the world) is what can and at the same time ought to be the ultimate human end."[161]

---

158. Kant's letter dated May 4, 1793 (*Correspondence*, Cambridge Edition of the Works of Immanuel Kant, trans. and ed., Arnulf Zweig [Cambridge: Cambridge University Press, 1999], 458). Carl Friedrich Stäudlin (1761–1826) reciprocated by sending Kant a copy of his *Geschichte und Geist des Skeptizismus, vorzüglich auf Moral und Religion* (Leipzig, 1794) (Kant's letter to Stäudlin, December 4, 1794, *Correspondence*, 490–92). Kant dedicated *Der Streit der Fakultäten* (1798) to Stäudlin.

Kant's new work was preceded by his major discussions of metaphysics and morals. Kant's *Kritik der reinen Vernunft* (1781; 2nd ed., 1787) explored the conditions and limits of knowledge, treating the idea of God as a "regulative principle." His *Kritik der praktischen Vernunft* (1788) made ethics independent of religion, making God, freedom and immortality "non-cognitive postulates of pure practical reason."

159. Kant, *Religion within the Boundaries of Mere Reason*, trans. George di Giovanni, in *Religion and Rational Theology*, Cambridge Edition of the Works of Immanuel Kant, ed. Allen W. Wood and George di Giovanni (Cambridge: Cambridge University Press, 1996), 39–216.

The more familiar version of Kant's title is *Religion within the Limits of Reason Alone*, trans. with introduction and notes by Theodore M. Greene and Hoyt Hudson [with an essay by John R. Silber, "The Ethical Significance of Kant's *Religion*"] (LaSalle, IL: Open Court, 1934; repr., New York: Harper, 1960). Di Giovanni preferred the words *boundaries* and *mere* as being closer to Kant's intentions and rhetoric (*Religion and Rational Theology*, 53).

160. Kant, *Religion and Rational Theology*, 57.
161. Kant, *Religion and Rational Theology*, 59–60.

Quests before Schweitzer

The nearest that Kant came to articulating a *Christology* is found in his discussion in the section on "The Personified Idea of the Good Principle."[162] Perhaps *Christology* is the wrong word; even though Kant's language was redolent with biblical intertextual allusions drawn from the New Testament, the title *Christ* was not used. Kant made it clear that rational religion did not require a historical Jesus.

> That which alone can make a world the object of divine decree and the end of creation is *Humanity* (rational being in general as pertaining to the world) *in its full moral perfection*, from which happiness follows in the will of the Highest Being directly as from its supreme condition.—This human being, alone pleasing to God, "is in him from all eternity" [John 1:1–2]; the idea of him proceeds from God's being; he is not therefore a created thing but God's only-begotten Son, "the *Word*" (the *Fiat!*) through which all other beings are, and without whom nothing that is made would exist [John 1:3] (since for him, that is for a rational being in the world, as can be thought according to its moral determination, everything was made).—"He is the reflection of his glory" [Heb. 1:3].—"In him God loved the world" [John 3:16], and only in him and through the adoption of his dispositions can we hope "to become children of God" [John 1:13] etc.[163]
>
> But, precisely because we are not its authors but the idea has established itself in the human being without our comprehending how human nature could have been receptive of it, it is better to say that that *prototype* has *come down* to us from heaven, that it has taken up humanity (for it is not just as possible to conceive how the *human being*, *evil* by nature, would renounce evil on his own and *raise* himself up to the ideal of holiness, as it is that the latter take up humanity—which is not evil in itself—by *descending* to it). This union with us therefore may be regarded as a state of *abasement* of the Son of God [Phil. 2:6–8] if we represent to ourselves this God-like human being, our prototype, in such a way that, though himself holy and hence not bound to submit to sufferings, he nonetheless takes these upon himself in the fullest measure for promoting the world's greatest good.[164]

---

162. Kant, *Religion and Rational Theology*, 103–17.
163. Kant, *Religion and Rational Theology*, 103–4.
164. Kant, *Religion and Rational Theology*, 104.

In discussing "The Objective Reality of this Idea," Kant hastened to add that "there is no need . . . of any example from experience to make the idea of a human being morally pleasing to God a model to us; the idea is present as a model already in our reason." Moreover, to ask for "miracles as credentials" is a confession of "moral *unbelief.*"[165] Nevertheless,

> if such a human being of such a truly divine disposition had descended, as it were, from heaven to earth at a specific time, and had he exhibited in his self, through teaching, conduct, and suffering, the *example* of a human well-pleasing to God . . . had he brought about all this, an incalculably great moral good in the world, through a revolution in the human race: even then we would have no cause to assume in him anything else except a naturally begotten human being (because he too feels to be under the obligation to exhibit such an example in himself).[166]

In dealing with the death of the archetypal figure, Kant showed himself aware of recent theological controversies from which he astutely distanced himself. In a footnote he noted the "fanciful fiction" of Karl Friedrich Bahrdt that Jesus "*sought* death in order to promote a worthy purpose through a shining and sensational example: that would be suicide"—which Kant rejected not on historical but on *moral* grounds.[167] In the same footnote Kant dismissed the view put forward in the *Wolfenbüttel Fragments* that Jesus staked "his life for just a political though illegal purpose, and not a moral one, perhaps that of overthrowing the rule of the priests in order to establish himself in their place with supreme temporal power." Such an act would have been "a worldly design" that would ultimately have been "self-defeating."[168] As it was,

---

165. Kant, *Religion and Rational Theology*, 105.
166. Kant, *Religion and Rational Theology*, 106.
167. Kant, *Religion and Rational Theology*, 120. Karl Friedrich Bahrdt (1741–92) was the author of one of the fictitious lives of Jesus that enjoyed notoriety at the turn of the century, *Ausführung des Plans und Zwecks Jesu. In Briefe an Wahrheit an suchende Leser*, 11 vols. (1784–92). The crucifixion was rigged by Nicodemus after Luke had given Jesus painkilling drugs. Luke resuscitated him in the coolness of the cave in which Joseph of Arimathea had arranged to have Jesus placed (see below, chap. 3; and Brown, *Jesus in European Protestant Thought*, 163).
168. Kant, *Religion and Rational Theology*, 120. In Kant's day it was not widely known that the author of the *Wolfenbüttel Fragments* was Heinrich Samuel Reimarus, whom Schweitzer wrongly identified as the originator of the quest of the historical Jesus (see below, chap. 5; and Brown, *Jesus in European Protestant Thought*, 1–55).

Quests before Schweitzer

the words "Do this in remembrance of me" could "just as well refer to the failure of a very good and purely moral design of the Master, namely, to bring about in his own lifetime a *public* revolution (in religion), by overthrowing a morally repressive ceremonial faith and the authority of its priests."[169]

The moral outcome of this conflict was not the conquering of the evil principle, which still grips the world, "but only the breaking up of its controlling power in holding against their will those who have been subject to it. . . . It is easy to see, once we divest it of its mystical cover [*von ihrer mystischen Hülle*] this vivid mode of representing things, apparently also the only one at the time *suited to the common people*, why it (its spirit and rational meaning) has been valid and binding practically, for the whole world and at all times: because it lies near enough to every human being for each to recognize his duty in it."[170] Kant concluded that "any attempt like the present to find a meaning in Scriptures in harmony with the *most holy* teachings of reason must be held not only as permissible but as a duty; and we may be reminded at this point of what the *wise teacher* said to his disciples regarding someone who went his own way, by which, however, he would have had eventually to come to the same goal: 'Forbid him not, for he who is not against us is for us [Mark 9:39–40].'"[171]

Kant saw "the coming kingdom of God" as "the gradual transition of ecclesiastical faith toward the exclusive dominion of pure religious faith."[172] As his work neared its climax Kant devoted a section to discussion of "The Christian Religion as Natural Religion."[173]

> Natural religion, as morality (with reference to the freedom of the subject), combined with the concept of that which can actualize its ultimate end (the concept of *God* as moral originator of the world), and referred to a duration of the human being proportionate to the entirety of this end (immortality), is a pure practical concept of reason which, despite its infinite fruitfulness, yet presuppose only so little a capacity for theoretical reason that, practically, we can

---

169. Kant, *Religion and Rational Theology*, 120.
170. Kant, *Religion and Rational Theology*, 121; cf. Ernst Troeltsch, *Gesammelte Schriften*, 4 vols. (Tübingen: Mohr Siebeck, 1912–25), 6:83.
171. Kant, *Religion and Rational Theology*, 122.
172. Kant, *Religion and Rational Theology*, 146.
173. Kant, *Religion and Rational Theology*, 179–84.

sufficiently convince every human being of it and everyone can expect its effect at least, as duty. This religion possesses the great prerequisite of the true church, namely the qualification for universality, inasmuch as by universality we mean validity for every human being (*universitas vel omnitudo distributiva*), i.e. communality of insight. To propagate and preserve itself as world religion in this sense, indeed it requires a staff of ministering (*ministerium*) to the purely invisible church, but no officials (*officials*), i.e. teachers but no dignitaries, for by virtue of the rational religion of single individuals no church in the sense of a universal union (*omnitudo collectiva*) is yet in place, nor is any such church really contemplated through that idea.[174]

Within this scheme Kant encouraged readers to suppose that Jesus, who remained unnamed, was a teacher of natural religion.

If we now assume a teacher of whom the story (or, at least, a general opinion which is not in principle disputable) has it that he was the first to advocate a pure and compelling religion, one within the grasp of the whole world (i.e. a natural religion) and of which the doctrines, as preserved for us, we can therefore test on our own. . . . After this description one will not fail to recognize the person who can be revered, not indeed as the *founder* of the *religion* which, free from every dogma, is inscribed in the heart of all human beings (for there is nothing arbitrary in the origin of this religion), but as the founder of the first true *church*.[175]

Following a brief account of the Sermon on the Mount and the parables of the kingdom, Kant saw in Jesus' teaching on the two great commandments an understanding of morality virtually identical with his own categorical imperative.

Finally, he sums up all duties (1) into one *universal* rule (which includes the internal as well as the external moral relation of human beings), namely, Do your duty from no other incentive except the

---

174. Kant, *Religion and Rational Theology*, 179–80.
175. Kant, *Religion and Rational Theology*, 180–81.

unmediated appreciation of duty itself, i.e. love God (the Legislator of all duties) above all else; (2) and into a *particular* rule, one namely that concerns the human being's external relation to other human beings as universal duty, Love everyone as yourself, i.e. promote his welfare from an unmediated good-will, one not derived from selfish incentives. And these commands are not merely laws of virtue but precepts of *holiness* which we ought to strive after, yet in view of them the striving itself is called *virtue*.[176]

Toward the end of the book Kant denounced *priestcraft* in a section entitled "Concerning Priestcraft as a Regime in the Counterfeit Service of the Good Principle."[177]

For some time religious conservatives—including King Friedrich Wilhelm II of Prussia (1786–97)—had grown increasingly alarmed over the German Enlightenment. On July 3, 1788, the king appointed the evangelical theologian Johann Christoff Wöllner (1732–1800) as *Staatsminister* for spiritual affairs and education. Within less than a week Wöllner introduced his notorious *Edikt, die Religionsverfassung in den preussischen Staaten betreffend* warning against those who revived "the miserable, long refuted errors of the Socinians, deists, naturalists and other sectarians" and spread "among the people the impertinent impudence under the much abused banner of 'enlightenment'! They denigrate the respect in which the Bible has hitherto been held as the revealed word of God. . . . They throw suspicion on the mysteries of revealed religion, shaking the faith of Christians and indeed making Christianity appear ridiculous in the world."[178] Preachers who deviated from the creed were threatened with prompt dismissal, and new appointments of preachers,

---

176. Kant, *Religion and Rational Theology*, 182; cf. Matt 22:34–40; Mark 12:28–34; Luke 10:25–28. Kant distinguished between maxims and laws. Laws were objective principles that were universally valid and binding. Maxims were subjective practical rules according to which one acts. He observed: "There is only one categorical imperative. It is: Act only according to that maxim by which you can at the same time will that it should become a law of nature. . . . The universality of law according to which effects are produced constitutes what is properly called nature in the most general sense (as to form), i.e., the existence of things so far as it is determined by universal laws. [By analogy], then, the universal imperative of duty can be expressed as follows: Act as though the maxim of your action were by your will to become a universal law of nature" (*Foundations of the Metaphysics of Morals*, trans. Lewis White Beck [Indianapolis: Bobbs-Merrill, 1956], 39).

177. Kant, *Religion and Rational Theology*, 194–202.

178. Kant, *Religion and Rational Theology*, xv–xxii, 41–54; text of the edict in Klaus Epstein, *The Genesis of German Conservatism* (Princeton, NJ: Princeton University Press, 1966), 143–44. The edict was based on Wöllner's *Abhandlung von der Religion*. The edict did not introduce new

teachers, and university professors would be "limited to subjects who provide no ground for questioning their inner adherence to the creed they are employed to teach."

In 1790 Wöllner's Immediate Commission introduced a new system for testing the orthodoxy of theological students under solemn oath. Kant was outraged and wrote an essay *On the Miscarriage of All Philosophical Trials in Theodicy* (1791).[179] It paved the way for the first part of *Religion within the Boundaries of Mere Reason*, which Kant submitted to the Berlin censorship. It was rejected. Kant then submitted the entire work to the philosophical faculties of Königsberg and Jena, who approved it on the grounds that since the work was philosophical in character, they had the appropriate jurisdiction.

On October 1, 1794, Wöllner sent to Kant a *Kabinettsorder* in the name of Friedrich Wilhelm II, which contained the following accusation:

> Our gracious greetings, first of all. Worthy and most learned, dear loyal subject! Our most high person has long observed with great displeasure how you misuse your philosophy to distort and disparage many of the cardinal and foundation teachings of the Holy Scriptures and of Christianity; how you have done this specifically in your book "Religion within the Limits of Reason Alone," and similarly in other shorter treatises. We expected better of you, since you yourself must see how irresponsibly you have acted against your duty as a teacher of youth and against our sovereign purposes, of which you are well aware. We demand that you immediately give a conscientious vindication of your actions, and we expect that in the future, to avoid our highest disfavor, you will be guilty of not such fault, but rather, in keeping with your duty, apply your authority and your talents to the progressive realization of our sovereign purpose. Failing this, you must expect unpleasant measures for your continuing obstinacy.
>
> With our gracious regards. By the most gracious *special* order of his royal majesty.[180]

---

censorship provisions that were not already enacted but put liberal pastors in a threatening situation. Throughout, Wöllner concealed his heterodoxy.

179. Kant, *Religion and Rational Theology*, 19–37.

180. §177 (*Correspondence*, 485–86). On October 14, 1795, an order was issued to the academic senate in Königberg forbidding all professors to lecture on Kant's book.

Kant received the letter on October 12, 1794, and proceeded to draft a reply defending himself of having misused his philosophy to "disparage Christianity."[181] As an educator of the youth, Kant denied having used his academic lectures even to discuss the subject of Christianity. Nor had he as the author of *Religion within the Limits of Reason Alone* "opposed the highest purposes of the sovereign that were known to me. For since those purposes concern the state religion, I would have had to write as a teacher of the general public, a task for which this book along with my other little essays is ill-suited. They were written only as scholarly discussions for specialists in theology and philosophy, in order to determine how religion may be inculcated most clearly and forcefully into the hearts of men."

Kant pleaded "not guilty of disparaging Christianity in that book, since it contains no assessment of any actual revealed religion. It is intended merely as an examination of rational religion, an assessment of its priority as the highest condition of all true religion, of its completeness and of its practical aim (namely, to show what we are obligated to do. . .). Consequently the need for revealed doctrine is not obscured, and rational religion is related to revealed religion in general, without specifying which one it is (where Christianity, for example, is regarded as the mere idea of a conceivable revelation)." It was incumbent on Kant's accusers to point out cases where he had profaned Christianity "either by arguing against its acceptance as a revelation or by showing it to be unnecessary." To the contrary, Kant's respect for Christianity was demonstrated by his "extolling the Bible as the best available guide for the grounding and support of a truly moral state religion, perennially suitable for public instruction in religion."

Kant concluded by insisting that his conscience was clear and that he had never let "the divine Judge" out of his sight when writing on religion. To avoid falling under further suspicion, Kant declared that it would be "the surest way for me to abstain entirely from all public lectures on religious topics, whether on natural or revealed religion, and not only from lectures but also from publications. I hereby promise this. I am eternally Your Royal Majesty's most submissive and obedient servant." However, upon the death of Friedrich Wilhelm II, Kant saw himself released from this obligation and published the correspondence in the preface to *Der*

---

181. §178 (*Correspondence*, 486–89).

Streit der Fakultäten (1798).[182] Kant's *Opus posthumum*, which was concerned with the metaphysical foundations of natural science to physics, shows that the ideas of God and freedom continued to play an integral part in Kant's thought to the end of his life.[183]

4. Retrospect

The quests of Jesus before the quest narrated by Schweitzer were not a unified quest. But neither was Schweitzer's quest and those that followed it. Like Schweitzer's, it was a quest about the real Jesus. The quests that we have traced back to the sixteenth century exhibit varieties of skepticism. Servetus and the early Socinians were skeptical about the orthodox constructions placed on the Jesus of Scripture, but they were not skeptical about the veracity of Scripture. They believed that the real Jesus was not the Jesus of orthodoxy, and that the doctrines of the Trinity and of the divinity of Christ were unscriptural. For the Socinians and their Unitarian successors, integrity required repudiation of orthodoxy.

It was otherwise with the eighteenth-century Anglican "Arians," who were more anti-Athanasius and anti-Nicea than pro-Arius. They too believed that the real Jesus was different from the constructions placed on him by the Niceno-Constantinopolitan Creed. They endeavored to remain within the Church of England in the hope of a more flexible

---

182. Kant, *The Conflict of the Faculties*, in *Religion and Rational Theology*, 233–327, here 239–42. The work consists of three essays, the first of which on "The Conflict of the Philosophy Faculty with the Theology Faculty" was written between June and October 1794. In light of his undertaking to Friedrich Wilhelm II, Kant declined C. F. Stäudlin's offer to publish the essay in Göttingen.

Kant divided university faculties into two "ranks": three higher faculties concerned with professional training, and which therefore had obligations to the state (theology, law, and medicine). Accordingly, the state had the right to *sanction* the teachings of those faculties. The lower faculty was that of philosophy, whose function was directed to the world of learning and scholarship. Its concern was with "public use of reason," and thus it should be free from regulation. The division between higher and lower was adopted "with reference to the government rather than the learned professions" (*Religion and Rational Theology*, 248).

183. The following is just one of many references. "The concept of God is the idea that man, as a moral being, forms of the highest moral being in relation according to the principles of right, insofar as he, according to the categorical imperative, regards all duties as commands of this being. *Concept of freedom. Moral-practical reason is one of the moving forces of nature* and all sense-objects. These form a particular field: for *ideas*" (*Opus posthumum*, Cambridge Edition of the Works of Immanuel Kant, ed. Eckart Förster, trans. Eckart Förster and Michael Rosen [Cambridge: Cambridge University Press, 1993], 198–99).

interpretation of his formularies. With Newton, Whiston, and Clarke, we see the beginnings of a historical consciousness with its repudiation of dogmatic interpretation of Scripture and reinterpretation of the emergence of orthodoxy. Attention was paid to philology, but it lacked a developed historical-critical approach to the New Testament. Clarke's method seems more akin to the scientific methods of his day with its rigorous assembling of data, formulation of propositions, and endeavor to demonstrate the propositions by drawing logical deductions from the data.

In *A View of the Principal Deistical Writers* (including David Hume), John Leland observed that "there is scarce anything in which the Deistical writers have been more generally agreed than in bending their force against the proof from miracles."[184] As R. M. Burns pointed out, their major concern was not to deny the possibility of miracles in themselves but to nullify the evidentialist appeal to miracles in order to legitimate belief systems.[185] Ultimately, this concern went back beyond the deists to Pyrrhonism and the role that miracles played in competing belief systems in the sixteenth and seventeenth centuries. Neither the orthodox nor their opponents appear to be deeply interested in the miracle stories themselves and what they might convey about Jesus. Rather, miracles functioned as extrinsic legitimation for Jesus and his teaching and ultimately for the Christian belief system at large. In challenging that belief system, Hume and the deists effectively disposed of the historical Jesus. Some of them called themselves Christian deists, but the Jesus that survives in their writings is a shadowy figure who teaches nothing that could not be discovered from natural religion.

With the exception of Collins and Woolston, whose purposes were entirely negative, no one in the deist controversy was particularly concerned with biblical exegesis in any sense that could be called critical. The debate was about hermeneutics rather than exegesis. It was a conflict over what was rational and plausible in a world that was becoming increasingly aware of scientific explanation. At the heart of it was the question of analogy and its role in making judgments. One further element appears almost like a speck on the horizon. Blount's translation of Philostratus's

---

184. Leland, *A View of the Principal Deistical Writers* (1754), 1:444.
185. Burns, *The Great Debate on Miracles*, 70.

Life of Apollonius of Tyana, Woolston's use of it, and Hume's reference to Tacitus and Lucian to locate miracle stories in the context of the Graeco-Roman world foreshadowed the history of religions school. It would take more than a century before the implications of this context would become a serious issue.

It is now clear that the effects of British deism were felt as far afield as the New World and Germany. It provided the initial impulse for Thomas Jefferson's thinking about Jesus the moralist and for Herman Samuel Reimarus's politically driven Jesus. In the nineteenth century Kant was hailed as the philosopher of Protestantism.[186] But it would be more accurate to see him as the philosopher of deism. Admittedly Kant distanced himself from the author of the *Wolfenbüttel Fragments* and proclaimed himself a theist.[187] However, the wide variety of deistic thinking and Kant's own pronouncements point in a different direction. These pronouncements include Kant's denunciation of priestcraft. Above all, the great teacher of natural religion who figures in *Religion within the Boundaries of Mere Reason* is more a project of thought embodying an ideal morality than a historical figure in Second Temple Judaism. In this light, Kant seems more a deist than a Christian theist.[188]

---

186. Julius Kaftan, *Die Religionsphilosophie Kants in ihrer Bedeutung für die Apologetik* (Detloff: Bahnmaier, 1874); Friedrich Paulsen, *Kant der Philosoph des Protestantismus* (Berlin: Reuther & Reichard, 1899); cf. Werner Schultz, *Kant als Philosoph des Protestantimus*, Theologische Forschung 22 (Hamburg-Bergstedt: Reich, 1961), 19–20.

187. Kant observed: "Hence the deist's God is wholly idle and useless and makes no impression on me if I assume it alone. But if transcendental theology is used as a propaedeutic or introduction to the two other kinds of theology, it is of great and wholly excellent utility. For in transcendental theology we think of God in a wholly pure way; and this prevents anthropomorphism from creeping into the other two forms of theology. Hence transcendental theology is of the greatest negative utility in keeping us safe from errors" ("Lectures on the Philosophical Doctrine of Religion," *Religion and Rational Theology*, 348).

188. To Allen W. Wood the decisive factor was Kant's exclusion of revelation from the boundaries of human reason ("Kant's Deism," *Kant's Philosophy of Religion Reconsidered*, 1–21). Wood saw Kant's rejection of revealed faith as resting on two premises: the theoretical premise that we have no cognition of the supersensible; and the practical premise that we have a duty to think for ourselves. Such a view is consistent with Kant's answer to the question "What is Enlightenment?" "Enlightenment is man's release from his self-incurred tutelage. . . . *Sapere aude!* 'Have courage to use your own reason!'—that is the motto of enlightenment" ("Beantwort der Frage: Was ist Aufklärung?" *Berlinische Monatsschrift* 4, no. 12 [1784]: 481–94; *Foundations of the Metaphysics of Morals and What Is Enlightenment?*, trans. Beck, 85).

Sapere aude! derives from Horace, *Epistles* 1.2.40 and was adopted in 1735 by the Gesellschaft der Wahrheitsfreunden who pledged themselves not to accept or reject any belief except for a "sufficient reason."

PART 2

THE EUROPEAN SCENE

CHAPTER 5

SCHWEITZER AND THE OLD QUEST

THE IDEA of a concerted quest of the historical Jesus gained currency through Albert Schweitzer's book *Von Reimarus zu Wrede. Geschichte der Leben-Jesu-Forschung* ("From Reimarus to Wrede: History of Research into the Life of Jesus," 1906). The title of the English translation introduced the word *Quest* and relegated the names of Reimarus and Wrede to the subtitle: *The Quest of the Historical Jesus: A Critical History of Its Progress from Reimarus to Wrede*.[1] In so doing, it added drama to Schweitzer's narrative of numerous scholars, including himself, who attempted to write a *truly historical* life of Jesus. The title change heightened the impression

---

1. References below are to Albert Schweitzer, *The Quest of the Historical Jesus: A Critical Study of Its Progress from Reimarus to Wrede* (London: Black, 1910; repr. with introduction by James M. Robinson, New York: Macmillan, 1968). The sixth German edition, entitled simply *Geschichte der Leben-Jesu-Forschung* (Tübingen: Mohr Siebeck, 1951), was based on the expanded 1913 edition. Reference is also given to *The Quest of the Historical Jesus*, 1st complete ed., ed. John Bowden (London: SCM, 2000; Minneapolis: Fortress, 2001), which is based on the 1913 German edition. Schweitzer gave his personal account in *My Life and Thought: An Autobiography*, trans. C. T. Campion (1933; repr., London: Guild, 1955), 44–51. Studies include Werner Picht, *The Life and Thought of Albert Schweitzer*, trans. Edward Fitzgerald (London: Allen & Unwin; New York: Harper & Row, 1964), 46–78, 203–53; James Brabazon, *Albert Schweitzer: A Biography* (New York: Putnam, 1975); Helmut Groos, *Albert Schweitzer, Grösse und Grenzen. Eine kritische Würdigung des Forschers und Denkers* (Munich: Reinhardt, 1974); Erich Gräßer, *Albert Schweitzer als Theologe*, BHT 60 (Tübingen: Mohr Siebeck, 1979), 8–154; Walter P. Weaver, *The Historical Jesus in the Twentieth Century*, 1900–1950 (Harrisburg, PA: Trinity Press International, 1999), 25–44; Erich Gräßer, *TRE*, 30: 675–82; Simon J. Gathercole, "The Critical and Dogmatic Agenda of Albert Schweitzer's *The Quest of the Historical Jesus*," *TynBul* 51 (2000): 261–83; C. R. Mercer, *DMBI*, 2nd ed., 899–902; Nils Ole Oermann, *Albert Schweitzer: A Biography* (Oxford: Oxford University Press, 2017). For a selection of texts relating to the Quest, see Gregory W. Dawes, *The Historical Jesus Quest: Landmarks in the Search for the Jesus of History* (Louisville: Westminster John Knox, 2000).

The European Scene

that scholarly research showed that the *Jesus of history* was different from the Christ of the creeds, orthodox theology, traditional piety, and the gospel narratives.

Rather than attempt to condense over 600 pages of Schweitzer's German text, this chapter will focus on the origin of Schweitzer's *Quest* and the four phases of its course that he detected. Note will also be taken of scholars who did not fit into Schweitzer's scheme. The term *Old Quest* is used partly because Schweitzer contended that he had traced the quest to its origin and partly to distinguish it from other quests.

1. The Origin of Schweitzer's *Quest*
2. The Course of Schweitzer's *Quest*
   2.1. Reimarus, Lessing, and the *Wolfenbüttel Fragments*
   2.2. Strauss and the "Purely Historical" Jesus
   2.3. The Triumph of the Synoptic Jesus
   2.4. The "Eschatological" versus the "Noneschatological" Jesus
3. Schweitzer's Jesus

1. The Origin of Schweitzer's *Quest*

In order to appreciate Schweitzer's *Quest of the Historical Jesus* in perspective, three facts should be noted. The first is the course of Schweitzer's studies. Albert Schweitzer (1875–1965) was born in Alsace, which had recently been annexed by Germany through the Franco-Prussian War. When he entered the University of Strassburg at the age of eighteen, Schweitzer studied both theology and philosophy. This dual interest stayed with him for life. Schweitzer took his first theological examination in 1898 but earned his first doctorate in *philosophy* with a dissertation on Kant's philosophy of religion.[2] The dissertation was written in Paris, where Schweitzer was also studying the organ. Remuneration for his organ recitals helped to pay expenses. The regulations of the reading room of the Bibliothèque Nationale proved so irksome that Schweitzer

---

2. Albert Schweitzer, *Die Religionsphilosophie Kants von der "Kritik der reinen Vernunft" bis zur "Religion innerhalb der Grenzen der blossen Vernunft"* (Freiburg: Mohr, 1899).

decided to bury himself in Kant's primary sources without troubling about secondary literature.[3]

Schweitzer noticed important discrepancies in Kant's vocabulary. In many sections of the *Critique of Pure Reason* (1781) Kant used the word *intelligibel*, which accorded with his critical philosophy. But elsewhere Kant used the vague term *übersinnlich* (supersensible, transcendent), which Schweitzer traced to Kant's precritical philosophy. This discovery led Schweitzer to the conclusion that the three postulates of God, freedom, and immortality developed in the *Critique of Practical Reason* (1778) were inconsistent with Kant's critical philosophy. He observed that the postulates disappeared entirely in Kant's *Religion within the Boundaries of Mere Reason* (1793).[4]

Instead of proceeding to a career in philosophy, Schweitzer decided to embark on a licentiate in theology. However, it was not the end of Schweitzer's interest in philosophy, for philosophy supplied the parameters for his critical theology. To borrow a phrase from Kant, Schweitzer's research methods and subsequent account of Jesus were thoroughly within the boundaries of mere reason.

The second fact to note is that *The Quest of the Historical Jesus* was actually Schweitzer's *second* attempt to deal with the historical Jesus. His first was his licentiate dissertation at Strassburg on the overarching topic of *The Problem of the Lord's Supper according to the Scholarly Research of the Nineteenth Century and the Historical Accounts*. The project was published in two parts with separate titles.

---

3. Schweitzer, *My Life and Thought*, 24–29.

4. Kant, *Religion within the Limits of Reason Alone* is the familiar translation of Kant's title. See Colin Brown, *Jesus in European Protestant Thought, 1778–1860*, Studies in Historical Theology 1 (Durham: Labyrinth, 1985; repr., Pasadena: Fuller Seminary Press, 2008), 58–73. However, in the Cambridge edition of the Works of Immanuel Kant, the title is translated as *Religion within the Boundaries of Mere Reason* (see above, chap. 4).

Later Schweitzer remarked: "To establish the ideas of God and immortality as equally 'postulates,' Kant has to abandon all respectable logic and argue with bold and ever bolder sophisms" (*The Philosophy of Civilization*, vol. 2, *Civilization and Ethics*, trans. C. T. Campion, 3rd ed. revised by Mrs. Charles E. B. Russell [1923; London: Black, 1946], 111).

Schweitzer's conclusion was given support by Erich Adickes, who argued that Kant eventually abandoned the moral proof for the existence of God (*Kants Opus Postumum. Dargestellt und beureteilt*. Kant-Studien Ergänzungshefte im Auftrag der Kant-Gesellschaft, 50). But his thesis has been rejected by other scholars. See Colin Brown, *Jesus in European Protestant Thought, 1778–1860*, Studies in Historical Theology 1 (Durham: Labyrinth, 1985; repr., Pasadena: Fuller Theological Seminary Press, 2008), 297. It is not supported by the Cambridge edition of *Kants Opus Postumum*, 198–99.

The European Scene

Part 1 dealt with *The Lord's Supper in Relationship to the Life of Jesus and the History of the Early Church* (Ger., 1901; ET, 1982).[5] Schweitzer concluded that interpretations of the Lord's Supper from the Reformation down to modern times were generally misguided. The key was to be found in Mark 14:22–25, which alone presented an authentic report of what went on in the upper room. The climactic saying of Mark 14:25 was the key that unlocked the problem: "Truly I tell you, I will never again drink of the fruit of the vine until that day when I drink it new in the kingdom of God." Schweitzer took it to mean that Jesus never intended to inaugurate a rite to be passed on down the centuries. Rather, Jesus expected that his imminent death as God's Messiah would inaugurate the eschatological kingdom of God on earth.[6]

It was an accident of history that Schweitzer's two-part work was published in English at an interval of some sixty-eight years between the parts. Moreover, their publication in English reversed the order of the German original. Part 1 (1982) dealing with the Last Supper posed the *question* of Jesus' intentions. Part 2 (1914) gave the *answer* by tracing the events that led up to the Last Supper.

The English title of Part 2 was *The Mystery of the Kingdom of God: The Secret of Jesus's Messiahship and Passion*.[7] The German original work enabled Schweitzer to gain the entry-level qualification of *Privatdozent* at the University of Strassburg (1902).[8] Jesus' actions and motives had fascinated Schweitzer from the beginning of his theological studies. *The Mystery of the Kingdom of God* outlined the conclusions repeated in

---

5. Albert Schweitzer, *Das Abendmahlsproblem auf Grund der wissenschaftlichen Forschung des 19. Jahrhunderts und der historischen Berichte*, Heft 1, *Das Abendmahl im Zusammenhang mit dem Leben Jesu und der Geschichte des Urchristentums* (Tübingen: Mohr, 1901); ET: *The Problem of the Lord's Supper*, trans. A. J. Mattill Jr., ed. John Reumann (Macon, GA: Mercer University Press, 1982).

6. Schweitzer, *The Problem of the Lord's Supper*, 1:131–37. The thought first occurred to Schweitzer when writing a paper on Schleiermacher's teaching about the Last Supper (*My Life and Thought*, 19). Schleiermacher noted that in Mark Jesus did not charge the disciples to repeat the meal. However, Schleiermacher did not follow it through.

7. Albert Schweitzer, *The Mystery of the Kingdom of God: The Secret of Jesus' Messiahship and Passion*, trans. Walter Lowrie (London: Black, 1914). The English title relegates Schweitzer's original title to a subtitle, *Das Messianitäts- und Leidenschaftsgeheimnis. Eine Skizze des Lebens Jesu* (Tübingen: Mohr, 1902). It omits the German subtitle ("A Sketch of the Life of Jesus").

8. Schweitzer, *My Life and Thought*, 36. Schweitzer lectured in the Protestant faculty at Strassburg from 1902 to 1912. During part of that period he served in the Protestant seminary and as a pastor. In the latter part of the period he studied medicine in order to prepare for his life's work as a missionary doctor in West Africa.

The Quest of the Historical Jesus. In fact, *The Quest of the Historical Jesus* was written in vindication of Schweitzer's earlier work. What follows is a brief summary.

In sending out his disciples to proclaim the kingdom Jesus believed that their mission would inaugurate the messianic woes, and that they would not have gone through all the towns of Israel before the Son of Man would come (Matt 10:23).[9] When the disciples returned unscathed, Jesus realized that he himself was called to be the Son of Man who would initiate the messianic woes by giving his life as a ransom for many (Mark 10:45).[10] The mystery of the kingdom was Jesus' conviction about his vocation to be the messianic Son of Man, foretold in Daniel 7:13. His death as a ransom would inaugurate the kingdom of God on earth. Initially, Jesus revealed this mystery only to Peter, James, and John. Later, Peter told the rest of the Twelve. Judas told the secret to the high priest, who intended to use it as the grounds for Jesus' condemnation and execution. This plan was thwarted by Judas's suicide. However, Jesus was convicted on the basis of his own claim to be the messianic Son of Man (Mark 14:61–64; cf. Dan 7:13).[11]

Schweitzer had begun to form his ideas as early as 1894.[12] Building on Johannes Weiss's eschatological interpretation of the kingdom of God (though eschewing references), Schweitzer proposed what he called the "eschatological-historical" solution.[13] In a postscript he declared his aim

---

9. Schweitzer, *The Mystery of the Kingdom of God*, 88–89.
10. Schweitzer, *The Mystery of the Kingdom of God*, 230–36.
11. Schweitzer, *The Mystery of the Kingdom of God*, 214–18. "*He was condemned as Messiah although he had never appeared in that role*" (218, Schweitzer's emphasis; cf. *Quest*, 396–97). Schweitzer stressed that the only witness that the authorities had was Judas, who had committed suicide. In his absence they tried to secure condemnation on other grounds. But it was Jesus' own admission of messiahship that provided the proof needed for condemnation.
12. Schweitzer, *My Life and Thought*, 13–16. In 1894 Schweitzer began his year of compulsory military service in the German army. He kept up his study of Greek by reading his Greek New Testament in his free time. One day, reading Matthew 10–11, he began to question the view of his teacher, H. J. Holtzmann, that the life of Jesus could be understood solely from Mark. Jesus apparently expected the coming of the kingdom before the return of the disciples from their mission (Matt 10:23). He declared that John the Baptist was the greatest of all who are born of women, but the least in the kingdom of heaven was greater than John (11:11). Schweitzer took it to mean that John was the greatest man in the history of the natural world. But the kingdom about to come would introduce a supernatural order.
13. Schweitzer, *The Mystery of the Kingdom of God*, 83. Weiss's work on the *Kingdom of God* was published in 1892. Schweitzer expressed his appreciation in *My Life and Thought*, 49. The mystery of the kingdom was Jesus' growing, but secret, conviction about his vocation to be the messianic Son of Man, who would inaugurate the kingdom of God on earth as foretold in Daniel 7:13.

The European Scene

"to depict the figure of Jesus in its overwhelming heroic greatness and to impress it upon the modern age and upon the modern theology."[14]

The third fact that we need to appreciate in order to see Schweitzer's work in perspective is the coincidence that on the same day[15] that Schweitzer published *The Mystery of the Kingdom of God*, a book dealing with the same subject titled *The Messianic Secret* appeared from the pen of William Wrede, a renowned scholar at the University of Breslau.[16] In German both titles contained the word *Geheimnis*. Whereas Schweitzer's translator took the word to mean "mystery," in Wrede's work it meant "secret." It was a secret bound up with Jesus' injunctions not to tell anyone that he was the Messiah. In the hindsight of Schweitzer's *Quest* the climactic debate to which everything led was the clash with Wrede over thoroughgoing skepticism versus thoroughgoing eschatology. It focused on two issues: method and eschatology. The two principal contestants were Wrede and Weiss. But it soon became apparent that Weiss (who was given credit for pioneering eschatology alongside Reimarus) was a surrogate for Schweitzer himself.

The two issues, method and eschatology, were entwined. Wrede's method was literary. His literary approach to the gospel narratives led to the conclusion that Jesus' public activity did not turn on messianic claims. Mark's account of Jesus forbidding people to say that he was the Messiah suggested that Mark (or Mark's community) invented the "messianic secret." The confession of Jesus as the Messiah/Christ was made retrospectively in light of resurrection faith. Wrede's solution was diametrically opposed to that of Schweitzer, who insisted that his *method* was based on *history*. His historical hypothesis that Jesus came to believe that Jesus was the Messiah, who must experience the messianic woes in order to establish the kingdom, was the vital clue for interpreting the narratives.

We shall return to Weiss and Wrede in due course. For now it must suffice to note that the scholarly world's acceptance of Wrede at the expense of the twenty-six-year-old Schweitzer set the latter on a course

---

14. Schweitzer, *The Mystery of the Kingdom of God*, 274.
15. Schweitzer, *Quest*, 330.
16. William Wrede, *The Messianic Secret*, trans. J. C. G. Greig (London: Clarke, 1971). In the original German Wrede's work was entitled *Das Messiasgeheimnis in den Evangelien. Zugleich in Beitrag zum Verständnis des Markusevangeliums* (Göttingen: Vandenhoeck & Ruprecht, 1901; 3rd unchanged ed., 1963).

of self-vindication that resulted in *The Quest of the Historical Jesus*. It would show the world that the course of the quest led inevitably to the ultimate choice: either Wrede's thoroughgoing skepticism or Schweitzer's thoroughgoing eschatology.

2. The Course of Schweitzer's *Quest*

2.1. Reimarus, Lessing, and the *Wolfenbüttel Fragments*. Schweitzer's *Quest of the Historical Jesus* was constructed like a lawn tennis championship, in which competitors progressed through successive rounds by knocking out opponents until the victor triumphed in the final duel. The simile may be pressed even further by observing that certain "seeded" scholars were identified as winners of early rounds, though not necessarily the championship.

Reimarus. Hermann Samuel Reimarus (1694–1768) was the "seeded player" who won the opening round. He appeared like a bolt from the blue, without predecessors or successors.[17] His work was "perhaps the most splendid achievement in the whole course of the historical investigation of the life of Jesus, for he was the first to grasp the fact that the world of thought in which Jesus moved was essentially eschatological."[18] In view of the subsequent neglect of eschatology, "the whole movement of theology, down to Johannes Weiss, appears retrograde." Every sentence of Weiss's work "is a vindication, a rehabilitation, of Reimarus as a historical thinker."[19]

As the tournament progressed other "seeded players" won decisive rounds. They were D. F. Strauss, F. C. Baur and the Tübingen School,

---

17. Schweitzer, *Quest*, 26. The nearest that Schweitzer came to acknowledging the possibility of earlier work preparing the ground for Reimarus's work was tantamount to a repudiation: "We have no right simply to dismiss it in a word, as a Deistic production, as Otto Schmiedel, for example, does; it is time that Reimarus came into his own, and that we should recognize a historical performance of no mean order in this piece of Deistic polemics" (*Quest*, 22; cf. Schmiedel, *Die Hauptprobleme der Leben-Jesu Forschung* [Tübingen: Mohr Siebeck, 1902], 2). The second edition (1906), quoted here with page references supplied by the author, observes that Schweitzer valued Reimarus as a *historian* on account of an eschatology, which made Reimarus the direct predecessor of Johannes Weiss (2–3n1). Schmiedel rejected Schweizer's criticism, claiming that almost all critics agreed with his evaluation (2, 67–75). He concluded with a critique of *Von Reimarus zu Wrede* (119–24), which again drew attention of the equation of "eschatological" with "historical."

18. Schweitzer, *Quest*, 22–23.

19. Schweitzer, *Quest*, 22–23.

and Schweitzer's own mentor, H. J. Holtzmann. But none of them made it to the final round in view of their neglect of eschatology. The final round was the contest between Wrede's "thoroughgoing skepticism," based on *The Messianic Secret*, and Schweitzer's "thoroughgoing eschatology," based on *The Mystery of the Kingdom of God*.[20]

A sketch of Reimarus and his writings was given in the previous chapter. His *Apologie* may have eventually been discovered in the Hamburg University Library by researchers investigating eighteenth-century thought, but it would not have made the impact that it achieved but for the intervention of Gotthold Ephraïm Lessing (1729–81).

Lessing. Lessing was the son of a Lutheran pastor, who hoped that his son would follow him in his vocation. At the University of Leipzig Lessing pursued a range of studies, which included classics, philosophy, theology, philology, and medicine. He went on to earn an MA at Wittenberg. From 1748 to 1767 Lessing lived chiefly in Leipzig, Berlin, and Breslau. During this period he established a lifelong friendship with Moses Mendelssohn, who would become the grandfather of the composer Felix Mendelssohn, and who was widely acknowledged as the leading Jewish scholar in the Age of Enlightenment. Mendelssohn is remembered as a "Jewish Socrates," who combined Enlightenment philosophy with traditional Judaism. In the meantime, Lessing built up a national reputation as a dramatist and essayist. He pioneered the model of drama based on middle-class characters, rejecting rigid French interpretations of classical drama.

Lessing came to Hamburg in 1767—the year before Reimarus's death—as resident critic and dramatic theorist of the newly founded National Theater. Lessing consulted Reimarus's son professionally as a doctor and became a friend of the family. Lessing's *Hamburgische Dramaturgie* further enhanced his reputation through analysis of plays and acting. Lessing's plays modeled the ideal of bourgeois drama. However, the National Theater went bankrupt, and in 1770 Lessing moved to Wolfenbüttel as librarian to the duke of Brunswick-Lüneburg. The duchy was situated south of Hamburg, with Wolfenbüttel as the ducal seat.

In 1771 Lessing was initiated into Freemasonry. His patron, the duke of Brunswick, was the German grand master. Between 1774 and 1778 Lessing published extracts from Reimarus's *Apologie*, which will be

---

20. Schweitzer, *Quest*, 330–97.

explained shortly. In 1776 Lessing married a widow, Eva König. Their son died within hours of his birth, and Eva died shortly after in 1778. Lessing himself died in 1781 at the age of 52.

The *Wolfenbüttel Fragments*. On leaving Hamburg to take up his position at Wolfenbüttel, Lessing took with him a copy of an early draft of Reimarus's *Apologie*, which subsequently disappeared. His attempts to publish the complete manuscript failed because of the prospect of censorship.[21] However, Lessing procured exemption from censorship for his series of "Contributions to History and Literature from the Treasures of the Ducal Library at Wolfenbüttel"—*Beyträge zur Geschichte und Literatur. Aus den Schätzen der Herzoglichen Bibliothek zu Wolfenbüttel.*

Lessing took the opportunity to insert into this series his extracts from Reimarus's manuscript. He identified them as *Fragmente eines Ungenannten*. In order to put heresy hunters off the scent, Lessing conjectured that the author might have been the deist Johann Lorenz Schmidt, who had ended his days in poverty at Wolfenbüttel.[22] However, Lessing added that the identification of Schmidt as the author would be hasty speculation.

Lessing presented the first *Fragment* as an extension of the Reformation tradition of free speech. It was entitled *Von der Duldung der Deisten* ("On Toleration of the Deists," 1774). It provoked little comment. Things changed with the publication in 1777 of five *Fragments*, which introduced criticism of biblical revelation. *Von Verschreyung der Vernunft von den Kanzeln* ("The Decrying of Reason from the Pulpit") criticized preachers for treating adults like children. *Unmöglichkeit einer Offenbarung, die allen Menschen auf eine gegründete Art glauben könnten* ("The Impossibility of a Revelation That All Human Beings Could Believe as Basic") questioned the divine justice of giving a particular revelation a privileged position.

---

21. Lessing's *Fragments* appear to represent stages that increasingly approximate to Reimarus's second draft. See Dietrich Klein, *Hermann Samuel Reimarus (1694–1768)*, Beiträge zur historischen Theologie 145 (Tübingen: Mohr Siebeck, 2009), 169; cf. Hermann Samuel Reimarus, *Apologie oder Schutzschrift für die vernünftigen Verehrer Gottes*, Im Auftrag der Joachim Jungius-Gesellschaft der Wissenschaften in Hamburg herausgegeben von Gerhard Alexander (Frankfurt: Suhrkamp, 1972), 1:9–38, here 27–28. Lessing attempted publication as early as 1770 and again in 1772 (Dietrich Klein, *Hermann Samuel Reimarus*, 173).

22. J. L. Schmidt (1702–49) was the author of the notorious *Wertheimer Bibel* (1735), a free translation with rationalistic notes. Like the English deists, he rejected miracles and prophecy as vindication of Christianity. Schmidt was imprisoned (1737), but escaped to Hamburg, where he translated Tindal's *Christianity as Old as the Creation*. He died at Wolfenbüttel. See further Dietrich Klein, *Hermann Samuel Reimarus*, 37–41.

Durchgang der Israeliten durchs Rothe Meer ("The Passage of the Israelites through the Red Sea") ridiculed the statistics of the biblical narratives. *Dass die Bücher des Alten Testaments nicht geschrieben worden, eine Religion zu offenbaren* ("That the Books of the Old Testament Were Not Written to Reveal a Religion") drew attention to the absence of clear teaching on immortality in the Old Testament. Since the immortality of the soul was recognized by natural religion, the Old Testament's lack of clarity seriously compromised the absolute claims that were made on its behalf.

Only the last two *Fragments* dealt explicitly with Jesus. *Über die Auferstehungsgeschichte* ("On the Resurrection Story") was the last of the *Fragments* published in 1777. It exploited discrepancies in the gospel narratives, which Reimarus drew from Woolston and Sherlock.[23] Since the narratives were mistaken in detail, they must be mistaken about the fact. The issue would be raised again in Lessing's rejoinder to J. J. Ress, *Eine Duplik* (1778).[24] By this time the controversy was near boiling point.

The final *Fragment* was entitled *Vom Zwecke Jesu und seiner Jünger. Noch ein Fragment des Wolfenbüttelschen Ungenannten* ("On the Intention of Jesus and His Disciples, One More Fragment of the Wolfenbüttel Unnamed Author," 1778).[25] Jesus was depicted as a Jewish reformer who had no intention of establishing a new religion. His call to repentance was a call for Brownmoral purity. In a manner evocative of the British deists, Reimarus insisted that Jesus' teaching contained no "mysteries."[26] The title *Son of God* meant no more than what it meant in the Hebrew Scriptures: God's Beloved.[27] The Jewish nation bore the title, as did their kings. In the case of Jesus, it was a messianic title, not a designation of deity. The Last Supper was a Passover meal.[28]

---

23. Klein, *Hermann Samuel Reimarus*, 134–35.
24. Ress wrote anonymously, but Lessing detected his identity. Ress was the Lutheran superintendent at Wolfenbüttel. For details of the debate with see Brown, *Jesus in European Protestant Thought*, 25–26, 284–85.
25. Translations of the final *Fragment* include *The Goal of Jesus and His Disciples*, trans. George Wesley Buchanan (Leiden: Brill, 1970); and *Reimarus: Fragments*, trans. Ralph S. Fraser, ed. Charles H. Talbert (Philadelphia: Fortress, 1970; London: SCM, 1971). References below are to Fraser's translation. See further Ernst Bammel, "The Revolution Theory from Reimarus to Brandon," in *Jesus and the Politics of His Day*, ed. Ernst Bammel and C. F. D. Moule (Cambridge: Cambridge University Press, 1984), 11–68.
26. *Reimarus: Fragments*, 72–76.
27. *Reimarus: Fragments*, 76–88.
28. *Reimarus: Fragments*, 118–22.

Schweitzer and the Old Quest

To the Jewish mind, the transition from repenting to preparing for an earthly theocratic kingdom to be inaugurated by a messiah was but slight. Jesus' fatal mistake was to embrace political messianism and push through his program at all costs.[29] Jesus had come to think that the kingdom of God could be established on earth through his own death. But his dying words, "My God, my God, why have you forsaken me?" attest his bitter disillusion.[30]

The resurrection was a fraud perpetrated by the disciples who pretended to the credulous populace that they had encountered Christ alive from the tomb and that he would return again to earth.[31] Both claims were fraudulent, but together they constitute the foundation of Christianity. Continual postponement of the second coming of Christ merely underscored the point.

The above account indicates that eschatology did not occupy the same place in the mind of Reimarus that it did in Schweitzer's. Nor was Lessing's agenda identical with Schweitzer's.

Schweitzer paid scant attention to Lessing, other than to his importance in editing and publishing the *Fragments*. However, Lessing had his own agenda, which became clearer through the subsequent turn of events.[32] Reimarus played a major part in the deconstruction of the Gospel narratives—but less so in the construction of Lessing's theology.

Dietrich Klein saw Lessing's initial stance more as a rejection of current theological options than as a positive statement.[33] Three issues stood out. The first was the conventional orthodox view of the historicity of the Bible and its infallibility. The second was the position of the Neologians

---

29. *Reimarus: Fragments*, 136–50.
30. *Reimarus: Fragments*, 150.
31. *Reimarus: Fragments*, 153–227.
32. On Lessing and his circle, see Henry Chadwick, ed. and trans., *Lessing's Theological Writings* (London: Black, 1956); Georges Pons, *Gotthold Ephraim Lessing et le Christianisme*, Germanica 5 (Paris: Didier, 1964); Henry E. Allison, *Lessing and the Enlightenment: His Philosophy of Religion and Its Relation to Eighteenth-Century Thought* (Ann Arbor: University of Michigan Press, 1966); Alexander Altmann, *Moses Mendelssohn: A Biographical Study* (New York: Routledge: 1973); Brown, *Jesus in European Protestant Thought*, 1–55; Harald Schultze, "Reimarus, Hermann Samuel," in *TRE*, 28:470–73; Leonard P. Wessel, *G. E. Lessing's Theology, A Reinterpretation: A Study in the Problematic Nature of the Enlightenment* (The Hague: Mouton, 1977); Gottfried Hornig, "Lessing," in *TRE*, 21: 20–33; Toshimasa Yasukata, *Lessing's Philosophy of Religion and the German Enlightenment: Lessing on Christianity and Religion* (Oxford: Oxford University Press, 2002); H. B. Nisbet, ed., *Lessing: Philosophical and Theological Writings*, Cambridge Texts in the History of Philosophy (Cambridge: Cambridge University Press, 2009).
33. Klein, *Hermann Samuel Reimarus*, 170–72.

with their pretensions to orthodoxy and Socinian leanings. The third was anti-Semitism and treatment of Jews as second-class citizens. Even before his friendship with Moses Mendelssohn, Lessing had written a one-act play *The Jews* (1749) exposing anti-Jewish prejudice. All three options were antithetical to Enlightenment. The writings of the deists may not have provided the ultimate solution. At the same time they could not be ignored.

The Pamphlet War. The *Wolfenbüttel Fragments* provoked a bitter pamphlet war, which gave Lessing opportunity to air his own views. At the center of the fray was Johann Melchior Goeze (1717–86), senior pastor of the Church of St. Catharine in Hamburg. Goeze was an authority on German editions and translations of the Bible, a seasoned polemicist, and self-appointed defender of Lutheran orthodoxy. In the background were Goeze's threats of invoking legal intervention in the form of appeal to the Corpus Evangelicorum in order to quell Lessing.[34] The name *Goeze* was phonetically identical with *Götze*, meaning "idol." In earlier usage it carried the sense of *Dummkopf*. Lessing was not usually given to abusing people by their names. But readers could make what they wished of Lessing's profusely respectful addresses to Goeze and his delight in plays on words.[35] As tensions mounted, Lessing wrote a total of eleven anti-Goeze polemical pamphlets, which were somewhat repetitive.

More substantial were his succinct *Necessary Answer to a Very Unnecessary Question of Herr-Pastor Goeze in Hamburg*[36] and the lengthier *Axioms (If There Are Any in Matters Such as This)*.[37] Both were dated 1778, a time when Lessing was grieving over the loss of his son and wife. To the same date belongs the publication of a scholarly treatise in the form of brief, unambiguous paragraphs on which Lessing had been working for many years: *New Hypothesis on the Evangelists as Merely Human Historians*.[38] The source criticism of the Gospels was unexplored territory for other participants in the *Fragments* controversy.

---

34. The Corpus Evangelicorum was the authority that represented Protestant interests within the Holy Roman Empire.

35. Pons, *Gotthold Ephraïm Lessing et le Christianisme*, 310.

36. Nisbet, ed., *Lessing: Philosophical and Theological Writings*, 172–77. Lessing's concise but comprehensive list of historical definitions was in response to Goeze's demand for an answer to the question of what Lessing meant by "the Christian religion." It may have left Goeze more exasperated than before.

37. Nisbet, ed., *Lessing: Philosophical and Theological Writings*, 120–47.

38. Nisbet, ed., *Lessing: Philosophical and Theological Writings*, 148–71. An analysis is given by Brown, *Jesus in European Protestant Thought*, 26–28.

Lessing's *On the Proof of the Spirit and of Power* (1777) broke new ground by its formulation of the question of God in history. It was written in response to Johann Daniel Schumann, a headmaster and clergyman.[39] Lessing presented himself as a doubter who was undecided about the truths of Christianity. He began by drawing a distinction between events and reports of events. A miracle that he had seen for himself was different from reports of miracles. It led to Lessing framing the question of God in history in terms of the dilemma posed by the alternative: either the contingent truths of history or the necessary truths of reason. "If no historical truth can be demonstrated, then nothing can be demonstrated *by means of* historical truths. That is, *contingent truths of history [zufällige Geschichtswahrheiten] can never become the proof of necessary truths of reason [nothwendigen Vernunftwahrheiten]*."[40]

Even if events were accepted as reliable history, they did not warrant deductions from them of truths of a different kind. "If I have no historical objection to the fact that this Christ himself rose from the dead, must I therefore regard it as true that this same risen Christ was the Son of God?"[41]

> But to make the leap from this historical truth into a quite different class of truths, and to require me to revise all my metaphysical and moral concepts accordingly; to expect me to change all my basic ideas on the nature of the deity because I cannot offer any credible evidence against the resurrection of Christ—if this is not a "transition to another category", I do not know what Aristotle meant by that phrase. . . .
>
> This, this is the broad and ugly ditch which I cannot get across, no matter how often and earnestly I have tried to make the leap. If anyone can help me over it, I beg and implore him to do so. He will earn a divine reward for this service.[42]

---

39. It was written in response to the headmaster and clergyman, Johann Daniel Schumann, who entered the fray with his book *On the Evidence for the Truth of Christianity* (1777); cf. Nisbet, ed., *Lessing: Philosophical and Theological Writings*, 83–94. Lessing's title was an allusion to 1 Cor 2:4, where Paul referred to the demonstration of the Spirit and power that accompanied his preaching of Jesus Christ "and him crucified" (2:2). Paul's reference to the Jesus Christ, the crucified one—with what it implied in the Jewish and Greco-Roman worlds—indicates that his *kerygma* was anchored in the Jesus of history.

40. Nisbet, ed., *Lessing: Philosophical and Theological Writings*, 85. Italics original. Henry Chadwick has "accidental truths of history" (*Lessing's Theological Writings*, 53).

41. Nisbet, ed., *Lessing: Philosophical and Theological Writings*, 86.

42. Nisbet, ed., *Lessing: Philosophical and Theological Writings*, 87; cf. Aristotle, *Posterior Analytics* 1.6–7.

The European Scene

Lessing's broad and ugly ditch, over which he found it impossible to jump, was constituted by categories recognized by Aristotle and philosophers down the centuries. One could not prove anything by crossing from one genus to another (e.g., from arithmetic to geometry, to quote Aristotle's example). In fact, Lessing chose not to jump at all. His recommended course of action depended neither on necessary truths of reason nor on contingent truths of history. As his appended apocryphal *Testament of St. John* and later drama *Nathan the Wise* made clear—what mattered was to love one another.

Lessing's identification of two kinds of statements corresponded to the distinction made by Kant between "analytic" and "synthetic" judgments in *A Critique of Pure Reason* (1781). Lessing's formulation was like a "heads I win, tails you lose" argument. It was plausible but misleading because of the implication that necessary truths were rational yet the contingent truths of history fell short of rationality. The only strictly necessary truths are analytic statements that are true by definition. However, recognition of historical truth implies (like all statements about the world) that they have a rational component. Subsequent discussions of the broad, ugly ditch have reframed it in terms of God and humanity, the "wholly other" and human contingent reality, and the distance between the world of Jesus and Second Temple Judaism and our world.[43]

Lessing's argument provided the starting point for the *Philosophical Fragments* (1844) and *Concluding Unscientific Postscript to the Philosophical Fragments* (1846) by the Danish philosopher Søren Kierkegaard (1813–55). The term *fragments* echoed the controversy unleashed by Lessing. It also expressed Kierkegaard's alternative approach to truth and philosophy. The full title of the first work was *Philosophical Fragments, Or a Fragment of Philosophy by Johannes Climacus, Edited by S. Kierkegaard*. The title page stated the problem raised by Lessing: "Can a historical point of departure be given for an eternal consciousness; how can such a point of departure be of more than historical interest; can an eternal happiness be built of historical knowledge?"[44] Like Lessing, Kierkegaard was the "editor" of the *Philosophical Fragments*.

---

43. Gordon E. Michalson Jr., *Lessing's "Ugly Ditch": A Study of Theology and History* (University Park, PA: Pennsylvania State University Press, 1985).

44. Kierkegaard, *Philosophical Fragments*, ed. and trans. Howard V. Hong and Edna H. Hong (Princeton, NJ: Princeton University Press, 1985); cf. Brown, *Jesus in European Protestant Thought*, 140–59, here 146–51. In naming himself as the editor, Kierkegaard implied that he had a role similar to that of Lessing with regard to the *Fragments*.

The *Philosophical Fragments* were followed by the much larger *Concluding Unscientific*

Kierkegaard sought answers to his questions through "projects of thought," in which he considered how human beings might know God. He concluded that since God was wholly other metaphysically and morally, the gulf could only be bridged from God's side. It could happen only if God became human. However, the incarnation of God involved a paradoxical impenetrable incognito because God cannot be recognized directly.

A passage that has often been cited erroneously as an example of Kierkegaard's historical minimalism makes the point:

> Even if the contemporary generation had not left anything behind except these words, "We have believed that in such and such a year the god appeared in the humble form of a servant, lived and taught among us, and then died"—that is more than enough. The contemporary generation would have done what is needful, for this little announcement, this world-historical *nota bene*, is enough for someone who comes later, and the most prolix report can never in all eternity become more for the person who comes later.[45]

Kierkegaard explained that he was defining not the minimum of recoverable objective history but the role of history in relation to faith. In fact, this minimal definition may be seen as a concise summary of what was left by the Wolfenbüttel fragmentist in his examination of the intensions of Jesus and his disciples. Whereas Lessing concluded that the ditch could not be jumped, the metaphor suggested to Kierkegaard that the gulf between God and humankind was bridged by the divine incognito of God's incarnation in Christ and the corresponding leap of faith on the part of human beings.[46] Kierkegaard gave the following summary of the

---

Postscript to the Philosophical Fragments. A Mimi-Pathetic-Dialectical Composition. An Existential Contribution by Johannes Climacus. Responsible for Publication: S. Kierkegaard (1846), trans. D. F. Swenson and W. Lowrie (Princeton, NJ: Princeton University Press, 1941). It asked how the eternal could be related to temporal in the objective Christ. The *Postscript* acknowledged Kierkegaard's debt to Lessing, though it was not the kind of debt that Lessing envisaged.

45. Kierkegaard, *Philosophical Fragments*, 104.

46. Alistair Hannay traced Kierkegaard's leap of faith to Lessing and his observations about the broad, ugly ditch. See Alistair Hannay, *Kierkegaard* (London: Routledge & Kegan Paul, 1982), 98.

Kierkegaard's *Journals and Papers* contain numerous references to Lessing. An early instance is the entry entitled "The Dialectic Oriented toward Becoming a Christian." Lessing began by reflection on the method of Socrates, who did not begin by collecting proofs. He staked this

role of historical knowledge: "*By means of* the contemporary's report (the occasion), the person who comes later believes by virtue of the condition he himself receives from the god."[47]

Lessing took it as self-evident that historical factual claims belonged to a genus that was distinct from that of theological assertions. His view was virtually axiomatic in Enlightenment thought. However, twentieth-century thinking questions the claim that "facts" are independent objective entities and insists that they are inseparable from interpretation and judgment. Among his theses concerning the resurrection, Wolfhart Pannenberg stipulated: "If Jesus has been raised, this for a Jew can only mean that God himself has confirmed the pre-Easter activity of Jesus. . . . If Jesus really has been raised, this claim has been visibly and unambiguously confirmed by the God of Israel, who was allegedly blasphemed by Jesus. This was done by Israel's God."[48] In short, God's raising of Jesus overturned the verdict of blasphemy passed by the Sanhedrin. It installed him as the messianic Son of God.

The most comprehensive review of the situation is the discussion by Gerd Theissen and Dagmar Winter, which they describe as: "Criteria in Jesus Research and the 'Wide Ugly Ditch' of History."[49] They saw the chasm as the gulf "between hypothetical knowledge and unconditional

---

upon the possibility of immortality. "Used with discrimination, this may be applied to becoming a Christian. But first of all comes, quite properly, Lessing's doubt that one cannot base an eternal happiness on something historical." Against this is "the story of Jesus Christ. But is it historically entirely certain? The answer to this must be that even if it were the surest things in all history, this does not help; no *direct* transition can be made as a basis for an eternal happiness. What do we do now? . . . Something historical teaches me that I must turn to Jesus Christ. I must beware of taking the wrong turn into scientific rummaging and reconnoitering to see if it is entirely historically certain—that is, even if it were ten times as certain even to the minutest detail, it still would not help me—for I cannot be helped *directly*. . . . But with regard to becoming a Christian there is a dialectical difference from Socrates that must be remembered. Specifically in relation to immortality—a person relates himself to himself and the idea—no further. But when a man chooses upon an *if* to believe in Christ—that is, chooses to wager his life upon that, then he has permission to address himself to Christ in prayer. Thus the historical is the occasion and still also the object of faith" (*Søren Kierkegaard's Journals and Papers*, ed. and trans. Howard V. Hong and Edna H. Hong, with Gregor Malantschuk [Bloomington, IN: Indiana University Press, 1967], §73, dated 1850, 1:27–28).

47. Kierkegaard, *Philosophical Fragments*, 104.

48. Wolfhart Pannenberg, *Jesus—God and Man*, trans. Lewis L. Wilkins (London: SCM, 1968), 67. See also the discussion by Jürgen Moltmann of the resurrection as a historical and theological problem in *The Way of Jesus Christ: Christology in Messianic Dimensions*, trans. Margaret Kohl (San Francisco: HarperSanFrancisco, 1990), 234–52.

49. Gerd Theissen and Dagmar Winter, *The Quest for the Plausible Jesus: The Question of Criteria*, trans. M. Eugene Boring (Louisville: Westminster John Knox, 2002), 226–59.

faith."[50] It is wider, deeper, and longer than Lessing imagined on account of the development of historical resources, the complexity of the issues, and the sheer strangeness of Jesus' world. "Jesus the exorcist and prophet of the end of the world belongs to a submerged world of antiquity, a world that every day recedes further from our world."[51] Because the ditch is full of water, the challenge is to swim across, perhaps with the help of someone on the other side to pull us to dry land. Ultimately, the answer rests on religious faith. "All knowledge consists of hypotheses—and all life is a not-yet-validated hypothesis, a not-yet fulfilled promise from God. Everything hypothetical runs the risk of defeat. But Christian faith is convinced that God also accepts the defeated variations of life. From the divine side, God confers that validation of the hypothetical toward which all life strives. In the gospel, God offers the fulfilled validation and concord with himself, without qualification, unconditional and unlimited."[52]

We shall return to Theissen in due course and discuss his views on criteria and method in chapter 18. For now we must offer some concluding observations on the first phase of Schweitzer's *Quest*.

Semler. The weightiest reply to the *Fragments* came from the pen of Johann Salomo Semler (1725–91), professor of theology at the University of Halle. During his tenure there, Halle became the center of liberal critical theology in the eighteenth century. His *Abhandlung von freier Untersuchung des Canon* ("Treatise on Free Examination of the Canon," 1771–75) differentiated between "Holy Scripture" and the "Word of God." Not every part of Scripture taught moral truth for every generation. Even Jesus and his apostles accommodated their teaching to their hearers.

Semler resisted initial entreaties to enter the *Fragments* controversy. In the end, he delivered a sledge-hammer blow. Semler's *Beantwortung der Fragmente eines ungenannten insbesondere vom Zweck Jesu und seiner Jünger* ("Answer to the Fragments of an Unnamed Author, in Particular on the Intentions of Jesus and His Disciples," 1779) numbered 452 pages. It was accompanied by a thirty-two-page appendix. Although he regarded the Fragmentist's manner as repugnant, he paid him the compliment of answering him almost sentence by sentence in the manner of Origen's *Contra Celsum*.

---

50. Theissen and Winter, *The Quest for the Plausible Jesus*, 259.
51. Theissen and Winter, *The Quest for the Plausible Jesus*, 229.
52. Theissen and Winter, *The Quest for the Plausible Jesus*, 259.

Semler conceded that the Fragmentist was broadly correct in his interpretation of *Son of God* in the Old Testament. However, it had specialized meaning outside Palestinian Judaism. The early church was justified in its use of the term. Part of Semler's strategy was to show not only that Jesus transcended Palestinian Judaism but that messianic expectation did so too. "I have shown above that the Jews expected exactly from the messiah *a new and special religion*. The Unnamed Author wanted, however, to denigrate equally the Christian and Jewish religions by his work, in order to promote himself as a Deist."[53]

Semler was cautious in handling Old Testament prophecy. What was legitimate for the early church was not necessarily legitimate for educated readers of the eighteenth century. Christianity was vindicated not by fulfillment of predictions but by its fundamental truth.

> The *New Covenant* has already partly overthrown Judaism and paganism and partly superseded it, certainly with regard to its content. Thus it is increasingly spreading among humankind.... *We do not prove from prophecy the teaching of Christianity*, or the *basic truths* that constitute the Christian religion, and elevate it above Judaism and paganism. We hear and know them from the teaching of Jesus and the apostles. And now people either accept this teaching or not.[54]

On the subject of the resurrection of Jesus, Semler replied that many of the Fragmentist's objections were superficial. They would be fatal to the old doctrine of the verbal inspiration of Scripture. However, Semler was not interested in harmonizing every detail.[55] Some discrepancies should be expected in documents written some thirty years after Jesus' death. In any case the resurrection of Jesus was "no mere physical event" capable of being seen by the human eye. "It is a *supernatural event*, the intrinsic possibility of which was granted by the Pharisees and many others. But it does not at all follow that the Risen One must necessarily strike the senses, just as a tree, a mountain, a bird, etc.... The resurrection of Jesus was no natural event, subject to the laws of motion and

---

53. J. S. Semler, *Beantwortung*, 161 (author's translation, as are subsequent quotations).
54. Semler, *Beantwortung*, 355–56.
55. Semler, *Beantwortung*, 359.

the senses. It constituted an act of the living Jesus which he himself determined and ordered for his ultimate purpose."[56]

In his concluding remarks Semler declared: "We compel no Deist to this faith, because it is utterly impossible. But neither can any Deist tear from our soul this true Christian faith."[57]

Lessing did not reply. Already his health was declining, and circumstances were changing rapidly.

Lessing after the *Fragments*. In July 1778, the Duke of Brunswick was persuaded by traditionalist elements of this court to bar Lessing from further religious publication unless his work was approved by the censor. In a Letter to Elise Reimarus, Lessing expressed his resolve to return to his former "pulpit, the theater."[58] This resolve found expression in Lessing's last play, the poetic drama of ideas *Nathan the Wise* (1779).[59] It was set in the time of the Crusades, when Jerusalem was under Muslim rule. The play was an allegory in which the three main characters, Nathan the wealthy Jewish merchant, Saladin the sultan ruler of Jerusalem, and the Knight Templar who was a crusader, represented the three major religions. Nathan was modeled on Lessing's longstanding Jewish friend Moses Mendelssohn. The unnamed Knight Templar represented Lessing himself. Saladin bore traits of Frederick the Great.[60] Other characters were recognizable as participants in the *Fragments* controversy.[61]

The convoluted plot defies brief summary. It begins with Nathan returning home to Jerusalem after a lengthy absence on business. He is told that his adopted daughter, Recha,[62] has been rescued from a fire by the Knight Templar. The audience is led to suspect that this event might be the beginning of a romantic drama with a happy ending. To cut a long story short, there is a happy ending, but not what the audience is led to expect. The Knight and Recha turned out to be brother and sister.

---

56. Semler, *Beantwortung*, 261–62.
57. Semler, *Beantwortung*, 432.
58. Lessing's letter dated September 6, 1778 (Lessing, *Sämtliche Schriften*, ed. Karl Lachmann and Franz Muncker, 23 vols. ([Leipzig: Goschen, 1886–1924], 13:285).
59. There are several English translations. One of the most accessible, with informative material, is the edition by Ronald Schechter, *Nathan the Wise by Gotthold Ephraim Lessing, With Related Documents* (New York: St. Martins, 2004).
60. Saladin was like Frederick the Great, the philosopher king of Prussia, who was skeptical about religion and believed that human happiness depended on good government.
61. Hendrik Birus, *Poetische Namengebung. Zur Bedeutung der Namen in Lessings "Nathan der Weise"* (Göttingen: Vandenhoeck & Ruprecht, 1978).
62. Recha believes that she is Jewish. Later it is revealed that her parents were Christian.

Their father was the brother of Saladin. The leading characters—except for Nathan—are blood-related. Without Nathan, the climactic joyful resolution is not possible.

The message of the play is epitomized as a parable in act 3, scene 7. It is told by Nathan to Saladin, who demands to be informed which is the true religion. Nathan does not want to offend. At the same time, he cannot deny his own Jewishness or claim it to be the only true religion. When he and Saladin are alone, Nathan relates the parable of three rings. Many years ago there lived a man who owned a ring of inestimable worth. Whoever wore it was pleasing to God and his fellow human beings. He bequeathed the ring to his favorite son. This went on for several generations until one of his descendants had three sons, whom the father loved equally.

The father turned to a wise judge, who advised him to have three copies made and give each son a ring. Each son would possess a ring and show by his life of uncorrupted love that he possessed the true ring. Thus, the life of love would show which is the true religion. Saladin is overwhelmed by Nathan's answer to his question, with its potential for transformation.[63]

Lessing did not live to see a public performance of *Nathan the Wise*. It was first published in book form. Following the productions by Schiller and Goethe the play obtained its standard place in the repertoire of the German theatre. Its ban by the Nazi government enhanced its prestige.

Among Lessing's later writings were the Masonic dialogues *Ernst and Falk* (written in 1776–78, and published in 1780), which reflected on the meaning of history. Lessing saw Freemasonry as comparable with the institutional church, whose true aim was to promote human brotherhood.[64]

The Education of the Human Race was published in Berlin (1780).[65] Lessing proclaimed himself merely to be the editor—a stance that he consistently adopted with regard to his philosophical and theological

---

63. Lessing acknowledged that the primary source for his parable was Boccacio's *Decameron*. See Pons, *Gotthold Ephraim Lessing et le Christianisme*, 413–14. It stands in contrast with the parable of the Old Testament prophet Nathan (2 Sam 12:1–12). See Elena Volkova, "The Bible in Literature," in *The New Cambridge History of the Bible*, vol. 4, *From 1750 to the Present*, ed. John Riches (Cambridge: Cambridge University Press, 2015), 651–67, here 652. The Old Testament prophet's parable was one of judgment, in consequence of King David's adultery and murder.

64. Nisbet, ed., *Lessing: Philosophical and Theological Writings*, 184–216.

65. Nisbet, ed., *Lessing: Philosophical and Theological Writings*, 217–40.

works. It was the product of a lengthy gestation period and took the form of one hundred numbered reflections. Section 50 viewed Matthew, Mark, and Luke as traceable to "the so-called Hebrew Gospel of Matthew."[66] Christ "became the first *reliable* and *practical* teacher of the immortality of the soul" (§58). Lessing went on to explain this claim in succeeding paragraphs (§59–61).[67]

> (§59) The first *reliable* teacher.—Reliable through the prophecies which seemed fulfilled in him; reliable through the miracles he performed; reliable through his own revival after a death by which he had set his seal on his own doctrine. Whether we can still prove this revival and the miracles now is a question which I leave open—just as I leave it open who the person of this Christ was. All this may have been important then for the *acceptance* of this doctrine; but it is no longer important now for the recognition of its truth.
>
> (§60) The first *practical* teacher.—For it is one thing to conjecture, desire, and believe in the immortality of the soul as a philosophical speculation, and another to direct one's inner life and outer actions accordingly.

Jesus may not have been the first actual person to have taught the immortality of the soul. However, (§61) "To recommend an inner purity of the heart with a view to another life was reserved for him alone."

Toward the end of his life, Lessing was visited by the theistic philosopher and statesman F. H. Jacobi.[68] In a series of conversations Jacobi quizzed Lessing about his thoughts on Spinoza and determinism. Jacobi showed Lessing a poem by Goethe titled "Prometheus" and asked what he thought of it. Lessing confessed that he agreed with Goethe's point of view. He had no taste for orthodox concepts of deity. ""Ἐν καὶ Πᾶν' [*hen kai pan*, 'One and All']! I know nothing else. That's also the sense of this poem; and I must confess that I like it very much. . . . There is no other

---

66. Lessing's conclusions reflected the earlier view that he had elaborated in his *New Hypothesis on the Evangelists as Merely Human Historians* (1778); cf. Nisbet, ed., *Lessing: Philosophical and Theological Writings*, 148–71.
67. Cited from Nisbet, ed., *Lessing: Philosophical and Theological Writings*, 217–40, here 232.
68. Friedrich Heinrich Jacobi (1743–1819) was a philosopher and politician. He rejected pantheistic determinism, and stressed the role of belief in philosophy. He was critical of Mendelssohn's attachment to the Enlightenment. See further Samuel Atlas, "Friedrich Heinrich Jacobi," in *EP*, 4:235–38.

philosophy than that of Spinoza."[69] The Greek formula was repeated in subsequent conversations.

Jacobi came away thinking that Lessing did not believe in a cause of reality outside nature and that Lessing was indeed a Spinozist. He published the conversations along with commentary in *Briefe über die Lehre Spinozas* ("Letters on the Teaching of Spinoza," 1783; enlarged, 1785). Mendelssohn was deeply shocked by the disclosure, not least because Lessing had not informed him. Mendelssohn replied with *Morgenstunden, oder Vorlesungen über das Daseyn Gottes* (1785) and his final work *An die Freunde Lessings* (1786). Eventually other leading figures, including Goethe, Kant, and Hamann, were drawn into the pantheism controversy.[70]

The debate continues about what Lessing really thought. It may be that Lessing was simply being Lessing, the inveterate provocateur. His writings are remote from the deductive analysis of propositions contained in Spinoza's *Ethics*. On the other hand, the formula Ἓν καὶ Πᾶν expresses Lessing's fundamental commitment to the connectedness of human life transcending particular religious forms.[71]

2.2. Strauss and the "Purely Historical" Jesus. Before considering the contribution of David Friedrich Strauss, it may be helpful to return to what was said earlier about the structure of Schweitzer's *Quest*.

The Structure of Schweitzer's Narrative. Schweitzer's *Quest* was like a lawn tennis tournament in which "seeded" competitors knocked out rivals in successive rounds until a final winner emerged. We have just reviewed the preliminary round in which Reimarus eliminated Semler. Schweitzer credited Reimarus's victory to his insight into eschatology. After that there was a hiatus. Debate about the historical Jesus went into a kind of limbo, which Schweitzer attributed more to the prestige of Semler than to the effectiveness of his arguments.

---

69. Nisbet, ed., *Lessing: Philosophical and Theological Writings*, 243–44.

70. For details, see Altmann, *Moses Mendelssohn*, 582–759. Lessing's citation of the Greek formula and allusion to Spinoza were enigmatic. For more than a century after his death, Spinoza was viewed as an atheist. John Toland is credited with coining the term *pantheism*. With the pantheism controversy, *pantheism* was seen as an alternative to *theism*. See further Pierre-François Moreau, "Spinoza's Reception and Influence," in *The Cambridge Companion to Spinoza*, ed. Don Garrett (Cambridge: Cambridge University Press, 1996), 408–33.

71. It may be noted that ἕν is the neuter singular of the nominative masculine form εἷς, meaning "one." The word εἷς appears during the opening of the Shema daily prayer: "Hear O Israel: The Lord our God is one [εἷς]" (Deut 6:4 LXX). καί is a conjunction meaning "and." πᾶν is the neuter form of the nominative masculine πᾶς, meaning "all," "each and every."

Schweitzer and the Old Quest

The ensuing quest was like a tournament with knock-out rounds. Each was marked by a confrontation, which eliminated rivals from further participation. Each round was decisive for the course of the tournament. It must be admitted that Schweitzer himself did not use the simile of a tennis tournament. He described the quest in terms of *great alternatives*, which decided once and for all key critical issues. These alternatives were each won by heroic figures.

> The first [great alternative] was laid down by Strauss: *either* purely historical *or* purely supernatural. The second had been worked out by the Tübingen school and Holtzmann: *either* Synoptic *or* Johannine. Now came the third: *either* eschatological [Johannes Weiss] *or* non-eschatological!
>
> Progress always consists in taking of one or other of two alternatives, in abandoning the attempt to combine them.[72]

However, this was not the end. There remained the final championship round with two remaining combatants and their rival theories: Wrede with his "thoroughgoing scepticism" and Schweitzer himself with his "thoroughgoing eschatology." Schweitzer's eschatology replaced that of Weiss as more *thoroughgoing*.[73]

---

72. Schweitzer, *Quest*, 238 (Schweitzer's italics). The statement is retained in the first complete edition, which also explains why Weiss made the cut and not Reimarus. Reimarus was "still primitive" and "not as constructive" (*Quest*, 241; 1st complete ed., 200).

73. Schweitzer, *Quest*, 330–97. In the first edition chapter 19 is entitled "Thoroughgoing Scepticism and Thoroughgoing Eschatology." Two books are noted: Wrede's and Schweitzer's.

The "first complete edition" gives a more nuanced expanded statement. Chapter 19 is retitled "The Criticism of the Modern View by Wrede and Thoroughgoing Eschatology." Chapter 20 is devoted entirely to Wrede under the title "Description and Criticism of Wrede's Hypothesis." Chapter 21 is entitled "The Solution of Thoroughgoing Eschatology."

Schweitzer faulted Johannes Weiss and his followers for concentrating on Jesus' messianic preaching and reducing it to its "dogmatic element." In so doing Weiss made himself vulnerable to Wrede's attack on "community theology." But eschatology was not simply "dogmatic history." Eschatology was the key to Jesus' activity, including his messianic suffering. "What is certain is that for [Jesus], suffering was always associated with the messianic secret, since he placed his parousia at the end of the pre-messianic tribulations in which he was to have a part. . . . The tribulation, so far as Jesus is concerned, is now connected with a historical event: he will go to Jerusalem, there to suffer death at the hands of the authorities" (347). "The new notion of his passion therefore has its basis in Jesus' authority to bring in the tribulation" (349).

The conclusions of the two editions of Schweitzer's *Quest* were substantially the same. No one outside the twelve disciples knew the secret of Jesus' messiahship. He was convicted on his own admission to being the messianic Son of Man. Public opinion changed immediately when

Schweitzer's account was determined by the cumulative outcome of these critical engagements: elimination of the supernatural, elimination of John as a historical source, and thoroughgoing eschatology. If this conclusion turned out to be paradoxical, it must be remembered that for Schweitzer the key to understanding the historical Jesus was the fact that Jesus was possessed by the notion of the imminent kingdom of God. But this did not mean that the notion had objective reality. We shall now look more closely at these great alternatives. Rather than looking at them solely through Schweitzer's eyes, it will be more illuminating to examine the issues in light of more recent scholarship.

Strauss and His Contemporaries. The first of Schweitzer's *great alternatives* was forced upon the theological world by David Friedrich Strauss (1808–74). Strauss completed the work begun by Reimarus (whom he greatly admired) by forcing the question of either a historical or a supernatural Jesus. By a single stroke, *The Life of Jesus Critically Examined* deprived Strauss of an academic career and secured his place in the history of scholarship.

Strauss came to Berlin from Tübingen in 1831 after studying with F. C. Baur.[74] He wanted to pursue postdoctoral studies with Hegel,[75] only to have his hopes dashed by the latter's untimely death. Strauss had to make do with attending the lectures of Schleiermacher and acquainting

---

priests persuaded the crowds that Jesus was not a worthy prophet but a deluded enthusiast and blasphemer. Execution quickly followed.

74. Strauss was awarded his doctorate for a brief essay about the doctrine of the universal return of things in its religious development, "Die Lehre von der Widerbringung aller Dinge in ihrer religionsgeschichtlichen Entwicklung." The essay was discovered during World War II and is reproduced in Gotthold Müller, *Identität und Immanenz. Zur Genese von David Friedrich Strauss, Eine theologie- und philosophiegeschitliche Studie* (Zürich: EVZ-Verlag, 1968), 50–82; cf. Brown, *Jesus in European Protestant Thought*, 184, 326.

75. With the growing hegemony of Prussia, Berlin was emerging as the center of national life. Its newly founded university was already attracting scholars of the stature of Schleiermacher and Hegel. The two presented competing worldviews. Georg Wilhelm Friedrich Hegel (1770–1831) emerged as the most formidable critic of Kant, although his early views were strongly influenced by Kant. Whereas Kant was concerned with the critical foundations of knowledge, Hegel viewed the facts of history as the material that philosophy must explain. Reality was the outworking of the Absolute Mind (*Geist*). Current discussions of Hegel include Peter Singer, *Hegel* (Oxford: Oxford University Press, 1983); Frederick C. Beiser, ed., *The Cambridge Companion to Hegel* (Cambridge: Cambridge University Press, 1993); Frederick C. Beiser, ed., *The Cambridge Companion to Hegel and Nineteenth-Century Philosophy* (Cambridge: Cambridge University Press, 2008). I have undertaken a more detailed examination of the thought of Fichte, Hegel, and Schelling and their perspectives on Jesus in *Jesus in European Protestant Thought, 1778–1860*, 78–103.

himself with members of the Hegelian School. Before we examine Strauss's contribution, it will be useful to sketch some background.[76]

Schleiermacher. Friedrich Schleiermacher (1768–1834) was the founding dean of the new theological faculty at Berlin. Over the years he lectured on hermeneutics, philosophy, ethics, dialectics, and various branches of theology. In each field he sought to restate orthodoxy for the modern world.

Schleiermacher was the first German professor to give courses on the life of Jesus. Strauss hoped to hear these lectures, but the course was not to be offered again until the following summer, and Strauss could not wait. He did the next best thing by obtaining a set of notes and making his own draft. The notes proved to be a disappointment. Dissatisfied with the "supernaturalism" of Schleiermacher and the "vulgar rationalism" of H. E. G. Paulus, Strauss resolved to write his own version, which would take account of the "mythical element in the history of Jesus." He would offer a Hegelian reinterpretation, which saw in the life of Jesus "the consciousness which the church has of the human spirit objectified as the divine spirit."[77]

---

76. David Friedrich Strauss, *Das Leben Jesu kritisch Bearbeitet* was published in Tübingen by C. F. Osiander in two volumes, each having two parts, dated 1835–36 but actually published in 1835. The translation by George Eliot (London, 1846; repr., 3 vols. in 1, with introduction by Peter C. Hodgson [Philadelphia: Fortress, 1972; London: SCM, 1973]) was based on the fourth German edition of 1840.

Strauss defended himself, modifying but finally endorsing his original position in *Streitschriften zur Vertheidigung meiner Schrift über das Leben Jesu und zur Charakteristik der gegenwärtigen Theologie. (Erster Band), Erstes bis drittes Heft* (Tübingen: Osiander, 1837; repr., in 1 vol. [Hildesheim: Olms, 1980]; partial trans. by Marilyn Chapin Massey, *In Defence of My Life of Jesus against the Hegelians* [Hamden: Archon, 1983]).

For some twenty years Strauss turned his back on theology, but his *Hermann Samuel Reimarus und seine Schutzschrift für die vernünftigen Verehrer Gottes* (Leipzig: Brockhaus, 1862; repr. Hildesheim: Olms, 1991) led to his return. Responding to the success of Renan's *Vie de Jésus*, Strauss wrote *Das Leben Jesu für das deutsche Volk bearbeitet* (Leipzig: Brockhaus, 1864; trans., *A New Life of Jesus*, 2nd ed., 2 vols. [London: Williams and Norgate, 1879]). It was more in line with Kant compared with his earlier *Life of Jesus*.

For background, discussion, and literature, see Horton Harris, *David Friedrich Strauss and His Theology*, Monograph Supplements to *SJT* (Cambridge: Cambridge University Press, 1973); Franz Courth, "Die Evangelienkritik des David Friedrich Strauß im Echo seiner Zeitgenossen. Zur Breitungwirkung seines Werkes," in *Historische Kritik in der Theologie. Beiträge zu ihrer Geschichte*, ed. Georg Schwaiger (Göttingen: Vandenhoeck & Ruprecht, 1980), 60–98; Brown, *Jesus in European Protestant Thought*, 183–203; Gerhard Maier, "Zur Neutestamentlichen Wunderexegese im 19. und 20. Jahrhundert," in *Gospel Perspectives*, vol. 6, *The Miracles of Jesus*, ed. David Wenham and Craig Blomberg (Sheffield: JSOT, 1986), 49–88; Robert Morgan, "A Straussian Question to 'New Testament Theology,'" *NTS* 23 (1977): 43–65; Thomas K. Kuhn, *TRE*, 32:241–46.

77. D. F. Strauss, letter to Christian Märklin dated February 6, 1832; cf. Harris, *David Friedrich Strauss*, 32–35.

Schleiermacher's "supernaturalism" had already received systematic exposition in *The Christian Faith* (1821; 2nd ed., 1831–32).[78] Jesus was presented as a man like all others, sharing the same human nature "but distinguished from the all by the constant potency of His God-consciousness, which was a veritable existence of God in Him."[79]

The Christian Faith was Schleiermacher's interpretation of the common faith of the Lutheran and Reformed Churches as a basis for reuniting them in a church of Prussian national unity. At the same time it sought to bypass the strictures that Kant placed on religious knowledge. Instead of trying to prove God's existence by natural theology, Schleiermacher saw religious experience as his starting point. A component of human self-awareness was the sense of the absolute dependence (*das schlechthinnige Abhängigkeitsgefühl*) on ultimate reality outside ourselves. This awareness of absolute dependence was basic to Christian experience and theological understanding.

God was the name given to this ultimate reality. On this basis Schleiermacher undertook to restate Christian doctrine in terms of religious self-consciousness. Attributes ascribed to God should not be taken as something in God but as expressions of this awareness in relation to God. Sin was the endeavor to be autonomous—the rejection of divinely constituted dependence. Redemption through Christ involved the restoration of this relationship. Schleiermacher's reinterpretation of the offices of Christ focused on spiritual achievement.[80]

Schleiermacher's lectures on *The Life of Jesus* (1864)[81] were not to be published for a generation after his death. When they finally appeared, Strauss commented:

---

78. F. D. E. Schleiermacher, *Der christliche Glaube nach den Grundsätzen der christlichen Kirche im Zusammenhange dargestellt* (repr. of the 1st ed., ed. Hermann Peiter, as vol. 7 of the *Kritische Gesamtausgabe* [Berlin: de Gruyter, 1980–81]; critical ed. of the 2nd ed., ed. Martin Redeker, 2 vols. [Berlin: de Gruyter, 1960]; ET: *The Christian Faith*, trans. and ed. H. R. Mackintosh and J. S. Stewart [Edinburgh: T&T Clark, 1928]); cf. Brown, *Jesus in European Protestant Thought*, 105–32; Hermann Fischer, *TRE*, 30:143–89.

79. Schleiermacher, *The Christian Faith*, §94 thesis, 389.

80. Schleiermacher reinterpreted Calvin's doctrine of the three offices of Christ as prophet, priest, and king (*Insitutes* 2.15). The prophetic office consisted in "teaching, prophesying, and working miracles" (*The Christian Faith*, thesis of §103, 441), but this last activity could not be fitted into a modern worldview, and the external marvel is superseded by the "spiritual miracle," which means that Christ is the end of all miracles (449).

81. Friedrich Schleiermacher, *Das Leben Jesu. Vorlesungen an der Universität zu Berlin im Jahr 1832*, ed. K. A. Rutenik (Berlin: Reimer, 1864); ET *The Life of Jesus*, trans. S. Maclean Gilmour, ed. Jack C. Verheyden (Philadelphia: Fortress, 1975).

Schleiermacher, we can say, is a supernaturalist in Christology but in criticism and exegesis a rationalist. His Christ, however many of the miraculous attributes of the old confession may have been removed, still remains essentially a superhuman, supernatural being. In contrast, his exegesis, as far as it pertains to the miraculous in Scripture, is distinguished from that of Paulus only by somewhat more spirit and subtlety—a difference which precisely in the main points, such as the resurrection story, becomes imperceptible.[82]

Strauss's verdict was actually a kind of compliment, although it was not intended as such. Schleiermacher's aim was to combine the essence of Christian tradition with current biblical interpretation. It involved restatement of creedal orthodoxy, as the following comments make clear.

If we wish to ascribe to [Jesus] such a self-consciousness as the creedal conception usually requires, a consciousness of a singular, pretemporal preexistence of the divine in him, then we must wholly do away with the human element. The exegetical basis of this assumption is very weak. If we hold fast to our canon, namely, the analogy of the Holy Spirit in us, then we find this only in what is most inward, as the principle of the pure volition of the divine will, consequently back of the actual consciousness, for every individual decision always involves human imperfection. Now Christ became aware of this in himself as a living being of God in him. . . . So he was able to say, I am the Son of God. According to the creedal conception he would have had to say, I have the Son of God in me.[83]

Paulus. The "vulgar rationalism" that Strauss sneered at represented the most consistent attempt to date to desupernaturalize the life of Jesus.[84] H. E. G. Paulus (1761–1851) taught theology at Heidelberg. He had been a friend of Goethe at Jena, where he had made a study of Kant and had

---

82. D. F. Strauss, *Der Christus des Glaubens und der Jesus der Geschichte. Eine Kritik des Schleiermacherschen Lebens Jesu* (Berlin: Duncker, 1865); ET *The Christ of Faith and the Jesus of History: A Critique of Schleiermacher's Life of Jesus*, trans. and ed. Leander E. Keck (Philadelphia: Fortress, 1977), 160.

83. Schleiermacher, *The Life of Jesus*, 94–95.

84. There had been earlier fictitious lives by Bahrdt and Venturini, and the more restrained rationalism of K. A. von Hase, whose work was contemporary with that of Paulus; cf. Brown, *Jesus in European Protestant Thought*, 163–72.

The European Scene

edited Spinoza's *Opera* (1802). Schleiermacher had given courses on the life of Jesus since 1819. Paulus's *Life of Jesus as the Foundation of a Pure History of Early Christianity* (1828)[85] brought naturalistic interpretation to a wider public. Paulus declared that his "greatest wish" was that his views on the miracle narratives should not be taken for "the chief matter." "The miraculous about Jesus is himself, his pure and serenely holy disposition, but which nevertheless was a genuinely human example for human spirits to imitate and emulate."[86]

Paulus discussed the Gospels synoptically, dividing them into separate episodes, which were treated as substantially historical but given natural explanations. Jesus' miraculous cures resulted either from his spiritual power or skillful use of medicines, known only to him, and the faith of the healed.[87] Simple explanations of the nature miracles were at hand. The five thousand were fed by those who had brought provisions—they were shamed into following the example of Jesus and the disciples, who shared their own food with those sitting nearest to them.[88] Jesus was not walking on the waves but standing on the shore, his features and position being obscured by the mist.[89] The resurrection was really a temporary resuscitation, effected by the cool of the tomb, the earthquake, and the spices.[90] Jesus finally succumbed some forty days later. Sensing that the end was near, he summoned his disciples, blessed them, and went away into the mist. Shortly afterward two Galilean disciples brought news that Jesus was now in a state of eternal bliss.

Schweitzer judged that Paulus's approach was doomed to failure because his strained exegesis saved his own integrity at the expense of his subject's. But, warned Schweitzer, if the theologians dragged Paulus before the Lord, he would command, as of old, "Let him that is without sin among you cast the first stone at him," and Paulus would go forth unharmed.[91] Nevertheless, Paulus had missed the point: he had failed to

---

85. H. E. G. Paulus *Das Leben Jesu als Grundlage einer reinen Geschichte des Urchristentums*, 2 vols. (Heidelberg: C. F. Winter, 1828). Each volume had two parts numbered separately. Quotations are translated by the author. Paulus developed his views originally set out in his *Philologisch-kritischer Commentar über das Neue Testament*, 2nd rev. ed., 3 vols. (Lübeck: J. F. Bohn, 1804–1805). See further Baird, *History of New Testament Research*, 1:201–8.
86. Paulus, *Das Leben*, 1, 1, x.
87. Paulus, *Das Leben*, 1, 1, xii–xiii.
88. Paulus, *Das Leben*, 1, 1, 349–56.
89. Paulus, *Das Leben*, 1, 1, 357–59.
90. Paulus, *Das Leben*, 1, 2, 266–315.
91. Schweitzer, *Quest*, 57.

grasp the significance of myth and the part that it played in the formation of beliefs and religious narratives.

Strauss's *Life of Jesus*. Strauss prefaced his *Life of Jesus* with a lengthy introduction reviewing the "Development of the Mythical Point of View in Relation to the Gospel Histories." At the close of this review, he proposed two negative criteria for identifying an account as unhistorical. "*First.* When the narration is irreconcilable with the known and universal laws which govern the course of events. . . . *Secondly.* An account which shall be regarded as historically valid, must neither be inconsistent with itself, nor in contradiction with other accounts."[92]

In principle, Strauss was following Hume and anticipating Ernst Troeltsch in the use of analogy as a critical tool. At the same time he was laying down criteria for scientific history, which were independent of the Hegelian philosophy that he would invoke at the end of his work to provide a hermeneutic for Christology.[93] This move was a precondition for "the mythical view," which steered a middle course between the absurdities of supernaturalism and crude naturalism.

> [It is] the mythical view which leaves the substance of the narrative unassailed; and instead of venturing to explain the details, accepts the whole, not indeed as true history, but as a sacred legend. This view is supported by the analogy of all antiquity, political and religious, since the closest resemblance exists between many of the narratives of the Old and New Testament, and the mythi of profane antiquity. But the most convincing argument is this: if the mythical view be once admitted, the innumerable, and never otherwise to be harmonized, discrepancies and chronological contradictions in the gospel histories disappear, as it were, at one stroke.[94]

---

92. Strauss, *The Life of Jesus*, introduction §16, 88.

93. Christian Hartlich and Walter Sachs, *Der Ursprung des Mythosbegriffes in der modernen Bibelwissenschaft*, Schriften der Studiengemeinschaft der Evangelischen Akademien 2 (Tübingen: Mohr Siebeck, 1952), 147. Peter C. Hodgson argues that Strauss was not interested in critical philosophy or constructive historiography: "Rather he moved from a rationalist historiography to a speculative transfiguration of historical data into philosophical truths. It is difficult to escape the suspicion that a marriage of convenience existed between these operations" (Strauss, *The Life of Jesus*, xxix); cf. Theissen and Winter, *The Quest for the Plausible Jesus*, 265 and passim.

94. Strauss, *The Life of Jesus*, introduction, §8, 56–57.

Strauss's use of analogy was twofold. On the one hand, to qualify as historical, reported events of the past should bear analogy to those within contemporary experience. On the other hand, biblical narratives were judged to bear analogies with known myths of antiquity.

Strauss distinguished between pure myths, which were generated by messianic expectations, and historical myths, in which fact was entwined with myth. He conceded that beneath the miraculous histories there might have been some bedrock of "natural occurrences."[95] When myths, legends, and authorial additions were removed, there remained a historical core, which coincided with thoroughgoing rationalism and which was not all that different from the conclusions of Reimarus and Schweitzer.

The "simple historical framework of the life of Jesus" consisted in the following: "That he grew up at Nazareth, let himself be baptized by John, collected disciples, went about teaching in the Jewish land, opposed Pharisaism everywhere and invited men into the messianic kingdom, but that in the end he fell victim to the hatred and envy of the Pharisaic party and died on the cross."[96]

Although Strauss drew occasionally on secular parallels, his main contention was that the gospel narratives were shaped by beliefs drawn from the Hebrew Scriptures. In this respect, Strauss differed from the later history of religions school. The miracle stories of the Gospels were predetermined by popular expectation of how the Messiah should act.

> That the Jewish people in the time of Jesus expected miracles from the Messiah is in itself natural, since the Messiah was a second Moses and the greatest of the prophets, and to Moses and the prophets the national legend attributed miracles of all kinds: by later Jewish writings it is rendered probable; by our gospels, certain. When Jesus on one occasion had (with natural means) cured a blind and dumb demoniac, the people were hereby led to ask: *Is not this the son of David?* (Matt. xii. 23), a proof that a miraculous power of healing was regarded as an attribute of the Messiah. John the Baptist, on hearing of the *works* of Jesus (*erga*), sent to him with the inquiry, *Art thou he that should come (erchomenos)?* Jesus, in proof

---

95. Strauss, *The Life of Jesus*, introduction, §15, 87.
96. Strauss, *Das Leben Jesu*, 1st ed. §12, 72 (author's translation). In later life Strauss published a study of Reimarus, *Hermann Samuel Reimarus und seine Schutzschrift für die vernünftigen Verehrer Gottes* (Leipzig: F. A. Brockhaus, 1862).

of the affirmative, merely appealed again to his miracles (Matt. xi. 2ff. parall.). At the Feast of Tabernacles, which was celebrated by Jesus in Jerusalem, many of the people believed on him, saying, in justification of their faith, *When Christ cometh, will he do more miracles than these which this man hath done?* (John vii. 31).[97]

Messianic expectation not only determined that the Messiah should perform miracles; it predetermined the particular kinds of miracles that the Messiah should perform. They included supernatural dispensation of food (Exod 16:17), opening the eyes of the blind (2 Kgs 6), and raising the dead (1 Kgs 17:17–24; 2 Kgs 4). Thus Jesus was made to fulfil the prophecy of Isaiah 35:5–6. Strauss detected a clue as to whether such events really had occurred in Jesus' reluctance to perform miracles (Mark 8:12; Matt 12:39; 16:4; Luke 9:29–30). This clue was confirmed by the relative infrequency of reference to them in apostolic preaching.

Strauss examined the stories one by one, searching for discrepancies that would demonstrate unreliability. He resisted explanations, which attributed healing to recovery from "nervous weakness," or "rapid psychical cure," preferring (like Hume) to say that "it is always incomparably more probable that histories of cures of the lame and paralytic in accordance with messianic expectation, should be formed by legend, than that they really should have happened."[98] It is almost superfluous to add that for Strauss the resurrection of Jesus was mythical.[99] The essential difference between Hume and Strauss lay in their objectives: in attacking miracles Hume was undermining Christianity as a belief system, whereas Strauss was undermining supernatural Christology.

Strauss invoked a Hegelian hermeneutic to rescue what his historical criticism had deconstructed. The "key to the whole of Christology" lay in recognizing the significance of the "idea" (not in a Kantian sense, existing only in the mind, but in the Hegelian sense of existing in reality).[100]

---

97. Strauss, *Life of Jesus*, §91, 413. This statement introduces Strauss's chapter on the miracles of Jesus.
98. Strauss, *Life of Jesus*, §96, 457; cf. David Hume, *An Enquiry Concerning Human Understanding: A Critical Edition*, trans. and ed. Tom L. Beauchamp, Clarendon Edition of the Works of David Hume (Oxford: Clarendon, [2000] 2007), §98.
99. Strauss, *Life of Jesus*, §§137–40, 709–44.
100. In his introduction, Peter C. Hodgson noted some inconsistencies regarding terminology in George Eliot's translation. Hodgson suggested that the German *Begriff* should be translated as "conception" or "concept," and *Vorstellung* as "imagery" or "image" (Strauss, *The Life of Jesus Critically Examined*, 1 vol., Lives of Jesus [Philadelphia: Fortress, 1972; London: SCM, 1973], l).

In an individual, a God-man, the properties and functions which the church ascribes to Christ contradict themselves; in the idea of the race they perfectly agree. Humanity is the union of the two natures—God become man, infinite manifesting itself in the finite, and the finite spirit remembering its infinitude; it is the child of the visible Mother and the invisible Father, Nature and Spirit; it is the worker of miracles, in so far in the course of history the spirit more and more completely subjugates nature, both within and around man, until it lies before him as the inert material on which he exercises his active power.[101]

In reply to critics, Strauss explained his debt to Hegel. He acknowledged that Hegel's concept of the "idea" was helpful in understanding the nature of historical reality, but it was not a critical tool for exploring history.[102] He insisted that his critical results were entirely the product of criticism. Strauss anticipated form criticism in his interest in the pre-literary development of the tradition and the history of religions school in his attempt to locate early Christianity in the context of the ancient world and show that it was shaped by a general myth-making process.[103]

Peter C. Hodgson concluded that there were two aspects to Strauss's method: negative and positive.[104] Negatively, it consisted in rejecting the *prima facie* supernaturalism of the Gospels and all attempts to provide rational explanations. Positively, it consisted in applying the mythical interpretation as the universal explanation of the Gospel texts. Ironically, Strauss held the same worldview as the rationalists in their common rejection of supernaturalism. The difference between them lay in the way they interpreted the Gospel narratives. The rationalists sought to preserve the stories associated with Jesus but to give them a rational explanation. Strauss's rationalism dictated that the stories should be treated as myth.[105]

---

101. Strauss, *The Life of Jesus*, §151, 780.
102. Strauss, *Streitschriften*, 3:57–58; cf. Brown, *Jesus in European Protestant Thought*, 203. In the second *Life of Jesus*, Strauss dropped his Hegelianism and presented Jesus as a rational teacher.
103. "In contrast to Baur, whose *Tendenzkritik* foreshadows modern redaction criticism, Strauss's work was more the precursor of modern form-criticism, with its main interest in the *pre*-literary development of the tradition"; C. M. Tuckett, "The Griesbach Hypothesis in the 19th Century," *JSNT* 3 (1979): 32; cf. Brown, *Jesus in European Protestant Thought*, 187–88.
104. Peter C. Hodgson's comments in Strauss, *The Life of Jesus*, xxv–xxix; cf. Hartlich and Sachs, *Der Ursprung des Mythosbegriffes*, 121–47; F. C. Baur, *Kritische Untersuchungen über die kanonischen Evangelien* (Tübingen: Fues, 1847), 41–46.
105. Thomas Fabiak has drawn attention to Strauss's interest in nineteenth-century

2.3. The Triumph of the Synoptic Jesus. The second of Schweitzer's *alternatives* was the question of whether the life of Jesus should be based on the Synoptic Gospels or on John. It was forced on theology in two phases, first by F. C. Baur and the Tübingen School, and then by Schweitzer's mentor, H. J. Holtzmann, to whom Schweitzer dedicated *The Mystery of the Kingdom of God.*

The Gospels and the Early Church. In the early church the basic test of whether a Scripture was canonical was apostolicity. "Unless a book could be shown to come from the pen of an apostle, or at least to have the authority of an apostle behind it, it was peremptorily rejected, however edifying or popular with the faithful it might be."[106] While the broad outline of the canon was fixed by the end of the second century, opinions differed among the fathers as to how the Gospels came to be written.

Clement of Alexandria believed that the Gospels with genealogies were written before those without.[107] John was written last of all. Conscious that "the bodily facts" were set forth in the other Gospels, John "urged on by his disciples, and, divinely moved by the Spirit, composed a spiritual Gospel."[108]

Augustine held that the Gospels were written in the order that we have them, and that the later evangelists knew of the existence of the earlier ones. Mark was the epitomizer of Matthew.[109] Papias, on the other hand, believed that Mark was the interpreter of Peter, and that his gospel contained, although not in order, all that Peter recalled about Jesus. Matthew compiled the *logia* in the Hebrew language, but everyone interpreted them as he was able.[110] Until the eighteenth century it was

---

expressions of the paranormal. See Fabiak, *The "Nocturnal Side of Science" in David Friedrich Strauss's* Life of Jesus *Critically Examined*, Emory Studies in Early Christianity 17 (Atlanta: SBL Press, 2015). Strauss explored the issue in various studies, e.g., *Charakteristiken und Kritiken. Eine Sammlung zerstreuten Aufsätze aus den Gebieten der Theologie, Anthroplogie und Aesthetik* (Leipzig: Wigand, 1839). His interest lay in rational interpretation of the phenomena. It belonged to his historical empirical investigation, rather than to his Hegelian attempts to salvage Christianity.

106. J. N. D. Kelly, *Early Christian Doctrines*, rev. ed. (New York: Harper, 1978), 60. The following discussion draws on several sections of my *Jesus in European Protestant Thought*. See also Werner Georg Kümmel, *The New Testament: The History of the Investigation of Its Problems*, trans. S. McClean Gilmour and Howard C. Kee (Nashville: Abingdon, 1972); Baird, *History of New Testament Research*, vol. 1; David Laird Dungan, *A History of the Synoptic Problem: The Canon, the Text, the Composition, and the Interpretation of the Gospels* (New York: Doubleday, 1999).

107. Eusebius, *Hist. eccl.* 6.14.5.
108. Eusebius, *Hist. eccl.* 6.14.7.
109. *De consensu evangelistarum* 1.2.3–4.
110. Eusebius, *Hist. eccl.* 3.39.15–16.

assumed that the four canonical Gospels could readily be harmonized to produce an authentic, historical, and indeed inspired record of the words and works of Jesus.[111]

Pioneers of Modern Criticism. In the half-century that followed the *Fragments* controversy, wildly contradictory theories about the composition and authorship of the Gospels were put forward. Lessing argued for a single, primitive Hebrew or Aramaic source.[112] Johann Gottfried von Herder (1744–1803) rejected the idea of an ultimate single primitive gospel—an *Urevangelium*—in favor of oral tradition.[113] Neither writer set store by the historicity of the Fourth Gospel. Schleiermacher also rejected the *Urevangelium* theory in favor of oral tradition, but he came down firmly for the priority and fundamental historicity of John.[114]

Early pioneers of a thoroughly historical approach to Scripture were Johann David Michaelis (1717–91) and his pupil at Göttingen, Johann

---

111. The first known Gospel harmony was Tatian's *Diatessaron* in the second century, which was still in use at the time of Eusebius (*Hist. eccl.* 4.29.6) and was translated in Old High German. Augustine's *De consensu evangelistarum* (c. 400) was also a harmony. Calvin's commentary on John (1553) was followed by his *Commentarii in Harmonium ex Matthaeo, Marco et Luca* (1555). Other harmonies of the Reformation period include Osiander's *Harmoniae Evangelicae Libri Quattuor* (1537) and Chemnitz's *Harmonia Quattuor Evangelistarum* (1593). See further D. Wünsch, "Evangelienharmonie," *TRE*, 10:626–36.

On the beginnings of biblical criticism see Henning Graf Reventlow, "Richard Simon und seine Bedeutung für die kritische Erforschung der Bibel," and Otto Merk, "Anfänge neutestamentlicher Wissenschaft im 18. Jahrhundert," in *Historische Kritik in der Theologie. Beiträge zu ihrer Geschichte*, 11–36, 37–59.

112. *Neue Hypothese über die Evangelisten als bloss menschliche Geschichtsschreiber betrachtet* (1778); ET: in Chadwick, *Lessing's Theological Writings*, 65–81; Nisbet, ed., *Lessing: Philosophical and Theological Writings*, 148–71; cf. Brown, *Jesus in European Protestant Thought*, 26–28.

113. Johann Gottfried Herder, *Vom Erlöser der Menschen. Nach unsern drei ersten Evangelien* (Riga: Hartknoch, 1796); Herder, *Vom Gottes Sohn, der Welt Heiland. Nach Johannes Evangelium. Nebst einer Regel der Zusammenstimmung unsrer Evangelien aus ihrer Entstehung und Ordnung* (Riga: Hartknoch, 1797); cf. Brown, *Jesus in European Protestant Thought*, 67–73. The Fourth Gospel was not to be regarded as history but as a series of "speaking pictures" revealing Jesus' spiritual significance. Herder's views on oral tradition are comparable with those of F. A. Wolf's *Prolegomena to Homer* (1795). He is credited with being the first to recognize the form-critical problems of the Gospels (Werner Georg Kümmel, *The New Testament: The History of the Investigation of Its Problems*, 82). Herder's view of the fatherhood of God and the brotherhood of human beings anticipated that of Harnack.

114. Friedrich Schleiermacher, *Einleitung in das Neue Testament* (Berlin: Reimer, 1845); cf. Brown, *Jesus in European Protestant Thought*, 125–30. For Schleiermacher, there were only two different sources: "The Gospel of John is the one, and the other three taken together are the other" (*The Life of Jesus*, 37). "I know no rule except this: The Gospel of John is an account by an eyewitness, and the whole Gospel was written by one man. The first three Gospels are compilations of many accounts that earlier stood by themselves" (*The Life of Jesus*, 433).

Gottfried Eichhorn (1752–1827).[115] Michaelis questioned whether Mark and Luke were inspired in the same way as the apostles Matthew and John. On the whole the evangelists were good historians, but Matthew may have been corrupted in the process of translation into Greek. Michaelis rejected the idea of literary dependence among the evangelists, and traced their shared characteristics to common use of "apocryphal gospels." Eichhorn brought into focus two critical questions. On the one hand, there was the problem of the original form of Jesus' words, which he sought to solve by positing an original Aramaic (or Hebrew source). On the other hand, there were the agreements of Matthew and Luke that suggested a common, written source. The suggestion paved the way for the idea of Q.

Gospel criticism took a major step forward through the work of Johann Jakob Griesbach (1745–1812). Following study with Semler at Halle, Griesbach made an extensive European tour to acquaint himself with the methods of leading scholars and study manuscripts at first hand in the great libraries of Paris, London, Oxford, and Cambridge. On his return he moved to Jena. Griesbach's synopsis, which set out the text of the first three gospels in parallel columns, originally appeared as the first volume of a critical edition of the Greek New Testament. In 1776 it was published as a separate volume with the title *Synopsis Evangeliorum Matthaei, Marci et Lucae, Textum Graecum adfidem codicum, versionum etpatrum emendavit et lectionis varietatem adiecit Io. Iac. Griesbach, Prof. Publ. Halae.* The significance of Griesbach's work was far reaching. The mere fact that Griesbach had produced a critical text to rival the Received Text was a signal of the impending overthrow of the latter. In Griesbach's opinion it was impossible to produce a gospel harmony without first making a precise study of the text on the basis of a synopsis. Even then it was impossible to fit every detail into a chronological pattern, for the Gospels themselves did not provide the necessary information.

Griesbach went on to propound what came to be known as "the Griesbach hypothesis," which held that "Mark when writing his book had in front of his eyes not only Matthew but Luke as well, and that he extracted from them whatever he committed to writing of the deeds,

---

115. Rudolf Smend, "Johann David Michaelis und Johann Gottfried Eichhorn—zwei Orientalisten am Rande der Theologie," in *Theologie in Göttingen. Ein Vorlesungsreihe*, ed. Bernd Moeller, Göttinger Universitätsschriften, Serie A, 1 (Göttingen: Vandenhoeck & Rupprecht, 1987), 58–81.

speeches and sayings of the Saviour."[116] Griesbach set out his thesis in fifteen propositions, which may be summarized as follows:

1. Mark generally followed Matthew.
2. But occasionally he preferred Luke.
3. Where he stuck closely to Matthew he did not lose sight of Luke, and vice versa.
4. Mark sought brevity.
5. This goal led Mark to omit things that did not pertain to Jesus' public office as a teacher.
6. Mark passed over the longer sermons contained in Matthew and Luke, omitting a third of Luke.
7. Mark wrote for non-Jewish readers, for whom the rules and regulations of Palestinian Jews hardly were known.
8. For this reason Mark cut out matters concerning Jews alone.
9. Mark was sparing in his quotation of the Hebrew Scriptures.
10. But Mark added for the sake of illustration things that he found useful.
11. Mark often preserved the same formulas, phrases, and constructions.
12. Mark did not copy their books word for word, but he related material in his own way.
13. Mark frequently paraphrased and said in his own words more briefly and distinctly what was handed down to him.
14. However, Mark added details that he thought would be of interest to his readers.
15. Mark also added a few brief stories of his own for reasons that the reader could readily discern.[117]

The Griesbach hypothesis was popular in the early nineteenth century. It was embraced by Strauss, Baur, W. M. L. de Wette (1780–1849),[118]

---

116. Bernard Orchard and Thomas R. W. Longstaff, eds., *J. J. Griesbach: Synoptic and Text-Critical Studies*, SNTSMS 34 (Cambridge: Cambridge University Press, 1978), 106; cf. Brown, *Jesus in European Protestant Thought*, 175–80; Sherman E. Johnson, *The Griesbach Hypothesis and Redaction Criticism* (Atlanta: Scholars, 1991).

117. C. M. Tuckett, "The Griesbach Hypothesis in the 19th Century," *JSNT* 3 (1979): 29–60; Tuckett, *The Revival of the Griesbach Hypothesis: An Analysis and Appraisal*, SNTSMS 44 (Cambridge: Cambridge University Press, 1983); Bruce M. Metzger, *TRE*, 14:253–56.

118. Brown, *Jesus in European Protestant Thought*, 179–83; John W. Rogerson, *W. M. L. de*

and Friedrich Bleek (1793–1859). Part of its appeal was that it fitted Augustine's view that Mark was the epitomizer of Matthew. But as scholarship began to abandon the view that the first gospel was written by the apostle Matthew, the argument lost attraction.

F. C. Baur and the Tübingen School. Traditions of apostolic authorship did not carry any weight with Ferdinand Christian Baur (1792–1860), the founder of the Tübingen School. In a tribute to Baur, Heinz Liebing remarked: "There has been historical critical theology in the full sense only since Ferdinand Christian Baur."[119] Baur's voluminous writings included early studies of Gnosticism, Apollonius of Tyana, and major studies of Paul, Christian doctrine, and church history.[120] Baur is commonly depicted as the scholar who applied Hegelian philosophy to New Testament study, but Baur's critical views were developed independently of Hegel. His views were characterized by resolve to follow a purely historical approach,[121] using *Tendenzkritik*—tendency criticism—as a primary critical tool.

With regard to the synoptic problem, Baur observed, "As the shortest of the three Gospels [Mark] can equally well be the first as the last of them: equally well the first still hardly developed sketch of gospel history as an abstract from already existing more comprehensive Gospels. Storr made it the first of all the Gospels, Griesbach the last."[122] To Baur the

---

Wette, Founder of Modern Biblical Criticism: An Intellectual Biography, JSOTSS 126 (Sheffield: Sheffield Academic Press, 1992); Rogerson, *DMBI*, 2nd ed., 355–58.

119. Heinz Liebing, "Historical Critical Theology. In Commemoration of the Death of Ferdinand Christian Baur, December 2 1860," *JTC* 3 (1967): 55–69, here 55–56. There is no complete edition of Baur's works, but several have been reprinted in the five-volume edition of Baur's *Ausgewählte Werke in Einzelausgaben*, ed. Klaus Scholder (Stuttgart: Fromann, 1963–75).

Recent studies containing bibliographies include Wolfgang Geiger, *Spekulation und Kritik. Die Geschichtstheologie Ferdinand Christian Baurs* (Munich: Kaiser, 1964); Peter C. Hodgson, *The Formation of Historical Theology: A Study of Ferdinand Christian Baur* (New York: Harper & Row, 1966); Peter Friedrich, *Ferdinand Christian Baur als Symboliker*, STGNJ 12 (Göttingen: Vandenhoeck & Rupprecht, 1975); Horton Harris, *The Tübingen School* (Oxford: Clarendon, 1975); Klaus Scholder, *TRE*, 5:352–59; S. J. Hafemann, *DMBI*, 2nd ed., 177–81. Peter C. Hodgson has edited and translated *Ferdinand Christian Baur on the Writing of Church History* (Oxford: Oxford University Press, 1968). Hodgson has also edited Baur's *Lectures on New Testament Theology*, trans. Robert F. Brown (Oxford: Oxford University Press, 2016).

120. Fuller details and discussion in Brown, *Jesus in European Protestant Thought*, 204–19.

121. "My standpoint is in one word the purely historical one: namely, that the one thing to be aimed at is to place before ourselves the materials given in the history as they are objectively, and otherwise, as far as that is possible." F. C. Baur, *The History of the Church of the First Three Centuries*, ed. Allan Menzies, 3rd ed. (London: Williams and Norgate, 1878), 1:x.

122. F. C. Baur, *Kritische Untersuchungen über die kanonischen Evangelien, ihr Verhältnis zu einander, ihren Charakter und Ursprung* (Tübingen: Fues, 1851), 36 (author's translation).

The European Scene

problem could only be resolved by *Tendenzkritik*, which analyzed the tendencies in documents in order to locate them in historical context.

Baur identified Matthew as the earliest gospel on the grounds of its Judaizing tendencies, which interpreted history "from the viewpoint of the Old Testament Messiah-ideal and its realization in the person of Jesus."[123] Behind Matthew was the gospel of the Hebrews mentioned by Papias and Hegesippus. It was originally written in Hebrew and went through various recensions before reaching its present form around 130–34 CE.[124] Luke was written in Greek by a Paulinist who revised Matthew in order to soften its Judaizing tendency. Mark avoided the special interests of Matthew and Luke in order to give a rounded harmonious picture. The author was an unknown writer working in the second half of the second century.[125] John "does not intend to be a strictly historical Gospel, but rather subordinates its historical content to an idea imposed upon the whole."[126] This idea was that of the incarnation of the divine Logos, the principle of light in a world of darkness.[127] John's dualism represents the conflict with Gnosticism and cannot be dated before the end of the second century.[128]

Lachmann and the Priority of Mark. In the meantime an essay on the order of the narratives in the Synoptic Gospels, written in Latin by the philologist Karl Lachmann (1793–1851), marked the beginning of the overthrow of the Griesbach hypothesis.[129]

Lachmann noted, "The ordering of the stories does not vary as much as people think. The variation appears greatest if all three writers are compared together, or if Luke is compared with Matthew: it is less if Mark is compared with the others one by one."[130] Lachmann concluded, "There is such precise and comprehensive agreement between both Matthew and Luke and the order of the gospel according to Mark that

---

123. Baur, *Kritische Untersuchungen*, 609.
124. Baur, *Kritische Untersuchungen*, 571–72; cf. Eusebius, *Hist. eccl.* 3.39; 4.22.
125. F. C. Baur, *Das Markusevangelium nach ihrem Urprung und Charakter. Nebst einem Anhang über das Evangelium Marcions* (Tübingen: Fues, 1851).
126. Baur, *Kritische Untersuchungen*, 108.
127. Baur, *Kritische Untersuchungen*, 310.
128. Baur, *Kritische Untersuchungen*, 373–74.
129. Karl Lachmann, "De ordine narrationum in evangeliis synopticis," *TSK* 8 (1835): 570–90; repr. in Lachmann's *Novum Testamentum Graece et Latine* 2 (1850). Key sections are translated by N. H. Palmer in "Lachmann's Argument," *NTS* 13 (1966–67): 368–78; cf. also Palmer, *The Logic of Gospel Criticism* (London: Macmillan, 1968).
130. Palmer, "Lachmann's Argument," 370.

what little variations there are can be supposed made by them each for his own purposes, and if it is clear, in spite of this complete agreement, that they did not have before them a copy of Mark to imitate, the only remaining possibility is to say that the more or less prescribed order which all three follow was settled and established by some authority and tradition of the gospel, before they themselves wrote."[131]

H. J. Holtzmann. From this point onward the view that Mark was the first (and most historically reliable) gospel steadily gained ground. It was furthered through the work of C. G. Wilke and C. H. Weisse, but it was Schweitzer's teacher, Heinrich Julius Holtzmann (1832–1910), who established the two-source hypothesis.[132]

The Q theory postulates that the two earliest sources of the synoptic tradition were a sayings source, now known as Q, and the gospel of Mark and that both Matthew and Luke made independent use of these sources. Holtzmann's work set the pattern for the liberal portrait of Jesus from the 1860s to the early twentieth century through Holtzmann's psychological reconstruction of Mark's Jesus.[133]

From Schweitzer's point of view, the two-source theory was tainted with liberalism. He welcomed Holtzmann's relegation of John[134] but

---

131. Palmer, "Lachmann's Argument," 377.

132. Schweitzer, *Quest*, 121–36, 202–6; Brown, *Jesus in European Protestant Thought*, 221–27. Holtzmann set out his views in *Die synoptische Evangelien. Ihr Ursprung und geschichtlicher Charakter* (Leipzig: Engelmann, 1863); Holtzmann, *Lehrbuch der historisch-kritischen Einleitung in das Neue Testament* (Freiburg: Mohr, 1885; 3rd ed., 1982); Holtzmann, *Lehrbuch der neutestamentlichen Theologie*, 2 vols. (Freiburg: Mohr, 1896–97; rev. by A. Jülicher and W. Bauer, 1911); Holtzmann, *Die Synoptiker*, HNT (Tübingen: Mohr Siebeck, 1901); Holtzmann, *Das Johannesevangelium untersucht und erklärt*, 3rd ed. (Darmstadt: Waitz, 1908); Holtzmann, *Die Entstehung des Neuen Testaments* (Halle: Gebauer-Schwetschke, 1904); and Holtzmann, *Das messianische Bewusstsein Jesu. Ein Beitrag zur Leben-Jesu-Forschung* (Tübingen: Mohr, 1907).

In deference to Papias' allusion to *logia* (Eusebius, *Hist. eccl.* 3.39), Holtzmann designated the source by the Greek letter Λ. Today Q, generally believed to stand for the German *Quelle* ("source"), is used. See Franz Neirynck, "The Symbol Q (= Quelle)," and "Once More: the Symbol Q," in *Evangelica. Études d'Évangile*, BETL 60 (Leuven: Leuven University Press, 1982), 683–89 and 689–90, respectively. See also David Barrett Peabody, "H. J. Holtzmann and His European Colleagues: Aspects of the Nineteenth-Century European Discussion of Gospel Origins," in *Biblical Studies and the Shifting of Paradigms, 1850–1914*, ed. Henning Graf Reventlow and William Farmer, JSOTSup 192 (Sheffield: Sheffield Academic Press, 1995), 50–131; Otto Merk, *TRE*, 15:5–22.

133. John S. Kloppenborg, "Holtzmann's Life of Jesus according to the 'A' Source," *JSHJ* 4, nos. 1 and 2 (2006): 75–108 and 203–23, respectively. Holtzmann posited seven stages in Jesus' psychological development. He based his portrait of Jesus not on Mark but on the "A" source on which Mark was based, an *Urmarkus*. Jesus was elevated by God to be the Christ, and Matthew introduced the idea of supernatural conception.

134. Schweitzer, *Quest*, 202–3. However, the welcome was tinged with regret that Holtzmann was still willing to make use of John.

regretted his attempt to interpret the kingdom in Mark idealistically.[135] Holtzmann sought to dissociate the imagery of Jesus' prophetic imagination from the literalism of *Schwärmerei*, or fanaticism. Jesus' thought world was not to be traced to that destination "where the picture of the fulfilled kingdom of God is painted with the crude colors of the apocalyptic world, but to that other pole where an already present, but hidden kingdom, growing towards fulfillment is discernible."[136] Schweitzer concluded (with his mentor doubtless in mind) that the victory of Markan priority "belonged, not to the Markan hypothesis pure and simple, but to the Markan hypothesis as psychologically interpreted by a liberal theology."[137]

Ernest Renan. The most widely read life of Jesus by a liberal scholar was that of French academic Ernest Renan (1823–92).[138] Renan had been destined for the priesthood, but by the time he wrote *Vie de Jésus*, that goal was long behind him. In a sense, he was indebted to German Protestant criticism, but it was less for any particular theory than for its stimulus in trying to reconstruct the life of Jesus in nonsupernatural terms. The result was a tale told with considerable verve and feeling, which avoided equally the vagaries of the fictitious lives[139] and the painstaking discussions of critical historiography.

---

135. Schweitzer, *Quest*, 203. On the question of messianic consciousness, Holtzmann maintained: "It is not a matter of banishing Messianism from history, but of correctly determining its relationship to the train of ideas bound up with those terms [Son of God and Son of Man]. It can be shown that the concept of the Son of man originally designated the bringer of the Kingdom of God, just as Son of God designated the immediate, untrammeled experience of God in the innermost being [*Gemütsgrund*]. He who, proceeding from the thought of the Kingdom, knew himself to be the chosen organ of its realization, found as a counterpart to the thought of God as Father the complementary idea in his own inner being which constituted his consciousness as Son." Holtzmann, *Das messianische Bewusstsein Jesu*, 98 (author's translation).

136. Holtzmann, *Lehrbuch der neutestamentlichen Theologie*, 1:337 (author's translation); cf. 221–22 for discussion of the parables of Jesus.

137. Schweitzer, *Quest*, 204.

138. Discussions include Schweitzer, *Quest*, 180–92; Jean G. H. Hoffmann, *Les Vies de Jésus et le Jésus de l'Histoire*, ASNU 17 (Paris: Messageries Evangéliques, 1947), 29–51; M. J. Lagrange, *Christ and Renan: A Commentary on Ernest Renan's "The Life of Jesus"*, trans. Maisie Ward (London: Sheed & Ward, 1928); W. H. Wardman, *Ernest Renan: A Critical Biography* (London: University of London; Athlone, 1964); Brown, *Jesus in European Protestant Thought*, 233–38; Robert D. Priest, *The Gospel according to Renan: Reading, Writing, and Religion in Nineteenth-Century France* (Oxford: Oxford University Press, 2015).

Renan was reinstated in 1870 during the Franco-Prussian war. He wrote extensively, and was elected to the Académie Française (1878), admitted to the Legion of Honor (1880), and was buried in the Panthéon alongside the tombs of Rousseau and Voltaire.

139. On the works of K. H. Venturini, K. F. Bahrdt, and Bruno Bauer, see Schweitzer, *Quest*, 38–47, 137–60; Brown, *Jesus in European Protestant Thought*, 162–64, 227–33.

Schweitzer and the Old Quest

In 1860 Renan sailed for the Middle East in charge of an archaeological expedition to Byblos. Inspired by the scenery of the Holy Land, Renan decided to write a biography of Jesus. On his return to Paris, Renan was appointed to the chair of Hebrew, Chaldaic, and Syriac at the Collège de France. In his inaugural lecture Renan described Jesus as an incomparable man, so great that he would not contradict those who called him God. The remark led to Renan's suspension. The publication of *The Life of Jesus* in 1863 performed the double function of bringing about the termination of Renan's appointment and establishing his popular reputation.

The book was filled with touches of local color designed to evoke feelings of realism. Joseph's house at Nazareth "no doubt closely resembled those poor shops, lighted by the door, which serve at once as workshop, kitchen, and bedroom, the furniture consisting of a mat, some cushions on the ground, one or two earthenware pots, and a painted chest."[140] From such conjecture, Renan moved on to the original gospel of Jesus, which he stated with an even greater certainty and even less critical evaluation. "The revolution that he sought to bring about was a moral revolution . . . and it was exalted sentiment rather than fixed design which urged him on to the sublime work he had conceived, though in a manner quite different from what he imagined. . . . It is in fact the kingdom of God, I mean, the kingdom of mind, that he founded."[141]

Renan wrote with the calm assurance of a man who has gotten to the bottom of things. The work went through the life of Jesus, explaining incidents and the motives behind them. But despite the footnotes added to later French editions, there is an almost complete absence of scholarly exegesis to support his interpretations.

Jesus' outlook was transformed through contact with the Samaritans. He received a brilliant illumination when he realized that true worship did not depend on places and ritual but upon spirit and truth (John 4:23). "The day on which he uttered this saying, he was in reality Son of God. He uttered for the first time the sentence upon which will repose the edifice of eternal religion."[142] Jesus returned to Galilee "filled

---

140. E. Renan, *The Life of Jesus* (London: Mathieson, 1890), 14. The work appears as the first volume of Renan's *History of the Origins of Christianity*.

141. Renan, *The Life of Jesus*, 70–71. The translation conveys a more rationalistic sense than does the French. It translates both *esprit* and *âme* as "mind."

142. Renan, *The Life of Jesus*, 136.

The European Scene

with revolutionary ardour.... The Law must be abolished, and it is to be abolished by him. The Messiah has come, and he it is who is the Messiah. The kingdom of God is soon to be revealed; and it is he who will reveal it."[143] Although it will not be established without suffering, the Son of Man will return in glory after his death, accompanied by legions of angels, and those who have rejected him will be confounded. "For the historian, the life of Jesus finishes with his last sigh. But such was the impression he had left in the hearts of his disciples and of a few devoted females, that during some weeks more it was as if he were living and consoling them."[144]

By the end of 1863, the book had gone through ten editions of 5,000 copies, and by 1864 it had been translated into most European languages. It was still going strong in the 1920s, although by then its literary and antiquarian interest had eclipsed its sensationalism. In the first few years counterattacks were selling almost equally well. The spate of literature exceeded the works provoked a generation earlier by Strauss's first *Life*, and Strauss himself took note of Renan's work in his second *Life*, which appeared the following year. To the end, Renan received a steady stream of letters ranging from hostile abuse to adulation. While there was clearly a market for Renan's blend of rationalism and romanticism, the younger generation of French critical scholars were unenthusiastic.

Timothée Colani. Writing in the *Revue de Théologie* (1864) and claiming to speak on behalf of the new Protestant Strasbourg school, Timothée Colani complained that Renan's Christ was not the Christ of history or the Synoptics but that of the Fourth Gospel, though without a metaphysical halo, and painted in the melancholy blue of modem poetry, the pink of the eighteenth-century idyll, and the gray of a moral philosophy that seemed to derive from La Rochefoucauld.[145] To Schweitzer, Renan's book had "imperishable charm," but it was written by an author

---

143. Renan, *The Life of Jesus*, 137.
144. Renan, *The Life of Jesus*, 249.
145. Colani's article was subsequently published separately: *Examen de la Vie de Jésus de M. Renan* (Strasbourg: Treutel et Wirtz, 1864). Colani presented his own views in *Jésus Christ et les Croyances Messianiques de son Temps* (Strassburg: Treutel et Würtz, 1864; 2nd. ed. also 1864). He argued that there was no connection between Jesus and Jewish messianic beliefs and that the apocalyptic teaching of Mark 13 was an interpolation. To the disciples question as to when these things shall be accomplished (Mark 13:4), Jesus had replied that only the Father knew (Mark 13:32). All that came between these verses was the invention of Christian apocalyptists. See further George R. Beasley-Murray, *Jesus and the Last Days: The Interpretation of the Olivet Discourse* (Peabody, MA: Hendrickson, 1993), 13–20.

who had to "perfume [the New Testament] with sentimentality in order to feel himself at home in it."[146]

Martin Kähler. Before we turn to the third and final "round" in Schweitzer's narrative—the "eschatological" versus the "noneschatological" Jesus—it is necessary to make a detour in order to listen to Martin Kähler's protest that the quest of the historical Jesus was "a blind alley."[147] It is perhaps no accident that the name of Martin Kähler does not appear in Schweitzer's *Quest of the Historical Jesus*, for ideologically Kähler did not fit into Schweitzer's scheme of things.

Martin Kähler (1835–1912) received his early education at Königsberg. On turning to theology, he was deeply influenced by the Mediating Theologians. Among them was the Halle professor, Friedrich August Gottreu Tholuck, who hired Kähler as his secretary-assistant and later served as his mentor.[148] Kähler spent most of his professional career at the University of Halle, where he became professor of systematic theology and New Testament in 1879. His chief works were a dogmatics, which took the doctrine of justification by faith as its center,[149] and a posthumous history of Protestant dogmatics in the nineteenth century.[150] Today Kähler is remembered for a lecture delivered at the Wuppertal Pastoral Conference, published in 1892 under the title *Der sogenannte historische Jesus und der geschichtliche, biblische Christus* ("The So-Called Historical Jesus and the Historic Biblical Christ").[151]

---

146. Schweitzer, *Quest*, 192.
147. Martin Kähler, *Der sogenannte historische Jesus und der geschichtliche, biblische Christus* (Leipzig: Deichert, 1892), 5; ET: *The So-Called Historical Jesus and the Historic Biblical Christ*, trans. and ed. Carl E. Braaten, foreword by Paul Tillich, Fortress Texts in Modern Theology (Philadelphia: Fortress, 1964), 46. An extract is reprinted in J. D. G. Dunn and Scot McKnight, eds., *The Historical Jesus in Recent Research*, Sources for Biblical and Theological Study 10 (Winona Lake, IN: Eisenbrauns, 2005), 67–84. See also Carl E. Braaten, "Martin Kähler on the Historic Biblical Christ," *The Historical Jesus and the Kerygmatic Christ: Essays on the New Quest of the Historical Jesus*, ed., Carl E. Braaten and Roy A. Harrisville (Nashville: Abingdon, 1964), 79–105; Hans-Joachim Kraus, *TRE*, 17:511–15; D. B. Peabody, *DMBI*, 2nd ed., 594–601.
148. On the Mediating Theologians and Tholuck see Brown, *Jesus in European Protestant Thought*, 240–41, 254–76. An abiding influence were the writings of the Königsberg private scholar J. G. Hamann.
149. Martin Kähler, *Die Wissenschaft der christlichen Lehre von den evangelischen Grundartikel aus im Abriss dargestellet* (Leipzig: A. Deichert, 1883; 3rd ed., 1905).
150. Martin Kähler, *Geschichte der protestantischen Dogmatik im 19. Jahrhundert*, with a list of his father's writings compiled by Ernst Kähler, TB 16 (München: Chr. Kaiser Verlag: 1962).
151. Kähler, *Der sogenannte historische Jesus und der geschichtliche, biblische Christus* (see n147 above). The work was subsequently enlarged in 1896 and reprinted in 1926. The modern edition, ed. E. Wolf, 3rd ed., TB 2 (München: Chr. Kaiser Verlag, 1961), contains the original lecture and the first paper of the 1896 edition. The English translation noted above is based on Wolf's edition.

The European Scene

The "Life-of-Jesus" movement was right to set the Bible against abstract dogmatism, but the sources are insufficient for a biography, which would "stand up to the standards of contemporary historical science. A trustworthy picture of the Savior for believers is a very different thing."[152] Carl E. Braaten set out Kähler's problem as follows:

> How can the Bible be a trustworthy normative document of revelation when biblical criticism has shattered our confidence in its historical reliability? And how can Jesus Christ be the authentic basis and content of Christian faith when historical science can never attain to indisputably certain knowledge of the historical Jesus? Underlying both of these questions is the existential quest for a sure foundation, for what Kähler called an "invulnerable area" (*sturmfreies Gebiet*, lit. "storm-free zone"). In other words, how can theology explicate the access of faith to a final historical revelation without being imprisoned in a thoroughgoing historical relativism?[153]

The answer lay in the distinction between the terms *historisch* ("historical," in the sense of critical history) and *geschichtlich* ("historic," in the sense that one may speak of a historic event).[154] The *sturmfreies Gebiet* was to be found in the *historic* proclamation of Scripture and the response of faith.

> The real Christ, that is, the Christ who has exercised an influence in history, with whom millions have communed in childlike faith, and with whom the great witnesses of faith have been in communion—while striving, apprehending, triumphing, and proclaiming—*this real Christ is the Christ who is preached*. The Christ who is preached, however, is precisely the Christ of faith. He is the Jesus whom the eyes of faith behold at every step he takes and through every syllable he utters—the Jesus whose image we

---

152. Martin Kähler, *The So-Called Historical Jesus and the Historic Biblical Christ*, 48.
153. Carle E. Braaten, introduction to *The So-Called Historical Jesus and the Historic Biblical Christ*, by Kähler, 10.
154. Kähler, *The So-Called Historical Jesus and the Historic Biblical Christ*, 21. I should note that the German word *Geschichte* is derived from *geschehen*, meaning something that has "happened." The word *Historie* is derived from the Latin *historia*, which in turn is derived from the Greek ἱστορία.

impress upon our minds because we both would and do commune with him, our risen, living Lord. The person of our living Savior, the person of the Word incarnate, of God revealed, gazes upon us from the features of that image which has deeply impressed itself on the memory of his followers—and which was finally disclosed and perfected through the illumination of his Spirit.[155]

Kähler's statement has been applauded as a return to a balanced perspective. But it is not without problems. Kähler seems to be speaking on behalf of orthodoxy, insisting that one cannot set aside Christian experience in favor of positivistic research. But Kähler can be understood in other ways, as he was by his famous pupil Paul Tillich. For Tillich, Kähler's contribution lay in his insistence on "the necessity to make the certainty of faith independent of the unavoidable incertitudes of historical research."[156] Tillich himself achieved this by appropriating the gospel stories for their *symbolic* value and transposing them in his philosophical theology as a means of relating to the ground of being.[157]

Wolfhart Pannenberg agreed with Kähler's protest against positing a discontinuity between the church's faith and the historical Jesus. However, it did not follow "(1) that the effects of the person Jesus are to be found only in the apostolic preaching, or (2) that what is 'truly historic' about Jesus is only his 'personal effect.'"[158] "Christology is concerned . . . not only with *unfolding* the Christian community's confession of Christ, but above all with *grounding* it in the activity and fate of Jesus in the past."[159]

For this reason Pannenberg put forward three cogent reasons starting with a Christology "from below."

1. A Christology from above presupposes the divinity of Jesus. The most important task of Christology is, however, precisely to present reasons for the confession of Jesus' divinity. Instead of

---

155. Kähler, *The So-Called Historical Jesus and the Historic Biblical Christ*, 66–67.
156. Kähler, *The So-Called Historical Jesus and the Historic Biblical Christ*, viii.
157. Paul Tillich, *Systematic Theology* (Chicago: University of Chicago Press, 1957), 2:107–35. See further chapter 15, §2.1.
158. Wolfhart Pannenberg, *Jesus—God and Man*, trans. Lewis L. Wilkins and Duane A. Priebe (Philadelphia: Westminster; London: SCM, 1968), 22–23.
159. Pannenberg, *Jesus—God and Man*, 28.

presupposing it, we must first inquire about how Jesus' appearance in history led to the recognition of his divinity.[160]
2. A Christology that takes the divinity of the Logos as its point of departure and finds its problems only in the union of God and man in Jesus recognizes only with difficulty the determinative significance inherent in the distinctive features of the real, historical man, Jesus of Nazareth. The manifold relationships between Jesus and the Judaism of his time, which are essential to an understanding of his life and message, must appear as less important to such a Christology, even when it discusses the offices of Christ as well as his humiliation and exaltation.[161]
3. There remains one final reason why the method of Christology "from above" is closed to us: one would have to stand in the position of God himself in order to follow the way of God's Son into the world.[162]

To Pannenberg's critique I would add two observations. First, Kähler's contention begs the question of which Christ is it that we have such direct and certain knowledge: The Lutheran Christ? The Reformed Christ? The Roman Catholic Christ? The Jewish Christ? Second, the historic proclamation of Scripture and the response of faith cannot have the privileged position of being a unique *sturmfreies Gebiet*—a storm-free zone of certitude—when all other areas of life involve doubt, conflict, and questioning. The common Christian experience is that we walk by faith and not by sight (2 Cor 5:7), and the kerygma is no exception. Indeed, we cannot appreciate the kerygma without also appreciating the opposition, which generated the kerygma. I suggest that the Gospels need to be read "with the grain" (in which we try to grasp what the evangelists are contending) and "against the grain" (in which we endeavor to appreciate the standpoints of Jesus' adversaries).[163] Otherwise, we end up with the pious platitudes that characterize Kähler's pronouncements.

---

160. Pannenberg, *Jesus—God and Man*, 34.
161. Pannenberg, *Jesus—God and Man*, 34–35.
162. Pannenberg, *Jesus—God and Man*, 35.
163. Colin Brown, "With the Grain and against the Grain—A Strategy for Reading the Synoptic Gospels," in *HSHJ*, ed. Tom Holmén and Stanley E. Porter, 4 vols. (Leiden: Brill, 2010), 2: 619–48.

2.4. The "Eschatological" versus the "Noneschatological" Jesus.

The scene was now set for the final confrontation. Liberalism was still in ascendance, typified by the theology of Ritschl.

Ritschl. Albrecht Benjamin Ritschl (1822–89)[164] became professor of theology at Göttingen in 1864. Ritschl saw Christianity as a spiritual and moral religion. It was not like a circle with a single center but "an ellipse which is determined by two *foci*."[165] Unfortunately, the Reformed traditions had emphasized the spiritual and doctrinal at the expense of the moral. Ritschl's theology sought to redress the balance. "Christ made the universal moral Kingdom of God His end, and thus He came to know and decide for that kind of redemption which He achieved through the maintenance of fidelity in His calling and of His blessed fellowship through suffering unto death."[166] It was Jesus' "unique vocation [*Beruf*] to establish the kingdom of God."[167] And "a universal ethical kingdom of

---

164. Ritschl rejected the view of his mentor, F. C. Baur, that Christianity arose out of a conflict between Petrine and Pauline theology. He also rejected metaphysical speculation, preferring to stress the moral, practical aspects of Christian conduct (*Lebensführung*). Ritschl distinguished between judgments of fact (*Sachurteile*) and judgments of value (*Werturteile*). Theological judgments belong to the latter category and represent the "revelational value" (*Offenbarungswert*) of the beliefs of the Christian community. Discussions include Gösta Lundström, *The Kingdom of God in the Teaching of Jesus: A History of Interpretation from the Last Decades of the Nineteenth Century to the Present Day*, trans. Joan Bulman (Edinburgh: Oliver and Boyd, 1963), 3–9; Paul Wrzecionko, *Die philosophischen Würzeln der Theologie Albrecht Ritschls. Ein Beitrag zum Problem des Verhältnisses von Theologie und Philosophie im 19. Jahrhundert* (Berlin: Töpelmann, 1964); Philip J. Hefner, *Faith and the Vitalities of History: A Theological Study Based on the Work of Albrecht Ritschl* (New York: Harper & Row, 1966); Rolf Schäfer, *Ritschl*, BHT 41 (Tübingen: Mohr Siebeck, 1968); Jörg Baur, "Albrecht Ritschl—Herrschaft und Versöhnung," in Moeller, *Theologie in Göttingen*, 256–70; Clive Marsh, *Albrecht Ritschl and the Problem of the Historical Jesus* (San Francisco: Mellen Research University Press, 1992); Darrell Jodock, ed., *Ritschl in Retrospect: History, Community, and Science* (Minneapolis: Fortress, 1995); Rolf Schäfer, *TRE*, 29:220–38; Eckhard Lessing, *Geschichte der deutschsprachigen evangelischen Theologie von Albrecht Ritschl bis zur Gegenwart*, vol. 1, *1870–1918* (Göttingen: Vandenhoeck & Ruprecht, 2000).

165. A. B. Ritschl, *The Christian Doctrine of Justification and Reconciliation: The Positive Development of the Doctrine*, trans. H. R. Mackintosh and A. B. Macaulay (Edinburgh: T&T Clark, 1900), 11.

166. Ritschl, *The Christian Doctrine of Justification and Reconciliation*, 10; cf. 448. Whereas *The Christian Doctrine of Justification and Reconciliation* gives a prolix account, Ritschl's *Instruction in the Christian Religion* gives a concise, closely argued account. "The kingdom of God is the overall purpose of the community constituted through God's revelation in Christ, and is the social product of the same, while its members bind themselves through a mutually determined mode of behavior.... Right conduct in which members of Christ's community bring about the kingdom of God has its general law and personal motivation in love for God and for one's neighbor." A. B. Ritschl, *Unterricht in der christlichen Religion* (Bonn: Marcus, 1875; repr., ed. Gerhard Ruhbach; Gütersloh: Gütersloher Verlagshaus Gerd Mohn, 1966), 15 (author's translation).

167. Ritschl, *The Christian Doctrine of Justification and Reconciliation*, 450.

God is the supreme end of God Himself in the world." As "the Founder of the Kingdom of God in the world," Jesus was "the Bearer of God's ethical lordship over men."[168]

Johannes Weiss. As a member of the Ritschlian circle—and Ritschl's son-in-law—Johannes Weiss (1863-1914) was troubled by the discrepancy between Ritschl's position and what he believed to be the historical truth. As he explained in the preface to the second edition of *Die Predigt Jesu vom Reiche Gottes* ("Jesus' Proclamation of the Kingdom of God," 1900), he was aware of the grief and pain that the publication of his own research would bring. "I am still of the opinion that [Ritschl's] system and particularly this central thought represents that form of belief that is best suited to bring the Christian religion to our generation, and rightly understood and rightly presented to awake and nourish a sound and strong religious life, as we need it today. But even early on I was troubled by the clear impression that Ritschl's notion of the kingdom of God and the idea which bears the same name in the teaching of Jesus were two very different things."[169] Further study convinced Weiss that the roots of Ritschl's notion lay in Kant and the theology of the Enlightenment. He waited three years after Ritschl's death before publishing *Jesus' Proclamation of the Kingdom of God* (1892).[170]

For Weiss it was fundamental that "the Kingdom of God as Jesus thought of it is never something subjective, inward, or spiritual, but it is

---

168. Ritschl, *The Christian Doctrine of Justification and Reconciliation*, 451.

169. Johannes Weiss, *Die Predigt Jesu vom Reiche Gottes*, xi (Hahn's edition, see next note); cf. also Weiss, *Die Idee des Reiches Gottes in der Theologie* (Giessen: J. Ricker'sche Buchhandlung, 1901).

170. Johannes Weiss, *Die Predigt Jesu vom Reiche Gottes* (1892; 2nd ed., 1900; 3rd ed., ed. Ferdinand Hahn, preface by Rudolf Bultmann; Göttingen: Vandenhoeck & Ruprecht, 1964); trans. of 1st ed. with introduction by R. H. Hiers and D. Larrimore Holland, *Jesus' Proclamation of the Kingdom of God* (Philadelphia: Fortress, 1971). Weiss studied at Marburg, Berlin, Göttingen, and Breslau, before his appointment to teach New Testament at Göttingen (1888). He became a full professor at Marburg (1895) and Heidelberg (1898).

Bibliography and discussion in Schweitzer, *Quest*, 238-41, 330-97; F. C. Burkitt, "Johannes Weiss: In Memoriam," *HTR* 8 (1915): 291-97; D. L. Holland, "History, Theology and the Kingdom of God: A Contribution of Johannes Weiss to Twentieth Century Theology," *Biblical Research* 13 (1968): 54-66; W. Willis, "The Discovery of the Eschatological Kingdom: Johannes Weiss and Albert Schweitzer," in *The Kingdom of God in 20th-Century Interpretation*, ed. Willis (Peabody, MA: Hendrickson, 1987), 1-14; M. J. Borg, "Jesus and Eschatology: A Reassessment," in *Images of Jesus Today*, ed. J. H. Charlesworth and W. P. Weaver (Valley Forge, PA: Trinity Press International, 1994), 42-67; Bruce Chilton, "The Kingdom of God in Recent Discussion," in *Studying the Historical Jesus: Evaluations of the State of Current Research*, ed. Bruce Chilton and Craig A. Evans, NTTS 19 (Leiden: Brill, 1994), 255-80; Berthold Lannert, *TRE*, 35:523-26; Brown, *DMBI*, 1026-30.

Schweitzer and the Old Quest

always the objective messianic Kingdom, which is usually pictured as a territory into which one enters, or as a land in which one has a share, or as a treasure which comes down from heaven."[171] At the end of the first edition Weiss summarized ten conclusions.[172]

1. "Jesus activity is governed by the strong and unwavering feeling that the messianic time is imminent" (Mark 1:15; Matt 10:7; Luke 10:9, 11). From time to time Jesus sensed that his exorcisms denoted the advent of the kingdom (Matt 12:28; Luke 11:20)[173]—a point downplayed by Schweitzer.
2. The actualization had yet to take place. Jesus urged his disciples to "pray for the coming of the Kingdom, but men could do nothing to establish it."[174]
3. "Not even Jesus can bring, establish, or found the Kingdom of God. God himself must take control. In the meantime, Jesus can only battle against the devil with the power imparted to him by the divine Spirit, and gather a band of followers who, with a new righteousness, with repentance, humility and renunciation await the Kingdom of God."[175]
4. Jesus' messianic consciousness consisted of the certainty that when God established the kingdom, both judgment and rule would be transferred to him.[176] Jesus' activity was not messianic but preparatory. "Since Jesus is now a rabbi, a prophet, he has nothing in common with the Son of man, except the claim that he will *become* the Son of man. Thus, he cannot intervene in the development of the Kingdom of God. He has to wait, just as the people have to wait, until God once again definitively takes up the rule."[177]
5. Although Jesus hoped to see the kingdom, the disciples' mission made it apparent that their preaching had not produced the necessary repentance. "Since sin which will cause his death is at the same

---

171. Weiss, *Jesus' Proclamation of the Kingdom*, 133.
172. Weiss, *Jesus' Proclamation of the Kingdom*, 129–31. The conclusions were expanded and their number was doubled in the 2nd ed. (*Die Predigt Jesu vom Reiche Gottes*, 65–126).
173. Weiss, *Jesus' Proclamation of the Kingdom*, 65–67.
174. Weiss, *Jesus' Proclamation of the Kingdom*, 129; cf. 73.
175. Weiss, *Jesus' Proclamation of the Kingdom*, 129–30; cf. 74–81.
176. Weiss, *Jesus' Proclamation of the Kingdom*, 73.
177. Weiss, *Jesus' Proclamation of the Kingdom*, 82–83. Weiss saw the idea of future exaltation in John 3:14; 5:27; Acts 2:36.

time the obstacle to the coming of the Kingdom, he seized upon the audacious and paradoxical idea—or the idea seized him—that his death should be the ransom for the people otherwise destined to destruction (Mark 10:45). He must give his life ὑπὲρ πολλῶν as a λύτρον [for many as a ransom] which the many, the people themselves, could not offer."[178] After that he will return on the clouds at the establishment of the kingdom within the lifetime of those who rejected him. Jesus did not fix the time because it could not be determined by observation of signs or calculation.[179]

6. When the kingdom comes, God will destroy the old world, which is ruled by the devil, and create a new world. Humankind will participate and become like the angels (Matt 5:9; 19:28; Mark 12:25; 1 Cor 15:52).[180]
7. Judgment will take place for the living and the dead, for Jew and gentile.[181]
8. The land of Palestine will be renewed as the center of the new kingdom. Aliens will no longer rule over it but will acknowledge God as the Lord. Sadness and sin will be abolished, and members of the kingdom shall behold the living God, serving him in eternal righteousness and bliss.[182]
9. Jesus and his faithful ones will rule over the newborn twelve tribes, which include gentiles.[183]
10. The rule of God is not suspended but is actualized by the Messiah, reigning together side by side, or by Jesus under God's higher sovereignty.[184]

Although Schweitzer declared that Weiss's book had "an importance equal to that of Strauss's first Life of Jesus," he devoted only three pages to it, compared with the sixty-eight devoted to Wrede.[185] As noted

---

178. Weiss, *Jesus' Proclamation of the Kingdom*, 87–88. This contrasts with Schweitzer's view that Jesus deliberately sent his disciples on a suicide mission that resulted in the messianic woes and the coming of the Son of Man.
179. Weiss, *Jesus' Proclamation of the Kingdom*, 130; cf. 92–96.
180. Weiss, *Jesus' Proclamation of the Kingdom*, 130; cf. 92–96.
181. Weiss, *Jesus' Proclamation of the Kingdom*, 130; cf. 96–101.
182. Weiss, *Jesus' Proclamation of the Kingdom*, 130–31.
183. Weiss, *Jesus' Proclamation of the Kingdom*, 131; cf. 114–27.
184. Weiss, *Jesus' Proclamation of the Kingdom*, 131; cf. 128–29.
185. Schweitzer, *Quest*, 238–41, 330–67.

earlier, Schweitzer and Wrede published their books on the messiahship of Jesus on the same day.[186] *The Quest of the Historical Jesus* was a rematch. As Schweitzer depicted it, the entire quest led inexorably to this final showdown: either the "thoroughgoing skepticism" of Wrede or "the thoroughgoing eschatology" (*konsequente Eschatologie*)[187] of Schweitzer.

William Wrede. William Wrede (1859–1906) had been professor of New Testament at Breslau since 1895. His monograph on *The Task and Method of So-Called New Testament Theology*[188] reduced the discipline to a purely historical account of primitive Christianity. *The Messianic Secret* (1901) applied this method to the Gospels—in particular to Mark.[189]

Wrede began with the various injunctions to secrecy in Mark.[190] After reviewing possible explanations, Wrede pronounced them all unsatisfactory, for the narratives themselves were "unhistorical, each and every one of them."[191] Wrede saw two basic themes in Mark. "(1) Jesus keeps his messiahship a secret as long as he is on earth; (2) He does, of course, reveal himself to the disciples in contrast to the people, but to them

---

186. Schweitzer, *Quest*, 330.

187. Schweitzer, *Quest*, 329–67. The bibliography at the beginning of the chapter lists only the titles of Wrede's book and Schweitzer's. Schweitzer saw his own account of Jesus' attitude to eschatology as more consistent than Weiss's. He describes Weiss's account of Jesus role as passive. "When Weiss asserts that the part played by Jesus was not the active role of establishing the Kingdom, but the passive role of waiting for the coming of the Kingdom; and that it was, in a sense, only by accepting His sufferings that He emerged from that passivity; he is only asserting what Ghillany had maintained thirty years before with the same arguments and the same decisiveness. But Weiss places the assertion on an unassailable basis" (Schweitzer, *Quest*, 241). In the "first complete edition" (315) Schweitzer blamed Weiss and his school for applying eschatology only to the messianic preaching of Jesus and not seeing it as the "dogmatic" element in the history of Jesus. Thus Wrede could leave out eschatology from his account of the life of Jesus. In light of our discussion above, Schweitzer is not entirely correct about Jesus' passivity. However, Schweitzer's attribution of Jesus' decision, following the safe return of the disciples from their mission, to go to Jerusalem in order to inaugurate the kingdom by his own death differs from Weiss's passive reading of the incident.

188. William Wrede, *Über Aufgabe und Methode der sogenannten neutestatemenlichen Theologie* (Göttingen: Vandenhoeck & Ruprecht, 1897), trans. Robert Morgan, in *The Nature of New Testament Theology: The Contributions of William Wrede and Adolf Schlatter*, SBT Second Series 25 (London: SCM, 1973), 68–116. For appraisal of Wrede and bibliography, see Georg Strecker, "William Wrede. Zur hundertsten Wiederkehr seines Geburtstags," *ZTK* 57 (1960): 67–91; Werner Zager, *TRE*, 36: 337–41; H. Rollmann, *DMBI*, 2nd ed., 1056–60.

189. The English title is a condensation of the German original. See n16 above.

190. Wrede identified five classes of prohibitions: prohibitions to demons (1:25, 34; 3:12), prohibitions following other miracles (1:43–45; 5:43; cf. 5:37, 40; 7:36; cf. 7:33; 8:26; cf. 8:23), prohibitions after Peter's confession (8:30; 9:9; cf. 9:2, 3), intentional preservation of Jesus' incognito (7:24; 9:30–31), and a prohibition that did not originate with Jesus (10:47–48). Wrede, *The Messianic Secret*, 34–36.

191. Wrede, *The Messianic Secret*, 49.

The European Scene

too he remains in his revelations incomprehensible for the time being."[192] The two ideas overlap, but behind them is "the common view that real knowledge of what Jesus is begins with his resurrection. This idea of the secret messiahship covers a significant field in Mark. It dominates many sayings of Jesus, numerous miracle stories, and the entire course of the narrative as a whole."[193]

Wrede was led to "two differentiated ideas" that were to be held apart.

> The one is an idea about Jesus and it rests on the fact that Jesus became messiah—so far as the belief of his followers was concerned—with the Resurrection, and the other is an idea about the disciples which rests upon the fact that they acquire a new understanding about Jesus as a *result* of the Resurrection. But the starting-point manifests itself in the end to be one and the same. Both ideas rest on the fact that the Resurrection is the decisive event for the messiahship and that Jesus' earthly life was not to begin with regarded as messianic.[194]

The messianic secret in Mark was "a transitional idea and *it can be characterised as the after-effect of the view that the resurrection is the beginning of the messiahship at the time when the life of Jesus was already being filled materially with messianic content.* Or else it proceeded from the impulse to make the earthly life of Jesus messianic, but one inhibited by the older view, which was still potent."[195] This led to the further suggestion. "If our view could only arise where nothing is known of an open messianic claim on Jesus' part, then we would seem to have in it *a positive historical testimony for the idea that Jesus actually did not give himself out as messiah.*"[196]

The net result of Wrede's argument was to identify the Gospels as *Gemeindetheologie*, theology produced by the church. They could be used for reconstructing the theology of the church, but not the life of Jesus. Wrede's path would be beaten by many in the years to come, especially by

---

192. Wrede, *The Messianic Secret*, 113.
193. Wrede, *The Messianic Secret*, 114.
194. Wrede, *The Messianic Secret*, 236.
195. Wrede, *The Messianic Secret*, 229.
196. Wrede, *The Messianic Secret*, 230. The argument stops short of saying that Jesus never thought of himself as messiah. At the 1997 Annual Meeting of the Society of Biblical Literature Gerd Lüdemann stated that Wrede's unpublished correspondence indicated that Wrede did in fact trace the rise of Christianity to Jesus' messianic consciousness.

the more radical form critics. In the dictum of R. H. Lightfoot, "It seems, then, that the form of the earthly no less than that of the heavenly Christ is for the most part hidden from us."[197] Jesus' messiahship was the fruit of resurrection faith retroactively projected onto Jesus. As Schweitzer remarked, "'The resurrection' is for Wrede the real Messianic event in the Life of Jesus."[198] But a creative tradition "would have carried the theory of the Messianic secret in the life of Jesus much more boldly and logically."[199] Wrede's account poses the difficulty of explaining how Jesus could be thought to be the Messiah when even to his intimates he gave no hint of the dignity.[200] It involves removing the revelation of messiahship from the resurrection in order to insert it into the public ministry.[201]

To Schweitzer, Jesus' secret messiahship was the key to understanding Jesus historically and to making sense of the Synoptic Gospels as history. What needed to be done was "to make a critical examination of the dogmatic element in the life of Jesus on the assumption that the atmosphere of the time was saturated with eschatology," and "to proceed not from the particular to the general, but from the general to the particular, carefully considering whether the dogmatic element is not precisely the historical element."[202] Mark alone gives "an inadequate basis."[203] Matthew fills in the details, not least in the mission discourse of chapter 10. It is a mistake of modern theology to talk about the new ethic of the kingdom. "There is for Jesus no ethic of the Kingdom of God, for in the Kingdom of God all natural relations . . . are abolished."[204] "The self-consciousness of Jesus cannot in fact be illustrated or explained; all that can be explained is the eschatological view, in which the Man who possessed that self-consciousness saw reflected in advance the coming events, both those of a more general character, and those which especially related to Himself."[205]

---

197. R. H. Lightfoot, *History and Interpretation in the Gospels*, Bampton Lectures 1934 (London: Hodder & Stoughton, 1935), 225. Lightfoot had gone to Germany 1931 to study form criticism, which he introduced to English readers in his book. Lightfoot's work was "strongly indebted to Wrede"; John Riches, *DMBI*, 2nd ed., 665–68, here 666.
198. Schweitzer, *Quest*, 339.
199. Schweitzer, *Quest*, 30.
200. Schweitzer, *Quest*, 344.
201. Schweitzer, *Quest*, 346.
202. Schweitzer, *Quest*, 350.
203. Schweitzer, *Quest*, 360.
204. Schweitzer, *Quest*, 365.
205. Schweitzer, *Quest*, 367.

The passion of Jesus cannot be understood if the kingdom is not understood. "In order to understand Jesus' resolve to suffer, we must first recognise that the mystery of this suffering is the mystery of the Kingdom of God, since the Kingdom cannot come until the πειρασμός has taken place."[206] As in his earlier sketch of Jesus' life, the turning point is the mission of the disciples. Jesus had thought that the mission would "let loose the final tribulation and so compel the coming of the Kingdom."[207] When it did not, Jesus resolved to go to Jerusalem to "make in His own blood the atonement which they would have had to render in the tribulation. The Kingdom could not come until the debt which weighed upon the world was discharged."[208]

Jesus died because two of his disciples broke his command to silence: Peter told the Twelve the secret of Jesus' messiahship, and Judas communicated it to the high priest.[209] But the betrayal was useless because Judas was the sole witness. Other charges were tried and failed. Armed with the knowledge that Jesus believed himself to be the Christ, the high priest asked Jesus if he was the Christ. Jesus' admission, strengthened by allusion to prophetic signs of his coming as the Son of Man (Matt 26:63–66; Mark 14:61–64; Luke 22:66–71), secured his condemnation as a blasphemer.

3. Schweitzer's Jesus

The *Quest* was not Schweitzer's last word on Jesus. To complete his medical doctorate, Schweitzer wrote a thesis that formed the basis of *The Psychiatric Study of Jesus: Exposition and Criticism* (1913).[210] It was

---

206. Schweitzer, *Quest*, 387. The term πειρασμός (*peirasmos*), which occurs in the Lord's Prayer (Matt 6:13; Luke 11:4), was understood by Schweitzer as the eschatological time of trial preceding the establishment of the kingdom (Matt 26:41; Mark 14:38; Luke 4:13; 22:28, 40, 46). Schweitzer understood the passion predictions as prophecies of this eschatological trial. His interpretation was endorsed by Brant Pitre, *Jesus, the Tribulation, and the End of the Exile: Restoration Eschatology and the Origin of the Atonement*, WUNT 204 (Tübingen: Mohr Siebeck; Grand Rapids: Baker Academic, 2005), 9–12, 132–59, 504–7. Joachim Jeremias took a similar view (*Jesus, the Tribulation, and the End of the Exile*, 14–15. See also below, chap. 8, §2). However, πειρασμός may be understood in the more general senses of "temptation," "enticement" (BDAG, 793).

207. Schweitzer, *Quest*, 389.
208. Schweitzer, *Quest*, 390.
209. Schweitzer, *Quest*, 397.
210. Schweitzer, *My Life and Thought*, 101–2; Albert Schweitzer, The *Psychiatric Study of Jesus: Exposition and Criticism*, trans. Charles R. Joy (Boston: Beacon, 1948). An earlier translation

Schweitzer and the Old Quest

a defense against charges of paranoia, characterized by hallucinations, delusions of grandeur, morbidity, and fanaticism. Schweitzer was prepared to admit that the charges might fit the Johannine Jesus.[211] But at this point in time no clinical diagnosis could be made.[212] Moreover, the eschatological ideas of Jesus belonged to the common stock of late Jewish belief and could not simply be dismissed as signs of Jesus' mental illness.[213] Schweitzer concluded: "The only symptoms to be accepted as historical and possibly to be discussed from the psychiatric point of view—the high estimate which Jesus has of himself and perhaps also the hallucination at the baptism—fall far short of proving the existence of mental illness."[214]

In 1913 Schweitzer went to Lambaréné in French Equatorial Africa to work as a medical missionary. He continued to work on Paul[215] and on a manuscript on the history of belief in the kingdom of God in Judaism, the teaching of Jesus, and primitive Christianity.[216] Essentially it was a reaffirmation of the opinions he had reached over half a century earlier.

Schweitzer concluded the *Quest* on a lyrical, almost mystical, note.

> He comes to us as One unknown, without a name, as of old, by the lake-side, He came to those men who knew Him not. He speaks to us the same word: 'Follow thou me!' and sets us the task which He has to fulfil for our time. He commands. And to those who obey Him, whether they be wise or simple, He will reveal Himself in the toils, the conflicts, the sufferings which they shall pass through in

---

by W. Montgomery appeared in *The Expositor* 8, no. 6, under the title of "The Sanity of the Eschatological Jesus."

For further discussion see Donald Capps, "Beyond Schweitzer and the Psychiatrists: Jesus as Fictive Personality"; and James H. Charlesworth, "Should Specialists in Jesus Research Include Psychobiography?," in *Jesus Research: New Methodologies and Perceptions*, ed. James H. Charlesworth with Brian Rhea and Petr Pokorný, Second Princeton-Prague Symposium on Jesus Research (Grand Rapids: Eerdmans, 2014), 399–435 and 436–66, respectively.

211. Schweitzer, *The Psychiatric Study of Jesus*, 45.
212. Schweitzer, *The Psychiatric Study of Jesus*, 56.
213. Schweitzer, *The Psychiatric Study of Jesus*, 61.
214. Schweitzer, *The Psychiatric Study of Jesus*, 72.
215. Schweitzer, *My Life and Thought*, 108–24. Schweitzer applied his methodology to Paul in *Paul and His Interpreters: A Critical History* [German: 1912], trans. W. Montgomery (London: Black, 1912), which was followed by *The Mysticism of the Apostle Paul* [German: 1930], trans. W. Montgomery (London: Black, 1931).
216. Albert Schweitzer, *The Kingdom of God and Primitive Christianity*, ed. Ulrich Neuenerschwander, trans. L. A. Garrard (London: Black, 1968); for full text, see *Reich Gottes und Christentum*, ed. Ulrich Luz, Ulrich Neuenerschwander, and Johann Zürcher (Munich: Beck, 1995).

His fellowship, and, as an ineffable mystery, they shall learn in their own experience Who He is.[217]

More bleakly Schweitzer confessed that "those who are fond of talking about negative theology can find their account here. There is nothing more negative than the result of the critical study of the Life of Jesus."[218] What Schweitzer meant was that his research showed that the Jesus of liberal, rationalistic, and orthodox theologies were fiction. "The Jesus of Nazareth who came forward publicly as the Messiah, who preached the ethic of the Kingdom of God, who founded the Kingdom of Heaven upon earth, and died to give His work its final consecration, never had any existence. He is a figure designed by rationalism, endowed with life by liberalism, and clothed by modern theology in an historical garb."[219]

"The true historical Jesus"—Schweitzer's Jesus—had overthrown "the Modern Jesus." Jesus was neither teacher nor casuist. He was "an imperious ruler,"[220] who had sent out his disciples to proclaim the eschatological kingdom in the belief that it would come, with him being installed as Son of Man, before they had gone through all the towns of Israel (Matt 10:23). When the disciples returned, and the kingdom had not yet come, Jesus came to the realization that he must experience the messianic woes in order to bring it about. In *The Mystery of the Kingdom of God* Schweitzer represents Jesus as saying, "'The Son of Man must suffer and will then rise from the dead:' that is to say, 'As the one who is to be Son of Man at the resurrection of the dead I must suffer' [Mark 10:45]."[221] In the first edition of *The Quest of the Historical Jesus* Schweitzer reflected on the futility and greatness of Jesus' enterprise.

> Jesus . . . in the knowledge that He is the coming Son of Man lays hold of the wheel of the world to set it moving on that last revolution which is to bring all history to a close. It refuses to turn, and He throws Himself upon it. Then it does turn; and crushes Him. Instead of bringing in the eschatological conditions, He has destroyed them. The wheel rolls onward, and the mangled body of

---

217. Schweitzer, *Quest*, 403.
218. Schweitzer, *Quest*, 398.
219. Schweitzer, *Quest*, 398; 1st complete ed., 478.
220. Schweitzer, *Quest*, 403.
221. Schweitzer, *The Mystery of the Kingdom of God*, 193.

the one immeasurably great Man, who was strong enough to think of Himself as the spiritual ruler of mankind and to bend history to His purpose, is hanging upon it still. That is His victory and His reign.[222]

Titles like Messiah, Son of Man, and Son of God are "merely historical parables. We can find no designation which expresses what He is for us."[223]

If eschatology was the key to understanding the actions of the historical Jesus, it was no more credible to Schweitzer than it had been to Ritschl and Weiss. "But the truth is, it is not Jesus as historically known, but Jesus as spiritually arisen within men, who is significant for our time and can help it. Not the historical Jesus, but the spirit which goes forth from him and in the spirits of men strives for new influence and rule, is that which overcomes the world."[224]

Schweitzer's Jesus turned out to be (as B. H. Streeter perceptively observed more than a century ago) Nietzsche's "superman" in Galilean garb, the *Übermensch*, revaluing all values.[225] Jesus was "the one immeasurably great Man, who was strong enough to think of Himself as the spiritual ruler of mankind and to bend history to His purpose."[226]

Schweitzer had long been fascinated by Nietzsche and his concept of greatness. Schweitzer adopted it as his own model.[227] At the time of Nietzsche's death in 1900, Schweitzer was working on a lecture on

---

222. Schweitzer, *Quest*, 370–71.
223. Schweitzer, *Quest*, 403.
224. Schweitzer, *Quest*, 401.
225. The similarity between Schweitzer's Jesus and Nietzsche's "superman" was noted by B. H. Streeter in *Foundations: A Statement of Christian Belief in Terms of Modern Thought by Seven Oxford Men* (London: Macmillan, 1912), 111; cf. A. M. Hunter, *The Work and Words of Jesus* (London: SCM, 1950), 13; James Brabazon, *Albert Schweitzer*, 141; Walter P. Weaver, *The Historical Jesus in the Twentieth Century*, 44. More recently Michael J. Thate has drawn attention to further connections with Nietzsche (*Remembrance of Things Past? Albert Schweitzer, the Anxiety of Influence, and the Untidy Jesus of Markan Memory*, WUNT 351 (Tübingen: Mohr Siebeck, 2013), esp. 150–51.
226. Schweitzer, *Quest*, 371.
227. Picht, *Albert Schweitzer*, 25, 269. With his piercing eyes and flowing moustache Schweitzer bore a striking physical resemblance to Nietzsche. He lived out his creed through his heroic career as a missionary doctor at Lambaréné in West Africa, interspersed with virtuoso organ tours in the Western world, and the writing of wide-ranging works on music, literature, theology, and civilization.
 As early as 1896 Schweitzer resolved that, "I would consider myself justified in living till I was thirty for science and art, in order to devote myself from that time forward to the direct service of humanity. Many a time I had tried to settle what meaning lay hidden for me in the saying of Jesus! 'Whosoever would save his life shall lose it, and whosoever shall lose his life for My sake

Nietzsche for the Paris Société des Langues Étrangères.[228] Later he reflected on Nietzsche's significance in *The Philosophy of Civilization*.

> Stripped of all its passion, then, Nietzsche's criticism means that only that system of ethics deserves to be accepted which springs from independent reflection on the meaning of life, and arrives at a straightforward understanding with reality. . . . [Nietzsche] was not the first to put forward in Western thought the theory of living one's own life to the full. . . . [He] brings to the theory the much deeper thought that by living one's own life victoriously to the full, life itself is honoured, and that by the enhancement of life the meaning of existence is realized. Men of genius and strong individuality, therefore, should be intent only on allowing the greatness that is in them to have free play.[229]

Schweitzer saw his own philosophy of reverence for life as a superior version of Nietzsche's. The heroic individualism honored by Nietzsche and exemplified in Schweitzer's career was embodied supremely in Jesus.[230]

This picture of Schweitzer's Jesus is reinforced by the publication of *The Quest of the Historical Jesus*, first complete edition, edited by John Bowden (2001).[231] Bowden has corrected and emended Montgomery's version to bring it closer to Schweitzer's German. In so doing, he toned down Montgomery's rhetoric and included changes that Schweitzer

---

and the Gospel's shall find it.' Now the answer was found. In addition to the outward, I now had inward happiness"; Schweitzer, *My Life and Thought*, 80–81.

We might also note that Schweitzer, like Nietzsche, was interested in Zarathustra (*The Kingdom of God and Primitive Christianity*, 33–41; cf. Nietzsche, *Thus Spake Zarathustra* [1883–1892]). Nietzsche was notorious for his scathing denunciation of Christianity, but he admired Jesus as a free spirit as against the Christ of religion. See Brend Magnus, "Jesus, Christianity and Superhumanity," in *Studies in Nietzsche and the Judeo-Christian Tradition*, ed. James C. O'Flaherty, Timothy E. Sellner, and Robert M. Helm (Chapel Hill: University of North Carolina Press, 1985), 295–318; Tyler T. Roberts, *Contesting Spirit: Nietzsche, Affirmation, Religion* (Princeton: Princeton University Press, 1998), 61–66; Nils Ole Oermann, *Albert Schweitzer: A Biography*, 116–19. See also below, chap. 17.

228. Schweitzer, *My Life and Thought*, 32.
229. Schweitzer, *The Philosophy of Civilization*, 2 *Civilization and Ethics*, 174, 176.
230. It does not seem coincidental that in the year following his Paris address on Nietzsche, Schweitzer concluded *The Mystery of the Kingdom of God* commending "the overwhelming heroic greatness" of Jesus (274).
231. See n1. Schweitzer himself made no changes after the 1913 German edition, which (apart from the addition of a new preface, now included in the "first complete edition") was reprinted in Gothic type in the 6th edition of 1951.

himself made to the text. I considered basing the present discussion on the "first complete edition" but decided against it on the grounds that the Schweitzer who shaped understanding of the quest in the English-speaking world for more than ninety years is not the Schweitzer of the "first complete edition" but that of Montgomery's translation. Nevertheless, some reflections on the "first complete edition" are in order.

Montgomery's translation, which ended with a duel of the Titans—Wrede battling for thoroughgoing skepticism and Schweitzer repelling the onslaught in the name of thoroughgoing eschatology—is now spun out into three chapters. In both editions the narrative ended with a terse account of the death of Jesus, the Nietzschean *Übermensch* who disdained pain: "At midday of the same day—it was 14 Nisan, and in the evening the Passover lamb would be eaten—Jesus cried aloud and expired. He had chosen to remain fully conscious to the last."[232]

The original edition closed with six pages of "results." The "complete edition" inserts three new chapters (amounting to 142 pages) before moving to a somewhat lengthier conclusion (*Schlussbetrachtung*). The three chapters deal respectively with "The Most Recent Disputing of the Historicity of Jesus," "The Debate about the Historicity of Jesus," and "1907 to 1912." As such, they fill a gap in our knowledge of some of the more recondite aspects of the original quest. In so doing, they bear testimony to the ongoing character of the debate, giving the lie to the view that once Schweitzer had spoken there was nothing more to say.

Schweitzer's conclusions were stated with less flamboyance but with greater precision and defiant certitude. He reiterated his acknowledgement of the negative character of his conclusions.[233] The new conclusion made it even clearer that Schweitzer used criticism and "scientific" method to overthrow criticism as it had come to be understood. The result was a *Sachkritik*—a criticism of the texts and of historical method in light of its subject matter (*Sache*)—which purported to get to the reality and enduring significance of Jesus, while discounting the particular concerns of the historical Jesus.

The conclusions lend further weight to the claim that Schweitzer may be considered the first postmodern theologian, in that he utterly

---

232. Schweitzer, *Quest*, 397. The "first complete edition" rewrites the final sentence: "He had refused the sedative drink (Mark 15.23) in order to remain conscious" (354).
233. Schweitzer, *Quest*, 1st complete ed., 478; cf. *Quest*, 398.

repudiated liberal values and all attempts to assimilate Jesus and his teaching in the modern world. "Nor will [Jesus] be a figure who by a popular historical treatment can be made as sympathetic and universally intelligible to the multitude. With the specific characteristics of his notions and actions, the historical Jesus will be to our time a stranger and an enigma."[234] "If, as has been attempted almost without exception in the past, Jesus' world-view is harmonized with ours as far as that is possible, this only weakens all that is characteristic in it, and affects the will manifested in that view as well. It loses its original quality and is no longer able to influence us in a fundamental way. That is why the Jesus of modern theology is so exceptionally lifeless. He is greater if he is allowed to remain in his own eschatological setting and, despite all that is strange to us in that way of thinking, can influence us then at a more elementary and powerful level than otherwise."[235]

At this point, Schweitzer, like Nietzsche (and Schopenhauer before him), called for a revisionary view of ethics in which the will played a primary role.

> The truth is that he cannot be an authority for us at the level of understanding, but only at the level of the will. His role can only be that of a powerful influence which elicits hopes and longings inherent in us and inspires us to heights and to a clarity we could not achieve if dependent on our own devices and without the influence of his personality. Thus he moulds our world-view to conform with his own, despite the great disparity in basic categories, and awakens in us those forces which are active in his own thinking.
>
> The ultimate and deepest knowledge of all things comes from the will. This means thinking that attempts to produce the final synthesis of observation and understanding in order to arrive at a world-view is directed by the will, which is the primary and irreducible essence of the personalities or periods concerned.[236]

---

234. Schweitzer, *Quest*, 1st complete ed., 478.
235. Schweitzer, *Quest*, 1st complete ed., 481–82. "That Jesus expected the final consummation to be realized supernaturally, whereas we can understand it only in terms of the result of moral effort, is merely the result of the change in fundamental thought-forms" (485).
236. Schweitzer, *Quest*, 1st complete ed., 482. The concept of *Wille zur Macht* ("will to power") is central to Nietzsche's philosophy and is characteristic of the *Übermensch*. In this regard Nietzsche was indebted to Schopenhauer (see below, chap. 17).

Schweitzer and the Old Quest

The virtues Schweitzer admired in Jesus were not the humility and love of the teacher revered by liberals but despised by Nietzsche. Schweitzer instead celebrated Jesus' determination to pursue his goals regardless of the cost. In the end, what mattered was not the historical recovery of Jesus but shared aspiration—not so much a Jesus-cult as a Jesus-mysticism.

> Our relationship to Jesus is ultimately of a mystical kind. No personality of the past can be transported alive into the present by means of historical observation or by discursive thought about his historical significance. We can achieve a relation to such a personality only when we become united with him in the knowledge of shared aspiration, when we feel that our will is clarified, enriched and enlivened by his will and when we rediscover ourselves through him. In this sense absolutely any deeper human relationship is of a mystical kind. Our religion, in so far as it proves to be specifically Christian, is therefore not as much a Jesus-cult as a Jesus-mysticism.[237]

The "first complete edition" contains an appreciation by Marcus J. Borg, a note by John Bowden the editor, and a foreword by Dennis Nineham. Together they constitute a reaffirmation of Schweitzer, bordering on hagiography. What is missing is in-depth reappraisal of Schweitzer's account of the quest and consideration of the vast literature since 1913, which has enlarged and challenged Schweitzer's perspectives on many matters. The "first complete edition" does not even update us on Schweitzer's own subsequent thinking on the kingdom of God.[238]

---

237. Schweitzer, *Quest*, 1st complete ed., 486.

238. Perhaps the nearest that it comes to an updating of Schweitzer's thought is the inclusion of the preface that Schweitzer wrote for the sixth (1950) edition (xxxv–xiv). In it Schweitzer acknowledged that he had not made any changes to the second edition of 1913. He did, however, offer clarification and reaffirmation of the first edition of 1906.

With regard to his relationship to Weiss, Schweitzer commented, "Johannes Weiss shows the thoroughly eschatological character of Jesus' preaching about the kingdom of God. My contribution is to find the eschatological clue, not only to his preaching, but also to his life and work" (xxxviii). Schweitzer maintained that it is "scarcely possible to answer" which of the two oldest gospels comes first. "The historical problem of the life of Jesus cannot be recognized, much less solved, from the fragmentary record of Mark. The differing narratives of the two oldest Gospels are equally valuable., but Matthew's fullness gives it greater importance, and Baur and his school rightly give it preference" (xli). Schweitzer left it to others to introduce order "into the chaos of modern lives of Jesus" and perform the task that he had performed for "the earlier period," though he did not believe that further advances would be made (xliiii).

The European Scene

The result is the virtual canonization of Schweitzer's text of 1913 as the definitive account of the original quest of the historical Jesus.

Schweitzer's work was a tour de force, but it was flawed. It was a celebration of heroes who swam against the stream. The book itself and Schweitzer's subsequent life were exemplifications. But the book did not meet with unqualified admiration. The leading authority on parables, Adolf Jülicher, complained that Schweitzer's Jesus had "sprung from his own head." Schweitzer was practicing "dogmatic, not historical criticism."[239] In the new edition of his great work on eschatology R. H. Charles commented: "Since Schweitzer's Eschatological studies show no knowledge of original documents and hardly any of firsthand works on the documents, and since further they make no fresh contribution to the subject, no notice is taken of him in this edition."[240]

More recently, James M. Robinson observed that the position that Schweitzer took on sources "only makes sense if he considered the canonical Gospel of Matthew to be the product of an eyewitness, which amounts to treating it as a definitive work of the apostle Matthew, the prevalent precritical view ever since Papias."[241] T. F. Glasson asked whether Schweitzer's literalistic eschatology had been a blessing or bane.[242]

---

239. Adolf Jülicher, *Neue Linien in der Kritik der evangelischen Überlieferung* (Giessen: Alfred Töpelmann, 1906), 5–6; cited from Walter P. Weaver, *The Historical Jesus in the Twentieth Century, 1900–1950*, 33. Weaver gives a survey of responses to Schweitzer (31–38).

240. R. H. Charles, *A Critical History of the Doctrine of a Future Life in Israel, in Judaism, and in Christianity, or Hebrew, Jewish, and Christian Eschatology from Pre-Prophetic Times till the Close of the New Testament Canon*, Jowett Lectures 1898–99, 2nd ed. (London: Black, 1913), viii.

241. James M. Robinson, "The Image of Jesus in Q," in *Jesus Then and Now: Images of Jesus in History and Christology*, Marvin Meyer and Charles Hughes (Harrisburg, PA: Trinity Press International, 2001), 7–25, here 10. Robinson noted that Schweitzer dismissed as absurd efforts to identify sources. He treated Matthew 10 as an authentic continuous discourse. Robinson also noted that Matthew 10:23, which played such a crucial part in Schweitzer's construction, was special Matthaean material absent from the mission discourses of Q and Mark.

242. T. F. Glasson, "Schweitzer's Influence: Blessing or Bane?" *JTS* 28 (1977) 289–302; reprinted in Bruce Chilton, ed. *The Kingdom of God*, Issues in Religion and Theology 5 (Philadelphia: Fortress; London, SPCK, 1984), 107–20. Glasson concluded that examination of four principal texts to which Schweitzer appealed—the Psalms of Solomon, Enoch, 2 Baruch and 4 Ezra (Schweitzer, *Quest*, 321)—lent no support for Schweitzer's eschatology. "The mystery is the astonishing way in which this baseless theory had dominated the interpretation of the Gospels for seventy years" (111).

Despite such strictures, cosmic eschatology has found enthusiastic support especially among the younger generation of scholars: Dale C. Allison Jr., *The End of the Ages Has Come: An Early Interpretation of the Passion and Resurrection of Jesus* (Philadelphia: Fortress, 1985), 115–41; Brant Pitre, *Jesus, The Great Tribulation and the End of the Exile: Restoration Eschatology and the Origin of Atonement*, WUNT 204 (Tübingen: Mohr Siebeck; Grand Rapids: Baker Academic, 2005); Scot McKnight, *Jesus and His Death: Historiography, the Historical Jesus and Atonement Theory*

Norman Perrin called for a deeper appreciation of the symbolic nature of the language of the kingdom.[243] N. T. Wright questioned whether Jews in Jesus' day ever expected an eschatology involving the end of the space-time universe. For Wright, eschatology is "the climax of Israel's history, involving events for which end-of-the-world language is the only set of metaphors adequate to express the significance of what will happen, but resulting in a new and different phase *within* space-time history."[244]

From the standpoint of critical history of the quest of the historical Jesus, Schweitzer's work raises questions. Unsuspecting readers would not guess that the origin of the modern quest was not to be found in Reimarus, but in the British deists whose work Reimarus had appropriated and whose ideas were already well known in France and Germany.[245] Schweitzer paid scant attention to philosophy and culture,[246] the contributions of theologians, or—in the first edition—of writers outside the borders of Germany and France.[247] Schweitzer read Reimarus through the eyes of Lessing. He knew that Reimarus's manuscript was accessible in Hamburg but was apparently content to take Lessing's extracts at face value. Lessing's part in the *Fragments* controversy was glossed over.

Schweitzer's work, like the quest in general, was characterized by scant interest in Jewish literature, religion, and culture and neglect of Jewish scholarship.[248] No mention is made of the work of Abraham

---

(Waco, TX: Baylor University Press, 2005), 58, 77–101; Edward Adams, *The Stars Will Fall from Heaven: Cosmic Catastrophe in the New Testament and Its World*, LNTS 347 (New York: T&T Clark International, 2007).

243. Norman Perrin, *Jesus and the Language of the Kingdom: Symbol and Metaphor in New Testament Interpretation* (Philadelphia: Fortress; London: SCM, 1976).

244. N. T. Wright, *Jesus and the Victory of God*, Christian Origins and the Question of God 2 (Minneapolis: Fortress, 1996), 208.

245. See above, chap. 4.

246. Vincent A. McCarthy, *Quest for a Philosophical Jesus: Christianity and Philosophy in Rousseau, Kant, Hegel, and Schelling* (Macon, GA: Mercer University Press, 1968); Brown, *Jesus in European Protestant Thought*, 57–104, 133–60.

247. An exception is Charles Christian Hennell's *An Inquiry concerning the Origin of Christianity* (1838), which was translated into German with a preface by Strauss, *Untersuchungen über den Ursprung des Christentums* (1840). Perhaps it was Strauss's involvement in the work and the fact that Hennell was instrumental in procuring Mary Ann Evans, better known as George Eliot, as Strauss's English translator that caught Schweitzer's attention.

Schweitzer acidly commented: "Strauss can hardly be said to have done himself honour by contributing a preface to Hennell's work, which is nothing more than Venturini's 'Non-miraculous History of the Great Prophet of Nazareth' tricked out with a fantastic paraphernalia of learning" (Schweitzer, *Quest*, 161). See further chap. 10, §1.1.

248. The 1913 edition of *The Quest* contained an augmented but unenthusiastic discussion of literature on rabbinics and the mention of Jesus by Josephus (*Ant.* 18.3.3). The latter is said to be

The European Scene

Geiger (1810–74), the leader of Reform Judaism and admirer of Strauss and Baur, who sought to reclaim Jesus for Judaism.[249] Ultimately, the reasons for these omissions might be traced to Schweitzer's aims and organizing principles. The *Quest* was a study in self-vindication, regarding the indifferent reception given to Schweitzer's 1901 dissertation on *Das Messianitäts- und Leidensgeheimnis*. In the interests of accuracy the *Quest* might have been properly titled, as Paul Wernle suggested in an early review, *From Reimarus to Schweitzer*.[250]

"either inauthentic or so extravagantly interpolated that it can no longer be presented as credible evidence" (Schweitzer, *Quest*, 1st complete ed., 359).

249. Abraham Geiger sought to apply the critical methods of Baur and Strauss to the Jewish understanding of Jesus. He practiced a form of *Sachkritik* that sought to identify the essentials of Judaism. The Pharisees were Jews par excellence in their struggle for equality and inner religious character. Their leader, Hillel, was a restorer and reformer, a calm and gentle teacher, in whose footsteps Jesus followed. Thus, Jesus was a Pharisee whose message became corrupted by Galilean influences.

The teachings of Jesus of which Geiger approved were Pharisaic, while those of which he disapproved were discounted as Galilean apocalyptic fantasy. The primary opponents of Jesus were the Sadducees. Passages in the Gospels critical of the Pharisees were judged by Geiger to be late interpolations. Absence of references to Pharisees in John was an indication of its late composition at a time when the Sadducees were no longer important.

On Geiger and his role in historical Jesus research, see Susannah Heschel, *Abraham Geiger and the Jewish Jesus*, Chicago Studies in the History of Judaism (Chicago: University of Chicago Press, 1998); reviewed by Colin Brown in *Shofar* 18, no. 4 (2000): 138–41.

250. Paul Wernle's review of Schweitzer's *Von Reimarus zu Wrede*, TLZ 31 (1906): 502–6; cited by Weaver, *The Historical Jesus in the Twentieth Century, 1900–1950*, 32.

CHAPTER 6
FROM OLD QUEST TO NEW

THE GREAT GERMAN classicist Ulrich von Wilamowitz-Moellendorff wryly recalled the regret of a fellow classicist over the discovery of the Greek magical papyri. The trouble was that they "deprived antiquity of the noble splendor of classicism."[1] The same could be said about gospel miracles, exorcisms, and first-century worldviews in the time frame marked by the history of religions school from the 1890s to the death of Rudolf Bultmann in 1976. The narratives deprived Christianity of noble splendor.[2]

This chapter examines the history of religions school and its influence on twentieth-century Jesus studies in Europe. It focuses on the following:

1. Wilhelm Bousset and the History of Religions School
   1.1. The History of Religions School
   1.2. Bousset's *Kyrios Christos*

---

1. Ulrich von Wilamowitz-Moellendorff, *Reden und Vorträge*, 2nd ed. (Berlin: Weidmann, 1902), 254–55, cited from Hans Dieter Betz's introduction to *The Greek Magical Papyri in Translation, Including the Demotic Spells*, 2nd ed. (Chicago: University of Chicago Press, 1922), xliii and li. Wilamowitz-Moellendorff admitted the blemish but did not regret the find. "For I do not want to admire my Greeks, but to understand, so that I can judge them justly."

2. Surveys of New Testament scholarship indicate marginal interest in miracles, healing, and the demonic for much of the twentieth century. Among others, see A. Roy Eckhardt, *Reclaiming the Jesus of History: Christology Today* (Minneapolis: Fortress, 1991); C. J. den Heyer, *Jesus Matters: 150 Years of Research* (Harrisburg, PA: Trinity Press International, 1998); Walter P. Weaver, *The Historical Jesus in the Twentieth Century—1900–1950* (Harrisburg, PA: Trinity Press International, 1999).

2. Bultmann, Form Criticism, and Demythologizing
  2.1. Theological Formation
  2.2. Form Criticism and Jesus
  2.3. John and Jesus
  2.4. Demythologizing the Kerygma
3. The New Quest of the Historical Jesus
  3.1. Unexpected Rise
  3.2. Abrupt Demise

1. Wilhelm Bousset and the History of Religions School

1.1. The History of Religions School. From the 1920s to the 1970s the Bultmann School set the theological agenda for much of European theology, but it was the history of religions school that set Bultmann's agenda, at least in gospel criticism. The German term *die Religionsgeschichtliche Schule* was given to a group of young researchers at the University of Göttingen in the 1890s, where they formed a "little faculty." Initially the term had a negative undertone, but it was quickly embraced by its members.[3] Theologically they were heirs to Albrecht Benjamin Ritschl; methodologically their research focused on the ancient world. The school had two major concerns. One was to situate the history and literature of Judaism and early Christianity in the context of Egyptian, Babylonian, and Greco-Roman religion and culture. Theological perspectives were to be replaced by strictly historical and cultural criteria. The other concern was to highlight the gulf separating the ancient world from the modern world and to identify what was of enduring value.

We have already encountered members who came to the fore toward the end of the old quest: Johannes Weiss, William Wrede, and Ernst Troeltsch. To this list must be added the names of Hermann Gunkel, Hugo Gressmann, Wilhelm Heitmüller, Hans Windisch, Richard Reitzenstein, Paul Fiebig, and Wilhelm Bousset. Larry W. Hurtado

---

3. Gerd Lüdemann, "Die Religionsgeschichtliche Schule," in *Theologie in Göttingen. Eine Vorlesungsreihe*, Göttinger Universitätsschriften, Serie A: Schriften 1, ed. Bernd Moeller (Göttingen: Vandenhoeck & Ruprecht, 1987), 325–61; Gerd Lüdemann and Martin Schröder, *Die Religionsgeschichtliche Schule in Göttingen. Eine Dokumentation* (Göttingen: Vandenhoeck & Ruprecht, 1987); Gerd Lüdemann and Alf Özen, *TRE*, 28:618–24.

commented: "Wilhelm Bousset's *Kyrios Christos* not only is the highwater mark of the German history-of-religions school of the early twentieth century but has determined the agenda for the scholarly study of NT Christology since the publication of the book in 1913."[4] Before discussing Bousset, note should be taken of the research of those who together built up databases for the work of Bousset and Bultmann.

The research of Richard Reitzenstein (1861–1931) on gnostic hymns led him to think that miracle stories likewise derived from pagan origins. His *Hellenistische Wundererzählungen* ("Hellenistic miracle stories") was divided into two parts.[5] The first part was devoted to aretalogy, drawing on accounts by Lucian, Horace, Damis, Philostratus, and others. The second part discussed the Wedding Hymn and the Hymn of the Pearl in the Acts of Thomas. Reitzenstein went on to study the mystery religions.[6] Also appearing at about the same time was *Antike Heilungswunder* by Otto Weinreich (1886–1972), which proved to be an influential anthology of Greco-Roman healing miracles.[7]

Paul Fiebig (1876–1949) edited several collections of miracle stories from the ancient world and Judaism, insisting on their relevance for the interpretation of the Gospels.[8] Fiebig's work drew a sharp reply from

---

4. Larry W. Hurtado, "New Testament Christology: A Critique of Bousset's Influence," *Theological Studies* 40 (1979): 306–17, here 306, referring to Bousset, *Kyrios Christos. Geschichte des Christusglaubens von den Anfängen des Christentums bis Irenaeus* (Göttingen: Vandenhoeck & Ruprecht, 1913; 5th ed., 1965); ET: *Kyrios Christos: A History of the Belief in Christ from the Beginnings of Christianity to Irenaeus*, trans. John E. Steely, with introductory word by Rudolf Bultmann (Nashville: Abingdon, 1970). Bousset replied to critics in *Jesus der Herr. Nachträge und Auseinandersetzungen zu Kyrios Christos* (Göttingen: Vandenhoeck & Ruprecht, 1916).

Several of Bousset's essays have been collected in *Religionsgeschtliche Studien. Aufsätze zur Religionsgeschichte des Hellenistischen Zeitalters*, ed. Anthonie F. Verheule, NovTSup 50 (Leiden: Brill, 1979). The most comprehensive account of Bousset's life and work is Anthonie F. Verheule, *Wilhelm Bousset. Leben und Werk* (Amsterdam: Uitgeverij Ton Bolland, 1973). See also Johann Michael Schmidt, *TRE*, 7:97–101. Some of the material in the following discussion previously appeared in Brown, *Miracles and the Critical Mind*, 130–33.

5. Richard Reitzenstein, *Hellenistische Wundererzählungen* (Stuttgart: Teubner, [1906]; 3rd ed., 1974). Reitzenstein taught at several universities before moving to Göttingen. See Peter Nagel, *RGG*[4], 7:255–56.

6. Richard Reitzenstein, *Die hellenistischen Mysterienreligionen nach ihren Grundgedanken und Wirkungen* (Stuttgart: Teubner, 1910; 3rd ed., 1927); ET: *Hellenistic Mystery Religions: Their Basic Ideas and Significance*, trans. John E. Steely, Pittsburgh Theological Monograph Series 15 (Pittsburgh: Pickwick, 1978).

7. Otto Weinreich, *Antike Heilungswunder. Untersuchungen zum Wunderglauben der Griechen und Römer* (Giessen: Töpelmann, 1909; repr., Berlin: de Gruyter, 1969).

8. Paul Fiebig served as acting director of the Institum Delitzschianum (1902) and became professor of New Testament at Leipzig (1930) (*BBK*, 2:31–32). His anthology of classical texts was subsequently expanded by Gerhard Delling, *Antike Wundertexte. Zweite völlig neu gestaltete Auflage*

The European Scene

Adolf Schlatter, who strenuously denied any connection between Jewish miracle stories and the New Testament.[9] Schlatter refused to date any rabbinic miracle stories before the time of Jesus and urged that a distinction be drawn between Palestinian and Babylonian stories. Fiebig's other contributions focused attention on the relevance of rabbinic parables for the study of Jesus' parables and the Sermon on the Mount.[10]

Wilhelm Bousset (1865–1920) taught as assistant professor of New Testament at Göttingen before moving to Giessen as full professor in 1916. He coedited the *Theologische Rundschau* (1897–1917) with his student Wilhelm Heitmüller. Herrmann Gunkel (1862–1932), the Old Testament scholar began his career at Göttingen, moved to Halle, and then Berlin. He became a full professor at Giessen (1907) before moving back to Halle, where he retired. Bousset and Gunkel were colleagues at Giessen. Together they edited the important series Forschungen zur Religion und Literatur des Alten und Neuen Testaments ("Investigations

---

des vorher von Paul Fiebig bearbeiteten Heftes (Berlin: de Gruyter, 1960). A rabbinic counterpart was his *Rabbinische Wundergeschichten des neutestamentlichen Zeitalters in vokalisiertem Text mit sprachlichen und sachlichen Bermerkungen* (Bonn: Marcus und Weber, 1911; repr., Berlin: de Gruyter, 1933).

Fiebig's analysis of *Jüdische Wundergeschichten des Neutestamentlichen Zeitalters unter besonderer Berücksichtigung ihres Verhältnisses zum Neuen Testament bearbeitet. Ein Beitrag zum Streit um die "Christusmythe"* (Tübingen: Mohr Siebeck, 1911) classified Jewish miracle stories according to type and date (Tannaitic pre-200 CE and Amoraic post-200 CE) and assessed their relevance to the New Testament.

Fiebig complained about failure to perceive the relevance of this material to the study of Jesus. The existence of rabbinic miracles demonstrated the mistake of linking miracles to messiahship (72). "In style of narrative the New Testament miracle stories show kinship with Jewish miracle stories in many details and in concise reporting, use of direct speech, frequent adornment of the narrative by Old Testament quotations, weight placed on authorship of the story, the words of the persons involved, whereas the dating of the story by day, month, and year totally recedes, as does locality" (74, author's translation).

In response to Arthur Drews's *Die Christusmythe*, 2 vols. (Jena: Diederichs, 1910–11); ET: *The Christ Myth*, trans. C. DeLisle Burns (London: Unwin, 1911), Fiebig claimed that legendary material in the life of Apollonius of Tyana was no reason to dismiss either Apollonius or Jesus as mythical (82–89). Fiebig dismissed the feeding and sea miracles of the Gospels (94–95). Jesus' awareness of his healing powers was alien to the modern mind. "For us today the most valuable element in the Gospels lies not in the miracle stories, but in the words of Jesus" (97–98).

9. Adolf Schlatter, *Das Wunder in der Synagoge*, BFCT (Gütersloh: Bertelsmann, 1912).

10. Paul Fiebig, *Die Gleichnisreden Jesu im Lichte der rabbinischen Gleichnisse des neutestamentlichen Zeitalters. Ein Beitrag zum Streit um die "Christusmythe," und eine Widerlegung der Gleichnistheorie Jülichers* (Tübingen: Mohr Siebeck: 1912, 1914); Fiebig, *Jesu Bergpredigt. Rabbinische Texte zum Verständnis der Bergpredigt ins Deutsche übersetzt, in ihren Ursprachen dargeboten und mit Erläuterungen und Lesearten versehen* (Göttingen: Vandenhoeck & Ruprecht, 1924); Fiebig, *Der Erzählungstil der Evangelien im Lichte des rabbinischen Erzählungstils untersucht zugleich ein Beitrag zum Streit um die "Christusmythe"* (Leipzig: Hinrichs, 1925).

in the Religion and Literature of the Old and New Testaments") from 1903.

Bousset's first book discussed the preaching of Jesus and criticized Johannes Weiss's eschatological interpretation of the kingdom of God. Bousset stressed the difference between Jesus' proclamation and Judaism.[11] Bousset went on to emulate Harnack with a book based on popular lectures. Whereas Harnack had sought to analyze the essence of Christianity, Bousset expanded his scope to the essence of religion.[12] "Above all Jesus frees religion from nationalism. In Judaism is bondage, here is liberation."[13]

In *Jesus* (1904) Bousset maintained that Jesus' "healing activity lies entirely within the bounds of what is psychologically conceivable, and this feature of the life of Jesus has absolutely nothing unique about it. The history of religion offers countless analogies to it down to the most recent times. . . . There are in fact but very few stories which record an absolutely miraculous and impossible event, or one for which no analogy can be found. These few must then be cast aside as the mere outgrowths of legend."[14]

Two seminal studies laid the foundations of Bousset's later work and that of the Bultmann school. *Die Religion des Judentums im Späthellenistichen Zeitalter* ("The Religion of Judaism in the Late Hellenistic Age") gave a comprehensive account of Judaism from the time of the Maccabees to the fall of Jerusalem.[15] Bousset, declared

---

11. Wilhelm Bousset, *Jesu Predigt in ihrem Gegensatz zum Judentum. Ein religionsgeschichtlicher Versuch* (Göttingen: Vandenhoeck & Ruprecht, 1892). Bousset insisted that the task of research was to understand the personality of Jesus as an outgrowth of late Judaism (6). In contrast with late Judaism, Jesus had a childlike trust in God (43), which was alien to the breathless, sickly longing for Jerusalem of late apocalyptic (44). Jesus' preaching with its emphasis on love of God and of one's neighbor renewed ancient prophecy (50). Jesus was concerned with real life, not speculative eschatology. The apocalyptic features noted by Weiss were to be explained as residual elements embedded in the language of Jesus' times (79).

12. Wilhelm Bousset, *Das Wesen der Religion* (Halle: Gebauer-Schwetszke, 1903; 4th ed. Tübingen: Mohr Siebeck, 1920); F. B. Low, trans., *What Is Religion?* (London: T. Fisher Unwin, 1907). As with Harnack's book, the title of the translation distorted the German. On Harnack's view of the essence of Christianity (*Das Wesen des Christentums*, 1901) see below, chap. 7, §1.

13. Wilhelm Bousset, *Das Wesen der Religion*, 161 (author's translation). "Jesus is the liberator. From all national pretensions, from national ties, from ceremony, from the letter, and from subservience to pedantry, Jesus liberates religion" (165).

14. Wilhelm Bousset, *Jesus* (Halle: Gebauer-Schwetszke, 1904); Janet Penrose Trevelyan, trans., *Jesus* (New York: Putman; London: Williams and Norgate, 1906), 48, 54.

15. Wilhelm Bousset, *Die Religion des Judentums im Späthellenistichen Zeitalter*, HNT 21 (Tübingen: Mohr Siebeck, 1903; 4th ed., with foreword by Eduard Lohse, 1966).

The European Scene

Eduard Lohse, showed that "pre-Christian Judaism was bound through many ties with the syncretistically determined surrounding world and contained fundamental presuppositions, which were taken up in primitive Christian proclamation."[16] Among them was Jewish apocalyptic with its message of the coming end, tribulation, dualism, conflict between God and the devil, the messianic Son of Man, judgment, hell, and new creation.[17] Late Judaism represented a transition from a national cultic religion to a universal spiritual religion. But it had not yet rid itself of national particularism and the alien influence of apocalyptic Persian religion. "There must come one who was greater than the apocalyptists and the rabbinic theologians, there must come about a reconstruction through the gospel, before the unity and vitality of a genuine and true piety could arise."[18]

The second of Bousset's seminal studies, *Hauptprobleme der Gnosis* ("Principal Problems of Gnosticism") gave an account of Bousset's research into Gnosticism, which among other things explored the idea of the primeval man and the figure of the gnostic redeemer.[19] Bousset's view that the latter predated Christianity was basic to Bultmann's understanding of New Testament Christology.

1.2. Bousset's *Kyrios Christos*. In the brief introduction to a reprint of Bousset's book, Rudolf Bultmann stated his belief that the central theme of Bousset's *Kyrios Christos* was also that of New Testament theology—the history of belief in Christ. In extending his account to Irenaeus, Bousset was seeking to tear down the wall separating New Testament theology from the early church.[20]

Bousset identified two stages of development in pre-Pauline theology.

---

16. Bousset, *Die Religion des Judentums* (4th ed.), v (author's translation). Lohse noted that Bousset saw impulses that led to the formation of Talmudic Judaism. However, Bousset was faulted for his lack of attention to this question. See Leander E. Keck, *Who Is Jesus? History in Perfect Tense* (Minneapolis: Fortress, 2001), 25–26. The editorial work of Hugo Gressmann in the third edition (1926) sought to remedy this defect.

17. Bousset, *Die Religion des Judentums*, 242–86.

18. Bousset, *Die Religion des Judentums*, 524 (author's translation). Gerd Lüdemann saw in Bousset's account of Judaism the powerful influence of Julius Wellhausen, who was a professor at Göttingen (1892–1913). See Lüdemann, *Theologie in Göttingen*, 343, 347. Anthonie F. Verheule (*Wilhelm Bousset*, 95) noted that for Bousset apocalyptic Judaism was the Judaism of Jesus and was thus to be considered as first step to the gospel.

19. Wilhelm Bousset, *Hauptprobleme der Gnosis*, FRLANT 10 (Göttingen: Vandenhoeck & Ruprecht, 1907; repr. 1973).

20. Bultmann's "Introductory Word" to the 5th German ed. of *Kyrios Christos*, 8–9, alluding to Bousset's subtitle.

The first stage was that of Jewish Christianity, which in turn was divided into two phases. The first phase was that of the primitive Palestinian community, which venerated Jesus as the apocalyptic Son of Man, appropriating not only the term but also the imagery of Daniel 7, as well as the pictures of the parousia in the Similitudes of Enoch.[21] The second phase saw the formation of the first three gospels, characterized by the dogma of the Messiah, miracle stories, the messianic secret, prophecy, and the sacrificial death of Jesus.[22]

The second stage of pre-Pauline theology witnessed the emergence of Hellenistic Christianity characterized by the bestowal on Jesus of the title *Kyrios*, "Lord," derived from the mystery cults. Thus, Jesus was turned into a cult-hero.[23]

The Christology of Paul introduced a "Christ mysticism" in which "Christ becomes the supra-terrestrial power which supports and fills with its presence his whole life. . . . Paul does not proclaim the faith of Jesus, but faith in Jesus."[24] Baptism "serves as an act of initiation in which the mystic is merged with the deity, or is clothed with the deity" (Rom 6:1–11; Gal 3:26–27).[25] In this cult mysticism the Lord and the Spirit are ultimately identical (2 Cor 3:17).[26] In Paul's Christ-Adam typology, "the first man Adam became a living being" in contrast to "the last Adam," who became "a life-giving Spirit" (1 Cor 15:45).[27] The source of these "perilous" speculations was not the Old Testament, but Jewish apocalyptic, Babylonian and Egyptian myths of the dying and rising god, and Gnosticism.[28] With Paul, faith in Christ, which was foreign to the primitive Palestinian community, "first appears as the center of religious life."[29]

John reconstructed the life of Christ, focusing on Jesus as the Son of God, while permitting the Pauline view of the Spirit to fade.[30]

---

21. Bousset, *Kyrios Christos*, 45–49. The idea of Jesus being the Son of David plays no significant part.
22. Bousset, *Kyrios Christos*, 69–118.
23. Bousset, *Kyrios Christos*, 136; cf. 152.
24. Bousset, *Kyrios Christos*, 154–55.
25. Bousset, *Kyrios Christos*, 158.
26. Bousset, *Kyrios Christos*, 160–63.
27. Bousset, *Kyrios Christos*, 172–81.
28. Bousset, *Kyrios Christos*, 181–200.
29. Bousset, *Kyrios Christos*, 200.
30. Bousset, *Kyrios Christos*, 211–45. "The concept of σάρξ is found in some few general expressions [John 1:13; 8:15; 1 John 2:16] and then in the favorite ideas of the Johannine writings

Christ is the supra-terrestrial Son of God who is in the Father's bosom and for this reason is in a position to reveal the divine secrets, who testifies of what he beheld and speaks what he has heard, whom the Father has sent into the world, in order to give eternal life to believers, who has come forth from the Father, who alone is from above, while all others are from below, the Son to whom the Father has given all his words, even including the greatest of them, judgment and resurrection. To him God gave the Spirit without measure; him God has consecrated and sealed. Christian faith is fully and totally faith in him (πιστεύειν τὸν υἱόν, εἰς αὐτόν).[31]

The "estrangement from the person of Jesus of Nazareth" in "the Johannine circle" is nothing short of docetism.[32]

It falls beyond our scope to trace the developments of the Christ cult that Bousset saw in the postapostolic age. However, it is important to note the role of Gnosticism as "a pre-Christian movement which has its roots in itself."[33] "Basically Gnosticism is the native soil of all bluntly supernaturalistic theory of revelation."[34] From Gnosticism derived Paul's pessimistic assessment of the flesh, his angelology, pneumatology, and spiritualizing of the resurrection.

Gnosticism contributed to Paul's redemption theology and was in turn fed by it. "*In Gnostic redemption theology, myth everywhere takes the place of the historical.* The development which began with Paul is completed here with uncanny speed. *If Paul has already woven a redemption myth around the historical figure of Jesus of Nazareth, here now the historical is altogether swallowed up by the myth.*"[35]

[John 1:14; 6:51–56, 63; 1 John 4:2; 2 John 7], that Christ has come in the flesh, and that he gives his flesh in the sacrament; and this heavy stressing of the flesh is very un-Pauline. Thus at this point the fire of Pauline Christ mysticism has almost completely disappeared. The Spirit has become the Spirit of the sacrament, Spirit of the office and of the confession, third person in the Godhead; the impetuous fire of elementary experience has burned down to slag"; Bousset, *Kyrios Christos*, 221.

31. Bousset, *Kyrios Christos*, 213–14.
32. Bousset, *Kyrios Christos*, 216.
33. Bousset, *Kyrios Christos*, 245.
34. Bousset, *Kyrios Christos*, 252. Matt 11:27 ("No one knows the Son except the Father, and no one knows the Father except the Son and anyone to whom the Son chooses to reveal him") is unparalleled in the Synoptic Gospels and is rooted in "Hellenistic piety." It became a *shibboleth* of the gnostics.
35. Bousset, *Kyrios Christos*, 267 (Bousset's emphasis).

In this trajectory of the development of early Christology Bousset located the miracle stories in the first stage of pre-Pauline theology, though not in the earliest phase of the primitive Palestinian community. They belong to the gospel phase that was characterized by a tendency to attribute miracles to the historical Jesus. Bousset believed that they could be separated from the earliest tradition.

> We are still able to see clearly how the earliest tradition of Jesus' life was still relatively free from the miraculous. It is characteristic that the older part of the evangelical tradition, as over against the narrative portion, was probably a collection of the words of the Lord (or a gospel consisting essentially of the Lord's words), in which miracle naturally played no role. At the most, here and there a catena of Logia was joined to a briefly told miracle story (e.g., the Beelzebul saying). Certainly when the Logia were collected there were many miracle legends of the life of Jesus already in circulation. But people did not consider these things to be the truly and important decisive matters.[36]

This conclusion was bound up with Bousset's evolutionary view of Christology predicated on the premise that the original gospel material was free from miracles. Bousset confidently separated the teaching and controversy narratives in Mark from the healing and miracle stories. Where Jesus' pronouncements were attached to miracle stories, the miraculous element was deemed to be a later embellishment. Bousset was reluctant to follow Strauss in attributing the supernatural elements in the Gospels to the myth-making desire of the early church to make Jesus fulfil the Old Testament. In a manner recalling David Hume, he suggested that "the fabrication of miracles in the life of Jesus probably took place as such procedures usually take place." But whereas Hume was content to attribute this phenomenon to a common human tendency to enlarge upon the truth, Bousset claimed, "People transferred to Jesus all sorts of stories which were current about this or that wonderworker and decorated gospel narratives that were already at hand with current miraculous motifs."[37]

---

36. Bousset, *Kyrios Christos*, 98.
37. Bousset, *Kyrios Christos*, 100.

The European Scene

Bousset's procedure consisted in drawing attention to putative parallels in pagan writings, with the implication that the gospel writers had drawn on them. It scarcely needed saying that such stories could be dismissed as incredible. Bousset felt no need to point out that the sources of the stories he cited were chiefly post-Christian or to dwell on differences. Nor did he feel it necessary to offer any account of how these particular stories might have influenced the gospel narratives. He was content to draw on the work of others[38] and take it as self-evident that the ostensible parallels furnished proof of borrowing, in order to enhance the stature of Jesus.

Bousset saw similarities between the gospel story of Jesus healing a paralytic and the story of Midas the vinedresser as told by Lucian of Samosata (c. 120–c. 180 CE) in his dialogue about credulity, *The Lover of Lies, or the Doubter*. The statement that "Midas himself picked up the litter on which he had been carried and went off to the farm"[39] was clear "proof" of borrowing. However, in Lucian's story the dying Midas had been bitten by a poisonous viper. He was healed by "a Babylonian, one of the so-called Chaldeans" who cast a spell and bound his foot with "a fragment which he broke from the tombstone of a dead maiden." The Babylonian went on to charm the snakes of the farm by ritual incantation and destroy them by breathing on them. Quite apart from its lateness, the story bears little resemblance to Jesus' healing of the paralytic, which focuses on Jesus' forgiving the man's sins and the skeptical attitude of the onlookers, who question whether Jesus has committed blasphemy since only God could forgive sins (Matt 9:1–8; Mark 2:1–12; Luke 5:17–26).

Whereas Lucian was patently skeptical of the stories he related, Pliny the Elder (c. 23–79 CE) uncritically assembled a vast and variegated lore in *Natural History*. An example was the physician Asclepiades of Prusa, who discovered a method of preparing "medicated wine for the sick" and "brought back a man from burial and saved his life."[40] Bousset did not make it clear whether he saw here a parallel to the raising of Jairus's daughter (Matt 9:18–26; Mark 5:21–43; Luke 8:40–56), to the widow

---

38. Bousset, *Kyrios Christos*, 101, where Bousset refers to Otto Weinreich, *Antike Heilungswunder*; Paul Fiebig, *Jüdische Wundergeschichten*; and Johannes Weiss, *RGG*¹ 3:2188.

39. Lucian, *The Lover of Lies, or the Doubter (Philopseudes sive Incredulus)*, 11 (Harmon, LCL) 3:337. Lucian may have been satirizing Christian miracle stories. The call to Midas to "Cheer up [θάρρει]" may echo Jesus' "Take heart [θάρσει]" (Matt 9:2). The Attic form θάρρει also had associations with the Eleusinian mysteries.

40. Pliny, *Natural History*, 7, 37, 124 (Rackham, LCL) 2:589.

of Nain's son (Luke 7:11–17), or to the centurion's servant (Matt 8:5–13; Luke 7:1–10; John 4:46–54). He appears to have conflated the stories in the interests of discerning common patterns: the coming of the healer, his appearance at the head of the bed, meeting the corpse on the bier, disparagement of the futile efforts of the previous healers, and the sudden accomplishment of the miracle.

In Pliny's account the intention was not to relate a miracle but to stress the skill of the physician. This point is emphasized in the account of the same event given by Celsus (14–37 CE). "Asclepiades, when he met a funeral procession, recognized that a man who was being carried out to burial was alive; and it is not primarily a fault of the art if there is a fault on the part of its professor."[41]

Bousset's discovery of parallels to the nature miracles of Jesus followed the same pattern. Stories of Rabbi Gamaliel II and an unnamed Jewish boy who prayed for deliverance in storms at sea suggested parallels to Jesus' stilling of the storm. But whereas Jesus stilled the storm with his word, in the Talmudic stories it was God answering the prayers of the devout.[42] Bousset omitted to point out that Lucian's story of the Hyperborean walking on water wearing peasant brogues also mentions him walking through fire and soaring through the air in broad daylight.[43] In the case of the Gadarene swine and other stories, Bousset admitted that proof was lacking, and that one was left to conjecture. Nevertheless, he had no hesitation in saying that the original form concerned "an amusing story of poor deluded devils who against their wills do what they most earnestly wish to avoid doing."[44] This story about an unknown exorcist was transferred to Jesus who, according to Bousset, never traveled to Gadara or to Gerasa.

The wine miracle at Cana (John 2:1–11) presented "a demonstrable

---

41. Celsus, *De Medicina*, 2, 6, 16 (Spencer, LCL) 1:115. The observation occurs in a passage commenting on the faulty and premature diagnosis of death. In Apuleius, *Florida*, 19, the story is treated as an absolute miracle. However, this work is dated much later (c. 160–70 CE).

42. Bousset, *Kyrios Christos*, 101; cf. *b. B. Mezia* 59b; *y. Ber.* 9.1; Matt 8:23–27; Mark 4:34–41; Luke 8:22–25.

43. Lucian, *The Lover of Lies*, 13 (3:339). The Hyperboreans were a legendary race of Apollo worshipers living in the far north who were revered by the Greeks. If Lucian was satirically identifying the Christians with them, the reference to the peasant brogues might be an allusion to Jesus' background. Similarly, the reference to flying through the air might allude to the ascension. The calling of "mouldy corpses" to life and the implication of magic might also reflect on incidents in the Gospels.

44. Bousset, *Kyrios Christos*, 101.

parallel" from the cult of Dionysos. A temple fountain of Dionysos on the island of Andros was said to flow all year long with wine. A similar story was told of a sacred place in Teos. In Elis on the eve of a festival three jugs were put in a sacred place and were filled overnight with wine behind locked doors. Bousset concluded, "Here, we may surmise, is the genesis of the wine miracle at Cana! People set the epiphany of the new God over against the epiphany of the god Dionysos and its miracle: And he revealed his glory and his disciples believed on him!"[45]

In his foreword to the 1965 reprint of *Kyrios Christos*, Bultmann pronounced Bousset's work "indispensable" for introducing "in incomparable fashion the questions which today are stirring New Testament scholarship." The demands of the history of religions school were brought "to fulfillment in a coherent and comprehensive presentation."[46] Bousset's convictions and agenda became the convictions and agenda of the Bultmann school. Bultmann's *History of the Synoptic Tradition* (1921) led the way.[47]

From then on it became axiomatic to separate Palestinian Christianity from Hellenistic Christianity and draw far-reaching conclusions.[48] Bousset's view of the Son of Man as an eschatological figure, different

---

45. Bousset, *Kyrios Christos*, 103. Bousset noted that the water-into-wine stories associated with Dionysos are related by Pliny, *Natural History* 31.13; Diodorus Siculus 3.66; Pausanias 6.26.1–2; Athenaios 1.61. He also noted that the early Christian festival of the Epiphany coincided with the beginning of the festival of Dionysos on the night of January 5–6. In early Christian liturgy January 6 was recognized as the anniversary of the wedding at Cana. The possible connection between the story in John 2:1–11 and Dionysos has been much discussed. Some see in the story an attempt on the part of the evangelist to claim superiority for Christ over Dionysos, while others see the story as symbolic of salvation through Christ.

For further discussion, see H. Van der Loos, *The Miracles of Jesus*, NovTSup 9 (Leiden: Brill, 1965), 590–618; J. D. M. Derrett, "Water into Wine," in *Law in the New Testament* (London: Darton, Longman & Todd, 1970), 228–46; Martin Hengel, "The Dionysiac Messiah," in *Studies in Early Christology* (Edinburgh: T&T Clark, 1995), 293–332. Bousset's account of the miracle's origin was followed by Rudolf Bultmann, *The Gospel of John: A Commentary*, trans. G. R. Beasley-Murray (Philadelphia: Westminster, 1971), 117.

46. Bousset, *Kyrios Christos*, 7.

47. Rudolf Bultmann, *Die Geschichte der synoptischen Tradition*, FRLANT 12 (Göttingen: Vandenhoeck & Ruprecht, 1921; 4th ed., 1958). The series was the organ of the History of Religions School for biblical studies. Its New Testament editor was Bousset. Bultmann's title was a concise statement of the School's program.

48. Works belonging to the era of the New Quest that make use of distinctions between Palestinian and Hellenistic Christianity include Ferdinand Hahn, *The Titles of Jesus in Christology: Their History in Early Christianity* (1963), trans. Harold Knight and George Ogg (London: Lutterworth, 1969); and Reginald H. Fuller, *The Foundations of New Testament Christology* (London: Lutterworth, 1965).

from Jesus, was further developed in the age of the New Quest.[49] His contention that the Kyrios title derived from the mystery cults found a modern defender in Siegfried Schultz.[50] Bousset's depiction of the Johannine Jesus anticipated by half a century that of Ernst Käsemann.[51] Bousset's identification of the Logia or sayings of Jesus as the earliest part of the Jesus-tradition free from miracle stories presaged the contemporary focus on Q as the earliest record of Jesus and his community.[52]

Outside the Bultmann tradition, Bousset's legacy has worn less well. Already in the 1920s Bousset's derivation of the Kyrios title from the mystery cults was subjected to devastating criticism by A. E. J. Rawlinson[53]

---

49. H. E. Tödt, *The Son of Man in the Synoptic Tradition*, trans. Dorothea M. Barton (London: SCM, 1965), 40–46; Hahn, *The Titles of Jesus in Christology*, 15–67; A. J. B. Higgins, *Jesus and the Son of Man* (London: Lutterworth, 1964); Fuller, *The Foundations of New Testament Christology*, 33–43, 142–50. Cf. Hurtado, "New Testament Christology," 310–12, who questioned this interpretation.

50. Siegfried Schultz defended Bousset's view in "Maranatha und Kyrios Jesus," *ZNW* 53 (1962): 125–44, claiming that *Mara* arose in Diaspora settings where pagan influence was strong. He argued that first-century Greek translations of the Old Testament did not use *Adonay* ("Lord") as a substitute for the tetragrammaton YHWH and that the Aramaic *Mara* ("Lord") was never so used. Thus, when the Aramaic church addressed Jesus *Mara*, it was an honorific and not a divine title, perhaps referring to the royal Son of Man. However, Hurtado questioned this interpretation, partly because of modern doubts over whether Son of Man was a pre-Christian title, partly because the evidence for Kyrios being a dominant cult-deity title is tenuous, and partly because, unlike *Mara*, Son of Man was never used in eschatological petitions (Hurtado, "New Testament Christology," 313–16). In Philo and Josephus, Kyrios is used as a divine title.

51. Ernst Käsemann, *The Testament of Jesus: A Study of the Gospel of John in the Light of Chapter 17* (1966), trans. Gerhard Krodel (London: SCM, 1968).

52. Leif E. Vaage, *Galilean Upstarts: Jesus' First Followers according to Q* (Valley Forge, PA: Trinity Press International, 1994); Christopher M. Tuckett, *Q and the History of Early Christianity* (Peabody, MA: Hendrickson, 1996); James M. Robinson, Paul Hoffmann, John S. Kloppenborg, eds., *The Critical Edition of Q* (Minneapolis: Fortress; Leuven: Peeters, 2000); John S. Kloppenborg Verbin, *Excavating Q: The History and Setting of the Sayings of Q* (Minneapolis: Fortress, 2000); Jon Ma. Asgeirsson, Kristin de Troyer, and Marvin W. Meyer, eds., *From Quest to Q: Festschrift James M. Robinson*, BETL 146 (Leuven: Leuven University Press, 2000); James M. Robinson, "The Image of Jesus in Q," in *Jesus Then and Now: Images of Jesus in History and Christology*, ed. Marvin Meyer and Charles Hughes (Harrisburg, PA: Trinity Press International, 2001), 7–25; William E. Arnal, *Jesus and the Village Scribes: Galilean Conflicts and the Setting of Q* (Minneapolis: Fortress, 2001).

53. "The phrase *Marana tha* [Come, Lord! 1 Cor. 16:22] is in fact the Achilles' heel of the theory of Bousset." A. E. J. Rawlinson, *The New Testament Doctrine of Christ*, The Bampton Lectures for 1926 (London: Longmans, 1926), 235. Rawlinson ridiculed Bousset's explanations. In the first edition of *Kyrios Christos* Bousset suggested that Aramaic-speaking Christians in Antioch imitated their Greek-speaking brethren and translated the Hellenistic title Kyrios into Aramaic. In *Jesus der Herr* (22–23) he suggested that it was used by Paul as a Jewish curse ("Our Lord will come and judge you!"). In the second edition of *Kyrios Christos*

and Ernst Lohmeyer.[54] More recently, Martin Hengel[55] and Joseph A. Fitzmyer[56] elaborated the argument that κύριος was a substitute for the divine name YHWH and that application of the term to Jesus amounted to divine honor.

Hengel also examined the theories of the history of religions school regarding the term Son of God, and found scant evidence in the Greco-Roman antiquity for the sending of a preexistent divine redeemer into the world.[57] No less fundamental is the work of Hengel and others in showing that the rigid distinction between Judaism and Hellenism is untenable and that the Palestinian Judaism of Jesus' day embraced Hellenism in varying degrees.[58] Not even Galilee escaped this influence. In short,

---

(84) Bousset returned to his former suggestion of a bilingual origin as "a possibility which cannot be ignored."

54. Ernst Lohmeyer, *Kyrios Jesus. Eine Untersuchung zu Phil. 2,5–11*, Sitzungsberichte der Heidelberger Akademie der Wissenschaften. Philosophisch-historische Klasse, Jahrgang 1927/1928, 4. (Heidelberg: Winter-Universitätsverlag, 1961); Ralph P. Martin, *Carmen Christi. Philippians ii. 5–11 in Recent Interpretation and in the Setting of Early Christian Worship*, SNTSMS 4 (Cambridge: Cambridge University Press, 1967); revised with new title *The Hymn of Christ* (Downers Grove, IL: InterVarsity Press, 1997); Colin Brown, "Ernst Lohmeyer's *Kyrios Jesus*," in *Where Christology Began: Essays on Philippians 2*, ed. Ralph P. Martin and Brian J. Dodd (Louisville: Westminster John Knox, 1998), 6–42; J. R. Edwards, *DMBI*, 671–73.

Lohmeyer's *Kyrios Jesus* was a reply to Bousset's *Kyrios Christos*. Lohmeyer argued that the only way to tell whether the title *Kyrios* was derived from Hellenistic mystery religions or from the familiar designation for God in the Hebrew Scriptures was to examine how it was used. Phil 2:6–11, which Lohmeyer identified as a Christian hymn, provided the earliest documentation. Lohmeyer contended that the hymn was thoroughly Jewish in orientation and that *Kyrios* was a title of divinity.

55. Hengel claimed that "the name that is above every name" (Phil 2:9) was the tetragrammaton YHWH, for which κύριος was substituted in the LXX; Hengel, "'Sit at My Right Hand!' The Enthronement of Christ at the Right Hand of God and Psalm 110:1," in *Studies in Early Christology*, 119–225. "God gave his unspeakable name to the Crucified and Exalted One. If the Exalted One is given the same unique name as God in Phil. 2:9, so also—presumably already in Rom. 8:34, but in any case in later texts, which speak of '*sitting* at the right hand of God'—he participates in the unique throne of God, the *kisse' hak-kabôd*, that is, also in the kingdom of God" (156–57). Hengel rejected the suggestion that the use of κύριος for the tetragrammaton in the LXX was due to Christian influence, and insisted that the LXX played a significant role in the introduction of the title κύριος into Christology (156n81). The practice of reading κύριος for the written יהוה (YHWH) was well established in pre-Christian times.

56. Joseph A. Fitzmyer, "New Testament *Kyrios* and *Maranatha* and their Aramaic Background," *To Advance the Gospel: New Testament Studies* (New York: Crossroad, 1981), 218–35. Fitzmyer concluded that use of the Kyrios title for Jesus "gives evidence of a veneration of Jesus by early Jewish Christians as the 'Lord,' as a figure associated with Yahweh of the Old Testament, even as one on the same level with him, without saying explicitly that he is divine" (229).

57. Martin Hengel, *The Son of God: The Origin of Christology and the History of Jewish-Hellenistic Religion*, trans. John Bowden (London: SCM, 1976), 34.

58. Martin Hengel, *Judaism and Hellenism: Studies in Their Encounter in Palestine during*

Bousset's attempt to differentiate between Palestinian and Hellenistic Christologies was based on faulty assumptions and oversimplified the realities of Palestinian life.[59]

In the meantime, Bultmann himself proved to be Bousset's heir in a double sense. Bultmann began his teaching career at Breslau, where he wrote *Die Geschichte der synoptischen Tradition*. Bultmann's stratification of the New Testament, his treatment of Jesus and the miracle stories, his account of myth and the New Testament's debt to Jewish apocalyptic and Gnosticism, and his desire to make the Gospel intelligible to the modern world followed the paths marked out by Bousset.

On Bousset's death in 1920, hastened by the privations of World War I, Bultmann succeeded to his chair in New Testament at Giessen.[60] He returned to Marburg, the center of radical theology in 1921, to assume the chair of his mentor, Wilhelm Heitmüller, and remained there until his retirement in 1951. In one important respect Bultmann and Bousset differed: Bousset belonged to the world of cultural Protestantism and religious liberalism, whereas Bultmann was committed to a radical Evangelical Lutheranism, which interpreted the kerygma of the death and resurrection of Jesus existentially.[61]

---

the *Early Hellenistic Period*, 2 vols., trans. John Bowden (London: SCM; Philadelphia: Fortress, 1974); cf. Hurtado, "New Testament Christology," 308–9. See also John J. Collins and Gregory E. Sterling, eds., *Hellenism in the Land of Israel*, Christianity and Judaism in Antiquity Series 13 (Notre Dame, IN: University of Notre Dame Press, 2001), which includes Hengel's "Judaism and Hellenism Revisited" (6–37).

59. Richard A. Horsley, *Archaeology, History, and Society in Galilee; The Social Context of Jesus and the Rabbis* (Valley Forge, PA: Trinity Press International, 1996), 178; cf. Eric M. Myers, ed., *Galilee through the Centuries* (Winona Lake, IN: Eisenbrauns, 1999); Jürgen Zangenberg, Harold W. Attridge, Dale B. Martin, eds., *Religion, Ethnicity and Identity in Ancient Galilee: A Region in Transition*, WUNT 210 (Tübingen: Mohr Siebeck, 2007); Seán Freyne, *The Jesus Movement and Its Expansion: Meaning and Mission* (Grand Rapids: Eerdmans, 2014); David E. Fiensy and James Riley Strange, eds., *Galilee in the Late Second Temple and Mishnaic Periods*, vol. 1, *Life, Culture, and Society* (Minneapolis: Fortress, 2014).

60. Bultmann finished writing *Die Geschichte der synoptischen Tradition* in December 1919. Originally, Bultmann wanted to dedicate the book to David Friedrich Strauss. He decided not to do so on the advice of Wilhelm Heitmüller. Eventually it was dedicated to Heitmüller and the Marburg faculty. From the second edition (1931) it was dedicated "To the Memory of Wilhelm Heitmüller."

Hermann Gunkel played a significant part in the appointment of Bultmann to Giessen. In turn, the appointment and Bultmann's appointment as coeditor with Gunkel for the FRLANT series swayed the publishing house of Vandenhoeck & Ruprecht to publish *Die Geschichte der synoptischen Tradition*. See Hamann, *Rudolph Bultmannn*, 105–6, 117–19; see below, n64.

61. Verheule, *Wilhelm Bousset*, 231–32.

2. Bultmann, Form Criticism, and Demythologizing

2.1. Theological Formation. In Britain scholars who adopted a radical view of the Bible were generally radical in their theology. In Germany it was possible to be radically liberal on Scripture and radically traditional in theology. Rudolf Bultmann (1884–1976) was heir to this tradition.[62] In 1956 Bultmann wrote a brief matter-of-fact review of his life.[63] The information that Bultmann gave is supplemented by the enthralling biography by Konrad Hammann. Not only does it give unique insight into Bultmann as a person; it also illuminates his close associates and contemporaries.[64]

---

62. Studies of Bultmann include John Macquarrie, *An Existentialist Theology: A Comparison of Heidegger and Bultmann* (London: SCM, 1955); Macquarrie, *The Scope of Demythologizing* (London: SCM, 1961); Carl A. Braaten and Roy A. Harrisville, *Kerygma and History: A Symposium on the Theology of Rudolf Bultmann* (Nashville: Abingdon, 1962); Pierre Barthel, *Interprétation du langage mythique et théologie biblique. Étude de quelques étapes de l'évolution du problème de l'interprétation des représentations d'origine et de structure mythique de la foi Chrétienne* (Leiden: Brill, 1967); Walter Schmithals, *An Introduction to the Theology of Rudolf Bultmann*, trans. John Bowden (London: SCM, 1968); Thomas F. O'Meara and Donald M. Weisser, eds., *Rudolf Bultmann in Catholic Thought* (New York: Herder and Herder, 1968); André Malet, *The Thought of Rudolf Bultmann*, trans. Richard Strachan with preface by Bultmann (Shannon: Irish University Press, 1969); Roger A. Johnson, *The Origins of Demythologizing: Philosophy and Historiography in the Theology of Rudolf Bultmann*, SHR 28 (Leiden: Brill, 1974); Günther Bornkamm, "In Memoriam Rudolf Bultmann," *NTS* 23 (1977): 235–42; Walter Schmithals, *TRE*, 7:387–96; Bernd Jaspert, ed., *Rudolf Bultmanns Werk und Wirkung* (Darmstadt: Wissenschaftliche Buchgesellschaft, 1984); John Painter, *Theology as Hermeneutics: Rudolf Bultmann's Interpretation of the History of Jesus*, Historical Texts and Interpreters in Biblical Scholarship (Sheffield: Almond, 1987); Martin Evang, *Rudolf Bultmann in seiner Frühzeit*, BHT 74 (Tübingen: Mohr Siebeck, 1988); Gareth Jones, *Bultmann: Towards a Critical Theology* (Oxford: Polity, 1991); David Fergusson, *Bultmann* (Collegeville, MN: Liturgical, 1992); David Fergusson, *DMBI*, 261–67; Russell Morton, in *EHJ*, 80–84; William Baird, *History of New Testament Research*, vol. 2, *From Jonathan Edwards to Rudolf Bultmann* (Minneapolis: Fortress, 2003), 280–86; Roy A. Harrisville, *Pandora's Box: An Examination and Defense of Historical-Critical Method and Its Master Practitioners* (Grand Rapids: Eerdmans, 2014), 182–98.

Bultmann was honored by his former students, the "Old Marburgers," on his eightieth birthday with the Festschrift *Zeit und Geschichte. Dankesgabe an Rudolf Bultmann zum 80. Geburtstag*, ed. Erich Dinkler (Tübingen: Mohr Siebeck, 1964). Extracts were published in English under the title *The Future of Our Religious Past*, ed. James M. Robinson, trans. Charles E. Carlston and Robert P. Scharlemann (London: SCM, 1971). Bultmann's essays have been collected in *Exegetica. Aufsätze zur Erforschung des Neuen Testaments* (1919–64), ed. Erich Dinkler (Tübingen: Mohr Siebeck, 1967); and *Glauben und Verstehen. Gesammelte Aufsätze* (1924–65), 4 vols., 8th ed. (Tübingen: Mohr Siebeck, 1980). The minutes of Bultmann's seminars have been published as *Sachgemässe Exegese. Die Protokolle aus Rudolf Bultmanns Neutestamentliche Seminaren 1921–1951* (Marburg: Elwert, 1996).

63. Rudolf Bultmann, "Autobiographical Reflections," in *The Theology of Rudolf Bultmann*, ed. Charles W. Kegley (London: SCM, 1966), xix–xxv. It was later updated to bring into the 1960s.

64. Konrad Hammann, *Rudolf Bultmann: A Biography*, trans. Philip E. Devenish (Salem, OR: Polebridge, 2013).

Rudolf Bultmann was the son of a Lutheran pastor. In his school years he was fascinated by the study of religion, Greek, and German literature. He began study of academic theology at Tübingen, where the professor that most impressed him was the Ritschlian church historian Karl Müller. He found Adolf Schlatter a boring disappointment but endeavored to keep this impression from his mother. In later life he became more appreciative.

After three semesters Bultmann transferred to Berlin, where he attended classes in Old Testament given by Herrmann Gunkel and church history by Adolf Harnack. The teaching of both, contrasting in content and style, made a lifelong impression. In Berlin he enjoyed the theatre, music, and culture. But the more intimate dynamic academic life of Marburg was more congenial. Bultmann returned to Marburg for his remaining semesters, concentrating on theology and philosophy.

The Marburg scholars who impressed him most were his future colleague Adolf Jülicher, his first mentor Johannes Weiss, and the systematic theologian Wilhelm Herrmann. Jülicher and Weiss figure elsewhere in this discussion. It is appropriate here to make brief comment on the impact of Hermann on both Barth and Bultmann. Some students at Marburg complained that Hermann's classes were like "advanced confirmation instruction." To Barth, Hermann was the most influential teacher of his student days because of his christological emphasis.[65] For Bultmann, Hermann's *Ethics* ranked among the six most important books in his life.[66]

In these years at Marburg an important role in the lives of Barth and Bultmann was played by Martin Rade (1857–1940), editor of the journal *Die christliche Welt* ("The Christian World"). Both were frequent visitors to Rade's home, and eager readers of the journal, which was an organ of Marburg theology. Bultmann was a member of its association, and

---

65. Eberhard Busch, *Karl Barth: His Life from Letters and Autobiographical Texts*, trans. John Bowden (London: SCM, 1976), 44–45.

66. Hammann, *Rudolf Bultmann*, 466. A work better known to English readers was Hermann's *The Communion of the Christian with God. Described on the Basis of Luther's Statements*, ed. Robert T. Voelkel, Lives of Jesus Series, ser. ed. Leander E. Keck (Philadelphia: Fortress, 1971). Voelkel saw the work as a polemic against metaphysics, which were "not the way into religion, but the way out of it" (xxv). The book was an appraisal of Jesus' significance in the Lutheran tradition.

James M. Robinson wrote his doctoral dissertation at Basel under Karl Barth, arguing that Herrmann became disenchanted with Ritschl; James M. Robinson, *Das Problem des Heiligen Geistes bei Wilhelm Herrmann* (Marburg: Gleiser, 1952).

in 1909 Barth, who at the time was theologically somewhere between Kant and the younger Schleiermacher, became assistant editor, reading manuscripts submitted by such eminences as Troeltsch, Bousset, Wernle, and Gunkel. The ethos of Marburg was a heady mix of liberalism and orthodoxy, which was worked out differently as Barth and Bultmann went their separate ways.

Johannes Weiss encouraged Bultmann to undertake graduate work. For his licentiate theology, he wrote a dissertation on the style of Pauline preaching and the Cynic-Stoic diatribe.[67] For his habilitation research qualification, which gave him the right to teach in the theology faculty, Bultmann wrote on a topic proposed by Adolf Jülicher: the exegesis of the Antiochene school, especially that of Theodore of Mopsuestia. In evaluating Bultmann's dissertation, Jülicher commented that the dissertation might well have been submitted to the church history department. Nevertheless, Bultmann had paid close attention to Paul's letters and should be granted the *venia legendi*. The other examiner, Wilhelm Heitmüller, concurred, as did the rest of the faculty. The degree was conferred, but the dissertation was published only posthumously.[68]

Life as a university tutor was not exactly easy, partly because of World War I, and partly because of Jülicher's antipathy to radical liberalism.[69] Although Bultmann was sorry to leave Marburg, he saw the call to Breslau as the opening of a new door. During his time at Breslau (1916–21), Bultmann married his fiancée Helene Feldmann and began his pioneering work on form criticism *Die Geschichte der Synoptische Tradition* (1921; ET: *The History of the Synoptic Tradition*, 1963).[70]

---

67. Bultmann was awarded the degree *cum laude*. His primary examiner, Heitmüller, had reservations but nevertheless recommended it for publication: Rudolf Bultmann, *Der Stil der paulinischen Predigt und die kynisch-stoische Diatribe*, FRLANT 13 (Göttingen: Vandenhoeck & Ruprecht, 1910; repr., 1984). Jülicher's report commended Bultmann's useful analysis of Paul and Greek culture. See Hammann, *Rudolf Bultmann*, 44–46. Later critics objected to the conflation of Stoicism and Cynicism.

68. Rudolf Bultmann, *Die Exegese des Theodor von Mopsuestia* (1912), ed. Helmut Feld and Karl Hermann Schelkle (Stuttgart: Kohlhammer, 1984); cf. Hammann, *Rudolf Bultmann*, 48–52.

69. Hammann, *Rudolf Bultmann*, 79–82.

70. Bultmannn, *The History of the Synoptic Tradition*, trans. John Marsh [from *Die Geschichte der Synoptischen Tradition*, 2nd ed.] (Göttingen: Vandenhoeck & Ruprecht, 1931) with additions and supplement, rev. ed. (Oxford: Basil Blackwell, 1972). Quotations below are taken from this edition.

Bultmann went on to produce a summary *Die Erforschung der synoptischen Evangelien*, 4th ed. (Berlin: Töpelmann, 1961); ET: "The Study of the Synoptic Gospels" (1934), trans. Frederick C. Grant, in *Form Criticism: Two Essays on New Testament Research*, by Rudolf Bultmann and Karl Kundsin (New York: Harper, 1962), 7–76.

We shall examine this work shortly. For now it is important to recognize that in the 1920s Bultmann welcomed the dialectical theology of Karl Barth with its protest against the liberal view that the Christian faith was a phenomenon of the history of religion. Looking back at his life's work, Bultmann reflected:

> It seemed to me that, distinguished from such a view, the new theology correctly saw that Christian faith is the answer to the Word of the transcendent God which encounters man, and that theology has to deal with this Word and the man who has been encountered by it. This judgment, however, has never led me to a simple condemnation of "liberal" theology; on the contrary I have endeavoured throughout my entire work to carry further the tradition of historical-critical research as it was practiced in "liberal" theology and to make our recent theological knowledge the more fruitful as a result.[71]

In 1925 Bultmann explained his critical method, which came to be known as *Sachkritik* ("subject-matter criticism"). This method "distinguishes what is said by what is meant and measures what is said by its meaning."[72] "Since exegetical work is work with concepts, and since the word of the text is never the subject matter itself, but its expression, this subject matter becomes available to the exegete only if he understands the word."[73]

Barth shared this basic assumption but worked it out differently. Barth practiced *Sachexegese* ("subject exegesis" or "theological exegesis"), which interpreted the text in light of what he considered to be its central concern. Barth's theology took the form of a reconfigured orthodoxy.

---

71. "Autobiographical Reflections," in Kegley, *The Theology of Rudolf Bultmann*, xxiv. Bultmann and Barth met as students at Marburg. Their lifelong correspondence is published in *Karl Barth—Rudolf Bultmann. Briefwechsel 1911–1966*, ed. Bernd Jaspert, Karl Barth. Gesamtausgabe, vol. 5, *Briefe*, 2nd ed. (Zürich: Theologischer, 1996); partial trans. by Geoffrey W. Bromiley, *Karl Barth—Rudolf Bultmann Letters, 1922–1966* (Grand Rapids: Eerdmans, 1981). Barth's *Römerbrief* (1922; 2nd ed.) ranked among the six most important books on Bultmann's thinking (see n66). See further David W. Congdon, *The Mission of Demythologizing: Rudolf Bultmann's Dialectical Theology* (Minneapolis: Fortress, 2015).

72. Bultmann, "The Problem of Theological Exegesis," in *The Beginnings of Dialectic Theology*, ed. James M. Robinson, trans. Keith R. Crim and Louis De Grazia (Richmond: John Knox, 1968), 236–56, here 241. Bultmann's article first appeared in *Zwischen den Zeiten* 3 (1925): 334–57.

73. Bultmann, "The Problem of Theological Exegesis," 255.

In the later volumes of *Church Dogmatics* Barth identified the pervasive theme of Scripture as the self-revelation of God in Jesus Christ, who embodies God's covenant with humankind and is the ground and goal of creation and reconciliation.[74]

Bultmann insisted that the *Sache* of Scripture was the Word of the transcendent God, the meaning of which had to be separated from the forms and myths of religion and culture. *Sachkritik* set Bultmann on a path that led from form criticism to demythologization of the Kerygma.

2.2. Form Criticism and Jesus. Bultmann saw himself building on the foundations laid by Weiss, Wrede, Schmidt, Wellhausen, and Gunkel, who had already applied form criticism to the Hebrew Bible. Together with two earlier works, Martin Dibelius's *Die Formgeschichte des Evangeliums* ("The History of the Forms of the Gospel," 1919)[75] and K. L. Schmidt's *Der Rahmen der Geschichte Jesu* ("The Framework of the History of Jesus," 1919),[76] Bultmann's *The History of the Synoptic Tradition* shaped gospel scholarship for the next half century.

---

74. Colin Brown, *Karl Barth and the Christian Message* (London: Tyndale, 1968; 2nd ed., Portland: Wipf & Stock, 1998). On this period of Bultmann's life, see Hammann, *Rudolf Bultmann*, 89–104.

75. Martin Dibelius, *Die Formgeschichte des Evangeliums*, 5th ed., with postscript by Gerhard Iber (Tübingen: Mohr Siebeck, 1966); ET from the 2nd ed. by Bertram Lee Woolf in collaboration with the author, *From Tradition to Gospel* (New York: Scribner's, 1935, 1971; Cambridge: Clarke, 1971).

Martin Franz Dibelius (1883–1947) was a pioneer of form criticism and an advocate of the history of religions school. He learned both from his teacher Hermann Gunkel (1862–1932) at Berlin, where he completed his ThD. Earlier he had obtained a PhD from Tübingen. Dibelius succeeded Johannes Weiss at Heidelberg. Dibelius stressed the importance of oral tradition prior to receiving fixed form in written texts.

Other works by Dibelius include *Die Botschaft von Jesu Christi. Die alte Überlieferung der Gemeinde in Geschichten, Sprüchen und Reden. Wiederhergestellt und verdeutscht* (Tübingen: Mohr Siebeck, 1935); ET: *The Message of Jesus Christ: The Tradition of the Early Christian Communities*, trans. Frederick C. Grant (New York: Scribner's, 1939); *Jesus*, 3rd ed., with addendum by Werner Georg Kümmel (Berlin: de Gruyter, 1939; repr. 1960; *Jesus*, trans. Charles B. Hedrick and Frederick C. Grant (Philadelphia: Westminster, 1949). See also Werner Georg Kümmel, "Martin Dibelius als Theologe," in *Heilsgeschen und Geschichte. Gesammelte Aufsätze 1933–1964*, ed. Erich Grässer, Otto Merk, and Adolf Fritz (Marburg: Elwert, 1965), 192–206; Kümmel, *TRE*, 8:726–29; D. B. Peabody, *DMBI*, 365–71; Michael Labahn, in *EHJ*, 157–60.

76. Karl Ludwig Schmidt (1891–1956), *Der Rahmen der Geschichte Jesu: Literarkritische Untersuchungen zur ältesten Jesusüberlieferung* (Berlin: Trowitzsch & Sohn, 1919; repr., Darmstadt: Wissenschaftliche Buchgesellschaft, 1964). *Der Rahmen der Geschichte Jesus* was based on Schmidt's *Habilitationsschrift* at the University of Berlin. The work was dedicated to Adolf Deissmann, who had greatly influenced Schmidt in his studies, and whose assistant Schmidt became. Deissmann's stress on locating Christianity in the Greco-Roman world left an abiding impression on Schmidt. Schmidt served as a *Privatdozent* in Berlin until he left for Giessen to succeed Bultmann in 1921. He moved to Jena (1925) and Bonn (1929).

On being dismissed from his chair at Bonn in 1933, Schmidt immigrated to Switzerland,

Whereas earlier critics held that Mark was the oldest source representing more or less a historical portrait of Jesus, Bultmann maintained that Mark was made up of disconnected units, which had themselves been shaped (and in many cases created) by the faith of the church. It was necessary to analyze the forms in which the stories and sayings had been preserved in order to detect their "life situation" (or to use Gunkel's immortal phrase *Sitz im Leben*[77]) in the early church.

In the second edition of *Die Geschichte der synoptischen Tradition* Bultmann expressed full agreement with the goal described by Dibelius. Form criticism was "not simply an exercise in aesthetics nor yet simply a process of description and classification: that is to say, it does not consist of identifying the individual units of the tradition according to various categories. It is much rather 'to rediscover the origin and the history of the particular units and thereby throw some light on the history of the tradition before it took literary form.'"[78]

The first part of *The History of the Synoptic Tradition* dealt with "The Tradition of the Sayings of Jesus." Bultmann divided the sayings into two main categories: apophthegms and dominical sayings. Apophthegms are "such units as consist of sayings of Jesus set in a brief context."[79] A typical example is the Sabbath healing of the man with the withered hand, which includes the saying: "Is it lawful to do good or to do harm on

---

where he held the chair of New Testament at Basel from 1935 until his death in 1956. In 1935 Karl Barth was dismissed from his chair at Bonn and moved to Basel, where he and Schmidt continued to be colleagues. Schmidt became the principal editor of the *Theologische Zeitschrift* (1945–53).

Schmidt's starting point in *Der Rahmen der Geschichte Jesu* was the question of the locations in which Jesus operated and the length of his public activity. The answer was complicated by the divergent topographical and geographical information given by the Gospels. On the basis of his minute examination of Gospel passages Schmidt concluded that "seen as a whole, only ruined fragments of an itinerary can be worked out. . . . The oldest Jesus tradition is conditioned by cult, and is therefore symbolic and super-historical [*bildhaft und übergeschtlich*]" (*Der Rahmen*, vi, author's translation).

Other studies include *Die Stellung der Evangelien in allgemeinen Literaturgeschichte* (Göttingen: Vandenhoeck & Ruprecht, 1923); ET: *The Place of the Gospels in the General History of Literature*, trans. Byron R. McCane, with introduction by John Riches (Columbia: University of South Carolina Press, 2002). See also K. L. Mühling, *TRE*, 30:231–32; E. Krentz, *DMBI*, 891–95; Byron R. McCane, *EHJ*, 549–50.

77. Martin J. Buss, "The Idea of Sitz im Leben—Critique and History," *ZAW* 90 (1978): 157–70; cf. Buss, *DMBI*, 499–503.

78. Bultmann, *The History of the Synoptic Tradition*, 3–4, citing Martin Dibelius, "Zur Formgeschichte der Evangelien," *TRu* Neue Folge 1 (1929): 185–216, here 187. See also Craig A. Evans, "Form Criticism," *EHJ*, 204–8.

79. Bultmann, *The History of the Synoptic Tradition*, 11; cf. 11–69. On the difference between Bultmann and Dibelius on apophthegms, see *Handbook of Biblical Criticism*, ed. Richard N. Soulen and R. Kendall Soulen, 4th ed. (Louisville: Westminster John Knox, 2011), 13–14.

the sabbath, to save life or to kill?" (Mark 3:4). Bultmann concluded: "Its language confirms what its content suggests as probable, that its formulation took place in the early Palestinian Church."[80] Matthew and Luke added characteristic embellishments.

Dominical sayings, which lacked the context of apophthegms, fell into five categories. Like the apophthegms, they reflected the circumstances of the early church. (1) Logia or Wisdom sayings had affinities with Hebrew wisdom literature, such as "Sufficient unto the day is the evil thereof" (Matt 6:34 KJV) and "Let the dead bury their own dead" (Matt 8:22; Luke 9:60).[81] (2) Prophetic and apocalyptic sayings included sayings created by the church about the blessedness of those persecuted for the sake of the Son of Man (Luke 6:22–23; Matt 5:10–12).[82] (3) Legal sayings and church rules were formulated to direct the practices of the early church. The saying about the founding of the church in Matthew 16:18–19 could not be genuine, for it deprived the church of "its radically eschatological character."[83] (4) The "I"-sayings of Jesus were predominantly the work of the Hellenistic churches, though a beginning had already been made in the Palestinian church. Christian prophets filled by the Spirit spoke in the name of the ascended Lord sayings like Revelation 16:15.[84] (5) Whereas the material so far noted grew out of an Aramaic environment, certain similitudes and similar forms may have grown out of a Hellenistic environment (e.g., Mark 7:20–23; Matt 11:27, par. Luke 10:22; Luke 21:34–36).[85]

The ultimate test of whether a saying was genuine turned on double dissimilarity between it and Jewish and Christian traditions. "We can only count on possessing a genuine similitude of Jesus where, on the one hand, expression is given to the contrast between Jewish morality and piety and the distinctive eschatological temper which characterized the preaching of Jesus; and where on the other hand we find no specifically Christian features."[86]

The second part of *The History of the Synoptic Tradition* was devoted

---

80. Bultmann, *The History of the Synoptic Tradition*, 12.
81. Bultmann, *The History of the Synoptic Tradition*, 73, 77.
82. Bultmann, *The History of the Synoptic Tradition*, 110.
83. Bultmann, *The History of the Synoptic Tradition*, 140.
84. Bultmann, *The History of the Synoptic Tradition*, 163.
85. Bultmann, *The History of the Synoptic Tradition*, 166.
86. Bultmann, *The History of the Synoptic Tradition*, 205; cf. Gerd Theissen and Dagmar Winter, *The Quest for the Plausible Jesus: The Question of Criteria*, trans. M. Eugene Boring (Louisville: Westminster John Knox, 2002), 103–12.

to analysis of narratives and legends. The latter consisted of those parts of the tradition, which "instead of being historical in character are religious and edifying."[87] Sometimes they include the miraculous, but they need not. The "cult legends" of the Last Supper do not contain anything distinctly miraculous.

A number of miracle stories occur in apophthegms (e.g., Mark 3:1–6; Luke 13:10–17; 14:1–6; 17:11–19).[88] Some miracles began merely as sayings and were converted into events. The healing of the paralytic (Mark 2:1–12) is a "miracle story proper," drawing attention to the faith that overcomes material difficulties and directing attention to the miracle worker who merits such trust. The story lacks any psychological interest in the sufferer. "The miracle working word, Jesus' command and its execution which demonstrates its effectiveness are typical characteristics, as is the impression made upon the onlookers."[89]

Similarly, the exorcism in Mark 1:21–28 "is plainly meant to give paradigmatic illustration of the ministry of Jesus."[90] The passage "exhibits the typical characteristics of a miracle story, and especially of an exorcism; (1) the demon recognizes the exorcist and puts up a struggle; (2) a threat and a command by the exorcist; (3) the demon comes out, making a demonstration; (4) an impression is made on the spectators."[91] By contrast Luke's handling of the incident (Luke 4:35) "shows that Luke no longer understands the motif, but instead emphasizes the healing itself as much as possible."[92]

Unlike Strauss who looked to the Old Testament as the quarry from which the early church dug its myths about Jesus, Bultmann turned to non-Christian literature and later rabbinic writings.[93] Although he saw broad analogies in other forms of literature, including the stories of the miracle worker Apollonius of Tyana,[94] Bultmann insisted that the Gospels were a unique form of literature.

---

87. Bultmann, *The History of the Synoptic Tradition*, 244.
88. Bultmann, *The History of the Synoptic Tradition*, 209.
89. Bultmann, *The History of the Synoptic Tradition*, 213.
90. Bultmann, *The History of the Synoptic Tradition*, 209.
91. Bultmann, *The History of the Synoptic Tradition*, 210.
92. Bultmann, *The History of the Synoptic Tradition*, 210.
93. Cf. Christian Hartlich and Walter Sachs, *Der Ursprung des Mythosbegriffes in der modernen Bibelwissenschaft*, Schriften der Studiengemeinschaft der evangelischen Akademien 2 (Tübingen: Mohr Siebeck, 1952); Günther Backhaus, *Kerygma und Mythos bei David Friedrich Strauss und Rudolf Bultmann* (Hamburg-Bergstedt: Herbert Reich, 1956).
94. Bultmann, *The History of the Synoptic Tradition*, 211, 221.

Bultmann's discussion of miracle stories is characterized by academic precision and wholesale allusions to tales of wonder from Ovid to the brothers Grimm. He observed that "the process of transferring some available miracle story to a hero (or healer or even a god) is frequently to be found in the history of literature and religion."[95] Bultmann's words might have been lifted straight out of Bousset.[96]

The third and final part of *The History of the Synoptic Tradition* dealt with the editing of the traditional material into their present forms as gospels. Mark was a collector of random stories with the result that "Mark was not sufficiently master of his material to be able to venture on a systematic construction himself."[97] The gospel of Mark was the first product of a new literary genre, which emerged in the Hellenistic church. In no sense could Mark be regarded as a biography recording historical events.

Mark was the creator of this sort of Gospel; the Christ myth gives his book, the book of secret epiphanies, not indeed a biographical

---

95. Bultmann, *The History of the Synoptic Tradition*, 228.
96. Cf. Bousset, *Kyrios Christos*, 100.
97. *The History of the Synoptic Tradition*, 350. Mark's gospel belonged to the genre of *Kleinliteratur*, "lesser literature" (372).
  Recent scholarship has challenged Bultmann's verdict on two counts. On the one hand, scholars now recognize that the canonical Gospels belong to the genre of ancient biography: David E. Aune, *The New Testament and Its Literary Environment* (Philadelphia: Westminster, 1987), 17–76; Graham N. Stanton, *The Gospels and Jesus* (Oxford: Oxford University Press, 1989); Dirk Frickenschmidt, *Evangelium als Biographie. Die vier Evangelien im Rahmen antiker Erzählerkunst* (Tübingen: Francke, 1997); David E. Aune, *The Westminster of the New Testament and Early Christian Literature and Rhetoric* (Louisville: Westminster John Knox, 2003); Richard A. Burridge, *What Are the Gospels? A Comparison with Graeco-Roman Biography*, 2nd ed. (Grand Rapids: Eerdmans, 2004).
  On the other hand, Mark is increasingly recognized as having tragic-epic structure with a prologue and epilogue with features that follow the canons of Aristotle's *Poetics* and Horace's *Ars Poetica*: Gilbert Bilezikian, *The Liberated Gospel: A Comparison of Mark and Greek Tragedy* (Grand Rapids: Baker, 1977); Friedrich Gustav Lang, "Kompositionsanalyse des Markusevangeliums," *ZTK* 74 (1977): 1–24; Benoit Standaert, *L'Évangile selon Marc. Composition et genre littéraire* (Nijmegen: Stichting Studenpers, 1978; repr. Brugge: Zevenkerken, 1984); Martin Hengel, *Studies in the Gospel of Mark*, trans. John Bowden (Philadelphia: Fortress, 1985); Dennis R. MacDonald, *The Homeric Epics and the Gospel of Mark* (New Haven, CT: Yale University Press, 200); Colin Brown, "The Jesus of Mark's Gospel," in *Jesus Then and Now*, 26–53. I see Mark as a tragic epic in five acts, with a prologue (1:1–15) and epilogue (15:40–16:8). The epilogue transforms the tragedy of Jesus' death into a triumph. The narrative epic form anchors Mark in the world of Greco-Roman literature. While it is broadly chronological, its form makes exact chronology difficult. The argument above in chap. 1 is based on this contention.
  It is ironical that Bultmann, an authority in the history of religion and culture, failed to explore the Gospels as ancient biography and Mark as an example of that genre.

unity, but a unity based upon the myth of the kerygma. . . . Matthew and Luke strengthened the mythical side of the gospel at points by many miracle stories and by their infancy narratives and Easter stories. But generally speaking they have not really developed the Mark type any further, but have simply made use of an historical tradition not accessible to Mark but available to them.[98]

The History of the Synoptic Tradition leaves the impression that while much can be known about the early church, relatively little can be known about Jesus himself. This impression was strengthened five years later, when Bultmann published his book on *Jesus* (1926; ET: *Jesus and the Word*, 1934), which initiated a series on "The Immortals: The Spiritual Heroes of Humanity in their Life and Work." In the meantime, Bultmann had formed a friendship with his Marburg colleague existentialist philosopher Martin Heidegger. Already the book on Jesus showed traces of existentialist interpretation, which was to characterize Bultmann's later work.[99]

Jesus is therefore the bearer of the word, and in the word he assures man of the forgiveness of God. . . . But if we return to the real significance of "word," implying as it does a relationship between speaker and hearer, then the word can become an event to the hearer, because it brings him into this relationship. But this presupposes ultimately a wholly different conception of man, namely that the possibilities for man and humanity are not marked out from the beginning and determined in the concrete situation by character or circumstances; rather, that they stand open, that in every concrete situation new possibilities appear, that human life throughout is characterized by successive decisions. Man is constrained to decision by the word which brings a new element into his situation, and the word therefore become to him an event; for it to become an event, the hearer is essential.

Therefore the attestation of the truth of the word lies wholly in what takes place between word and hearer. This can be called

---

98. Bultmann, *The History of the Synoptic Tradition*, 371.
99. Günther Bornkamm pointed out that it was not the case that Heidegger influenced Bultmann in writing the book but that the book attracted Heidegger to Bultmann. See Bornkamm, "*In memoriam* Rudolf Bultmann 20.8.1884–30.7.1976," *NTS* 23 (1977): 235–42, here 239.

subjective only by him who either has not understood or has not taken seriously the meaning of "word." Whoever understands it and takes it seriously knows that there is no other possibility of God's forgiveness becoming real for man than the word. In the word, and not otherwise, does Jesus bring forgiveness. Whether his word is truth, whether he is sent from God—that is the decision to which the hearer is constrained, and the word of Jesus remains: "Blessed is he who finds no cause of offence in me."[100]

2.3. John and Jesus. Twenty years after the first edition of *The History of the Synoptic Tradition* Bultmann published *The Gospel of John* (1941). It is widely regarded as one of the great commentaries on the Fourth Gospel written in the twentieth century. The commentary had been more than twenty years in preparation.[101] In 1880 Bernhard Weiss had published a relatively conservative commentary in Meier's series *Kritisch-exegetsicher Kommentar über das Neue Testament* (Critical Exegetical Commentary on the New Testament). It was planned that his son Johannes Weiss would undertake a revision of the gospel and letters of John. However, Johannes Weiss died in 1914. On the recommendation of Heitmüller, the publishers Vandenhoeck & Ruprecht reassigned the commentaries to Bultmann. The first installment was due in 1920. However, Bultmann completed the assignment on the Fourth Gospel in installments between 1937 and 1941. It was dedicated to Old Marburg Friends. Bultmann's commentary on *Die drei Johannesbriefe*, KEK 14 (1967), was published in retirement.

Bultmann's break with tradition began in the 1920s. John was not to be traced the to the eyewitness of John the son of Zebedee. Neither was John a mystical, spiritual gospel, written under the influence of Philo of Alexandria. Bultmann also rejected F. C. Baur's contention that the Fourth Gospel represented the ultimate Hellenization of the original Jewish prototype of Matthew.

Bultmann devoted relatively few pages to critical introduction. His

---

100. Bultmann, *Jesus and the Word*, 217–19. The translators changed the title with the approval of the author because they felt it better conveyed Bultmann's intentions.

101. Rudolf Bultmann, *Das Evangelium des Johannes*, KEK 2 (Göttingen: Vandenhoeck & Ruprecht, 1941); ET: *The Gospel of John: A Commentary*, trans. G. R. Beasley-Murray, ed. R. W. N. Hoare and J. K. Riches (Oxford: Blackwell; Philadelphia: Westminster, 1971); cf. Hammann, *Rudolf Bultmann*, 300–323.

From Old Quest to New

method became clear as the commentary proceeded. The gospel of John exhibited many of the features as the Synoptic Gospels.[102] It covered the same time frame. Many of the names and places were the same. Like the Synoptics, John consisted of miracle stories together with traditions of sayings and narratives. There were substantial common elements: the passion story, John the Baptist, individual logia, miracle stories, and narratives. John's style was even more Semitic than most parts of the Synoptics. No translation errors could be established. John was written in Greek, perhaps by a Semite who lived in a bilingual area like Syria.[103]

However, the polemical situation was considerably different from the synoptic controversy narratives. Admittedly there was the same continued opposition, but the Palestinian background had faded away. Opponents are described simply as *the Jews*, whereas "Jesus and his disciples appear as non-Jews" (8:17; 10:34). In John "the Jews represent the unbelieving world generally."[104]

From the perspective of form criticism, the isolated logia of the Synoptics are brought together in "sermonic compositions and parables," such as the I-am sayings that frequently introduce discourses like the good shepherd (chap. 10) and the vine (chap. 15). "Jesus does not act *like* a good shepherd, and is not *like* the real vine etc.: he is *himself* the Way, the Resurrection, as he is Truth and Life."[105] The conversations in the Synoptics more or less follow the rules of rabbinic discussion and debate. In John they are developed through misunderstandings of Jesus' utterances that have double meanings: being born anew (chap. 3), the Bread of Life (chap. 6), Jesus' departure (chap. 12). The technique is almost foreign to the Synoptics.

Miracles play an important part but have lost their formal independence. In John they are bound up with addresses and discourses. John "fundamentally contains but a single theme: the Person of Christ. The entire Gospel is concerned with the fact of his presence, the nature of his claim, whence he comes and whither he goes, and how men relate themselves to him. The miracles supply information about Jesus himself; the

---

102. Bultmann, *The Gospel of John*, 3–5.
103. Bultmann, *The Gospel of John*, 12. The argument for Syrian origin was developed in the course of the commentary. It was linked with Bultmann's case that John was a Christian response to Mandaean Gnosticism, which he traced to the region of Syria.
104. Bultmann, *The Gospel of John*, 4.
105. Bultmann, *The Gospel of John*, 4.

speeches are concerned with the speaker; the discussions revolve around the person of Jesus."[106] John's structure is determined by his understanding of Jesus, not *vice versa*.

Bultmann believed that John drew on two main sources. The first was a miracle or signs source. John recounted seven miracles, including two that have no parallel with the Synoptic Gospels: the wine miracle at the wedding at Cana and the raising of Lazarus. John identified the wine miracle at Cana and the healing at Capernaum as Jesus' first and second signs (2:11; 4:54). Bultmann took this fact, together with the precise number of seven miracles described in John, as indicative of a signs source upon which the author of the Fourth Gospel may have drawn.[107]

In addition to the signs source, Bultmann suggested that the author of John probably drew on a special source for his discourses. Often individual sentences within a discourse have "a peculiar poetic form" involving antithetic parallelism. An example is John 3:18.

> He who believes in him will not be judged;
> He who does not believe is already judged.

The discourses display three motifs. (1) The revealer presents himself and his significance. (2) Hearers are invited to come to him. (3) The consequence of accepting or rejecting the revealer is made known in promise and threat. The prologue (1:1–18), which was based on an existing hymn, sets out the themes of the gospel.[108] In addition, it must be noted that Bultmann proposed substantial rearrangements of the Fourth Gospel, which were reflected in the order in which he commented on the passages.[109]

---

106. Bultmann, *The Gospel of John*, 5.
107. Bultmann, *The Gospel of John*, 6–7.
108. Bultmann, *The Gospel of John*, 7, 13–83.
109. A list of passages in the order of the gospel text and the corresponding page numbers of Bultmann's discussion is set out in *The Gospel of John*, xiii. A comprehensive discussion is given by Dwight Moody Smith, *The Composition and Order of the Fourth Gospel: Bultmann's Literary Theory* (New Haven, CT: Yale University Press, 1965).

Bultmann's rearrangement has met with a mixed reception. Raymond E. Brown is among those who have proposed the alternative of several stages in writing (*The Gospel according to John*, AB 29 [New York: Doubleday, 1966], 1:xxi–xxviii). See also J. Louis Martyn, *History and Theology in the Fourth Gospel*, 3rd ed. (Louisville: Westminster John Knox, 2003); Urban C. von Wahlde, *The Gospel and Letters of John*, 3 vols. (Grand Rapids: Eerdmans, 2010).

Part 1 of the first edition of John Ashton's *Understanding the Fourth Gospel* (Oxford: Clarendon, 1991), 3–117, gives a comprehensive review of Bultmann. It is omitted in the second edition (2007).

At this point, Bultmann's form-critical approach to structure connected with his history-of-religions approach to the content and theology of John. It raised the question of John's relation to Gnosticism. Gnosticism was based on cosmic dualism: life and death, truth and falsehood, salvation and perdition.

John's relation to this world was complex. On the one hand, Bultmann detected close parallels with Mandaean Gnosticism. The Mandaeans may have been expelled from Judaism early in the Common Era. Their present-day descendants live in the territory between Iraq and Iran. Bultmann noted in their writings the figure of a redeemer "who is sent by the Father mostly in the primeval time, to impart the knowledge. Under his word men separate themselves into the children of the light, who are from above, and the children of darkness, who do not bear any soul of light in themselves. After his completed work of redemption the Redeemer ascends again and so make a way for the elements of light that follow him."[110] In addition, Bultmann saw links with the gnostic Odes of Solomon, and the Christology of Ignatius of Antioch was strongly influenced by Syrian Gnosticism.

On the other hand, John's theology was *anti-Gnostic*. There is no cosmic dualism in John. The divine *glory* is manifested precisely through the Redeemer becoming *flesh* (1:14).

> Man's lostness in the world is not the lost condition of a heavenly substance in the power of darkness, but the sinful turning of the creature from the Creator. In place of cosmic dualism steps a dualism of decision: life and death are not determined for all time on natural grounds, but depend on the decision of faith and unbelief. The Redeemer therefore does not bring a knowledge that illuminates men as to their true nature; rather he reveals to man his sin, and sets him before to live on the basis of the created world or from the Creator. John thus uses the language current in Gnostic circles to give expression to the Christian understanding of faith.[111]

---

110. Bultmann, *The Gospel of John*, 8. For Mandaean texts, see Werner Foerster, *Gnosis: A Selection of Gnostic Texts*, vol. 2, *Coptic and Mandi Sources*, trans. R. McL. Wilson (Oxford: Clarendon, 1974); cf. Kurt Rudolph, *Gnosis: The Nature and History of Gnosticism*, ed. Robert McLachlan Wilson (San Francisco: Harper & Row, 1987); Burton H. Throckmorton, *The New Testament and Mythology* (London: Darton, Logman & Todd, 1959).

111. Bultmann, *The Gospel of John*, 9.

John and Paul have much in common. Both replace the gnostic idea of substance with the historical dialectic of judgment and grace. But John was not dependent on Paul. John contains no discussion of law and righteousness. In John "the Jews" are not representatives of Jewish orthodoxy but "representatives of the unbelieving world."[112] John does not present a salvation history or furnish proofs from Scripture. "In reality Paul and John, independently of one another and in their respective concrete situations, give clear expression to the early Christian understanding of time and existence that in its essentials was already in existence before both."[113]

The Fourth Gospel originally ended at 20:30–31. Chapter 21 is clearly an addition. The reference in 21:24–25 to other works and deeds of Jesus indicates sources outside John. The arrangement of material is dictated by John's theological interest. Nevertheless, the gospel is given the appearance of a historical narrative.[114] Bultmann divided John into two main sections prefaced by the prologue (1:1–18), the martyrdom of John the Baptist, and the calling of the first disciples (1:19–51). Chapter 21 constituted a postscript. The first main part narrated "The revelation of the δόξα [glory] to the World" (chaps. 2–12). The second main part was "The Revelation of the δόξα [glory] before the Community" (chaps. 13–20).

A passage that captures the mood and spirit of Bultmann, the interpreter of John, is the following comment on John 3:18: "He who believes on me is not judged, he who does not believe is judged already":

> Thus the judgement is not a special contrived sequel to the coming and the departure of the Son. It is not a drastic cosmic event which is yet to come and which we must still await. Rather, the mission of the Son, complete as it is in his descent and exaltation, *is* the judgement. This means that the earlier naive eschatology of Jewish Christianity and Gnosticism has been abandoned, certainly not in favour of a spiritualizing of the eschatological process within man's

---

112. Bultmann, *The Gospel of John*, 10.
113. Bultmann, *The Gospel of John*, 10.
114. Bultmann, *The Gospel of John*, 130. The theme of Jesus the Revealer (2:23–4:42) begins by noting a visit to Jerusalem at the Passover and the effectiveness of Jesus' signs. Bultmann's exposition followed his thematic analysis of John (cf. vii–xiii). A characteristic of John is his account of multiple visits to Jerusalem in contrast with the Markan tradition, which describes only one climactic visit (Mark 11:1–15:39 par.).

soul, but in favour of a radical understanding of Jesus' appearance as the eschatological event. This event puts an end to the old course of the world. As from now on there are only believers and unbelievers, so there are also now only saved and lost, those that have life and those who are in death. This is because the event is grounded in the love of God, that love which gives life to faith, but must become judgement in the face of unbelief.[115]

Bultmann's *Gospel of John* was a *tour de force* of scholarship and insight. It was also vulnerable at its pivotal points: the question of sources[116] and the premise of the prior existence of Gnosticism. Theologically the commentary turned on its role as John's response to Mandaean Gnosticism. Yet as D. Moody Smith pointed out, the problem with the assumption of a Mandaean background is that "the Mandaean literature in its present form is centuries later than the New Testament, and it cannot be shown that they or their traditions antedate early Christianity."[117]

C. H. Dodd concluded his substantial review of Mandaeanism with a similar verdict.

> It seems that we must conclude that the Mandaean literature has not that direct and outstanding importance for the study of the Fourth Gospel which has been attributed to it by Lidzbarski, Reitzenstein and Bultmann, since it is hazardous in the presence of obvious and pervasive Christian influence, to use any part of it as direct evidence for a pre-Christian cult or mythology. . . . Alleged parallels drawn

---

115. Bultmann, *The Gospel of John*, 155. Bultmann quoted John in Greek, as he did throughout his commentary. I have given my own translation. The NRSV renders it in the plural so as to avoid male sexist language.

116. See above, n109. See also Robert T. Fortna, *The Gospel of Signs: A Reconstruction of the Narrative Source Underlying the Fourth Gospel*, SNTSMS 11 (Cambridge: Cambridge University Press, 1970); Fortna, *The Fourth Gospel and Its Predecessor: From Narrative Source to Present Gospel* (Edinburgh: T&T Clark, 1988); Robert Kysar, "The Fourth Gospel. A Report on Recent Research," *ANRW*, 2.25.3 (1985): 2390–2480; Kysar, *John: The Maverick Gospel*, 3rd ed. (Louisville: Westminster John Knox, 2007). The most extensive review of signs source scholarship is Gilbert van Belle, *The Signs Source in the Fourth Gospel: Historical Survey and Critical Evaluation of the Semeia Hypothesis*, BETL 116 (Leuven: Leuven University Press; Peeters, 1994). Van Belle concluded that despite its stimulus in promoting research, he was "inclined to refuse the semeia hypothesis as a valid working hypothesis in the study of the Fourth Gospel" (376).

117. D. Moody Smith, *The Theology of the Gospel of John* (Cambridge: Cambridge University Press, 1995), 14.

from this medieval body of literature have no value for the study of the Fourth Gospel unless they can be supported by earlier evidence.[118]

2.4. Demythologizing the Kerygma. Bultmann published *The Gospel of John* in 1941 at the height of World War II. He had been a member of the anti-Nazi Confessing Church from its founding in 1934.[119] During this period Bultmann had been contemplating writing a paper on Christian self-reflection. He was prompted by Wilhelm Kamlah's challenge to theology to grapple with existence and nonexistence in wartime Nazi Germany. The shape of Bultmann's response was indebted to the work that he had been doing on Mandaean Gnosticism and its rejection in the gospel of John. It took the form of a lecture on *Neues Testament und Mythologie* ("New Testament and Mythology") at a regional meeting of the Society for Protestant Theology in Frankfurt am Main on April 21, 1941, that was repeated at a general meeting of the Society in Alpirsbach on June 4, 1941. The lecture and its printed version ignited controversy from the start.[120] With its publication in German and English after World War II, the conflagration spread internationally.

The full title in English is "New Testament and Mythology: The Mythological Element of the New Testament and the Problem of Its Reinterpretation." It was published as the introductory essay in *Kerygma and Myth*.[121] The essay brought into sharp focus the implications of the work of the history of religions school and the picture of Christianity that Bultmann had been working on during the previous quarter century. Bultmann himself remarked that everything he said about the task of demythologizing could have been said thirty or forty years earlier.[122]

Bultmann dissociated himself from previous liberalism. Earlier liberals had held that some elements in the gospel story—the virgin birth, the magi, and the empty tomb—were mythical. Bultmann argued

---

118. C. H. Dodd, *The Interpretation of the Fourth Gospel* (Cambridge: Cambridge University Press, 1953), 115–30, here 130.
119. Hammann, *Rudolf Bultmann*, 267–310.
120. Hammann, *Rudolf Bultmann*, 323–36.
121. Bultmann, "New Testament and Mythology," trans. Reginald H. Fuller (1953), in *Kerygma and Myth: A Theological Debate*, ed. Hans-Werner Bartsch, vols. 1–2 combined with enlarged bibliography (London: SPCK, 1972), 1–44. In Germany the series from which these essays were taken, *Kerygma und Mythos*, continued into the 1970s, embracing a widening variety of topics.
122. Hammann, *Rudolf Bultmann*, 336. Hammann notes that Bultmann probably first used the term *demythologizing* in 1934.

that the entire thought world of the New Testament was mythical. The three-decker universe of heaven, earth, and hell, angels and demons, divine interventions, the heavenly redeemer, salvation, resurrection, and judgment were all mythical concepts used by the first-century church to express their faith. These mythical elements were drawn from the thought worlds of Jewish apocalyptic and Hellenistic Gnosticism.[123]

This mythological way of looking at the world is rendered obsolete by modern science, which does not admit divine interventions. What was once regarded as supernatural is now explained in terms of chemistry, physics, and psychology. Nevertheless, there was a point to myth. Although it did not represent an objective picture of the world as it is, it was a vehicle for expressing human awareness of an intangible reality.

> Myth is an expression of man's conviction that the origin and purpose of the world in which he lives are to be sought not within it but beyond it—that is, beyond the realm of known and tangible reality—and that this realm is perpetually dominated and menaced by those mysterious powers which are its source and limit. Myth is also an expression of man's awareness that he is not lord of his own being. It expresses his sense of dependence not only within the visible world, but more especially on those forces which hold sway beyond the confines of the known. Finally, myth expresses man's belief that in this state of dependence he can be delivered from the forces within the visible world. . . . The importance of the New Testament mythology lies not in its imagery but in the

---

123. Bultmann's understanding of Gnosticism, myth, and human existence changed radically through reading Hans Jonas. See Johnson, *The Origins of Demythologizing*, 116–23, 170–76, 240–54; James M. Robinson, "The Pre-history of Demythologization," *Interpretation* 20 (1966): 65–77; Anthony C. Thiselton, *The Two Horizons: New Testament Hermeneutics and Philosophical Description with Special Reference to Heidegger, Bultmann, Gadamer and Wittgenstein* (Grand Rapids: Eerdmans, 1980), 222–23, 256–57. For critique, see C. H. Talbert, "The Myth of a Descending-Ascending Redeemer in Mediterranean Antiquity," *NTS* 222 (1975–76): 418–40.

Jonas's dissertation on "Der Begriff der Gnosis" (1928) was supervised by Heidegger and was apparently read by Bultmann. It was later published as *Gnosis und spätantiker Geist*, vol. 2.1, *Von der Mythologie zur mystischen Philosophie*, FRLANT 45 (Göttingen: Vandenhoeck & Ruprecht, 1954; 2nd ed., 1966). Bultmann's earlier understanding of myth focused on its influence on the formation of the New Testament. Under the influence of Jonas, Bultmann widened the scope of myth criticism to become a tool of existential analysis of human existence.

On hermeneutical issues, see also Anthony Thiselton, *New Horizons in Hermeneutics* (Grand Rapids: Zondervan, 1992); Thiselton, *The Hermeneutics of Doctrine* (Grand Rapids: Eerdmans, 2007), 376–413; Thiselton, *Hermeneutics: An Introduction* (Grand Rapids: Eerdmans, 2009).

understanding of existence which it enshrines. The real question is whether this understanding of existence is true. Faith claims that it is, and faith ought not to be tied down to the imagery of New Testament mythology.[124]

This statement was, in effect, an application of the concept of *Sachkritik*, which Bultmann had formulated in the 1920s.[125] It was based on the distinction between what was *said* (the concepts of the mythical thought world) and what was *meant* (Bultmann's existential interpretation of their meaning). In his reinterpretation of the New Testament message Bultmann drew on the categories of Heidegger's existentialism. Paul's contrast between the life of faith and living according to the flesh was in fact a first-century anticipation of Heidegger's distinction between authentic and inauthentic existence.[126] The life of faith meant liberation from self-contrived, tangible security. As such it enabled human beings to be genuinely open to the future.

As in *Jesus and the Word*, the message of the Word was not something that we could question or prove objectively.

> The word of preaching confronts us as the word of God. It is not for us to question its credentials. It is we who are questioned, we who are asked whether we will believe the word or reject it. But in answering this question, in accepting the word of preaching as the word of God and the death and resurrection of Christ as the eschatological event, we are given an opportunity of understanding ourselves. Faith and unbelief are never blind arbitrary decisions. They offer us the alternative between accepting or rejecting that which alone can illuminate our understanding of ourselves.
>
> The real Easter faith is faith in the word of preaching which brings illumination. If the event of Easter Day is in any sense an event additional to the event of the cross, it is nothing else than the rise of faith in the risen Lord, since it was this faith which led to the apostolic preaching. The resurrection itself is not an event of past history.[127]

---

124. Bultmann, *Kerygma and Myth*, 10–11.
125. See above, nn72–73.
126. Bultmann, *Kerygma and Myth*, 25–26. Bultmann claimed that existentialism was indebted to Kierkegaard and Luther and thus indirectly to the New Testament.
127. Bultmann, *Kerygma and Myth*, 41–42.

From Old Quest to New

Bultmann's subsequent writings elaborated this theme. It dominated his remaining years of teaching and continued after his retirement in 1951. *Primitive Christianity in Its Contemporary Setting* was in some ways a counterpart to Bousset's *Kyrios Christos*, locating (as its German title indicated) Christian beliefs in the contextual framework of ancient religions.[128] Like Bousset's work, it predated the discovery of the Dead Sea Scrolls and the Nag Hammadi writings. Bultmann's eschatology was shaped by the exegesis of history of religions school and an existential hermeneutic. *Primitive Christianity* differed from Bousset's work in that it was written for a wider public than the world of technical scholarship.[129]

> [Jesus'] eschatological preaching is not the outcome of wishful thinking or speculation, but of his sense of the utter nothingness of man before God. . . . His claim that the destiny of men is determined by their attitude to him was taken up by the early Church and expressed in their proclamation of Jesus as "Messiah"—particularly in their expectation that he was to come on the clouds of heaven as the "Man," bringing judgement and salvation. His preaching was thus taken up in a new form, thus becoming specifically "Christian" preaching. Jesus proclaimed the message. The Church proclaims *him*.[130]

Bultmann's Christology was summed up in a previously unpublished essay on "The Christology of the New Testament."

> When the *primitive community* calls him Messiah, they are showing in their own fashion that they have understood him. The great enigma of New Testament theology, *how the proclaimer became the proclaimed*, why the community proclaimed not only the content of his preaching, but also and primarily Christ himself, why Paul

---

128. Bultmann, *Primitive Christianity in Its Contemporary Setting*, trans. R. H. Fuller (London: Thames & Hudson, 1956; reprint Collins, 1960), from *Das Urchristentum im Rahmen der antiken Religionen* (Zürich: Artemis Verlag, 1949).

129. Bultmann was awarded the Reuchlin Prize (1958) in connection with *Das Urchristentum im Rahmen der antiken Religionen*, which was his first postwar book. Later he was admitted to the Order *Pour le Mérite* (1969). The only theologians prior to him to receive the order were Adolf von Harnack, Albert Schweitzer, and Gerhard von Rad. See further Hammann, *Rudolf Bultmann*, 497–506.

130. Bultmann, *Primitive Christianity*, 110.

and John almost wholly ignore the content of his preaching—that enigma is solved by the realization that it is the fact, "*that* he proclaimed," which is decisive.[131]

Bultmann made the message of Jesus the presupposition of his *Theology of New Testament*, which began with the kerygma of the early church.

> *The message of Jesus* is a presupposition for the theology of the New Testament rather than a part of that theology itself. For New Testament theology consists in the unfolding of those ideas by means of which Christian faith makes sure of its own object, basis, and consequences. But Christian faith did not exist until there was a Christian *kerygma;* i.e., a *kerygma* proclaiming Jesus Christ—specifically Jesus Christ the Crucified and Risen One—to be God's eschatological act of salvation. He was first so proclaimed in the kerygma of the earliest Church, not in the message of the historical Jesus, even though that Church frequently introduced into its account of Jesus' message, motifs of its own proclamation. Thus, theological thinking—the theology of the New Testament—begins with the *kerygma* of the earliest Church and not before.[132]

Lectures delivered in 1951 at Yale, Vanderbilt, and other academic centers in the United States were published in *Jesus Christ and Mythology*.[133]

> What God has done in Jesus Christ is not an historical fact which is capable of historical proof. The objectifying historian as such

---

131. Bultmann, "The Christology of the New Testament," in *Faith and Understanding*, ed. Robert W. Funk, trans. Louise Pettibone Smith (London: SCM, 1969), 262–85, here 283. Bultmann had already articulated the theme in an article on "The Significance of the Historical Jesus for the Theology of Paul" (1929), in Funk, *Faith and Understanding*, 220–46.

In another previously unpublished essay on "The Question of Wonder" (in Funk, *Faith and Understanding*, 247–61), Bultmann maintained that "there is therefore only *one* wonder: the wonder of the *revelation*, the revelation of the grace of God for the godless, the revelation of forgiveness" (254).

132. *Theology of the New Testament* (1948), trans. Kendrick Grobel (New York: Scribner's; London; SCM, 1952) 1:3; cf. Hammann, *Rudolf Bultmann*, 417–30.

133. Rudolf Bultmann, *Jesus Christ and Mythology* (London: SCM, 1958); cf. Hammann, *Rudolf Bultmann*, 435–42. During this lecture tour Bultmann also delivered his Gifford Lectures at Edinburgh University (*History and Eschatology: The Presence of Eternity* [New York: Harper, 1957]).

cannot see that an historical person (Jesus of Nazareth) is the eternal Logos, the Word. It is precisely the mythological description of Jesus Christ in the New Testament which makes it clear that the figure and the work of Jesus Christ must be understood in a manner which is beyond the categories by which the objective historian understands world-history, if the figure and work of Jesus Christ are to be understood as the divine work of redemption.[134]

Bultmann went on to say:

> The invisibility of God excludes every myth which tries to make God and his action visible; God withholds himself from view and observation. We can believe in God only in spite of experience, just as we can accept justification only in spite of conscience. Indeed, de-mythologizing is a task parallel to that performed by Paul and Luther in their doctrine of justification by faith alone without the works of law. More precisely, de-mythologizing is the radical application of the doctrine of justification by faith to the sphere of knowledge and thought."[135]

In a manner echoing the apostle Paul (1 Cor 7:29–31), Bultmann concluded: "Let those who have the modern world-view live as though they had none."[136]

3. The New Quest of the Historical Jesus

Rudolf Bultmann made a deep and lasting impression on the lives of his students and colleagues. A case in point was his *Graeca*—Thursday evening meetings in his home devoted to reading classics in Greek with German translation, followed by a social hour of wine and academic gossip. Participants included Günther Bornkamm, Heinrich Schlier, Erich Dinkler, Gerhard Krüger, and Hans-Georg Gadamer. At the time Gadamer was studying philosophy under Martin Heidegger and

---

134. Bultmann, *Jesus Christ and Mythology*, 80.
135. Bultmann, *Jesus Christ and Mythology*, 84.
136. Bultmann, *Jesus Christ and Mythology*, 85.

was depressed over whether he was suited for a career in philosophy. In later life he expressed his debt to Bultmann for encouraging him to stay on course.[137]

The *Graeca* was an elite group that lasted some fifteen years. A larger group, drawn from a wider range of contemporaries, was the "Old Marburgers." Its roots reached back to 1924, when Bultmann and his colleague, Heinrich von Soden, founded the *Theologische Rundschau* ("Theological Review"). It was envisaged as a more theological successor to *Die Christliche Welt*.

From 1926 on, Bultmann invited graduates in theology to an annual reunion. Later the group was enlarged by the inclusion of philosophers—Gerhard Krüger, Hans-Georg Gadamer, and Karl Löwith. In addition to Marburg faculty, outside speakers were invited. They included Karl Barth, Friedrich Gogarten, and Martin Heidegger (who had moved from Marburg to Freiburg in 1928).

The annual meetings of the "Old Marburgers" became a forum for theological discussion. For many years they were convened by Erich Dinkler, who edited *Zeit und Geschichte* (1964). The volume sponsored by the "Old Marburgers" as a *Gift of Gratitude* to Bultmann on his eightieth birthday.[138] It was not so much a reflection of the Bultmann School as a spectrum of response to Bultmann's legacy. The "Old Marburgers" included members who were to figure in the New Quest: Ernst Käsemann, Günther Bornkamm, Ernst Fuchs, and Gerhard Ebeling. In retirement (1951), Bultmann continued to attend meetings until 1962. From then on he remained involved, but his declining years and ill health put attendance out of the question.

The remainder of this chapter will focus on the New Quest in Germany and Switzerland within the Bultmann School. The responses of Ethelbert Stauffer, Joachim Jeremias, and Oscar Cullmann will be reviewed in chapter 8. Reception of Bultmann and the New Quest in the United Kingdom is discussed in chapter 11. The rise and fall of the New Quest in America is discussed in chapter 14. The fact that publishers on both sides of the Atlantic published translations and replies ensured that readers were able to keep up with all sides of the debate. On neither side of the ocean did the New Quest succeed in displacing the Old.

---

137. Hammann, *Rudolf Bultmann*, 244.
138. See above, n62.

3.1. Unexpected Rise. The day before Bultmann's eightieth birthday he was presented at his home with a copy of the Festschrift *Zeit und Geschichte* by a delegation consisting of Erich Dinkler, Ernst Fuchs, Werner Georg Kümmel, and Hartwig Thyen.[139] Bultmann was gratified by the gift and its reception by the wider public. However, a rift on a range of issues began between Bultmann and one of his most prominent students in the 1950s.[140] Only later did it become recognized that one of the issues marked the beginning of a New Quest of the Historical Jesus. It was initiated at the 1953 meeting of the "Old Marburgers" by Ernst Käsemann's paper on "The Problem of the Historical Jesus."[141]

Ernst Käsemann. Ernst Käsemann (1906–98) received his doctorate from Marburg with a dissertation under Bultmann on *Leib und Leib Christi* (1933) ("Body and Body of Christ").[142] His radical opposition to the Nazis led to his arrest (1937). In prison Käsemann was able to work on a manuscript for his habilitation on the pilgrim people of God in Hebrews.[143] His writings brought theology to bear on church life. In World War II Käsemann was drafted. After the war, he held academic appointments at Mainz (1946–51), Göttingen (1951–59), and Tübingen (1959–71).

Käsemann's paper on "The Problem of the Historical Jesus" protested fidelity to Bultmannian methodology and disavowed any attempt

---

139. Hammann, *Rudolf Bultmann*, 497–98.

140. Hammann, *Rudolf Bultmann*, 473–79.

141. Ernst Käsemann, *Essays on New Testament Themes*, SBT 41, trans. W.J. Montague (London: SCM; Naperville, IL: Allenson, 1964), 15–47. On the New Quest, see James M. Robinson, *A New Quest of the Historical Jesus*, SBT 25 (London: SCM; Naperville, IL: Allenson, 1959); repr. in *A New Quest of the Historical Jesus and Other Essays* (Philadelphia: Fortress, 1983); Anthony C. Thiselton, "Hermeneutical Approaches to Christology," *The Hermeneutics of Doctrine* (Grand Rapids: Eerdmans, 2007), 376–413; R. P. Martin, *DMBI*, 601–6; Michael Labahn, *EHJ*, 352–54.

The term *New Quest* was not coined by Robinson but by his British publisher (*A New Quest of the Historical Jesus*, 5). On Robinson and the New Quest in America, see below, chap. 14. A bibliography of Käsemann's writings is given in *Rechtfertigung. Festschrift für Ernst Käsemann*, ed. Johannes Friedrich, Wolfgang Pöhlmann, and Peter Stuhlmacher (Tübingen: Mohr Siebeck; Göttingen: Vandenhoeck & Ruprecht, 1976), 593–604. Paul F. M. Zahl, "A Tribute to Ernst Käsemann and a Theological Testament," *ATR* 80 (1998): 382–94, contains personal letters written in Käsemann's last years. The disclosure that Käsemann's personal heroes were F. C. Baur and Martin Luther helps to explain Käsemann's potent blend of radical criticism and radical faith.

142. Ernst Käsemann, *Leib und Leib Christi. Eine Untersuchung zur Paulinischen Begrifflichkeit*, BHTh 9 (Tübingen: Mohr Siebeck, 1933).

143. Ernst Käsemann, *Das wandernde Gottesvolk. Eine Untersuchung zum Hebräerbrief*, FRLANT 55 (Göttingen: Vandenhoeck & Ruprecht, 1939; 2nd ed., 1957); ET: *The Wandering People of God: An Investigation of the Letter to the Hebrews*, trans. Roy A. Harrisville and Irving L. Sandberg (Minneapolis: Augsburg, 1984).

to write a biography of Jesus. Nevertheless, Käsemann feared relapse into docetism, if the exalted Lord of the kerygma was detached from the humiliated Lord in history. The way forward was to discover the earthly Jesus through the kerygma. "Jesus did not come to proclaim general religious and moral truths, but to tell of the *basileia* [kingdom] that had dawned in grace and demand."[144] Jesus did not preach realized eschatology; he inaugurated it.

> The problem of the historical Jesus is not our invention, but the riddle which he himself sets us. The historian may establish the existence of this riddle, but he is unable to solve it. It is solved by those who since the Cross and Resurrection confess him as that which, in the days of his flesh, he never claimed to be and yet was—their Lord, and the bringer of the liberty of the children of God, which is the correlate of the kingdom of God. For to his particularity there corresponds the particularity of faith, for which the real history of Jesus is always happening afresh; it is now the history of the exalted Lord, but it does not cease to be the earthly history it once was, in which the call and the claim of the Gospel are encountered.[145]

In an encyclopedia article, Käsemann linked the miracle stories of the Gospels with eschatology, though not in a simplistic way.[146] Käsemann noted, "The most dependable tradition testifies to Jesus' gift of healing (Mk 1:30). He saw his inspiration and message confirmed in the power of the exorcist, and on that account got into conflict with family and the Jewish authorities (Mk 3:20ff.)."[147] Jesus differed from John the Baptist, the Qumran leadership, and Hanina ben Dosa, who was mighty in prayer, in that only Jesus linked miracles and eschatology.

The miracle narratives were shaped by Jewish-Hellenistic aretalogy. They reflect more than any other genre the complex path from oral tradition to redaction. Mark delights in miracle stories. He presents Jesus as a "divine man," whose miracles anticipate the glory of the risen Christ.

---

144. Käsemann, *Essays on New Testament Themes*, 45. On Käsemann and the criterion of dissimilarity see Theissen and Winter, *The Quest for the Plausible Jesus*, 122–24.
145. Käsemann, *Essays on New Testament Themes*, 46–47.
146. Ernst Käsemann, "Wunder," in *RGG*³ (1962) 6:1835–37.
147. Käsemann, "Wunder," 1835 (my translation).

Matthew reduces the miraculous element, linking it with prophecy of the servant and God's mercy to his people. He allegorizes the stilling of the storm. John was the first evangelist to link miracles with Jesus' fate (John 11:45–53; 12:9–10). John's selection (20:30–31) drew on a source, depicting miracles as signs of the creator and redeemer. For Luke, the miracles point to Jesus as Son of God and the apostles as his delegates propagating his kingdom in the power of the Spirit.

"Historical criticism shows that there are no demonstrable miracles." *Sachkritik*, which distinguishes between what is said by what is meant and judges the former by the latter, is essential, particularly with regard to the depiction of Jesus as a "divine man." On the other hand, the miraculous is embedded in the kerygma, pointing to the fact that God wills to be grasped eschatologically and in the physicality of creation.

In 1966 Käsemann delivered the Schaffer Lectures at Yale on *The Testament of Jesus*.[148] It was a study of John 17. The lectures were delivered in the wake of Bultmann's rebuke to Käsemann and other colleagues associated with the New Quest in an address he gave at the Heidelberg Academy of Sciences in 1959. Bultmann's address will be discussed shortly. In the meantime, we may note that the dominant motif in John 17 was the glory of Christ. The dominant theme of Bultmann's Commentary on *The Gospel of John* was the revelation of *glory* to the world, followed by the revelation of *glory* before the community of believers.

Käsemann observed: "If the formula of [Jesus'] commission through the Father and his unity with the Father are isolated from each other, the result will be subordinationism or ditheism. Both formulae are correlative and complementary, because only together do they describe the truth that Jesus is nothing but the revealer of God and therefore belongs totally on the side of God while he is on earth."[149]

The road traveled by Jesus, according to John, was not a paradox of glory hidden in lowliness. Bultmann correctly saw that the divine hiddenness in John was the *consequence* of God's self-revelation.[150] Käsemann was led to the conclusion:

---

148. Ernst Käsemann, *The Testament of Jesus: A Study of the Gospel of John in the Light of Chapter 17*, trans. Gerhard Grobel (London: SCM, 1968). The German text was entitled *Jesu letzte Wille nach Johannes 17* (Tübingen: Mohr Siebeck, 1966).
149. Käsemann, *The Testament of Jesus*, 11.
150. Käsemann, *The Testament of Jesus*, 12; cf. Bultmann, *Theology of the New Testament*, 2:47–48.

One can hardly fail to recognize the danger of [John's] christology of glory, namely the danger of docetism. It is present in a still naïve, unreflected form and it has not yet been recognized by the Evangelist or his community. The following Christian generations were enchanted with John's christology of glory. Consequently the question 'Who is Jesus?' remained alive among them. . . . We too have to give an answer to the question at the centre of the Christian message. From John we must learn that this is the question of the right christology, and we have to recognize that he was able to give an answer only in the form of a naïve docetism. Thus we are forced to engage in dogmatics. An undogmatic faith is, at the very least, a decision against the Fourth Gospel.[151]

Käsemann's logic led him to conclude that, "From the historical point of view, the Church committed an error when it declared [John's] Gospel to be orthodox." Whether we regard it as a theological error depends on who Jesus is for us.[152] Käsemann's view of John's naïve docetic Christology prompted numerous replies that John's narrative also stressed the humanity of Jesus.[153] Like Käsemann, they were also critical of Bultmann.

Ernst Fuchs. The proposal to encounter the historical Jesus through faith in response to the kerygma was further developed by Ernst Fuchs (1903–83), who became professor of New Testament and hermeneutics at Marburg (1961–70).[154] Fuchs devoted a guest lecture at Zürich in 1956 to "The Question of the Historical Jesus."[155] Working backward from the

---

151. Käsemann, *The Testament of Jesus*, 26.
152. Käsemann, *The Testament of Jesus*, 77–78.
153. W. Nicol, *The Sēmeia in the Fourth Gospel: Tradition and Redaction*, NovTSup 32 (Leiden: Brill, 1972); Marianne Meye Thompson, *The Humanity of Jesus in the Fourth Gospel: An Investigation of the Place of the Fourth Gospel in the Johannine School* (Philadelphia: Fortress, 1988); Udo Schnelle, *Antidocetic Christology in the Gospel of John*, trans. Linda M. Maloney (Minneapolis: Fortress, [1987] 1992).
154. Fuchs completed his studies at Marburg (1924–25, 1927–29), where he was strongly influenced by Bultmann. His doctoral thesis was on *Glaube und Tat in der Mandata des Hirten des Hermas* ("Faith and Deed in the Mandates of the Shepherd of Hermas") (Marburg: Bauer, 1931). While serving as assistant to Karl Ludwig Schmidt in Bonn, Fuchs completed his *Christus und der Geist bei Paulus. Eine biblisch-theologische Untersuchung* ("Christ and the Spirit in Paul: A Biblical and Theological Study") UNT 23 (Leipzig: Hinrichs, 1932). Like Barth, who was also teaching at Bonn at the time, Fuchs was dismissed from his position by the Nazis in 1933. For several years Fuchs served as a pastor. Fuchs returned to academic life in 1949 when he moved to Tübingen. He came into conflict with other faculty on account of his Bultmannian stance. In 1955 he moved to the Kirchliche Hochschule in Berlin, where he remained until his appointment to Marburg.
155. Ernst Fuchs, "Die Frage nach dem historischen Jesus," in *Zur Frage nach dem historische*

Pauline concept of faith in Christ, Fuchs observed that, strictly speaking, it was impossible to speak of the preaching of Jesus. "Apart from the parables or similitudes we have only isolated sayings. They are most consonant with Jesus' conduct. This conduct is neither that of a prophet nor of a teacher of wisdom, but that of a man who dares to act in God's stead, and who, it must always be remembered, draws to himself sinners who, but for him, would have to flee from God."[156] What Jesus did was to "grasp the *time* of the rule of God in a new way,"[157] gathering together the unorganized group of the eschatological community in table fellowship. The disputes about Sabbath-breaking, fasting, and such could be traced back to Jesus.

Fuchs introduced a psychological element suggesting motives behind Jesus' actions. After the martyrdom of John the Baptist, Jesus began to envisage the possibility of his own suffering and death. Jesus transformed the Mosaic law into a law of suffering. The way of salvation was not by works of the law but by suffering for the faith. "God comes to meet man on the very way on which, as a rule, man has to expect God's judgment, and Paul, too, could say that whoever loses his life will gain it." "Faith knows that in the proclamation of the resurrection the historical Jesus himself *has* come to us. The so-called Christ of faith is none other than the historical Jesus. But what is more important is the statement that God himself *wants to be encountered* by us in the historical Jesus. The quest of the historical Jesus is now essentially transformed into the quest of the reality of the encounter with God in *preaching*."[158]

Fuchs's large number of articles exploring the themes of faith, the historical Jesus, and hermeneutics[159] go well beyond Bultmann in allowing what can be known about the historical Jesus. His lectures on Jesus'

Jesus. Gesammelte Aufsätze (Tübingen: Mohr Siebeck, 1960): 143–67; partial ET in *Studies in the Historical Jesus*, trans. Andrew Scobie, SBT 42 (London: SCM; Naperville, IL: Allenson, 1964). The lecture (11–31) is given the misleading title "The Quest of the Historical Jesus," whereas Fuchs entitled it "The Question of the Historical Jesus."

156. Fuchs, *Studies in the Historical Jesus*, 22.

157. Fuchs, *Studies in the Historical Jesus*, 23. This theme is further developed in "Jesus' Understanding of Time," 104–66.

158. Fuchs, *Studies in the Historical Jesus*, 30–31.

159. Fuchs, *Zum hermeneutischen Problem in der Theologie. Die existentiale Interpretation*, Gesammelte Aufsätze 1 (Tübingen: Mohr Siebeck, 1959); *Glaube und Erfahrung. Zum christologischen Problem im Neuen Testament*, Gesammelte Aufsätze 3 (Tübingen: Mohr Siebeck, 1965); *Hermeneutik* (Tübingen: Mohr Siebeck, 1954; 4th ed., 1970). The *Festschrift für Ernst Fuchs*, ed. Gerhard Ebeling, Eberhard Jüngel, and Gerd Schunack (Tübingen: Mohr Siebeck, 1973) contains a bibliography (347–61).

words and deeds contain a discussion of miracles, faith, and demons. The latter denote "the everyday experience of the human encounter with the non-human." "To know who Jesus is, means for Mark to know not only what Jesus can do (9:22b), but beyond that to know what Jesus did."[160] In the Gospels, "Jesus himself is by no means depicted as a traditional miracle worker. The common characterization of him as a *theios aner* [divine man] is mistaken. . . . Jesus' power brings faith to light, but in such a way that *he himself* establishes faith, declared to be lacking or explained as necessary."[161] In this regard, Fuchs was carrying on the tradition of Wilhelm Herrmann.[162]

Günther Bornkamm. A further step was taken by Günther Bornkamm (1905–90), whose *Jesus von Nazareth* (1956; ET: *Jesus of Nazareth*, 1960)[163] was the first book on Jesus in the Bultmann school since Bultmann's study thirty years earlier. Whereas Bultmann had stressed the future coming of the kingdom in Jesus' teaching, Bornkamm underlined the present element: the new age was already breaking in through Jesus' words and actions. His work proved to be closer to that of his predecessor at Heidelberg, Martin Dibelius, than to Bultmann's. Although the Gospels do not provide enough information "to paint a biographical picture of Jesus,"[164] Bornkamm gave more credence than Bultmann to the substratum of history in the Gospels but nevertheless paid tribute to Bultmann's achievements.[165]

---

160. Ernst Fuchs, *Jesus. Wort und Tat*, Vorlesungen zum Neuen Testament 1 (Tübingen: Mohr Siebeck, 1971), 52–53.

161. Fuchs, *Jesus. Wort und Tat*, 55.

162. Robert T. Voelkel, introduction to *The Communion of the Christian with God*, by Wilhelm Herrmann, xliii.

163. *Jesus of Nazareth*, trans. of the 3rd edition (Stuttgart: Kohlhammer Verlag, 1959) by Irene McLuskey and Fraser McLuskey with James M. Robinson (New York: Harper; London: Hodder & Stoughton, 1960); cf. Theissen and Winter, *The Quest for the Plausible Jesus*, 136–41.

An early pupil of Bultmann, Bornkamm wrote his dissertation on a typically Bultmannian theme: *Mythos und Legende in den apokryphen Thomas-Akten. Beiträge zur Geschichte der Gnosis und zur Vorgeschichte des Manichäismus* ["Myth and Legend in the Apocryphal Acts of Thomas: Contributions to the History of Gnosis and the Pre-History of Manichaeism"], FRLANT 49 (Göttingen: Vandenhoeck & Ruprecht, 1933). He went on to earn his licentiate at Königsberg. As a member of the Confessing Church, Bornkamm was deprived of his right to teach in a state university (Heidelberg). He subsequently taught in seminaries at Bielefeld and Bethel. After the War he moved to Göttingen (1946) and then to Heidelberg as successor to Martin Dibelius (1949). See further Robert Morgan, *DMBI*, 210–16; Michael Labahn, *EHJ*, 76–78.

164. Bornamm, *Jesus of Nazareth*, 53.

165. Günther Bornkamm, "The Theology of Rudolf Bultmann," in *The Theology of Rudolf Bultmann*, ed. Charles W. Kegley, 3–20.

"Quite clearly what the Gospels' report concerning the message, the deeds and the history of Jesus is still distinguished by an authenticity, a freshness, and a distinctiveness not in any way effaced by the Church's Easter faith. These features point us directly to the earthly figure of Jesus."[166] On the other hand, Jesus stands out from the world of Judaism. The latter was like "a soil hardened and barren through its age-long history and tradition." But it was also "a volcanic and eruptive ground, out of whose cracks and crevices breaks forth again and again the fire of a burning expectation. However, both torpidity and convulsion, petrifaction and blazing eruption [Pharisaism and apocalypticism] have at bottom, the same origin: they are the outcome and expression of a faith in a God who is beyond the world and history. . . . Jesus belongs to this world. Yet in the midst of it he is of unmistakable otherness."[167] Bornkamm's application of the criterion of double dissimilarity reveals a historical Jesus characterized by a unique sense of the divine present and its authority. "The reality of God and the authority of his will are always directly present, and are fulfilled in him."[168]

Bornkamm's account focused on the dawn of the kingdom of God, the will of God, discipleship, and Jesus' suffering and death. Miracle stories played virtually no part. The traditions accompanying Jesus' death—the darkness over the land and the tearing of the temple curtain—were "an expression and a symbol of the fact that an old, senile order of things has now come to an end, and that a new divine order has been founded."[169] It is not surprising that Bornkamm had no time for Jewish and pagan traditions about Jesus. They served merely to confirm that even the fiercest adversaries of Christianity never doubted the historical existence of Jesus. The report in the Talmud betrays "no independent knowledge whatsoever and is nothing but a polemical and tendentious representation of the Christian tradition. It makes Jesus into a magician, seducer and political agitator, and tries to justify his condemnation."[170]

---

166. Bornkamm, *Jesus of Nazareth*, 24; cf. Dibelius, *Jesus* (1939; ET: 1949), which showed how the gospel traditions related to the historical Jesus.
167. Bornkamm, *Jesus of Nazareth*, 55–56.
168. Bornkamm, *Jesus of Nazareth*, 57.
169. Bornkamm, *Jesus of Nazareth*, 167.
170. Bornkamm, *Jesus of Nazareth*, 28; cf. *b. Sanh.* 43a. A more penetrating view is given by Peter Schäfer, *Jesus in the Talmud* (Princeton, NJ: Princeton University Press, 2007). Schäfer contends that the Yerushalmi (Jerusalem Talmud) shows relative restraint toward Jesus, which he attributes to the growing impact of Christianity in the Holy Land and to the legal status of

The European Scene

Leander E. Keck applauded Bornkamm for highlighting the sense of authority that marked Jesus' teaching but deplored his distortion and denigration of Judaism so that "in the name of 'facts prior to any pious interpretation,' the authority of Jesus becomes historical evidence for his manifest superiority."[171] I would add that in rejecting the Talmudic tradition Bornkamm was turning a blind eye to an important strand of evidence that reached back to the gospel tradition.[172]

Gerhard Ebeling. The ethos of the New Quest was captured by the Zürich systematic theologian and Luther scholar Gerhard Ebeling (1912–2001).[173] In his dialogue with Bultmann on *Theology and Proclamation*, Ebeling wrote, "Now if we can say of the man Jesus that God comes to expression in such a way that we come to know Jesus himself as the Word which brings certainty and therefore as the point where reality is radically challenged; if this is so, then we have the clearest indication of how it is that the kerygma, as the homology of certainty, finds its support in Jesus."[174] Ebeling added, "Christian faith can be seriously accepted as faith in *Jesus* only where we properly accept Jesus himself as example."[175] The difference with Bultmann was summed up by Robert T. Voelkel, who observed that Ebeling's *The Nature of Faith* "more than any other [book] in recent theology resembles the intention of Herrmann's *The Communion of the Christian with God.*"[176]

Christianity in the age of Constantine. The Bavli (Babylonian Talmud) was produced under fewer constraints in a situation where Christians and Jews were in process of defining themselves. The Bavli shows greater knowledge of the New Testament but also more distortions. A more detailed discussion is given above in chap. 2, §2.2.

171. Keck, *Who Is Jesus?*, 29 citing Bornamm, *Jesus of Nazareth*, 53; cf. Keck, "Bornkamm's *Jesus of Nazareth* Revisited," *JR* 49 (1969): 1–17. On the continued exchange between Keck and Bornkamm, see below, chap. 15, §3.2–3.

172. Colin Brown, "Synoptic Miracle Stories: A Jewish Religious and Social Setting," *Foundations & Facets Forum* 2, no. 4 (1986): 55–76. See also above, chap. 1.

173. Ebeling studied in Marburg with Bultmann and also in Zürich and Berlin. He served as a pastor in the Confessing Church, before being drafted as a medical orderly during the War. He obtained his habilitation in 1946 and became a professor of church history before becoming professor of systematic theology at Tübingen in 1954. He moved to Zürich in 1954 but returned to Tübingen in 1965. He served on the editorial board that produced a new edition of Luther's works and as editor of the *Zeitschrift für Theologie und Kirche*. See Hans Jürgen Schultz, "Gerhard Ebeling," in *Tendenzen der Theologie im 20. Jahrhundert. Eine Geschichte in Porträts*, ed. Hans Jürgen Schultz, 2nd ed. (Stuttgart: Kreuz-Verlag; Olten: Walter-Verlag, 1967), 589–95.

174. Ebeling, *Theology and Proclamation: Dialogue with Rudolf Bultmann* (1962), trans. John Riches (Philadelphia: Fortress; London: Collins, 1966), 79; cf. Ebeling, *Word and Faith*, trans. James W. Leitch (Philadelphia: Fortress, 1963).

175. Ebeling, *Theology and Proclamation*, 89.

176. Robert T. Voelkel, introduction to Wilhelm Herrmann, *The Communion of the Christian*

Hans Conzelmann. The most concise—and perhaps the most negative—account of Jesus produced in the New Quest came from Ebeling's Zürich colleague Hans Conzelmann (1915–89).[177] It first took the form of an encyclopedia article and later expanded into a small book.[178] Conzelmann's *Jesus* was firmly based on the criterion of double dissimilarity.

> Whatever fits neither into Jewish thought nor the views of the later church can be regarded as authentic. This is the case, above all, for the sayings which express a consciousness of the uniqueness of [Jesus'] own situation. To this principle one can add certain observations about form. Such observations guarantee above all the genuineness of the core of the parables. These are clearly distinguished from all Jewish parables through style (narrative form, imagery) as well as thought, and reflect a sharply defined self-understanding in which teaching and action (miracle) are comprehended as an indissoluble unity.[179]

Conzelmann went on to say that "Jesus moved almost exclusively within the framework of Palestinian Judaism" and that "in the oldest stratum of the Synoptic tradition one observes no influence from Hellenistic

---

with God, liii, writing of Ebeling, *Das Wesen des chistlichen Glaubens*, ET: *The Nature of Faith*, trans. Ronald Gregor Smith (Philadelphia: Fortress, 1961).

177. Conzelmann studied theology at Tübingen and Marburg, where he got to know Hans von Soden and Rudolf Bultmann. Like others engaged in the New Quest, he was opposed to the Nazi dominated German Christians. Conzelmann's studies were interrupted by World War II, in which he received serious injuries. His Tübingen dissertation (1951) published as *Die Mitte der Zeit* ("The Center of Time") (Tübingen: Mohr Siebeck, 1953; 2nd ed., 1957) was translated by Geoffrey Buswell with the title *The Theology of St Luke* (London: Faber and Faber, 1960). Conzelmann contended that Luke was concerned with the delay of the parousia. He used redaction criticism to eliminate from his Markan source references to an imminent end, which he replaced by a history of salvation in which Jesus Christ was the center of history. In 1954 Conzelmann became professor of New Testament at Zürich, but spent most of his career at Göttingen (1960–78). See C. H. Talbert, *DMBI*, 324–28; Michael Labahn, *EHJ*, 122–24.

178. Hans Conzelmann, "Jesus Christus," in *Die Religion in Geschichte und Gegenwart*, eds. Kurt Galling et al. (3rd ed., Tübingen: Mohr Siebeck, 1959), 3:619–53; ET: *Jesus*, trans. J. Raymond Lord, ed. John Reumann (Philadelphia: Fortress, 1973).

179. Conzelmann, *Jesus*, 16; cf. Hans Conzelmann, "The Method of Life-of-Jesus Research," in *The Historical Jesus and the Kerygmatic Christ: Essays on the New Quest of the Historical Jesus*, ed. Carl E. Braaten and Roy A. Harrisville (Nashville: Abingdon, 1964), 54–68. Conzelmann spoke of "indirect Christology" as the presupposition of "direct Christology," and inferred that the kerygma itself required the historical portrayal of Jesus and his message; cf. Theissen and Winter, *The Quest of the Plausible Jesus*, 119.

ideas."[180] The saying in Matthew 23:37 and Luke 13:34 ("Jerusalem . . . how often would I have gathered together your children. . . .") cannot be a historical saying of Jesus because the speaker was "a suprahistorical subject, Wisdom."[181] The various titles ascribed to Jesus were largely the creation of the church. Peter's confession of Jesus as the Christ, which traditionally was seen as a turning point in Jesus' ministry, "is a pictorial narrative representation of the post-Easter faith of the church."[182] Likewise the trial scene—and with it the high priest's question about whether Jesus was the Christ—is "not authentic." The fact that Jesus went to Jerusalem seems to indicate that he was "a messianic pretender," but actually all it proves is that Jesus wished to call the people and their leaders "inescapably to repentance."[183]

The Son of Man sayings fell into three groups: the present activity, the coming suffering, and the parousia of the Son of Man. Those that link the Son of Man with suffering are *vaticinia ex eventu*, or prophecies made after the event. Unlike Bultmann, Conzelmann did not think that the Son of Man sayings referred to someone other than Jesus. The three groups of sayings were a synthesis produced by the church, a product of *Gemeindetheologie*, church theology. Jesus did not present his relationship to the kingdom by means of titles. "Rather he does so in the indirectness which characterizes his entire ministry—hence through his preaching and his miracles, through his call to repentance, his interpretation of the command of God, through the disclosure of God's immediacy [*Unmittelbarkeit*] for sinners and the poor. His 'Christology' then is an indirect one."[184]

At the heart of Jesus' teaching is "the absoluteness of the promise of salvation," which took shape in the recovery of immediacy to God through the proclamation of forgiveness. "Precisely from this follows the radical understanding of the demand of God which—in its unconditional nature—carries with it its fulfillment, and the understanding of the present time as the last hour, which opens up access to the kingdom of God. Salvation in its unconditional nature is the crisis of all security."[185]

---

180. Conzelmann, *Jesus*, 17.
181. Conzelmann, *Jesus*, 22–23.
182. Conzelmann, *Jesus*, 42.
183. Conzelmann, *Jesus*, 42.
184. Conzelmann, *Jesus*, 42.
185. Conzelmann, *Jesus*, 51.

Jesus had no idea of natural law and thus no concept of miracle. "In purview lie only the deeds which he himself does.... Further, miracle is a way in which God makes himself intelligible, and it happens *hic et nunc*. In this way the very fact that Jesus is present [*das Da-Sein Jesu*] is drawn into the proclamation about God. Miracle is a present 'sign,' not an objective proof."[186]

"Politics is visible only marginally.... Because one must obey [God] unconditionally, [Jesus] cannot use God's name in order to cover over a worldly political program. One cannot use God's name as a given entity, nor can one use him for the benefit of the 'chosen people.'"[187] Jesus' ethical instructions were not a retreat from the world but sought "the restoration of freedom of the children of God in the world." Jesus did not abolish the practice of fasting (Matt 6:16–18). On the other hand, his reputation as a glutton and a drunkard (Matt 11:19) indicates that he did not follow the asceticism of John the Baptist.[188] Jesus stood in the tradition of Jewish eschatology. As the history of religions school pointed out, the kingdom of God is not the result of a process. In Jesus' teaching "the kingdom is future, pressing near and now active in Jesus' deeds and preaching (cf. the figure of the sower)."[189]

The narrative of the passion contains historical elements (e.g., Mark 14:51; 15:21), but the institution of the Lord's Supper is "a cult legend, a *hieros logos* of the celebration of the Christian sacrament."[190] The trial scene is essentially "a witness of faith."[191] What happened after the crucifixion of Jesus "is no longer the history of Jesus but the history of its consequences."[192] Bultmann's program of "demythologizing" and "existential interpretation" poses the question of "How can a historical event be the *eschatological* event and encounter a person as such today? The answer is given by referring to proclamation: it can be present when *preached*. This possibility is then to be distinguished in principle from

---

186. Conzelmann, *Jesus*, 55.
187. Conzelmann, *Jesus*, 67.
188. Conzelmann, *Jesus*, 67.
189. Conzelmann, *Jesus*, 74. "In eschatology, too, we meet with 'indirect' Christology. There are still poverty, sickness, sin, demons. When the kingdom comes, there will be an end to these things. Thus it is not yet here. But it already casts its light in that it becomes operative in Jesus. Through the signs which he performs, the truth of his proclamation, the imminence of the kingdom, is guaranteed" (*Jesus*, 70).
190. Conzelmann, *Jesus*, 83.
191. Conzelmann, *Jesus*, 86.
192. Conzelmann, *Jesus*, 88.

the historically comprehensible consequences of a personality."[193] This does not foreclose historical inquiry but rather points up the differences and the connection. "Maintaining the historical reference opposes the mythologizing of the object of faith as well as dogmatic objectivising in which a series of statements about him takes the place of Jesus Christ. Statements cannot be an object of faith but only its explication."[194]

Eduard Schweizer. A dozen years after Bornkamm's *Jesus of Nazareth*, Eduard Schweizer (1913–2007)[195] produced a book on *Jesus* (1968).[196] It reflected the post–New Quest situation. It was based on lectures originally drafted in Japan, where the author had scant library resources. The lectures were subsequently given to general audiences in the University of Zürich. The book is characterized by both continuity and discontinuity with Bultmann.

> On the one hand, only a post-Easter witness speaking in faith can testify to us concerning what really took place in the life and death and resurrection of Jesus, as he recounts them. Only such a witness can tell us that Jesus is the *Christ*. On the other hand, the disciple knows from the very outset that he is saying these things about Jesus, in other words, about the man from Nazareth whom he accompanied, to whom he listened, and whose ministry he saw. He knows, in other words, that *Jesus* is the Christ. The former tells

---

193. Conzelmann, *Jesus*, 89.
194. Conzelmann, *Jesus*, 90.
195. Eduard Schweizer enjoyed a long and prolific career. He was born in Switzerland and studied theology in Basel before moving to Marburg in the early 1930s. Bultmann introduced Schweizer to existentialist interpretation, which spoke to many in the dark days of the Nazi era. He was impressed by Rudolf Otto's *The Idea of the Holy* (discussed below, chap. 7, §3), which posited "the holy" as a common feature of religions. But he also learned from Emil Brunner's concern for the communication of the gospel and from Barth's emphasis on the priority of grace.

Schweizer served as professor of New Testament theology and exegesis at Zürich, where he served two terms as president of the university. Honors included the presidency of the Society of New Testament Studies, the British Academy's award of the Burkett Medal (1996), and a Festschrift whose title both echoes and modifies Conzelmann: *Die Mitte des Neuen Testaments. Einheit und Vielfalt neutestamentlicher Theologie. Festschrift für Eduard Schweizer zum siebzigsten Gebutstag*, ed. Ulrich Luz and Hans Weder (Göttingen: Vandenhoeck & Ruprecht, 1983). The latter's bibliography lists 219 publications up to 1984. Articles by Eduard Schweizer appear in *Neotestamentica. Deutsche und Englische Aufsätze 1951–1963* (Zürich: Zwingli, 1963); and *Beiträge zur Theologie des Neuen Testaments. Neutestamentliche Aufsätze (1955–1970)* (Zürich: Zwingli, 1970). See further Edwin K. Broadhead, "The Historical Jesus in the World of Eduard Schweizer," *Perspectives in Religious Studies* 30 (2003): 21–28; Warren Carter, *DMBI*, 902–6.

196. Eduard Schweizer, *Jesus Christus* (Munich: Siebenstern, 1968); ET: *Jesus*, trans. David E. Green, NTL (London: SCM, 1971).

us who the man Jesus is, namely, he through whom God himself would speak to us; the latter tells us who this Christ of God is, namely, the man from Nazareth who died on the cross, not the national hero who drove out the Romans and established a kingdom of Israel to rule the world.[197]

Jesus was "the man who fits no formula."[198] He did not use titles like Messiah or Son of Man in order not to limit God's action.[199] Whereas the rabbis used parables as illustrations, Jesus uttered them with the authority of God "to lead the way along the path on which he wants his listeners to follow."[200] He spoke of the coming and present kingdom of God.[201] His healings and meals with the marginalized were manifestations of that kingdom. He was ambivalent toward the law.[202] It was "God's great gift to Israel," yet Jesus demanded "radical obedience" that brought freedom. "Only the man who lives on God's infinite love can and must be the channel toward his neighbor (Matt 18.21–25)."[203]

Schweizer was "certain that Jesus called disciples to follow him." "While the disciples walked with Jesus they were more and more entrusted with a commission, and . . . this commission filled lives that were empty, gave purpose to lives frittered away in daily routine, gave meaning to lives condemned to be meaningless."[204] Jesus' miracles were not proofs but signs, which pointed away from themselves to encounter with God.[205] "Easter was the sign which said 'yes' to the path taken by Jesus."[206] "While the community remained the community of Jesus Christ, it could never forget

---

197. Schweizer, *Jesus*, 11.
198. Schweizer, *Jesus*, 13–51.
199. Schweizer, *Jesus*, 13–22.
200. Schweizer, *Jesus*, 30. In his eighties Schweizer responded to the New Quest and to (among others) E. P. Sanders, Maurice Casey, and John Dominic Crossan. He went on to discuss Jesus, the parable teller, the preacher, healer, friend of tax collectors and sinners, the crucified and the resurrected Jesus. He sided with Käsemann and Barth against Bultmann. Schweizer argued that "the central data of Jesus' ministry, his death, and resurrection appearances are reported in a trustworthy way by our texts. . . . I tried to understand Jesus as *the* parable of God. As far as it concerns God's act, this is true for all humanity, whether they believe it or not, and whether they say so or not." Eduard Schweizer, *Jesus the Parable of God: What Do We Really Know about Jesus?* (Allison Park, PA: Pickwick, 1994), 93–95.
201. Schweizer, *Jesus*, 22–26.
202. Schweizer, *Jesus*, 29–34.
203. Schweizer, *Jesus*, 38.
204. Schweizer, *Jesus*, 39, 41.
205. Schweizer, *Jesus*, 43–45.
206. Schweizer, *Jesus*, 45.

The European Scene

that Jesus was wholly man, to the point of an ignominious death on the cross. Neither could it forget that God had recalled this crucified Jesus to life and appointed him Lord. This duality determined the entire story that we have been following, which often seems so confused."[207]

Toward the end of his book Schweizer offered thoughts on the character of the New Testament. Q, the presumed source of sayings common to Matthew and Luke,[208] seems to presuppose an understanding of Jesus as a divine miracle worker. It contains no reference to the cross and resurrection, though probably an allusion to the eschatological coming of Jesus as Son of Man, judge, and savior.[209] The collection appears to have been rooted in the Palestinian community. Q had a true vision of Jesus as the presence of God's approaching kingdom, but it lacked an understanding of Easter. Mark is "a theological accomplishment of the first order," having no models to follow. Mark focuses on God's revelation in the passion of Jesus and in the call to discipleship.[210] Matthew presents Jesus as the interpreter and fulfiller of the law.[211] Luke depicts Jesus' earthly ministry and its significance for the community, which consists in God's gracious love for the world and Jesus' gracious lordship over it.[212] "John concentrates everything in the figure of Jesus of Nazareth, in whom alone we encounter God's Logos, who created the world."[213] Without Jesus no one can see God (John 14:6). Without his coming there would be no sin, because rejection of Jesus is the only real sin (15:22).

3.2. Abrupt Demise. In July 1959 Bultmann came out of retirement to offer reflections on the contemporary situation. He did so in an address to the Heidelberg Academy of Sciences on "The Relationship of the Primitive Christian Message to the Historical Jesus."[214] He began by

---

207. Schweizer, *Jesus*, 190.
208. Schweizer, *Jesus*, 122–28.
209. Cf. P. Vielhauer, "Jesus und der Menschensohn. Zur Diskussion mit Heinz Eduard Tödt und Eduard Schweitzer," *ZTK* 60 (1963): 133–77.
210. Schweizer, *Jesus*, 128–32.
211. Schweizer, *Jesus*, 132–37.
212. Schweizer, *Jesus*, 137.
213. Schweizer, *Jesus*, 157.
214. Rudolf Bultmann, *Das Verhältnis der urchristlichen Botschaft zum historischen Jesus*, Sitzungsberichte der Heidelberger Akademie der Wissenschaften, Philosophisch-historische Klasse, Jahrgang 1960, 3. Abhandlung (Heidelberg: Carl Winter Universitätsverlag, 1960); ET: "The Primitive Christian Kerygma and the Historical Jesus," in *The Historical Jesus and the Kerygmatic Christ: Essays on the New Quest of the Historical Jesus*, trans. and ed. Carl E. Braaten and Roy A. Harrisville (Nashville: Abingdon, 1964), 15–42. See, further, Hammann, *Rudolf Bultmann*, 459–64.

drawing attention to the changed situation. The Old Quest sought to get behind the kerygma in order to discover the historical Jesus. Today the situation was reversed. "The emphasis lies on elaborating the unity of the historical Jesus and the Christ of the kerygma."[215] The problem for research arose from the difference between the historical Jesus and the Christ kerygma.

> 1. In the kerygma the mythical form of the Son of God has appeared in place of the historical person of Jesus (as the Synoptic Gospels present it to the historical eye).
> 2. While the preaching of Jesus is the eschatological message of the coming—more, of the breaking-in of the kingdom of God—in the kerygma Jesus Christ is proclaimed as the one who died vicariously on the cross for the sins of men and was miraculously raised by God for our salvation. In Pauline and Johannine theology the decisive eschatological event has thereby already occurred.
> 3. For Jesus the eschatological proclamation goes hand in hand with the proclamation of the will of God, with the call to radical obedience to God's demands culminating in the commandment of love.... The confessional formulations of the kerygma (the first Christian symbols) do not take up this exposition at all, and in the typical primitive Christian doctrinal and hortatory writings the ethical paraenesis takes second place.
>
> How then shall we determine the relationship between these two phenomena—Jesus and the Christ-kerygma?[216]

For Bultmann, "It is the Christ of the kerygma and not the person of the historical Jesus who is the object of faith, that the man whom the kerygma addresses may not inquire behind the kerygma for a legitimation offered by historical research."[217] This did not mean that Bultmann destroyed continuity between the historical Jesus and the kerygma. "The kerygma presupposes the historical Jesus, however much it may have mythologized him. Without him there would be no kerygma."[218]

---

215. Bultmann, "The Primitive Christian Kerygma," 15.
216. Bultmann, "The Primitive Christian Kerygma," 16–17.
217. Bultmann, "The Primitive Christian Kerygma," 17.
218. Bultmann, "The Primitive Christian Kerygma," 18.

The European Scene

Jesus was a Jew but (as Wellhausen observed[219]) definitely not a "Christian." Jesus did not demand faith in himself as the Christ. Jesus is the presupposition of the kerygma—the *that* (German *dass*) not the *what* (German *was*).

Bultmann granted that we may cautiously identify facets of Jesus' activity.

> Characteristic for him are exorcisms, the breach of the Sabbath commandment, the abandonment of ritual purifications, polemic against Jewish legalism, fellowship with outcasts such as publicans and harlots, sympathy for women and children; it can also be seen that Jesus was not an ascetic like John the Baptist, but gladly ate and drank a glass of wine. Perhaps we may add that he called disciples and assembled about himself a small company of followers—men and women. . . . [He] doubtless appeared conscious of being commissioned by God to preach the eschatological message of the breaking-in of the kingdom of God and the demanding but also inviting will of God. We may thus ascribe to him a prophetic consciousness, indeed, a "consciousness of authority."[220]

However, Bultmann denied that we can know how Jesus faced his death because the synoptic accounts were influenced by the kerygma.[221]

At this point Bultmann assumed the air of a headmaster lining up his best pupils—Käsemann, Bornkamm, Fuchs, Ebeling, Conzelmann, and Robinson[222]—to explain why they had flunked the test. Two factors stood out: losing sight of the existential character of the kerygma, which precludes objective legitimization of faith, and the fact that in the kerygma the proclaimer has become the one who is proclaimed.[223] Fuchs, Ebeling, Bornkamm, and Käsemann were all faulted for their inconsistent interest in the historical Jesus, when it was the Christ proclaimed by the kerygma

---

219. See below, chap. 7, §1.1.
220. Bultmann, "The Primitive Christian Kerygma," 22–23.
221. Bultmann, "The Primitive Christian Kerygma," 24.
222. Although Bultmann explicitly dealt with what he considered to be the shortcomings of those named here, he also gave detailed references to their writings throughout the footnotes of the printed version of his lecture. The printed version of Bultmann's lecture added discussion of works by Fuchs, Ebeling, and Conzelmann, to which Bultmann did not have access when he delivered his lecture.
223. Bultmann, "The Primitive Christian Kerygma," 38.

that was the saving event.[224] Even Robinson's attempt to demonstrate continuity between Jesus and the kerygma "may so blur the difference between them that in effect it will make the kerygma unnecessary."[225]

The solution to the problem of the proclaimer becoming the proclaimed lay in the fact that "the kerygma has changed the 'once' of the historical Jesus into the 'once-for-all.' In other words, the earliest community (with ever greater clarity) understood the history of Jesus as the decisive eschatological event which as such can never become mere past remains present, and of course, in the preaching."[226]

In closing, Bultmann remarked that "it has often been said, most of the time in criticism, that according to my interpretation of the kerygma Jesus has risen in the kerygma. I accept this proposition. It is entirely correct, assuming that it is properly understood. It presupposes that the kerygma itself is an eschatological event, and it expresses the fact that Jesus is really present in the kerygma, that it is *his* word which involves the hearer in the kerygma. . . . To believe in the Christ present in the kerygma is the meaning of the Easter faith."[227]

Karl Barth expressed his endorsement of Bultmann's treatment of the advocates of the New Quest in terms starker than mine. In a letter expressing his agreement with Bultmann, Barth remarked: "A true cemetery of honor, you buried your students, together, each one with a small cross, helmet, and nameplate!"[228] Bultmann's address to the Heidelberg Academy marked the beginning of the end. The New Quest continued for another decade, but Bultmann had defined the limits of what could be done on Bultmannian lines. Already the practitioners of the New Quest were looking for fresh woods and pastures new.

Bornkamm turned increasingly to redaction criticism and the study of Paul.[229] On moving from Zürich to Göttingen, Conzelmann announced

---

224. Bultmann, "The Primitive Christian Kerygma," 31–35.
225. Bultmann, "The Primitive Christian Kerygma," 39, citing R. H. Fuller's review of Bultmann's *Jesus Christ and Mythology*, and Robinson's *A New Quest*, in *ATR* 41 (1959): 234.
226. Bultmann, "The Primitive Christian Kerygma," 40. The passage in single quotation marks was actually a quotation from Käsemann's "The Problem of the Historical Jesus." It was intended to illustrate the fundamental inconsistency of the New Quest.
227. Bultmann, "The Primitive Christian Kerygma," 42.
228. Hammann, *Rudolf Bultmann*, 461, citing Barth's letter to Bultmann (3.1.1961); Jaspert, ed., *Karl Barth—Rudolf Bultmann*, 201.
229. Günther Bornkamm, Gerhard Barth, and H. J. Held, *Tradition and Interpretation in Matthew*, (1960), trans. Percy Scott (London: SCM, 1963); *Early Christian Experience*, trans. Paul L. Hammer (London: SCM, 1969), based on articles from *Das Ende des Gesetzes* (5th ed.,

his withdrawal from the quests on the grounds that it was irrelevant to faith.[230] Käsemann's riposte on John has already been noted. It was, in effect, a redoubling of the charge against Bultmann of docetism. Käsemann's later work increasingly focused on Paul and justification.[231]

Bultmann's account of the demythologized kerygma was based on a *Sachkritik* that enabled him to extrapolate the Reformation doctrine of *sola fide* from the context of justification by faith and apply it to the message of the cross and resurrection. To Bultmann this was a virtue;[232] to others it was a category mistake to abstract the cross from the historical events that surrounded it.

In hindsight two interrelated problems characterized Bultmann's scholarship. The first was *Sachkritik*, which took it as self-evident truth that what was *meant* could be readily separated from what was *said* and that this could be done *prior to* examining texts as a whole. However, meaning and context mutually determine each other, as I have endeavored to show in chapter 1. My personal recommendation is that we should be cautious about determining meaning apart from study of

---

1966) and *Studien zu Antike und Christentum* (2nd ed., 1963). Bibliography in *Kirche. Festschrift für Günther Bornkamm zum 75. Geburtstag*, ed. D. Lührmann and G. Strecker (Tübingen: Mohr Siebeck, 1980), 491–506; cf. Robert Morgan, *DMBI*, 439–444.

230. Robinson, *A New Quest of the Historical Jesus and Other Essays*, 159. Conzelmann's works include *The Theology of St Luke*, trans. Geoffrey Buswell (London: Faber and Faber; New York: Harper, 1960); *An Outline Theology of the New Testament*, trans. John Bowden (London; SCM; New York: Harper, 1969); *History of Primitive Christianity*, trans. John E. Steely (Nashville: Abingdon, 1973); *Theologie als Schriftauslegung* (München: Kaiser, 1974); *1 Corinthians*, Hermeneia, trans. James W. Leitch (Philadelphia: Fortress, 1975); *Acts of the Apostles*, Hermeneia, trans. James Limburg, A. Thomas Kraabel, and Donald H. Juel (Philadelphia: Fortress, 1987); *Interpreting the New Testament: An Introduction to the Principles and Methods of New Testament Exegesis*, with Andreas Lindemann, trans. Siegfried S. Schatzmann (Peabody, MA: Hendrickson, 1988); *Gentiles, Jews, Christians: Polemics and Apologetics in the Greco-Roman Era*, trans. M. Eugene Boring (Minneapolis: Fortress, 1992). Bibliography in *Jesus Christus in Historie und Theologie. Neutestamentliche Festschrift für Hans Conzelmann zum 60. Geburtstag*, ed. Georg Strecker (Tübingen: Mohr Siebeck, 1975), 549–57; cf. C. H. Talbert, *DMBI*, 325–28.

231. Käsemann's studies include *New Testament Questions of Today*, trans. W. J. Montague (London: SCM, 1969); *Perspectives on Paul*, trans. Margaret Kohl (London: SCM, 1971); and *Commentary on Romans*, trans. Geoffrey W. Bromiley (Grand Rapids: Eerdmans, 1980). Käsemann's "Blind Alleys in the 'Jesus of History' Controversy" (*New Testament Questions of Today*, 23–65) contains a critique of Joachim Jeremias and a reply to Bultmann.

232. "Indeed, de-mythologizing is a task parallel to that performed by Paul and Luther in their doctrine of justification by faith alone without the works of the law. More precisely, de-mythologizing is the radical application of the doctrine of justification by faith to the sphere of knowledge and thought. Like the doctrine of justification, de-mythologizing destroys every longing for security. There is no difference between security based on good works and security built on objectifying knowledge" (Bultmann, *Jesus Christ and Mythology*, 84).

texts as a whole. This applies especially to the interpretation of gospels, canonical and noncanonical. Prior determinations of meaning are best treated as provisional and subject to revision.

The second problem that is characteristic of Bultmann's scholarship is his attachment to dialectical theology. In hindsight, Bultmann seems more attached to it than Barth! Bultmann's criticism of his former students and their involvement in the New Quest was not faulty critical scholarship but theological failure. The point is graphically illustrated by the way that Bultmann understood how the proclaimer had become the proclaimed, and how the kerygma had changed the *once* of the historical Jesus into the *once and for all* of proclamation. To New Questers like Käsemnn, Bornkamm, and Fuchs—as well as outsiders like Joachim Jeremias—there was a self-evident link between the Jesus of history and the Christ of faith. There would be kerygma without the events that produced it. To Bultmann, the kerygma made the Jesus of history redundant.

In Bultmann's theology the cross and resurrection became symbols, detached from historical context and invested with ineffable salvific power. The result was too rarified to sustain faith for all but an intellectual minority. In launching the New Quest, Käsemann feared that Bultmannianism would lead to a relapse into docetism. In old age he accused Bultmann of idealism on account of his proclivity for abstraction.[233] It was an abstraction that stripped Jesus of his Jewishness. In this regard Bousset, Bultmann, and their followers were heirs to a theological tradition that universalized Jesus at the expense of his Jewishness.[234] With the discovery of the Dead Sea Scrolls beginning in late 1946 or early 1947, knowledge of the world of Second Temple Judaism changed forever.[235] Increasingly, scholars felt the need to locate Jesus in that world, and almost overnight Bultmann and advocates of a New Quest were figures of the past.

---

233. Käsemann, letter to Paul F. M. Zahl, August 22, 1995 (*ATR* 80 [1998]: 386).

234. Susannah Heschel, *Abraham Geiger and the Jewish Jesus*, Chicago Studies in the History of Judaism (Chicago: University of Chicago Press, 1998), 127–61, 229–42; Keck, *Who Is Jesus?*, 23–47.

235. A harbinger of the changing awareness was Nils Alstrup Dahl, "Eschatologie und Geschichte im Lichte der Qumrantexte," in *Sein und Zeit*, 3–18.

CHAPTER 7
THE NO QUEST IN EUROPE TO WORLD WAR II

THE PERIOD FOLLOWING the publication of Schweitzer's *Quest* down to the post-Bultmannian New Quest is sometimes dubbed the "No Quest."[1] Three factors were responsible for the impression that the quest of the historical Jesus had come to a dead end. The first was the belief that Schweitzer had said all that was to be said. Conservatives, who had not read Schweitzer closely, believed that Schweitzer had rehabilitated eschatology and only liberal intransigence blocked the way to wider acceptance. The second factor, potent in the German-speaking world, was the dominance of Bultmann in New Testament studies. Bultmann's program of form criticism and demythologizing exalted the kerygma of the cross and resurrection at the expense of the historical Jesus. The sputtering New Quest posited a historical Jesus behind the kerygma, but it soon expired. It had demonstrated the limits of what could be done on Bultmannian lines. The third factor was the dominance of Karl Barth in theology. Barth's stress on the otherness of God and revelation as the sole means of knowing God made the quest of the historical Jesus seem irrelevant.[2]

---

1. John Reumann, "Jesus and Christology," in *The New Testament and Its Modern Interpreters*, ed. Eldon J. Epp and George W. MacRae (Atlanta: Scholars, 1989), 501–64, here 502; Stanley E. Porter, *The Criteria for Authenticity in Historical Jesus Research*, JSNTSup 191 (Sheffield: Sheffield Academic Press, 2000), 45; cf. Leander E. Keck, *A Future for the Historical Jesus: The Place of Jesus in Preaching and Theology* (Nashville: Abingdon, 1971; London: SCM, 1972), 9.

2. Colin Brown, *Karl Barth and the Christian Message* (London: Tyndale, 1968; 2nd ed. Portland, OR: Wipf & Stock, 1998); Eberhard Busch, *Karl Barth: His Life from Letters and Autobiographical Texts*, trans. John Bowden (London: SCM; Philadelphia: Fortress, 1976); Bruce L. McCormack, *Karl Barth's Critically Realistic Dialectical Theology: Its Genesis and Development, 1909–1936* (Oxford: Clarendon, 1995).

The European Scene

Reports of the demise of the quest turned out to have been greatly exaggerated. The second edition of Schweitzer's *Geschichte der Leben-Jesu-Forschung* (1913), which contained additional chapters tracking the quest from 1905 to 1912, bore eloquent testimony to its continued vigor. Readers of journals like *Theologische Rundschau*, *Theologische Literaturzeitung*, *Journal of Theological Studies*, and *The Expository Times* were kept abreast of continuing developments. The extent of these developments is set out in Walter P. Weaver's *The Historical Jesus in the Twentieth Century, 1900–1950*.[3] Weaver's definitive survey traces the fortunes of Jesus studies decade by decade, culminating in the Jewish quest for Jesus. It concluded with a review of the state of debate on key topics like Son of Man, kingdom of God, parables, and a survey of Jesus as an icon in popular literature.

This chapter is more narrowly focused. It covers roughly the same period as the previous chapter, from the beginning of the twentieth century up to the 1950s. Whereas chapter 6 discussed the history of religions school and the Bultmann School, the next six chapters focus on scholarship mainly outside those schools, looking first at the continent of Europe (chaps. 7 and 8), then Britain (chaps. 9–11), and finally North America (chaps. 12–15). This chapter reviews three developments in Europe up to period of World War II (1939–45).

1. Early Reclamations of Jesus
    1.1. Harnack, Wellhausen, and the Liberal Protestant Jesus
    1.2. Loisy and the Catholic Modernist Jesus
    1.3. Baeck, Klausner, and the Jewish Reclamation of Jesus
2. The Recovery of Jesus' World
    2.1. Schürer and the Jewish People
    2.2. Strack-Billerbeck and the Relevance of Talmud and Midrash
    2.3. Dalman and the Languages of Jesus
    2.4. Deissmann and the Ancient East
    2.5. Kittel, Politics, and the *Theological Word Book*

---

3. Walter P. Weaver, *The Historical Jesus in the Twentieth Century, 1900–1950* (Harrisburg, PA: Trinity Press International, 1999). Weaver's work supersedes previous surveys, which sought to update Schweitzer: Chester C. McCown, *The Search for the Real Jesus: A Century of Historical Study* (New York: Scribner's, 1940); H. G. Wood, *Jesus in the Twentieth Century* (London: Lutterworth, 1960); Hugh Anderson, *Jesus and Christian Origins: A Commentary on Modern Viewpoints* (Oxford: Oxford University Press, 1964); Gustaf Aulén, *Jesus in Contemporary Historical Research*, trans. Ingalill H. Hjelm (Philadelphia: Fortress, 1976).

3. Later Reclamations of Jesus
  3.1. Schlatter and the Jewish Christ of Faith
  3.2. Otto and the Jewish Charismatic Jesus
  3.3. Grundmann and the Anti-Semitic Jesus

1. Early Reclamations of Jesus

1.1. Harnack, Wellhausen, and the Liberal Protestant Jesus. Schweitzer presented his thoroughgoing eschatology as the wave of the future, leaving readers with the thoroughgoing skepticism of Wrede as the bleak alternative. But the Ritschlian liberal tradition was far from dead. It had been presented in a compelling way by the greatest church historian of the age, Adolf Harnack (1851–1930).

Adolf Harnack. Harnack's lectures had drawn Albert Schweitzer to Berlin in 1899.[4] During the Winter semester 1899–1900 Harnack gave a series of sixteen popular lectures on the essence of Christianity. The title given to the English translation was *What Is Christianity?*[5] By 1901

---

4. Schweitzer, letter of condolence (July 19, 1930) to the Harnack family on Harnack's death; Albert Schweitzer, *Letters, 1905–1965*, ed. Hans Walter Bähr, trans. Joachim Neugroschel (New York: Macmillan, 1972), 111–12. Harnack invited Schweitzer to his home, and the two maintained a friendship from then on.

5. Adolf Harnack, *What Is Christianity?*, trans. T. B. Saunders (London: Williams and Norgate, 1901). The German title better conveys the author's attempt to identify the essence of Christianity, *Das Wesen des Christentums. Sechszehn Vorlesungen vor Studierenden aller Facultäten im Wintersemester 1899/1900 an der Universität Berlin* (Leipzig: Hinrichs, 1900). Harnack had delivered the lectures extemporarily, but they were taken down in shorthand by a theology student, Walter Becker, and became the text of Harnack's book (German edition, iii).

Harnack taught at the universities of Leipzig, Giessen, Marburg, and Berlin. He was cofounder and editor of the *Theologische Literaturzeiting* and served as director of the Königliche Bibliothek in Berlin and as president of the Kaiser-Wilhelm Gesellschaft zur Förderung der Wissenschaften. Harnack's celebrated *Lehrbuch der Dogmengeschichte* (3 vols., 1886–89; ET: *History of Dogma*, 7 vols., 1894–99) reflected Harnack's Ritschlianism. Metaphysics was the alien intrusion of "Hellenism" into Christian theology. Harnack's later work on *Marcion. Das Evangelium vom fremden Gott* (1921; ET: *Marcion: The Gospel of the Alien God*, trans. John E. Seely and Lyle D. Bierma [Durham, NC: Labyrinth, 1990]) argued that Marcion's New Testament God of redeeming love was more relevant to modern culture that the wrathful God of the Old Testament.

Harnack was closely associated with the Kaiser and national affairs. In recognition for his services he was given the title *von Harnack* in 1914. After the First World War he was offered, but declined, the post of German ambassador to the United States. Harnack's daughter, Agnes von Zahn-Harnack, wrote his biography, *Adolf von Harnack* (Berlin: de Gruyter, 1936; 2nd ed., 1951).

On Harnack's thought, see G. Wayne Glick, *The Reality of Christianity: A Study of Adolf von Harnack as Historian and Theologian* (New York: Harper & Row, 1967); Wilhelm Pauck, *Harnack*

(the year Schweitzer's *The Mystery of the Kingdom of God* was published), the fourth printing of Harnack's book reached 20,000 copies. By 1927 there had been fourteen printings, amounting to 71,000 copies.[6] From the outset Schweitzer's book had been eclipsed not only by Wrede's but also by Harnack's.

Harnack scorned Strauss's denial of the credibility of the Gospels on account of miracle stories.[7] "Miracles, it is true, do not happen; but of the marvellous and the inexplicable there is plenty. In our present state of knowledge we have become more careful, more hesitating in our judgment, in regard to the stories which we have received from antiquity.... That a storm was quieted by a word, we do not believe, and we shall never again believe; but that the lame walked, the blind saw, and the deaf heard, will not be summarily dismissed as an illusion."[8]

For Harnack, Jesus was first and foremost a teacher whose message was summed up under three headings:

Firstly, the kingdom of God and its coming.
Secondly, God the Father and the infinite value of the human soul.
Thirdly, the higher righteousness and the commandment of love.[9]

The historian's task of distinguishing "between the kernel and the husk in Jesus' message of the kingdom of God is a difficult and responsible one."[10] Jesus himself distinguished between the traditional elements in the ideas of his time: "He left out none in which there was a spark of moral force, and he accepted none in which there was a spark of the self expectations of his nation."[11]

---

and Troeltsch: *Two Historical Theologians* (Oxford: Oxford University Press, 1968); H. Martin Rumscheidt, *Revelation and Theology: An Analysis of the Barth-Harnack Correspondence of 1923*, Monograph Supplements to the Scottish Journal of Theology (Cambridge: Cambridge University Press, 1972); E. P. Meijering, *Theologische Urteile über die Dogmengeschichte. Ritschls Einfluss auf von Harnack*, BZRGG 20 (Leiden: Brill, 1978); E. P. Meijering, *Die Hellenisierung des Christentums im Urteil Adolf von Harnacks* (Amsterdam: North Holland, 1985); H. Martin Rumscheidt, *Adolf von Harnack: Liberal Theology at Its Height* (Minneapolis: Fortress, 1989); H. Martin Rumscheidt, *DMBI*, 104–07; Stephen G. Dempster, *EHJ*, 273–75.

6. Zahn-Harnack, *Adolf von Harnack*, 183.
7. Harnack, *What Is Christianity?*, 24.
8. Harnack, *What Is Christianity?*, 28.
9. Harnack, *What Is Christianity?*, 51 (Harnack's emphasis).
10. Harnack, *What Is Christianity?*, 55.
11. Harnack, *What Is Christianity?*, 56.

The No Quest in Europe to World War II

If anyone wants to know what the kingdom of God and the coming of it meant in Jesus' message, he must read and study his parables. He will then see what it is that he meant. The kingdom of God comes by coming to the individual, by entering into his soul and laying hold of it. True, the kingdom of God is the rule of God; but it is the rule of the holy God in the hearts of individuals; *it is God himself in his power*. From this point of view everything that is dramatic in the external and historical sense has vanished; and gone, too, are all the external hopes for the future.[12]

Echoing the language of Friedrich Nietzsche (1844–1900), but inverting its meaning, Harnack insisted that Jesus' understanding of the fatherhood of God and the infinite value of the human soul amounted to "a transvaluation of all values."[13]

The Gospel, as Jesus proclaimed it, has to do with the Father only and not with the Son. . . . But no one had ever yet known the Father in the way in which Jesus knew him, and to this knowledge of Him he draws other men's attention. . . . He leads them to God, not only by what he says, but still more by what he is and does, and ultimately by what he suffers. . . . He is the way to the Father, and as he is the appointed by the Father, so he is the judge as well. . . . He was [the] personal realization [of the Gospel] and its strength, and this he is felt to be still.[14]

This portrait of Jesus was reinforced by Harnack's study of Q, the sayings source behind Matthew and Luke.[15] Q represents "our Lord's own rule of life and all His promises—a summary of genuine ordinances

---

12. Harnack, *What Is Christianity?*, 56 (Harnack's emphasis).
13. Harnack, *What Is Christianity?*, 68. Nietzsche's atheistic philosophy repudiated the values of Christianity, and called for an *Umwertung aller Werte*, a "revaluation of all values." Nietzsche planned to use the term as the overall title of his *magnum opus*, which was to consist of four books. 1. The Antichrist: Attempt at a Critique of Christianity. 2. The Free Spirit: Critique of Philosophy as a Nihilistic Movement. 3. The Immoralist: Critique of the Most Fatal Kind of Ignorance, [Current] Morality. 4. Dionysus: Philosophy of Eternal Recurrence. Only the first was written; Walter Kaufmann, *Nietzsche: Philosopher, Psychologist, Antichrist* (3rd ed., Princeton, NJ: Princeton University Press, 1968), 102–15. On Nietzsche and Jesus, see below, chap. 17.
14. Harnack, *What Is Christianity?*, 144–45 (Harnack's emphasis), citing Matt 11:28 and Mark 10:45.
15. Harnack, *New Testament Studies*, vol. 2, *The Sayings of Jesus, the Second Source of St. Matthew and St. Luke*, trans. J.R. Wilkinson (New York: Putnam; London: Williams and Norgate, 1908).

transforming the life, such as is not to be found elsewhere in the Gospel."[16] The kingdom of God appears frequently in Q, where it clearly is not the eschatological kingdom of Schweitzer. Deliverance from the power of evil spirits "implies that the Kingdom of God had already come among the people. In the parables of the Mustard Seed and the Leaven . . . it is represented as a growing power, an influence gradually leavening mankind, and this conception makes it possible to regard the new epoch which dawned with the active ministry of our Lord, succeeding the mission of the Baptist, as already the epoch of the Kingdom."[17] Q provides the best "portrait" of Jesus: *"The collection of sayings and St. Mark must remain in power, but the former* [Q] *takes precedence."*[18]

Julius Wellhausen. Harnack's view of the essence of Christianity found widespread approval among liberal Protestants. A somewhat different view was taken by the leading Old Testament scholar Julius Wellhausen (1844–1918), who turned to New Testament studies later in his career.

Wellhausen famously stressed that Jesus was not a Christian but a *Jew*.

> Jesus was not a Christian but a Jew. . . . His teaching, according to Mark, is almost entirely a polemic directed against the scribes and Pharisees. He thought that they choked the Law with their additions and pushed aside the commandments of God by means of human ordinances. But through this distinction he undermined the uniform binding authority of the Law. He gave priority to the Decalogue and reduced its scope to love of God and one's neighbor. . . . He demanded purity of heart and of actions, which were directed not to God but to human beings. For God sees such actions as directed to himself, and in this lies the essence of true worship—morality remains religiously motivated and is independent of the changing idols of culture.[19]

---

16. Harnack, *New Testament Studies*, 2:231.
17. Harnack, *New Testament Studies*, 2:232; cf. 242.
18. Harnack, *New Testament Studies*, 2:250 (Harnack's emphasis). "And yet again how different are these two sources! On the one hand, St. Mark—wherein page by page the student is reduced to despair by the inconsistencies, the discrepancies, and the incredibilities of the narrative—and yet without this gospel we should be deprived of every thread of consistent and concrete historical information concerning the life of Jesus; and on the other hand, this compilation of sayings, which alone affords us a really exact and profound conception of the teaching of Jesus, and is free from bias, apologetic or otherwise, and yet gives us no history" (250).
19. Julius Wellhausen, *Einleitung in die drei ersten Evangelien* (Berlin: Reimer, 1905; 2nd ed., 1911), 102 (author's translation). Herder had rightly stressed oral tradition as the ultimate

The No Quest in Europe to World War II

Wellhausen differed from Harnack in refusing to draw a sharp line between Jesus' preaching and later developments. The kingdom of God was not something that would suddenly drop from heaven but was a present growing reality. "This present kingdom is now none other than the church, and indeed not merely in the invisible sense of Dr. Martin Luther. Jesus lays the foundation for the church in his preaching. He shows the disciples from whom the church will grow its ideal and also the external dangers and internal hindrances."[20] "As the Crucified, Risen, and Returning One, Jesus is the Christian Messiah." Harnack had gone too far. "The pronouncement ostensibly formulated by Harnack—'not the Son but only the Father belongs in the gospel'—is fundamentally false, if it is presented as a fact, and not merely as a postulate."[21]

Wellhausen also differed from Harnack over Q, which he dated later than Mark. "As Mark has priority for the narrative material, so he has for the discourse material. He is the oldest gospel writer. This explains his preservation in the catholic church."[22] In Mark Christianizing influence was concentrated in the passion and resurrection narratives. In Matthew and Luke it had permeated the entire narratives.[23] Wellhausen's position prompted James M. Robinson to see an analogy between Wellhausen's view of Q and Wrede's view of Mark and to see Harnack's reconstruction of Q as a refutation of Wellhausen.[24]

---

source (32). Unlike Harnack, Wellhausen gave Mark priority over Q as the most important source (32, 64–79, 159–63).

Schweitzer possessed a copy of Wellhausen's work. The signed copy dated 1913 is currently in the author's possession. The following comment is underlined with exclamation points: "Above all one must renounce the attempt to extract Ur-Mark cleanly and demonstrate the stages of redaction. It is a different matter in the narrative books of the Old Testament" (48).

Wellhausen wrote commentaries on Matthew (1904; 2nd ed., 1914), Mark (1905; 2nd ed., 1909), Luke (1904), and John (1908). They are reprinted together with *Einleitung* with the title *Evangelienkommentare*, with introduction by Martin Hengel (Berlin: de Gruyter, 1987). Quotations from Wellhausen's *Einleitung* have been translated by the author.

20. Wellhausen, *Einleitung*, 152; cf. Wellhausen, *Israelitische und Jüdische Geschichte* (Berlin: Reimer, 1894), 308–21.

21. Wellhausen, *Einleitung*, 153.

22. Wellhausen, *Einleitung*, 78.

23. Wellhausen, *Einleitung*, 75.

24. James M. Robinson, Paul Hoffmann, and John S. Kloppenborg, eds., *The Critical Edition of Q*, Hermeneia (Minneapolis: Fortress; Leuven: Peeters, 2000), xxxix. Robinson noted Harnack's comment: "I, on the contrary, believe that I can show in the following pages that Wellhausen in his characteristic of Q has unconsciously allowed himself to be influenced by the tendencies of St. Matthew and St. Luke, that he has attributed to Q what belongs to these gospels, and that in not a few passages he has preferred Mark on insufficient grounds. The conclusions at which I

1.2. Loisy and the Catholic Modernist Jesus. Harnack's lectures drew a swift reply from Alfred Loisy (1857–1940), priest, professor at the École Pratique des Hautes-Études de la Sorbonne, and leader of the modernist movement in the Roman Catholic Church.[25]

Alfred Loisy. Loisy's modernist agenda included wholesale adoption of the critical study of Scripture, the rejection of scholastic theology, and a developmental approach to dogma. In this last respect Loisy was following in the footsteps of John Henry Newman, who solved the problem of the divergence between church teaching and practice in his day and that of the primitive church with his theory of doctrinal development. What mattered was not identity but continuity as the church adapted to changing cultures.[26]

---

have arrived stand therefore in strong opposition to the results of his criticism" (Harnack, *New Testament Studies*, 2:194).

Harnack believed that Q was composed in Palestine, while Mark with its traces of "Paulinism" was composed in Rome. In light of Eusebius' claim that Matthew composed the *logia* in the Hebrew dialect, Harnack thought that Matthew was very probably the author of Q (248; cf. Eusebius, *Hist. eccl.* 3.39). In response, Wellhausen hardened his position in the second edition of his *Einleitung*.

25. On Loisy, see Maude Petre, *Alfred Loisy: His Religious Significance* (Cambridge: Cambridge University Press, 1944); Albert Houtin and Félix Sartiaux, *Alfred Loisy. Sa Vie, son Oeuvre*, with bibliography of Loisy's works and a bio-bibliography of persons connected with his life compiled by Émile Poulat (Paris: Centre Nationale de la Recherche Scientifique, 1960). Loisy entitled his autobiography *Mémoires pour servir à l'histoire religieuse de notre temps*, 3 vols. (Paris: Nourry, 1930–31).

On modernism, see A. Leslie Lilley, *Modernism: A Record and a Review* (New York: Scribner's, 1908); H. D. A. Major, *English Modernism: Its Origin, Methods, Aims* (Cambridge, MA: Harvard University Press, 1927); Émile Poulat, *Histoire, Dogme et Critique dans la Crise Moderniste* (Paris: Casterman, 1962); John Ratté, *Three Modernists: Alfred Loisy, William L. Sullivan, George Tyrrell* (London: Sheed and Ward, 1968); B. M. G. Reardon, ed., *Roman Catholic Modernism* (London: Black, 1970); Alec R. Vidler, *A Variety of Catholic Modernists* (Cambridge: Cambridge University Press, 1970); Alan H. Jones, *Independence and Exegesis: The Study of Early Christianity in the Work of Alfred Loisy (1857–1940), Charles Guignebert (1857–1939), and Maurice Goguel (1880–1955)*, BGBE 26 (Tübingen: Mohr Siebeck, 1983); B. M. G. Reardon, "Roman Catholic Modernism," in *Nineteenth Century Religious Thought in the West*, ed. Ninian Smart, John Clayton, Steven T. Katz, and Patrick Sherry (Cambridge: Cambridge University Press, 1985), 2:141–77; Lester R. Kurtz, *The Politics of Heresy: The Modernist Crisis in Roman Catholicism* (Berkeley: University of California Press, 1986); David G. Schultenover, *A View from Rome: On the Eve of the Modernist Crisis* (New York: Fordham University Press, 1993); Marvin R. O'Connell, *Critics on Trial: An Introduction to the Catholic Modernist Crisis* (Washington, DC: Catholic University of America Press, 1994); C. J. T. Talar, *DMBI*, 675–79.

On modernism in Germany, see Otto Weiss, *Der Modernismus in Deutschland. Ein Beitrag zur Theologiegeschichte*, with introduction by Heinrich Fries (Regenburg: Pustet, 1994).

26. John Henry Newman, *An Essay on the Development of Christian Doctrine* (1845), ed. J. M. Cameron (Harmondsworth: Penguin, 1974). Just as a mature adult is not an enlarged baby,

Loisy's reply to Harnack, *L'Évangile et L'Église* ("The Gospel and the Church") (1902), denounced Harnack's attempt to found religion on a "sole and unchangeable principle" extracted from the Gospel and used "as a touchstone to test the whole Christian development."[27] Harnack's "definition of Christianity is not based on the totality of authentic texts, but rests, when analyzed, on a very small number of texts, practically indeed on two passages:—'No man knoweth the Son, but the Father: neither knoweth any man the Father, save the Son' [Matt. 11:27], and 'The kingdom of God is within you' [Luke 17:21], both of them passages that might well have been influenced, if not produced, by the theology of early times."[28] By contrast, Loisy contended that "whatever we think, theologically, of tradition, whether we trust it or regard it with suspicion, we know Christ only by the tradition of the primitive Christians. . . . The attempt to define the essence of Christianity according to the pure gospel of Jesus, apart from tradition cannot succeed."[29]

Loisy agreed with Harnack—up to a point—that Jesus' proclamation centered on the kingdom of God. "Jésus annonçait le royaume, et c'est l'Église qui est venue [Jesus announced the kingdom, and what came was the church]."[30] His famous remark is frequently taken out of context to imply that the emergence of the institutional church was an anticlimax.

---

so the church cannot be expected to be the same as it was in the first century. Newman identified seven marks of true doctrinal development: preservation of type, continuity of principles, power of assimilation, logical sequence, anticipation of the future, conservation of the past, and chronic vigor.

Frank M. Turner commented on the *Essay*, which was written in justification for moving from Anglicanism to Roman Catholicism: "The perplexingly narrow focus of the *Essay on Development*, which defended only a limited Catholic vision rather than one of expansive Catholic reform, arose from his personally self-contained religious goal. He embraced development for the purpose of justifying devotional practices that he either wished to embrace himself or that his coterie wished to undertake." Frank M. Turner, *John Henry Newman: The Challenge to Evangelical Religion* (New Haven, CT: Yale University Press, 2002), 639.

27. Alfred Loisy, *The Gospel and the Church*, trans. Christopher Home (New York: Scribner's, 1903); repr. with introduction by Bernard B. Scott, Lives of Jesus (Philadelphia: Fortress, 1976), 3.

28. Loisy, *The Gospel and the Church*, 11–12; cf. Harnack, *What Is Christianity?* 127–28. Perusal of Harnack's text reveals Loisy's misrepresentation of Harnack's use of the Gospels and Loisy's omission to point out that Harnack's work was divided into two parts: 1. The Gospel, and 2. The Gospel in History.

29. Loisy, *The Gospel and the Church*, 13.

30. Loisy, *L'Évangile et L'Église* (Bellevue: Chez le'auteur, 1902; 5th ed., Paris: Nourry 1929), 153 (author's translation); cf. *The Gospel and the Church*, 166. Loisy presented his letters defending his book in *Autour d'un petit livre* (Paris: Picard, 1903).

For Loisy it was a frank admission not only of historical facts but also of historical necessity. The only way for the proclamation of Jesus to be realized was through the church.[31]

> In all Christian communities there is a service of the gospel which ensures the transmission and application of the Master's word. The Catholic Church is such a service formed by the centuries and continuous from the beginning. To be identical with the religion of Jesus, it has no more need to reproduce exactly the forms of the Galilean gospel, than a man has need to preserve at fifty the proportions, features, and manner of life of the day of his birth, in order to be the same individual. The identity of the man is not ensured by making him return to his cradle.[32]

George Tyrrell. In *Christianity at the Cross-Roads* (1909) the Jesuit modernist George Tyrrell (1861–1909) summed up Loisy's case. "The Christ that Harnack sees, looking back through nineteen centuries of Catholic darkness, is only the reflection of a Liberal Protestant face, seen at the bottom of a deep well."[33] If Harnack had been so minded, he might have replied in kind: the Christ that Loisy imagines, buried beneath nineteen centuries of Catholic tradition, is a shadowy, romantic construct designed to fit the modernist theory of development. Harnack had not done away with tradition, but as a Protestant he wanted to evaluate traditions by comparing them with the essence of Christianity, which he found in the teaching and practice of Jesus.

At this stage in his career, Loisy appeared ready to accept all traditions of the Catholic Church as legitimate expressions of Jesus'

---

31. Loisy, *The Gospel and the Church*, xxxvii–xlii, 59–60, 147–51, 165–66.

32. Loisy, *The Gospel and the Church*, 170; cf. Newman's illustration noted above in n26. "Here the most ready test is suggested by the analogy of physical growth, which is such that the parts and proportions of the developed form correspond to those which belong to its rudiments.... Unity of type is certainly the most obvious characteristic of a faithful development." Newman, *An Essay on the Development of Christian Doctrine*, 117.

33. George Tyrrell, *Christianity at the Cross-Roads* (London: Longmans, Green, 1909; repr., London: Allen & Unwin, 1963), 49. Having read Schweitzer's *Quest*, Tyrrell wrote to Baron von Hügel (April 9, 1909): "Having finished Schweitzer and re-read J. Weiss very carefully... I realize better the full depth of the Loisy-Harnack controversy" (9). On Tyrrell, see Maude D. Petre, *Autobiography and Life of George Tyrrell*, 2 vols. (London: Arnold, 1912); Ellen Leonard, *George Tyrrell and the Catholic Tradition* (New York: Paulist, 1982); David G. Schultenover, *George Tyrrell: In Search of Catholicism* (Shepherdstown, WV: Patmos, 1981); Nicholas Sagovsky, *On God's Side: A Life of George Tyrrell* (Oxford: Clarendon, 1990); Nicholas Sagovsky, *ODNB*, 55:802–4.

proclamation of the kingdom. In retrospect, Loisy's postulation of a historical Jesus behind tradition looks curiously like a Catholic counterpart to the historical Jesus posited by the Protestant New Quest. Catholic tradition pointed back to Loisy's Jesus; the kerygma of the cross and resurrection pointed back to the Jesus of the New Quest. Tyrrell's jibe highlights the problem of subjectivity and the danger of reconstructing Jesus in our image and with our values. At the same time it overlooks the process embedded in all historical interpretation—the interplay between the horizons of the interpreter and the horizons of the text. Without what Hans-Georg Gadamer called "the fusion of horizons," no historical understanding is possible.[34]

By the time that *Christianity at the Cross-Roads* appeared, modernism had been formally condemned, and Tyrrell, who had been alienated from the church, was dead.[35] Loisy responded to the condemnation with *Simples réflexions sur le Décret du Saint Office Lamentabili sane exitu et sur l'Encyclique Pascendi domini gregis* (1908). He was excommunicated on March 7, 1908. From 1909 to 1930 he taught the history of religions at the Collège de France. A prolific author, his writings include studies of the Gospels, Jesus, and Christian origins.[36] His final position was that the Gospels should be treated as catechetical and cultural literature but not as history.

1.3. Baeck, Klausner, and the Jewish Reclamation of Jesus. From a Jewish standpoint, Harnack's book drew a sharp reply from the twenty-seven-year-old Reform rabbi Leo Baeck (1873–1956).[37] In the

---

34. Hans-Georg Gadamer, *Truth and Method*, trans. Joel Weinsheimer and Donald G. Marshall (London: T&T Clark, 2004; repr., 2013), 317. See above, chap. 1, §2.2.

35. The decree of the Holy Office *Lamentabili* (July 3, 1907) condemned sixty-five modernist propositions. It was followed by the encyclical of Pius X *Pascendi* (September 8, 1907) and the oath against modernism *Sacrorum Antistites* (September 1, 1910). Texts in Denzinger-Schönmetzer, *Enchiridion* §3401–66, §3475–3502, §3537–52.

36. Alfred Loisy, *Le Quatrième Évangile* (Paris: Picard, 1903); *Les Évangiles Synoptiques*, 2 vols. (Ceffonds: self-published, 1907-8); *Jésus et la tradition évangélique* (Paris: Nourry, 1910); *L'Évangile selon Marc* (Paris: Nourry, 1912); *La Naissance du Christianisme* (Paris: Nourry, 1933); *Les Origines du Nouveau Testament* (Paris: Nourry, 1936); ET: *The Origins of the New Testament*, trans. L. P. Jacks (London: Allen & Unwin, 1950); *Histoire et mythe à propos de Jésus-Christ* (Paris: Nourry, 1938).

37. "Harnacks Vorlesungen über das Wesen des Christentums," *Monatsschrift für Geschichte und Wissenschaft des Judentums* 45 (Neue Folge 9) (1901): 97–98, 117–20; partial translation with introduction by J. Louis Martyn in Fritz A. Rothschild, ed., *Jewish Perspectives on Christianity: Leo Baeck, Martin Buber, Franz Rosenzweig, and Abraham J. Heschel* (New York: Continuum, 1996), 42–45; cf. Akiba Ernst Simon, Yehoyada Amir, *EJ* 2nd ed., 3:50–52.

Baeck's subsequent works included *Das Wesen des Judentums*, ([1905] 6th ed. Frankfurt am

1920s Joseph Klausner wrote the first full-scale life of Jesus by a Jewish scholar, which saw Jesus in a positive light.

Leo Baeck. Baeck claimed that although Harnack presented himself as an objective historian, he was an apologist who was woefully ignorant of Jewish sources. Harnack had stressed the gulf between Jesus and the rabbis but had overlooked the fact that the rabbis included haggadists as well as Torah experts—a point underscored by recent scholarship.[38] Jesus' teaching show him as a storyteller in the rabbinic haggadic tradition. "Most writers about the life of Jesus fail to point out that Jesus, in every one of his traits, was a *thoroughly Jewish character*, that a man such as he could arise only from the soil of Judaism. . . . This matrix of the personality of Jesus has not been regarded by Harnack."[39] Baeck inverted Harnack's argument about the universal significance of Jesus. Instead of transcending Judaism, "the day had come when [pagans] could begin to absorb Israel's teaching, and God let his own people rise to the occasion. And if only for that reason, Judaism has nothing but love and respect for the founder of Christianity."[40]

Baeck viewed Christianity as a "romantic," abstract, spiritual religion, sharply distinguished from Judaism, which was the classical religion of concrete, daily life. As such, Baeck was an early advocate of "the Jewish reclamation of Jesus."[41]

Joseph Klausner. The most thoroughly researched and most influential book on Jesus by a Jewish scholar from early times to the mid-twentieth century came from the pen of Joseph Gedaliah Klausner (1874–1960).[42] Klausner was born near Vilnius in Lithuania but grew up

---

Main: Kaufmann, 1932); ET: *The Essence of Judaism*, trans. Irving Howe, based on the translation by V. Grubenwieser and L. Pearl (New York: Macmillan, 1936; repr., New York: Schocken, 1948); *Judaism and Christianity: Essays*, trans. Walter Kaufmann (Philadelphia: Jewish Publication Society of America, 1954).

Baeck was sent by the Nazis to a concentration camp but survived. After World War II he settled in London. In the 1950s he served as visiting professor at the Hebrew Union College, Cincinnati.

38. Geza Vermes, *The Religion of Jesus the Jew* (London: SCM, 1993), 76–118; Bruce D. Chilton, *Judaic Approaches to the Gospels*, USF International Studies in Formative Christianity and Judaism 2 (Atlanta: Scholars, 1994); Craig A. Evans, *Jesus and His Contemporaries*, AGJU 25 (Leiden: Brill, 1995), 251–97.

39. Rothschild, ed., *Jewish Perspectives on Christianity*, 44.

40. Rothschild, ed., *Jewish Perspectives on Christianity*, 45.

41. Donald A. Hagner, *The Jewish Reclamation of Jesus: An Analysis and Critique of Modern Jewish Study of Jesus*, with a foreword by Gösta Lindeskog (Grand Rapids: Zondervan, 1984), 36.

42. Donald A. Hagner, *The Jewish Reclamation of Jesus*, 30–31 and passim; Gösta Lindeskog,

in Odessa on the Black Sea. Early on he came under the influence of "Ahad-ha-Am" (Asher Ginsberg), the Zionist editor of the periodical *Ha-Shiloach*. In 1897 Klausner entered the University of Heidelberg, where he studied philosophy and Semitic languages. He wrote his doctorate on "Die messianischen Vorstellungen des jüdischen Volkes im Zeitalter der Tannaiten" ("The Messianic Ideas of the Jewish People in the Age of the Tannaites"—the authorities of the first two centuries CE, whose teachings are preserved in the Mishnah). Klausner went on to make a lifelong study of the messianic idea.[43] In 1905 Klausner succeeded Ginsberg as editor of *Ha-Shiloach*, and from 1904 to 1919 he held various academic posts in Jewish institutions in Odessa. In 1920 he emigrated to Palestine, where he taught modern Hebrew and literature at the Hebrew University.

Klausner's main contribution to Jesus studies was *Jesus of Nazareth: His Life, Times, and Teaching* (1925).[44] It was divided into eight "books" dealing respectively with the sources, the period, the early life of Jesus, the beginning of Jesus' ministry, Jesus' revelation of himself as Messiah, Jesus in Jerusalem, the trial and crucifixion of Jesus, and the teaching of Jesus. Within the confines of this brief section it is impossible to do justice to the rich exactness of Klausner's work. It demonstrates a rare thoroughness and a deep appreciation of his subject, as well as a clear account of why Klausner could not embrace the teaching of Jesus.

Klausner dismissed Harnack's *Das Wesen des Christentums* in a single paragraph. "There, the historical Jew, Jesus, disappears totally. Virtually every word he taught is made to be of permanent and universal humanitarian interest.... It is not without cause that Harnack devoted his last book to that extremist of early Christian opponents of Judaism, Marcion.... Harnack's Jesus is altogether a modernist and philosopher,

---

Die Jesusfrage im neuzeitlichen Judentum. Ein Beitrag zur Geschichte der Leben-Jesu-Forschung (1938; 2nd ed., Darmstadt: Wissenschaftliche Buchgesellscht, 1973); Samuel Sandmel, "Into the Fray: Joseph Klausner's Approach to Judaism and Christianity in the Greco-Roman World" (PhD diss., University of Pennsylvania, 2002); David Flusser, Samuel Werses, Meir Meda, *EncJudJ* 2nd ed., 12: 215–17; Reidar Hvalvik, *EHJ*, 358–60.

43. Joseph Klausner, *The Messianic Idea in Israel*, trans W. F. Stinespring (London: Allen & Unwin, 1956). It was originally published in German in 1904.

44. Joseph Klausner, *Jesus of Nazareth: His Life, Times, and Teaching* (London: Allen & Unwin, 1925). The book was translated from the Hebrew by Herbert Danby, who gave a brief sketch of Klausner's life in his preface. The above account is indebted to Danby's sketch. Danby was residentiary canon of the Anglican Cathedral of St. George in Jerusalem. His translation of *The Mishnah* (Oxford: Oxford University Press, 1922) was for many years the standard edition in English. He went on to become Regius Professor of Hebrew at Oxford.

the Jesus of the liberal anti-Jewish Germany of the early twentieth century."[45]

Wellhausen fared scarcely better. Klausner began his summing up of "the Jewishness of Jesus" with the following comment:

> Despite the animus which Julius Wellhausen usually showed in treating of Pharisaic, *Tannaitic* and even Prophetic Judaism, he was responsible for the following bold estimate: *"Jesus was not a Christian: he was a Jew*. He did not preach a new faith, but taught men to do the will of God; and in his opinion, as also in that of the Jews, the will of God was to be found in the Law of Moses and in the other books of Scripture." How could it have been otherwise? . . . [Jesus] was a product of Palestine alone, a product of Judaism unaffected by any foreign admixture. There were many gentiles in Galilee, but Jesus was in no way influenced by them.[46]

Jesus' quarrel was not with the law *per se* but with those who regarded the ceremonial laws as more important than the moral laws.[47] "Jesus was a Jew and a Jew he remained until his last breath. His one idea was to implant within this nation the idea of the coming of the Messiah and, by repentance and good works hasten the 'end.'"[48] In some respects, Jesus was "the most Jewish of Jews, more Jewish than Simeon ben Shetah, more Jewish even than Hillel. Yet nothing is more dangerous to national Judaism than [Jesus'] *exaggerated* Judaism; it is the ruin of national culture, the national state, and national life. Where there is no call for the enactment of laws, for justice, for national statecraft, where belief in God and the practice of an extreme and one-sided ethic is in itself enough—there we have the negation of national life and of the national state."[49]

Nevertheless, if miracles and mystical sayings deifying the Son of Man were omitted, "the Gospels would count as one of the most

---

45. Klausner, *Jesus of Nazareth*, 96.
46. Klausner, *Jesus of Nazareth*, 363; cf. Wellhausen, *Einleitung*, 113.
47. Klausner, *Jesus of Nazareth*, 367; cf. Matt 23:23; Luke 11:42.
48. Klausner, *Jesus of Nazareth*, 368.
49. Klausner, *Jesus of Nazareth*, 374. A case in point of this regard for national law was Jesus' refusal to speak to a man's brother in the interests of dividing their inheritance (Luke 12:13–14). Klausner commented: "Jesus disregards justice generally, even when it is a case of natural civil interest, free of any ill motive; he thus ignores anything concerned with material civilization: in this sense he does not belong to civilization" (375).

wonderful collections of ethical teaching in the world."[50] "Yet with Geiger and Graetz, we can aver, without laying ourselves open to the charge of subjectivity and without any desire to argue in defence of Judaism, that *throughout the Gospels there is not one item of ethical teaching which can not be paralleled either in the Old Testament, the Apocrypha, or in the Talmudic and Midrashic literature of the period nearer to the time of Jesus.*"[51]

Klausner saw a profound paradox in Jesus—superb ethical teaching alongside indifference to the needs of Jewish national life. It was for the latter reason that Judaism could not embrace Jesus of Nazareth.

> Jesus surpassed Hillel in his ethical ideals: he changed Hillel's "Golden Rule" from the negative form ("What thou thyself hatest do not do unto thy neighbour"—in which the *Book of Tobit* anticipates Hillel) to the positive form ("What thou wouldest that men should do unto thee, do thou also unto them"—in which the "Letter of Aristeas" anticipates Jesus), and concerns himself more with ethical teaching than did Hillel; but his teaching has not proved possible in practice.
>
> Therefore he left the course of ordinary life untouched—wicked, cruel, pagan, and his exalted ethical teaching was relegated to a book, or at most, became a possession of monastics and recluses who lived far apart from the paths of ordinary life.
>
> Beyond this ethical teaching Jesus gave nothing to his nation. He cared not for reforming the world or civilization: therefore to adopt the teaching of Jesus is to remove oneself from the whole of ordered national and human existence—from law, learning and civics (all three of which were absorbed into the codes of the *Tannaim-Pharisees*), from life within the State, and from wealth in all its forms. How could Judaism accede to *such* an ethical ideal?—that Judaism to which the monastic ideal had ever been foreign![52]

---

50. Klausner, *Jesus of Nazareth*, 381.

51. Klausner, *Jesus of Nazareth*, 384 (Klausner's emphasis).

52. Klausner, *Jesus of Nazareth*, 397. Klausner traced the Golden Rule to Tobit 4:15; Philo as quoted by Eusebius, *Praeparatio Evangelica* 8.7.6; and the *Didache* 1.2, which he regarded as a mainly Jewish work. Recent discussions of the Golden Rule include P. S. Alexander, "Jesus and the Golden Rule," in *Hillel and Jesus: Comparative Studies of Two Major Religious Leaders*, ed. James H. Charlesworth and Loren L. Johns (Minneapolis: Fortress, 1997), 363–88; and Jacob Neusner and Bruce Chilton, eds., *The Golden Rule: Analytical Perspectives* (Lanham, MD: University Press of America, 2008).

Despite these differences, it was Pilate, not the Jews—except possibly a small section of the Sadducees—who were responsible for Jesus' crucifixion.[53] This tragedy had an "epilogue" in the resurrection that alone made Christianity possible.[54] The resurrection was not an imposture, for a religion with millions of adherents could not be based on imposture. However, the bulk of the Jewish nation could not found its belief on such a cornerstone.

In comparing *Jesus of Nazareth* with contemporary Protestant writing, especially that of Bousset and Bultmann, I am struck by two issues. The first is that Klausner was much more ready than they to treat the Gospels as credible, historical narratives of Jesus and his teaching. The second issue is that whereas Bousset and Bultmann worked with the criterion of double dissimilarity, Klausner anticipated the criteria of double similarity and double dissimilarity of the Third Quest. Klausner's Jesus was doubly similar to the world and teachings of both Judaism and Christianity. Jesus' teaching was drawn entirely from Jewish teaching, and it formed the basis of Christian belief and practice. But it was also doubly dissimilar to both Judaism and Christianity. Although Jesus was a Jew and not a Christian, his ethical teaching was too alien to Jewish public life to be embraced by the Jewish nation. On the other hand, the Christian church abstracted Jesus and his teaching from their Jewish horizons in order to form the basis of a gentile religion.

Some years after *Jesus of Nazareth*, Klausner wrote *From Jesus to Paul* (1939),[55] which traced the rise of Christianity and the parting of the ways between Christianity and Judaism. For this break the prime responsibility must lie with Paul, whose Jewish beliefs "took on a new, half-pagan complexion from foreign influences, and thus became non-Judaism and anti-Judaism."[56] A Jewish minority followed Paul, but a great number of gentiles accepted his teaching, paving the way for Christianity to become a gentile religion in which Paul's dogmas replaced the ceremonial laws.[57]

---

53. Klausner, *Jesus of Nazareth*, 340–55.

54. Klausner, *Jesus of Nazareth*, 356–59.

55. Joseph Klausner, *From Jesus to Paul*, trans. William F. Stinespring (New York: Macmillan, 1943; London: Allen & Unwin, 1944; repr., New York: Beacon, 1961). Quotations below are taken from the London edition; cf. W. G. Kümmel, "Jesus und Paulus. Zu Joseph Klausners Darstellung des Christentums," *Heilsgeschehen und Geschichte. Gesammelte Aufsätze, 1933–1964* (Marburg: Elwert, 1965), 439–56.

56. Klausner, *From Jesus to Paul*, 591.

57. Klausner, *From Jesus to Paul*, 596.

"[By] means of exaggerated words of adoration which Paul applied to 'Christ Jesus,' this Christ became more and more a supernatural figure, and after a little while an actual son of God."[58] Separation was inevitable.

2. The Recovery of Jesus' World

2.1. Schürer and the Jewish People. The task of recovering the Jewish world of Jesus began in earnest with Emil Schürer (1844–1910).[59] Schürer studied theology at Erlangen, Berlin, and Heidelberg, but he was not ordained and apparently preached only one sermon in his life. At Heidelberg he came under the influence of the mediating theologian Richard Rothe (1799–1867), who directed him to the study of Schleiermacher and Baur. He was also influenced by Schweitzer's future mentor H. J. Holtzmann (1832–1910), whom Martin Hengel described as "the true founder of historical-critical scholarship in Germany."[60] Schürer held positions at Leipzig (1873)—where he formed a lifelong friendship with Harnack, with whom he cofounded the *Theologische Literaturzeitung* (1876)—Giessen (1878), Kiel (1890), and Göttingen (1895). On Schürer's death, Harnack remarked that the most enduring influence on Schürer was Ritschl, who stimulated him to reduce theology to its most basic elements.[61] By that time the *Theologische Literaturzeitung* had become the organ of historical critical theology in the Ritschlian tradition.

Schürer's main contribution was his magisterial *History of the Jewish People in the Time of Jesus Christ*. It began modestly as a textbook on the historical background of New Testament times (1877) but was retitled

---

58. Klausner, *From Jesus to Paul*, 597.
59. George Foot Moore, "Christian Writers on Judaism," *HTR* 14 (1921): 197–254; Martin Hengel, "Der alte und der neue 'Schürer.' Mit einem Anhang von Hanswulf Bloedhorn," *JSS* 35 (1990): 19–79; repr. in Martin Hengel, *Judaica, Hellenistica et Christiana*, WUNT 109 (Tübingen: Mohr Siebeck, 1999), 157–99; Rainer Riesner, "Schürer," *TRE*, 30:565–68; Christoph Dahm, "Schürer," in *Biographisch-Bibliographisches Kirchenlexikon*, 9:1050–53.
60. Hengel, *Judaica, Hellenistica et Christiana*, 158. John S. Kloppenborg has made a cogent case for claiming that Holtzmann's *Die synoptischen Evangelien* (1863) not only established Mark's priority and the basic contours of the two-source hypothesis but also represented the starting point for the "liberal lives of Jesus" that prevailed until the early 1900s. Kloppenborg, "Holtzmann's Life of Jesus according to the 'A' Sources: Part 1," *JSHJ* 4 (2006): 75–108; Kloppenborg, "Holtzmann's Life of Jesus according to the 'A' Sources: Part 2," *JSHJ* 4 (2006): 203–23.
61. Adolf Harnack, "Nachruf für Emil Schürer," *TLZ* 35, no. 10 (1910): 289–90. Harnack noted that Schürer had reached his position on theology and history by about the age of twenty-seven. "He never abandoned it or hardly modified it. . . . He was more often right than wrong."

for the second edition (1886–87) on which the original English translation was based.[62] Eventually it ran to 2,297 pages. The third and fourth editions (1901–09) began with the observation: "In the fullness of time Christianity sprang from the womb of Judaism, admittedly as a fact of divine revelation, yet bound through countless threads to the thousand-year history of Israel. No fact of Gospel history, no word in the preaching of Jesus is thinkable without the presupposition of Jewish history and the entire thought-world of the Jewish people."[63]

The first volume covered political history from Antiochus Epiphanes to the disastrous Bar Kokhba revolt against Rome (175 BCE–135 CE). The second volume analyzed "the internal situation"—that is, the spread of Hellenistic culture, the Sanhedrin, high priests, priesthood, temple cult, scribes, Pharisees, Sadducees, life under the law, messianic expectation, and the Essenes. The third volume dealt with the Diaspora and postbiblical literature. Schürer's work became the standard authority for over half a century.

In the 1960s Matthew Black of St. Andrews University put together a team to translate and update the final German edition. Schürer's basic structure was retained, but the text was virtually rewritten to account for new archaeological, epigraphical, and literary evidence, including the Dead Sea Scrolls and the Bar Kokhba documents. In its new form, *The History of the Jewish People in the Age of Jesus Christ* (1973–1987), edited by Geza Vermes, Fergus Millar, and Martin Goodman, with organizing editor Matthew Black and literary editor Pamela Vermes,[64] was greeted by Martin Hengel as "an astonishing achievement."[65]

Schürer's view of the Pharisees[66] and his reduction of Jewish piety

---

62. The work was originally entitled *Lehrbuch der Neutestamentlichen Zeitgeschichte* (1874). In its second edition it was retitled *Geschichte des jüdischen Volkes im Zeitalter Jesus Christi* (Leipzig: Hinrichs, 1886–87); ET: *A History of the Jewish People in the Time of Jesus Christ*, trans. J. Macpherson, S. Taylor, and P. Christie (Edinburgh: T&T Clark, 1890–91).

63. Schürer, *Geschichte*, 1:1 (author's translation).

64. The revision followed Schürer's division of three volumes, but the third volume is divided into two parts (Edinburgh: T&T Clark, 1973–1987); cf. Heinz Schreckenberg and Geza Vermes, *EJ*, 2nd ed., 18:215–18.

65. Hengel, *Judaica, Hellenistica et Christiana*, 157. Hengel subjected the work to a detailed critique, noting *inter alia* the fact that the full text of the Dead Sea Scrolls was not available at the time of publication. His comments on the number of printing errors, especially in Greek quotations, and numerous observations make his appraisal a valuable supplement.

66. Schürer, *Geschichte*, 4th ed., §26, 456–75; cf. Roland Deines, *Die Pharisäer. Ihr Verständnis im Spiegel der christlichen und jüdischen Forschung seit Wellhausen und Graetz*, WUNT 101

to two themes—life under the law[67] and messianic hope[68]—reflected liberal Protestant views. The preface of the *New Schürer* noted that "in the domain of value judgments, the editors have endeavoured to clear the notorious chap. 28, *Das Leben unter dem Gesetz* ['Life under the Law']— here re-styled as 'Life and the Law'—and the section on the Pharisees (§26 I) of the dogmatic prejudices of nineteenth-century theology."[69]

Schürer's work was like a background without a portrait. Although Jesus featured in the title, Jesus himself did not appear in the book. This omission was partially rectified in Schürer's lecture on the essence of the Christian revelation, which was almost contemporary with Harnack's lectures on the essence of Christianity.[70] The negative view of Jewish piety in the *History* served as the backdrop for Jesus' significance. God had revealed himself through the prophets, but since the time of Ezra, religion "had become codified in a book of laws, and this book of laws become elevated as the norm of religious behavior."[71] Jesus was conscious of the fact that "the true being of God the father is first revealed through him" (Matt 11:27; Luke 10:22).[72]

Schürer went on to review the contents of the New Testament. Anticipating Bultmann's theme of the proclaimer becoming the proclaimed, Schürer declared that, "For Paul the gospel is the word of the

---

(Tübingen: Mohr Siebeck, 1997), 68–95; Hans-Günther Waubke, *Die Pharisäer in der protestantischen Bibelwissenschaft des 19. Jahrhunderts*, BHT 107 (Tübingen: Mohr Siebeck, 1998), 226–49.

Schürer depicted Palestinian Judaism as a unified entity, dominated by the Pharisees and scribes. He was heavily dependent on Josephus for his reconstruction and used rabbinic sources uncritically in his picture of daily life. The later editions of the *Geschichte* drew on apocalyptic pseudepigrapha primarily to depict popular piety as a preparation for the gospel. Pharisaic influence was identified with growing legalism in Palestinian Judaism. Schürer recognized more clearly than his predecessors or successors the importance of halakhah for the Pharisees, but he tended to treat it negatively, failing to recognize its positive role.

67. Schürer, *Geschichte*, 4th ed., §28, 537–79.
68. Schürer, *Geschichte*, 4th ed., §29, 579–650.
69. Schürer, *The History of the Jewish People in the Age of Jesus*, 2:v. In a lengthy footnote at the beginning of §28 the editors explain their reasons for the new version, which is now treated "from a historical rather than a theological vantage point. Moreover, the purpose of the Pharisees and their rabbinic heirs is obviously no longer represented as a trivialization of religion, but identified as an attempt to elevate everyday Jewish life as a whole, and in its minute details, to the sphere of cultic worship" (2:464).
70. Schürer, "Das Wesen der christlichen Offenbarung nach dem Neuen Testament. Vortrag gehalten im wissenschaftlichen Predigerverein zu Hannover am 3. Mai 1899," *ZTK* 10 (1900): 1–39. English translations below are by the author.
71. Schürer, "Das Wesen der christlichen Offenbarung," 2.
72. Schürer, "Das Wesen der christlichen Offenbarung," 5.

cross (1 Cor. 1:18). . . . But the death of Christ on the cross is the ground of salvation only because Christ is also risen."[73] "Paul and John are the theologians of the New Testament."[74] Whereas the earthly activity of Jesus is almost without significance for Paul, it is the reverse for John who "places all emphasis on the activity of the historical Jesus."[75]

Schürer's conclusion was reminiscent of Schleiermacher's portrait of Jesus as the mediator of human awareness of God. "According to Christ's own testimony as in the account of the Fourth Gospel, he himself has brought us the full revelation of the Father, indeed not only through his word but in his entire activity—through his living, God-filled personality. In him we behold the Father, and his Spirit, which works in the church, continues and brings again and again understanding of this revelation. . . . The significance of Scripture consists in the fact that it paints the portrait of Christ living before our eyes—it replaces his physical presence for us as it proclaims Christ to us. Thus we participate in revelation as we receive Christ into our inner selves, just as Scripture depicts him to us. *His* life thus becomes *our* life, *his* fellowship with God becomes *our* fellowship with God. God is revealed to us as the gracious one, and this life in God makes us free from sin and the world."[76]

2.2. Strack-Billerbeck and the Relevance of Talmud and Midrash.

A more positive view of the religion of Judaism was given by the *Kommentar zum Neuen Testament aus Talmud und Midrasch* ("Commentary to the New Testament from Talmud and Midrash").[77] The project was conceived by Hermann L. Strack (1848–1922).[78] Strack became head of the Institutum Judaicum at Berlin in 1866 and was made an honorary university professor in 1910. His *Introduction to the Talmud and Midrash* (1920; ET 1931) provided introduction to the sources used in the commentary.[79] Strack's endeavors to promote understanding for the Jewish

---

73. Schürer, "Das Wesen der christlichen Offenbarung," 10.
74. Schürer, "Das Wesen der christlichen Offenbarung," 24.
75. Schürer, "Das Wesen der christlichen Offenbarung," 18.
76. Schürer, "Das Wesen der christlichen Offenbarung," 39; cf. Schleiermacher, *The Christian Faith*, §94; Brown, *Jesus in European Protestant Thought*, 116–23.
77. H. L. Strack and Paul Billerbeck, *Kommentar zum Neuen Testament aus Talmud und Midrasch*, 4 vols. (Munich: Beck, 1924–28). An English translation by Lexham Press is in preparation.
78. Christof Dahm, *BBK*, 11:5–8.
79. The work has been extensively revised to incorporate new material and new perspectives on Judaism and is now published as H. L. Strack and G. Stemberger, *Introduction to the Talmud and Midrash*, trans. Markus Bockmuehl, foreword by Jacob Neusner (Minneapolis: Fortress, 1992).

people provoked the ire of anti-Semites. At the same time his support for the evangelism of Jews earned him the reputation of being "a wolf in sheep's clothing." His vision for the *Kommentar* was to provide a basis for understanding the New Testament within the world of Judaism. Strack saw to the planning, funding—no small matter in a period of galloping inflation—and publication, but the compilation of the material was the work of Pastor Paul Billerbeck (1853–1932).[80]

Billerbeck's interest in Judaism sprang from a sermon he was preparing on the kingdom of God (Matt 4:17) as a young minister. Existing commentaries had plenty to say about Jesus' understanding of the kingdom but nothing about that of his hearers. Billerbeck was led to the study of rabbinic sources. A series of articles for the missionary journal *Nathanael*, edited by Strack, led to the invitation to collect and translate rabbinic material with a view to illuminating the New Testament from the standpoint of Jewish belief and practice. In the quiet of his country parsonage Billerbeck worked on the project from 1906 to 1922.

The first volume of 1,055 pages was devoted to Matthew. The second (867 pages) covered the other three gospels and Acts, and the third (857 pages) the rest of the New Testament. Volume 4 (in two parts; 1,323 pages) consisted of thirty-three excurses on sundry topics and an index. Volumes 5 and 6 containing further indexes were added later and were produced by Joachim Jeremias, to whom Billerbeck had entrusted the work on his deathbed. In this work, Jeremias was aided by Kurt Adolph. The work was not strictly a commentary but a compilation of more than 40,000 annotations. The principal sources were the Mishnah (c. 200 CE), and works exegeting the Mishnah: the Tosefta, the Talmud of the Land of Israel (Palestinian Talmud or Yerushalmi, c. 400 CE), and the Talmud of Babylonia (Babylonian Talmud or Bavli, c. 600 CE). In addition, the *Kommentar* drew on the interpretative commentaries on the Hebrew Bible known as Midrash.

Jeremias summed up the importance of the *Kommentar* with the comment: "A research area of fundamental importance for understanding the New Testament, that hitherto was unknown territory accessible to only a few specialists—the Jewish world of Jesus and the early church—has been opened up to the theological world since 1922 for common use.

---

80. Joachim Jeremias, "Paul Billerbeck in Memoriam," *TBl* 12 (1932): 33–35; cf. Jeremias, *TRE*, 8:640–42; S. S. Schatzmann, *DMBI*, 937–41; *Kommentar* 1:v; 2:vii–viii.

Thereby a new basis for New Testament exegesis, in particular for that of the Gospels, has been created."[81]

The work became a prime source for initiating scholars into the world of Judaism. But there were problems. It was easy to assume parallels between the Gospels and Rabbinic Judaism on the basis of *apparent* parallels.[82] Strack-Billerbeck could mislead those who, in the words of Anthony J. Saldarini, "lacked the expertise to consult the sources for the context, genre, and relevance of the parallels adduced to illuminate the NT."[83] Perhaps the biggest difficulty was the assumption that rabbinic Judaism represented normative Judaism,[84] in contrast to Hellenism, Diaspora Judaism, and sectarian Judaism, not to mention Philo and Josephus. Any commentary written today from the perspective of Jewish sources would have to take into account the diversity of Judaisms, including the Dead Sea Scrolls, whose discovery still lay in the future.[85]

2.3. Dalman and the Languages of Jesus. Gustaf Dalman (1855–1941) is best known for his study of Aramaic and his research into the world of Second Temple Judaism.[86] A student of Franz Delitzsch,

---

81. Jeremias, *TRE*, 8:642.

82. Samuel Sandmel, "Parallelomania," *JBL* 81 (1962): 1–13.

83. Anthony J. Saldarini, "Judaism and the New Testament," in Epp and MacRae, *The New Testament and Its Modern Interpreters*, 27–54, here 29.

84. Saldarini cited as an example of this limitation (p. 27) George Foot Moore's *Judaism in the First Centuries of the Christian Era: The Age of the Tannaim*, 3 vols. (Cambridge, MA: Harvard University Press, 1927–30).

85. At the time of writing, the first volume of a replacement commentary, which addresses these issues, has been published. It is entitled *A Comparative Handbook to the Gospel of Mark: Comparisons with the Pseudepigrapha, the Qumran Scrolls, and Rabbinic Literature*, New Testament Gospels in their Judaic Contexts, general editor Bruce Chilton, assistant editor Darrell Bock, editor for Apocrypha, Pseudepigrapha, Philo, and Josephus Daniel M. Gurtner, editor for Rabbinic Literature Jacob Neusner, editor for the literature of Qumran Lawrence H. Schiffmann, assistant editor for the literature of Qumran Daniel Oden, vol. 1 (Leiden: Brill, 2010). The second volume, which is on the gospels of Matthew and Luke, appeared in 2021. A third volume, on the gospel of John, is planned.

86. Dalman's linguistic work includes *Grammatik des jüdisch-palästinischen Aramäisch nach den Idiomen des palästinischen Talmud des Onkelostargum und der Jerusalemischen Targume* (Leipzig: Hinrichs, 1894; 2nd ed., 1905); repr. with *Aramäische Dialektproben* (Leipzig: Hinrichs, 1896; 2nd ed., 1927; Darmstadt: Wissenschaftliche Buchgesellschaft, 1960); *Aramäisch-neuhebräisches Handwörterbuch zu Targum, Talmud und Midrasch* (1897; 3rd ed., Göttingen: E. Pfeiffer, 1938). Dalman's studies in topography and culture include *Sacred Sites and Ways: Studies in the Topography of the Gospels* (1919), trans. Paul P. Levertoff (London: SPCK, 1929; New York: Macmillan, 1935); *Jerusalem und seine Gelände* (Gütersloh: Gerd Mohn, 1930; repr., Hildesheim: Olms, 1972); and 7 volumes of *Arbeit und Sitte in Palästina* (Gütersloh: Bertelsmann, 1928–42; repr., Hildesheim: Georg Olms, 1964). An eighth volume on family life, edited by Julia Männchen, L. Rogler, and S. Schorch, was published by the Gustaf-Dalman-Institut (Berlin: de Gruyter, 2000). Tribute by Albrecht Alt in *Palästinajahrbuch für Altertumswissenschaft des deutschen evangelischen Instituts*

Dalman was made a professor at the Institutum Delitzschianum at Leipzig in 1895. He traveled in the Holy Land and Syria (1899–1900) and became the first director of the Deutsche Evangelische Institut für Altertumswissenschaft des Heiligen Landes in Jerusalem (1902). In 1917 he became professor of Old Testament and Palestine studies at Greifswald, and in 1925 he assumed the directorship of the Gustaf-Dalman-Institut für Palästinawissenschaft at Greifswald.

Dalman was a Moravian. His writings are characterized by reverent piety, but Dalman never confused piety with scholarship. An early work on the Suffering Servant of Isaiah 53 in Jewish literature stressed fulfillment of the prophecy by Jesus. Further study led Dalman to think that the servant envisaged by the prophet was not the messianic king but a collective figure who stood over against Israel as her servant.[87] He finally concluded that the servant was a personification of Israel from the standpoint of Israel's prophetic calling to serve the nations. No other Israelite prophet had such a vision of winning the world for God.

The Words of Jesus (1898; 2nd ed., 1930)[88] sought to ascertain the meaning of Jesus' words, as they would have been heard by Aramaic-speaking hearers. It examined concepts of the sovereignty of God, the present age and the age to come, life, the world, ways of speaking about God (including heaven and use of the passive voice), and titles given to Jesus. Dalman's careful, probing discussion marked a turning point in scholarship. From now on, serious investigation of Jesus' world had to take Aramaic into account. *The Words of Jesus* was followed by *Jesus-Jeshua* (1922).[89] The title reminded readers that Jesus was not known as

---

für Altertumswissenschaft des heiligen Landes zu Jerusalem 37 (1941): 5–18. For bibliography, see K. H. Rengstorf and W. Müller, "Das Schrifttum Gustaf Dalmans," *Wissenschaftliche Zeitschrift der Ernst Moritz Arndt-Universität Greifswald* 4 (1955): 209–32. Further literature in *Biographisch-Bibliographisches Kirchenlexikon*, 1:1197–98. See further Irene Garbel and Markus Pyke, *EJ*, 2nd ed., 5:383–84.

87. Gustaf H. Dalman, *Der leidende und der sterbende Messias der Synagoge im ersten nachchristlichen Jahrtausend* (Berlin: Reuther & Reichard, 1888), supplemented by *Jesaja 53: das Prophetenwort vom Sühnleiden des Gottesknechtes mit besonderer Berücksichtigung der jüdischen Literatur*, Schriften des Institutum Judaicum in Berlin 13 (Leipzig: J. C. Hinrichs, 1894; 2nd ed., 1914).

88. Gustaf H. Dalman, *Die Worte Jesu* (Leipzig: Hinrichs, 1898); ET: *The Words of Jesus, Considered in the Light of Post-Biblical Jewish Writings and the Aramaic Language*, trans. D. M. Kay (Edinburgh: T&T Clark, 1902; repr. Eugene, OR: Wipf & Stock, 1997).

89. D. Gustaf H. Dalman, *Jesus-Jeschua. Die drei Sprachen Jesu. Jesus in der Synagoge, auf dem Berge, beim Passachmahl, am Kreuz* (Leipzig: Hinrichs, 1922; repr., Darmstadt: Wissenschaftliche Buchgesellschaft, 1967); ET: *Jesus-Jeshua: Studies in the Gospels*, trans. Paul P. Levertoff (London: SPCK, 1929). The German title emphasizes Dalman's claim that Jesus knew three languages.

"Jesus" to his contemporaries but as "Jeshua." Dalman claimed that Jesus knew three languages: Aramaic his mother tongue, Greek the language of government, and Hebrew the language of Scripture and theological discourse. When Jesus stood up to read from the Isaiah scroll in the synagogue at Nazareth (Luke 4:16), he would have read it in Hebrew.[90] Dalman focused on Jesus and the fulfillment of Isaiah 61:1–2,[91] what it meant to seek righteousness higher than that of the scribes,[92] the Passover context of the Last Supper,[93] and the words from the cross.[94] The work concluded with an appendix identifying parallels in Jewish literature to Jesus' sayings, showing their thoroughly Jewish character.[95]

2.4. Deissmann and the Ancient East. As a graduate student at Marburg, Adolf Deissmann (1866–1937)[96] discovered the two driving themes of his scholarship: the Christ-mysticism in Paul, which found expression in his dissertation on the formula "in Christ," and the importance of inscriptions, ostraca, and papyri from the Hellenistic world for the study of the New Testament. Deissmann went on to occupy chairs at Heidelberg (1897) and Berlin (1908), where he served as rector (1930–31).

Deissmann's knowledge of the ancient world was deepened by extensive travel in the Middle East. His studies culminated in *Licht vom Osten* (1908; ET: *Light from the Ancient East: The New Testament Illustrated by Recently Discovered Texts from the Graeco-Roman World*, 1910).[97] After a chapter dealing with inscriptions, papyri, and ostraca, Deissmann devoted the rest of the book to the language and literature of the New

---

90. Dalman, *Jesus-Jeshua*, 37. Dalman claims that there is no proof that an Aramaic Targum was used in divine service (40). For a modern reassessment that endorses the claim that Jesus knew and used Greek, see Stanley E. Porter, "Jesus and the Use of Greek in Galilee," in *Studying the Historical Jesus: Evaluations of the State of Current Research*, ed. Bruce Chilton and Craig A. Evans, NTTS 19 (Leiden: Brill, 1994), 123–54; James Barr, "Which Language Did Jesus Speak? Some Remarks of a Semitist," in *Bible and Interpretation: The Collected Essays of James Barr*, ed. John Barton (Oxford: Oxford University Press, 2013), 2:231–46.

91. Dalman, *Jesus-Jeshua*, 38–55.
92. Dalman, *Jesus-Jeshua*, 67–86.
93. Dalman, *Jesus-Jeshua*, 87–184.
94. Dalman, *Jesus-Jeshua*, 185–222.
95. Dalman, *Jesus-Jeshua*, 223–36.
96. Hans Lietzmann, "Adolf Deissmann zum Gedächtnis," *ZNW* 35 (1936): 299–306; Eckhard Plümmacher, *TRE*, 8:406–8.
97. Adolf Deissmann, *Light from the Ancient East*, trans. Lionel R. M. Strachan (Edinburgh: T&T Clark, 1910, and subsequently updated; repr., Grand Rapids: Baker, 1978). Other works include two series of *Bibelstudien* (1895, 1897), trans. Alexander Grieve (Edinburgh: T&T Clark, 1901; 2nd ed., 1903), and sundry writings on the language of the Greek Bible, including *Die Urgeschichte des Christentums im Lichte der Sprachungforschung* (Tübingen: Mohr Siebeck, 1910).

Testament in light of newly discovered texts. Deissmann showed, to the satisfaction of most,[98] that the language of the New Testament was not a form of Semitic Greek barely understandable in the Hellenistic world but was the everyday Greek known as Koine Greek. A planned dictionary of New Testament Greek failed to come to fruition. It fell to Walter Bauer (1877–1960)[99] to produce the standard work used by scholars the world over, *A Greek-English Lexicon of the New Testament and Other Early Christian Literature* (1928; 3rd English ed., 2000, based on the 6th German ed., ed. Kurt and Barbara Aland).[100]

The First World War brought an end to Deissmann's creative research. His later years were devoted to church affairs, university administration, and to the ecumenical movement, where he worked for the reconciliation of former enemies. Deissmann's lectures at Selly Oak, Birmingham, England, *The Religion of Jesus and the Faith of Paul* (1923), fell into two parts: "Communion with God in the Experience of Jesus" and "Communion with Christ in the Experience of Paul." In the former Deissmann saw three stages in the inner life of Jesus. "The basal groundwork is the quiet piety of His communion with God the Father and God the Lord; to this there comes a specific consciousness of prophetic endowment for His Mission; and finally, the prophetic consciousness culminates in the Messianic consciousness."[101] As Harnack and Wellhausen had shown, "The originality of Jesus lies in the comprehensive uniqueness of His inner life; the new, the epoch-making thing is Himself."[102] In turning to Paul, Deissmann returned to the theme of his

---

98. Moisés Silva, "Bilingualism and the Character of Palestinian Greek," *Biblica* 61 (1980): 198–219. Silva concluded that there is a semiticized Greek style and a Christian Greek style, but that did not overthrow Deissmann's basic contentions. Much of the critique of Deissmann stemmed from a failure to distinguish between language (*langue*) and speech (*parole*).

99. M. E. Boring, *DMBI*, 172–77. Bauer's *Rechtgläubigkeit und Ketzerei im ältesten Christentum* (BHT 10 [Tübingen: Mohr Siebeck, 1934]; ET: *Orthodoxy and Heresy in Earliest Christianity*, trans. and ed. Robert A. Kraft and Gerhard Krodel [London: SCM, 1971]) argued that the various responses to Jesus in early Christianity called for a revision of views of orthodoxy and heresy. A recent discussion is Paul A. Hartog, ed., *Orthodoxy and Heresy in Early Christian Contexts: Reconsidering the Bauer Thesis* (Eugene, OR: Pickwick, 2015).

100. Walter Bauer, *A Greek-English Lexicon of the New Testament and Other Early Christian Literature*. The third English edition is edited by Frederick William Danker (Chicago: University of Chicago Press, 2000). The acronym BDAG denotes its editors' surnames: Bauer, Danker, Arndt, and Gingrich.

101. Adolf Deissmann, *The Religion of Jesus and the Faith of Paul*, trans. William E. Wilson (London: Hodder & Stoughton, 1923), 125–26.

102. Deissmann, *The Religion of Jesus and the Faith of Paul*, 149.

early research, that of being "in Christ," an expression found 164 times in Paul. It means the same as being in the Spirit: "in Christ who is the Spirit" (2 Cor 3:17).[103] The key to Paul was his "Christ-mysticism."

A fruit of Deissmann's ecumenical labors was a conference in 1928 at the historic Wartburg castle, where Luther had found refuge from the imperial ban. The papers were edited by Deissmann and G. K. A. Bell, the Anglican bishop of Chichester, and published under the title *Mysterium Christi: Christological Studies by British and German Theologians* (1930).[104] Deissmann was a man of deep personal faith and humanity, a token of which was shown earlier by his regular and arduous visits to his English translator Lionel Strachan, who spent most of World War I as a prisoner of war in Berlin.[105] In his memorial address for Deissmann, Hans Lietzmann called him "the teacher and exemplary *Führer*" of thousands of students, learned colleagues, and the entire Christian world, a man "who was truly in Jesus Christ."[106]

2.5. Kittel, Politics, and the *Theological Word Book*. After studies in Leipzig, Tübingen, and Berlin, Gerhard Kittel (1888–1948)[107] obtained his doctorate for work on the Odes of Solomon and habilitation in New Testament at Kiel. He gained a further habilitation at Leipzig, where he got his first teaching position. After a professorship at Greifswald (1922), Kittel moved to Tübingen (1926) where he taught until 1945, while simultaneously holding a chair in Vienna (1939–43).

Kittel was recognized in both Jewish and Christian circles as a leading authority on Judaism. His work fell into three phases.[108] The first

---

103. Deissmann, *The Religion of Jesus and the Faith of Paul*, 175.

104. Adolf Deissmann and G. K. A. Bell, eds., *Mysterium Christi: Christological Studies by British and German Theologians* (London: Longmans, Green, 1930). A German edition was also published. Contributors included Paul Althaus, G. K. A. Bell, J. M. Creed, Deissmann, C. H. Dodd, Heinrich Frick, Sir Edwyn C. Hoskyns, Gerhard Kittel, Nathaniel Micklem, J. K. Mozley, A. E. J. Rawlinson, and Hermann Sasse.

105. Deissmann, *Light from the Ancient East*, xix.

106. Hans Lietzmann, "Adolf Deißmann zum Gedächtnis," *ZNW* 35 (1936): 306.

107. Max Weinreich, *Hitler's Professors: The Part of Scholarship in Germany's Crimes against the Jewish People* (New York: Yiddish Scientific Institute, 1946), 40–45; J. R. Porter, "The Case of Kittel," *Theology* 50 (1947): 401–6; Otto Michel, "Das wissenschaftliche Vermächtnis Gerhard Kittels. Zur 70. Wiederkehr seines Geburtstages," *Deutsches Pfarrerblatt* 58 (1958): 415–17; Robert P. Ericksen, *Theologians under Hitler: Gerhard Kittel, Paul Althaus and Emmanuel Hirsch* (New Haven, CT: Yale University Press, 1985), 28–78; Gerhard Friedrich and Johannes Friedrich, *TRE*, 19:221–25; S. S. Schatzmann, *DMBI*, 614–18; A. Gerdmar, *Roots of Theological Antisemitism: German Interpretation and the Jews, from Herder and Semler to Kittel and Bultmann*, SJHC 20 (Leiden: Brill, 2009).

108. *TRE*, 19:222.

was marked by publication of texts and studies showing the importance of rabbinic literature for understanding the message of Jesus. The parting of the ways between Christianity and Judaism had its origin in Jesus' confrontation with the scribes. Since their outlook and methods were not essentially different from the later rabbis, rabbinic literature was valuable for illuminating the New Testament. Kittel sought to remedy the lack of accessible texts, beginning with his edition of Sifre Deuteronomy.[109]

In a study comparing Judaism and Christianity, Kittel concluded that "*among the ethical demands of Jesus there was no single one that was or needed to be as such absolutely unique.*"[110] Both Jesus and Judaism had their roots in Old Testament piety. What made Jesus different was "a *concentration* such as we find nowhere in Judaism."[111] Jewish ethics were directed at the practicalities of everyday life, but the demands of Jesus were directed beyond the present. A second component of Jesus' message was his consciousness of the absolute character of the demands of the kingdom of God and his own role in its fulfillment. "Here arose what was the ultimate, crowning piece of Israelite-Jewish religious history, out of which emerged the *new* religion and the *new* ethic. At the point where Jesus' consciousness of mission coincided with the claim to *fulfillment* in his own person, he ceased to be a Jew, and his proclamation ceased to be part of this Judaism."[112] This separation of Jesus from Judaism proved to be an ominous portent of things to come.

The second phase in Kittel's career began with his move to Tübingen in 1926, where he turned increasingly to the Hellenistic world and its importance for the New Testament. The standard theological dictionary, Hermann Cremer's *Biblisch-theologisches Wörterbuch der neutestamentlichen Gräzität*, was defective in its attention to both Judaism and Hellenism, even in the edition updated by Julius Kögel (11th ed., 1923). In 1927 Kögel invited Kittel to take part in a fresh revision. When Kögel died, Kittel took charge but decided that an entirely new work was needed. The result was Kittel's major contribution to theology, *Theologisches Wörterbuch zum Neuen Testament*, which is often simply referred to as

---

109. Gerard Kittel, *Sifre zu Deuteronomium. Übersetzt und erläutert* (Stuttgart: Kohlhammer, 1922).
110. Kittel, *Die Probleme des palästinischen Spätjudentums und das Urchristentum*, BWANT 3. Folge, Heft 1 (Stuttgart: Kohlhammer, 1926), 96 (Kittel's emphasis); cf. Kittel, *Jesus und die Juden* (Berlin: Furche-Verlag, 1926).
111. Kittel, *Die Probleme*, 124.
112. Kittel, *Die Probleme*, 131.

"Kittel." Kittel edited the first four volumes (1933–42). When publication resumed after the war, Gerhard Friedrich led the team of contributors.[113]

Kittel was guided by the program outlined by Deissmann, who saw the first task of a future lexicon as the placing of "the New Testament vocabulary in living linguistic connexion with the contemporary world. . . . An author who undertakes a New Testament Lexicon at the present day without sketching in each article the history and statistics of words and meanings, is tearing the world-apostle from his world and the gospel from history, shutting off the New Testament from the light of research."[114]

The contribution of the *Theologisches Wörterbuch* to the quest of the historical Jesus was largely indirect. The article on Ἰησοῦς (Jesus) by Werner Foerster[115] focused on the history and derivation of the name, noting its wide use in the form of יְהוֹשׁוּעַ (*yehoshua* = Joshua), and after the Exile mostly יֵשׁוּעַ (*yeshua*). The name continued to be common until the second century CE but then virtually disappeared. Foerster took Matthew 1:21 ("You are to name him Jesus, for he will save his people from their sins") to imply that the choice of the name was connected with the verb יָשַׁע (*yasha'* = save) rather than the figure of Moses' successor who led the Israelites into the promised land. Joshua was never a prototype of the Messiah in late Judaism.[116]

Since Kittel's day, the assumptions and methods of his great dictionary have been called into question, as its second editor, Gerhard Friedrich, well recognized.[117] Whereas Deissmann had written at length about popular speech, questions began to be raised about what

---

113. *Theologisches Wörterbuch zum Neuen Testament*, 10 vols. [vol. 10 containing index and supplement in 2 parts] (Stuttgart: Kohlhammer, 1933–78); ET: *Theological Dictionary of the New Testament*, trans. Geoffrey W. Bromiley, 10 vols. (Grand Rapids: Eerdmans, 1964–76). Vol. 10 also contains a "Pre-History of the Theological Dictionary of the New Testament" (613–61) by Gerhard Friedrich. Kittel edited the first four volumes. The rest were edited by Friedrich.

114. Deissmann, *Light from the Ancient East*, 407; cf. Gerhard Friedrich, *TDNT*, 10:649. When the first fascicle appeared, Deissmann sent his congratulations, adding: "It gives me great pleasure, then, that without breaking respectful continuity with Kremer and Kögel you have succeeded in giving to biblical research a work in which powerful traces of the rhythm of modern scholarship may everywhere be seen."

115. Werner Foerster, *TWNT* 3:284–94.

116. For a contrary view that argues that Mark depicts Jesus as a second Joshua engaged in religious conquest of the land and its people, see Colin Brown, "The Jesus of Mark's Gospel," in *Jesus Then and Now: Images of Jesus in History and Christology*, ed. Marvin Meyer and Charles Hughes (Harrisburg, PA: Trinity Press International, 2001), 26–53.

117. See the review by Gerhard Friedrich in *TDNT*, 10:650–61.

The No Quest in Europe to World War II

popular speech really was, especially in light of the Greek of the papyri. Grammatical features of the New Testament are also found in Hellenistic scientific writings. The LXX may have shaped New Testament Greek far more than previously realized. Greek culture and language had penetrated Palestine more than earlier scholars had assumed. In addition, objections have been raised about the structure of the dictionary. The grouping of words by a common stem led to interpretations based on etymology that do not do justice to textual usage.[118] In the end, it must be recognized that even the best dictionaries are imperfect tools.

To Jewish readers, there were disturbing features of a different kind. Strack-Billerbeck and Kittel were

> just two examples of major scholarly projects that were also major anti-Jewish tracts.... Liberal Protestants' identification of Jesus with the progressive values of their own society resulted in the creation of a Jesus figure who was, above all, a religious teacher, a moral exhorter, and an upstanding citizen. *Kulturprotestantismus*, as the theological movement was called, saw itself as theologically progressive, rejecting all elements of supernaturalism, dogma, and apocalypticism. Their Jesus was the ideal person for Imperial German society—decidedly not a Jew.[119]

The third phase of Kittel's career was marked by tragedy. In 1933 he joined the National Socialist Party, believing that he could exercise a moderating influence on the party, which that year made all other political parties illegal. The following year, on the death of Hindenburg, Hitler was given supreme power by the Reichstag. In 1933 at the request of the theology faculty, Kittel delivered a public lecture on "The Jewish Question," which was published as *Die Judenfrage*. Turning his back on his early work, which saw close affinities between Judaism and Christianity, Kittel now charged the Jews with responsibility for many of the ills of German society. He outlined four possible solutions: extermination (pogroms); the creation of a Jewish state in Palestine (Zionism); assimilation; and the deliberate preservation of alien status (*Fremdlingschaft*).

---

118. James Barr, *The Semantics of Biblical Language* (Oxford: Oxford University Press, 1962); cf. Gerhard Friedrich, *TDNT*, 10:659.

119. Susannah Heschel, *Abraham Geiger and the Jewish Jesus*, Chicago Studies in the History of Judaism (Chicago: University of Chicago Press, 1998), 231.

Kittel saw the last as the sole feasible possibility, claiming that it was consistent with the message of the Old Testament.[120] "One of the fundamental laws that the *Old Testament prophets* did not tire of proclaiming is this, that *interbreeding [Vermischung] with other nations was the worst sin for Israel.*"[121]

In its striving for dominance in this world, Judaism had become uprooted and decadent. Jews should be treated as guests and be encouraged to follow their own traditions. *"From the standpoint of the German people it is the Jew who preserves and honors his own traditions and customs who is a much better guest than the uprooted Jew who no longer knows and would like to forget that he ever had anything to do with them.* For this reason, synagogue, circumcision, sabbath, feasts, and rites are to be preserved like all genuine religious confessions."[122] Mixed marriages should not be allowed.[123] Jews who convert to Christianity should be welcomed as Christian brothers. But the converted Jew would not be a German. He would be a Jewish Christian (*Judenchrist*). Such a person should follow Jewish-Christian theology and customs. He should not be allowed to be a pastor or elder in a German congregation.[124]

Further pronouncements followed in *Forschungen zur Judenfrage*, the journal of Walter Frank's Reichsinstitut. In the meantime, Kittel's political views were repudiated by (among others) Martin Buber, Karl Barth, and Ernst Lohmeyer.[125] At the end of World War II Kittel was interned by the French occupying forces and deprived of his professorship and pension. He was permitted to live in the Abbey at Beuron, and in 1947 was invited by the Papal Archaeological Institute in Rome to edit the second volume of the *Corpus Inscriptionum Judicarum*. In 1948 he was permitted to return to Tübingen, but not to his chair or to the editorship of the *Theologisches Wörterbuch*. He died a few months later. The theology that began by stressing Jesus' Jewishness, then his transcending of Judaism, and ended by advocating total separation had reaped a terrible harvest.

---

120. Gerard Kittel, *Die Judenfrage* (Stuttgart: Kohlhammer, 1933), 13–37.
121. Kittel, *Die Judenfrage*, 36–37 (Kittel's emphasis).
122. Kittel, *Die Judenfrage*, 40–41 (Kittel's emphasis).
123. Kittel, *Die Judenfrage*, 57.
124. Kittel, *Die Judenfrage*, 70–71.
125. Martin Buber, *TBl* 12 (1933): 248–50, 370–71; Ericksen, *Theologians under Hitler*, 59–62; *TRE*, 19:223. Barth and Kittel published an exchange of letters; cf. Karl Barth and Gerhard Kittel, *Ein theologischer Briefwechsel* (Stuttgart: Kohlhammer, 1934).

3. Later Reclamations of Jesus

3.1. Schlatter and the Jewish Christ of Faith. An early Christian advocate of understanding the Jewishness of Jesus was Adolf Schlatter (1852–1938).[126] Schlatter, who was the predecessor of Kittel,[127] enjoyed the reputation of being able to read "unpointed" rabbinic texts with the ease with which other people read newspapers.[128] He studied at Basel and Tübingen, where he obtained his *Licentiat* and doctorate in theology. Schlatter became a professor at Greifswald (1898) and taught systematic theology alongside Harnack at Berlin (1893–98) before returning to Tübingen as professor of New Testament (1898–1922), where he continued to teach in both fields. Schlatter's distinguished students included Karl Barth, Ernst Käsemann, Ernst Fuchs, and Gerhard Kittel. The latter dedicated the first volume of the *Theologisches Wörterbuch zum Neuen Testament* (1933) to "Adolf Schlatter the octogenarian." Schlatter greeted Kittel's National Socialism with dismay[129] and urged that only a new and profound turning to Jesus Christ could help both church and nation.

Early in his career Schlatter made a journey to the Holy Land. On returning, he published a book of nearly 400 pages on the topography and history of Palestine.[130] The book sought to interpret Schlatter's travels in

---

126. Studies of Schlatter include Ulrich Luck, *Kerygma und Tradition*, Arbeitsgemeinschaft für Forschung des Landes Nordrhein-Westfalen 45 (Köln: Westdeutscher, 1955); Karl Gerhard Steck, *Die Idee der Heilsgeschichte. Hoffmann, Schlatter, Cullmann*, TS 56 (Zollikon: Evangelischer, 1959); Gottfried Egg, *Adolf Schlatters kritische Position gezeigt an seiner Matthäusinterpretation*, Arbeiten zur Theologie 2.14 (Stuttgart: Calwer, 1968); Johannes Heinrich Schmid, *Erkenntnis des geschichtlichen Christus bei Martin Kähler und bei Adolf Schlatter*, TZ Sonderband 5 (Basel: Reinhardt, 1978); Peter Stuhlmacher, "Adolf Schlatter's Interpretation of Scripture," *NTS* 24 (1978): 433–46; Werner Neuer, *Adolf Schlatter. Ein Leben für Theologie und Kirche* (Stuttgart: Calwer, 1996) [with extensive bibliography]; ET: *Adolf Schlatter: A Biography of Germany's Premier Biblical Theologian*, trans. Robert W. Yarbrough (Grand Rapids: Baker, 1996); see also *Vom Dienst an Theologie und Kirche. Festgabe für Adolf Schlatter zum 75. Geburtstag 16. August 1927* (Berlin: Furche, 1927); Robert W. Yarborough, *The Salvation History Fallacy? Reassessing the History of New Testament Theology* (Leiden: Deo, 2004); Yarborough, *DMBI*, 881–85.

127. On retirement in 1922 Schlatter had hoped that Kittel would succeed him. However, the history-of-religions scholar and Bultmann's mentor Wilhelm Heitmüller (1869–1926) was appointed. On Heitmüller's death, Kittel was called (Neuer, *Adolf Schlatter*, 592, 621).

128. Remark by Martin Hengel in a seminar attended by the author. "Unpointed" refers to the fact that the texts, like the earliest texts of the Hebrew Bible, lacked "points" or vowels. It was up to the reader to supply them.

129. Neuer, *Adolf Schlatter*, 731. In conversation with Schlatter, Kittel replied, "You stand too much under pressure of anxiety, you exaggerate the struggle between the party and the church" (Schlatter, in a letter to his son Theodor, October 26, 1933).

130. Adolf Schlatter, *Zur Topographie und Geschichte Palästinas* (Stuttgart: Calwer, 1893).

light of Jewish sources. Almost half of it was devoted to Jerusalem. It was welcomed by the Jerusalem expert Conrad Schick but was trashed by the reviewer who mattered most, Emil Schürer, coeditor with Harnack of the *Theologische Literaturzeiting*. Schürer charged Schlatter with substituting "bold imagination" for "sound method," making everything appear like a personal revelation.[131] Sales plummeted, and the Deutsche Palästinaverein noted that Schürer had pronounced the book unscientific. Though deeply wounded, Schlatter felt that Schürer was prompted less by animosity than by differing methodology. The complaint that Schlatter largely ignored the viewpoints of other scholars dogged him throughout his career. For his part, Schlatter felt it more important to address the primary sources.

Schlatter's writings ranged from a history of philosophy since Descartes to studies of the Pharisees and rabbinics.[132] He wrote numerous commentaries on the New Testament, including major works (written in retirement) on Matthew, Luke, and John.[133] These commentaries are characterized by absence of critical introduction and lack of interaction with other scholars. This deficit reinforced Schlatter's reputation for being out of touch with the scholarship of his day. On the other hand, the commentaries are crammed with citations in Greek and Hebrew from Josephus, the Mishnah, the Talmuds, and other primary sources. They show the Jesus of the Gospels deeply rooted in the world of Judaism and the importance of Jewish literature for understanding him.

It is characteristic of Schlatter that the book that promises to deal most directly with the historical Jesus was the first volume of *Die Theologie des Neuen Testaments* (1909). Its title in English is *The History of Christ: The Foundation for New Testament Theology*.[134] Schlatter began

---

131. Neuer, *Adolf Schlatter*, 280–84.
132. Adolf Schlatter, *Die philosophische Arbeit seit Descartes. Ihr ethischer und religiöser Ertrag* (Stuttgart: Calwer, 1906; repr. 1959); Schlatter, *Synagoge und Kirche bis zum Barkochba-Aufstand. Vier Studien zur Geschichte des Rabbinats und der jüdischen Christenheit in den ersten zwei Jahrhunderten. Mit einem Geleitwort von Joachim Jeremias* (Stuttgart: Calwer, 1966); cf. Roland Deines, *Die Pharisäer. Ihr Verständnis im Spiegel der christlichen und jüdischen Forschung seit Wellhausen und Graetz*, WUNT 101 (Tübingen: Mohr Siebeck, 1997), 262–99.
133. Schlatter, *Der Evangelist Matthäus. Seine Sprache, sein Ziel, seine Selbstständigkeit. Ein Kommentar zum ersten Evangelium* (Stuttgart: Calwer, 1929; 6th unchanged ed., 1963); *Das Evangelium des Lukas. Aus seinen Quellen erklärt* (Stuttgart: Calwer, 1931; 2nd unchanged ed., 1960); *Der Evangelist Johannes. Wie er spricht, denkt, und glaubt. Ein Kommentar zum vierten Evangelium* (Stuttgart: Calwer, 1930; 3rd unchanged ed., 1960).
134. Schlatter, *Die Theologie des Neuen Testaments*, vol. 1, *Das Wort Jesu* (Stuttgart: Calwer,

The No Quest in Europe to World War II

with the declaration: "Knowledge of Jesus is the first, indispensable, principal part of 'New Testament Theology.' If we endeavor to perceive the convictions which the New Testament represents, and understand how they arose, we take the first step to this goal, by making it clear to ourselves what Jesus carried as a certainty in himself, and how what he did arose from it."[135] What followed was a harmony of the Gospels, retold in Schlatter's words. As with the commentaries, there was no interaction with current scholarship or reference to the quest of the historical Jesus.

For Schlatter the historical Jesus was the Christ of faith, who was to be found by entering into the world of the text. Peter Stuhlmacher, who carried on the Schlatter tradition at Tübingen, observes: "According to Schlatter Jesus of Nazareth appeared precisely as the Gospels record— with the claim to be the Son of God and Israel's Messiah. For Schlatter, the fundamental difference between the historical Jesus and the Christ of faith arises only when one is not able and willing to conceptualize that the human Jesus already appeared as the Messiah."[136] It is not for nothing that scholars have seen similarities with Martin Kähler (1835–1912)[137] and his famous protest against the whole idea of a quest for the historical Jesus.

> The real Christ, that is, the Christ who has exercised an influence in history, with whom millions have communed in childlike faith, and with whom the great witnesses of faith have been in communion— while striving, apprehending, triumphing, and proclaiming—*this*

1909); 2nd ed. *Die Geschichte des Christus*, 1920; trans. Andreas J. Köstenberger (Grand Rapids: Baker, 1997).

Schlatter's earlier article, "The Theology of the New Testament and Dogmatics" (1909), was edited and translated by Robert Morgan in *The Nature of New Testament Theology: The Contributions of William Wrede and Adolf Schlatter*, SBT Second Series 25 (London: SCM; Naperville, IL: Allenson, 1973), 117–66.

135. Schlatter, *Die Geschichte des Christus*, 2nd ed., 5 (author's translation).

136. Peter Stuhlmacher, *Jesus of Nazareth—Christ of Faith*, trans. Siegfried S. Schatzmann (Peabody, MA: Hendrickson, 1993), 2–3.

137. See the works by Luck and Schmid noted above (n. 126) and Stuhlmacher, *Jesus of Nazareth—Christ of Faith*, 2–3. Schmid, who had studied the similarities in great detail, concluded: "We are of the opinion that we must designate the theology of both scholars as outspokenly a-philosophical and anti-intellectual. However, the rejection of the epistemological and ontological question should be more thoroughly explored in both. . . . The task was to present with the help of the New Testament and on the basis of its pronouncements the fact that Jesus as the Christ of God was a historical person and was thus capable of being understood historically" (429).

real Christ is the Christ who is preached. The Christ who is preached, however, is precisely the Christ of faith.[138]

In his commentary on Matthew, Schlatter reiterated his approach.

> It is right and proper that we read the Gospel for the sake of Jesus, for it was written for his sake. To reach Jesus we must listen to the evangelist. Were he to disappear from us, we would be severed from the course of history and left to our own imaginations. Jesus speaks to humanity through his disciples. For this reason every encounter with the Gospel poses for us the question: "What was the evangelist and what did he want?" It is this question—to which our contemporary academic tradition has only shaky answers—which the reading of the First Gospel serves, and to which I here invite my readers.[139]

Fifty years after the publication of Schlatter's Matthew commentary, Martin Hengel observed that with good reason one could describe Schlatter's work as "the most significant and original commentary on Matthew written in our century. Schlatter combines here in a unique way an acute gift for philological-historical observation with a deeply penetrating power for theological interpretation."[140]

3.2. Otto and the Jewish Charismatic Jesus. Although he wanted to locate Jesus within his Jewish context, Rudolf Otto (1869–1937)[141] approached his task from a diametrically opposite perspective—the phenomenology of religion. Otto began his studies with the conservative faculty at Erlangen to arm himself against the "liberals" before moving to Göttingen. Even before completing his studies, he undertook the first of his many world travels. In 1895 on a trip to the Middle East he contracted malaria, which resulted in ailments that plagued him for life. In 1915 he accepted a call to Breslau, where he remained for two years

---

138. Martin Kähler, *Der sogenannte historische Jesus und der christliche, biblische Christus* (Leipzig: Deichert, 1892; 2nd ed., 1896); ET: *The So-Called Historical Jesus and the Historic Biblical Christ*, trans. Carl E. Braaten, foreword by Paul Tillich (Philadelphia: Fortress, 1964), 66.

139. Schlatter, *Der Evangelist Matthäus*, x (author's translation).

140. Neuer, *Adolf Schlatter*, 635 (author's translation).

141. Ernst Benz, ed., *Rudolf Ottos Bedeutung für die Religionswissenschaft und die Theologie heute. Zur Hundertjahrsfeier seines Geburtstags 25. September 1969* (Leiden: Brill, 1971); Karl Heinz Ratschow, *TRE*, 25:559–62; Melissa Raphael, *Rudolf Otto and the Concept of Holiness* (Oxford: Clarendon, 1997).

before transferring to Marburg, where he spent the rest of his career teaching systematic theology and the world's religions. At Marburg, Otto founded a museum of world religions and published extensively in that field, especially in Indian religions. His ramrod military bearing belied his character. Karl Barth described him as "looking just like an Indian rajah."[142] Otto's relationship with Bultmann became increasingly strained.[143] While they were colleagues at Breslau, they got on. But at Marburg, there was no meeting of minds or personality. Perpetual ill health contributed to Otto's depression, and he took early retirement at the age of sixty.

Otto's seminal work *Das Heilige* (1917; ET: *The Idea of the Holy*, 1923)[144] sought to recover the dimension of the holy and its place in religious epistemology. As such, it stands in the tradition of scholarship, which sought to distill the essence of Christianity. A Kantian in philosophy, Otto sought to apply Kantian principles to give recognition to the holy as an irreducible category of thought and experience. Otto regarded the holy "on the one hand as an *a priori* category of the mind, and on the other as manifesting itself in outward appearance."[145] There were three factors in the process by which religion comes into being in history.

> First, the interplay of predisposition and stimulus, which in the historical development of man's mind actualizes the potentiality in the former, and at the same time helps to determine its form. Second, the groping recognition, by virtue of this very disposition, of specific portions of history as the manifestation of "the holy," with consequent modification of the religious experience already attained in its quality and degree. And third, on the basis of the other two, the achieved fellowship with "the holy" in knowing, feeling, and willing.[146]

---

142. Eberhard Busch, *Karl Barth: His Life from Letters and Autobiographical Texts*, trans. John Bowden (London: SCM, 1976), 136.
143. Hammann, *Rudolf Bultmann*, 134–35; cf. 91–92, 166–69.
144. Rudolf Otto, *The Idea of the Holy*, trans. John W. Harvey (London: Oxford University Press, 1923; 2nd ed., New York: Oxford University Press, 1958). The edition cited here is the reprint published by Penguin (Harmondsworth, 1959). See also Otto, *Religious Essays: A Supplement to "The Idea of the Holy"*, trans. Brian Lunn (London: Oxford University Press, 1931).
145. Otto, *The Idea of the Holy*, 192.
146. Otto, *The Idea of the Holy*, 193–94. The philosophical underpinning of Otto's thought was given in *Kantisch-Fries'sche Religionsphilosophie und ihre Anwendung auf die Theologie* (Tübingen:

Otto saw his work as a corrective to Schleiermacher, who had argued for recognition of feeling (*Gefühl*) alongside knowing and doing as fundamental components of human nature. Otto maintained that Schleiermacher's feeling or sense of absolute dependence (*Abhängigkeitsgefühl*)[147] did not do justice to the element of the *numinous*, which was experience "as objective and outside the self."[148] Otto adopted a word coined from the Latin *numen* (a divinity, daemon, spirit) to denote experience of the *mysterium tremendum et fascinans*, the mystery which produces awe and fear, while it also attracts and exalts.[149] In protest against attempts to interpret Jesus' proclamation of the fatherhood of God and the kingdom in moral, rational terms, Otto declared that the kingdom was "the 'wholly other' 'heavenly' thing set in contrast to the world here and now, 'the mysterious' itself in its dual character as awe-compelling yet all-attracting an atmosphere of genuine 'religious awe.'"[150]

In Jesus' experience in the garden of Gethsemane, "there is more here than the fear of death; there is the awe of the creature before the *mysterium tremendum*, before the shuddering secret of the numen."[151] In Otto's eyes, the prophet corresponded in the religious sphere to the creative artist in that of art. "He is the man in whom the Spirit shows itself alike as the power to hear the 'voice within' and the power of divination, and in each case appears as a creative force."[152] But above the prophet there is "one in whom is found the Spirit in all its plenitude, and who at the same time in His person and in His performance is become most completely the object of divination, in who Holiness is recognized apparent. Such a one is more than Prophet. He is the Son."[153]

This picture was a far cry from Otto's early depiction of Jesus on Kantian lines as a preacher of morals.[154] Otto's last major work *The*

Mohr Siebeck, 1909); ET: *The Philosophy of Religion, Based on Kant and Fries*, trans. E. B. Dicker (London: Williams & Norgate, 1931).

147. Schleiermacher, *The Christian Faith*, §3–4; cf. Otto's introduction to Schleiermacher, *On Religion: Speeches to Its Cultured Despisers*, trans. John Oman (repr., New York: Harper, 1958) vii–xx; Brown, *Jesus in European Protestant Thought*, 115–17.

148. Otto, *The Idea of the Holy*, 25.

149. Otto, *The Idea of the Holy*, 26–55.

150. Otto, *The Idea of the Holy*, 90.

151. Otto, *The Idea of the Holy*, 101.

152. Otto, *The Idea of the Holy*, 194–95.

153. Otto, *The Idea of the Holy*, 195.

154. Rudolf Otto, *Leben und Wirken Jesu nach historisch-kritischer Auffassung* (Göttingen: Vandenhoeck & Ruprecht, 1902).

Kingdom of God and the Son of Man: A Study in the History of Religion (1934; 2nd ed. 1940; ET, 1938)[155] built on the portrait in *The Idea of the Holy*. Jesus was a Galilean charismatic itinerant preacher and healer. "As a Galilean, Jesus belonged to unofficial Judaism, which was certainly not typically Jewish."[156] He lived in a land which had been Judaized only relatively recently since the Maccabean rising.

Otto agreed with Walter Bauer, who observed, "Galileans grew up outside the jurisdiction of scribalism and Pharisaism in considerable freedom from the Law and without the torturing anxiety that the proximity of the Gentiles would contaminate them. . . . No proof is needed that Jesus, who spent his childhood in Nazareth, scarcely four miles from Sepphoris, was not and never would be a Pharisaic zealot."[157] It was a scenario that also fitted into the scheme of Walter Grundmann, as we shall see presently.

John the Baptist and Jesus were "borne along by the eschatological movement of their time." Whereas John was a preacher of repentance, "Jesus was a charismatic evangelist who was also an exorcist."[158] Instead of preaching the menacing day of the Lord, Jesus came with the message of the kingdom of God. For Jesus the kingdom was always "the future kingdom of the new age. . . . It was to follow the Messianic woes and the divine judgment. But what distinguished his own eschatology from previous forms was, on the one side, that he already lived in the miracle of the new age which was active even in the present . . . on the other side, that through works, speech, parable, and charismatic bestowing power, he mediated contact with this miracle of the transcendental to a circle of adherents who came into his train."[159]

The concept of the Son of Man derived from teaching preserved in Slavonic Enoch.[160] Jesus let it be known "not only to his more intimate disciples, that he was the personal representative of the Son of Man.

---

155. Rudolf Otto, *The Kingdom of God and the Son of Man: A Study in the History of Religion*, trans. Floyd V. Filson and Bertram Lee Woolf (London: Lutterworth, 1938).
156. Otto, *The Kingdom of God and the Son of Man*, 15.
157. Otto, *The Kingdom of God and the Son of Man*, 17, citing Walter Bauer, "Jesus der Galiläer," in *Festgabe für Adolf Jülicher zum 70. Geburtstag 26. Januar 1927*, ed. Rudolf Bultmann and Hans von Soden (Tübingen: Mohr Siebeck, 1927), 27. I have modified the quotation to bring it into line with Bauer's text; cf. Walter Bauer, *Aufsätze und kleine Schriften*, ed. Georg Strecker (Tübingen: Mohr Siebeck, 1967), 102.
158. Otto, *The Kingdom of God and the Son of Man*, 67.
159. Otto, *The Kingdom of God and the Son of Man*, 155.
160. Otto, *The Kingdom of God and the Son of Man*, 176–218.

The cause of Jesus was the cause of the Son of Man (Lk. xii. 8): 'Every one who shall confess me before men, him also shall the Son of Man confess before the angels of God.'"[161] However, Jesus came to use *Son of Man* as a self-designation.[162] Believing that "he would depart and be exalted like Enoch, and, from the time when he recognized that 'the Son of Man' must suffer,' he thought of death itself as a direct gateway to exaltation."[163] The Last Supper was a prophetic sign, signifying Jesus' willingness to be broken and take upon himself "the Messianic obligation to suffer."[164]

In conclusion, Otto reiterated his conviction that the records about Jesus were "typical of the religious historical genus in being of a hagiological character; the figure which they describe is a holy man, and, as such, belonging to a certain class."[165] But Jesus was not merely a charismatic. The operations of the Spirit through Jesus' healings and exorcisms (Matt 12:27; Luke 11:10) are "the operations of the power of the dawning kingdom of God itself."[166] The kingdom was for Jesus "the in-breaking power of God into salvation." Jesus was not a rabbi but "an eschatological redeemer, who was an integral part of the eschatological order itself. Charisma and kingdom belong together by their very nature and they illuminate one another."[167]

3.3. Grundmann and the Anti-Semitic Jesus. For some time after World War II there seemed to be a tacit agreement among editors of reference works and historians of New Testament scholarship to blot out the memory of Walter Grundmann (1906–76).[168] If so, it was on account

---

161. Otto, *The Kingdom of God and the Son of Man*, 227.
162. Otto, *The Kingdom of God and the Son of Man*, 230–36.
163. Otto, *The Kingdom of God and the Son of Man*, 237. For recent assessment of the Enoch literature see *Enoch and the Messiah Son of Man*, ed. Gabriele Boccaccini et al. (Grand Rapids: Eerdmans, 2007).
164. Otto, *The Kingdom of God and the Son of Man*, 300–301. Otto saw the Last Supper as a sign in the tradition of Ezek 4 and Isa 30. In Jer 19:10–11 the prophet is instructed to break a jar in the presence of the people to illustrate the prophecy, "Thus says the Lord of hosts: So will I break this people and this city, as one breaks a potter's vessel, so that it can never be mended."
165. Otto, *The Kingdom of God and the Son of Man*, 333.
166. Otto, *The Kingdom of God and the Son of Man*, 336; cf. 346–56. The narratives of Jesus walking on the sea belong to the genre of "charismatic apparition," which "is not intended to exhibit supernatural powers, but to grant a presence that will reassure and help" (371).
167. Otto, *The Kingdom of God and the Son of Man*, 375.
168. An exception to the virtual exclusion of Grundmann is his article on "The Decision of the Supreme Court to Put Jesus to Death (John 11:47–57) in Its Context: Tradition and Redaction in the Gospel of John," in *Jesus and the Politics of His Day*, ed. Ernst Bammel and C. F. D. Moule (Cambridge: Cambridge University Press, 1984; repr., 1992), 295–318.
Another exception is the discussion of Paul Fiebig and Walter Grundmann by Maurice

of his anti-Semitism under the Third Reich coupled with doubts about his postwar views and political activities. But if history is concerned with understanding the realities of the past, Grundmann cannot be left out of the picture. The chief resources for reconstructing his life and thought are studies of Nazi anti-Semitism[169] and Grundmann's own writings.

Although the claim that Jesus was not Jewish has a lengthy history,[170] Walter Grundmann did more than anyone to bolster the pro-Nazi *Deutsche Christen*, "German Christians," in the belief that Jesus had no Jewish blood in him. Grundmann joined the Nazi Party in 1930. He worked for his doctorate under Kittel and assisted him from 1930 to 1932 in preparing the *Theologisches Wörterbuch*, for which he wrote some twenty articles. Although lacking the mandatory habilitation and less qualified than his rival candidate Günther Bornkamm, Grundmann was appointed professor of New Testament and *völkische Theologie* at

---

Casey in his survey of the history of the quest of the historical Jesus. See Casey, *Jesus of Nazareth: An Independent Historian's Account of His Life and Teaching* (London: T&T Clark, 2010), 4–9. Fiebig used his study of ancient texts (see above, chap. 6, n8) in support of the Nazi view of a non-Jewish Jesus. He declared his support of National Socialism in a series of lectures; cf. Grundmann, *Neues Testament und Nationalsozialismus. Drei Universitätsvorlesungen über das Führerprinzip—Rassenfrage—Kampf*, Schriften der Deutschen Christen (Dresden: Deutsch-Christliche, 1935).

169. Information on Grundmann may be found in Weinreich, *Hitler's Professors*, 62–67; Susannah Heschel, "Nazifying Christian Theology: Walter Grundmann and the Institute for the Study and Eradication of Jewish Influence on German Church Life," *Church History* 63 (1994): 587–605; Heschel, "When Jesus Was an Aryan: The Protestant Church and Antisemitic Propaganda," in *Betrayal: German Churches and the Holocaust*, ed. Robert P. Ericksen and Susannah Heschel (Minneapolis: Fortress, 1999), 68–89; Uwe Hossfeld, *Kämpferische Wissenschaft. Studien zur Universität Jena im Nationalsozialismus* (Köln: Böhlau, 2003); Roland Deines, Volker Lippin, and Karl-Wilhelm Niebuhr, eds., *Walter Grundmann. Ein Neutestamentler im dritten Reich* (Leipzig: Evangelischer Verlagsanstalt, 2007). The most comprehensive discussion in English is Susannah Heschel, *The Aryan Jesus: Christian Theologians and the Bible in Nazi Germany* (Princeton: Princeton University Press, 2008).

170. Heschel (*Betrayal*, 77–78, 203–4) noted J. G. Fichte, *Werke*, ed. Fritz Medicus, 6 vols. (Leipzig: Meiner, 1914; repr. 1922), 4:105; Fichte, *Addresses to the German Nation*, trans. R. F. Jones and G. H. Turnbull (Chicago: Open Court, 1922), 68–69; Ernest Renan, *La Vie de Jésus* (Paris: Calman-Levy, 1863); Renan, *Essai psychologique sur Jésus Christ* (Paris: La Connaissance, 1921), 55–57; Theodor Keim, *Geschichte von Jesus von Nazara* (Zürich: Orell, Füssli, 1920); Friedrich Delitzsch, *Die grosse Täuschung. Kritische Beobachtungen zu den alttestamentliche Berichten über Israels Eindringungen in Kanaan, die Gottesoffenbarung von Sinai und die Wirksamkeit der Propheten* (Stuttgart: Deutsche Verlagsanstalt, 1920); Edmond Picard, *L'Aryano-sémitisme* (Brussels: Lacomblez, 1899); Houston Stewart Chamberlain (an English emigrant), *Die Grundlagen des neunzehnten Jahrhunderts* (München: Bruckmann, 1902). See also Brown, *Jesus in European Protestant Thought*, 78–83 (on Fichte), 83–97 (on Hegel), and 233–38 (on Renan).

Heschel also noted Ernst Lohmeyer's theory of a twofold development of Christianity: in Galilee characterized by a universalistic Son-of-Man eschatology; and in Jerusalem dominated by nationalistic Jewish eschatology: Lohmeyer, *Galiläa und Jerusalem* (Göttingen: Vandenhoeck & Ruprecht, 1936); cf. Otto, *The Kingdom of God and the Son of Man* (1934; ET: 1938).

the University of Jena in 1936. He resided on Adolf Hitler Strasse. Hitler himself signed Grundmann's tenure in 1938. Grundmann was also the *Wissenschaftlicher Leiter* (director of research) of the Institut zur Erforschung und Beiseitigung des jüdischen Einflusses auf das deutsche kirchliche Leben (Institute for Investigation into Jewish Influence on German Church Life and Its Eradication), the largest of five Nazi research institutes.

Bishop Martin Sasse of Thuringia had proposed that the Institute should come under the aegis of the University of Jena, but the university rector, though a Nazi, opposed expansion of its small theological faculty, which Grundmann dominated. The institute eventually was located in the *Predigerseminar* in neighboring Eisenach. Notable scholars linked with the institute included Paul Fiebig, Karl Georg Kuhn, Georg Bertram (a Kittel student who replaced Grundmann in 1943 when he was drafted), and Georg Beer. The Institute was formally opened in May 1939 with celebrations at the Wartburg Castle overlooking the city. Here in seclusion Luther had translated the New Testament into German. In 1928 German and British theologians had met in ecumenical solidarity at the Wartburg, reading papers later published in *Mysterium Christi*. In his address on "The Dejudaization of Religious Life as the Task of German Theology and the Church,"[171] Grundmann outlined the program of the institute. It was depicted as carrying forward the work of Martin Luther.[172]

The systematic theologian Emmanuel Hirsch (1888–1972) anticipated Grundmann in his account of the essence of Christianity.[173] In 1940 Grundmann published *Jesus der Galiläer und das Judentum* (Jesus the Galilean and Judaism) with a view to giving "inquiring Germans an answer to the burning and momentous question of the relationship of Jesus of Nazareth to Judaism, indeed, an answer that is based on serious scientific scholarship."[174]

---

171. It was published in pamphlet form, Walter Grundmann, *Die Entjudung des religiösen Lebens als Aufgabe der deutschen Theologie und Lebens* (Weimar, 1940).

172. Heschel, *Betrayal*, 71–76. Bishop Sasse published a pamphlet, *Martin Luther über die Juden. Weg mit Ihnen*, urging that the Kristallnacht pogrom of November 1938 was in full accord with Luther's view of the Jews.

173. Emmanuel Hirsch, *Das Wesen des Christentums* (Weimar: Deutsche Christen, 1939); Ericksen, *Theologians under Hitler*, 163–65; Ericksen and Heschel, *Betrayal*, 28–29.

174. Walter Grundmann, *Jesus der Galiläer und das Judentum* (Leipzig: Weigand, 1940), foreword (author's translation, as are the following citations; italics indicate Grundmann's emphasis).

Hans von Soden, professor of New Testament and church history at Marburg and a member of the Confessing Church, criticized Grundmann for his sloppy scholarship; cf. *Deutsches*

Grundmann explored two avenues. The first was Jesus' message and his clash with Judaism. Citing Rudolf Otto, Grundmann described Jesus as a "charismatic" who possessed an inner vision. "It belongs to the unique way of Jesus Christ that he was a charismatic, both in the absolute authority [*Vollmacht*] of his proclamation [*Verkündigung*] and in his deeds."[175] Inevitably, Jesus came into conflict with the Jews. "Their charges against him of impurity, being in league with the devil, barring the way to the kingdom of God through teaching that led astray, Jesus throws back at them, declaring that they are murderers of the prophets, full of uncleanness, opponents of the will of God, and have no share in God's kingdom and knowledge of him."[176]

For a Jew to declare himself the Son of God was blasphemous, but it was not so to the Romans. The Jews adopted the cynical ploy of representing Jesus as a dangerous political messiah. Jesus was not "worthy" of a Jewish execution by means of stoning. The act of handing Jesus over to the Romans for execution revealed the chasm between Jesus and Judaism.[177]

The other avenue that Grundmann explored was Jesus' ethnic background. He built up a case for claiming that for most of its history Galilee had been separate politically and ethnically from Judea.[178] Grundmann concluded: "If then the Galilean origin of Jesus is beyond doubt, it follows with the greatest probability, on the basis of our previous discussion,

---

Pfarrerblatt 46 (1942): 49; Heschel, *Betrayal*, 85, 205; Heschel, *The Aryan Jesus*, 160. In the political climate it was perhaps as far as anyone could go. Von Soden's criticism of Grundmann and German Christians as "Jewish" was akin to Bultmann's use of *Jew* and *Jewish* in his commentary on *The Gospel of John*. Bultmann used the terms to describe the unbelieving world, regardless of ethnicity (see above, chap. 6, n103).

175. Grundmann, *Jesus der Galiläer und das Judentum*, 128; cf. Otto, *The Kingdom of God and the Son of Man*, 285–87, 292–93, 296, 324–25.

176. Grundmann, *Jesus der Galiläer und das Judentum*, 150.

177. Grundmann, *Jesus der Galiläer und das Judentum*, 161–62.

178. Grundmann, *Jesus der Galiläer und das Judentum*, 166–75. Grundmann argued that only under David was there a united kingdom. By 733/32 BCE Galilee was an Assyrian province. Papyri from the third century were written in Greek. Herod the Great settled veterans of his cavalry—including Germans (Josephus, *Ant.* 17.198)—in Galilee. "As royal territory Galilee was open to foreign governors, who brought their families and slaves with them, and to settlers of official and military rank. Socio-politically this meant the penetration by different ethnic elements" (168). Galilee was reunited with Judea only under the Maccabeans, Hasmoneans, and Romans. "The Judeans had always striven for Galilee, but never had the land firmly under their control. The ethnic identity of a Galilean leaves open the most divergent possibilities" (168). "The subjection of the Galileans to the Judeans was accomplished by forced circumcision and forced acceptance of Judean religion. Whoever refused was driven from his land" (169). Greek was widely spoken, and Hellenistic culture flourished (172).

that he was not a Jew, but rather belonged to one of the ethnic streams already existing in Galilee."[179]

Grundmann considered those strands in the gospel narratives that linked Jesus with Judea, such as his birth in Bethlehem, childhood visits to Jerusalem, and the genealogies, to be untenable fabrications devised to foster acceptance of Jesus' Davidic descent and messiahship.[180] Confession of Jesus as "the Son of David" originated in "the Palestinian Judean Christian community which saw Jesus as the Messiah, who according to the promises of the prophets and the expectation of Judaism would come from David's line."[181] But the historical Jesus undermined Jewish expectations of an earthly ruler. "Jesus did not appear as an earthly ruler, but as servant.... His calling belongs to that of a servant and not that of a ruler. But the idea of the messiah sprang fundamentally from the thought of domination."[182]

In the tradition of liberal Protestantism, Grundmann presented his portrait of Jesus as the spiritual alternative to Jewish legalistic, belligerent religion. It originated in Hellenistic Galilee. "Above all, there are two factors in which those 'Hellenistic original components of the gospel' consist: on the one hand, the thought of the proximity of God as Father, and on the other hand, that of a morality free from the law corresponding to the inner being of humanity. Here too Jesus brings the thought of self-giving love for society, from which flows morality, a thought new and transforming to Hellenism, which was eagerly seized by the citizens of the Hellenistic world."[183] "What in him sprang from different roots appeared in complete contrast to Jewish positions in the whole range of religious and human life. From our contemporary knowledge of the unity of spiritual disposition and ethnic bloodlines it necessarily follows in all probability that on the basis of his spirituality [*seelischen Artung*] Jesus could not have been a Jew, and also was not so by blood."[184] Grundmann concluded with a quotation from the Fourth Gospel: "The light shines in the darkness, and the darkness did not overcome it" (John 1:5).

---

179. Grundmann, *Jesus der Galiläer und das Judentum*, 175.
180. Grundmann, *Jesus der Galiläer und das Judentum*, 175–200.
181. Grundmann, *Jesus der Galiläer und das Judentum*, 175.
182. Grundmann, *Jesus der Galiläer und das Judentum*, 56; cf. Walter Grundmann, "Das Problem des hellenistischen Christentums innerhalb der Jerusalemer Urgemeinde," *ZAW* 38 (1939): 45–73.
183. Grundmann, *Jesus der Galiläer und das Judentum*, 204.
184. Grundmann, *Jesus der Galiläer und das Judentum*, 205.

The No Quest in Europe to World War II

In 1938 Grundmann urged the elimination of the study of Hebrew from the theological curriculum on the grounds that the LXX was the Scripture of the early church. It was decided to make Hebrew optional. Doctoral students who did not toe the party line were denied their degrees. *Die Botschaft Gottes* ("God's Message"), a dejudaized version of the New Testament appeared in 1940 together with a dejudaized hymnal, *Grosser Gott Wir Loben Dich* ("We Praise You, Great God"). They were followed in 1941 by a catechism, *Deutsche mit Gott. Ein deutsches Glaubensbuch* ("German with God: A German Book of Belief"). Links between Jesus and Judaism were severed, and the hymnal "expunged words such as *amen, hallelujah, Hosannah,* and *Zebaoth.*"[185]

At the end of the war Grundmann was released from a Russian prisoner of war camp. He returned to Jena but was not reinstated in his chair. His pleas for retaining the institute on the grounds that it sought to save the church from Nazi oppression were heard but denied. He professed acceptance of the Barmen Declaration's assertion of the sovereignty of Christ but was not asked to repudiate anti-Semitism. He did not mention the Holocaust in his many subsequent publications,[186] and there are grounds for thinking that he had ties with the STASI.[187] Grundmann was appointed rector of the *Predigerseminar* at Eisenach (then in East Germany). Shortly before his death in 1976, he was given the honorary title of Kirchenrat (counselor of the church).

Grundmann's postwar writings included major commentaries on Matthew, Mark, and Luke[188] and *Die Geschichte Jesu Christi* ("The History of Jesus Christ"),[189] a work that ran to nearly 500 pages. In appearance

---

185. Heschel, *Betrayal*, 73.
186. Heschel, *Betrayal*, 84.
187. The STASI (*Staatssicherheitsdient*, State Security Service of East Germany) was made up of former members of the Gestapo.
188. Grundmann's publications include: "Verkündigung und Geschichte in der Bericht vom Eingang der Geschichte Jesu im Johannes-Evangelium," in *Der historische Jesus und der kerygmatische Christus. Beiträge zum Christusverständnis in Forschung und Verkündigung*, ed. Helmut Ristow und Karl Matthiae (Berlin: Evangelische Verlagsanstalt, 1962), 289–309; *Das Evangelium nach Matthäus*, THKNT 1 (Berlin: Evangelische Verlagsanstalt, 1968); *Das Evangelium nach Markus*, THKNT 2 (Berlin: Evangelische Verlagsanstalt, 1968); *Das Evangelium nach Lukas*, THKNT 3 (Berlin: Evangelische Verlagsanstalt, 1961).
189. Walter Grundmann, *Die Geschichte Jesu Christi* (Berlin: Evangelische Verlagsanstalt, 1956; 3rd ed., 1961). In the following discussion, quotations from the German are translated by the author. The second and third editions are reprints of the first supplemented by additional explanations, references, and corrections (425–48). The Evangelische Verlagsanstalt, with Grundmann as advisor, was the leading theological publisher in the DDR.

it was mainstream moderate, engaging with the current literature of the day, and mediating to many their first encounter with the Dead Sea Scrolls. It gave no hint that its author was also the author of *Jesus der Galiläer und das Judentum*. In the second edition Grundmann expressed gratification at the reception of his work at home and abroad. It helped to make Grundmann the leading New Testament scholar in the Deutsche Demokratische Republik.

Grundmann began with a brief review of Jesus studies, concluding that Harnack was right in maintaining the thesis in his licentiate oral defense: "*Vita Christi scribi nequit*"—"The life of Christ cannot be written."[190] What we have to work with are individual *pericopae* that must be studied with the tools of form and redaction criticism. Even if a history of Jesus cannot be written, certain themes may be identified: John the Baptist and Jesus; the hour of dawning fulfillment; the Father and the Son; loving one's neighbor; disputes with Jewish parties; possessions; the kingdom of God; disciples, Israel, and the gentiles; Jesus as the Christ; the way to the cross; the answer of the Father; and the birth narratives.

Leaving aside his former speculations regarding Galilee, Grundmann began with Mark's account of John the Baptist, which encapsulated the mission of Jesus.

> *For Mark the baptism story constitutes the message: Jesus is the Messianic High Priest. His way was shown beforehand by Isaiah in the vision of the Servant of the Lord. As Messianic High Priest, Jesus is God's Son. It is his office to act for God among men, as he bestows upon them the new eschatological fellowship with God in the Holy Spirit, and acts for men before God as he stands on their side and takes their sins upon himself. Therefore, God's good pleasure rests upon him.* Heaven is open and the Spirit comes down upon him for men. Mark arranges this message in a narrative formed in the style of sacred history.[191]

Jesus was "the herald of the coming kingdom."[192] But the hour of fulfillment also unleashed conflict with demonic powers. Grundmann

---

190. Grundmann, *Die Geschichte Jesu Christi*, 5; cf. Agnes von Zahn-Harnack, *Adolf von Harnack*, 2nd ed. (Berlin: de Gruyter, 1951), 46. The second and third editions were reprints of the first, supplemented by additional explanations, references, and corrections (425–48).
191. Grundmann, *Die Geschichte Jesu Christi*, 37 (Grundmann's emphasis).
192. Grundmann, *Die Geschichte Jesu Christi*, 45.

reversed his former high opinion of Hellenism. Following Adolf Schlatter, he now attributed the outbreak of demonism among the Jewish populace to "a vexatious consequence of Hellenism."[193] The cry of the unclean spirit, "What have you to do with us, Jesus of Nazareth? Have you come to destroy us? I know who you are, the Holy One of God" (Mark 1:24), was a magical formula invoked to gain power over Jesus.[194] At the same time "it reveals Jesus as the Messianic High Priest." It belonged to messianic expectation that "the Lord will raise up a new priest. . . . The spirit of holiness shall be upon them. And Beliar shall be bound by him. And he shall grant to his children the authority to trample upon wicked spirits" (T. Levi 18:1, 11–12; cf. *OTP* 1:794–95).

Grundmann asserts, "Not judgment, but salvation stands at the center of Jesus' proclamation and determines his appearance and activity in contrast to that of the Baptist. The salvation proclaimed by him is universal. This means: *Jesus did not come with a preconceived attitude toward the Pharisees.* Since he considered his mission to be universal, he could not exclude the Pharisees in advance."[195] The conflict was no longer between the Galilean Jesus and Judaism but over issues and practices within Israel. A crucial question was purity and purification. "Israel was to be a pure and holy people, and live in a pure and holy land, separate in such purity and holiness from the Gentiles. In the world of ancient Israel purity was both cultic and above all ethical under the influence of prophetic preaching."[196] Citing Friedrich Hauck's article on καθαρός (*katharos*, clean, pure) in the *Theologisches Wörterbuch*, Grundmann pronounced, "It became the defect of late Jewish official religion that it conceded to the demand for cultic purity a highly exaggerated preponderance over against the innermost concern of religion, and that it remained incapable of repelling the primitive."[197] For the Pharisees and the Essenes, separation from all who were considered unclean was essential.

---

193. Grundmann, *Die Geschichte Jesu Christi*, 57; cf. Adolf Schlatter, *Der Evangelist Matthäus* (Stuttgart: Calver Verlag, 1929; 6th ed. 1963), 229. Grundmann noted that the Old Testament was frugal in its references to Satan and demons.
194. Grundmann, *Die Geschichte Jesu Christi*, 58; cf. Graham H. Twelftree, *Jesus the Exorcist: A Contribution to the Study of the Historical Jesus*, WUNT 54 (Tübingen: Mohr Siebeck, 1993), 57–71.
195. Grundmann, *Die Geschichte Jesu Christi*, 109.
196. Grundmann, *Die Geschichte Jesu Christi*, 142–43.
197. Grundmann, *Die Geschichte Jesu Christi*, 144 (author's translation); cf. *TWNT* 3:420.

The European Scene

If we look at Jesus in this connection, it is immediately apparent that the question of impurity plays no role at all for him. He has table fellowship with sinners and tax collectors, who counted as unclean, requires no cultic purification, and has apparently no fear or horror that he might become unclean through contact with them. He speaks with the leper and touches him. He lets himself be touched by the menstruating woman who is impure in the highest degree. He speaks with her and no word of rebuke comes from his mouth, because she is impure and has made him impure by touching him. Time and time again we encounter Jesus' lack of concern for the possibility of becoming impure.[198]

While some of the disputes were compositions of the evangelist in the manner of the Fourth Gospel, the way of Jesus was clear. "Service to God at the expense of love for human beings, especially at the expense of obligation of children to their parents, is for Jesus empty lip service."[199] "*In the coming of Jesus an authority can be seen, which transcended that of the authorities of his time, the scribes.* 'For he taught as one who had authority and not as the scribes' (Mark 1:22; Matt 7:29). This authority was understood as *prophetic*, for which reason people considered him a prophet (Mark 8:28; Luke 7:39)."[200] Drawing once more on Rudolf Otto, Grundmann described Jesus as "the archetypal charismatic [*der Urcharismatiker*]" and primitive Christianity as "a charismatic movement [*eine charismatische Bewegung*]."[201]

> The spiritual gifts of wisdom and knowledge, of prophecy and of the word are his, and he sees through the spirits of men and powers. In his dealings with the sick and possessed, but also with his disciples and his adversaries this is clear. John's Gospel sums it up: "He had no need of testimony from men, for he knew what was in man" (John 2:25). Whether he knows of the sin of the paralytic, who was brought to him (Mark 2:5), or of the state of Jairus's daughter and the woman with the flow of blood (Mark 5:29ff., 39), whether he

---

198. Grundmann, *Die Geschichte Jesu Christi*, 144.
199. Grundmann, *Die Geschichte Jesu Christi*, 145.
200. Grundmann, *Die Geschichte Jesu Christi*, 261; cf. Otto, *The Kingdom of God and the Son of Man*, 333–76.
201. Grundmann, *Die Geschichte Jesu Christi*, 265.

knows how to free the demonically possessed, whether he assigns disciples in the kingdom of God with a new name (Mark 3:16f.), or sees through the intentions of his adversaries (Mark 2:8; 3:5; and often) in each case he knows what is in men. Jesus is a charismatic.[202]

Die Geschichte Jesu Christi depicted the passion as a divine necessity. The sayings to the sons of Zebedee (Mark 10:35–45) about baptism and the cup spoke of purification. "This baptism is the bath of purification. Its link with the cup in the reply to the sons of Zebedee leads one to think . . . that his suffering purifies for the eternal banquet, while he takes the cup of judgment and drinks on behalf of those whom he prepares for the eternal banquet. The cup is mentioned again in connection with the Last Supper and the events in Gethsemane."[203]

In the hearing before the Sanhedrin Jesus was condemned out of his own mouth. In answer to the high priest's question, "Are you the Messiah, the Son of the Blessed One?" Jesus replied with the divine revelatory "I am" (Mark 14:61–62; cf. Exod 3:14). Since Jesus' sonship was known only to the circle of the disciples, the sole explanation for its appearance here was that Judas had betrayed it to the Sanhedrin. However, it could not be used because there were not two witnesses who could testify to it. "Thus the high priest had to make the entire Sanhedrin witnesses. *Jesus' blasphemy consists in the name of the Son, from which the sentence of death follows.*"[204]

Grundmann suspected that there might have been collusion between Pilate and the Sanhedrin in the arrest of Jesus.[205] Pilate had been sent to Judea by Sejanus to whom, on retiring to Capri, Tiberius had committed government. Pilate had carried out Sejanus's hostile policy against the Jews. But following the fall and execution of Sejanus in 31 CE, Pilate appears to have adopted a more conciliatory attitude. Grundmann attributed Pilate's eventual readiness to allow Jesus to be executed to this change of attitude.[206] "After the people had clamored for Barabbas, Jesus

---

202. Grundmann, *Die Geschichte Jesu Christi*, 266.
203. Grundmann, *Die Geschichte Jesu Christi*, 299.
204. Grundmann, *Die Geschichte Jesu Christi*, 335.
205. Grundmann, *Die Geschichte Jesu Christi*, 336, where Grundmann noted John's account of the presence of Roman soldiers (John 18:3, 12).
206. Grundmann, *Die Geschichte Jesu Christi*, 337. Pilate may have acquired the title *amicus Caesaris* through his connections with Sejanus. Tacitus observed, "quisque Sejano intimus, ita Caesaris amicitia validus"—"the closer a man's intimacy with Sejanus, the stronger his claim to the

appeared to Pilate as an obstacle that stood in the way and must be done away with."[207]

In trying to assess *Die Geschichte Jesu Christi*, two questions loom large: "How does it relate to *Jesus der Galiläer und das Judentum?*" and "What contribution does it make to understanding the historical Jesus?" In answer to the first question, it must be acknowledged that it did not renew the attempt to make Jesus an Aryan. It contained nothing on the ethnic make-up of Galilee. Nor did it attribute Jesus' *seelische Artung* to bloodlines. But if the excrescences of the past were removed, the underlying contours remain. The conflict was still between the Galilean Jesus and the Judeans in the south. It was mitigated by the claim that Jesus proclaimed a universal salvation, which did not exclude *a priori* the Pharisees. Together with the Essenes, the Pharisees had a high regard for cultic purity, and Jesus had none. Conflict was inevitable. Repeating Hauck's offensive phraseology, Grundmann endorsed the view that "the defect of late Jewish official religion" consisted in its exaggerated demand for "cultic purity" at the expense of "the innermost concern of religion" and was thus unable to repel "the primitive."

As in *Jesus der Galiläer und das Judentum*, Grundmann relegated the birth and infancy narratives, with their links to Judea and Davidic messiahship, to the end of the book, dismissing them as "theological-christological pronouncements—not historical reports."[208] As in the earlier book, Grundmann posited two centers of early Christianity. He thought it "not improbable" that the resurrection appearances to the apostles took place mainly in Galilee and those to Jesus' relatives in and around Jerusalem.[209] Once more, and again invoking the authority of Rudolf Otto, Grundmann represented Jesus as a charismatic whose possession of the Spirit led him to disregard the high value set upon "cultic purity" by "late official Jewish religion."

With this last point, we come to our second question regarding *Die Geschichte Jesu Christi*: What contribution does it make to understanding the historical Jesus? First, it may be noted that not long after

---

emperor's friendship" (*Annales* 6.8; LCL 3, 167). John 19:12 indicates that the title was invoked to pressure Pilate into compliance: "From then on Pilate tried to release him, but the Jews cried out, 'If you release this man, you are no friend of the emperor. Everyone who claims to be a king sets himself against the emperor.'"

207. Grundmann, *Die Geschichte Jesu Christi*, 340.
208. Grundmann, *Die Geschichte Jesu Christi*, 409.
209. Grundmann, *Die Geschichte Jesu Christi*, 370.

the appearance of Grundmann's book the Jewish scholar Geza Vermes also represented Jesus as a Galilean charismatic. "The representation of Jesus in the Gospels as a man whose supernatural abilities derived, not from secret powers, but from immediate contact with God, proves him to be a genuine charismatic, the true heir of an age-old prophetic religious line."[210] Vermes saw affinity between Jesus, Honi the Circle Drawer, and Hanina ben Dosa. While Galilean charismatics enjoyed a more relaxed attitude to the law, Vermes located Jesus firmly in the world of Judaism noting many similarities of style, idiom, and teaching.[211] Jesus' place within Judaism has been affirmed by both Christian and Jewish scholars. Among them are David Flusser,[212] E. P. Sanders,[213] Leander E. Keck,[214] James H. Charlesworth,[215] and Paula Fredriksen.[216] At the same time current scholarship recognizes the variety of Judaisms and their messiahs in Second Temple Judaism.[217]

---

210. Geza Vermes, *Jesus the Jew: A Historian's Reading of the Gospels* (London: Collins; Philadelphia: Fortress, 1973; 2nd ed. 1981), 69; see also Vermes, "Hanina ben Dosa," in *Post-Biblical Jewish Studies*, SJLA 8 (Leiden: Brill, 1975), 178–214; and Vermes, *Jesus and the World of Judaism* (Philadelphia: Fortress, 1984), esp. 5–11.

211. Vermes, *Jesus and the World of Judaism*; revised as *Jesus in His Jewish Context* (Minneapolis: Fortress, 2003); *The Religion of Jesus the Jew* (Minneapolis: Fortress, 1993); *The Changing Faces of Jesus* (London: Allen Lane; Penguin, 2000); *The Authentic Gospel of Jesus* (London: Allen Lane; Penguin, 2003).

212. David Flusser, in collaboration with R. Steven Notley, *Jesus* (Jerusalem: Hebrew University; Magness Press, 1997).

213. E. P. Sanders, *Jesus and Judaism* (Philadelphia: Fortress; London: SCM, 1985); Sanders, *Jewish Law from Jesus to the Mishnah: Five Studies* (London: SCM; Philadelphia: Trinity Press International, 1990); Sanders, *Judaism, Practice and Belief, 63 BCE–66 CE* (London: SCM; Philadelphia: Trinity Press International, 1992); Sanders, *The Historical Figure of Jesus* (London: Allen Lane; Penguin, 1992).

214. Leander E. Keck, *Who Is Jesus? History in Perfect Tense* (Minneapolis: Fortress, 2001).

215. James H. Charlesworth, *Jesus within Judaism: New Light from Exciting Archaeological Discoveries* (New York: Doubleday, 1988); Charlesworth, ed., *Jesus' Jewishness: Exploring the Place of Jesus within Early Judaism* (New York: American Interfaith Institute; Crossroad, 1991); Charlesworth, ed., *Jesus and the Dead Sea Scrolls* (New York: Doubleday, 1992); James H. Charlesworth and Loren L. Johns, eds., *Hillel and Jesus: Comparisons of Two Major Religious Leaders* (Minneapolis: Fortress, 1997).

216. Paula Fredriksen, *From Jesus to Christ: The Origins of the New Testament Images of Jesus* (New Haven, London: Yale University Press, 1988); *Jesus of Nazareth, King of the Jews: A Jewish Life and the Emergence of Christianity* (New York: Knopf, 2000).

217. Jacob Neusner, William S. Green, and Ernest Frerichs, eds. *Judaisms and Their Messiahs at the Turn of the Christian Era* (Cambridge: Cambridge University Press, 1987); James H. Charlesworth, ed., *The Messiah: Developments in Earliest Judaism and Christianity*, The First Princeton Symposium on Judaism and Christian Origins (Minneapolis: Fortress, 1992); John J. Collins, *The Scepter and the Star: The Messiahs of the Dead Sea Scrolls and Other Ancient Literature* (New York: Doubleday, 1995); Timo Eskola, *Messiah and Throne: Jewish Merkabah Mysticism and Early Christian Exaltation Discourse*, WUNT 142 (Tübingen: Mohr Siebeck, 2001); Andrew

The European Scene

A tradition dating back to Luther and beyond saw Jesus as high priest and king.[218] Grundmann focused exclusively on Jesus, who was made high priest by the coming of the Spirit upon him after his baptism. Two observations may be made. On the one hand, the citation of the Testament of Levi as evidence of messianic expectation is questionable in light of Christian reworking of passages in the Testaments of the Twelve Patriarchs.[219] On the other hand, Grundmann's linking of Jesus' sonship with high priestly office downplays the allusions to messianic *kingship* in the words of the voice from heaven (Mark 1:11; cf. Isa 42:1; Ps 2:7; 4Q174). It ignores the political undercurrents in the opening words of Mark: "The beginning of the good news [εὐαγγελίου] of Jesus Christ, the Son of God" (1:1). Both εὐαγγέλιον and *Son of God* are terms used in inscriptions in emperor worship,[220] and Mark's gospel presents Jesus as Caesar's rival and superior.[221]

Finally, comment must be made on Grundmann's disparagement of cultic purity, and his claim that Jesus was utterly indifferent to it. Recent study has indicated that cultic purity plays a major part in Mark. The story that Mark tells is how Jesus communicated different facets of purity, beginning with expelling the unclean spirits, cleansing the leper, and declaration of God's forgiveness to the paralytic and ending with cleansing the grave.[222] As we shall see in later discussion, there is reason to link these narratives with allusions to Jesus' kingly priesthood exaltation after the order of Melchizedek (Mark 12:36; Matt 22:44; Luke 20:42; cf. Ps 110:1–4).[223]

Chester, *Messiah and Exaltation: Jewish Messianic and Visionary Traditions and New Testament Christology*, WUNT 207 (Tübingen: Mohr Siebeck, 2007).

218. Ian D. Kingston Siggins, *Martin Luther's Doctrine of Christ* (New Haven, CT: Yale University Press, 1970).

219. Howard Clark Kee, *OTP* 1:775–80.

220. Hans-Josef Klauck, *The Religious Context of Early Christianity: A Guide to Graeco-Roman Religions*, trans. Brian McNeil (Edinburgh: T&T Clark, 2000), 289–330.

221. Craig A. Evans, *Mark 8:27–16:20*, WBC 34B (Nashville: Nelson, 2001), lxxx–xciii.

222. See my argument in chap. 1.

223. See chap. 21, §1.2; §4.2; §5.2.

CHAPTER 8

THE NO QUEST IN EUROPE AFTER WORLD WAR II

FROM ITS SECOND YEAR (1899) the *Theologische Rundschau*, under the editorship of Wilhelm Bousset, published regular progress reports on the quest of the historical Jesus. In 1929 Rudolf Bultmann took over and launched a new series. The stream of reports dried up. Bultmann continued to edit the journal, assisted by Erich Dinkler, until his death in 1976. The 1950s saw an article by Peter Biehl (Bultmann's teaching assistant) on the question of the historical Jesus. It focused on Käsemann and ended by endorsing Bultmann.[1]

When Werner Georg Kümmel (1905–95), Bultmann's successor at Marburg, joined the editorial team, the *Theologische Rundschau* resumed the practice of giving regular reports on Jesus research. Kümmel's reports of successive decades of research around the world are models of comprehensive, concise analysis. They were published together in book form as *Thirty Years of Jesus Research (1950–1980)*. Subsequently, it was enlarged in a second edition, *Vierzig Jahre Jesusforschung (1950–1990)*.[2] As a

---

1. Peter Biehl, "Zur Frage des historischen Jesus," *TRu* 24 (1957–58): 54–76.
2. Kümmel began with "Jesusforschung seit 1950," *TRu* 31 (1965–66), 15–46, 289–315. The period between 1960 and 1965 was omitted on account of personal reasons. Kümmel resumed with "Ein Jahrzehnt Jesusforschung (1965–75)," *TRu* 40 (1975): 289–336; 41 (1976): 197–258, 295–363; 45 (1980): 40–84, 293–337; "Jesusforschung seit 1965: Nachträge 1975–1980," *TRu* 46 (1981): 317–63; 47 (1982): 136–65, 348–83; "Jesusforschung seit 1981," *TRu* 53 (1988): 229–49; 54 (1989): 1–53; 55 (1990): 21–45; 56 (1991): 27–53, 391–420.

These articles were collected and edited by Helmut Merklein with an epilogue and

comprehensive, classified, analytic review of Jesus research in the second half of the twentieth century, Kümmel's work is unrivalled. Rather than try to emulate it, I shall focus on three European scholars who attracted international attention.

1. Ethelbert Stauffer
   1.1. A History of Jesus
   1.2. Stauffer in Retrospect
2. Joachim Jeremias
   2.1. Jeremias's Plea for Renewal of the Quest
   2.2. The Eucharistic Words of Jesus
   2.3. The Death of Jesus
   2.4. The Gentile Mission
   2.5. The Parables of Jesus
   2.6. The Prayers of Jesus
   2.7. Jeremias in Retrospect
3. Oscar Cullmann
   3.1. The Origin of Christmas
   3.2. The Quest of the Historical Peter
   3.3. New Testament Christology
   3.4. Time and Salvation History
   3.5. The Johannine Circle
   3.6. Cullmann in Retrospect

---

bibliographical supplement in Werner Georg Kümmel, *Vierzig Jahre Jesusforschung (1950–1990)*, 2nd ed., BBB 91 (Weinheim: Beltz Athenäum, 1994). The reports were organized in a more or less uniform pattern. That was typical for the decade 1965–75: (1) reports of research, sources outside the Gospels, questions of method; (2) nonacademic and scholarly accounts; (3) Jesus' teaching; (4) Sermon on the Mount, parables, miracle stories; (5) personal claims of Jesus; (6) trial and crucifixion of Jesus.

Kümmel became a full professor at Zürich in 1946 and assumed Bultmann's chair at Marburg in 1952, retiring in 1973. Kümmel's numerous works include *Promise and Fulfillment: The Eschatological Message of Jesus*, trans. Dorothea M. Barton, SBT 23 (London: SCM, 1957); *Das Neue Testament. Geschichte der Erforschung seiner Probleme* (Freiburg: Alber, 1970); ET: *The New Testament: The History and Investigation of Its Problems*, trans. S. MacLean Gilmour and Howard Clark Kee (Nashville: Abingdon, 1972); *Heilsgeschehen und Geschichte. Gesammelte Aufsätze 1933–1964*, ed. Erich Grässer, Otto Merk and Adolf Fritz, Marburger Theologische Studien 3 (Marburg: Elwert, 1965); *Introduction to the New Testament*, rev. ed., trans. Howard Clark Kee (Nashville: Abingdon, 1975). See also *Jesus und Paulus. Festschrift für Werner Georg Kümmel zum 70. Geburtstag*, ed. E. Earle Ellis and Erich Grässer (Göttingen: Vandenhoeck & Ruprecht, 1975); Otto Merk, *DMBI*, 625–27.

1. Ethelbert Stauffer

In the period following World War II, Ethelbert Stauffer (1902–79), professor of New Testament at Erlangen,[3] wrote a series of books designed to locate Jesus in the worlds of Rome and Judaism for the benefit of general readers. *Christ and the Caesars: Historical Sketches* (1955) used Roman coins to illustrate gospel incidents and track the rise of Christianity in the imperial world.[4]

Stauffer's study of Jerusalem and Rome in the age of Jesus Christ focused predominantly on the world of Judaism.[5] It introduced readers to Jewish apocalyptic, the Dead Sea Scrolls, scribes and Pharisees, the men of the Great Sanhedrin, Jewish eschatology, liturgy, laws against heretics, and the death penalty in ancient Palestine. It concluded with a sketch of Jesus, the crucified Torah teacher. Though popular in style, the book's endnotes were full of references to primary sources.

The two books on background were accompanied by three books on Jesus, one of which—*Jesus and His Story*—was published in English in two separate translations.[6] In addition Stauffer wrote a *New Testament Theology*,[7]

---

3. Stauffer came from a Mennonite background. He studied at Tübingen and worked with Dobschütz and Klostermann at Halle, where he became a Privatdozent. He taught at Bonn (1934–46), where concerns were raised about alleged Nazi sympathies during the war. He was cleared but chose to move to a new chair of New Testament at Erlangen (1948–67). Stauffer was honored by the Festschrift *Donum Gratulatorium. Ethelbert Stauffer dem sechzigjährigen in dankbarer Verehrung* (Leiden: Brill, 1962). An incomplete bibliography was compiled by Hanna Stauffer, *JSNTS* 11 (1981): 21–38. For Stauffer's life and full bibliography, see Klaus-Gunther Wesseling, *BBK*, 10: 1245–50.

4. Ethelbert Stauffer, *Christus und die Caesaren: Historische Skizzen*, 3rd ed. (Hamburg: Wittig, 1952); ET: *Christ and the Caesars: Historical Sketches*, trans. K. and R. Gregor Smith (London: SCM; Philadelphia: Westminster, 1955).

5. Stauffer, *Jerusalem und Rom im Zeitalter Jesu Christi* (Bern: Francke, 1957).

6. Stauffer, *Jesus. Gestalt und Geschichte* (Bern: Franke, 1957); ET: *Jesus and His Story*, trans. Richard and Clara Winston (New York: Knopf, 1959); trans. Dorothea M. Barton (London: SCM, 1960). The endnotes are curiously different in the two translations. References below are to the American edition, which reproduces (205–10) from Stauffer, *Jerusalem und Rom*, 113–22, the references to provisions against heretics in rabbinic writings, which were omitted from the German and English editions.

Stauffer, *Die Botschaft Jesu. Damals und Heute* ("The Message of Jesus, Then and Today") (Bern: Francke, 1959), gave a summary of Jesus' teaching. Stauffer, *Jesus war ganz anders* ("Jesus Was Quite Different") (Hamburg: Wittig, 1967), brought together themes from earlier books.

7. Stauffer, *Die Theologie des Neuen Testaments*, 5th ed. (Stuttgart: Bertelsmann, 1955); ET: *New Testament Theology*, trans. John Marsh (London: SCM, 1955). The original was completed in 1938 and first published in 1941. In a review of the English translation C. K. Barrett (*ExpTim* 72 [1961]: 356–60) noted various problems but welcomed Stauffer's treatment of the theology

a major encyclopedia article on "Jesus, History and Proclamation,"[8] and numerous shorter pieces.[9]

1.1. A History of Jesus. In an age when the Bultmannian school saw Jesus as the presupposition of the *kerygma*, Stauffer embarked on "a *history* of Jesus." He did not mean a biography in the nineteenth-century sense but "a strict clarification of those facts which can be ascertained." "I shall proceed along pragmatic lines, refraining from any psychologizing. Chronology will be my guide. I shall synchronize but not invent or speculate."[10] Stauffer "barred" from his work all interpretations, including his own. He would stick to "presentation of facts and causal relationships." "However, the oldest and most important interpretation must be treated: Jesus' own interpretation of himself."[11]

It was not possible to fit the gospel of John into synoptic chronology, but it was possible "to fit the Synoptic frame into John's structure."[12] By using allusions to seasons and events like the death of Herod (4 BCE)[13] and the fifteenth year of Tiberius (Luke 3:1–2), Stauffer set up a framework for a four-year ministry of Jesus. He went on to describe Jesus' appearance on the basis of what would be normal for a Palestinian male.[14] Stauffer placed John the Baptist's arrest shortly before the Feast of

---

of martyrdom and the need for systematic theologians to learn from Stauffer's "quasi systematic work" in framing theological questions.

8. Stauffer, "Jesus, Geschichte und Verkündigung," *ANRW*, 2.25.1:3–130.

9. Stauffer's shorter works include *Jesus and the Wilderness Community at Qumran*, trans. Hans Spalteholz, Facet Books Biblical Series 10 (Philadelphia: Fortress, 1964), and a study of Paul and Jesus directed at his Erlangen colleagues, *Jesus, Paulus und Wir. Antwort auf einen Offenen Brief von Paul Althaus, Walter Künneth und Wilfried Joest* (Hamburg: Wittig, 1961).

10. Stauffer, *Jesus and His Story*, xiii.

11. Stauffer, *Jesus and His Story*, xiii.

12. Stauffer, *Jesus and His Story*, 7.

13. The year 4 BCE is the commonly accepted date for the death of Herod (Schürer, *The History of the Jewish People in the Age of Jesus Christ*, 1:326–27). In view of the allusions to Herod in connection with the birth of Jesus (Matt 2:1–29) it is assumed that Jesus was born while Herod was still alive (i.e., c. 5/4 BCE). Josephus mentions an eclipse of the moon shortly before Herod's death (*Ant.* 17.167) and the Passover that followed (*War* 2.10; *Ant.* 17.213).

Jack Finegan revised the traditional dating of Herod's death. He placed it in the time frame between the total eclipse of the moon on the night of January 9–10 and the full paschal moon on Nisan 14/April 8, 1 BCE. See Finegan, *Handbook of Biblical Chronology: Principles of Time Reckoning in the Ancient World and the Problems of Chronology in the Bible*, rev. ed. (Peabody, MA: Hendrickson, 1998), 295–301. If so, Jesus would have been born c. 3/2 BCE. These revised dates for Herod and Jesus seem to correlate with the tradition in Luke 3:23, which says Jesus began his public activities, when he "was about thirty." If the Passion occurred in 30 CE, as many think, then the public ministry of Jesus may have begun in 28 CE.

14. Stauffer, *Jesus and His Story*, 58–62.

Tabernacles in 30 CE[15] and Jesus' proclamation of the kingdom between November of 30 CE and March of 31 CE.[16] His narrative reads like a harmony of the Gospels in which John provided the framework.

Stauffer traced the Sanhedrin's decision to liquidate Jesus to the raising of Lazarus (John 11:46–50)[17] but used Mark for the events leading to Jesus' conviction for blasphemy.

> Caiaphas plays his last card: "Are you the Christ, the son of the Blessed?" This, for Jesus, was the point at which he had to make his statement. More than that, it was the moment of revelation. His time had come [cf. John 2:4, 24]. And Jesus replied: "I am [ἐγώ εἰμι; *egō eimi*]; and you will see the Son of Man sitting at the right hand of Power, and coming with the clouds of heaven." Whereupon the high Priest rent his garments and said: "Why do we still need witnesses? You have heard his blasphemy? And they all pronounced against him a sentence of death [Mark 14:61–64]."[18]

Following an account of the crucifixion and resurrection appearances, Stauffer turned to "Jesus' witness to himself." Jesus did not preach the end of the world.[19] There are no allusions to it in Q. Jesus proclaimed the kingdom of God in the present (Mark 1:15). In his encyclopedia article, Stauffer elaborated the point, giving lengthy quotations from Wellhausen, "the most brilliant biblical scholar of the past hundred years," in rebuttal of Schweitzer. Stauffer ruefully remarked that Wellhausen "remained like

---

15. Stauffer, *Jesus and His Story*, 73. "Apparently Jesus first heard of the imprisonment of John when he arrived in Jerusalem for 'the feast' [John 5:1]."
16. Stauffer, *Jesus and His Story*, 70–71.
17. Stauffer, *Jesus and His Story*, 100–108.
18. Stauffer, *Jesus and His Story*, 124. Stauffer was emphatic on the question of the religious character of Jesus' condemnation. In a review article on Paul Winter, *On the Trial of Jesus*, Judaica 1 (Berlin: de Gruyter, 1961; 2nd ed. revised by T. A. Burkill and Geza Vermes, 1974), Stauffer criticized Winter's claims that Jesus was a Pharisee, that Jesus was not condemned by the Sanhedrin, and that Jesus was condemned by Pilate in order to placate the Jews. Stauffer, "Die Heimholung Jesu in das jüdische Volk," *TLZ* 88 (1963): 98–102. "The death sentence of the Sanhedrin," says Stauffer, "was in order from the judicial point of view, from the religious point of view, and from the theological point of view. Here faith stood against faith. Between the faith of Jesus and the faith of his judges there was only one either-or" (102).

For a response, see Hans-Werner Bartsch, "Wer verurteilte Jesus zum Tode? Zu der Rezension des Buches von Paul Winter *On the Trial of Jesus*, durch Ethelbert Stauffer," *NovT* 7 (1964): 210–16.

19. Stauffer, *Jesus and His Story*, 154–60.

a lonely bird on the roof. His words have made no impression on Albert Schweitzer or on the younger generation who could not free themselves for decades from fascination with the apocalyptic picture of Jesus."[20]

On the question of Jesus' identify, Stauffer argued that Jesus did not refer to himself as the Messiah.[21] He used Son of Man more frequently than any other title, often as a direct counter to Messiah.[22] The fact that Son of Man did not figure in the theology of the early church argued for it being unique to Jesus, as did its diminished use by the rabbis. Stauffer took the remark by Rabbi Abbahu in the Jerusalem Talmud to be "an unmistakable allusion to Jesus": "If a man says, I am the Son of Man, he will come to an end that he will rue."[23] When used by Jesus, the term expresses "the transcendent authority of a great stranger from another world."[24]

The logion about the Father's unique knowledge of the Son, and the Son's unique knowledge of the Father, and ability to reveal that knowledge (Matt 11:25–27) was an authentic word, which sheds light on Jesus' solitary hours of prayer.[25] The most important self-designation was the "I am He." It led to Jesus' condemnation for blasphemy. It was the divine self-designation found in the Hebrew Scriptures used in the Torah (Deut 5:6), the Passover Hallel Psalms (115–118), Isaiah 43:1–5, and numerous other places.[26] On the lips of Jesus (Mark 6:50; 14:62; John 4:26; 8:24, 58; 13:19) it was the "historical epiphany of God."[27]

1.2. Stauffer in Retrospect. Susannah Heschel noted affinities between Stauffer's portrait of Jesus in *Jesus and His Story* and that of Walter Grundmann. "Basing his argument on the Gospel of John, which had been favored by the German Christians for its hostility to the Jews, Stauffer reiterated the German Christian view of Jesus as a lonely fighter

---

20. Stauffer, *ANRW*, 2.25.1:78, citing Julius Wellhausen, *Einleitung in die drei ersten Evangelien* (Berlin: Reimer, 1905), 98, 107. Wellhausen argued that Jesus did not predict the parousia and that Jesus should be freed from fanaticism and false prophecy. Eschatological expectation derived from enthusiasts who saddled Jesus with their fanaticism. Among the "younger generation" fascinated by apocalyptic, Stauffer named Bultmann and Martin Werner.
21. Stauffer, *Jesus and His Story*, 160–62.
22. Stauffer, *Jesus and His Story*, 162–65.
23. Stauffer, *Jesus and His Story*, 164, citing *y. Ta'anit* 2.1.
24. Stauffer, *Jesus and His Story*, 165.
25. Stauffer, *Jesus and His Story*, 165–70.
26. Stauffer, *Jesus and His Story*, 174–95.
27. Stauffer, *Jesus and His Story*, 194.

against the Jewish pseudo-piety he opposed."[28] At the same time it should be noted that a significant body of Jewish and Christian scholars regard as anachronistic and erroneous English translations of Ἰουδαῖος (*Ioudaios*) as "Jew." A more precise translation is "Judean"—a member of the tribe of Judah living in the region of Judea; a person living in Judea on account of its proximity to Jerusalem and the temple.[29]

To some reviewers, Stauffer had fallen back into the errors of the old "Lives of Jesus."[30] His use of John to establish chronology for his composite portrait harkened back to precritical Gospel harmonies. Stauffer paid no attention to genre and composition, which further weakened his case.[31] Stauffer's claim to bar all interpretation and present only the facts and causal relationships appears naïve and positivistic in an age

---

28. Heschel, *The Aryan Jesus*, 264. Heschel noted Grundmann's favorable review of *Jesus. Gestalt und Geschichte* in *Theologische Literaturzeitung* (1958). She identified Stauffer as a "former German Christian colleague" of Grundmann.

29. BDAG, 478–79; Urban von Wahlde, "The Johannine 'Jews'—A Critical Survey," *NTS* 28 (1982): 33–60. See also the American Interfaith Institute's *Explorations: Rethinking Relationships among Christians and Jews* 9, no. 1 (1995).

The NRSV translation of John 7:1 is incoherent: "After this Jesus went about in Galilee. He did not wish to go about in Judea because the Jews [Ἰουδαῖοι] were looking for an opportunity to kill him." If the Galileans were generic Jews, the reason for going to Galilee did not make sense. However, if Ἰουδαῖοι is translated as "Judeans," the reason becomes evident. It was more prudent to return to Galilee rather than remain in Judea and the hostility of the Judeans.

John mentions Ἰουδαῖοι who were followers of Jesus (8:52; 10:19–21; 11:45; 12:11).

Josephus's use of Ἰουδαῖοι to include Galileans is an inadequate counterargument in light of his underlying apologetic purposes. Josephus sought to vindicate the actions of Rome in the Jewish War as divine judgment on the actions of a rebellious faction. He presented the history of the Jews as the history of a great people with its religious traditions.

In the corpus of Pauline letters, the apostle never called himself a Jew. He described himself as "a member of the people of Israel, of the tribe of Benjamin, a Hebrew born of Hebrews; as to the law, a Pharisee; as to zeal, a persecutor of the church; as to righteousness under the law, blameless" (Phil 3:5–6).

30. James M. Robinson, *A New Quest of the Historical Jesus and Other Essays* (Philadelphia: Fortress, 1983), 14; Paul J. Achtemeier, "The Historical Jesus: A Dilemma," *Theology and Life* 4 (1961): 107–19.

31. In my judgment, Mark was written in the form of a tragic epic history in the traditions of Aristotle's *Poetics*. Its arrangement in five acts follows dramatic necessity rather than exact chronology. See Colin Brown, "The Jesus of Mark's Gospel," in *Jesus Then and Now*, ed. Marvin Meyer and Charles Hughes, 26–53. See also above, chap. 1.

Ernst Lohmeyer had already demonstrated that John had a numerical structure based on the numbers seven and three; cf. Lohmeyer, "Über Aufbau und Gliederung des vierten Evangeliums," *ZNW* 27 (1928): 11–36; ET: "The Structure and Organization of the Fourth Gospel," trans. Colin Brown, *Journal of Higher Criticism* 5 (1998): 113–38. The structure of the Fourth Gospel in the form of a lawsuit militates against taking its chronology as strictly literal; cf. Andrew T. Lincoln, *Truth on Trial: The Lawsuit Motif in the Fourth Gospel* (Peabody, MA: Hendrickson, 2000).

when philosophers recognize that all "facts" are "theory-laden."[32] To claim without more ado that Jesus' "self-interpretation" can be lifted directly from the Gospels ignores the fact that the Gospels themselves were interpretations of Jesus, written for apologetic purposes. To say all this, is not to deny that Stauffer's work raises important issues. Among them is the question of why Jesus aroused such hostility.[33]

2. Joachim Jeremias

The most concerted attempt to recover the historical Jesus within the context of Judaism was made by Joachim Jeremias (1900–1979).[34] Jeremias had lived in Jerusalem from 1910 to 1915, while his father served as provost to the German Lutheran Church. The foundations of his later career were laid in his doctoral dissertation at Leipzig on *Jerusalem in the Time of Jesus* (1923).[35] When Paul Billerbeck lay on his deathbed in 1932, he entrusted to Jeremias care of the *Kommentar*. Aided by Kurt Rudolf, Jeremias oversaw publication of the fifth and sixth volumes, together

---

32. See, e.g., Sir Karl R. Popper, *The Logic of Scientific Discovery* (London: Hutchinson, 1959).

33. Stauffer traced hostility to Jesus to the early perception of him as an apostate preacher, a pseudo-prophet whose healings and exorcisms were demonic miracles designed to lead Israel astray. Evidence for this is furnished by the Beelzebul charge (Matt 10:25; 12:24-27; Mark 3:22; Luke 11:15-19; cf. *Jesus and His Story*, 74, 84-88, and the references to categories of heretics in rabbinic literature, 205-10).

Stauffer was criticized for uncritical use of this material; cf. Børge Salomonsen, "Einige kritische Bemerkungen zu Stauffers Darstellung der spätjüdischen Ketzergestzgebung," *Studia Theologica* 17 (1963): 91-118. Salomonsen noted that there was no single tractate dealing exclusively with heresy. Many rabbinic pronouncements should be treated as hypothetical and not as first-century practice. Despite these criticisms, it is possible to trace trajectories from pronouncements in the Torah to rabbinic pronouncements, which illuminate incidents in the Gospels.

34. Matthew Black, "Theologians of Our Time: Joachim Jeremias," *ExpTim* 74 (1962-63): 115-19; Eduard Lohse, "Joachim Jeremias in Memoriam," *ZNW* 70 (197): 139-40; L. D. Vander Broek, *DMBI*, 560-65; Michael Labahn, *EHJ*, 318-20. See also *Judentum, Christentum, Urkirche, Festschrift für Joachim Jeremias*, ed. Walther Eltester, 2nd ed., BZNTW 26 (Berlin: Töpelmann, 1964), containing Black's tribute, ix-xviii; *Der Ruf Jesu und die Antwort der Gemeinde. Exegetische Untersuchungen Joachim Jeremias zum 70. Geburtstag gewidmet von seinen Schülern*, ed. Eduard Lohse, with Christoph Burchard and Berndt Schaller (Göttingen: Vandenhoeck & Ruprecht, 1970), with bibliography from 1923 to 1970 (11-38).

35. Joachim Jeremias, *Jerusalem zur Zeit Jesu* (Göttingen: Vandenhoeck & Ruprecht, 1962; 3rd ed., 1962); ET: *Jerusalem in the Time of Jesus: An Investigation into Economic and Social Conditions during the New Testament Period*, trans. F. H. and C. H. Cave (London: SCM, 1967), with author's revisions to 1967. While Jeremias's use of rabbinic sources from different periods has been faulted as uncritical, Jeremias did not make Schlatter's mistake of ignoring contemporary scholarship.

with the index. Jeremias taught at Greifswald (1929–34) before moving to Göttingen, where he spent the rest of his professional career (1935–62).

2.1. Jeremias's Plea for Renewal of the Quest. In 1956 Jeremias delivered a lecture as part of the celebrations of the 500th anniversary of the theological faculty at Greifswald. He took the opportunity to review "The Present State of the Debate about the Problem of the Historical Jesus." Later it became the introductory chapter in a massive volume designed to review the state of the debate, *Der historische Jesus und der kerygmatische Christus* ("The Historical Jesus and the Kerygmatic Christ"). Eventually, it was published as a separate monograph, *The Problem of the Historical Jesus* (ET: 1964).[36]

Jeremias began by sketching the course of the quest from Reimarus to Kähler. Reimarus's portrayal of Jesus was "clearly absurd and amateurish." However, he raised the question that was more sharply defined by Kähler of a difference between the historical Jesus of Nazareth and the Christ proclaimed by the church. Kähler dismissed academic reconstructions of Jesus in favor of the Christ of faith, who was far more significant in the long run. The Jesus of history belonged to Judaism. Unwittingly, Kähler had prepared the way for Bultmann, who made the history of Jesus part of the history of Judaism—not of Christianity.

Jeremias recognized positive gains in the Bultmann school's focus on the kerygma, but he also recognized "very grave dangers." "We are in danger of surrendering the affirmation 'the Word became flesh' and of dissolving 'salvation history' [*Heilsgeschichte*], God's activity in the man Jesus of Nazareth and in his message; we are in danger of Docetism, where Christ becomes an idea; we are in danger of putting the proclamation of the apostle Paul in the place of the good tidings of Jesus."[37]

---

36. Joachim Jeremias, "Der gegengwärtige Stand der Debatte um das Problem des historischen Jesus," in *Der historische Jesus und der kerygmatische Christus. Beiträge zum Christusverständnis in Forschung und Verkündigung*, ed. Helmut Ristow und Karl Matthiae (Berlin: Evangelische Verlagsanstalt, 1960; 2nd ed., 1961), 12–25. The vast list of contributors included members of the Bultmann school, such as Bultmann himself, Conzelmann, Bornkamm, Fuchs, and Schweizer, as well as conservatives like Cullmann, Riesenfeld, Michel, Schnackenburg, and Stauffer. An earlier version of Jeremias's paper was published in *ExpTim* 69 (1957): 333–39.

Jeremias's contribution was published separately as *The Problem of the Historical Jesus*, trans. Norman Perrin, Facet Books, Biblical Series 13 (Philadelphia: Fortress, 1964). It was reedited as "The Search for the Historical Jesus," in *Jesus and the Message of the New Testament*, ed. K. C. Hanson (Minneapolis: Fortress, 2002), 1–17. This volume also contained Jeremias's studies of "The Sermon on the Mount," "The Lord's Prayer," and "The Central Message of the New Testament."

37. Jeremias, *The Problem of the Historical Jesus*, 11.

The European Scene

Jeremias proposed a different course: "We *must* continually return to the historical Jesus and his message. The sources demand it; the kerygma, which refers us back from itself, also demands it. To put it in theological terms, the Incarnation implies that the story of Jesus is not only a possible subject for historical research, study, and criticism, but demands all of these."[38] We need to avoid the risk of "modernizing Jesus and fashioning him in our own likeness."[39]

Jeremias urged five considerations in the case against Bultmann's modernizing of Jesus:[40]

1. The positive gains of literary criticism must be preserved, thus enabling us to distinguish between tradition and redaction and to trace tradition back to its preliterary stage.
2. The "essential significance" of form criticism is that it has enabled us "to remove a Hellenistic layer which had overlaid an earlier Palestinian tradition."
3. Study of rabbinic literature, late Jewish apocalyptic, and life in ancient Palestine "has helped us to realize afresh the sharpness of Jesus' opposition to the religiosity of his time."
4. Study of Aramaic enables us to identify better the original form behind the Greek of the New Testament. "In this connection it is of special importance to note that this kind of study reveals peculiarities in the utterances of Jesus which are without contemporary parallels. As a form of address to God the word *abba* is without parallel in the whole of Late Jewish devotional literature. Similarly there is no contemporary analogy to Jesus' use of 'Amen' as an introduction to his own utterances. It may be maintained that these two characteristic features of the *ipsissima vox* [authentic voice] of Jesus contain in a nutshell his message and his consciousness of his authority."[41]

---

38. Jeremias, *The Problem of the Historical Jesus*, 11; cf. 4–15.
39. Jeremias, *The Problem of the Historical Jesus*, 20.
40. Jeremias, *The Problem of the Historical Jesus*, 16–20.
41. Jeremias, *The Problem of the Historical Jesus*, 18. Jeremias expressed his conviction that Gustaf Dalman had established that Jesus spoke Galilean Aramaic; cf. Dalman, *Die Worte Jesu mit Berücksichtigung des nachkanonischen jüdischen Schrifttums und der aramäischen Sprache erörtert* (Leipzig: J. C. Hinrichs, 1898, 2nd ed. 1930); ET: *The Words of Jesus Considered in the Light of Post-Biblical Jewish Writings and the Aramaic Language*, trans. D. M. Kay (Edinburgh: T&T Clark, 1902).

5. Especially significant "against a psychological modernizing of Jesus is the rediscovery of the eschatological character of his message.... The whole message of Jesus flowed from an awareness that God was about to break into history, an awareness of the approaching crisis, the coming judgment.... It was against this background that he proclaimed the present in-breaking in his own ministry of the kingdom of God."[42]

These five considerations amounted to a distillation of the convictions that ran through Jeremias's explorations of different facets of the question of the historical Jesus. In particular, the fifth consideration provided the keystone, which held together the different aspects of Jeremias's work. It was the *control belief* in the interpretation of the sundry parts and brought them into a unity.

2.2. The Eucharistic Words of Jesus. Jeremias's first major investigation was devoted to the words of Jesus at the Last Supper (1935) and went through several stages of amplification. In English it bore the title *The Eucharistic Words of Jesus*.[43]

Drawing on his knowledge of Philo and rabbinic traditions, Jeremias cogently argued that the Last Supper was a Passover meal. The meal had a fourfold structure: (1) a preliminary course with blessing and the first cup; (2) the Passover liturgy with the *haggadah* narrated by the head of the house, the first part of the *hallel*, and the second cup; (3) the main meal with grace, the Passover lamb, unleavened bread, bitter herbs (Exod 12:8), fruit purée, and the cup of blessing; and (4) the conclusion, consisting of the second part of the *hallel* and praise over the fourth cup, the *hallel* cup.

Jesus spoke the word of interpretation over the bread in connection with the grace before the beginning of the main meal. Only at this point was a grace said over bread, since no bread was eaten with the

---

42. Jeremias, *The Problem of the Historical Jesus*, 18–19. Earlier Jeremias noted that, despite Schweitzer's ruthless exposure of "psychological reconstruction," Schweitzer himself was "ensnared" by it. His interpretation of Matt 10:23 posited a state of mind, which led to the decision to go to Jerusalem to die in order to force the coming of the kingdom of God (6).

43. The first English edition (1955) was based on the second German edition of *Die Abendmahlsworte Jesu* (Göttingen: Vandenhoeck & Ruprecht, 1949). It was replaced by Norman Perrin's translation (London: SCM, 1966) of the greatly enlarged third edition (1960). References here are to this edition.

preliminary course at a passover meal. So far as the word of interpretation over the wine is concerned, this must have been spoken in connection with the grace (Mark 14.23: "having given thanks") *after* the main meal, since according to Mark it was *after* the breaking of bread (14.22) but *before* the passover *hallel* (14.26). This setting of these words is supported by two things found in Paul: the very archaic "after supper" (I Cor. 11.25) and "the cup of blessing" (I Cor. 10.16). *Jesus, therefore, used the prayers before and after the main course of the passover meal to add his words of interpretation concerning the bread and the wine.* Both prayers of Jesus were preceded by the passover meditation; this is an important observation because it justifies the conclusion that the disciples were thereby prepared for the words of interpretation, in themselves puzzling. Jesus' vow of abstinence came . . . either at the very beginning of the meal (Luke 22.15f.) or at the taking of the first cup (Luke 22.17f.).[44]

This was more than a matter of antiquarian or chronological interest. "It is much more a question of the setting of the Last Supper within the context of the *Heilsgeschichte* [salvation history]."[45]

Jeremias proceeded with a minute comparison of the traditions, showing the influence of worship in the transmission of the narratives.[46] The wording of Mark, followed by Matthew, was more original than that of Paul and Luke.[47] Detecting Semitisms, Jeremias concluded that we may hear the *ipsissima vox* of Jesus with "no less than three peculiarities which present the most distinctive manner of Jesus' speaking."[48] (1) The phrase ἀμὴν λέγω ὑμῖν, "Truly I tell you" (Mark 14:25), an introductory

---

44. Jeremias, *The Eucharistic Words of Jesus*, 87–88; cf. 160–61. For a summary of Jeremias's argument, see I. Howard Marshall, *Last Supper and Lord's Supper* (Grand Rapids: Eerdmans, 1980), 58–62. Marshall gave an extensive review of later scholarship in "The Last Supper," in *Key Events in the Life of the Historical Jesus: A Collaborative Exploration of Context and Coherence*, ed. Darrell Bock and Robert L. Webb, WUNT 247 (Tübingen, Mohr Siebeck, 2009), 481–588.

45. Jeremias, *The Eucharistic Words of Jesus*, 88.

46. Jeremias, *The Eucharistic Words of Jesus*, 106–37.

47. Jeremias, *The Eucharistic Words of Jesus*, 164–73.

48. Jeremias, *The Eucharistic Words of Jesus*, 201; cf. Jeremias, "Kennzeichen der ipssisma vox Jesu," in *Synoptische Studien Alfred Wikenhauser zum siebzigsten Geburtstag am 22. Februar dargebracht* (Munich: Zink, 1954), 86–93; ET: "Characteristics of the *Ipsissima Vox Jesu*," trans. John Bowden, in Jeremias, *The Prayers of Jesus*, SBT Second Series 6 (London: SCM, 1967), 108–15. Jeremias believed that the gospel tradition does not permit us to speak of the *ipsissima verba* (the actual words) of Jesus in view of the way the traditions were adapted to differing situations. But we may speak of the *ipsissima vox* of Jesus (the actual voice, Jesus' original way of speaking), which

formula emphasizing Jesus' pronouncements, was "a completely new idiom of Jesus, which is without parallel in the entire Jewish literature and in the New Testament outside the Gospels."[49] (2) The use of the theological passive as a reverent circumlocution for the activity of God was characteristic of Jesus (e.g., Matt. 5:4, 6, 7; Mark 2:5; Luke 22:16). It is seldom found in rabbinic literature. (3) "The predilection for similitudes, comparisons, and parabolic expressions which is presupposed in the words of interpretation is likewise a peculiarity of Jesus."[50]

The Passover narrative of Exodus 12 (further illuminated by *Mek. Exod.* 12.13 par. 12.23; *Exod. Rab.* 15.12 on 12:10; *Exod. Rab.* 15.12 on 12:2) provided the salvation history context for the Last Supper.

> As a reward for the Israelites' obedience to the commandment to spread blood on their doors, God manifested himself and spared them, "passing over" their houses. For the sake of the passover blood God revoked the death sentence against Israel; he said: "I will see the blood of the passover and make atonement for you." In the same way the people of God of the End time will be redeemed by the merits of the passover blood. Jesus describes his death as this eschatological passover sacrifice: *his vicarious* (ὑπέρ [for]) *death brings into operation the final deliverance*, the new covenant of God. Διαθήκη (covenant) is a correlate of βασιλεία τῶν οὐρανῶν ("kingdom of heaven"). The content of this gracious institution which is mediated by Jesus' death is perfect communion with God (Jer. 31.33–34a) in his reign, based upon remission of sins (31.34b).[51]

Jeremias broke new ground with his interpretation of the injunction τοῦτο ποιεῖτε εἰς τὴν ἐμὴν ἀνάμνησιν (lit. "Do this in remembrance of me," Luke 22:19; 1 Cor 11:24, cf. 25). He suggested that it should not be taken in a Hellenistic sense of a meal commemorating the dead, but in the Palestinian tradition of doing something to ensure God's

---

is preserved in the traditions. The ἀμὴν λέγω formula is found seventy-five times in the Gospels including the double formula ἀμὴν ἀμὴν λέγω in John.

49. Jeremias, *The Eucharistic Words of Jesus*, 201–2.
50. Jeremias, *The Eucharistic Words of Jesus*, 202. Jeremias noted that we possess only two comparisons (*Lev. Rab.* 34.3 on 25:35) from Hillel (c. 20 BCE), though he was the one pre-Christian scholar whose parables were transmitted in rabbinic literature (Strack-Billerbeck 1:654).
51. Jeremias, *The Eucharistic Words of Jesus*, 226.

merciful remembrance.⁵² In Palestinian usage "(1) εἰς ἀνάμνησιν is said *for the most part in reference to God* and (2) it then designates, always and without exception, *a presentation before God intended to induce God to act.*"⁵³ Jeremias linked remembrance with the Maranatha cry (1 Cor. 16:22) and the eucharist as proclamation of the Lord's death until he comes (1 Cor. 11:23–25). *"As often as the death of the Lord is proclaimed at the Lord's supper, and the maranatha rises upwards, God is reminded of the unfulfilled climax of the work of salvation* 'until (the goal is reached, that) he comes.'"⁵⁴

2.3. The Death of Jesus. Jeremias further explored the significance of Jesus' death in the article he coauthored with Walter Zimmerli on Παῖς Θεοῦ for *Theologisches Wörterbuch zum Neuen Testament*, which was subsequently published separately under the title *The Servant of God*.⁵⁵ Some passages, which identified Jesus with the servant of Deutero-Isaiah, may have been the work of the church. But the fact that Jesus reckoned with the possibility of violent death "has the strongest probability behind it."⁵⁶ If so, Jesus could well have pondered its meaning. "The assertion in the sources that Jesus found in Isa. 53 the clue to the necessity and meaning of his passion can also claim strong historical probability."⁵⁷

The Maccabean martyrs furnished precedent for death having atoning significance (4 Macc 6:29; 2 Macc 7:37–38).⁵⁸ Some of Jesus' predictions are couched in such general terms that they could hardly have been shaped after the event. Absence of reference to Easter argued against invention by the church (Mark 9:12; 14:8; Luke 9:44; 12:50; 13:32–33; 17:25; 23:37). The "oldest and most reliable stratum of tradition" contains clear allusion to Isaiah 53 in the eucharistic words of Jesus referring to Jesus' blood "poured out for many" (Mark 14:24).

The number of texts in which Jesus related Isaiah 53 to himself was

---

52. Jeremias, *The Eucharistic Words of Jesus*, 244–49. See, e.g., Lev 24:7; Pss 37(38):1; 69(70):1–2; Eccl 50:16; Mark 14:9 par. Matt 26:13; Acts 10:4.

53. Jeremias, *The Eucharistic Words of Jesus*, 249.

54. Jeremias, *The Eucharistic Words of Jesus*, 253.

55. Joachim Jeremias, *The Servant of God*, trans. Harold Knight et al., SBT 20 (London: SCM; Naperville, IL: Allenson, 1957).

56. Jeremias, *The Servant of God*, 100, where Jeremias noted that charges of blasphemy (Mark 2:7 par.; John 10:33–36; cf. 5:18) and Sabbath-breaking (Mark 2:23–3:7) were both capital offences. As a prophet, Jesus could expect martyrdom (Luke 13:33; Matt. 23:34–36 par.).

57. Jeremias, *The Servant of God*, 102.

58. The point is also supported by the noncanonical psalms of the Dead Sea Scrolls. See Bruce Chilton, ed., *A Comparative Handbook to the Gospel of Mark: Comparisons with the Pseudepigrapha, the Qumran Scrolls, and Rabbinic Literature*, New Testament Gospels in their Judaic Contexts 1 (Leiden: Brill, 2010), 320–21.

not great. The fact that they are altogether absent from the *logia* peculiar to Matthew and Luke may be attributed to Jesus' decision not to make it part of his public preaching. "Only to his disciples did he unveil the mystery that he viewed the fulfilment of Isa. 53 as his God-appointed task, and to them alone did he interpret his death as a vicarious dying for the countless multitude . . . of those who lay under the judgement of God (Mark 10.45; 14.24). Because he goes to his death innocently, voluntarily, patiently in accordance with the will of God (Isa. 53) his dying has boundless atoning virtue. It is life flowing from God, and life in God which he outpours."[59]

2.4. The Gentile Mission. In *Jesus' Promise to the Nations* (1956) Jeremias addressed the question of the gentile mission.[60] Three negative conclusions argue against the historicity of such a mission: Jesus pronounced stern judgment on the Jewish mission; he forbade his disciples to preach to non-Jews; he limited his own activity to Israel.[61] Three positive conclusions seem to contradict the negative conclusions: Jesus removed the idea of vengeance from eschatological expectation; he promised gentiles a share in salvation; the redemptive activity and lordship of Jesus includes the gentiles.[62]

Resolution of this tension is indicated by the logion "I tell you, many will come from east and west and will eat with Abraham and Isaac and Jacob in the kingdom of heaven, while the heirs of the kingdom will be thrown into the outer darkness, where there will be weeping and gnashing of teeth" (Matt 8:11–12; cf. Luke 13:28–29, which includes "and all the prophets of the kingdom of God," but reverses the word order).[63]

---

59. Jeremias, *The Servant of God*, 104. Jeremias saw a connection between Isa 53:12 ("he poured out himself to death") and Phil 2:7 ("he emptied himself [ἑαυτὸν ἐκένωσεν] taking the form of a slave, being born in human likeness").

Phil 2:7 is widely taken as a proof text for the preexistent sonship of Christ. However, Jeremias regarded the passage a literal equivalent of the Hebrew underlying Isa 53:12. The passage referred to the death of Jesus rather than his birth (*TDNT*, 5:708–11).

Jeremias's argument would have been stronger if the LXX had used a form of κενόω (*kenoō*, "empty"). Instead, it gave a paraphrase: παρεδόθη εἰς θάνατον ἡ ψυχὴ αὐτοῦ ("his soul/life was handed over to death"). For further discussion of Phil 2:6–11, see below, chap. 9, §1.2.2; and chap. 21, §6.2 regarding the significance of κενόω.

60. Joachim Jeremias, *Jesu Verheissung für die Völker* (Franz Delitzsch-Vorlesung, 1953; Stuttgart: Kohlhammer, 1956); ET: *Jesus' Promise to the Nations*, trans. S. H. Hooke (London: SCM, 1958; rev., 1967).

61. Jeremias, *Jesus' Promise to the Nations*, 11–39.

62. Jeremias, *Jesus' Promise to the Nations*, 40–54.

63. Jeremias, *Jesus' Promise to the Nations*, 55–56. Jeremias noted the Semitic features of the

The European Scene

The picture envisages "the *eschatological pilgrimage of the Gentiles to the Mountain of God*," which synthesizes five strands of prophetic hope: the epiphany of God, the call of God, the journey of the gentiles, worship at the world-sanctuary, and the messianic banquet on the world mountain.[64] In prophecy, "the Gentiles will not be evangelized where they dwell, but will be summoned to the holy Mount by the divine epiphany. Zion is always the appointed centre for their gathering," where they will be included in God's redeemed community.[65] The inclusion of the nations belongs to the *eschaton*, which had not yet arrived in the days of Jesus' public ministry (Matt 10:5–6).[66]

2.5. The Parables of Jesus. Modern study of the parables began with the Marburg professor Adolf Jülicher (1857–1938), whose work on the parable discourses of Jesus reversed the ancient tradition of allegorical interpretation. Jülicher declared, "Despite the authority of so many centuries, despite the greater authority of the evangelists, I cannot regard the parables of Jesus as allegories."[67] "If the Master is not identical with the evangelists, and gives us more than the evangelists, then we must make every endeavor to understand him better than the evangelists."[68] There was no need to set aside the general authenticity of the parables. Jülicher felt compelled to ascribe to them "a relative authenticity." "Almost without exception they have an authentic kernel going back to Jesus himself." This kernel was to be found by separating it from allegory and taking

---

logion: (1) mention of the patriarchs and prophets, the messianic banquet, and the idea that the damned will see the blessed, (2) antithetic parallelism, and (3) Semitisms.

64. Jeremias, *Jesus' Promise to the Nations*, 57–60. 1. The epiphany of God (Isa 2:2; 11:10; 40:5; 51:4–5; 52:10; 60:3; 62:10; Zech 2:13). 2. The call of God (Ps 96:3, 10; Isa 42:6; 45: 20, 22; 49:6; 55:5; 66:19–20). 3. The journey of the gentiles (Ps 68:30–32; Isa 2:3; 18:7; 19:23; 60:5–14 [often quoted in rabbinic literature]; Hag 2:7; Zech 8:21, 23; 14:16). 4. Worship at the world sanctuary as the goal of the journey (Pss 22:28; 72:9–11; 86:10; 96:8; Isa 19:24–25; 45:14, 23–24; 56:7 [cited in Mark 11:17]; Jer 16:19; Zeph 3:9). 5. The messianic banquet on the world mountain (Isa 25:6–8; Dan 7:14; Zech 2:11; 9:10). For extracanonical references, see *Jesus' Promise to the Nations*, 61.

65. Jeremias, *Jesus' Promise to the Nations*, 60.

66. Jeremias, *Jesus' Promise to the Nations*, 62–73.

67. Adolf Jülicher, *Die Gleichnisreden Jesu* (Tübingen: Mohr Siebeck, 1888; 2nd ed., 1899), 1:61 (author's translation). The first volume discussed parables in general, culminating in a history of interpretation (203–322). The second volume gave interpretation of the synoptic parables. See further Hans-Josef Klauck, "Adolf-Jülicher—Leben, Werk und Wirkung," in *Historische Kritik in der Theologie. Beiträge zu ihrer Geschichte*, ed. Georg Schwaiger, Studien zur Theologie und Geistesgeschichte des neunzehnten Jahrhunderts 32 (Göttingen: Vandenhoeck & Ruprecht, 1980), 99–150.

68. Jülicher, *Die Gleichnisreden Jesu*, 1:11.

from the parable "only *one* thought."⁶⁹ "The parable is always there to illuminate only that one point, one law, one idea, one experience, that is valid in the spiritual life just as in the earthly."⁷⁰

In writing *The Parables of Jesus*⁷¹ Jeremias followed in the footsteps of Jülicher. Like Jülicher, he found allegory in the Gospels' text, and his prime concern was to hear the voice of Jesus through that text. "What did Jesus intend to say at this or that particular moment? What must have been the effect of his word upon his hearers? These are questions we must ask, in order, so far as possible, to recover the original meaning of the parables of Jesus, to hear again his authentic voice."⁷²

The first part of the book was devoted to methodological issues: translation from Aramaic to Greek, representational changes, embellishment, influence of Old Testament and folklore, change of audience, the church's hortatory use, influence of the church's situation—delay of the parousia, mission, church order—allegorization, collection and conflation, redactional setting.⁷³ These factors were formulated as "ten laws of transformation" to aid "the recovery of the original meaning of the parables of Jesus."⁷⁴ The outcome was the identification of ten themes that characterized the message of the parables: now is the day of salvation, God's mercy for sinners, the great assurance, the imminence of catastrophe, it may be too late, the challenge of the hour, realized discipleship, the Via Dolorosa and the exaltation of the Son of Man, the consummation, and parabolic actions.⁷⁵ The point of the parables was to compel Jesus' hearers to come to a decision about his person and mission. "They are all full of 'the secret of the Kingdom of God' (Mark 4.11), that is to say, the recognition of 'an eschatology that is in process of realization [*sich realisierende Eschatologie*].'"⁷⁶

---

69. Jülicher, *Die Gleichnisreden Jesu*, 1:74.
70. Jülicher, *Die Gleichnisreden Jesu*, 1:317.
71. Joachim Jeremias, *Die Gleichnisse Jesu*, ATANT 11 (Zürich: Zwingli, 1947; 6th ed., Göttingen: Vandenhoeck & Ruprecht, 1962); ET: *The Parables of Jesus*, trans. S. H. Hooke (London: SCM, 1963).
72. Jeremias, *The Parables of Jesus*, 22.
73. Jeremias, *The Parables of Jesus*, 23–114.
74. Jeremias, *The Parables of Jesus*, 114.
75. Jeremias, *The Parables of Jesus*, 115–229.
76. Jeremias, *The Parables of Jesus*, 230. In a footnote Jeremias added that the term was communicated to him in a letter by Ernst Haenchen, and to his joy C. H. Dodd had agreed with it in preference to Dodd's earlier term *realized eschatology*. Dodd liked Jeremias's term, but could find no way of turning *sich realisierende Eschatologie* (lit. "self-realizing eschatology") into felicitous

The European Scene

2.6. The Prayers of Jesus. Jeremias made notable contributions in two other areas: the term *Abba*, and the Lord's Prayer.[77] The Greek word ἀββα (*abba*) is a transliteration of the Aramaic אַבָּא (*abba*). *Abba*, followed by the Greek translation, occurs in Jesus' prayer in Gethsemane: "Abba, Father [ἀββα ὁ πατήρ], for you all things are possible; remove this cup from me; yet, not what I want, but what you want" (Mark 14:36). Jeremias contended that when *Father* is used for *God* in the Gospels, the underlying Aramaic word would have been אַבָּא.[78] *Abba* is also found in Paul as a traditional form of Christian prayer: "For you did not receive a spirit of slavery to fall back into fear, but you have received a spirit of adoption. When we cry, 'Abba! Father! [ἀββα ὁ πατήρ].' . . ." (Rom 8:15); "And because you are children, God has sent the Spirit of his Son into our hearts, crying, 'Abba! Father! [ἀββα ὁ πατήρ]'" (Gal 4:6). Jeremias argued that this was a unique form of prayer, originating with Jesus. There was no evidence of *my Father* used as a personal address in early Palestinian literature. "We can say quite definitely that there is *no analogy at all* in the whole literature of Jewish prayer for God being addressed as Abba. . . . We have here a quite unmistakable characteristic of the *ipsissima vox Jesu*."[79]

Jeremias suggested that Abba derived from children's speech. The Talmud says, "When a child experiences the taste of wheat [i.e., when it is weaned], it learns to say *abba* and *imma* [*Dada* and *Mama*]."[80] By the time of Jesus the use of *abba* was no longer limited to children, but it was not used as an address to God, for it was "inconceivable to address

---

English; cf. C. H. Dodd, *The Interpretation of the Fourth Gospel* (Cambridge: Cambridge University Press, 1953), 447.

77. Joachim Jeremias, *Abba. Studien zur neutestamentlichen Theologie und Zeitgeschichte* (Göttingen: Vandenhoeck & Ruprecht, 1966), 1–80; ET: *The Prayers of Jesus*, trans. John Bowden (London: SCM, 1967), 11–65. See also Jeremias, *Neutestamentliche Theologie. Erster Teil, Die Verkündigung Jesu* (Gütersloh: Mohn, 1971; 2nd ed., 1973); ET: *New Testament Theology*, vol. 1, *The Proclamation of Jesus*, trans. John Bowden, SBT 6 (London: SCM, 1971), 36–37, 61–68; *Jesus and the Message of the New Testament*, 39–62, 68–75.

78. Jeremias, *The Prayers of Jesus*, 29–57.

79. Jeremias, *The Prayers of Jesus*, 57. Jeremias rejected the suggestion that *Abba* was an emphatic state in Aramaic meaning "the Father." The final -*a* was not an appended article, as in the emphatic state. *Abba* was in origin an exclamation (58).

80. Jeremias, *The Prayers of Jesus*, 59, citing *b. Ber.* 40a par. *b. Sanh.* 70b; cf. *Tg. Isa.* 8:4, "Before the child learns to call *abba* and *imma*." The story was told of Hanin ha-Nehba that when rain was needed, children tugged his coat and said "Daddy, daddy [*abba, abba*] give us rain." Hanin ha-Nehba prayed to God: "Master of the world, grant [the rain] for the sake of these who are not yet able to distinguish between an *abba* who has the power to give rain and an *abba* who has not." Cf. Jeremias, *The Prayers of Jesus*, 61, citing *b. Ta'an* 23b.

God with this familiar word."[81] Jeremias stopped short of saying that Jesus' use of *Abba* was a sign of casual familiarity with God. Rather, "it shows the complete surrender of the Son in obedience to the Father (Mark 14.36; Matt 11.25f.)."[82] Moreover, the saying connecting the Son's unique knowledge of the Father with revelation (Matt 11:25–27 par. Luke 10:21–22) invests the term with authority.[83]

As an observant Jew, Jesus would have prayed three times a day: at sunrise a combination of the Tefillah or Eighteen Benedictions with the Shema, in the afternoon at the time of the temple sacrifice the Tefillah, and the Shema and the Tefillah before going to sleep.[84] Two prayers of Jesus are recorded in the Synoptic Gospels, and three in John.[85] In addition, Jesus taught the disciples the prayer known as the Lord's Prayer. The different forms in Matthew 6:9–13 and Luke 11:2–4 pose problems. Matthew's version is set in the context of the Sermon on the Mount. Luke's is given in response to a request by the disciples to be taught how to pray. Matthew begins with an address that a pious Jew might make, setting distance between himself and God: "Our Father in heaven." Luke begins with "Father [Πάτερρ]," which suggests that it is a more direct rendering of ἀββα.

Matthew has a balanced structure of three "Thou-petitions" concerning God (the hallowing of his name, the coming of his kingdom, and the doing of his will) followed by three "We-petitions" concerning human needs (for bread, forgiveness, and not being led into temptation/ deliverance from evil). Luke omits the final petition from both lists. Matthew's three "Thou-petitions" recall the ancient Aramaic prayer known as the Kaddish.

> Exalted and hallowed be his great name
>   In the world which he created according to his will.
> May he let his kingdom rule
>   In your lifetime and in your days and in the lifetime

---

81. Jeremias, *The Prayers of Jesus*, 62.
82. Jeremias, *The Prayers of Jesus*, 62. This reversed an earlier position which held that *abba* implied childlike intimacy.
83. Jeremias, *The Prayers of Jesus*, 62–63.
84. Jeremias, *The Prayers of Jesus*, 72, 75; cf. Mark 1:35; 6:46; Luke 6:12.
85. The cry of jubilation (Matt 11:25 par.), the prayer in Gethsemane (Mark 14:36 par.), the prayer in the Lazarus story (John 11:41–41), the prayer in the temple forecourt (John 12:27–28), and the high priestly prayer (John 17) (*The Prayers of Jesus*, 72–73).

of the whole house of Israel, speedily and soon.
And to this, say: Amen.[86]

Luke omits Matthew's third petition ("Your will be done, on earth as it is in heaven") and his sixth ("but rescue us from the evil one"). Matthew asks to be forgiven our debts (ὀφειλήματα), which appears to translate an Aramaic word for both debt and sin. Luke uses the common Greek word for sins (ἁμαρτίας).[87]

Jeremias resolved the differences by suggesting that Luke's form had been assimilated to Greek usage, concluding that "the Lucan version has preserved the oldest form with regard to *length*, but the Matthaean text is more original with regard to *wording*."[88] The conclusion is not as paradoxical as it sounds, if we see Matthew's additional words as liturgical parallelism which say in other words what is already said in the petitions "your kingdom come" and "do not bring us to the time of trial." The differences between the two forms of the Lord's Prayer are to be explained by the fact that they are primers on prayer directed at different groups. Matthew transmits "instruction on prayer directed at Jewish-Christians, Luke at Gentile-Christians."[89]

Comparison with the Kaddish and its focus on the coming of the kingdom indicated the eschatological character of the Lord's Prayer.[90] The new material added by the Lord's Prayer was seen by Jeremias to reinforce this eschatological thrust. The prayer for "our daily bread [τὸν ἄρτον ἡμῶν τὸν ἐπιούσιον]" is really "our bread for tomorrow." It means "Our bread for tomorrow give us today."[91] It includes "daily bread" but also asks to be fed now with the bread of the kingdom. The petition for forgiveness refers to the messianic age, for the "age of the Messiah is the age of forgiveness."[92] The familiar "Lead us not into temptation" is amplified by "And do not bring us to the time of trial [εἰς πειρασμόν]." The word πειρασμός does not mean everyday testing but "the final persecution

---

86. Jeremias, *The Prayers of Jesus*, 98. For Aramaic text, see Gustaf Dalman, *Die Worte Jesu* (Leipzig: Hinrichs, 1898), 305.
87. On this issue and the forms of the Lord's Prayer, see *A Comparative Handbook to the Gospel of Mark*, ed. Bruce Chilton, Darrell Bock, et al., 52–59.
88. Jeremias, *The Prayers of Jesus*, 93.
89. Jeremias, *The Prayers of Jesus*, 88–89.
90. Jeremias, *The Prayers of Jesus*, 98.
91. Jeremias, *The Prayers of Jesus*, 100.
92. Jeremias, *The Prayers of Jesus*, 103.

and testing of God's saints by pseudo-prophets and false saviours."[93] It means: "O Lord, preserve us from falling away, from apostasy." Likewise, the Matthaean petition to be delivered from evil seeks "final deliverance from the power of evil, which seeks to plunge men into eternal ruin."[94] In sum, the Lord's Prayer (like the parables) is about "eschatology becoming actualized [*sich realiseierende Eschatologie*]."[95]

2.7. Jeremias in Retrospect. In retirement Jeremias planned to write a *New Testament Theology*, but he lived to publish only the first volume. Whereas Bultmann's *New Testament Theology* treated Jesus as the presupposition of the *kerygma*, Jeremias made Jesus' proclamation the subject matter of New Testament theology—*New Testament Theology*, volume 1, *The Proclamation of Jesus* (1971).[96] For Bultmann, the apostolic kerygma of the cross and resurrection was the way to encountering the *eschaton* in the here and now. For Jeremias the Gospels' record of the proclamation of Jesus was the way of hearing the *ipsissima vox* of Jesus and through it the message of salvation. Jeremias's *New Testament Theology* was a succinct recapitulation of the themes of Jeremias's earlier books.

In the years that followed, Jeremias's *oeuvre* has been subjected to scrutiny. The most vitriolic critique came from E. P. Sanders,[97] who questioned Jeremias's knowledge of Jewish sources and berated Ben F. Meyer for defending him.[98] Of the secondary literature read by scholars and students, the work by Jeremias "does the most harm."[99] Jeremias knew little beyond what he found in Billerbeck, whose work was characterized

---

93. Jeremias, *The Prayers of Jesus*, 105–6. *A Comparative Handbook to the Gospel of Mark*, ed. Chilton et al., 58, is less dogmatic than Jeremias. "Without an apocalyptic context *nisyona'* [*peirasmos*, temptation] cannot be assumed to demand an apocalyptic meaning. The Matthean gloss, 'Deliver us from the evil one,' provides an unequivocally apocalyptic sense, but at the same time demonstrates the necessity of gloss to make that meaning unmistakable. As in the case of the clause concerning God's will, the Matthean version explains what would be a difficult clause to understand."

94. Jeremias, *The Prayers of Jesus*, 106.

95. Jeremias, *The Prayers of Jesus*, 107.

96. Joachim Jeremias, *New Testament Theology*, vol. 1, *The Proclamation of Jesus*, trans. John Bowden (London: SCM, 1971).

97. E. P. Sanders, "Jesus and the Kingdom: The Restoration of Israel and the New People of God," in *Jesus, the Gospels and the Church: Essays in Honor of William R. Farmer*, ed. E. P. Sanders (Macon, GA: Mercer University Press, 1987), 225–39; Sanders, "Defending the Indefensible," *JBL* 110 (1991): 463–77.

98. Ben F. Meyer, "A Caricature of Joachim Jeremias and his Scholarly Work," *JBL* 110 (1991): 451–62.

99. E. P. Sanders, "Jesus and the Kingdom," *JBL* 110 (1991): 463.

The European Scene

by "miscategorization and incorrect summaries."[100] But there was an even deeper problem. Jeremias never "distanced 'what Christians now should think' from the sayings of Jesus."[101] For his part, Meyer cited authorities who personally knew Jeremias's familiarity with Jewish sources, his pro-Jewish stance against the Nazis, and the honors awarded Jeremias, including honorary degrees and the Burkitt medal conferred on him by the British Academy.

I personally think contemporary theology owes a great debt to Jeremias, not least to his call for a renewal of the quest of the historical Jesus and the arguments that he put forward for its renewal. At the same time, scholarship has not stood still. In what follows I wish to draw attention to discussion of some of the fundamental issues that he raised, following broadly the preceding account of his teaching.

The Last Supper. Jeremias's discussion of the Last Supper was based on the synoptic accounts and Paul, since the account in John focuses on Jesus washing the disciples' feet rather than the meal that followed (John 13:1–20). John records a discourse about bread from heaven and a dispute about eating Jesus' flesh and drinking his blood (John 6:25–59). However, it is separate from the Last Supper. Another difference between John and the synoptic accounts is their chronologies. John places the Last Supper, the trials, and crucifixion before the official Passover (John 19:14, 31). The Synoptic Gospels depict the meal but not the footwashing.

The most convincing attempt to reconcile the dating by proposing that John and the Synoptics were using different calendars is Colin Humphries, *The Mystery of the Last Supper* (2011).[102] Another major issue is the use of the term *covenant* (διαθήκη, *diathēkē*) in Matthew, Mark, Luke, and Paul, but not John. Moreover, in the synoptic narratives the only occurrence of the word on the lips of Jesus was during this final Passover meal. It was not part of Jesus' earlier teaching. Elsewhere, the term is found in the Pauline corpus and most notably in the epistle to the Hebrews—but not in the public or private teaching of Jesus.

---

100. Sanders, "Jesus and the Kingdom," 471. "One should *never* believe the generalizations of the man who wrote those pages in *Jesus' Promise to the Nations*. The original basis of Jeremias's false generalization, however, was Billerbeck's summary, which he unhesitatingly accepted here and elsewhere."

101. Sanders, "Jesus and the Kingdom," 476.

102. Colin Humphries, *The Mystery of the Last Supper: Reconstructing the Final Days of Jesus* (Cambridge: Cambridge University Press, 2011).

The relevant passages in the synoptic and Pauline narratives of the Last Supper are:

> This is my blood of the covenant [τὸ αἷμά μου τῆς διαθήκης], which is poured out for many for the forgiveness of sins. (Matt 26:28)

> This is my blood of the covenant [τὸ αἷμά μου τῆς διαθήκης] which is poured out for many. (Mark 14:24)

> And he did the same with the cup after supper, saying, "This cup that is poured out for you is the new covenant in my blood [τοῦτο τὸ ποτήριον ἡ καινὴ διαθήκη ἐν τῷ αἵματί μου τὸ ὑπὲρ ὑμῶν ἐκχυννόμενον]." (Luke 22:20)

> In the same way he took the cup also, after supper, saying, "This cup is the new covenant in my blood [τοῦτο τὸ ποτήριον ἡ καινὴ διαθήκη ἐστὶν ἐν τῷ ἐμῷ αἵματι]. Do this, as often as you drink it, in remembrance of me." (1 Cor 11:25)

Jeremias gave a *salvation-history theological* interpretation. He compared Jesus' words with rabbinic interpretation of the Passover narratives of Exodus 12.

> As a reward for the Israelites' to the commandment to spread blood on their doors, God manifested himself and spared them, "passing over" their houses. For the sake of the passover blood God revoked the death sentence against Israel; he said, "I will see the blood of the Passover and make atonement for you." In the same way the people of God in the End time will be redeemed by the merits of the passover blood. Jesus describes his death as this eschatological Passover sacrifice: *his vicarious (ὑπέρ) death brings into operation the final deliverance*, the new covenant of God. Διαθήκη ("covenant") is a correlate of *βασιλεία τῶν οὐρανῶν* ("kingdom of heaven").[103]

On the historical level, the synoptic narratives described Jesus' activity as a succession of *ad hoc* encounters involving response or rejection.

---

103. Jeremias, *The Eucharistic Words of Jesus*, 226.

To those who responded the situations led to disclosure. The Last Supper represented a climax. It took the form that it did because of the response of the temple authorities to Jesus' action in the temple. It marked the end of one era and the beginning of another.

Parables. In *Jesus and the Language of the Kingdom* (1976) Norman Perrin discussed Jeremias in more measured tones than those of Sanders. However, Perrin, who obtained his doctorate under Jeremias[104] and translated several of his works, could not resist saying that Jeremias's account of the message of the parables "looks very much like a summary of rather conservative Lutheran piety."[105] Jeremias's contribution was on the level of textual criticism and historical criticism.

Perrin now denied that parables had a message. "They tease the mind into ever new perceptions of reality; they startle the imagination; they function like symbols in that they 'give rise to thought.'"[106] Perrin advocated a literary approach to the parables, which distinguished two types of symbols. The "steno-symbol" has a one-to-one relationship to that which it represents, like the mathematical sign π. The "tensive symbol" has a set of meanings that cannot be exhausted or adequately represented by any one referent.[107]

The kingdom of God was a "tensive symbol"—"a narrative means of demonstrating the inner meaning of the universe and of human life," or "a means of verbalizing one's basic understanding of the historicity of human existence in the world in language meant to be taken seriously but not necessarily literally." We shall return to Perrin in connection with the discussion of the New Quest in America in chapter 14. In the meantime, his negative overreaction to Jeremias seems to have led him to conclude that the "tensive symbol" of kingdom of God could not carry

---

104. Norman Perrin, *The Kingdom of God in the Teaching of Jesus* (London: SCM, 1963), was a revision of his D.Theol. dissertation under Jeremias. It was dedicated to Perrin's two under teachers, T. W. Manson at Manchester and Jeremias at Göttingen. The book contained respectful discussions of both, as well as Oscar Cullmann. However, hints of change were also given, including reference to James M. Robinson, who read the original while a visiting professor at Göttingen.

105. Norman Perrin, *Jesus and the Language of the Kingdom: Symbol and Metaphor in New Testament Interpretation* (Philadelphia: Fortress, 1976), 106.

106. Perrin, *Jesus and the Language of the Kingdom*, 106.

107. Perrin, *Jesus and the Language of the Kingdom*, 30; cf. Philip Wheelwright, *Metaphor and Reality* (Bloomington, IN: Indiana University Press, 1962). See further Wendell Willis, ed., *The Kingdom of God in 20th-Century Interpretation* (Peabody, MA: Hendrickson, 1987); Mark Saucy, *The Kingdom of God in the Teaching of Jesus in 20th-Century Theology* (Dallas: Word, 1997).

any reference to the meaning of human existence except for the situations in which the Jesus of history was involved.

John W. Sider thought that Jeremias's approach was flawed by not allowing literary criticism to precede reconstruction.[108] "To determine the original setting Jeremias usually depends on two kinds of correspondence: between the gospel version and his view of the evangelists in the church; and between his general understanding of Jesus' message and the reconstructed parable."[109] Part of the problem was that Jeremias's method rested on too many assumptions. It was characterized, in words adopted from Humphrey Palmer, by a failure to "distinguish evidence which proves (which cannot be otherwise explained) from evidence which merely fits."[110] A case in point is Jeremias's eschatology, which he got "as much from Schweitzer as from the gospels."[111]

Another issue is the view of allegory, which Jeremias inherited from Jülicher, inspiring his determination to cleanse the parables from allegory. More recent scholars see this resolve as alien to the world of Jesus and his contemporaries.[112] The term παραβολή (*parabolē*), parable, is found twenty-two times in the LXX to translate the Hebrew מָשָׁל, plural מְשָׁלִים (*mashal, meshalim*), a saying, a mocking byword, similitude, riddle, allegory, oracle, fable, proverb.[113] Arland J. Hultgren contended that "the parables of Jesus fit more precisely in form and content within the context of various *meshalim* known from rabbinic sources."[114] He went on to say that while we cannot go back to the old allegorical method, "parable and allegory were not sharply differentiated in the world of Jesus and his contemporaries; the term *mashal* covers both. Terms like 'father' and

---

108. John W. Sider, "Rediscovering the Parables: The Logic of the Jeremias Tradition," *JBL* 102 (1983): 61–83.
109. Sider, "Rediscovering the Parables," 67.
110. Sider, "Rediscovering the Parables," 72, 77; cf. Humphrey Palmer, *The Logic of Gospel Criticism: An Account of the Methods, and Arguments used by Textual, Documentary, Source, and Form Critics of the New Testament* (London: Macmillan; New York: Saint Martin's Press, 1968), 152.
111. Sider, "Rediscovering the Parables," 74.
112. Raymond E. Brown, "Parable and Allegory Reconsidered," in *New Testament Essays* (Garden City, NY: Doubleday Image, 1968), 321–33; John Drury, *The Parables in the Gospels: History and Allegory* (New York: Crossroad, 1985); Arland J. Hultgren, *The Parables of Jesus: A Commentary* (Grand Rapids: Eerdmans, 2000), 12–14; Klyne R. Snodgrass, *Stories with Intent: A Comprehensive Guide to the Parables of Jesus* (Grand Rapids: Eerdmans, 2008), 1–59, 567–77. Snodgrass's work is much closer to Jeremias than Norman Perrin's *Jesus and the Language of the Kingdom*.
113. Hultgren, *The Parables of Jesus*, 5.
114. Hultgren, *The Parables of Jesus*, 6.

'servant' have metaphorical meanings in the parables of Jesus that are to be noticed by the interpreter, and as soon as that is done, a given parable may well be seen to have some allegorical elements in it."[115]

An issue that Jeremias overlooked in his preoccupation with salvation history is the contemporary social and political aspects of Jesus' parables, which recently have been highlighted by William R. Herzog II[116] and Luise Schottroff.[117] A case in point is Schottroff's contention that "Mark 4:32 expresses a political vision: God will reign over all peoples. But that means that there will be no more great empires like those that have dominated little Israel for centuries. At the time of the Gospel of Mark, 4:32 was a political prophecy that announced the end of the Roman empire and its Pax Romana. There will no longer be any nation that subjects other nations; all the nations are subject, in the same way to God's dominion, and by it they will be protected."[118]

On the other hand, an insight of Jeremias that today is frequently overlooked is his observation, "All the Gospel parables are a defence of the Good News. The actual proclamation of the Good News to sinners took a different form: in the offer of forgiveness, in Jesus' invitation to the guilty to taste his hospitality, in his call to follow him. It was not to sinners that he addressed the Gospel parables, but to his critics: to those who rejected him because he gathered the despised around him."[119] The parables were not sermon illustrations but riddles, challenging their hearers and their worldviews. Even if we have to modify Jeremias's contention by noting that some parables were addressed to disciples, they remain defences of Jesus' actions in view of the hostility that his actions provoked.[120]

---

115. Hultgren, *The Parables of Jesus*, 13.
116. William R. Herzog II, *Parables as Subversive Speech: Jesus as Pedagogue of the Oppressed* (Louisville: Westminster John Knox, 1994); Herzog, *Prophet and Teacher: An Introduction to the Historical Jesus* (Louisville: Westminster John Knox, 2005).
117. Luise Schotroff, *The Parables of Jesus*, trans. Linda M. Maloney (Minneapolis: Fortress, 2006).
118. Schotroff, *The Parables of Jesus*, 120.
119. Jeremias, *The Parables of Jesus*, 145.
120. Colin Brown, "The Unjust Steward: A New Twist?," in *Worship, Theology and Ministry in the Early Church: Essays in Honor of Ralph P. Martin*, ed. Michael J. Wilkins and Terence Paige, JSNTSS 87 (Sheffield: Sheffield Academic Press, 1992), 121–45; Brown, "The Parable of the Rebellious Son(s)," *SJT* 1 (1998): 391–405. In the former article I argue that the unjust steward represents Jesus, whose actions of forgiving debts are judged by adversaries to be improper, but who is ultimately commended. In the second article, I argue that the parable known as the parable of the prodigal son is modeled on the concepts of the stubborn and rebellious son (Deut 21:18–21) and the wise and foolish son in wisdom literature. It challenges those who criticize Jesus with the riddle: who actually is the stubborn and rebellious son?

The No Quest in Europe after World War II

At the end of *The Parables of Jesus* Jeremias devoted a couple of pages to what he called "parabolic actions."[121] By that he meant that Jesus performed deliberately symbolic and kerygmatic actions throughout his public activity. "His most significant parabolic action was his extension of hospitality to the outcasts (Luke 19.5f.) and their reception into his house (Luke 15.1–2) and even into the circle of his disciples (Mark 2.14 par. Matt. 10:3). These feasts for publicans are prophetic signs, more significant than words, silent proclamations that the Messianic Age is here, the Age of forgiveness."[122] The Last Supper was such a symbolic act. Also symbolic of the messianic age were Jesus' healings, his rejection of fasting (Mark 2:19–20), the bestowal on Simon the name *Kēpha*, designating him as the foundation stone of the eschatological temple of God (Matt 16:17–18). The symbolic number of the Twelve signified the eschatological people of God. Jesus' kingly entry into Jerusalem and his cleansing of the temple were "inseparably connected as symbol of the coming of the New Age."[123] The peaceful purpose of his mission was symbolized by the choice of an ass on which to make his entry (Zech 9:9).

Other symbolic actions were the setting of a child amid the disciples, the footwashing (John 13:1ff.), writing in the sand (John 7:53ff.; cf. Jer 17:13), and cursing of the fig tree. These actions were all symbols of the arrival of the messianic age. In the words of C. Maurer, "Jesus not only utters the message of the kingdom of God, he himself is the message."[124]

Jeremias is saying something important here, but was he entirely correct? His conclusion reverses Harnack's conclusion that Jesus' message was all about the Father and not about the Son and Bultmann's view that Jesus was initially the proclaimer who became the proclaimed only in the kerygma. I have no doubt that Jesus taught by deed as well as by word. The Gospels attribute Jesus' actions to the power of God working through him: in the case of the Synoptic Gospels, the Spirit of God (Matt 12:28; Luke 11:20; Mark 3:28–30); in the case of John, the Father performing his works (John 5:36; 10:37–38; 14:9–11). There is something paradoxical about Jeremias's choice of the word *parabolic* for

---

121. *The Parables of Jesus*, 227–29. The term appears to have originated with Gustav Stählin, "Die Gleichnishandlungen Jesu," in *Kosmos und Ekklesia. Festschrift für Wilhelm Stählin zu seinem siebzigsten Geburtstag, 24. September 1953*, ed. Heinz-Dietrich Wendland (Kassel: Johannes Stauda-Verlag, 1953), 9–22.

122. Jeremias, *The Parables of Jesus*, 227.

123. Jeremias, *The Parables of Jesus*, 228.

124. Jeremias, *The Parables of Jesus*, 229, citing C. Maurer, *Judaica* 4 (1948): 147.

The European Scene

Jesus' actions. By Jeremias's own definition, the parables did not serve to preach the gospel, which was done by Jesus' forgiveness and hospitality to the outcasts, but to defend it from criticism. But now Jeremias describes those acts of hospitality as Jesus' "most significant parabolic action."

A better choice of term, one which Jeremias also used, is *prophetic sign*. Jesus' actions fit into the tradition of the sign-working prophet, whose signs embodied and illustrated his message. But perhaps there was in the signs an element of "riddle," which—like the "riddles" in the spoken parables—were designed to challenge those who saw them to ponder their significance. In particular, the Last Supper was not simply a Passover celebration but a Passover meal transformed by Jesus' use of bread and wine as signs prophetic of the meaning of his death.[125]

Prayer. Jeremias's views on prayer have come under scrutiny, regarding the Lord's Prayer and its function as well as its component parts. We shall look at these issues in turn.

Michael D. Goulder proposed that the Lord's Prayer was composed by the author of Matthew from the traditions of prayer in Mark, who lacks the Lord's Prayer but preserves fragmentary parallels.[126] *Abba* was used by Jesus in his Gethsemane prayer (Mark 14:36), where Jesus prayed that the Father's will may be done. He urged Peter to pray that he might not come into temptation (πειρασμόν) (Mark 14:38). Earlier Jesus linked prayer with forgiveness: "Whenever you stand praying, forgive, if you have anything against anyone; so that your Father in heaven may also forgive you your trespasses" (Mark 11:25).

Absence of the Lord's Prayer from Mark is not decisive since Mark omits much of the teaching attributed to Jesus. As suggested in chapter 1, Mark was written in dramatic-epic form to be declaimed during liturgical worship, extensive didactic material may have been omitted lest it hinder the narrative flow. Goulder's argument depended on the nonexistence of Q and the claim that Luke abbreviated Matthew.

The fragments on prayer in Mark (also found in Matthew and Luke) indicate that Jesus did use petitions that are contained in the Lord's

---

125. See below, chap. 19, §6.
126. Michael D. Goulder, *Midrash and Lection in Matthew*, Speaker's Lectures in Biblical Studies 1969–71 (London: SPCK, 1974), 296–301. More recently, Marc Philonenko has suggested that the first three petitions of the Lord's Prayer represent the prayer of Jesus himself and the last three the prayer that he taught the disciples. Cf. Marc Philonenko, *Le Notre Père. De la prière de Jésus à la prière des disciples* (Paris: Gallimard, 2001).

The No Quest in Europe after World War II

Prayer. The existence of the Kaddish indicates that such formal prayers existed prior to Jesus. It provides a Jewish precedent for the plausibility of Jeremias's proposal regarding its forms in Matthew and Luke.[127]

In *The Historical Jesus* (1991) Crossan doubted whether Jesus ever composed the prayer that we know as the Lord's Prayer. If Jesus had taught a special prayer, it would have been more widely attested than Matthew 6:9–13; Luke 11:2–4; and Didache 8:2.[128] There was nothing apocalyptic about the Lord's Prayer. Nor should it be interpreted too spiritually. However, it serves "as a beautiful summary of the themes and emphases in Jesus' vision of the kingdom of God." This theme was expanded in what is perhaps Crossan's most moving book, *The Greatest Prayer* (2011).[129]

Crossan skirted questions about the prayer's different forms, preferring to base his remarks on Matthew's version as the one most commonly known. He noted the connection between prayer and forgiveness in Mark 11:25 (cf. Matt. 18:15, 21–35) and traced what he called Jesus' *Abba* prayer to his words in Gethsemane regarding submission to his Father's will (Mark 14:36). The Aramaic word *Abba* suggested the Fatherhood of God in terms of a benevolent householder and humanity as his household. His Son was his heir. Human beings were his stewards, and the Lord's Prayer turned on their needs and their role in exercising their stewardship in justice and righteousness. The Prayer came from the heart of Judaism through the mouth of Christianity, pleading for the establishment of God's will on earth.

Jeremias's views on components of the Lord's Prayer and their function have also been challenged. The consensus of Aramaic experts has concluded, in the words of James H. Charlesworth, that "there is no compelling evidence that Jesus used *Abba* [in the sense of Daddy] nor are we warranted in concluding that Jesus, in contrast to his contemporaries, thought of removing God from heaven and placing him on earth."[130] It is

---

127. Jeremias, *The Prayers of Jesus*, 98. For updated research see Andreas Lehnhardt, *Qaddish. Untersuchungen zur Entsehung und Rezeption eines rabbinischen Gebets*, TSAJ 87 (Tübingen: Mohr Siebeck, 2002).

128. John Dominic Crossan, *The Historical Jesus: The Life of a Mediterranean Peasant* (San Francisco: HarperSanFrancisco, 1991), 294.

129. John Dominic Crossan, *The Greatest Prayer: Rediscovering the Revolutionary Message of the Lord's Prayer* (San Francisco: HarperOne, 2011).

130. James H. Charlesworth, "A Caveat on Textual Transmission and the Meaning of *Abba*: A Study of the Lord's Prayer," in *The Lord's Prayer and Other Prayer Texts from the Greco-Roman*

now recognized that there is no distinctive word for "Daddy" in Hebrew or Aramaic, and it is incorrect to translate πατήρ as "Daddy." Geza Vermes showed that, if the story about Hanin ha-Nehba and the children using Abba proves anything, it is that Jesus was not alone in using Abba for God.[131] Charlesworth's alternative was that, rather than proving unique communion with God, Jesus' use of Abba probably reminded his hearers of the ancient Scriptures, where God called his son Israel out of slavery in Egypt (Exod 4:22–23; Hos 11:1) and adopted Israel's king as his special son at his enthronement.[132]

Recent scholarship has also shown that the petition for our daily bread did not have the eschatological overtones that Jeremias read into it but simply meant "daily."[133] This conclusion is reinforced if the subtext of the prayer is the exodus wanderings of God's people and if the petition contained an allusion to the daily supply of manna (Exod 16:4, 16–21).[134]

Crossan portrayed Jesus as a Jewish peasant Cynic engaged in indirect protest against Roman rule through healing and shared meals.[135] In *Jesus, Debt, and the Lord's Prayer* (2014) Douglas E. Oakman presented a compelling case for situating the Lord's Prayer in the context of Jesus' social and economic teaching.[136] Debt was a major problem in Judea, as instanced by Josephus's reports of the seizure and burning of debt records

---

Era, ed. James H. Charlesworth, with Mark Harding and Mark Kiley (Valley Forge, PA: Trinity Press International, 1994), 9; cf. J. C. G. Greig, "Abba and Amen: Their Relevance to Christology," in *Studia Evangelica* 5, ed. F. L. Cross, (Berlin: Akademie-Verlag, 1968), 3–13; Joseph A. Fitzmyer, *"Abba* and Jesus' Relation to God," in *À Cause de l'Évangile. Études sur les Synoptiques et les Actes offert au P. Jacques Dupont, O.S.B. à l'occasion de son 70e anniversaire* (Paris: Cerf, 1985), 15–38; James Barr, "Abba Isn't Daddy," *JTS* 39 (1988): 28–47; repr. in *Bible and Interpretation: The Collected Essays of James Barr*, ed. John Barton, (Oxford: Oxford University Press, 2013), 2:262–80; Barr, "'Abba, Father' and the Familiarity of Jesus' Speech," *Theology* 91 (1998): 173–79; BDAG, 1, 786–88.

131. *Jesus the Jew: A Historian's Reading of the Gospels* (London: Collins; Philadelphia: Fortress, 1973; Philadelphia: Fortress, 1981), 211.

132. Charlesworth, "A Caveat on Textual Transmission," 10–11.

133. Colin Hemer, "ἐπιούσιος," *JSNT* 22 (1984): 81–94. Arland J. Hultgren took it to mean "the bread that comes upon [us]," that is, from the Father. Cf. Hultgren, "The Bread Petition of the Lord's Prayer," in *Christ and His Communities: Essays in Honor of Reginald H. Fuller*, ed. Arland J. Hultgren and Barbara Hall, *ATR Supplementary Series* 11 (1990): 41–54. See further BDAG, 376–77.

134. Brown, *NIDNTT*, 2:871–72.

135. Crossan, *The Historical Jesus*, 303–53.

136. Douglas E. Oakman, *Jesus, Debt, and the Lord's Prayer: First-Century Debt and Jesus' Intentions* (Eugene, OR: Cascade, 2014). Chap. 2 of this book (17–41) is a revised version of Oakman, "The Lord's Prayer in Social Perspective," in *Authenticating the Words of Jesus*, ed. Bruce Chilton and Craig A. Evans, NTTS 28.1 (Leiden: Brill, 1999), 137–86.

in the war with Rome (*War* 2.247; 7.61). Galilee was burdened by two competing tax systems: Roman and Judean.[137]

Debt played a major part in Jesus' teaching. The parable of the unforgiving servant (Matt 18:23–35) depicted a case where an entire family was imprisoned for insolvency. The sayings in Matthew 5:25–26 and Luke 12:58–59 refer to settling out of court to avoid incarceration until the debt was paid in full. The Torah prohibited Israelites from lending at interest to fellow Israelites but allowed loans at interest to gentiles (Deut 23:19–20). To circumvent this prohibition, a procedure was devised that allowed interest in the form of commodities. The *prozbul* was a legal device for securing loans. In default of repayment, foreclosure could be accomplished through a court. Financial stress on rural lower classes meant the loss of their inherited land and an accumulation of wealth by the upper classes.[138]

Oakman proposed that the original form of the prayer consisted of address to God as Father plus petitions four, five, and six.[139] *Father* denoted the head of the household, the one who ruled as benevolent king. The petitioner interceded as his heir and member of his household. The fourth petition was for basic bread. The fifth asked for removal of debt. And petition six sought deliverance from rigged courts and evil judges.

---

137. Oakman, *Jesus, Debt, and the Lord's Prayer*, 17.

138. The parable of the unjust steward (Luke 16:1–8) relates to this situation. Oakman, *Jesus, Debt, and the Lord's Prayer*, 37. Oakman suggested that the "rich man" owned whole villages. The tenants paid rent through their produce. The steward ingratiated himself with the debtors by reducing their payment. However, there are alternative interpretations that may fit better the social, economic, and religious milieu.

It should be noted that before the steward made the reductions he had already been accused of squandering his master's property. The first part of the parable depicts the steward being called to account for this charge. J. D. M. Derrett cogently argued that the steward realized that sums owed were illegal, usurious interest, presumably sanctioned by others acting for the rich man. The steward used his authority to cancel them, leaving only the principal to be repaid. In so doing he restored the rich man's status as regards the law. This explains why the master commended the astute action of the steward (Luke 16:8; J. D. M. Derrett, "The Parable of the Unjust Steward," *Law in the New Testament* (London: Darton, Longman & Todd, 1970), 48–77. The steward was more faithful to his master than his accusers by removing the wrong that had been perpetrated in the master's name.

In light of Jeremias's assertion that the parables were taught to defend the gospel, Derrett's interpretation may be carried further. The parable may belong to the cycle of parables in which Luke relates Jesus' response to the complaints of the Pharisees and scribes (Luke 15:1–2). The steward represents Jesus himself, who was seen as unfit to act on behalf of God in remitting sin as debt (Luke 5:20–21; 7:47–49). Cf. Brown, "The Unjust Steward," in Wilkins and Paige, *Worship, Theology and Ministry in the Early Church*, 121–45.

139. Oakman, *Jesus, Debt, and the Lord's Prayer*, 62–91.

The European Scene

> Central to the concerns of Jesus' original Prayer was the reality of oppression, indebtedness, hunger, and social insecurity. When early Christian groups moved out of the immediate context of such social realities, the concrete and immediate meaning of Jesus' Prayer was led in the direction of theological abstractions and aligned with Israelite traditions and early rabbinic forms of prayer. Twenty-first century Christian communities might reflect on the meaning and consequences of that transition as they confront social and economic realities at the beginning of a new millennium.[140]

In his recent study *The Disciples' Prayer* (2015) Jeffrey B. Gibson reopened the whole question and concluded that it was not a prayer that Jesus regularly used himself. "Its aim from start to finish was to keep his band of disciples from straying from that path through their securing divine aid to help them remain faithful to God's ways as Jesus understood them."[141]

The gospel narratives record eight prayers attributed to Jesus. None of them depict Jesus uttering the Lord's Prayer. The nearest is the petition in Gethsemane: "And going a little farther, he threw himself on the ground and prayed that, if it were possible, the hour might pass from him. He said, 'Abba, Father, for you all things are possible; remove this cup from me; yet, not what I want, but what you want'" (Mark 14:35–36 par. Matt 26:39).[142] Alongside this quotation, we may place the exhortation, which follows Jesus' action in the temple, linking prayer and forgiveness. "Whenever you stand praying, forgive, if you have anything against anyone; so that your Father in heaven may also forgive you your trespasses" (Mark 11:25). This exhortation is substantially parallel to that in the Sermon on the Mount (Matt 6:14–15).

Gibson argued (persuasively in my opinion) that the prayer that Jesus taught was intended to be the Disciples' Prayer for use in face of the hazards of daily life. His argument is based not on literary relations between the fragments noted above but on his construal of Jesus' aims in calling disciples. Jesus called disciples not to revolution and retaliation but to be υἱοὶ θεοῦ, "sons of God" (Matt 5:9 RSV). The prayer was addressed to

---

140. Oakman, *Jesus, Debt, and the Lord's Prayer*, 90–91.
141. Jeffrey B. Gibson, *The Disciples' Prayer: The Prayer Jesus Taught in Its Historical Setting* (Minneapolis: Fortress, 2015), 162.
142. The other prayers noted by Gibson are Matt 11:25–26 par. Luke 10:21; Mark 15:34; Luke 23:34; 23:46; John 11:41–42; 12:27–28; 17:1–26. See Gibson, *The Disciples' Prayer*, 5–7.

God as Father so that disciples might live like "sons of God." "They were the faithful remnant of Israel that, among other things, was to hallow God's name and bring knowledge of him to the world (Matt 5:11, 13–14; Luke 6:12, 22–23) by conforming their lives to what Jesus taught them to see was the pattern of faithfulness that such υἱοί owe to their Father."[143] On these grounds Gibson rejected eschatological interpretations of the prayer as a whole, and also of individual petitions.[144]

Regarding the version of the Lord's Prayer in Didache 8, Peter J. Tomson makes an impressive case for locating it at the parting of the ways of Judaism and Christianity. He argues that "from being one among many Jewish prayers, the Lord's Prayer became a Christian boundary marker at the rupture that occurred between Jews and Christians under Trajan and Hadrian and that the institution of rabbinic daily prayer of Eighteen Benedictions played a crucial role in this development."[145] Matthew and the Didache both belong to the time frame of early "rabbinic" reform under Gamaliel the Younger. They both lack echoes of the cursing of heretics contained in the Eighteen Benedictions or hints of Christian excommunication that are found in rabbinic traditions and the gospel of John.

Luke's simpler version, which lacks suggestion of polemics, indicates an earlier date. Matthew's version sounds more "rabbinic." However, there is no fundamental theological difference in the prayers. "Theologically the continuity of Judaism and Christianity depicted by Luke carries as much weight as the rupture reflected by Matthew. Judging by the way the prayer of Jesus is transmitted in the New Testament, the relationship of Jews and Christians remains an undecided issue. It is the extra canonical text of the Didache that helps us realize this."[146]

The most succinct, but still detailed, account of modern discussions of the Lord's Prayer is given by Robert J. Karris in *Prayer and the New Testament* (2000). His opening chapter on "Prayer and the Historical Jesus" situates the petitions of the Lord's Prayer in the context of Jewish

---

143. Gibson, *The Disciples' Prayer*, 67.
144. Gibson, *The Disciples' Prayer*, 102–60.
145. Peter J. Tomson, "The Lord's Prayer (Didache 8) at the Faultline of Judaism and Christianity," in *The Didache: A Missing Piece of the Puzzle in Early Christianity*, ed. Jonathan A. Draper and Clayton N. Jefford, Early Christianity and Its Literature 14 (Atlanta: SBL Press, 2015), 165–87, here 165.
146. Tomson, "The Lord's Prayer," 187.

The European Scene

prayers of his day.[147] Jesus put his life on the line for these petitions, which relate to the state of the world.

If we reflect on the petitions of the Lord's Prayer, it becomes apparent that they embody intertextual echoes of the *Torah*—what Christian translations of Scripture call the Law but in Judaism means *instruction*, *teaching*, or *guidance*. In its wider sense, the term applies to the entire body of sacred writings, but in a more specific sense it refers to the first five books, Genesis to Deuteronomy. This latter sense is applicable here. *Torah* contains what rabbinic tradition called *Haggadah* (nonlegal narratives, sayings, and stories) and *Halakhah* (legal instruction about the way that Israel should "go"; Exod 18:20). The Lord's Prayer contains echoes of both *Haggadah* and *Halakhah*.

Haggadah is echoed in the petitions regarding the provision of daily bread and temptation as well as the narratives regarding Israel's wilderness wanderings, which involved manna and multiple trials and temptations. *Halakhah* echoes the Ten Commandments (Exod 20:2–17; Deut 5:6–21) with petitions regarding the hallowing of God's name and deliverance from trial and temptation. The specific imperatives of the Ten Commandments regarding murder, adultery, stealing, and covetousness are subsumed in the Lord's Prayer by "Your kingdom come, your will be done on earth as it is in heaven" (Matt 6:10). Anyone who sincerely utters these petitions and sincerely asks forgiveness of past sins cannot commit the sins specified in the Ten Commandments.

Mark records that when Jesus was himself tested by a scribe on which was the first commandment, Jesus replied by citing the opening words of the Shema: "Hear O Israel: the Lord our God, the Lord is one; you shall love the Lord your God with all your heart, and with all your soul, and with all your mind, and with all your strength" (Mark 12:29–30 par. Matt 22:37; cf. Deut 6:4–5). Jesus immediately supplemented his answer by adding a *second* commandment with a citation from Leviticus 19:18: "The second is this, 'You shall love your neighbor as yourself.' There is no commandment greater than these" (Mark 12:31; par. Matt 22:39–40; cf. Luke 10:25–28).[148]

---

147. Robert J. Karris, *Prayer and the New Testament* (New York: Herder and Herder, 2000), 1–39, 64–67. An appendix to chap. 1 gives Jewish prayers of Jesus' time in translation: the Shema, the Eighteen Benedictions or Tefillah, Grace at Meals, 'Ahabah Rabbah (Great Love), 'Alenu (Our Duty), Qaddish ("Hallowed"), 33–39.

148. In Mark's narrative the scribe acknowledged that Jesus was right and that observance

The two Great Commandments and the Lord's Prayer epitomize the teaching and activity of Jesus. From opposite but converging viewpoints they represent the central reality of the kingdom of God—God's reign on earth. The Great Commandments represent the divine imperative. The Lord's Prayer represents that imperative in the form of a human response, asking God that his will may be done, that his kingdom come on earth, and that he would provide what is needed to bring his will about. As such, it expressed what Jeremiah prophesied regarding a new covenant.

> The days are surely coming says the LORD, when I will make a new covenant with the house of Israel and the house of Judah. It will not be like the covenant that I made with their ancestors when I took them by the hand to bring them out of the land of Egypt. . . . But this is the covenant that I will make with the house of Israel after those days, says the LORD: I will put my law within them, and I will write it on their hearts; and I will be their God, and they shall be my people. . . . For I will forgive their iniquity, and remember their sin no more. (Jer 31:31–34)

In the observations made above in connection with Jeremias's discussion of the Last Supper, it was noted that the term *covenant* (διαθήκη) occurs in Matthew, Mark, Luke, and Paul in their account of Jesus' words at the meal. The word διαθήκη was not used previously by Jesus. In Hellenistic times it carried the sense of a last will and testament. It was used in this sense in Hebrews 9:16–17. In the LXX διαθήκη was used of covenants initiated by God.[149] An integral part of God's covenant with Israel under Moses was the shedding of animal blood (Exod 24:8). However, consumption of blood was prohibited by the Noahic Laws (Gen 9:4).

Jesus' final Passover was celebrated against the background of impending arrest and execution (Mark 14:1–2; Matt 26:1–5; Luke 22:1–2). The underlying reason was his teaching and conduct, which amounted

---

of these commandments was more important than sacrifice. Jesus replied that he had answered wisely and was not far from the kingdom of God (Mark 12:32–34).

In rabbinic discussion of prayer and entrance to the Temple (*m. Ber.* 9:5), Deut 6:4–5 was explained as follows: *With all your heart* meant with both your inclinations—good and evil. *With all your soul* meant even if God takes away your life. *With all your might* meant with all your money. It may be noted that these themes all figure in the synoptic accounts of Jesus in the temple court and the events leading to his death.

149. BDAG, 228–29.

to the implementation of a new covenant. Eating the bread and drinking the wine were symbolic signs and acts of participation in his life and death. They embodied both Jesus' last will and the new covenant that he initiated. Thus, the cup symbolized "the blood of the διαθήκης (*tēs diathēkēs*), which is poured out for many" (Mark 14:24; cf. Matt 26:28; Luke 22:20; 1 Cor 11:27).

Jesus and the Gentile Nations. Finally, comment may be made on Jeremias's *Jesus' Promise to the Nations*, in which Jeremias argued that Jesus envisaged the incorporation of the gentiles into Israel at the *eschaton*, but not the evangelization of the gentiles in the lands in which they lived. The question of Jesus' relations with the gentiles is once more a debated issue.[150]

The most serious challenge to Jeremias is the study of *Jesus and the Origins of the Gentile Mission* by Michael F. Bird.[151] Bird sees a direct connection between Jesus and the gentile mission, since "Jesus conception of the restoration of Israel was intrinsically bound up with the fate of the nations. Jesus operated with a view of restoration eschatology which made the salvation of the Gentiles wholly compatible with a view of Israel's salvation."[152]

In contrast with Jeremias's salvation-history approach, Bird argues that Jesus held a distinct form of eschatology that he labels "*symbolic restoration*, according to which the fate of the Gentile world hung on the salvation of Israel. Furthermore, this paradigm provides the presupposition and platform for the salvation of the Gentiles and for a Gentile mission."[153] Although Jesus shared contemporary Jewish critiques of gentile immorality and idolatry, he did not exclude the gentiles.[154] Jesus' parables envisage inclusion of the gentiles. For example, the mustard seed (Mark 4:30–32) envisages a restored Israel (the tree) in which birds (the gentiles) would nest in its branches.[155]

Jesus' encounter with the Syrophoenician woman and the remark about the children's crumbs falling from the table (Mark 7:24–30) indicated the priority of Israel but also the possibility of gentiles sharing Israel's benefits.[156]

---

150. Cf. Leander E. Keck, *Who Is Jesus? History in Perfect Tense* (Minneapolis: Fortress, 2001).
151. Michael F. Bird, *Jesus and the Origins of the Gentile Mission*, Library of New Testament Studies 331 (New York: T&T Clark International, 2007).
152. Bird, *Jesus and the Origins of the Gentile Mission*, 173.
153. Bird, *Jesus and the Origins of the Gentile Mission*, 174; cf. 26–45.
154. Bird, *Jesus and the Origins of the Gentile Mission*, 46–57.
155. Bird, *Jesus and the Origins of the Gentile Mission*, 73–76.
156. Bird, *Jesus and the Origins of the Gentile Mission*, 51–52. More recently this passage has been examined in depth by Pablo Alonso, *The Woman Who Changed Jesus: Crossing the Boundaries*

The centurion in Capernaum (Lk. 7.1–10; Mt. 8.5–12) exhibits the faith that Israel was meant to possess in the face of restoration, and so warrants inclusion in the present blessings of the kingdom.... In a purity system defined by holiness, sacred space, contamination and cleansing, Jesus' interaction with Gentiles implied the relativizing of traditional barriers that demanded Jewish-Gentile separation. Jesus' encounters with Gentiles are then a visible parable that Israel's restoration can and will effect the Gentile world.[157]

Bird's account of Jesus, the disciples, and the temple culminated in the judgment: "It is because Jesus' disciples are already the vanguard of the new Israel and that they are already the new temple that they can already project the universal purposes of Israel's God into the world of the present and so effect the salvation of the Gentiles."[158] In short, "Jeremias' proposal concerning Jesus' relationship to the Gentiles, important as it has been in scholarship, is fundamentally flawed and should no longer be the default position for scholars who wish to address the question of Jesus and the Gentiles."[159]

3. Oscar Cullmann

Oscar Cullmann (1902–99)[160] was the last of the generation of European scholars that shaped the course of New Testament study in the mid-twentieth century. He was born in Strassburg, then a German city, and

---

in Mk 7:34–30, Biblical Tools and Studies 11 (Leuven: Peeters, 2011). Following a history of interpretation, and a comparison with the parallel, Matt 15:21–28, which is seen as a redaction, Alonso presents a synchronic and contextual reading of the narrative.
    157. Bird, *Jesus and the Origins of the Gentile Mission*, 175; cf. 95–124.
    158. Bird, *Jesus and the Origins of the Gentile Mission*, 161; cf. 125–72.
    159. Bird, *Jesus and the Origins of the Gentile Mission*, 176.
    160. Karlfried Fröhlich, autobiographical sketch in *Oscar Cullmann. Vorträge und Aufsätze, 1925–1962*, ed. Karlfried Fröhlich (Tübingen: Mohr Siebeck; Zürich: Zwingli, 1966), 683–87; David H. Wallace, "Oscar Cullman," in *Creative Minds in Contemporary Theology*, ed. Philip Edgcumbe Hughes, 2nd ed. (Grand Rapids: Eerdmans, 1969), 163–202; Karl-Heinz Schlaudraff, *"Heil als Geschichte"? Die Frage nach dem heilsgeschichtlichen Denken, dargestellt anhand der Konzeption Oscar Cullmanns*, BGBE 29 (Tübingen: Mohr Siebeck, 1988); Theodore M. Dorman, *The Hermeneutics of Oscar Cullmann* (San Francisco: Mellen Research University Press, 1991); T. M. Dorman, *DMBI*, 333–38. In addition to the *Vorträge und Aufsätze*, Cullmann was presented with *Oikonomia. Heilsgeschichte als Thema der Theologie. Oscar Cullmann zum 65. Geburtstage gewidmet*, ed. Felix Christ (Hamburg-Bergstedt: Reich, 1967).

after World War I when it reverted to France (and reassumed its French name Strasbourg), Cullmann studied at the university. He grew up bilingual. He recalled that "the reading of *The Quest of the Historical Jesus* by my fellow countryman A. Schweitzer opened my eyes for seeing that historical-critical research on the Bible was thoroughly corrupted not only by orthodoxy but also in modern times even more strongly by then the prevailing philosophy."[161]

The advent of form criticism proved liberating. Cullmann's advocacy of form criticism in his first publication was welcomed by Bultmann.[162] After graduation, Cullmann taught Greek and German in Paris, where he took the opportunity to study theology under Goguel,[163] Guignebert, and Loisy. At the time he had no idea that he would succeed to their posts.

In 1930 Cullmann was appointed professor of New Testament at Strasbourg. He resolved to put aside modern conceptions of Christianity, and gradually through "purely academic endeavor" attained a deeper theological understanding of the alien element of which the New Testament speaks.[164] In 1938 Cullmann received a call to Basel, where he was a colleague of Karl Barth, K. L. Schmidt, and later Bo Reicke. In subsequent years Cullmann combined his teaching at Basel with appointments at the École des Hautes-Études, the philosophical faculty at the Sorbonne, and the Free Protestant Faculty. Cullmann had little in common with Barth, except a shared "obedient listening to the strangeness of the Bible."[165] Cullmann appreciated Schmidt's positive approach to form criticism,[166] but his eschatology and hermeneutics were developed in conscious opposition to the schools of Schweitzer[167] and Bultmann.[168] Cullmann's work

---

161. Oscar Cullmann, *Vorträge und Aufsätze*, 683–84.

162. Cullmann, "Die neuen Arbeiten zur Geschichte der Evangelientradition" (1925), *Vorträge und Aufsätze*, 41–89; cf. 684.

163. Cullmann, "Maurice Goguel (1880–1955)" (1955), *Vorträge und Aufsätze*, 667–74.

164. Cullmann, *Vorträge und Aufsätze*, 685.

165. Cullmann, *Vorträge und Aufsätze*, 686.

166. Cullmann, *Vorträge und Aufsätze*, 687; "Karl Ludwig Schmidt 1891–1956," *Vorträge und Aufsätze*, 675–82.

167. Cullmann, "Neutestamentliche Eschatologie und Entstehung des Dogmas" (1942), "Die Hoffnung der Kirche auf die Wiederkunft Christi nach dem Neuen Testament" (1944), "Das wahre durch die ausgebliebene Parousie gestellte neutestamentliche Problem" (1947), *Vorträge und Aufsätze*, 361–77, 378–402, 414–26.

168. Cullmann, "Mythos und 'Entmythologisierung' im Neuen Testament" (1954), "Unzeitgemässe Bemerkungen zum 'historischen Jesus' der Bultmannschule" (1960), "Parousieverzögerung und Urchristentum" (1958), "Das ausgebliebene Reich Gottes als theologisches Problem" (1961), *Vorträge und Aufsätze*, 125–40, 141–58, 427–44, 445–55.

ranged widely over the New Testament and church history, including a penetrating analysis of the Gospel of Thomas,[169] which I heard him give at University of Nottingham when I was a graduate student. Here I will focus on five issues that bear on the historical Jesus: Christmas, Peter, Christology, Time and *Heilsgeschichte*, and Cullmann's late study of *The Johannine Circle*.

3.1. The Origin of Christmas. One of Cullmann's investigations—albeit negative in its conclusions—concerned the origin of Christmas.[170] Christian celebration of December 25 was unknown in the first three centuries. The only hint given in the New Testament of the time of Jesus' birth is the reference to shepherds in the fields (Luke 2:8). Since shepherds watched over sheep during the warmer months (March-April to November), Luke's narrative seems to preclude a winter date for the birth of Jesus.

Cullmann concluded that the decisive factor in the adoption of December 25 was Constantine's policy of uniting the worship of Christ with that of the sun. The chief festival fell on December 25, in connection with the winter solstice. The decision was comparable with Constantine's earlier edict of 321, which made the day of the sun (which coincided with the Lord's Day) the authorized day of rest throughout the empire. Over time the pagan term *Sunday* replaced the distinctly Christian term *The Lord's Day*.

In a Christmas Day sermon Ambrose of Milan adopted a pragmatic approach: "Well do Christian people call this holy day, on which our Lord was born, the day of the new sun. . . . For if the sun withdrew its light when Christ suffered, it must shine at his birth with greater splendour than before."[171]

3.2. The Quest of the Historical Peter. Cullmann's *Peter: Disciple, Apostle, Martyr*[172] was a contribution to the quest of the historical Peter. It was thus indirectly a contribution to the quest of the historical Jesus. The first part was devoted to the three aspects of Peter's life noted in the title.

---

169. Cullmann, "Das Thomasevangelium und die Frage nach dem Alter der in ihm enthaltenen Tradition" (1960), *Vorträge und Aufsätze*, 566–88.

170. Cullmann, "The Origin of Christmas," *The Early Church*, trans. A. J. B. Higgins and Stanley Godman (London: SCM, 1956; abridged ed., 1966), 21–36.

171. Cullmann, *The Early Church*, 36, citing Ambrose Sermon 6 (Migne, PL 17:614).

172. Cullmann, *Petrus: Jünger–Apostel–Märtyrer. Das historische und das theologische Petrusproblem* (Zürich: Zwingli-Verlag, 1952); ET: *Peter: Disciple, Apostle, Martyr; A Historical and Theological Study*, trans. Floyd V. Filson (London: SCM, 1953; 2nd ed., 1962).

Cullmann concluded that recent excavations in Rome did not permit either an affirmative or a negative answer to the question of Peter's stay in Rome. However, literary evidence pointed to the probability that Peter was martyred in Rome under Nero.[173]

The second part of the book was devoted to the question of the authenticity and implications of the sayings regarding Peter, the church, and the rock (Matt 16:17–19). The case for rejecting authenticity was summed up by Günther Bornkamm: "This is because [the words attributed to Jesus] have no parallel in the other Gospels, and because this is the only place in the whole synoptic tradition where the word '*ekklesia*' appears in the sense of the church as a whole. (Only in Mt. xviii.17 do we come across the word '*ekklesia*' again, in connection with Church regulations, but used here in the sense of an assembly of the Church.) But the authenticity of the passage in Matthew xvi is questioned chiefly because it is not easily compatible with Jesus' proclamation of the imminent coming of the kingdom of God."[174] Cullmann denied that the infrequency of ἐκκλησία (*ekklēsia*, "church") in the Gospels was decisive, for the term aptly fitted Jesus' community of followers. The term "*does not designate anything like a Christian creation*, but belongs to the Jewish sphere."[175] In the LXX ἐκκλησία occurs about 100 times, usually to translate קָהָל (*qāhāl*) to denote the assembly or congregation of Israel.[176] It is found in this sense in Acts 7:38, where Moses is said to have been "in the congregation [ἐν τῇ ἐκκλησίᾳ] in the wilderness with the angel who spoke to him at Mount Sinai." In short, ἐκκλησία refers to "the people of God." "Above all, the Jewish Messianic expectation includes the conception of a Messianic community and is inconceivable without it."[177]

> Jesus speaks of *his ekklesia*. To me this does not seem, as has been claimed, irreconcilable with the fact that in Judaism the concept

---

173. Cullmann, *Peter*, 156.
174. Bornkamm, *Jesus of Nazareth*, 187; cf. Cullmann, *Peter*, 171–76 for recent interpretations. Those who supported authenticity included K. L. Schmidt, Joachim Jeremias, A. Oepke, and M.-J. Lagrange.
175. Cullmann, *Peter*, 194.
176. The underlying Aramaic word is presumed to be בְּנִשְׁתָּא (*kenishta*) (Cullmann, *Peter*, 195). In the LXX συναγωγή (*synagoge*) is used even more frequently but was generally rejected by the church as it parted ways from Israel. It is used in Jas 2:2 for an assembly of the church: "For if a person with gold rings and in fine clothes comes into your assembly [εἰς συναγωγὴν ὑμῶν], and if a poor person in dirty clothes also comes in . . ."
177. Cullmann, *Peter*, 195.

involved was the people *of God*, the *qʰhal Yahweh*, the *ekklesia* of the Lord (Num. 16:3; Deut. 7:6). It is possible, in fact, for the Messiah-Son of Man to speak of his *ekklesia*. In this capacity he also can say that he will "build" this people. There is no contradiction here with the fact that this building is the work of God.[178]

Cullmann concluded that traditional Catholic exegesis was correct. Peter, as Jesus' designated successor, was the rock on which the church would be built.[179] However, the passage contained no allusions to successors of Peter.[180] Cullmann's work brought him to the forefront of ecumenical affairs, prompting Karl Barth to comment that Cullmann's tombstone would bear the words *Advisor to Three Popes*.

3.3. New Testament Christology. *The Christology of the New Testament* (1957; ET: 1959) called for a return to form criticism as a means to recovering the historical Jesus. "The knowledge that the Gospels are confessions of faith and that the early Church's faith in Christ is the real creator of the Gospel tradition does not justify an absolute historical scepticism which refuses to use these confessions of faith as historical sources at all. On the contrary, this knowledge should encourage us to use the Church's faith in Christ positively as a means of discovering historical reality."[181] Cullmann proceeded to develop a functional Christology based on the titles of Jesus, which he arranged chronologically, using form criticism to "arrive at Jesus' self-consciousness."[182] By distinguishing passages where writers express their own view from those that report "the words of Jesus himself," Cullmann believed that he had found "an objective criterion."

Cullmann identified four categories of titles applied to Jesus: (1) titles that referred to his earthly work, such as prophet, (suffering) servant of

---

178. Cullmann, *Peter*. 197.
179. In Matt 16:18 both the English and the Greek differentiate between Peter and the rock: "And I tell you, you are Peter [Πέτρος], and on this rock [πέτρᾳ] I will build my church." Cullmann maintained that both words translated the Aramaic *kepha*. It is transliterated as Κηφᾶς (Cephas) in some passages in John and Paul (John 1:42; 1 Cor 1:12; 3:22; 9:5; 15:5; Gal 1:18; 2:9, 11, 14). In other contexts *kepha* was not used as a name, but was a common noun meaning "stone" (Cullmann, *Peter*, 20–21).
180. Cullmann, *Peter*, 213.
181. Oscar Cullmann, *Die Christologie des Neuen Testaments* (Tübingen: Mohr Siebeck, 1957); ET: *The Christology of the New Testament*, trans. Shirley C. Guthrie and Charles A. M. Hall (London: SCM, 1959; 2nd ed., 1963), 7.
182. Cullmann, *The Christology of the New Testament*, 7.

God, and high priest; (2) titles that referred to his future work, such as Messiah and Son of Man; (3) titles that referred to his present work, such as Lord and savior; and (4) titles that referred to preexistence, such as Logos, Son of God, and his designation as God. Cullmann concluded, "Whatever particular function may be under consideration, the identity of the pre-existent, present or coming Christ with Jesus of Nazareth is certain only when it is recognized that the real centre of all revelation is the Incarnate One."[183]

> Because the first Christians see God's redemptive revelation in Jesus Christ, for them it is his very nature that can be known only in his work—fundamentally in the central work accomplished in the flesh. Therefore, in the light of the New Testament witness, all mere speculation about his nature is an absurdity. Functional Christology is the only kind which exists. Therefore all Christology is *Heilsgeschichte*, and all *Heilsgeschichte* is Christology.[184]

3.4. Time and Salvation History. The idea of *Heilsgeschichte* gained currency in the nineteenth century through the Erlangen confessional theologian J. C. K. Hofmann (1810–77). Hofmann saw world history rooted in the Trinitarian character of God and the predestination of humankind to be one with God.[185] For Cullmann, God's saving actions in Christ were the dominant theme of theology.

The foundations of Cullmann's position were laid in *Christ and Time: The Primitive Christian Conception of Time and History*,[186] which was published in German a year after the end of the World War II. In conscious opposition to Schweitzer, Bultmann, and Barth, Cullmann developed a linear view of time. The decisive point in that line was the resurrection of Christ. With the war fresh in mind, Cullmann argued that "hope for the future can now be supported by faith in the past, faith in the already concluded decisive battle. That which has already happened offers the solid guarantee for that which will still take place.

---

183. Cullmann, *The Christology of the New Testament*, 323–24.
184. Cullmann, *The Christology of the New Testament*, 326.
185. Brown, *Jesus in European Protestant Thought*, 244–48. Hofmann wrote extensively on prophecy and fulfillment.
186. Cullmann, *Christus und Zeit* (Zollikon-Zürich: Evangelischer, 1946; 3rd ed., 1962); ET: *Christ and Time: The Primitive Christian Conception of Time and History*, trans. Floyd V. Filson (Philadelphia: Westminster; London: SCM, 1951; rev. ed., 1964).

The hope of the final victory is so much the more vivid because of the unshakably firm conviction that the battle that decides the victory has already taken place."[187]

Cullmann replied to critics and reiterated his theme in *Heil als Geschichte. Heilsgeschichtliche Existenz im Neuen Testament* (1965).[188] The English title *Salvation in History*[189] is a précis of the German, which literally means "Salvation as History: Salvation-History Existence in the New Testament." Schweitzer's "consistent eschatology" amounted to "the progressive abandonment of eschatology, that is, a 'consistent de-eschatologizing.'"[190] "In Bultmann's interpretation, the essence of Jesus' expectation is seen as something other than the end of all things soon to come in the temporal sense. For the Bultmann school it is rather an 'always standing in the situation of decision.'"[191] Neither here nor in the earlier book was it Cullmann's intention to treat the New Testament concept of time in and of itself; his aim was to examine the temporal situation in the New Testament.[192]

Eschatology embraces all the saving events beginning with the incarnation and concluding with the *parousia*. Drawing on the D-day and V-day terminology of World War II, Cullmann reiterated: "The decisive battle has already been won. But the war continues until a certain, though not as yet definite, Victory Day when the weapons will at last be still. The decisive battle would be Christ's death and resurrection, and Victory Day his *parousia.*"[193]

To the Bultmann school, Cullmann was uncritical and misguided in adopting Luke's eschatology as the eschatology of the entire New Testament.[194] Cullmann conceded, "The faith making the proclaimer an object of the *kerygma* . . . allowing the proclaimer to become the one

---

187. Cullmann, *Christ and Time*, 86–87 (Cullmann's emphasis).

188. Cullmann, *Heil als Geschichte. Heilsgeschichtliche Existenz im Neuen Testament* (Tübingen: Mohr Siebeck, 1965).

189. Cullmann, *Salvation in History*, draft translation prepared by Sidney G. Gowers and completed by the staff of the SCM (London: SCM, 1967).

190. Cullmann, *Salvation in History*, 29.

191. Cullmann, *Salvation in History*, 31.

192. Cullmann, *Salvation in History*, 11–16.

193. Cullmann, *Salvation in History*, 44.

194. Philipp Vielhauer, "Zum 'Paulinismus' der Apostelgeschichte," *EvT* 10 (1950–51): 1–16; ET: "On the Paulinism of Acts," trans. Wm. C. Robinson Jr. and V. P. Furnish, in *Studies in Luke-Acts*, ed. L. E. Keck and J. L. Martyn (London: SPCK, 1966), 33–50; Hans Conzelmann, *Die Mitte der Zeit* (Tübingen: Mohr Siebeck, 1953, 1957); ET: *The Theology of St Luke*, trans. Geoffrey Buswell (London: Faber and Faber, 1960); cf. Cullmann, *Salvation in History*, 45–46.

proclaimed, arose for the first time in the early Church."[195] But in light of the Easter events "it becomes clear to the disciples that not only the events, but also the revelation *that* these were really saving events, could already have been available to them at the time. It becomes evident that there was *already an interpretation, a kerygma*, reaching back to Jesus himself."[196] The tension between the "already" and the "not yet" goes back to Jesus himself. "We conclude that in Jesus' preaching the present which extends beyond his death is *already the end*. But this does not in any was justify asserting that Jesus is the end of all salvation history. *The end time is, on the contrary, understood as belonging completely to salvation history, since each of its periods, short as they may be, has its own significance and is distinguished from others.*"[197]

3.5. The Johannine Circle. Cullmann formally retired in 1972. Retirement gave him opportunity to pull together ideas regarding the Fourth Gospel developed over many years and produce a sketch of how John's Gospel might relate to the historical Jesus. An invitation from the Protestant faculty of the Ludwig-Maximilians-University of Munich gave Cullmann the opportunity to outline these ideas in a book on *The Johannine Circle* (1976).[198] He proposed the following timeline of developmental stages, which pointed back to Jesus himself: "special Hellenist group in the early community in Jerusalem—Johannine circle of disciples—disciples of the Baptist—heterodox marginal Judaism."[199]

Cullmann remarked that he was not alone in observing that the Synoptic Gospels "have a saying in Q with a 'Johannine' ring (Matt. 11:27; Luke 10:22), which stands out like an erratic block." The NRSV translation of Matthew reads: "All things have been handed over to me by my Father; and no one knows the Son except the Father, and no one knows the Father except the Son and anyone to whom the Son chooses to reveal him." Cullmann asked, "Is there not a recollection even in the synoptics that Jesus spoke about some things only rarely, and in a special way?"[200]

---

195. Cullmann, *Salvation in History*, 107.
196. Cullmann, *Salvation in History*, 105.
197. Cullmann, *Salvation in History*, 230 (Cullmann's emphasis).
198. Cullmann, *Die johanneische Kreis, sein Platz im Spätjudentum, in der Jüngerschaft Jesu und im Urchristentum* (Tübingen: Mohr Siebeck, 1975); ET: *The Johannine Circle: Its Place in Judaism, among the Disciples of Jesus and in Early Christianity—A Study in the Origin of John*, trans. John Bowden (London: SCM, 1975; repr., 1976).
199. Cullmann, *The Johannine Circle*, 87.
200. Cullmann, *The Johannine Circle*, 94; cf. 81.

The No Quest in Europe after World War II

Cullmann rejected the proposal that Jesus might have taught secret doctrines. On the other hand, it was probable that Jesus spoke to his disciples in different ways at different times. As death became an increasing probability Jesus may have become more explicit. Cullmann hypothesized that *two* groups of disciples emerged, one linked with Peter and Galilee and another linked with "the beloved disciple." Cullmann called it the "Johannine circle." "One would be more important by virtue of its number and the continuity of its common life, and would be represented by Peter; the other represented by the beloved disciple, would be smaller and rest upon a more inward relationship. Were this to be so, our customary picture of the beginnings of Christianity would have to be revised in this direction."[201]

3.6. Cullmann in Retrospect. To conservatives on both sides of the Atlantic, Cullmann was a heroic defender of the faith. However, aspects of his work provoked criticism. James Barr criticized Cullmann's methodology in dealing with time. The root trouble was that Cullmann was working from "a lexical structure of hypostatized words."[202] More recently Bruce J. Malina urged the need for a socially oriented perspective in his article "Christ and Time: Swiss or Mediterranean?"[203] In some ways Cullmann appears to anticipate the "Third Quest of the historical Jesus" in his rejection of Bultmannian skepticism and in his global hypotheses designed to throw light on the historicity of the gospel tradition. In the end he was closer to Kähler in merging *Heilsgeschichte* with the Jesus of history. Perhaps Cullmann's most enduring legacy was

---

201. Cullmann, *The Johannine Circle*, 94. Cullmann insisted that the date of the composition and redaction of John must be distinguished from the origin of the Johannine circle (95–99). The text of John indicates that the gospel was edited a while after it was written (John 21:24). The passage also mentions "the disciple whom Jesus loved," a potential rival to Peter, who vouched for the truth of the narrative (John 21:20–24). Cullmann thought that tradition was probably wrong in identifying John the son of Zebedee as the author of the gospel. But the original author may have been the "beloved disciple" of Jesus who lived to an old age.

Cullmann suggested that the original composition was as early as that of the Synoptic Gospels. It represented tradition of "heterodox Judaism" not far removed from that of Jesus himself (93). Cullmann noted that Luke especially with his narrative of the mission of seventy (seventy-two) disciples (Luke 10) reflected Gen 10 and a concern with the nations beyond Israel (93).

John was widely circulated in gnostic circles, though its redaction should not be placed as contemporary with the emergence of the major gnostic schools (96). Cullmann favored Syria as the place of origin, though Samaria, Transjordan, and Asia were also possible (98–99).

202. James Barr, *Biblical Words for Time*, SBT 33 (London: SCM; Naperville, IL: Allenson, 1962), 146.

203. Bruce J. Malina, *The Social World of Jesus and the Gospels* (New York: Routledge, 1996), 179–214.

The European Scene

in his work drawing attention to the importance of Peter in Matthew and to development of Johannine tradition.

Peter, the Rock, and the Church. The interpretation and significance of the sayings about the rock and the church (Matt 16:17–19) has been hotly disputed both before and after the Protestant Reformation.[204] Contemporary Catholic exegetes explore the question with caution. John P. Meier reminded readers that in context *ekklēsia* suggested the community of Israel in its wilderness wanderings rather than the post-Easter church.[205] Cullmann departed from Protestant tradition, when he identified Simon as Peter—*petros*—the rock on which Christ would build his church.

Since his groundbreaking book on *Peter*, discussions of Peter and New Testament passages concerning his role have become less adversarial and more ecumenical. They include the report sponsored by the United States Lutheran–Roman Catholic dialogue *Peter in the New Testament* (1973)[206] and major biblical commentaries on Matthew. Among them are the reception critical studies of Ulrich Luz.[207] Major monographs on Peter are Martin Hengel's *Saint Peter: The Underestimated Apostle* (2010),[208] and the two studies by Markus Bockmuehl, *The Remembered Peter in Ancient Reception and Modern Debate* (2010) and *Simon Peter in Scripture and Memory* (2012).[209] These works are supplemented by the Edinburgh conference on Peter (2013) and the papers edited by Helen K. Bond and Larry W. Hurtado under the title *Peter in Early Christianity* (2015).[210]

---

204. See, e.g., H. Burn-murdoch, *The Development of the Papacy* (London: Faber & Faber, 1954).

205. John P. Meier, *A Marginal Jew: Rethinking the Historical Jesus*, vol. 3, *Companions and Competitors*, ABRL (New York: Doubleday, 2001), 221–38, esp. 229–30.

206. Raymond E. Brown, Karl P. Donfried, and John Reumann, eds., *Peter in the New Testament: A Collaborative Assessment by Protestant and Catholic Scholars* (Minneapolis: Augsburg, 1973).

207. Ulrich Luz, *Das Evangelium nach Matthäus*, EKKNT 1.1–2 (Zürich: Benziger; Neukirchen-Vluyn: Neukirchener, 1985–89); ET: *Matthew*, Hermeneia, 3 vols., trans. J. E. Crouch (Minneapolis: Augsburg, 2001–7); Luz, "Das Primatwort Matthäus 16.17–19 aus wirkungsgeschichtlicher Sicht," *NTS* 37 (1991): 415–33; ET: "The Primacy Saying of Matthew 16:17–19 from the Perspective of Its Effective History," in *Studies in Matthew*, trans. R. Selle (Grand Rapids: Eerdmans, 2005), 165–82.

208. Martin Hengel, *Saint Peter: The Underestimated Apostle*, trans. Thomas H. Trapp (Grand Rapids: Eerdmans, 2010).

209. Markus Bockmuehl, *The Remembered Peter in Ancient Reception and Modern Debate*, WUNT 262 (Tübingen: Mohr Siebeck, 2010); Bockmuehl, *Simon Peter in Scripture and Memory: The New Testament Apostle in the Early Church* (Grand Rapids: Baker Academic, 2012).

210. Helen K. Bond and Larry W. Hurtado, eds., *Peter in Early Christianity* (Grand Rapids: Eerdmans, 2015).

The No Quest in Europe after World War II

Hengel's investigation of Peter is marked by the meticulous encyclopedic scholarship that characterized his other writings. He acknowledged Cullmann's work as *remaining foundational*.[211] The first part of Hengel's book was devoted to Peter, the Rock, Paul, and the Gospel Tradition. Matthew 16:17–19 raised three questions: Who was responsible for this textual unit? When did it come into existence? Why did the evangelist insert it as a "special unit" or conceptualize it himself?

In answering his first question, Hengel showed how the passage was integral to Matthew's gospel. *Binding* and *loosing* were rabbinic terms used in disciplinary situations. The author of Matthew was a first-century Jewish Christian scribe who recognized the importance of discipline in the post-70 CE situation. He recognized the authority given to Peter that would have validity on "earth" and in "heaven." The keys had to do with the proclamation and confession of Jesus as "'the Messiah, the son of the living God' (16:16) and the one who brings the reign of God."[212]

In answer to his second question about the time of origin of Matthew 16:17–19, Hengel located the gospel's composition between 90 and 100 CE in southern Syria or on the border between Syria and Palestine. The author looked back on Peter "as someone who was for him, a unique authority of the past, one who had a martyr's death in Rome approximately one generation earlier, presumably within the context of Nero's persecution."[213] The "gates of Hades" (πύλαι ᾅδου, *pulai hadou*) through which Jesus himself, and in due course Peter and others passed, would not overpower (οὐ κατισχύσουσιν, *ou katischysousin*) "my community" (μου τὴν ἐκκλησίαν, *mou tēn ekklēsian*). The "gates of Hades" were the "gates of the realm of death."[214]

Hengel's third question was about whether Matthew 16:17–19 was a "special unit" inserted in the gospel or a free composition of the author. Hengel observed that the saying about Simon as the "Man of Rock" presented the climax of the entire gospel and along with the starkly contrasting first passion prediction was unique in the entire New Testament. "In no other passage is any particular disciple selected for particular

---

211. Hengel, *Saint Peter*, 1.
212. Hengel, *Saint Peter*, 4.
213. Hengel, *Saint Peter*, 5.
214. Hengel, *Saint Peter*, 6; cf. Pss. Sol. 16:2; Wis. 16:13; 3 Macc. 5:51. An additional Old Testament reference is the allusion to being confined to the "gates of Sheol" (Isa 38:10). "Gates of death" corresponds to "death's door" in modern parlance. A further aspect of the "gates of Hades" will be discussed below.

emphasis in any comparable way."[215] The force of Hengel's remark is made evident by Matthew's narrative of what followed Jesus' injunction "not to tell anyone that he was the Messiah" (16:20).

> From that time on, Jesus began to show his disciples that he must go to Jerusalem and undergo great suffering at the hands of the elders and chief priests and scribes, and be killed, and on the third day be raised. And Peter took him aside and began to rebuke him, saying, "God forbid it, Lord! This must never happen to you." But he turned and said to Peter, "Get behind me, Satan! You are a stumbling block to me; for you are setting your mind not on divine things but on human things. (Matt 16:21–23)

The Aramaic name *kepha* was a nickname Jesus gave to Simon.[216] The Greek form Πέτρος (*Petros*) superseded the given name Simon at an early date (possibly beginning with the Hellenists in Jerusalem). It signified Peter's unique role rather than his character or spiritual qualities.[217] Also important was the role of Mark as the disciple of Peter and as transmitter of Peter's reminiscences in the gospel of Mark. Mark's gospel was basic to the synoptic tradition of Matthew and Luke.[218] In the second part of *Saint Peter* Hengel explored "The Family of Peter and Other Apostolic Families." It contains an overview of narratives in which families, especially women, played an important part in Jesus' activity.[219]

In *Simon Peter in Scripture and Memory* Markus Bockmuehl cautioned against a hasty, overoptimistic quest of a "historical Peter" on the grounds that so much of the information about Peter is fragmentary

---

215. Hengel, *Saint Peter*, 8. Hengel noted that despite the prominence given to the Beloved Disciple in the Fourth Gospel, it was Peter who was given the threefold mandate to "feed my sheep" (John 21:15–17).

216. There may even be an implied contrast between the names Cephas and Caiaphas, suggesting that Simon would supersede the Jewish high priest in the new people of God.

217. Hengel, *Saint Peter*, 22–36; cf. 100–102.

218. Hengel, *Saint Peter*, 36–48; cf. Hengel, *Studies in the Gospel of Mark*, trans. John Bowden (Philadelphia: Fortress, 1985); Hengel, "Probleme des Markusevangeliums," in *Das Evangelium und die Evangelien. Vorträge vom Tübinger Symposion 1982*, WUNT 28, ed. Peter Stuhlmacher (Tübingen: Mohr Siebeck, 1983), 221–65; ET: "Literary, Theological, and Historical Problems in the Gospel of Mark," in *The Gospel and the Gospels*, ed. Peter Stuhlmacher, trans. John Bowden and John Vriend (Grand Rapids: Eerdmans, 1991), 209–51. Hengel vigorously defended the traditions reported by Papias and Irenaeus regarding Peter and Mark (Eusebius, *Hist. eccl.* 3.39; 5.8).

219. Hengel, *Saint Peter*, 103–10.

and vague.[220] His approach rested on two principles: the text's implied readers and its early effective history.[221] The apostle is always *somebody's* Peter, whether friend or opponent, "rather than neutrally or objectively recoverable figure. And from the earliest days, that somebody turns out to be, above all, the ecclesial community in all its remarkable diversity of practice, belief, and understanding."[222]

Simon Peter in Scripture and Memory has three parts. Part 1 is devoted to canon and memory. Bockmuehl noted differences, omissions, and convergence. Among the differences are the accounts of Simon's initial call.[223] Matthew 4:18–22 and Mark 1:16–20 are in substantial agreement. Both depict Simon and his brother Andrew casting their nets into the Sea of Galilee. Jesus calls them to follow him, and he will make them "fishers of men [ἁλιεῖς ἀνθρώπων]." Bockmuehl detected an intertextual echo of Jeremiah 16:15–16. Luke's version (5:1–11) features two boats, a massive catch of fish (to which Jesus has directed Peter, entirely omitting Andrew). However, in the Fourth Gospel Andrew, having discovered Jesus as the Messiah, introduced Peter to Jesus, whereupon Jesus named him Cephas, which John translated as Peter (1:42).

By way of personal comment, I would like to add that Bockmuehl's account of the call of the first disciples represents Christian reception, which saw nothing untoward in Jesus' charismatic call to radical discipleship. It suggested the model response of total commitment, even if it meant abandoning one's job and security for oneself and one's family. The reception by outsiders was not so sanguine. The call of disciples sounded alarm bells, warning of the formation of an apostate splinter group in Israel. As noted above in chapter 1, the rejection of Jesus by the Jerusalem authorities was rooted in the fear that Jesus might fit the profile of the apostate prophet that performed signs and wonders in order to lead astray. This fear resulted in the Beelzebul charge, which followed the calling of the Twelve (Mark 3:22; cf. Deut 13:1–16). From that point on, Jesus' relations with the Jerusalem authorities went irrevocably downhill.

Bockmuehl went on to discuss accounts of Peter as confidant and representative, Peter in the passion narrative, Peter in the Acts of the Apostles, Peter in the letters of Paul, and the Petrine letters. He drew the

---

220. Bockmuehl, *Simon Peter in Scripture and Memory*, 3.
221. Bockmuehl, *Simon Peter in Scripture and Memory*, 17.
222. Bockmuehl, *Simon Peter in Scripture and Memory*, xv.
223. Bockmuehl, *Simon Peter in Scripture and Memory*, 71; cf. 64.

general conclusion that "the formative picture is surprisingly vague and incomplete in biographical terms, considering his prominence in the original circle of the Twelve. Yet there is enough to identify Peter as the premier disciple of Jesus, however flawed, and as a leading figure in the Jerusalem church and in Christianity's outreach beyond Palestine."[224] Yet the New Testament was remarkably silent about what happened to Peter.[225]

Bockmuehl's focus was primarily on internal Christian reception even in conflicts, such as the tensions between Peter and Paul. Paul's comments about Cephas and "pillars" of the church in Galatians 1–2 were not invented by Paul. They rested on tradition in the Syrian church that was also echoed in Matthew 16:17–19.[226] "Matthew's profile of Peter's place in the universal church closely dovetails with the significance of the Jesus tradition itself in all mainstream Christian circles."[227]

Parts 2 and 3 of *Simon Peter in Scripture and Memory* focused on Peter in the traditions of Christian churches of the East and the West, with the two case studies of history and memory. The work was characterized by considerable erudition and lucidity in marshaling and interpreting data on the reception of Peter and preservation of his memory. However, the focus remained on Christian perceptions. It left undone the attempt to understand the memories of opponents.

The issue on which Bockmuehl differed most from Cullmann was over Cullmann's insistence that Peter's office died with him. Rather, "Peter's memory embodies the archetype of an apostolic ministry that serves the entire church, a task of pastoral service that continues while the church continues. It is in this sense, above all, that Peter is remembered as the rock on which the church is built, as nourisher and pastor of Christ's sheep, as a caretaker of the kingdom's keys, as binder and looser."[228]

---

224. Bockmuehl, *Simon Peter in Scripture and Memory*, 32.

225. Robert Gundry has recently argued that according to the Matthean evangelist, Peter became an apostate. See Robert H. Gundry, *Peter: False Disciple and Apostate according to Saint Matthew* (Grand Rapids: Eerdmans, 2015). Although I appreciate Gundry's perceptive exegesis and insights, I remain utterly unconvinced by his thesis. At the end of the Matthean gospel, the Eleven meet the risen Jesus and receive from him his commission to evangelize the world (Matt 28:16–20). The Eleven must include Peter, for Judas Iscariot, who betrayed Jesus and committed suicide, is the only one of the Twelve who no longer exists. Readers of the gospel of Matthew would assume that Peter was one of the eleven and as such had been restored to his place among the apostles.

226. Bockmuehl, *Simon Peter in Scripture and Memory*, 75.

227. Bockmuehl, *Simon Peter in Scripture and Memory*, 77; cf. Luz, *Matthew*, 2:482; W. D. Davies and Dale C. Allison Jr., *Matthew*, 3 vols, ICC (Edinburgh: T&T Clark, 1988–97), 2:602–52, here 651.

228. Bockmuehl, *Simon Peter in Scripture and Memory*, 183.

The No Quest in Europe after World War II

Bockmuehl passed over the importance of Psalm 118. Hengel noted Psalm 118:2 only in a footnote on terminology regarding stone.[229] Yet there is reason to think that Psalm 118 had wider significance.[230] Joachim Jeremias recognized it as one of the Hallel Psalms (i.e., Pss 114–118) recited during the Passover meal, which he interpreted eschatologically.[231]

In the history of interpretation, Catholic exegetes interpreted the gates of hell as an allusion to heretics and schismatics who sought to undermine the church. Protestant exegetes saw them as a picture of the onslaught of pope and emperor on the Reformation. Both interpretations exemplified hermeneutics without exegesis. Hades/Sheol was not the abode of Satan but the realm of the dead. Gates do not attack; they open to allow entry and exit and close to deny them. As Hengel and others recognized, *gates of hades* was an idiom for what today we might call "death's door."

Jerusalem had gates. So had the temple. The opening of the temple gates symbolized admission to the holy presence of God, the rock of salvation (Pss 18:1–6, 46; 24:3–7). Psalm 118 was a psalm of thanksgiving uttered by one, perhaps a king, who once was like a stone that the builders rejected but now was the chief cornerstone (v. 22). Psalm 118 was a psalm of ritual admission in which the supplicant sought admission to the temple in order to give thanks (vv. 28–29). Standing outside the supplicant cried: "Open to me the gates of righteousness, that I may enter through them and give thanks to the Lord" (v. 19). The priests from inside the temple replied: "This is the gate of the Lord; the righteous shall enter through it" (v. 20).

My hypothesis for explaining the course of events from Peter's confession to Jesus' action in the temple suggests that Jesus himself planned a reenactment of Psalm 118. The hypothesis suggests that Psalm 118:18 contains the clue that connects Peter's confession with the sequence of events that led to Jesus' action in the temple, the decision to arrest Jesus, the blasphemy charge, and the crucifixion. It began with Peter's confession of Jesus as the Christ, which initiated the pilgrimage from Caesarea

---

229. Hengel, *Saint Peter*, 73n71.

230. Colin Brown, "The Gates of Hell and the Church," in *Church, Word, and Spirit: Historical and Theological Essays in Honor of Geoffrey W. Bromiley*, ed. James E. Bradley and Richard A. Muller (Grand Rapids: Eerdmans, 1987), 15–44; Brown, "The Gates of Hell: An Alternative Approach," *SBL 1987 Seminar Papers*, ed. Kent Harold Richards (Atlanta: Scholars, 1987), 357–67.

231. Jeremias, *The Eucharistic Words of Jesus*, 255–62.

Philippi in the north to Jerusalem in the south. The intended goal was to enact the ritual prescribed in Psalm 118. However, in the background was the virtually certain knowledge—based on past encounters with temple authorities—that Jesus would be rejected. Instead of being "the gates of righteousness," the temple gates would prove to be "the gates of Sheol." Nevertheless, they would "not prevail" over Christ's community.

In other words, the saying in Matthew 16:18 was a cryptic, oracular form of the passion prediction that is spelled out in the paraphrase that is generally called the first passion prediction: "From that time on, Jesus began to show his disciples that he must go to Jerusalem and undergo great suffering at the hands of the elders and chief priests and scribes, and be killed, and on the third day be raised" (Matt 16:21; cf. Mark 8:31; Luke 9:22). Matthew preserved the cryptic oracle and the paraphrase. Mark and Luke preserved the paraphrase.

Some scholars interpret the words "Blessed is the one who comes in the name of the Lord" (Matt 21:9; Mark 11:9; Luke 19:38; John 12:13; Ps 118:26 RSV) as part of the liturgical chanting used by Passover pilgrims as they approached the temple.[232] Perhaps they implied nothing more than that Jesus' presence heightened expectations. In Psalm 118 these words formed part of the thanksgiving *by the welcoming priests* prior to the festal sacrifice: "Blessed is the one who comes in the name of the LORD. We bless you from the house of the LORD" (Ps 118:26). However, when Jesus went into the temple, there was no welcome from the priests inside.

In Mark's narrative Jesus entered the temple, "and when he looked around at everything, as it was already late, he went out to Bethany with the twelve" (Mark 11:11). On this reading, what is called the cleansing of the temple or Jesus' temple action (Matt 21:12–13; Mark 11:15–17; Luke 19:45–46) occurred on the following day and was a symbolic sign of judgment. It led to the decision to destroy Jesus (Mark 11:18–19; Luke 19:47–48), which in turn led to his arrest and the blasphemy accusation on which Jesus was charged and executed.[233]

There is a further aspect of the bearing of Psalm 118 on the actions of Jesus. It may help to elucidate Jesus' stern warning to the disciples "not

---

232. Anthony Harvey, *Jesus and the Constraints of History*, Bampton Lectures 1980 (Philadelphia: Westminster, 1982), 126–27; Brent Kinman, "Jesus Royal Entry into Jerusalem," in *Key Events in the Life of the Historical Jesus*, ed. Darrell L. Bock and Robert L. Webb, WUNT 247 (Tübingen: Mohr Siebeck, 2009), 383–427, here 406–9.

233. For literature, see chap. 1, n167.

to tell anyone that he was the Messiah" (Matt 16:20; Mark 8:30; Luke 9:21) and Jesus' sharp rebuke of Peter (Matt 16:22–23; Mark 8:32–33). Both episodes involve the possibility that Jesus might be deflected from his intended course of action, which had the ultimate goal of entering and being received in the temple. In the former case, recognition of Jesus as the Lord's Anointed based merely on the disciples' word would have been premature and a diversion from Jesus' goal. Likewise, Peter's well-intentioned endeavor to spare Jesus from rejection and suffering would have preempted the goal of entering the temple.

Jesus' sharp response to Peter appears abrupt and puzzling in light of Jesus' previous affirmation of Peter as the rock on which he would build his *ekklēsia*. On closer inspection, it presents a verbal parallel to Matthew's narrative of the temptation regarding the temple. Both episodes contain the phrase ὕπαγε . . . σατανᾶ ("go away . . . Satan")[234] followed by an explanation regarding God's will (Matt 4:10; 16:23; Mark 8:33). Peter had unwittingly become the mouthpiece of Satan.

The above explanation deviates from tradition. However, it presents a hypothesis that links three otherwise disparate puzzling episodes: Peter's confession and the decision to go to Jerusalem, the so-called "Messianic Secret," and Jesus' harsh rebuke of Peter, which followed so soon after his affirmation of Peter.

The Johannine Community and the Gospel of John. Finally, attention may be drawn to discussion of what Cullmann called the "Johannine circle," which he believed might elucidate the differences between John and the synoptic tradition and possibly provide a biblical basis for belief in the preexistence of Christ.[235] It raised two important questions: the meaning and implications of the Father-Son language and the part played by a Johannine community in the composition of the Fourth Gospel.

In connection with the first question, Cullmann drew attention to the Johannine ring of the Q passage (Matt 11:27; Luke 10:22), claiming unique relationship of Jesus with the Father regarding his activities. However, speculation about Jesus as the incarnation of the preexistent Son has scant support from current Johannine scholarship.

---

234. English translations tend to translate the Greek differently in the two passages, presumably in the interests of giving idiomatic translations. The NRSV translates Matt 4:10 as "Away with you, Satan!" and Matt 16:23 as "Get behind me, Satan!" In doing so they obscure the fact that the underlying Greek verb is the same.

235. Cullmann, *The Johannine Circle*, 81, 94.

The European Scene

John 1:1 proclaims the preexistence of the Word (λόγος), not the Son. Craig A. Evans sums up the prologue in John 1:1–18:

> In it Jesus is presented as the fleshly dwelling of the *logos*, that which has existed with God from eternity and that which enlightens the world. As such Jesus represents the fulfillment of eschatological hopes that God (or perhaps his "extensions" such as Word, Glory, Wisdom or Spirit) would someday "tabernacle" among humankind. As the human tabernacle in which the glory of God could be witnessed Jesus conducts his ministry as God's agent, an aspect of his ministry clarified by *shaliach* traditions associated with Moses. But Jesus is an agent vastly superior to Moses, for unlike Moses who only beheld glimpses of God's glory, Jesus *is* God's glory.[236]

With regard to John 10:30—"I and the Father are one"—which occurs in the context of the discourse on the good shepherd, Raymond E. Brown (1928–98) commented:

> It seems worth while to pause for a moment to summarize what we have heard thus far in John about the relations between Father and Son. The Son comes from the Father (viii 42); yet the Father who sent him is with him (viii 29). The Father loves the Son (iii 35); the Son knows the Father intimately (viii 55, x 15). In his mission on earth, the Son can do only what he has seen the Father do (v 19), can judge and speak only as he hears from the Father (v 30). The Son was taught from the Father (viii 28) and has received from Him powers such as that of judgment (v 22) and of giving and possessing life (v 21, 26, vi 57). The Son does the will of the Father (iv 34, vi 38) and has received a command from the Father that concerns his

---

236. Craig A. Evans, *Word and Glory: On the Exegetical and Theological Background of John's Prologue*, JSNT Sup 89 (Sheffield: JSOT Press, 1993), 185–86; cf. Peder Borgen, "God's Agent in the Fourth Gospel" (1968), in *The Interpretation of John*, ed. John Ashton, Issues in Religion and Theology 9 (Philadelphia: Fortress, 1986; 2nd ed., Edinburgh: T&T Clark, 1997), 83–96. The verb translated by the RSV in the phrase "lived among us" is ἐσκήνωσεν (*eskēnosen*). It is perhaps better rendered "dwelt among us." Literally it means "tabernacled among us." It evokes images of the wilderness wanderings of Israel, during which the *glory* of God's presence dwelt in the *tabernacle* (cf. Exod 40:34 "the glory of the LORD filled the tabernacle [ἡ σκηνή]"). The word can also be used in reference to Wisdom (Sophia). God commands Wisdom: "Dwell [κατασκήνωσον] in Jacob" (Sir 24:8).

death and resurrection (x 18). It will be noted that all these relationships between Father and Son are described in function of the Son's dealings with men. It would be the work of later theologians to take this gospel material pertaining to the mission of the Son *ad extra* and draw from it a theology of the inner life of the Trinity.[237]

Rudolf Schnackenburg (1914–2012), whom Pope Benedict XVI described as "probably the most prominent Catholic exegete writing in German in the second half of the twentieth century,"[238] made the comment: "All the passages which have been cited since the Fathers to prove the 'procession' of the Son within the Trinity refer, in the mind of the evangelist, to the temporal mission in the world (8:42; 13:3; 16:27f.; 17:8)."[239]

In the game-changing study *Rhetoric and Reference in the Fourth Gospel* (1992), Margaret Davies situated the Father-Son language that runs throughout John in the social-economic situation of first-century times. The son was the apprentice learning his father's trade by observing what he did. This idea underlies John 5:19: "The Son can do nothing on his own, but only what he sees the Father doing; for whatever the Father does, the Son does likewise." Davies summed up John's scenario as follows:

> When the Gospel uses the father-son metaphor to depict the relationship between God and a human being, it is clear that first-century social conventions are being taken for granted. The Son of God is entirely dependent on his Father. He lives only for the Father (6.57). He does nothing on his own authority but only what he sees or hears the Father doing (8.38; 10:18; 12.49–50; 14:24; 15.15). The Father is his teacher (8.28). The Son is his Father's apprentice . . . (5.19–20). . . .
>
> The Gospel depicts the Son's activity as that of a human agent, acting on the Father's behalf. The Father 'sent' the Son into the

---

237. Raymond E. Brown, *The Gospel according to John*, AB 29 (Garden City, NY: Doubleday, 1966), 407.

238. Joseph Ratzinger, Pope Benedict XVI, *Jesus of Nazareth: From the Baptism in the Jordan to the Transfiguration*, trans. Adrian J. Walker (New York: Doubleday, 2007), xii–xiii.

239. Rudolf Schnackenburg, *The Gospel according to John*, trans. Kevin Smyth (London: Burns & Oates; New York: Herder and Herder, 1968), 1:271.

world to achieve his purpose (5.36–37; 8.16; 10.36; 12.49). Hence the Son has come 'in the Father's name' (5.43; 10.25), and the Father has set his seal on his mission (6.27). He does the Father's works (5.17; 10.25, 37; 14.10), fulfills his commands (15.10), speaks his words (8.38; 12.50; 14.24), does what the Father wills (6.40), looks after his interests (2.16), and drinks from the cup he has given him (18.11). It is therefore appropriate that the Son should be accorded the same honour as the Father (1.14; 5.23; 12.28). Those who hate the Son hate the Father (15.23–24), those who love the Son are loved by the Father (14.21–23; 16.27). To see the Son doing the Father's work is therefore tantamount to seeing the Father (14.9), since the Father dwells in the Son, his agent, as the Son dwells in the Father (10.38; 14.10–11; 17.21). In this sense the Father and the Son are one (10.30) in spite of the fact that the Son acknowledges the Father's superiority (14.28).

The Son can rely upon the Father's support (16.32). It is the Father who bears witness to him (5.37; 8.18) because the Son is making the Father known (8.19; 10.15; 14.7, 10–11; 16.3). The Father honors him (8.54; 12.26; 17.5) and is honoured by him (8.49; 14.13; 15.8). Since the Son is the Father's representative in the world, no one comes to the Father except through him (14.6).[240]

In connection with our second question regarding the Johannine circle, Raymond Brown made an investigation into *The Community of the Beloved Disciple* (1979). In it he offered his interpretation of John 1:14: "And the Word became flesh [ὁ λόγος σὰρξ ἐγένετο] and lived among us, and we have seen his glory, the glory as of the father's only son, full of grace and truth." Brown commented: "Too often we read John 1:14, 'The Word became flesh,' in the light of the Matthean and Lucan infancy narratives and assume that the moment of becoming flesh should be interpreted as the conception/birth of Jesus. There is reason to believe that the evangelist himself regarded the whole human life of Jesus *from its beginning* as the career of the Word-become-flesh."[241]

Brown discussed Cullmann in an appendix on recent reconstructions

---

240. Margaret Davies, *Rhetoric and Reference in the Fourth Gospel*, JSNTSup 69 (Sheffield: Sheffield Academic Press, 1992), 131–32.
241. Raymond E. Brown, *The Community of the Beloved Disciple* (New York: Paulist, 1979), 152–53 (Brown's italics).

of Johannine community.[242] He saw himself close to Cullmann on a number of points: the importance of the Beloved Disciple, the disciples of John the Baptist, the Samaritans, and a core of historical tradition behind the gospel of John. However, Cullmann had oversimplified the situation. (1) It was inadequate to solve the issue by invoking differences of speech without taking account of editorial and theological development. (2) The differences cannot be explained by claiming that John represented different eyewitnesses. (3) The issue could not be reduced by a vague appeal to heterodoxy. (4) More needed to be said about the shaping of Johannine thought by struggle with other Christians and internal division.

Martin Hengel recognized the importance of Cullmann's Johannine-circle hypothesis, but proposed an alternative theory regarding the decisive contribution of "John the Elder" during the decisive period between 30 and 60 CE.[243] James H. Charlesworth made a good case for identifying the anonymous disciple whom Jesus loved (John 13:23; 19:26) with Thomas, who was the disciple who vouched for the truth of the Fourth Gospel (19:35; 21:24).[244] From time to time Lazarus, the first person in the Johannine narrative said to be loved by Jesus (John 11:3: "Lord, he whom you love is ill"), is also mentioned as possibly the Beloved Disciple.[245]

Regretfully this is not the place to pursue discussion of the roles and importance of "John the Elder" and the "Beloved Disciple." What is important is recognition of a band of Jesus' disciples who produced John and who were more or less contemporary with another band who followed Peter and—through Peter's disciple Mark—shaped the synoptic tradition.

---

242. Brown, *The Community of the Beloved Disciple*, 177–78.

243. Martin Hengel, *The Johannine Question*, trans. John Bowden (London: SCM; Philadelphia: Trinity Press International, 1989), 133. This edition has been expanded and published in German in Hengel, *Die Johanneische Frage. Ein Lösungsversuch*, WUNT 67 (Tübingen: Mohr Siebeck, 1993), 324.

244. James H. Charlesworth, *The Beloved Disciple: Whose Witness Validates the Truth of the Gospel of John?* (Valley Forge, PA: Trinity Press International, 1995).

245. For a few examples, see F. V. Filson, "Who Was the Beloved Disciple?," *JBL* 68 (1949): 83–88; J. N. Sanders, "Those Whom Jesus Loved (John XI,5)," *NTS* 1 (1954): 29–41; B. Witherington, "What's in a Name? Rethinking the Historical Figure of the Beloved Disciple in the Fourth Gospel," in *John, Jesus, and History*, vol. 2, *Aspects of Historicity in the Fourth Gospel*, ed. Paul N. Anderson, Felix Just, and Tom Thatcher, Society of Biblical Literature Early Christianity and Its Literature 2 (Atlanta: SBL Press, 2009), 203–12.

ABBREVIATIONS

FOR MOST ABBREVIATIONS, see *The SBL Handbook of Style: For Biblical Studies and Related Disciplines*, 2nd ed. (Atlanta: Society of Biblical Literature, 2014). Additional abbreviations are listed below and provided after the bibliographical entries of works not listed in *The SBL Handbook*.

DJG   *Dictionary of Jesus and the Gospels*
DMBI   *Dictionary of Major Biblical Interpreters*
EHJ   *Encyclopedia of the Historical Jesus*
EP   *Encyclopedia of Philosophy*
HSHJ   *Handbook for the Study of the Historical Jesus*
KGW   *Friedrich Nietzsche, Sämtliche Werke. Kritische Gesamtausgabe*
KSA   *Friedrich Nietzsche, Kritische Studien-Ausgabe*
ODJR   *Oxford Dictionary of the Jewish Religion*
ODNB   *Oxford Dictionary of National Biography*

BIBLIOGRAPHY

NOTE: The following bibliographical entries are listed alphabetically by author's last name. Multiple entries for the same author are listed chronologically by publication year.

Adams, Edward. *The Stars Will Fall from Heaven: Cosmic Catastrophe in the New Testament and Its World*. LNTS 347. New York: T&T Clark, 2007.

———. *Parallel Lives of Jesus: A Guide to the Four Gospels*. London: SPCK; Louisville: Westminster John Knox, 2011.

Adams, Jim W. *The Performative Nature and Function of Isaiah 40–55*. Library of Hebrew Bible/Old Testament Studies 448. New York: T&T Clark, 2006.

Adams, Samuel L. *Social and Economic Life in Second Temple Judea*. Louisville: Westminster John Knox, 2014.

Agnew, Francis H. "The Origin of the NT Apostle-Concept: A Review of Research." *JBL* 105 (1986): 75–96.

Aharoni, Yohanan, Michael Avi-Yonah, Anson F. Rainey, and Ze'ev Safrai. *The Macmillan Bible Atlas*, 3rd ed. New York: Macmillan, 1993.

Ahlstrom, Sydney E., ed. *Theology in America: The Major Protestant Voices from Puritanism to Neo-Orthodoxy*. Indianapolis: Bobbs-Merrill, 1967.

Aichele, George, and Richard Walsh, eds. *Those Outside: Noncanonical Readings of the Canonical Gospels*. New York: T&T Clark International, 2005.

Akala, Adesola Joan. *The Son-Father Relationship and Christological Symbolism in the Gospel of John*. LNTS 505. London: T&T Clark, 2014.

Aland, Kurt, ed. *Synopsis Quattuor Evangeliorum, Locis parallelis evangeliorum apocryphorum et partum adhibitis*. 15th revised ed. Stuttgart: Deutsche Bibelgesellschaft, 2001.

Alberti, G. W. *Briefe betreffend den allerneuesten Zustand der Religion und der Wissenschaften in Gross-Britanien*. Hanover: Johann Christoph Richter, 1752–54.

Alexander, H. G., ed. *The Leibniz-Clarke Correspondence: Together with Extracts from Newton's Principia and Opticks*. New York: Philosophical Library, 1956.

A History of the Quests for the Historical Jesus

Alexander, Philip S. "Rabbinic Biography and the Biography of Jesus: A Survey of the Evidence." In *Synoptic Studies: The Ampleforth Conferences of 1982–1983*, edited by C. M. Tuckett, JSNTSup 7, 19–50. Sheffield: JSOT, 1984.

———. "Jesus and the Golden Rule." In *Hillel and Jesus*, edited by James H. Charlesworth and Loren L. Johns, 363–88. Minneapolis: Fortress, 1997.

Allen, Ethan. *Reason the Only Oracle of Man*. Bennington, VT: Haswell, 1784. Reprint, New York: Kraus Reprint Company, 1970.

Alexander, Loveday. "Ancient Book Production and the Circulation of the Gospels." In *The Gospels for All Christians*, edited by Richard J. Bauckham, 71–105. Grand Rapids: Eerdmans, 1998.

Allen, Leslie C. *Psalms 101–150*. WBC 21. Waco, TX: Word, 1983.

Allen, David M. *The Historical Character of Jesus: Canonical Insights from Outside the Gospels*. Minneapolis: Fortress, 2014.

Allison, Dale C., Jr. *The End of the Ages Has Come: An Early Interpretation of the Passion and Resurrection of Jesus*. Philadelphia: Fortress, 1985.

———. *The New Moses: A Matthean Typology*. Minneapolis: Fortress, 1993.

———. *The Jesus Tradition in Q*. Harrisburg, PA: Trinity Press International, 1997.

———. *Jesus of Nazareth: Millenarian Prophet*. Minneapolis: Fortress, 1998.

———. "Jesus and the Victory of Apocalyptic." In *Jesus and the Restoration of Israel: A Critical Assessment of N. T. Wright's Jesus and the Victory of God*, edited by Carey C. Newman, 126–41. Downers Grove, IL: InterVarsity Press, 1999.

———. *The Intertextual Jesus: Scripture in Q*. Harrisburg, PA: Trinity Press International, 2000.

———. *Resurrecting Jesus: The Earliest Christian Tradition and Its Interpreters*. London and New York: T&T Clark, 2005.

———. *The Historical Christ and the Theological Jesus*. Grand Rapids: Eerdmans, 2009.

———. *Constructing Jesus: Memory, Imagination, and History*. Grand Rapids: Baker Academic, 2010.

Allison, Henry E. *Lessing and the Enlightenment: His Philosophy of Religion and Its Relation to Eighteenth-Century Thought*. Ann Arbor: University of Michigan Press, 1966.

Alonso, Pablo. *The Woman Who Changed Jesus: Crossing Boundaries in Mk 7.24–30*. BTS 11. Leuven: Peeters, 2011.

Altaner, Berthold. *Patrology*. Translated by Hilda C. Graef. Freiburg: Herder; Edinburgh: Nelson, 1958.

Altmann, Alexander. *Moses Mendelssohn: A Biographical Study*. London: Routledge & Kegan Paul, 1973.

Anderson, Hugh. *Jesus and Christian Origins: A Commentary on Modern Viewpoints*. New York: Oxford University Press, 1964.

Anderson, Janice Capel. *Matthew's Narrative Web: Over, and Over, and Over Again*. JSNTSup 91. Sheffield: Sheffield Academic Press, 1994.

Bibliography

Anderson, Janice Capel, and Stephen D. Moore. *Mark and Method: New Approaches to Biblical Studies.* 2nd ed. Minneapolis: Fortress, 2008.

Anderson, Paul N. *The Christology of the Fourth Gospel: Its Unity and Disunity in Light of John 6.* Valley Forge, PA: Trinity Press International, 1996. Reprint, 1997.

Anderson, Paul N., Felix Just, and Tom Thatcher, eds. *John, Jesus, and History.* Vol. 1, *Critical Appraisals of Critical Views.* Atlanta: SBL Press, 2007.

———. *John, Jesus, and History.* Vol. 2, *Aspects of History in the Fourth Gospel.* Atlanta: SBL Press, 2009.

———. *John, Jesus, and History.* Vol. 3, *Glimpses of Jesus through the Johannine Lens.* Atlanta: SBL Press, 2016.

Aner, Karl. *Die Theologie des Lessingzeit.* Halle: Niemeyer, 1929. Reprint, Hildesheim: Georg Olms, 1964.

Angami, Zhodi. *Tribals, Empire and God: A Tribal Reading of the Birth of Jesus in Matthew's Gospel.* New York: T&T Clark, 2017.

Annas, Julia, and Jonathan Barnes. *The Modes of Scepticism: Ancient Texts and Modern Interpretations.* Cambridge: Cambridge University Press, 1985.

Anrich, Ernst, ed. *Die Idee der deutschen Universität. Die fünf Grundschriften aus der Zeit ihrer Neubegründung durch klassischen Idealismus und romantischen Realismus.* Darmstadt: Wissenschaftliche Buchgesellschaft, 1956. Reprint, 1964.

———. *Die Idee der deutschen Universität und die Reform der deutschen Universitäten.* Darmstadt: Wissenschaftliche Buchgesellschaft, 1960.

Anselm. *A Scholastic Miscellany: Anselm to Ockham.* Edited by Eugene R. Fairweather. LCC 10. London: SCM; Philadelphia: Westminster, 1956.

Apperloo-Borsma, Karla, and Herman J. Selderhuis. *Power of Faith: 450 Years of the Heidelberg Catechism.* Göttingen: Vandenhoeck & Ruprecht, 2013.

Aquinas, Thomas. *Summa Theologiae.* Latin text and English translation by Blackfriars. 60 vols. London: Eyre & Spottiswoode; New York: McGraw-Hill, 1963–66.

Aristotle. *The Complete Works of Aristotle.* Revised Oxford Translation. Edited by Jonathan Barnes. 2 vols. Princeton / Bollingen Series LXXI.2. Princeton: Princeton University Press, 1984.

———. *Poetics.* Translated by Stephen Halliwell. LCL 199. Cambridge, MA: Harvard University Press, 1995.

———. *The "Art" of Rhetoric.* Translated by John Henry Freese. LCL 193. Cambridge, MA: Harvard University Press, 1926. Reprint, 2006.

Arminius. *The Works of Arminius.* Translated by James and Williams Nichols. 3 vols. 1825–75. Reprint, with introduction by Carl Bangs. Grand Rapids: Baker, 1999.

Arnal, William E. *Jesus and the Village Scribes: Galilean Conflicts and the Setting of Q.* Minneapolis: Fortress, 2001.

Arnal, William E., and Michael Desjardins, eds. *Whose Historical Jesus?* Waterloo, Ontario: Wilfred Laurier University Press, 1997.

Arnold, Charles Harvey. *Near the Edge of Battle: A Short History of the Divinity School and the "Chicago School of Theology"*. Chicago: Divinity School Association, University of Chicago, 1966.

Arnold, Clinton E. *Ephesians: Power and Magic; The Concept of Power in Ephesians in Light of Its Historical Setting*. SNTSMS 63. Cambridge: Cambridge University Press, 1989.

Aslan, Reza. *Zealot: The Life and Times of Jesus of Nazareth*. New York: Random House, 2013.

Asgeirsson, Jón Ma., Kristin de Troyer, and Marvin W. Meyer, eds. *From Quest to Q: Festschrift James M. Robinson*. BETL 146. Leuven: Leuven University Press; Peeters, 2000.

Ashton, John. *Understanding the Fourth Gospel*. Oxford: Clarendon, 1991; 2nd ed., Oxford: Oxford University Press, 2007.

———. *The Gospel of John and Christian Origins*. Minneapolis: Fortress, 2014.

Ashton, John, ed. *The Interpretation of John*. Issues in Religion and Theology 9. Philadelphia: Fortress, 1986; 2nd ed., Studies in New Testament Interpretation. Edinburgh: T&T Clark, 1997.

Astour, Michael C. "Melchizedek." In *ABD*, 4:684–86.

———. "Salem." In *ABD*, 5:905.

Athanasius. *Contra Gentes and De Incarnatione*. Edited and translated by Robert W. Thomson. Oxford: Clarendon, 1971.

Attridge, Harold W., and Gohei Hata, eds. *Eusebius, Christianity and Judaism*. Detroit: Wayne State University Press, 1992.

Auerbach, Erich. *Mimesis*. Princeton: Princeton University Press, 1968.

Aulén, Gustaf. *Jesus in Contemporary Historical Research*. Translated by Ingalill H. Hjelm. Philadelphia: Fortress, 1976.

Aune, David E. "Magic in Early Christianity." *ANRW*, 2.23.2 (1980), 1507–57. Reprint in *Apocalypticism, Prophecy, and Magic in Early Christianity: Collected Essays*, 368–420. WUNT 199. Tübingen: Mohr Siebeck, 2006; Grand Rapids: Baker Academic, 2008.

———. *Prophecy in Early Christianity and the Ancient Mediterranean World*. Grand Rapids: Eerdmans, 1983.

———. *The New Testament in Its Literary Environment*. Philadelphia: Westminster, 1987.

———. "Jesus and the Cynics in First-Century Palestine: Some Critical Considerations." In *Hillel and Jesus*, edited by James H. Charlesworth and Loren L. Johns, 176–92. Minneapolis: Fortress, 1997.

———. *Revelation*. 3 vols. WBC 53A, 53B, 53C. Dallas: Word; Nashville: Nelson, 1997–98.

———. *The Westminster Dictionary of New Testament and Early Christian Literature and Rhetoric*. Louisville: Westminster John Knox, 2003.

Bibliography

———. "Genre Theory and the Genre-Function of Mark and Matthew." In *Jesus, Gospel Tradition and Paul in the Context of Jewish and Greco-Roman Antiquity: Collected Essays II*, 25–56. WUNT 303. Tübingen: Mohr Siebeck, 2013.

———. "Prolegomena to the Study of Oral Tradition in the Hellenistic World." In *Collected Essays II*, 220–55.

Aune, David E., Torrey Seland, and Jarl Henning Ulrichsen, eds. *Neotestamentica et Philonica: Studies in Honor of Peder Borgen*. NovTSup 106. Leiden: Brill, 2003.

Aus, Roger David. *"Caught in the Act," Walking on the Sea, and the Release of Barabbas Revisited*. South Florida Studies in the History of Judaism 157. Atlanta: Scholars, 1998.

Avery-Peck, Alan, Bruce Chilton, William Scott Green, and Gary G. Porton, eds. *A Legacy of Learning: Essays in Honor of Jacob Neusner*. BRLJ 43. Leiden: Brill, 2014.

Bacon, Benjamin Wisner. *An Introduction to the New Testament*. New York: Macmillan, 1902.

———. *The Beginnings of Gospel Story: A Historic-Critical Inquiry into the Sources and Structure of the Gospel according to Mark, with Expository Notes upon the Text, for English Readers*. New Haven, CT: Yale University Press, 1909.

———. *The Fourth Gospel in Research and Debate: A Series of Essays on Problems Concerning the Origin and Value of the Anonymous Writings Attributed to the Apostle John*. New York: Moffat, Yard and Company, 1910.

———. *Jesus the Son of God or Primitive Christology: Three Essays and a Discussion*. New Haven, CT: Yale University Press; London: Oxford University Press, 1911. [The three essays on the titles of Jesus had been previously published in *HTR* (1909–11).]

———. *Is Mark a Roman Gospel?* HTS 15. Cambridge, MA: Harvard University Press; London: Oxford University Press, 1919.

———. *Jesus and Paul: Lectures Given at Manchester College, Oxford, for the Winter Term 1920*. London: Hodder & Stoughton, 1921.

———. *The Gospel of Mark: Its Composition and Date*. New Haven, CT: Yale University Press; London: Oxford University Press, 1925.

———. *The Story of Jesus and the Beginnings of the Church: A Valuation of the Synoptic Record for History and for Religion*. New York: Century, 1927; London: Allen & Unwin, 1928.

———. *Jesus the Son of God*. New York: Holt, 1930.

———. *Studies in Matthew*. New York: Holt, 1930.

———. "Enter the Higher Criticism." In *Contemporary American Theology: Theological Autobiographies*, edited by Vergilius Ferm, 1:1–50.

———. *The Gospel of the Hellenists*. Edited by Carl H. Kraeling. New York: Holt, 1933.

Bacon, Margaret Hope. *Let This Life Speak: The Legacy of Henry Joel Cadbury*. Philadelphia: University of Pennsylvania Press, 1987.

Baeck, Leo. "Harnacks Vorlesungen über das Wesen des Christentums," *Monatsschrift für Geschichte und Wissenschaft des Judentums* 45, Neue Folge 9 (1901): 97–98, 117–20.

Partial translation with introduction by J. Louis Martyn in *Jewish Perspectives on Christianity: Leo Baeck, Martin Buber, Franz Rosenzweig, and Abraham J. Heschel*, edited by Fritz A. Rothschild, 42–45. New York: Continuum, 1996.

———. *Das Wesen des Judentums*. Berlin: Rathausen & Lamm, 1905. 6th ed. Frankfurt am Main: Kaufmann, 1932.

———. *The Essence of Judaism*. Translated by Irving Howe. Based on the translation by V. Grubenwieser and L. Pearl. London: Macmillan, 1936. Reprint, New York: Schocken, 1948.

———. *Judaism and Christianity: Essays*. Translated by Walter Kaufmann. Philadelphia: Jewish Publication Society of America, 1954.

Bagchi, David, and David C. Steinmetz, eds. *The Cambridge Companion to Reformation Theology*. Cambridge: Cambridge University Press, 2004.

Bahrdt, Karl Friedrich. *Ausführung des Plans und Zwecks Jesu. In Briefe an Wahrheit suchende Leser*. 11 vols. Berlin: Mylius, 1784–92.

Bailey, Kenneth E. *Poet and Peasant* (1976); *Through Peasant Eyes* (1980). Combined Edition, *Poet and Peasant and Through Peasant Eyes: A Literary-Cultural Approach to the Parables in Luke*. Grand Rapids: Eerdmans, 1983.

———. *Jacob and the Prodigal: How Jesus Retold Israel's Story*. Downers Grove, IL: IVP Academic, 2003.

———. *Jesus through Middle Eastern Eyes: Cultural Studies in the Gospels*. Downers Grove, IL: IVP Academic, 2008.

———. *The Good Shepherd: A Thousand-Year Journey from Psalm 23 to the New Testament*. Downers Grove, IL: IVP Academic, 2014.

Baillie, D. M. *God Was in Christ: An Essay on Incarnation and Atonement*. London: Faber and Faber; New York: Scribner's, 1948. [The undated paperback reprint contains an appendix on "Christology and Mythology" composed by John Baillie, which was included in the German translation published by Vandenhoeck & Ruprecht.]

Bainton, Roland. *Yale and the Ministry: A History of Education for the Christian Ministry at Yale from the Founding in 1701*. San Francisco: Harper & Row, [1957]; 2nd ed., 1985.

Baird, William. *History of New Testament Research*. 3 vols. Vol. 1, *From Deism to Tübingen*. Vol. 2, *From Jonathan Edwards to Rudolf Bultmann*. Vol. 3, *From C. H. Dodd to Hans Dieter Betz*. Minneapolis: Fortress, 1992–2013.

Baker, A. E. *William Temple and His Message*. Harmondsworth: Penguin, 1946.

Ball, David Mark. *'I Am' in John's Gospel: Literary Function, Background and Theological Implications*. JSNTSup 124. Sheffield: Sheffield Academic Press, 1996.

Bammel, Ernst. "The *Titulus*." In *Jesus and the Politics of His Day*, edited by Ernst Bammel and C. F. D. Moule, 353–64.

Bammel, Ernst, ed. *The Trial of Jesus: Cambridge Studies in Honour of C. F. D. Moule*. SBT Second Series 13. London: SCM, 1970.

Bammel, E., C. K. Barrett, and W. D. Davies eds. *Donum Gentilicium: New Testament Studies in Honour of David Daube*. Oxford: Clarendon, 1978.

Bibliography

Bammel, Ernst, and C. F. D. Moule, eds. *Jesus and the Politics of His Day*. Cambridge: Cambridge University Press, 1984. Reprint, 1992.

Bangs, Carl. *Arminius: A Study in the Dutch Reformation*. 1985. Reprint, Eugene, OR: Wipf & Stock, 1998.

Barber, Michael. "The Historical Jesus and Cultic Restoration Eschatology: The New Temple, the New Priesthood and the New Cult." PhD diss., Fuller Theological Seminary, 2010.

Barbour, Ian G. *Myths, Models, and Paradigms: The Nature of Scientific and Religious Language*. London: SCM; New York: Harper & Row, 1974.

Barclay, John, and John Sweet, eds. *Early Christian Thought in Its Jewish Context*. Studies in Honour of Morna D. Hooker. Cambridge: Cambridge University Press, 1996.

Barker, Margaret. *The Gate of Heaven: The History and Symbolism of the Temple in Jerusalem*. London: SPCK, 1991.

Barnes, Jonathan, ed. *The Cambridge Companion to Aristotle*. Cambridge: Cambridge University Press, 1995. [Barnes is the author of the chapter on "Rhetoric and Poetics," 259–85.]

Barnes, Michael R., and Daniel H. Williams, eds. *Arianism after Arius: Essays on the Development of the Fourth Century Trinitarian Conflicts*. Edinburgh: T&T Clark, 1993.

Barr, James. *The Semantics of Biblical Language*. Oxford: Oxford University Press, 1962.

———. *Biblical Words for Time*. SBT 33. London: SCM; Naperville, IL: Allenson, 1962.

———. *Bible and Interpretation: The Collected Essays of James Barr*. 3 vols. Edited by John Barton. Oxford: Oxford University Press, 2013–14.

———. "Which Language Did Jesus Speak? Some Remarks of a Semitist." In *Bible and Interpretation*, 2:231–46.

———. "Abba Isn't Daddy." In *Bible and Interpretation*, 2:262–80.

Barrett, C. K. *The Gospel according to John: An Introduction with Commentary and Notes on the Greek Text*. London: SPCK; Philadelphia: Westminster, 1955; 2nd ed., 1978.

———. *The New Testament Background: Selected Documents*. London: SPCK; San Francisco: Harper & Row, 1956. Reprint, 1987.

———. *The Gospel of John and Judaism*. Franz Delitzsch Lectures 1967. London: SPCK, 1975.

———. "*Shaliach* and Apostle." In *Donum Gentilicium*, edited by Ernst Bammel et al., 88–102.

Barth, Karl, *Karl Barth: Gesamtausgabe*. Vol. 5, *Karl Barth—Rudolf Bultmann. Briefwechsel 1911–1966*. Edited by Bernd Jaspert. 2nd ed. Zürich: Theologischer, 1996. Partial translation in Geoffrey W. Bromiley, *Karl Barth—Rudolf Bultmann Letters, 1922–1966*. Grand Rapids: Eerdmans, 1981.

Barthel, Pierre. *Interprétation du langage mythique et théologie biblique. Étude de quelques étapes de l'évolution du problème de l'interprétation des représentations d'origine et de structure mythique de la foi Chrétienne*. Leiden: Brill, 1967.

A History of the Quests for the Historical Jesus

Bartholomew, Craig G., Joel B. Green, and Anthony C. Thiselton, eds. *Reading Luke: Interpretation, Reflection, Formation*. Grand Rapids: Zondervan, 2005.

Barton, Stephen C., ed. "Social Values and Structures." In *Dictionary of New Testament Background*, edited by Craig A. Evans and Stanley E. Porter, 1127–34.

———. *The Cambridge Companion to the Gospels* (Cambridge: Cambridge University Press, 2006).

Bartsch, Hans-Werner, ed. *Kerygma and Myth: A Theological Debate*. Translated by Reginald H. Fuller. London: SPCK, 1953.

———. *Kerygma and Myth: A Theological Debate*. Translated by Reginald H. Fuller. 2 vols. London: SPCK, 1962.

———. *Kerygma and Myth: A Theological Debate*. Translated by Reginald H. Fuller. 2 vols. in 1 vol. with enlarged bibliography. London: SPCK, 1972.

Basinger, David, and Randall Basinger. *Philosophy and Miracle: The Contemporary Debate*. Problems in Contemporary Philosophy 2. Lewiston: Mellon, 1986.

Bates, Matthew W. *The Birth of the Trinity: Jesus, God, and Spirit in the New Testament and Early Christian Interpretations of the Old Testament*. Oxford: Oxford University Press, 2015.

Bauckham, Richard. *The Theology of Jürgen Moltmann*. Edinburgh: T&T Clark. 1995.

———. *God Crucified: Monotheism and Christology in the New Testament*. Grand Rapids: Eerdmans, 1998.

———. *The Testimony of the Beloved Disciple: Narrative, History, and Theology in the Gospel of John*. Grand Rapids: Baker Academic, 2007.

———. "The 'Most High' God and the Nature of Early Jewish Monotheism." In *Israel's God and Rebecca's Children*, edited by David B. Capes et al., 39–53.

———. *Jesus and the God of Israel: God Crucified and Other Studies on the New Testament's Christology of Divine Identity*. Grand Rapids: Eerdmans, 2008.

———. *The Jewish World around the New Testament*. WUNT 233. Tübingen: Mohr Siebeck, 2008. Reprint, Grand Rapids: Baker Academic, 2010.

———. *Jesus and the Eyewitnesses: The Gospels as Eyewitness Testimony*. Grand Rapids: Eerdmans, 2006; 2nd ed., 2017.

Bauckham, Richard, ed. *The Gospels for All Christians: Rethinking the Gospel Audiences*. Grand Rapids: Eerdmans, 1998.

Bauckham, Richard, and Carl Mosser, eds. *The Gospel of John and Christian Theology*. Grand Rapids: Eerdmans, 2008.

Bauer, David R. *The Structure of Matthew's Gospel: A Study in Literary Design*. Sheffield: Almond, 1989.

Bauer, David R., and Mark Allan Powell, eds. *Treasures Old and New: Contributions to Matthean Studies*. SBL Symposium Series 1. Atlanta: Scholars, 1996.

Bauer, Walter. *Rechtgläubigkeit und Ketzerei im ältesten Christentum*. BHT 10. Tübingen: Mohr Siebeck, 1934. ET: *Orthodoxy and Heresy in Earliest Christianity*. Edited

Bibliography

by Georg Strecker. Translated by Robert A. Kraft and Gerhard Krodel. NTL. Philadelphia: Fortress, 1971; London: SCM, 1972.

———. *Aufsätze und kleine Schriften*. Edited by Georg Strecker. Tübingen: Mohr Siebeck, 1967.

———. *A Greek-English Lexicon of the New Testament and Other Early Christian Literature*. 3rd ed. Revised and Edited by Frederick William Danker. Based on the earlier English editions by W. F. Arndt and F. W. Gingrich. Chicago, London: University of Chicago Press, 2000. Abbreviated as BDAG.

Baum, Armin D. *Der mündliche Faktor und seine Bedeutung für die synoptische Frage: Analogien aus der antiken Literatur, der Experimentalpsychologie, der Oral Poetry-Forschung und dem rabbinischen Traditionswesen*. Texte und Arbeiten zum neutestamentlichen Zeitalter 49. Tübingen: Francke, 2008.

Baumgarten, Joseph M. "Damascus Document." In *Encyclopedia of the Dead Sea Scrolls*, edited by Lawrence H. Schiffman and James C. VanderKam, 1:16–70.

Baumgarten, S. J. *Nachrichten von einer Hallischen Bibliothek*. 8 vols. Halle: Verlegts Joh. Justinus Gebauer, 1748–51.

———. *Nachrichten von merkwürdigen Büchern*. 12 vols. Halle: Verlegts Joh. Justinus Gebauer, 1752–58.

Baur, Ferdinand Christian. "Apollonius von Tyana und Christus, oder das Verhältnis des Pythagoreismus zum Christenthum." *Tübinger Zeitschrift für Theologie* (1832): 4:3–235. Reprinted in *Drei Abhandlungen zur Geschichte der alten Philosophie und ihres Verhältnisses zum Christentum*, edited by Eduard Zeller, 1–227. Aalen: Scientia, 1876. Reprint, 1978.

———. *Kritische Untersuchungen über die kanonischen Evangelien, ihr Verhältnis zueinander, ihrem Charakter und Ursprung*. Tübingen: Fues, 1847.

———. *Kritische Untersuchungen über die kanonischen Evangelien, ihr Verhältnis zu einander, ihren Charakter und Ursprung*. Tübingen: Fues, 1851.

———. *Das Markusevangelium nach ihrem Urprung und Charakter. Nebst einem Anhang über das Evangelium Marcions*. Tübingen: Fues, 1851.

———. *Das Christentum und die christliche Kirche der drei ersten Jahrhunderte*. 1853. *Kirchengeschichte der drei ersten Jahrhunderte*. Tübingen: Fues, 1860.

———. *Vorlesungen über Neutestamentliche Theologie*. Edited by Ferdinand Friedrich Baur. Leipzig: Fues, 1864.

———. *Paulus, Der Apostel Jesus Christi. Sein Leben und Wirken, seine Briefe and seine Lehre. Ein Beitrag zur kritschen Geschichte des Urchristentums*. 2nd ed. Edited by Eduard Zeller. 2 vols. Leipzig: Fues, 1866.

———. *The Church History of the First Three Centuries*. Edited and translated by Allan Menzies. 2 vols. London: Williams and Norgate, 1878–79.

———. *Ausgewählte Werke in Einzelausgaben*. Edited by Klaus Scholder. 5 vols. Stuttgart and Bad Cannstatt: Fromann, 1963–75.

———. *On the Writing of Church History*. Edited and translated by Peter C. Hodgson. New York: Oxford University Press, 1968.

———. *Lectures on New Testament Theology*. Edited by Peter C. Hodgson. Translated by Robert F. Brown. Oxford: Oxford University Press, 2016.

Bauspiess, Martin, Christof Landmesser, David Linicum, eds. *Ferdinand Christian Baur and the History of Early Christianity*. Translated by Peter C. Hodgson and Robert F. Brown. Oxford: Oxford University Press, 2017.

Beal, Todd S. "Essenes." In *Encyclopedia of the Dead Sea Scrolls*, edited by Lawrence H. Schiffman and James C. VanderKam, 1:62–69.

Beasley-Murray, George R. *Jesus and the Kingdom*. Grand Rapids: Eerdmans, 1986.

———. "The Vision on the Mount: The Eschatological Discourse of Mark 13." *Ex Auditu* 6 (1990): 39–52.

———. *Jesus and the Last Days: The Interpretation of the Olivet Discourse*. Peabody, MA: Hendrickson, 1993.

Beavis, Mary Ann. *Mark's Audience: The Literary and Social Setting of Mark 4:11–12*. JSNTSup 33. Sheffield: Sheffield Academic Press, 1989.

———. *Jesus and Utopia: Looking for the Kingdom of God in the Roman World*. Minneapolis: Fortress, 2006.

Becker, Michael. *Wunder und Wundertätenr im früh rabbinischen Judentum*. WUNT 144. Tübingen: Mohr Siebeck, 2002.

Beeby, C. E. "Doctrinal Significance of a Miraculous Birth." *The Hibbert Journal* 2 (1903–1904): 125–40.

Behr, John. *Irenaeus of Lyons: Identifying Christianity*. Christian Theology in Context. Oxford: Oxford University Press, 2013.

Beilby, James K., and Paul Rhodes Eddy, eds. *The Historical Jesus: Five Views*. [Essays by Robert M. Price, John Dominic Crossan, Luke Timothy Johnson, James D. G. Dunn, Darrell L. Bock.] Downers Grove, IL: IVP Academic, 2009.

Beiser, Frederick C., ed. *The Cambridge Companion to Hegel*. Cambridge: Cambridge University Press, 1993.

———. *The Cambridge Companion to Hegel and Nineteenth-Century Philosophy*. Cambridge: Cambridge University Press, 2008.

Bell, G. K. A. *Randall Davidson, Archbishop of Canterbury*. 2 vols. London: Oxford University Press, 1935; 3rd ed., 1952.

Bell, G. K. A., and D. Adolf Deissmann, eds. *Mysterium Christi: Christological Studies by British and German Theologians*. London: Longmans, Green, 1930.

Bellinger, William H., Jr., and William R. Farmer, eds. *Jesus and the Suffering Servant: Isaiah 53 and Christian Origins*. Harrisburg, PA: Trinity Press International, 1998.

Bendroth, Margaret Lamberts. *A School for the Church: Andover Newton across Two Centuries*. Grand Rapids: Eerdmans, 2008.

Ben-Eliyahu, Eyal, Yehudah Cohn, and Fergus Millar, eds. *Handbook of Jewish Literature*

Bibliography

from Late Antiquity, 135–700 CE. Foreword by Philip Alexander. Oxford: Oxford University Press for the British Academy, 2012.

Ben Ezra, Daniel Stökl. *The Impact of Yom Kippur on Early Christianity: The Day of Atonement from Second Temple Judaism to the Fifth Century*. WUNT 163. Tübingen: Mohr Siebeck, 2003.

Bennett, Zoë, and David B. Gowler, eds. *Radical Christian Voices and Practice: Essays in Honour of Christopher Rowland*. Oxford: Oxford University Press, 2012.

Benson, Bruce Ellis. *Pious Nietzsche: Decadence and Dionysian Faith*. Bloomington, IN: Indiana University Press, 2008.

Benz, Ernst, ed. *Rudolf Ottos Bedeutung für die Religionswissenschaft und die Theologie heute. Zur Hundertjahrsfeier seines Geburtstags 25. September 1969*. Leiden: Brill, 1971.

Berger, Klaus. "Jesus als Pharisäer und frühe Christen als Pharisäer." *NovT* 30 (1988): 231–62.

———. *Im Anfang war Johannes: Datierung und Theologie des vierten Evangeliums*. Stuttgart: Quell, 1997.

———. *Jesus*. Munich: Pattloch, 2007.

———. "The Reliability of the Gospels." In *The Gospels: History and Christology. The Search of Joseph Ratzinger-Benedict XVI–I Vangeli: Storia e Cristologia. La ricerca di Joseph Ratzinger-Benedetto XVI*, edited by Bernardo Estrada, Ermenegildo Manicardi, and Armand Puig i Tàrrech, 2 vols., 1:229–36. Città del Vaticano: Libreria Editrice Vaticana, 2013.

Berkey, Robert E., and Sarah A. Edwards, eds. *Christological Perspectives: Essays in Honor of Harvey K. MacArthur*. New York: Pilgrim, 1982.

Berman, David. "Deism, Immortality, and the Art of Theological Lying." In *Deism, Masonry, and the Enlightenment: Essays Honoring Alfred Owen Aldridge*, edited by J. A. Leo Lemay, 61–78. Newark: University of Delaware Press; London: Associated University Presses, 1987.

———. *A History of Atheism in Britain: From Hobbes to Russell*. New York: Croom Helm, 1988.

Bernier, Jonathan. *Aposynagogos and the Historical Jesus in John: Rethinking the Historicity of the Expulsion Passages*. BibInt Series 122. Leiden: Brill, 2013.

———. *The Quest of the Historical Jesus after the Demise of Authenticity: Toward a Critical Realist Philosophy of History in Jesus Studies*. LNTS 540. New York: T&T Clark, 2016.

Bethune-Baker, James Franklin. *The Miracle of Christianity*. London: Longmans, 1914.

———. *The Faith of the Apostles' Creed*. London: Macmillan, 1918. Abridged edition, edited by W. Norman Pittinger. Greenwich, CT: Seabury, 1955.

Bettenson, Henry. *The Early Christian Fathers: A Selection from the Writings of the Fathers from St. Clement of Rome to St. Athanasius*. London: Oxford University Press, 1956.

Betz, Hans Dieter. *Lukian von Samosata und das Neue Testament. Religionsgeschichtliche und paränetische Parallelen*. TU 76. Berlin: Akademie, 1961.

A History of the Quests for the Historical Jesus

———. "Jesus as Divine Man." In *Jesus and the Historian: Written in Honor of Ernest Cadman Colwell*, edited by F. Thomas Trotter, 114–33. Philadelphia: Westminster, 1978.

———. *Synoptische Studien*. Tübingen: Mohr Siebeck, 1992.

———. *The Sermon on the Mount: A Commentary on the Sermon on the Mount, Including the Sermon on the Plain (Matthew 5:3–7:27 and Luke 6:20–49)*. Hermeneia. Minneapolis: Fortress, 1995.

Betz, Hans Dieter, ed. *Christology and a Modern Pilgrimage: A Discussion with Norman Perrin*. Missoula, MT: Scholars, 1974.

———. *The Greek Magical Papyri in Translation, Including the Demotic Spells*. Chicago: University of Chicago Press, 1986; 2nd ed., 1992. [For Greek texts see Karl Preisendanz.]

Betz, Otto. "Probleme des Prozesses Jesu." *ANRW*, 2.25.1 (1982), 565–647.

———. "Jesus and the Temple Scroll." In *Jesus and the Dead Sea Scrolls*, edited by James H. Charlesworth, 75–103.

Beutler, Johannes. *Martyria. Traditionsgeschichtliche Untersuchungen zum Zeugnisthema bei Johannes*. Frankfurt: Josef Knecht, 1972.

———. *Neue Studien zu den Johanneischen Schriften*. BBB 167. Göttingen: Vandenhoeck & Ruprecht, 2012.

Bieler, Ludwig. θεῖος ἀνήρ: *Das Bild des "Göttlichen Menschen" in Spätantike und Frühchristentum*. 2 vols. 1935–36. Reprinted in one volume. Darmstadt: Wissenschaftliche Buchgesellschaft, 1976.

Bieringer, Reimund, Didier Pollefeyt, Frederique Vandecasteele-Vanneuvlle, eds. *Anti-Judaism and the Fourth Gospel*. Louisville: Westminster John Knox, 2001.

Bilde, Per. *The Originality of Jesus: A Critical Discussion and a Comparative Attempt*. Studia Aarhusiana Neotestamentica 1. Göttingen, Bristol, CT: Vandenhoeck & Ruprecht, 2013.

Bilezikian, Gilbert G. *The Liberated Gospel: A Comparison of the Gospel of Mark and Greek Tragedy*. Grand Rapids: Baker, 1977.

Binns, L. Elliott, J. W. Hunkin, and J. F. Bethune-Baker. *The Rise of the Christian Church*. Cambridge: Cambridge University Press, 1929.

Bird, Michael F. *Jesus and the Origins of the Gentile Mission*. LNTS 331. New York: T&T Clark International, 2007.

———. *The Saving Righteousness of God: Studies on Paul, Justification, and the New Perspective*. Milton Keynes: Paternoster; Eugene, OR: Wipf & Stock, 2007).

———. *Are You the One Who Is to Come? The Historical Jesus and the Messianic Question*. Grand Rapids: Baker Academic, 2009.

———. *Jesus the Eternal Son: Answering Adoptionist Christology*. Foreword by Richard Bauckham. Grand Rapids: Eerdmans, 2017.

Bird, Michael F., ed. *How God Became Jesus: The Real Origins of Belief in Jesus' Divine Nature*. Grand Rapids: Zondervan, 2014.

Bird, Michael F., and Preston M. Sprinkle. *The Faith of Jesus Christ: Exegetical, Biblical, and Theological Studies*. Milton Keynes: Paternoster; Peabody, MA: Hendrickson, 2009.

Birus, Hendrik. *Poetische Namengebung. Zur Bedeutung der Namen in Lessings "Nathan der Weise"*. Göttingen: Vandenhoeck & Rupprecht, 1978.

Black, C. Clifton. *The Disciples according to Mark: Markan Redaction in Current Debate*. JSNTSup 27. Sheffield: Sheffield Academic Press, 1989.

———. *Mark: Images of an Apostolic Interpreter*. Studies on Personalities in the New Testament. Columbia: University of South Carolina Press, 1994.

Black, Matthew. *An Aramaic Approach to the Gospels and Acts*. Oxford: Oxford University Press, 1946; 3rd ed., 1967. Reprinted with an introduction by Craig A. Evans titled "An Aramaic Approach Thirty Years Later." Peabody, MA: Hendrickson, 1967.

Blackburn, Barry L. "Miracle Working ΘΕΟΙ ΑΝΔΡΕΣ in Hellenism (and Hellenistic Judaism)." In *Gospel Perspectives*. Vol. 6, *The Miracles of Jesus*, edited by David Wenham and Craig Blomberg, 185–218. (Sheffield: JSOT, 1986).

———. *Theios Aner and the Markan Miracle Traditions: A Critique of the Theios Aner Concept as an Interpretative Background of the Miracle Traditions Used by Mark*. WUNT 40. Tübingen: Mohr Siebeck, 1991.

———. "The Miracles of Jesus." *Studying the Historical Jesus: Evaluations of the State of Current Research*, edited by Bruce Chilton and Craig A. Evans, 353–94. NNTS 19. Leiden: Brill, 1994.

Blankenberg, Birgit. *Gottes Geist in der Theologie Piet Schoonenbergs*. Mainz: Matthias-Grünewald, 2000.

Blanton, Ward, and Hent de Vries, eds. *Paul and the Philosophers*. New York: Fordham University Press, 2013.

Blasi, Anthony J., Jean Duhaime, Paul-André Turcotte, eds. *Handbook of Early Christianity: Social Science Approaches*. Walnut Creek, CA: Altamira, 2002.

Blass, F., and A. Debrunner. *A Greek Grammar of the New Testament and Other Early Christian Literature: A Translation and Revision of the Ninth-Tenth German Edition, Incorporating Supplementary Notes of A. Debrunner*. Translated and edited by Robert W. Funk. Cambridge: Cambridge University Press; Chicago: University of Chicago Press, 1961.

Blount, Charles, *The First Two Books of Philostratus, Concerning the Life of Apollonius Tyaneus: Written Originally in Greek, And Now Published in English; Together with Philological Notes upon Each Chapter*. London: Thompson, 1680. Facsimile reprint, Early English Books Online Editions.

———. *Miracles, No Violations of the Laws of Nature*. London: Sollers, 1683. Facsimile reprint, Early English Books Online Editions.

———. *The Miscellaneous Works of Charles Blount, Esq . . . To Which Is Prefixed the Life of the Author, and an Account and Vindication of His Death*. Edited by Charles Gilden. London, 1695.

Boccaccini, Gabriele. *Beyond the Essene Hypothesis: The Parting of the Ways between Qumran and Enochic Judaism*. Grand Rapids: Eerdmans, 1998.

———. *The Roots of Rabbinic Judaism: An Intellectual History from Ezekiel to Daniel*. Grand Rapids: Eerdmans, 2002.

Boccaccini, Gabriele, ed. *Enoch and the Messiah Son of Man: Revisiting the Messiah Son of Man*. Grand Rapids: Eerdmans, 2007.

Bock, Darrell L. *Proclamation from Prophecy and Pattern: Lucan Old Testament Christology*. JSNTSS 12. Sheffield: Sheffield Academic Press, 1987.

———. *Blasphemy and Exaltation in Judaism and the Final Examination of Jesus: A Philological Study of the Key Jewish Themes Impacting Mark 14:61–64*. WUNT 106. Tübingen: Mohr Siebeck, 1998.

———. "Trial of Jesus." In *EHJ*, 656–62.

———. "Blasphemy and the Jewish Examination of Jesus." In *Key Events in the Life of the Historical Jesus*, edited by Darrell L. Bock and Robert L. Webb, 589–667.

Bock, Darrell L., and Benjamin J. Simon. *Jesus according to the Scripture: Restoring the Portrait from the Gospels*. 2nd ed. Grand Rapids: Baker Academic, 2016.

Bock, Darrell L., and Robert L. Webb, eds. *Key Events in the Life of the Historical Jesus: A Collaborative Exploration of Context and Coherence*. WUNT 247. Tübingen: Mohr Siebeck, 2009.

Bockmuehl, Markus. *Revelation and Mystery in Ancient Judaism and Pauline Christianity*. WUNT 36. Tübingen: Mohr Siebeck, 1990; Grand Rapids: Eerdmans, 1997.

———. *This Jesus: Martyr, Lord, Messiah*. Edinburgh: T&T Clark; Downers Grove, IL: InterVarsity Press, 1994.

———. *Jewish Law in Gentile Churches: Halakhah and the Beginning of Public Christian Ethics*. Edinburgh: T&T Clark, 2000.

———. *Seeing the Word: Refocusing New Testament Study*. Studies in Theological Interpretation. Grand Rapids: Baker Academic, 2006.

———. *The Remembered Peter in Ancient Reception and Modern Debate*. WUNT 262. Tübingen: Mohr Siebeck, 2010.

———. *Simon Peter in Scripture and Memory: The New Testament Apostle in the Early Church*. Grand Rapids: Baker Academic, 2012.

———. *Ancient Apocryphal Gospels*. Interpretation: Resources for the Use of Scripture in the Church. Louisville: Westminster John Knox, 2017.

Bockmuehl, Markus, ed. *The Cambridge Companion to Jesus*. Cambridge: Cambridge University Press, 2001.

Bohak, Gideon. *Ancient Jewish Magic: A History*. Cambridge: Cambridge University Press, 2008. Reprint, 2011.

Bolingbroke, Henry St. John. *The Philosophical Works of the Late Right Honorable Henry St. John, Lord Viscount Bolingbroke*. 5 vols. 1754–77. Facsimile reprint, London: Garland, 1977.

Bibliography

Bolt, Peter G. "Mark 13: An Apocalyptic Precursor to the Passion Narrative." *Reformed Theological Review* 54 (1995): 10–32.

———. "Jesus, the Daimons and the Dead." In *The Unseen World*, edited by A. N. S. Lane, 75–102.

———. *Jesus' Defeat of Death: Persuading Mark's Early Readers*. SNTSMS 125. Cambridge: Cambridge University Press, 2003.

———. *The Cross from a Distance: Atonement in Mark's Gospel*. Downers Grove, IL: InterVarsity Press, 2004.

Bond, Helen K. *Pontius Pilate in History and Interpretation*. SNTSMS 100. Cambridge: Cambridge University Press, 1998.

———. *Caiaphas: Friend of Rome and Judge of Jesus?* Louisville: Westminster John Knox, 2004.

———. "Barabbas Remembered." In *Jesus and Paul*, edited by B. J. Oropeza et al., 59–71.

———. *The Historical Jesus: A Guide for the Perplexed*. London, New York: T&T International, 2012.

Bond, Helen K., and Larry W. Hurtado, eds. *Peter in Early Christianity*. Grand Rapids: Eerdmans, 2015.

Bonhoeffer, Dietrich. *Letters and Papers from Prison*. Enlarged ed. Edited by Eberhard Bethge. London: SCM, 1971.

Boomershine, Thomas E., and Gilbert L. Bartholomew. "The Narrative Technique of Mark 16:8." *JBL* 100 (1981): 213–23.

Boomershine, Thomas E. "Mark 16:8 and the Apostolic Commission." *JBL* 100 (1981): 225–39.

Borg, Marcus J. "Jesus and Eschatology: A Reassessment." In *Images of Jesus Today*, edited by James H. Charlesworth and Walter P. Weaver, 42–67.

———. *Jesus, A New Vision: Spirit, Culture and the Life of Discipleship*. San Francisco: Harper & Row, 1987.

———. *Jesus in Contemporary Scholarship*. Valley Forge, PA: Trinity Press International, 1994.

———. *Jesus at 2000*. Boulder, CO: Westview, 1997.

———. *Conflict, Holiness, and Politics in the Teachings of Jesus*. Lewiston: Mellen, 1984. Reprint, Harrisburg, PA: Trinity Press International, 1998.

Borg, Marcus J., and N. T. Wright. *The Meaning of Jesus: Two Visions*. San Francisco: HarperSanFrancisco, 1999.

Borgen, Peder. *Bread from Heaven: An Exegetical Study of the Concept of Manna in the Gospel of John and the Writings of Philo*. NovTSup 10. Leiden: Brill, 1965.

———. "God's Agent in the Fourth Gospel." In *Religions in Antiquity*, edited by J. Neusner, 137–48. Leiden: Brill, 1968. Reprinted in *Logos Was the True Light and Other Essays on the Gospel of John*, 121–32. Relieff 9. Trondheim Tapir, University of Trondheim, 1983; and in *The Interpretation of John*, edited by John Ashton, 83–95.

———. *Early Christianity and Hellenistic Judaism*. Edinburgh: T&T Clark, 1996.
Borgen, Peder, and Søren Giversen, eds. *The New Testament and Hellenistic Judaism*. Peabody, MA: Hendrickson, 1997.
Bornkamm, Günther. *Mythos und Legende in den apokryphen Thomas-Akten. Beiträge zur Geschichte der Gnosis und zur Vorgeschichte des Manichäismus*. FRLANT 49. Göttingen: Vandenhoeck & Ruprecht, 1933.
———. *Jesus von Nazareth*. Stuttgart: Kohlhammer, [1956]; 10th ed., 1975.
———. *Jesus of Nazareth*. Translation of the 3rd ed. (1959) by Irene McLuskey and Fraser McLuskey with James M. Robinson. New York: Harper; London: Hodder & Stoughton, 1960.
———. "The Theology of Rudolf Bultmann." In *The Theology of Rudolf Bultmann*, edited by Charles W. Kegley, 3–20.
———. *Early Christian Experience*. Translated by Paul L. Hammer. London: SCM, 1969.
Bornkamm, Günther, Gerhard Barth, and Heinz Joachim Held. *Tradition and Interpretation in Matthew*. Translated by Percy Scott. London: SCM, 1963.
Botha, Pieter J. J. *Orality and Literacy in Early Christianity*. Biblical Performance Criticism 5. Eugene, OR: Cascade, 2012.
Böttrich, Christfried, and Jens Herzer, assisted by Torsten Reiprich, eds. *Josephus und das Neue Testament. Wechselseitige Wahrnehmungen. II. Internationales Symposium zum Corpus Judaeo-Hellenisticum 25.-28 Mai 206, Greifswald*. WUNT 209. Tübingen: Mohr Siebeck, 2007.
Bousset, Wilhelm. *Jesu Predigt in ihrem Gegensatz zum Judentum. Ein religionsgeschichtlicher Versuch*. Göttingen: Vandenhoeck & Ruprecht, 1892.
———. *Das Wesen der Religion*. Halle, 1903; 4th ed. Tübingen: Mohr Siebeck, 1920. ET: F. B. Low. *What Is Religion?* London: Unwin, 1907.
———. *Die Religion des Judentums im Späthellenistichen Zeitalter*. HNT 21. Tübingen: Mohr Siebeck, 1903; 4th ed. with foreword by Eduard Lohse, 1966.
———. *Jesus*. Halle: Gebauer-Schwetszke, 1904. ET: *Jesus*. Translated by Janet Penrose Trevelyan. New York: Putman; London: Williams and Norgate, 1906.
———. *Hauptprobleme der Gnosis*. FRLANT 10. Göttingen: Vandenhoeck & Ruprecht, 1907. Reprint, 1973.
———. *Kyrios Christos. Geschichte des Christusglaubens von den Anfängen des Christentums bis Irenaeus*. Geleitwort, Rudolf Bultmann. Göttingen: Vandenhoeck & Ruprecht, [1913]; 5th ed. 1965.
———. *Kyrios Christos: A History of the Belief in Christ from the Beginnings of Christianity to Irenaeus*. Introduction by Rudolf Bultmann. Translated by John E. Steely. Nashville: Abingdon, [1913]; 1970.
———. *Jesus der Herr. Nachträge und Auseinandersetzungen zu Kyrios Christos*. Göttingen: Vandenhoeck & Ruprecht, 1916.
———. *Religionsgeschtliche Studien. Aufsätze zur Religionsgeschichte des Hellenistischen Zeitalters*. Edited by Anthonie F. Verheule. *NovTSup* 50. Leiden: Brill, 1979.

Bibliography

Bowen, Desmond. *The Idea of the Victorian Church: A Study of the Church of England, 1833–1889.* Montreal: McGill University Press, 1968.

Bowersock, Glen W. *Greek Sophists of the Roman Empire.* Oxford: Oxford University Press, 1969.

Bowie, Ewen Lyall. "Apollonius of Tyana: Tradition and Reality." *ANRW*, 2.16.2 (1978), 1653–99.

Boyarin, Daniel. *The Jewish Gospels: The Story of the Jewish Christ.* Foreword by Jack Miles. New York: New Press, 2012.

Boyd, Gregory A. *Cynic Sage or Son of God?* Wheaton: Bridgepoint, 1995.

Braaten, Carl E. "Martin Kähler on the Historic Biblical Christ." In *The Historical Jesus and the Kerygmatic Christ*, edited by Carl Braaten and Roy A. Harrisville, 79–105.

Braaten, Carl A., and Roy A. Harrisville. *Kerygma and History: A Symposium on the Theology of Rudolf Bultmann.* Nashville: Abingdon, 1962.

Braaten, Carl E., and Roy A. Harrisville, trans. and eds., *The Historical Jesus and the Kerygmatic Christ: Essays on the New Quest of the Historical Jesus.* Nashville: Abingdon, 1964.

Brabazon, James. *Albert Schweitzer: A Biography.* New York: Putnam, 1975.

Brandon, S. G. F. *The Fall of Jerusalem and the Christian Church: A Study of the Effects of the Jewish Overthrow of A.D. 70 on Christianity.* London: SPCK, 1951.

———. *Jesus and the Zealots: A Study of the Political Factor in Primitive Christianity.* Manchester: Manchester University Press; New York: Scribner's, 1967.

Branham, Robert Bracht, and Marie-Odile Goulet-Cazé, eds. *The Cynics: The Cynic Movement in Antiquity and Its Legacy.* Berkeley: University of California Press, 1996.

Braun, F. M. *Jean le théologien et son évangile dans l'Église ancienne.* Paris: Gabalda, 1959.

———. *Jean le théologien. Les Grandes traditions d'Israël, l'accord des Écritures d'après le Quatrième Évangile.* Paris: J. Gabalda, 1964.

Brawley, Robert. "Vincent Taylor." In *DMBI*, 960–63.

Breech, James. *The Silence of Jesus: The Authentic Voice of the Historical Man.* Philadelphia: Fortress, 1983.

Breisach, Ernst. *Historiography, Ancient, Medieval, and Modern.* Chicago: University of Chicago Press, 1983; 3rd ed., 2007.

Briggman, Anthony. *Irenaeus of Lyons and the Theology of the Holy Spirit.* Oxford Early Christian Studies. Oxford: Oxford University Press, 2012.

Briggs, Charles Augustus. *The Defence of Professor Briggs before the Presbytery of New York, December 13, 14, 19 and 22, 1882.* New York: Scribner's, 1892.

Briggs, Richard S. *Words in Action: Speech Act Theory and Biblical Interpretation. Toward a Hermeneutic of Self-Involvement.* Edinburgh: T&T Clark, 2001.

Broadhead, Edwin K. *Teaching with Authority: Miracles and Christology in the Gospel of Mark.* JSNTSup 74. Sheffield: Sheffield Academic Press, 1994.

Broadie, Alexander, ed. *The Cambridge Companion to the Scottish Enlightenment.* Cambridge: Cambridge University Press, 2003.

Brodd, Jeffrey, and Jonathan L. Reed, eds. *Rome and Religion: A Cross-Disciplinary Dialogue on the Imperial Cult.* WGRWSup 5. Atlanta: SBL Press, 2011.

Brodie, Thomas L. *The Quest for the Origin of John's Gospel: A Source-Oriented Approach.* Oxford: Oxford University Press, 1993.

———. *The Gospel according to John: A Literary and Theological Commentary.* Oxford: Oxford University Press, 1993.

———. *Beyond the Quest for the Historical Jesus: Memoir of A Discovery.* Sheffield: Phoenix, 2012.

Bromiley, Geoffrey W. "The Reformers and the Humanity of Christ." In *Perspectives on Christology: Essays in Honor of Paul K. Jewett,* edited by Marguerite Shuster and Richard Muller, 79–104. Grand Rapids: Zondervan, 1991.

Brooke, George J. *The Dead Sea Scrolls and the New Testament.* London: SPCK; Minneapolis: Fortress, 2005.

Brooke, George J., ed. *Exegesis at Qumran: 4QFlorilegium in Its Jewish Context.* JSOTSup 29. Sheffield: Sheffield Academic Press, 1985.

———. "Melchizedek (11QMelch)." In *ABD,* 4:687–88.

———. *The Birth of Jesus: Biblical and Theological Reflections.* Edinburgh: T&T Clark, 2000.

———. "Florilegium." In *Encyclopedia of the Dead Sea Scrolls,* edited by Lawrence H. Schiffman and James C. VanderKam, 1:297–98.

Brower, K. E., and M. W. Elliott, eds. *'The Reader Must Understand': Eschatology in Bible and Theology.* Leicester: Apollos, 1997.

Brown, Colin. *Karl Barth and the Christian Message.* London: Tyndale, 1967.

———. "Charles Gore." In *Creative Minds in Contemporary Theology,* edited by Philip Edgcumbe Hughes, 2nd ed., 341–76. Grand Rapids: Eerdmans, 1969.

———. *Miracles and the Critical Mind.* Grand Rapids: Eerdmans, 1984. Reprint, Pasadena, CA: Fuller Theological Seminary, 2006.

———. *Jesus in European Protestant Thought, 1778–1860.* Studies in Historical Theology 1. Durham, NC: Labyrinth, 1985. Reprint, Pasadena, CA: Fuller Theological Seminary, 2008.

———. "Synoptic Miracle Stories: A Jewish Religious and Social Setting." *Foundations and Facets Forum* 2, no. 4 (1986): 55–76.

———. *History and Faith: A Personal Exploration.* Grand Rapids: Zondervan, 1987.

———. "The Gates of Hell and the Church." In *Church, Word, and Spirit: Historical and Theological Essays in Honor of Geoffrey W. Bromiley,* edited by James E. Bradley and Richard A. Muller, 15–43. Grand Rapids: Eerdmans, 1987.

———. "The Gates of Hell: An Alternative Approach." In *SBLSP 1987,* edited by Kent Harold Richards, 357–67. Atlanta: Scholars, 1987.

———. *Christianity and Western Thought: A History of Philosophers, Ideas and Movements.* Vol. 1, *From the Ancient World to the Age of Enlightenment.* Downers Grove, IL: InterVarsity Press, 1990.

Bibliography

———. "Trinity and Incarnation: In Search of Contemporary Orthodoxy." *Ex Auditu* 7 (1991): 83–100.

———. "*Scripture and Christology*: A Protestant Look at the Work of the Pontifical Biblical Commission." In *Perspectives on Christology: Essays in Honor of Paul K. Jewett*, edited by Marguerite Shuster and Richard Muller, 39–76. Grand Rapids: Zondervan, 1991.

———. "The Unjust Steward: A New Twist?" In *Worship, Theology and Ministry in the Early Church: Essays in Honor of Ralph P. Martin*, edited by Michael J. Wilkins and Terence Paige, 121–45. JSNTSup 87. Sheffield: Sheffield Academic Press, 1992.

———. "The Hermeneutics of Confession and Accusation." *CTJ* 30 (1995): 460–71.

———. "What Was John the Baptist Doing?" *BBR* 7 (1997): 37–50.

———. "Ernst Lohmeyer's *Kyrios Jesus*." In *Where Christology Began: Essays on Philippians 2*, edited by Ralph P. Martin and Brian J. Dodd, 6–42. Louisville: Westminster John Knox, 1998.

———. "The Parable of the Rebellious Son(s)." *SJT* 51 (1998): 391–405.

———. "The Jesus of Mark's Gospel." In *Jesus Then and Now*, edited by Marvin Meyer and Charles Hughes, 26–53.

———. "Enlightenment Period." In *Dictionary of Biblical Criticism and Interpretation*, edited by Stanley E. Porter, 91–101.

———. "With the Grain and against the Grain: A Strategy for Reading the Synoptic Gospels." In *HSHJ*, 1:619–49.

———. "The Quest of the Unhistorical Jesus and the Quest of the Historical Jesus." In *HSHJ*, 2:855–86.

———. "Why Study the Historical Jesus?" In *HSHJ*, 2:1411–38.

———. "Issues in the History of Debates on Miracles." In *The Cambridge Companion to Miracles*, edited by Graham H. Twelftree, 273–90.

Brown, David. *The Divine Trinity*. London: Duckworth; LaSalle, IL: Open Court, 1985.

———. *Continental Philosophy and Modern Theology: An Engagement*. New York: Blackwell, 1987.

Brown, Raymond E. "Parable and Allegory Reconsidered." In *New Testament Essays*, 321–33. Garden City, NY: Doubleday Image, 1968.

———. *The Gospel according to John*. 2 vols. AB 29. New York: Doubleday, 1966, 1971.

———. *The Virginal Conception and Bodily Resurrection of Jesus*. London: Geoffrey Chapman, 1973.

———. *The Birth of the Messiah: A Commentary on the Infancy Narratives in the Gospels of Matthew and Luke*. New York: Doubleday, 1977; 2nd ed., 1993.

———. *The Community of the Beloved Disciple*. New York: Paulist, 1979.

———. *The Death of the Messiah: From Gethsemane to the Grave; A Commentary of the Passion Narratives in the Four Gospels*. 2 vols. New York: Doubleday, 1994.

———. *An Introduction to New Testament Christology*. New York: Paulist, 1994.

A History of the Quests for the Historical Jesus

Brown, Raymond E., Joseph A. Fitzmyer, and Roland E. Murphy, eds. *The New Jerome Biblical Commentary*. Englewood Cliffs, NJ: Prentice Hall, 1990.

Brown, Raymond E., Karl P. Donfried, and John Reumann, eds. *Peter in the New Testament: A Collaborative Assessment by Protestant and Catholic Scholars*. Minneapolis: Augsburg, 1973.

Brown, Raymond E., Joseph A. Fitzmyer, and John Reumann, eds. *Mary in the New Testament*. Philadelphia: Fortress, 1978.

Brown, Robert E. *Jonathan Edwards and the Bible*. Bloomington: Indiana University Press, 2002.

Bruce, A. B. *The Humiliation of Christ in Its Physical, Ethical, and Official Aspects*. Cunningham Lectures. Edinburgh: T&T Clark, 1876; 5th ed. 1905.

Bruce, F. F. "The Speeches in Acts: Thirty Years After." In *Reconciliation and Hope: New Testament Essays on Atonement and Eschatology. Presented to L. L. Morris on His 60th Birthday*, edited by Robert Banks, 53–68. Exeter: Paternoster, 1974.

———. *Paul and Jesus*. London: SPCK, 1974.

———. *Paul: Apostle of the Free Spirit*. Exeter: Paternoster, 1979.

———. "Render to Caesar." In *Jesus and the Politics of His Day*, edited Ernst Bammel and C. F. D. Moule, 249–63.

Brucker, Ralph. *'Christushymnen' oder 'epideiktishe Passagen'? Studien zum Stilwechsel im Neuen Testament und seiner Umwelt*. FRLANT 176. Göttingen: Vandenenhoeck & Ruprecht, 1997.

Brueggemann, Walter. *The Theology of the Old Testament: Testimony, Dispute, Advocacy*. Minneapolis: Fortress, 1997.

Brunson, Andrew C. *Psalm 118 in the Gospel of John: An Intertextual Study on the New Exodus Pattern in the Theology of John*. WUNT 158. Tübingen: Mohr Siebeck, 2003.

Bryan, Christopher. *A Preface to Mark: Notes on the Gospel in Its Literary and Cultural Settings*. Oxford: Oxford University Press, 1993.

———. *Render to Caesar: Jesus, the Early Church, and the Roman Superpower*. Oxford: Oxford University Press, 2007.

Buchanan, Anne L., and Jean-Pierre V. M. Hérubel, eds. *The Doctor of Philosophy Degree: A Selective, Annotated Bibliography*. Bibliographies and Indexes in Education 15. Westport, CT: Greenwood, 1995.

Büchner, Dirk. "ἐξιλάσασθαι: Appeasing God in the Septuagint Pentateuch." *JBL* 129 (2010): 237–60.

Bühner, Jan-Adolf. *Der Gesandte und sein Weg im 4. Evangelium. Die kultur- und religionsgeschichtlichen Grundlagen der Johanneischen Sendungschristologie sowie ihre traditionsgeschichtliche Entwicklickung*. WUNT 2. Tübingen: Mohr Siebeck, 1977.

Bulman, Raymond F., and Frederick J. Parrela, eds. *Paul Tillich: A New Catholic Assessment*. Collegeville, MN: Liturgical, 1994.

Bultmann, Rudolf. *Der Stil der Paulinischen Predigt und die kynisch-stoische Diatribe*. FRLANT 13. Göttingen: Vandenhoeck & Ruprecht, 1910. Reprint, 1984.

———. *Die Exegese des Theodor von Mopsuestia* (1912). Edited by Helmut Feld and Karl Hermann Schelkle. Stuttgart: Kohlhammer, 1984.

———. *Die Geschichte der synoptischen Tradition*. FRLANT 29. Göttingen: Vandenhoeck & Ruprecht, 1921.

———. "Das Problem einer theologischen Ezegese des Neuen Testaments." In *Zwischen den Zeiten* 3, 334–57. Munich: Christian Kaiser, 1925. ET: "The Problem of Theological Exegesis." In *The Beginnings of Dialectic Theology*, edited by James M. Robinson, translated by Keith R. Crim and Louis De Grazia, 236–56. Richmond, VA: John Knox, 1968.

———. *Jesus*. Die Unsterblichen: Die geistigen Heroen der Menschheit in ihrem Leben und Wirken. Berlin: Deutsche Bibliothek, 1926.

———. *Jesus and the Word*. Translated by Louise Pettibone Smith and Erminie Huntress Lantero. New York: Scribner's, 1934. Reprint, 1958.

———. *Die Erforschung der synoptischen Evangelien*. Berlin: Töpelmann, 1934; 4th ed., 1961. ET: Frederick C. Grant, trans. "The Study of the Synoptic Gospels." In Rudolf Bultmann and Karl Kundsin, *Form Criticism: Two Essays on New Testament Research*, 11–76. New York: Harper, 1962.

———. *Das Evangelium des Johannes*. KEK 2. Göttingen: Vandenhoeck & Ruprecht, 1941.

———. *Das Urchristentum im Rahmen der antiken Religionen*. Zürich: Artemis, 1949.

———. *Theology of the New Testament*. Translated by Kendrick Grobel. 2 vols. New York: Scribner's; London: SCM, 1951–55.

———. "New Testament and Mythology." In *Kerygma and Myth*, edited by Hans-Werner Bartsch, 1:1–44.

———. *History and Eschatology: The Presence of Eternity*. Gifford Lectures. New York: Harper, 1957.

———. *Jesus Christ and Mythology*. London: SCM, 1958.

———. *Primitive Christianity in Its Contemporary Setting*. Translated by R. H. Fuller. London: Thames & Hudson, 1956. Reprint, London: Collins, 1960.

———. *Existence and Faith: Shorter Writings of Rudolf Bultmann*. Selected, translated, and introduced by Schubert M. Ogden. New York: Meridien, 1960; London: Hodder & Stoughton, 1961.

———. *Das Verhältnis der urchristlichen Botschaft zum historischen Jesus*. Sitzungsberichte der Heidelberger Akademie der Wissenschaften. Philosophisch-historische Klasse, Jahrgang 1960, 3. Abhandlung. Heidelberg: Carl Winter Universitätsverlag, 1962.

———. *Das Verhältnis der urchristlichen Christusbotschaft zum historischen Jesus*. 3rd ed. Heidelberg: Carl Winter, 1962. ET: "The Primitive Christian Kerygma and the Historical Jesus." In *The Historical Jesus and the Kerygmatic Christ*, translated and edited by Carl E. Braaten and Roy A. Harrisville, 15–42.

———. *The History of the Synoptic Tradition*. Translated by John Marsh from the 2nd German edition (1931) with additions and supplement. Oxford: Blackwell, 1963; rev. ed., 1972.

———. "Autobiographical Reflections." In *The Theology of Rudolf Bultmann*, edited by Charles W. Kegley, xix–xxv.

———. *Exegetica. Aufsätze zur Erforschung des Neuen Testaments*. Edited by Erich Dinkler. Tübingen: Mohr Siebeck, 1967.

———. *Faith and Understanding*. Edited by Robert W. Funk. Translated by Louise Pettibone Smith. London: SCM, 1969.

———. *The Gospel of John: A Commentary*. Translated by G. R. Beasley-Murray. General editors, N. Hoare and J. K. Riches. Oxford: Blackwell; Philadelphia: Westminster, 1971.

———. *Glauben und Verstehen. Gesammelte Aufsätze*. 4 vols. 8th ed. Tübingen: Mohr Siebeck, 1980.

———. *Sachgemässe Exegese. Die Protokolle aus Rudolf Bultmanns Neutestamentliche Seminaren 1921–1951*. Marburg: Elwert, 1996.

Burke, Tony. *Secret Scriptures Revealed: A New Introduction to the Christian Apocrypha*. Grand Rapids: Eerdmans, 2013.

Burke, Tony, and Brent Landau, eds. *More New Testament Apocryphal Gospels*. Vol. 1. Grand Rapids: Eerdmans, 2016.

Burkett, Delbert. *The Son of Man Debate: A History and Evaluation*. SNTSMS 107. Cambridge: Cambridge University Press, 1999.

Burkett, Delbert, ed. *The Blackwell Companion to Jesus*. Chichester: Wiley-Blackwell, 2011. Reprint, 2014.

Burkitt, F. Crawford. *The Gospel History and Its Transmission*. Edinburgh: T&T Clark, 1906.

———. *The Earliest Sources for the Life of Jesus*. London: Constable, 1910.

———. "Johannes Weiss: In Memoriam." *HTR* 8 (1915): 291–97.

———. *Jesus Christ: An Historical Outline*. London and Glasgow: Blackie, 1932.

Burn-murdoch, H. *The Development of the Papacy*. London: Faber & Faber, 1954.

Burns, David. *The Life and Death of the Radical Historical Jesus*. Oxford: Oxford University Press, 2013.

Burns, R. M. *The Great Debate on Miracles: From Joseph Glanvill to David Hume*. Lewisburg: Bucknell University Press; London: Associated University Presses, 1981.

Burridge, Richard A. *What Are the Gospels? A Comparison with Graeco-Roman Biography*. SNTSMS 70. Cambridge: Cambridge University Press, 1992; 2nd ed., with foreword by Graham Stanton; Grand Rapids: Eerdmans, 2004.

———. "Gospel Genre, Christological Controversy and the Absence of Rabbinic Biography: Some Implications of the Biographical Hypothesis." In *Christology, Controversy and Community: New Testament Essays in Honour of David Catchpole*, edited by David G. Horrell and Christopher M. Tuckett, 137–56. Leiden: Brill, 2000.

———. "Gospel: Genre." In *DJG*, edited by Joel B. Green et al., 335–42.

Bibliography

———. "The Gospel of Jesus: Graham Stanton, Biography and the Genre of Matthew." In *Jesus, Matthew's Gospel and Early Christianity*, edited by Gurtner et al., 5–22.

———. *Four Gospels, One Jesus? A Symbolic Reading*. Grand Rapids: Eerdmans, 1994; 3rd ed., 2014.

Burridge, Richard A., and Grahahm Gould. *Jesus Now and Then*. Grand Rapids: Eerdmans, 2004.

Burton, Ernest DeWitt. *Syntax of the Moods and Tenses in New Testament Greek*. Chicago: University of Chicago Press, 1898. Reprint, Grand Rapids: Kregel, 1976.

———. *Some Principles of Literary Criticism and Their Application to the Synoptic Problem*. Decennial Publications 5. Chicago: University of Chicago Press, 1904.

———. *Galatians*. ICC. Edinburgh: T&T Clark; New York: Scribner's, 1920.

———. *A Short Introduction to the Gospels*. Edited by Harold R. Willoughby. Chicago: University of Chicago Press, 1926.

———. *New Testament Word Studies*. Edited by Harold R. Willoughby. Chicago: University of Chicago Press, 1927.

Burton, Ernest DeWitt, and Edgar Johnson Goodspeed. *A Harmony of the Synoptic Gospels for Historical and Critical Study*. New York: Scribner's, 1917.

———. *A Harmony of the Synoptic Gospels in Greek*. Chicago: University of Chicago Press, 1922.

Burton, Ernest DeWitt, and Shailer Mathews. *The Life of Christ*. Chicago: University of Chicago Press, 1901; rev. ed., New York: Harper, 1927.

Burton, Ernest DeWitt, and W. Arnold Stevens. *A Harmony of the Gospels for Historical Study: An Analytical Synopsis of the Four Gospels*. New York: Scribner's, 1893; rev. ed., 1904.

Busch, Eberhard. *Karl Barth: His Life from Letters and Autobiographical Texts*. Translated by John Bowden. London: SCM, 1976.

Bushnell, Horace. *God in Christ: Three Discourses Delivered at New Haven, Cambridge and Andover with a Preliminary Dissertation on Language*. Hartford: Brown and Parsons, 1849.

———. *The Character of Jesus, Forbidding His Possible Classification with Men*. New York: Scribner's, 1860. Reprint, New York: Chautauqua, 1888.

Bushnell Cheney, Mary A., ed. *Life and Letters of Horace Bushnell*. New York: Harper, 1880.

Buss, Martin J. "The Idea of Sitz im Leben: Critique and History." *ZAW* 90 (1978): 157–70.

Buth, Randall. "A More Complete Semitic Background for בר־נאשא, 'Son of Man.'" In *The Function of Scripture in Early Jewish and Christian Tradition*, edited by Craig A. Evans and James A. Sanders, 176–89. JSNTSip 154. Sheffield: Sheffield Academic Press, 1998.

Butler, Joseph. *The Works of Joseph Butler, D.C.L.* Edited by W. E. Gladstone. 2 vols. Oxford: Clarendon; New York: Macmillan, 1896.

Butler, Perry, ed. *Pusey Rediscovered*. London: SPCK, 1983.

Byrskog, Samuel. *Story as History—History as Story: The Gospel Tradition in the Context of Ancient History*. WUNT 123. Tübingen: Mohr Siebeck, 2000. Reprint, Boston, Leiden: 2002.

Byrskog, Samuel, Tom Holmén, Matti Kankaanniemi, eds. *The Identity of Jesus: Nordic Voices*. Turku/Åbo Symposium 2010. WUNT 373. Tübingen: Mohr Siebeck, 2014.

Byrskog, Samuel, and Tobias Hägerland, eds. *The Mission of Jesus*. Second Nordic Symposium on the Historical Jesus, Lund, 7–10 October 2012. WUNT 391. Tübingen: Mohr Siebeck, 2015.

Cadbury, Henry Joel. *The Style and Literary Method of Luke*. 2 vols. HTS 6. Cambridge, MA: Harvard University Press, 1919–20. Reprinted in one vol., New York: Kraus, 1969.

———. *The Making of Luke-Acts*. New York: Macmillan, 1927. Reprint, London: SPCK, 1961.

———. *The Peril of Modernizing Jesus*. New York: Macmillan, 1937. Reprint, Eugene, OR: Wipf & Stock, 2006.

———. *Jesus: What Manner of Man*. Shaffer Lectures Yale 1946. New York: Macmillan, 1947.

———. *The Book of Acts in History*. New York: Harper, 1955. Reprint, Eugene, OR: Wipf & Stock, 2004.

———. *The Eclipse of the Historical Jesus*. Haverford Library Lectures at Haverford College, April 1963. Haverford: Pendle Hill, 1964.

Caird, G. B. *Jesus and the Jewish Nation*. London: University of London, the Athlone Press, 1965.

———. *The Language and Imagery of the Bible*. London: Duckworth; Philadelphia: Westminster, 1980. Reprint, Grand Rapids: Eerdmans, 1997.

———. *New Testament Theology*. Completed and edited by L. D. Hurst. Oxford: Clarendon, 1995.

Calvin, John. *John Calvin: Institutes of the Christian Religion*. Edited by John T. McNeill. Translated by Ford Lewis Battles. 2 vols. LCC 21–22. London: SCM; Philadelphia: Westminster, 1961.

———. *Calvin: Theological Treatises*. Edited and translated by J. K. S. Reid. LCC 22. London: SCM; Philadelphia: Westminster, 1964.

———. *Calvin: Commentaries*. Edited by Joseph Haroutunian and Louise Pettibone Smith. LCC 23. London: SCM; Philadelphia: Westminster, 1969.

———. *The Gospel according to St. John*. Translated by T. H. L. Parker. 2 vols. Grand Rapids: Eerdmans, 1961.

———. *A Harmony of the Gospels, Matthew, Mark and Luke*. Translated by A. W. Morrison and T. H. L. Parker. 3 vols. Grand Rapids: Eerdmans, 1972.

Cameron, Euan, ed. *The New Cambridge History of the Bible*. Vol. 3, *From 1450 to 1750*. Cambridge: Cambridge University Press, 2016.

Bibliography

Campbell, Douglas A. *The Rhetoric of Righteousness in Romans 3.21–26.* JSNTSS 65. Sheffield: Sheffield Academic Press, 1992.

———. *Framing Paul: An Epistolary Biography.* Grand Rapids: Eerdmans, 2014.

Campbell, George. *Dissertation on Miracles: Containing an Examination of the Principle Advanced by David Hume, Esq; in an Essay on Miracles.* Edinburgh: Kincaid and Bell, 1762.

Campbell, J. MacCleod. *The Nature of Atonement.* London: Macmillan, [1856]. Reprint with new introduction by James B. Torrance, Edinburgh: Handsel; Grand Rapids, Eerdmans, 1996.

Campbell, Richard. "History and Bultmann's Structural Inconsistency." *Religious Studies* 9, no. 1 (1973): 63–79.

Campbell, R. J. *The New Theology.* New York: MacMillan, 1907.

———. *A Spiritual Pilgrimage.* New York: Appleton, 1916.

———. *The Life of Christ.* New York: Appleton, 1921.

Campenhausen, Hans von. *The Virgin Birth in the Theology of the Ancient Church.* Translated by Frank Clarke. Studies in Historical Theology 2. London: SCM; Naperville, Allenson, 1964.

Capel Anderson, Janice and Stephen D. Moore, eds. *Mark and Method: New Approaches in Biblical Studies.* 2nd ed. Minneapolis: Fortress, 2008.

Capes, David B. *Old Testament Yahweh Texts in Paul's Christology.* WUNT II/47. Tübingen: Mohr Siebeck, 1992.

Capes, David B., April DeConick, Helen K. Bond, Troy A. Miller, eds. *Israel's God and Rebecca's Children, Christology and Community in Early Judaism and Christianity: Essays in Honor of Larry W. Hurtado and Alan F. Segal.* Waco, TX: Baylor University Press, 2007.

Capps, Donald. "Beyond Schweitzer and the Psychiatrists: Jesus as Fictive Personality." *Jesus Research: New Methodologies and Perceptions,* edited by James H. Charlesworth with Brian Rhea and Petr Pokorný, Second Princeton-Prague Symposium on Jesus Research, 399–435. Grand Rapids: Eerdmans, 2014.

Caragounis, Chrys C. *The Son of Man: Vision and Interpretation.* WUNT 38. Tübingen: Mohr Siebeck, 1986.

———. *The Development of Greek and the New Testament.* WUNT 167. Tübingen: Mohr Siebeck, 2004.

———. *New Testament Language and Exegesis: A Diachronic Approach.* WUNT 323. Tübingen: Mohr Siebeck, 2014.

Carey, Holly J. *Jesus' Cry from the Cross: Towards a First-Century Understanding of the Intertextual Relationship between Psalm 22 and the Narrative of Mark's Gospel.* LNTS 398. London: T&T Clark International, 2009.

Carlson, Jeffrey, and Robert A. Ludwig, eds. *Jesus and Faith: A Conversation on the Work of John Dominic Crossan.* Maryknoll, NY: Orbis, 1994.

Carlson, Stephen C. *The Gospel Hoax: Morton Smith's Invention of Secret Mark.* Waco, TX: Baylor University Press, 2005.

Carlston, Charles E. *The Parables of the Triple Tradition*. Philadelphia: Fortress, 1975.

———. "Transfiguration and Resurrection." *JBL* 80 (1961): 233–40.

Carlston, Charles E., and Craig A. Evans. *From Synagogue to Ecclesia: Matthew's Community at the Crossroads*. WUNT 334. Tübingen: Mohr Siebeck, 2014.

Carmichael, Calum. *Ideas and the Man: Remembering David Daube*. Studien zur europäischen Rechtsgeschichte 177. Frankfurt am Main: Vittorio Klostermann, 2004.

Carpenter, Edward. *Thomas Sherlock, 1678–1761: Bishop of Bangor 1728; of Salisbury 1734; of London 1748*. London: SPCK, 1936.

Carpenter, James. *Gore: A Study in Liberal Catholic Thought*. London: Faith, 1960. [Contains an extensive bibliography.]

Carr, David. *Time, Narrative, and History*. Bloomington, IN: Indiana University Press, [1986], 1991.

Carroll, John T., and Joel B. Green, eds. *The Death of Jesus in Early Christianity*. Peabody, MA: Hendrickson, 1995.

Carson, D. A., ed. *From Sabbath to Lord's Day: A Biblical, Historical, and Theological Investigation*. Grand Rapids: Zondervan, 1982.

Carson, D. A., Peter T. O'Brien, and Mark A. Seifrid, eds. *Justification and Variegated Nomism*. Vol. 1, *The Complexities of Second Temple Judaism*. WUNT 140. Tübingen: Mohr Siebeck; Grand Rapids: Baker Academic, 2001.

———. *Justification and Variegated Nomism*. Vol. 2, *The Paradoxes of Paul*. WUNT 181. Tübingen: Mohr Siebeck; Grand Rapids: Baker Academic, 2004.

Carter, Warren. *John and Empire: Initial Explorations*. New York: T&T Clark, 2008.

Cartlidge, David R., and David L. Dungan. *Documents for the Study of the Gospels*. Philadelphia: Fortress, 1980.

Case, Shirley Jackson. *The Historicity of Jesus: A Criticism of the Contention That Jesus Never Lived, A Statement of the Evidence for His Existence, An Estimate of His Relation to Christianity*. Chicago: University of Chicago Press, 1912.

———. *The Evolution of Early Christianity*. Chicago: University of Chicago Press, 1914.

———. "The Historical Study of Religion" [1921]. Reprint, *JR* 29 (1949): 5–14.

———. *The Social Origins of Christianity*. Chicago: University of Chicago Press, 1923.

———. "The Life of Jesus." In *Religious Thought in the Last Quarter Century*, edited by Gerald Birney Smith, 26–42. Chicago: University of Chicago Press, 1927.

———. *Jesus: A New Biography*. Chicago: University of Chicago Press, 1927.

———. *Jesus through the Centuries*. Chicago: University of Chicago Press, 1932.

———. "Education in Liberalism." *Contemporary American Theology*, 2:106–25.

———. *Christianity in a Changing World*. New York: Harper, 1941.

———. *The Christian Philosophy of History*. Chicago: University of Chicago Press, 1943.

Case, Shirley Jackson, ed. *Studies in Early Christianity, Presented to Frank Chamberlin Porter and Benjamin Wisner Bacon by Friends and Fellow-Teachers in America and Europe*. New York: Century, 1928.

Bibliography

Casey, Maurice. *Son of Man: The Interpretation and Influence of Daniel 7*. London: SPCK, 1979.

———. *From Jewish Prophet to Gentile God: The Origins and Development of New Testament Christology*. Edward Cadbury Lectures in the University of Birmingham, 1985–86. Cambridge: James Clarke; Louisville: Westminster John Knox, 1991.

———. *Is John's Gospel True?* New York: Routledge, 1996.

———. *Aramaic Sources of Mark's Gospel*. SNTSMS 102. Cambridge: Cambridge University Press, 1998.

———. "Where Wright Is Wrong: A Critical Review of N. T. Wright's *Jesus and the Victory of God*." *JSNT* 69 (1998): 74–94, 95–103.

———. *An Aramaic Approach to Q: Sources for the Gospels of Matthew and Luke*. SNTSMS 122. Cambridge: Cambridge University Press, 2002.

———. *The Solution to the 'Son of Man' Problem*. LNTS 343. New York: T&T Clark International, 2007.

———. "Prophetic Identity and Conflict in the Historic Ministry of Jesus." In *Israel's God and Rebecca's Children*, edited by David B. Capes et al., 121–34.

———. *Jesus of Nazareth: An Independent Historian's Account of His Life and Teaching*. New York: T&T Clark International, 2010.

———. "The Role of Aramaic in Reconstructing the Teaching of Jesus." In *HSHJ*, 2:1343–75.

———. *Jesus: Evidence and Argument or Mythicist Myths?* New York: T&T Clark, 2014.

Cashdollar, Charles D. *The Transformation of Theology, 1830–1890: Positivism and Protestant Thought in Britain and America*. Princeton: Princeton University Press, 1989.

Cassidy, Richard J. *John's Gospel in New Perspective: Christology and the Realities of Roman Power*. Eugene, OR: Wipf & Stock, [1992], 2015.

Catchpole, David R. *The Quest for Q*. Edinburgh: T&T Clark, 1993.

———. *Jesus People: The Historical Jesus and the Beginnings of Community*. London: Darton, Longman & Todd; Grand Rapids: Baker Academic, 2006.

Celsus. *On the True Doctrine: A Discourse against the Christians*. Translated by R. Joseph Hoffmann. New York: Oxford University Press, 1987.

Chadwick, Owen. *Westcott and the University*. Cambridge: Cambridge University Press, 1963.

———. *The Victorian Church*. 2 vols. London: Black, 1966–70. Reprint, 1972.

———. *The Secularization of the European Mind in the Nineteenth Century*. Gifford Lectures in the University of Edinburgh, 1973–74. Cambridge: Cambridge University Press, 1975.

———. *Hensley Henson: A Study of the Friction between Church and State*. Oxford: Clarendon, 1983.

———. *From Bossuet to Newman: The Idea of Doctrinal Development*. Cambridge: Cambridge University Press, 2nd ed., 1987.

———. *The Spirit of the Oxford Movement: Tractarian Essays.* Cambridge: Cambridge University Press, 1990.

Chamberlain, Houston Stewart. *Die Grundlagen des neunzehnten Jahrhunderts.* 2 vols. München: Bruckmann, 1899.

———. *The Foundations of the Nineteenth Century.* Translated by John Lees. 2 vols. New York: John Lane, 1910.

Champion, J. A. I. *John Toland: Nazarenus.* British Deism and Free Thought 1. Oxford: Voltaire Foundation, 1999.

———. *Republican Learning: John Toland and the Crisis of Christian Culture.* Manchester, NY: Manchester University Press, 2003.

———. *The Pillars of Priestcraft Shaken: The Church of England and Its Enemies, 1660–1730.* Cambridge Studies in Early Modern History. Cambridge: Cambridge University Press, [1992], 2014.

Chancey, Mark A. *The Myth of a Gentile Galilee.* SNTSMS 118. Cambridge: Cambridge University Press, 2002.

———. "The Ethnicities of Galileans." In *Galilee in the Late Second Temple and Mishnaic Periods.* Vol. 1, *Life, Culture, and Society*, edited by David E. Fiensy and James Riley Strange, 112–28. Minneapolis: Fortress, 2014.

Chang, Dongshin Don. *Phinehas, the Sons of Zadok, and Melchizedek: Priestly Covenant in Late Second Temple Texts.* LSTS 90. New York: T&T Clark, 2016.

Chanikuzhy, Jacob. *Jesus, the Eschatological Temple: An Exegetical Study of Jn 2, 13–22 in the Light of the Pre-70 C.E., Eschatological Temple Hopes, and the Synoptic Temple Action.* CBET 58. Walpole, MA: Peeters, 2012.

Chapman, David W. *Ancient Jewish and Christian Perceptions of Crucifixion.* WUNT 244. Tübingen: Mohr Siebeck, 2008; Grand Rapids: Baker, 2010.

Chapman, David W., and Eckhard J. Schnabel. *The Trial and Crucifixion of Jesus: Texts and Commentary.* WUNT 344. Tübingen: Mohr Siebeck, 2015.

Chapman, Mark D. "The Socratic Subversion of Tradition: William Sanday and Theology, 1900–1920." *JTS* 45 (1994): 94–116.

———. *The Coming Crisis: The Impact of Eschatology on Theology in Edwardian England.* JSNTSS 208. Sheffield: Sheffield Academic Press, 2001.

Chappell, Vere, ed. *The Cambridge Companion to Locke.* Cambridge: Cambridge University Press, 1994.

Charles, R. H. *A Critical History of the Doctrine of a Future Life in Israel, in Judaism, and in Christianity, or Hebrew, Jewish, and Christian Eschatology from Pre-Prophetic Times till the Close of the New Testament Canon.* Jowett Lectures 1898–99. 2nd ed. London: Black, 1913.

Charlesworth, James H. *The Old Testament Pseudepigrapha and the New Testament: Prolegomena for the Study of Christian Origins.* SNTSMS 54. Cambridge: Cambridge University Press, 1985.

Bibliography

———. *Jesus' Jewishness: Exploring the Place of Jesus in Early Judaism.* New York: Crossroad, 1991.

———. *Jesus' Jewishness: Exploring the Place of Jesus within Early Judaism.* New York: Crossroad, 1991.

———. *John and the Dead Sea Scrolls.* New York: Crossroad, 1991.

———. *Jesus and the Dead Sea Scrolls.* ABRL. New York: Doubleday, 1992.

———. *The Messiah: Developments in Earliest Judaism and Christianity.* First Princeton Symposium on Judaism and Christian Origins. Minneapolis: Fortress, 1992.

———. *The Beloved Disciple: Whose Witness Validates the Gospel of John?* Valley Forge, PA: Trinity Press International, 1995.

———. *Jesus within Judaism: New Light from Exciting Archaeological Discoveries* New York: Doubleday, 1998.

———. *Jesus Two Thousand Years Later.* Harrisburg, PA: Trinity Press International, 2000.

———. *The Bible and the Dead Sea Scrolls.* The Second Princeton Symposium on Judaism and Christian Origins. 3 vols. Vol. 1, *Scripture and the Scrolls.* Vol. 2, *The Dead Sea Scrolls and the Qumran Community.* Vol. 3, *The Scrolls and Christian Origins.* Waco, TX: Baylor University Press, 2006.

———. *The Historical Jesus.* Essential Guide. Nashville: Abingdon, 2008.

———. "Should Specialists in Jesus Research Include Psychobiography?" In *Jesus Research: New Methodologies and Perceptions*, edited by James H. Charlesworth with Brian Rhea and Petr Pokorný, Second Princeton-Prague Symposium on Jesus Research, 436–66. Grand Rapids: Eerdmans, 2014.

———. *Jesus and Temple: Textual and Archaeological Explorations.* Minneapolis: Fortress, 2014.

———. "Preface: Herod the Great, Hillel, Jesus, and Their Temple." In *Jesus and Temple*, edited by Charlesworth, xi–xv.

———. "Introduction: Devotion to and Worship in Jerusalem's Temple." In *Jesus and Temple*, edited by Charlesworth, 1–18.

———. "Jesus and the Temple." In *Jesus and Temple*, edited by Charlesworth, 145–82.

———. "The Temple and Jesus' Followers," In *Jesus and Temple*, edited by Charlesworth, 183–212.

Charlesworth, James H., ed. *The Old Testament Pseudepigrapha.* 2 vols. Vol. 1, *Apocalyptic Literature and Testaments.* Vol. 2, *Expansions of the "Old Testament" and Legends, Wisdom and Philosophical Literature, Prayers, Psalms and Odes, Fragments of Lost Judeo-Hellenistic Works.* Garden City, NY: Doubleday, 1982, 1985.

Charlesworth, James H., with Mark Harding and Mark Kiley, eds. *The Lord's Prayer and Other Prayer Texts from the Greco-Roman Era.* Valley Forge, PA: Trinity Press International, 1994.

Charlesworth, James H., and Walter P. Weaver, eds. *The Old and New Testaments: Their*

Relationship and the "Intertestamental" Literature. Valley Forge, PA: Trinity Press International, 1993.

———. *Images of Jesus Today.* Valley Forge, PA: Trinity Press International, 1994.

———. *Jesus Two Thousand Years Later.* Harrisburg, PA: Trinity Press International, 2000.

Charlesworth, James H., and Loren J. Johns, eds. *Hillel and Jesus: Comparisons of Two Major Leaders.* Minneapolis: Fortress, 1997.

Charlesworth, James H., and Petr Pokorný, eds. *Jesus Research: The First Princeton-Prague Symposium on Jesus Research.* Grand Rapids: Eerdmans, 2009.

Charlesworth, James H., ed., with Bryan Rhea and Petr Pokorný. *Jesus Research: New Methodologies and Perceptions.* Second Princeton-Prague Symposium on Jesus Research, Princeton 2007. Grand Rapids: Eerdmans, 2014.

Chester, Andrew. *Messiah and Exaltation: Jewish Messianic and Visionary Traditions and New Testament Christology.* WUNT 207. Tübingen: Mohr Siebeck, 2007.

Chilton, Bruce D. *God in Strength: Jesus' Announcement of the Kingdom.* Sheffield: JSOT, 1979. Reprint, 1987.

———. *The Glory of Israel: The Theology and Provenience of the Isaiah Targum.* JSOTSS 23. Sheffield: JSOT, 1982.

———. *A Galilean Rabbi and His Bible: Jesus' Use of the Interpreted Scripture of His Time.* Good News Studies 8. Wilmington, DE: Michael Glazier, 1984.

———. *Profiles of a Rabbi: Synoptic Opportunities for Reading about Jesus.* Brown Judaic Studies 177. Atlanta: Scholars, 1989.

———. *The Temple of Jesus: His Sacrificial Program within a Cultural History of Sacrifice.* University Park, PA: Pennsylvania State University Press, 1992.

———. *Judaic Approaches to the Gospels.* Atlanta: Scholars Press for the University of South Florida, 1994.

———. "John the Purifier." In *Judaic Approaches to the Gospels*, 1–30.

———. *A Feast of Meanings: Eucharistic Theologies from Jesus through Johannine Circles.* NovTSup 72. Leiden: Brill, 1994.

———. "The Kingdom of God in Recent Discussion." *Studying the Historical Jesus: Evaluations of the State of Current Research*, edited by Bruce Chilton and Craig A. Evans, 255–80. NTTS 19. Leiden: Brill, 1994.

———. *Pure Kingdom: Jesus' Vision of God.* Studying the Historical Jesus. London: SPCK; Grand Rapids: Eerdmans, 1996.

———. *Jesus' Prayer and Jesus' Eucharist: His Personal Practice of Spirituality.* Valley Forge, PA: Trinity Press International, 1997.

———. *Jesus' Baptism and Jesus' Healing: His Personal Practice of Spirituality.* Valley Forge, PA: Trinity Press International, 1998.

———. *Rabbi Jesus: An Intimate Biography.* New York: Doubleday, 2000.

Chilton, Bruce, ed. *The Kingdom of God in the Teaching of Jesus.* Issues in Religion and Theology 5. London: SPCK; Philadelphia: Fortress, 1984.

Bibliography

Chilton, Bruce, ed. *A Comparative Handbook to the Gospel of Mark: Comparisons with the Pseudepigrapha, the Qumran Scrolls, and Rabbinic Literature.* New Testament Gospels in their Judaic Contexts 1. Leiden: Brill, 2010.

Chilton, Bruce and Craig A. Evans, eds. *Studying the Historical Jesus: Evaluations of the State of Current Research.* NTTS 9. Leiden: Brill, 1994.

———. *Jesus in Context: Temple, Purity, and Restoration.* AGJU 39. Leiden: Brill, 1997.

———. *Authenticating the Words of Jesus.* NTTS 28.1. Leiden: Brill, 1999.

———. *Authenticating the Activities of Jesus.* NTTS 28.2. Leiden: Brill, 1999.

Chilton, Bruce, and Jacob Neusner. *Judaism and the New Testament: Practices and Beliefs.* New York: Routledge, 1995.

Chilton, Bruce, Craig A. Evans, and Jacob Neusner, eds. *The Missing Jesus: Rabbinic Judaism and the New Testament.* Boston, Leiden: Brill, 2002.

Chilton, Bruce, Anthony Le Donne, and Jacob Neusner, eds. *Soundings in the Religion of Jesus: Perspectives and Methods in Jewish and Christian Scholarship.* Minneapolis: Fortress, 2012.

Christ, Felix, ed. *Oikonomia. Heilsgeschichte als Thema der Theologie. Oscar Cullmann zum 65. Geburtstag gewidmet.* Hamburg-Bergstedt: Herbert Reich, 1967.

Christensen, Torben. *The Divine Order: A Study in F. D. Maurice's Theology.* Acta Theologica Danica 11. Leiden: Brill, 1973.

Chubb, Thomas, *Posthumous Works*, 2 vols. (1748).

Clark, David. *On Earth as in Heaven: The Lord's Prayer from Jewish Prayer to Christian Ritual.* Minneapolis: Fortress, 2017.

Clark Wire, Antoinette. *The Case for Mark Composed in Performance.* Biblical Performance Criticism 3. Eugene, OR: Cascade, 2011.

Clarke, Desmond M. *Descartes: A Biography.* Cambridge: Cambridge University Press, 2006.

Clarke, Samuel. *A Discourse Concerning the Being and Attributes of God, the Obligations of Natural Religion, and the Truth and Certainty of the Christian Revelation.* London: Botham, 1716.

———. *The Works of Samuel Clarke, D.D.* 4 vols. London: John and Paul Knapton, 1738. Reprint, New York: Garland, 1978.

Clayton, John Powell. *The Concept of Correlation: Paul Tillich and the Possibility of a Mediating Theology.* New York: De Gruyter, 1980.

Cleave, Richard. *The Holy Land Satellite Atlas: Student Map Manual Illustrated Supplement.* Nicosia, Cyprus: Rohr, 1994.

Clements, Keith W. *Lovers of Discord: Twentieth-Century Theological Controversies in England.* London: SPCK, 1988.

Clooney, Francis X. "The Future of the *Harvard Theological Review* in a Global and Interreligious Age." *HTR* 10 (2008): 339–49.

Coady, C. A. J. *Testimony: A Philosophical Study.* Oxford: Clarendon, [1992]. Reprint, 2002.

Coakley, Sarah. *Christ without Absolutes: A Study of the Christology of Ernst Troeltsch.* Oxford: Clarendon, 1988.

Coakley, Sarah, and David Pailin, eds. *The Making and Remaking of Christian Doctrine: Essays in Honour of Maurice Wiles.* Oxford: Clarendon, 1993.

Cobb, James Harrel, and Louis B. Jennings. *A Biography and Bibliography of Edgar Johnson Goodspeed.* Chicago: University of Chicago Press, 1948.

Coffey, John, and Paul C. H. Lim, eds. *The Cambridge Companion to Puritanism.* Cambridge: Cambridge University Press, 2008.

Cohen, I. Bernard, and George E. Smith, eds. *The Cambridge Companion to Newton.* Cambridge: Cambridge University Press, 2002.

Cohen, Shaye J. D. *From the Maccabees to the Mishnah.* 3rd ed. Louisville: Westminster John Knox, 2014.

Colani, Timothée. *Jésus Christ et les Croyances Messianiques de son Temps.* Strassburg: Treutel et Würtz, 1864; 2nd. ed. also 1864.

Collins, Adela Yarbro. *The Beginnings of the Gospel: Probings of Mark in Context.* Minneapolis: Fortress, 1992.

———. "The Charge of Blasphemy in Mark 14.64." *JSNT* 26 (2004): 379–401.

———. *Mark: A Commentary.* Edited by Harold W. Attridge. Hermeneia. Minneapolis: Fortress, 2007.

———. "'How on Earth Did Jesus Become a God?' A Reply." In *Israel's God and Rebecca's Children*, edited by David B. Capes et al., 55–66.

———. "Apocalypticism and Christian Origins." In *The Oxford Handbook of Apocalyptic Literature*, edited by J. J. Collins, 326–39.

Collins, Adela Yarbro, and John J. Collins. *King and Messiah as Son of God: Divine, Human, and Angelic Messianic Figures in Biblical and Related Literature.* Grand Rapids: Eerdmans, 2008.

Collins, Anthony. *A Discourse of Free Thinking.* 1713. Facsimile reprint together with Richard Bentley's *Remarks* and Collins's *Philosophical Inquiry.* New York: Garland, 1978.

———. *A Philosophical Inquiry Concerning Human Liberty.* 1717.

———. *A Discourse on the Grounds and Reasons of the Christian Religion.* 1724. Facsimile reprint, New York: Garland, 1976.

———. *The Scheme of Literal Prophecy Consider'd; In a View of the Controversy, Occasion'd by a late Book, intitled, A Discourse of the Grounds and Reasons of the Christian Religion.* "London" [The Hague], 1726.

Collins, Derek. *Magic in the Ancient Greek World.* Malden, MA: Blackwell, 2008.

Collins, Jeffrey R. "Thomas Hobbes: 'Father of Atheists.'" In *Atheism and Deism Revalued: Heterodox Religious Identities in Britain, 1650–1800*, edited by Wayne Hudson, Diego Lucci, and Jeffrey R. Wigglesworth, 25–43. Farnham, Surrey: Ashgate, 2014.

Collins, John J. *Daniel: With an Introduction to Apocalyptic Literature.* Grand Rapids: Eerdmans, 1984.

———. *Daniel: A Commentary on the Book of Daniel*, with an essay by Adela Yarbro Collins, "The Influence of Daniel on the New Testament." Edited by Frank Moore Cross. Hermeneia. Minneapolis: Fortress, 1993.

———. *The Scepter and the Star: Messianism in Light of the Dead Sea Scrolls*. 2nd ed. Grand Rapids: Eerdmans, [1995], 2010.

———. *Apocalypticism in the Dead Sea Scrolls*. New York: Routledge, 1997.

———. *Beyond the Qumran Community: The Sectarian Movement of the Dead Sea Scrolls*. Grand Rapids: Eerdmans, 2010.

———. *The Dead Sea Scrolls: A Biography*. Princeton: Princeton University Press, 2013.

———. *Apocalypse, Prophecy, and Pseudepigraphy: On Jewish Apocalyptic Literature*. Grand Rapids: Eerdmans, 2015.

———. *The Apocalyptic Imagination: An Introduction to Jewish Apocalyptic Literature*. Grand Rapids: Eerdmans, [1984]; 3rd ed. 2016.

Collins, John J., ed. *Apocalypse: The Morphology of a Genre*. Semeia 14. Missoula, MT: Scholars, 1979.

———. *The Encyclopedia of Apocalypticism*. Vol. 1, *The Origins of Apocalypticism in Judaism and Christianity*. New York: Continuum, 2000.

———. *The Oxford Handbook on Apocalyptic Literature*. Oxford: Oxford University Press, 2014.

Collins, John J., Peter W. Flint, and Cameron VanEpps, eds. *The Book of Daniel: Composition and Reception*. 2 vols. VTSup 83. Leiden: Brill, 2001.

Collins, John J., and Daniel C. Harlow, eds. *The Eerdmans Dictionary of Early Judaism*. Grand Rapids: Eerdmans, 2010.

Collins, John J., and Robert A. Kugler, eds. *Religion in the Dead Sea Scrolls*. Studies in the Dead Sea Scrolls and Related Literature. Grand Rapids: Eerdmans, 2000.

Collins, John J., and Gregory E. Sterling, eds. *Hellenism in the Land of Israel*. Christianity and Judaism in Antiquity 13. Notre Dame, IN: University of Notre Dame Press, 2001.

Collins, Nina L. *Jesus, the Sabbath and the Jewish Debate: Healing on the Sabbath in the 1st and 2nd Centuries CE* LNTS 474. London: T&T Clark, 2014.

Coloe, Mary L., and Tom Thatcher, eds. *John, Qumran, and the Dead Sea Scrolls: Sixty Years of Discovery and Debate*. SBL EJL 32. Atlanta: SBL Press, 2011.

Commission Biblique Pontificale. *Bible et Christologie*. Paris: Les Éditions du Cerf, 1984.

Compton, Jared. *Psalm 110 and the Logic of Hebrews*. LNTS 537. London: T&T Clark, 2015.

Congdon, David W. *The Mission of Demythologizing: Rudolf Bultmann's Dialectical Theology*. Minneapolis: Fortress, 2015.

Conway, Colleen M. *Behold the Man: Jesus and Greco-Roman Masculinity*. Oxford: Oxford University Press, 2008.

Conzelmann, Hans. *Die Mitte der Zeit*. Tübingen: Mohr Siebeck, 1953; 2nd ed., 1957. ET: *The Theology of St Luke*. Translated by Geoffrey Buswell. New York: Harper; London: Faber and Faber, 1960.

———. "Jesus Christus." *Die Religion in Geschichte und Gegenwart*. 3rd ed., edited by Kurt Galling et al., 3: 619–53. Tübingen: Mohr Siebeck, 1959. ET: *Jesus*. Translated by J. Raymond Lord. Edited by John Reumann. Philadelphia: Fortress, 1973.

———. "The Method of Life-of-Jesus Research." In *The Historical Jesus and the Kerygmatic Christ: Essays on the New Quest of the Historical Jesus*, edited by Carl E. Braaten and Roy A. Harrisville, 54–68.

———. *An Outline Theology of the New Testament*. Translated by John Bowden. London; SCM; New York: Harper, 1969.

———. *History of Primitive Christianity*. Translated by John E. Steely. Nashville: Abingdon, 1973.

———. *Theologie als Schriftauslegung*. München: Chr. Kaiser, 1974.

———. *1 Corinthians*. Translated by James W. Leitch. Hemeneia. Philadelphia: Fortress, 1975.

———. *Acts of the Apostles*. Translated by James Limburg, A. Thomas Kraabel, and Donald H. Juel. Hermeneia. Philadelphia: Fortress, 1987.

———. *Interpreting the New Testament: An Introduction to the Principles and Methods of New Testament Exegesis*. With Andreas Lindemann. Translated by Siegfried S. Schatzmann. Peabody, MA: Hendrickson, 1988.

———. *Gentiles, Jews, Christians: Polemics and Apologetics in the Greco-Roman Era*. Translated by M. Eugene Boring. Minneapolis: Fortress, 1992.

Cook, James I. *Edgar Johnson Goodspeed: Articulate Scholar*. Chico, CA: Scholars, 1981.

Cook, M. J. *Mark's Treatment of the Jewish Leaders*. NovTSup 51. Leiden: Brill, 1978.

Cooper, John W. *Panentheism: The Other God of the Philosophers; From Plato to the Present*. Grand Rapids: Baker Academic, 2006.

Copan, Paul, ed. *Will the Real Jesus Please Stand Up? A Debate between William Lane Craig and John Dominic Crossan*. Grand Rapids: Baker, 1998.

Copan, Paul, and Craig A. Evans, eds. *Who Was Jesus? A Jewish-Christian Dialogue*. Louisville: Westminster John Knox, 2001.

Copenhaver, Brian P. *Hermetica: The Greek* Corpus Hermeticum *and the Latin* Asclepius *in a New English Translation, with Notes and Introduction*. Cambridge: Cambridge University Press, 1992.

Corley, Kathleen E., *Private Women, Public Meals: Social Conflict in the Synoptic Tradition*. Peabody, MA: Hendrickson, 1993.

Cotter, Wendy. *Miracles in the Greco-Roman World: A Sourcebook*. London: Routledge, 1999.

Cottingham, John, ed. *The Cambridge Companion to Descartes*. Cambridge: Cambridge University Press, 1992.

Cottingham, John, ed. *Descartes*. Oxford Readings in Philosophy. Oxford: Oxford University Press, 1998.

Courth, Franz. "Die Evangelienkritik des David Friedrich Strauss im Echo seiner Zeitgenossen. Zur Breitungwirkung seines Werkes." In *Historische Kritik in*

Bibliography

der Theologie. Beiträge zu ihrer Geschichte, edited by Georg Schwaiger, 60–98. Göttingen: Vandenhoeck & Ruprecht, 1980.

Cowdell, Scott. *Is Christ Unique?* New York: Paulist, 1996.

Craig, William Lane. *The Historical Argument for the Resurrection of Jesus during the Deist Controversy.* Texts and Studies in Religion 23. Lewiston: Mellon, 1985.

Crawford, Barry S. *Redescribing the Gospel of Mark.* Atlanta: SBL Press, 2017.

Crawford, Sidnie White. *Rewriting Scripture in Second Temple Times.* Grand Rapids: Eerdmans, 2008.

———. "A View from the Caves: Who Put the Scrolls in There?" *BAR* 37, no. 5 (2011): 30–39, 69–70.

Creed, John Martin. *The Gospel according to St. Luke: The Greek Text with Introduction, Notes, and Indices.* London: Macmillan, 1930. Reprint, 1950.

———. *The Divinity of Christ.* [1938]. Reprint with introduction by D. M. Mackinnon, London: Collins, 1964.

Creed, John Martin, and J. S. Boys Smith. *Religious Thought in the Eighteenth Century, Illustrated from Writers of the Period.* Cambridge: Cambridge University Press, 1934.

Crisp, Oliver D. *Divinity and Humanity: The Incarnation Reconsidered.* Current Issues in Theology. Cambridge: Cambridge University Press, 2007.

———. "Incarnation." In *The Oxford Handbook of Systematic Theology,* edited by John Webster, Kathryn Tanner, Iain Torrance, 160–75. Oxford: Oxford University Press, 2007.

———. *God Incarnate: Explorations in Christology.* New York: T&T Clark, 2009.

———. "Donald Baillie (1887–1954): Paradox and Christology." In *Revisioning Christology: Theology in the Reformed Tradition,* 1–22. Burlington, VT: Ashgate, 2011.

Crisp, Oliver D., and Fred Sanders, eds. *Christology Ancient and Modern: Explorations in Constructive Dogmatics.* Grand Rapids: Zondervan, 2013.

Crosby, Donald A. *Horace Bushnell's Theory of Language: In the Context of Other Nineteenth-Century Theories of Language.* The Hague: Mouton, 1975.

Cross, Barbara M. *Horace Bushnell: Minister to a Changing America.* Chicago: University of Chicago Press, 1958.

Cross, F. L. *The Oxford Dictionary of the Christian Church.* Oxford: Oxford University Press, [1957]; 3rd ed., edited by E. A. Livingstone, 1997.

Cross, F. L., ed. *Studia Evangelica.* Vols. 2 and 3, *Papers Presented to the Second International Congress on New Testament Studies, Oxford, 1961.* Part 1, *The New Testament Scriptures.* Part 2, *The New Testament Message.* TUGAL 87–88. Berlin: Akademie-Verlag, 1964.

———. *Studia Evangelica.* Vols. 4 and 5, *Papers Presented to the Third International Congress on New Testament Studies, Oxford, 1965.* Part 1, *The New Testament Scriptures.* Part 2, *The New Testament Message.* TUGAL 102–3. Berlin: Akademie-Verlag, 1964. [Vol. 5 contains a cumulative index for vols. 1–5.]

A History of the Quests for the Historical Jesus

Crossan, John Dominic. *In Parables: The Challenge of the Historical Jesus.* New York: Harper & Row, 1973.

———. *Cliffs of Fall: Paradox and Polyvalence in the Parables of Jesus.* New York: Seabury, 1980.

———. *The Cross That Spoke: The Origins of the Passion Narrative.* San Francisco: Harper & Row, 1988.

———. *The Historical Jesus: The Life of a Mediterranean Peasant.* San Francisco: HarperSanFrancisco, 1991.

———. *Jesus: A Revolutionary Biography.* San Francisco: HarperSanFrancisco, 1994.

———. *Who Killed Jesus? Exposing the Roots of Anti-Semitism in the Gospel Story of the Death of Jesus.* San Francisco: HarperSanFrancisco, 1995.

———. "Itinerants and Householders in the Earliest Jesus Movement." In *Whose Historical Jesus?*, edited by William E. Arnal and Michael Desjardins, 7–24.

———. *The Birth of Christianity: Discovering What Happened in the Years Immediately After the Execution of Jesus.* San Francisco: HarperSanFrancisco, 1998.

———. *A Long Way from Tipperary.* San Francisco: HarperSanFrancisco, 2000.

———. *God and Empire: Jesus Against Rome, Then and Now.* San Francisco: HarperSanFrancisco, 2007.

———. *The Greatest Prayer: Rediscovering the Revolutionary Message of the Lord's Prayer.* San Francisco: HarperOne, 2010.

———. "Context and Text in Historical Jesus Methodology." In *HSHJ*, 1:159–79.

Crossan, John Dominic, Luke Timothy Johnson, and Werner H. Kelber. *The Jesus Controversy: Perspective in Conflict.* Harrisburg, PA: Trinity Press International, 1999.

Crossan, John Dominic, and Jonathan L. Reed. *Excavating Jesus: Beneath the Stones, Behind the Texts.* 2nd ed. San Francisco: HarperSanFrancisco, 2001.

Crossley, James G. *The Date of Mark's Gospel: Insight from the Law in Earliest Christianity.* JSNTSS 266. London: T&T Clark International, 2004.

———. *Jesus in an Age of Neoliberalism: Quests, Scholarship and Ideology.* Sheffield: Equinox, 2012.

———. *Jesus and the Chaos of History: Redirecting the Life of the Historical Jesus.* Biblical Reconfigurations. Oxford: Oxford University Press, 2015.

Crossley, James G., ed. *Judaism, Jewish Identities and the Gospel Tradition: Essays in Honour of Maurice Casey.* London: Equinox, 2010.

Crouzel, Henri. *Origen: The Life and Thought of the First Great Theologian.* Translated by A. S. Worrall. Edinburgh: T&T Clark; San Francisco: Harper & Row, 1989.

Crowe, Frederick E. *Lonergan.* Outstanding Christian Thinkers. Collegeville, MN: Liturgical, 1992.

Cullmann, Oscar. *Oscar Cullmann. Vorträge und Aufsätze, 1925–1962.* Edited by Karlfried Fröhlich. Tübingen: Mohr Siebeck; Zürich: Zwingli, 1966.

———. *The Early Church.* Translated by A. J. B. Higgins and Stanley Godman. London: SCM, [1956]; abridged ed., 1966.

Bibliography

———. "The Origin of Christmas." In *The Early Church*, abridged ed., 21–36.

———. *Peter: Disciple, Apostle, Martyr; A Historical and Theological Study*. Translated by Floyd V. Filson. 2nd ed. London: SCM, 1962.

———. *The Christology of the New Testament*. Translated by Shirley C. Guthrie and Charles A. M. Hall. London: SCM, 1959; 2nd ed., 1963.

———. *Christ and Time: The Primitive Christian Conception of Time and History*. Translated by Floyd V. Filson. Philadelphia: Westminster; London: SCM, 1951; rev. ed., 1964.

———. *Heil als Geschichte. Heilsgeschichtliche Existenz im Neuen Testament*. Tübingen: Mohr Siebeck, 1965.

———. *Salvation in History*. Draft translation prepared by Sidney G. Gowers and completed by the staff of the SCM. London: SCM, 1967.

———. *The Johannine Circle: Its Place in Judaism, among the Disciples of Jesus and in Early Christianity; A Study in the Origin of John*. Translation by John Bowden. London: SCM, 1976.

Culpepper, R. Alan. *Anatomy of the Fourth Gospel: A Study in Literary Design*. Foundations and Facets: New Testament. Philadelphia: Fortress, 1973.

———. *John the Son of Zebedee: The Life of a Legend*. Columbia: University of South Carolina Press, 1994.

Culpepper, R. Alan and C. Clifton Black, eds. *Exploring the Gospel of John: In Honor of D. Moody Smith*. Louisville: Westminster John Knox, 1996.

Cunning, David, ed. *The Cambridge Companion to Descartes' Meditations*. Cambridge: Cambridge University Press, 2014.

Curtis, Philip. *A Hawk among the Sparrows: A Biography of Austin Farrer*. London: SPCK, 1985. [Includes a chapter by Michael Goulder on "Farrer the Biblical Scholar," 192–212.]

Cyril of Alexandria. *Select Letters*. Edited and translated by Lionel R. Wickham. Oxford Early Christian Texts. Oxford: Clarendon, 1983.

Dahl, N. A. *The Crucified Messiah and Other Essays*. Minneapolis: Augsburg, 1974.

Dalman, Gustaf. *Der leidende und der sterbende Messias der Synagoge im ersten nachchristlichen Jahrtausend*. Berlin: Reuther & Reichard, 1888; supplemented by *Jesaja 53. Das Prophetenwort vom Sühnleiden des Gottesknechtes mit besonderer Berücksichtigung der jüdischen Literatur*. Schriften des Institutum Judaicum in Berlin 13. Leipzig: J. C. Hinrichs, 1894; 2nd ed., 1914.

———. *Die Grammatik des jüdisch-palästinischen Aramäisch nach den Idiomen des palästinischen Talmud des Onkelostargum und der Jerusalemischen Targume*. Leipzig: Hinrichs, 1894; 2nd ed., 1905. Reprint with *Aramäische Dialektproben*. Leipzig: Hinrichs, 1896; 2nd ed., 1927. In Darmstadt: Wissenschaftliche Buchgesellschaft, 1960.

———. *The Words of Jesus, Considered in the Light of Post-Biblical Jewish Writings and the Aramaic Language*. 1898; 2nd ed. 1930. Translated by D. M. Kay. Edinburgh: T&T Clark, 1902. Reprint, Eugene OR: Wipf & Stock, 1997.

———. *Aramäisch-neuhebräisches Handwörterbuch zu Targum, Talmud und Midrasch.* Göttingen: Pfeiffer, 1897; 3rd ed., 1938.

———. *Orte und Wege Jesu.* Gütersloh: Bertelsmann, 1919; 3rd ed., 1924. ET: *Sacred Sites and Ways: Studies in the Topography of the Gospels.* Translated by Paul P. Levertoff. London: SPCK, 1929; New York: Macmillan, 1935.

———. *Jesus-Jeschua. Die drei Sprachen Jesu. Jesus in der Synagoge, auf dem Berge, beim Passachmahl, am Kreuz.* Leipzig: Hinrichs, 1922. Reprint, Darmstadt: Wissenschaftliche Buchgesellschaft, 1967. ET: *Jesus-Jeshua: Studies in the Gospels.* Translated by Paul P. Levertoff. London: SPCK, 1929.

———. *Jerusalem und seine Gelände.* Gütersloh: Bertelsmann, 1930. Reprint, Hildesheim: Olms, 1972.

———. *Arbeit und Sitte in Palästina.* 7 vols. Gütersloh: Bertelsmann, 1928–42. Reprint, Hildesheim: Olms, 1964.

Damm, Alex. *Ancient Rhetoric and the Synoptic Problem: Clarifying Markan Priority.* BETL 252. Leuven: Peeters, 2013.

Danby, Herbert, trans. *The Mishnah.* London: Oxford University Press, 1933.

Daniel, Stephen H. *John Toland: His Methods, Manners, and Mind.* Montreal: McGill Queen's University Press, 1984.

Daube, David. *The New Testament and Rabbinic Judaism.* Jordan Lectures at the School of Oriental and African Studies, University of London. London: Athlone, 1956.

———. *The Deed and the Doer in the Bible.* Gifford Lectures 1962. Edited by Calum Carmichael. Philadelphia, PA: Templeton Foundation Press, 2008.

———. *Law and Wisdom in the Bible.* Gifford Lectures 1964. Edited by Calum Carmichael. Philadelphia, PA: Templeton Foundation Press, 2011.

Davidson, Edward H., and William J. Scheick. *Paine, Scripture and Authority: The Age of Reason as Religious and Political Idea.* Bethlehem, PA: Lehigh University Press; London: Associated University Presses, 1994.

Davidson, Randall T., ed. *The Lambeth Conferences of 1867, 1878, 1888.* London: SPCK, 1889.

Davies, Margaret. *Rhetoric and Reference in the Fourth Gospel.* JSNTSup 69. Sheffield: Sheffield Academic Press, 1992.

Davies, Philip R. "War of the Sons of Light against the Sons of Darkness." In *Encyclopedia of the Dead Sea Scrolls*, edited by Lawrence H. Schiffman and James C. VanderKam, 2:965–68.

Davies, Stevan L. *Jesus the Healer: Possession, Trance, and the Origin of Christianity.* New York: Continuum, 1995.

Davies, W. D. *Paul and Rabbinic Judaism: Some Rabbinic Elements in Pauline Theology.* London: SPCK, 1948; 4th ed., Philadelphia: Fortress, 1980.

———. *Torah in the Messianic Age and/or the Age to Come.* JBL Monograph Series 7. Philadelphia: SBL Press, 1952.

Bibliography

———. *The Setting of the Sermon on the Mount*. Cambridge: Cambridge University Press, 1964.

———. *The Sermon on the Mount*. Cambridge: Cambridge University Press, 1966.

———. *The Gospel and the Land: Early Christianity and Jewish Territorial Doctrine*. Berkeley: University of California Press, 1974.

———. *The Territorial Dimensions of Judaism*. Berkeley: University of California Press, 1982. [The 2nd ed. contains *A Symposium and Further Reflections*. Minneapolis: Fortress, 1991.]

Davies, W. D., and Dale C. Allison Jr. *Matthew*. 3 vols. ICC. Edinburgh: T&T Clark, 1988–97.

Davies, W. D., and D. Daube, eds. *The Background of the New Testament and Its Eschatology: In Honour of Charles Harold Dodd*. Cambridge: Cambridge University Press, 1954. Reprint, 1964.

Davies, W. D., Louis Finkelstein, William Horbury, and John Sturdy, eds. *The Cambridge History of Judaism*. 4 vols. Cambridge: Cambridge University Press, 1984–2006. [The first two volumes were edited by W. D. Davies and Louis Finkelstein. Vol. 3 contains W. D. Davies and E. P. Sanders, "Jesus: From the Jewish Point of View," 618–67, and Davies on "Paul: From the Jewish Point of View," 678–730.]

Davis, Stephen T. *Logic and the Nature of God*. Grand Rapids: Eerdmans, 1983.

———. "Was Jesus Mad, Bad, or God?" In *The Incarnation*, edited by Davis et al., 221–45.

Davis, Stephen T., Daniel Kendall, and Gerald O'Collins, eds. *The Trinity: An Interdisciplinary Symposium on the Trinity*. Oxford: Oxford University Press, 1999.

———. *The Incarnation: An Interdisciplinary Symposium on the Incarnation of the Son of God*. Oxford: Oxford University Press, 2002.

Davies, W. Merlin. *An Introduction to F. D. Maurice's Theology*. London: SPCK, 1964.

Dawe, Donald G. "A Fresh Look at the Kenotic Christologies." *SJT* 15 (1962): 337–49.

Dawes, Gregory W. *The Historical Jesus Quest: Landmarks in the Search for the Jesus of History*. Louisville: Westminster John Knox, 2000.

Dean, William E. *American Religious Empiricism*. Albany: State University of New York Press, 1986.

De Beer, E. S., ed. *The Correspondence of John Locke*. 9 vols. Oxford: Clarendon, 1989.

De Boer, Martinus C., ed. *From Jesus to John: Essays on Jesus and New Testament Christology in Honour of Marinus de Jonge*. JSNTSup 84. Sheffield: Sheffield Academic Press, 1993.

Deines, Roland. *Jüdische Steingefässe und pharisäische Frömmigkeit. Ein archäologisch-historischer Beitrag zum Verständnis von Joh 2,6 und der jüdischen Reinheithalacha zur Zeit Jesu*. WUNT 52. Tübingen: Mohr Siebeck, 1993.

———. *Die Pharisäer. Ihr Verständnis im Spiegel der christlichen und jüdischen Forschung seit Wellhausen und Graetz*. WUNT 101. Tübingen: Mohr Siebeck, 1997.

---. "Martin Hengel: A Life in the Service of Christology." *TynBul* 58 (2007): 25–42.

---. "Galilee and the Historical Jesus in Recent Research." In *Galilee in the Late Second Temple and Mishnaic Periods*, vol. 1, edited by David E. Fiensy and James Riley Strange, 11–48. Minneapolis: Fortress, 2014.

---. "Religious Practices and Religious Movements in Galilee: 100 BCE–200 CE." In *Galilee in the Late Second Temple and Mishnaic Periods*, vol. 1, *Life, Culture and Society*, edited by David E. Fiensy and James Riley Strange, 78–111. Minneapolis: Fortress, 2014.

Deines, Roland, Volker Lippin, and Karl-Wilhelm Niebuhr, eds. *Walter Grundmann. Ein Neutestamentler im dritten Reich*. Leipzig: Evangelischer Verlagsanstalt, 2007.

De la Potterie, Ignace. *La Vérité dans Saint Jean*. AnBib 73. Rome: Biblical Institute Press, 1977.

D'Elia, John A. *A Place at the Table: George Eldon Ladd and the Rehabilitation of Evangelical Scholarship in America*. Oxford: Oxford University Press, 2008.

Deissmann, Adolf. *Bibelstudien*. Marburg: Elwert, 1895. Reprint with *Neue Bibelstudien*. Marburg: Elwert, 1897. ET: *Bible Studies*. Translated by Alexander Grieve. Edinburgh: T&T Clark, 1901; 2nd ed. 1903.

---. *Licht vom Osten*. Tübingen: Mohr Siebeck, 1908; 4th ed., 1923. ET: *Light from the Ancient East*. Translated by Lionel R. M Strachan. Edinburgh: T&T Clark, 1910. Reprint, Grand Rapids: Baker, 1978.

---. *The Religion of Jesus and the Faith of Paul*. Translated by William E. Wilson. London: Hodder & Stoughton, 1923.

De Jonge, Marinus. *Christology in Context: The Earliest Christian Response to Jesus*. Philadelphia: Westminster, 1988.

---. "Jesus' Death for Others and the Death of the Maccabean Martyrs." *Text and Testimony: Essays on New Testament and Apocryphal Literature in Honour of A. F. J. Klijn*. Edited by T. Baarda, A. Hilhorst., G. P. Luttikhuizen, A. S. van der Woude. Kampen: J. H. Kok, 1988.

De Labriolle, Pierre. *La Réaction Païenne. Étude sur la Polémique antichrétienne du Ier au VIe Siècle*. Paris: L'Artisan du Livre, 1942.

De la Roche, Michael. *Memoirs of Literature. Containing a Large Account of Many Valuable Books, Letters and Dissertations upon Several Subjects, Miscellaneous Observations, etc.* London: Kaplock, 1722.

Del Colle, Ralph. *Christ and Spirit: Spirit-Christology in Trinitarian Perspective*. Oxford: Oxford University Press, 1994.

Delitzsch, Friedrich. *Die grosse Täuschung. Kritische Beobachtungen zu den alttestamentliche Berichten über Israels Eindringungen in Kanaan, die Gottesoffenbarung von Sinai und die Wirksamkeit der Propheten*. Stuttgart: Deutsche Verlagsanstalt, 1920.

Demson, David E. *Hans Frei and Karl Barth: Different Ways of Reading Scripture*. Eugene, OR: Wipf & Stock, 1997.

Bibliography

Den Heyer, C. J. *Jesus Matters: 150 Years of Research.* Harrisburg PA: Trinity Press International, 1998.

Denton, Donald L. Jr. *Historiography and Hermeneutics in Jesus Studies: An Examination of the Work of John Dominic Crossan and Ben F. Meyer.* JSNTSup 262. New York: T&T Clark International, 2004.

Denzey Lewis, Nicola, and Justine Ariel Blount. "Rethinking the Origins of the Nag Hammadi Codices." *JBL* 133 (2014): 399–419.

Denzinger, Heinrich. *Enchiridion symbolorum definitionum et declarationum de rebus fidei et morum.* 36th ed. by A. Schönmetzer. Freiburg: Herder, 1976. Abbreviated as Denzinger-Schönmetzer.

Deppe, Dean B. *The Theological Intentions of Mark's Literary Devices: Markan Intercalations, Frames, Allusionary Repetitions, Narrative Surprises, and Three Types of Mirroring.* Eugene OR: Wipf & Stock, 2015.

Derrett, J. Duncan M. *Law in the New Testament.* London: Darton, Longman & Todd, 1970. [Among the articles reprinted are "The Parable of the Unjust Steward" (1961), 48–77; "The Parable of the Wicked Vinedressers" (1963), 286–312; and "Render to Caesar ... ," 313–38.]

———. *Jesus' Audience: The Social and Psychological Environment in which He Worked, Prolegomena to a Restatement of the Teaching of Jesus.* Lectures at Newquay 1971. London: Darton, Longman & Todd, 1973.

———. *Studies in the New Testament.* 6 vols. Leiden: Brill, 1977–95. [The following articles are discussed in the text in connection with Derrett: "Cursing Jesus (1 Cor. Xii. 3): The Jews as Religious 'Persecutors.'" *Studies in the New Testament,* 2:194–204. "Why and How Jesus Walked on the Sea." *NovT* 23 (1981): 331–48. Reprint, *Studies in the New Testament* 4:92–110. "The Upper Room and the Dish." *HeyJ* 26 (1985): 373–81. Reprint, *Studies in the New Testament,* vol. 5 (1989): 119–28.]

———. *The Anastasis: The Resurrection as an Historical Event.* Shipston-on-Stour: Drinkwater, 1982.

———. *The Making of Mark: The Scriptural Basis of the Earliest Gospel.* 2 vols. Shipston-on-Stour: Drinkwater, 1985.

———. *New Resolutions of Old Conundrums: A Fresh Insight into Luke's Gospel.* Shipston-on-Stour: Drinkwater, 1986.

———. *The Victim: The Johannine Passion Narrative Reexamined.* Shipston-on-Stour: Drinkwater, 1993.

———. *The Sermon on the Mount: A Manual for Living.* Northampton: Pilkington, 1994.

———. *Two Masters: The Buddha and Jesus.* Northampton: Pilkington, 1995.

———. *Law and Morality.* Northampton: Pilkington, 1998.

DeSilva, David A. *The Jewish Teachers of Jesus, James, and Jude: What Earliest Christianity Learned from the Apocrypha and Pseudepigrapha.* Oxford: Oxford University Press, 2012.

Descartes, René. *Mediatationes de Prima Philosophiae.* Paris: Soly, 1641.

———. *The Philosophical Writings of Descartes*. 2 vols. Translated by John Cottingham, Robert Stoothoff, and Dugald Murdoch. Cambridge: Cambridge University Press, 1984–85.

———. *The Correspondence*. Translated by John Cottingham, Robert Stoothoff, Dugald Murdoch, and Anthony Kenny. Cambridge: Cambridge University Press, 1991.

Despland, Michel. *Kant on History and Religion, with a Translation of Kant's "On the Failure of All Attempted Philosophical Theodicies*. Montreal: McGill-Queen's University Press, 1973.

Detweiler, Robert, and William G. Doty, eds. *The Daemonic Imagination: Biblical Text and Secular Story*. AARSR 60. Atlanta: Scholars, 1990.

Devenish, Philip E., and George L. Goodwin, eds. *Witness and Existence: Essays in Honor of Schubert M. Ogden*. Chicago: University of Chicago Press, 1989.

Dewey, Joanna. *Markan Public Debate: Literary Technique, Concentric Structure, and Theology in Mark 2:1–3:6*. SBLDS 48. Chico, CA: Scholars, 1980.

———. *The Oral Ethos of the Early Church: Speaking, Writing, and the Gospel of Mark*. Biblical Performance Criticism 8. Eugene, OR: Cascade, 2013.

Dibelius, Martin. *From Tradition to Gospel*. Translated by Bertram Lee Woolf. New York: Scribner, 1935, 1971; Cambridge: Clarke, 1971.

———. *Die Botschaft von Jesu Christi. Die alte Überlieferung der Gemeinde in Geschichten, Sprüchen und Reden. Wiederhergestellt und verdeutscht*. Tübingen: Mohr Siebeck, 1935.

———. *The Message of Jesus Christ: The Tradition of the Early Christian Communities*. Translated by Frederick C. Grant. New York: Scribner's, 1939.

———. *Jesus*. 3rd ed. Addendum by Werner Georg Kümmel. Berlin: De Gruyter, [1939], 1960.

———. *Jesus*. Translated by Charles B. Hedrick and Frederick C. Grant. Philadelphia: Westminster, 1949.

———. *Die Formgeschichte des Evangeliums*. 5th ed. With postscript by Gerhard Iber. Tübingen: Mohr Siebeck, 1966.

Dickie, Matthew. *Magic and Magicians in the Greco-Roman World*. New York: Routledge, 2001.

Dillistone, F. W. *C. H. Dodd: Interpreter of the New Testament*. Grand Rapids: Eerdmans, 1977.

Dinkler, Erich, ed. *Zeit und Geschichte. Dankesgabe an Rudolf Bultmann zum 80. Geburtstag im Auftrage der Alten Marburger, und in Zusammenarbeit mit Hartwig Thyen*. Tübingen: Mohr Siebeck, 1964.

Diogenes Laertius. *Lives of Eminent Philosophers*. 2 vols. Translated by R. D. Hicks. LCL. Cambridge, MA: Harvard University Press, 1925. Reprint, 1972.

Do, Toan. *Re-thinking the Death of Jesus: An Examination and Theological Study of* Hilasmos *and* Agape *in 1 John 2:1–2 and 4:7–10*. Leuven: Peeters, 2014.

Dobschütz, Ernst von. *The Eschatology of the Gospels*. London: Hodder & Stoughton, 1910.

Bibliography

———. "Matthäus als Rabbi und Katechet." *ZNW* 37 (1928): 338–48. ET: "Matthew as Rabbi and Catechist." Translated by Robert Morgan. In *The Interpretation of Matthew*, edited by Graham N. Stanton, 2nd ed., 27–38.

Dodd, Charles Harold. "Jesus as Teacher and Prophet." In *Mysterium Christi*, edited by G. K. A. Bell and D. Adolf Deissmann, 53–66.

———. "ΙΛΑΣΚΕΣΘΑΙ, Its Cognates, Derivatives and Synonyms in the Septuagint," *JTS* 32 (1931): 352–60. Reprint with the title, "Atonement." In *The Bible and the Greeks*, 82–95. London: Hodder & Stoughton, 1935.

———. *The Parables of the Kingdom*. London: Nisbet, 1935; rev. ed. 1936.

———. *The Present Task in New Testament Studies: An Inaugural Lecture Delivered in the Divinity School on Tuesday, 2 June 1936*. Cambridge: Cambridge University Press, 1936.

———. *The Apostolic Preaching and Its Development: Three Lectures with an Appendix on Eschatology and History*. London: Hodder & Stoughton, 1936. New Edition, 1944.

———. *New Testament Studies*. Manchester: Manchester University Press, 1953.

———. *The Interpretation of the Fourth Gospel*. Cambridge: Cambridge University Press, 1953.

———. *Historical Tradition in the Fourth Gospel*. Cambridge: Cambridge University Press, 1963.

———. *History and the Gospel*. London: Hodder & Stoughton, [1938]; rev. ed., 1964.

———. *More New Testament Studies*. Manchester: Manchester University Press, 1968.

———. *The Founder of Christianity*. Foreword by John A. T. Robinson. London: Collins, 1971.

Dorman, Theodore M. *The Hermeneutics of Oscar Cullmann*. San Francisco: Mellen Research University Press, 1991.

Dorrien, Gary J. *The Making of American Liberal Theology: Idealism, Realism, Modernity, 1900–1950*. Louisville: Westminster John Knox, 2003.

Dostal, Robert J., ed. *The Cambridge Companion to Gadamer*. Cambridge: Cambridge University Press, 2002.

Douglas, Mary. *Purity and Danger: An Analysis of the Concepts of Pollution and Taboo*. London: Routledge & Kegan Paul, 1966.

———. *Natural Symbols: Explorations in Cosmology*. New York: Random House, 1970.

———. *Implicit Meanings: Essays in Anthropology*. London: Routledge & Kegan Paul, 1975.

Downing, Gerald F. *Christ and the Cynics: Jesus and Other Radical Preachers in First-Century Tradition*. JSOT Manuals 4. Sheffield: Sheffield Academic Press, 1988.

———. *Cynics and Christian Origins*. Edinburgh: T&T Clark, 1992.

———. "Deeper Reflections on the Jewish Cynic Jesus." *JBL* 117 (1998): 97–104.

———. "The Jewish Cynic Jesus." In *Jesus, Mark and Q*, edited by Labahn and Schmidt, 184–214.

———. "Jesus and Cynicism." In *HSHJ*, 2:1105–36.

Draper, Jonathan A., Richard A. Horsley, and John Miles Foley, eds. *Performing the Gospel: Orality, Memory, and Mark; Essays Dedicated to Werner Kelber.* Minneapolis: Fortress, 2006.

Draper, Jonathan A., and Clayton N. Jefford, eds. *The Didache: A Missing Piece of the Puzzle in Early Christianity.* Early Christianity and Its Literature 14. Atlanta: SBL Press, 2015.

Drews, Arthur. *Die Christusmythe.* 2 vols. Jena: Diederichs, 1909–11. ET: *The Christ Myth.* Translation of the 3rd German edition by C. Delisle Burns. London: Unwin, 1910.

———. *Die Zeugnisse für die Geschichtlichkeit Jesu. Eine Antwort an die Schriftgelehrten mit besonderer Berücksichtigung der theologischen Methode.* Jena: Eugen Diederichs, 1911. ET: *The Witnesses of the Historicity of Jesus.* Translated by Joseph McCabe. London: Watts, 1912. Reprint, New York: Arno, 1972.

Drury, John. *The Parables in the Gospels: History and Allegory.* New York: Crossroad, 1985.

Duhaime, Anthony Jean, J. Blasi, and Paul-André Turcotte, eds. *Handbook of Early Christianity: Social Science Approaches.* Oxford: Alta Mira, 2002.

Duke, James O. *Horace Bushnell on the Vitality of Biblical Language.* Chico, CA: SBL Centennial Publications, 1984.

Dunderberg, Ismo. *The Beloved Disciple in Conflict? Revisiting the Gospels of John and Thomas.* Oxford: Oxford University Press, 2006.

Dungan, David Laird. *A History of the Synoptic Problem: The Canon, the Text, the Composition, and the Interpretation of the Gospels.* New York: Doubleday, 1999.

Dunn, James D. G. *Baptism in the Holy Spirit: A Re-examination of the New Testament Teaching on the Gift of the Spirit in Relation to Pentecostalism Today.* SBT 13. London: SCM, 1970.

———. *Jesus and the Spirit: A Study of the Religious and Charismatic Experience of Jesus and the First Christians as Reflected in the New Testament.* London: SCM, 1975.

———. *Romans.* WBC 38A, 38B, 2 vols. Dallas, TX: Word, 1988.

———. *Christology in the Making: A New Testament Inquiry into the Origins of the Doctrine of the Incarnation.* 2nd ed. Grand Rapids: Eerdmans, 1989.

———. *Unity and Diversity in the New Testament: An Inquiry into the Character of Earliest Christianity.* London: SCM; Valley Forge PA: Trinity Press International, 1977; 2nd ed., 1990.

———. *Jesus, Paul and the Law: Studies in Mark and Galatians.* London: SPCK, 1990.

———. *The Partings of the Ways, Between Christianity and Judaism and Their Significance for the Character of Christianity.* London: SCM; Philadelphia: Trinity Press International, 1991.

———. *The Christ and the Spirit: Collected Essays.* Vol. 1, *Christology.* Vol. 2, *Pneumatology.* Grand Rapids: Eerdmans, 1998.

———. "Christ, Adam, and Preexistence." In *Where Christology Began*, edited by Ralph P. Martin and Brian J. Dodd, 74–83.

Bibliography

———. "Let John Be John: A Gospel for Its Time." In *The Christ and the Spirit*, 345–75.

———. *The Theology of Paul the Apostle*. Grand Rapids: Eerdmans, 1998.

———. *Jesus Remembered*. Christianity in the Making 1. Grand Rapids: Eerdmans, 2003.

———. *A New Perspective on Jesus: What the Quest for the Historical Jesus Missed*. Grand Rapids: Baker Academic, 2005.

———. "C. H. Dodd and New Testament Studies." In *Biblical Scholarship in the Twentieth Century: The Rylands Chair of Biblical Criticism and Exegesis at the University of Manchester, 1904–2004*, edited by Timothy Larsen, 55–75. Manchester: University of Manchester Press, 2007. [Reprinted from *BJRL* 86, no. 3 (2004).]

———. *The New Perspective on Paul*. Revised ed. Grand Rapids: Eerdmans, 2008.

———. "ΕΚ ΠΙΣΤΕΩΣ: A Key to the Meaning of ΠΙΣΤΙΣ ΧΡΙΣΤΟΥ." In *The Word Leaps the Gap: Essays on Scripture and Theology in Honor of Richard B. Hays*, edited by J. R. Wagner et al., 351–66. Grand Rapids: Eerdmans, 2008.

———. "Son of God." In *EHJ*, 587–93.

———. *Beginning from Jerusalem*. Christianity in the Making 2. Grand Rapids, Eerdmans, 2009.

———. *Did the First Christians Worship Jesus? The New Testament Evidence*. London: SPCK; Louisville: Westminster John Knox, 2010.

———. *Jesus, Paul, and the Gospels*. Grand Rapids: Eerdmans, 2011.

———. *The Oral Gospel Tradition*. Grand Rapids: Eerdmans, 2013.

———. *Neither Jew Nor Greek: A Contested Identity*. Christianity in the Making 3. Grand Rapids: Eerdmans, 2015.

Dunn, James D.G., ed. *Jews and Christians: The Parting of the Ways A.D. 70 to 135*. Second Durham-Tübingen Research Symposium on Earliest Christianity and Judaism [Durham, September, 1989]. WUNT 66. Tübingen: Mohr Siebeck, 1992.

Dunn, James D. G., and James H. Charlesworth. "Qumran's *Some Works of Torah* (4Q394–399 [4QMMT]) and Paul's Galatians." In *The Bible and the Dead Sea Scrolls*, edited by Charlesworth, 3:187–201.

Dunn, James D. G., and Scot McKnight, eds. *The Historical Jesus in Recent Research*. Sources for Biblical and Theological Study 10. Winona Lake, IN: Eisenbrauns, 2005.

Dunn, James D. G., and James P. Mackey. *New Testament Theology in Dialogue: Christology and Ministry*. Philadelphia: Westminster, 1987.

Du Toit, David S. *Theios Anthropos. Zur Verwendung von "Theios Anthropos" und sinnverwandten Ausdrücken in der Literatur der Kaiserzeit*. WUNT 91. Tübingen: Mohr Siebeck, 1997.

Dyer, Bryan R. *Suffering in the Face of Death: The Epistle to the Hebrews and Its Context of Situation*. LNTS 568. New York: T&T Clark, 2017.

Dyer, Keith D. "'But concerning *that* day . . .' (Mark 13:32). 'Prophetic' and 'Apocalyptic' Eschatology in Mark 13." In *SBL 1999 Seminar Papers*, 104–22.

A History of the Quests for the Historical Jesus

Easterling, P. E., and Bernard M. W. Knox, eds. *The Cambridge History of Classical Literature*. Vol. 1, *Greek Literature*. Cambridge: Cambridge University Press, 2008. Abbrev: *CHCL*.

Ebeling, Gerhard. *Wort und Glaube*. Tübingen: Mohr Siebeck, 1960.

———. *Word and Faith*. Translated by James W. Leitch. Philadelphia: Fortress, 1963.

———. *Theologie und Verkündigung: Ein Gespräch mit Rudolf Bultmann*. Tübingen: Mohr Siebeck, 1962. ET: *Theology and Proclamation: Dialogue with Rudolf Bultmann*. Translated by John Riches. Philadelphia: Fortress; London: Collins, 1966.

Ebeling, Gerhard, Eberhard Jüngel, and Gerd Schunack, eds. *Festschrift für Ernst Fuchs*. Tübingen: Mohr Siebeck, 1973. [Fuchs bibliography, 347–61.]

Eckhardt, A. Roy. *Reclaiming the Jesus of History: Christology Today*. Minneapolis: Fortress, 1991.

Edersheim, Alfred. *The Life and Times of Jesus the Messiah*. 2 vols. London: Longmans, 1883.

———. *Prophecy and History in Relation to the Messiah: The Warburton Lectures for 1880–1884 with Two Appendices on the Arrangement, Analysis, and Recent Criticism of the Pentateuch*. London: Longmans, Green, 1901. Reprint, Grand Rapids: Baker, 1955.

Eddy, Paul Rhodes. "Jesus as Diogenes? Reflections on the Cynic Jesus Thesis." *JBL* 115 (1996): 449–69.

Eddy, Paul Rhodes, and Gregory A. Boyd. *The Jesus Legend: A Case for the Historical Reliability of the Synoptic Jesus Tradition*. Grand Rapids: Baker Academic, 2007.

Edwards, David L. *Leaders of the Church of England, 1828–1944*. London: Oxford University Press, 1971.

Edwards, Douglas R., and C. Thomas McCollough, eds. *Archaeology and the Galilee: Texts and Contexts in the Graeco-Roman and Byzantine Periods*. South Florida Studies in the History of Judaism 143. Atlanta: Scholars, 1997.

Edwards, J. Christopher. *The Ransom Logion in Mark and Matthew*. WUNT 327. Tübingen: Mohr Siebeck, 2012.

Edwards, Paul, ed. *The Encyclopedia of Philosophy*. 8 vols. New York: Macmillan; London: Collier Macmillan, 1967. Abbreviated as *EP*.

Egg, Gottfried. *Adolf Schlatters kritische Position gezeigt an seiner Matthäusinterpretation*. Arbeiten zur Theologie 2.14. Stuttgart: Calwer, 1968.

Ehrhardt, Arnold. *The Beginning: A Study in the Greek Philosophical Approach to the Concept of Creation from Anaximander to St John*. Manchester: Manchester University Press, 1968.

Ehrman, Bart D. *Jesus: Apocalyptic Prophet of the New Millennium*. Oxford: Oxford University Press, 1999.

———. *Lost Christianities: The Battles for Scripture and the Faith We Never Knew*. Oxford: Oxford University Press, 2003.

———. *Lost Scriptures: Books That Did Not Make It into the New Testament*. Oxford: Oxford University Press, 2003.

Bibliography

———. *The Apostolic Fathers*. 2 vols. LCL. Cambridge, MA: Harvard University Press, 2003.

———. *Truth and Fiction in* The Da Vinci Code*: A Historian Reveals What We Really Know about Jesus, Mary Magdalene and Constantine*. Oxford: Oxford University Press, 2004.

———. *Misquoting Jesus: The Story Behind Who Changed the Bible and Why*. San Francisco: HarperSanFrancisco, 2005.

———. *Did Jesus Exist? The Historical Argument for Jesus of Nazareth*. San Francisco: HarperOne, 2012.

———. *How Jesus Became God: The Exaltation of a Jewish Preacher from Galilee*. San Francisco: HarperOne, 2014.

———. *Jesus before the Gospels: How the Earliest Christians Remembered, Changed, and Invented Their Stories of the Savior*. San Francisco: HarperOne, 2016.

Ehrman, Barth D., and Zlatko Pleše, eds. *The Apocryphal Gospels: Texts and Translations*. Oxford: Oxford University Press, 2011.

———. *The Other Gospels: Accounts of Jesus from Outside the New Testament*. New York: Oxford University Press, 2014.

Eitrem, S. *Some Notes on the Demonology in the New Testament*, Symbolae Osloenses Fasc. Supplet. 12. Oslo: Brøgger, 1950.

Elisheva Fonrobert, Charlotte, and Martin S. Jaffee, eds. *The Cambridge Companion to the Talmud and Rabbinic Literature*. Cambridge: Cambridge University Press, 2007.

Elledge, Roderick. *Use of the Third Person for Self-Reference by Jesus and Yahweh: A Study of Illeism in the Bible and Near Eastern Texts and Its Implications for Christology*. LNTS 575. New York: T&T Clark, 2017.

Elliott, J. K., ed. *The Apocryphal Jesus: Legends of the Early Church*. Oxford: Oxford University Press, 1996; 2nd ed., 2008.

Ellis, E. Earle, and Erich Grässer, eds. *Jesus und Paulus. Festschrift für Werner Georg Kümmel zum 70. Geburtstag*. Göttingen: Vandenhoeck & Ruprecht, 1975.

Ellis, Ieuan. *Seven against Christ: A Study of 'Essays and Reviews'*. Studies in the History of Christian Thought 23. Leiden: Brill, 1980.

Emery, Giles, and Matthew Levering, eds. *The Oxford Handbook of the Trinity*. Oxford: Oxford University Press, 2011.

Emmet, C. W. *The Eschatological Element in the Gospels*. Edinburgh: T&T Clark, 1911.

Engberg-Pedersen, Troels. *John and Philosophi: A New Reading of the Fourth Gospel*. Oxford: Oxford University Press, 2017.

Ensor, Peter W. *Jesus and His "Works": The Johannine Sayings in Historical Perspective*. WUNT 85. Tübingen: Mohr Siebeck, 1996.

Epp, Eldon Jay. "Norman Perrin on the Kingdom of God." In *Christology and a Modern Pilgrimage: A Discussion with Norman Perrin*, edited by Hans Dieter Betz, 113–22. Missoula, MT: Scholars, 1971; rev. ed., 1974.

———. "Mediating Approaches to the Kingdom: Werner Georg Kümmel and George

Eldon Ladd." In *The Kingdom of God in 20th-Century Interpretation*, edited by Wendell Willis, 35–52. Peabody, MA: Hendrickson, 1987.

Epp, Eldon Jay, and George W. MacRae, eds. *The New Testament and Its Modern Interpreters*. Atlanta: Scholars, 1989.

Eppstein, Victor. "The Historicity of the Gospel Account of the Cleansing of the Temple." *ZNW* 55 (1964): 42–58.

Epstein, Klaus. *The Genesis of German Conservatism*. Princeton: Princeton University Press, 1966.

Epstein, Israel, trans. and ed. *The Babylonian Talmud*. 18 vols. London: Soncino, 1948.

Ericksen, Robert P. *Theologians under Hitler: Gerhard Kittel, Paul Althaus and Emmanuel Hirsch*. New Haven, CT: Yale University Press, 1985.

Ericksen, Robert P., and Susannah Heschel, eds. *Betrayal: German Churches and the Holocaust*. Minneapolis: Fortress, 1999.

Eshel, Esther. "Jesus the Exorcist in Light of Epigraphic Sources." In *Jesus and Archaeology*, edited by James H. Charlesworth, 178–85. Grand Rapids: Eerdmans, 2006.

Eskola, Timo. *Messiah and the Throne. Jewish Merkabah Mysticism and Early Christian Exaltation Discourse*. WUNT 142. Tübingen: Mohr Siebeck, 2001.

Esler, Philip F., ed. *Modelling Early Christianity: Social-Scientific Studies of the New Testament in Its Context*. New York: Routledge, 1995.

Estrada, Bernardo, Ermenegildo Manicardi, and Armand Puig i Tàrrech, eds. *The Gospels: History and Christology; The Search of Joseph Ratzinger-Benedict XVI–I Vangeli; Storia e Cristologia. La ricerca di Joseph Ratzinger-Benedetto XVI*. 2 vols. Città del Vaticano: Libreria Editrice Vaticana, 2013.

Eubank, Nathan. *Wages of Cross-Bearing and Debt of Sin: The Economy of Heaven in Matthew's Gospel*. BZNW 196. Berlin: de Gruyter, 2013.

Eusebius. *The Ecclesiastical History*. Translated by J. E. L. Oulton, based on the text of H. J. Lawlor. 2 vols. LCL. London: Heinemann; Cambridge MA: Harvard University Press, 1932.

———. *The Proof of the Gospel*. Translated by W. J. Farrar. London: SPCK, 1920. Reprint, Grand Rapids, Baker, 1981.

Evang, Martin. *Rudolf Bultmann in seiner Frühzeit*. BHT 74. Tübingen: Mohr Siebeck, 1988.

Evans, C. Stephen. "The Self-Emptying of Love: Some Thoughts on Kenotic Christology." In *The Incarnation*, edited by Steven Davis et al., 246–72.

———. *The Historical Christ and the Jesus of Faith: The Incarnational Faith as History*. Oxford: Clarendon, 1996.

———. *Exploring Kenotic Christology: The Self-Emptying of God*. Oxford: Oxford University Press, 2006.

Evans, Craig A. *Noncanonical Writings and New Testament Interpretation*. Peabody, MA: Hendrickson, 1992. Updated version: *Ancient Texts for New Testament Studies:*

Bibliography

A Guide to the Background Literature. Peabody MA: Hendrickson, 2005. Reprint, Grand Rapids: Baker Academic, 2011.

———. *Word and Glory: On the Exegetical and Theological Background of John's Prologue*. JSNTSup 89. Sheffield: JSOT Press, 1993.

———. *Jesus and His Contemporaries: Comparative Studies*. AGJU 25. Leiden: Brill, 1995.

———. "Excursus Two: Jesus and Apollonius of Tyana." In *Jesus and His Contemporaries*, 245–50.

———. "In What Sense 'Blasphemy'? Jesus Before Caiaphas in Mark 14:61–64." In *Jesus and His Contemporaries*, 407–34.

———. "From Anointed Prophet to Anointed King." In *Jesus and His Contemporaries*, 437–56.

———. *Life of Jesus Research: An Annotated Bibliography*. NTTS 24. Leiden: Brill, 1996.

———. "From 'House of Prayer' to 'Cave of Robbers': Jesus' Prophetic Criticism of the Temple Establishment." In *The Quest for Context and Meaning: Studies in Biblical Intertextuality in Honor of James A. Sanders*, edited by Craig A. Evans and Shemaryahu Talmon, 417–42. BibIntS 28. Leiden: Brill, 1997.

———. "Jesus and the Continuing Exile of Israel." In *Jesus and the Restoration of Israel*, edited by Carey C. Newman, 77–100.

———. "Mark's Incipit and the Priene Calendar Inscription: From Jewish Gospel to Greco-Roman Gospel." *Journal of Greco-Roman Christianity and Judaism* 1 (2000): 67–81.

———. *Mark 8:27–16:20*. WBC 34B. Nashville: Nelson, 2001.

———. *Jesus and the Ossuaries: What Jewish Burial Practices Reveal about the Beginning of Christianity*. Waco, TX: Baylor University Press, 2003.

———. "The Messiah in the Dead Sea Scrolls." In *Israel's Messiah in the Bible and the Dead Sea Scrolls*, edited by Richard S. Hess and M. Daniel Carroll R., 85–191.

———. "Inaugurating the Kingdom of God and Defeating the Kingdom of Satan." *BBR* 15 (2005): 49–75.

———. *Fabricating Jesus: How Modern Scholars Distort the Gospels*. Downers Grove, IL: InterVarsity Press, 2006.

———. "Der Sieg über Satan und die Befreiung Israels: Jesus und die Visionen Daniels." *Studien zum Neuen Testament und seiner Umwelt* 34 (2009): 147–58.

———. "Prophet, Sage, Healer, Messiah, and Martyr: Types and Identities of Jesus." In *HSHJ*, 2:1217–43.

———. *Jesus and His World*. London: SPCK; Louisville: Westminster John Knox, 2012.

———. *From Jesus to Church: The First Christian Generation*. Louisville: Westminster John Knox, 2014.

———. *Jesus and the Remains of His Day: Studies in Jesus and the Evidence of Material Culture*. Peabody MA: Hendrickson, 2015.

———. "'Hang Him on a Tree until Dead': Hanging and Crucifixion in Second Temple Israel." In *Jesus and the Remains of His Day*, 109–30.

---. "Was Jesus a Zealot? Finding the Right Context for an Ambiguous Concept." In *Treasures New and Old: A Festschrift Presented to Donald A. Hagner in Celebration of His 80th Birthday*, edited by Clifford B. Kvidahl and Carl S. Sweatman, 19–35. Glossa House Festschrift Series 1. Wilmore, KY: GlossaHouse, 2017.

Evans, Craig A., ed. *Encyclopedia of the Historical Jesus*. New York: Routledge, 2008. Abbreviated as *EHJ*.

---. *The World of Jesus and the Early Church: Identity and Interpretation in Early Communities of Faith*. Peabody, MA: Hendrickson, 2011.

Evans, Craig A., and Peter W. Flint, eds. *Eschatology, Messianism, and the Dead Sea Scrolls*. Studies in the Dead Sea Scrolls and Related Literature. Grand Rapids: Eerdmans, 1997.

Evans, Craig A., and Donald A. Hagner, eds. *Anti-Semitism and Early Christianity: Issues of Polemic and Faith*. Minneapolis: Fortress, 1993.

Evans, Craig A., Robert L. Webb, and Richard A. Wiebe, eds. *Nag Hammadi Texts and the Bible: A Synopsis and Index*. NTTS 18. Leiden: Brill, 1993.

Evans, Craig A., and Stanley E. Porter, eds. *The Historical Jesus*. Biblical Seminar 33. Sheffield: Sheffield Academic Press, 1995.

---. *Dictionary of New Testament Background*. Downers Grove, IL: InterVarsity Press, 2000.

Evans, Craig A., and H. Daniel Zacharias, eds. *"What Does the Scripture Say?" Studies in the Function of Scripture in Early Judaism and Christianity*. Vol. 1, *The Synoptic Gospels*. LNTS 469. New York: T&T Clark International, 2012.

Evans, Craig A., and Jeremiah J. Johnston, eds. *Searching the Scriptures: Studies in Context and Intertextuality*. LNTS 543. New York: T&T Clark, 2015.

Evans, Christopher F. "The Central Section of St. Luke's Gospel." In *Studies in the Gospels*, edited by D. E. Nineham, 37–53.

Evans, Owen. "A List of the Published Writings of Vincent Taylor." In *New Testament Essays*, edited by Robert Banks, 141–46. London: Epworth, 1974.

Evans, Robert. *Reception History, Tradition and Biblical Interpretation: Gadamer and Jauss in Current Practice*. Scriptural Traces: Critical Perspectives on the Reception and Influence of the Bible 4. LNTS 510. New York: T&T Clark, 2014.

Eve, Eric. *The Jewish Context of Jesus' Miracles*. JSNTSup 231. London: Sheffield Academic Press, 2002.

---. *The Healer from Nazareth: Jesus' Miracles in Historical Context*. London: SPCK, 2009.

---. *Behind the Gospels: Understanding the Oral Tradition*. London: SPCK; Minneapolis: Fortress, 2014.

Faber, Geoffrey. *Jowett: Portrait with a Background*. London: Faber and Faber, 1957.

Fabiak, Thomas. *The "Nocturnal Side of Science" in David Friedrich Strauss's Life of Jesus Critically Examined*. Emory Studies in Early Christianity 17. Atlanta: SBL Press, 2015.

Bibliography

Fackenheim, Emil L. *The Religious Dimension of Hegel's Thought*. Bloomington, IN: Indiana University Press, 1967.

Falk, Harvey. *Jesus the Pharisee: A New Look at the Jewishness of Jesus*. [1985.] Reprint, Portland, OR: Wipf & Stock, 2003.

Farmer, William R. *Maccabees, Zealots, and Josephus: An Inquiry into Jewish Nationalism in the Greco-Roman Period*. New York: Columbia University Press, 1956.

———. *The Synoptic Problem: A Critical Analysis*. New York: Macmillan, 1962.

———. *The Last Twelve Verses of Mark*. SNTSMS 25. Cambridge: Cambridge University Press, 1974.

———. *Jesus and the Gospel: Tradition, Scripture, and Canon*. Philadelphia: Fortress, 1982.

Farmer, W. R., C. F. D. Moule, and R. R. Niebuhr, eds. *Christian History and Interpretation: Studies Presented to John Knox*. Cambridge: Cambridge University Press, 1967.

Farrar, Fredric William. *Life of Christ*. London: Cassell, 1874.

Farrer, Austin. *The Glass of Vision*. Bampton Lectures 1948. London: Dacre, 1948.

———. *A Rebirth of Images: The Making of St. John's Apocalypse*. London: Dacre, 1949.

———. *A Study in St. Mark*. London: Dacre, 1951.

———. "On Dispensing with Q." In *Studies in the Gospels: Essays in Memory of R. H. Lightfoot*, edited by D. E. Nineham, 55–88. Oxford: Blackwell, 1953.

———. *St. Matthew and St. Mark*. Edward Cadbury Lectures, Birmingham 1953–1954. London: Dacre, 1954.

———. *The Freedom of the Will*. Gifford Lectures, Edinburgh 1957. London: Black, 1958.

Feenstra, Ronald J. "Reconsidering Kenotic Christology." In *Trinity, Incarnation, and Atonement: Philosophical and Theological Essays*, edited by Ronald J. Feenstra and Cornelius Plantinga Jr., 48–78. Library of Religious Philosophy 1. Notre Dame, IN: University of Notre Dame Press, 1989.

———. "Incarnation." In *A Companion to Philosophy of Religion*, edited by Philip L. Quinn and Charles Taliaferro, 532–40. Oxford: Blackwell, 1997. Reprint, 1999.

Feldman, Louis H. *Jew and Gentile in the Ancient World: Attitudes and Interactions from Alexander to Justinian*. Princeton: Princeton University Press, 1993.

Ferguson, Everett, *Backgrounds of Early Christianity*. Grand Rapids: Eerdmans, 1987; 2nd ed., 1993.

Ferguson, John. *The Religions of the Roman Empire*. London: Thames and Hudson, 1970.

Fergusson, David. *Bultmann*. Collegeville, MN: Liturgical, 1992.

Fergusson, David, ed. *Christ, Church and Society: Essays on John Baillie and Donald Baillie*. Edinburgh: T&T Clark, 1993.

Ferm, Vergilius, ed. *Contemporary American Theology: Theological Autobiographies*. 2 vols. New York: Round Table, 1932–33.

Feuerbach, Ludwig. *Das Wesen des Christentums*. Leipzig: Wigand, 1854. ET: *The Essence of Christianity*. Translated by George Eliot. Foreword by H. Richard Niebuhr. New York: Harper Torchbook, 1957.

A History of the Quests for the Historical Jesus

Fewell, Danna Nolan, ed. *The Oxford Handbook of Biblical Narrative*. Oxford: Oxford University Press, 2016.

Fichte, J. G. *Addresses to the German Nation*. Translated by R. F. Jones and G. H. Turnbull. Chicago: Open Court, 1922.

Fiebig, Paul. *Rabbinische Wundergeschichten des neutestamentlichen Zeitalters in vokalisiertem Text mit sprachlichen und sachlichen Bermerkungen*. Bonn: Marcus and Weber, 1911. Reprint, Berlin: de Gruyter, 1933.

———. *Jüdische Wundergeschichten des Neutestamentlichen Zeitalters unter besonderer Berücksichtigung ihres Verhältnisses zum Neuen Testament bearbeitet. Ein Beitrag zum Streit um die "Christusmythe"*. Tübingen: Mohr Siebeck, 1911.

———. *Die Gleichnisreden Jesu im Lichte der rabbinischen Gleichnisse des neutestamentlichen Zeitalters. Ein Beitrag zum Streit um die "Christusmythe," und eine Widerlegung der Gleichnistheorie Jülichers*. Tübingen: Mohr Siebeck: 1912, 1914.

———. *Jesu Bergpredigt. Rabbinische Texte zum Verständnis der Bergpredigt ins Deutsche übersetzt, in ihren Ursprachen dargeboten and mit Erläuterungen und Lesearten versehen*. Göttingen: Vandenhoeck & Ruprecht, 1924.

———. *Der Erzählungstil der Evangelien im Lichte des rabbinischen Erzählungstils untersucht zugleich ein Beitrag zum Streit um die "Christusmythe"*. Leipzig: Hinrichs, 1925.

———. *Neues Testament und Nationalsozialismus. Drei Universitätsvorlesungen über das Führerprinzip—Rassenfrage—Kampf*. Schriften der Deutschen Christen. Dresden: Deutsch-Christliche, 1935.

———. *Antike Wundertexte. Zweite völlig neu gestaltete Auflage des vorher von Paul Fiebig bearbeiteten Heftes*. Edited by Gerhard Delling. Berlin: de Gruyter, 1960.

Fiensy, David A. *Christian Origins and the Ancient Economy*. Eugene, OR: Cascade, 2014.

Fiensy, David A., and James Riley Strange, eds. *Galilee in the Late Temple and Mishnaic Periods*. Vol. 1, *Life, Culture and Society*. Vol. 2, *The Archaeological Record from Cities, Towns, and Villages*. Minneapolis: Fortress, 2014–15.

Finegan, Jack. *Handbook of Biblical Chronology: Principles of Time Reckoning in the Ancient World and Problems of Chronology in the Bible*. Princeton: Princeton University Press, 1964; rev. ed., Peabody MA: Hendrickson, 1998.

Fiorenza, Elisabeth Schüssler. *In Memory of Her: A Feminist Theological Reconstruction of Christian Origins*. New York: Crossroad, 1983.

———. *Miriam's Child, Sophia's Prophet: Critical Issues in Feminist Theology*. New York: Continuum, 1994.

———. *Changing Horizons: Explorations in Feminist Interpretation*. Minneapolis: Fortress, 2013.

Firestone, Chris L., and Stephen R. Palmquist, eds. *Kant and the New Philosophy of Religion*. Indiana Series in the Philosophy of Religion. Bloomington, IN: Indiana University Press, 2006.

Fitzmyer, Joseph A. *To Advance the Gospel: New Testament Studies*. New York: Crossroad, 1981.

---. *The Gospel according to Luke*. 2 vols. AB 28, 28A. New York: Doubleday, 1981–85.

---. *A Christological Catechism: New Testament Answers*. New York: Paulist, 1982.

---. "Abba and Jesus' Relation to God." In *À Cause de l'Évangile. Études sur les Synoptiques et les Actes offert au P. Jacques Dupont, O.S.B. à l'occasion de son 70e anniversaire*, 15–38. Paris: Cerf, 1985.

---. *Scripture and Christology: A Statement of the Biblical Commission with a Commentary*. New York: Paulist, 1986.

---. *Romans: A New Translation with Introduction and Commentary*. AB 33. New York: Doubleday, 1993.

---. *Essays on the Semitic Background of the New Testament*. London: Geoffrey Chapman, 1971. Reprint, SBLSBS 5. Missoula: Scholars, 1974. [Combined with *A Wandering Aramean: Collected Aramaic Essays*. SBLMS 25. Missoula: Scholars, 1979. Reprinted as *The Semitic Background of the New Testament: Combined Edition of Essays on the Semitic Background of the New Testament*. Grand Rapids: Eerdmans; Livonia, MI: Dove, 1997.

---. *The Dead Sea Scrolls and Christian Origins*. Studies in the Dead Sea Scrolls and Related Literature. Grand Rapids: Eerdmans, 2000.

Flender, Helmut. *Heil und Geschichte in der Theologie des Lukas*. Munich: Kaiser, 1965. ET: *St Luke: Theologian of Redemptive History*. Translated by Reginald H. and Ilse Fuller. London: SPCK, 1967.

Fletcher-Louis, Crispin H. T. "The Destruction of the Temple and the Relativization of the Old Covenant: Mark 13:31 and Matthew 5:18." In *"The Reader Must Understand": Eschatology in Bible and Theology*, edited by K. E. Brower and M. W. Elliott, 145–69. Leicester: Apollos, 1997.

---. *All the Glory of Adam: Liturgical Anthropology in the Dead Sea Scrolls*. STDJ 42. Leiden: Brill, 2002.

---. "Jesus as the High Priestly Messiah." *JSHJ* 4 (2006): 155–75; *JSHJ* 5 (2007): 57–79.

---. *Jesus Monotheism*. Vol. 1, *Christological Origins: The Emerging Consensus and Beyond*. Eugene, OR: Cascade, 2015.

Flew, Antony. *Hume's Philosophy of Belief: A Study of His First Enquiry*. New York: Humanities, 1961.

Flew, Anthony, and Alasdair MacIntyre, eds. *New Essays in Philosophical Theology*. London: SCM, 1955.

Flint, Peter W., and James C. VanderKam, eds. *The Dead Sea Scrolls after Fifty Years: A Comprehensive Assessment*. 2 vols. Leiden: Brill, 1998.

Flusser, David. *Jesus*. Jerusalem: Magness Press and Hebrew University, 1968. Revised in collaboration with R. Steven Notley, 1997.

Foakes-Jackson, F. J., and Kirsopp Lake. *The Beginnings of Christianity*. 5 vols. London: Macmillan, 1920–33.

Foerster, Werner. *Gnosis: A Selection of Gnostic Texts.* 2 vols. Vol. 1, *Patristic Evidence.* Vol. 2, *Coptic and Mandi Sources.* Translated by R. McL. Wilson. Oxford: Clarendon, 1974.

Fogarty, Gerald P. *American Catholic Biblical Scholarship: A History from the Early Republic to Vatican II.* San Francisco: Harper & Row, 1989.

Fogelin, Robert J. *Hume's Skepticism in the Treatise of Human Nature.* London: Routledge, 1985.

———. *A Defense of Hume on Miracles.* Princeton: Princeton University Press, 2003.

Force, James E. *William Whiston: Honest Newtonian.* Cambridge: Cambridge University Press, 1985.

Force, James E., and Richard Popkin, eds. *The Books of Nature and Scripture: Recent Essays on Natural Philosophy, Theology, and Biblical Criticism in the Netherlands of Spinoza's Time and the British Isles of Newton's Time.* International Archives of the History of Ideas 139. Dordrecht and London: Kluwer Academic Publishers, 1994.

Ford, David F., with Rachel Muers, eds. *The Modern Theologians: An Introduction to Christian Theology since 1918.* 3rd ed. Oxford: Blackwell, 2005.

Forlines, F. Leroy. *Classical Arminianism: A Theology of Salvation.* Nashville: Randall House, 2011.

Forsyth, Peter Taylor. *The Old Faith and the New Theology.* Edited by C. H. Vine. London: Sampson Low, 1907.

———. *The Person and Place of Jesus Christ.* London: Independent, [1909], 1961.

Fortman, E. J. *The Triune God: A Historical Study of the Doctrine of the Trinity.* Philadelphia: Westminster, 1972.

Fortna, Robert T. *The Gospel of Signs: A Reconstruction of the Narrative Source Underlying the Fourth Gospel.* SNTSMS 11. Cambridge: Cambridge University Press, 1970.

———. *The Fourth Gospel and Its Predecessor: From Narrative Source to Present Gospel.* Edinburgh: T&T Clark, 1988.

Fortna, Robert T., and Tom Thatcher, eds. *Jesus in Johannine Tradition.* Louisville: Westminster John Knox, 2001.

Fossum, Jarl. "The New *Religionsgeschichtliche Schule*: The Quest for Jewish Christology." In *SBL 1991 Seminar Papers*, 638–46.

Foster, George Burman. "Kaftan's Dogmatik." *AJT* 2 (1898): 802–27.

———. *The Finality of the Christian Religion.* Decennial Publications. Second Series 16. Chicago: University of Chicago Press, 1906; 2nd ed., 1909.

———. *The Function of Religion in Man's Struggle for Existence.* Chicago: University of Chicago Press, 1909.

———. *Christianity in Its Modern Expression.* Edited by Douglas Clyde Macintosh. New York: Macmillan, 1921.

———. *Friedrich Nietzsche.* Edited by Curtis W. Reese. Introduction by A. Eustace Haydon. New York: Macmillan, 1931.

Foster, Paul, ed. *The Non-Canonical Gospels.* New York: T&T Clark, 2008.

Bibliography

Foster, P., A. Gregory, J. S. Kloppenborg, and J. Verheyden, eds. *New Studies in the Synoptic Problem, Oxford Conference, April 2008: Essays in Honour of Christopher M. Tuckett.* BETL 239. Leuven: Peeters, 2011.

Fowl, Stephen E. *The Story of Christ in the Ethics of Paul: An Analysis of the Function of the Hymnic Material in the Pauline Corpus.* JSNTSup 36. Sheffield: JSOT, 1990.

Fox, Richard Wightman. *Jesus in America: Personal Savior, Cultural Hero, National Obsession.* San Fancisco: HarperSanFrancisco, 2004.

Franzmann, Majella. *Jesus in the Nag Hammadi Writings.* Edinburgh: T&T Clark, 1996.

Fredriksen, Paula. *From Jesus to Christ: The Origins of the New Testament Images of Jesus.* New Haven, CT: Yale University Press, 1988.

———. *Jesus of Nazareth, King of the Jews: A Jewish Life and the Emergence of Christianity.* New York: Knopf, 2000.

Freedman, David Noel. *The Unity of the Hebrew Bible.* Ann Arbor: University of Michigan Press, 1993.

Freedman, David Noel, ed. *The Anchor Bible Dictionary.* 6 vols. New York: Doubleday, 1992.

Frei, Hans. "The Mystery of the Presence of Jesus Christ." *Crossroads* 17 (1967): 69–96.

———. *The Eclipse of Biblical Narrative: A Study in Eighteenth and Nineteenth Century Hermeneutics.* New Haven, CT: Yale University Press, 1974.

———. *The Identity of Jesus Christ: The Hermeneutical Bases of Dogmatic Theology.* Philadelphia: Fortress, 1975.

———. "David Friedrich Strauss." In *Nineteenth-Century Religious Thought in the West*, edited by Ninian Smart and John Clayton et al., 1:215–60.

———. *Types of Christian Theology.* New Haven, CT: Yale University Press, 1992.

———. *Theology and Narrative: Selected Essays.* Edited by George Hunsinger and William C. Placher. Oxford: Oxford University Press, 1993.

———. *The Identity of Jesus Christ: The Hermeneutical Bases of Dogmatic Theology.* Edited by Mark Alan Bowland. Foreword by Mike Higton. Introduction by Joshua B. Davis. Eugene, OR: Cascade, 2013.

Frey, Jörg, and Jens Schröter, eds. *Deutungen des Todes Jesu im Neuen Testament.* WUNT 181. Tübingen: Mohr Siebeck, 2005.

Frey, Jörg, and Jens Schröter, assisted by Jakob Spaeth, eds. *Jesus in apokryphen Evangelienüberlieferungen. Beiträge zu ausserkanonischen Jesusüberlieferungen aus verschiedenen Sprach- und Kulturtraditionen.* WUNT 254. Tübingen: Mohr Siebeck, 2010.

Friedrich, Johannes, Wolfgang Pöhlmann, and Peter Stuhlmacher, eds. *Rechtfertigung. Festschrift für Ernst Käsemann.* Tübingen: Mohr Siebeck; Göttingen: Vandenhoeck & Ruprecht, 1976. [Bibliography of Käsemann's works (1933–75), 593–604.]

Freyne, Séan. "The Charismatic." In *Ideal Figures in Ancient Judaism: Profiles and Paradigms*, edited by John J. Collins and George W. E. Nickelsburg, 223–58. Septuagint and Cognate Studies Series 12. Chico, CA: Scholars, 1980.

———. *Galilee, Jesus and the Gospels: Literary Approaches and Historical Investigations.* Philadelphia: Fortress, 1988.

A History of the Quests for the Historical Jesus

———. *Galilee: From Alexander the Great to Hadrian; A Study of Second Temple Judaism.* Edinburgh: T&T Clark, [1980], 1998.
———. *Jesus: A Jewish Galilean; A New Reading of the Jesus-Story.* Edinburgh: T&T Clark, 2004.
———. "Galilean Studies: Old Issues and New Questions." In *Religion, Ethnicity, and Identity in Ancient Galilee*, edited by Jürgen Zangenberg et al., 13–29.
———. *The Jesus Movement and Its Expansion: Meaning and Mission.* Grand Rapids: Eerdmans, 2014.
Frickenschmidt, Dirk. *Evangelium als Biographie. Die vier Evangelien im Rahmen der antiken Erzählerkunst.* Tübingen: Francke, 1997.
Friedrich, Peter. *Ferdinand Christian Baur als Symboliker.* STGNJ 12. Göttingen: Vandenhoeck & Ruprecht, 1975.
Fuchs, Ernst. *Christus und der Geist bei Paulus. Eine biblisch-theologische Untersuchung.* UNT 23. Leipzig: Hinrichs, 1932.
———. *Hermeneutik.* Tübingen: Mohr Siebeck, 1954; 4th ed., 1970.
———. *Zum hermeneutischen Problem in der Theologie. Die existentiale Interpretation.* Gesammelte Aufsätze 1. Tübingen: Mohr Siebeck, 1959.
———. *Zur Frage nach dem historische Jesus. Gesammelte Aufsätze.* Gesammelte Aufsätze 2. Tübingen: Mohr Siebeck, 1960. ET: *Studies in the Historical Jesus.* Translated by Andrew Scobie. SBT 42. London: SCM; Naperville, IL: Allenson, 1964.
———. *Glaube und Erfahrung. Zum christologischen Problem im Neuen Testament.* Gesammelte Aufsätze 3. Tübingen: Mohr Siebeck, 1965.
———. *Jesus: Wort und Tat. Vorlesungen zum Neuen Testament.* Vol. 1. Tübingen: Mohr Siebeck, 1971.
Fuller, Reginald H. *The Mission and Achievement of Jesus: An Examination of the Presuppositions of New Testament Theology.* SBT 12. London: SCM; Naperville: Allenson, 1954.
———. *Interpreting the Miracles.* London: SCM; Philadelphia: Westminster, 1963.
———. *The Foundations of New Testament Christology.* London: Lutterworth, 1965.
———. *Preaching the Lectionary: The Word of God for the Church Today.* Collegeville, MN: Liturgical, 1984.
———. "Sir Edwyn Hoskyns and the Contemporary Relevance of 'Biblical Theology.'" *NTS* 30 (1984): 321–44. Reprint in Fuller, *Christ and Christianity*, edited by Robert Kahl (1994).
———. *Christ and Christianity: Studies in the Formation of Christology.* Edited by Robert Kahl. Valley Forge, PA: Trinity Press International, 1994.
Fuller, Reginald H., ed. and trans. *Kerygma and Myth: A Theological Debate.* German editor Hans Werner Bartsch. 2 vols. London: SPCK, 1953–62. [Combined volume with preface by Bultmann and enlarged bibliography, 1972.]

Bibliography

Fuller, Reginald H., and Pheme Perkins. *Who Is This Christ? Gospel Christology and Contemporary Faith*. Philadelphia: Fortress, 1983.

Funk, Robert W. *Jesus the Precursor*. SBL Supplements to *Semeia* 2. Missoula, MT: Scholars; Fortress, 1975.

———. "The Watershed of the American Biblical Tradition: The Chicago School, First Phase, 1892–1920." *JBL* 95 (1976): 4–22.

———. *Language, Hermeneutic, and the Word of God: The Problem of Language in the New Testament and Contemporary Theology*. New York: Harper & Row, 1966. Reprint, Chico, CA: Scholars, n.d.

———. *New Gospel Parallels*. 2 vols. Foundations and Facets: New Testament. Philadelphia: Fortress, 1985.

———. *Honest to Jesus: Jesus for a New Millennium*. San Francisco: HarperSanFrancisco, 1996.

———. "The Jesus Seminar and the Quest." In *Jesus Then and Now*, edited by Marvin Meyer and Charles Hughes, 130–39.

Funk, Robert W., Bernard Brandon Scott, James R. Butts, and the Jesus Seminar, eds. *The Parables of Jesus: Red Letter Edition*. Sonoma, CA: Polebridge, 1988.

Funk, Robert W., Roy W. Hoover, and the Jesus Seminar. *The Five Gospels: The Search for the Authentic Words of Jesus*. New Translation and Commentary. Sonoma, CA: Polebridge, 1993; San Francisco: HarperSanFrancisco, 1997.

Funk, Robert W., et al. *The Acts of Jesus: The Search for the Authentic Deeds of Jesus*. Sonoma, CA: Polebridge, 1998.

Funk, Robert W., et al. *The Gospel of Jesus: According to the Jesus Seminar*. Sonoma, CA: Polebridge, 1999.

Gadamer, Hans-Georg. *Wahrheit und Methode*. 2nd ed. Tübingen: Mohr Siebeck, 1965. ET: *Truth and Method*. Translated by Joel Weinsheimer and Donald G. Marshall. Reprint, New York: Bloomsbury Academic, 2013.

———. *Philosophical Hermeneutics*. Translated and edited by David E. Linge. Berkeley: University of California Press, 1977.

Gagarin, Michael, ed. *The Oxford Encyclopedia of Ancient Greece and Rome*. 7 vols. Oxford: Oxford University Press, 2010.

Gallagher, Eugene V. *Divine Man or Magician? Celsus and Origen on Jesus*. SBLDS 64. Chico, CA: Scholars, 1982.

Garber, Zev, ed. *Teaching the Historical Jesus: Issues and Exegesis*. Routledge Studies in Religion 42. New York: Routledge, 2015.

García Martínez, Florentino. *The Dead Sea Scrolls Translated: The Qumran Text in English*. Translated from Spanish by Wilfred G. E. Watson. Leiden: Brill; Grand Rapids: Eerdmans, 1994; 2nd ed., 1996.

———. "Temple Scroll." In *Encyclopedia of the Dead Sea Scrolls*, edited by Lawrence H. Schiffman and James C. VanderKam, 2:927–33.

A History of the Quests for the Historical Jesus

Gardner-Smith, Percival. *Saint John and the Synoptic Gospels*. Cambridge: Cambridge University Press, 1938.

Garrett, Don, ed. *The Cambridge Companion to Spinoza*. Cambridge: Cambridge University Press, 1996.

Garrett, Susan R. *The Demise of the Devil: Magic and the Demonic in Luke's Writings*. Minneapolis: Fortress, 1989.

———. *The Temptations of Jesus in Mark's Gospel*. Grand Rapids: Eerdmans, 1998.

Gärtner, Bertil. *The Temple and the Community in Qumran and the New Testament: A Comparative Study in the Temple Symbolism of the Qumran Texts and the New Testament*. SNTSMS 1. Cambridge: Cambridge University Press, 1965.

Gaskin, J. C. A. *Hume's Philosophy of Religion*. Atlantic Highlands, NJ: Humanities, 1978; 2nd ed., 1988.

Gasque, W. Ward. *A History of the Criticism of the Acts of the Apostles*. Grand Rapids: Eerdmans, 1975.

Gathercole, Simon J. "The Critical and Dogmatic Agenda of Albert Schweitzer's *The Quest of the Historical Jesus*." *TynBul* 51 (2000): 261–83.

———. *The Preexistent Son: Recovering the Christologies of Matthew, Mark, and Luke*. Grand Rapids: Eerdmans, 2006.

———. *The Composition of the Gospel of Thomas: Original Language and Influences*. SNTSMS 151. Cambridge: Cambridge University Press, 2012.

———. *The Gospel of Thomas: Introduction and Commentary*. TENTS 11. Leiden: Brill, 2014.

———. *Defending Substitution: An Essay on Atonement in Paul*. Grand Rapids: Baker, 2015.

———. "The Gospel of Thomas: Jesus Said *What*?" *BAR* 41, no. 4 (2015): 50–56.

Gawlick, Günter. "Der Deismus als Grundzug der Religionsphilosophie der Aufklärung." In *Hermann Samuel Reimarus (1694–1768). Ein "bekannter Unbekannte" der Aufklärung in Hamburg*, 15–43. Vorträge der Tagung der Joachim Jungius-Gesellschaft der Wissenschaften. Hamburg am 12. und 13. Oktober 1972. Göttingen: Vandenhoeck & Ruprecht, 1973.

Gay, Peter. *The Enlightenment*. 2 vols. Vol. 1, *The Rise of Modern Paganism*. Vol. 2, *The Science of Freedom*. London: Weidenfeld and Nicolson, 1967, 1970.

Gebauer, Gunter, and Christoph Wulf. *Mimesis: Culture—Art—Society*. Translated by Don Reneau. Berkeley: University of California Press, 1995.

Geiger, Abraham. *Das Judenthum und seine Geschichte von der Zerstörung des zweiten Tempels bis zum Ende des zwölften Jahrhunderts*. 1864–71. Reprint in 3 vols., Breslau: Jacobson, 1910. Translated by Charles Newburgh with the title *Judaism and Its History* [1911]. Reprint, Lanham MD: University Press of America, 1985.

Geiger, Wolfgang. *Spekulation und Kritik. Die Geschichtstheologie Ferdinand Christian Baurs*. Munich: Kaiser, 1964.

Geivett, R. Douglas, and Gary R. Habermas, eds. *In Defense of Miracles: A Comprehensive Case for God's Action in History*. Downers Grove, IL: InterVarsity Press, 1997.

Bibliography

Gemser, B. "The *Rib*—or Controversy—Pattern in Hebrew Mentality." In *Wisdom in Israel and in the Ancient Near East*, edited by Martin Noth and D. Winton Thomas, Festschrift for H.H. Rowley, 120–37. VTSup 3. Leiden: Brill, 1965.

Georgi, Dieter. "Socioeconomic Reasons for the 'Divine Man' as a Propagandistic Pattern." In *Aspects of Religious Propaganda in Judaism and Early Christianity*, edited by Elisabeth Schüssler Fiorenza, 27–42. Notre Dame: University of Notre Dame Press, 1976.

Gerdmar, Anders. *Roots of Theological Antisemitism: German Interpretation and the Jews, from Herder and Semler to Kittel and Bultmann*. SJHC 20. Leiden: Brill, 2009.

Gerhardsson, Birger. *Memory and Manuscript: Oral Tradition and Written Transmission in Rabbinic Judaism and Early Christianity*. Translated by Eric J. Sharpe. Lund: Gleerup, 1961.

———. *Tradition and Transmission in Early Christianity*. Translated by Eric J. Sharpe. Lund: Gleerup, 1964.

———. *The Testing of God's Son: (Matt 4:1–11 & Par.)*. Translated by John Toy. ConBNT 2:1. Lund: Gleerup, 1966.

———. *The Mighty Acts of Jesus according to Matthew*. Translated by Robert Dewsnap. Scripta Minora. Lund: Gleerup, 1979.

———. *The Origins of the Gospel Traditions*. Philadelphia: Fortress, 1979.

———. *Memory and Manuscript* and *Tradition and Transmission*. Combined with new preface by Gerhardsson. Foreword by Jacob Neusner. Biblical Resource Series. Grand Rapids: Eerdmans; Livonia: Dove, 1998.

———. *The Reliability of the Gospel Tradition*. Peabody, MA: Hendrickson, 2001.

———. "Illuminating the Kingdom: Narrative Meshalim in the Synoptic Gospels." In *Jesus and the Oral Tradition*, edited by Henry Wansbrough, 266–309.

Gero, S. "The Spirit as a Dove at the Baptism of Jesus." *NovT* 18 (1977): 17–35.

Geyer, Paul, ed. *The Cambridge Companion to Kant and Modern Philosophy*. Cambridge: Cambridge University Press, 2006.

———. *The Cambridge Companion to Kant's Critique of Pure Reason*. Cambridge: Cambridge University Press, 2010.

Gibbon, Edward. *The Decline and Fall of the Roman Empire* (1776–81), edited by J. B. Bury. New York: Macmillan, 1914.

Gibson, Jeffrey B. *The Disciples' Prayer: The Prayer Jesus Taught in Its Historical Setting*. Minneapolis: Fortress, 2015.

Gilkey, Langdon. *Gilkey on Tillich*. New York: Crossroad, 1990.

Gilley, Sheridan. *Newman and His Age*. London: Darton, Longman & Todd; Westminster, MD: Christian Classics, 1990.

Glanvill, Joseph. *Saducismus Triumphatus*. London: Bettesworth and Batley, 1689. Reprint, Gainesville, FL: Scholar's Facsimiles and Reprints, 1966.

Glasson, T. F. "Schweitzer's Influence: Blessing or Bane?" *JTS* 28 (1977): 289–302. Reprint in *The Kingdom of God*, edited by Bruce Chilton, 107–20. Issues in Religion and Theology 5. Philadelphia: Fortress; London, SPCK, 1984.

Gleaves, G. Scott. *Did Jesus Speak Greek? The Emerging Evidence of Greek Dominance in First-Century Palestine.* Eugene, OR: Pickwick, 2015.

Glick, G. Wayne. *The Reality of Christianity: A Study of Adolf von Harnack as Historian and Theologian.* New York: Harper & Row, 1967.

Godbey, John Charles. "A Study of Faustus Socinus's De Jesu Christo Servatore." PhD diss., University of Chicago, 1968.

Golb, Norman. *Who Wrote the Dead Sea Scrolls? The Search for the Secret of Qumran.* New York: Scribner's, 1995.

Gomez, Alan W. "Faustus Socinus' *De Jesu Christo Servatore*. Part III, Historical Introduction, Translation, and Notes." PhD diss., Fuller Theological Seminary, 1990.

Goodspeed, Edgar J. *A Life of Jesus.* New York: Harper & Brothers, 1950.

———. *As I Remember.* New York: Harper & Brothers, 1953.

Goodacre, Mark. *Goulder on the Gospels: An Examination of a New Paradigm.* JSNTSup 133. Sheffield: Sheffield Academic Press, 1996.

———. *The Case against Q: Studies in Markan Priority and the Synoptic Problem.* Harrisburg, PA: Trinity Press International, 2002.

———. *Thomas and the Gospels: The Case for Thomas's Familiarity with the Synoptics.* Grand Rapids: Eerdmans, 2012.

———. "How Reliable Is the Story of the Nag Hammadi Discovery?" *JSNT* 35 (2013): 303–22.

Goodacre, Mark, and Nicholas Perrin, eds. *Questioning Q: A Multicultural Critique.* Downers Grove, IL: InterVarsity Press, 2004.

Goodman, Martin. *The Ruling Class of Judaea: The Origins of the Jewish Revolt against Rome, A.D. 66–70.* Cambridge: Cambridge University Press, 1987.

Goodman, Martin, with the assistance of Jane Sherwood. *The Roman World 44 B.C.–A.D. 180.* New York: Routledge, 1997.

Gore, Charles. *The Incarnation of the Son of God.* Bampton Lectures 1891. London: John Murray, 1891.

———. *Dissertations on Subjects Connected with the Incarnation.* London: Murray, 1895.

———. *The New Theology and the Old Religion, Being Eight Lectures, Together with Five Sermons.* London: Murray; New York: Dutton, 1907.

———. *The Basis of Anglican Fellowship in Faith and Organization.* London: Mowbray, 1914.

———. *The Reconstruction of Belief.* London: Murray, 1926. [Consisting of reprints of *Belief in God* (1921), *Belief in Christ* (1922), and *The Holy Spirit and the Church* (1926).]

———. *Can We Then Believe? Summary of the Volumes on "Reconstruction of Belief" and Reply to Criticisms.* London: Murray, 1926.

———. *Jesus of Nazareth.* London: Thornton, Butterworth, 1929.

Gore, Charles, ed. *Lux Mundi: A Series of Studies in the Religion of the Incarnation.* London: Murray, 1889.

Bibliography

Gottlieb, Michah. *Faith and Freedom: Moses Mendelssohn's Theological-Political Thought*. Oxford: Oxford University Press, 2011.

Goulder, Michael D. *Midrash and Lection in Matthew*. Speaker's Lectures in Biblical Studies 1969–71. London: SPCK, 1974.

Goulder, Michael, ed. *Incarnation and Myth: The Debate Continued*. London: SCM; Grand Rapids, Eerdmans, 1979.

Gowler, David B. *Host, Guest, Enemy and Friend: Portraits of the Pharisees in Luke and Acts*. New York: Peter Lang, 1991. Reprint, Portland: Wipf & Stock, 2007.

Grabbe, Lester L. *Priests, Prophets, Diviners, Sages: A Socio-Historical Study of Religious Specialists in Ancient Israel*. Valley Forge, PA: Trinity Press International, 1995.

Gragg, Alan. *George Burman Foster: Religious Humanist*. Perspectives in Religious Studies, Special Series 3. Danville, VA: Perspectives in Religious Studies, 1978.

Graham, R. W. *Charles Harold Dodd 1884–1973: A Bibliography of His Published Writings*. Lexington Theological Library Occasional Studies. Lexington, KY: Lexington Theological Library, 1974.

Grant, Robert M. *Greek Apologists of the Second Century*. Philadelphia: Westminster, 1988.

———. *Jesus after the Gospels: The Christ of the Second Century*. Louisville: Westminster John Knox, 1990.

Grass, Hans, and Werner Georg Kümmel, eds. *Jesus Christus. Das Christusverständnis im Wandel der Zeiten*. Marburger theologische Studien 1. Marburg: Elwert, 1963.

Grässer, Erich. *Albert Schweitzer als Theologe*. BHT 60. Tübingen: Mohr Siebeck, 1979.

Gray, Brett. *Jesus in the Theology of Rowan Williams*. T&T Clark Studies in English Theology. New York: T&T Clark, 2016.

Gray, Patrick. *Paul as a Problem in History and Culture: The Apostle and His Critics through the Centuries*. Grand Rapids: Baker Academic, 2016.

Gray, Rebecca. *Prophetic Figures in Late Second Temple Jewish Palestine: The Evidence from Josephus*. Oxford: Oxford University Press, 1993.

Gray, Timothy C. *The Temple in the Gospel of Mark: A Study in Its Narrative Role*. WUNT 242. Tübingen: Mohr Siebeck, 2008.

Green, Garrett, ed. *Scriptural Authority and Narrative Interpretation*. Minneapolis: Augsburg, 1987. Reprint, Eugene, OR: Wipf & Stock, 2000.

Green, Joel B. *The Death of Jesus: Tradition and Interpretation in the Passion Narratives*. WUNT 33. Tübingen: Mohr Siebeck, 1988.

———. *The Theology of the Gospel of Luke*. New Testament Theology. Cambridge: Cambridge University Press, 1995.

———. *The Gospel of Luke*. NICGT. Grand Rapids: Eerdmans, 1997.

Green, Joel B., and Max Turner, eds. *Jesus of Nazareth: Essays on the Historical Jesus and New Testament Christology*. Grand Rapids: Eerdmans; Carlisle: Paternoster, 1994.

Green, Joel B., ed. *Hearing the New Testament: Strategies for Interpretation*. Grand Rapids: Eerdmans, 1995; 2nd ed., 2010.

———. *Methods for Luke*. Cambridge: Cambridge University Press, 2010.

Green, Joel B., and Lee Martin McDonald, eds. *The World of the New Testament: Cultural, Social, and Historical Contexts*. Grand Rapids: Baker Academic, 2013.

Green, Joel B., Jeannine K. Brown, and Nicholas Perrin, eds. *Dictionary of Jesus and the Gospels*. 2nd ed. Downers Grove, IL: IVP Academic, 2013. Abbreviated as *DJG*.

Green, Steven K. *Inventing a Christian America: The Myth of the Religious Founding*. Oxford: Oxford University Press, 2015.

Green, V. H. H. *Religion at Oxford and Cambridge*. London; SCM, 1964.

Gregersen, Niels Henrik, ed. *Incarnation: On the Scope and Depth of Christology*. Minneapolis: Fortress, 2015.

Gregg, Robert C., and Dennis E. Groh. *Early Arianism: A View of Salvation*. Philadelphia: Fortress, 1981.

Gregory, Andrew, and Christopher Tuckett, eds., with Tobias Nicklas and Joseph Verheyden, consulting eds. *The Oxford Handbook of Early Christian Apocrypha*. Oxford: Oxford University Press, 2015.

Greig, J. C. G. "Abba and Amen: Their Relevance to Christology." In *Studia Evangelica*, vol. 5, edited by F. L. Cross, 3–13. Berlin: Akademie-Verlag, 1968.

Grell, Ole Peter, Jonathan I. Israel, and Nicholas Tyacke, eds. *From Persecution to Toleration: The Glorious Revolution in England*. Oxford: Clarendon, 1991.

Grensted, L. W. *A Short History of the Doctrine of Atonement*. Manchester: Manchester University Press; London: Longmans, Green, 1920.

Griffth-Jones, Trevor. *The Four Witnesses: The Rebel, the Rabbi, the Chronicler, the Mystic*. San Francisco: HarperSanFrancisco, 2000.

Grillmeier, Aloys, and Heinrich Bacht, eds. *Das Konzil von Chalkedon: Geschichte und Gegenwart*. 3 vols. Würzburg: Echter-Verlag, 1951.

Grillmeier, Aloys. *Christ in Christian Tradition*. Vol. 1, *From the Apostolic Age to Chalcedon (451)*. Translated by John Bowden. London: Mowbrays, [1965]; 2nd ed., 1975. Vol. 2, *From Chalcedon to Justinian (451) to Gregory the Great (590–604)*. Translated by Pauline Allen and John Cawte. London: Mowbrays; Atlanta: John Knox, 1987.

Groos, Helmut. *Albert Schweitzer, Grösse und Grenzen. Eine kritische Würdigung des Forschers und Denkers*. Munich: Ernst Reinhardt, 1974.

Grotius, Hugo. *Defensio Fidei Catholicae de Satisfactione Christi adversus Faustum Socinum Senensem*. 1617.

———. *Annotationes in Novum Testamentum*. 3 parts. 1641–50, edited by E. de Windheim. 1755–57.

———. *The Truth of the Christian Religion, with Jean Le Clerc's Notes and Additions*. Translated by John Clarke [1742]. Edited with introduction by Maria Ross Antognazza. Indianola, IA: Liberty Fund, 2012.

Gruen, Erich S. *Heritage and Hellenism: The Reinvention of Jewish Tradition*. Hellenistic Culture and Society 30. Berkeley: University of California Press, 1998.

Gruenwald, Ithamar, Shaul Shaked, and Gedaliahu G. Stroumsa, eds. *Messiah and*

Christos. Studies in the Jewish Origins of Christianity, Presented to David Flusser on the Occasion of His Seventy-Fifth Birthday. TSAJ 32. Tübingen: Mohr Siebeck, 1992.

Grundmann, Walter. *Jesus der Galiläer und das Judentum*. Leipzig: Weigand, 1940.

———. *Die Entjudung des religiösen Lebens als Aufgabe der deutschen Theologie und Lebens*. Weimar: Verlag Deutsche Christen, 1940.

———. *Die Geschichte Jesu Christi*. Berlin: Evangelische Verlagsanstalt, 1956; 3rd ed., 1961.

———. *Das Evangelium nach Lukas*. THKNT 3. Berlin: Evangelische Verlagsanstalt, 1961.

———. "Verkündigung und Geschichte in der Bericht vom Eingang der Geschichte Jesu im Johannes-Evangelium." In *Der historische Jesus und der kerygmatische Christus*, edited by Helmut Ristow und Karl Matthiae, 289–309.

———. *Das Evangelium nach Matthäus*. THKNT 1. Berlin: Evangelische Verlagsanstalt, 1968.

———. *Das Evangelium nach Markus*. THKNT 2. Berlin: Evangelische Verlagsanstalt, 1968.

———. "The Decision of the Supreme Court to Put Jesus to Death (John 11:47–57) in Its Context: Tradition and Redaction in the Gospel of John." In *Jesus and the Politics of His Day*, edited by Ernst Bammel and C. F. D. Moule, 295–318.

Guelich, Robert A. *The Sermon on the Mount: A Foundation for Understanding*. Waco TX: Word, 1982.

———. *Mark 1:1–8:26*. WBC 34A. Dallas: Word, 1989.

Guelich, Robert A., ed. *Prophetic and/or Apocalyptic Eschatology*. Ex Auditu 6. Eugene, OR: Pickwick, 1990.

Gundry, Robert H. *Matthew: A Commentary on His Handbook for a Mixed Church under Persecution*. Grand Rapids: Eerdmans, 1982; 2nd ed., 1994.

———. *Mark: A Commentary on His Apology for the Cross*. Grand Rapids: Eerdmans, 1993.

———. "Excursus on the Secret Gospel of Mark." In *Mark*, 603–23.

———. *The Old Is Better*. WUNT 178. Tübingen: Mohr Siebeck, 2005.

———. *Peter: False Disciple and Apostate according to Saint Matthew*. Grand Rapids: Eerdmans, 2015.

Gunter, W. Stephen. *Arminius and His Declaration of Sentiments: An Annotated Translation with Introduction and Theological Commentary*. Waco TX: Baylor University Press, 2012.

Gurtner, Daniel M., Joel Willitts, and Richard A. Burridge, eds. *Jesus, Matthew's Gospel and Early Christianity: Studies in Memory of Graham N. Stanton*. LNTS 435. London: T&T Clark International, 2011.

Gurtner, Daniel M., Grant Macaskill, and Jonathan T. Penngton, eds. *In the Fullness of Time: Essays on Christology, Creation, and Eschatology in Honor of Richard Bauckham*. Grand Rapids: Eerdmans, 2016. [List of Bauckham's publications through 2015, 229–48.]

A History of the Quests for the Historical Jesus

Guyer, Paul, ed. *The Cambridge Companion to Kant and Modern Philosophy*. Cambridge: Cambridge University Press, 2006.

Guyer, Paul, ed. *The Cambridge Companion to Kant's Critique of Pure Reason*. Cambridge: Cambridge University Press, 2010.

Hagner, Donald A. *The Jewish Reclamation of Jesus: An Analysis and Critique of Modern Jewish Study of Jesus*. Foreword by Gösta Lindeskog. Grand Rapids: Zondervan, 1984.

———. *Matthew 1–13* and *Matthew 14–28*, WBC 33A, 33B. Dallas: Word, 1993–95.

———. "The Jesus Quest and Jewish-Christian Relations." In *HSHJ*, 2:1055–77.

———. *The New Testament: A Historical and Theological Introduction*. Grand Rapids: Baker Academic, 2012.

Hahn, Fredinand. *Christologische Hoheitstitel*. Göttingen: Vandenhoeck & Ruprecht, 1963. ET: *The Titles of Jesus in Christology: Their History in Early Christianity*. Translated by Harold Knight and George Ogg. London: Lutterworth, 1969.

Hahn, Scott W., and Benjamin Wiker. *Politicizing the Bible: The Roots of Historical Criticism and the Secularization of Scripture, 1300–1700*. New York: Herder and Herder, 2013.

Haight, Roger. *Jesus, Symbol of God*. Maryknoll NY: Orbis, 1999.

Halliwell, Stephen. *The Aesthetics of Mimesis: Ancient Texts and Modern Problems*. Princeton: Princeton University Press, 2002.

Halyburton, Thomas. *Natural Religion Insufficient, and Revealed Necessary to Man's Happiness in His Present State*. Edinburgh: Published by the Heirs of the Author, 1714.

———. *Works of Thomas Halyburton*. Glasgow: Blackie, 1837.

Hamilton, Kenneth. *The System and the Gospel: A Critique of Paul Tillich*. Grand Rapids: Eerdmans; London: SCM, 1963.

Hammann, Konrad. *Rudolf Bultmann: Eine Biographie*. 2nd ed. Tübingen: Mohr Siebeck, 2009. ET: *Rudolf Bultmann: A Biography*. Translated by Philip E. Devenish. Salem, OR: Polebridge, 2013.

Hammerton-Kelly, R.G. *Pre-Existence, Wisdom, and the Son of Man: A Study of the Idea of Pre-Existence in the New Testament*. SNTSMS 21. Cambridge: Cambridge University Press, 1973.

Hammerton-Kelly, Robert G., and Robin Scroggs, eds. *Jews, Greeks and Christians: Religious Cultures in Late Antiquity, Essays in Honor of William David Davies*. Leiden: Brill, 1976.

Hammond, Nicholas. *The Cambridge Companion to Pascal*. Cambridge: Cambridge University Press, 2003.

Han, Kyu Sam. *Jerusalem and the Early Jesus Movement: The Q Community's Attitude toward the Temple*. JSNTSup 207. New York: T&T Clark, 2002.

Hannay, Alistair. *Kierkegaard*. London: Routledge & Kegan Paul, 1982.

Hanson, K. C., and Douglas E. Oakman. *Palestine in the Time of Jesus: Social Structures and Social Conflicts*. Minneapolis: Fortress, 1998.

Bibliography

Hanson, Paul D. *The Dawn of Apocalyptic.* Philadelphia: Fortress, 1975.

Hanson, R. P. C. *Allegory and Event: A Study of the Sources and Significance of Origen's Interpretation of Scripture.* London: SCM, 1959.

———. *The Search for the Christian Doctrine of God: The Arian Controversy, 318–381.* Edinburgh: T&T Clark, 1988.

Harnack, Adolf. *Lehrbuch der Dogmengeschichte.* 3 vols. Tübingen: Mohr Siebeck: [1886–89]; 4th ed. 1909. ET: *A History of Dogma.* Edited by A. B. Bruce. 7 vols. London: Williams and Norgate, 1894–99.

———. *Das Wesen des Christentums. Sechszehn Vorlesungen vor Studierenden aller Facultäten im Wintersemester 1899/1900 an der Universität Berlin.* Leipzig: J. C. Hinrichs, 1900. ET: *What Is Christianity?* Translated by T. B. Saunders. London: Williams and Norgate, 1901.

———. *Luke the Physician: The Author of the Third Gospel and the Acts of the Apostles.* New Testament Studies 1. Translated by J. R. Wilkinson. New York: Putman; London: Williams and Norgate, 1907.

———. *Sprüche und Reden Jesu: Die zweite Quelle des Matthäus und Lukas.* Beiträge zur Einleitung in das Neue Testament 2. Leipzig: Hinrichs, 1907. ET: *The Sayings of Jesus: The Second Source of St. Matthew and St. Luke.* Translated by J. R. Wilkinson. New Testament Studies 2. New York: Putnam; London: Williams and Norgate, 1908.

———. *Marcion. Das Evangelium vom fremden Gott.* Leipzig: Hinrichs, 1921. ET: *Marcion: The Gospel of the Alien God.* Translated by John E. Seely and Lyle D. Bierma. Durham, NC: Labyrinth, 1990.

Harrington, Hannah K. *The Impurity Systems of Qumran and the Rabbis: Biblical Foundations.* SBLDS 143. Atlanta: Scholars, 1993.

———. *Holiness: Rabbinic Judaism and the Graeco-Roman World.* New York: Routledge, 2001.

———. *The Purity Texts.* Companion to the Qumran Scrolls 5. London: T&T Clark, 2004.

Harris, Elizabeth. *Prologue and Gospel: The Theology of the Fourth Evangelist.* New York: T&T Clark International, 1994.

Harris, Horton. *David Friedrich Strauss and His Theology.* Monograph Supplements to *SJT.* Cambridge: Cambridge University Press, 1973.

———. *The Tübingen School.* Oxford: Clarendon, 1975.

Harrisville, Roy A. *Benjamin Wisner Bacon: Pioneer in American Biblical Criticism.* Studies in American Biblical Scholarship 2. Missoula, MT: Scholars, 1976.

———. *Pandora's Box Opened: An Examination and Defense of Historical-Critical Method and Its Master Practitioners.* Grand Rapids: Eerdmans, 2014.

Hart, Darryl G. *Calvinism: A History.* New Haven, CT: Yale University Press, 2013.

Hart, Trevor. *Faith Thinking: The Dynamics of Christian Theology.* Downers Grove, IL: InterVarsity Press, 1996.

Hart, Trevor, ed. *Justice and the Only Mercy: Essays on the Life and Theology of Peter Taylor Forsyth*. Edinburgh: T&T Clark, 1995.

Hart, H. "The Coin of 'Render unto Caesar . . .' (A Note of Some Aspects of Mark 12:13–17; Matt. 22:1–22; Luke 20:20–26)." In *Jesus and the Politics of His Day*, edited by Ernst Bammel and C. F. D. Moule, 241–48.

Hartlich, Christian, and Walter Sachs. *Der Ursprung des Mythosbegriffes in der modernen Bibelwissenshaft*. Schriften der Studiengemeinschaft der Evangelischen Akademien 2. Tübingen: Mohr Siebeck: 1952.

Hartog, Paul A., ed. *Orthodoxy and Heresy in Early Christian Contexts: Reconsidering the Bauer Thesis*. Eugene OR: Pickwick, 2015.

Harvey, Anthony E. *Jesus on Trial: A Study in the Fourth Gospel*. London: SPCK, 1976.

———. *Jesus and the Constraints of History*. Bampton Lectures 1980. London: Duckworth; Philadelphia: Westminster, 1982.

———. "Christ as Agent." In *The Glory of Christ in the New Testament*, edited by L. D. Hurst and N. T. Wright, 239–250.

Harvey, Van A., and Schubert M. Ogden. "How New Is the 'New Quest of the Historical Jesus'?" In *The Historical Jesus and the Kerygmatic Christ*, edited by Carl E. Braaten and Roy A. Harrisville, 197–242.

Hastings, A. W., and E. Hastings, eds. *Theologians of Our Time*. Edinburgh: T&T Clark, 1966.

Hatch, Carl E. *The Charles A. Briggs Heresy Trial: Prologue to Twentieth-Century Protestantism*. New York: Exposition, 1969.

Hauge, Matthew Ryan, and Christopher W. Skinner, eds. *Character Studies in the Gospel of Mark*. LNTS 483. London: T&T Clark, 2014.

Hawkins, Sir John C. *Horae Synopticae: Contributions to the Study of the Synoptic Problem*. Oxford: Clarendon, 1899; 2nd ed. 1909. Reprint, Grand Rapids: Baker, 1968.

Hawthorne, Gerald F. *Philippians*. WBC 43. Dallas: Word, 1983.

———. *The Presence and the Power*. Dallas: Word, 1991.

———. "In the Form of God and Equal with God (Philippians 2:6)." In *Where Christology Began*, edited by Ralph P. Martin and Brian J. Dodd, 96–110.

———. *Philippians*. Revised and expanded by Ralph P. Martin. WBC 43. Nashville: Nelson, 2004.

Hay, David M. *Glory at the Right Hand: Psalm 110 in Early Christianity*. SBLMS 18. Nashville: Abingdon, 1973.

Hayman, Ronald. *Nietzsche: A Critical Life*. Oxford: Oxford University Press, 1980.

Hays, Christopher M., et al. *When the Son of Man Didn't Come: A Constructive Proposal on the Delay of the Parousia*. Minneapolis: Fortress, 2016.

Hays, Richard B. *The Faith of Jesus Christ: The Narrative Substructure of Galatians 3:1–4:11*. SBLDS 56. Chico, CA: Scholars, 1983; 2nd ed., Grand Rapids: Eerdmans, 2003.

———. *Reading Backwards: Figural Christology and the Fourfold Witness*. Waco, TX: Baylor University Press, 2014.

Bibliography

Hayward, C. T. R. *The Jewish Temple: A Non-Biblical Sourcebook.* New York: Routledge, 1996.

Headlam, Arthur Cayley. *The Life and Teaching of Jesus the Christ.* London: Murray, 1923.

———. *Jesus Christ in History and Faith.* William Beldon Noble Lectures at Harvard 1924. Cambridge, MA: Harvard University Press, 1925.

———. *The Fourth Gospel as History.* With a biographical essay by Agnes Headlam-Morley. Oxford: Blackwell, 1948.

Hearon, Holly E., and Philip Ruge-Jones, eds. *The Bible in Ancient and Modern Media: Story and Performance.* Biblical Performance Criticism 1. Eugene OR: Cascade, 2009.

Hebblethwaite, Brian. *The Incarnation: Collected Essays on Christology.* Cambridge: Cambridge University Press, 1987.

Hedrick, Charles W. *Unlocking the Secrets of the Gospel according to Thomas: A Radical Faith for a New Age.* Eugene, OR: Cascade, 2010.

Hedrick, Charles W. *The Wisdom of Jesus: Between the Sages of Israel and the Apostles of the Church.* Eugene, OR: Cascade, 2014.

Hefner, Philip J. *Faith and the Vitalities of History: A Theological Study Based on the Work of Albrecht Ritschl.* New York: Harper & Row, 1966.

Hegel, G. W. F. *System der Wissenschaft. Erster Theil, Die Phänomenologie des Geistes.* Bamberg and Würzburg: Goebhardt, 1807. ET: *Phenomenology of Spirit.* Translated by A. V. Miller. Foreword by J. N. Findlay. Oxford: Oxford University Press, 1977. Reprint, 1981.

———. *Vorlesungen über die Philosophie der Religion.* Berlin: Duncker und Humblot, 1832. ET: *Lectures on the Philosophy of Religion, The Lectures of 1827.* Edited by Peter C. Hodgson. Berkeley: University of California Press, 1988.

———. *Vorlesungen über die Geschichte der Philosophie.* Berlin: Duncker und Humblot, 1833–42. ET: *Lectures on the History of Philosophy.* Translated by E. S. Haldane and F. H. Simson. 3 vols. Reprint, New York: Humanities, 1974.

Heidegger, Martin. *Being and Time.* Translated by John Macquarrie and Edward Robinson. London: SCM; New York: Harper & Row, 1962; 2nd ed., Oxford: Blackwell, 1973.

Heil, John Paul. *Jesus Walking on the Sea: Meaning and Gospel Functions of Matt 14:22–33, Mark 6:45–52 and John 6:15b–2.* AnBib 87. Rome: Pontifical Biblical Institute, 1981.

Hellholm, David, ed. *Apocalypticism in the Mediterranean World and the Near East. Proceedings of the International Colloquium on Apocalypticism, Uppsala, August 12–17, 1979.* Tübingen: Mohr Siebeck, 1983.

Hendricks, Obery M., Jr. *The Politics of Jesus: Discovering the True Revolutionary Nature of the Teachings of Jesus and How They Have Been Corrupted.* New York: Doubleday, 2006.

A History of the Quests for the Historical Jesus

Hendrickx, Herman. *The Miracle Stories: Studies in the Synoptic Gospels*. London: Geoffrey Chapman; San Francisco: Harper & Row, 1987.

Hengel, Martin. *Die Zeloten: Untersuchungen zur jüdischen Freiheitsbewegung in der Zeit von Herodes I. bis 70 n. Chr.* AGJU 1. Leiden: Brill, 1961; 2nd ed., 1976. ET: *The Zealots: Investigations into the Jewish Freedom Movement in the Period from Herod I until 70 A.D.* Translated by David Smith from the 2nd German ed. Edinburgh: T&T Clark, 1989.

———. *War Jesus Revolutionär?* CH 110. Stuttgart: Calwer, 1970. ET: *Was Jesus a Revolutionist?* Translated by William Klassen. Facet Books Biblical Series 28. Philadelphia: Fortress, 1971.

———. *Victory Over Violence: Jesus and the Revolutionists*. Translated by David E. Green with introduction by Robin Scroggs. Philadelphia: Fortress, 1973.

———. *Judaism and Hellenism: Studies in Their Encounter in Palestine during the Early Hellenistic Period*. 2 vols. Translated by John Bowden from the 2nd German ed. 1973. London: SCM, 1974.

———. *The Son of God: The Origin of Christology and the History of Jewish-Hellenistic Religion*. Translated by John Bowden. London: SCM, 1976.

———. *Christ and Power*. Translated by Everett R. Kalin. Philadelphia: Fortress, 1977.

———. *Crucifixion: In the Ancient World and the Folly of the Message of the Cross*. Translated by John Bowden. London: SCM; Philadelphia: Fortress, 1977.

———. *The Atonement: The Origins of the Doctrine in the New Testament*. Translated by John Bowden. London: SCM; Philadelphia: Fortress, 1981.

———. *The Charismatic Leader and His Followers*. Translated by James Greig. New York: Crossroad, 1981.

———. *Between Jesus and Paul: Studies in the Earliest History of Christianity*. Translated by John Bowden. London: SCM; Philadelphia: Fortress, 1983.

———. *Studies in the Gospel of Mark*. Translated by John Bowden. Philadelphia: Fortress, 1985.

———. *The Johannine Question*. Stone Lectures at Princeton Theological Seminary in 1987. Translated by John Bowden. London: SCM; Philadelphia: Trinity Press International, 1989. [Expanded German edition: *Die johanneische Frage: Ein Lösungsversuch*. WUNT 67. Tübingen: Mohr Siebeck, 1993.]

———. *The "Hellenization" of Judaea in the First Century after Christ*. Translated by John Bowden. London: SCM; Philadelphia: Trinity Press International, 1989. Reprint, Eugene, OR: Wipf & Stock, 2003.

———. *The Pre-Christian Paul*. In collaboration with Roland Deines. Translated by John Bowden. London: SCM; Philadelphia: Trinity Press International, 1991.

———. *Studies in Early Christology*. Edinburgh: T&T Clark, 1995.

———. "Jesus, the Messiah of Israel." In *Studies in Early Christology*, 1–72.

———. "'Sit at My Right Hand!' The Enthronement of Christ at the Right Hand of God and Psalm 110:1." In *Studies in Early Christology*, 119–225.

Bibliography

———. *The Septuagint as Christian Scripture: Its Prehistory and the Problem of Its Canon.* With the assistance of Roland Deines. Translated by Mark E. Biddle. Edinburgh: T&T Clark, 2002. Reprint, Grand Rapids: Baker Academic, 2004.

———. *Der unterschätzte Petrus: Zwei Studien.* Tübingen: Mohr Siebeck, 2006. ET: *Saint Peter: The Underestimated Apostle.* Translated by Thomas H. Trapp. Grand Rapids: Eerdmans, 2010.

Hengel, Martin, and Anna Maria Schwemer. *Paul between Damascus and Antioch: The Unknown Years.* Translated by John Bowden. London: SCM; Louisville: Westminster John Knox, 1997.

Hennell, Charles Christian. *An Inquiry Concerning the Origin of Christianity.* London: Smallfield and Son, 1838; 2nd ed., 1840. Facsimile reprint, Scholar's Choice and Primary Source Edition, n.d.

———. *Untersuchung über den Ursprung des Christenthums.* Aus dem Englischem. Translated by Ludwig Georgii. Introduction by David Friedrich Strauss. Stuttgart: Hallberger'sche Verlagshandlung, 1840. Reprint, Nabu Public Domain Reprints, n.d.

———. *Christian Theism.* London: John Chapman, 1839. Reprint, 1852. Facsimile reprint, ULAN Press, n.d.

Hennell, Sara S., *A Memoir of Charles Christian Hennell.* Published privately, 1899.

Henson, Herbert Hensley. *The Creed in the Pulpit.* New York: Hodder & Stoughton, 1912.

———. *Retrospect of an Unimportant Life.* 3 vols. London: Oxford University Press, 1942–50.

Henze, Matthias, ed. *Biblical Interpretation at Qumran.* Studies in the Dead Sea Scrolls and Related Literature. Grand Rapids: Eerdmans, 2005.

Herder, Johann Gottfried. *Vom Erlöser der Menschen. Nach unsern drei ersten Evangelien.* Riga: Hartknoch, 1796.

———. *Vom Gottes Sohn, der Welt Heiland. Nach Johannes Evangelium. Nebst einer Regel der Zusammenstimmung unsrer Evangelien aus ihrer Entstehung und Ordnung.* Riga: Hartknoch, 1797.

Herbert, Edward, Lord Herbert of Cherbury. *De Veritate, prout distinguitur a revelatione, a verisimili, a possibili, et a falso.* Paris, 1624; 3rd ed., 1645. French translation, 1639. ET: *On Truth, as It Is Distinguished from Revelation, the Probable, the Possible, and the False.* Translated by Merrick H. Carré. [Translation of the 3rd ed.] University of Bristol Studies 6. Bristol: Arrowsmith, 1937.

Herbst, Jürgen. "Francis Greenwood Peabody: Harvard's Theologian of the Social Gospel." *HTR* 54 (1961): 4–60.

———. *The German Historical School in American Scholarship.* New York: Cornell University Press, 1965.

Herrenbrück, Fritz. *Jesus und die Zöllner. Historische und neutestamentlich-exegetische Untersuchungen.* WUNT 41. Tübingen: Mohr Siebeck, 1990.

A History of the Quests for the Historical Jesus

Herrick, James A. *The Radical Rhetoric of the English Deists: The Discourse of Skepticisim, 1680–1750.* Columbia: University of South Carolina Press, 1997.

Hermann, Wilhelm. *The Communion of the Christian with God. Described on the Basis of Luther's Statements.* Edited by Robert T. Voelkel. Lives of Jesus Series. Philadelphia: Fortress, 1971.

Herzog, William R., II. *Parables as Subversive Speech: Jesus as Pedagogue of the Oppressed.* Louisville: Westminster John Knox, 1994.

———. *Jesus, Justice, and the Reign of God: A Ministry of Liberation.* Louisville: Westminster John Knox, 2000.

———. *Prophet and Teacher: An Introduction to the Historical Jesus.* Louisville: Westminster John Knox, 2005.

Heschel, Susannah. *Abraham Geiger and the Jewish Jesus.* Chicago Studies in the History of Judaism. Chicago: University of Chicago Press, 1998.

———. *The Aryan Jesus: Christian Theologians and the Bible in Nazi Germany.* Princeton: Princeton University Press, 2008.

Hess, Richard S., and M. Daniel Carroll R., eds. *Israel's Messiah in the Bible and the Dead Sea Scrolls.* Grand Rapids: Baker Academic, 2003.

Hezser, Catherine, ed. *The Oxford Handbook of Jewish Daily Life in Roman Palestine.* Oxford: Oxford University Press, 2010.

Hick, John. "The Christology of D. M. Baillie." *SJT* 11 (1958): 1–12.

———. "Christology at the Crossroads." In *Prospect for Theology; Essays in Honour of H. H. Farmer*, edited by F. G. Healey, 137–66. Digswell Place: Nisbet, 1966.

———. *An Autobiography.* Oxford: Oneworld, 2002.

———. *The Metaphor of God Incarnate: Christology in a Pluralistic Age.* London: SCM; Louisville: Westminster John Knox, 1993. Reprint, 2005.

———. "Literal and Metaphorical Christologies." In *Jesus Then and Now*, edited by Marvin Meyer and Charles Hughes, 143–53.

Hick, John, ed. *The Myth of God Incarnate.* London: SCM, 1977.

Higgins, A. J. B. *Jesus and the Son of Man.* London: Lutterworth, 1964.

Higgins, A. J. B., ed. *New Testament Essays: Studies in Memory of Thomas Walter Manson, 1893–1958.* Manchester: Manchester University Press, 1959. [Select Manson bibliography, xi–xiv.]

Higgins, Kathleen. *Nietzsche's "Zarathustra".* Philadelphia: Temple University Press, 1987.

Hill, Wesley. *Paul and the Trinity: Persons, Relations, and the Pauline Letters.* Grand Rapids: Eerdmans, 2015.

Hillerbrand, H. J. *The Reformation in Its Own Words.* New York: Harper & Row; London: SCM, 1964.

Hinchliff, Peter. *John William Colenso: Bishop of Natal.* London: Nelson, 1964.

———. *Benjamin Jowett and the Christian Religion.* Oxford: Clarendon, 1987.

———. *God and History: Aspects of British Theology, 1875–1914.* Oxford: Clarendon, 1992.

Bibliography

———. *Frederick Temple, Archbishop of Canterbury: A Life*. Oxford: Clarendon, 1998.
Hirsch, Emmanuel. *Das Wesen des Christentums*. Weimar: Verlag Deutsche Christen, 1939.
———. *Geschichte der neueren evangelischen Theologie im Zusammenhang mit den allgemeinen Bewegungen des europäischen Denkens*. 5 vols. Gütersloh: Güterslohe Verlagshaus, [1949], 1960.
Hodgson, Peter C. *The Formation of Historical Theology: A Study of Ferdinand Christian Baur*. New York: Harper & Row, 1966.
Hoffecker, W. Andrew. "Benjamin B. Warfield." In *Reformed Theology in America*, vol. 1, *The Princeton Theology*, edited by David F. Wells, 63–91.
———. *Piety and the Princeton Theologians: Archibald Alexander, Charles Hodge, and Benjamin Warfield*. Grand Rapids: Baker, 1981.
Hoffmann, Jean G. H. *Les Vies de Jésus et le Jésus de l'Histoire*. ASNU 17. Paris: Messageries Evangéliques, 1947.
Hogan, John P. *Collingwood and Theological Hermeneutics*. New York: University Press of America, 1989.
Holifield, E. Brooks. *The Gentlemen Theologians: American Theology in Southern Culture, 1795–1860*. Durham, NC: Duke University Press, 1978.
———. *Theology in America: Christian Thought from the Age of the Puritans to the Civil War*. New Haven, CT: Yale University Press, 2003.
Holladay, Carl H. *Theios Aner in Hellenistic Judaism: A Critique of the Use of This Category in New Testament Christology*. SBLDS 40. Missoula: Scholars, 1977.
Holland, D. L. "History, Theology and the Kingdom of God: A Contribution of Johannes Weiss to Twentieth Century Theology." *BR* 13 (1968): 54–66.
Hollenbach, Paul W. "Jesus, Demoniacs, and Public Authorities: A Socio-Historical Study." *JAAR* 81 (1981): 567–88.
———. "Recent Historical Jesus Studies and the Social Sciences." In *SBL 1983 Seminar Papers*, 61–78.
———. "Help for Interpreting Jesus' Exorcisms." In *SBL 1993 Seminar Papers*, 119–28.
Hollingdale, R. J. *Nietzsche: The Man and His Philosophy*. Cambridge: Cambridge University Press, 1965; rev. ed., 1999.
Holmberg, Bengt. *Sociology and the New Testament: An Appraisal*. Minneapolis: Fortress, 1990.
Holmén, Tom. *Jesus and Jewish Covenant Thinking*. BibIntS 55. Leiden: Brill, 2001.
———. "A Theologically Disinterested Quest? On the Origins of the 'Third Quest' of the Historical Jesus." *Studia Theologica* 55 (2001): 175–97.
———. "Doubts about Double Dissimilarity: Restructuring the Main Criterion of Jesus-of-History Research." In *Authenticating the Words of Jesus*, edited by Bruce Chilton and Craig A. Evans, 48–80.
———. "The Jewishness of Jesus in the 'Third Quest.'" In *Jesus, Mark and Q*, edited by Michael Labahn and Andreas Schmidt, 143–62.

———. "A Theologically Disinterested Quest? On the Origins of the 'Third Quest' for the Historical Jesus." *Studia Theologica* 55 (2001): 175–97.
———. "Jesus, Judaism and the Covenant." *JSHJ* 2 (2004): 3–27.
———. "Jesus and the Purity Paradigm." *HSJS* 3 (2011): 2709–44.
Holmén, Tom, ed. *Jesus from Judaism to Christianity: Continuum Perspectives to the Historical Jesus*. London: T&T Clark, 2007.
———. *Jesus in Continuum*. WUNT 289. Tübingen: Mohr Siebeck, 2012.
Holmén, Tom, and Stanley E. Porter, eds. *Handbook for the Study of the Historical Jesus*. 4 vols. Leiden: Brill, 2011. [Vol. 1, *How to Study the Historical Jesus*; vol. 2: *The Study of Jesus*; vol. 3: *The Historical Jesus*; vol. 4: *Individual Studies*.] Abbreviated as *HSHJ*.
Holtzmann, Heinrich Julius. *Die synoptische Evangelien. Ihr Ursprung und geschichtlicher Charakter*. Leipzig: Engelmann, 1863.
———. *Lehrbuch der historisch-kritischen Einleitung in das Neue Testament*. Freiburg: Mohr Siebeck, 1885; 3rd ed., 1982.
———. *Lehrbuch der neutestamentlichen Theologie*. 2 vols. Freiburg and Leipzig: Mohr Siebeck, 1896–97; rev. by Adolf Jülicher and Walter Bauer, 1911.
———. *Die Synoptiker*. HNT. Tübingen: Mohr Siebeck, 1901.
———. *Die Entstehung des Neuen Testaments*. Halle: Gebauer-Schwetschke, 1904.
———. *Das messianische Bewusstsein Jesu. Ein Beitrag zur Leben-Jesu-Forschung*. Tübingen: Mohr, 1907.
———. *Das Johannesevangelium untersucht und erklärt*. 3rd ed. Darmstadt: Waitz, 1908.
Homolka, Walter. *Jewish Identity in Modern Times: Leo Baeck and German Protestantism*. Providence, RI: Berghahn, 1995.
———. *Jesus Reclaimed: Jewish Perspectives on the Nazarene*. Translated by Ingrid Shafer. New York: Berghahn, 2009; rev. enlarged ed., 2015.
Honderich, Ted, ed. *The Oxford Companion to Philosophy*. 2nd ed. Oxford: Oxford University Press, 2005.
Hook, Sidney, ed. *Religious Experience and Truth: A Symposium*. New York: New York University Press, 1961; London: Oliver and Boyd, 1962.
Hooker, Morna D. *The Son of Man in Mark: A Study of the Background of the Term "Son of Man" and Its Use in St Mark's Gospel*. London: SPCK, 1967.
———. "Christology and Methodology." *NTS* 17 (1971): 480–87.
———. *The Gospel according to Saint Mark*. Black's New Testament Commentaries. London: Black; Peabody, MA: Hendrickson, 1991.
———. "Chalcedon and the New Testament." In *The Making and Remaking of Christian Doctrine: Essays in Honour of Maurice Wiles*, edited by Sarah Coakley and David Pailin, 73–93. Oxford: Clarendon, 1993.
———. "The Beginning of the Gospel." In *The Future of Christology*, edited by Abraham J. Malherbe and Wayne A. Meeks, 18–28.
———. *Beginnings: Keys That Open the Gospels*. London: SCM; Harrisburg PA: Trinity Press International, 1997.

Bibliography

———. *The Signs of a Prophet: The Prophetic Actions of Jesus*. Harrisburg PA: Trinity Press International, 1997. [Plus an appendix by David Stacey on "The Lord's Supper as Prophetic Drama."]

———. *Endings: Invitations to Discipleship*. London: SCM; Peabody, MA: Hendrickson, 2003.

———. "T. W. Manson and the Twentieth-Century Search for Jesus." In *Biblical Scholarship in the Twentieth Century: The Rylands Chair of Biblical Criticism and Exegesis at the University of Manchester, 1904–2004*. Edited by Timothy Larsen. Manchester: University of Manchester Press, 2007. [Originally appeared in *BJRL* 86, no. 3 (2004): 77–98.]

Hoover, R. W. "The Harpagmos Enigma: A Philological Solution." *HTR* 64 (1971): 95–119.

Horace (Quintos Horatius Flaccus). *Opera*. Edited by Edward C. Wickham. Revised by H. W. Garrod. Oxford Classical Texts. Oxford: Oxford University Press, 1901. [The Latin text of the *Ars Poetica* is given on pp. 253–68. C. H. Sisson has given a modern idiomatic English rendering in *The Poetic Art*. Cheadle, UK; Carcanet Press, 1975.]

Horbury, William, *Jewish Messianism and the Cult of Christ*. London: SCM, 1998.

———. *Jews and Christians in Contact and Controversy*. Edinburgh: T&T Clark, 1998.

Horbury, William, W. D. Davies, and John Sturdy, eds. *The Cambridge History of Judaism*. Vol. 3, *The Early Roman Period*. Cambridge: Cambridge University Press, 1999.

Hornblower, Simon, and Antony Spawforth, and Esther Eidinow, eds. *The Oxford Classical Dictionary*. 4th ed. Oxford: Oxford University Press, 2012.

Hornig, Gottfried. *Die Anfänge der historisch-kritischen Theologie. Johann Salomo Semlers Schriftverständnis und seiner Stellung zu Luther*. Forschungen zur Systematischen Theologie und Religionsphilosophie 8. Göttingen: Vandenhoeck & Ruprecht, 1961.

Horrell, David G., ed. *Social-Scientific Approaches to New Testament Interpretation*. Edinburgh: T&T Clark, 1999.

Horsley, Richard A. "Josephus and the Bandits." *JSJ* 10 (1979): 37–63.

———. "The Zealots: Their Origin, Relationships, and Importance to the Jewish Revolt." *NovT* 27 (1986): 159–92.

———. *Jesus and the Spiral of Violence: Popular Resistance in Roman Palestine*. San Francisco: Harper & Row: 1987.

———. *Sociology and the Jesus Movement*. New York: Crossroad, 1989.

———. *The Liberation of Christmas: The Infancy Narratives in Social Context*. New York: Crossroad, 1989.

———. "Jesus, Itinerant Cynic or Israelite Prophet?" In *Images of Jesus Today*, edited by James H. Charlesworth and Walter P. Weaver, 868–907.

———. *Galilee: History, Politics, People*. Valley Forge PA: Trinity Press International, 1995.

A History of the Quests for the Historical Jesus

———. *Archaeology, History, and Society in Galilee: The Social Context of Jesus and the Rabbis*. Valley Forge PA: Trinity Press International, 1996.

———. *Jesus and Empire: The Kingdom of God and the New World Disorder*. Minneapolis: Fortress, 2003.

———. "The Dead Sea Scrolls and the Historical Jesus." In *The Bible and the Dead Sea Scrolls*, edited by James H. Charlesworth, 3:37–60.

———. *Jesus and the Politics of Roman Palestine*. Columbia: University of South Carolina Press, 2013.

———. *Text and Tradition in Performance and Writing*. Text and Tradition in Performance and Writing 9. Eugene, OR: Cascade, 2013.

———. *Jesus and Magic: Freeing the Gospel Stories from Modern Misconceptions*. Eugene, OR: Cascade, 2014.

Horsley, Richard A., and John S. Hanson. *Bandits, Prophets, and Messiahs: Popular Movements in the Time of Jesus*. New Voices in Biblical Studies. Minneapolis: Winston, 1985. Reprint, San Francisco: Harper & Row, 1988.

Horsley, Richard A., and Neil Asher Silberman. *The Message of the Kingdom: How Jesus and Paul Ignited a Revolution and Transformed the Ancient World*. New York: Penguin Putnam, 1997.

Horsley, Richard A., with Jonathan A. Draper. *Whoever Hears You Hears Me: Prophets, Performance, and Tradition in Q*. Harrisburg PA: Trinity Press International, 1999.

Hort, Arthur Fenton. *Life and Letters of Fenton John Anthony Hort*. 2 vols. London: Macmillan, 1896.

Hoskyns, Edwyn Clement. *Cambridge Sermons*. London: SPCK, 1938. Reprint, 1970.

———. "The Christ of the Synoptic Gospels." In *Essays Catholic and Critical, by Members of the Anglican Communion*, edited by E. G. Selwyn, 151–78. London: SPCK; New York: Macmillan, 1926.

———. *The Fourth Gospel*. Edited by Francis Noel Davey. London: Faber, 1940; rev. ed., 1947.

Hoskyns, Edwyn Clement, and Francis Noel Davey. *The Riddle of the New Testament*. London: Faber and Faber, 1936; 3rd ed., 1947.

———. *Crucifixion-Resurrection: The Pattern of Theology and Ethics of the New Testament*. Edited by Gordon S. Wakefield. London: SPCK, 1981.

Hossfeld, Uwe. *Kämpferische Wissenschaft. Studien zur Universität Jena im Nationalsozialismus*. Köln: Böhlau, 2003.

Houston, J. *Reported Miracles: A Critique of Hume*. Cambridge: Cambridge University Press, 1994.

Hovey, Craig. *Nietzsche and Theology*. New York: T&T Clark, 2008.

Howatson, M. C., ed. *The Oxford Companion to Classical Literature*. 3rd ed. Oxford: Oxford University Press, 2011.

Howerzyl, Timothy. "Imaging Salvation: A Methodological Inquiry into the Function of Metaphor in Christian Soteriology, with Application to the Metaphor of Ransom." PhD diss., Fuller Theological Seminary, 2015.

Hudson, Wayne, Diego Lucci, and Jeffrey R. Wigglesworth, eds. *Atheism and Deism Revalued: Heterodox Religious Identities in Britain, 1650–1800*. Farnham: Ashgate, 2014.

Hughes, Philip Edgcumbe, ed. *Creative Minds in Contemporary Theology*. 2nd ed. Grand Rapids: Eerdmans, 1969.

Hull, John M. *Hellenistic Magic and the Synoptic*. SBT 28. London: SCM; Naperville, IL: Allenson, 1974.

Hultgren, Arland J. *Jesus and His Adversaries: The Form and Function of the Conflict Stories in the Synoptic Tradition*. Minneapolis: Augsburg, 1979.

———. *New Testament Christology: A Critical Assessment and Annotated Bibliography*. Bibliographies an Indexes in Religious Studies 12. New York: Greenwood, 1988.

———. "The Bread Petition of the Lord's Prayer." *Christ and His Communities*, edited by Arland J. Hultgren and Barbara Hall, 41–54.

———. *The Parables of Jesus: A Commentary*. Grand Rapids: Eerdmans, 2000.

Hultgren, Arland J., and Barbara Hall, eds. *Christ and His Communities: Essays in Honor of Reginald H. Fuller*. Cincinnati: Forward Movement, 1990.

Hume, David. *A Treatise of Human Nature*. Edited by L. A. Selby-Bigge. Oxford: Clarendon, 1888.

———. *Dialogues Concerning Natural Religion*. Edited by Norman Kemp Smith. New York: Nelson, 1935; 2nd ed., 1947. Reprint, Indianapolis: Bobbs-Merrill, n.d.

———. *The Natural History of Religion*. Edited by H. E. Root. London: Black, 1956.

———. *Enquiries Concerning Human Understanding and Concerning the Principles of Morals*. Edited by L. A. Selby-Bigge. 3rd ed. Revised by P. H. Nidditch. Oxford: Clarendon, 1975.

———. *The Letters of David Hume*. Edited by J. Y. T. Greig. Oxford: Clarendon, 1932. Reprint, New York: Garland, 1983.

———. *A Treatise of Human Nature*. Edited by David Fate Norton and Mary J. Norton. Clarendon Edition of the Works of David Hume. Oxford: Clarendon, 2000.

———. *An Enquiry Concerning Human Understanding: A Critical Edition*. Edited by Tom L. Beauchamp. Clarendon Edition of the Works of David Hume. Oxford: Clarendon, 2000. Reprint, 2007.

Humphries, Colin. *The Mystery of the Last Supper: Reconstructing the Final Days of Jesus*. Cambridge: Cambridge University Press, 2011.

Hunsinger, George. "Hans Frei as a Theologian." *Modern Theology* 8 (1992): 103–28.

Hunter, Michael, and David Wootton, eds. *Atheism from the Reformation to the Enlightenment*. Oxford: Clarendon, [1992], 2003.

Hur, Ju. *A Dynamic Reading of the Holy Spirit in Luke-Acts*. New York: T&T Clark International, 2001. Reprint, 2004.

Hurst, L. D., and N. T. Wright, eds. *The Glory of Christ in the New Testament: Studies in Christology in Memory of George Bradford Caird.* Oxford: Clarendon, 1987.

Hurtado, Larry W. "New Testament Christology: A Critique of Bousset's Influence." *TS* 40 (1979): 306–17.

———. "The Origin of *Nomina Sacra*: A Proposal." *JBL* 117 (1998): 655–73.

———. *One God, One Lord: Early Christian Devotion and Ancient Jewish Monotheism.* Philadelphia: Fortress, 1988; 2nd ed., Edinburgh: T&T Clark, 1998.

———. *At the Origins of Christian Worship: The Context and Character of Earliest Christian Devotion.* Carlisle: Paternoster, 1999; Grand Rapids: Eerdmans, 2000.

———. *Lord Jesus Christ: Devotion to Jesus in Earliest Christianity.* Grand Rapids: Eerdmans, 2003.

———. *How on Earth Did Jesus Become a God? Historical Questions about Earliest Devotion to Jesus.* Grand Rapids: Eerdmans, 2005.

———. *God in New Testament Theology.* Nashville: Abingdon, 2010.

Hurtado, Larry W., and Paul L. Owen, eds. *"Who Is This Son of Man?" The Latest Scholarship on a Puzzling Expression of the Historical Jesus* LNTS 390. New York: T&T Clark International, 2011.

Hyatt, J. Philip, ed. *The Bible in Modern Scholarship: Papers Read at the 100th Meeting of the Society of Biblical Literature, December 28–30, 1964.* Nashville: Abingdon, 1964; London: Carey Kingsgate, 1966.

Hylson-Smith, Kenneth. *High Churchmanship in the Church of England: From the Sixteenth Century to the Late Twentieth Century.* Edinburgh: T&T Clark, 1993.

Hynes, William J. *Shirley Jackson Case and the Chicago School: The Socio-Historical Method.* SBLSNA 5. Chico, CA: Scholars, 1981.

Iggers, Georg G. *Historiography in the Twentieth Century: From Scientific Objectivity to the Postmodern Challenge.* Hanover, NH: Wesleyan University Press, 1997.

Iliffe, Rob. *Priest of Nature: The Religious Worlds of Isaac Newton.* New York: Oxford University Press, 2017.

Illingworth, John Richardson. *Personality, Human and Divine.* Bampton Lectures for 1894. London: Macmillan, 1894.

———. *Divine Immanence: An Essay on the Spiritual Significance of Matter.* London: Macmillan, 1898.

———. *The Doctrine of the Trinity Apologetically Considered.* London: Macmillan, 1907.

———. *Divine Transcendence and Its Reflection in Religious Authority.* London: Macmillan, 1911.

Iremonger, F. A. *William Temple, Archbishop of Canterbury: His Life and Letters.* London: Oxford University Press, 1948.

Irons, Charles Lee. *The Righteousness of God.* WUNT 386. Tübingen: Mohr Siebeck, 2015.

Israel, Jonathan I. *Radical Enlightenment: Philosophy and the Making of Modernity 1650–1750.* Oxford, New York: Oxford University Press, 2001.

Bibliography

Iverson, Kelly R., ed. *From Text to Performance: Narrative and Performance Criticism in Dialogue and Debate*. Biblical Performance Criticism 10. Eugene OR: Cascade, 2014.
Jacob, W. M. *The Making of the Anglican Church Worldwide*. London: SPCK, 1997.
James, Susan. *Spinoza on Philosophy, Religion, and Politics: The Theologico-Political Treatise*. Oxford: Oxford University Press, 2012.
James, William. *The Varieties of Religious Experience: A Study of Human Experience*. Gifford Lectures at Edinburgh, 1901–1902. London: Longmans, Green, 1902.
Janowitz, Naomi. *Magic in the Roman World*. New York: Routledge, 2001.
Janse, Sam. *"You Are My Son": The Reception History of Psalm 2 in Early Judaism and the Early Church*. Contributions to Biblical Exegesis and Theology. Leuven: Peeters, 2009.
Jarrett, James L., ed. *Nietzsche's "Zarathustra": Notes of the Seminar Given in 1934–1939 by C. G. Jung*. 2 vols. Princeton: Princeton University Press, 1988.
Jasper, Ronald. *Arthur Cayley Headlam: The Life and Letters of a Bishop*. London: Faith Press, 1960.
Jaspert, Bernd, ed. *Rudolf Bultmanns Werk und Wirkung*. Darmstadt: Wissenschaftliche Buchgesellschaft, 1984.
Jauss, Hans Robert. *Toward an Aesthetic of Reception*. Translated by Timothy Bahti. Introduction by Paul de Man. Theory and History of Literature 2. Minneapolis: University of Minnesota Press, 1982.
———. *Aesthetic Experience and Literary Hermeneutics*. Translated by Michael Shaw. Introduction by Wlad Godzich. Theory and History of Literature 3. Minneapolis: University of Minnesota Press, 1982.
Jefferson, Thomas. *The Life and Morals of Jesus of Nazareth. Extracted Textually from the Gospels in Greek, Latin, French, and English*. Published in facsimile with an introduction by Cyrus Adler. Washington, DC: Government Printing Office, 1904.
———. *Jefferson's Extracts from the Gospels: "The Philosophy of Jesus" and "The Life and Morals of Jesus"*. Edited by Dickinson W. Adams and Ruth W. Lester. Introduction by Eugene R. Sheridan. The Papers of Thomas Jefferson, Second Series. Princeton, NJ: Princeton University Press, 1983.
———. *The Jefferson Bible: The Life and Morals of Jesus of Nazareth, Extracted Textually from the Gospels in Greek, Latin, French & English*. With essays by Harry R. Rubenstein, Barbara Clark Smith, and Janice Stagnitto Ellis. Washington, DC: Smithsonian, 2011.
Jeffery, Peter. *The Secret Gospel of Mark Unveiled: Imagine Rituals of Sex, Death, and Madness in a Biblical Forgery*. New Haven, CT: Yale University Press, 2007.
Jenkins, Philip. *Hidden Gospels: How the Search for Jesus Lost Its Way*. New York: Oxford University Press, 2001.
Jennings, Louis B. "Bibliography of the Writings of Shirley Jackson Case." *JR* 29 (1949): 47–58.

A History of the Quests for the Historical Jesus

Jensen, Morten Hørning. *Herod Antipas in Galilee: The Literary and Archaeological Sources on the Reign of Herod Antipas and Its Socio-Economic Impact on Galilee*. WUNT II/215. Tübingen: Mohr Siebeck, 2006; 2nd ed., 2010.

———. "The Political History in Galilee from the First Century BCE to the End of the Second Century CE." In *Galilee*, edited by David A. Fiensy and James Riley Strange, 1:51–77. Minneapolis: Fortress, 2014.

Jeremias, Joachim. *Jerusalem zur Zeit Jesu*. 2 vols. Leipzig: Pfeiffer, 1923–37; 3rd ed., Göttingen: Vandenhoeck & Ruprecht, 1962. ET: *Jerusalem in the Time of Jesus: An Investigation into Economic and Social Conditions during the New Testament Period*. Translated by F. H. and C. H. Cave, based on the 3rd German ed. (1962) with author's revisions to 1967. London: SCM, 1967; Philadelphia: Fortress, 1969.

———. *Die Gleichnisse Jesu*. ATANT 11. Zürich: Zwingli, 1947; 6th ed., Göttingen: Vandenhoeck & Ruprecht, 1962. ET: *The Parables of Jesus*. Translated by S. H. Hooke, based on the 6th German ed. 1962. London: SCM, 1963.

———. *Die Abendmahlsworte Jesu*. Göttingen: Vandenhoeck & Ruprecht, 1949. ET: *The Eucharistic Words of Jesus*. Translated by Norman Perrin, based on the enlarged 3rd German ed. (1960). London: SCM, 1966.

———. *Jesu Verheissung für die Völker*. Franz Delitzsch-Vorlesung 1953. Stuttgart: Kohlhammer, 1956. ET: *Jesus' Promise to the Nations*. SBT 24. Translated by S. H. Hooke. London: SCM, 1958; rev. ed., 1967.

———. *The Servant of God*. SBT 20. Translated by Harold Knight et al. London: SCM; Naperville, IL: Allenson, 1957.

———. *Das Problem des historischen Jesus*. CH 32. Stuttgart: Calwer, 1960. Reprint in *Der historische Jesus und der kerygmatische Christus*, edited by H. Ristow and K. Matthiae, 12–26. Berlin: Evangelische Verlagsanstalt, 1962. ET: *The Problem of the Historical Jesus*. Translated by Norman Perrin. FBBS 13. Philadelphia: Fortress, 1964. Reedited as "The Search for the Historical Jesus." In *Jesus and the Message of the New Testament*, edited by K. C. Hanson, 1–17. Minneapolis: Fortress, 2002. [This volume also contains Jeremias's studies of "The Sermon on the Mount," "The Lord's Prayer," and "The Central Message of the New Testament."]

———. *Abba. Studien zur neutestamentlichen Theologie und Zeitgeschichte*. Göttingen: Vandenhoeck & Ruprecht, 1966.

———. *The Prayers of Jesus*. Translated by John Bowden. SBT 6. London: SCM, 1967.

———. *Neutestamentliche Theologie*. Erster Teil, *Die Verkündigung Jesu*. Gütersloh: Mohn, 1971; 2nd ed., 1973. ET: *New Testament Theology*. Vol. 1, *The Proclamation of Jesus*. Translated by John Bowden. London: SCM, 1971.

Jewett, Robert, assisted by Roy D. Kotansky. *Romans: A Commentary*. Edited by Eldon J. Epp. Hermeneia. Minneapolis: Fortress, 2007.

———. *Romans: A Short Commentary*. Minneapolis: Fortress, 2014.

Jewett, Robert, and John Shelton Lawrence. *Captain America and the Crusade against Evil: The Dilemma of Zealous Nationalism*. Grand Rapids: Eerdmans, 2004.

Bibliography

Jipp, Joshua W. *Christ Is King: Paul's Royal Ideology*. Minneapolis: Fortress, 2015.

Jöcher, Christian Gottloeb. *Allgemeines Gelehrten-Lexicon*, 4 vols. Leipzig: Deutsche Gesellschaft, 1750. Reprint, Hildesheim: Olms, 1960.

Jodock, Darrell, ed. *Ritschl in Retrospect: History, Community, and Science*. Minneapolis: Fortress, 1995.

Johnson, Luke Timothy. *The Real Jesus: The Misguided Quest of the Historical Jesus and the Truth of the Traditional Gospels*. San Francisco: HarperSanFrancisco, 1996.

———. *Living Jesus: Learning the Heart of the Gospel*. San Francisco: HarperSanFrancisco, 1998.

———. "A Historiographical Response to Wright's Jesus." In *Jesus and the Restoration of Israel*, edited by Carey C. Newman, 206–24.

Johnson, Marshall D. *The Purpose of the Biblical Genealogies with Special Reference to the Setting of the Genealogies of Jesus*. SNTSMS 8. Cambridge: Cambridge University Press, 1969; 2nd ed. 1988.

Johnston, John Octavius. *Life and Letters of Henry Parry Liddon*. London: Longmans, 1904.

Jones, Alan H. *Independence and Exegesis: The Study of Early Christianity in the Work of Alfred Loisy (1857–1940), Charles Guignebert (1857–1939), and Maurice Goguel (1880–1955)*. BGBE 26. Tübingen: Mohr Siebeck, 1983.

Jones, Mary Hoxie. "Henry Joel Cadbury: A Biographical Sketch." In *Then and Now: Quaker Essays: Historical and Contemporary, by Friends of Henry Joel Cadbury On His Completion of Twenty-Two Years as Chairman of the American Friends Service Committee*, edited by Anna Brinton, 11–70. Philadelphia: University of Pennsylvania Press, 1960.

Johnson, Roger A. *The Origins of Demythologizing: Philosophy and Historiography in the Theology of Rudolf Bultmann*. SHR 28. Leiden: Brill, 1974.

Johnson, Gary L.W., ed. *B. B. Warfield: Essays on His Life and Thought*. Foreword by David B. Calhoun. Introduction by Mark A. Noll. Phillipsburg, NJ: P&R, 2007.

Johnson, Sherman E. *The Griesbach Hypothesis and Redaction Criticism*. Atlanta: Scholars, 1991.

Jonas, Hans. *Gnosis und spätantiker Geist*. Vol. 2.1, *Von der Mythologie zur mystischen Philosophie*. FRLANT 45. Göttingen: Vandenhoeck & Ruprecht, 1954; 2nd ed., 1966.

Jones, F. Stanley, ed. *The Rediscovery of Jewish Christianity: From Toland to Baur*. HBS 5. Atlanta: SBL Press, 2012.

Jones, Gareth. *Bultmann: Towards a Critical Theology*. Oxford: Polity, 1991.

Jónsson, Jakob. *Humour and Irony in the New Testament: Illuminated by Parallels in Talmud and Midrash*. Foreword by Krister Stendahl. BZRGG 28. Leiden: Brill, 1985.

Joseph, Simon J. *The Nonviolent Messiah: Jesus, Q, and the Enochic Tradition*. Minneapolis: Fortress, 2014.

Josephus, Loeb Classical Library, 10 vols. Cambridge, MA: Harvard University Press, 1926–65.

Juel, Donald. *Messianic Exegesis: Christological Interpretation of the Old Testament in Early Christianity*. Philadelphia: Fortress, 1988.

Jülicher, Adolf. *Die Gleichnisreden Jesu*. 2 vols. Tübingen: Mohr Siebeck, 1888; 2nd ed., 1899.

Jüngel, Eberhard. *Paulus und Jesus. Eine Untersuchung zur Präzisierung der Frage nach dem Ursprung der Christologie*. HUT 2. Tübingen: Mohr Siebeck, 1962.

Justin Martyr. *Selections from Justin Martyr's Dialogue with Trypho*. Edited by R. P. C. Hanson. London: Lutterworth, 1963.

———. *The First and Second Apologies*. Translated by Leslie William Barnard. Ancient Christian Writers 56. New York: Paulist, 1997.

———. *Dialogue with Trypho*. Edited by Michael Slusser. Translated by Thomas B. Falls. Revised by Thomas P. Halton. Washington, DC: Catholic University Press of America, 2003.

Kaftan, Julius Wilhelm Martin. *Das Wesen der christlichen Religion*. Basel: Bahnmeier, 1881.

———. *The Truth of the Christian Religion*. Translated by George Ferries. 2 vols. Edinburgh: T&T Clark, 1894.

Kähler, Martin. *Die Wissenschaft der christlichen Lehre von den evangelischen Grundartikel aus im Abriss dargestellet*. Leipzig: Deichert, 1883; 3rd ed., 1905.

———. *Der sogenannte historische Jesus und der geschichtliche, biblische Christus*. Leipzig: Deichert. 1892; 2nd ed., 1896. [The modern edition edited by E. Wolf. TB 2 (München: Chr. Kaiser Verlag; 3rd ed., 1961) contains the original lecture and the first paper of the 1896 edition.] ET: *The So-Called Historical Jesus and the Historic Biblical Christ*. Translated and edited by Carl E. Braaten. Foreword by Paul Tillich. Fortress Texts in Modern Theology. Philadelphia: Fortress, 1964.

———. *Geschichte der protestantischen Dogmatik im 19. Jahrhundert*. With a list of his father's writings compiled by Ernst Kähler. TB 16. Munich: Kaiser, 1962.

Kaiser, Christopher Barina. *Seeing the Lord's Glory: Kyriocentric Visions and the Dilemma of Early Christology*. Minneapolis: Fortress, 2014.

Kampen, John, and Moshe J. Bernstein, eds. *Reading 4QMMT: New Perspectives on Qumran Law and History*. SBL Symposium Series 2. Atlanta: Scholars, 1996.

Kant, Immanuel. *Kritik der reinen Vernunft*. Riga: Hartknoch, 1781; 2nd ed., 1787. ET: *Critique of Pure Reason*. Translated and edited by Paul Guyer and Allen W. Wood. Cambridge Edition of the Works of Immanuel Kant. Cambridge: Cambridge University Press, [1998], 2016.

———. *Religion within the Limits of Reason Alone*. Translated with introduction and notes by Theodore M. Greene and Hoyt Hudson. [With an essay by John R. Silber, "The Ethical Significance of Kant's *Religion*."] LaSalle: Open Court, 1934. Reprint, New York: Harper, 1960.

———. *Religion and Rational Theology*. Edited by Allen W. Wood and George di Giovanni. Cambridge Edition of the Works of Immanuel Kant. Cambridge:

Bibliography

Cambridge University Press, 1996. [Contents include *Religion within the Boundaries of Mere Reason* (1793) and *The Conflict of the Faculties* (1798).]

———. *Correspondence*. Translated and edited by Arnulf Zweig. Cambridge Edition of the Works of Immanuel Kant. Cambridge: Cambridge University Press, 1999.

Karris, Robert J. *Prayer and the New Testament*. New York: Herder and Herder, 2000.

Käsemann, Ernst. *Leib und Leib Christi. Eine Untersuchung zur Paulinischen Begrifflichkeit*. BHTh 9. Tübingen: Mohr Siebeck, 1933.

———. *Das wandernde Gottesvolk. Eine Untersuchung zum Hebräerbrief*. FRLANT 55. Göttingen: Vandenhoeck & Ruprecht, 1939; 2nd ed., 1957. ET: *The Wandering People of God: An Investigation of the Letter to the Hebrews*. Translated by Roy A. Harrisville and Irving L. Sandberg. Minneapolis: Augsburg, 1984.

———. *Essays on New Testament Themes*. Translated by W. J. Montague. SBT 41. London: SCM; Naperville, IL: Allenson, 1964.

———. "Wunder." *RGG*³ (1962) 6:1835–37.

———. *Jesu letzte Wille nach Johannes 17*. Tübngen: Mohr Siebeck, 1966. ET: *The Testament of Jesus: A Study of the Gospel of John in the Light of Chapter 17*. Translated by Gerhard Grobel. London: SCM, 1968.

———. *Exegetische Versuche und Besinnungen*. 2 vols. Göttingen: Vandenhoeck & Ruprecht, 1965. ET (selections): *New Testament Questions of Today*. Translated by W. J. Montague. London: SCM, 1969.

———. *Perspectives on Paul*. Translated by Margaret Kohl. London: SCM, 1971.

———. *An die Römer*. Tübingen: Mohr Siebeck, 1980. ET: *Commentary on Romans*. Translated by Geoffrey W. Bromiley. Grand Rapids: Eerdmans, 1980.

Kasser, Rodolphe, Marvin Meyer, and Gregor Wurst, eds., with additional commentary by Bart D. Ehrman. *The Gospel of Judas from Codex Tchacos*. Washington, DC: National Geographic, 2006; rev. ed., 2008.

Kaufmann, Walter. *Nietzsche: Philosopher, Psychologist, Antichrist*. Princeton: Princeton University Press; New York: Random House, 1950; 3rd ed., 1968.

———. *The Portable Nietzsche*. New York: Viking, 1954. Reprint, 1968.

Kazen, Thomas. *Jesus and Purity Halakah: Was Jesus Indifferent to Impurity?* ConBNT 38. Stockholm: Almqvist & Wicksell, 2002.

Keck, Leander E. "Which Way to Jesus of Nazareth?" [Reviews of Bornkamm and Stauffer] *Foundations* 5 (1962): 173–83.

———. "Bornkamm's *Jesus of Nazareth* Revisited." *JR* 49 (1969): 1–17.

———. "The Spirit and the Dove." *NTS* 17 (1970): 41–67.

———. *A Future for the Historical Jesus: The Place of Jesus in Preaching and Theology*. Nashville: Abingdon, 1971; London: SCM, 1972.

———. Review of Hans Frei's *The Eclipse of Biblical Narrative*. In *Theology Today* 31 (1974–75): 367–70.

———. Review of Hans Frei's *The Identity of Jesus Christ*. In *Theology Today* 32 (1976): 312–30.

———. *Who Is Jesus? History in Perfect Tense*. Columbia: University of South Carolina, 2000. Reprint, Minneapolis: Fortress, 2001.
———. *Why Christ Matters: Toward a New Testament Christology*. Waco TX: Baylor University Press, 2015.
———. *Christ's First Theologian: The Shape of Paul's Thought*. Waco TX: Baylor University Press, 2015.
———. *Echoes of the Word*. Eugene OR: Wipf & Stock; Cambridge: Lutterworth, 2015.
Keck, Leander E., and J. Louis Martyn, eds. *Studies in Luke-Acts: Essays Presented in Honor of Paul Schubert, Buckingham Professor of New Testament Criticism and Interpretation at Yale University*. Louisville: Abingdon, 1966; London: SPCK, 1968.
Kee, Alistair. *Nietzsche against the Crucified*. London: SCM, 1999.
Kee, Alistair, and Eugene T. Long, eds. *Being and Truth: Essays in Honour of John Macquarrie*. London: SCM, 1986.
Kee, Howard Clark. *Miracle in the Early Christian World: A Study in Sociohistorical Method*. New Haven, CT: Yale University Press, 1983.
———. *Medicine, Miracle and Magic in New Testament Times*. SNTSMS 55. Cambridge: Cambridge University Press, 1986.
———. *What Can We Know about Jesus?* Cambridge: Cambridge University Press, 1990.
———. "Medicine and Healing." In *ABD* 4 (1992), 659–64.
Keener, Craig S. *The Spirit in the Gospels and Acts: Divine Purity and Power*. Peabody MA: Hendrickson, 1997.
———. *A Commentary on the Gospel of Matthew*. Grand Rapids: Eerdmans, 1999.
———. *The Gospel of John: A Commentary*. 2 vols. Peabody MA: Hendrickson, 2003.
———. *The Historical Jesus of the Gospels*. Grand Rapids: Eerdmans, 2009.
———. *Miracles: The Credibility of the New Testament Accounts*. 2 vols. Grand Rapids: Baker Academic, 2012.
———. *Acts: An Exegetical Commentary*. 4 vols. Grand Rapids: Baker Academic, 2012–15.
Kegley, Charles W., ed. *The Theology of Paul Tillich*. New York: Pilgrim, 1952; rev. ed., 1982.
———. *The Theology of Rudolf Bultmann*. London: SCM, 1966.
Keim, Theodor. *Geschichte von Jesus von Nazara*. Zürich: Orell, Füssli, 1920.
Keith, Chris. *Jesus' Literacy: Scribal Culture and the Teacher from Galilee*. LNTS 413. New York: T&T Clark, 2011.
———. *Jesus against the Scribal Elite: The Origins of the Conflict*. Grand Rapids: Baker Academic, 2014.
Keith, Chris, and Larry W. Hurtado, eds. *Jesus among Friends and Enemies: A Historical and Literary Introduction to Jesus in the Gospels*. Grand Rapids: Baker Academic, 2011.
Keith, Chris, and Anthony Le Donne, eds. *Jesus, Criteria, and the Demise of Authenticity*. New York: T&T Clark, 2012.

Bibliography

Kelber, Werner H. *The Oral and the Written Gospel: The Hermeneutics of Speaking and Writing in the Synoptic Tradition, Mark, Paul, and Q.* Voices in Performance and Text. Foreword by Walter J. Ong. Philadelphia: Fortress, 1983. Reprint, with new introduction. Bloomington, IN: Indiana University Press, 1997.

Kelber, Werner H., and Samuel Byrskog. *Jesus in Memory: Traditions in Oral and Scribal Perspectives.* Waco TX: Baylor University Press, 2009.

Kelly, J. N. D. *Early Christian Creeds.* London: Longmans, Green, 1950.

———. *Early Christian Doctrines.* New York: Harper & Row, 1960; rev. ed., 1978.

Kelsey, David H. *The Fabric of Paul Tillich's Theology.* New Haven, CT: Yale University Press, 1967.

———. *The Uses of Scripture in Recent Theology.* Philadelphia: Fortress, 1975.

Kent, John. *William Temple: Church, State and Society in Britain.* Cambridge: Cambridge University Press, 1992.

Ker, Ian. *John Henry Newman: A Biography.* Oxford: Clarendon, 1988.

Kerényi, Carl. *Dionysos: Archetypal Image of Indestructible Life.* Bollingen Series 15/2. Translated by Ralph Mannheim. Princeton: Princeton University Press, 1976.

Khalidi, Tarif, ed. and trans. *The Muslim Jesus: Sayings and Stories in Islamic Literature.* Cambridge, MA: Harvard University Press, 2001.

Kidger, Mark, *The Star of Bethlehem: An Astronomer's View.* Princeton, NJ: Princeton University Press, 1999.

Kieft, Lester, and Bennett R. Willeford Jr., eds. *Joseph Priestley, Scientist, Theologian, and Metaphysician: A Symposium Celebrating the Two Hundredth Anniversary of the Discovery of Oxygen by Joseph Priestley in 1774.* Lewisburg, PA: Bucknell University Press, 1980.

Kierkegaard, Søren. *Philosophical Fragments.* Edited and translated by Howard V. Hong and Edna H. Hong. Princeton: Princeton University Press, 1985.

———. *Either/Or.* Part 1. Translated by Howard V. Hong and Edna H. Hong. Kierkegaard's Writings 3. Princeton: Princeton University Press, 1987.

———. *Concluding Unscientific Postscript to the Philosophical Fragments: A Mimic-Pathetic-Dialectical Composition; An Existential Contribution by Johannes Climacus. Responsible for Publication: S. Kierkegaard* (1846). Translated by D. F. Swenson and W. Lowrie. Princeton: Princeton University Press, 1941.

———. *Søren Kierkegaard's Journals and Papers.* Edited and translated by Howard V. Hong and Edna H. Hong, with Gregor Malantschuk et al. 7 vols. Bloomington, IN: Indiana University Press, 1967–78.

Kim, Seyoon. *The Origin of Paul's Gospel.* Grand Rapids: Eerdmans, 1981. Reprint, 1982.

———. *Paul and the New Perspective: Second Thoughts on the Origin of Paul's Gospel.* Grand Rapids: Eerdmans, 2002.

———. *Christ and Caesar: The Gospel and the Roman Empire in the Writings of Paul and Luke.* Grand Rapids: Eerdmans, 2008.

King, John Benjamin. *Newman and the Alexandrian Fathers.* Changing Paradigms in Historical and Systematic Theology. Oxford: Oxford University Press, 2009.
King, Karen L. *What Is Gnosticism?* Cambridge, MA: Harvard University Press, 2003.
Kingsbury, Jack Dean. *Matthew: Structure, Christology, Kingdom.* Minneapolis: Fortress, 1975. Reprint, 1989.
Kirk, J. R. Daniel. *A Man Attested by God: The Human Jesus of the Synoptic Gospels.* Grand Rapids: Eerdmans, 2016.
Kittel, Gerhard. *Die Probleme des palästinischen Spätjudentums und das Urchristentum.* BWANT 3. Folge, Heft 1. Stuttgart: Kohlhammer, 1926.
———. *Jesus und die Juden.* Berlin: Furche-Verlag, 1926.
———. *Theologisches Wörterbuch zum Neuen Testament.* Vols. 1–4. Stuttgart: Kohlhammer, 1933–42. [Subsequent 6 vols. ed. by Gerhard Friedrich.]
———. *Theological Dictionary of the New Testament.* Translated by Geoffrey W. Bromiley. 10 vols. Grand Rapids: Eerdmans, 1964–76.
Kittel, Gerhard. *Die Judenfrage.* Stuttgart: Kohlhammer, 1933.
Klassen, William. "Judas Iscariot." In *ABD*, 3:1091–96.
Klauck, Hans-Josef. *The Religious Context of Early Christianity: A Guide to Graeco-Roman Religions.* Translated by Brian MacNeil. Edinburgh: T&T Clark, 2000.
———. *Magic and Paganism in Early Christianity: The World of the Acts of the Apostles.* Translated by Brian McNeil. Edinburgh: T&T Clark, 2000.
———. *Apocryphal Gospels: An Introduction.* Translated by Brian McNeil. New York: T&T International, 2003.
Klausner, Joseph. הרעיון המשיחי בישראל מראשיתו ועד חתימת־המשנה. Jerusalem: Sifriya Historit-Filogit al yad Yehuda Yunovits, 1926. ET: *The Messianic Idea in Israel: From Its Beginning to the Completion of the Mishnah.* Translated by William F. Stinespring. New York: Macmillan, 1955; London: Allen & Unwin, 1956. [The doctoral dissertation was written in German and was published as *Die messianischen Vorstellungen des jüdischen Volkes im Zeitalter der Tannaiten.* Translated by Friedrich Thieberger. Krakow: Joseph Fischer, 1903.]
———. ישו הנוצרי: זמנו, חייו ותורתו. Jerusalem: Shibi, 1921. ET: *Jesus of Nazareth: His Life, Times, and Teaching.* Translated by Herbert Danby. London: Allen & Unwin, 1925.
———. מישו עד פאולוס. Tel Aviv: Mada, 1940. ET: *From Jesus to Paul.* Translated by William F. Stinespring. New York: Macmillan, 1943; London: Allen & Unwin, 1944. Reprint, Boston: Beacon, 1961. German translation: *Von Jesus zu Paulus.* Jerusalem: Jewish Publishing House, 1950.
Klein, Dietrich. *Hermann Samuel Reimarus (1694–1768). Das theologische Werk.* BHT 145. Tübingen: Mohr Siebeck, 2009.
Klein, Hans. *Lukasstudien.* FRLANT 209. Göttingen: Vandenhoeck & Ruprecht, 2009.
Kloppenborg, John S. *The Formation of Q: Trajectories in Ancient Wisdom Collections.*

Bibliography

Studies in Antiquity & Christianity. Foreword by James M. Robinson. Philadelphia: Fortress, 1987.

———. "Holtzmann's Life of Jesus according to the 'A' Source." *JSHJ* 4 (2006): 75–108, 203–23.

Kloppenborg, John S., ed. *The Shape of Q: Signal Essays on the Sayings Gospel*. Minneapolis: Fortress, 1994.

Kloppenborg Verbin, John S. *Excavating Q: The History and Setting of the Sayings of Q*. Minneapolis: Fortress, 2000.

Kloppenborg, John S., with John W. Marshall, eds. *Apocalypticism, Anti-Semitism and the Historical Jesus*. JSNTSup 275. New York: T&T Clark International, 2005.

Knox, Ronald Arbuthnott. *Some Loose Stones: Being a Consideration of Certain Tendencies in Modern Theology; Illustrated by Reference to the Book Called "Foundations"*. New York: Longmans, 1913.

———. *Essays in Satire*. London: Sheed and Ward, 1928.

———. *A Spiritual Aeneid*. Westminster MD: Newman, 1918. Reprint, 1948.

Koch, Gustav Adolf. *Religion of the American Enlightenment*. New York: Holt, 1933. Reprint, New York: Crowell, 1969.

Koester, Craig R. *Symbolism in the Fourth Gospel: Meaning, Mystery, Community*. Minneapolis: Fortress, 1995; 2nd ed., 2003.

Koester, Helmut. *Einführung in das Neue Testament*. Berlin: de Gruyter, 1980. ET: *Introduction to the New Testament*. 2 vols. Berlin: de Gruyter; Philadelphia: Fortress, 1982.

———. *Ancient Christian Gospels: Their History and Development*. Philadelphia: Trinity Press International; London: SCM, 1990.

———. "An Intellectual Biography of James M. Robinson." In *From Quest to Q*, edited by Jón Ma. Asgeirsson, xiii–xxi.

———. "New Testament Scholarship through One Hundred Years of the *Harvard Theological Review*." *HTR* 101 (2008): 311–22.

Koistinen, Olli, ed. *The Cambridge Companion to Spinoza's Ethics*. Cambridge: Cambridge University Press, 2009.

Kolb, Robert, Irene Dingel, and L'Ubomír Batka, eds. *The Oxford Handbook of Martin Luther's Theology*. Oxford: Oxford University Press, 2014.

Kolenkow, Anitra Bingham. "A Problem of Power: How Miracle Workers Counter Charges of Magic in the Hellenistic World." In *SBL 1976 Seminar Papers*, 105–11.

Korte, Anne-Marie, ed. *Women and Miracle Stories: A Multidisciplinary Exploration*. SHR 88. Leiden: Brill, 2001.

Kortholt, Christian. *De Matthaeo Tindalio dissertation*. Leipzig: Breitkopf, 1734.

Koskenniemi, Erkki. *Der philostratische Apollonios*. Commentationes Humanorum Litterarum 94. Helsinki: Societas Scientarium Fennica, 1991.

———. *Apollonius von Tyana in der neutestamentlichen Exegese. Forschungsbericht und Weiterführung der Diskussion*. WUNT 61. Tübingen: Mohr Siebeck, 1994.

———. "Apollonius of Tyana: A Typical θεῖος ἄνθρωπος?" *JBL* 117 (1998): 455–67.
Kreiser, Robert B. *Miracles, Convulsions, and Ecclesiastical Politics in Early Eighteenth-Century Paris*. Princeton: Princeton University Press, 1978.
Krosney, Herbert. *The Lost Gospel: The Quest for the Gospel of Judas Iscariot*. Washington, DC: National Geographic, 2006.
Krueger, Derek. "The Bawdy and Society: The Shamelessness of Diogenes in Roman Imperial Culture." In *The Cynics: The Cynic Movement in Antiquity and Its Legacy*, edited by R. B. Branham and M.-O. Goulet-Cazé, 222–39.
Kugler, Robert A., and Eileen M. Schuller, eds. *The Dead Sea Scrolls at Fifty*. SBL Early Judaism and Its Literature 15. Atlanta: Scholars, 1999.
Kuhn, Heinz-Wolfgang. "The Impact of Selected Qumran Texts on the Understanding of Pauline Theology." In *The Bible and the Dead Sea Scrolls*, edited by James H. Charlesworth, 3:153–85.
———. "Jesus im Licht der Qumrangemeinde." In *HSHJ*, 2:1245–85.
Kuhn, Thomas S. *The Structure of Scientific Revolutions*. Chicago: University of Chicago Press, 1962; 2nd ed., 1970.
Kümmel, Werner Georg. *Verheissung und Erfüllung: Untersuchungen zur eschatologischen Verkündigung Jesu*. ATANT 6. Zürich: Zwingli, 1945; 3rd ed., 1956. ET: *Promise and Fulfillment: The Eschatological Message of Jesus*. Translated by Dorothea M. Barton. SBT 23. London: SCM, 1957.
———. *Heilsgeschehen und Geschichte. Gesammelte Aufsätze 1933–1964*. Edited by Erich Grässer, Otto Merk, and Adolf Fritz. MTS 3. Marburg: Elwert, 1965.
———. *Das Neue Testament. Geschichte der Erforschung seiner Probleme*. Freiburg: Alber, 1970. ET: *The New Testament: The History and Investigation of Its Problems*. Translated by S. MacLean Gilmour and Howard Clark Kee. Nashville: Abingdon, 1972.
———. *Einleitung in das Neue Testament*. Heidelberg: Quelle & Meyer, 1963; 2nd ed., 1973. ET: *Introduction to the New Testament*. Translated by Howard Clark Kee. Rev. ed., Nashville: Abingdon, 1975.
———. *Dreißig Jahre Jesusforschung (1950–1980)*. BBB 60. Bonn: Hanstein, 1985.
———. *Vierzig Jahre Jesusforschung (1950–1990)*. Edited by Helmut Merklein. 2nd ed. BBB 91. Weinheim: Beltz Athenäum, 1994.
Kurtz, Lester R. *The Politics of Heresy: The Modernist Crisis in Roman Catholicism*. Berkeley: University of California Press, 1986.
Kysar, Robert. "The Fourth Gospel. A Report on Recent Research." *ANRW*, 2.25.3 (1985): 2390–2480.
———. *John, the Maverick Gospel*. Louisville: Westminster John Knox, 1976; 3rd ed., 2007.
———. "Anti-Semitism in the Gospel of John." *Anti-Semitism and Early Christianity: Issues of Polemic and Faith*, edited by Craig A. Evans and Donald A. Hagner, 113–27.
Labahn, Michael and Andreas Schmitt, eds. *Jesus, Mark and Q: The Teaching of Jesus and Its Earliest Records*. JSNTSup 214. Sheffield: Sheffield Academic Press, 2001.

Bibliography

LacCocque, André. *Jesus the Central Jew: His Times and His People*. Early Christianity and Its Literature 15. Atlanta: SBL Press, 2015.

Lachmann, Karl. *Novum Testamentum Graece et Latine*, 2 vols. (1842–50). [*See* N. H. Palmer.]

Ladd, George Eldon. *Jesus and the Kingdom: The Eschatology of Biblical Realism*. New York: Harper and Row, 1964; London: SPCK, 1966.

———. "The Problem of History in Contemporary New Testament Interpretation." In *Studia Evagelica*, vol. 5, *Papers Presented to the Third International Congress on New Testament Studies Held at Christ Church, Oxford, 1965*, edited by F. L. Cross, 88–100. Berlin: Akademie-Verlag, 1968.

———. "Historic Premillennialism." In *The Meaning of the Millennium: Four Views*, edited by Robert G. Clouse, 17–40. Downers Grove, IL: InterVarsity Press, 1977.

Lagrange, Marie-Joseph. *Christ and Renan: A Commentary on Ernest Renan's "The Life of Jesus"*. Translated by Maisie Ward. London: Sheed & Ward, 1928.

Lamberth, David C. "Original and Ongoing Theological Issues through One Hundred Years of the *Harvard Theological Review*." *HTR* 101 (2008): 323–38.

Lampe, G. W. H. *God as Spirit*. Bampton Lectures 1976. Oxford: Clarendon, 1977.

———. "The 1938 Report in Retrospect." In *Doctrine in the Church of England: The Report of the Commission on Christian Doctrine Appointed by the Archbishops of Canterbury and York*, ix–xl. London: SPCK, 1982.

Lane, Anthony N. S., ed. *The Unseen World: Christian Reflections on Angels, Demons and the Heavenly Realm*. Carlisle, UK: Paternoster; Grand Rapids: Baker, 1996.

Lampert, Laurence. *Nietzsche's Teaching: An Interpretation of "Thus Spoke Zarathustra"*. New Haven, CT: Yale University Press, 1986.

Lane Fox, Robin. *Pagans and Christians*. New York: Knopf, 1987.

Lang, Bernhard. "The Roots of the Eucharist in Jesus' Praxis." In *SBL 1992 Seminar Papers*, 467–72.

Lang, Friedrich Gustav. "Kompositionsanalyse des Markusevangeliums." *ZTK* 74 (1977): 1–24.

Lange, Armin, Hermann Lichtenberger, and K. F. Diethard Römheld, eds. *Die Dämonen/ Demons. Die Dämonologie der israelisch-jüdischen und frühchristlichen Literatur im Kontext ihrer Umwelt / The Demonology of Israelite-Jewish and Early Christian Literature in Context of Their Environment*. Tübingen: Mohr Siebeck, 2003.

Lange, Armin, Eric M. Meyers, Bennie H. Reynolds III, and Randall Styers, eds. *Light against Darkness: Dualism in Ancient Mediterranean Religion and the Contemporary World*. JAJS 2. Göttingen: Vandenhoeck & Ruprecht, 2011.

Lange, Friedrich Albert. *Geschichte des Materialismus und seiner Bedeutung in der Gegenwart*, 3 vols. Leipzig: Iserloh, 1866. ET: *History of Materialism and Critique of Its Present Significance*. 3 vols. Translated by Ernest Chester Thomas. Boston: James R. Osgood, 1877–81. Reprinted with introduction by Bertrand Russell. Edinburgh: Kegan Paul, Trench, Trubner, 1925.

Lapide, Pinchas. *Der Rabbi von Nazereth. Wandlungen des jüdischen Jesusbildes*. Trier: Spee-Verlag, 1974.

———. *Auferstehung: Ein jüdisches Glaubenserlebnis*. Stuttgart: Calwer, 1977. ET: *The Resurrection of Jesus: A Jewish Perspective*. Translated by Wilhelm C. Linss. Introduction by Carl E. Braaten. Minneapolis: Augsburg, 1983.

———. *Der Jude Jesus. Thesen eines Juden, Antworten eines Christen*. Zürich: Benzinger, 1980.

Larmer, Robert A. H. *Water into Wine? An Investigation of the Concept of Miracle*. Montreal: McGill-Queen's University Press, 1988.

Law, Timothy Michael. *When God Spoke Greek: The Septuagint and the Making of the Christian Bible*. Oxford: Oxford University Press, 2013.

Lawrence, Louise J. *Sense and Stigma in the Gospels: Depictions of Sensory-Disabled Characters*. Biblical Reconfigurations. Oxford: Oxford University Press, 2013.

LeBeau, Bryan F., Leonard Greenspoon, and Dennis Hamm, eds. *The Historical Jesus through Catholic and Jewish Eyes*. Harrisburg, PA: Trinity Press International, 2000.

Lechler, Gotthard Victor. *Geschichte des englischen Deismus*. Tübingen: Gotta, 1841. Reprinted with foreword by Günter Gawlick. Hildesheim: Olms, 1965.

Lee, Doohee. *Luke-Acts and "Tragic History:" Communicating Gospel with the World*. WUNT 346. Tübingen: Mohr Siebeck, 2013.

Le Donne, Anthony. *The Historiographical Jesus: Memory, Typology, and the Son of David*. Waco, TX: Baylor University Press, 2009.

———. *Historical Jesus: What Can We Know and How Can We Know It?* Foreword by Dale C. Allison Jr. Grand Rapids: Eerdmans, 2011.

———. *The Wife of Jesus: Ancient Texts and Modern Scandals*. London: Oneworld, 2013.

Le Donne, Anthony, and Tom Thatcher, eds. *The Fourth Gospel in First-Century Media Culture*. LNTS 426. New York: T&T Clark, 2011.

Lehnhardt, Andreas. *Qaddish. Untersuchungen zur Entstehung und Rezeption eines rabbinischen Gebets*. TSAJ 87. Tübingen: Mohr Siebeck, 2002.

Leland, John. *A View of the Principal Deistical Writers That Have Appeared in England in the Last and Present Century; with Observations upon Them, and Some Account of the Answers That Have Been Published against Them. in Several Letters to a Friend*. 2 vols. London: Benjamin Dod, 1744; 3rd ed. 1757.

———. *A Supplement to the First and Second Volume of the View of the Deistical Writers. Containing Additions and Illustrations Relating to Those Volumes. in Several Letters to a Friend. to Which Is Added, Reflections on the Late Lord Bolingbroke's Letters on the Study and Use of History, as It Relates to the Holy Scriptures . . . with a Large Index to the Three Volumes*. 3rd ed. London: Benjamin Dod, 1756.

Lemker, Heinrich Christian. *Historische Nachrichten von Thomas Woolstons Schicksal, Schriften und Streitigkeiten*. Leipzig: Johann Friedrich Gleditsch, 1740.

Leonard, Ellen. *George Tyrrell and the Catholic Tradition*. New York: Paulist, 1982.

Lessing, Eckhard. *Geschichte der deutschsprachigen evangelischen Theologie von Albrecht*

Bibliography

Ritschl bis zur Gegenwart. Vol. 1, *1870–1918*. Göttingen: Vandenhoeck & Ruprecht, 2000.

Lessing, Gotthold Ephraïm. *Sämtliche Schriften*. Edited by Karl Lachmann and Franz Muncker. 23 vols. Leipzig: Göschen, 1886–1924.

———. *Lessing's Theological Writings*. Edited and translated by Henry Chadwick. London: Black, 1956.

———. *Lessing: Philosophical and Theological Writings*. Edited and translated by H. B. Nisbet. Cambridge Texts in the History of Philosophy. Cambridge: Cambridge University Press, 2009.

———. *Nathan the Wise by Gotthold Ephraim Lessing, With Related Documents*. Edited by Ronald Schechter. Boston: Bedford; New York: St. Martins, 2004.

Levenson, Jon D. *Sinai and Zion: An Entry into the Jewish Bible*. Minneapolis: Winston, 1985.

Levine, Amy-Jill. *The Misunderstood Jew: The Church and the Scandal of the Jewish Jesus*. San Francisco: HarperSanFrancisco, 2006.

———. *Short Stories by Jesus: The Enigmatic Parables of a Controversial Rabbi*. San Francisco: HarperOne, 2014.

Levine, Amy-Jill, with Marianne Blickenstaff, eds. *A Feminist Companion to the New Testament and Early Christian Writings*. London: T&T Clark International; Cleveland: Pilgrim. [The 14 vols. include *Matthew* (2001); *Mark* (2001); *Luke* (2001); *John*, 2 vols. (2003).]

Levine, Amy-Jill, Dale C. Allison Jr., and John Dominic Crossan, eds. *The Historical Jesus in Context*. Princeton: Princeton University Press, 2006.

Levine, Amy-Jill, and Marc Zvi Brettler, eds. *The Jewish Annotated New Testament: New Revised Standard Bible Translation*. Oxford: Oxford University Press, 2011.

Levine, Lee I., ed. *The Galilee in Late Antiquity*. New York: Jewish Theological Seminary of America; Cambridge, MA: Harvard University Press, 1992.

Levison, John R. *The Spirit in First Century Judaism*. AGJU 29. Leiden: Brill, 1997.

Lewis, Nicola Denzey. *Introduction to "Gnosticism": Ancient Voices, Christian Worlds*. Oxford: Oxford University Press, 2013.

Licona, Michael R. *Why Are There Differences in the Gospels? What We Can Learn from Ancient Biography*. Foreword by Craig A. Evans. Oxford: Oxford University Press, 2017.

Liddell, Henry George, and Robert Scott. *A Greek-English Lexicon*. Revised by Sir Henry Stuart Jones, assisted by Robert McKenzie, with supplement. Oxford: Clarendon, 1996. Abbreviated as LSJ.

Liddon, Henry Parry. *The Divinity of Our Lord and Saviour*. Bampton Lectures 1866. London: Rivingtons, 1867; 4th ed., 1869.

———. *Life of Edward Bouverie Pusey*. 4 vols. London: Longmans, 1893–97.

Lieb, Michael, Emma Mason, Jonathan Roberts, and Christopher Rowland, eds. *The Oxford Handbook of the Reception History of the Bible*. Oxford: Oxford University Press, 2011.

Liebing, Heinz. "Historical Critical Theology: In Commemoration of the Death of Ferdinand Christian Baur, December 2, 1860," *JTC* 3 (1967): 55–69.
Lieu, Judith M. *Marcion and the Making of a Heretic: God and Scripture in the Second Century*. Cambridge: Cambridge University Press, 2015.
Lightfoot, R. H. *History and Interpretation in the Gospels*. Bampton Lectures 1934. London: Hodder & Stoughton, 1935.
———. *The Gospel Message of St. Mark*. Oxford: Clarendon, 1950.
———. "St. Mark's Gospel: Complete or Incomplete?" In *The Gospel Message of St. Mark*, 80–97.
Lilley, A. Leslie. *Modernism: A Record and a Review*. New York: Scribner's, 1908.
Lim, Paul C. H. *Mystery Unveiled: The Crisis of the Trinity in Early Modern England*. Oxford Studies in Historical Theology. Oxford: Oxford University Press, 2012.
Lim, Timothy H., and John J. Collins, eds. *The Oxford Handbook of the Dead Sea Scrolls*. Oxford: Oxford University Press, 2010.
Lincoln, Andrew T. "Trials, Plots and the Narrative of the Fourth Gospel." *JSNT* 56 (1994): 3–30.
———. *Truth on Trial: The Lawsuit Motif in the Fourth Gospel*. Peabody, MA: Hendrickson, 2000.
———. *Born of a Virgin? Reconceiving Jesus in the Bible, Tradition, and Theology*. Grand Rapids: Eerdmans, 2013.
Lincoln, Andrew T., and Angus Paddison, eds. *Christology and Scripture: Interdisciplinary Perspectives*. New York: T&T Clark, 2008.
Lindars, Barnabas. *New Testament Apologetic: The Doctrinal Significance of the Old Testament Quotations*. London: SCM, 1961.
Lindars, Barnabas, and Stephen S. Smalley, eds. *Christ and Spirit in the New Testament: Studies in Honour of Charles Francis Digby Moule*. Cambridge: Cambridge University Press, 1973. [List of Moule's publications, x–xvi.]
Lindbeck, George A. *The Nature of Doctrine: Religion and Theology in a Postliberal Age*. Philadelphia: Westminster, 1984.
Lindeskog, Gösta. *Die Jesusfrage im neuzeitlichen Judentum. Ein Beitrag zur Geschichte der Leben-Jesu-Forschung*. Stockholm: Almqvist & Wiksell, 1938; 2nd ed., Darmstadt: Wissenschaftliche Buchgesellscht, 1973.
Link, Christian. *Hegels Wort "Gott selbst ist tot"*. ThSt 114. Zürich: Theologischer, 1974.
Litwa, M. David. *Iesus Deus: The Early Christian Depiction of Jesus as a Mediterranean God*. Minneapolis: Fortress, 2014.
Litwa, M. David, trans. *Refutation of All Heresies*. WGRW 40. Atlanta: SBL Press, 2016.
Livingston, James C., and Francis Schüssler Fiorenza, with Sarah Coakley and James H. Evans Jr., eds. *Modern Christian Thought*. Vol. 2, *The Twentieth Century*. Upper Saddle River, NJ: Prentice Hall, 2000.
Livingstone, E. A., ed. *Studia Biblica 1978*. Vol. 2, *Papers on the Gospels*. Sixth

Bibliography

International Congress on Biblical Studies at Oxford. JSNTSup 2. Sheffield: JSOT, 1980.

Lloyd, Roger. *The Church of England, 1900–1965.* London: SCM, 1966.

Loader, William R. G. "The Apocalyptic Model of Sonship: Its Origin and Development in the Synoptic Tradition." *JBL* 97 (1978): 525–54.

———. *Jesus' Attitude towards the Law: A Study of the Gospels.* WUNT 97. Tübingen: Mohr Siebeck, 1997. Reprint, Grand Rapids: Eerdmans, 2002.

Loades, Ann, and Robert MacSwain, eds. *The Truth-Seeking Heart: Austin Farrer and His Writings.* Canterbury Studies in Spiritual Theology. Norwich, UK: Canterbury, 2006.

Locke, John. *An Essay Concerning Human Understanding* [1689]. Edited by A. S. Pringle-Pattison. Revised by Peter H. Nidditch. Oxford: Clarendon, 1974. [A version based on the posthumous 5th edition of 1706 was edited by Roger Woolhouse. London: Penguin, 1997 and 2004.]

———. *A Paraphrase and Notes on the Epistles of St. Paul.* 6 vols. London: Thomas Pyle, 1705–1707. Reprint, Rivington, 1824.

———. *The Reasonableness of Christianity with A Discourse of Miracles and Part of A Third Letter Concerning Toleration.* Edited by Ian T. Ramsey. London: Printed for Awnsham and John Churchill, 1695. Reprint, London: Black, 1958.

Lohmeyer, Ernst. *Kyrios Jesus. Eine Untersuchung zu Phil. 2,5–11.* Sitzungsberichte der Heidelberger Akademie der Wissenschaften. Philosophisch-historische Klasse, Jahrgang 1927/1928, 4. Abhandlung. Heidelberg: Winter-Universitätsverlag, 1961.

———. *Galiläa und Jerusalem.* Göttingen: Vandenhoeck & Ruprecht, 1936.

———. "Über Aufbau und Gliederung des vierten Evangeliums." *ZNW* 27 (1928): 11–36. ET: "The Structure and Organization of the Fourth Gospel." Translated by Colin Brown. *Journal of Higher Criticism* 5 (1998): 113–38.

Lohse, Eduard, with Christoph Burchard and Berndt Schaller, eds. *Der Ruf Jesu und die Antwort der Gemeinde. Exegetische Untersuchungen Joachim Jeremias zum 70. Geburtstag gewidmet von seinen Schülern.* Göttingen: Vandenhoeck & Ruprecht, 1970. [Bibliography 1923–70, 11–38.]

Loisy, Alfred. *L'Évangile et L'Église.* Paris: Nourry, 1902; 5th ed., 1929. ET: *The Gospel and the Church.* Translated by Christopher Home. London: Pitman & Sons, 1903. Reprinted with introduction by Bernard B. Scott. Lives of Jesus. Philadelphia: Fortress, 1976.

———. *Autour d'un petit livre.* Paris: Picard, 1903.

———. *Le Quatrième Évangile.* Paris: Picard, 1903.

———. *Les Évangiles Synoptiques.* 2 vols. Ceffonds: self-published, 1907–8.

———. *Jésus et la tradition évangélique.* Paris: Nourry, 1910.

———. *L'Évangile selon Marc.* Paris: Nourry, 1912.

———. *La Naissance du Christianisme.* Paris: Nourry, 1933.

———. *Les Origines du Nouveau Testament.* Paris: Nourry, 1936. ET: *The Origins of the New Testament.* Translated by L. P. Jacks. London: Allen & Unwin, 1950.

———. *Histoire et mythe à propos de Jésus-Christ*. Paris: Nourry, 1938.
Lombardo, Nicholas E. *The Father's Will: Crucifixion and the Goodness of God*. Oxford: Oxford University Press, 2013.
Lonergan, Bernard J. F. *Insight: A Study in Human Understanding*. 3rd ed. New York: Philosophical Library, 1970. 5th ed. Edited by Frederick E. Crowe and Robert M. Doran. Collected Works of Bernard Lonergan 3. Toronto: University of Toronto Press, 1992.
———. *Method in Theology*. London: Darton, Longman & Todd; New York: Herder and Herder, 1972.
———. *Collection*. 2nd ed. Edited by Frederick E. Crowe and Robert M. Doran. Collected Works of Bernard Lonergan 4. Toronto: University of Toronto, 1993.
Loubser, J. A. (Bobby). *Oral and Manuscript Culture in the Bible: Studies on the Media Texture of the New Testament; Explorative Hermeneutics*. Biblical Performance Criticism 7. Eugene, OR: Cascade, 2013.
Löwith, Karl. *From Hegel to Nietzsche: The Revolution in Nineteenth-Century Thought*. Translated by David E. Green. New York: Holt, Rinehart, and Winston; London: Constable, 1964.
———. *Nietzsches Philosophie der ewigen Wiederkehr des Gleichen*. Stuttgart: Kohlhammer, 1935. Reprint, 1956. ET: *Nietzsche's Philosophy of the Eternal Occurrence of the Same*. Berkeley: University of California Press, 1997.
Lüdemann, Gerd. "Die Religionsgeschichtliche Schule." In *Theologie in Göttingen. Eine Vorlesungsreihe*, Göttinger Universitätsschriften, Serie A: Schriften 1, edited by Bernd Moeller, 325–61. Göttingen: Vandenhoeck & Ruprecht, 1987.
———. *Jungfrauengeburt? Die Geschichte von Maria und ihrem Sohn Jesus*. Lüneburg: Klampen, 1997. ET: *Virgin Birth? The Real Story of Mary and Her Son Jesus*. Translated by John Bowden. Harrisburg, PA: Trinity Press International, 1998.
Lüdemann, Gerd, and Martin Schröder. *Die Religionsgeschichtliche Schule in Göttingen. Eine Dokumentation*. Göttingen: Vandenhoeck & Ruprecht, 1987.
Lührmann, Dieter. "Bornkamm's Response to Keck." In *The Future of Christology*, edited by Abraham J. Malherbe and Wayne A. Meeks, 66–78.
Lührmann, Dieter, and Georg Strecker, eds. *Kirche. Festschrift für Günther Bornkamm zum 75. Geburtstag*. Tübingen: Mohr Siebeck, 1980. [Bornkamm bibliography, 491–506.]
Lundsteen, A. C. *Hermann Samuel Reimarus und die Anfänge der Leben-Jesu-Forschung*. Copenhagen: Olsen, 1939.
Lundström, Gösta. *The Kingdom of God in the Teaching of Jesus: A History of Interpretation from the Last Decades of the Nineteenth Century to the Present Day*. Translated by Joan Bulman. Edinburgh: Oliver and Boyd, 1963.
Luther, Martin. *Werke*. Weimar: Böhlau, 1883–1993. In references this edition of Luther's works is referred to as WA (= *Weimarer Ausgabe*).

Bibliography

———. *Works*. Edited by Helmut T. Lehmann and Jaroslav Pelikan. 54 vols. St. Louis: Muhlenberg; Philadelphia: Concordia, 1955–76.

———. *Martin Luther: Selections from His Writings*. Edited by John Dillenberger. New York: Doubleday, 1961.

———. *Luther: Lectures on Romans*. Edited by Wilhelm Pauck. LCC 15. London: SCM; Philadelphia: Westminster, 1961.

———. *Luther and Erasmus: Free Will and Salvation*. Translated and edited by E. Gordon Rupp. LCC 17. London: SCM; Philadelphia: Westminster, 1969.

Lutheran Church. *Die Bekenntnisschriften der evangelisch-lutherischen Kirche, herausgegeben im Gedenkjahr der Augsburgischen Konfession 1530*. 3rd ed. Göttingen: Vandenhoeck & Ruprecht, 1956.

Luz, Ulrich. *Matthew: A Commentary*. Translated by James E. Crouch and Wilhelm C. Linss. Edited by Helmut Koester. 3 vols. Hermeneia. Minneapolis: Fortress, 2001–2007.

———. *Matthew in History: Interpretation, Influence, and Effects*. Minneapolis: Fortress, 2007.

Luz, Ulrich, and Hans Weder, eds. *Die Mitte des Neuen Testaments. Einheit und Vielfalt neutestamentlicher Theologie. Festschrift für Eduard Schweizer zum siebzigsten Gebutstag*. Göttingen: Vandenhoeck & Ruprecht, 1983.

Maccini, Robert Gordon. *Her Testimony Is True: Women as Witnesses according to John*. JSNTSup 125. Sheffield: Sheffield Academic Press, 1996.

MacCormac, Earl R. *Metaphor and Myth in Science and Religion*. Durham, NC: Duke University Press, 1976.

MacDonald, Dennis R. *The Homeric Epics and the Gospel of Mark*. New Haven, CT: Yale University Press, 2000.

———. *Two Shipwrecked Gospels: The Logoi of Jesus and Papias's Exposition of Logia about the Lord*. Atlanta: SBL Press, 2012.

———. *Mythologizing Jesus: From Jewish Teacher to Epic Hero*. Lanham, MD: Rowman & Littlefield, 2015.

———. *The Gospels and Homer: Imitations of Greek Epic in Mark and Luke-Acts*. The New Testament and Greek Literature 1. Lanham, MD: Rowman & Littlefield, 2015.

Machen, J. Gresham. "Christianity in Conflict." *Contemporary American Theology: Theological Autobiographies*, edited by Vergilius Ferm, 1:245–74. New York: Round Table, 1932.

———. *The Virgin Birth of Christ*. New York: Harper, 1930; 2nd ed., 1932. Reprint of 2nd ed., London: James Clarke, 1958.

MacIntyre, Alasdair. *Whose Justice? Which Rationality?* Notre Dame, IN: University of Notre Dame Press, 1998.

Mack, Burton L. *A Myth of Innocence: Mark and Christian Origins*. Philadelphia: Fortress, 1988.

———. *The Lost Gospel: The Book of Q and Christian Origins.* San Francisco: HarperSanFrancisco, 1993.

———. "Q and a Cynic-Like Jesus." *Whose Historical Jesus?*, edited by William E. Arnal and Michael Desjardins, 25–36.

Mackie, J. L. *The Miracle of Theism: Arguments for and against the Existence of God.* Oxford: Clarendon, 1982.

Mackintosh, Hugh Ross. *The Doctrine of the Person of Christ.* Edinburgh: T&T Clark, 1912.

———. *Types of Modern Theology.* Digswell Place: Nisbet, 1937.

MacMullen, Ramsay. *Enemies of the Roman Order: Treason, Unrest, and Alienation in the Empire.* Cambridge MA: Harvard University Press, 1966.

———. *Paganism in the Roman Empire.* New Haven, CT: Yale University Press, 1981.

———. *Christianizing the Roman Empire (A.D. 100–400).* New Haven, CT: Yale University Press, 1984.

———. *Christianity and Paganism in the Fourth to Eighth Centuries.* New Haven, CT: Yale University Press, 1997.

MacMullen, Ramsay, and Eugene N. Lane, eds. *Paganism and Christianity, 100–425 C.E.: A Sourcebook.* Minneapolis: Fortress, 1992.

Macquarrie, John. *An Existentialist Theology: A Comparison of Heidegger and Bultmann.* London: SCM; New York: Macmillan, 1955. 2nd ed. Foreword by Bultmann. London: SCM; New York: Harper & Row, 1965; 3rd ed., Harmondsworth: Penguin, 1972.

———. *The Scope of Demythologizing: Bultmann and His Critics.* London; SCM; New York: Harper & Row, 1960.

———. *Twentieth-Century Religious Thought: The Frontiers of Philosophy and Theology, 1900–1960.* New York: Harper & Row; London: SCM, 1963; 2nd edition with additional chapter covering 1960–70; 3rd edition with postscript, 1960–80, London: SCM; New York: Scribner's, 1981.

———. *Principles of Christian Theology.* London: SCM, 1966; 2nd ed., New York: Scribner's; London: SCM, 1977.

———. *Mary for All Christians.* Grand Rapids: Eerdmans, 1991.

———. *Jesus Christ in Modern Thought.* London: SCM, 1990.

———. *Christology Revisited.* Albert Cardinal Meyer Memorial Lectures 1998. Harrisburg, PA: Trinity Press International, 1998.

———. "The Theological Legacy of Maurice Wiles." *ATR* 88 (2006): 597–616.

Madden, Patrick J. *Jesus' Walking on the Sea: An Investigation of the Origin of the Narrative Account.* BZNW 81. Berlin, New York: De Gruyter, 1997.

Magness, Jodi. *The Archaeology of Qumran and the Dead Sea Scrolls.* Grand Rapids: Eerdmans, 2002.

———. *Stone and Dung, Oil and Spit: Jewish Daily Life in the Time of Jesus.* Grand Rapids: Eerdmans, 2011.

Bibliography

———. *The Archaeology of the Holy Land: From the Destruction of Solomon's Temple to the Muslim Conquest.* Cambridge: Cambridge University Press, 2012.

Magnus, Bernd. "Jesus, Christianity and Superhumanity." In *Studies in Nietzsche and the Judeo-Christian Tradition,* edited by James C. O'Flaherty, Timothy E. Sellner, and Robert M. Helm, 295–318. Chapel Hill: University of North Carolina Press, 1985.

Magnus, Bernd, and Kathleen M. Higgins, eds. *The Cambridge Companion to Nietzsche.* Cambridge: Cambridge University Press, 1996.

Maier, Gerhard. "Zur Neutestamentlichen Wunderexegese im 19. und 20. Jahrhundert." In *Gospel Perspectives,* vol. 6, *The Miracles of Jesus,* edited by David Wenham and Craig Blomberg, 49–88. Sheffield: JSOT, 1986.

Maier, Johann. *The Temple Scroll: An Introduction, Translation and Commentary.* JSOTSup 34. Sheffield: JSOT, 1985.

———. "Temple." In *Encyclopedia of the Dead Sea Scrolls,* edited by Lawrence H. Schiffman and James C. VanderKam, 2:921–27.

Major, H. D. A. *Reminiscences of Jesus by an Eye-Witness.* Modern Churchman's Library. London: Murray, 1925.

———. *English Modernism: Its Origin, Methods, Aims.* William Belden Noble Lectures at Harvard University, 1925–1926. Cambridge, MA: Harvard University Press, 1927.

Major, H. D. A., T. W. Manson, and C. J. Wright. *The Mission and Message of Jesus: An Exposition of the Gospels in the Light of Modern Research.* London: Macmillan, 1937. Reprint, 1940.

Malet, André. *The Thought of Rudolf Bultmann.* Translated by Richard Strachan. Preface by Rudolf Bultmann. Shannon: Irish University Press, 1969.

Malherbe, Abraham J. *Paul and the Popular Philosophers.* Minneapolis: Fortress, 1989.

Malherbe, Abraham J., and Wayne A. Meeks, eds. *The Future of Christology: Essays in Honor of Leander W. Keck.* Minneapolis: Fortress, 1993. [Keck's bibliography to 1991 compiled by Grace Pauls (239–46).]

Malina, Bruce J. *The New Testament World: Insights from Cultural Anthropology.* Louisville: Westminster John Knox, 1993; 3rd ed., 2001.

———. *The Social World of Jesus and the Gospels.* New York: Routledge, 1996.

———. *The Social Gospel of Jesus: The Kingdom of God in the Mediterranean World.* Minneapolis: Fortress, 2001.

Malina, Bruce J., and Jerome H. Neyrey. *Calling Jesus Names: The Social Value of Labels in Matthew.* Foundations and Facets. Sonoma, CA: Polebridge, 1988.

Malina, Bruce J., and Richard L, Rohrbaugh. *Social-Science Commentary on the Synoptic Gospels.* Minneapolis: Fortress, 1992.

———. *Social-Science Commentary on the Gospel of John.* Minneapolis: Fortress, 1998.

Manson, T. W. *The Teaching of Jesus: Studies in Its Form and Content.* Cambridge: Cambridge University Press, 1931. [Paperback 1963.]

———. *The Sayings of Jesus.* London: SCM, 1949. [Previously published as Part 2 of H. D. A. Major, T. W. Manson, and C. J. Wright. *The Mission and Message of*

Jesus: An Exposition of the Gospels in the Light of Modern Research, 301–639. London: Macmillan, 1937.]

———. *The Servant-Messiah: A Study of the Public Ministry of Jesus.* Saffer Lectures at Yale 1939. Cambridge: Cambridge University Press, 1953. Reprint with foreword by F. F. Bruce, Grand Rapids: Baker, 1977.

———. "The Life of Jesus: Some Tendencies in Present-day Research." In *The Background of the New Testament and Its Eschatology*, edited by W. D. Davies and D. Daube, 211–21.

———. *Jesus and the Non-Jews.* Ethel M. Wood Lecture, University of London, 1954. London: Athlone, 1955.

———. *Ethics and the Gospel.* London: SCM, 1960.

———. *Studies in the Gospels and Epistles.* Edited by Matthew Black. Memoir by H. H. Rowley. Manchester: Manchester University Press, 1962.

———. *On Paul and John: Some Selected Theological Themes.* Edited by Matthew Black. SBT 38. London: SCM, 1963.

Manuel, Frank E. *The Religion of Sir Isaac Newton.* Freemantle Lectures 1973. Oxford: Clarendon, 1974.

Marchal, Joseph A., ed. *The People Beside Paul: The Philippian Assembly and History from Below.* ECL 17. Atlanta: SBL Press, 2001.

Marcos, Natalio Fernandez. *The Septuagint in Context: Introduction to the Greek Version of the Bible.* Translated by Wilfred G. E. Watson. Boston, Leiden: Brill, 2001.

Marcus, Joel. *The Way of the Lord: Christological Exegesis of the Old Testament in the Gospel of Mark.* Louisville: Westminster John Knox, 1992.

———. *Mark 1–8.* AB 27. *Mark 8–16.* AB 27A. New York: Doubleday, 2000.

Marincola, John. *Authority and Tradition in Ancient Historiography.* Cambridge: Cambridge University Press, 1997. Reprint, 2004.

Markschies, Christoph, Jens Schröter, Andreas Heiser, eds. *Antike Christliche Apokryphen in Deutscher Übersetzung.* Tübingen: Mohr Siebeck, 2012.

Marmion, Declan, and Mary E. Hines, eds. *The Cambridge Companion to Karl Rahner.* Cambridge: University Press, 2005.

Marmodoro, Anna, and Jonathan Hill, eds. *The Metaphysics of the Incarnation.* Oxford: Oxford University Press, 2011.

Marsden, George M. *Reforming Fundamentalism: Fuller Seminary and the New Evangelicalism.* Grand Rapids: Eerdmans, 1987.

———. *The Soul of the American University: From Protestant Establishment to Established Nonbelief.* Oxford: Oxford University Press, 1994.

———. *Jonathan Edwards: A Life.* New Haven, CT: Yale University Press, 2003.

Marsh, Clive. *Albrecht Ritschl and the Problem of the Historical Jesus.* San Francisco: Mellen Research University Press, 1992.

Marsh, Herbert. *Introduction to the New Testament. by John David Michaelis, Late Professor in the University of Göttingen, &C. Translated from the Fourth Edition of the German,*

Bibliography

and Considerably Augmented by Notes, and a Dissertation on the Origin & Composition of the Three First Gospels by Herbert Marsh D.D., F.R.S., Lord Bishop of Peterborough. 4 vols. London: Rivington, 1793–1801; 4th ed., 1823.

———. *A Course of Lectures, Containing a Description and Systematic Arrangement of the Several Branches of Divinity.* Cambridge: Hilliard, 1812.

Marsh, P. T. *The Victorian Church in Decline: Archbishop Tait and the Church of England, 1868–1882.* London: Routledge, 1966.

Marshak, Adam Kolman. *The Many Faces of Herod the Great.* Grand Rapids: Eerdmans, 2015.

Marshall, I. Howard. *Luke: Historian and Theologian.* Exeter: Paternoster, 1970.

———. *The Gospel of Luke: A Commentary on the Greek Text.* NIGTC. Exeter: Paternoster; Grand Rapids, Eerdmans, 1978.

———. *Last Supper and Lord's Supper.* Grand Rapids: Eerdmans, 1980.

———. "The Last Supper." In *Key Events in the Life of the Historical Jesus*, edited by Darrell L. Bock and Robert L. Webb, 481–588.

Martin, Ralph P. *A Hymn of Christ: Philippians 2:5–11 in Recent Interpretation & in the Setting of Early Christian Worship.* Downers Grove, IL: InterVarsity Press, 1997. Expanded edition of *Carmen Christi: Philippians ii. 5–11 in Recent Interpretation and in the Setting of Early Christian Worship.* SNTSMS 4. Cambridge: Cambridge University Press, 1967.

Martin, Ralph P., and Brian J. Dodd, eds. *Where Christology Began: Essays on Philippians 2.* Louisville: Westminster John Knox, 1998.

Martin Nagy, Rebecca, Carol L. Myers, Eric M. Myers, and Zeev Weiss, eds. *Sepphoris in Galilee: Crosscurrents of Culture.* Winona Lake, IN: Eisenbrauns, 1996.

Martinich, A. P. *Hobbes: A Biography.* Cambridge: Cambridge University Press, 1999.

Martyn, J. Louis. *History and Theology in the Fourth Gospel.* New York: Harper & Row, 1968; 3rd ed., Louisville: Westminster John Knox, 2003.

Mascall, E. L. *Christ, the Christian and the Church: A Study of the Incarnation and Its Consequences.* London: Longmans, 1946.

Mason, Steve. *Flavius Josephus on the Pharisees: A Composition-Critical Study.* Leiden: Brill, 1991.

———. *Josephus and the New Testament.* Peabody, MA: Hendrickson, 1992.

———. "The Writings of Josephus: Their Significance for New Testament Study." In *HSHJ*, 2:1639–86.

Massa, Mark Stephen. *Charles Augustus Briggs and the Crisis of Historical Criticism.* Harvard Dissertations in Religion 29. Minneapolis: Fortress, 1990.

———. *Charles Augustus Briggs: Union Seminary and Twentieth-Century American Protestantism.* New York: Union Theological Seminary, 1994.

Master, Daniel M., ed. *The Oxford Encyclopedia of the Bible and Archaeology.* 2 vols. Oxford: Oxford University Press, 2013.

Matera, Frank J. *Passion Narratives and Gospel Theologies: Interpreting the Synoptics through Their Passion Stories.* New York: Paulist, 1986.

A History of the Quests for the Historical Jesus

———. *New Testament Christology*. Louisville: Westminster John Knox, 1999.

Mathews, Shailer. *Select Medieval Documents*. New York: Silver, Burdette, 1891. Reprint, 1900.

———. *The Social Teachings of Jesus*. New York: Macmillan, 1897.

———. *The French Revolution—A Sketch*. New York: Longmans, Green, 1901.

———. *The Messianic Hope in the New Testament*. Decennial Publications Second Series 12. Chicago: University of Chicago Press, 1905.

———. *The French Revolution (1789–1815)*. New York: Longmans, Green, 1924.

———. *The Faith of Modernism*. New York: Macmillan, 1924.

———. *Jesus on Social Institutions*. New York: Macmillan, 1928. Reprint with introduction by Kenneth Cauthen. Lives of Jesus Series. Philadelphia: Fortress, 1971.

———. *The Atonement and the Social Process*. Chicago: University of Chicago Press, 1930.

———. "Theology as Group Belief." In *Contemporary American Theology*, edited by Vergilius Ferm, 2:163–93.

———. *New Faith for Old: An Autobiography*. New York: Macmillan, 1936.

Maurice, Frederick Denison. *The Kingdom of Christ, Or Hints to a Quaker Respecting the Principles, Constitution, and Ordinances of the Catholic Church*. London: Darton & Clark, 1838. [New edition based on the second edition of 1842. Edited by A. R. Vidler. 2 vols. London: SCM, 1958.]

———. "On Eternal Life and Eternal Death." In *Theological Essays* [1853], 302–32. New edition with introduction by Edward F. Carpenter. London: James Clarke, 1957.

Maurice, Frederick. *The Life of Frederick Denison Maurice, Chiefly Told in His Own Letters*. 4th ed. 2 vols. London: Macmillan, 1885.

Maxey, James A., and Ernst R. Wendland, eds. *Translating Scripture for Sound and Performance: New Directions in Biblical Studies*. Biblical Performance Criticism 6. Eugene OR: Cascade, 2012.

May, Herbert F. *The Enlightenment in America*. New York: Oxford University Press, 1976.

May, Rollo. *Paulus: Reminiscences of a Friendship*. New York: Harper & Row, 1973.

McArthur, Harvey K. *The Quest through the Centuries*. Philadelphia: Fortress, 1966.

McArthur, Harvey K., ed. *In Search of the Historical Jesus*. New York: Scribner's, 1969; London: SPCK, 1970.

McCarthy, Vincent A. *Quest for a Philosophical Jesus: Christianity and Philosophy in Rousseau, Kant, Hegel, and Schelling*. Macon, GA: Mercer University Press, 1986.

McCauley, David. *Paul's Use of Scripture: Intertextuality and Rhetorical Situation in Philippians 2:10–16*. Eugene, OR: Pickwick, 2015.

McCook, John M., ed. *The Appeal in the Briggs Case before the General Assembly of the Presbyterian Church in the United States of America*. New York: Rankin, 1893.

McCown, Chester C. *The Promise of His Coming: A Historical Interpretation and Revolution of the Idea of the Second Coming*. New York: Macmillan, 1921.

Bibliography

———. *The Genesis of the Social Gospel: The Meaning of the Ideals of Jesus in the Light of Their Antecedents*. New York: Knopf, 1929.

———. *The Search for the Real Jesus: A Century of Historical Study*. New York: Scribner's, 1940.

———. "Shirley Jackson Case's Contribution to the Theory of Socio-Historical Interpretation." *JR* 29 (1949): 30–47.

McCormack, Bruce L. *Karl Barth's Critically Realistic Dialectical Theology: Its Genesis and Development, 1909–1936*. Oxford: Clarendon, 1995.

———. "Kenoticism in Modern Christology." *The Oxford Handbook of Christology*, edited by Francesca Aran Murphy and Troy A. Stefano, 444–57. Oxford: Oxford University Press, 2015.

McCown, Chester C. *The Search for the Real Jesus: A Century of Historical Study*. New York: Scribner's, 1940.

McDaniel, Karl. *Emerging Irony in the First Gospel: Suspense, Surprise, Curiosity*. LNTS 488. New York: T&T Clark, 2013.

McDonald, Lee Martin. *The Biblical Canon: Its Origin, Transmission, and Authority*. Grand Rapids: Baker Academic, 2011.

———. *The Story of Jesus in History and Faith: An Introduction*. Grand Rapids: Baker Academic, 2013.

———. *The Formation of the Biblical Canon*. 2 vols. New York: T&T Clark, 2017.

McGinn, Bernard J., ed. *The Encyclopedia of Apocalypticism*. Vol. 2, *Apocalypticism in Western History and Culture*. New York: Continuum, 2000.

McKelway, Alexander J. *The Systematic Theology of Paul Tillich: A Review and Analysis*. Introduction by Karl Barth. London: Lutterworth, 1964.

McKim, Donald K., ed. *The Westminster Handbook to Reformed Theology*. Louisville: Westminster John Knox, 2001.

———. *Dictionary of Major Biblical Interpreters*. Downers Grove, IL: IVP Academic, 2007. Abbreviated as *DMBI*.

McKnight, Edgar V. *Jesus Christ in History and Scripture: A Poetic and Sectarian Perspective*. Macon, GA: Mercer University Press, 1999.

McKnight, Scot. *Jesus and His Death: Historiography, the Historical Jesus and Atonement*. Waco, TX: Baylor University Press, 2005.

———. "Jesus as *MAMZER* ('Illegitimate Son')." In *Who Do My Opponents Say That I Am?*, edited by Scot McKnight and Joseph B. Modica, 133–63.

McKnight, Scot, and Joseph B. Modica, eds. *Who Do My Opponents Say That I Am? An Investigation into the Accusations against Jesus*. LNTS 327. London: T&T Clark, 2008.

———. *The Apostle Paul and the Christian Life: Ethical and Missional Implications of the New Perspective*. Grand Rapids: Baker Academic, 2016.

McLachlan, H. John. *Socinianism in Seventeenth-Century England*. Oxford: Oxford University Press, 1951.

A History of the Quests for the Historical Jesus

McLean, B. Hudson. *The Cursed Christ: Mediterranean Expulsion Rituals and Pauline Soteriology*. JSNTSup 126. Sheffield: Sheffield Academic Press, 1996.

McNeill, John T. *The History and Character of Calvinism*. Oxford: Oxford University Press, 1954.

Mead, George Robert Stowe. *Apollonius of Tyana*. London: Theosophical, 1901. Reprint with foreword by L. Shepard. New York: University Books, 1966.

Meeks, Wayne A. *The Prophet-King: Moses Traditions and the Johannine Christology*. NovTSup 17. Leiden: Brill, 1967.

———. "The Man from Heaven in Johannine Sectarianism." In *The Interpretation of John*, edited by John Ashton, 169–205.

———. *The First Urban Christians: The Social World of the Apostle Paul*. New Haven, CT: Yale University Press, 1983; 2nd ed., 2003.

———. *Christ is the Question*. Louisville: Westminster: John Knox, 2006.

Meeter, John E., and Roger Nicole. *A Bibliography of Benjamin Breckinridge Warfield, 1851–1921*. Nutley, NJ: P&R, 1974.

Meier, John P. "Jesus." In *The New Jerome Bible Commentary*, edited by Raymond E. Brown, Joseph A. Fitzmyer, and Roland E. Murphy, 1316–28. Englewood Cliffs, NJ: Prentice Hall, 1990.

———. *A Marginal Jew: Rethinking the Historical Jesus*. 5 vols. Vol. 1, *The Roots of the Problem of the Person*. New York, Doubleday, 1991. Vol. 2, *Mentor, Message, and Miracles*. New York: Doubleday, 1994. Vol. 3, *Companions and Competitors*. New York: Doubleday, 2001. Vol. 4, *Law and Love*. New Haven, CT: Yale University Press, 2009. Vol. 5, *Probing the Authenticity of the Parables*. New Haven, CT: Yale University Press, 2015.

———. "Basic Methodology and the Quest of the Historical Jesus." In *HSHJ*, 1:291–330.

———. "The Historical Figure of Jesus: The Historical Jesus and His Historical Parables." In *The Gospels: History and Christology. The Search of Joseph Ratzinger-Benedict XVI–I Vangeli: Storia e Cristologia. La ricerca di Joseph Ratzinger-Benedetto XVI*, edited by Bernardo Estrada, Ermenegildo Manicardi, and Armand Puig i Tàrrech, 2 vols., 1:237–60. Città del Vaticano: Libreria Editrice Vaticana, 2013.

Meijering, E. P. *Theologische Urteile über die Dogmengeschichte. Ritschls Einfluss auf von Harnack*. BZRGG 20. Leiden: Brill, 1978.

———. *Die Hellenisierung des Christentums im Urteil Adolf von Harnacks*. Amsterdam, NY: North Holland, 1985.

Meinhold, Peter. *Geschichte der kirchlichen Historiographie*. Orbis Academicus. 2 vols. Freiburg: Alber, 1967.

Melamed, Yitzhak Y., ed. *Spinoza's Ethics: A Critical Guide*. Cambridge Critical Guides. Cambridge: Cambridge University Press, 2017.

Melamed, Yitzhak Y., and Michael A. Rosenthal, eds. *Spinoza's Theological-Critical Treatise: A Critical Guide*. Cambridge: Cambridge University Press, 2010.

Bibliography

Melanchthon, *Melanchthon and Bucer.* Edited by Wilhelm Pauck. LCC 19. London: SCM; Philadelphia: Westminster, 1969.

Meland, Bernard E. "Introduction: The Empirical Tradition in Theology at Chicago." In *The Future of Empirical Theology*, edited by Meland, 1–62. Essays in Divinity 7. Chicago: University Press of Chicago, 1969.

Mendelson, Alan. "Jesus and the Posthumous Career of Apollonius of Tyana." In *Eusebius, Christianity and Judaism*, edited by Harold W. Attridge and Gohei Hata, 510–22.

Mercer, Calvin R. *Norman Perrin's Interpretation of the New Testament: From "Exegetical Method" to "Hermeneutical Process".* StABH 2. Macon, GA: Mercer University Press, 1986.

———. "ΑΠΟΣΤΕΛΛΕΙΝ and ΠΕΜΠΕΙΝ in John." *NTS* 36 (1990): 619–24.

———. "Jesus the Apostle: 'Sending and the Theology of John." *JETS* 35 (1992): 457–52.

Merkel, H., ed. "The 'Secret Gospel' of Mark." In *New Testament Apocrypha*, edited by Wilhelm Schneemelcher, 1:106–9.

Merrill, Walter M. *From Statesman to Philosopher: A Study in Bolingbroke's Deism.* New York: Philosophical Library, 1949.

Metzdorf, Christina. *Die Tempelaktion Jesu. Patristische und historisch-kritische Exegese im Vergleich.* WUNT 168. Tübingen: Mohr Siebeck, 2003.

Metzger, Bruce M. *A Textual Commentary on the Greek New Testament.* 2nd ed. New York: United Bible Societies, 1994.

Meye Thompson, Marianne. *The Humanity of Jesus in the Fourth Gospel.* Philadelphia: Fortress, 1988.

———. "The Historical Jesus and the Johannine Christ." In *Exploring the Gospel of John*, edited by R. Alan and Culpepper and C. Clifton Black, 21–42.

———. *The God of the Gospel of John.* Grand Rapids: Eerdmans, 2001.

———. "Jesus and the Victory of God Meets the Gospel of John." In *Jesus, Paul and the People of God*, edited by Nicholas Perrin and Richard B. Hays, 21–38.

Meyer, Ben F. *The Aims of Jesus.* London: SCM, 1979. Reprint with new introduction, Eugene, OR: Pickwick, 2002.

———. *The Early Christians: Their World Mission and Self-Discovery.* Wilmington, DE: Glazier, 1986.

———. *Critical Realism and the New Testament.* Princeton Theological Monograph Series 17. Allison Park, PA: Pickwick, 1989.

———. "A Caricature of Joachim Jeremias and his Scholarly Work." *JBL* 110 (1991): 451–62. [A reply to E. P. Sanders.]

———. *Christus Faber: The Master-Builder and the House of God.* Princeton Theological Monograph Series 29. Allison Park, PA: Pickwick, 1992.

———. "The Temple at the Navel of the Earth." In *Christus Faber*, 217–79.

———. *Reality and Illusion in New Testament Scholarship: A Primer in Critical Realist Hermeneutics.* Collegeville, MN: Glazier; Liturgical, 1995.

Meyer, Marvin. *The Ancient Mysteries, A Sourcebook: Sacred Text of the Mystery Religions of the Ancient Mediterranean World*. San Francisco: Harper & Row, 1987.

———. *The Gnostic Discoveries: The Impact of the Nag Hammadi Library*. San Francisco: HarperSanFrancisco, 2005.

———. *The Gnostic Gospels of Jesus: The Definitive Collection of Mystical Gospels and Secret Books about Jesus of Nazareth*. San Francisco: HarperSanFrancisco, 2005.

———. *Judas: The Definitive Collection of Gospels and Legends about the Infamous Apostle of Jesus*. San Francisco: HarperOne, 2007.

Meyer, Marvin, ed. *The Gospel of Thomas: The Hidden Sayings of Jesus*. With interpretation by Harold Bloom. San Francisco: HarperSanFrancisco, 1992.

———. *Secret Gospels: Essays on Thomas and the Secret Gospel of Mark*. Harrisburg, PA: Trinity Press International, 2003.

———. *The Nag Hammadi Scriptures: The International Edition*. San Francisco: HarperSanFrancico, 2007.

Meyer, Marvin, with Esther A. de Boer. *The Gospels of Mary: The Secret Tradition of Mary Magdalene the Companion of Jesus*. San Francisco: HarperSanFrancisco, 2004.

Meyer, Marvin, and Charles Hughes, eds. *Jesus Then and Now: Images of Jesus in History and Christology*. Harrisburg, PA: Trinity Press International, 2001.

Meyers, Eric M. "Roman Sepphoris in Light of New Archaeological Evidence and Recent Research." In *The Galilee in Late Antiquity*, edited by Lee I. Levine, 321–33.

Meyers, Eric M., ed. *Galilee through the Centuries*. Winona Lake, IN: Eisenbrauns, 1999.

Michalson, Gordon E., Jr. *Lessing's "Ugly Ditch": A Study of Theology and History*. University Park, PA: Pennsylvania State University Press, 1985.

Michaels, J. Ramsey. "John 18.31 and the 'Trial' of Jesus." *NTS* 36 (1990): 474–79.

Middleton, Conyers. *A Free Inquiry into the Miraculous Powers Which are supposed to have subsisted in the Christian Church, From the Earliest Ages through several successive Centuries*. London: Boone, 1749. Facsimile reprint, New York: Garland, 1976.

Milgrom, Jacob. *Cult and Conscience: The ASHAM and the Priestly Doctrine of Repentance*. SJLA 18. Leiden: Brill, 1976.

———. "Israel's Sanctuary: The Priestly 'Picture of Dorian Gray.'" *Revue Biblique* 83 (1976): 390–99.

———. *Leviticus*. 3 vols. AB 3, 3A, 3B. New York: Doubleday, 1991–2000.

Miller, Nicholas P. *The Religious Roots of the First Amendment: Dissenting Protestants and the Separation of Church and State*. Oxford: Oxford University Press, 2012.

Moberly, R. C. *Atonement and Personality*. London: John Murray, 1901.

Modica, Joseph B. "Jesus as Glutton and Drunkard: The 'Excesses' of Jesus." In *Who Do My Opponents Say That I Am?*, edited by Scot McKnight and Joseph B. Modica, 50–75.

Moeller, Bernd, ed. *Theologie in Göttingen. Ein Vorlesungsreihe*. Göttinger Universitätsschriften. Serie A, 1. Göttingen: Vandenhoeck & Ruprecht, 1987.

Moessner, David P. *Lord of the Banquet: The Literary and Theological Significance of the*

Bibliography

Lukan Travel Narrative. Foreword by Richard B. Hayes. Harrisburg, PA: Trinity Press International, 1989.

Molnar, Michael R. *The Star of Bethlehem: The Legacy of the Magi*. New Brunswick, NJ: Rutgers University Press, 1999.

Moltmann, Jürgen. *Theology of Hope: On the Ground and Implications of Christian Eschatology*. Translated by James W. Leitch from the 5th German ed. London: SCM, 1967.

———. *Hope and Planning*. Translated by Margaret Clarkson. London: SCM, 1971.

———. *The Crucified God: The Cross as the Foundation and Criticism of Christian Theology*. Translated from the 2nd German ed. [1974] by R. A. Wilson and John Bowden. New York: Harper & Row, 1974.

———. *The Church in the Power of the Spirit: A Contribution to Messianic Eschatology*. Translated by Margaret Kohl. New York: Harper & Row, 1977.

———. *The Trinity and The Kingdom: The Doctrine of God*. Translated by Margaret Kohl. San Francisco: Harper & Row, 1980. Reprint, 1981.

———. *God in Creation: A New Theology of Creation and the Spirit of God*. Gifford Lectures 1984–85. Translated by Margaret Kohl. London: SCM; San Francisco, Harper & Row, 1985.

———. *The Way of Jesus Christ: Christology in Messianic Dimensions*. Translated by Margaret Kohl. San Francisco: HarperSanFrancisco, 1989. Reprint, 1990.

———. *The Spirit of Life: A Universal Affirmation*. Translated by Margaret Kohl. Minneapolis: Fortress, 1992.

———. *The Coming of God: Christian Eschatology*. Translated by Margret Kohl. Minneapolis: Fortress, 1996.

———. *Experiences in Theology: Ways and Forms of Christian Theology*. Translated by Margaret Kohl. Minneapolis: Fortress, 2000.

———. *A Broad Place: An Autobiography*. Translated by Margaret Kohl. Minneapolis: Fortress, 2006. Reprint, 2008.

Moltmann, Jürgen, ed. *How I Have Changed: Reflections on Thirty Years of Theology*. Translated by John Bowden. Harrisburg, PA: Trinity Press International, 1997.

Montague, George T., SM. *The Holy Spirit: Growth of a Biblical Tradition*. New York: Paulist, 1976. Reprint, Peabody, MA: Hendrickson, 1993.

Montanari, Franco, Madeleine Goh, and Chad Schroeder, eds. *The Brill Dictionary of Ancient Greek*. [Under the auspices of the Center for Hellenic Studies, Harvard University. Advisory Editors, Gregory Nagy, Leonard Moellner.] Leiden: Brill, 2015.

Montefiore, Claude G. *The Synoptic Gospels*. Edited with an introduction and commentary. Additional notes by I. Abraham. 2 vols. London: Macmillan, 1909; 2nd ed., 1927.

———. *Rabbinic Literature and Gospel Teachings*. New York: Macmillan, 1930.

Moore, R. Laurence. *Touchdown Jesus: The Mixing of Sacred and Secular in American History*. Louisville: Westminster John Knox, 2003.

Morais, Herbert M. *Deism in Eighteenth Century America*. New York: Columbia University Press, 1934. Reprint, New York: Russell & Russell, 1960.

Morgan, Robert. *The Nature of New Testament Theology: The Contributions of William Wrede and Adolf Schlatter*. SBT Second Series 25. London: SCM; Naperville, IL: Allenson, 1973.

———. "A Straussian Question to 'New Testament Theology.'" *NTS* 23 (1977): 43–65.

———. *The Religion of the Incarnation: Anglican Essays in Commemoration of Lux Mundi*. Bristol: Bristol Classical, 1989.

Morgan, Robert, ed. *In Search of Humanity and Deity: A Celebration of John Macquarrie's Theology*. London: SCM, 2006.

Morgan, Teresa. *Roman Faith and Christian Faith:* Pistis *and* Fides *in the Early Roman Empire and Early Churches*. Oxford: Oxford University Press, 2015.

Morris, Jeremy N. "A Social Doctrine of the Trinity? A Reappraisal of F. D. Maurice on Eternal Life." *Anglican and Episcopal History* 69 (2000): 72–100.

Morris, Leon. *The Apostolic Preaching of the Cross*. London: Tyndale, 1955; 3rd ed., 1965.

Morrison, Samuel Eliot. *Three Centuries of Harvard, 1636–1936*. Cambridge, MA: Harvard University Press, 1936.

Mortimer, Sarah. *Reason and Religion in the English Revolution: The Challenge of Socinianism*. Cambridge Studies in Early Modern British History. Cambridge: Cambridge University Press, 2010.

Moser, Paul K., ed. *Jesus and Philosophy: New Essays*. Cambridge: Cambridge University Press, 2009.

Mosheim, John Lawrence. *Vindicia Antiquae Christianorum Disciplinae contra Tolandi Nazarenum* (1720).

Mossner, Ernest Campbell. *The Life of David Hume*. London: Nelson, 1954; 2nd ed., Oxford: Clarendon, 1980.

Moule, C. F. D. *The Origin of Christology*. Cambridge: Cambridge University Press, 1977.

———. *The Holy Spirit*. Oxford: Mowbray, 1978; Grand Rapids: Eerdmans, 1979.

———. "'The Son of Man': Some of the Facts." *NTS* 41 (1995): 277–79.

Moule, C. F. D., ed. *Miracles: Cambridge Studies in Their Philosophy and History*. London: Mowbray, 1965.

Mowery, R. L. "Pharisees and Scribes, Galilee and Jerusalem." *ZNW* 80 (1989): 266–68.

Moxnes, Halvor. *Putting Jesus in His Place: A Radical Vision of Household and Kingdom*. Louisville: Westminster John Knox, 2003.

Moxnes, Halvor, Ward Blanton, James G. Crossley, eds. *Jesus Beyond Nationalism: Constructing the Historical Jesus in a Period of Cultural Complexity*. London: Equinox, 2009.

Moyise, Steve. *Was the Birth of Jesus according to Scripture?* Eugene OR: Cascade, 2013.

Mozley, John Kenneth. "The Incarnation." In *Essays Catholic and Critical, by Members of the Anglican Communion*, edited by E. G. Selwyn, 179–202. London: SPCK; New York: Macmillan, 1926.

Bibliography

Muddiman, John. "The Glory of Jesus, Mark 10:37." In *The Glory of Christ in the New Testament*, edited by L. D. Hurst and N. T. Wright, 51–58.

Müller, Gotthold. *Identität und Immanenz. Zur Genese von David Friedrich Strauss, Eine theologie- und philosophiegeschitliche Studie*. Zürich: EVZ-Verlag, 1968.

Muller, Richard A. *Dictionary of Latin and Greek Theological Terms, Drawn Principally from Protestant Theology*. Grand Rapids: Baker, 1985.

———. *Christ and the Decree: Christianity and Predestination in Reformed Theology from Calvin to Perkins*. Studies in Historical Theology. Durham, NC: Labyrinth, 1986.

———. *God, Creation, and Providence in the Thought of Jacob Arminius: Sources and Directions of Scholastic Protestantism in the Era of Early Orthodoxy*. Grand Rapids: Baker, 1991.

———. *The Unaccommodated Calvin: Studies in the Foundation of a Theological Tradition*. Oxford: Oxford University Press, 2000.

———. *After Calvin: Studies in the Development of a Theological Tradition*. Oxford: Oxford University Press, 2003.

———. *Post-Reformation Reformed Dogmatics: The Rise and Development of Reformed Orthodoxy, ca. 1520 to ca. 1725*. 4 vols. Grand Rapids: Baker Academic, 2003.

———. *Calvin and the Reformed Tradition: On the Work of Christ and the Order of Salvation*. Grand Rapids: Baker Academic, 2012.

Mullin, Robert Bruce. *Miracles and the Modern Religious Imagination*. New Haven, CT: Yale University Press, 1996.

Murphy, Francesca Aran, with Troy A. Stefano, eds. *The Oxford Handbook of Christology*. Oxford: Oxford University Press, 2015.

Murphy-O'Connor, Jerome. *The Holy Land: An Archaeological Guide from Earliest Times to 1700*. Oxford: Oxford University Press, 1980; 5th ed., 2008.

———. *Jesus and Paul: Parallel Lives*. Collegeville, MN: Liturgical, 2007.

———. "What Really Happened at Gethsemane?" In *Keys to Jerusalem: Collected Essays*, 77–106. Oxford: Oxford University Press, 2012.

———. "Tracing the Via Dolorosa." In *Keys to Jerusalem*, 107–21.

———. *Paul: A Critical Life*. Oxford: Oxford University Press, 2014.

Myers, Alicia D., and Bruce G. Schuchard, eds. *Abiding Words: The Use of Scripture in the Gospel of John*. RBS 81. Atlanta: SBL Press, 2015.

Myers, Eric M., ed. *Galilee through the Centuries: Confluence of Cultures*. Winona Lake, IN: Eisenbrauns, 1999.

Myers, Susan E., ed. *Portraits of Jesus: Studies in Christology*. WUNT 321. Tübingen: Mohr Siebeck, 2012.

Nadler, Steven. *A Book Forged in Hell: Spinoza's Treatise and the Birth of the Secular Age*. Princeton: Princeton University Press, 2011.

Naumann, Gustav. *Zarathustra—Commentar*. 4 vols. Leipzig: Hassel, 1899–1901.

Neale, D. "Was Jesus a *Mesith*? Public Response to Jesus and His Ministry." *TynBul* 44 (1993): 89–101.

A History of the Quests for the Historical Jesus

Neel, Douglas E., and Joel L Pugh. *The Food and Feasts of Jesus: Inside the World of First-Century-Fare with Menus and Recipes.* Lanham, MD: Rowman & Littlefield, 2012.

Neill, Stephen, and Tom Wright. *The Interpretation of the New Testament, 1861–1986.* Oxford: Oxford University Press, 1964; 2nd ed., 1988.

Nebreda, Sergio Rosell. *Christ Identity: A Social-Scientific Reading of Philippians 2.5–11.* FRLANT 240. Göttingen: Vandenhoeck & Ruprecht, 2011.

Nestle, Eberhard, Barbara Erwin, Kurt Aland, Johannes Karavidopoulos, Carlo M. Martini, and Bruce M. Metzger, eds. *Novum Testamentum Graece.* 28th ed. Stuttgart: Deutsche Bibelgesellschaft, 2012.

Neudecker, Reinhard. *Moses Interpreted by the Pharisees and Jesus: Matthew's Antitheses in the Light of Early Rabbinic Literature.* SubBi 44. Rome: Pontifical Biblical Institute, Gregorian and Biblical Press, 2012.

———. *Adolf Schlatter. Ein Leben für Theologie und Kirche.* Stuttgart: Calwer, 1996. ET [of 1998 edition]: *Adolf Schlatter: A Biography of Germany's Premier Biblical Theologian.* Translated by Robert W. Yarbrough. Grand Rapids: Baker, 1995.

Neufeld, Dietmar. *Mockery and Secretism in the Social World of Mark's Gospel.* LNTS 503. New York: T&T Clark, 2014.

Neusner, Jacob. *The Rabbinic Traditions about the Pharisees before 70.* Leiden: Brill, 1971.

———. *The Idea of Purity in Ancient Judaism.* SJLA 1. Leiden: Brill, 1973.

———. *From Politics to Piety: The Emergence of Pharisaic Judaism.* Englewood Cliffs, NJ: Prentice-Hall, 1973.

———. *Talmud of the Land of Israel: A Preliminary Translation and Explanation.* 35 vols. Chicago: University of Chicago Press, 1983–.

———. *In Search of Talmudic Biography: The Problem of the Attributed Saying.* BJS 70. Chico, CA: Scholars, 1984.

———. *Why No Gospels in Rabbinic Judaism?* BJS 135. Atlanta: Scholars, 1988.

———. *The Mishnah: A New Translation.* New Haven, CT: Yale University Press, 1988.

———. *A Midrash Reader.* Minneapolis: Fortress, 1990.

———. *Introduction to Rabbinic Literature.* New York: Doubleday, 1994.

———. *Christianity and Judaism: The Formative Categories.* 3 vols. Valley Forge, PA: Trinity Press International, 1995–97.

———. *Jewish-Christian Debates: God, Kingdom, Messiah.* Harrisburg, PA: Trinity Press International, 1996.

———. *A Rabbi Talks with Jesus.* Montreal: McGill-Queen's University Press, 2000.

Neusner, Jacob et al., trans. *The Babylonian Talmud.* 75 vols. Atlanta: Scholars, 1984–95.

Neusner, Jacob, and Bruce D. Chilton, eds. *In Quest of the Historical Pharisees.* Waco, TX: Baylor University Press, 2007.

———. *The Golden Rule: Analytical Perspectives.* Studies in Religion and the Social Order. Lanham, MD: University Press of America, 2009.

Neusner, Jacob, William Scott Green, Ernest S. Frerichs, eds. *Judaism and Their Messiahs at the Turn of the Christian Era.* Cambridge: Cambridge University Press, 1987.

Bibliography

Newman, Carey C., ed. *Jesus and the Restoration of Israel: A Critical Assessment of N. T. Wright's Jesus and the Victory of God.* Downers Grove, IL: InterVarsity Press, 1999.

Newman, Carey C., James R. Davila, and Gladys S. Lewis, eds. *The Jewish Roots of Christological Monotheism: Papers from the St. Andrews Conference on the Historical Origins of the Worship of Jesus.* JSJSup 63. Leiden: Brill, 1999.

Newman, John Henry. "Apollonius of Tyana." *Encyclopaedia Metropolitana* (1826). Reprint in *Historical Sketches*, 1:305–31. Westminster, MD: Christian Classics, 1872. Reprint, 1970.

———. *An Essay on the Development of Christian Doctrine* (1845). Edited by J. S. Cameron. Harmondsworth: Penguin, 1974.

Newman, John Henry et al. *Tracts for the Times.* London: J. G. & F. Rivington, 1833–41. Reprint, *Tracts for the Times by Members of the University of Oxford.* New York: AMS, 1969.

Newman, Lex, ed. *The Cambridge Companion to Locke's "Essay Concerning Human Understanding".* Cambridge: Cambridge University Press, 2007.

Newport, John P. *Paul Tillich.* Makers of the Modern Theological Mind. Waco, TX: Word, 1984.

Newsome, James D. *Greeks, Romans, Jews: Currents of Culture and Belief in the New Testament World.* Philadelphia: Trinity Press International, 1992.

Newton, Sir Isaac. *Theological Manuscripts.* Edited by Herbert McLachlan. Liverpool: Liverpool University Press, 1950.

Neyrey, Jerome H. "The Idea of Purity in Mark's Gospel." *Semeia* 35 (1986): 91–128.

———. *An Ideology of Revolt: John's Christology in Social-Science Perspective.* Philadelphia: Fortress, 1988.

———. "A Symbolic Approach to Mark 7." *Foundations and Facets Forum* 4, no. 3 (1988): 63–91.

———. "Clean/Unclean, Pure/Polluted, and Holy/Profane: The Idea and the System of Purity." In *The Social Sciences and New Testament Interpretation*, edited by Richard Rohrbaugh, 80–104.

———. *Honor and Shame in the Gospel of Matthew.* Louisville: Westminster John Knox, 1998.

———. *The Gospel of John in Cultural and Rhetorical Perspective.* Grand Rapids: Eerdmans, 2009.

Neyrey, Jerome H., ed. *The Social World of Luke-Acts: Models for Interpretation.* Peabody, MA: Hendrickson, 1991.

Neyrey, Jerome H., and Eric C. Stewart, eds. *The Social World of the New Testament: Insights and Models.* Peabody, MA: Hendrickson, 2008.

Nickelsburg, George W. E. *Jewish Literature between the Bible and the Mishnah: A Historical and Literary Introduction.* Philadelphia: Fortress, 1981.

Nickelsburg, George W. E., and John J. Collins, eds. *Ideal Figures in Ancient Judaism: Profiles and Paradigms.* SBLSCS 12. Missoula, MT: Scholars, 1980.

Nickelsburg, George W. E., and Michael E. Stone. *Faith and Piety in Early Judaism: Texts and Documents*. Philadelphia: Fortress, 1983; Philadelphia: Trinity Press International, 1991.

Nicol, W. *The Sēmeia in the Fourth Gospel: Tradition and Redaction*. NovTSup 32. Leiden: Brill, 1972.

Nichols, Adrian. *From Newman to Congar: The Idea of Doctrinal Development from the Victorians to the Second Vatican Council*. Edinburgh: T&T Clark, 1990.

Niesel, Wilhelm, ed. *Bekenntnisschriften und Kirchenordnungen der nach Gottes Wort reformierten Kirche*. Zollikon-Zürich: Evangelischer, n.d.

Nietzsche, Friedrich Wilhelm. *Friedrich Nietzsche, Sämtliche Werke. Kritische Gesamtausgabe*. Edited by Georgio Colli and Mazzino Montinari. 30 vols. Berlin: de Gruyter, 1967–77. Abbreviated as *KGW*.

———. *Friedrich Nietzsche, Kritische Studien-Ausgabe*. Edited by G. Colli and M. Montinari. 15 vols. Berlin: de Gruyter, 1980. Abbreviated as *KSA*.

———. *Daybreak*. Edited by Maudemarie Clark and Brian Leiter. Translated by R. J. Hollingdale. CTHP. Cambridge: Cambridge University Press, 1982.

———. *Human, All Too Human*. Translated by R. J. Hollingdale. With introduction by Richard Schacht. CTHP. Cambridge: Cambridge University Press, 1986.

———. *On the Genealogy of Morality*. CTHP. Translated by Carol Diethe. Cambridge: Cambridge University Press, 1994.

———. *The Complete Works of Friedrich Nietzsche*. Edited by Bernd Magnus. 20 vols. Stanford, CA: Stanford University Press, 1995–.

———. *Human, All Too Human*. Translated by Gary Handwerk. Stanford, CA: Stanford University Press, 1995.

———. *Untimely Meditations*. Edited by Daniel Breazeale. Translated by R. J. Hollingdale. CTHP. Cambridge: Cambridge University Press, 1997.

———. *On the Genealogy of Morals: A Polemic by Way of Clarification and Supplement to My Last Book, Beyond God and Evil*. Translated by Douglas Smith. Oxford: Oxford University Press, 1998.

———. *The Birth of Tragedy and Other Writings*. Edited by Raymond Geuss and Ronald Speirs. Translated by Ronald Speirs. CTHP. Cambridge: Cambridge University Press, 1999. [The edition includes the unpublished essay on "The Dionysiac Worldview." The abbreviation CTHP stands for Cambridge Texts in the History of Philosophy.]

———. *The Gay Science: With a Prelude in German Rhymes and an Appendix of Songs*. CTHP. Edited by Bernard Williams. Translated by Josefine Nauckhoff. Poems translated by Adrian Del Caro. Cambridge: Cambridge University Press, 2001.

———. *Beyond Good and Evil: Prelude to a Philosophy of the Future*. Edited by Rolf-Peter Horstmann and Judith Norman. CTHP. Cambridge: Cambridge University Press, 2002.

———. *Writings from the Late Notebooks*. Edited by Rüdiger Bittner. Translated by Kate Sturge. CTHP. Cambridge: Cambridge University Press, 2003.

———. *Thus Spoke Zarathustra: A Book for All and None*. Edited by Adrian Del Caro and Robert B. Pippin. Translated by Adrian Del Caro. CTHP. Cambridge: Cambridge University Press, 2006.

———. *The Anti-Christ, Ecce Homo, Twilight of the Idols and Other Writings*. Edited by Aaron Ridley and Judith Norman. Translated by Judith Norman. CTHP. Cambridge: Cambridge University Press, 2005.

———. *Writings from the Early Notebooks*. Edited by Raymond Geuss and Alexander Nehamas. Translated by Ladislaus Löb. CTHP. Cambridge: Cambridge University Press, 2009.

Nockles, Peter Benedict. *The Oxford Movement in Context: Anglican High Churchmanship, 1760–1857*. Cambridge: Cambridge University Press, 1994.

Noll, Mark A. "The Founding of Princeton Seminary." *WTJ* 42 (1979): 72–110.

Noll, Mark A., ed. *The Princeton Theology 1812–1921: Scripture, Science, and Theological Method from Archibald Alexander to Benjamin Warfield*. Grand Rapids: Baker, 1983.

Norris, Frederick W. "Eusebius on Jesus as Deceiver and Sorcerer." In *Eusebius, Christianity and Judaism*, edited by Harold W. Attridge and Gohei Hata, 523–40.

North, Wendy E. S. *A Journey Round John: Tradition, Interpretation and Context in the Fourth Gospel*. LNTS 534. New York: T&T Clark, 2015.

Norton, David Fate, and Jacqueline Taylor, eds. *The Cambridge Companion to Hume*. Cambridge: Cambridge University Press, 1993; 2nd ed., 2009. [An appendix contains Hume's two autobiographical sketches: "A Kind of History of My Life" (1734), and "My Own Life" (1776), 515–29.]

Notley, R. Steven. *Jerusalem: City of the Great King*. Jerusalem: Carta, 2015.

Nouwen, Henri. *The Return of the Prodigal Son: A Story of Homecoming*. New York: Doubleday, 1992.

Novak, Ralph Martin Jr. *Christianity and the Roman Empire: Background Texts*. Harrisburg, PA: Trinity Press International, 2001.

Novakovic, Lidija. *Messiah, the Healer of the Sick*. WUNT 170. Tübingen: Mohr Siebeck, 2003.

Novenson, Matthew V. *Christ among the Messiahs: Christ Language in Paul and Messiah Language in Ancient Judaism*. Oxford: Oxford University Press, 2012.

———. *The Grammar of Messianism: An Ancient Jewish Political Idiom and Its Users*. Oxford: Oxford University Press, 2017.

Oakman, Douglas E. *The Political Aims of Jesus*. Minneapolis: Fortress, 2013.

———. *Jesus, Debt, and the Lord's Prayer: First-Century Debt and Jesus' Intentions*. Eugene, OR: Cascade, 2014.

Oberman, Heiko A. *The Virgin Mary in Evangelical Perspective*. Introduction by Thomas F. O'Meara. Facet Books Historical Series 20. Philadelphia: Fortress, 1971.

Obermann, Andreas. *Die christologische Erfüllung der Schrift im Johannesevangelium. Eine Untersuchung zur Johanneischen Hermeneutik anhand der Schriftzitate*. WUNT 83. Tübingen: Mohr Siebeck, 1996.

A History of the Quests for the Historical Jesus

O'Carroll, Michael, C.S.Sp. *Theotokos: A Theological Encyclopedia of the Blessed Virgin Mary.* Collegeville, MN: Liturgical; Glazier, 1982.

———. *Trinitas: A Theological Encyclopedia of the Holy Trinity.* Collegeville, MN: Liturgical; Glazier, 1987.

———. *Corpus Christi: An Encyclopedia of the Eucharist.* Collegeville, MN: Liturgical; Glazier, 1988.

———. *Veni Creator Spiritus: An Encyclopedia of the Holy Spirit.* Collegeville, MN: Liturgical; Glazier, 1990.

———. *Verbum Caro: An Encyclopedia on Jesus, the Christ.* Collegeville, MN: Liturgical; Glazier, 1992.

O'Collins, Gerald. *Christology: A Biblical, Historical, and Systematic Study of Jesus.* Oxford: Oxford University Press, 1995; 2nd ed., 2009.

O'Connell, Marvin R. *Critics on Trial: An Introduction to the Catholic Modernist Crisis.* Washington, DC: Catholic University of America Press, 1994.

Oegema, Gerbern S. *The Anointed and His People: Messianic Expectation from the Maccabees to Bar Kochba.* JSPSup 27. Sheffield: Sheffield Academic Press, 1998.

Oermann, Nils Ole. *Albert Schweitzer: A Biography.* Oxford: Oxford University Press, 2017.

O'Flaherty, James C., Timothy F. Sellner, and Robert M. Helm, eds. *Studies in Nietzsche and the Judaeo-Christian Tradition.* Chapel Hill: University of North Carolina Press, 1985.

Ogden, Daniel. *Magic, Witchcraft, and Ghosts in the Greek and Roman Worlds: A Sourcebook.* Oxford: Oxford University Press, 2002; 2nd ed., 2009.

Ogden, Schubert M. *Christ without Myth: A Study Based on the Theology of Rudolf Bultmann.* New York: Harper & Row, 1961.

———. *The Point of Christology.* San Francisco: Harper & Row; London, SCM, 1982.

———. *On Theology.* San Francisco: Harper & Row, 1986.

———. *Doing Theology Today.* Valley Forge, PA: Trinity Press International, 1996.

O'Higgins, James. *Anthony Collins: The Man and His Works.* International Archives of the History of Ideas 35. The Hague: Martinus Nijhoff, 1970.

Olbricht, Thomas H. "New Testament Studies at the University of Chicago: The First Decade 1892–1902." *ResQ* 22 (1979): 84–99.

O'Meara, Thomas F., and Donald M. Weisser, eds. *Rudolf Bultmann in Catholic Thought.* New York: Herder and Herder, 1968.

Olson, Roger E. *Arminian Theology: Myths and Realities.* Downers Grove, IL: InterVarsity Press, 2006.

———. *Against Calvinism.* Grand Rapids: Zondervan, 2011.

Orchard, Bernard, and Thomas R. W. Longstaff, eds. *J. J. Griesbach: Synoptic and Text-Critical Studies.* SNTSMS 34. Cambridge: Cambridge University Press, 1978.

Origen. *Contra Celsum.* Translated with introduction and notes by Henry Chadwick. Cambridge: Cambridge University Press, [1953]; 2003.

Bibliography

Oropeza, B. J., C. K. Robertson, and Douglas C. Mohrmann, eds. *Jesus and Paul: Global Perspectives in Honor of James D. G. Dunn. A Festschrift for His 70th Birthday*. LNTS 414. New York: T&T Clark, 2009.

Orr, Peter, *Christ Absent and Present: A Study in Pauline Christology*, WUNT 354. Tübinen: Mohr Siebeck, 2014.

Osiek, Carolyn, RSCJ. *What Are They Saying about the Social Setting of the New Testament?* New York: Paulist, 1984; rev. ed., 1992.

Otto, Rudolf. *Leben und Wirken Jesu nach historisch-kritischer Auffassung*. Göttingen: Vandenhoeck & Ruprecht, 1902.

———. *Kantische-Fries'sche Religionsphilosophie*. Tübingen: Mohr Siebeck, 1909. ET: *The Philosophy of Religion, Based on Kant and Fries*. Translated by E. B. Dicker. London: Williams & Norgate, 1931.

———. *The Idea of the Holy* [1917]. Translated by John W. Harvey. London: Oxford University Press, 1923; 2nd ed. 1958. [The edition cited in the present book is the reprint published by Penguin in 1959.]

———. *The Kingdom of God and the Son of Man: A Study in the History of Religion*. 1934. 2nd ed. 1940. Translated by Floyd V. Filson and Bertram Lee Woolf. London: Lutterworth, 1938.

Padilla, C. *Los Milagros de la "Vida de Apolonio de Tiana." Morfologia del relato y géneros afines*. Estudios de Filología Neotestamentaria 4. Córdoba: Ediciones El Almendro, 1991.

Paffenroth, Kim. *The Story of Jesus according to L*. JSNTSup 147. Sheffield: Sheffield Academic Press, 1997.

Pagels, Elaine. *Beyond Belief: The Secret Gospel of Thomas*. New York: Random House, 2003.

Paine, Thomas. *Collected Writings*. Edited by P. S. Foner. 2 vols. New York: Library of America, 1995.

Painter, John. *Theology as Hermeneutics: Rudolf Bultmann's Interpretation of the History of Jesus*. Historical Texts and Interpreters in Biblical Scholarship. Sheffield: Almond, 1987.

———. *The Quest for the Messiah: The History, Literature and Theology of the Johannine Community*. 2nd ed. Edinburgh: T&T Clark; Nashville: Abingdon, 1993.

Paley, William. *View of the Evidences of Christianity*. Cambridge: Hall & Son, 1794; 4th ed., 1864.

Palmer, N. H. "Lachmann's Argument." *NTS* 13 (1966–67): 368–78.

———. *The Logic of Gospel Criticism: An Account of the Methods, and Arguments used by Textual, Documentary, Source, and Form Critics of the New Testament*. London: Macmillan; New York: Saint Martin's Press, 1968.

Pals, Daniel L. *The Victorian "Lives" of Jesus*. Trinity University Monograph Series in Religion 7. San Antonio, TX: Trinity University Press, 1982.

Pancaro, S. *The Law in the Fourth Gospel*. NovTSup 42. Leiden: Brill, 1975.

A History of the Quests for the Historical Jesus

Pannenberg, Wolfhart. *Jesus: God and Man*. Translated by Lewis L. Wilkins and Duane A. Priebe. London: SCM, 1968.

———. *Basic Questions in Theology*. 3 vols. Vols. 1 and 2, translated by George H. Kehm. Vol. 3, translated by R. A. Wilson. London: SCM, 1970–73. [US editions: vols. 1 and 2, Philadelphia: Fortress; vol. 3, *The Idea of God and Human Freedom*, Philadelphia: Westminster.]

———. *Systematic Theology*. Translated by Geoffrey W. Bromiley. 3 vols. Grand Rapids: Eerdmans, 1991–98.

Parrinder, Geoffrey. *Son of Joseph: The Parentage of Jesus*. Edinburgh: T&T Clark, 1992.

Parsons, Michael C., and Joseph B. Tyson, eds. *Cadbury, Knox, and Talbert: American Contributions to the Study of Acts*. Atlanta: Scholars, 1991.

Parsons, Richard E. *Sir Edwyn Hoskyns as a Biblical Theologian*. London: Hurst; New York: St. Martin's, 1985.

Partee, Charles. *Calvin and Classical Philosophy*. Studies in the History of Christian Thought 14. Leiden: Brill, 1977.

Pascal, Blaise. *Pensées*. Translated by A. J. Krailsheimer. Penguin Classics. Harmondsworth: Penguin, 1966; rev. ed., 1995.

———. *Pensées and Other Writings*. Translated by Honor Levi. Introduction and notes by Anthony Levi. World's Classics. Oxford: Oxford University Press, 1995.

Patrick, Graham A. *F. J. A. Hort: Eminent Victorian*. Sheffield: Almond, 1988.

Patterson, Stephen J., James M. Robinson, Hans-Gebhard Bethge. *The Fifth Gospel: The Gospel of Thomas Comes of Age*. Harrisburg, PA: Trinity Press International, 1998.

Pauck, Wilhelm. *Harnack and Troeltsch: Two Historical Theologians*. Oxford: Oxford University Press, 1968.

Pauck, Wilhelm, and Marion Pauck. *Paul Tillich: His Life and Thought*. Vol. 1, *Life*. New York: Harper & Row, 1976.

Paul, Jean. "Die Rede des toten Christus vom Weltgebäude herab, dass kein Gott sei." *Siebenkäs*, 1796–97. Text in Günther Bornkamm, *Studien zu Antike und Christentum*, 2nd ed., vol. 2, 245–50. Beiträge zur evangelischen Theologie 28. Munich: Kaiser, 1983.

Paulus, H. E. G. *Das Leben Jesu als Grundlage einer reinen Geschichte des Urchristentums*. 2 vols. Heidelberg: Winter, 1828.

Peabody, David Barrett. "H. J. Holtzmann and His European Colleagues: Aspects of the Nineteenth-Century European Discussion of Gospel Origins." In *Biblical Studies and the Shifting of Paradigms, 1850–1914*, edited by Henning Graf Reventlow and William Farmer, 50–131. JSOTSup 192. Sheffield: Sheffield Academic Press, 1995.

Peabody, Francis G. *Jesus Christ and the Social Question: An Examination of the Teaching of Jesus in Its Relation to Some of the Problems of Modern Social Life*. New York: Grosset and Dunlap, 1900. Reprint, 1911.

———. *Jesus Christ and the Christian Character: An Examination of the Teaching of Jesus in Relation to Some of the Problems of Personal Life*. New York: Hodder & Stoughton, 1906.

Bibliography

———. *The Social Museum as the Instrument of University Teaching: A Classified List of the Collections in the Social Museum of Harvard University.* Publications of the Department of Social Ethics in Harvard University 1. Cambridge, MA: Harvard University Press, 1911.

———. *The Social Teaching of Jesus Christ: I. The Social Principle of Jesus: II. The Social Consequences of the Teaching of Jesus, Two Lectures Delivered before the University of Pennsylvania, April 22 and 23, 1924.* Philadelphia: Press of the University of Pennsylvania, 1924.

Pearson, Birger A. "The Gospel according to the 'Jesus Seminar'; On Some Recent Trends in Gospel Research." In *The Emergence of the Christian Religion: Essays on Early Christianity*, 23–57. Harrisburg, PA: Trinity Press International, 1997. An earlier version with a preface by the author and an afterword by James M. Robinson was published as Birger A. Pearson, *The Gospel according to the Jesus Seminar*. Institute for Antiquity and Christianity Occasional Papers 35. Claremont, CA: Claremont Graduate School, 1996.

———. *Ancient Gnosticism: Traditions and Literature.* Minneapolis: Fortress, 2007.

Peart-Binns, John S. *Herbert Hensley Henson: A Biography.* Cambridge: Lutterworth Press, 2013.

Peden, W. Creighton. *The Chicago School: Voices in Liberal Religious Thought.* Bristol, IN: Wyndham Hall, 1987.

Peden, W. Creighton, and Jerome A. Stone, eds. *The Chicago School of Theology: Pioneers in Religious Inquiry.* Vol. 1, *The Early Chicago School, 1906–1959.* Studies in American Religion 66a. Lewiston: Mellen, 1996.

Peirce, C. S. *Values in a Universe of Chance.* Edited by P. P. Wiener. New York: Doubleday Anchor, 1958.

Pelikan, Jaroslav. *The Christian Tradition: A History of the Development of Doctrine.* 5 vols. Chicago: University of Chicago Press, 1973–90.

———. *Jesus through the Centuries: His Place in the History of Culture.* New Haven, CT: Yale University Press, 1985. Reprint, 1999.

———. *Credo: Historical and Theological Guide to Creeds and Confessions of Faith in the Christian Tradition.* New Haven, CT: Yale University Press, 2003.

Pelikan, Jaroslav, and Valerie Hotchkiss, eds. *Creeds and Confessions of Faith in the Christian Tradition.* 3 vols. New Haven, CT: Yale University Press, 2003.

Pelle, Moshe. "The Impact of Deism on the Hebrew Literature of the Enlightenment in Germany." *Eighteenth-Century Studies* 6 (1972–73): 35–59.

Penelhum, Terence. *Hume.* London: Macmillan, 1975.

Peppard, Michael. *The Son of God in the Roman World: Divine Sonship in Its Social and Political Context.* Oxford: Oxford University Press, 2011.

Perdue, Leon G., Warren Carter, and Coleman A. Baker, ed. *Israel and Empire: A Postcolonial History of Israel and Early Judaism.* New York: T&T Clark, 2015.

Perrin, Nicholas. *Jesus the Temple.* London: SPCK; Grand Rapids, Baker, 2010.

A History of the Quests for the Historical Jesus

Perrin, Nicholas, and Richard B. Hays, eds. *Jesus, Paul and the People of God: A Theological Dialogue with N. T. Wright.* Downers Grove, IL: IVP Academic, 2011.

Perrin, Norman. *The Kingdom of God in the Teaching of Jesus.* London: SCM; Philadelphia: Westminster, 1963.

———. "Against the Current." *Interpretation* 19 (1965): 228–31.

———. *Rediscovering the Teaching of Jesus.* London: SCM; New York: Harper & Row, 1967.

———. *The Promise of Bultmann: The Promise of Theology.* Philadelphia: Lippincott, 1969. Reprint, Philadelphia: Fortress, 1979.

———. *What Is Redaction Criticism?* Edited by Dan O. Via Guides to Biblical Scholarship. Philadelphia: Fortress, 1969; London: SPCK, 1970.

———. *A Modern Pilgrimage in New Testament Christology.* Philadelphia: Fortress, 1974.

———. *The New Testament: An Introduction, Proclamation and Parenesis, Myth and History.* New York: Harcourt Brace, 1974. [Subsequently revised with Dennis C. Duling, 1982.]

———. *Jesus and the Language of the Kingdom: Symbol and Metaphor in New Testament Interpretation.* Philadelphia: Fortress, 1976.

———. *The Resurrection according to Matthew, Mark, and Luke.* Philadelphia: Fortress, 1977.

Peters, F. E. *Jesus and Muhammad: Parallel Tracks, Parallel Lives.* Oxford: Oxford University Press, 2011.

Petersen, William L., Johan S. Vos, and Henk J. de Jonge, eds. *Sayings of Jesus: Canonical and Non-Canonical, Essays in Honour of Tijitze Baarda.* Leiden: Brill, 1997.

Peterson, Brian Neil. *John's Use of Ezekiel: Understanding the Unique Perspective of the Fourth Gospel.* Minneapolis: Fortress, 2015.

Petre, Maude D. *Autobiography and Life of George Tyrrell.* 2 vols. London: Arnold, 1912.

Petzke, Gerd. *Die Traditionen über Apollonius von Tyana und das Neue Testament.* SCH 1. Leiden: Brill, 1970.

———. "Historizität und Bedeutsamkeit von Wunderberichte. Möglichkeiten und Grenzen des religionsgeschichtlichen Vergleiches." In *Neues Testament und christliche Existenz. Festschrift für Herbert Braun zum 70. Geburtstag am 4. Mai 1993*, edited by Hans Dieter Betz and Luise Schottroff, 367–85. Tübingen: Mohr Siebeck, 1973.

Pfizenmaier, Thomas C. "Was Isaac Newton an Arian?" *Journal of the History of Ideas* 58 (1997): 57–80.

———. *The Trinitarian Theology of Dr. Samuel Clarke (1675–1729): Context, Sources, and Controversy.* Studies in the History of Christian Thought 75. Leiden: Brill, 1997.

Philipp, Wolfgang. *Das Werden der Aufklärung in theologiegeschichtlicher Sicht.* FSTR 3. Göttingen: Vandenhoeck & Ruprecht, 1957.

Philonenko, Marc. *Le Notre Père. De la prière de Jésus à la prière des disciples.* Paris: Gallimard, 2001.

Philo. Loeb Classical Library. 12 vols. Cambridge, MA: Harvard University Press, 1929–87.

Bibliography

Philostratus. *Life of Apollonius of Tyana*. Abridged and translated by Christopher P. Jones. Introduction by G. W. Bowersock. Harmondsworth: Penguin, 1970.

———. *The Life of Apollonius of Tyana*. 2 vols. LCL. With Greek and English on facing pages. Edited and translated by Christopher P. Jones. Cambridge, MA: Harvard University Press, 2005. [Philostratus, *Apollonius of Tyana*, vol. 3 (2006), includes letters of Apollonius and Eusebius's *Reply to Hierocles* regarding Apollonius.]

Picard, Edmond. *L'Aryano-sémitisme*. Brussels: Lacomblez, 1899.

Picht, Werner. *The Life and Thought of Albert Schweitzer*. Translated by Edward Fitzgerald. London: Allen & Unwin; New York: Harper & Row, 1964.

Pickering, W. S. F. *Anglo-Catholicism: A Study in Religious Ambiguity*. New York: Routledge, 1989.

Pietsch, B. M. *Dispensational Modernism*. Oxford: Oxford University Press, 2015.

Pilch, John J. *Introducing the Cultural Context of the Old Testament*. New York: Paulist, 1991.

———. *Introducing the Cultural Context of the New Testament*. New York: Paulist, 1991.

———. *Healing and the New Testament: Insights from Medical and Mediterranean Anthropology*. Minneapolis: Fortress, 2000.

Pilch, John J., ed. *Social Scientific Models for Interpreting the Bible: Essays by the Context Group in Honor of Bruce J. Malina*. BibIntS 53. Leiden: Brill, 2001.

Pilgaard, Aage. "The Hellenistic *Theios Aner*—A Model for Early Christian Christology?" In *The New Testament and Hellenistic Judaism*, edited by Peder Borgen and Søren Giversen, 101–22. Peabody, MA: Hendrickson, 1997.

Pinnock, Clark, Richard Rice, John Sanders, William Hasker, and David Basinger. *The Openness of God: A Biblical Challenge to the Traditional Understanding of God*. Downers Grove, IL: InterVarsity Press, 1994.

Piper, John. *The Future of Justification: A Response to N. T. Wright*. Wheaton, IL: Crossway, 2007.

Pitre, Brant. *Jesus, the Tribulation, and the End of the Exile: Restoration Eschatology and the Origin of the Atonement*. WUNT 204. Tübingen: Mohr Siebeck; Grand Rapids: Baker Academic, 2005.

———. *Jesus and the Last Supper*. Grand Rapids: Eerdmans, 2015.

Pittinger, W. Norman. "The Christian Apologetics of James Franklin Bethune-Baker." *ATR* 37 (1955): 260–77.

Plantinga Pauw, Amy. *The Supreme Harmony of All: The Trinitarian Theology of Jonathan Edwards*. Grand Rapids: Eerdmans, 2002.

Plisch, Uwe-Karsten. *The Gospel of Thomas: Original Text with Commentary*. Translated by Gesine Schenke Robinson. Stuttgart: Deutsche Bibelgesellschaft, 2008.

Pobee, John. "The Cry of the Centurion—A Cry of Defeat." In *The Trial of Jesus*, edited by E. Bammel, 91–102.

Pokorný, Petr. *The Genesis of Christology: Foundations for a Theology of the New Testament*. Translated by Marcus Lefébure. Edinburgh: T&T Clark, 1987.

———. *A Commentary on the Gospel of Thomas: From Interpretations to the Interpreted.* New York: T&T International, 2009.
———. "Words of Jesus in Paul: On the Theology and Practice of the Jesus Tradition." In *HSHJ*, 4:3437–67.
Poland, Lynn M. "The New Criticism, Neoorthodoxy, and the New Testament." *JR* 65 (1985): 459–77.
———. *Literary Criticism and Biblical Hermeneutics: A Critique of Formalist Approaches.* AARSR 48. Chico, CA: Scholars Press, 1985.
Polkinghorne, John, and Michael Welker, eds. *The End of the World and the Ends of God: Science and Theology and Eschatology.* Harrisburg, PA: Trinity Press International, 2000.
Polanyi, Michael. *Personal Knowledge: Towards a Post-Critical Philosophy.* Gifford Lectures, Aberdeen, 1951–52. London: Routledge, 1958.
———. *The Tacit Dimension.* Terry Lectures, Yale, 1962. London: Routledge, 1967.
Pons, Georges. *Gotthold Ephraïm Lessing et le Christianisme.* Germanica 5. Paris: Marcel Didier, 1964.
Popkin, Richard H. *The History of Scepticism from Savonarola to Bayle.* Oxford: Oxford University Press, 2003.
Popper, Karl R. *The Logic of Scientific Discovery.* [1st German ed., 1934.] London: Hutchinson, 1959.
Porter, Roy. *The Creation of the Modern World: The Untold Story of the British Enlightenment.* New York: Norton, 2000.
Porter, Stanley E. *Idioms of the Greek New Testament.* Biblical Languages: Greek 2. Sheffield: Sheffield Academic Press, 1992; 2nd ed., 1999.
———. "Jesus and the Use of Greek in Galilee." In *Studying the Historical Jesus: Evaluations of the State of Current Research*, edited by Bruce Chilton and Craig A. Evans, 123–54. NTTS 19. Leiden: Brill, 1994.
———. *The Criteria for Authenticity in Historical-Jesus Research: Previous Discussion and New Proposals.* JSNTSup 191. Sheffield: Sheffield Academic Press, 2000.
———. "The Role of Greek Language Criteria in Historical Jesus Research." In *HSHJ*, 1:361–404.
———. "The Language(s) Jesus Spoke." In *HSHJ*, 3:2455–72.
———. *John, His Gospel, and Jesus: In Pursuit of the Johannine Voice.* Grand Rapids: Eerdmans, 2015.
———. *Sacred Tradition in the New Testament: Tracing Old Testament Themes in the Gospels and Epistles.* Grand Rapids: Baker Academic, 2016.
Porter, Stanley E., ed. *The Language of the New Testament: Classic Essays.* JSNTSup 60. Sheffield: Sheffield Academic Press, 1991.
———. *Handbook to Exegesis of the New Testament.* NTTS 25. Leiden: Brill, 1997.
———. *Reading the Gospels Today.* Grand Rapids: Eerdmans, 2004.
———. *Dictionary of Biblical Criticism and Interpretation.* New York: Routledge, 2007.

———. *The Apostle Paul: His Life, Thought, and Letters*. Grand Rapids: Eerdmans, 2016.
Porter, Stanley E., Michael A. Hayes, and David Tombs, eds. *Images of Christ: Ancient and Modern*. Roehampton Institute London Papers 2. Sheffield: Sheffield Academic Press, 1997.
Porter, Stanley E., and Jason C. Robinson, eds. *Hermeneutics: An Introduction to Interpretive Theory*. Grand Rapids: Eerdmans, 2011.
Porter, Stanley E., and Matthew R. Malcolm, eds., *Horizons in Hermeneutics: A Festschrift in Honor of Anthony C. Thiselton*. Grand Rapids: Eerdmans, 2013.
Porter, Stanley E., and Bryan R. Dyer, eds. *The Synoptic Problem: Four Views*. Grand Rapids: Baker, 2016.
Potolsky, Gary. *Mimesis*. New York: Routledge, 2006.
Poulat, Émile. *Histoire, Dogme et Critique dans la Crise Moderniste*. Paris: Casterman, 1962.
Powell, Mark Allan. *Jesus as a Figure in History: How Modern Historians View the Man from Galilee*. Louisville: Westminster John Knox, 1998; 2nd ed., 2013.
Powell, Mark Allan, and David R. Bauer, eds. *Who Do You Say That I Am? Essays on Christology; In Honor of Jack Dean Kingsbury*. Louisville: Westminster John Knox, 1999.
Powell, Mark Allan, ed. *Methods for Matthew*. Methods in Biblical Interpretation. Cambridge: Cambridge University Press, 2009.
Preisendanz, Karl. *Papyri Graecae Magicae / Die griechischen Zauberpapyri*. 2 vols. Stuttgart: Teubner, 1928–31; 2nd ed., 1973–74. [For updated English text, see H. D. Betz, ed. *The Greek Magical Papyri in Translation*. 2nd ed. Chicago: University of Chicago Press, 1992.]
Prestige, G. L. *The Life of Charles Gore: A Great Englishman*. London: Heinemann, 1935.
Preston, Ronald H., ed. *Theology and Change: Essays in Memory of Alan Richardson*. London: SCM, 1975. [Richardson bibliography, 205–11.]
Price, Mary Bell, and Lawrence Marsden Price. *English Literature in Germany*. Berkeley: University of California Press, 1934.
———. *The Publication of English Humaniora in Germany in the Eighteenth Century*. University of California Publications in Modern Philology 44. Berkeley: University of California Press, 1955.
Price, Robert M. "Second Thoughts about the Secret Gospel." *BBR* 14 (2004): 127–32.
Priest, Robert D. *The Gospel according to Renan: Reading, Writing, and Religion in Nineteenth-Century France*. Oxford: Oxford University Press, 2015.
Priestley, Joseph. *Socrates and Jesus Compared*. Philadelphia: Johnson, 1803.
Propp, Vladimir I. *Morphology of the Folktale*. Austin, TX: University of Texas Press, 1928; 2nd ed., 1968.
Prothero, Stephen R. *The American Jesus: How the Son of God Became a National Icon*. New York: Farrar, Straus and Giroux, 2003.
Pummer, Reinhard. *The Samaritans: A Profile*. Grand Rapids: Eerdmans, 2016.

Purdy, Vernon L. *The Christology of John Macquarrie*. Foreword by Colin Brown. New York: Peter Lang, 2009.

Pusey, Edward Bouverie. *An Historical Enquiry into the Probable Causes of the Rationalist Character lately predominant in the Theology of Germany*. 2 parts. London: Rivington, 1828, 1830.

Rahner, Karl. *Theological Investigations*. Various translators. 23 vols. London: Darton Longman, and Todd, 1961–84. [In the United States vols. 1–6 were published in Baltimore by Helicon; vols. 7–10 in New York by Herder and Herder; vols. 11–16 in New York by Seabury; vols. 17–23 in New York by Crossroad. For other works see *The Cambridge Companion to Karl Rahner*. Edited by Declan Marmion and Mary E. Hines. 2005.]

——. *The Trinity*. Translated by Joseph Donceel [1974]. Introduction by Catherine Mowry LaCugna. New York: Crossroad, 2010.

Rainey, Anson F., and R. Steven Notley. *The Sacred Bridge: Carta's Atlas of the Biblical World*. Jerusalem: Carta, 2006.

Räisänen, Heikki. *Beyond New Testament Theology: A Story and a Programme*. London: SCM; Philadelphia: Trinity Press International, 1990.

——. *The 'Messianic Secret' in Mark*. Translated by Christopher Tuckett. Studies in the New Testament and Its World. Edinburgh: T&T Clark, 1990.

Ramey, Margaret E. *The Quest for the Fictional Jesus: Gospel Rewrites, Gospel (Re)interpretation, and Christological Portraits within Jesus Novels*. Eugene, OR: Pickwick, 2013.

Raphael, Melissa. *Rudolf Otto and the Concept of Holiness*. Oxford: Clarendon, 1997.

Ramsey, Arthur Michael. *F. D. Maurice and the Conflicts of Modern Theology*. Cambridge: Cambridge University Press, 1951.

——. *From Gore to Temple: The Development of Anglican Theology between* Lux Mundi *and the Second World War*. Hale Memorial Lectures at Seabury-Western Theological Seminary 1959. London: Longmans, 1960.

Rashdall, Hastings. *The Universities of Europe in the Middle Ages*. 3 vols. Oxford: Clarendon, 1895. Revised by F. M. Powicke and A. B. Emden. Oxford: Clarendon, 1936.

——. *The Idea of Atonement*. Bampton Lectures 1915. London: Macmillan, 1919.

——. *God and Man*. Edited by H. D. A. Major and F. L. Cross. Oxford: Blackwell, 1930.

Ratté, John. *Three Modernists: Alfred Loisy, William L. Sullivan, George Tyrrell*. London: Sheed and Ward, 1968.

Ratzinger, Joseph, Pope Bendict XVI. *Jesus of Nazareth: From the Baptism in the Jordan to the Transfiguration*. Translated by Adrian J. Walker. New York: Doubleday, 2007.

——. *Jesus of Nazareth*. Part Two, *From the Entrance into Jerusalem to the Resurrection*. Translated by Philip J. Whitmore. San Francisco: Ignatius, 2011.

——. *Jesus of Nazareth: The Infancy Narratives*. Translated by Philip J. Whitmore. New York: Image, Random House, 2012.

Bibliography

Rawlinson, A. E. J. *The New Testament Doctrine of Christ*. Bampton Lectures 1926. London: Longmans, 1926.

Reardon, B. M. G., ed. *Roman Catholic Modernism*. London: Black, 1970.

———. *From Coleridge to Gore: A Century of Religious Thought in Britain*. London: Longmans, 1971.

Redman, Robert R., Jr. *Reformulating Reformed Theology: Jesus Christ in the Theology of Hugh Ross Mackintosh*. Lanham, MD: University Press of America, 1997.

Redwood, J. A. "Charles Blount (1654–1693), Deism and English Free Thought." *Journal of the History of Ideas* 35 (1974): 490–98.

———. *Reason, Ridicule and Religion: The Age of Enlightenment in England, 1660–1750*. London: Thames and Hudson, 1976.

Reed, Jonathan L. "Instability in Jesus' Galilee: A Demographic Perspective." *JBL* 129 (2010): 343–65.

Rees, Thomas, trans. *The Racovian Catechism, with Notes and Illustrations, Translated from the Latin, To which is Prefixed a Sketch of the History of Unitarianism in Poland and the Adjacent Countries*. London: Longman, 1818. Facsimile reprint, Kessinger Legacy Reprints, n.d.

Reid, Daniel G., Robert D. Linder, Bruce L. Shelley, and Harry S. Stout, eds. *Dictionary of Christianity in America*. Downers Grove, IL: InterVarsity Press, 1990.

Reimarus, Hermann Samuel. *Apologie oder Schutzschrift für die vernünftigen Verehrer Gottes*. Im Auftrag der Joachim Jungius-Gesellschaft der Wissenschaften in Hamburg herausgegeben von Gerhard Alexander. 2 vols. Frankfurt: Suhrkamp, 1972.

———. *De Vita Sua Commentarius*. Hamburg: Klotzii, 1815.

———. *The Goal of Jesus and His Disciples*. Translated by George Wesley Buchanan. Leiden: Brill, 1970.

———. *Reimarus: Fragments*. Translated by Ralph S. Fraser. Edited by Charles H. Talbert. Lives of Jesus Series. Philadelphia: Fortress, 1970; London; SCM, 1971.

Reimer, Andy M. *Miracle and Magic: A Study in the Acts of the Apostles and the Life of Apollonius of Tyana*. JSNTSup 235. Sheffield: Sheffield Academic Press, 2002.

Rein, Matthias. *Die Heilung des Blindgeborenen (Joh 9): Tradition und Redaktion*. WUNT 73. Tübingen: Mohr Siebeck, 1995.

Reiser, Marius. *Syntax und Stil des Markusevangeliums*. WUNT 11. Tübingen: Mohr Siebeck, 1984.

———. *Jesus and Judgment: The Eschatological Proclamation in Its Jewish Context*. Translated by Linda M. Maloney. Minneapolis: Fortress, 1997.

Reitzenstein, Richard. *Hellenistische Wundererzählungen*. Stuttgart: Teubner, [1906]; 3rd ed., 1974.

———. *Die hellenistischen Mysterienreligionen nach ihren Grundgedanken und Wirkungen*. Stuttgart: Teubner, 1910; 3rd ed., 1927. ET: John E. Steely, trans. *Hellenistic Mystery Religions: Their Basic Ideas and Significance*. Pittsburgh Theological Monograph Series 15. Pittsburgh: Pickwick, 1978.

Relton, H. M. *A Study in Christology: The Problem of the Relation of the Two Natures in the Person of Christ*. London: SPCK, 1917.

Remus, Harold. *Pagan-Christian Conflict over Miracle in the Second Century*. Patristic Monograph Series 10. Cambridge, MA: Philadelphia Patristic Foundation, 1983.

———. *Jesus as Healer*. Understanding Jesus Today. Cambridge: Cambridge University Press, 1997.

Renan, Ernest. *Vie de Jésus*. Paris: Calmann-Lévy, 1863; 16th ed., 1879. [Published as the 1st volume of Renan's *Histoire du Christianisme*.]

———. *The Life of Jesus*. London: Trübner, 1864. Reprint, London: Matheson, 1890. [And many more reprints.]

———. *Essai psychologique sur Jésus Christ*. Paris: La Connaissance, 1921.

———. *Oeuvres Complètes*. Edited by Henriette Psichari. 10 vols. Paris: Calmann-Lévy, 1947–61.

Reuben, Julie. *The Making of the Modern University: Intellectual Transformation and the Marginalization of Morality*. Chicago: University of Chicago Press, 1996.

Reumann, John. "Jesus and Christology." In *The New Testament and Its Modern Interpreters*. Edited by Eldon Jay Epp and George W. MacRae. Atlanta: Scholars, 1989.

Reventlow, Henning Graf. "Das Arsenal der Bibelkritik des Reimarus: Die Auslegung der Bibel, insbesondere des Alten Testaments, bei den englischen Deisten." In *Hermann Samuel Reimarus (1694–1768). Ein "bekannter Unbekannte" der Aufklärung in Hamburg*, 44–65.

———. *The Authority of the Bible and the Rise of the Modern World*. Translated by John Bowden. London: SCM, 1984; Philadelphia: Fortress, 1985.

———. *History of Biblical Interpretation*. 4 vols. Translated by Leo Perdue and James O. Duke. SBL Resources for Biblical Study 50, 61–63. Atlanta: SBL Press, 2009–10.

Rhoads, David. "Social Criticism: Crossing Boundaries." In *Mark and Method*, edited by Janice Capel Anderson and Stephen D. Moore [2nd ed., 2008], 145–79.

Rhoads, David, Joanna Dewey, and Donald Michie. *Mark as Story: An Introduction to the Narrative of a Gospel*. Minneapolis: Fortress, 1982; 3rd ed., 2012.

Richardson, Alan. *The Miracle Stories of the Gospels*. London: SCM, 1941.

———. *History Sacred and Profane*. Bampton Lectures 1962. London: SCM, 1964.

Riches, John K. *Conflicting Mythologies: Identity Formation in the Gospels of Mark and Matthew*. Studies of the New Testament and Its World. Edinburgh: T&T Clark, 2000.

Riches, John, ed. *The New Cambridge History of the Bible*. Vol. 4, *From 1750 to the Present*. Cambridge: Cambridge University Press, 2015.

Ricoeur, Paul. *The Symbolism of Evil*. Translated by E. Buchanan. Boston: Beacon, 1967.

Ricoeur, Paul. *Memory, History, Forgetting*. Translated by Kathleen Blamey and David Pellauer. Chicago: University of Chicago Press, 2004.

Riesenfeld, Harald. "The Gospel Tradition and Its Beginnings." *Studia Evangelica: Papers Presented to the International Congress on "The Four Gospels in 1957" Held*

Bibliography

at Christ Church, Oxford, 1957. Edited by Kurt Aland et al. Vol. 1. TUGAL 73. Berlin: Akademie-Verlag, 1959. Reprint, *The Gospels Reconsidered: A Selection of Papers Read at the International Conference on the Four Gospels Oxford 1957*, 131–53. Oxford: Basil Blackwell, 1960.

Riesner, Rainer. *Jesus als Lehrer*. WUNT II/7. Tübingen: Mohr Siebeck, 1981; 3rd ed., 1988.

Ristow, Helmut, and Karl Matthiae, eds. *Der historische Jesus und der kerygmatische Christus. Beiträge zum Christusverständnis in Forschung und Verkündigung*. Berlin: Evangelische Verlagsanstalt, 1962.

Ritmeyer, Leen. "Imagining the Temple Known to Jesus and to Early Jews." In *Jesus and Temple*, edited by James H. Charlesworth, 19–57.

Ritschl, Albrecht Benjamin. *Die christliche Lehre von der Rechfertigung und Versöhnung*. 3 vols. Bonn: Marcus, 1870–74. ET: *The Christian Doctrine of Justification and Reconciliation: The Positive Development of the Doctrine*. Translated by J. S. Black, 1872. Edited by H. R. Mackintosh and A. B. Macaulay. Edinburgh: T&T Clark, 1900.

———. *Unterricht in der christlichen Religion*. Bonn: Marcus, 1875. Reprint, edited by Gerhard Ruhbach. Gütersloh: Gerd Mohn, 1966.

Roberts, R. "Jesus or Christ? An Appeal for Consistency." In *Jesus or Christ? The Hibbert Journal Supplement for 1909*, 270–82. London: Williams and Norgate, 1909.

Roberts, Tyler T. *Contesting Spirit: Nietzsche, Affirmation, Religion*. Princeton: Princeton University Press, 1998.

Robinson, Daniel A. "Two Radical Christologies: John A. T. Robinson and Maurice Wiles." PhD diss., Fuller Theological Seminary, 2005.

Robinson, James M. *Das Problem des Heiligen Geistes bei Wilhelm Herrmann*. Marburg: Gleiser, 1952.

———. *The Problem of History in Mark*. SBT 21. London: SCM, 1957.

———. *A New Quest of the Historical Jesus*. SBT 25. London: SCM; Naperville, IL: Allenson, 1959.

———. "Albert Schweitzer's *Quest of the Historical Jesus* Today" (1966). Reprint in *A New Quest of the Historical Jesus and Other Essays*, 172–95. Reprint in the introduction to Schweitzer, *The Quest of the Historical Jesus*, xi–xxiii. New York: Macmillan, 1968.

———. *A New Quest of the Historical Jesus and Other Essays*. Philadelphia: Fortress, 1983.

———. "How My Mind Has Changed (or Remained the Same)." In *SBL 1985 Seminar Papers*, 481–504.

———. "Theological Autobiography—1998." Reprint in *The Sayings Gospel Q: Collected Essays*, edited by Christoph Heil and Joseph Verheyden, 3–34.

———. *The Sayings Gospel Q: Collected Essays*. Edited by Christoph Heil and Joseph Verheyden. BETL 189. Leuven: Leuven University Press; Peeters, 2005.

———. "Nag Hammadi: The First Fifty Years." In *The Fifth Gospel*, edited by Stephen J. Patterson et al., 77–110.

———. "The Image of Jesus in Q." In *Jesus Then and Now: Images of Jesus in History and Christology*, edited by Marvin Meyer and Charles Hughes, 7–25.

———. *The Gospel of Jesus: In Search of the Original Good News*. San Francisco: HarperSanFrancisco, 2005.

Robinson, James M., ed. *The Future of Our Religious Past: Essays in Honour of Rudolf Bultmann*. Translated by Charles E. Carlston and Robert P. Scharlemann. London: SCM, 1971.

———. *The Nag Hammadi Library in English, Translated and Introduced by Members of the Coptic Gnostic Library Project of the Institute for Antiquity and Christianity, Claremont, California*. Leiden: Brill; San Francisco: Harper & Row, 1977; 3rd ed., 1988.

Robinson, James M., and Helmut Koester. *Trajectories through Early Christianity*. Philadelphia: Fortress, 1971.

Robinson, James M., Paul Hoffmann, John S. Kloppenborg, eds. *The Critical Edition of Q: Synopsis Including the Gospels of Matthew, Mark, Luke and Thomas with English, German, and French Translations of Q and Thomas*. Hermeneia. Minneapolis: Fortress; Leuven: Peeters, 2000.

Robinson, John A. T. *Jesus and His Coming: The Emergence of a Doctrine*. London: SCM, 1957.

———. *Twelve New Testament Studies*. SBT 34. London: SCM; Naperville, IL: Allenson, 1962.

———. *Honest to God*. London: SCM, 1963. 40th anniv. ed. with essays by Douglas John Hall and Rowan Williams. Louisville: Westminster John Knox, 2002.

———. *Exploration into God*. London: SCM, 1967.

———. *The Human Face of God*. London: SCM, 1973.

———. *Redating the New Testament*. London: SCM, 1976.

———. *Twelve More New Testament Studies*. London: SCM, 1984.

———. *The Priority of John*. Bampton Lectures 1984. Edited by F. J. Coakley. London: SCM, 1985.

Robinson, John A. T., and David L. Edwards, eds. *The Honest to God Debate*. London: SCM, 1963.

Rocca, Samuel. *Herod's Judea: A Mediterranean State in the Classical World*. TSAJ 122. Tübingen: Mohr Siebeck, 2008; Eugene, OR: Wipf & Stock, 2015.

Robinson, William Childs, Jr. *Der Weg des Herrn: Studien zur Geschichte und Eschatologie im Lukas-Evangelium. Ein Gespräch mit Hans Conzelmann*. TF 36. Hamburg: Evangelischer, 1964.

Rodis-Lewis, Geneviève. *Descartes: His Life and Thought*. Translated by Jane Marie Todd. Ithaca, NY: Cornell University Press, 1998.

Rodríguez, Rafael. *Structuring Early Christian Memory: Jesus in Tradition, Performance, and Text*. LNTS 407. New York: T&T Clark, 2010.

———. *Oral Tradition and the New Testament: A Guide for the Perplexed*. New York: T&T Clark, 2014.

Rogers, G. A. J., ed. *Locke's Philosophy: Context and Content*. Oxford: Oxford University Press, 1994.
Rohrbaugh, Richard, ed. *The Social Sciences and New Testament Interpretation*. Peabody, MA: Hendrickson, 1996.
Rollston, Christopher A., ed. *The Gospels according to Goulder: A North American Response*. Harrisburg, PA: Trinity Press International, 2002.
Rossi, Philip J., and Michael Wreen, eds. *Kant's Philosophy of Religion Reconsidered*. Indiana Series in the Philosophy of Religion. Bloomington, IN: Indiana University Press, 1991.
Rousseau, John J., and Rami Arav. *Jesus and His World: An Archaeological and Cultural Dictionary*. Minneapolis: Fortress, 1995.
Rowell, Geoffrey. *Hell and the Victorians: A Study in Nineteenth-Century Theological Controversies concerning Eternal Punishment and the Future Life*. Oxford: Clarendon, 1974.
———. *The Vision Glorious: Themes and Personalities of the Catholic Revival of Anglicanism*. Oxford: Oxford University Press, 1986.
Rowland, Christopher. *The Open Heaven: A Study of Apocalyptic in Judaism and Early Christianity*. New York: Crossroad, 1982. Reprint, Eugene, OR: Wipf & Stock, 2002.
———. *Christian Origins: From Messianic Movement to Christian Religion*. Minneapolis: Augsburg, 1985.
Rowland, Christopher, and Crispin H. T. Fletcher-Louis, eds. *Understanding, Studying, and Reading: New Testament Essays in Honour of John Ashton*. JSNTSup 153. Sheffield: Sheffield Academic Press, 1998.
Rowland, Christopher, and Christopher Tuckett, eds. *The Nature of New Testament Theology: Essays in Honour of Robert Morgan*. Foreword by Rowan Williams on "Reading, Criticism, Performance." Malden, MA: Blackwell, 2006.
Rudolph, Kurt. *Gnosis: The Nature and History of Gnosticism*. Translated and edited by R. McLachlan Wilson. San Francisco: Harper & Row, 1987.
Rumscheidt, H. Martin. *Revelation and Theology: An Analysis of the Barth-Harnack Correspondence of 1923*. Monograph Supplements to the Scottish Journal of Theology. Cambridge: Cambridge University Press, 1972.
———. *Adolf von Harnack: Liberal Theology at Its Height*. Minneapolis: Fortress, 1989.
Rush, Osmond. *The Reception of Doctrine: An Appropriation of Hans Robert Jauss' Reception Aesthetics and Literary Hermeneutics*. TGST 19. Rome: Pontifical Gregorian University, 1997.
Rylaarsdam, J. Coert. "Introduction: The Chicago School—and After." In *Transitions in Biblical Scholarship*, edited by Rylaarsdam, 1–16. Chicago: University of Chicago Press, 1968.
Sabourin, Leopold. *The Divine Miracles Discussed and Defended*. Rome: Officium Libri Catholici, 1977.

Safranski, Rüdiger. *Nietzsche: A Philosophical Biography*. Translated by Shelley Frisch. New York: Norton, 2002.

Sagovsky, Nicholas. *On God's Side: A Life of George Tyrrell*. Oxford: Clarendon, 1990.

Saldarini, Anthony. *Pharisees, Scribes, and Sadducees in Palestinian Society*. Grand Rapids: Eerdmans, 2001.

Samely, Alexander, in collaboration with Philip Alexander, Rocco Bernasconi, and Robert Hayward. *Profiling Jewish Literature in Antiquity: An Inventory, from Second Temple Texts to the Talmuds*. Oxford: Oxford University Press, 2013.

Sampley, J. Paul, ed. *Paul in the Greco-Roman World: A Handbook*. 2 vols. New York: T&T Clark, [2003]; rev. ed., 2016.

Sanday, William. *The Authorship and Historical Character of the Fourth Gospel*. London: Macmillan, 1872.

———. *Inspiration: Eight Lectures on the Early History and Origin of the Doctrine of Biblical Inspiration*. Bampton Lectures 1893. London: Longmans, Green, 1893.

———. *Sacred Sites of the Gospels*. Oxford: Clarendon, 1903.

———. *The Criticism of the Fourth Gospel: Eight Lectures on the Morse Foundation, Delivered in the Union Seminary, New York in October and November, 1904*. Oxford: Clarendon, 1905.

———. *Outlines of the Life of Christ*. Edinburgh: T&T Clark, 1905; 2nd ed., 1906.

———. *The Life of Christ in Recent Research*. Oxford: Clarendon, 1907.

———. *Christologies Ancient and Modern*. Oxford: Clarendon, 1910.

———. *Christology and Personality: Containing I. Christologies Ancient and Modern; II. Personality in Christ and in Ourselves*. Oxford: Clarendon, 1911.

———. *Bishop Gore's Challenge to Criticism: A Reply to the Bishop of Oxford's Open Letter on the Basis of Anglican Fellowship*. London: Longmans, 1914.

———. *Spirit, Matter, and Miracles: A Friendly Discussion between T. B. Strong, D.D., Dean of Christ Church, and W. Sanday, Canon of Christ Church*. Published privately, 1916.

———. *Form and Content in the Christian Tradition: A Friendly Discussion between W. Sanday, D.D. and N.P. Williams, M.A.* London: Longmans, 1916.

———. *Dr. Sanday's Nunc Dimittis: The Position of Liberal Theology: a Friendly Examination of the Bishop of Zanzibar's Open Letter entitled 'The Christ and His Critics'*. London: Faith, 1920.

———. *Divine Overruling*. Edinburgh: T&T Clark, 1920.

———. *Essays in Biblical Criticism and Exegesis*. Edited by Craig A. Evans and Stanley E. Porter with the assistance of Scott N. Dolff. JSNTSup 225. Sheffield: Sheffield Academic Press, 2001.

Sanday, William, and Arthur Cayley Headlam. *The Epistle to the Romans*. ICC. Edinburgh: T&T Clark, 1895.

Sanday, William, ed. *Studies in the Synoptic Problem. By Members of the University of Oxford*. Oxford: Clarendon, 1911.

Bibliography

Sanders, E. P. *Paul and Palestinian Judaism: A Comparison of Patterns of Religion.* London: SCM, 1977.

———. "On the Question of Fulfilling the Law in Paul and Rabbinic Judaism." *Donum Gentilicium*, edited by E. Bammel et al., 103–26.

———. *Jesus and Judaism.* London: SCM; Philadelphia: Fortress, 1985.

———. "Jesus and the Kingdom: The Restoration of Israel and the New People of God." *Jesus, the Gospels and the Church*, edited by Sanders, 225–39.

———. *Jewish Law from Jesus to the Mishnah: Five Studies.* London: SCM; Philadelphia: Trinity Press International, 1990.

———. "Defending the Indefensible." *JBL* 110 (1991): 463–77. [Critique of Ben F. Meyer's defense of Joachim Jeremias.]

———. *Judaism, Practice and Belief: 63 BCE-66 CE.* Philadelphia: Trinity Press International, 1992. Reprint, Philadelphia: Augsburg, 2016.

———. *The Historical Figure of Jesus.* London: Lane, Penguin, 1993.

———. "Comparing Judaism and Christianity: An Academic Autobiography." In *Redefining First-Century Jewish and Christian Identities*, edited by Fabian E. Udoh et al., 11–41.

———. *Paul: The Apostle's Life, Letters, and Thought.* Minneapolis: Fortress, 2015.

———. *Comparing Judaism and Christianity: Common Judaism, Paul, and the Inner and Outer in Ancient Religion.* Philadelphia: Fortress, 2016.

Sanders, E. P., ed. *Jesus, the Gospels and the Church: Essays in Honor of William R. Farmer.* Macon, GA; Mercer University Press, 1987.

Saucy, Mark. *The Kingdom of God in the Teaching of Jesus in 20th-Century Theology.* Dallas: Word, 1997.

Saunders, Ernest W. *Searching the Scriptures: A History of the Society of Biblical Literature, 1880–1980.* SBLBSNA 8. Chico, CA: Scholars, 1982.

Schaberg, Jane. *The Illegitimacy of Jesus: A Feminist Theological Interpretation of the Infancy Narratives.* New York: Crossroad, 1990.

Schäfer, Peter. *The History of the Jews in the Greco Roman World.* London: Routledge, 2003.

———. *Jesus in the Talmud.* Princeton, NJ: Princeton University Press, 2007.

———. *The Jewish Jesus: How Judaism and Christianity Shaped Each Other.* Princeton, NJ: Princeton University Press, 2012.

Schäfer, Peter, Michael Meerson, Yaacov Deutsch, eds. *Toledot Yeshu ("The Life Story of Jesus") Revisited, A Princeton Conference.* TSAJ 143. Tübingen: Mohr Siebeck, 2011.

Schäfer, Peter, and Hans G. Kippenberg, eds. *Envisioning Magic.* A Princeton Seminar and Symposium. SHR 75. Leiden: Brill, 1997.

Schäfer, Rolf. *Ritschl.* BHT 41. Tübingen: Mohr Siebeck, 1968.

Schaff, Philip, ed. *Creeds of Christendom.* 3 vols. New York: Harper, 1877. Reprint, Grand Rapids: Baker, 1977.

Schams, Christine. *Jewish Scribes in the Second Temple Period.* JSOTSup 291. Sheffield: Sheffield Academic Press, 1998.

A History of the Quests for the Historical Jesus

Scharlemann, Robert P. *Reflection and Doubt in the Thought of Paul Tillich.* New Haven, CT: Yale University Press, 1969.

Scheeben, Matthias Joseph. *The Mysteries of Christianity.* Translated by Cyril Vollert. St. Louis: Herder, 1864. Reprint, 1947.

Schiffman, Lawrence H. *Qumran and Jerusalem: Studies in the Dead Sea Scrolls and the History of Judaism.* Studies in the Dead Sea Scrolls and Related Literature. Grand Rapids: Eerdmans, 2010.

———. "The Importance of the Temple for Ancient Jews." *Jesus and the Temple*, edited by James H. Charlesworth, 75–93.

Schiffman, Lawrence H., and James C. VanderKam, eds. *Encyclopedia of the Dead Sea Scrolls.* 2 vols. Oxford: Oxford University Press, 2000.

Schlatter, Adolf. *Zur Topographie und Geschichte Palästinas.* Stuttgart: Calwer, 1893.

———. *Die philosophische Arbeit seit Descartes. Ihr ethischer und religiöser Ertrag.* Stuttgart: Calwer, 1906. Reprint, 1959.

———. *Die Theologie des Neuen Testaments.* Vol. 1, *Das Wort Jesu.* Stuttgart: Calwer, 1909; 2nd ed., *Die Geschichte des Christus*, 1920.

———. *Das Wunder in der Synagoge.* BFCT. Gütersloh: Bertelsmann, 1912.

———. *Der Evangelist Matthäus. Seine Sprache, sein Ziel, seine Selbstständigkeit. Ein Kommentar zum ersten Evangelium.* Stuttgart: Calwer, 1929; 6th unchanged ed., 1963.

———. *Der Evangelist Johannes. Wie er spricht, denkt, und glaubt. Ein Kommentar zum vierten Evangelium.* Stuttgart: Calwer, 1930; 3rd unchanged ed., 1960.

———. *Das Evangelium des Lukas. Aus seinen Quellen erklärt.* Stuttgart: Calwer, 1931; 2nd unchanged ed., 1960.

———. *Synagoge und Kirche bis zum Barkochba-Aufstand. Vier Studien zur Geschichte des Rabbinats und der jüdischen Christenheit in den ersten zwei Jahrhunderten. Mit einem Geleitwort von Joachim Jeremias.* Stuttgart: Calwer, 1966.

———. *The History of Christ: The Foundation for New Testament Theology.* Translated by Andreas J. Köstenberger. Grand Rapids: Baker, 1997.

Schlaudraff, Karl-Heinz. *"Heil als Geschichte"? Die Frage nach dem heilsgeschichtlichen Denken, dargestellt anhand der Konzeption Oscar Cullmanns.* BGBE 29. Tübingen: Mohr Siebeck, 1988.

Schleiermacher, Friedrich Daniel Ernst. *Der christliche Glaube nach den Grundsätzen der christlichen Kirche im Zusammenhange dargestellt.* Halle: Otto Hendel, 1821–22. Reprint of the 1st ed., edited by Hermann Peiter, as vol. 7 of the *Kritische Gesamtausgabe*. Berlin: de Gruyter, 1980–81.

———. *Der christliche Glaube.* 2nd ed. Halle: Otto Hendel, 1830. Reprint, edited by Martin Redeker. 2 vols. Berlin: de Gruyter, 1960.

———. *Das Leben Jesu. Vorlesungen an der Universität zu Berlin im Jahr 1832.* Edited by K. A. Rutenik. Berlin: Reimer, 1864.

———. *The Christian Faith in Outline.* Translated by D. M. Baillie. Edinburgh: W. F. Henderson, 1922.

Bibliography

———. *The Christian Faith*. Translated and edited by H. R. Mackintosh and J. S. Stewart. Edinburgh: T&T Clark, 1928. Reprint with introduction by Paul T. Nimmo. New York: T&T Clark, 2016.

———. *The Life of Jesus*. Translated by S. Maclean Gilmour. Edited by Jack C. Verheyden. Lives of Jesus. Philadelphia: Fortress, 1975.

———. *Christian Faith: A New Translation and Critical Edition*. 2 vols. Translated by Terrence N. Tice, Catherine L. Kelsey, and Edwina Lawlor. Edited by Catherine L. Kelsey and Terrence N. Tice. Louisville: Westminster John Knox, 2016.

Schmid, Heinrich Gottlob. *Abriss der vornehmsten deistischen Schriften, die in dem vorigen und gegenwärtigen Jahrhunderte in Engeland bekandt geworden sind; nebst Anmerkungen über dieselben und Nachrichten von den gegen sie hearausgekommenen Antworten. In verschieden Briefen an einen guten Freund*. Hannover: Schmid, 1755–56. [Translation of John Leland's *View of the Principal Deistical Writings*.]

Schmid, Johannes Heinrich. *Erkenntnis des geschichtlichen Christus bei Martin Kähler und bei Adolf Schlatter*. TZ Sonderband 5. Basel: Friedrich Reinhardt, 1978.

Schmidt, Johann Lorenz. *Beweis, dass das Christenthum so ald wie die Welt sey, nebst Herrn Jacob Fosters Widerlegung desselben*. Frankfurt and Leipzig: self-published, 1741. [Translation of Tindal's *Christianity as Old as the Creation*.]

Schmidt, Karl Ludwig. *Der Rahmen der Geschichte Jesu. Literarkritische Untersuchungen zur ältesten Jesusüberlieferung*. Berlin: Trowitzsch & Sohn, 1919. Reprint, Darmstadt: Wissenschaftliche Buchgesellschaft, 1964.

———. *Die Stellung der Evangelien in allgemeinen Literaturgeschichte*. Göttingen: Vandenhoeck & Ruprecht, 1923. ET: *The Place of the Gospels in the General History of Literature*. Translated by Byron R. McCane. With an introduction by John Riches. Columbia: University of South Carolina Press, 2002.

Schmidt, Thomas. "Mark 15:16–32: The Crucifixion Narrative and the Roman Triumphal Procession." *NTS* 41 (1995): 1–18.

———. "Jesus' Triumphal March to Crucifixion." *Bible Review* 13, no. 1 (1997): 30–37.

Schmiedel, Paul Wilhelm. "Gospels." In *Encyclopaedia Biblica*. Edited by T. K. Cheyne, columns 1761–1898.

———. *Die Hauptprobleme der Leben-Jesu Forschung*. Tübingen: Mohr Siebeck, 1902; 2nd ed., 1906.

———. "Die Person Jesu im Streite der Meinungen der Gegenwart." *Protestantische Monatshefte* 10 (1906): 257–82. Later published separately as *Die Person Jesu im Streite der Meinungen der Gegengwart*. Leipzig: Hensius, 1906.

———. *Das vierte Evangelium gegebüber die drei ersten*. Religionsgeschichtliche Volksbücher für die deutsche chrstliche Gegenwart. Tübingen: Mohr Siebeck, 1906.

———. *Jesus in Modern Criticism: A Lecture*. Translated by Maurice A. Canney. London: Black, 1907.

Schmithals, Walter. *An Introduction to the Theology of Rudolf Bultmann*. Translated by John Bowden. London: SCM, 1968.

A History of the Quests for the Historical Jesus

Schnackenburg, Rudolf. *The Gospel according to John*. 3 vols. Translated by Kevin Smyth et al. London: Burns & Oates; New York: Herder and Herder, 1968–82.

Schneemelcher, Wilhelm, ed. *New Testament Apocrypha, Revised Edition of the Collection edited by Edgar Hennecke*. Translated by R. McL. Wilson. 2 vols. Cambridge: James Clarke; Louisville: Westminster John Knox, 1991–92.

Schnelle, Udo. *Antidoketische Christologie Im Johannesevangelium: Eine Untersuchung zur Stellung des vierten Evangeliums in der Johanneischen Schule*. FRLANT. Göttingen: Vendenhoeck & Ruprecht, 1987. ET: *Antidocetic Christology in the Gospel of John*. Translated by Linda M. Maloney. Minneapolis: Fortress, 1992.

Schoberg, Gerry. *Perspectives of Jesus in the Writings of Paul: A Historical Examination of Shared Core Commitments with a View to Determining the Extents of Paul's Dependence on Jesus*. Princeton Theological Monograph Series 190. Eugene, OR: Pickwick, 2013.

Schofield, Robert E. *The Enlightenment of Joseph Priestley: A Study of His Life and Work from 1733 to 1773*. University Park, PA: Pennsylvania State University Press, 1997.

Schoonenberg, Piet. *The Christ: A Study of the God-Man Relationship in the Whole Creation and in Jesus Christ*. Translated by Della Couling. New York: Herder and Herder, 1971.

———. *Der Geist, das Wort und der Sohn. Eine Geist-Christologie*. Regensberg: Pustet, 2000.

Schopenhauer, Arthur. *Die Welt als Wille und Vorstellung*. Leipzig: Brockhaus, 1859. ET: *The World as Will and Representation*. Translated by E. F. J. Payne. 3 vols. New York: Dover, 1966.

Schotroff, Luise. *The Parables of Jesus*. Translated by Linda M. Maloney. Minneapolis: Fortress, 2006.

Schröder, Winfried. *Spinoza in der deutschen Frühaufklärung*. Würzburg: Königshausen und Neumann, 1987.

Schröter, Jens. "Jesus of Galilee: The Role of Location in Understanding Jesus." In *Jesus Research*, edited by James H. Charlesworth and Petr Pokorný, 36–55.

Schröter, Jens, ed. *The Apocryphal Gospels within the Context of Early Christian Theology*. BETL 260. Leuven: Peeters, 2013.

Schröter, Jens, and Ralph Brucker, eds. *Der historische Jesus. Tendenzen und Perspektiven der gegenwärtigen Forschung*. BZNW 114. Berlin: de Gruyter, 2002.

Schröter, Jens, Stefan Krauter, and Hermann Lichtenberger, eds. *Heil und Geschichte. Die Geschichtsbezogenheit des Heils und das Problem der Heilsgeschichte in der biblischen Tradition und in der theologischen Deutung*. WUNT 248. Tübingen: Mohr Siebeck, 2009.

Schubert, Paul. "Shirley Jackson Case, Historian of Early Christianity: An Appraisal." *JR* 29 (1949): 30–46.

Schultenover, David G. *A View from Rome: On the Eve of the Modernist Crisis*. New York: Fordham University Press, 1993.

Bibliography

———. *George Tyrrell: In Search of Catholicism*. Shepherdstown, WV: Patmos, 1981.

Schürer, Emil. *Lehrbuch der Neutestamentlichen Zeitgeschichte*. 1874. Retitled, *Geschichte des jüdischen Volkes im Zeitalter Jesus Christi*. Leipzig: Hinrichs, 1886–87. ET: *A History of the Jewish People in the Time of Jesus Christ*. Translated by J. Macpherson, S. Taylor, and P. Christie. Edinburgh: T&T Clark, 1890–91.

———. *The History of the Jewish People in the Age of Jesus Christ (175 B.C.–A.D. 135)*. Rev. ed. Edited by Geza Vermes, Fergus Millar. Pamela Vermes, and Matthew Black. 3 vols. [Vol. 3 in 2 parts.] Edinburgh: T&T Clark, 1973–87. Reprint, New York: T&T Clark, 2014.

———. "Das Wesen der christlichen Offenbarung nach dem Neuen Testament. Vortrag gehalten im wissenschaftlichen Predigerverein zu Hannover am 3. Mai 1899." *ZTK* 10 (1900): 1–39.

Schüssler Fiorenza, Elisabeth. *Jesus—Miriam's Child, Sophia's Prophet: Critical Issues in Feminist Christology*. New York: Continuum, 1994.

———. *Changing Horizons: Explorations in Feminist Interpretation*. Minneapolis: Fortress, 2013.

Schüssler Fiorenza, Elisabeth, ed. *Aspects of Religious Propaganda in Judaism and Early Christianity*. University of Notre Dame Center for the Study of Judaism and Christianity in Antiquity 2. Notre Dame, IN: University of Notre Dame Press, 1976.

Schwaiger, Georg, ed. *Historische Kritik in der Theologie. Beiträge zu ihrer Geschichte*. Studien zur Theologie und Geistesgeschichte des neunzehnten Jahrhunderts 32. Göttingen: Vandenhoeck & Ruprecht, 1980.

Schwartz, Daniel B. *The First Modern Jew: Spinoza and the History of an Image*. Princeton, NJ: Princeton University Press, 2012.

Schwartz, Daniel R. *Studies in the Jewish Background of Christianity*. WUNT 60. Tübingen: Mohr Siebeck, 1992.

Schweitzer, Albert. *Die Religionsphilosophie Kants von der "Kritik der reinen Vernunft" bis zur "Religion innerhalb der Grenzen der blossen Vernunft"*. Freiburg: Mohr Siebeck, 1899.

———. *Das Abendmahlsproblem auf Grund der wissenschaftlichen Forschung des 19. Jahrhunderts und der historischen Berichte*. Heft 1, *Das Abendmahl im Zusammenhang mit dem Leben Jesu und der Geschichte des Urchristentums*. Tübingen: Mohr Siebeck, 1901.

———. *Das Messianitäts- und Leidenschaftsgeheimnis. Eine Skizze des Lebens Jesu*. Tübingen: Mohr Siebeck, 1902.

———. *Von Reimarus zu Wrede. Eine Geschichte der Leben-Jesu-Forschung*. Tübingen: Mohr Siebeck, 1906.

———. *Paul and His Interpreters: A Critical History*. Translated by W. Montgomery. [1911.] London: Black; New York: Macmillan, 1912.

———. *Geschichte der Leben-Jesu-Forschung*. 2nd ed. Tübingen: Mohr Siebeck, 1913; 6th reprint, 1951.

———. *The Mystery of the Kingdom of God: The Secret of Jesus' Messiahship and Passion*. Translated by Walter Lowrie. London: Black, 1914.

———. *The Philosophy of Civilization*. Translated by John Naish. Vol. 1, *The Decay and Restoration of Civilization*. Vol. 2, *Civilization and Ethics*. London: Black, 1923.

———. *The Mysticism of the Apostle Paul*. Translated by W. Montgomery. [1930.] London: Black, 1931.

———. *The Quest of the Historical Jesus: A Critical Study of Its Progress from Reimarus to Wrede*. Translated by W. Montgomery. Preface by F. C. Burkitt. London: Black, 1910. Reprint, 3rd ed. with introduction by Schweitzer, 1954. Reprint with introduction by James M. Robinson. New York: Macmillan, 1968.

———. *My Life and Thought: An Autobiography*. Translated by C. T. Campion. [1933.] Reprint, London: Guild Books, Allen & Unwin, 1955.

———. *The Psychiatric Study of Jesus: Exposition and Criticism*. Translated by Charles R. Joy. Foreword by Winfred Overholser. Boston: Beacon, 1958.

———. *The Kingdom of God and Primitive Christianity*. Edited by Ulrich Neuenerschwander. Translated by L. A. Garrard. London: Black, 1968. Full text, *Reich Gottes und Christentum*. Edited by Ulrich Luz, Ulrich Neuenerschwander, and Johann Zürcher. Munich: Beck, 1995.

———. *Letters, 1905–1965*. Edited by Hans Walter Bähr. Translated by Joachim Neugroschel. New York: Macmillan, 1972.

———. *The Problem of the Lord's Supper according to the Scholarly Research of the Nineteenth Century and the Historical Accounts*. Vol. 1, *The Lord's Supper in Relationship to the Life of Jesus and the History of the Early Church*. Translated by A. J. Mattill Jr. Edited by John Reumann. Macon, GA: Mercer University Press, 1982.

———. *The Quest of the Historical Jesus*. Edited by John Bowden. 1st complete ed. London: SCM, 2000; Minneapolis: Fortress, 2001.

Schweizer, Eduard, *Neotestamentica. Deutsche und Englische Aufsätze 1951–1963*. Zürich: Zwingli, 1963.

———. *Beiträge zur Theologie des Neuen Testaments. Neutestamentliche Aufsätze (1955–1970)*. Zürich: Zwingli, 1970.

———. *Jesus Christus*. Munich: Siebenstern, 1968. ET: *Jesus*. Translated by David E. Green. NTL. London: SCM, 1971.

Scott, James M., ed. *Exile: Old Testament, Jewish, and Christian Conceptions*. JSJSup 56. Leiden: Brill, 1997.

———. *Restoration: Old Testament, Jewish, and Christian Perspectives*. JSJSup 72. Leiden: Brill, 2001).

Scott, Martin. *Sophia and the Johannine Jesus*. JSNTSup 71. Sheffield: JSOT, 1992.

Seeley, David. "Jesus and the Cynics Revisited." *JBL* 116 (1997): 704–12.

Seeley, John R. *Ecce Homo: A Survey of the Life and Work of Jesus Christ*. London: Macmillan; Boston: Roberts, 1865; 2nd ed., 1866. Reprint, London: Dent; New York: Dutton, 1908. [Reprints lack the subtitle.]

Bibliography

Segovia, Fernando F., ed. *"What Is John?"* Vol. 1, *Readers and Readings of the Fourth Gospel.* Vol. 2, *Literary and Social Readings of the Fourth Gospel.* SymS 3 and 7. Atlanta: Scholars, 1996–98.

Seland, Torrey, ed. *Reading Philo: A Handbook to Philo of Alexandria.* Grand Rapids: Eerdmans, 2014.

Sell, Alan P. F. *John Locke and the Eighteenth-Century Divines.* Cardiff: University of Wales Press, 1997.

Sellers, R. V. *Two Ancient Christologies: A Study of the Christological Thought of the Schools of Alexandria and Antioch in the Early History of Christian Doctrine.* London: SPCK, 1940.

———. *The Council of Chalcedon: A Historical and Doctrinal Survey.* London: SPCK, 1953.

Selwyn, E. G., ed. *Essays Catholic and Critical, by Members of the Anglican Communion.* London: SPCK; New York: Macmillan, 1926.

Semler, Johann Salomo. *Abhandlung von freier Untersuchung des Canon.* [Halle, 1771–75.] Texte zur Kirchen- und Theologiegeschichte 5. Gütersloh: Gerd Mohn, 1967.

———. *Beantwortung der Fragmente eines ungenannten insbesondere vom Zweck Jesu und seiner Jünger. Andere verbesserte Auflage. Anhang zur Beantwortung des Ungenannten. Bekant gemacht von D. Joh. Salomo Semler.* Halle, 1780.

Servetus, M. *The Two Treatises of Servetus on the Trinity: On the Errors of the Trinity Seven Books, A.D. MCXXXI; Dialogues on the Trinity Two Books; On the Righteousness of Christ's Kingdom Four Chapters.* Translated by Earl Morse Wilbur. HTS 16. Cambridge, MA: Harvard University Press; London: Oxford University Press, 1932. Reprint, Eugene, OR: Wipf & Stock, 2013.

———. *The Restoration of Christianity.* Translated by Christopher A. Hoffman and Marian Hiller. Lewiston, NY; Queenston, ON: Mellen, 2007.

———. *Thirty Letters to Calvin, Preacher to the Genevans; And Sixty Signs of the Kingdom of the Antichrist which is Now at Hand.* Translated by Christopher A. Hoffman and Marian Hiller. Lewiston, NY; Queenston, ON: Mellen, 2010.

Sextus Empiricus. LCL. 4 vols. Translated by R. G. Bury. London: Heinemann; Cambridge, MA: Harvard University Press, 1933–4199.

———. *Outlines of Scepticism.* Edited and translated by Julia Annas and Jonathan Barnes. 2nd ed. Cambridge: Cambridge University Press, 2000.

Seybold, Klaus, and Ulrich B. Mueller. *Sickness and Healing.* Translated by Douglas W. Stott. Nashville: Abingdon, 1981.

Shea, Victor, and William Whitla, eds. *Essays and Reviews: The 1860 Text and Its Reading.* Charlottesville, VA: University of Virginia Press, 2000.

Sherlock, Thomas. *The Tryal of the Witnesses of the Resurrection of Jesus* [1743] and *The Use and Intent of Prophecy* [1728]. Combined facsimile reprint of *The Tryal* [11th ed.] and *The Use and Intent of Prophecy.* New York: Garland, 1978.

Sherwin-White, A. N. *Roman Society and Roman Law in the New Testament.* Sarum Lectures 1960–61. Oxford: Clarendon, 1963. Reprint, 1965.

Shieber, Joseph. *Testimony: A Philosophical Introduction.* New York: Routledge, 2015.

Shiner, Whitney Taylor. *Follow Me! Disciples in Markan Rhetoric.* SBLDS 145. Atlanta: Scholars, 1995.

Shillington, V. George. *James and Paul: The Politics of Identity at the Turn of the Ages.* Minneapolis: Fortress, 2015.

Shoemaker, Stephen. "The Emerging Distinction between Theology and Religion at Nineteenth-Century Harvard University." *HTR* Centennial Issue, 1908–2008, edited by François Bovon, 417–30.

Shoemaker, Stephen J. *Mary in Early Christian Faith and Devotion.* New Haven, CT: Yale University Press, 2016.

Shortt, Rupert. *Rowan's Rule: The Biography of the Archbishop of Canterbury.* Grand Rapids: Eerdmans, 2008.

Sider, John W. "Rediscovering the Parables: The Logic of the Jeremias Tradition." *JBL* 102 (1983): 61–83.

Siggins, I. D. K. *Martin Luther's Doctrine of Christ.* New Haven, CT: Yale University Press, 1970.

Siliezar, Carlos Raúl Sosa. *Creation Imagery in the Gospel of John.* LNTS 546. London: T&T Clark, 2015.

Silva, Moisés. "Bilingualism and the Character of Palestinian Greek." *Biblica* 61 (1980): 198–219.

Sim, David C. *The Gospel of Matthew and Christian Judaism: The History and Social Setting of the Matthean Community.* Studies of the New Testament and Its World. Edinburgh: T&T Clark, 1998.

Simon, Richard. *Histoire critique du Nouveau Testament.* Rotterdam, 1689.

———. *Nouvelles observations sur le texte et les versions du Nouveau Testament.* Paris, 1695.

Singer, Peter. *Hegel.* Oxford: Oxford University Press, 1983.

Skinner, Christopher W., and Kelly R. Iverson, eds. *Unity and Diversity in the Gospels and Paul: Essays in Honor of Frank J. Matera.* SBL Early Christianity and Its Literature 7. Atlanta: SBL Press, 2012.

Skinner, Christopher W., and Matthew Ryan Hauge, eds. *Character Studies and the Gospel of Mark.* LNTS 483. New York: T&T Clark, 2014.

Slocum, Robert Boak. *Light in a Burning Glass: A Systematic Presentation of Austin Farrer's Theology.* Columbia: University of South Carolina Press, 2007.

Smart, Ninian, John Clayton, Steven T. Katz, and Patrick Sherry, eds. *Nineteenth Century Religious Thought in the West.* 3 vols. Cambridge: Cambridge University Press, 1985.

Smedes, Lewis B. *The Incarnation: Trends in Modern Anglican Thought.* Kampen: Kok, 1953.

Smith, Carl B., II. *No Longer Jews: The Search for Gnostic Origins.* Peabody, MA: Hendrickson, 2004.

Smith, Dwight Moody. *The Composition and Order of the Fourth Gospel: Bultmann's Literary Theory.* New Haven, CT: Yale University Press, 1965.

———. "B. W. Bacon on John and Mark." *Perspectives in Religious Studies* 8 (1981): 201–18. Reprint in Smith, *Johannine Christianity: Essays on Its Setting, Sources, and Theology*, 106–27. Columbia: University of South Carolina Press, 1984.

———. *John among the Gospels: The Relationship in Twentieth-Century Research.* Minneapolis: Fortress, 1992; 2nd ed., Columbia: University of South Carolina Press, 2001.

———. *The Theology of the Gospel of John.* Cambridge: Cambridge University Press, 1995.

———. *The Theology of the Gospel of John.* Cambridge: Cambridge University Press, 1995.

———. "Redaction Criticism, Genre, and the Historical Jesus in the Gospel of John." In *Jesus Research*, edited by James H. Charlesworth, 624–33.

Smith, D. Moody, Jr. "The Historical Jesus in Paul Tillich's Christology." *JR* 46 (1966): 131–47. See also Paul Tillich, "Rejoinder," *JR* 46 (1966): 184–96.

Smith, Geoffrey S. *Guilt by Association: Heresy Catalogues in Early Christianity.* Oxford: Oxford University Press, 2015.

Smith, H. Maynard. *Frank, Bishop of Zanzibar: Life of Frank Weston, D.D., 1871–1924.* London: SPCK, 1926.

Smith, H. Shelton, ed. *Horace Bushnell.* Library of Protestant Thought. Oxford: Oxford University Press, 1965.

Smith, Jonathan Z. "No News Is Good News: Aretalogy and Gospel." In *Christianity, Judaism and Other Greco-Roman Cults: Studies for Morton Smith at Sixty*, edited by Jacob Neusner, 1:21–38. SJLA 12. Leiden: Brill, 1975. Reprint in Smith, *Map Is Not Territory: Studies in the History of Religions*, 190–207. Chicago: University of Chicago Press, 1993.

Smith, Morton. "A Comparison of Early Christian and Early Rabbinic Tradition." *JBL* 82 (1963): 169–76.

———. *Clement of Alexandria and a Secret Gospel of Mark.* Cambridge, MA: Harvard University Press, 1973.

———. *The Secret Gospel: The Discovery and Interpretation of the Secret Gospel according to Mark.* New York: Harper & Row, 1973.

———. *Jesus the Magician.* New York: Harper & Row, 1978.

———. "On the History of ΑΠΟΚΑΛΥΠΤΩ and ΑΠΟΚΑΛΥΨΙΣ." In *Apocalypticism in the Mediterranean World and the Near East*, edited by David Hellholm, 9–20.

Snodgrass, Klyne R. *Stories with Intent: A Comprehensive Guide to the Parables of Jesus.* Grand Rapids: Eerdmans, 2008.

Socinus, Faustus. *De Unigeniti filii Dei Existentia in Erasmum Iohannnis, et Faustum Socinum Disputatio.* [2nd ed. Racovia, 1626.] Facsimile reprint, Kessinger, n.d.

Sorell, Tom, ed. *The Cambridge Companion to Hobbes.* Cambridge: Cambridge University Press, 1996.

Soskice, Janet M. *Metaphor and Religious Language.* Oxford: Clarendon, 1985.

———. *The Sisters of Sinai: How Two Lady Adventurers Discovered the Hidden Gospels.* New York: Knopf, 2009.

Soulen, Richard N., and R. Kendall Soulen. *Handbook of Biblical Criticism.* 4th ed. Louisville: Westminster John Knox, 2011.

Sparrow, J. A. H. *Mark Pattison and the Idea of a University.* Cambridge: Cambridge University Press, 1967.

Spinoza, Baruch. *Tractatus Theologico-Politicus.* Edited by Carl Gebhard. Heidelberg: Winter, 1925. Reprint, translated by Samuel Shirley. With introduction by Brad S. Gregory. Leiden: Brill, 1989.

———. *Tractatus Theologico-Politicus* [1669]. ET: *Theological-Political Treatise.* Edited by Jonathan Israel. Translated by Michael Silverthorne and Jonathan Israel. Cambridge Texts in the History of Philosophy. Cambridge: Cambridge University Press, 2007.

———. *The Collected Works of Spinoza.* Translated and edited by Edwin Curley. 2 vols. Princeton, NJ: Princeton University Press, 1985, 2016. [Curley's edition of the *Theological-Political Treatise* is given in 2:65–354. The *Ethics* is in 1:408–617.]

Springborg, Patricia ed. *The Cambridge Companion to Hobbes's Leviathan.* Cambridge: Cambridge University Press, 2007.

Springs, Jason S. *Towards A Generous Orthodoxy: Prospects for Hans Frei's Postliberal Theology.* Oxford: Oxford University Press, 2010.

Stackhouse, Thomas. *A Fair State of the Controversy between Mr. Woolston and His Adversaries.* London, 1730.

Stählin, Gustav. "Die Gleichnishandlungen Jesu." In *Kosmos und Ekklesia. Festschrift für Wilhelm Stählin zu seinem siebzigsten Geburtstag, 24. September 1953*, edited by Heinz-Dietrich Wendland, 9–22. Kassel: Johannes Stauda-Verlag, 1953.

Standaert, Benoît. *L'Évangile selon Marc. Composition et genre littéraire.* Nijmegen: Stichting Studenpers, 1978. Reprint, Brugge: Zevenkerken, 1984.

———. *L'évgile selon Marc. Commentaire.* 12th ed. Paris: Les Éditions du Cerf, 1997.

Stanglin, Keith D., and Thomas H. McCall. *Jacob Arminius: Theologian of Grace.* Oxford: Oxford University Press, 2012.

Stanton, Graham N. *Jesus of Nazareth in New Testament Preaching.* SNTSMS 27. Cambridge: Cambridge University Press, 1974.

———. *A Gospel for a New People: Studies in Matthew.* Edinburgh: T&T Clark, 1992.

———. *Gospel Truth? New Light on Jesus and the Gospels.* London: HarperCollins, 1995.

———. *Jesus and the Gospel.* Cambridge: Cambridge University Press, 2004.

———. "Jesus of Nazareth: A Magician and a False Prophet Who Deceived God's People?" In *Jesus and the Gospel*, edited by J. B. Green, 227–47. Reprint in Stanton, *Jesus and the Gospel*, 127–47.

Bibliography

Stanton, Graham N., ed. *The Interpretation of Matthew*. Studies in New Testament Interpretation. 2nd ed. Edinburgh: T&T Clark, 1995.

Stanton, Graham N., Bruce W. Longenecker, and Stehen C. Barton, eds. *The Holy Spirit and Christian Origins: Essays in Honor of James D.G. Dunn*. Grand Rapids: Eerdmans, 2004. [List of Dunn's publications, 360–75.]

Stassen, Glenn H. "The Fourteen Triads of the Sermon on the Mount (Matthew 5:21–7:12)." *JBL* 122, no. 2 (2003): 267–308.

Stassen, Glenn H., and David P. Gushee. *Kingdom Ethics: Following Jesus in Contemporary Context*. Downers Grove, IL: InterVarsity Press, 2003.

Stauffer, Ethelbert. *Christ and the Caesars: Historical Sketches*. Translated by K. and R. Gregor Smith. London: SCM; Philadelphia: Westminster, 1955.

———. *New Testament Theology*. Translated by John Marsh. London: SCM, 1955.

———. *Jerusalem und Rom im Zeitalter Jesu Christi*. Bern: Francke, 1957.

———. *Jesus. Gestalt und Geschichte*. Bern: Franke, 1957.

———. *Jesus and His Story*. Translated by Richard and Clara Winston. New York: Knopf, 1959. Reprint, translated by Dorothea M. Barton. London: SCM, 1960.

———. *Die Botschaft Jesu. Damals und Heute*. Bern: Francke, 1959.

———. *Jesus, Paulus und Wir. Antwort auf einen Offenen Brief von Paul Althaus, Walter Künneth und Wilfried Joest*. Hamburg: Wittig, 1961.

———. *Jesus and the Wilderness Community at Qumran*. Translated by Hans Spalteholz. FBBS 10. Philadelphia: Fortress, 1964.

———. *Jesus war ganz anders*. Hamburg: Wittig, 1967.

———. "Jesus, Geschichte und Verkündigung." In *ANRW*, 2.25.1: 3–130.

Stead, Cristopher. *Divine Substance*. Oxford: Clarendon, 1977.

Steck, Karl Gerhard. *Die Idee der Heilsgeschichte. Hoffmann, Schlatter, Cullmann*. TS 56. Zollikon: Evangelischer, 1959.

Steenburg, Dave. "The Case against the Synonymity of ΜΟΡΦΗ and ΕΙΚΩΝ." *JSNT* 34 (1988): 77–86.

Stegemann, Ekkehard W., and Wolfgang Stegemann. *The Jesus Movement: A Social History of Its First Century*. Translated by O. C. Dean Jr. Minneapolis: Fortress, 1999.

Stegemann, Wolfgang, Bruce J. Malina, and Gerd Theissen, eds. *The Social Setting of Jesus and the Gospels*. Minneapolis: Fortress, 2002.

Stein, Stephen J., ed. *The Encyclopedia of Apocalypticism*. Vol. 3, *Apocalypticism in the Modern Period and the Contemporary Age*. New York: Continuum, 2000.

Steinmetz, David C. *Luther in Context*. Grand Rapids: Baker, 1995; 2nd ed., 2002.

Stemberger, Günter. *Jewish Contemporaries of Jesus: Pharisees, Sadducees, Essenes*. Translation by Allan W. Mahnke. Minneapolis: Fortress, 1995.

Stendahl, Krister. *The School of St. Matthew and Its Use of the Old Testament*. Lund: Gleerup, 1954; 2nd ed., 1968.

Stephen, Leslie. *History of English Thought in the Eighteenth Century*. 2 vols. [1876.] Reprint of 3rd ed., 1902. New York: Harcourt, Brace; London: Rupert-Hart Davis, 1962.

A History of the Quests for the Historical Jesus

Stephenson, Alan M. G. *The First Lambeth Conference 1867.* London: SPCK, 1967.

———. *Anglicanism and the Lambeth Conferences.* London SPCK, 1978.

———. *The Rise and Decline of English Modernism.* Hulsean Lectures 1979–1980. London: SPCK, 1984.

Steudel, Annette. "Melchizedek." In *Encyclopedia of the Dead Sea Scrolls*, edited by Lawrence H. Schiffman and James C. VanderKam, 1:535–37.

Stevenson, Kenneth, ed. *A Fallible Church.* London: Darton, Longman & Todd, 2008.

Stewart, John W., and James H. Moorhead, eds. *Charles Hodge Revisited: A Critical Appraisal of His Life and Work.* Grand Rapids: Eerdmans, 2002.

Stewart, Matthew. *Nature's God: The Heretical Origins of the American Republic.* New York: Norton, 2014.

———. *The Courtier and the Heretic: Leibniz, Spinoza, and the Fate of God in the Modern World.* New York: Norton, 2006.

Stewart, Robert B., ed. *The Message of Jesus: John Dominic Crossan and Ben Witherington III in Dialogue.* Minneapolis: Fortress, 2013.

Still, E. Todd, and David E. Wilhite, eds. *Tertullian and Paul.* Pauline and Patristic Scholars in Debate. New York: T&T Clark, 2017.

———. *The Apostolic Fathers and Paul.* Pauline and Patristic Scholars in Debate. New York: T&T Clark. 2013.

Stonehouse, N. B. *J. Gresham Machen: A Biographical Memoir.* Grand Rapids: Eerdmans, 1954.

Storr, Richard J. *The Beginnings of Graduate Education in America.* Chicago: University of Chicago Press, 1953.

Strack, H. L., and Paul Billerbeck. *Kommentar zum Neuen Testament aus Talmud und Midrasch.* 4 vols. Munich: Beck, 1924–28. [Vols. 5–6 and index edited by Joachim Jeremias, assisted by Kurt Rudolf.]

Strack, H. L., and G. Stemberger. *An Introduction to the Talmud and Midrash.* Translated by Markus Bockmuehl. Foreword by Jacob Neusner. Edinburgh: T&T Clark, 1991; Minneapolis: Fortress, 1992.

Strange, Roderick. *Newman and the Gospel of Christ.* Oxford: Oxford University Press, 1981.

Strauss, David Friedrich. *Das Leben Jesu kritisch Bearbeitet.* 2 vols. Tübingen: Osiander, dated 1835–36, but actually 1835.

———. *Charakteristiken und Kritiken. Eine Sammlung zerstreuten Aufsätze aus den Gebieten der Theologie, Anthroplogie und Aesthetik.* Leipzig: Wigand, 1839.

———. *The Life of Jesus Critically Examined.* Translated by George Eliot from 4th German ed., 1840. 3 vols. London: Allen, 1846.

———. *Streitschriften zur Vertheidigung meiner Schrift über das Leben Jesu und zur Charakteristik der gegenwärtigen Theologie. (Erster Band), Erstes bis drittes Heft.* Tübingen: Osiander, 1837. Reprint in one vol., Hildesheim: Olms, 1980.

———. *Hermann Samuel Reimarus und seine Schutzschrift für die vernünftigen Verehrer Gottes*. Leipzig: Brockhaus, 1862. Reprint, Hildesheim: Olms, 1991.

———. *Das Leben Jesu für das deutsche Volk bearbeitet*. Leipzig, 1864. ET: *A New Life of Jesus*. 2 vols. 2nd ed. London: Williams and Norgate, 1879.

———. *Der Christus des Glaubens und der Jesus der Geschichte. Eine Kritik des Schleiermacherschen Lebens Jesu*. Berlin: Franz Duncker, 1865. Reprint, edited by Hans Jürgen Geischer. Texte zur Kirchen- und Theologiegeschichte 14. Gütersloh: Gerd Mohn, 1971.

———. *Der alte und der neue Glaube. Ein Benkenntnis*. Leipzig: Wigand, 1872.

———. *The Old Faith and the New*. Translated by Mathilde Blind [1873]. 2 vols. Combined vol. with introduction and notes by G. A. Wells. Amherst, NY; Oxford: Prometheus, [1873], 1997.

———. *The Life of Jesus Critically Examined*. Reprint of Eliot's translation with corrections, 1 vol., with introduction by Peter C. Hodgson. Lives of Jesus. Philadelphia: Fortress, 1972; London: SCM, 1973.

———. *The Christ of Faith and the Jesus of History: A Critique of Schleiermacher's Life of Jesus*. Translated and edited by Leander E. Keck. Lives of Jesus. Philadelphia: Fortress, 1977.

———. *In Defence of My Life of Jesus against the Hegelians*. Partial translation of the *Streitschriften* by Marilyn Chapin Massey. Hamden: Archon, 1983.

Strauss, Leo. *Natural Right and History*. Chicago: University of Chicago Press, 1954.

Strecker, Georg, ed. *Jesus Christus in Historie und Theologie. Neutestamentliche Festschrift für Hans Conzelmann zum 60. Geburtstag*. Tübingen: Mohr Siebeck, 1975. [Conzelmann bibliography, 549–57.]

Streeter, Burnett Hillman. *The Four Gospels, A Study of Origins: Treating of the Manuscript Tradition, Sources, Authorship, & Dates*. London: Macmillan, 1924.

———. *Reality: A New Correlation of Science and Religion*. New York: Macmillan, 1926.

———. *The Primitive Church: Studied with Special Reference to the Origins of the Christian Ministry*. Hewett Lectures at Union Theological Seminary, New York, 1928. London: Macmillan, 1929.

———. *The Buddha and the Christ: An Exploration of the Meaning of the Universe and of the Purpose of Human Life*. Bampton Lectures for 1932. London: Macmillan, 1932.

Streeter, B. H., ed. *Foundations: A Statement of Christian Belief in Terms of Modern Thought by Seven Oxford Men*. London: Macmillan, 1912.

———. *The Spirit: God and His Relation to Man Considered from the Standpoint of Philosophy, Psychology and Art*. London: Macmillan, 1921.

Streett, R. Alan. *Subversive Meals: An Analysis of the Lord's Supper under Roman Domination during the First Century*. Eugene, OR: Pickwick, 2013.

Strobel, August. *Die Stunde der Wahrheit. Untersuchungen zum Strafverfahren gegen Jesu*. WUNT 21. Tübingen: Mohr Siebeck, 1980.

Strong, Rowan, and Carol Engelhardt Herringer, eds. *Edward Bouverie Pusey and the Oxford Movement*. London: Anthem, 2012.

Strousma, Guy G. *The Making of Abrahamic Religions in Late Antiquity*. Oxford Studies in Abrahamic Religions. Oxford: Oxford University Press, 2015.

Struthers Malbon, Elizabeth. *Narrative Space and Mythic Meaning in Mark*. New York: Harper & Row, 1986.

Stuckenbruck, Loren T. *Myth of Rebellious Angels: Studies in Second Temple Judaism and New Testament Texts*. Grand Rapids: Eerdmans, 2017.

Stuhlmacher, Peter. "Adolf Schlatter's Interpretation of Scripture." *NTS* 24 (1978): 433–46.

———. *Jesus of Nazareth—Christ of Faith*. Translated by Siegfried S. Schatzmann. Peabody, MA: Hendrickson, 1993.

Stuhlmacher, Peter, ed. *The Gospel and the Gospels*. Translated by John Bowden and John Vriend. Grand Rapids: Eerdmans, 1991.

Stump, Eleonore, and Norman Kretzmann, eds. *The Cambridge Companion to Augustine*. Cambridge: Cambridge University Press, 2001.

Suderman, Jeffrey M. *Orthodoxy and Enlightenment: George Campbell in the Eighteenth Century*. McGill-Queen's Studies in the History of Ideas 32. Montreal: McGill-Queen's University Press, 2001.

Suggs, M. Jack. *Wisdom, Christology, and Law in Matthew's Gospel*. Cambridge, MA: Harvard University Press, 1970.

Sullivan, Robert E. *John Toland and the Deist Controversy: A Study in Adaptation*. Cambridge, MA: Harvard University Press, 1982.

Surenhusius, Guilielmus. *Tractatus in quo secudum Veterum Theologorum Hebraeorum formulas allegandi, & modus interpretandi, conciliantur loca ex V. in Nov. Test. Allegata*. Amsterdam, 1713.

Swinburne, Richard. *The Concept of Miracle*. London: Macmillan, 1970.

Swinburne, Richard, ed. *Miracles*. New York: Macmillan, 1989.

Sykes, Norman. *William Wake, Archbishop of Canterbury 1657–1737*. 2 vols. Cambridge: Cambridge University Press, 1957.

Sykes, S. W., and J. P. Clayton, eds. *Christ, Faith and History: Cambridge Studies in Christology*. Cambridge: Cambridge University Press, 1972.

Sykes, Stephen W. "The Strange Persistence of Kenotic Christology." In *Being and Truth: Essays in Honour of John Macquarrie*, edited by Alistair Kee and Eugene T. Long, 349–75. London: SCM, 1986.

Sykes, Stephen, John Booty, and Jonathan Knight, eds. *The Study of Anglicanism*. London: SPCK; Minneapolis: Fortress, 1988; 2nd ed., 1998.

Tabb, Brian J. *Suffering in Ancient Worldview: Luke, Seneca and 4 Maccabees in Dialogue*. LNTS 569. New York: T&T Clark, 2017.

Tabor, James B. *Paul and Jesus: How the Apostle Transformed Christianity*. New York: Simon & Schuster, 2012.

Bibliography

Tait, Michael and Peter Oakes, eds. *Torah in the New Testament: Papers Delivered at the Manchester-Lausanne Seminar of June 2008.* LNTS 401. New York: T&T Clark, 2009.

Talbert, Charles H. "Biographies of Philosophers and Rulers as Instruments of Religious Propaganda in Mediterranean Antiquity." *ANRW,* 2.16.2 (1978): 1619–51.

Tanner, Norman P., ed. *Decrees of the Ecumenical Councils.* Original text established by G. Alberigo, J. A. Dosetti, P.-P. Joannou, C. Leonardi, and P. Prodi in consultation with H. Jedin. 2 vols. London: Sheed & Ward; Washington, DC: Georgetown University Press, 1990.

Tavard, George H. *Paul Tillich and the Christian Message.* London: Burns and Oates, 1962.

Taylor, Joan E. *The Immerser: John the Baptist within Second Temple Judaism.* Grand Rapids: Eerdmans, 1997.

Taylor, Mark Kline, ed. *Paul Tillich: Theologian of the Boundaries.* London: Collins, 1987.

Taylor, Vincent. *The Historical Evidence for the Virgin Birth.* Oxford: Clarendon, 1920.

———. *Behind the Third Gospel: A Study in the Proto-Luke Hypothesis.* Oxford: Clarendon, 1926.

———. *The Formation of the Gospel Tradition.* London: Macmillan, 1933; expanded 2nd ed., 1935.

———. *Jesus and His Sacrifice: A Study of the Passion-Sayings in the Gospels.* London: Macmillan, 1937.

———. *The Atonement in New Testament Teaching.* London: Epworth, 1940; 3rd ed., 1958.

———. *Forgiveness and Reconciliation: A Study in New Testament Theology.* London: Macmillan, 1941.

———. *The Gospel according to St. Mark: The Greek Text with Introduction, Notes, and Indexes.* London: Macmillan, 1952.

———. *The Names of Jesus.* London: Macmillan, 1953.

———. *The Life and Ministry of Jesus.* London: Macmillan, 1954; Nashville: Abingdon, 1955.

———. *The Person of Christ in New Testament Teaching.* London: Macmillan, 1958.

Telford, W. R. *The Theology of the Gospel of Mark.* New Testament Theology. Cambridge: Cambridge University Press, 1999.

Telford, William R., ed. *The Interpretation of Mark.* Studies in New Testament Interpretation. Edinburgh: T&T Clark, 1985; 2nd ed., 1995.

Temple, William. *Christus Veritas: An Essay.* London: Macmillan, 1924.

———. *Nature, Man and God.* Gifford Lectures, Glasgow, 1932–1933 and 1933–1934. London: Macmillan, 1934.

———. *Readings in St. John's Gospel.* New York: Macmillan, 1939–40.

Temple, William. *Doctrine in the Church of England: The Report of the Commission on Christian Doctrine Appointed by the Archbishops of Canterbury and York in 1922.* London: SPCK, 1938.

A History of the Quests for the Historical Jesus

Tertullian. *Treatise against Praxeas*. Translated and edited by Ernest Evans. London: SPCK, 1948.

Thatcher, Adrian. *The Ontology of Paul Tillich*. Oxford: Oxford University Press, 1978.

Thate, Michael J. *Remembrance of Things Past? Albert Schweitzer, the Anxiety of Influence, and the Untidy Jesus of Markan Memory*. WUNT 351. Tübingen: Mohr Siebeck, 2013.

Theissen, Gerd. *Sociology of Early Palestinian Christianity*. Translated by John Bowden. London: SCM; Philadelphia: Fortress, 1977. Reprint, 1978.

———. *The Miracle Stories of the Early Christian Tradition*. Translated by Francis McDonagh. Edited by John Riches. Philadelphia: Fortress, 1983.

———. *Biblical Faith: An Evolutionary Approach*. Translated by John Bowden. Minneapolis: Fortress, 1984. Reprint, 1985.

———. *The Gospels in Context: Social and Political History in the Synoptic Tradition*. Translated by Linda M. Maloney. Minneapolis: Fortress, 1989. Reprint, 1991.

———. *The Religion of the Earliest Churches: Creating a Symbolic World*. Translated by John Bowden. Minneapolis: Fortress, 1990. Reprint, 1999.

———. *Jesus als historische Gestalt. Beiträge zur Jesusforschung, Zum 60. Geburtstag von Gerd Theissen herausgegeben von Annette Merz*. FRLANT 202. Göttingen: Vandenhoeck & Ruprecht, 2003. [Collected studies by Theissen on Jesus as a historical figure.]

———. *The Shadow of the Galilean: The Quest of the Historical Jesus in Narrative Form*. Translated by John Bowden. Minneapolis: Fortress, 1986. Reprint, 1987. Updated ed., 2007.

———. *Von Jesus zur urchristlichen Zeichenwelt. "Neutestamentliche Grenzgänge" im Dialog*. SUNT 78. Göttingen: Vandoeck & Ruprecht, 2011. [Studies based on a symposium in honor of Theissen's 65th birthday. They are prefaced by Theissen's reflections on his work from 1969 to 2009.]

Theissen, Gerd, and Annette Merz. *The Historical Jesus: A Comprehensive Guide*. Translated by John Bowden. With bibliographies revised and updated by Robert Morgan. Minneapolis: Fortress, 1996. Reprint, 1998.

Theissen, Gerd, and Dagmar Winter. *The Quest for the Plausible Jesus: The Question of Criteria*. Translated by M. Eugene Boring. Louisville: Westminster John Knox, 1997. Reprint, 2002.

Thiselton, Anthony C. *The Two Horizons: New Testament Hermeneutics and Philosophical Description with Special Reference to Heidegger, Gadamer, Bultmann, and Wittgenstein*. Grand Rapids: Eerdmans, 1980.

———. *New Horizons in Hermeneutics: The Theory and Practice of Transforming Biblical Reading*. Carlisle, UK: Paternoster; Grand Rapids: Zondervan, 1992.

———. *The Hermeneutics of Doctrine*. Grand Rapids: Eerdmans, 2007.

———. *Hermeneutics: An Introduction*. Grand Rapids: Eerdmans, 2009.

———. *The Holy Spirit: In Biblical Teaching, through the Centuries, and Today*. Grand Rapids: Eerdmans, 2013.

Bibliography

———. *The Thiselton Companion to Christian Theology*. Grand Rapids: Eerdmans, 2015.

Thomas, John Christopher. *The Devil, Disease and Deliverance: Origins of Illness in New Testament Thought*. JSPSup 13. London: Sheffield Academic Press, 1998.

Thomas, John Heywood. *Paul Tillich: An Appraisal*. London: SCM, 1963.

Thomas, Owen C. *William Temple's Philosophy of Religion*. London: SPCK, 1961.

Thomasius, Gottfried. *Christi Person und Werk. Darstellung der Evangelisch-Lutherischen Dogmatik vom Mittelpunkt der Christologie aus*. 2 vols. 2nd ed. Erlangen: Bläser, 1856–63.

Thompson, J. M. *The Synoptic Gospels Arranged in Parallel Columns*. Oxford: Clarendon, 1910.

———. *Jesus according to S. Mark*. 2nd ed. New York: Dutton, 1910.

———. *Miracles in the New Testament*. London: Arnold, 1911.

Thompson, Robin. "Healing at the Pool of Bethesda: A Challenge to Asclepius?" *BBR* 27 (2017): 65–84.

Thorschmid, Urban Gottlob. *Critische Lebensgeschichte Anton Collins*. Leipzig: Harpeter, 1755.

———. *Versuch einer vollständigen Engelländischen Freydenker-Bibliothek, in welcher aller Schriften der berühmtesten Freydenker nebst dem Schutzschriften für die christliche Religion... aufgestellt werden*. 4 vols. Halle im Magdeburgischen: Hemmerde, 1765–67.

Throckmorton, Burton H. *The New Testament and Mythology*. London: Darton, Longman & Todd, 1959.

Tiede, David Lenz. *The Charismatic Figure as Miracle Worker*. SBLDS 1. Missoula, MT: Scholars, 1972.

Tillich, Hannah. *From Time to Time*. New York: Stein and Day, 1973.

Tillich, Paul. *The Shaking of the Foundations*. London: SCM, 1949; Harmondsworth: Pelican, 1962.

———. *The Courage to Be*. Terry Lectures. New Haven, CT: Yale University Press, 1952.

———. *Love, Power, and Justice: Ontological Analyses and Ethical Applications*. Firth Lectures Nottingham, Sprunt Lectures Union Seminary Richmond. London: Oxford University Press, 1954.

———. "Schelling und die Anfänge des existentialischen Protestes." In *Main Works/Hauptwerke*, edited by Gunther Wenz, vol. 1, 391–402.

———. *The New Being*. New York: Scribner, 1955; London: SCM, 1956.

———. *Systematic Theology*. 3 vols. Chicago: University of Chicago Press, 1951–63. [Republished in one volume, 1967. English edition in 3 vol. with different pagination. London: Nisbet. 1953, 1957, 1964. Volumes 2 and 3 based on Tillich's Gifford Lectures, Aberdeen, 1952–54.]

———. *The Eternal Now*. New York: Scribner's; London: SCM, 1963.

———. *Ultimate Concern: Tillich in Dialogue*. Edited by D. Mackenzie Brown. London: SCM, 1965.

———. *On the Boundary: An Autobiographical Sketch*. Introduction by J. Heywood Thomas. London: Collins, 1967.

———. *Perspectives on 19th and 20th Century Protestant Thought*. Edited by Carl E. Braaten. London: SCM, 1967.

———. *A History of Christian Thought*. Edited by Carl E. Braaten. London: Touchstone, 1968.

———. "Autobiographical Reflections." In *The Theology of Paul Tillich*, edited by Charles W. Kegley, 2nd ed., 3–21. New York: Pilgrim, 1982.

———. *Main Works/Hauptwerke*. Edited by Carl Heinz Ratschow. 6 vols. New York: de Gruyter, 1989–92.

———. "Die christliche Gewissheit und der historische Jesus." In *Main Works/Hauptwerke*, edited by Gert Hummel, vol. 6, 21–37.

Tilling, Chris. *Paul's Divine Christology*. With a foreword by Douglas Campbell. WUNT 323. Tübingen: Mohr Siebeck, 2012; Grand Rapids: Eerdmans, 2015.

Tindal, Matthew. *Christianity as Old as the Creation* [1730]. Facsimile reprint, New York: Garland, 1978.

Tödt, H. E. *The Son of Man in the Synoptic Tradition*. Translated by Dorothea M. Barton. NTL. London: SCM, 1965.

Toland, John. *Christianity Not Mysterious, Showing that there is Nothing in the Gospel Contrary to Reason, nor above it; And that no Christian Doctrine can properly be call'd a Mystery* [1695 with the imprint 1696]. Facsimile reprint, New York: Garland, 1978.

Tolbert, Mary Ann. *Perspectives on the Parables: An Approach to Multiple Interpretations*. Philadelphia: Fortress, 1979.

———. *Sowing the Gospel: Mark's World in Literary-Historical Perspective*. Minneapolis: Fortress, 1989. Reprint, 1996.

Torrance, James B. *The Nature of Atonement*. London: Macmillan, [1856]. Reprint with new introduction by James B. Torrance. Edinburgh: Handsel; Grand Rapids, Eerdmans, 1996.

———. "The Vicarious Humanity of Christ." In *The Incarnation: Ecumenical Studies in the Nicene-Constantinopolitan Creed, A.D. 381*, 127–47. Edinburgh: Handsel, 1981.

Torrey, Norman L. *Voltaire and the English Deists*. New Haven, CT: Yale University Press, 1930. Reprint, Hamden, CT: Archon, 1967.

Toulmin, Joshua. *Memoirs of the Life, Character, Sentiments and Writings, of Faustus Socinus*. [1777.] Facsimile reprint, Ecco Print Editions, n.d.

Trapnell, William H. *Thomas Woolston: Madman and Deist?* Bristol: Thoemmes, 1994.

———. *Thomas Woolston: Six discourse sur les miracles de Notre Sauveur. Deux traductions manuscrites du XVIIIe siècle don't une de Mme Du Châtelet*. Libre Pensée et Littérature Clandestine 8. Paris: Honoré Champion, 2001.

Trautmann, Maria. *Zeichenhafte Handlungen Jesu. Ein Beitrag zur Frage nach dem geschichtlichen Jesus*. Würzburg: Echter, 1980.

Treloar, Geoffrey R. *Lightfoot the Historian: The Nature and Role of History in the Life*

Bibliography

and Thought of J. B. Lightfoot (1828–1889) as Churchman and Scholar. WUNT 103. Tübingen: Mohr Siebeck, 1998.

Trinius. J. A. *Freydenker-Lexikon, oder Einleitung in die Geschichte der neueren Freygeister, ihrer Schriften, und deren Widerlegungen*. Leipzig: Cörner, 1759.

Trites, Allison A. *The New Testament Concept of Witness*. SNTSMS 31. Cambridge: Cambridge University Press, 1977.

Troeltsch, Ernst. *Gesammelte Schriften*. 4 vols. Tübingen: Mohr Siebeck, 1912–25. Reprint of 2nd ed., Aalen: Scientia, 1981.

———. *The Absoluteness of Christianity and the History of Religions*. Translated by David Reid. Introduction by James Luther Adams. Atlanta: John Knox, 1971; London: SCM, 1972.

———. *Ernst Troeltsch: Writings on Theology and Religion*. Translated and edited by Robert Morgan and Michael Pye. Atlanta: John Knox, 1977.

Tucker, J. Brian, and Coleman A. Baker. *T&T Clark Handbook to Social Identity in the New Testament*. New York: T&T Clark, 2014.

Tuckett, Christopher M. "The Griesbach Hypothesis in the 19th Century." *JSNT* 3 (1979): 29–60.

———. *The Revival of the Griesbach Hypothesis: An Analysis and Appraisal*. SNTSMS 44. Cambridge: Cambridge University Press, 1983.

———. *Q and the History of Early Christianity: Studies in Q*. Edinburgh: T&T Clark; Peabody, MA: Hendrickson, 1996.

———. "The Historical Jesus, Crossan and Methodology." In *Text und Geschichte. Facetten theologischen Arbeitens aus dem Freundes- und Schülerkreis. Dieter Lührmann zum 60. Geburtstag*, edited by Stefan Maser and Egbert Schlarb, 257–79. Marburger Theologische Studien 50. Marburg: Elwert, 1999.

———. *Christology and the New Testament: Jesus and His Earliest Followers*. Louisville: Westminster John Knox, 2001.

Tuckett, Christopher, ed. *The Messianic Secret*. Issues in Religion and Theology 1. London: SPCK; Philadelphia: Fortress, 1983.

———. *Synoptic Studies: The Ampleforth Conferences of 1982 and 1983*. JSNTSup 7. Sheffield: JSOT, 1984.

Tukasaki, Emmanuel O. *Determinism and Petitionary Prayer in John and the Dead Sea Scrolls: An Ideological Reading of John and the Rule of the Community (1QS)*. LSTS 66. New York: T&T Clark International, 2008.

Turner, Denys. *Thomas Aquinas: A Portrait*. New Haven, CT: Yale University Press, 2013.

Turner, Frank M. *John Henry Newman: The Challenge to Evangelical Religion*. New Haven, CT: Yale University Press, 2002.

Turner, Max. *Power from on High: The Spirit in Israel's Restoration and Witness in Luke-Acts*. Journal of Pentecostal Theology Supplement Series 9. Sheffield: Sheffield Academic Press, 1996.

Twelftree, Graham H. *Christ Triumphant: Exorcism Then and Now*. London: Hodder & Stoughton, 1985.

———. *Jesus the Exorcist: A Contribution to the Study of the Historical Jesus*. WUNT 54. Tübingen: Mohr Siebeck, 1993.

———. *Jesus the Miracle Worker: A Historical and Theological Study*. Downers Grove, IL: InterVarsity Press, 1999.

———. "Jesus the Exorcist and Ancient Magic." In *A Kind of Magic: Understanding Magic in the New Testament and Its Religious Environment*, edited by Michael Labahn and Bert Jan Lietaert Peerbolte, 57–86. European Studies in Christian Origins, LNTS 306. New York: T&T Clark, 2007.

———. *In the Name of Jesus: Exorcism among Early Christians*. Grand Rapids: Baker Academic, 2007.

Twelftree, Graham H., ed. *The Cambridge Companion to Miracles*. Cambridge: Cambridge University Press, 2011.

Tyrrell, George. *Christianity at the Cross-Roads* [1909]. Reprint, London: Allen & Unwin, 1963.

———. "The Point at Issue." In *Jesus or Christ? The Hibbert Journal Supplement for 1909*, 5–16. London: Williams and Norgate, 1909.

Tyson, Joseph B. *Luke, Judaism, and the Scholars: Critical Approaches to Luke-Acts*. Columbia: University of South Carolina Press, 1999.

Udoh, Fabian E., with Susannah Heschel, Mark Chancey, and Gregory Tatum. *Redefining First-Century Jewish and Christian Identities: Essays in Honor of Ed Parish Sanders*. Notre Dame, IN: University of Notre Dame Press, 2008. [Bibliography of Sanders's works, 391–96.]

Uro, Risto. *Thomas: Seeking the Historical Context of the Gospel of Thomas*. New York: T&T Clark, 2003.

Vaage, Leif E. *Galilean Upstarts: Jesus' First Followers according to Q*. Valley Forge, PA: Trinity Press International, 1994.

Van Belle, Gilbert. *The Signs Source in the Fourth Gospel: Historical Survey and Critical Evaluation of the Semeia Hypothesis*. BETL 116. Leuven: Leuven University Press; Peeters, 1994.

Van Belle, G., J. G. van der Watt, and P. Maritz, eds. *Theology and Christology in the Fourth Gospel: Essays by Members of the SNTS Johannine Writings Seminar*. BETL 184. Leuven: Peeters, 2005.

Van Belle, G., ed. *The Death of Jesus in the Fourth Gospel*. BETL 200. Leuven: Peeters, 2007.

Van Belle, G., M. Labahn, and P. Maritz, eds. *Repetitions and Variations in the Fourth Gospel: Style, Text, and Variation*. BETL 223. Leuven: Peeters, 2009.

VanderKam, James C. *The Dead Sea Scrolls Today*. Grand Rapids: Eerdmans; London: SPCK, 1994.

———. *From Joshua to Caiaphas: High Priests after the Exile*. Minneapolis: Fortress, 2004.

Bibliography

———. "The Dead Sea Scrolls and the New Testament." *BAR* 42, no. 2 (2015): 42–53, 78–79.

VanderKam, James C., and William Adler, eds. *The Jewish Apocalyptic Heritage in Early Christianity*. CRINT 4. Assen: Van Gorcum; Minneapolis: Fortress, 1996.

VanderKam, James C., and Peter Flint. *The Meaning of the Dead Sea Scrolls: Their Significance for Understanding the Bible, Judaism, Jesus, and Christianity*. San Francisco: HarperSanFancisco, 2002.

Van Iersel, B. M. F. "He Will Baptize You with the Holy Spirit: The Time Perspective of *baptisei*." In *Text and Testimony: Essays on New Testament and Apocryphal Literature in Honour of A.F.J. Klijn*, edited by T. Baarda, A. Hilhorst, G. P. Luttikhuizen, A. S. van der Woude, 132–41. Kampen: J. H. Kok, 1988.

———. *Mark: A Reader-Response Commentary*. Translated by W. H. Bisseroux. JSNTSS 164. Sheffield: Sheffield Academic Press, 1998.

Van Voorst, Robert E. *Jesus outside the New Testament: An Introduction to the Ancient Evidence*. Grand Rapids: Eerdmans, 2000.

Van Unnik, W. C. "Jesu Verhöhnung vor dem Senedrium (Marc xiv 65 par.)." *ZNW* 29 (1930): 310–11. Reprint in van Unnik. *Sparsa Collecta: The Collected Essays of W.C. van Unnik*. NovTSup 29, 1:3–5. Leiden: Brill, 1973.

Vattimo, Gianni. *Dialogue with Nietzsche*. Translated by William McCuaig. New York: Columbia University Press, 2006.

Verheule, Anthonie F. *Wilhelm Bousset. Leben und Werk*. Amsterdam: Uitgeverij Ton Bolland, 1973.

Verheyden, Joseph, Geert van Oyen, Michael Labahn, and Reimund Bieringer, eds. *Studies in the Gospel of John and Its Christology: Festschrift Gilbert van Belle*. BETL 265. Leuven: Peeters, 2014.

Verheyden, Joseph, and Gilbert Van Belle, eds. *An Early Reader of Mark and Q*. BTS. Leuven: Peeters, 2016.

Vermes, Geza. "The Use of בר נש/בר נשא in Jewish Aramaic." An appendix to Matthew Black, *An Aramaic Approach to the Gospels and Acts*, 310–28. [In response, Black endorsed Vermes's interpretation of the Aramaic as a circumlocution for *I*. He affirmed this use of the term in the Gospels, which he traced to Jesus himself (328–30).]

———. "Hanina ben Dosa." *Journal of Jewish Studies* 23 (1972): 28–50; and 24 (1974): 51–64. Reprint in Vermes, *Post-Biblical Jewish Studies*, 178–214. SJLA. Leiden: Brill, 1975.

———. *Jesus the Jew: A Historian's Reading of the Gospels*. London: Collins, 1973; 2nd ed., Philadelphia Fortress, 1981.

———. "The Jesus Notice of Josephus Re-Examined." *JJS* 38 (1987): 2–10.

———. *The Religion of Jesus the Jew*. London: SCM, 1993.

———. *Providential Accidents: An Autobiography*. London: SCM, 1998; Lanham MD: Rowman & Littlefield, 1999.

———. *The Changing Faces of Jesus*. London: Lane, Penguin, 2000.

———. *Jesus in His Jewish Context*. London: SCM; Minneapolis: Fortress, 2003. [An earlier edition appeared under the title of *Jesus and the World of Judaism*. London: SCM, 1983; Philadelphia: Fortress, 1984.]

———. *The Complete Dead Sea Scrolls in English*. London: Penguin: 1962; 5th ed., 2004.

———. *The Passion*. London: Lane, Penguin, 2005.

———. *The Nativity: History and Legend*. New York: Doubleday, 2006.

———. *The Resurrection: History and Myth*. New York: Doubleday, 2008.

———. *The Real Jesus: Then and Now*. Minneapolis: Fortress, 2010.

———. *Christian Beginnings: From Nazareth to Nicaea*. London: Penguin, 2012; New Haven, CT: Yale University Press, 2013.

———. *The True Herod*. New York: T&T Clark, 2014.

Via, Dan O. *The Parables: Their Literary and Existential Dimension*. Philadelphia: Fortress, 1967.

Vidler, Alec R. *F. D. Maurice and Company: Nineteenth Century Studies*. London: SCM, 1966. [The book contains Vidler's *The Theology of F. D. Maurice*, 1948.]

———. *A Variety of Catholic Modernists*. Cambridge: Cambridge University Press, 1970.

Vledder, Evert-Jan. *Conflict in the Miracle Stories: A Socio-Exegetical Study of Matthew 8 and 9*. JSNTSup 152. Sheffield: Sheffield Academic Press, 1997.

Voigt, Christopher. *Der englische Deismus in Deutschland. Eine Studie zur Rezeption englisch-deutscher Literatur in den Zeitschriften und Kompendien des 18. Jahrhunderts.* BHT 121. Tübingen: Mohr Siebeck, 2003.

Von Wahlde, Urban C. *The Gospel and Letters of John*. 3 vols. Grand Rapids: Eerdmans, 2010.

Von Zahn-Harnack, Agnes. *Adolf von Harnack*. Berlin: Bott, 1936; 2nd ed., Berlin: de Gruyter, 1951.

Votaw, Clyde Weber. "The Gospels and Contemporary Bibliographies." *The American Journal of Theology* 19 (1915): 45–73, 217–49. Reprint, *The Gospels and Contemporary Biographies in the Greco-Roman World*. Edited by John Reumann. Facet Books Biblical Series 27. Philadelphia: Fortress, 1970.

Voysey, Charles, ed. *Fragments from Reimarus, Consisting of Brief Critical Remarks on the Object of Jesus and His Disciples as Seen in the New Testament. Translated from the German of G. E. Lessing*. London: Williams and Norgate, 1879. Facsimile reprint, Bibliolife, n.d.

Wagner, Fritz. *Geschichts-Wissenschaft*. Orbis Academicus. Freiburg: Alber, 1951. Reprint, 1966.

Wahlen, Clinton. *Jesus and the Impurity of Spirits in the Synoptic Gospels*. WUNT 185. Tübingen: Mohr Siebeck, 2004.

Wainwright, Geoffrey, ed. *Keeping the Faith: Essays to Mark the Centenary of Lux Mundi*. Philadelphia: Fortress, 1988.

Walker, Brandon. *Memory, Mission, and Identity: Orality and the Apostolic Miracle*

Tradition. Studia Traditionis Theologiae. Explorations in Early and Medieval Theology 20. Turnhout, Belgium: Brepols, 2015.

Walls, Jerry L., ed. *The Oxford Handbook of Eschatology*. Oxford: Oxford University Press, 2008.

Wansbrough, Henry, ed. *Jesus and the Oral Tradition*. JSNTSup 64. Sheffield: Sheffield Academic Press, 1991.

Wardman, W. H. *Ernest Renan: A Critical Biography*. London: University of London; Athlone, 1964.

Warfield, Benjamin Breckinridge. *An Introduction to the Textual Criticism of the New Testament*. New York: Whittaker; London: Hodder & Stoughton, 1886. Reprint, 1889.

———. *The Lord of Glory*. New York: American Tract Society; London: Hodder & Stoughton, 1907. Reprint, Grand Rapids: Zondervan, 1952.

———. Review of *The Doctrine of the Person of Jesus Christ* by H. R. Mackintosh. *Princeton Theological Review* 11 (1913): 141–56.

———. "The Person of Christ." In *The International Standard Bible Encyclopedia*, edited by James Orr, 4:2338–48. Chicago: Howard-Severance, 1915. Reprints in Warfield, *Biblical Doctrines*, 175–209. Oxford: Oxford University Press, 1929; and in Warfield, *The Person and Work of Christ*, 37–70 [see below].

———. *Counterfeit Miracles*. New York: Scribner's, 1918. Republished as *Miracles: Yesterday and Today, True and False*. Grand Rapids: Eerdmans, 1954.

———. *The Collected Works of Benjamin Breckinridge Warfield*. 10 vols. New York: Oxford University Press, 1927–32.

———. *The Person and Work of Christ*. Edited by Samuel G. Craig. Philadelphia: Presbyterian and Reformed, 1950.

———. *The Inspiration and Authority of the Bible*. Edited by Samuel G. Craig. Philadelphia: Presbyterian and Reformed, 1951.

———. *Biblical and Theological Studies*. Edited by Samuel G. Craig. Philadelphia: Presbyterian and Reformed, 1952. [An account of Warfield's life and thought, xi–xlviii.]

Watson, Alan. *The Trial of Jesus*. Athens, GA: University of Georgia Press, 1995.

———. *Jesus and the Law*. Athens, GA: University of Georgia Press, 1996.

Watson, Francis. *The Fourfold Gospel: A Theological Reading of the New Testament Portraits of Jesus*. Grand Rapids: Baker Academic, 2016.

Watts, Joel L. *Mimetic Criticism and the Gospel of Mark*. Eugene, OR: Wipf & Stock, 2013.

Watts, Rikki E. *Isaiah's New Exodus and Mark*. WUNT 88. Tübingen: Mohr Siebeck, 1997.

Waubke, Hans-Günther. *Die Pharisäer in der protestantischen Bibelwissenschaft des 19. Jahrhunderts*. BHT 107. Tübingen: Mohr Siebeck, 1998.

Weaver, Walter P. *The Historical Jesus in the Twentieth Century: 1900–1950*. Harrisburg, PA: Trinity Press International, 1999.

Webb, Robert L. *John the Baptizer and Prophet: A Socio-Historical Study.* JSNTSup 62. Sheffield: JSOT, 1991.

———. "The Roman Examination and Crucifixion of Jesus: Their Historicity and Implications." In *Key Events in the Life of the Historical Jesus*, edited by Darrell L. Bock and Robert L. Webb, 669–773.

Wedderburn, Alexander J. M., ed. *Paul and Jesus: Collected Essays.* JSNTSup 37. Sheffield: JSOT, 1989. Reprint, New York: T&T Clark International, 2004.

Weeden, Theodore J., Sr. "The Heresy That Necessitated Mark's Gospel." *ZNW* 59 (1968): 145–58.

———. *Mark: Traditions in Conflict.* Philadelphia: Fortress, 1971. Reprint with new preface, 1979.

Weinberg, Kurt. "Patheismusstreit." In *The Encyclopedia of Philosophy*, edited by Paul Edwards, 6:35–37. New York: Macmillan, 1967.

Weinreich, Max. *Hitler's Professors: The Part of Scholarship in Germany's Crimes against the Jewish People.* New York: Yiddish Scientific Institute, 1946.

Weinreich, Otto. *Antike Heilungswunder. Untersuchungen zum Wunderglauben der Griechen und Römer.* Giessen: Töpelmann, 1909. Reprint, Berlin: de Gruyter, 1969.

Weinsheimer, Joel C. *Gadamer's Hermeneutics: A Reading of Truth and Method.* New Haven, CT: Yale University Press, 1985.

Weiss, Johannes. *Die Predigt Jesu vom Reiche Gottes.* Göttingen: Vandenhoeck & Ruprecht, 1892; 2nd ed., 1900. Reprint, edited by Ferdinand Hahn. Preface by Rudolf Bultmann. Göttingen: Vandenhoeck & Ruprecht, 1964. ET [of 1st German ed.]: *Jesus' Proclamation of the Kingdom of God.* Translated by R. H. Hiers and D. Larrimore Holland. Philadelphia: Fortress, 1971.

———. *Die Idee des Reiches Gottes in der Theologie.* Giessen: J. Ricker, 1901.

Weiss, Otto. *Der Modernismus in Deutschland. Ein Beitrag zur Theologiegeschichte.* Introduction by Heinrich Fries. Regensburg: Pustet, 1994.

Weissenberger, Michael. "Die jüdischen 'Philosophenschulen' bei Josephus: Variationen eines Themas." In *Josephus und das Neue Testament*, edited by Christfried Böttrich et al., 521–25.

Welch, Claude, ed. *God and Incarnation in Mid-Nineteenth Century German Theology: G. Thomasius, I. A. Dorner, A. E. Biedermann.* Oxford: Oxford University Press, 1965.

Welch, John W. "Miracles, *Maleficium*, and *Majestas* in the Trial of Jesus." In *Jesus and Archaeology*, edited by James H. Charlesworth, 349–83.

Wellhausen, Julius. *Israelitische und Jüdische Geschichte.* Berlin: Reimer, 1894.

———. *Einleitung in die drei ersten Evangelien.* Berlin: Reimer, 1905; 2nd ed., 1911.

———. *Evangelienkommentare.* Introduction by Martin Hengel. Berlin: de Gruyter, 1987.

Wells, David F., ed. *Reformed Theology in America.* 3 vols. Grand Rapids: Baker, 1989.

Wendel, Susan J., and David M. Miller, eds. *Torah Ethics and Early Christian Identity.* Grand Rapids: Eerdmans, 2016.

Bibliography

Wendland, Heinz-Dietrich. *Kosmos und Ekklesia. Festschrift für Wilhelm Stählin zu seinem siebzigsten Geburtstag.* Kassel: Johannes Stauda-Verlag, 1953.

Wenham, David, and Craig Blomberg, eds. *Gospel Perspectives.* Vol. 6, *The Miracles of Jesus.* Sheffield: JSOT, 1986.

Werblowsky, R. I. Zwi, and Geoffrey Wigoder, eds. *The Oxford Dictionary of the Jewish Religion.* Oxford: Oxford University Press, 1997. Abbreviated as *ODJR.*

Weren, Wim, Huub van de Sandt, and Joseph Verheyden, eds. *Life Beyond Death in Matthew's Gospel: Religious Metaphor or Bodily Reality.* BTS 13. Leeuven: Peeters, 2011.

Wessel, Leonard P. *G. E. Lessing's Theology, A Reinterpretation: A Study in the Problematic Nature of the Enlightenment.* The Hague: Mouton, 1977.

Westcott, Arthur. *Life and Letters of Brooke Foss Westcott.* 2 vols. London: Macmillan, 1903.

Westcott, B. F. *The Epistle to the Hebrews.* New York: Macmillan, 1889; 2nd ed., 1892.

Westcott, B. F., and F. J. A. Hort. *The New Testament in the Original Greek.* 2 vols. London: Macmillan, 1881.

Westerholm, Stephen, ed. *The Blackwell Companion to Paul.* Chichester: Wiley-Blackwell, 2011. Reprint, 2014.

Westfall, R. S. *Never at Rest: A Biography of Isaac Newton.* Cambridge: Cambridge University Press, 1980.

———. "Newton." *ODNB* (2004), 40:705–24.

Weston, Frank. *The One Christ: An Enquiry into the Manner of the Incarnation.* London: Longmans, 1907.

———. *Ecclesia Anglicana: For What Does She Stand? An Open Letter to Edgar, Lord Bishop of St. Albans.* London: Longmans, 1913.

———. *The Christ and His Critics: An Open Pastoral Letter to the European Missionaries of His Diocese.* London: Mowbray, 1919.

Wheelwright, Philip. *Metaphor and Reality.* Bloomington, IN: Indiana University Press, 1962.

Whiston, William. *A New Theory of the Earth from Its Original, to the Consummation of All Things.* London: Robert, 1696.

———. *A Short View of the Chronology of the Old Testament and of the Harmony of the Four Evangelists.* Cambridge: Cambridge University Press, 1702.

———. *Accomplishment of Scripture Prophecies.* Cambridge: Cambridge University Press, 1708.

———. *Primitive Christianity Revived.* 4 vols. London: self-published, 1711.

———. *An Account of the Convocation's Proceedings with Relation to Mr. Whiston.* London: Baldwin, 1711.

———. *Athanasius Convicted of Forgery: In a Letter to Mr. Thirlby.* London: self-published, 1712.

———. *Three Essays.* London: self-published, 1713.

———. *Essay towards Restoring the True Text of the Old Testament and for Vindicating the Citations thence made in the New Testament.* London: Senex, 1722.

———. *Historical Memoirs of the Life and Writings of Dr. Samuel Clarke.* London: Gyles and Roberts, 1730.

———. *The Genuine Works of Flavius Josephus the Jewish Historian.* London: Bowyer, 1737. Reprint, Peabody, MA: Hendrickson, 1987; 16th printing 2001.

———. *Memoirs of the Life and Writings of Mr. William Whiston.* London: self-published, 1749.

White, Benjamin L. *Remembering Paul: Ancient and Modern Contests over the Image of the Apostle.* Oxford: Oxford University Press, 2014.

White, L. Michael, and O. Larry Yarborough, eds. *The Social World of the First Christians: Essays in Honor of Wayne A. Meeks.* Minneapolis: Fortress, 1995.

Wilamowitz-Moellendorff, Ulrich von. *Reden und Vorträge.* 2nd ed. Berlin: Weidmann, 1902.

———. *Zukunftsphilosophie! Eine Erwiederung auf Friedrich Nietzsches Geburt der Tragödie. Die Schriften von F. Rohde, R. Wagners, U. v. Wilamowitz-Möllendorf.* Edited by Kalfried Gründer. Hildesheim: Olms, 1969.

Wilbur, Earl Morse. *A History of Unitarianism: Socinianism and Its Antecedents.* Cambridge, MA: Harvard University Press; London: Oxford University Press, 1945.

———. *A History of Unitarianism: In Transylvania, England, and America to 1900.* Cambridge, MA: Harvard University Press, 1952.

Wilder, Amos N. *Eschatology and Ethics in the Teaching of Jesus.* New York: Harper, 1939.

———. *The Language of the Gospel: Early Christian Rhetoric.* New York: Harper & Row; London: SCM, 1964.

———. *Jesus' Parables and the War of Myths: Essays on Imagination in the Scripture.* Edited by James Breech. Philadelphia: Fortress, 1982.

Wiles, Maurice. "The Christology of D.M. Baillie." *CQR* 164 (1963): 58–64.

———. *The Remaking of Christian Doctrine.* Hulsean Lectures 1973. London: SCM, 1974.

———. *Working Papers in Doctrine.* London: SCM, 1976. [See especially "Some Reflections on the Origins of the Doctrine of the Trinity," 1–17; and "Eternal Generation," 18–27.]

———. *Archetypal Heresy: Arianism through the Centuries.* Oxford: Oxford University Press, 1996.

Wilkinson, John. *The Bible and Healing.* Edinburgh: Handsel; Grand Rapids: Eerdmans, 1991.

Wilkinson Duran, Nicole. *The Power of Disorder: Ritual Elements in Mark's Passion Narrative.* LNTS 378. New York: T&T Clark, 2008.

Williams, Daniel Day. *The Andover Liberals: A Study in American Theology.* New York: Octagon, 1970.

Bibliography

Williams, George H. *The Radical Reformation*. Philadelphia: Westminster; London: Weidenfeld and Nicolson, 1962; 3rd ed., Kirksville, MO: Sixteenth Century Journal, 1992.

Williams, George Huntston, ed. *The Harvard Divinity School: Its Place in Harvard University and in American Culture*. Boston: Beacon, 1954.

Williams, Joel F. "Literary Approaches to the End of Mark's Gospel." *JETS* 42 (1999): 21–25.

Williams, Michael Allen. *Rethinking "Gnosticism": An Argument for Dismantling a Dubious Category*. Princeton: Princeton University Press, 1996.

Williams, Norman Powell. *The Ideas of the Fall and Original Sin*. Bampton Lectures 1924. London: Longmans, Green, 1930.

Williams, Rowan. *Arius: Heresy and Tradition*. Grand Rapids: Eerdmans, 1987. Reprint, 2002.

———. "Article Review: R. P. C. Hanson's *The Search for the Christian Doctrine of God*." *SJT* 45 (1992): 101–11.

———. *On Augustine*. New York: T&T Clark, 2016.

Williams, Stephen N. *The Shadow of the Antichrist: Nietzsche's Critique of Christianity*. Grand Rapids: Baker Academic; Carlisle: Paternoster, 2006.

Williams, T. C. *The Idea of the Miraculous: The Challenge to Science and Religion*. New York: St. Martin's, 1990.

Willis, E. David. *Calvin's Catholic Christology: The Function of the So-Called Extra Calvinisticum in Calvin's Theology*. Studies in Medieval and Reformed Thought 2. Leiden: Brill, 1966.

Willis, Wendell, ed. *The Kingdom of God in 20th-Century Interpretation*. Peabody, MA: Hendrickson, 1987.

Willis, Wendell. "The Discovery of the Eschatological Kingdom: Joahnnes Weiss and Albert Schweitzer." In *The Kingdom of God in 20th-Century Interpretation*, edited by Wendell Willis, 1–14.

Wilson, H. B., ed. *Essays and Reviews*. Oxford: Parker, 1860. [Later editions were published by Longmans.] Critical edition: Edited by Victor Shea and William Whitla. Charlottesville, VA: University of Virginia Press, 2000.

Windisch, Hans. *Johannes und die Synoptiker: Wollte der vierte Evangelist die älteren Evangelisten Ergänzen oder Ersetzen?* WUNT I/12. Leipzig: Hinrichs, 1926.

Wink, Walter. *Naming the Powers: The Language of Powers in the New Testament*. Philadelphia: Fortress, 1984.

———. *Unmasking the Powers: The Invisible Forces That Determine Human Existence*. Philadelphia: Fortress, 1986.

———. *Engaging the Powers: Discernment and Resistance in a World of Domination*. Minneapolis: Fortress, 1992.

Winn, Adam. *The Purpose of Mark's Gospel: An Early Christian Response to Roman Imperial Propaganda*. WUNT II/245. Tübingen: Mohr Siebeck, 2005.

———. *Mark and the Elijah-Elisha Narrative: Considering the Practice of Greco-Roman Imitation in the Search for Markan-Source Material.* Eugene, OR: Pickwick, 2010.
Winter, Dagmar. "The Burden of Proof in Jesus Research." In *HSHJ*, 1:843–51.
Winter, Paul. *On the Trial of Jesus.* Judaica 1. Berlin: de Gruyter, 1961; 2nd ed. revised by T. A. Burkill and Geza Vermes, 1974.
Wise, Michael Owen. *A Critical Study of the Temple Scroll from Qumran Cave 11.* Studies in Ancient Oriental Civilization 49. Chicago: Oriental Institute of the University of Chicago, 1990.
Witherington, Ben, III. *The Christology of Jesus.* Minneapolis: Fortress, 1990.
———. *Jesus, Paul and the End of the World: A Comparative Study in New Testament Eschatology.* Downers Grove, IL: InterVarsity Press, 1993.
———. *Jesus the Sage: The Pilgrimage of Wisdom.* Minneapolis: Fortress, 1994.
———. *The Jesus Quest: The Third Search for the Jew of Nazareth.* Downers Grove, IL: InterVarsity Press, 1995; 2nd ed., 1997.
———. *Jesus the Seer: The Progress of Prophecy.* Minneapolis: Fortress, 1999.
Witmer, Amanda. *Jesus, the Galilean Exorcist: His Social and Political Context.* LNTS 459. London: T&T Clark, 2012.
Wolterstoff, Nicholas. *Reason within the Bounds of Religion.* Grand Rapids: Eerdmans, 1976; 2nd ed., 1984.
Wood, Allen W. *Kant's Rational Theology.* Ithaca, NY: Cornell University Press, 1978.
Wood, H. G. *Jesus in the Twentieth Century.* London: Lutterworth, 1960.
Woods, Edward J. *The 'Finger of God' and Pneumatology in Luke-Acts.* JSNTSup 205. Sheffield: Sheffield Academic Press, 2001.
Woog, Carl Christian. *De Vita et Scriptis Thomae Woolstoni.* Leipzig: Langenheim, 1743.
Woolston, Thomas. *Six Discourses on the Miracles of Our Saviour and Defences of His Discourses, 1727–1730.* London: Self-published, 1728–1730. Facsimile reprint, New York: Garland, 1979.
———. *Works.* 5 vols. London: Self-published, 1733.
Wrede, William. *Über Aufgabe und Methode der sogenannten neutestatemenlichen Theologie.* Göttingen: Vandenhoeck & Ruprecht, 1897. ET: *The Nature of New Testament Theology: The Contributions of William Wrede and Adolf Schlatter.* Translated by Robert Morgan. SBT Second Series 25. London: SCM, 1973.
———. *Das Messiasgeheimnis in den Evangelien. Zugleich in Beitrag zum Verständnis des Markusevangeliums.* Göttingen: Vandenhoeck & Ruprecht, 1901; 3rd unchanged ed., 1963. ET: *The Messianic Secret.* Translated by J. C. G. Greig. Cambridge: Clarke, 1971.
Wright, C. C. "The Election of Henry Ware: Two Contemporary Accounts, Edited with Commentary." *Harvard Literary Bulletin* 17 (1969): 245–78.
Wright, N. T. *The Climax of the Covenant: Christ and the Law in Pauline Theology.* Edinburgh: T&T Clark, 1991; Minneapolis: Fortress, 1992.

———. "Jesus Christ is Lord: Philippians 2.5–11." In *The Climax of the Covenant*, 56–98.

———. *The New Testament and the People of God*. Christian Origins and the Question of God 1. London: SPCK; Minneapolis: Fortress, 1992.

———. *Jesus and the Victory of God*. Christian Origins and the Question of God 2. Minneapolis: Fortress, 1996.

———. "Theology, History, and Jesus: A Response to Maurice Casey and Clive Marsh." *JSNT* 69 (1998): 105–12.

———. *The Resurrection of the Son of God*. Christian Origins and the Question of God 3. Minneapolis: Fortress, 2003.

———. *Judas and the Gospel of Jesus: Have We Missed the Truth about Christianity?* Grand Rapids: Baker, 2006.

———. *Justification: God's Plan and Paul's Vision*. Downers Grove IL: IVP Academic, 2009.

———. *How God Became King: The Forgotten Story of the Gospels*. San Francisco: HarperOne, 2012.

———. *Paul and the Faithfulness of God*. Christian Origins and the Question of God 4. 2 vols. Minneapolis: Fortress, 2013.

———. *Pauline Perspectives: Essays on Paul, 1978–2013*. Minneapolis: Fortress, 2013.

———. *Paul and His Recent Interpreters: Some Contemporary Debates*. Minneapolis: Fortress, 2015.

Wrzecionko, Paul. *Die philosophischen Wurzeln der Theologie Albrecht Ritschls. Ein Beitrag zum Problem des Verhältnisses von Theologie und Philosophie im 19. Jahrhundert*. Berlin: Töpelmann, 1964.

Yadin, Yigael. *The Temple Scroll: The Hidden Law of the Dead Sea Sect*. New York: Random House, 1985.

Yammauchi, Edwin M. *Pre-Christian Gnosticism: A Survey of the Proposed Evidences*. London: Tyndale, 1973.

———. *Dictionary of Daily Life in Biblical and Post-Biblical Antiquity*. 4 vols. Peabody, MA: Hendrickson, 2017.

Yandell, Keith E. *Hume's "Inexplicable Mystery": His Views on Religion*. Philadelphia: Temple University Press, 1992.

Yang, Yong-Eui. *Jesus and the Sabbath in Matthew's Gospel*. JSNTSup 139. Sheffield: Sheffield Academic Press, 1997.

Yarborough, Robert W. *The Salvation History Fallacy? Reassessing the History of New Testament Theology*. Leiden: Deo, 2004.

Yasukata, Toshimasa. *Lessing's Philosophy of Religion and the German Enlightenment: Lessing on Christianity and Religion*. New York: Oxford University Press, 2002.

Yoder, John Howard. *The Politics of Jesus: Vicit Agnus Noster*. Grand Rapids: Eerdmans; Carlisle, UK: Paternoster, 1972; 2nd ed., 1994.

Yolton, Jean S., ed. *A Locke Miscellany: Locke Biography and Criticism for All.* Bristol: Thoemmes, 1990.

Yolton, John W., ed. *John Locke: Problems and Perspectives.* Cambridge: Cambridge University Press, 1969.

Young, Frances M., with Andrew Teal. *From Nicaea to Chalcedon: A Guide to the Literature and Its Background.* Grand Rapids: Baker Academic, 1983; 2nd ed., 2010.

Zahl, Paul F. M. "A Tribute to Ernst Käsemann and a Theological Testament." *ATR* 80 (1998): 382–94.

Zakai, Avihu. *Jonathan Edwards's Philosophy of History.* Princeton, NJ: Princeton University Press, 2003.

Zangenberg, Jürgen, Harold W. Attridge, and Dale B. Martin, eds. *Religion, Ethnicity and Identity in Ancient Galilee: A Region in Transition.* WUNT 210. Tübingen: Mohr Siebeck, 2007.

Zerwick, Maximilian, and Mary Grosvenor. *A Grammatical Analysis of the Greek New Testament.* 3rd ed. Rome: Pontifical Biblical Institute, 1988.

Zuckert, Michael P. *The Natural Rights Republic: Studies in the Foundation of the American Political Tradition.* Notre Dame, IN: University of Notre Dame Press, 1996.

———. *Launching Liberalism: On Lockean Political Philosophy.* Lawrence, KS: University Press of Kansas, 2002.

INDEX OF SUBJECTS

Abba, xxxiii–xxiv, 420, 428–29, 428n79, 438, 439–40
absolute paradox, the, xxxix
Adam, 309
Adolph, Kurt, 381
Adoptionism, 78, 95, 96
Ahaz, 83, 85, 88, 197
Allen, Ethan, 213
Allen, W. C., xxxvi
Amoraim, 69
Anabaptists, 122
analogy
    role of in determining possibility, 167, 181, 206, 234
    use of by Hume, 175n167, 181, 206, 206n87
    use of by Locke, 167, 206, 206n87
    use of in affirming the hypostatic union, 78, 106
Andover Newton Theological School, xli
Andover Theological Seminary, xl–xli
Andrew, 11, 28
Anglican Church, the. *See* Church of England, the
Annet, Peter, 210
anointing. *See* Jesus: anointing of
anti-Trinitarianism, xx, 134–40
Antipas, Herod, xlix, 25, 25n75
apocatastasis, 80
Apollinarianism, 95
Apollinaris, 95
Apollonius of Tyana, xxi, xliii, 187–88, 187n11, 306n8, 325
apologetics, Christian, twin pillars of, xxi, 175, 179, 193, 199

apologists, 74n37
Apology for the Augsburg Confession, 102
apophthegms, 323, 324, 325
apostasy, punishment for, xviii, 29
Apostles' Creed, the, 99–100, 99–100n106, 104, 121
Aquinas, Thomas, 110n135, 175n168
Archelaus, 90
Arian controversy, 73, 90–92, 140–46
Arianism, xxi, 90, 92, 95, 140, 142, 143, 145, 164
Aristotle, 47, 49–50, 147n80, 252
Arius, 90, 91, 92, 93, 94
Arminian controversy, the, xx, 126–34
Arminius, Jacobus, 126–30, 133–34
Athanasian Creed, the, 121
Athanasius, xxi, 91, 93–94, 99
atheism, 124, 156, 159, 185, 193, 194, 213
Augustine, 101, 149, 175n168, 271, 275
authority. *See* Jesus: authority of
Bacon, Benjamin W., xl
Baeck, Leo, xxviii, 371–72, 372n37
Bahrdt, Karl Friedrich, 227, 227n167
baptism
    believers' 122, 138
    creeds in, 92, 94, 99
    of Jesus, xix, 5–6, 7, 8, 78, 117, 309, 404, 410
    and purification, 407
    with the Holy Spirit, 7n9, 8, 9, 32, 33, 52, 404
Bar Kochba, Shimon, 65, 65n5
Barth, Karl
    and Adolf Schlatter, 391
    cyclical view of time of, xxxiv–xxxv

dialectical theology of, xx, 77, 77n48, 321, 361
as editor of *Die christliche Welt*, 319–20
influence of Wilhelm Hermann on, 319
and Karl Ludwig Schmidt, 323n76
later theology of, 77n48, 322
and Oscar Cullman, 448, 451
repudiation of Gerhard Kittel, xxx, 390
and Rudolf Bultmann, xxvi, 321, 340, 357
and *Sachexegese*, 321–22
Bartimaeus, healing of, 10, 11n21
Bathsheba, 85, 86n62
Bauer, Walter, xxix, 385, 397
Baur, Ferdinand Christian
influence on Albert Schweitzer, xxiv, 245
influence on David Friedrich Strauss, 262
and origin of Christianity, 285n164
and writing of the Gospels, 271, 274, 275–76, 328
Bayes, Thomas, 177n180
Bayle, Pierre, 164
Beer, Georg, 400
Beelzebul charge, the, xviii, 1, 4–5, 13, 28–30, 32–33, 57, 58, 161, 418n33, 459
Being, theology of, xlii
Belgic Confession, the, 128, 128n17, 130, 131, 133
belief vs. paradigm, 42–43, 43n129
Ben Dosa, Hanina, 114–15, 117–18, 409
Bertram Georg, 400
Beza, Theodore, 126
Bible, the
authority of, 100n107, 108, 121, 139, 160, 233, 248, 282
setting of canon of, 70, 271
writing of the gospels, 271–79
biblical performance criticism, 47
Biddle, John, 138–39
Biehl, Peter, 411
Billerbeck, Paul, xxix, 181–82, 418
Bird, Michael F., 446, 447
blasphemy
as based on Jesus's claim to be God's agent, 17, 20, 61
as based on Jesus's self-identification as messiah, 54, 407, 415, 416
as capital offense, li, 407, 424n56
Jesus convicted of, xxxii, li, 19, 55, 254, 407, 415, 416, 462
as purview of the scribes, 17, 19, 20, 26n77

Bleek, Friedrich, 275
Blount, Charles, xxi, 186–88, 186n9, 198
Boaz, 85–86n62
Bolingbroke, Viscount, 210
Book of Common Prayer, the, 155
Borg, Marcus, xii
Bornkamm, Günther, xxvi, 339, 340, 346–48, 346n163, 357, 359, 419n36
Bousset, Wilhelm
background of, 306
and the Bultmann School, 314
criticism of, 315–17
death of, 317
and double dissimilarity, 376
and Gnosticism, 308, 310
and the history of religions school, xxv, 304–17
influence on Bultmann, 307, 308, 314, 317
and Jesus as cult-hero, 309–10, 315
and Jesus as *Kyrios*, 309, 315, 315n50, 315–16n53, 316n54, 316n55
and Jesus as liberator of religion from nationalism, 307, 307n13, 308
and Jesus's healing activity, 307
and Jesus's preaching, 307, 307n11
and *Kyrios Christos*, 305, 308–17
and miracle stories, 311, 312–14, 313n43, 314n45, 315
and Palestinian vs. Hellenistic Christianity, 309, 314, 316
and the Son of Man as distinct from Jesus, 314–15, 316
and the *Theologische Rundschau*, 306, 411
works of, 306–8
Boyarin, Daniel, xlvii
Boyle, Robert, 165
Brenz, Johann, 112
Brès, Guido de, 128n17
British deism
decline of, 207–12
deism as alternative to orthodoxy and Pyrrhonism, 184–93
influence of, 183
and Jesus, 223
leading figures in, xxi
opposition of to institutional Christianity, xxi
Buber, Martin, xxx, 390
Bucer, Martin, 105, 110

Index of Subjects

Bullinger, Heinrich, 135
Bultmann, Rudolf
  Celsus as forerunner to, 81
  and the Confessing Church, 334
  and criterion for judging authenticity of traditions about Jesus, xiii–xiv
  cyclical view of time of, xxxiv
  death of, 303
  and demythologization of the kerygma, 322, 334–39, 358, 358n232, 359, 361
  and dialectical theology, xxvi, 321, 359
  and double dissimilarity, xiii, 324, 376
  as existentialist, 317, 327, 336, 337
  fascination of with the apocalyptic, 416n20
  and form criticism, xxv–xxvi, 320, 321, 322–28, 329, 331, 361, 448
  and the future coming of the kingdom, 346, 453
  and the Gospel of John, 328–33, 334, 343
  and the Gospel of Mark, 323, 326–27
  and the *Graeca*, 339–40
  and the history of Jesus as part of the history of Judaism, not Christianity, 419
  and the history of religions school, xxv, 304, 337
  influence of Bousset on, 307, 308, 314, 317, 326
  influence of Hermann on, 319
  influence of on next generation of scholars, xxxvii
  and Jesus, 327–28, 337–39, 346, 437
  and Jesus as the proclaimer who became the proclaimed, xxvii, 337–38, 355–59, 421, 437, 453–54
  and the kerygma as the presupposition of New Testament theology, xxvi, xxvii, xli, 338, 355–57, 359, 414, 431
  and the miracle stories, 326
  and the narratives and legends of Jesus, 325
  and the New Quest, xii, xxvi–xxvii, 343, 354–57, 359
  and the "Old Marburgers," 340
  and Paul as founder of Christianity, xli
  and the purpose of myth, 335–36
  and *Sachkritik*, 321, 322, 336, 358
  and the sayings of Jesus, 323–24
  theological formation of, 318–22, 320n67
  and the *Theologische Rundschau*, 340, 411
  works of, xxvi, 314, 317, 317n60, 320, 322–27, 334, 337, 338, 343, 419n36
Bultmann school, the, xii, 304, 307, 314, 414, 419, 453
Burkitt, F. C., xxxvi, xxxvii
Butler, Joseph, 206, 206n87, 211–12, 211n109
Cadbury, Henry Joel, xli
Calvin, John
  and credibility of Scripture, 108
  and divine vs. human natures of Christ, 110, 110n35, 111–12
  and Jesus, 106–13
  and Laelius Socinus, 135
  life of, 106–7
  and miracles, 111
  and predestination, 109
  Servetus and, 125
  theology of, 109–10
  and twofold knowledge of God, 107–8
  works of, 107, 109, 110
Calvinism
  emergence of, 121, 126
  vs. Lutheranism, 105–6, 111–13
Cambridge, xxv, xxxvii
Canons of Dort, 131
Capernaum
  as center of Jesus's operations, xix, 11–12, 56, 192
  end of activity in, 26, 37–40
  events at the synagogue in, 11, 13, 14, 18, 24
  fidelity to the Torah of, 15
  healings in, 18, 19, 24, 330
  location of, 11–12
  scribes in, 18
Cartesian doubt, 148
Cellarius, Martin, 123n4
Celsus, 81–84, 313
Chandler, Edward, 200, 202n70
Charlesworth, James H., 439–40
Chilton, Bruce, xlvii
Christ. *See* Jesus
Christianity
  Palestinian vs. Hellenistic, 309, 314
  parting of the ways with Judaism, xx, 65–67, 84, 376–77, 378, 387, 443
  twofold development of, 399n170
Christmas, dating of, xxxiv, 449

Christology
  a priori, xlii
  from below, 77n47, 283–84
  indirect, 349n179, 350, 351n189
  of John, 344
  Logos, 79, 93
  New Testament, 305, 308, 311, 337–38, 451–52
  patristic, 80, 99
  of Paul, 309
  Spirit, 5–9, 5n4, 58
  without the historical Jesus, xlii–xliii
  Word-Flesh (Alexandrian), 94, 95, 96, 97, 99
  Word-Man (Antiochene), 94, 95, 96, 97, 99
Chubb, Thomas, 209
Church of England, the, xxxv–xxxvi, 121, 155
Clarke, Samuel, xxi, 140, 143–46, 146n77, 170, 234
Clement of Alexandria, 271
Colani, Timothée, 280
Collins, Anthony
  as atheist, 199
  background of, xxi, 193–99
  as deist, xxi, 199, 210, 219
  and determinism, 195
  and free speech, 194–95
  and Jesus as fulfillment of prophecy, xxi, 193, 196–98
  and John Locke, 194, 194n35
  and John Toland, 194
  library of, 191n28, 194, 195, 195n43, 199n61
  and Matthew Tindale, 194
  and miracles, 195, 196, 199
  as positivist, 199
  and predictive prophecy, xxi, 193, 195, 196–98
  and theological lying, 198–99
  and William Whiston, 196
  works of, xxi, 194–95
Collins, Elizabeth, 199n61
Confessing Church, the, 334, 346n153, 348n173
Confession of Augsburg, 102, 104, 106
constructs, types of, xlvi
control beliefs, xlv, 42, 43, 48, 133
controversy dialogue, 24, 24n70

Conzelmann, Hans, xxvi, 349–52, 349n177, 419n36
Corpus Evangelicorum, the, 250, 250n34
Council of Chalcedon, 94, 95, 118
Council of Constantinople, 93, 94
Council of Ephesus. *See* Third Ecumenical Council
Council of Nicea, 92–94, 142
Council of Trent, 128
Couvet, Jacques, 135
Creed, J. M., xxxvii
criteria, link with conclusions, xlv–xlvi
Cromwell, Oliver, 138, 139
cross, the, 103, 104
cross-section evidence, 6
Crossan, John Dominic, xliv–xlv, 439, 440
Cudworth, Ralph, 164
Cullman, Oscar
  background of, 447–48
  Christology of, 451–52
  critical reception of, xxxv, 453, 455
  and dating of Christmas, xxxiv, 449
  and dating of the Gospel of Thomas, xxxiv
  and *ekklesia*, xxxiv, 450–51
  and form criticism, 448, 451
  and *Heilsgeschichte*, xxxiv, xxxv, 452–54, 455
  and Jesus's titles, 451
  and the Johannine circle, 454–56, 463–67
  linear view of time of, xxxv, 452
  and the parousia, xxxv, 453–54
  and preexistence of Christ, 473
  and the quest for the historical Peter, xxxiv, 449–51, 455, 456, 460
  works of, xxxiv, xxxv, 419n36, 449, 451, 452, 453, 454
Cyril, 96
Dalman, Gustaf, xxix, 382–84
Daniel, book of
  original language of, 34
  as part of canon, 70–71, 70n20
  Son of Man as concept derived from, xxxviii, xlviii, l, 20, 35, 55, 243, 243n13, 309
data background beliefs, xlv, 42, 48, 108, 133
data beliefs, xlv, 42, 48, 108, 133
Daube, David, xxxix
David, 86n62

Index of Subjects

Dávid, Francis, 136
Davies, W. D., xxxix
debt
   in Jesus's teaching, 441, 441n138, 442
   in Judea, 440–41
   and the Lord's Prayer, 441–42
deism
   as alternative to orthodoxy and Pyrrhonism, 184–93
   in America, xxii, 213–18
   assault of on prophecy and miracles, 193–207, 234
   and atheism, 185
   British. *See* British deism
   decline of, 207–12
   definition of, 184, 184n3
   in Germany, xxii, 218–33
   origination of, 185–86
   tenets of, 186
Deissmann, Adolf
   and Christ-mysticism in Paul, 384, 385–86
   influence on Karl Ludwig Schmidt, 322n76
   and language of the New Testament, xxix, xxx, 384–86, 388
   and the messianic consciousness, 385
Derrett, J. D. M., xxxix
Des Maizeaux, Pierre, 199n61
Descartes, René
   education of, 147–48, 172
   and existence of God, 149–50
   and Pascal, 151
   and philosophy based on doubt, 148–50
   and Pyrrhonism, xxi, 147–51
   works of, 147, 148, 150, 155n107
Diatessaron, the, 71n22
Dibelius, Martin Franz, 322n75, 323, 346
Diet of Augsburg, 102, 110
Diet of Worms, 101
Diets of Speyer, 101
Dinkler, Erich, 339, 340, 341, 411
disciples
   calling of, xix, 10, 11, 20–21, 26, 28, 50, 354, 442, 459
   commission of, 27
   as Jesus's agents, 20
   Jesus's aims in calling, 442–43
   and the Lord's Prayer, 442–43
   picking grain on the Sabbath, 22–24
   as the righteous remnant, xxxviii, xlviii, 20, 24, 27, 443
   role of, 20, 26–27
docetism
   Bultmann and, xvii, xxvi, xxxiii, 342, 344, 358, 359, 419
   in the Johannine circle, xxv, 310, 344
   Käsemann and, 342, 344, 358, 359
Dodd, C. H., xxxvi
dominical sayings, 323, 324
double dissimilarity, xiii, xlvi, 324, 347, 349, 376
double similarity and double dissimilarity, xiv, xlvi, 376
dream interpretation, 32
dreams, 32, 70n20, 89
Drews, Arthur, 81
Du Bose, Jacques, 155
Dynamic Monarchianism, 78
Ebeling, Gerhard, 340, 348, 348n173
Ebionites, 191, 192
Edwards, Jonathan, 209
Eichhorn, Johann Gottfried, 272–73
ekklesia, xxxiv, 450–51, 456
Elijah, 16, 39, 51, 58, 74, 197
Eliot, Charles William, xl
Elisha, 16, 58
embarrassment, as theme in the gospels, xlv, 41–42
empiricism, 147n80
Empiricus, Sextus, xxi, 146, 147
Enoch, 69
epics, xx, 47n151, 49
Er, 85n62
eschatology
   consistent, xxxvii, 453
   in the process of realization, xxxiii, 427, 431
   Jesus's, 261n73, 289n187, 291, 295, 397, 446
   Jewish, 193, 301, 332, 351, 399n170, 413
   miracles and, 342
   realized, xxxvii, 342, 427n76
   Reimarus as pioneering, 244, 245, 260
   restoration, 446
   thoroughgoing, xxiv, xxxvii, 244, 245, 246, 261–62, 261n73, 289, 297, 363
eternal generation, 81, 90
Eusebius of Caesarea, 92, 142–43n63
Eutyches, 95

exorcism
  episodes of as leading to Beelzebul charge, 1, 10, 11, 12n29, 15, 24, 26, 29, 418
  vs. healing, 10n20, 13
  as manifestation of the dawning of the kingdom of God, xxxi, 58, 287, 398
  naming and, 13, 14n36
  "rebuke" as used with, 40, 40n19
extra Calvinisticum, 112, 113n141
Fabricius, Johann Albert, 222
Farrer, Austin, xxxix
fasting, 22
Feldmann, Helene, 320
fiction, xix, 47n151
Fiebig, Paul, 304, 305–6, 305–6n8, 400
First Quest, the
  as clash over authority and hermeneutics, 32
  gospel of Mark as embodying, 48
  purpose of, xviii, 3, 4, 101
  verdict of, xviii
  when it happened, xviii, 3, 4
form criticism, xxv–xxvi, xxxvii, xxxviii, 270, 270n103, 321–22, 323, 329, 420, 448
Formula of Concord, the, 106, 112
Franklin, Benjamin, 213
Fredriksen, Paula, xlvii
Fourth Ecumenical Council, 96–99
Frei, Hans, xlii
Fuchs, Ernst
  and Adolf Schlatter, 391
  background of, 344, 344n154
  and *Der historische Jesus und der kerygmatische Christus*, 419n36
  and faith, 345, 346
  and the historical Jesus, 344–46, 359
  and the New Quest, xxvi, 340
  and the "Old Marburgers," 340
  and Rudolf Bultmann, 341, 344n154
Fuller, Reginald H., xli, xlii
Gadamer, Hans-Georg, 339–40
Galilee
  Antipas as ruler of, xlix, 11–12, 11n25, 25
  capital cities of, xlix, 12, 12n26, 12n27
  disciples linked with, 455, 459
  Hellenism in, 316, 401n178, 402
  as Jesus's place of origin, xix, xxxi, 5, 11, 402

  ministry of Jesus in, xix, 6, 10, 11, 12, 15, 56, 279, 417n29
  as politically and ethnically separate from Judea, xxxi, xlviii–xlix, 11, 316, 374, 399n170, 401, 401n178, 408
  resurrection appearances in, 408
  scribes sent to, xviii, li, 4, 18, 22–23, 33
  tax systems in, 441
Gassendi, Pierre, 151
gates of Hades, the, l, 457, 457n214, 461–62
Geiger, Abraham, 302, 302n249
genre-constancy, 6
Gentile mission, the, 425–26, 446–47
Gibson, Edmund, 201
Gibson, Jeffrey B., 442–43
Ginsberg, Asher, 373
Glanvill, Joseph, 165
gleaning, 23
Gnosticism, 308, 310, 310n34, 331, 332, 333, 334
God
  as author of Scripture, 108
  coming in judgment, li
  death of, xliv
  as the Father of the Son, 78, 90, 99
  immutability of, 94
  impassibility of, 78, 91, 94, 99
  Jesus as agent of, 16, 17, 19–28, 465–66
  kingdom of. *See* kingdom of God
  as nature, 159
  oneness of, 78, 80
  people of, xxxiv
  presence of with his people, xlii, xlvi, xlvii, li, 31n90, 67
  Son of. *See* Son of God
  Spirit of. *See* Holy Spirit, the
  suffering of. *See* God: impassibility of
  word of, 32, 38, 66, 108, 112
Goethe, Johann Wolfgang von, 163, 260
Goeze, Johann Melchior, 250
Gogarten, Friedrich, 340
Goguel, Maurice, 448
Golden Rule, the, 375, 375n52
Gomarus, Franciscus, 127, 130
Gore, Charles, xxxvi
Gospels, the. *See* Bible, the; John, Gospel of; Luke, Gospel of; Mark, Gospel of; Matthew, Gospel of
Goulder, Michael, xxxix
grace, 130, 131

Index of Subjects

Graeca, the, 339–40
Great Commandments, the, 444–45, 444–45n148
Gressmann, Hugo, 304
Griesbach, Johann Jakob, 273–74
Griesbach hypothesis, the, 273–75, 276
Grotius, Hugo, 131, 136n37, 155, 161, 187n11, 198
Grundmann, Walter
    anti-Semitism of, 399–401, 403
    background of, xxxi, 399–400, 403
    contribution of to understanding the historical Jesus, 408–9
    and demonic powers, 404–5
    and Hellenism, 402, 405
    and impossibility of writing the life of Jesus, 404
    and Jesus as charismatic, xxxi, 401, 406–7, 408
    and Jesus as high priest, 410
    and Jesus as no Jew, xxxi, 397, 399, 400–403
    and the passion as necessity, 407
    and purity, 405–6, 407, 408, 410
    and salvation, 405, 407, 408
    works of, xxxi, 400, 403–4, 407
Guignebert, Charles, 448
Gunkel, Hermann, 304, 306, 317n60, 319, 322, 322n75
Haggadah, 69, 444
Halakhah, 69, 444
Hamann, Johann Georg, 260
ha-Nasi', Yehudah, 67
Hare, Francis, 203n74
Harmenszoon, Jacobus. *See* Arminius, Jacobus
harmony, 216n127, 271, 271n111
Harnack, Adolf
    and Albert Schweitzer, 363, 363n4
    background of, 363n5
    and Emil Schürer, 377
    and the essence of Christianity, xxvii, 307, 363, 370
    and the God of redeeming love, 363n5
    and the infinite value of the human soul, xxvii, 365
    influence on Bultmann, 319
    and miracles, 364
    and Q, 365–66, 367, 367–68n24
    responses to teaching of, xxvii–xxviii, 367, 369–70, 371–72, 373–74
    and teaching of Jesus, xxvii, 364–66, 370, 437
    works of, 363–64, 363n5
Harper, William Rainey, xl
Harvard Divinity School, xxxix, xl
Hawkins, John, xxxvi
healing
    as basis of Beelzebul charge, 1, 10, 15, 16, 19, 24–25, 26, 29, 57, 161, 312, 342, 418n33
    as evidence of Jesus as the Messiah, xxxi, 1, 6, 268 269, 307, 325, 342, 353, 398, 437
    and forgiveness of sin, 17, 19, 312
    by Jesus, l, 10, 11n21, 14–16, 17, 19, 24–25, 26, 266, 268, 312, 325, 398, 437
    as mark of God's favor, 6, 16
    and the Pool of Bethesda, the, 202, 202n73, 203n73
    through prophets, 16
    and the Sabbath, 13n29, 24–25, 323–24
    trained physicians and, l, 16
    Vespasian and, 176, 187n11
Hegel, Georg Wilhelm Friedrich, 262, 262n75
Heidegger, Martin, 327, 327n99, 340
Heidelberg Catechism, the, 112, 112n114, 128, 128n17, 1288n18, 130, 131, 133
Heilsgeschichte, xxxiii, xxxiv, 419, 422, 452–53, 455
Heitmüller, Wilhelm, 304, 306, 320, 391n127
Herbert, Edward, xxi, 185–86, 187
Herbert of Cherbury. *See* Herbert, Edward
Herder, Johann Gottfried von, 272, 272n113
Hermann, Wilhelm, 319, 319n66, 346
hermeneutics, 31
Herod Antipas, xlix, 11, 12, 12n27, 25, 25n75, 25n76, 89, 414n13
Herod the Great, xlviii, 11, 12n26, 401n178
Herodians, the, 25, 33, 53
Hirsch, Emmanuel, 400
history, xix, 47–48n151, 49
history of religions school, the, xxv, 304–8
Hobbes, Thomas, 154–57, 155n107, 162, 187
Hoffmann, J. C. K., xxxiv, 452

631

Holmén, Tom, xlvii
Holtzmann, Heinrich Julius
   influence of Albert Schweitzer on, xxiv, 243n12, 246, 271, 377
   influence of on Emil Schürer, 377
   and messianic consciousness, 278n135
   and priority of the Gospel of Mark, xxiv, 243n12, 261, 271, 277, 377n60
   and psychological development of Jesus, 277, 277n133
   and the two-source theory, 277–78, 377n60
Holy Spirit, the
   and anointing of Jesus, xlviii, 5–7, 7n9, 9, 13, 17, 30, 32, 55, 58, 83, 117, 310, 404, 410
   and baptism of Jesus, xlviii, 5, 6, 7, 32
   blasphemies against as unforgivable sin, 30
   and conception of Jesus, 82, 85, 86–87, 90, 137
   lack of suffering of, 80
   purification by, 31n90
   reception of in baptism and conversion, 8
   and resurrection of Jesus, 86
   salvation through grace of, 130
   speaking, 78n49
   and temptation of Jesus, 10–11
   as third person of the Trinity, 78, 79, 80, 107, 110n135, 124, 310n30
   Unitarian view of, 137
   use of term, 30–31n90
   and the writing of Scripture, 108, 108n31, 271
Homolka, Walter, xlvii
Honi the rainmaker, 114, 117, 118
Hume, David
   as empiricist, xxi, 171
   and George Campbell, 179, 179n189
   and the historical Jesus, 234
   life of, 171–73
   and miracles, xxi, 172, 174–81, 176n172, 178n186, 208, 234, 269, 311
   and prophecy, 177
   and Pyrrhonism, xxi, 171, 171n155, 180
   and skepticism, 171n155, 173n162, 180
   use of analogy by, 175n167, 181, 206, 206n87, 267
   works of, 172, 173, 173n161, 173n162, 174

hypostatic union, the, 97, 106
Ilive, Jacob, 211n107
incarnation, of Jesus, xxxv, 77, 79, 81, 93, 95, 99, 103, 105, 106, 111, 112n141, 253, 276, 463
Institute for Investigation into Jewish Influence on German Church Life, the, 400
International Q Project, the, xlii
ipsissima verba, 54, 422n48
ipsissima vox, xxxiii, 19n53, 54, 420, 422, 422n48, 428, 431
Irenaeus, 75–76
Jacobi, Friedrich Heinrich, 162, 259, 259n68, 260
James, 11, 28, 243
Jansen, Cornelius, 151
Jansenism, 151
Jauss, Hans Robert, 45–46, 45n137
Jefferson, Thomas
   and the comparative method, 214–15
   and the divinity of Christ, 214
   and the historical Jesus, 213–14
   and the Holy Spirit, 217–18
   influence of deism on, xxii, 213, 214, 235
   and Jesus, 215–16, 215n122, 217, 217–18n136, 235
   and Joseph Priestley, xxii, 140, 214, 214n121, 215n122, 216
   Literary Bible of, xxii, 214
   rejection of miracles, 214
   and the supernatural, xxii, 217–18
   and the Trinity, 214, 217n136
   as Unitarian, xxii, 218, 218n137
   and Viscount Bolingbroke, 210, 214
   works of, xxii, 213–18
Jeremias, Joachim
   and *Abba*, xxxiii–xxxiv, 420, 428–29, 428n79
   background of, 418–19
   and the Commentary to the New Testament from Talmud and Midrash, 381
   critical reception of, xxxv, 431–32, 434–35, 438–47
   and the death of Jesus, significance of, 424–25, 425n59
   and eschatology being realized, 421, 431, 435, 437
   and form criticism, 420

Index of Subjects

and the Gentile mission, 425–26, 446–47
and *Heilsgeschichte*, xxxiii, 419, 422
and historical Jesus vs. Christ proclaimed
  by the church, 359, 419
and *ipsissima vox* vs. *ipsissima verba*,
  xxxiii, 19n53, 54, 422–23n48, 428, 431
and the Last Supper, xxxiii, 421–24,
  432–33, 437, 445
and the Lord's Prayer, xxxiv, 429–31, 440
and the parables, xxxiii, 426–27, 434–38
and parabolic actions, 437–38
and plea for the renewal of the quest
  of the historical Jesus, xxxii–xxxiii,
  419–21, 432
and the prayers of Jesus, 428–31
and Psalm, 118, 461
works of, xxxiii, 418–19, 421, 424, 425,
  427, 431
Jerusalem, history of, 65, 71
Jesse, 86n62
Jesus
  as adversary of Satan (and Satan), 9–10
  allusions to illegitimacy of, 71–72, 71n24,
    82
  anointing of, xix, xlviii, 5, 6, 7, 9, 13, 55,
    58, 83, 117, 404, 410
  appearance of, 414
  association of with sinners, 20–21
  authority of, xix, 13, 17, 19–20, 22, 24,
    33, 52, 354, 406, 416, 420
  baptism of. *See* baptism: of Jesus
  as bearer of the New Being, xlii
  as bridegroom, 22
  and calling of the disciples, xix, 10, 11,
    20–21, 26, 28, 50, 354, 442, 459
  Calvin and, 106–13
  in Capernaum. *See* Capernaum
  as casting out demons by Beelzebul, xviii,
    xlix, 4, 13, 29–30, 33, 39, 118, 418n33
  Catholic Modernist reclamation of,
    368–71
  as charismatic, xxxi, 64, 113, 116, 397,
    398, 401, 406–7, 408, 409
  commandment to love, xxvii
  as communicating holiness and purity,
    xlix, 16, 17, 56
  conception of, 74, 82–84, 85–87, 88–89,
    137
  conflict of with the authorities, 16–17, 19,
    20–21, 23, 25–26, 35, 52–55

continuity of with Jewish tradition, 12,
  17, 21
criteria for authenticating the words and
  actions of, xlv–xlvi, 41–43
critics of, 17–20, 24, 25–26, 39, 52–53
as cult-hero, 309–10, 315
dating of birth of, 414n13
dating of ministry of, 414–15, 414n13
and debt, 441
death of, l, 8, 424–25
and a demand for surplus, xli
divinity vs. humanity of, xxxix, 94–97,
  104, 105, 106, 110, 111–13, 112n141,
  118–19
early church fathers and, 73–90
eschatological, xxiii, xxiv, 242, 244, 245,
  249, 261n73, 262, 291–92, 337, 345,
  355, 356
eternal existence of, 90, 144, 463–64
ethnic background of, 401
exorcisms by, xix, xxx, 13, 15, 19, 26, 58,
  287, 397, 398
faith of vs. faith in, 309, 310
and fasting, 22, 437
as the fleshly dwelling of the logos (as
  tabernacle of God), xlvi, xlvii
and forgiveness of sin, 17, 19, 21
as fulfillment of prophecies of Hebrew
  Bible, 31, 82–83, 87, 88–89, 103,
  196–97, 269, 383, 384
as fulfillment of prophecies of John the
  Baptist, xix, 9, 10, 26n76, 31
and the Gentiles, 191, 192–93, 425,
  446–47
as God's agent, 16, 17, 19–28, 465–66
and the Great Commandments, 444
healings by, xix, xxx, xlix, 10, 11n21,
  14–16, 17, 19, 24–25, 26, 266, 268,
  398, 437
as high priest and king, 410
and impurity, 406, 408, 410
incarnation of, xxxv, 77, 79, 81, 93, 95,
  99, 103, 105, 106, 111, 112n141, 253,
  276, 463
as itinerant, xix, 38, 56–57, 58, 397
Jewish reclamation of, 371–77
Jewishness of, xiii, xxviii, 359, 372, 374,
  387, 390, 391
and Joshua, xlviii, 51, 66, 87, 388,
  388n116

633

and Judaism, 67–73, 372, 409
and kingdom of God. *See* kingdom of God
as *Kyrios*, 309, 315, 315n50, 315–16n53, 316n54, 316n55
languages spoken by, xxix, 382–84, 383n89, 420n41
as leading followers astray, xviii, 25, 29, 33, 55, 61, 74, 118, 262n73, 418n33, 459
liberal Protestant reclamation of, 363–67
Luther and, 100–106
messianic consciousness of, xxx, 278n135, 287, 290n196, 292, 385
mission of, xix, 10, 15, 20, 23, 38–39
name of, xlviii, 87, 88–89, 388
as Nazarene, 192
as new Moses, xl, 65–66, 268
as one with the father, xxxvii, 5n4, 79, 90–92, 93–94, 96, 97, 123–24, 248
as the parable of God, 354n200
parabolic actions by, 437
passion predictions of, 22, 39, 51, 72, 462
perception of as male witch, 58
politics of, xlix
prayer of, xxxiv, 15, 15n38, 429–31, 438–39, 442
as the proclaimer who became the proclaimed, xxvii, 337–38, 355–59, 421, 437, 453–54
and Psalm 118, 461–63
psychological development of, 277n133
quests for. *See* quests for Jesus
and radical obedience, 355
radical role of, 71
and raising of Lazarus, xxxii, 61, 204, 330, 415
real vs. historical vs. theological, xlv, 41
relationship of with biological family, xix, 15, 28, 36–37, 39, 50, 192
rescue miracles of, 39–40
response to Beelzebul charge, 4, 13, 30
resurrection of, 86, 93, 203–4, 249, 376
as revelation of God, 345
as the righteous remnant, xxxviii, xlviii, 20, 24, 27, 71
and the Sabbath, 22–25
and salvation, xxvi, 26, 129, 338, 355, 408
sayings of, 323–24, 345

as second God, 81–82
separation of from Judaism, 387, 389, 390
sinlessness of, 82
as the Son of God. *See* Son of God
as the Son of Man. *See* Son of Man
stilling of the sea by, 40, 343
as storyteller, 372
as stubborn and rebellious son, 36–37, 59–60
as successor to Jeremiah, 161, 162
as teacher, xix, xxvii, xli, xlviii, 12–13, 33–34, 161–62, 170n144, 364, 372
in the Talmud, 71–73, 347, 347–48n170
and the Torah, 9, 12, 24, 32, 53, 116
transfiguration of, 7, 51, 55
triadic structure of teaching of, 21
trial of, l–li
and unforgivable sin, 30
Unitarian view of, 137
as unjust steward, 60
veneration of, li
as virtual gentile, 73, 78, 87, 359
Jöcher, Christian Gottloeb, 219
Johannine circle, the, 454–55, 455n201, 463–67
John (disciple), 11, 28, 243
John, gospel of
  Bultmann and, 328–33
  calling of Simon in, 459
  commonalities of with Synoptic Gospels, 329
  as differing from Synoptic Gospels, xx, xlvii, 60–61, 276, 329, 432, 442, 459
  discourses in, 330
  emphasis on earthly activity of historic Jesus, 380
  Father-Son language in, 463–66
  form criticism of, 329
  and the incarnation, 276
  and Jesus as encounter with God, 354
  and Jesus as king of the Jews, 61
  and Jesus and the Son of God, 309
  Last Supper in, 432
  as legal case, xlvii
  links with Gnosticism, 331, 333, 334
  miracles in, 329, 330, 343
  narrative of, 60–61
  as not strictly literal chronology, 417n30

Index of Subjects

prologue of, 330, 332
structure of, 417n30
sources of, 330, 332
theme of, 329–30
as vindication of Jesus, xx
works of Jesus as signs in, 60
writing of, 271, 272, 328, 329, 330, 455n201, 467
John the Baptist, xix, xlix, 5–6, 8, 25n76, 50, 58, 197, 397, 414
Johnson, Samuel, 143
Jones, Christopher P., xliii
Jordan, River, 5–6
Joshua
  Jesus as new, xlviii, 51, 66, 87
  John the Baptist and, 6
  similarity to Moses, 66
Judah, 85n62
Judaism
  apocalyptic, 308, 308n18
  Daniel, book of, and, 70–71, 70n20
  Enochian, 69, 70
  four philosophies of, 27n81
  important texts to emergence of, 67–70
  Late, 308
  parting of the ways with Christianity, 65–67, 443
  prehistory of, 69–70
  separation of Jesus from, 387, 389, 390
  situation of within surrounding culture, 308
  teaching of about Jesus, 70–73
  Zadokite, 69–70
Judas Iscariot, 27, 27n82, 243, 292, 407
Jülicher, Adolf, xxxiii, 319, 320, 426, 427, 435
Justin Martyr, 74–75
Kähler, Martin, 281–84, 393, 419, 455
Kamlah, Wilhelm, 334
Kant, Immanuel
  and analytic and synthetic judgments, 252
  censorship of, 230–32
  Christianity as natural religion, 228–29
  and critical foundations of knowledge, 262n75, 264
  as deist, xxii, 224–33, 235
  influence on Albert Schweitzer, xxiii, 224, 240–41
  influence on Georg Wilhelm Friedrich Hegel, 262n75

and Jesus, xxii, 226, 227–28, 229, 235
and knowledge of God, xxii
and maxims vs. laws, 230n176
and miracles, 227
and morality, xxii, 224, 225, 226, 227, 229–30, 235
and the pantheism controversy, 161, 260
philosophical goals of, 224
and priestcraft, 230, 235
religious philosophy of, 224–29, 225n158, 233
and revelation, xxii, 235n188
works of, 224–30, 225n158, 231, 232–33, 233n182, 241
Karris, Robert J., 443
Käsemann, Ernst
  and Adolf Schlatter, 391
  after the New Quest, 358
  background of, 341
  and the Gospel of John, 343–44, 358
  and the Johannine Jesus, 315
  and justification, 358
  and the kerygma, 342, 343
  and link between historical Jesus and Christ of faith, 359
  and the miracle stories, 342–43
  and the New Quest, xxvi, 340, 341–44, 359
  and the "Old Marburgers," 340
  personal heroes of, 341n141
  and Rudolf Bultmann, 358, 359
  works of, 341
Keck, Leander E., xliii
kenosis, xxxvi, 105–6, 113
kerygma
  Bultmann and, xxvi, xxvii, xxxiii, xli, 102, 317, 322, 327, 334–39, 355–59, 361
  demythologizing, xxvi, 322, 334–39, 355–59, 361
  faith required for belief in, 284
  vs. the kingdom of Satan, 10n17, 288
  miraculous embedded in, 343
  as precursor to Christian faith, xxvi, xli, 338, 344, 356
  and the proclaimer becoming the proclaimed, xxvii, 337–38, 355–59, 359, 421, 437, 453–54
Kierkegaard, Soren, 252–54

635

kingdom of God
  as already present, 278, 346, 351, 397, 398, 421
  dating of, 415
  ethic of, 285–86, 285n166, 291, 294
  as imminent, xxxiii, xxviii, 10, 64, 114, 116, 243, 243n12, 262, 287, 294, 351, 354
  as inaugurated through Jesus's death, xxiii, 223, 242, 243, 243n13, 244, 249, 278n135, 280, 285, 288, 289n187, 292, 294, 342, 355–56, 397–98
  and love, nonviolence, and reconciliation, xlix
  meaning of in Jesus's message, 364–65
  miracles as manifestations of dawning of, xxxi, 57, 58, 351, 351n189
  republicanism as establishing on earth, 215n122
  as tensive symbol, 434
  as transition from ecclesiastical faith to pure religious faith 228
Kittel, Gerhard
  and Adolf Schlatter, 391, 391n129
  background of, 386, 390, 391n127
  and importance of rabbinic literature for understanding message of Jesus, 387, 390
  and "The Jewish Question," 389–90
  links of to the National Socialist Party, xxx, 389
  and the parting of the ways, 387
  and separation of Jesus from Judaism, 387, 389, 390
  works of, xxix–xxx, 387–88
Klausner, Joseph Gedaliah, xxviii, 372–77
  background of, xxviii, 372–73
  and double similarity and double dissimilarity, 376
  and the Gospels as credible historical narratives, 376
  and Jesus as indifferent to needs of Jewish life, xxviii, 374, 374 n49, 375
  and Jewishness of Jesus, 374, 376
  and the messianic idea, xxviii, 373, 374
  and the resurrection of Jesus, 376
  and the rise of Christianity, 376
  and teaching of Jesus, xxviii, 373, 374–75, 376
  works of, 373, 376

knowledge, innate vs, intuitive, 165–67
Kögel, Julius, 387
König, Eva, 247
Krüger, Gerhard, 339, 340
krypsis, 106, 112, 113
Kuhn, Karl Georg, 400
Kümmel, Werner Georg
  and festschrift for Rudolf Bultmann, 31
  and the *Theologische Rundschau*, 411–12, 411–12n2
  works of, 411, 411–12n2
Kyrios, as title for Jesus, 309, 315, 315n50, 315–16n53, 316n54, 316n55
Lalchmann, Karl, 276–77
Lambeth Quadrilateral, 99–100, 100n107
Last Supper, the
  as covenant, 432–33, 445–46
  and the cup, 407, 421, 433
  in the Gospel of John, 61, 432
  lack of miracles in, 325
  as parabolic action, 437
  as Passover meal, xxxiii, 61, 248, 384, 421, 438
  as precursor to the Lord's Supper, xxiii, 105, 242, 242n6
  as prophetic sign, xxx, 398, 398n164, 437, 438
  salvation history context of, 422, 423
  structure of, xxxiii, 421–22
  timing of, 432
Laud, Archbishop, 131
Lazarus, raising of, xxxii, 61, 204, 330, 415
Leibniz, Gottfried Wilhelm, 144, 162
Lessing, Gotthold Ephraïm
  and anti-Semitism, 250
  and authority of Scripture, 208–9n96
  and authorship of the Gospels, 272
  and contingent truths of history vs. necessary truths of reason, 251
  as dramatist, 246, 250, 252, 257
  and Freemasonry, 246, 258
  and immortality of the soul, 259
  and Johann Melchior Goeze, 250
  life of, 246–47, 257
  and objective historical facts vs. theological assertions, 254
  and the pantheism controversy, 162, 163, 259–60
  and publication of Reimarus's text, xxiii, 246, 247, 247n21, 249

Index of Subjects

works of, 250–51, 252, 257–59
Levi, 20, 30
Levine, Amy-Jill, xlvii
Levites, 20
Licensing Order, the, 187, 187n10, 204
Lindsey, Theophilus, 139
Locke, John, 147n80, 163–71
  and Anthony Collins, 194, 194n35
  as anti-Trinitarian, 164
  and the existence of God, 168, 170
  and knowledge, 165–67, 170
  life of, 163–64
  and miracles, 165, 168–69, 171
  and probability, 167
  and revelation, 167–69, 189
  and skepticism, 164, 170
  use of analogy by, 167, 206, 206n87
  works of, 163, 164, 165
Logos, 74, 79, 81–82, 93, 96
Lohmeyer, Ernst, xxx, 390, 399n170, 417n30
Loisy, Alfred, xxvii–xxviii, 368–71, 448
Lord's Prayer, the
  debt and, 440–42
  as Disciples' Prayer (purpose of), 442–43
  as echo of the Torah, 444
  eschatological interpretation of, xxxiv, 430–31
  and forgiveness, 439, 442
  in the Gospel of Luke, xxxiv, 429–30, 442, 443
  and the Gospel of Mark, 438
  in the Gospel of Matthew, xxxiv, 429–30, 438, 442, 443
  as human response to the divine imperative, 445
  and the parting of the ways, 443
Löwith, Karl, 340
Lucian of Samosata, 312
Luke, gospel of
  Beelzebul charge in, 4, 5, 58
  as built on framework of Mark's gospel, xx, 57
  and calling of Simon, 459
  conception of Jesus in, 85
  genealogy in, 57
  and Jesus as king of the Jews, 61
  and Jesus as the Son of God, 343
  and Jesus as stubborn and rebellious son, 59

  and Jesus's earthly ministry, 354
  Last Supper in, 433
  Lord's Prayer in, xxxiv, 429–30, 442, 443
  as Mary's story, 57
  miracle stories in, 343
  narrative of, 57–60
  parables in, 57, 59–60
  Sermon on the Mount in, 57
  sources of, 354, 365
  Spirit Christology of, 58
  writing of, 273, 276–77
Luke-Acts, xli, xliii
Luther, Martin
  and allegory, 103n18
  and the cross, 103, 104
  and free will, 101n113
  and Jesus, 100–106
  life of, 100–101
  and Marburg Colloquy, 105
  Ninety-Five Theses of, 100, 101
  and sin and grace, 101, 102, 103, 104
  theology of, 77, 103, 103n18, 104, 105, 106, 111–12
  and transubstantiation, 105
Lutheranism
  vs. Calvinism, 105–6, 111–13
  and divinity of Christ, 104, 105
  emergence of, 121
  and original sin, 104
  and salvation, 104
  tenets of, 102–6, 111–12
  and transubstantiation, 105
Macquarrie, John, xxxviii–xxxix
Magisterial Reformation, the, 121
Manson, T. W., xxxvii–xxxviii
Marburg Colloquy, 105
Mark, gospel of
  act 1 of, 50, 59
  act 2 of, 50–51
  act 3 of, 51–52
  act 4 of, 52–54
  act 5 of, 54–56
  and anointing of Jesus, xix, 5, 7, 9
  apocalyptic discourse in, 1
  and authority of Jesus, 17
  and baptism of Jesus, 5, 7
  Beelzebul charge in, 4–5
  call to discipleship in, 10, 11, 15, 20–21, 26, 459

637

contested ending of, 56
epilogue of, xix, 48, 50, 56, 326n97
exorcism and healing in, 10, 11, 13, 14–16, 24–25, 26
and First Quest, 4, 48
five-act format of, xix, 47n151, 48, 50, 326n97
as fulfillment of prophecy of Isaiah, 8, 31–32, 39n116
genre of, 49
healings in, 10, 11n21, 15
and Jesus as adversary of Satan, 9–10
and Jesus as king of the Jews, 61
and Jesus as Son of God, 7–8
and Jesus as stubborn and rebellious son, 36–37, 59–60
Last Supper in, 433
and the Lord's Prayer, 438
miracle stories in, 342
narrative of, xix, 49–57
as not strictly literal chronology, 417n30
as oldest historical portrait of Jesus, 323
as oral performance, xx, 46–47, 51
parables in, 21, 22, 28, 30, 32, 37–39, 50, 52
as Peter's reminiscences, 458
primary incidents in, 5
prologue of, xix, 48, 50, 56
prophecies in, 8
and purification and sanctification of Israel, 9, 16
rescue miracle in, 39
as revelation of God, 354
spirit Christology of, 5–9
theme of purity in, 50, 51, 410
as tragic epic, xix–xx, 48, 49, 50, 56, 326n97, 417n31, 438
viewpoints presented in, 9
as vindication of Jesus, xix, 49
writing of, 271, 273–74, 275, 276–77, 377n60
Matthew, gospel of
allusions in, 89
appeal to prophecy in, xxi
author of, 457
Beelzebul charge in, 4, 5, 57
birth and infancy narratives in, 84, 85–88
as built on framework of Mark's gospel, xx, 57
and calling of Simon, 459

dreams in, 89
as foundation document for Christianity, 66–67
fulfillment formulae in, 88–90
as fulfillment of prophecy of Isaiah, 57, 87–88
genealogy in, 57, 85–86, 89
and Jesus as fulfiller of the law, 354
and Jesus as king of the Jews, 61
and Jesus as new Moses, xl
and Jesus as stubborn and rebellious son, 59, 60
as Joseph's story, 57
Last Supper in, 433
Lord's Prayer in, xxxiv, 429–30, 438, 442, 443
miracle stories in, 343
narrative of, 57–60
as new Pentateuch, xl
parables in, 60, 197
and Peter as the rock, 457
Sermon on the Mount in, 57
and significance of Jesus, 67
sources of, 354, 365
stress of on continuity with Judaism, 84, 276
as written to prevent parting of the ways, 65–66, 88
writing of, 271, 273, 276–77, 457
Meier, John P., xliv, xlv
Meijer, Lodewijk, 162
Melanchthon, Philip, 102, 103, 105
Melchizedek secret, xlviii
memory, role of, in quest of the historic Jesus, xlviii
Mendelssohn, Moses, 162, 221, 246, 257, 260
Mersenne, Marin, 147, 151
messianic expectation, 256, 268, 269, 378, 405, 410, 450
messianic secret, the, xxiii, xlviii, 38–39, 243, 243n13, 244, 309, 458, 462–63
Methodist Church, the, 132
Meyer, Ben F., 431, 432
Michael, 70
Michaelis, Johann David, 272–73
Michel, Otto, 419n36
Middleton, Conyers, 172, 173–74, 173n160, 176n175, 180, 180n194
Midrash, 68, 381

Index of Subjects

miracles
  Aquinas's view of, 175n168
  Augustine's view of, 175n168
  definition of, 175, 175n168
  deistic assault on, 193–207
  as establishing Jesus's messiahship, 111, 212, 306n8
  Hobbes's view of, 156
  Hume's view of, xxi, 172, 174–81, 176n172, 178n186, 179n189, 208
  as legitimation of Christianity, xxi, 88, 212, 234, 247n22, 269
  Locke's view of, 165, 168–69
  and messianic expectation, 268–69
  natural explanations for, 266
  Paulus's view of, 266
  role of in belief systems, 88, 178, 178n186, 179n188, 179n181, 189, 208, 234, 266–67
  as sign of God's presence, 351, 353
  Toland's view of, 189
Mishnah, the, 67–68, 381
Modalism, 78, 123
Moltmann, Jürgen, 77, 77n48, 86–87, 100
Monarchianism, 78
Monophysitism, 95
Morgan, Thomas, 209–10
myths, pure vs. historical, 268
Nag Hammadi Library, the, xlii
naming, as quest for power, 13, 14
Nazarenes, 191, 192
Nestorius, 96
New Quest, the
  Bultmann and, xii, xxvi
  end of, xxvi, xli, 354–59, 361, 362
  participants in, xxvi, xli, 349–54
  rise of, xiii, xxvi, 341
  as unifying the historical Jesus and the Christ of the kerygma, 355, 361
Newman, John Henry, xxviii, 63–64, 368, 368–69n26
Newton, Isaac
  and Arianism, 140–42
  and Athanasius, xxi, 140
  and fulfilled prophecy as guarantee of reasonableness of Christianity, 168n138
  and intelligent design, 140
  and literal interpretation of prophecy, 141, 142
  theological beliefs of, 140–42, 234
  and the Trinity, 140
  writings of, xxi, 140, 141
Nicene Creed, the, 92–93, 94, 99–100, 121
Niebuhr, H. Richard, xlii
Nietzsche, Friedrich, xliii–xliv, 365n13
Noetus, 78
No Quest, the
  after World War II, 411–67
  before World War II, 361–410
  definition of, xiv, xvii
Noahic laws, 191, 191n28, 193
Oakman, Douglas E., 440–41
Obed, 86n62
Ochino, Bernardino, 123n4
Oecolampadius, Johannes, 105
Ogden, Schubert M., xli, xlii
"Old Marburgers," the, 340
Oldenbarnevelt, J. van, 131
Olevianus, Caspar, 128n18
Onan, 85n62
Origen
  and apocatastasis, 80
  and double origin of Jesus, 80, 90
  and eternal generation, 81, 90
  and humans as fallen souls, 81
  and incarnation of Jesus, 81, 82, 88, 90
  and Jesus as fulfillment of prophecies, 82–83, 88
  and Jesus as second God, 81–82, 90
  life of, 80
  and preexistence of souls, 81, 82
  and virgin birth of Jesus, 82–83, 88, 90
  works of, 80–81
original sin, 104
orthodoxies, Christological
  break between Christianity and Judaism, 65–67
  formation of, 65–100
Osiander, Andreas, 110
Otto, Rudolf
  background of, 394–95
  and the holy, xxx, 395
  and the *numen*, 396
  and Jesus, xxx, 396–98, 406, 408
  and Rudolf Bultmann, 395
  works of, 395, 396–97
Oxford
  studies of the historical Jesus at, xxxvi, xxxvii
  ties to the Church of England, xxxv

639

Paine, Thomas, 210, 213
Palmer, Elihu, 213
pantheism, 190, 190n21, 260n70
pantheism controversy, the, 162, 260, 260n70
Pantheismusstreit, 162
Panthera, 82, 82n57
Papias, 271
parables, the
   and allegory, xxxiii, 426, 427, 435–36
   contemporary social and political aspects of, 436
   as defenses of Jesus's actions, xxxiii, 21, 22, 436, 436n120, 438, 441n138
   as farewell address to Capernaum, 37–39
   as fulfillment of prophecy, 198
   and the Gentiles, 446
   and kingdom of God as eschatology in the process of realization, xxxiii, 427
   meaning of, 426–27, 434
   relevance of rabbinic to study of Jesus's, 306
   symbolism of, 434
   themes of, xxxiii, 427
   to lead the way for followers, 353
parabolic actions, xxxiii, 437
paradigms, 42–43, 43n129
Pâris, François de, 176n175
parousia, the, xxxv, 116, 261n73, 309, 349n177, 350, 416n20, 427, 453
Pascal, Blaise, 151–54, 152n99, 154n102
Pascal, Jacqueline, 152
Pascal's Wager, 154
Patripassianism, 78, 79–80, 99
Paul
   break of with Judaism, 376
   covenant in, 432
   and faith in Christ vs. faith of Jesus, xxv, 102, 308, 309, 345, 384, 386
   as founder of Christianity, xli
   and Jesus as the tabernacle, 47
   and justification by faith, 102, 127, 332, 339, 345, 358n232
   and the Last Supper, 422, 432, 433, 445
   and miracles, 111
   as Nazarene, 192
   and Peter, 460
   prayer in, 428
   redemption theology of, 310, 332, 355
   and supernaturalization of Jesus, xxv, 114, 309, 377
   and the women at the tomb of Jesus, 56, 56n175
Paulus, H. E. G., 263, 265–67
Pax Romana, the, xliv
Perez, 85n62
Périer, Etienne, xli, xlii, 152, 434
Perrin, Norman, 434
Peshitta, the, 71n22
Petavius, Dionysius, 145, 145n77
Peter
   as apostate, 460n225
   calling of, 27, 459
   and confession of Christ as the messiah, 457
   Jesus's rebuke of, 458, 463
   Mark as disciple of, 458, 467
   martyrdom of, 450, 457
   and messianic secret, 243, 292
   naming of, 458, 459
   quest of the historical, 449–51, 455, 456
   as the rock, 456, 457, 460, 461
   works on, 456
   See also Simon
Pharisees
   criticism of Jesus, 18, 22, 23, 25, 25–26n76, 35, 53
   and purity, 16–17, 18, 25, 26n77, 405, 408
   and the Sabbath, 23, 25
   who they were, 18–19
Phinehas, 27n81
Pilate, xx, 2, 61, 115, 192, 376, 407–8, 407–8n206, 415n18
plausibility, importance of, xlvi
Pliny the Elder, 312
Polycarp, 75
Pool of Bethesda, 202, 202–3n73
Pontius Pilate. *See* Pilate
Porter, Stanley E., xlvii
possession, 13–14
postliberalism, xlii
Potter, John, 204n80
prayer
   and forgiveness, 442
   of Jesus, xxxiv, 15, 15n38, 429–31, 438–39, 442
   Lord's, xxxiv, 429–31, 438–45
predestination
   Arminius and, 127–30
   Canons of Dort and, 131, 134
   doctrine of, 128, 134

Index of Subjects

double, 129, 134
Franciscus Gomarus and, 127
Westminster Confession of Faith and, 132
Presbyterian Church, the, 132
Priestley, Joseph, xxii, 139–40, 214–16, 215n122
priests, as public health inspectors, 16
Princeton Theological Seminary, xxxix
principle of context, the, 165
probability, 167, 177n180
prodigal son, parable of, 59–60
prophecy
  in Acts, 8
  by Jesus, li, 34, 55
  cosmic language in, 1
  deistic assault on, 193–207
  as dreamlike experience, 32
  fulfillment of as legitimation of Christianity, 88
  of Isaiah, 8, 8n13, 31, 34, 39, 39n116, 57, 82–83, 87–88, 197–98, 269, 383
  of Jeremiah, 161, 162, 445
  Jesus's baptism and anointing as fulfillment of, xix, 8
  of John the Baptist, 8, 8n14, 9, 26n76, 31, 33, 54n164
  political, 436
  skepticism about, 122, 256
  as validation, xxi, 88, 111, 168, 168n138, 177, 212
prophetic hope, five strands of, 426
prophetic office, 137–38, 264n80
prophetic signs, xxx, xlv, xlviii, 21, 55, 292, 398, 398n164, 437, 438
prophets
  Elijah and Elisha, 114, 197
  Former, 24n71
  healing through, 16
  Jesus as false, xviii, 25, 29, 33, 55, 61, 74, 118, 262n73, 418n33, 459
  penalties for false, xviii, 29, 160, 424n56
  Torah as taking priority over, 31
Protestant, origin of term, 101
Protestant Reformation, the, 121
proto-orthodoxy, 3
prozbul, the, 441
purification, forgiveness of sin as, 17, 19, 312
purity
  Jesus as conveying, xlix, 16, 17

Pharisees' concern with, 16–17, 18, 25, 26n77
  as root of Jesus's conflict with the authorities, 16–17
  Torah system of, 16–17
Pyrrhonism
  Descartes and, 147–51
  Hume and, xxi, 171, 171n155, 180
  Locke and, 163
  and miracles, 234
  Pascal and, 151–54
  rise of, xxi, 122, 146–47
  and skepticism, xxi, 122, 146–47
Q, xxxix, xlii, 273, 277, 315, 354, 365, 367, 415, 454, 463
Q theory, the, 277
Quest of the Historical Jesus (Schweitzer)
  based on synoptic gospels vs. John, 261, 271–84
  course of, 245–91
  criticism of, 300–301
  eschatological vs. non-eschatological Jesus, 261, 285–92
  first complete edition, 296–97
  great alternatives of, 261, 262, 271
  historical vs. supernatural Jesus, 261, 262–70
  omissions from, 301–2
  turning points in, xxiv
  as vindication of earlier work, xxiii, 243, 245–46, 302
  structure of, 241–42, 245–46, 260–62
quests for Jesus
  First. *See* First Quest, the
  New. *See* New Quest, the
  No. *See* No Quest, the
  number of, xiv, xv
  old, 240
  original, xii–xiii
  Third, xii, xiii, xiv, 33n98
  possibility of authenticity in, 42–43
  reception of, 43–48
  when they began, xviii, 3, 4
Rachel, 89–90
Racovian Catechism, the, 137–38
Rade, Martin, 319
Radical Reformation, the, 121–22
Rahab, 85, 85n62
rationalism, 21, 123, 134, 154, 263, 265, 268, 270, 280, 294

641

Raymond, Robert, 201n65
realized eschatology, 427n76
reception theory, 45, 46
Reformed Church, the, 112, 112n121, 128n17, 128n18, 131, 134, 141
Reicke, Bo, 448
Reimarus, Elise, 222
Reimarus, Hermann Samuel, 3
   criticism of biblical revelation, 247
   criticism of preaching, 247
   and deity of Jesus, 248
   and eschatology, 244, 245, 260
   and immortality, 248
   influence of John Toland on, 189, 223
   and intentions of Jesus vs. those of his disciples, 223, 235, 248–49
   knowledge of British deism, xxii, 222, 223, 223n155, 223n156, 235
   and the Last Supper, 248
   life of, 221–23
   as originator of quest of the historical Jesus, xxiii, 3, 183, 227n168, 245–46
   publication of by Schweitzer, xxiii
   and resurrection of Jesus, 223, 249
   works of, 221, 222–23, 227n168, 246
Reimarus, Johann Albert Hinrich, 222
Reitzenstein, Richard, 304, 305
Renan, Ernest, 278–80, 278n138
rescue miracle, 39
resurrection
   adoptionism and, 78
   as beginning of Jesus's messiahship, 290
   bodily, 84
   in the gospel of Mark, xix, 50
   husbands and wives in, 53
   as mythical, 269
   Paulus's view of, 266
   as proof of Jesus as Son of God, 254
   as supernatural event, 256
   witnesses to, 56, 56n175
Riesenfeld, Harald, 419n36
Ritschl, Albrecht Benjamin, 285–86, 285n164, 304
Robinson, James M.
   and the *Nag Hammadi Library*, xlii
   and the New Quest, xiii, xli, xlii, 357
   and Q, xlii
Rothe, Richard, 377
Royal Society, the, 164–65
Rush, Benjamin, 215n122

Ruth, 85, 85–86n62
Sabbath, the
   activity allowed on, 23, 25, 323–24
   breaking as capital offense, 424n56
   disciples plucking grain on, 22, 23
   healings and miracles on, 11–12, 13n29, 24–25, 323
   Jesus and, 22–25, 323–24, 345
Sabellius, 78
Sachkritik, 321, 322, 336, 343, 358
Sadducees, 53
Sanday, William, xxxvi
Sanders, E.P., xliv, xlv, 431
Sanhedrin, the, 33, 22n97, 54, 55
Satan, xviii, 4, 9, 9–10n17
Savonarola, 147n80
Savoy Declaration, the, 132
Schlatter, Adolf
   background of, 391
   and demonism, 405
   and Gerhard Kittel, xxx, 391, 391n127
   and the historical Jesus as the Jesus of the Gospels, 393–94
   and importance of Jewish literature for understanding Jesus, 392, 393
   and Jewishness of Jesus, xxx, 391, 392
   and rabbinic miracle stories, 306
   students of, 391
   works of, 391–93
Schleiermacher, Friedrich
   and components of human nature, 396
   concern with discovering author's original intent, 44
   and Jesus as the mediator of human awareness of God, 380
   and the gospel of John, 272, 272n114
   and the Last Supper, 242n6
   and the offices of Christ, 264, 264n80
   and religious self-consciousness as basis of Christian doctrine, 264, 265
   and sin, 264
   and the supernatural, 263, 264, 264n80, 265
   works of, 264
Schlier, Heinrich, 339
Schmidt, Johann Lorenz, 219, 219–20n144, 247, 247n22, 322
Schmidt, Karl Ludwig, 322–23n76, 448
Schnackenburg, Rudolf, 419n36, 465
Schultz, Siegfried, 315, 315n50

Index of Subjects

Schürer, Emil, xxviii, 377–80
  and Adolf Harnack, 377
  background of, 377
  and God as revealed through Jesus, 379, 380
  and the history of the Jewish people, 377–80, 379n66
  and the Pharisees, 378, 379n66
  works of, xxviii–xxix, 377–78
Schweitzer, Albert
  and Adolf Harnack, 363, 363n4
  background of, xi, xxiii, 240–42, 242n8, 292, 293
  cyclical view of time of, xxxiv
  and elimination of John's gospel from historical study, xxiv, xxv, 262
  as father of historical-Jesus studies, xi–xii, xxiii, 239, 300
  as first postmodern theologian, 297–98
  influence of Immanuel Kant on, xxiii, 224, 240–41
  influence of Nietzsche on, xxv, xliii–xliv, 295–96
  influence of on next generation of scholars, xxxvii
  and Jesus as heroic, xxv, 244, 295, 296, 297, 299
  and the kingdom of God, xxiii, 287, 294
  and the Last Supper, xxiii, 241–44
  and the messianic secret, 291
  method of, 244
  omissions of, xiv
  philosophy as parameters for theology of, 241
  and psychiatric study of Jesus, 292–93
  quest of for historical Jesus. *See Quest of the Historical Jesus* (Schweitzer)
  as skeptic, xxiv
  and the supernatural, xxv, 262
  thoroughgoing eschatology of, xxiii, xxiv, xxxvii, 243n12, 244, 245, 249, 261, 262, 289, 291–92, 294–95, 297, 363, 421n42, 453
  and the two-source theory, 277–78
  and the will in ethics, 298
  works of, xi, xii, 241–42, 243, 292, 296–97, 364, 419n36
Schweizer, Eduard, 352–54, 352n195
Scott, Walter, 206n87

scribes
  and apostasy and blasphemy, 26n77
  classes of, 18
  criticism of Jesus by, xviii, 4, 19–21, 35, 37, 39
  and the First Quest, xviii, 4
  who they were, 4, 17–18, 19
scripture. *See* Bible, the
Semler, Johann Salomo, 255–57, 260
Sepphoris, 12, 12n26
Sermon on the Mount, the, xxix, 7, 21, 57, 138, 161, 218, 229, 306, 429, 442
Servetus, Michael, xx, 123–26. *See also* Villeneuve, Michael de
  and Calvin, 125
  and divinity of Jesus, 233
  trial and execution of, 125–26, 135
  and the Trinity, xx, 123–26, 223
  works of, 123, 125
Sherlock, Thomas, 204, 205–6, 206n87
sickness, as God's punishment, 16
Sider, John W., 435
Sigismund, John, 136
Simon, 11, 14–15, 27, 27n80, 28, 437, 456, 457, 458, 459. *See also* Peter
Simon, Richard, 146, 146n78
Simon the Zealot, 27, 27n81
sin
  as endeavor to be autonomous from God, 264
  original, 104
skepticism
  impact of on belief and society, 154–81
  rise of, xxi, 146–54
Smallbroke, Richard, 202n72
Socinianism, xx, 134–38, 140, 233
Socinus, Faustus, 135
  and Jesus, 136, 137
  life of, 135–37
  and unity of God, 137
Socinus, Laelius, 135
  and Arianism, 135
  confession of faith of, 135
  life of, 135
sociology, importance of to study of Jesus, xlix
Solomon, 86n62
Son of God
  anointing as, xix, xlvii, 5, 7, 55, 67
  as equivalent to God the Son, 78

evidence of Jesus as, 165, 343
as God's beloved, 248
in the gospel of Mark, 7–8
Hasidim as, 115
as immediate experience of God, 278n135
self-identification as, 54, 124, 265
and the transfiguration, 7, 51
Son of Man
  as applying to the disciples, xxxviii, xlviii, 20, 24, 27
  Aramaic scholarship regarding, 113–14, 115, 117n156, 315n50
  authority of, 19
  as bringer of the kingdom of God, 278n135
  as derived from 1 Enoch, 35, 35n108, 69n16, 309, 397
  as derived from Daniel 7:13, xxxviii, xlviii, xlx, 20, 35, 55, 309
  eschatological purpose of, 51, 52, 243, 280, 292, 315, 354, 398
  Jesus self-references as, xxxii, xxxviii, li, 19, 54, 71, 115, 243, 261n73, 292, 397–98, 415, 416
  in Q, 354
  as righteous remnant, xxxviii, xlviii, 20, 24, 27, 71
  sayings, 324, 350
  as vocational title, xxxii, xxxviii, xlviii, 20, 55, 71, 115, 243, 243n13, 315n50, 451–52
Sorbière, Samuel, 155
Sozini, Lelio Francesco Maria. *See* Socinus, Laelius
Sozzini, Fausto Paolo. *See* Socinus, Faustus
Spanish Armada, the, 155
Spinoza, Baruch
  and authority of Scripture, 160
  background of, 157–58
  and God as nature, xxi, 159, 159n119, 160, 260n70
  and miracles, xxi, 159–61, 160n122, 161n123
  and skepticism, 158
  works of, 158–59, 158n115, 162
Spinoza, Benedictus de. *See* Spinoza, Baruch
Spirit Christology, 5–9, 58
Stauffer, Ethelbert, xxxii, 413–18
  and appearance of Jesus, 414
  background, xxxii, 413n3

critical reception of works of, 416–18, 418n33
  and dating of Jesus's ministry, 414–15, 414n13
  and the gospel of John, 415, 416, 417
  and Jesus's self-identity, xxxii, 414, 415, 416, 418
  and locating Jesus in the Roman and Judaic worlds, 413–16
  and roots of hostility aroused by Jesus, xxxii, 415, 415n18, 416, 418n33
  and Walter Grundmann, 416, 417n28
  works of, xxxii, 413–14, 419n36
steno-symbol, 434
Stillingfleet, Edward, 170, 170n145
Strack, Hermann L., xxix, 380–81
Strauss, David Friedrich
  background of, xxiv, 262–63
  Celsus as forerunner to, 81
  criteria of for identifying historical and unhistorical accounts, 267, 268
  and form criticism, 270, 270n103
  and the Griesbach hypothesis, 274
  and Hegel, 270
  and Jesus as purely historical, xxiv, 245, 261, 262, 268, 269
  and miracles, xxiv, 268, 269
  and the mythical view, 267, 268, 270, 325
  and Reimarus, 262
  and resurrection of Jesus, 269
  and Schleiermacher, xxiv, 262, 263
  and the supernatural, 270, 270–71n105
  use of analogy by, 267, 268
  works of, xxiv, 262, 267
Streeter, B. H., xxxvi
Sunday, as day of rest, xxxiv, 449
supralapsarianism, 127
Surenhusius, 196, 198, 198n56
Swinburne, Richard, 178n185, 178n186
symbolic restoration, 446
Synod of Dort, the, 131, 147
Talmud
  allusions to Jesus in as counternarrative to the gospels, 71–73, 347
  Bavli (Babylonian), 68, 69, 71, 72, 73, 348n170, 381
  Yerushalmi (Palestinian), 68, 69, 71, 347–48n170, 381
Tamar, 85, 85n62
Tannaim, 67–68, 69

Index of Subjects

Tannaites, the, 373
tax collectors, Jesus association with, 12n29, 20, 21, 60, 353n200, 406
Taylor, Vincent, xxxvii, xxxviii
temple, cleansing of, 52, 60
tendency criticism, 275, 276
Tendenzkritik, 275, 276
tensive symbol, 434
Tertullian, 78–80, 99
Testimonium Flavianum, xlvii, 115
theism, 184n3
theologia crucis, 103, 104, 105
theologia gloriae, 103, 105
theological interpretation, 76–77
theological lying, xxii, 187, 192, 198–99, 207
Theologische Rundschau, 340, 411
theotokos, 96, 97
Third Ecumenical Council, 96, 99
Thirty Years' War, the, 155
Tholuck, Friedrich August Gottreu, 281
Thomas, 467
Thyen, Hartwig, 341
Tiberius, 12, 12n27
Tillich, Paul, xlii, 283
Tindal, Matthew, xxi, 194, 198, 207–9, 207–8n90, 208–9n96
Titus, 73
Toland, John
  as atheist, 193, 194
  and Anthony Collins, 194
  and authenticity of the New Testament, 190
  background of, 188, 219
  and Christianity vs. nature, 211
  and early Jewish Christianity, 190–93, 190n22
  influence on Reimarus, 189
  and introduction of deism in Germany, 219
  and Jesus, 189, 190, 191, 191n23
  and miracles, 189
  and mysteries in religion, xxi, 189, 192n29
  pantheism of, xxi, 190, 192n29, 193, 194, 260n70
  and priestcraft, 189–90
  and Spinoza, xxi, 190
  and theological lying, 192, 192n29, 198
  works of, 188–92, 193

Tomson, Peter J., 443
Torah, the
  Capernaum fidelity to, 15
  Fasting and, 22
  importance of to Orthodox Jews, 31, 32
  Jesus as upholder of, 9, 12, 24, 32, 53, 116
  and healings by Jesus as going against, 16
  and Levirate marriage, 53
  and lending, 441
  and punishment for blasphemy and false prophets, xviii, li, 29, 72
  purity system in, 16–17
  scholars of as Jesus's adversaries, l, 4, 18, 24
  supplementary materials related to, 68
  what it is, 4n2, 444
Tosefta, the, 67, 68, 381
tragedies, xix, 47n151, 49, 50, 56
transfiguration, the, 7, 51, 55
transubstantiation, 105
Transylvanian Confession of Faith, 136
Trinity, the
  and the incarnation, 99
  Isaac Newton and, 140
  John Biddle and, 139
  John Calvin and, 108, 110n135
  Lutheran Church and, 105
  origination of the term, 99
  Rudolf Schnackenburg and, 465
  Samuel Clarke and, 142–44, 174–75
  Servetus and, xxi, 123–26, 233
  Tertullian and, 79–80, 99
  Thomas Jefferson and, 214, 217n136
  William Whiston and, 142
Troeltsch, Ernst
  and the history of religions school, 304
  use of analogy by, 267
true doctrine, 83
Twelve Years Truce, the, 128n17
two-source hypothesis, the, 277–78, 377n60
Tyrrell, George, xxviii, 370–71
Uitenbogaert, Johannes, 130
Union of Utrecht, the, 128n17
Union Symbol, 96
Unitarianism, xx, xxi, xxii, 134, 137–39, 233
University of Chicago Divinity School, xxxix, xl
unjust steward, parable of, 60
Urevangelium, 272
Uriah, 85, 86n62
Valdés, Juan de, 123n4

645

A History of the Quests for the Historical Jesus

Vermes, Geza, 64, 64n2, 113–17, 116–17n154, 404, 409, 440
Vespasian, 176
Villeneuve, Michael de, 125. *See also* Servetus, Michael
Viret, Pierre, 184
Voltaire, 218–19
Von Soden, Heinrich, 340
Warfield, Benjamin B., xxxix, xl
Washington, George, 213
Weinreich, Otto, 305
Weiss, Bernhard, 328
Weiss, Johannes
  death of, 328
  and eschatological view of the kingdom of God, xxiii, xxiv, 243, 244, 261, 261n73, 286–88
  and form criticism, 322
  and the history of religions school, 304
  influence of on Albert Schweitzer, xxiii, xxiv, 243, 243n13, 244, 261, 261n73, 288
  influence of on Rudolf Bultmann, 319, 320, 322
Weisse, C. H., 277
Wellhausen, Julius
  and form criticism, 322
  and Jesus as not a Christian but a Jew, xxvii, 356, 366, 374
  and Jesus as not predicting parousia, 416n20
  and the kingdom of God, 367
  and Q, 367, 367n19
  and teaching of Jesus, xxvii, 366–67
  works of, 367n19
Werner, Martin, 416n20
Wesley, John, 132, 174, 176n175
Westminster Confession of Faith, 132, 132n26, 139, 139n48
Wette, W. M. L. de, 274
Whiston, William, xxi, 140, 142–43, 196, 234

Whitefield, George, 132
Wilke, C. G., 277
Windisch, Hans, 304
Wolf, Johann Christoph, 222
Wöllner, Johann Christoff, 230, 231
Woolston, Thomas
  allegorical interpretation of Scripture of, 200, 200n63, 201, 202, 203, 207
  and Anthony Collins, 199, 200–201
  attacks of on orthodox Christianity, 200, 201, 203
  critique of literalism, 207
  as deist, xxi, 207, 210
  and Edward Chandler, 200, 201
  influence of Origen on, 200, 203
  life of, xxii, 199–205
  and miracles, xxii, 199, 201–4, 208
  and prophecy, 199
  and resurrection, 203–4
  and theological lying, 207
  works of, xxii, 200, 201–5
Wrede, William
  and form criticism, 322
  and the Gospels as theology produced by the church, 290
  and the history of religions school, 304
  and the messianic secret, xxiii, 244, 289–90, 289n190, 291
  method of, 244
  and the resurrection as revelation of Jesus's messiahship, 290, 291
  thoroughgoing skepticism of, xxiv, 244, 245, 261, 289, 297, 363
  works of, xxiii, 244, 289
Wright, N. T., xii, xiii, xiv, xlvi, 300
Yale Divinity School, xxxix
Yale theology, xlii
Zahn-Harnack, Agnes von, 363n5
Zadokites, 69–70
Zealots, the, xlix
Zwingli, Ulrich, 105

INDEX OF NAMES

Adams, Edward, 301
Adickes, Erich, 241
Alberti, G. W., 220
Alexander, H. G., 144
Alexander, P. S., 375
Alexander, Philip, 67
Alexandre, Yardenna, 11
Allen, Ethan, 213
Allison, Henry E., 249
Allison Jr., Dale C., 21, 65, 66, 300
Alonso, Pablo, 51
Altaner, Berthold, 74, 95
Altmann, Alexander, 221, 249, 260
Amir, Yehoyada, 371
Anderson, Hugh, 362
Aner, Karl, 219
Annas, Julia, 147
Annet, Peter, 210
Apperloo-Boersma, Karla, 128
Aquinas, Thomas, 110, 175
Arav, Rami, 11, 12
Ariew, Roger, 152
Arnal, William E., 315
Asgeirsson, Jon Ma., 315
Ashton, John, 330
Atlas, Samuel, 259
Attridge, Harold W., 317
Aulén, Gustaf, 362
Aune, David E., 3, 326
Bacht, Heinrich, 98
Backhaus, Günther, 325
Baeck, Leo, 371, 372
Bagchi, David, 100, 121
Bahrdt, Karl Friedrich, 227
Baillie, D. M., 118, 119

Baird, William, 184, 266, 271, 318
Bammel, Ernst, 248
Bangs, Carl, 126
Barbour, Ian G., 43
Barclay, John, 99
Barnes, Jonathan, 147
Barnes, Michael R., 91
Barr, James, 384, 389
Barth, Gerhard, 357
Barth, Karl, 321, 390
Barth, P., 110
Barthel, Pierre, 318
Basinger, David, 132, 174
Basinger, Randall, 174
Bates. Matthew W., 73, 78
Batka, L'Ubomir, 101
Bauer, Walter, xxix, 385, 397
Baumgarten, S. J., 220
Baur, F. C., 270, 275, 276
Baur, Jörg, 285
Baxter, Donald L. M., 171
Beasley-Murray, George R., 280
Beauchamp, Tom L., 171, 172, 175
Behr, John, 75
Beiser, Frederick C., 262
Bell, G. K. A., 386
Bell, Richard H., 9, 10
Ben-Eliyahu, Eyal, 67
Bennett, Zoë, 46
Benz, Ernst, 394
Berger, Klaus, 16, 17
Berman, David, 156, 186, 192, 198, 199
Bernasconi, Rocco, 67
Bettenson, Henry, 76
Betz, Hans Dieter, 13, 59

Betz, Otto, 55
Bilezikian, Gilbert, 326
Billerbeck, Paul, 380
Birus, Hendrik, 257
Black, C. Clifton, 26
Black, Matthew, 113
Blankenberg, Birgit, 5
Blomberg, Craig L., 21
Blount, Charles, 186, 187, 188
Boccaccini, Gabriele, 69, 70, 398
Bock, Darrell L., 12, 13, 19, 55
Bockmuehl, Marcus, 11
Bodmer, Martin, 141
Bohak, Gideon, 59
Bolt, Peter G., 14
Borg, Marcus J., xii, 286
Boring, M. E., 385
Bornkamm, Günther, 318, 327, 346, 347, 348, 357
Bousset, Wilhelm, xxv, 305, 307, 308, 309, 310, 311, 312, 313, 314, 315, 316, 326
Boyle, Robert, 165
Braaten, Carl E., 281, 282, 318, 354
Brabazon, James, 239, 295
Brawley, Robert, xxxviii
Brettler, Marc Zvi, 36
Briggman, Anthony, 76
Broadhead, Edwin K., 47, 352
Broadie, Alexander, 171
Bromiley, Geoffrey W., 112
Brooke, George J., 84
Brown, Colin, xv, 3, 6, 8, 9, 26, 47, 48, 51, 52, 54, 55, 56, 59, 60, 77, 146, 168, 171, 173, 174, 180, 181, 185, 211, 219, 224, 227, 241, 248, 249, 250, 252, 262, 263, 264, 265, 270, 271, 272, 274, 275, 277, 278, 281, 284, 286, 301, 302, 305, 316, 322, 326, 348, 361, 380, 388, 399
Brown, Raymond E., xlvi, 55, 84, 86, 89, 90, 330
Buber, Martin, 390
Bultmann, Rudolf, xiii, xiv, xxvi, 24, 314, 317, 318, 320, 321, 323, 324, 325, 326, 327, 328, 329, 330, 331, 332, 333, 334, 336, 337, 338, 339, 343, 354, 355, 356, 357, 358, 401
Burkitt, F. C., xi-xii, 286
Burns, R. M., 165, 174, 180, 201, 234
Burridge, Richard A., 67, 326
Busch, Eberhard, 319, 361, 395

Buss, Martin J., 323
Butler, Joseph, 206, 211, 212
Calvin, John, 107, 108, 109, 272
Campbell, George, 179
Campenhausen, Hans von, 84
Capps, Donald, 293
Carpenter, Edward, 205
Carré, Merrick H., 185
Carson, D. A., 23
Carter, Warren, 352
Casey, Maurice, 23, 399
Celsus, 81, 313
Chadwick, Henry, 81, 82, 83, 209, 249, 251, 272
Chamberlain, Houston Stewart, 399
Champion, J. A. I., 184, 189, 190
Chandler, Edward, 200
Chapman, John, 180
Chappell, Vere, 163, 167
Charles, R. H., 300
Charlesworth, James H., 9, 49, 202, 293, 409
Chester, Andrew, 410
Chilton, Bruce D., 18, 34, 53, 67, 286, 372, 375
Chinard, Gilbert, 214
Chubb, Thomas, 209
Clarke, Desmond M., 148, 149
Clarke, Samuel, 143, 144, 145, 146, 170, 210
Cohen, I. Bernard, 141
Cohen, Shaye J. D., 65
Cohick, Lynn H., 18
Cohn, Yehudah, 67
Colani, Timothée, 280
Collins, Adela Yarbro, 7, 28, 30, 34, 117
Collins, Anthony, 194, 195, 196, 197, 198, 199
Collins, Jeffrey R., 156
Collins, John J., 7, 9, 34, 49, 67, 317, 409
Collins, Nina L., 25
Congdon, David W., 321
Conzelmann, Hans, 349, 350, 351, 352, 358
Cook, M. J., 18
Corbo, Virgilio C., 11
Cotter, Wendy, 59
Cottingham, John, 148
Courth, Franz, 263
Craig, William Lane, 205
Crouzel, Henri, 80
Cullman, Oscar, xxxiv
Cunliffe, Christopher, 211
Cunning, David, 148

Index of Names

Curley, Edwin, 157, 158
Dahl, Nils Alstrup, 359
Dahm, Christoph, 377, 380
Dalman, Gustaf H., xxix, 382, 383, 384
Dan, Joseph, 32
Daniel, Stephen H., 189, 190, 219
Dark, Ken, 28
Darwin, Charles, 63
Davidson, Edward H., 213
Davies, Stevan L., 58
Davies, W. D., 17, 21
Davis, Stephan T., 98
Dawes, Gregory W., 239
De Beer, E. S., 194
Defoe, Daniel, 204
Deines, Roland, 5, 378, 392, 399
Deissmann, Adolf, xxix, 384, 385, 386, 388
de la Roche, Michael, 198
Del Colle, Ralph, 5
Delitzsch, Friedrich, 399
Delling, Gerhard, 305
De Luca, Stephano, 11
de Molina, Luis, 133, 134
Dempster, Stephen G., 364
Derrett, J. D. M., 51, 57, 60, 314
Descartes, René, 147, 148, 149, 150, 155, 162
deSilva, David A., 34, 35
Despland, Michel, 224
Detweiler, Robert, 59
Deutsch, Yaacov, 73
Dewey, Joanna, 47
Dibelius, Martin Franz, 322, 323, 347
Dickie, Matthew, 59
Dickinson, H. T., 210
Dillenberger, John, 100
Dingel, Irene, 101, 106
Dinkler, Erich, 318
DiTommaso, Lorenzo, 34
Dodd, C. H., 334
Donagan, Alan, 158
Donahue, John R., 20
Donfred, Karl P., 84
Doran, Robert, 49
Dostal, Robert J., 43
Doty, William G., 59
Drew, Arthur, 306
Duncan, J., 57
Dungan, David Laird, 271
Dunn James D. G., 5, 8, 18, 65, 134, 281
Dybikowski, J., 193, 199

Dyce, Alexander, 185
Ebeling, Gerhard, 348, 349
Eckhardt, A. Roy, 303
Edwards, A. W. F., 154
Edwards, J. R., 316
Edwards, Jonathan, 209
Egg, Gottfried, 391
Elster, Jon, 154
Epstein, Isadore, 69
Epstein, Klaus, 230
Ericksen, Robert P., 386, 390, 400
Eskola, Timo, 409
Evang, Martin, 318
Evans, Craig A., xlvi, 10, 52, 55, 323, 372, 410
Evans, Ernest, 79, 80
Evans, Robert, 45
Eve, Eric, 3
Fabiak, Thomas, 270–71
Farrer, Austin, 10
Fergusson, David, 318
Fichte, J. G., 399
Fiebig, Paul, 306, 312
Fiensy, David E., 317
Fiorenza, Elisabeth Schüssler, 84
Firestone, Chris L., 224
Fischer, Hermann, 264
Fitzmyer, Joseph A., 84, 316
Fletcher-Louis, Crispin H. T., 17, 46
Flew, Antony, 43, 174, 178, 181
Flint, Peter W., 34
Flusser, David, 117, 373, 409
Foerster, Werner, 331, 388
Fogelin, Robert J., 171, 174
Fonrobert, Charlotte Elisheva, 68
Force, James E., 141, 142, 168
Forlines, F. Leroy, 132
Fortman, E. J., 98
Fortna, Robert T., 333
Fowler, Robert M., 47
Fox, Richard Wightman, xiv
Franks, Robert S., 136
Fredriksen, Paula, 409
Freedman, David Noel, 24, 36, 70
Frerichs, Ernest, 9, 409
Freyne, Séan, 117, 317
Frickenschmidt, Dirk, 326
Friedrich, Gerhard, 386, 388
Friedrich, Johannes, 386
Friedrich, Peter, 275

649

Fuchs, Ernst, 344, 345, 346
Fuller, Reginald H., 314, 315, 357
Gadamer, Hans-Georg, 43, 44, 45, 46, 371
Garbel, Irene, 383
Garrels, Scott R., 49
Garrett, Don, 157
Garrett, Susan R.
Gascoigne, John, 143
Gaskin, J. C. A., 174, 179, 206
Gassendi, Pierre, 186
Gathercole, Simon J., 78, 239
Gawlick, Günter, 220
Gebauer, Gunter, 49
Gebhard, Carl, 157
Geiger, Wolfgang, 275
Geivett, R. Douglas, 174
Gerdmar, A., 386
Geyer, Paul, 224
Gilden, Charles, 186
Gladstone, W. E., 211
Glanvill, Joseph, 165
Glasson, T. F., 300
Glick, G. Wayne, 363
Godbey, John Charles, 136
Gomez, Alan W., 136
Good, E. M., 66
Gottlieb, Micah, 162
Gowler, David B., 46
Grabbe, Lester L., 13, 17, 18
Grant, Robert N., 74
Grässer, Erich, 239
Gray, Rebecca, 115
Green, Steven K., 213
Green, William Scott, 9, 409
Gregersen, Niels Henrik, 73
Gregg, Robert C., 91
Greig, J. Y. T., 179
Grensted, L. W., 136
Griesbach, Johann Jakob, 273
Grillmeier, Aloys, 98
Groh, Dennis E., 91
Groos, Helmut
Grotius, Hugo, 161, 187, 198
Gruen, Erich S., 49
Grundmann, Walter, xxxi, 398, 399, 400, 401, 402, 403, 404, 405, 406, 407, 408
Gunter, W. Stephen, 126, 128, 129, 130
Gurtner, Daniel M., 67
Habermas, Gary R., 174
Hafemann, S. J., 275

Hagner, Donald A., 24, 372
Hahn, Ferdinand, 314, 315
Haight, Roger, 5
Halliwell, Stephen, 49
Hamann, J. G., 317
Hammann, Konrad, 318, 319, 320, 322, 328, 334, 338, 340, 341, 354, 357, 395
Hammond, Nicholas, 152
Hannay, Alistair, 253
Hanson, R. P. C., 74, 75, 80, 91, 92
Hare, Francis, 203
Harlow, Daniel C., 67
Harnack, Adolf, 363, 364, 365, 366, 368, 369, 377
Haroutunian, Joseph, 106
Harris, Horton, 263, 275
Harrison, Peter, 209
Harrisville, Roy A., 318, 354
Hart, Darryl G., 126
Hart, Trevor, 42
Hartlich, Christian, 267, 270, 325
Hartog, Paul A., 385
Harvey, Anthony E., 7, 9
Hasker, William, 132
Hauge, Matthew Ryan, 47
Hawthorne, Gerald F., 5
Haydon, Colin, 205
Hayward, Robert, 67
Hefner, Philip J., 285
Heitzenrater, Richard P., 174
Held, H. J., 357
Hendrix, Scott, 103
Hengel, Martin, xlix, 11, 27, 47, 49, 54, 314, 316, 317, 326, 377
Hennell, Charles Christian, 301
Herbert, Edward, 185, 186
Herder, Johann Gottfried, 272
Hermann, Wilhelm, 319
Herrenbrück, Fritz, 20
Herrick, James A., 185, 210, 211
Heschel, Susannah, 302, 359, 389, 399, 400, 401, 403
Heyer, C. J. den, 303
Hick, John, 98
Higgins, A. J. B., 315
Hill, Jonathan, 73
Hillerbrand, H. J., 100, 101, 103, 106, 121, 122, 124, 125, 126
Hirsch, Emmanuel, 400
Hobbes, Thomas, 155, 156, 158, 162

Index of Names

Hodgson, Peter C., 267, 269, 270, 275
Hoffmann, Jean G. H., 278
Hoffmann, Paul, 315, 367
Hoffmann, R. Joseph, 81
Holland, D. L., 286
Hollenbach, Paul W., 13, 14
Holmén, Tom, 12
Holtzmann, Heinrich Julius, 277, 278
Hooker, Morna D., 50, 98, 99
Horbury, William, 17
Hornig, Gottfried, 249
Horsley, Richard A., 47, 84, 317
Hossfeld, Uwe, 399
Hotchkiss, Valerie, 102, 104, 106, 112, 121, 128, 130, 131, 132, 135, 136, 137, 139
Houston, J., 174
Houtin, Albert, 368
Hudson, Wayne, 183, 185
Hughes, Charles, 315
Hume, David, 171, 172, 173, 174, 175, 176, 177, 178, 179, 180, 206, 269
Hunter, A. M., 295
Hunter, Michael, 147, 184
Hurtado, Larry W., 304, 305, 315, 317
Hvalvik, Reidar, 373
Iliffe, Rob, 141
Isaac, Ephraim, 69
Israel, Jonathan I., 154, 157, 158, 159, 160, 161, 185, 207
Jackson-McCabe, Matt, 193
Jacobi, F. H., 260
Jaffee, Martin S., 68
James, Susan, 157
Janowitz, Naomi, 59
Janse, Sam, 7
Jaspert, Bernd, 318, 357
Jauss, Hans Robert, 45, 46
Jefferson, Thomas, 214, 215, 216, 217, 218
Jensen, Gordon A., 105
Jensen, Morton Horning, 11
Jeremias, Joachim, 19, 21, 24, 193, 292, 381, 382
Jewett, Robert, 134
Jöcher, Christian Gottloeb, 219
Jodock, Darrell, 285
Johns, Loren L., 409
Johnson, Roger A., 318, 335
Johnson, Samuel, 184
Johnson, Sherman E., 274
Jonas, Hans, 335
Jones, Alan H., 368
Jones, F. Stanley, 190, 220
Jones, Gareth, 318
Jones, Richard M., 15
Jülicher, Adolf, 300
Kaftan, Julius, 235
Kähler, Martin, xiv, 281, 282, 283, 394
Kant, Immanuel, 224, 225, 226, 227, 228, 229, 230, 231, 232, 233, 235, 241, 252
Käsemann, Ernst, 315, 341, 342, 343, 344, 358, 359
Kaufmann, Walter, 365
Keck, Leander E., xliii, 6, 308, 348, 359, 361, 409
Kee, Howard Clark, 16, 17, 60, 178, 410
Keener, Craig S., 59, 203
Kegley, Charles W., 321
Keim, Theodor, 399
Keith, Chris, 35, 41
Kelly, J. N. D., 76, 78, 80, 90, 95, 96, 99, 100, 271
Kendall, Daniel, 98
Kidger, Mark, 89
Kieft, Lester, 139
Kierkegaard, Søren, 171, 252, 253, 254
Kittel, Gerhard, xxix, 387, 388, 390
Klassen, William, 27
Klauck, Hans-Josef, 410
Klausner, Joseph, xxviii, 33, 373, 374, 375, 376, 377
Klein, Dietrich, 221, 223, 247, 248, 249
Klibansky, Raymond, 179
Kloppenborg, John S., 277, 315, 367, 377
Koch, Gustav Adolf, 213
Koch, Klaus, 70
Koistinen, Olli, 157
Kolb, Robert, 101
Koperski, Veronica, 26
Kortholt, Christian, 219
Kovacs, Judith, 46
Kraft, Robert A., 385
Krailsheimer, A. J., 152
Kreiser, Robert B., 176
Krentz, E., 323
Krodel, Gerhard, 385
Kuhn, Thomas K., 263
Kuhn, Thomas S., 43
Kümmel, Werner Georg, xxxii, 271, 272, 322, 376
Kurtz, Lester R., 368

651

Kysar, Robert, 333
Labahn, Michael, 30, 322, 349
Lachmann, Karl, 276
Lafuma, Louis, 152
Lagrange, M. J., 278
Lampe, G. W. H., 5
Lang, Friedrich Gustav, 326
Lange, Armin, 10, 59
Larmer, Robert A. H., 174
Larmore, Charles, 150
Le Donne, Anthony, 41
Leask, Ian, 189
Lechler, Gotthard Victor, 219
Lehmann, Helmut T. 101
Leland, John, 184, 220, 234
Lemker, Heinrich Christian, 219
Leonard, Ellen, 370
Lessing, Eckhard, 285
Lessing, Gotthold Ephraïm, 219, 220, 221, 247, 248, 249, 250, 251, 252, 257, 258, 259, 272
Levi, Anthony, 152, 153, 154
Levine, Amy-Jill, 36
Levine, Lee I., 13
Levison, John R., 31
Lichtenberger, Hermann, 59
Lieb, Michael, 46
Liebing, Heinz, 275
Lienhart, J., 142
Lietzmann, Hans, 384, 386
Lightfoot, R. H., 291
Lilley, A. Leslie, 368
Lim, Paul C. H., 138
Lincoln, Andrew T., 84, 86
Lindars, Barnabas, 39
Lindeskog, Gösta, 372
Locke, John, 163, 164, 165, 166, 167, 168, 169, 206, 210
Loeser, M., 223
Lohmeyer, Ernst, 316, 399
Loisy, Alfred, xxviii, 368, 369, 370, 371
Longstaff, Thomas R. W., 274
Lucci, Diego, 185
Lucian of Samosata, 176, 312, 313
Luck, Ulrich, 391, 393
Lüdemann, Gerd, 84, 304, 308
Lührmann, D., 358
Lundsteen, A. C., 223
Lundström, Gösta, 285
Lurbe, Pierre, 191

Luz, Ulrich, 46, 352
MacCormac, Earl R., 43
MacDonald, Dennis R., xix, 49, 326
Mackie, J. L., 174, 179
Macquarrie, John, 92, 318
Magnus, Brand, 296
Maier, Gerhard, 263
Major, H. D. A., 368
Malet, André, 318
Malina, Bruce J., 58
Mamiani, Maurizio, 141
Mandelbrote, Scott, 141
Manson, T. W., 20, 27
Manuel, Frank E., 141, 168
Marcus, Joel, 7, 8, 18, 20, 22, 27, 28
Marki, Peter, 149
Markschies, Christoph, 49
Marmodoro, Anna, 73
Marsh, Clive, 285
Martin, Dale B., 317
Martin, Ralph P., 316, 341
Martinich, A. P., 154, 155, 156
Martyn, J. Louis, 330
Mason, Emma, 46
Mason, Steve, 18
Matthews, Gareth B., 149
May, Herbert F., 213
McCall Thomas H., 126
McCane, Byron R., 323
McCarthy, Vincent A., xiv, 301
McCormack, Bruce L., 361
McCown, Chester, C., 362
McIntyre, Alasdair, 42
McKim, Donald K., 132
McKnight, Scot, 72, 281, 300
McLachlan, H. John, 138
McLachlan, Herbert, 140, 141
McNeill, John T., 106, 126
Meda, Meir, 373
Meerson, Michael, 73
Meier, John P., 18, 26, 39, 41, 86, 87
Meijer, Lodewijk, 162
Meijering, E. P., 364
Melamed, Yitzhak Y., 157
Meli, Domenico Bertoloni, 144
Mendelssohn, Moses, 260
Mercer, C. R., 239
Merk, Otto, 272, 277
Merrill, Walter M., 210
Mersenne, Marin, 151, 186

Index of Names

Merz, Annette, 11, 25
Metzger. Bruce M., 26, 274
Meyer, Marvin W., 27, 315
Meyers, Carol L., 12
Meyers, Eric A., 10
Meyers, Eric M., 12
Michalson, Gordon E., Jr., 252
Michel, Otto, 386
Michie, Donald, 47
Middleton, Conyers, 172, 173, 174, 180
Milgrom, Jacob, 16, 36
Mill, J. S., 206
Millar, Fergus, 67
Miller, Shulamit, 12
Milton, J. R., 163, 164
Modica, Joseph B., 36
Molnar, Michael R., 89
Moltmann, Jürgen, 77, 87, 100, 254
Montgomery, William, xii
Moore, George Foot, 377, 382
Moore, R. Laurence, xiv
Morais, Herbert M. 213
Moreau, Pierre-François, 260
Morgan, Robert, 263, 346, 358
Morgan, Thomas, 209, 210
Morrill, John, 139
Mortimer, Sarah, 136, 138
Morton, Russell, 318
Moser, Paul K., xiv
Mosheim, J. L., 219
Mossner, Ernest Campbell, 171, 172, 179, 188, 193, 199, 210
Moyise, Steve, 84
Mueller, Ulrich B., 58
Mühling, K. L., 323
Müller, Gotthold, 262
Muller, Richard A., 105, 112, 126, 133, 134
Müller, W., 383
Mullin, Robert Bruce, 174
Murphy, Francesca Aran, 73
Myers, Eric M., 317
Nadler, Steven, 157, 162
Nagy, Rebecca Martin, 12
Naphy, William G., 125
Neale, D., 57, 58
Neill, Stephen, xiii
Neirynck, Franz, 277
Neuer, Werner, 391, 392, 394
Neusner, Jacob, 9, 18, 53, 67, 69, 117, 375, 409

Newman, John Henry, 63, 64, 368, 370
Newman, Lex, 163
Newton, Isaac, 140, 141, 143, 168
Neyrey, Jerome H., 16, 58
Nichols, Adrian, 64
Nicol, W., 344
Niesel, Wilhelm, 110, 128
Nietzsche, Friedrich, 296
Nineham, Dennis, xii
Nisbet, H. B., 249, 250, 251, 258, 259, 260, 272
Norton, David Fate, 171
Notley, R. Steven, 117
Oakes, Peter, 4
Oberman, Heiko A., 84, 126
O'Collins, Gerald, 64, 98
O'Connell, Marvin R., 368
O'Daly, Gerard, 149
Oermann, Nils Ole, 239, 296
Ogden, Daniel, 59
O'Higgins, James, 193, 194, 195, 196, 199
Olson, Roger E., 132
O'Meara, Thomas F., 318
Orchard, Bernard, 274
Osiander, Andreas, 109, 110, 272
Otto, Rudolf, xxx, 352, 395, 396, 397, 398, 399, 401, 406
Owen, David, 177, 178
Özen, Alf, 304
Paige, Terence, 26
Pailin, David A., 186
Paine, Thomas, 213
Painter, John, 318
Paley, William, 178
Palmer, N. H., 276, 277
Palmquist, Stephen R., 224
Pannenberg, Wolfhart, 77, 110, 111, 254, 283, 284
Parish, Richard, 152
Parrinder, Geoffrey, 84
Partee, Charles, 107
Pauck, Wilhelm, 103, 104, 363
Paulsen, Friedrich, 235
Paulus, H. E. G., 266
Peabody, David Barrett, 277, 281, 322
Peirce, C. S., 181
Pelikan, Jaroslav, 101, 102, 104, 106, 112, 121, 128, 130, 131, 132, 135, 136, 137, 139
Pelle, Moshe, 220, 221

653

A History of the Quests for the Historical Jesus

Penelhum, Terence, 179
Peppard, Michael, 7
Perrin, Norman, 301
Petre, Maude D., 368, 370
Pfanner, Dario, 186, 188
Pfizenmaier, Thomas C., 141, 143, 145
Philipp, Wolfgang, 219
Philips, Henry, 151
Philostratus, xliii
Picard, Edmond, 399
Picht, Werner, 239, 295
Pinnock, Clark, 132
Pitre, Brant, 12, 292, 300
Plümmacher, Eckhard, 384
Pobee, John, 56
Polanyi, Michael, 42
Pons, Georges, 249, 250, 258
Popkin, Richard H., 141, 146, 147, 149, 150, 151, 154, 157, 158, 163, 167, 170, 184, 185, 186
Porter, J. R., 386
Porter, Roy, 154
Porter, Stanley E., 361, 384
Potolsky, Gary, 49
Poulat, Émile, 368
Price, Lawrence Marsden, 219
Price, Mary Bell, 219
Priest, Robert D., 278
Priestley, Joseph, 214, 215, 216, 217
Pringle-Pattison. A. S., 163
Probyn, Clive, 209
Pyke, Markus, 383
Rahner, Karl, xvi, 110
Ramey, Margaret E., xiv
Ramsey, Ian T., 164
Raphael, Melissa, 394
Ratschow, Karl Heinz, 394
Ratté, John, 368
Ratzinger, Joseph, 84
Rawlinson, A. E. J., 315
Reardon, B. M. G., 368
Redwood, John A., 184, 186, 188
Reid, J. K. S., 106
Reimarus, Hermann Samuel, 221, 222, 223, 227, 246, 247
Reimarus, J. A. H., 222
Reitzenstein, Richard, 305
Renan, Ernest, 278, 279, 280, 399
Rengstorf, K. H., 383
Reumann, John, 84, 361

Reventlow, Henning Graf, 103, 107, 109, 146, 184, 185, 222, 223, 272
Reynolds III, Bennie H., 10
Rhoads, David, 47
Rice, Richard, 132
Richardson, Alan, 193
Riches, John, 291
Riesner, Rainer, 22, 34, 377
Ritschl, Albrecht Benjamin, 285, 286
Roberts, Jonathan, 46
Roberts, Tyler T., 296
Robinson, James M., xii, xiii, 300, 315, 319, 335, 341, 357, 358, 367
Rodis-Lewis, Geneviève, 148
Rogers, Ben, 151
Rogers, G. A. J., 163
Rogerson, John W., 274–75
Rollmann, H., 289
Römheld, K. F. Diethard, 59
Root, H. E., 173
Rosenthal, Michael A., 157
Rossi, Philip J., 224
Rothschild, Fritz A., 372
Rousseau, John J., 11, 12
Rowland, Christopher, 46
Rudolph, Kurt, 331
Rumscheidt, H. Martin, 364
Runesson, Anders, 13
Rupp, E. Gordon, 101
Rush, Osmond, 45
Sachs, Walter, 267, 270, 325
Sagovsky, Nicholas, 370
Saldarini, Anthony J., 18, 382
Samely, Alexander, 67
Sanders, E. P., 18, 22, 25, 33, 34, 409
Sanders, John, 132
Sandmel, Samuel, 373, 382
Sartiaux, Félix, 368
Schaberg, Jane, 84
Schäfer, Peter, 65, 71, 72, 73, 347
Schäfer, Rolf, 285
Schaff, Philip, 127
Schams, Christine, 18
Schatzmann, S. S., 381, 386
Schechter, Ronald, 257
Scheeben, Matthias J., 87
Scheick, William J., 213
Scherrer, Steven J., 176
Schlatter, Adolf, 306, 391, 392, 393, 394, 405

Index of Names

Schleiermacher, F. D. E., 264, 265, 272, 380, 396
Schmid, Johannes Heinrich, 391, 393
Schmidt, Johann Lorenz, 219, 247
Schmidt, Johann Michael, 305
Schmidt, Karl Ludwig, 322, 323
Schmidt, Thomas, 55
Schmiedel, Otto, 245
Schmithals, Walter, 318
Schnabel, Eckhard J., 26
Schnelle, Udo, 344
Schofield, Robert E., 139
Schoonenberg, Piet, 5
Schreckenberg, Heinz, 378
Schröder, Martin, 304
Schröder, Winfried, 157
Schultenover, David G., 368, 370
Schultz, Hans Jürgen, 348
Schultz, Siegfried, 315
Schultz, Werner, 235
Schultze, Harald, 249
Schumann, Johann Daniel, 251
Schürer, Emil, xxviii, 4, 31, 33, 378, 379, 380
Schwartz, Daniel R., 18
Schweitzer, Albert, xi, xii, xiii, 38, 118, 119, 183, 221, 239, 240, 241, 242, 243, 244, 245, 246, 261, 266, 277, 278, 281, 286, 288, 289, 291, 292, 293, 294, 295, 296, 297, 298, 299, 300, 301, 302, 362, 363
Schweizer, Eduard, 352, 353, 354
Scott, Walter, 206
Selderhuis, Herman J., 128
Sell, Alan P. F., 163, 170
Sellier, Philippe, 152
Sellers, R. V., 94
Semler, Johann Salomo, 146, 255, 256, 257
Servetus, M., 124, 125
Seybold, Klaus, 58
Shapiro, Alan E., 143
Shapiro, Marc, 191
Sheets, Dwight D., 30
Sherlock, Thomas, 205, 206
Siggins, Ian D. Kingston, 100, 410
Silva, Moisés, 385
Simon, Akiba Ernst, 371
Simon, Richard, 146
Sinclair, Daniel, 36, 72, 82
Singer, Peter, 262
Skinner, Christopher W., 47

Smend, Rudolf, 273
Smith, Dwight Moody, 330, 333
Smith, George E., 141
Smith, Louise Pettibone, 106
Smith, Morton, 3
Smith, Norman Kemp, 173
Snobelen, Stephen D., 142
Sorrell, Tom, 154
Soulen, R. Kendall, 76, 323
Soulen, Richard N., 76, 323
Sperber, Daniel, 32
Spinoza, Baruch, 157, 158, 159, 160, 161, 162
Springborg, Patricia, 155
St. John, Henry, 210
Stackhouse, Thomas, 199
Standaert, Benoit, 326
Stanglin, Keith D., 126
Stanton, Graham N., 66, 67, 74, 75, 326
Stassen, Glen H., 21
Stäudlin, Carl Friedrich, 225
Stead, Christopher, 98
Steck, Karl Gerhard, 391
Stefano, Troy A., 73
Steinmetz, David C., 100, 121
Stemberger, Günter, 68, 380
Stephen, Leslie, 184, 209
Sterling, Gregory E., 49, 317
Stewart, Matthew, 162, 170, 213
Stillingfleet, Edward, 170
Strack, Hermann L., 68, 380
Strange, James F., 12
Strange, James Riley, 317
Strauss, David Friedrich, 262, 263, 265, 267, 268, 269, 270, 271, 280
Strauss, Leo, 170
Strecker, Georg, 289, 358
Streeter, B. H., xxv, 295
Strobel, August, 55
Sturdy, John, 17
Stuhlmacher, Peter, 391, 393
Styers, Randall, 10
Suderman, Jeffrey M., 179
Sullivan, Robert E., 188
Surenhusius, Guilielmus, 198
Swain, Scott R., 104
Sweet, John, 99
Swinburne, Richard, 174, 178, 179
Sykes, Norman, 144
Tait, Michael, 4

A History of the Quests for the Historical Jesus

Talar, C. J. T., 368
Talbert, C. H., 335, 349, 358
Tanner, Norman P., 93
Tarantino, Giovanni, 191, 195
Taylor, Jacqueline, 171
Teal, Andrew, 93
Telford, John, 174
Thate, Michael J., 295
Theissen, Gerd, 6, 11, 25, 39, 56, 57, 254, 255, 267, 324, 342, 346, 349
Thellman, Gregory, 18, 19
Thigpen, T. P., 213
Thiselton, Anthony C., 31, 43, 44, 45, 46, 335, 341
Thomas, John Christopher, 58
Thompson, Marianne Meye, 344
Thompson, Robin, 203
Thomson, Robert W., 93
Thorschmid, Urban Gottlob, 220
Throckmorton, Burton H., 331
Tillich, Paul, 283
Tindal, Matthew, 207, 208, 210
Tiwald, Markus, 32
Tödt, H. E., 315
Toland, John, 188, 189, 190, 191, 192, 193
Torrey, Norman L., 184, 199, 209, 219
Toulmin, Joshua, 135
Trapnell, William H., 199, 200, 205, 219
Trinius, J. A., 220
Troeltsch, Ernst, 228
Troyer, Kristin de, 315
Tuck, Richard, 156, 157
Tuckett, Christopher M., 7, 12, 13, 39, 270, 274, 315
Turner, Denys, 110
Turner, Frank M., 64, 369
Twelftree Graham H., 13, 33, 58, 405
Tyrrell, George, xxviii, 370
Vaage, Leif E., 315
Van Belle, Gilbert, 333
Van der Loos, H.,
VanEpps, Cameron, 34
Van Voorst, Robert E., 115
Veleck, Ceslaus, 110
Verbin, John S. Kloppenborg, 315
Verheule, Anthonie F., 305, 308, 317
Vermes, Geza, xxix, 64, 113, 114, 115, 116, 117, 372, 378, 409
Vidler, Alec R., 368
Vielhauer, P., 354

Viret, Pierre, 184
Voelkel, Robert T., 346, 348
Voigt, Christoph, 220
Volkova, Elena, 258
Von Soden, Hans, 400–401
Von Wahlde, Urban C., 203, 330
Wahlen, Clinton, 13
Ward, W. Reginald, 174
Wardman, W. H., 278
Waterland, Daniel, 145
Watts, Joel L., 49
Watts, Rikki E., 8, 38
Waubke, Hans-Günther, 379
Weaver, Walter P., 239, 295, 300, 302, 303, 362
Weder, Hans, 352
Weinandy, Thomas G., 93, 94
Weinberg, Kurt, 162
Weinreich, Max, 386, 399
Weinreich, Otto, 305
Weinsheimer, Joel C., 43, 44
Weiss, Johannes, 243, 286, 287, 288
Weiss, Otto, 368
Weiss, Zeev, 12
Weisser, Donald M., 318
Wellhausen, Julius, xxvii, 366, 367, 374
Wernle, Paul, 302
Wessel, Leonard P., 249
Westhelle, Vitor, 103, 104
Werblowsky, R. I. Zwi, 15–16, 22
Werses, Samuel, 373
Wesley, John, 174, 176
Westfall, Richard S., 141
Whiston, William, 142, 143, 145, 200, 209
Wickham, Lionel R., 113
Wigglesworth, Jeffrey R., 185, 208, 209
Wigoder, Geoffrey, 16, 22
Wilamowitz-Moellendorff, Ulrich von, 303
Wilbur, Earl Morse, 123, 124
Wilckens, Ulrich, 46
Wiles, Maurice, 90, 91, 92, 141, 142, 145
Wilkins, Michael J., 26
Wilkinson, John, 58
Willeford, Bennett R., Jr., 139
Williams, Daniel H., 91
Williams, George H., 122, 124, 136
Williams, Rowan, 91, 92
Williams, T. C., 174
Willis, E. David, 112
Willis, W., 286

Index of Names

Willitts, Joel, 67
Winter, Dagmar, 6, 254, 255, 267, 324, 342, 346, 349
Wire, Antoinette Clark, 47
Witherington III, Ben, 34
Witmer, Amanda, 59
Wolterstorff, Nicholas, 42, 43, 48
Wood, Allen W., 235
Wood, H. G., 362
Woods, Edward J., 58
Woog, Carl Christian, 219
Woolhouse, Roger, 163
Woolston, Thomas, 199, 200, 201, 202, 203, 204, 205
Wootton, David, 147, 177, 184
Wrede, William, 38, 244, 246, 289, 290
Wreen, Michael, 224
Wright, David P., 15
Wright, N. T., xii, xiii, xiv, 301
Wright, Tom, xiii
Wrzecionko, Paul, 285
Wulf, Christoph, 49
Wünsch, D., 272
Yandell, Keith E., 174
Yarborough, Robert W., 391
Yasukata, Toshimasa, 249
Young, B. W., 207
Young, Frances M., 93, 94, 95, 96
Zangenberg, Jürgen, 317
Zerwick, Maximilian, 19
Zager, Werner, 289
Zahl, Paul F. M., 341
Zahn-Harnack, Agnes von, 363, 364, 404
Zuckert, Michael P., 170

INDEX OF ANCIENT WRITINGS

OLD TESTAMENT
Genesis
1:3 79
2:2–3 24
2:9 136
3:22–24 136
5:21–23 69
5:24 69
6:2 . . . . 7, 83
6:6 109
9:4 445
10 455
22:18 89
37–50 89
38 85

Exodus
3:14 407
4:22 . . . . 7, 89
4:22–23 440
12 . . . . 423, 433
15:26 16
16:4, 16–21 440
16:17 269
18:20 444
20:2–17 . . . . 28, 444
20:8–11 23
20:12 36
23:20 8
24:8 445
24:9–11 26
40:34 464

Leviticus
13–14 15
14:2–32 16
16:29–31 22
19:9 23
19:18 . . . . 53, 444
19:27 30
20:27 30
21:1–2, 11–12 56
23:26–32 22
24:7 424
24:8–9 23
24:10–11, 14–16, 23 19
26:12 xlvii

Numbers
6:6 56
12:6–7 32
16:3 451
19:11–22 12
19:14–22 56
24:17 65
25 27
27:17 51
27:18 51
35:30 37

Deuteronomy
4:34 25
5:6 416
5:6–21 . . . . 28, 444
5:12–15 23

5:15 25
5:16 36
5:29 56
6:4 260
6:4–5 . . . . 53, 444, 445
7:6 451
7:19 25
11:2 25
13 29, 55, 156, 160, 161, 187
13:1–2 196
13:1–5 . . xviii, 25, 29, 32, 84
13:1–6 55
13:1–16 459
13:2–6 111
13:4 56
13:12–18 29
17:6 37
18 156
18:15, 18 66
19:15 37
21 36
21:18–21 . . . . . . 36, 59, 436
21:22–23 72
23:2–6 72
23:19–20 441
25:5–10 . . . . 53, 85
26:6 25
30:12 32
31:12–13 56
32:5–6 7
32:8 7
32:39 16

Index of Ancient Writings

Joshua
3–4 6

Ruth
1:16 153
3:4 85
4:1–12 85
4:17, 22 86
4:18–22 85

1 Samuel
15:1 109
15:22 53
17:12 89
21:1–6 23

2 Samuel
5:2 89
7:14 7
11:3 86
12:1–12 258
12:24 86

1 Kings
8:42 25
17:8–24 51
17:17–24 . . . . 16, 269
19 39

2 Kings
4 269
5 16
5:1–15 16
6 269

2 Chronicles
6:32 25

Job
3:8 156
41:1 156

Psalms
2 7
2:7 . . . . 7, 410
2:11 56
17:8 87
18:1–6, 46 461
22:28 426
24:1 7
24:3–7 461
33:6 92
36:7 87
37:1 424
41:9 27
51:11 31
57:1 87
63:7 87
68:30–32 426
69:1–2 424
72:9–11 426
74:14 156
86:10 426
89:7 7
89:9 40
89:26–27 7
91:1 87
96:3 426
96:8 426
96:10 426
104:26 156
110 55
110:1 . . . . li, 19, 54
110:1–4 410
110:3 90
110:4 111
114–18 461
115–18 416
115:3 109
118 . . . . 1, 52, 461, 462
118:2 461
118:18 461
118:19 461
118:20 461
118:22 461
118:22–23 52
118:26 462
118:28–29 461
136:12 25

Proverbs
1:7 56
8:22 . . . . 79, 92
8:25 . . . . 79, 90

Isaiah
1:2 8
2:2 426
2:3 426
5:1–7 8
6:9 . . . . 39, 197
6:9–10 38
6:13 38
7:6 8
7:6–7 8
7:10–14 82
7:10–17 83
7:14 . . . . 85, 87, 88, 196
7:14–17 89
7:16–17 88
11:10 426
12:1–6 8
12:12 8
18:7 426
19:23 426
19:24–25 426
25:6–8 426
27:1 156
28:21 103
29:13 8
30 398
35:5–6 269
38:10 457
40:3 . . . . 8, 39
40:5 426
42:1 . . . . 7, 410
42:1–4 57
42:6 426
43:1–5 416
45:14 426
45:20, 22 426
45:23–24 426
49:6 426
51:4–5 426
52:10 426
53 . . . . 383, 424, 425
53:8 90
53:12 425
54:5 22
55:5 426
56:7 426
58:6 58
60:3 426
60:5–14 426
61:1–2 . . . . 58, 384
62:5 22
62:10 426
63:10–11 31
66:19–20 426

A History of the Quests for the Historical Jesus

Jeremiah
2:2 22
16:15–16 459
16:19 426
17:13 437
18:8 109
19:10–11 398
21:5 25
23. 32
31:9 7
31:15 90
31:20 7
31:31–34 445
31:33–34a 423
31:34b 423
32:21 25

Lamentations
3. 162

Ezekiel
4. 398
16. 22
20:33–34 25

Daniel
2:4b–7:28 34
3:25 7
7. 309
7:9–10 35
7:13 .... l, li, 20, 54, 55,
                117, 243
7:13–14 .... 19, 35
7:14 426

Hosea
2. 22
6:6 53
11:1 .... 7, 89, 197, 440

Joel
2:28 8

Jonah
1:5 40
3:7–8 22

Micah
5:1 89
6:6–8 53

Zephaniah
3:9 426

Haggai
2:7 426

Zechariah
2:11 426
2:13 426
8:21, 23 426
9:9 437
9:10 426
14:6 426

Malachi
3:1 8
4:5 197

DEUTEROCANONICAL WORKS

Tobit
4:15 375

Wisdom of Solomon
2:13 7
2:17–18 7
16:13 457

Sirach (Ecclesiasticus)
4:10 7
24:8 464
38:2 16
38:24–39:11 18
46:1 66

2 Maccabees
7:37–38 424

OLD TESTAMENT PSEUDEPIGRAPHA

1 Enoch
37–71 69
46:1 35
46:3 35
47:3 35
48:2 35
70:1–4 35
71:8–14 35

Jubilees
1:24–25 7

3 Maccabees
5:51 457

4 Maccabees
6:29 424

Psalms of Solomon
16:2 457

DEAD SEA SCROLLS

CD
5:11–13 31
7:4 31
12:2–3 30

1QHa
20:11–12 30

4Q174
4Q174 410

11QTemple
55:2–19 29

ANCIENT JEWISH WRITERS

Josephus
Against Apion
2.206 36

Jewish Antiquities
4.263–264 36
13.300 111
17.167 414
17.198 401
17.213 414
17.289 12
18.3 115
18.3.3 301
18.23–25 27
18.27 12
18.36 12
18.37 12
18.64 115
18.65–80 .... xlvii, 115
18.117–19 11
18.118–19 25

660

Index of Ancient Writings

Jewish War
2.10 414
2.68 12
2.117 33
2.247 441
7.61 441

Life
197–98 23

Philo of Alexandria
Life of Moses
1.277 29

On Dreams
LCL 275 32

On Drunkenness
14 36

The Special Laws
1.315–16 29
1.318 29
2.232 36
4.50–52 29

NEW TESTAMENT
Matthew
1:1 89
1:1–16 85
1:2 85
1:3 85
1:5 85
1:5–6 86
1:6 . . . . 85, 86, 89
1:9 85
1:15–16 82
1:16 85
1:17 85
1:18 86
1:18–25 82
1:19 72
1:20 . . . . 67, 82, 86, 89
1:21 . . . . 87, 88, 388
1:22–23 196
1:23 . . . . 67, 82, 88, 89
2:1–2 89
2:1–29 414
2:12 89
2:13 89
2:15 . . . . 89, 197
2:18 90
2:23 . . . . 90, 192, 197
3:1 39
3:17 . . . . 5, 7, 67
4:10 463
4:17 381
4:18 27
4:18–22 459
5:4, 6, 7 423
5:9 . . . . 7, 288, 442
5:10–12 324
5:11, 13–14 443
5:16 7
5:17 . . . . 161, 189
5:25–26 441
6:9 7
6:9–13 . . . . . xxxiv, 429, 439
6:10 444
6:13 292
6:14–15 442
6:16–18 351
6:34 324
7:29 406
8:5–12 447
8:5–13 313
8:11–12 425
8:22 324
8:23–27 . . . . 39, 67, 313
9:1–8 312
9:2 312
9:18–26 . . . . 204, 312
9:34 30
10 300
10–11 243
10:3 437
10:4 27
10:5–6 426
10:5–14 57
10:7 287
10:23 . . . 243, 294, 300, 421
10:24–25 34
10:25 418
10:40 67
10:45 243
11:2 269
11:5 191
11:14 197
11:19 . . . . 59, 351
11:25 429
11:25–26 442
11:25–27 . . . . 117, 416, 429
11:25–71 67
11:27 . . . 310, 324, 369, 379, 454, 463
11:28 365
12:18–21 57
12:22–32 4
12:23 268
12:24 . . . . 5, 30, 33
12:24–27 418
12:27 . . . . 33, 398
12:28 . . . . 33, 287, 437
12:39 269
12:46–50 59
13:11 39
13:13 39
13:34–35 197
14:22–33 67
15:17–20 73
15:21–28 447
15:34 80
16:4 269
16:16 457
16:17 67
16:17–18 437
16:17–19 . . . . 450, 456, 457, 460
16:18 . . . . . . xxxiv, 451, 462
16:18–19 324
16:20 . . . . 458, 463
16:21 462
16:21–23 458
16:22–23 463
16:23 463
17:5 . . . . 67, 87
18:15 439
18:16 37
18:17 450
18:20 67
18:21–25 353
18:21–35 439
18:23–35 441
19:28 288
21:9 462
21:12–13 . . . . 60, 462
21:28–32 60
21:37 67
22:34–40 230
22:37 444

661

A History of the Quests for the Historical Jesus

22:39–40 444	1:27 . . . . 13, 17	3:10 26
22:44 410	1:29–31 . . . . 14, 20	3:11–12 . . . . 13, 26
23:8 111	1:30 342	3:12 289
23:15 58	1:31 11	3:13–19 26
23:23 374	1:32–34 15	3:14–15 26
23:27 56	1:33 15	3:15 17
23:34–36 424	1:34 . . . . 13, 15, 289	3:16 . . . . 11, 27, 407
23:37 350	1:35 . . . . 15, 429	3:18 . . . . 20, 27
24:3 1	1:38 15	3:19 15
24:24 . . . . 84, 111, 161	1:39 15	3:20 342
25:1–12 22	1:40 16	3:20–21 . . . . 27, 28
26:1–5 445	1:40–42 9	3:20–35 . . . . 28, 37
26:13 424	1:40–45 15	3:21 192
26:28 . . . . 433, 446	1:41 . . . . 11, 16	3:22 . . . . 4, 5, 13, 18, 30, 33,
26:39 442	1:43–45 289	48, 192, 418, 459
26:41 292	1:44 16	3:24–26 30
26:63 59	1:45 17	3:27 30
26:63–66 292	2:1 . . . . 11, 15, 28	3:28–29 30
27:37 61	2:1–12 . . . . 17, 19, 312, 325	3:28–30 437
27:46 80	2:5 . . . . 17, 19, 406, 423	3:30 . . . . 30, 33, 54
27:63–64 59	2:5–11 9	3:31 15
28:16–20 460	2:6 18	3:31–35 . . . . 36, 59, 192
28:30 67	2:7 . . . . . 17, 19, 26, 55, 424	3:33–35 . . . . 15, 36
	2:8 407	4 32
Mark	2:10 . . . . 17, 19	4:1 37
1:1 410	2:11 11	4:1–33 . . . . 21, 48, 50
1:1–13 50	2:12 18	4:3–9 37
1:1–15 . . . . 48, 326	2:13–17 20	4:9 38
1:2 39	2:14 437	4:10–20 38
1:2–3 8	2:15 . . . . 20, 21	4:11 . . . . . xxxii, 37, 39, 427
1:4 10	2:16 . . . . 18, 21	4:12 38
1:8 . . . . . 8, 9, 30, 33, 52, 54	2:17 . . . . 16, 21	4:15 38
1:9 11	2:18–22 22	4:16 38
1:10 . . . . 6, 30	2:19–20 437	4:17 38
1:11 . . . . 5, 7, 410	2:20 22	4:18–19 38
1:12–13 . . . . 10, 52	2:21 22	4:20 38
1:14–15 10	2:22 22	4:21 58
1:14–3:35 50	2:23–28 22	4:21–25 . . . . 37, 38
1:15 . . . . 287, 415	2:23–3:7 424	4:26–29 37
1:16 27	2:26 23	4:26–31 39
1:16–20 . . . . 11, 459	2:27 24	4:30–32 . . . . 37, 446
1:16–3:35 48	2:27–28 24	4:32 436
1:17 11	2:35–37 24	4:33 37
1:21 11	3:1 11	4:34 37
1:21–28 . . . . 11, 325	3:1–6 . . . . 24, 325	4:34–41 313
1:22 . . . . 13, 17, 18, 406	3:4 . . . . 25, 324	4:35–36 39
1:23 . . . . 9, 33, 54	3:5 . . . . 11, 25, 407	4:35–41 . . . . 39, 48
1:23–26 13	3:6 . . . . 25, 33	4:35–6:56 50
1:24 . . . . 13, 14, 405	3:7–12 26	4:38 40
1:25 . . . . 11, 40, 289	3:9 26	4:39 40

Index of Ancient Writings

4:41 . . . . 40, 56	9:2 289	12:10–11 52
5:2 . . . . 33, 54	9:2–8 51	12:12 52
5:8 11	9:3 289	12:13 . . . . 18, 25, 53
5:21–43 . . . . 204, 312	9:7 . . . . 7, 8, 87	12:13–44 21
5:23 11	9:9 289	12:13–17 26
5:26 16	9:12 424	12:13–34 52
5:29 . . . . 11, 406	9:22b 346	12:14–17 53
5:33 56	9:25 . . . . 11, 40	12:18–27 53
5:37 289	9:30–31 289	12:24 58
5:39 406	9:34 58	12:25 288
5:40 289	9:35–10:45 51	12:28 57
5:43 289	9:39–40 228	12:28–34 . . . . 53, 230
6:1 28	9:43–48 8	12:29–30 . . . . 53, 444
6:1–2 25	10:1–45 21	12:31 . . . . 53, 444
6:1–6 . . . . 56, 192	10:2–9 . . . . 24, 25	12:32–34 445
6:1–6a 28	10:7 36	12:33 53
6:3 . . . . 27, 36	10:18 92	12:34 53
6:6–13 57	10:19 36	12:36 . . . . 54, 410
6:7 17	10:25 58	12:43–45 58
6:14–20 11	10:29 36	13 280
6:34 51	10:33 19	13:1–37 54
6:46 . . . . 15, 429	10:35–45 407	13:3–37 1
6:50 416	10:38 58	13:4 280
7:1 . . . . 5, 18	10:38–39 52	13:22 . . . . 29, 84
7:1–13 24	10:39 8	13:32 280
7:1–23 . . . . 21, 25, 51	10:45 . . . 288, 294, 365, 425	13:38–39 58
7:10–12 36	10:46 . . . . 10, 11	14:1 19
7:18–23 73	10:46–12:44 52	14:1–2 445
7:19 51	10:47–48 . . . . 24, 289	14:1–15:39 54
7:20–23 324	10:52 10	14:8 424
7:24 289	11:1–15:39 332	14:9 424
7:24–30 446	11:9 462	14:14 34
7:24–9:34 51	11:10 24	14:22 422
7:29 11	11:11 . . . . 52, 462	14:22–25 242
7:33 289	11:15–17 462	14:23 422
7:34 11	11:15–18 60	14:24 . . . 424, 425, 433, 446
7:36 289	11:15–19 19	14:25 . . . . 242, 422
8:11–12 25	11:17 426	14:26 422
8:12 269	11:18 . . . . 19, 58	14:35 15
8:23 289	11:18–19 462	14:35–36 442
8:25 11	11:25 . . . . 438, 439, 442	14:36 . . . 428, 429, 438, 439
8:26 289	11:27 . . . . 19, 53	14:38 . . . . 292, 438
8:27–29 9	11:27–33 19	14:39 15
8:28 406	11:27–12:11 24	14:51 351
8:29 . . . . 51, 54	11:28 17	14:53 19
8:30 . . . . 289, 463	11:28–33 54	14:59 37
8:31 . . . . 19, 462	11:29 17	14:61 54
8:31–32 51	11:30 52	14:61–62 . . . . 54, 407
8:32–33 463	11:31 52	14:61–64 . . . . 26, 243,
8:33 . . . . 51, 463	11:33 17	292, 415

14:62 . . . . li, 416	9:22 462	21:34–36 324
14:63–64 55	9:29–30 269	22:1–2 445
14:64 19	9:34 87	22:15 422
15:1 19	9:44 424	22:16 423
15:21 351	9:58 58	22:17 422
15:23 297	9:60 324	22:19 423
15:26 61	10 455	22:20 . . . . 433, 446
15:31 19	10:9, 11 287	22:28 292
15:34 . . . . 116, 442	10:21 442	22:28–30 26
15:39 . . . . 8, 56	10:21–22 429	22:40, 46 292
15:40–16:8 . . . . . 50, 56, 326	10:22 . . . 324, 379, 454, 463	22:66–71 292
16:8 56	10:25–28 . . . . 230, 444	23:34 442
16:16 59	11:2 7	23:37 424
	11:2–4 . . . . . xxxiv, 429, 439	23:38 . . . . 61, 62
Luke	11:4 292	23:46 442
1:26–38 86	11:10 398	24:19 . . . . 6, 114
1:35 86	11:14–23 4	
2:8 449	11:15 . . . . 5, 30, 33, 58	**John**
2:39–40 192	11:15–19 418	1:1 464
2:52 112	11:18–19 . . . . 33, 58	1:1–2 226
3:1–2 414	11:20 . . . . 58, 287, 437	1:1–18 . . . 60, 330, 332, 464
3:4 39	11:42 374	1:3 226
3:22 . . . . 5, 7	11:44 56	1:5 402
3:23 414	12:8 398	1:13 . . . . 226, 309
4:13 292	12:10 4	1:14 . . . . xlvi, 110, 310,
4:16 384	12:13–14 374	331, 466
4:16–30 58	12:49–50 8	1:19–51 332
4:18–19 58	12:50 424	1:33–34 7
4:28–30 192	12:58–59 441	1:42 . . . . 451, 459
4:35 325	13 202	2–12 332
5:1–11 459	13:10–17 325	2:1–11 . . . . 61, 313
5:17–26 312	13:28–29 425	2:4 415
5:20–21 441	13:32–33 424	2:11 330
6:12 . . . . 429, 443	13:33 424	2:13–25 60
6:13 26	13:34 350	2:16 466
6:14 27	14:1–6 325	2:23–4:42 332
6:15 27	15 60	2:24 415
6:22–23 . . . . 324, 443	15:1–2 . . . . 60, 437, 441	2:25 406
6:40 34	15:11–32 59	3 329
7:1–10 . . . . 313, 447	16:1–8 . . . . 60, 441	3:2 169
7:11–17 . . . . 204, 313	16:8 441	3:14 287
7:34 59	17:11–19 325	3:16 . . . . 130, 226
7:39 406	17:21 369	3:18 . . . . 330, 332
7:47–49 441	17:25 424	3:34 7
8:10 39	18:37 192	3:35 464
8:19–21 59	19:5 437	4:23 279
8:22–25 . . . . 39, 313	19:38 462	4:26 416
8:40–56 . . . . 204, 312	19:45–46 . . . . 60, 462	4:34 464
9:1–6 57	19:47–48 462	4:46–54 . . . . 61, 313
9:21 463	20:42 410	4:54 330

Index of Ancient Writings

5. 202	8:42 . . . . 464, 465	12:50 466
5:1 415	8:48–49 61	13–20 332
5:1–18 61	8:49 466	13:1 437
5:14 61	8:52 417	13:1–11 61
5:17 466	8:54 466	13:1–20 432
5:18 424	8:55 464	13:3 465
5:19 . . . . 464, 465	8:58 416	13:19 416
5:19–20 465	8:59 61	13:23 467
5:21 464	9. 160	14:1–30 61
5:22 464	9:1–41 61	14:6 . . . . 354, 466
5:23 466	9:6 202	14:7 466
5:26 464	9:13–16 li	14:9 466
5:27 287	10. 329	14:9–11 437
5:30 464	10:1–30 61	14:10 . . . . 61, 466
5:36 437	10:15 466	14:10–11 466
5:36–37 466	10:18 465	14:13 466
5:37 466	10:19–21 417	14:21–23 466
5:43 466	10:22–23 61	14:24 . . . . 465, 466
6. . . . . 73, 329	10:25 466	14:28 466
6:1–15 61	10:28 130	15. 329
6:16–21 61	10:30 . . . . 464, 466	15:1–11 61
6:21, 23 12	10:33 61	15:5 130
6:25–59 432	10:33–36 424	15:8 466
6:27 466	10:34 329	15:10 466
6:35–65 61	10:36 . . . . 61, 466	15:15 465
6:38 464	10:37 466	15:22 354
6:40 466	10:37–38 . . . . 61, 437	15:23–24 466
6:51–56 310	10:38 466	16:3 466
6:57 . . . . 464, 465	11:1–44 . . . . 61, 204	16:27 . . . . 465, 466
6:63 . . . . 102, 310	11:3 467	16:32 466
7:1 417	11:11 243	17. 429
7:12 61	11:38–50 xxxii	17:1–26 . . . . 61, 442
7:14, 28 61	11:41 429	17:3 . . . . 81, 92, 153
7:31 269	11:41–42 442	17:5 466
7:37–39 61	11:45 417	17:8 465
7:53 437	11:45–53 343	17:21 466
8:2 61	11:46–50 415	18:3 407
8:12–20 61	11:47–48 61	18:5–7 192
8:15 309	11:47–57 398	18:11 466
8:16 466	11:56 61	18:12 407
8:17 329	12. 329	18:19–24 61
8:18 466	12:9–10 343	18:20 61
8:19 466	12:11 417	18:28 61
8:20 61	12:13 462	18:31 33
8: 21–59 61	12:26 466	19:12 . . . . 61, 408
8:24 416	12:27–28 . . . . 429, 442	19:14 432
8:28 464	12:28 466	19:19 . . . . 62, 192
8:29 464	12:28–30 7	19:26 467
8:38 . . . . 465, 466	12:49 466	19:31 432
8:41–42 72	12:49–50 465	19:35 467

665

20:17 153	9:5 451	**James**
20:30–31 . . . . 332, 343	9:19–20 56	2:2 450
21 332	10:16 322	2:5 191
21:1 12	11:23–25 424	
21:1–24 60	11:24 423	**2 Peter**
21:15–17 458	11:25 . . . . . . 422, 423, 433	1:4 94
21:20–24 455	11:27 446	
21:24 . . . . 455, 467	15:3–9 56	**1 John**
21:24–25 332	15:5 451	2:2 130
	15:45 309	2:16 309
Acts	15:52 288	4:2 310
1:5 8	16:22 . . . . 315, 424	4:13 159
1:13 27		
2:22 . . . . 6, 192	**2 Corinthians**	**2 John**
2:36 287	3:17 . . . . 309, 386	7 310
3:6 192	5:7 284	
4:10 192	5:19 xlvii	**Revelation**
6:14 192	6:16 xlvii	16:15 324
7 130	13:1 37	
7:38 450		**RABBINIC**
10:4 424	**Galatians**	**LITERATURE**
10:37–38 6	1–2 460	**'Abot**
11:16 8	1:18 451	3:9–10 114
11:26 191	2:9, 11, 14 451	
15 193	3:26–27 309	**Mishnah**
15:19–20 . . . . 191, 193	4:6 428	*Berakhot*
22:8 192		5:5 . . . . 20, 114
24:5 192	**Philippians**	9:5 . . . . 53, 57, 445
26:9 192	2:5–11 92	
	2:6–8 226	*Sanhedrin*
Romans	2:6–11 . . . . li, 316, 425	7:4 29
1:3–4 86	2:7 . . . . 95, 112, 425	7:5 . . . . 19, 55
6:1–11 309	2:8 76	7:7 30
8:11 86	2:9 316	10:4 29
8:15 428	3:5–6 417	
8:28–39 134		*Shabbat*
8:34 316	**2 Thessalonians**	7:2 23
9:1–33 134	2:9 111	
10:4 189		*Sotah*
16:27 92	**1 Timothy**	9:15 . . . . 6, 114, 117
	5:19 37	
1 Corinthians	6:15–16 92	*Ta'anit*
1 111		3:8 114
1:12 451	**Hebrews**	
1:18 380	1:3 226	*Tohorot*
2:2 251	1:8–9 92	7:6 20
2:4 251	3:6 92	
3:22 451	9:16–17 445	**Babylonian Talmud**
7:29–31 339	10:28 37	*Bava Metzia*
8:6 92	11:31 85	59b 32, 313

Index of Ancient Writings

Berakot
40a 428

Sanhedrin
43a 72, 347
43b 116
67a 71
70b 428
103a 72

Shabbat
104b 71

Ta'anit
23b 428

Jerusalem Talmud
Berakot
9.1 33

Ta'anit
2.1 414

Targum Isaiah
8:4 428

EARLY CHURCH FATHERS
Apostolic Fathers
Didache
1.2 375
8 439
8:2 439

Ignatius
To the Ephesians
7 91

Irenaeus
Heresies
1.22.1 76
2.30.9 90
3.16.6 76
3.22.4 76
4.20.3 90
5.16.3 76
5.17.3 76

Justin Martyr
Dialogue with Trypho
7.3 74

8 74

First Apology
5 74
21 74

Origen
Contra Celsum
1.32 . . . . 71, 82
1.33 82
1.34 82
1.35 . . . . 83, 88
1.38 83
1.39 83
1.41 84
1.53 84
1.57 84
5.39 . . . . 81, 82

De Principiis
1.2.4 90

Homilies on Jeremiah
9.4 90

Tatian
Diatessaron 216

Tertullian
Adversus Judaeos
9 83

Adversus Marcionem
3.13 83

Against Praxeas
1 79
2 80
6 79
7 79
8 79
29 79
30 80

LATER MAJOR WRITERS
Anselm of Canterbury
Cur deus homo
1.3–4 77

Athanasius
On the Incarnation of the Word
7–9 91
54:3 94
268–69 94

Augustine
Against Faustus
26.3 175

Against the Academicians
3.11.25–26 149

City of God
11.26 149
21.8 175

De consensus evangelistarum
1.2.3–4 271

The Literal Meaning of Genesis
6:13–14, 18 175

On Free Will
2.3.7 149

On the Blessed Life
2.2.7 149

On the Trinity
10.10 149
15.12.21

On True Religion
73 149

Eusebius
Ecclesiastical History
3.39 . . . . 276, 277, 368, 458
3.39.15–16 271
4.29.6 272
4.33 276
5:8 458
6.14.5 271
6.14.7 271

Preparation Evangelica
8.7.6............... 375

Gregory of Nazianzus
Epistle
101................. 95

T. Levi
18:1, 11–12 405

GRECO-ROMAN SOURCES
Apuleius
Florida
19.................. 313

Aristotle
Poetics 326

Posterior Analytics
1.6–7 251

Cicero
On the Nature of the Gods
1.16.43............. 108

Horace
Ars Poetica 326

Epistles
1.2.40 235

Pausanias
6.26.1–2............ 314

Pliny the Elder
Natural History
7................... 312
31.13 314
37, 124.............. 312

Suetonius
Lives: The Deified Vespasian
7................... 176

Tacitus
Annales
6.8................. 408

Histories
4................... 187
4.81 176